to You

More Powerful Interaction
In Your Classroom Out of Your Classroom

For you. For your students. What better way to learn about marketing than to see it in action, both in and out of the classroom. BusinessNow Video Shorts and Video Segments enable you and your students to interact with the real world anywhere and anytime.

Video Shorts appear at the end of each chapter. Students are asked to watch a 4-minute video featuring an entrepreneurial company and then answer 3-4 related questions. Show the shorts in class or go to www.prenhall.com/kotler to watch them anytime.

SENSABLE TECHNOLOGIES:
DESIGNING PRODUCTS DIGITALLY

With the new emphasis on cyber-retailing, what's a traditional brick-and-mortar retailer to do? Hire a consultant! The consultants at Online Retail Partners (ORP), recently renamed Accordia, work with traditional retailers to create an online presence that builds customer relationships, promotes products and services, and enhances sales. In addition to providing Web technology expertise, ORP educates clients about how to use existing brick-and-mortar resources to drive new customers to the online retail marketplace.

After viewing the Online Retail Partners video, answer the following questions about retailing and wholesaling:

1. Executives at ZanyBrainy assert that it's important to maintain a balance between online and traditional retailing. How do the two channels interact and support one another? How might building an online presence influence the place decision for retailers? How might it influence other marketing decisions?

2. Should Online Retail Partners consider expanding its services to wholesalers? How would the services required by wholesalers interested in building an online presence differ from those required by retailers? Which types of wholesalers are most likely to find success online?

3. How does the growth of e-commerce affect or interact with the retailing trends discussed in the chapter?

Video Segments are based on well-known large and small companies that students can identify with. Each 8-10 minute segment features an in-depth, behind-the-scenes look at the marketing issues faced by a particular company. Show the entire shorts in class on VHS or DVD, or highlight quick clips right from the PowerPoint lectures. Even choose to include the segments in your online course.

More Power

More Powerful Content

Simply put, marketing is the science and art of building and managing profitable customer relationships. Today's marketers must attract new customers by promising superior customer value. They must keep and grow current customers by delivering superior satisfaction and effectively managing the company-customer interface. Today's outstanding marketing companies are connecting more selectively, directly, and deeply with customers to form profitable customer relationships and to build customer equity. But marketers cannot go it alone. They also must be good at managing relationships with partners inside and outside the company, working together to build strong customer relationships. In the tenth edition of *Principles of Marketing*, we build on four powerful themes that go to the heart of modern marketing theory and practice.

- *Building and managing profitable customer relationships:* This framework is introduced in the first two chapters and then built upon throughout the book.
- *Building strong brands and brand equity:* Strong brands provide the basis upon which to build profitable customer relationships.
- *Marketing in a socially responsible way around the globe:* As the world becomes an increasingly smaller place, marketers must be good at marketing their brands globally and in socially responsible ways.
- *Harnessing marketing technology in the new digital age:* The Internet and other technological developments have redefined marketing strategy and customer relationship building.

Connecting with Customers

We've already discussed the critical importance of customer relationship management. The most profound new developments in marketing involve the ways in which today's companies are relating to their customers. Yesterday's companies focused on mass marketing to all comers at arm's length. Today's companies are building more direct and lasting relationships with more carefully selected customers.

Connecting with More Carefully Selected Customers

Few firms today still practice true mass marketing—selling in a standardized way to an who comes along. Today, most marketers realize that they don't want to connect wi customers. Instead, most are targeting fewer, more profitable customers.

The United States—in fact, the world—has become more of a "salad bowl" of di cultural, social, and locational groups. The greater diversity has meant greater mark tion. In response, most firms have moved from mass marketing to segmented which they target carefully chosen submarkets or even individual buyers. They build huge cust ing" has become the order of the day for some marketers. They build huge custo containing rich information on individual customer preferences and purchases. T these databases to gain insights by which they can "mass-customize" their offe greater value to individual buyers.

At the same time that companies are finding new ways to deliver more va they are also beginning to assess carefully the value of customers to the firm. The

SOLUTIONS FROM DELL, MICROSOFT AND INTEL. GIVING IMPOSSIBLE AN INFERIORITY COMPLEX.

DELL

Strategic alliances: Dell recently ran ads telling how it partners with Microsoft and Intel to provide cus tomized e-business solutions. "At Dell, Microsoft, and Intel, we specialize in solving the impossible."

Principles
of Marketing

Principles of Marketing

Tenth Edition

PHILIP KOTLER
Northwestern University

GARY ARMSTRONG
University of North Carolina

PEARSON

Prentice
Hall

PEARSON EDUCATION INTERNATIONAL

Acquisitions Editor: Wendy Craven and Katie Stevens
Editor-in-Chief: Jeff Shelstad
Assistant Editor: Melissa Pellerano
Editorial Assistant: Danielle Serra
Media Project Manager: Anthony Palmiotto
Marketing Manager: Michelle O'Brien
Marketing Assistant: Amanda Fisher
Managing Editor (Production): Judith Leale
Production Editor: Virginia Somma
Production Assistant: Joe DeProspero
Permissions Coordinator: Suzanne Grappi
Associate Director, Manufacturing: Vincent Scelta
Manufacturing Buyer: Arnold Vila
Design Manager: Maria Lange
Art Director: Blair Brown
Interior Design: Blair Brown
Cover Design: Blair Brown
Manager, Print Production: Christy Mahon
Composition: Carlisle Communications
Full-Service Project Management: Lynn Steines, Carlisle Communications
Printer/Binder: RR Donnelley—Willard

Credits and acknowledgments borrowed from other sources and reproduced,
with permission, in this textbook appear on page C-1.

If you purchased this book within the United States or Canada you should be aware that it has been wrongfully imported without
the approval of the Publisher or the Author.

Pearson Prentice Hall™ is a trademark of Pearson Education, Inc.
Pearson® is a registered trademark of Pearson plc
Pearson® is a registered trademark of Pearson Education, Inc.

Pearson Education LTD.
Pearson Education Australia PTY, Limited
Pearson Education Singapore, Pte., Ltd
Pearson Education North Asia Ltd
Pearson Education, Canada, Ltd
Pearson Educaión de Mexico, S.A. de C.V.
Pearson Education-Japan
Pearson Education Malaysia, Pte. Ltd
Pearson Education Upper Saddle River, New Jersey

10 9 8 7 6 5 4 3 2 1
ISBN 0-13-121276-1

About the Authors

As a team, Philip Kotler and Gary Armstrong provide a blend of skills uniquely suited to writing an introductory marketing text. Professor Kotler is one of the world's leading authorities on marketing. Professor Armstrong is an award-winning teacher of under-graduate business students. Together they make the complex world of marketing practical, approachable, and enjoyable.

Philip Kotler is the S. C. Johnson & Son Distinguished Professor of International Marketing at the Kellogg Graduate School of Management, Northwestern University. He received his master's degree at the University of Chicago and his Ph.D. at M.I.T., both in economics. Dr. Kotler is author of Marketing Management: Analysis, Planning, Implementation, and Control (Prentice Hall), now in its eleventh edition and the most widely used marketing textbook in graduate schools of business. He has authored several successful books and has written over 100 articles for leading journals. He is the only three-time winner of the coveted Alpha Kappa Psi award for the best annual article in the Journal of Marketing. Dr. Kotler's numerous major honors include the Paul D. Converse Award given by the American Marketing Association to honor "outstanding contributions to science in marketing" and the Stuart Henderson Britt Award as Marketer of the Year. He was named the first recipient of two major awards: the Distinguished Marketing Educator of the Year Award given by the American Marketing Association and the Philip Kotler Award for Excellence in Health Care Marketing presented by the Academy for Health Care Services Marketing. He has also received the Charles Coolidge Parlin Award which each year honors an outstanding leader in the field of marketing. In 1995, he received the Marketing Educator of the Year Award from Sales and Marketing Executives International. Dr. Kotler has served as chairman of the College on Marketing of the Institute of Management Sciences (TIMS) and a director of the American Marketing Association. He has received honorary doctorate degrees from DePaul University, the University of Zurich, and the Athens University of Economics and Business. He has consulted with many major U.S. and foreign companies on marketing strategy.

Gary Armstrong is Crist W. Blackwell Distinguished Professor of Undergraduate Education in the Kenan-Flagler Business School at the University of North Carolina at Chapel Hill. He holds undergraduate and masters degrees in business from Wayne State University in Detroit, and he received his Ph.D. in marketing from Northwestern University. Dr. Armstrong has contributed numerous articles to leading business journals. As a consultant and researcher, he has worked with many companies on marketing research, sales management, and marketing strategy. But Professor Armstrong's first love is teaching. His Blackwell Distinguished Professorship is the only permanent endowed professorship for distinguished undergraduate teaching at the University of North Carolina at Chapel Hill. He has been very active in the teaching and administration of Kenan-Flagler's undergraduate program. His recent administrative posts include Chair of the Marketing Faculty, Associate Director of the Undergraduate Business Program, Director of the Business Honors Program, and others. He works closely with business student groups and has received several campus-wide and Business School teaching awards. He is the only repeat recipient of the school's highly regarded Award for Excellence in Undergraduate Teaching, which he won three times.

Brief Contents

Contents

Part II   DEVELOPING MARKETING OPPORTUNITIES AND STRATEGIES   104

CHAPTER 6:   Consumer Markets and Consumer Buyer Behavior   177

CHAPTER 7:   Business Markets and Business Buyer Behavior   213

Part IV MANAGING MARKETING   564

A Message from the Authors

Welcome to the tenth edition of **Principles of Marketing**! With each new edition, we've worked hard to bring you the freshest and most authoritative insights into the fascinating world of marketing. As we present this new edition, we want to take a moment to thank you and the millions of other marketing students and professors who have used our text over the years. Without you, this book would never have become the international best seller that it is today. You've been our inspiration. Thank you.

Our goal for the tenth edition is to **bring more power to you**. Before we launch into a full "tour," we'd like to give you a quick preview of what we mean by a more **powerful** edition. First, the new edition builds upon a powerful theme: Marketing is the science and art of creating and managing profitable customer relationships. But marketers cannot do this alone. They must also be good at managing relationships with partners inside and outside the company, working together to connect with customers. In this new edition, we develop this **customer and partner relationship-building framework** in the first two chapters, and then expand upon it throughout the book.

Beyond the strengthened customer relationships framework, we emphasize three additional powerful themes. First, we expand our emphasis on **building strong brands and brand equity**. After all, profitable customer relationships are built upon strong brands. Next, we emphasize the importance of **socially responsible marketing around the globe**. As the world becomes an increasingly smaller place, marketers must be good at marketing their brands globally and in socially responsible ways. Finally, we include all the latest material on **harnessing marketing technology in the new digital age**. We've added a new chapter, "Marketing in the Digital Age," and lots of new information on digital developments throughout the book.

To bring even more power to you, while providing the latest marketing coverage, we make learning about and teaching marketing easier and more exciting for both students and instructors. The tenth edition presents marketing in a practical, exciting, and easy to digest way. For example, to help bring marketing to life, we've filled the text with interesting examples and stories about real companies and their marketing practices. Moreover, the integrated, cutting edge teaching and learning package gives you the power to customize your learning and teaching experience. The tenth edition's many new features and interactive enhancements are highlighted in the pages that follow.

So, **more marketing power to you**—more power in content, more power in supplements, and more power in YOUR classroom. We think that the tenth edition is the best edition yet. We hope that you'll find **Principles of Marketing** the very best text from which to learn about and teach marketing.

Sincerely,

Philip Kotler
Northwestern University

Gary Armstrong
University of North Carolina - Chapel Hill

Why Marketing Is Powerful

The goal of *Principles of Marketing, Tenth Edition*, is to introduce new marketing students to the fascinating world of modern marketing in an enjoyable and practical way. Many people see marketing only as advertising or selling. But real marketing does not involve the art of selling what you make, so much as knowing *what* to make! Organizations gain market leadership by understanding consumer needs and finding solutions that delight customers. If customer value and satisfaction are absent, no amount of advertising or selling can compensate.

Simply put, the aim of marketing is to **build and manage profitable customer relationships.** Marketers study consumer needs and wants, select target markets they can serve best, and design products, services, and programs to serve these markets. They attract new customers by promising superior value, and keep and grow current customers by delivering superior satisfaction.

16   Part 1   Understanding Marketing and the Marketing Process

Customer relationship management
The overall process of building and maintaining profitable customer relationships by delivering superior customer value and satisfaction.

"touchpoints" in order to maximize customer loyalty. We will discuss this narrower CRM activity in a later chapter dealing with marketing information.

More recently, however, customer relationship management has taken on a broader meaning. In this broader sense, **customer relationship management** is the overall process of building and maintaining profitable customer relationships by delivering superior customer value and satisfaction. Thus, today's companies are going beyond designing strategies to *attract* new customers and create *transactions* with them. They are using customer relationship management to *retain* current customers and build profitable, long-term *relationships* with them. The new view is that marketing is the science and art of finding, retaining, *and* growing profitable customers.

Why the new emphasis on retaining and growing customers? In the past, many companies took their customers for granted. Facing an expanding economy and rapidly growing markets, companies could practice a "leaky bucket" approach to marketing. Growing markets meant a plentiful supply of new customers. Companies could keep filling the marketing bucket with new customers without worrying about losing old customers through holes in the bottom of the bucket.

However, companies today face some new marketing realities. Changing demographics, more-sophisticated competitors, and overcapacity in many industries—all of these factors mean that there are fewer customers to go around. Many companies are now fighting for shares of flat or fading markets. Thus, the costs of attracting new consumers are rising. In fact, on average, it costs 5 to 10 times as much to attract a new customer as it does to keep a current customer satisfied. Sears found that it costs 12 times more to attract a customer than to keep an existing one.[13]

Customer lifetime value
The value of the entire stream of purchases that the customer would make over a lifetime of patronage.

Companies are also realizing that losing a customer means losing more than a single sale. It means losing the entire stream of purchases that the customer would make over a lifetime of patronage. For example, here is a dramatic illustration of **customer lifetime value:**

Stew Leonard, who operates a highly profitable three-store supermarket, says that he sees $50,000 flying out of his store every time he sees a sulking customer. Why? Because his average customer spends about $100 a week, shops 50 weeks a year, and remains in the area for about 10 years. If this customer has an unhappy experience and switches to another supermarket, Stew Leonard's has lost $50,000 in revenue. The loss can be much greater if the disappointed customer shares the bad experience with other customers and causes them to defect. To keep customers coming back,

Customer lifetime value: To keep customers coming back, Stew Leonard's has created the "Disneyland of dairy stores," Rule #1—the customer is always right. Rule #2—if the customer is ever wrong, reread rule #1!

Marketing is much more than just an isolated business function—it is a philosophy that guides the entire organization toward sensing, serving, and satisfying consumer needs. The marketing department cannot accomplish the company's customer relationship-building goals by itself. It must partner closely with other departments in the company and with other organizations throughout its entire value-delivery network to provide superior customer value and satisfaction. Thus, marketing calls upon everyone in the organization to "think customer" and to do all they can to help build and manage profitable customer relationships.

Marketing is all around us, and we all need to know something about it. Marketing is used not only by manufacturing companies, wholesalers, and retailers, but also by all kinds of individuals and organizations. Lawyers, accountants, and doctors use marketing to manage demand for their services. No politician can get the needed votes, and no resort the needed tourists, without developing and carrying out marketing plans.

People throughout these organizations need to know how to define and segment markets, develop attractive value propositions, and build strongly positioned brands. They must know how to price their offerings to make them attractive and affordable, and how to choose and manage intermediaries to make their products available to customers. They need to know how to advertise and promote products so that customers will know about and want them. Moreover, they must know how to adapt their marketing strategies and management to a host of new technological and global realities. Clearly, marketers need a broad range of skills in order to build profitable relationships with customers.

---

company case

Botox: Almost Trouble-Free New Faces

In the movie virgule *Face/Off*, John Travolta got a new look by exchanging faces with Nicholas Cage. Unfortunately, he got a lot of trouble along with it. Today, John could receive a much less troublesome new look by using Botox, from Allergan Laboratories in Irvine, California. Not only has Botox smoothed the visage of aging actors, it has also come to the rescue of countless comedians and late-night talk-show hosts. Beyond perhaps doing wonders for their appearance, it's also given them a slew of new jokes as the "next Viagra."

In 1990, Allergan was just a small specialty pharmaceutical firm selling little-known eye and skin drugs and over-the-counter contact lens cleaners. The introduction of Botox wasn't such a big deal initially. After all, typical of Allergan specialty products, it was just another specialty drug aimed at a small market (treatment of cross-eye) supported by little marketing effort.

That was before doctors discovered that injecting Botox around eyes not only eliminated ocular problems, it erased frown lines as well. Once that happened, the buzz was on between doctors and patients. Before long, doctors in most major U.S. cities were giving patients off-label (not approved by the FDA for this use) Botox injections. Even though Allergan could not openly market the product for cosmetic purposes, by 2001 sales of Botox rocketed to $310 million and were growing between 25 percent and 35 percent per year. That translates into over 1.6 million Botox cosmetic procedures performed on roughly 850,000 patients. FDA approval, granted in April 2002, only accelerated this sales bonanza.

The good news for Allergan does not end with wiping out frown lines. Botox also effectively treats migraine headaches, chronic neck and back pain, excessive sweating, and possibly spastic disorders. With all those target markets, Botox could become a blockbuster drug—with more than a billion dollars in sales—bringing Allergan out of the backwaters of the pharmaceutical business.

Botox Cosmetic is botulinum toxin A, a heavily diluted version of the feared botulinum toxin found in spoiled canned soups and vegetables. It contains only 20 units of the toxin compared to the thousands of units found in spoiled food, but it works in the same way—by paralyzing facial muscles to the point where they can no longer contract.

Frown lines are definitely a sign of age, use, and wear. They occur when facial muscles contract, drawing the skin up. When the muscles relax, the lines disappear. As we get older, it becomes more difficult to relax, so that we seldom fully relax our facial muscles.

Although eliminating frown lines sounds great, there is at least one small problem. Totally relaxed forehead muscles leave you incapable of rendering any expression at or above the eyes. For the celebrities and stars that were among the first to use Botox, this resulted in "performance" problems. One TV star commented that when the director kept telling her to show anger, she replied, "I am, I am." Unfortunately, nothing was moving on the upper half of her face. As a consequence, she stopped using Botox except for Emmy awards night!

For others, however, the loss of expression might be a positive. Business people seeking a softer look might want to eliminate frown lines that make them look so irritated or impatient. Trial lawyers attempting to establish rapport with juries might want to eliminate expressions of annoyance and anger. And sales representatives might want to appear unperturbed by what their clients and customers are saying. But while some observers think Botox could give us a kinder, gentler-looking America, others think it could turn us into a nation of zombies.

Besides loss of expression, Botox produces additional side effects. When used on the forehead and around the eyes, Botox can cause drooping eyelids (you won't be able to close or open them completely—this could be either a sexy or a dopey look). Used around the mouth, Botox may cause slurred speech, a droopy mouth, and constant drooling. Other possible side effects include nausea, allergic reactions, headaches, respiratory infections, flu symptoms, and redness and swelling around the injections. The redness and swelling usually go away in a couple of days.

Because Botox Cosmetic lasts only three to six months, all side effects are temporary. This also means, however, that Botox treatments must be repeated when the effects wear off. While that is bad news for consumers, it's good news for doctors. The margins on Botox are quite high—around 80 percent. A vial of Botox Cosmetic costs about $400 and can be used for four treatments. Depending on the doctor's pricing scheme, each treatment can be $500 to $1,000. That's quite a nifty profit for a treatment that usually takes less than 15 minutes, and it's quite a bill for the patient, because insurance companies don't pay for Botox Cosmetic treatments.

Botox has become so lucrative and the demand so great that the treatments are sometimes offered in a party atmosphere—sort of like a Tupperware party. Doctors usually ask a current patient to invite 10 to 15 prospective clients to a party at his or her home, where the partygoers are offered such tidbits as chocolates, brie, and champagne. After a brief social period, the doctor gives a short lecture on Botox and invites the partygoers to sign up for treatment. Patients take turns leaving the room, to the applause of other partygoers, and the doctor gives the injections in private. Parties provide a nonclinical atmosphere more conducive to patient receptivity and reduce the time and costs incurred by the doctor. Even good champagne costs less than nurses, receptionists, and rent, and the doctor can give patients a price break—maybe charging only $250 per treatment at a party. Thus, parties are "good" for everyone. Some doctors, however, object to the "party scene" on the basis that this is a medical treatment and not a social gimmick. Therefore, they hold multiple client sessions in their offices in the evening with the same benefits of price breaks for patients and lower costs and less time for themselves.

---

decide to serve only one or a few special segments or "market niches." This strategy limits sales but can be very profitable. Or a company might choose to serve several related segments—perhaps those with different kinds of customers but with the same basic wants. A large company might also decide to offer a complete range of products to serve all market segments.

Most companies enter a new market by serving a single segment, and if this proves successful, they add segments. Large companies eventually seek full market coverage. They want to be the General Motors of their industry. GM says that it makes a car for every "person, purse, and personality." The leading company normally has different products designed to meet the special needs of each segment.

Market Positioning

After a company has decided which market segments to enter, it must decide what positions it wants to occupy in those segments. A product's *position* is the place the product occupies relative to competitors in consumers' minds. Marketers want to develop unique market positions for their products. If a product is perceived to be exactly like others on the market, consumers would have no reason to buy it.

Market positioning is arranging for a product to occupy a clear, distinctive, and desirable place relative to competing products in the minds of target consumers. Thus, marketers plan positions that distinguish their products from competing brands and give them the greatest strategic advantage in their target markets. For example, the Ford Taurus is "built to last"; Chevy Blazer is "like a rock"; Toyota's economical Echo states, "It's not you. It's the car"; and Saturn is "a different kind of company, different kind of car." Lexus avows "the passionate pursuit of excellence." Jaguar is positioned as "the art of performance," and Mercedes says, "In a perfect world, everyone would drive a Mercedes." The luxurious Bentley promises "18 handcrafted feet of shameless luxury." Such deceptively simple statements form the backbone of a product's marketing strategy.

In positioning its product, the company first identifies possible competitive advantages upon which to build the position. To gain competitive advantage, the company must offer greater value to target consumers. It can do this either by charging lower prices than competitors do or by offering more benefits to justify higher prices. But if the company positions the product as offering greater value, it must then *deliver* that greater value. Thus, effective positioning begins with actually differentiating the company's marketing offer so that it gives consumers more value.

Market positioning
Arranging for a product to occupy a clear, distinctive, and desirable place relative to competing products in the minds of target consumers.

Positioning: Bentley promises "18 handcrafted feet of shameless luxury." In contrast, Toyota promises, "At 41 miles per gallon ... it's not you. It's the car." Such deceptively simple statements form the backbone of a product's marketing strategy.

More Powerful Content

Welcome to the Tenth Edition of *Principles of Marketing*!

Principles of Marketing, Tenth Edition, provides an authoritative, comprehensive, innovative, managerial, and practical introduction to marketing. It is designed to help students learn about and apply the basic concepts and practices of modern marketing as they are used in a wide variety of settings.

POWERFUL Themes in *Principles of Marketing*

Technological advances, rapid globalization, economic shifts, and cultural and environmental developments are causing profound changes in the marketplace. As the marketplace changes, so must the marketers who serve it. These new developments signify a brand new world of opportunities for forward-thinking marketers.

In light of these new developments, *Principles of Marketing, Tenth Edition* builds on four major, powerful themes that go to the heart of modern marketing theory and practice.

1. ***Building and managing profitable customer relationships***. Today's marketers must be good at ***managing customer relationships***. They must attract customers with strong value propositions, then keep and grow customers by delivering superior customer value and satisfaction and effectively managing the company-customer interface. Today's outstanding marketing companies are connecting more selectively, directly, and deeply with customers to form profitable customer relationships and build customer equity.

   Marketers must also execute ***partner relationship management***. They must work closely with partners inside and outside the company to jointly build profitable customer relationships. Successful marketers are now connecting effectively with other company departments to build strong company value chains, and with outside partners to build effective demand and supply chains and effective customer-focused alliances.

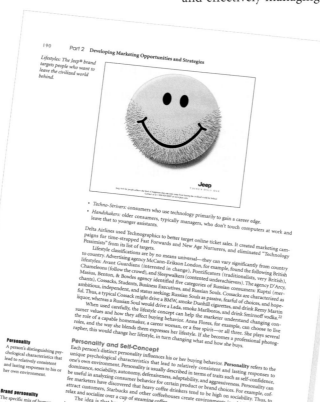

190   Part 2   Developing Marketing Opportunities and Strategies

Lifestyles: The Jeep® brand targets people who want to leave the civilized world behind.

- *Techno-Strivers*: consumers who use technology primarily to gain a career edge.
- *Handshakers*: older consumers, typically managers, who don't touch computers at work and leave that to younger assistants.

Delta Airlines used Technographics to better target online ticket sales. It created marketing campaigns for time-strapped Fast Forwards and New Age Nurturers, and eliminated "Technology Pessimists" from its list of targets.

Lifestyle classifications are by no means universal—they can vary significantly from country to country. Advertising agency McCann-Erikson London, for example, found the following British lifestyles: Avant Guardians (interested in change), Pontificators (traditionalists, very British), Chameleons (follow the crowd), and Sleepwalkers (contented underachievers). The agency D'Arcy, Masius, Benton, & Bowles agency identified five categories of Russian consumers: Kuptsi (merchants), Cossacks, Students, Business Executives, and Russian Souls. Cossacks are characterized as ambitious, independent, and status seeking; Russian Souls as passive, fearful of choices, and hopeful. Thus, a typical Cossack might drive a BMW, smoke Dunhill cigarettes, and drink Remy Martin liquor, whereas a Russian Soul would drive a Lada, smoke Marlboros, and drink Smirnoff vodka.[22]

When used carefully, the lifestyle concept can help the marketer understand changing consumer values and how they affect buying behavior. Anna Flores, for example, can choose to live the role of a capable homemaker, a career woman, or a free spirit—all three. She plays several roles, and the way she blends them expresses her lifestyle. If she becomes a professional photographer, this would change her lifestyle, in turn changing what and how she buys.

Personality and Self-Concept

Personality
A person's distinguishing psychological characteristics that lead to relatively consistent and lasting responses to his or her own environment.

Each person's distinct personality influences his or her buying behavior. **Personality** refers to the unique psychological characteristics that lead to relatively consistent and lasting responses to one's own environment. Personality is usually described in terms of traits such as self-confidence, dominance, sociability, autonomy, defensiveness, adaptability, and aggressiveness. Personality can be useful in analyzing consumer behavior for certain product or brand choices. For example, coffee marketers have discovered that heavy coffee drinkers tend to be high on sociability. Thus, to attract customers, Starbucks and other coffeehouses create environments in which people can relax and socialize over a cup of steaming coffee.

Brand personality
The specific mix of human traits that may be attributed to a particular brand.

The idea is that brands also have personalities, and that consumers are likely to choose brands whose personalities match their own. A **brand personality** is the specific mix of human traits that may be attributed to a particular brand. One researcher identified five brand personality traits:[23]

2. ***Building and managing strong brands***. Well-positioned brands with strong brand equity provide the basis upon which to build profitable customer relationships. Today's marketers must be good at positioning their brands powerfully and managing them well.

3. ***Harnessing new marketing technologies in this digital age***. New digital and other high-tech marketing developments, including the explosion of the Internet, are having a dramatic impact on both buyers and the marketers who serve them. Today's marketers must know how to leverage new computer, information, communication, and transportation technologies to connect more effectively with customers and marketing partners in this new digital age.

4. ***Marketing in a socially responsible way around the globe***. As technological developments make the world an increasingly smaller place, marketers must market their brands globally and in socially responsible ways.

More Powerful *Real Marketing* Applications

Principles of Marketing, Tenth Edition tells the stories that reveal the drama of modern marketing. While the majority of vignettes and *Real Marketing* exhibits are brand-new to this edition, we also retain some of the popular classics from previous editions. We think it's important to show how strategies at best-practice and up-and-coming companies change and continuously evolve. Some real marketing examples from the tenth edition include the following:

- **MTV**'s phenomenal success in international markets

- **Google**'s survival amid the dot-com meltdown

- **AT&T**'s focus on brand and value rather than price in its through the mLife campaign

- **Ritz-Carlton**'s zeal for taking care of customers

- **Home Depot**'s penchant for taking care of those who take care of customers

- **Kmart**'s BlueLight strategy and how it started a price war only Wal-Mart could win

- **Charles Schwab Corporation**'s transformation from a traditional "brick-and-mortar" marketer to a full-fledged, industry-leading "click-and-mortar" marketer

- **Microsoft**'s passion for innovation and its quest for "the Next Big Thing"

- **Dell Computer**'s stunning direct selling formula

- **Coca-Cola**'s international marketing prowess

After studying this chapter you should be able to

1. discuss how the international trade system, economic, political-legal, and cultural environments affect a company's international marketing decisions
2. describe three key approaches to entering international markets
3. explain how companies adapt their marketing mixes for international markets
4. identify the three major forms of international marketing organization

592

real marketing 3.2

"We Love You, Google Users"—and Advertisers, Too!

When you think back to the early dot-com boom, you probably think of brash, fast-growing startups led by offbeat, young entrepreneurs offering unique work environments to attract creative and talented employees. Google, the Web search services provider, is no different. Founded in September 1998 by Sergey Brin and Larry Page, then 25 and 29 years old, Google got its start in a rented garage, complete with a washer, dryer, and hot tub. Since then, it has grown from three employees to nearly 300. And like many dot-coms, Google offers a relaxed and friendly environment to woo and keep the best employees.

There's no official starting time at Google—or ending time for that matter. It's not about rules here. Far from it. No, workers . . . set their own hours, get back-rubs from a company masseuse, even bake bread from scratch if the mood strikes them. When he does arrive, [co-founder] Brin skates into the Googleplex, as headquarters is called—past the undulating red, blue, and yellow lava lamps, the crimson couch, and the self-playing ebony grand piano with Muppet-theme sheet music. . . . At any moment, Yoshka, a 100-plus pound Leonberger (think Saint Bernard), might come trotting around the corner with his owner.

Although this start-up story mirrors that of previous dot-coms, for Google there is one big difference. Whereas other dot-coms have struggled, Google is growing at a phenomenal rate: some 20 percent a month. More than 365 million unique visitors use Google's search engine each month to search 2 billion Web pages. They spend nearly 13 million hours a month searching on Google; second-place Yahoo! logs less than half that figure. Google users make more than 150 million queries each day—2,000 per second during peak hours. Half of the queries originate from outside of the United States, where Google offers search services in 28 different languages. Even more amazing, most of these searches are answered within half a second.

Perhaps more surprising, unlike most other dot-coms, Google turns a profit. In fact, Google is three times more profitable than eBay was at the same stage in its development. What's behind this incredible success? Google's technology is an important part of the equation. Page and Brin started the company to promote their PageRank search technology, which has revolutionized Internet searching. The Google search engine returns results that are usually more reliable and more useful than those of other search engines.

Beyond this revolutionary technology, Google has triumphed because it has focused heavily on helping users search. Unlike Yahoo! and other competitors, Google opted not to offer e-mail, shopping, and other services. Its Web site promises "a laser-like focus on finding the right answer for each and every inquiry." In fact, the name of the company is a play on the word googol, a mathematical term for a 1 followed by 100 zeros. It's a very large number. Google chose the name to reflect its mission to organize and make accessible the immense amount of information available on the Web. By focusing only on Internet searching, Google positions itself as "the World's Best Search Engine—accurate and easy to use." Users rave about Google's simple, search-only home page, uncluttered with news reports or banner ads.

The best part is that Google's extraordinary services are free to users. But how, then, does Google make money? About half of Google's revenues come from contracts with corporate partners to provide search services for their own Internet and intranet sites. Today, more than 130 companies in 30 different countries rely on Google's WebSearch and SiteSearch technologies to power the search services on their Web sites. These partners include companies such as Yahoo!, the Washington Post, Cisco, Red Hat, Palm, Nextel, Virgin, Netscape, Sony, and Cingular Wireless.

The other half of Google's revenues come from advertising sales. By attracting the largest online audience in the world, Google has made itself a very attractive advertising medium. Here's how it works. Through constant data mining, Google determines which search terms are most popular. It then approaches companies who sell in those categories and offers them space for sponsored ad messages and links for a fee. Then, when someone searches Google for a topic related to the sponsor's product or service, a tasteful ad box appears at the top or side of the Google results page, containing a short ad message and links to the sponsor's Web site.

Try it yourself. Go to the Google site (www.google.com), type in a search word or phrase, and see what advertiser messages and links appear. For example, if you search "Disneyland," you'll see ads and links at the top of the search list for online travel services Expedia and Orbitz. The ads promise "Save up to 70% on Disneyland Hotels with Expedia!" and "Incredible deals on Disneyland at Orbitz!" Search "barbeque grills" and you're greeted with "Shop Sears for brand name grills

With the world's largest online search audience, Google has become a very attractive advertising medium. It's highly targeted ads reach users when they are already searching for related information.

After studying this chapter you should be able to

1. explain how companies find and develop new-product ideas
2. list and define the steps in the new-product development process
3. describe the stages of the product life cycle
4. describe how marketing strategies change during the product's life cycle

312

What's New. . . What's Changed

1. ***A powerful new "customer relationships" framework:*** This new edition is organized around a powerful *managing profitable customer relationships* framework for teaching and learning marketing.

   - A retitled and heavily revised Chapter 1—"Marketing: Managing Profitable Customer Relationships"—establishes this *customer relationships* theme at the start of the text. A new Chapter 1 section, *Managing Customer Relationships,* pulls together the latest thinking on creating superior customer value and satisfaction in order to attract, retain, and grow customers and maximize customer equity. The closing section of Chapter 1 presents a final relationships theme—*connecting*—that summarizes how changes in technology have impacted how companies connect with customers, marketing partners, and the world around them.

   - A retitled and streamlined "Managing Marketing Information" Chapter 5 includes a major new section on Customer Relationship Management (CRM), and software and analytical techniques for organizing and applying customer information from all customer touchpoints to build stronger customer relationships.

   - The customer and marketing partner relationships theme is carried forward into later chapters. In all, from the first chapter to the last, *Principles of Marketing* is organized around a powerfully enhanced theme: *developing and managing profitable customer and marketing partner relationships.*

2. ***A new chapter: "Marketing in the Digital Age":*** The new Chapter 3 addresses the impact of the Internet and other developments in today's high-tech marketing environment on marketing strategy and customer relationship building. The new digital age is having a dramatic impact on both buyers and the marketers who serve them. To succeed—even to survive—marketers must rethink their strategies and practices. The new chapter explores the major forces shaping the digital age; major e-marketing developments in B2C, B2B, C2C, and C2B domains; and strategies and tactics for setting up a successful e-commerce presence. Unlike most other texts, which treat this material as an end-of-book afterthought, *Principles of Marketing* presents it up front, where it becomes an important part of the underlying fabric of marketing. This early coverage sets a platform for countless examples of digital developments integrated throughout the remainder of the text.

3. ***Building strong brands and brand equity:*** Chapter 9— "Product, Services, and Branding Strategies" —now includes a separate and expanded section: *Building Strong Brands.* The section includes new material on brand equity, brand positioning, managing brands, and rebranding. Chapter 8— "Segmentation, Targeting, and Positioning: Building the Right Relationships with the Right Customers" —presents a new discussion on developing brand positioning statements.

4. *Socially responsible marketing around the globe:* The tenth edition of *Principles of Marketing* continues its strong coverage of socially responsible marketing and global marketing.

- *Marketing ethics, environmentalism, and social responsibility:* This coverage appears in almost every chapter, plus in a full chapter on social responsibility and marketing ethics.

- *Global marketing:* This important topic is integrated chapter-by-chapter plus featured in a full chapter focusing on global marketing considerations.

5. *Other additions and enhancements:* The tenth edition contains new material on a wide range of subjects, including customer relationship management and partner relationship management; the digital age and Internet marketing; customer lifetime value and customer equity; brand equity, brand building, brand management, and rebranding; value propositions, positioning, and positioning statements; demand chain and supply chain management; the new direct marketing model and database marketing; customized and customerized marketing; online marketing research; value pricing and dynamic pricing; integrated marketing communications and buzz marketing; Web selling and online sales training; marketing and diversity; environmental sustainability; global marketing strategy; and much more.

Chapter 9 Product, Services, and Branding Strategies 291

product lines are consistent insofar as they are consumer products that go through the same distribution channels. The lines are less consistent insofar as they perform different functions for buyers.

These product mix dimensions provide the handles for defining the company's product strategy. The company can increase its business in four ways. It can add new product lines, thus widening its product mix. In this way, its new lines build on the company's reputation in its other lines. The company can lengthen its existing product lines to become a more full-line company. Or it can add more versions of each product and thus deepen its product mix. Finally, the company can pursue more product line consistency—or less—depending on whether it wants to have a strong reputation in a single field or in several fields.

Branding Strategy: Building Strong Brands

Some analysts see brands as the major enduring asset of a company, outlasting the company's specific products and facilities. John Stewart, co-founder of Quaker Oats, once said, "If this business were split up, I would give you the land and bricks and mortar, and I would keep the brands and trademarks, and I would fare better than you." The CEO of McDonald's agrees:

A McDonald's board member who worked at Coca-Cola once talked to us about the value of our brand. He said if every asset we own, every building, and every piece of equipment were destroyed in a terrible natural disaster, we would be able to borrow all the money to replace it very quickly because of the value of our brand. And he's right. The brand is more valuable than the totality of all these assets.[19]

Thus, brands are powerful assets that must be carefully developed and managed. In this section, we examine the key strategies for building and managing brands.

Brand Equity

Brands are more than just names and symbols. Brands represent consumers' perceptions and feelings about a product and its performance—everything that the product or service *means* to consumers. As

A strong brand is a valuable asset. How many familiar brands and brand symbols can you find in this picture?

162 Part 2 Developing Marketing Opportunities and Strategies

Siebel's CRM software integrates individual customer data from every touch point to help build customer relationships. Using CRM, the Siebel customer shown in this ad increased customer satisfaction 86 percent and revenues per customer 20 percent.

about individual customers to provide a 360-degree view of the customer relationship. It pulls together, analyzes, and provides easy access to customer information from all of the various touch points. Companies use CRM analysis to assess the value of individual customers, identify the best ones to target, and customize the company's products and interactions to each customer.

CRM analysts develop *data warehouses* and use sophisticated *data mining* techniques to unearth the riches hidden in customer data. A data warehouse is a companywide electronic storehouse of customer information—a centralized database of finely detailed customer data that needs to be sifted through for gems. The purpose of a data warehouse is not to gather information—many companies have already amassed endless stores of information about their customers. Rather, the purpose is to allow managers to integrate the information the company already has. Then, once the data warehouse brings the data together for analysis, the company uses high-powered data-mining techniques to sift through the mounds of data and dig out interesting relationships and findings about customers.

Companies can gain many benefits from customer relationship management. By understanding customers better, they can provide higher levels of customer service and develop deeper customer relationships. They can use CRM to pinpoint high-value customers, target them more effectively, cross-sell the company's products, and create offers tailored to specific customer requirements. Consider the following examples:[18]

FedEx recently launched a multimillion-dollar CRM system in an effort to cut costs, improve its customer support, and use its existing customer data to cross-sell and up-sell services to potential or existing customers. The new system gives every member of FedEx's 3,300-person sales force a comprehensive view of every customer, detailing each one's needs and suggesting services that might meet those needs. For instance, if a customer who does a lot of international shipping calls to arrange a delivery, a sales rep will see a detailed customer history on his or her computer screen, assess the customer's needs, and determine the most appro-

Chapter 3 Marketing in the Digital Age: Making New Customer Connections 91

Gillette used viral marketing to introduce the three-bladed Venus razor for women, greatly expanding the audience reached by its "Celebrate the Goddess in You" truck tour and beach-site promotions.

sion and print media. Many marketers still question the value of Internet advertising as an effective tool. Costs are reasonable compared with those of other advertising media, but Web surfers can easily ignore such advertising and often do. Although many firms are experimenting with Web advertising, it plays only a minor role in most promotion mixes.

As a result, online advertising expenditures still represent only a small fraction of overall advertising media expenditures. Last year, online advertising spending amounted to just $7.2 billion, a mere 3.1 percent of the total spent offline. Moreover, in spite of its early promise, the growth of online advertising spending has slowed recently. According to one account:

The Internet was supposed to be the ultimate ad medium, the killer app that would eclipse newspapers, magazines, even television. But it's become increasingly clear that the online ad boom was largely a mirage, one created by the unfettered spending of the dot-coms themselves. Those days are over.[40]

Despite the recent setbacks, some industry insiders remain optimistic about the future of online advertising.[41] And some Web sites, such as Google, have been successful in creating effective online advertising processes and environments (see Real Marketing 3.2). Whatever its future, companies are now seeking more effective forms and uses for Web advertising and marketing.

Creating or Participating in Web Communities

The popularity of forums and newsgroups has resulted in a rash of commercially sponsored Web sites called **Web communities**, which take advantage of the C2C properties of the Internet. Such sites allow members to congregate online and exchange views on issues of common interest. They are the cyberspace equivalent to a Starbucks coffeehouse, a place where everybody knows your address.

Web communities
Web sites upon which members can congregate online and exchange views on issues of common interest.

For example, iVillage.com is a Web community in which women can exchange views and obtain information, support, and solutions on families, food, fitness, relationships, relaxation, home and garden, news and issues, or just about any other topic. The site draws 393 million page views per month, putting it in a league with magazines such as *Cosmopolitan, Glamour,* and *Vogue.* Another example is MyFamily.com, which aspires to be the largest and most active online community in the world for families. It provides free, private Web discussions, share family news, create online family members can connect online to hold family discussions, share family news, create online family photo albums, maintain a calendar of family events, share family history information, jointly build

A More Powerful Look and Feel

- Countless new chapter-opening examples and *Real Marketing* exhibits have been added to illustrate important concepts using real business applications.

- A brand-new design and redrawn figures give this edition a fresh, new feel. All tables, figures, examples, and references throughout the text have been thoroughly updated.

- New photos and advertisements have been added. These illustrations appear larger and more vivid than ever before.

- All of the real-life company cases are new or revised, as are the videos that accompany the text. These cases and videos help to bring the real world directly to the student and into the classroom.

More Powerful Learning Aids

- *Looking Ahead: Previewing the Concepts.* A section at the beginning of each chapter briefly previews chapter concepts, links them to concepts in previous chapters, presents chapter learning objectives, and introduces the chapter-opening marketing story.

- *Looking Back: Reviewing the Concepts.* A summary at the end of each chapter reviews major chapter concepts and chapter objectives.

- *Chapter-opening marketing stories.* Each chapter starts with a dramatic marketing story that introduces the chapter material and sparks student interest.

- *Real Marketing highlights.* Go behind the scenes for an in-depth look at real marketing practices at large and small companies.

- *Visuals.* Marketing is a visual subject matter, so throughout each chapter we feature plenty of colorful figures, photographs, advertisements, and illustrations to help reinforce key concepts and applications.

- *Discussing the Concepts* and *Applying the Concepts.* Each chapter contains a set of discussion questions and application exercises covering major chapter concepts.

- *Digital Connections.* Each chapter ends with an interactive Internet exercise that relates to important chapter concepts.

- *Reviewing the Key Terms.* Key terms are highlighted within the text, clearly defined in the margins of the pages in which they appear, and listed at the end of each chapter.

- *Company Cases.* Company cases for class or written discussion are provided at the end of each chapter. These cases challenge students to apply marketing principles to real companies in real situations.

- *Case Pilot Cases.* This new feature is designed to help students to develop the fundamentals of case study analysis. Case projects appear at the end of each part and students can visit **www.prenhall.com/kotler** to use a free interactive case analysis tool.

- *Video Shorts.* These short vignettes and discussion questions appear at the end of every chapter. They are designed for use with the brand-new 3-to-4 minute videos clips that accompany this edition. The video clips can be accessed at **www.prenhall.com/kotler** or in the Instructor's Video Library.

- *Appendixes.* Two appendixes, "Measuring and Forecasting Demand" and "Marketing Arithmetic" appear at the end of the text and provide additional, practical information for students.

- *Glossary and Indexes.* At the end of the book, an extensive glossary provides quick reference to the key terms found in the book. Subject, company, and author indexes reference all information and examples in the book.

More Powerful Supplements:
In Your Class, Everywhere, Anywhere

FOR THE INSTRUCTOR

NEW **Prentice Hall Asset Library (PAL):** Portable case that includes Instructor Course Organizer CD, DVD format of videos, and all art from the text.

Instructor's Manual: This teaching guide contains chapter overviews and objectives, plus detailed lecture outlines and incorporates figures and assignments from the text. It includes suggested discussion questions and exercises, plus review questions and answers along with extra projects.

Test Item File: This test bank is brand-new and completely revamped since the last edition! It includes thousands of questions of varying type—multiple-choice, true/false, and short-answer. Page references and level of difficulty indicators are provided for each question.

New TestGen–EQ Software: The new TestGen–EQ test generation software, a computerized package that allows instructors to custom design, save, and generate classroom tests. The test program permits instructors to edit, add, or delete questions from the test bank; analyze test results, and organize a database of tests and students results. The new software allows for greater flexibility and ease of use. It provides many options for organizing and displaying tests, along with a search and sort feature.

PowerPoint Express: Easily customizable for even the most novice user, this presentation package includes basic chapter outlines and key points from each chapter. It's the best option if you want to incorporate your own material or print to use as handouts.

PowerPoint Expanded: This expanded presentation package includes the basics found in the Express version but also advertisements and art from the text, plus Web links and video bytes. It's the best option if you want a complete presentation solution! Both PowerPoint presentation formats are available at www.prenhall.com/kotler and on the Instructor Course Organizer CD-ROM.

Color Overhead Transparencies: This supplement includes key figures from the text, key concepts, and various print advertisements and photos.

 Instructor Course Organizer CD-ROM: This CD provides one source for all of your supplement needs. This Instructor CD contains art and advertisements from the book plus the text's print and technology supplements on a single CD-ROM. Enjoy the freedom to transport the entire supplements package from your home, to your office, to your classroom. The Instructor CD-ROM enables you to customize any of the ancillaries, print only the chapters or materials you wish to use, or access any item from the package within the classroom.

 PH Marketing Video Gallery: Video Segments and Video Shorts

Available on VHS, DVD and Online!

All New Video Segments: In cunjunction with BusinessNow, bring large and small companies into your classroom. Each 8- to 10-minute segment features an in-depth, behind-the-scenes look at marketing issues faced by a best-practice or up-and-coming company. Sample companies include: Sony, Honest Tea, Marriott, and Swiss Army.

All New Video Shorts: At the end of each chapter, students are asked to watch a 4-minute video featuring an entrepreneurial company and then answer 3 to 4 related questions. Show the Video Shorts in class or go to www.prenhall.com/kotler to watch them anytime.

Innovative Online Courses and Teaching/Learning Support: Online course content is available with text adoption for Blackboard, WebCT, and CourseCompass platforms. You need no technical expertise. Teach a complete online course or a Web-enhanced course. Add your own materials, take advantage of online testing and Gradebook features, and use innovative bulletin board and discussion-thread functions. All course content and access is free upon adoption of this text.

FOR THE INSTRUCTOR AND STUDENT

www.prenhall.com/kotler

Go beyond the text. Our acclaimed Web resource provides professors and students with a customized course Website that features a complete array of teaching and learning material.

For Instructors: Download the Instructor's Resource Manual, PowerPoint slides, video transcripts, and additional resources such as *Marketing ADventure*. Or, try the Syllabus Builder to plan your own course! Contact your Prentice Hall representative about securing a password.

For the Instructor and Student: View online all of the video segments that accompany this text.

Access a free interactive Study Guide that includes self-quizzes and immediate feedback.

FOR THE STUDENT:

The Marketing Plan: A Handbook **by Marian Burk Wood**. Concise and user-friendly, this new text guides students through the process of developing a realistic, customized marketing plan by applying concepts learned in the classroom. It includes Marketing PlanPro, an award-winning commercial software package that leads students through the entire marketing plan process. The Marketing PlanPro CD-ROM features various sample marketing plans, step-by-step guides, help wizards, and customizable charts. Ask your Prentice Hall representative how this new handbook can be value-packaged with this textbook at a deep discount.

Navigating WebCT or Navigating BlackBoard—A Student's Guide. Beginning with a brief introduction to the Internet and the World Wide Web, these lively guides help students understand and master the basic navigation path through a WebCT or BlackBoard Online Course. The guides cover WebCT 3.7 or BlackBoard 5.0+. It's the definitive offline tool for the online student! These guides are available as a value-package option.

WWW.PRENHALL.COM/KOTLER

Acknowledgments

No book is the work only of its authors. We owe much to the pioneers of marketing who first identified its major issues and developed its concepts and techniques. Our thanks also go to our colleagues at the J. L. Kellogg Graduate School of Management, Northwestern University, and at the Kenan-Flagler Business School, University of North Carolina at Chapel Hill, for ideas and suggestions. We owe special thanks to Lew Brown and Martha McEnally, both of the University of North Carolina at Greensboro, for their valuable work in preparing high-quality company cases. We also thank Andrea Meyer of WorkingKnowledge for her fine contributions. A note of gratitude to our supplement authors, Rusty Brooks, and others who helped coordinate supplements.

Instructor's Manual — John R. Brooks, Jr. *Houston Baptist University*

Test Item File — David Murphy *Madisonville Community College*

PowerPoints — Karen E. James *Louisiana State University, Shreveport*

Internet Study Guide — Thomas Paczkowski *Cayuga Community College*

Video Guide — Howard Olsen *University of Nevada, Reno*

Kotler's Marketing ADventure Exercises — Patricia M. Bernson *County College of Morris*

Finally, we thank Mandy Roylance for her dedicated and high quality editorial and developmental assistance.

Many reviewers at other colleges provided valuable comments and suggestions. We are indebted to the following colleagues:

Simon Walls *University of Tennessee*

David J. Burns *Youngstown State University*

Tamara Mangleburg *Florida Atlantic University*

Alicia Cooper *Morgan State University*

Sana Akili *Iowa State University*

Laurie Babin *University of Southern Mississippi*

Howard W. Olsen *University of Nevada, Reno*

Thomas Brashear *Isenberg School of Management, University of Massachusetts, Amherst*

We would also like to thank the many colleagues who reviewed previous editions of this book:

Sang T. Choe *University of Southern Indiana*

Mark Alpert *University of Texas at Austin*

Patricia M. Manninen *North Shore Community College*

Martin Meyers *University of Wisconsin, Stevens Point*

Andrew Yap *Florida International University*

Irvin A Zaenglein *Northern Michigan University*

Martin St. John *Westmoreland County Community College*

Preyas Desai *Purdue University*

Carl Obermiller *Seattle University*

Richard Leventhal *Metropolitan State College, Denver*

Allan L. Appell *San Francisco State University*

John Stovall *University of Illinois, Chicago*

Jeff Streiter *SUNY Brockport*

H. Lee Meadow *Northern Illinois University*

Alan T. Shao *University of North Carolina, Charlotte*

David M. Nemi *Niagra County Community College*

J. Ford Laumer, Jr. *Auburn University*

Donna Tillman *California State Polytechnic University*

We also owe a great deal to the people at Prentice Hall who helped develop this book. Editors Wendy Craven and Katie Stevens provided energetic support and ably managed the many facets of this complex revision project. Bruce Kaplan provided early feedback and necessary nudging. We also owe much thanks to Judy Leale and Virginia Somma, who helped shepherd the project smoothly through production. Additional thanks go to Executive Marketing Manager Michelle O'Brien, who provided many good ideas, a keen design eye, and a positive attitude.

Finally, we owe many thanks to our families—Kathy, KC, Keri, Mandy, and Matt; and Nancy, Amy, Melissa, and Jessica—for their constant support and encouragement. To them, we dedicate this book.

Philip Kotler

Gary Armstrong

After studying this chapter you should be able to

1. define what marketing is and discuss its core concepts
2. define marketing management and compare the five marketing management orientations
3. discuss customer relationship management and strategies for building lasting customer relationships
4. analyze the major challenges facing marketers heading into the new "connected" millennium

Marketing

MANAGING PROFITABLE CUSTOMER RELATIONSHIPS

LOOKING AHEAD: PREVIEWING THE CONCEPTS

Welcome to the exciting world of marketing! In this chapter, to start you off, we will introduce you to the basic concepts of marketing. We'll first define marketing and its key concepts. Then, we'll look at the various orientations that guide marketing management. Next, we'll examine perhaps the most important concept of modern marketing—customer relationship management. Above all else, marketing seeks to create and manage profitable customer relationships by delivering superior value to customers. Finally, we'll outline the challenges marketing faces in the twenty-first century. Understanding these basic concepts, and forming your own ideas about what they really mean to you, will give you a solid foundation for all that follows.

To set the stage, let's first look at Amazon.com. In only a few years, Amazon.com has blossomed from an obscure dot-com upstart into one of the best-known names on the Internet. In the process, it has forever changed the practice of marketing. It pioneered the use of Web technology to build strong, one-to-one customer relationships based on creating genuine customer value. The only problem: This seemingly successful company has yet to prove that it can turn long-term profit. As you read on, ask yourself: Will Amazon.com eventually become the Wal-Mart of the Internet? Or will it become just another dot-com has-been?

Chances are, when you think of shopping on the Web, you think first of Amazon.com. Amazon.com first opened its virtual doors in mid-July 1995, selling books out of founder Jeff Bezos's garage in suburban Seattle. It still sells books—by the millions. But it now sells products in a dozen other categories as well: from music, videos, consumer electronics, and computers to tools and hardware, kitchen and housewares, and toys and baby products. "We have the Earth's Biggest Selection," declares the company's Web site.

In only a few short years, upstart Amazon.com has become the best-known name on the Net. In the process, it is also rewriting the rules of marketing. "By pioneering—and darn near perfecting—the art of selling online, . . . [Amazon.com has caused] a wrenching shift to a new way of doing business," asserts business analyst Robert Hof. Its most ardent fans view Amazon.com as *the* model for New Economy businesses of the twenty-first century. If any dot-com can make it, they believe, Amazon.com will.

But not everything is clicking smoothly for Amazon.com. If you believe the skeptics, the company may already be out of business by the time you read this story. Attracting customers and sales hasn't been a problem. In just the past two years, Amazon.com's customer base has grown more than eightfold to 35 million customers in more than 220 countries. Sales have rocketed from a modest $15 million a year in 1996 to more than $3.6 billion today. So, what's the problem? Profits—or a lack thereof. Amazon.com's losses have mounted almost as fast as its sales. Although Amazon.com turned its first quarterly profit in 2002, doubters say that Amazon.com's Web-only model can never be truly profitable.

No matter what your view on its future, there's little doubt that Amazon.com is an outstanding marketing company. To its core, the company is relentlessly customer driven. "The thing that drives everything is creating genuine value for customers," says founder Jeff Bezos. "Nothing happens without that." A few years back, when asked when Amazon.com would start putting profits first rather than growth, Bezos replied, "Customers come first. If you focus on what customers want and build a relationship, they will allow you to make money."

The relationship with customers is the key to the company's future. Anyone at Amazon.com will tell you that the company wants to do much more than just sell books or DVDs or digital cameras. It wants to deliver a special *experience* to every customer. "The customer experience really matters," says Bezos. "We've focused on just having a better store, where it's easier to shop, where you can learn more about the products, where you have a bigger selection, and where you have the lowest prices. You combine all of that stuff together and people say, 'Hey, these guys really get it.'"

And they do get it. Most Amazon.com regulars feel a surprisingly strong and personal relationship with the company, especially given the almost complete lack of actual human interaction. Last year, the American Customer Satisfaction Index rated Amazon the highest ever in customer satisfaction for a service company, regardless of industry. Analyst Geoffrey Colvin comments:

> I travel a lot and talk with all kinds of people, and I'm struck by how many of them speak passionately about their retail experience with Amazon.com. . . . How can people get so cranked up about an experience in which they don't see, touch, or hear another soul? The answer is that Amazon.com creates a more human relationship than most people realize. . . . The experience has been crafted so carefully that most of us actually enjoy it. It results from many people at headquarters obsessing over what customers want in a fundamentally new kind of relationship, the online experience.

Amazon.com really does obsess over making each customer's experience uniquely personal. For example, the site's "Recommendations" feature prepares personalized product recommendations, and its "New for You" feature links customers through to their own personalized home pages. Amazon.com was first to use "collaborative filtering" technology, which sifts through each customer's past purchases and the purchasing patterns of customers with similar profiles to come up with personalized site content. "We want Amazon.com to be the right store for you as an individual," says Bezos. "If we have 35 million customers, we should have 35 million stores."

Visitors to Amazon.com's Web site receive a unique blend of benefits: huge selection, good value, convenience, and what Amazon vice president Jason Kilar calls "discovery." In books alone, for example, Amazon.com offers an easily searchable virtual selection of more than 3 million titles, 15 times more than any physical bookstore. Good value comes in the form of reasonable prices, with everyday discounts off suggested retail. And at Amazon.com, it's irresistibly convenient to buy. You can log on, find what you want, and order with a single mouse click, all in less time than it takes to find a parking space at the local mall.

But it's the "discovery" factor that makes the Amazon.com experience really special. Once on the Web site, you're compelled to stay for a while—looking, learning, and discovering. Amazon.com has become a kind of online community, in which customers can browse for products, research purchase alternatives, share opinions and reviews with other visitors, and chat online with authors and experts.

In addition to the ability to develop personalized relationships with millions of customers, selling on the Internet gives Amazon.com some real advantages over brick-and-mortar rivals. By selling direct, Amazon.com avoids the huge costs of building and operating stores and carrying large inventories. And whereas traditional retailers must continually build new stores to grow revenues, Amazon.com can boost sales by simply attracting more customers to its single existing Web store.

Selling on the Web also presents serious challenges. Although it doesn't face store costs, Amazon.com has had to make large initial investments in such things as computer systems, distribution centers, and customer acquisition. Perhaps more important, many people still like shopping in a real store, where they can rub elbows with other shoppers, touch and try out the merchandise, buy goods on the spot, and easily return purchases that don't work out.

Many experts predict that the future will belong to retailers who offer *both* "clicks" and "bricks." In fact, almost 60 percent of consumer online revenues are now captured by companies that sell both online and through traditional stores. In response to these new realities, Amazon.com is partnering with real-world retailers such as Target, Toys "R" Us, Circuit City, and Borders. The brick-and-mortar partners handle purchasing and inventory; Amazon.com oversees the customer experience—maintaining the Web site, attracting customers, filling orders, and managing customer service. Thus, the upstart Web seller that once threatened to replace the giant brick-and-mortar retailers is now becoming their best friend.

So, what do you think? Does Amazon.com really create superior value for customers? Will it eventually become the Wal-Mart of the Web? Or will it end up as just another dot-com has-been? Here's one analyst's conclusion:

> I'm betting on Amazon.com. . . . In the old days, only small outfits could keep track of customers: your local tailor, the local barber, the butcher at the grocery store. [Lately,] we've bemoaned the loss of that personal touch. The Net can bring it back. Amazon.com [understands] that the real opportunity is in using the technology to build long-term relationships. . . . What Amazon.com has done is invent and implement a model for interacting with millions of customers, one at a time. Old-line companies can't do that. . . . Amazon.com's technology gives me exactly what I want, in an extraordinarily responsive way.

Whatever its fate, Amazon.com has forever changed the face of marketing. "No matter what becomes of Amazon," says the analyst, "it has taught us something new."[1]

Today's successful companies at all levels have one thing in common: Like Amazon.com, they are strongly customer focused and heavily committed to marketing. These companies share a passion for understanding and satisfying the needs of customers in well-defined target markets. They motivate everyone in the organization to help build lasting customer relationships through superior customer value and satisfaction. As co-founder Bernie Marcus of Home Depot asserts, "All of our people understand what the Holy Grail is. It's not the bottom line. It's an almost blind, passionate commitment to taking care of customers."

What Is Marketing?

Marketing, more than any other business function, deals with customers. Building customer relationships based on customer value and satisfaction is at the very heart of modern marketing. Although we will soon explore more detailed definitions of marketing, perhaps the simplest definition is this one: Marketing is managing profitable customer relationships. The twofold goal of marketing is to attract new customers by promising superior value and to keep and grow current customers by delivering satisfaction.

Wal-Mart has become the world's largest retailer by delivering on its promise, "Always low prices. Always!" Ritz-Carlton promises—and delivers—truly "memorable experiences" for its hotel guests. AT&T says, "It's all within your reach—one connection: across town, across the country, across the world." At Disney theme parks, "imaginers" work wonders in their quest to create fantasies and "make a dream come true today." Dell leads the personal computer industry by consistently making good on its promise to "be direct," making it easy for customers to custom-design their own computers and have them delivered quickly to their doorsteps or desktops. These and other highly successful companies know that if they take care of their customers, market share and profits will follow.

Sound marketing is critical to the success of every organization—large or small, for-profit or not-for-profit, domestic or global. Large for-profit firms such as Microsoft, Sony, Wal-Mart, IBM, Charles Schwab, and Marriott use marketing. But so do not-for-profit organizations such as colleges, hospitals, museums, symphony orchestras, and even churches. Moreover, marketing is practiced not only in the United States but also in the rest of the world.

You already know a lot about marketing—it's all around you. You see the results of marketing in the abundance of products in your nearby shopping mall. You see marketing in the advertisements that fill your TV, spice up your magazines, stuff your mailbox, or enliven your Web pages. At home, at school, where you work, and where you play, you see marketing in almost everything you do. Yet, there is much more to marketing than meets the consumer's casual eye. Behind it all is a massive network of people and activities competing for your attention and purchases.

This book will give you a more complete and formal introduction to the basic concepts and practices of today's marketing. In this chapter, we begin by defining marketing and its core concepts.

Marketing Defined

What does the term *marketing* mean? Many people think of marketing only as selling and advertising. And no wonder—every day we are bombarded with television commercials, newspaper ads, direct-mail offers, sales calls, and Internet pitches. However, selling and advertising are only the tip of the marketing iceberg. Although they are important, they are only two of many marketing functions and are often not the most important ones.

Today, marketing must be understood not in the old sense of making a sale—"telling and selling"—but in the new sense of *satisfying customer needs*. If the marketer does a good job of understanding consumer needs, develops products that provide superior value, and prices, distributes, and promotes them effectively, these products will sell very easily. Thus, selling and advertising are only part of a larger "marketing mix"—a set of marketing tools that work together to affect the marketplace.

Marketing

A social and managerial process whereby individuals and groups obtain what they need and want through creating and exchanging products and value with others.

We define **marketing** as a social and managerial process by which individuals and groups obtain what they need and want through creating and exchanging products and value with others.[2] To explain this definition, we will examine the following important core marketing concepts: *needs, wants, and demands; marketing offers (products, services, and experiences); value and*

FIGURE 1.1
Core marketing concepts

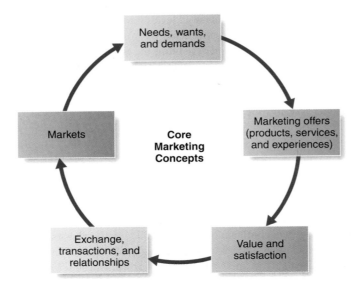

satisfaction; exchanges, transactions, and relationships; and markets. Figure 1.1 shows that these core marketing concepts are linked, with each concept building on the one before it.

Needs, Wants, and Demands

Needs
A state of felt deprivation.

The most basic concept underlying marketing is that of human needs. Human **needs** are states of felt deprivation. They include basic *physical* needs for food, clothing, warmth, and safety; *social* needs for belonging and affection; and *individual* needs for knowledge and self-expression. These needs were not created by marketers; they are a basic part of the human makeup.

Wants
The form taken by a human need as shaped by culture and individual personality.

Demands
Human wants that are backed by buying power.

Wants are the form human needs take as they are shaped by culture and individual personality. An American *needs* food but *wants* Big Mac, french fries, and a soft drink. A person in Mauritius *needs* food but *wants* a mango, rice, lentils, and beans. Wants are shaped by one's society and are described in terms of objects that will satisfy needs. When backed by buying power, wants become **demands.** Given their wants and resources, people demand products with benefits that add up to the most value and satisfaction.

Outstanding marketing companies go to great lengths to learn about and understand their customers' needs, wants, and demands. They conduct consumer research and analyze mountains of customer sales, warranty, and service data. Their people at all levels—including top management—stay close to customers. For example, top executives from Wal-Mart spend two days each week visiting stores and mingling with customers. At Disney World, at least once in his or her career, each manager spends a day touring the park in a Mickey, Minnie, Goofy, or other character costume.

At consumer products giant Procter & Gamble, top executives even visit with ordinary consumers in their homes and on shopping trips. "We read the data and look at the charts," says one P&G executive, "but to shop [with consumers] and see how the woman is changing retailers to save 10 cents on a loaf of bread [so she can] spend it on things that are more important—that's important to us to keep front and center."[3]

Marketing Offers—Products, Services, and Experiences

Marketing offer
Some combination of products, services, information, or experiences offered to a market to satisfy a need or want.

Companies address needs by putting forth a *value proposition,* a set of benefits that they promise to consumers to satisfy their needs. The value proposition is fulfilled through a **marketing offer**—some combination of products, services, information, or experiences offered to a market to satisfy a need or want. Marketing offers are not limited to physical *products*. In addition to tangible products, marketing offers include *services,* activities or benefits offered for sale that are essentially intangible and do not result in the ownership of anything. Examples include banking, airline, hotel, tax preparation, and home repair services. More broadly, marketing offers also include other entities, such as *persons, places, organizations, information,* and *ideas.*

Many sellers make the mistake of paying more attention to the specific products they offer than to the benefits and experiences produced by these products. They see themselves as selling a

Marketing offers do not have to be physical objects. Here, the "product" is an idea: protecting animals.

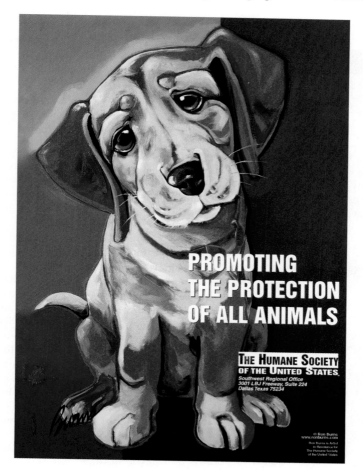

product rather than providing a solution to a need. A manufacturer of quarter-inch drill bits may think that the customer needs a drill bit. But what the customer *really* needs is a quarter-inch hole. These sellers may suffer from "marketing myopia." They are so taken with their products that they focus only on existing wants and lose sight of underlying customer needs.[4] They forget that a product is only a tool to solve a consumer problem. These sellers will have trouble if a new product comes along that serves the customer's need better or less expensively. The customer with the same *need* will *want* the new product.

Thus, smart marketers look beyond the attributes of the products and services they sell. They create brand *meaning* and brand *experiences* for consumers. For example, Coca-Cola means much more to consumers than just something to drink—it has become an American icon with a rich tradition and meaning. And Nike is more than just shoes, it's what the shoes do for you and where they take you. The familiar Nike swoosh stands for high sports performance, famous athletes, and a "Just Do It!" attitude (see Real Marketing 1.1). By orchestrating several services and products, companies can create, stage, and market brand experiences. Disney World is an experience; so is a ride on a Harley-Davidson motorcycle. You experience a visit to Barnes & Noble or surfing Sony's playstation.com Web site. In fact, as products and services increasingly become commodities, experiences have emerged for many firms as the next step in differentiating the company's offer. Consider, for example, a restaurant that doesn't even serve food:

[One] entrepreneur in Israel has entered the experience economy with the opening of Cafe

Ke'ilu, which roughly translates as "Cafe Make Believe." Manager Nir Caspi told a reporter that people come to cafes to be seen and to meet people, not for the food; Cafe Ke'ilu pursues that observation to its logical conclusion. The establishment serves its customers empty plates and mugs and charges guests $3 during the week and $6 on weekends for the social experience.[5]

"What consumers really want is [offers] that dazzle their senses, touch their hearts, and stimulate their minds," declares one expert. "They want [offers] that deliver an experience."[6]

real marketing 1.1

Nike: It's Not So Much the Shoes but Where They Take You!

The "swoosh"—it's everywhere! Just for fun, try counting the swooshes whenever you pick up the sports pages or watch a pickup basketball game or tune in to a televised golf match. Nike has built the ubiquitous swoosh into one of the best-known brand symbols on the planet. And the swoosh has come to

The ever-present Nike swoosh has come to stand for all that Nike means to those who wear it all around the world. "It's not so much the shoes but where they take you."

stand for all of the things that Nike means to those who wear it all around the world.

The power of its brand and logo speaks loudly of Nike's superb marketing skills. The company's strategy of building superior products around popular athletes and its classic "Just Do It!" ad campaign have forever changed the face of sports marketing. Nike spends hundreds of millions of dollars each year on big-name endorsements, splashy promotional events, and lots of attention-getting ads. Over the years, Nike has associated itself with some of the biggest names in sports, from Michael Jordan, Tiger Woods, Pete Sampras, and Mike Schmidt to Mia Hamm, Lance Armstrong, and Ronaldo. No matter what your sport, chances are good that one of your favorite athletes wears the Nike swoosh.

Nike knows, however, that good marketing is more than promotional hype and promises—it means consistently building strong relationships with customers based on real value. Nike's initial success resulted from the technical superiority of its running and basketball shoes, pitched to serious athletes who were frustrated by the lack of innovation in athletic equipment. To this day, Nike leads the industry in research-and-development spending.

But Nike gives its customers more than just good athletic gear. Customers don't just wear their Nikes, they *experience* them. As the company states on its Web page (www.nike.com), "Nike has always known the truth—it's not so much the shoes but where they take you." Beyond shoes, apparel, and equipment, Nike markets a way of life, a sports culture, a "just do it" attitude. That's the real meaning of Nike to its customers. Says Phil Knight, Nike's founder and chief executive, "Basically, our culture and our style is to be a rebel." The company was built on a genuine passion for sports, a maverick disregard for convention, and a belief in hard work and serious sports performance. Notes the Web page: "Just Do It" is "both universal and intensely personal. It speaks of sports. It invites dreams. It is a call to action, a refusal to hear excuses, and a license to be eccentric, courageous, and exceptional. It is Nike."

The strong relationships between customers and its brand paid off handsomely for Nike. Over the decade ending in 1997, Nike's revenues grew at an incredible annual rate of 21 percent; annual return to investors averaged 47 percent. In the mid-1990s, Nike levered its brand strength, moving aggressively into new product categories, sports, and regions of the world. Its sports apparel business grew explosively. The company slapped its familiar swoosh logo on everything from sunglasses and soccer balls to batting gloves and hockey sticks. Nike invaded a dozen new sports, including baseball, golf, ice and street hockey, in-line skating, wall climbing, and hiking.

In the late 1990s, however, Nike stumbled and its sales slipped. Many factors contributed to the company's sales woes. The whole industry suffered a setback, as a "brown shoe" craze for hiking and outdoor shoe styles ate into the athletic sneaker business. Competition improved: A revitalized Adidas saw its U.S. sales surge as Nike's sales declined. To make matters worse, college students on many campuses protested against Nike for its alleged exploitation of child labor in Asia and its commercialization of sports.

But Nike's biggest obstacle may be its own incredible success—it may have over-swooshed America. The brand appeared to suffer from big-brand backlash, and the swoosh may have become too common to be cool. According to one analyst, "When Tiger Woods made his debut in Nike gear, there were so many logos on him that he looked as if he'd got caught in an embroidering machine." A Nike executive admits, "There has been a little bit of backlash about the number of swooshes that are out there." Moreover, with sales of more than $9.5 billion, Nike has moved from maverick to mainstream. Today, rooting for Nike is like rooting for Microsoft.

To address these problems, Nike has returned to the basics—focusing on innovation, developing new product lines, creating subbrands, and focusing once again on product performance. And despite its recent ups and downs, Nike still flat out dominates the athletic shoe market. It captures a 42 percent market share in the United States and more than 25 percent abroad.

Competitors can hope that Nike's slump will continue, but few are counting on it. Most can only sit back and marvel at Nike's marketing prowess. One market analyst comments, "Nike remains one of the great American brands, as well known around the world as Coke or McDonald's." The sports giant also appears to be returning to its creative, rebellious roots. According to another analyst, recent advertising is bringing Nike's image back to hip:

Remember when Nike was unhip? It didn't last long . . . maybe three years at the end of the '90s, but the conquistadors of cool undoubtedly had a little swoon. But spot by spot, campaign by campaign, . . . good things began to happen. [The comeback culminated in Nike's stunning "Freestyle" ad, which featured five NBA stars performing remarkable moves, stunts, and dribbles, the sounds of which were mixed into an original song that served as the ad's soundtrack. The ad won last year's

Advertising Age Ad of the Year award and restored] the sports apparel marketer to its previous place at the creative summit.

Still, to stay on top, Nike will have to find new ways deliver the kind of innovation and value that built the brand so powerfully in the past. No longer the rebellious, antiestablishment upstart, huge Nike must continually reassess and rekindle its meaning to customers. Says Knight, "Now that we've [grown so large], there's a fine line between being a rebel and being a bully. [To our customers,] we have to be beautiful as well as big."

Sources: Quotes from Bill Saporito, "Can Nike Get Unstuck?" *Time,* March 30, 1998, pp. 48–53; Jolie Solomon, "When Cool Goes Cold," *Newsweek,* March 30, 1998, pp. 36–37; Jerry Edgerton, "Can Nike Still Play Above the Rim?" *Money,* May 1999, p. 48; Louise Lee, "Can Nike Still Do It?" *Business Week,* February 21, 2000, pp. 121–128; and Bob Garfield, "Best of Show; and Apparel/Accessories: Nike." *Advertising Age,* May 6, 2002, p. S2. Also see Douglas Robson, "Just Do . . . Something," *Business Week,* July 2, 2001, pp. 70–71; and Maureen Tkacik, "Nike Net Rises 30% on Corrected Glitch to Its Supply Chain," *Wall Street Journal,* March 22, 2002, p. B2.

Value and Satisfaction

Consumers usually face a broad array of products and services that might satisfy a given need. How do they choose among these many marketing offers? Consumers make choices based on their perceptions of the value and satisfaction that various products and services deliver.

Customer value is the difference between the values the customer gains from owning and using a product and the costs of obtaining the product. Customers form expectations about the value of various marketing offers and buy accordingly. How do buyers form their expectations? Customer expectations are based on past buying experiences, the opinions of friends, and marketer and competitor information and promises.

Customer satisfaction with a purchase depends on how well the product's performance lives up to the customer's expectations. Customer satisfaction is a key influence on future buying behavior. Satisfied customers buy again and tell others about their good experiences. Dissatisfied customers often switch to competitors and disparage the product to others.

Marketers must be careful to set the right level of expectations. If they set expectations too low, they may satisfy those who buy but fail to attract enough buyers. If they raise expectations too high, buyers will be disappointed. Customer value and customer satisfaction are key building blocks for developing and managing customer relationships. We will revisit these core concepts later in the chapter.

Exchange, Transactions, and Relationships

Exchange
The act of obtaining a desired object from someone by offering something in return.

Transaction
A trade of values between two parties.

Marketing occurs when people decide to satisfy needs and wants through exchange. **Exchange** is the act of obtaining a desired object from someone by offering something in return. Whereas exchange is the core concept of marketing, a transaction, in turn, is marketing's unit of measurement. A **transaction** consists of a trade of values between two parties: One party gives X to another party and gets Y in return. For example, you pay Sears $350 for a television set.

In the broadest sense, the marketer tries to bring about a response to some marketing offer. The response may be more than simply buying or trading products and services. A political candidate, for instance, wants votes, a church wants membership, and a social-action group wants idea acceptance.

Marketing consists of actions taken to build and maintain desirable *exchange relationships* with target audiences involving a product, service, idea, or other object. Beyond simply attracting new customers and creating transactions, the goal is to retain customers and grow their business with the company. Marketers want to build strong economic and social connections by promising and consistently delivering superior value. We will discuss the important concept of customer relationship management in more detail later in the chapter.

Markets

Market

The set of all actual and potential buyers of a product or service.

The concepts of exchange and relationships lead to the concept of a market. A **market** is the set of actual and potential buyers of a product. These buyers share a particular need or want that can be satisfied through exchange relationships. The size of a market depends on the number of people who exhibit the need, have resources to engage in exchange, and are willing to exchange these resources for what they want.

Originally the term *market* stood for the place where buyers and sellers gathered to exchange their goods, such as a village square. Economists use the term *market* to refer to a collection of buyers and sellers who transact in a particular product class, as in the housing market or the grain market. Marketers, however, see the sellers as constituting an industry and the buyers as constituting a market.

Marketers are keenly interested in markets. Each nation's economy and the whole world economy consist of complex, interacting sets of markets that are linked through exchange processes. Marketers work to understand the needs and wants of specific markets and to select the markets that they can serve best. In turn, they develop products and services that create value and satisfaction for customers in these markets. The result is profitable long-term customer relationships.

Marketing

The concept of markets finally brings us full circle to the concept of marketing. Marketing means managing markets to bring about profitable exchange relationships by creating value and satisfying needs and wants. Thus, we return to our definition of marketing as a process by which individuals and groups obtain what they need and want by creating and exchanging products and value with others.

Creating exchange relationships involves work. Sellers must search for buyers, identify their needs, design good marketing offers, set prices for them, promote them, and store and deliver them. Activities such as product development, research, communication, distribution, pricing, and service are core marketing activities. Although we normally think of marketing as being carried on by sellers, buyers also carry on marketing. Consumers do marketing when they search for the goods they need at prices they can afford. Company purchasing agents do marketing when they track down sellers and bargain for good terms.

Figure 1.2 shows the main elements in a modern marketing system. In the usual situation, marketing involves serving a market of end users in the face of competitors. The company and the competitors send their respective offers and messages to consumers, either directly or through marketing intermediaries. All of the actors in the system are affected by major environmental forces (demographic, economic, physical, technological, political/legal, social/cultural).

Each party in the system adds value for the next level. Thus, a company's success depends not only on its own actions but also on how well the entire system serves the needs of final consumers. Wal-Mart cannot fulfill its promise of low prices unless its suppliers provide merchandise at low costs. And Ford cannot deliver high quality to car buyers unless its dealers provide outstanding service.

FIGURE 1.2

Elements of a modern marketing system

Environment

Marketing Management

Marketing management
The art and science of choosing target markets and building profitable relationships with them.

We define **marketing management** as the art and science of choosing target markets and building profitable relationships with them. This involves getting, keeping, and growing customers through creating, delivering, and communicating superior customer value. Thus, marketing management involves managing demand, which in turn involves managing customer relationships.

Customer and Demand Management

Some people think of marketing management as finding enough customers for the company's current output. But this view is too limited. Marketing management is not concerned with serving all customers in every way. Instead, marketers want to serve selected customers that they can serve well and profitably.

The organization has a desired level of demand for its products. At any point in time, there may be no demand, adequate demand, irregular demand, or too much demand. Marketing management must find ways to deal with these different demand states. It may be concerned not only with finding and increasing demand but also with changing or even reducing it.

Demarketing
Marketing to reduce demand temporarily or permanently; the aim is not to destroy demand but only to reduce or shift it.

For example, the Golden Gate Bridge sometimes carries an unsafe level of traffic, and Yosemite National Park is badly overcrowded in the summer. Power companies sometimes have trouble meeting demand during peak usage periods. In these and other cases of excess demand, **demarketing** may be required to reduce the number of customers or to shift their demand temporarily or permanently.[7] For example, to reduce demand for space on congested expressways in Washington, D.C., the Metropolitan Washington Council of Governments has set up a Web site encouraging commuters to carpool and use mass transit. Thus, marketing management seeks to affect the types of customers served and the level, timing, and nature of their demand in a way that helps the organization achieve its objectives. Simply put, marketing management is *customer management* and *demand management*.

Demarketing: To reduce demand for space on already congested expressways in Washington, D.C., the Metropolitan Washington Council of Governments has set up a Web site encouraging commuters to carpool or use mass transit.

Marketing Management Orientations

We describe marketing management as carrying out tasks to build profitable relationships with target consumers. What *philosophy* should guide these marketing efforts? What weight should be given to the interests of the organization, customers, and society? Very often these interests conflict.

There are five alternative concepts under which organizations conduct their marketing activities: the *production, product, selling, marketing,* and *societal marketing concepts.*

The Production Concept

Production concept
The idea that consumers will favor products that are available and highly affordable.

The **production concept** holds that consumers will favor products that are available and highly affordable. Therefore, management should focus on improving production and distribution efficiency. This concept is one of the oldest orientations that guides sellers.

The production concept is still a useful philosophy in two types of situations. The first occurs when the demand for a product exceeds the supply. Here, management should look for ways to increase production. The second situation occurs when the product's cost is too high and improved productivity is needed to bring it down. For example, Henry Ford's whole philosophy was to perfect the production of the Model T so that its cost could be reduced and more people could afford it. He joked about offering people a car of any color as long as it was black.

Although useful in some situations, the production concept can lead to marketing myopia. Companies adopting this orientation run a major risk of focusing too narrowly on their own operations and losing sight of the real objective—satisfying customers' needs.

The Product Concept

Product concept
The idea that consumers will favor products that offer the most quality, performance, and features and that the organization should therefore devote its energy to making continuous product improvements.

The **product concept** holds that consumers will favor products that offer the most in quality, performance, and innovative features. Thus, an organization should devote energy to making continuous product improvements. Some manufacturers believe that if they can build a better mousetrap, the world will beat a path to their door.[8] But they are often rudely shocked. Buyers may well be looking for a better solution to a mouse problem but not necessarily for a better mousetrap. The solution might be a chemical spray, an exterminating service, or something that works better than a mousetrap. Furthermore, a better mousetrap will not sell unless the manufacturer designs, packages, and prices it attractively; places it in convenient distribution channels; brings it to the attention of people who need it; and convinces buyers that it is a better product.

Thus, the product concept also can lead to marketing myopia. For instance, railroad management once thought that users wanted *trains* rather than *transportation* and overlooked the growing challenge of airlines, buses, trucks, and automobiles. Kodak assumed that consumers wanted photographic film rather than a way to capture and share memories and at first overlooked the challenge of digital cameras. Although it now leads the digital camera market in sales, it has yet to make significant profits from this business.

The Selling Concept

Selling concept
The idea that consumers will not buy enough of the organization's products unless the organization undertakes a large-scale selling and promotion effort.

Many companies follow the **selling concept,** which holds that consumers will not buy enough of the firm's products unless it undertakes a large-scale selling and promotion effort. The concept is typically practiced with unsought goods—those that buyers do not normally think of buying, such as insurance or blood donations. These industries must be good at tracking down prospects and selling them on product benefits.

Most firms practice the selling concept when they face overcapacity. Their aim is to sell what they make rather than make what the market wants. Such marketing carries high risks. It focuses on creating sales transactions rather than on building long-term, profitable customer relationships. It assumes that customers who are coaxed into buying the product will like it. Or, if they don't like it, they will possibly forget their disappointment and buy it again later. These are usually poor assumptions. Most studies show that dissatisfied customers do not buy again. Worse yet, whereas the average satisfied customer tells three others about good experiences, the average dissatisfied customer tells ten others about his or her bad experiences.[9]

The Marketing Concept

Marketing concept
The marketing management philosophy that holds that achieving organizational goals depends on determining the needs and wants of target markets and delivering the desired satisfactions more effectively and efficiently than competitors do.

The **marketing concept** holds that achieving organizational goals depends on knowing the needs and wants of target markets and delivering the desired satisfactions better than competitors do. Under the marketing concept, customer focus and value are the *paths* to sales and profits.

FIGURE 1.3
The selling and marketing
concepts contrasted

Instead of a product-centered "make and sell" philosophy, the marketing concept is a customer-centered "sense and respond" philosophy. It views marketing not as "hunting," but as "gardening." The job is not to find the right customers for your product, but the right products for your customers. As stated by famed direct marketer Lester Wunderman, "The chant of the Industrial Revolution was that of the manufacturer who said, 'This is what I make, won't you please buy it.' The call of the Information Age is the consumer asking, 'This is what I want, won't you please make it.' "[10]

Figure 1.3 contrasts the selling concept and the marketing concept. The selling concept takes an *inside-out* perspective. It starts with the factory, focuses on the company's existing products, and calls for heavy selling and promotion to obtain profitable sales. It focuses primarily on customer conquest—getting short-term sales with little concern about who buys or why.

In contrast, the marketing concept takes an *outside-in* perspective. As Herb Kelleher, Southwest Airlines's colorful CEO, puts it, "We don't have a Marketing Department; we have a Customer Department." And in the words of one Ford executive, "If we're not customer driven, our cars won't be either." The marketing concept starts with a well-defined market, focuses on customer needs, and integrates all the marketing activities that affect customers. It turn, it yields profits by creating long-term customer relationships based on customer value and satisfaction.

Many successful and well-known companies have adopted the marketing concept. Procter & Gamble, Disney, Wal-Mart, Marriott, Nordstrom, Dell Computer, and Southwest Airlines follow it faithfully. The goal is to build customer satisfaction into the very fabric of the firm. L.L. Bean, the highly successful catalog retailer, was founded on the marketing concept. In 1912, in his first circulars, L.L. Bean included the following notice: "I do not consider a sale complete until goods are worn out and the customer still is satisfied. We will thank anyone to return goods that are not perfectly satisfactory. . . . Above all things we wish to avoid having a dissatisfied customer." To this day, Today, L.L. Bean dedicates itself to giving perfect satisfaction in every way.

In contrast, many companies claim to practice the marketing concept but do not. Implementing the marketing concept often means more than simply responding to customers' stated desires and obvious needs. *Customer-driven* companies research current customers deeply to learn about their desires, gather new product and service ideas, and test proposed product improvements. Such customer-driven marketing usually works well when a clear need exists and when customers know what they want.

In many cases, however, customers *don't* know what they want or even what is possible. For example, 20 years ago, how many consumers would have thought to ask for cell phones, fax machines, home copiers, 24-hour Internet brokerage accounts, DVD players, handheld global satellite positioning systems, or wearable PCs? Such situations call for *customer-driving* marketing—understanding customer needs even better than customers themselves do and creating products and services that will meet existing and latent needs, now and in the future.

"Customers should not be trusted to come up with solutions," says the CEO of an innovation management firm, "they aren't expert enough for that. . . . Rather, customers should be asked only [about] what they want a new product or service to do for them." As Sony's visionary leader, Akio Morita, puts it: "Our plan is to lead the public with new products rather than ask them what kinds of products they want. The public does not know what is possible, but we do." And according to an executive at 3M, "Our goal is to lead customers where they want to go before *they* know where they want to go."[11]

Customer-driving market-ing: In many cases, how-ever, customers don't know what they want or even what is possible. How many of us would have thought to ask for a "wearable PC."

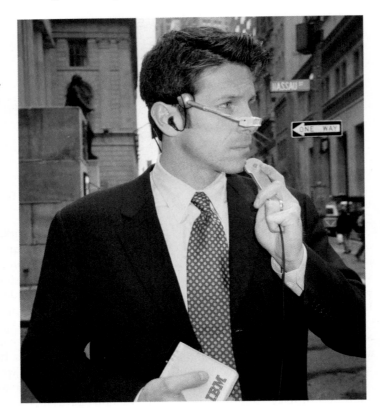

The Societal Marketing Concept

Societal marketing concept

The idea that the organiza-tion should determine the needs, wants, and interests of target markets and deliver the desired satisfactions more effectively and efficiently than do competitors in a way that maintains or improves the consumer's and society's well-being.

The **societal marketing concept** holds that the organization should determine the needs, wants, and interests of target markets. It should then deliver superior value to customers in a way that maintains or improves the consumer's *and the society's* well-being. It questions whether the pure marketing concept overlooks possible conflicts between consumer *short-run wants* and consumer *long-run welfare*. Is a firm that senses, serves, and satisfies individual short-term wants always doing what's best for consumers and society in the long run?

Consider the fast-food industry. Most people see today's giant fast-food chains as offering tasty and convenient food at reasonable prices. Yet many consumer and environmental groups have voiced concerns. Critics point out that hamburgers, fried chicken, french fries, and most other foods sold by fast-food restaurants are high in fat and salt. The products are wrapped in convenient packaging, but this leads to waste and pollution. Thus, in satisfying short-term consumer wants, the highly success-ful fast-food chains may be harming consumer health and causing environmental problems.

As Figure 1.4 shows, the societal marketing concept calls on marketers to balance three con-siderations in setting their marketing policies: company profits, consumer wants, *and* society's interests. Originally, most companies based their marketing decisions largely on short-run com-

FIGURE 1.4
Three considerations underlying the societal marketing concept

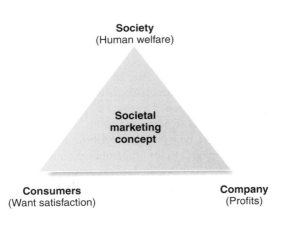

Society
(Human welfare)

Societal
marketing
concept

Consumers
(Want satisfaction)

Company
(Profits)

Johnson & Johnson's concern for society is summarized in its credo and in the company's actions over the years.

Our Credo

We believe our first responsibility is to the doctors, nurses and patients,
to mothers and fathers and all others who use our products and services.
In meeting their needs everything we do must be of high quality.
We must constantly strive to reduce our costs
in order to maintain reasonable prices.
Customers' orders must be serviced promptly and accurately.
Our suppliers and distributors must have an opportunity
to make a fair profit.

We are responsible to our employees,
the men and women who work with us throughout the world.
Everyone must be considered as an individual.
We must respect their dignity and recognize their merit.
They must have a sense of security in their jobs.
Compensation must be fair and adequate,
and working conditions clean, orderly and safe.
We must be mindful of ways to help our employees fulfill
their family responsibilities.
Employees must feel free to make suggestions and complaints.
There must be equal opportunity for employment, development
and advancement for those qualified.
We must provide competent management,
and their actions must be just and ethical.

We are responsible to the communities in which we live and work
and to the world community as well.
We must be good citizens — support good works and charities
and bear our fair share of taxes.
We must encourage civic improvements and better health and education.
We must maintain in good order
the property we are privileged to use,
protecting the environment and natural resources.

Our final responsibility is to our stockholders.
Business must make a sound profit.
We must experiment with new ideas.
Research must be carried on, innovative programs developed
and mistakes paid for.
New equipment must be purchased, new facilities provided
and new products launched.
Reserves must be created to provide for adverse times.
When we operate according to these principles,
the stockholders should realize a fair return.

Johnson & Johnson

pany profit. Eventually, they recognized the long-run importance of satisfying consumer wants, and the marketing concept emerged. Now many companies are beginning to think of society's interests when making their marketing decisions.

One such company is Johnson & Johnson, rated each year in a *Fortune* magazine poll as one of America's most admired companies. Johnson & Johnson's concern for societal interests is summarized in a company document called "Our Credo," which stresses honesty, integrity, and putting people before profits. Under this credo, Johnson & Johnson would rather take a big loss than ship a bad batch of one of its products.

Consider the tragic tampering case in which eight people died from swallowing cyanide-laced capsules of Tylenol, a Johnson & Johnson brand. Although Johnson & Johnson believed that the pills had been altered in only a few stores, not in the factory, it quickly recalled all of its product. The recall cost the company $240 million in earnings. In the long run, however, the company's swift recall of Tylenol strengthened consumer confidence and loyalty, and Tylenol remains the nation's leading brand of pain reliever.

In this and other cases, Johnson & Johnson management has found that doing what's right benefits both consumers and the company. Says Johnson & Johnson's chief executive, "The Credo should not be viewed as some kind of social welfare program. . . it's just plain good business. If we keep trying to do what's right, at the end of the day we believe the marketplace will reward us." Thus, over the years, Johnson & Johnson's dedication to consumers and community service has made it one of America's most-admired companies *and* one of the most profitable.[12]

Customer Relationship Management

No matter what its orientation, marketing management's crucial task is to create profitable relationships with customers. Until recently, *customer relationship management (CRM)* has been defined narrowly as a customer database management activity. By this definition, it involves managing detailed information about individual customers and carefully managing customer "touchpoints" in order to maximize customer loyalty. We will discuss this narrower CRM activity in a later chapter dealing with marketing information.

More recently, however, customer relationship management has taken on a broader meaning. In this broader sense, **customer relationship management** is the overall process of building and maintaining profitable customer relationships by delivering superior customer value and satisfaction. Thus, today's companies are going beyond designing strategies to *attract* new customers and create *transactions* with them. They are using customer relationship management to *retain* current customers and build profitable, long-term *relationships* with them. The new view is that marketing is the science and art of finding, retaining, *and* growing profitable customers.

Why the new emphasis on retaining and growing customers? In the past, many companies took their customers for granted. Facing an expanding economy and rapidly growing markets, companies could practice a "leaky bucket" approach to marketing. Growing markets meant a plentiful supply of new customers. Companies could keep filling the marketing bucket with new customers without worrying about losing old customers through holes in the bottom of the bucket.

However, companies today face some new marketing realities. Changing demographics, more-sophisticated competitors, and overcapacity in many industries—all of these factors mean that there are fewer customers to go around. Many companies are now fighting for shares of flat or fading markets. Thus, the costs of attracting new consumers are rising. In fact, on average, it costs 5 to 10 times as much to attract a new customer as it does to keep a current customer satisfied. Sears found that it costs 12 times more to attract a customer than to keep an existing one.[13]

Companies are also realizing that losing a customer means losing more than a single sale. It means losing the entire stream of purchases that the customer would make over a lifetime of patronage. For example, here is a dramatic illustration of **customer lifetime value:**

> Stew Leonard, who operates a highly profitable three-store supermarket, says that he sees $50,000 flying out of his store every time he sees a sulking customer. Why? Because his average customer spends about $100 a week, shops 50 weeks a year, and remains in the area for about 10 years. If this customer has an unhappy experience and switches to another supermarket, Stew Leonard's has lost $50,000 in revenue. The loss can be much greater if the disappointed customer shares the bad experience with other customers and causes them to defect. To keep customers coming back,

Customer relationship management

The overall process of building and maintaining profitable customer relationships by delivering superior customer value and satisfaction.

Customer lifetime value

The value of the entire stream of purchases that the customer would make over a lifetime of patronage.

Customer lifetime value: To keep customers coming back, Stew Leonard's has created the "Disneyland of dairy stores," Rule #1—the customer is always right. Rule #2—if the customer is ever wrong, reread rule #1!

Stew Leonard's has created what the *New York Times* has dubbed the "Disneyland of Dairy Stores," complete with costumed characters, scheduled entertainment, a petting zoo, and animatronics throughout the store. From its humble beginnings as a small dairy store in 1969, Stew Leonard's has grown at an amazing pace. It's built 29 additions onto the original store, which now serves more that 250,000 customers each week. This legion of loyal shoppers is largely a result of the store's passionate approach to customer service. Rule #1 at Stew Leonard's—The customer is always right. Rule #2—If the customer is ever wrong, reread rule #1![14]

Similarly, the customer lifetime value of a Taco Bell customer exceeds $12,000. Lexus estimates that a single satisfied and loyal customer is worth $600,000 in lifetime sales.[15] Thus, working to retain and grow customers makes good economic sense. In fact, a company can lose money on a specific transaction but still benefit greatly from a long-term relationship.

Attracting, Retaining, and Growing Customers

The key to building lasting customer relationships is to create superior customer value and satisfaction. Satisfied customers are more likely to be loyal customers, and loyal customers are more likely to give the company a larger share of their business. We now look more closely at the concepts of customer value and satisfaction, loyalty and retention, and share of customer.

Relationship Building Blocks: Customer Value and Satisfaction

Attracting and retaining customers can be a difficult task. Customers often face a bewildering array of products and services from which to choose. To attract and keep customers, a company must constantly seek ways to deliver superior customer value and satisfaction.

Customer perceived value
The difference between total customer value and total customer cost.

Customer Value.   A customer buys from the firm that offers the highest **customer perceived value**—the customer's evaluation of the difference between all the benefits and all the costs of a marketing offer relative to those of competing offers. For example, FedEx customers gain a number of benefits. The most obvious is fast and reliable package delivery. However, by using FedEx, customers also may receive some status and image values. Using FedEx usually makes both the package sender and the receiver feel more important. When deciding whether to send a package via FedEx, customers will weigh these and other perceived values against the money, effort, and psychic costs of using the service. Moreover, they will compare the value of using FedEx against the value of using other shippers—UPS, Airborne, the U.S. Postal Service. They will select the service that gives them the greatest perceived value.

Customers often do not judge product values and costs accurately or objectively. They act on *perceived* value. For example, does FedEx really provide faster, more reliable delivery? If so, is this better service worth the higher prices FedEx charges? The U.S. Postal Service argues that its express service is comparable, and its prices are much lower. However, judging by market share, most consumers perceive otherwise. Each day, they entrust FedEx with 50 percent more next-day air packages than they give to nearest competitor UPS. The Postal Service's challenge is to change these customer value perceptions.[16]

Customer satisfaction
The extent to which a product's perceived performance matches a buyer's expectations.

Customer Satisfaction.   **Customer satisfaction** depends on the product's perceived performance relative to a buyer's expectations. If the product's performance falls short of expectations, the customer is dissatisfied. If performance matches expectations, the customer is satisfied. If performance exceeds expectations, the customer is highly satisfied or delighted. Outstanding marketing companies go out of their way to keep their customers satisfied. Satisfied customers make repeat purchases and tell others about their good experiences with the product. The key is to match customer expectations with company performance. Smart companies aim to *delight* customers by promising only what they can deliver, then delivering *more* than they promise.[17] (See Real Marketing 1.2.) The American Customer Satisfaction Index, which tracks customer satisfaction in more than two dozen U.S. manufacturing and service industries, shows that overall customer satisfaction has been declining slightly in recent years.[18] It is unclear whether this has resulted from a decrease in product and service quality or from an increase in customer expectations. In either case, it presents an opportunity for companies that can consistently deliver superior customer value and satisfaction.

However, although the customer-centered firm seeks to deliver high customer satisfaction relative to competitors, it does not attempt to *maximize* customer satisfaction. A company can always increase customer satisfaction by lowering its price or increasing its services. But this may

real marketing 1.2

Customer Relationships: Delighting Customers

Top-notch marketing companies know that delighting customers involves more than simply opening a complaint department, smiling a lot, and being nice. These companies set very high standards for customer satisfaction and often make seemingly outlandish efforts to achieve them. Consider the following examples:

A man bought his first new Lexus—a $45,000 piece of machinery. He could afford a Mercedes, a Jaguar, or a Cadillac,

Delighting customers: Top-notch marketing companies set very high standards for customer satisfaction and often make seemingly outlandish efforts to achieve them.

but he bought the Lexus. He took delivery of his new honey and started to drive it home, luxuriating in the smell of the leather interior and the glorious handling. On the interstate, he put the pedal to the metal and felt the Gs in the pit of his stomach. The lights, the windshield washer, the gizmo cup holder that popped out of the dashboard, the seat heater that warmed his bottom on a cold winter morning—he tried all of these with mounting pleasure. On a whim, he turned on the radio. His favorite classical music station came on in splendid quadraphonic sound that ricocheted around the interior. He pushed the

second button; it was his favorite news station. The third button brought his favorite talk station that kept him awake on long trips. The fourth button was set to his daughter's favorite rock station. In fact, every button was set to his specific tastes. The customer knew the car was smart, but was it psychic? No. The mechanic at Lexus had noted the radio settings on his trade-in and duplicated them on the new Lexus. The customer was delighted. This was his car now—through and through! No one told the mechanic to do it. It's just part of the Lexus philosophy: Delight a customer and continue to delight that customer, and you will have a customer for life. What the mechanic did cost Lexus nothing. Not one red cent. Yet it solidified the relationship that could be worth high six figures to Lexus in customer lifetime value.

Don and Betts Jackson are two of the most fun and outgoing people around. And Betts is one of the great chefs of the world. Their holiday party at their farmhouse in Delaware—usually filled to overflowing with friends, relatives, neighbors, and members of the local chamber of commerce—is a stunner with an array of foods, drinks, and wines that would shame a Michelin four-star restaurant in Lyons. Several years ago, the Jacksons gave each other $1,500 worth of kitchen gear from Williams-Sonoma as their main gifts to go under the Christmas tree. Don placed the order in plenty of time for Christmas delivery. The order never arrived. It was a bleak sight under the tree, made bleaker by the knowledge that Betts needed the new implements for the upcoming holiday party. The next day, Jackson got a Williams-Sonoma sales rep on the phone and told him the sad story. A combination of factors was involved: a

Federal Express slowdown, a computer glitch in Williams-Sonoma's eastern distribution center, and unexpected snow all conspired to delay the order. The rep took instant action. "Here's what I'm going to do for you," he said. "First, I'm going to reassemble the order and get it out to you by FedEx overnight, so you'll have it tomorrow morning. Second, I'm going to enclose merchandise return labels, so when the old order arrives, you can slap the labels on the packages and call Fed Ex to take them away. Third, I'm going to forgive all shipping costs for the original order, for the returns, and for this new order that you'll get tomorrow morning. And fourth, I'm going to send you a present—a thank-you for your patience and for being a customer of Williams-Sonoma." Jackson hung up the phone feeling better. The next day, the merchandise arrived as promised, together with the return labels and a giant, top-of-the-line, blue-glass turkey baster as the free gift. Despite the original goof, the Jacksons were delighted.

When a customer arrived early one winter morning at an Enterprise Rent-A-Car office in Cambridge, Massachusetts, to pick up an SUV to drive on a ski vacation to the Sugarbush resort in Vermont (a three-hour-plus drive away), there was no vehicle and no record of his reservation. Cambridge's customer service representative apologized profusely and called nearby branches until he found the car the customer wanted, a Chevy Trailblazer at a location several miles away. So far, so good. But then Lowery drove the customer back to his house to pick up his ski gear, and to the other branch to retrieve the Trailblazer. He knocked 20 percent off the rental price, provided the customer the two-dollar toll he would have to pay to get on the highway (which he wouldn't have had to pay leaving from Cambridge), and gave him a half-tank of gas. Within a month, the delighted customer had rented twice more from Enterprise and "will probably rent more," he says.

Studies show that going to extremes to keep customers happy, although sometimes costly, goes hand in hand with good financial performance. Satisfied customers come back again and again. Thus, in today's highly competitive marketplace, companies can well afford to lose money on one transaction if it helps to cement a profitable long-term customer relationship.

For companies interested in delighting customers, exceptional value and service are more than a set of policies or actions—they are a companywide attitude, an important part of the overall company culture. American Express loves to tell stories about how its people have rescued customers from disasters ranging from civil wars to earthquakes, no matter what the cost. The company gives cash rewards of up to $1,000 to "Great Performers," such as Barbara Weber, who moved mountains of U.S. State Department and Treasury Department bureaucracy to refund $980 in stolen traveler's checks to a customer stranded in Cuba.

Southwest Airlines is well known for its low fares and prompt arrivals. But its friendly and often funny flight staff goes to great lengths to delight customers. In one instance, after pushing away from the departure gate, a Southwest pilot spied an anguished passenger, sweat streaming from her face, racing down the jetway only to find that that she'd arrived too late. He returned to the gate to pick her up. Says Southwest's executive vice president for customers, "It broke every rule in the book, but we congratulated the pilot on a job well done."

Four Seasons Hotels, long known for its outstanding service, tells its employees the story of Ron Dyment, a doorman in Toronto, who forgot to load a departing guest's briefcase into his taxi. The doorman called the guest, a lawyer in Washington, D.C., and learned that he desperately needed the briefcase for a meeting the following morning. Without first asking for approval from management, Dyment hopped on a plane and returned the briefcase. The company named Dyment Employee of the Year.

Similarly, the Nordstrom department store chain thrives on stories about its service heroics, such as employees dropping off orders at customers' homes or warming up cars while customers spend a little more time shopping. In one case, a salesclerk reportedly gave a customer a refund on a tire—Nordstrom doesn't carry tires, but the store prides itself on a no-questions-asked return policy. There's even a story about a man whose wife, a loyal Nordstrom customer, died with her Nordstrom account $1,000 in arrears. Not only did Nordstrom settle the account, it also sent flowers to the funeral.

There's no simple formula for taking care of customers, but neither is it a mystery. According to the president of L.L. Bean, "A lot of people have fancy things to say about customer service . . . but it's just a day-in, day-out, ongoing, never-ending, unremitting, persevering, compassionate type of activity." For the companies that do it well, it's also very rewarding.

Sources: See Bill Kelley, "Five Companies That Do It Right—and Make It Pay," *Sales & Marketing Management,* April 1988, pp. 57–64; Patricia Sellers, "Companies That Serve You Best," *Fortune,* May 31, 1993, pp. 74–88; and Len Ellis, "Customer Loyalty," *Executive Excellence,* July 2001, pp. 13–14. The Lexus and Williams-Sonoma examples are adapted from Denny Hatch and Ernie Schell, "Delight Your Customers," *Target Marketing,* April 2002, pp. 32–39. The Enterprise example is from and Dana James, "Lighting the Way," *Marketing News,* April 1, 2002, pp. 1, 11.

result in lower profits. Thus, the purpose of marketing is to generate customer value profitably. This requires a very delicate balance: The marketer must continue to generate more customer value and satisfaction but not "give away the house."

Customer Loyalty and Retention

Highly satisfied customers produce several benefits for the company. Satisfied customers are less price sensitive. They talk favorably to others about the company and its products and remain loyal for a longer period. However, the relationship between customer satisfaction and loyalty varies greatly across industries and competitive situations.

Figure 1.5 shows the relationship between customer satisfaction and loyalty in five different markets.[19] In all cases, as satisfaction increases, so does loyalty. Highly competitive markets, such as those for automobiles and personal computers, show surprisingly little difference between the loyalty of less satisfied customers and those who are somewhat satisfied. However, they show a tremendous difference between the loyalty of satisfied customers and *completely* satisfied customers.

Even a slight drop from complete satisfaction can create an enormous drop in loyalty. For example, one study showed that completely satisfied customers are nearly 42 percent more likely to be loyal than merely satisfied customers. Another study, by AT&T, showed that 70 percent of customers who say they are satisfied with a product or service are still willing to switch to a competitor; customers who are *highly* satisfied are much more loyal. Xerox found that its totally satisfied customers are six times more likely to repurchase Xerox products than are its satisfied customers.[20]

This means that companies must aim high if they want to hold on to their customers. Customer *delight* creates an emotional relationship with a product or service, not just a rational preference. This, in turn, creates high customer loyalty. Hanging on to customers is "so basic, it's scary," claims one marketing executive. "We find out what our customers' needs and wants are, and then we overdeliver."[21]

FIGURE 1.5

The relationship between customer satisfaction and customer loyalty

Source: Thomas O. Jones and W. Earl Sasser Jr., "Why Satisfied Customers Defect," *Harvard Business Review,* November–December 1995, p. 91. Copyright © 1997 by the President and Fellows of Harvard College; all rights reserved. Reprinted by permission of *Harvard Business Review.*

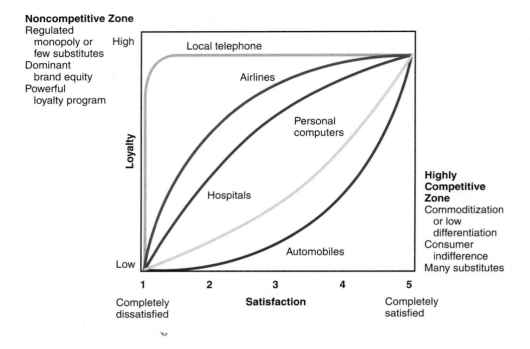

Figure 1.5 also shows that in noncompetitive markets, such as those served by regulated monopolies or dominated by powerful or patent-protected brands, customers tend to remain loyal no matter how dissatisfied. This might seem like an ideal situation for the protected or dominant firm. However, such firms may pay a high price for customer dissatisfaction in the long run. If a firm loses its monopoly, disaster can result. For example, when Xerox lost patent protection on its copiers in the late 1970s, dissatisfied customers gleefully defected to the new competitors. Xerox's share of the world copier market plunged from more than 80 percent to less than 35 percent in just five years. Thus, even highly successful companies must pay close attention to customer satisfaction and its relationship to customer loyalty.

Growing "Share of Customer"

Beyond simply retaining good customers, marketers want to constantly increase their *share of customer*—the share they get of the customer's purchasing in their product categories. They may do this by becoming the sole supplier of products the customer is currently buying. Or they may persuade the customer to purchase additional company products. Thus, banks want a greater "share of wallet." Supermarkets want to increase their "share of stomach." Car companies want a greater "share of garage" and airlines want a greater "share of travel."

One of the best ways to increase share of customer is through cross-selling. Cross-selling means getting more business from current customers of one product by selling them additional offerings. For example, the merger between Citibank and Travelers helped both units of the Citibank Group to cross-sell the company's services.[22] A new Travelers Financial Edge program let independent Travelers agents introduce Citibank products to their insurance clients, such as credit cards and student loans. Similarly, a new Citibank Partners program let Citibank representatives offer more financial services to their customers, such as insurance from Travelers and mutual funds from Salomon Smith Barney (another Citibank Group unit). To support cross-selling of a broader range of services, Citibank's personal bankers became "client financial analysts." Its branches were renamed "Citibank Financial Centers." As a result, Citibank Group obtained a larger share of each customer's financial services dollars.

Building Customer Relationships and Customer Equity

We can now see the importance of not just finding customers, but of keeping and growing them as well. Customer relationship management is oriented toward the long term. Today's smart companies not only want to create customers, they want to "own" them for life, capture their customer lifetime value, and build overall customer equity.

Customer Equity

Customer equity

The total combined customer lifetime values of all of the company's customers.

The aim of customer relationship management is to produce high **customer equity.**[23] Customer equity is the total combined customer lifetime values of all of the company's customers. Clearly, the more loyal the firm's customers, the higher the firm's customer equity. Customer equity may be a better measure of a firm's performance than current sales or market share. Whereas sales and market share reflect the past, customer equity suggests the future. Consider Cadillac:

In the 1970s and 1980s, Cadillac had some of the most loyal customers in the industry. To an entire generation of car buyers, the name "Cadillac" defined American luxury. Cadillac's share of the luxury car market reached a whopping 51 percent in 1976. Based on market share and sales, the brand's future looked rosy. However, measures of customer equity would have painted a bleaker picture. Cadillac customers were getting older (average age 60) and average customer lifetime value was falling. Many Cadillac buyers were on their last car. Thus, although Cadillac's market share was good, its customer equity was not. Compare this with BMW. Its more youthful and vigorous image didn't win BMW the early market share war. However, it did win BMW younger customers with higher customer lifetime values. The result: Cadillac now captures only about a 15 percent market share, lower than BMW's. And BMW's customer equity remains much higher—it has more customers with a higher average customer lifetime value. Thus, market share is not the answer. We should care not just about current sales but also about future sales. Customer lifetime value and customer equity are the name of the game.[24]

Customer Relationship Levels and Tools

Companies can build customer relationships at many levels, depending on the nature of the target market. At one extreme, a company with many low-margin customers may seek to develop *basic relationships* with them. For example, Procter & Gamble does not phone all of its Tide customers to get to know them personally. Instead, P&G creates relationships through brand-building advertising, sales promotions, a 1-800 customer response number, and its Tide FabricCare Network Web site (www.Tide.com).

At the other extreme, in markets with few customers and high margins, sellers want to create *full partnerships* with key customers. For example, P&G customer teams work closely with Wal-Mart, Safeway, and other large retailers. And Boeing partners with American Airlines, Delta, and other airlines in designing its airplanes that fully satisfy their requirements. In between these two extreme situations, other levels of customer relationships are appropriate.

Today, most leading companies are developing customer loyalty and retention programs. Beyond offering consistently high value and satisfaction, marketers can use specific marketing tools to develop stronger bonds with consumers.[25] First, a company might build value and satisfaction by adding *financial benefits* to the customer relationship. For example, many companies now offer *frequency marketing programs* that reward customers who buy frequently or in large amounts. Airlines offer frequent-flier programs, hotels give room upgrades to their frequent guests, and supermarkets give patronage discounts.

A second approach is to add *social benefits* as well as financial benefits. For example, many companies sponsor *club marketing programs* that offer members special discounts and create member communities. For example:[26]

Swiss watchmaker, Swatch, uses its club to cater to collectors, who on average buy nine of the company's quirky watches every year. "Swatch: The Club" members get additional chances to buy limited-edition Swatch specials. They also receive the *Swatch World Journal,* a magazine filled with Swatch-centric news from the four corners of the globe. And the club's Web site is the ultimate meeting place for Swatch enthusiasts. Swatch counts on enthusiastic word of mouth from club members as a boost to business. "Our members are like walking billboards," says the manager of Swatch's club, Trish O'Callaghan. "They love, live, and breathe our product. They are ambassadors for Swatch."

Harley-Davidson sponsors the Harley Owners Group (H.O.G.), which gives Harley riders "an organized way to share their passion and show their pride." H.O.G. membership benefits include two magazines (*Hog Tales* and *Enthusiast*), a *H.O.G. Touring Handbook,* a roadside assistance program, a specially designed insurance program, theft reward service, a travel center, and a "Fly & Ride" program enabling members to rent Harleys while on vacation. The

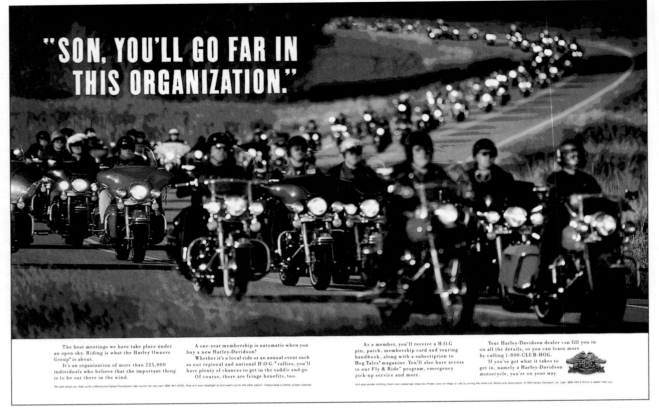

Building customer relationships: Harley-Davidson sponsors the Harley Owners Group (H.O.G.),
which gives Harley owners "an organized way to share their passion and show their pride." The
worldwide club now numbers more than 1,300 local chapters and 700,000 members.

company also maintains an extensive H.O.G. Web site, which offers information on H.O.G. chapters, rallies, events, and benefits. The worldwide club now numbers more than 1,300 local chapters and 700,000 members.

A third approach to building customer relationships is to add *structural ties* as well as financial and social benefits. For example, a business marketer might supply customers with special equipment or computer linkages that help them manage their orders, payroll, or inventory. McKesson Corporation, a leading pharmaceutical wholesaler, has invested millions of dollars to set up direct computer links with drug manufacturers and an online system to help small pharmacies manage their inventories, their order entry, and their shelf space. FedEx offers Web links to its customers to keep them from defecting to competitors such as UPS. Customers can use the Web site to arrange shipments and track the status of their FedEx packages anywhere in the world.

Customer relationship management means that marketers must focus on managing their customers as well as their products. At the same time, they don't want relationships with every customer. In fact, there are undesirable customers for every company. Ultimately, marketing involves attracting, keeping, and growing *profitable* customers.

Marketing Challenges in the New, "Connected" Millennium

As the world spins into the first decade of the twenty-first century, dramatic changes are occurring in the marketing arena. Richard Love of Hewlett-Packard observes, "The pace of change is so rapid that the ability to change has now become a competitive advantage." Yogi Berra, the legendary New York Yankees catcher, summed it up more simply when he said, "The future ain't what it used to be." Technological advances, rapid globalization, and continuing social and economic shifts—all are causing profound changes in the marketplace. As the marketplace changes, so must those who serve it.

FIGURE 1.6
Today's marketing
connections

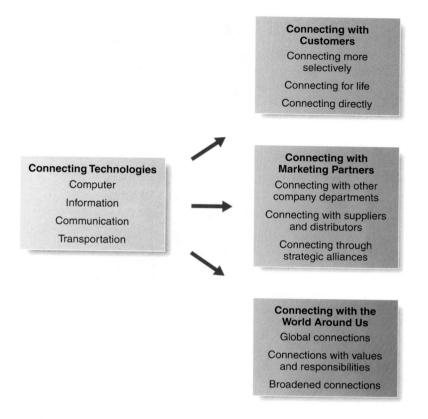

The major marketing developments as we enter the new millennium can be summed up in a single theme: *connecting.* Now, more than ever before, we are all connected to each other and to things near and far in the world around us. Moreover, we are connecting in new and different ways. Where it once took weeks or months to travel across the United States, we can now travel around the globe in only hours or days. Where it once took days or weeks to receive news about important world events, we now see them as they are occurring through live satellite broadcasts. Where it once took weeks to correspond with others in distant places, they are now only moments away by phone or the Internet.

In this section, we examine the major trends and forces that are changing the marketing landscape and challenging marketing strategy in this new, connected millennium. As Figure 1.6 shows, sweeping changes in connecting technologies are causing marketers to redefine how they connect with the marketplace. Marketers are rethinking their relationships with customers, with marketing partners inside and outside the company, and with the world around them. We first look at the dramatic changes occurring in the connecting technologies. Then, we examine how these changes are affecting marketing connections.

Technologies for Connecting

The major force behind the new connectedness is explosive advances in computer, telecommunications, information, transportation, and other connecting technologies. The technology boom has created exciting new ways to learn about and track customers and create products and services tailored to individual customer needs. Technology is helping companies to distribute products more efficiently and effectively and to communicate with customers in large groups or one-to-one. For example, through videoconferencing, marketing researchers at a company's headquarters in New York can look in on focus groups in Chicago or Paris without ever stepping onto a plane. With only a few clicks of a mouse button, a direct marketer can tap into online data services to learn anything from what car you drive to what you read to what flavor of ice cream you prefer.

Using today's vastly more powerful computers, marketers create detailed databases and use them to target individual customers with offers designed to meet their specific needs and buying patterns. With a new wave of communication and advertising tools—ranging from cell phones, fax machines, CD-ROM, and interactive TV to video kiosks at airports and shopping malls—marketers can zero in on selected customers with carefully targeted messages. Through

Explosive advances in connecting technologies have created exciting ways to learn about customers and to create tailored products, distribute them more effectively, and communicate with customers in large groups or one-to-one.

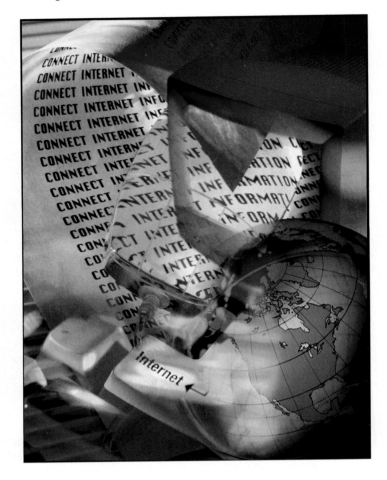

electronic commerce, customers can design, order, and pay for products and services—without ever leaving home. Then, through the marvels of express delivery, they can receive their purchases in less than 24 hours. From virtual reality displays that test new products to online virtual stores that sell them, the technology boom is affecting every aspect of marketing.

The Internet

Internet
The vast and burgeoning global web of computer networks with no central management or ownership.

Perhaps the most dramatic new technology driving the connected age is the **Internet.** The Internet is a vast and burgeoning global web of computer networks with no central management or ownership. Today, the Internet links individuals and businesses of all types to each other and to information all around the world.

The Internet has been hailed as the technology behind a New Economy. It allows anytime, anywhere connections to information, entertainment, and communication. Companies are using the Internet to build closer relationships with customers and marketing partners and to sell and distribute their products more efficiently and effectively. Beyond competing in traditional marketplaces, they now have access to exciting new market*spaces*.

Internet usage surged in the 1990s with the development of the user-friendly World Wide Web. Entering the new millennium, Internet penetration in the United States has reached close to 66 percent, with some 160 million people accessing the Web in any given month. The Internet is truly a global phenomenon—the number of Internet users worldwide is expected to approach 1 billion by 2004.[27] This growing and diverse Internet population means that all kinds of people are now going to the Web for information and to buy products and services. Notes one analyst, "In just [a few short years], the Net has gone from a playground for nerds into a vast communications and trading center where . . . people swap information and do deals around the world. . . . [More and more] companies have hung www.shingle.com atop their digital doorways with the notion that being anywhere on the Net means selling virtually everywhere."[28]

Companies of all types are now attempting to snare new customers on the Web. Many traditional "brick-and-mortar" companies have now become "click-and-mortar" companies. They are venturing online in an effort to attract new customers and build stronger relationships with existing ones. The Internet also spawned an entirely new breed of "click-only" companies—the so-called "dot-coms." During the Web frenzy of the late 1990s, dot-coms popped up everywhere, selling everything from books, toys, and CDs to furniture, home mortgages, and 100-pound bags of dog food via the Internet. The frenzy cooled during the "dot-com meltdown" of 2000, when many poorly conceived e-tailers and other Web start-ups went out of business. Today, despite its turbulent start, online consumer buying is growing at a healthy rate, and many of the dot-com survivors face promising futures.[29]

If consumer e-commerce looks promising, business-to-business e-commerce is just plain booming. Business-to-business transactions online are expected to reach $4.3 trillion in 2005, compared with only $107 billion in consumer purchases. By 2005, more than 500,000 businesses will engage in e-commerce as buyers, sellers, or both. It seems that almost every major business has set up shop on the Web. Giants such as GE, IBM, Dell, Cisco Systems, Microsoft, and many others have moved quickly to exploit the power of the Internet.[30]

Thus, changes in connecting technologies are providing exciting new opportunities for marketers. We will explore the impact of the new Internet age in more detail in Chapter 3. Here, we look at the ways these technological changes are affecting how companies connect with their customers, marketing partners, and the world around us (see Figure 1.6).

Connecting with Customers

We've already discussed the critical importance of customer relationship management. The most profound new developments in marketing involve the ways in which today's companies are relating to their customers. Yesterday's companies focused on mass marketing to all comers at arm's length. Today's companies are building more direct and lasting relationships with more carefully selected customers.

Connecting with More Carefully Selected Customers

Few firms today still practice true mass marketing—selling in a standardized way to any customer who comes along. Today, most marketers realize that they don't want to connect with just *any* customers. Instead, most are targeting fewer, more profitable customers.

The United States—in fact, the world—has become more of a "salad bowl" of diverse ethnic, cultural, social, and locational groups. The greater diversity has meant greater market fragmentation. In response, most firms have moved from mass marketing to segmented marketing, in which they target carefully chosen submarkets or even individual buyers. "One-to-one marketing" has become the order of the day for some marketers. They build huge customer databases containing rich information on individual customer preferences and purchases. Then, they mine these databases to gain insights by which they can "mass-customize" their offerings to deliver greater value to individual buyers.

At the same time that companies are finding new ways to deliver more value *to* customers, they are also beginning to assess carefully the value *of* customers to the firm. They want to connect only with customers that they can serve *profitably*. In a process called *selective relationship management,* many companies now use customer profitability analysis to weed out losing customers and target the winning ones for pampering. Once they identify profitable customers, firms can create attractive offers and special handling to capture these customers and earn their loyalty.

But what should the company do with unprofitable customers? If it can't turn them into profitable ones, it may even want to "fire" customers that are too unreasonable or that cost more to serve than they are worth. For example, the banking industry has led the way in assessing customer profitability. After decades of casting a wide net to lure as many customers as possible, many banks are now mining their vast databases to identify winning customers and weed out losing ones.

Banks now routinely calculate customer value based on such factors as an account's average balances, account activity, services usage, branch visits, and other variables. A bank's customer service reps use such customer ratings when deciding how much—or how little—leeway to give a customer who wants, say, a lower credit-card interest rate or to escape the bank's bounced-check fee. Profitable customers often get what they want; for customers whose accounts lose money for the bank, the reps rarely budge. This sorting-out process, of course, has many risks. For one, future profits are hard to predict. A high school student on his or her way to a Harvard MBA and a plum job on Wall Street might be unprofitable now

Selective relationship management: BankOne in Lousiana lets its "Premier One" customers know that they are "special, exclusive, privileged, and valued." For example, after presenting a special gold card to the "concierge' near the front door, they are whisked away to a special teller window with no line or to the desk of a specially trained bank officer.

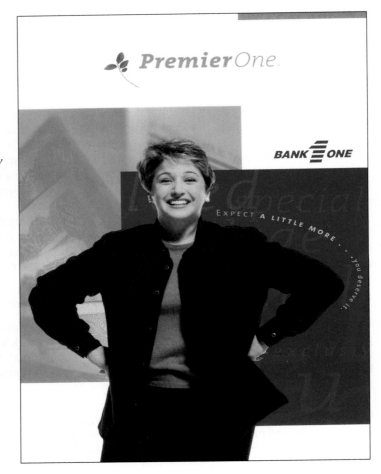

but worth courting for the future. Or that shabby-looking guy might actually be or become an eccentric billionaire—so you may not want to give him the bum's rush. Still, most banks believe that the benefits outweigh the risks. For example, after First Chicago imposed a three-dollar teller fee in 1995 on some of its money-losing customers, 30,000 of them—or close to 3 percent of the bank's customers—closed their accounts. However, many marginal customers became profitable by boosting their account balances high enough to avoid the fee or by visiting ATMs instead of tellers. On balance, imposing the fee improved the profitability of the bank's customer base.[31]

Connecting for a Customer's Lifetime

Just as companies are being more selective about which customers they choose to serve, they are serving those they choose in a deeper, more lasting way. As we discussed earlier, the goal is shifting from making a profit on each sale to making long-term profits by managing the lifetime value of a customer and the firm's total customer equity. Marketers now spend less time figuring out how to increase "share of market" and more time trying to grow "share of customer." They offer greater variety to current customers and train employees to cross-sell and up-sell in order to market more products and services to existing customers. For example, Amazon.com began as an online bookseller, but now offers music, videos, gifts, toys, consumer electronics, home improvement items, and an online auction. In addition, based on each customer's purchase history, the company recommends related books, CDs, or videos that might be of interest. In this way, Amazon.com captures a greater share of each customer's leisure and entertainment budget.

Connecting Directly

Beyond connecting more deeply with their customers, many companies are also connecting more *directly*. In fact, direct marketing is booming. Consumers can now buy virtually any product without going to a store—by telephone, mail-order catalogs, kiosks, and e-commerce. Business

New customer connections: P&G uses its www.Pampers. com Web site to build relationships with young parents by providing information and advice on diapering, baby care, and even child development.

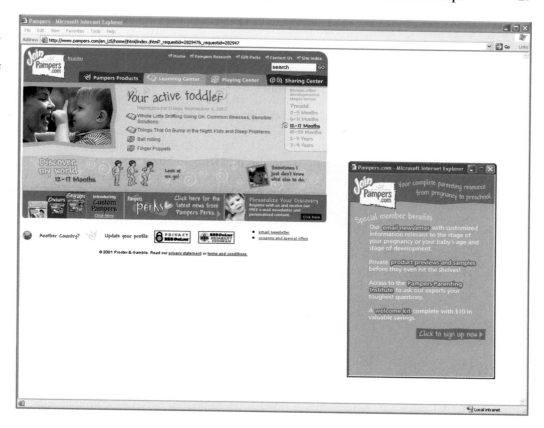

purchasing agents routinely shop on the Web for items ranging from standard office supplies to high-priced, high-tech computer equipment.

Some companies sell *only* via direct channels—firms such as Dell Computer, Expedia, 1-800-Flowers, and Amazon.com, to name only a few. Other companies use direct connections to supplement their other communications and distribution channels. For example, Procter & Gamble sells Pampers disposable diapers through retailers, supported by millions of dollars of mass-media advertising. However, P&G uses its www.Pampers.com Web site to build relationships with young parents by providing information and advice on diapering, baby care, and even child development. Similarly, you can't buy crayons from the Crayola Web site (www.crayola.com). However, you can find out how to remove crayon marks from your new carpeting or freshly painted walls.

Some marketers have hailed direct marketing as the "marketing model of the next millennium." They envision a day when all buying and selling will involve direct connections between companies and their customers. Others, although agreeing that direct marketing will play a growing and important role, see it as just one more way to approach the marketplace. We will take a closer look at world of direct marketing in Chapters 3 and 17.

Connecting with Marketing Partners

Partner relationship management

Working closely with partners in other company departments and outside the company to jointly bring greater value to customers.

In addition to *customer relationship management,* marketers must also be good at **partner relationship management.** In these ever more connected times, major changes are occurring in how marketers partner with others inside and outside the company to jointly bring greater value to customers.

Connecting Inside the Company

Traditionally, marketers have been charged with understanding customers and representing customer needs to different company departments. The old thinking was that marketing is done only by marketing, sales, and customer support people. However, in today's connected world, marketing no longer has sole ownership of customer interactions. Every functional area can interact with customers, especially electronically. The new thinking is that every employee must be customer focused. David Packard, co-founder of Hewlett-Packard, wisely said, "Marketing is far too important to be left only to the marketing department."[32]

Today, rather than letting each department go its own way, firms are linking all departments in the cause of creating customer value. Rather than assigning only sales and marketing people to customers, they are forming cross-functional customer teams. For example, Procter & Gamble assigns "customer development teams" to each of its major retailer accounts. These teams—consisting of sales and marketing people, operations and logistics specialists, market and financial analysts, and others—coordinate the efforts of many P&G departments toward helping the retailer be more successful.

Connecting with Outside Partners

Rapid changes are also occurring in how marketers connect with their suppliers, channel partners, and even competitors. Most companies today are networked companies, relying heavily on partnerships with other firms.

Supply Chain Management.   Marketing channels consist of distributors, retailers, and others who connect the company to its buyers. The *supply chain* describes a longer channel, stretching from raw materials to components to final products that are carried to final buyers. For example, the supply chain for personal computers consists of suppliers of computer chips and other components, the computer manufacturer, and the distributors, retailers, and others who sell the computers to businesses and final customers. Each member of the supply chain creates and captures only a portion of the total value generated by the supply chain.

Through *supply chain management,* many companies today are strengthening their connections with partners all along the supply chain. They know that their fortunes rest not only on how well they perform. Success also rests on how well their entire supply chain performs against competitors' supply chains. They don't just treat suppliers as vendors and distributors as customers. They treat both as partners in delivering customer value. For example, Wal-Mart works with suppliers such as Procter & Gamble, Rubbermaid, and Black & Decker to streamline logistics and reduce joint distribution costs, resulting in lower prices to consumers. Lexus, on the one hand, works closely with carefully selected suppliers to improve quality and operations efficiency. On the other hand, it works with its franchise dealers to provide top-grade sales and service support that will bring customers in the door and keep them coming back.

Strategic Alliances.   Beyond managing the supply chain, today's companies are also discovering that they need *strategic* partners if they hope to be effective. In the new, more competitive global environment, going it alone is going out of style. *Strategic alliances* are booming across almost all industries and services. For example, Dell Computer recently ran advertisements telling how it partners with Microsoft and Intel to provide customized e-business solutions. The ads ask: "Why do many corporations choose Windows running on Dell PowerEdge servers with Intel Pentium processors to power their e-business solutions?" The answer: "At Dell, Microsoft, and Intel, we specialize in solving the impossible."

Companies need to give careful thought to finding partners who might complement their strengths and offset their weaknesses. Well-managed alliances can have a huge impact on sales and profits. A recent study found that one in every four dollars earned by the top 1,000 U.S. companies flows from alliances, double the rate in the early 1990s. As Jim Kelly, former CEO at UPS, puts it, "The old adage 'If you can't beat 'em, join 'em,' is being replaced by 'Join 'em and you can't be beat.'"[33]

Connecting with the World Around Us

As they are redefining their relationships with customers and partners, marketers are also taking a fresh look at the ways in which they connect with the broader world around them. Here we look at trends toward increasing globalization, more concern for social and environmental responsibility, and greater use of marketing by nonprofit and public-sector organizations.

Global Connections

In an increasingly smaller world, many marketers are now connected *globally* with their customers and marketing partners. The world economy has undergone radical change during the past two decades. Geographical and cultural distances have shrunk with the advent of jet planes, fax machines, world satellite television broadcasts, global Internet hookups, and other technical

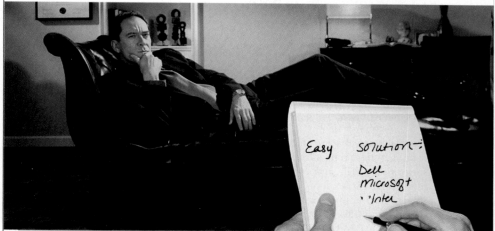

Strategic alliances: Dell recently ran ads telling how it partners with Microsoft and Intel to provide customized e-business solutions. "At Dell, Microsoft, and Intel, we specialize in solving the impossible."

advances. This has allowed companies to greatly expand their geographical market coverage, purchasing, and manufacturing. The result is a vastly more complex marketing environment for both companies and consumers.

Today, almost every company, large or small, is touched in some way by global competition. A neighborhood florist buys its flowers from Mexican nurseries, while a large U.S. electronics manufacturer competes in its home markets with giant Japanese rivals. A fledgling Internet retailer that finds itself receiving orders from all over the world at the same time that an American consumer-goods producer introduces new products into emerging markets abroad.

American firms have been challenged at home by the skillful marketing of European and Asian multinationals. Companies such as Toyota, Siemens, Nestlé, Sony, and Samsung have often outperformed their U.S. competitors in American markets. Similarly, U.S. companies in a wide range of industries have found new opportunities abroad. Coca-Cola, General Motors, ExxonMobil, IBM, General Electric, DuPont, Motorola, and dozens of other American companies have developed truly global operations, making and selling their products worldwide. Even MTV has joined the elite of global brands, delivering localized versions of its pulse-thumping fare to teens in 140 countries around the globe (see Real Marketing 1.3).

Today, companies are not only trying to sell more of their locally produced goods in international markets, they also are buying more supplies and components abroad. For example, Bill Blass, one of America's top fashion designers, may choose cloth woven from Australian wool with designs printed in Italy. He will design a dress and e-mail the drawing to a Hong Kong agent, who will place the order with a Chinese factory. Finished dresses will be air-freighted to New York, where they will be redistributed to department and specialty stores around the country.

Thus, managers in countries around the world are increasingly taking a global, not just local, view of the company's industry, competitors, and opportunities. They are asking: What is global marketing? How does it differ from domestic marketing? How do global competitors and forces affect our business? To what extent should we "go global"? Many companies are forming strategic alliances with foreign companies, even competitors, who serve as suppliers or marketing partners. Winning companies in the next century may well be those that have built the best global networks.

MTV Global: Music Is the Universal Language

Some say love is the universal language. But for MTV, the universal language is *music*. In 1981, MTV began offering its unique brand of programming for young music lovers across the United States. The channel's quirky but pulse-thumping lineup of shows soon attracted a large audience in its targeted 12-to-34 age group. MTV quickly established itself as the nation's youth-culture network, offering up "everything young people care about." With success in the United States secured, MTV went global in 1986, selling a few hours of programming to Japan's Asahi network. A short time later, in 1987, it launched MTV Europe, and the network has experienced phenomenal global growth ever since.

MTV now offers programming in 140 countries, including Brazil, Canada, China, France, Germany, Holland, India, Italy, Japan, Korea, Latin America, Poland, Russia, Southeast Asia, Spain, Taiwan, Hong Kong, and the United Kingdom. The result of this global expansion? Today, MTV reaches twice as many people around the world as CNN, and 8 out of 10 MTV viewers live outside of the United States. All together, MTV reaches into an astounding 384 million households in 19 different languages on 33 different channels and 17 Web sites.

What is the secret to MTV's roaring international success? Of course, it offers viewers around the globe plenty of what made it so popular in the United States. Tune in to the network in Paris, or Beijing, or Moscow, or Tierra del Fuego, or anywhere else and you'll see all of the elements that make it uniquely MTV anywhere in the world—the global MTV brand symbols, fast-paced format, veejays, rockumentaries, and music, music, music. But rather than just offering a carbon copy of its U.S. programming to international viewers, MTV carefully localizes its fare. Each channel serves up a mix that includes 70 percent local programming tailored to the specific tastes on viewers in local markets. A *Business Week* analyst notes:

> [MTV is] shrewd enough to realize that while the world's teens want American music, they really want the local stuff, too. So, MTV's producers and veejays scour their local markets for the top talent. The result is an endless stream of overnight sensations that keep MTV's global offerings

fresh. Just over a year ago, for example, Lena Katina and Yulia Volkova were no different than most Moscow schoolgirls. Today, Katina, 16, and Volkova, 15, make up Tatu, one of the hottest bands ever to come out of Russia.

Tatu is just one of a slew of emerging local music groups gaining international exposure through MTV and a wider audience in the United States, too. Colombian rock singer Shakira, unknown outside Latin America until 1999 when she recorded an MTV Unplugged CD—the acoustic live concerts recorded by MTV—is now the winner of one U.S. Grammy and two Latin Grammy awards. Her CD has gone platinum, selling more than 2 million copies worldwide.

[MTV's] policy of 70 percent local content has resulted in some of the network's most creative shows, such as MTV Brazil's monthlong *Rockgol*, a soccer championship that pits Brazilian musicians against record industry executives. In Russia, the locally produced *Twelve Angry Viewers* was voted one of Russia's top three talk programs. In a colorful studio amid bright blue steps and large green cushions, a dozen teens watch and discuss the latest videos. Periodically, they break into spontaneous dance or pop one another over the head with inflatable lollipops. Okay, it's not Chekhov. But Russian groups beg to be featured on it.

Ceding so much control to local channels does result in the occasional misstep. While watching MTV in Taiwan, [MTV executives were] aghast to see nude wrestling. That was one time [they] had to intervene. And when MTV first entered the Indian market in 1996, Hindi film music—the romantic soundtracks of Bollywood movies—was wildly popular, but [MTV's] locally hired programmers disdained it as uncool. Viewers abandoned the channel, forcing it to [relent and] air Bollywood music. Since then its ratings have soared by some 700 percent. To give kids their dose of rock, [Roedy] has breakfasted with former Israeli Prime Minister Shimon Peres, dined with Singapore founder Lee Kuan Yew, and

chewed the fat with Chinese leader Jiang Zemin. [He] even met with El Caudillo himself—Cuban leader Fidel Castro—who wondered if MTV could teach Cuban kids English. Says Roedy: "We've had very little resistance once we explain that we're not in the business of exporting American culture."

At the center of MTV's global growth machine is Bill Roedy, president of MTV Networks International. He's a nonstop ambassador on a mission to make MTV available in every last global nook and cranny.

MTV's unique blend of international and local programming is not only popular, it's also highly profitable. The network's hold on a young, increasingly wealthy population makes its programming especially popular with advertisers. Altogether, its mix of local and international content, combined with early entry in international markets, makes it tough to beat. "MTV Networks International makes buckets of money year after year from a potent combination of cable subscriber fees, advertising, and, increasingly, new media," concludes the analyst. "Revenues at MTV Networks International increased 19 percent [last year] . . . while operating profits grew a hefty 50 percent. They are expected to more than double by 2004." Meanwhile, the competition struggles just to break even. VIVA, MTV's strongest competitor in Europe, has yet to turn a profit.

Thus, in only two decades, MTV has joined the ranks of the global brand elite, alongside such icons as Coke, Levi's, and Sony. Concludes the analyst: "MTV's version of globalization rocks."

Sources: Excerpts from Kerry Capell, "MTV's World: Mando-Pop. Mexican Hip Hop. Russian Rap. It's All Fueling the Biggest Global Channel," *Business Week*, February 18, 2002, pp. 81–84. Also see Lynn Elber, "US TV Networks Expand Interests Overseas," *Marketing News*, November 7, 1994, p. 7; Alkman, Granitsas, "MTV Is Launching a 24-Hour Network in Indonesian Cities," *Wall Street Journal*, March 13, 2002, p. B7; the MTV Worldwide Web site, www.mtv.com/mtvinternational; and the Viacom Corporate Web site, www.viacom.com.

Connections with Our Values and Social Responsibilities

Marketers are reexamining their connections with social values and responsibilities and with the very Earth that sustains us. As the worldwide consumerism and environmentalism movements mature, today's marketers are being called upon to take greater responsibility for the social and environmental impact of their actions. Corporate ethics and social responsibility have become hot topics for almost every business. And few companies can ignore the renewed and very demanding environmental movement.

The social responsibility and environmental movements will place even stricter demands on companies in the future. Some companies resist these movements, budging only when forced by legislation or consumer outcries. More forward-looking companies, however, readily accept their responsibilities to the world around them. They view socially responsible actions as an opportunity to do well by doing good. They seek ways to profit by serving the best long-run interests of their customers and communities. Some companies—such as Ben & Jerry's, Saturn, The Body Shop, and others—are practicing "caring capitalism" and distinguishing themselves by being more civic-minded and caring. They are building social responsibility and action into their company value and mission statements. For example, the Ben & Jerry's mission statement challenges all employees, from top management to ice cream scoopers in each store, to include concern for individual and community welfare in their day-to-day decisions.[34]

Broadening Connections

Many different kinds of organizations are using marketing to connect with customers and other important constituencies. In the past, marketing has been most widely applied in the for-profit business sector. In recent years, however, marketing also has become a major part of the strategies of many not-for-profit organizations, such as colleges, hospitals, museums, symphony orchestras, and even churches. Consider the following example:

Want to feed your soul?" implores a subway ad for Marble Collegiate Church in New York City. "We've got a great menu." Indeed, Marble Collegiate has something on its plate for almost every type of hungering spiritual consumer. It has ministries targeting senior citizens; young singles; older singles; gays and lesbians; entrepreneurs; artists, actors, and writers; men; women; children; and people who love singing gospel music, to name a few. The church has been at work on yet another program. Called the New Spirit Cafe, it's a hip kind of spiritual eatery designed to feed the souls—and stomachs—of those who may be disillusioned by organized religion. The New Spirit Cafe aimed to establish Marble Collegiate's "brand" with spiritually minded people in their twenties and thirties who may be wary of conventional religious organizations. It was purposely located several blocks from the sanctuary and offered its fare of hot food, snacks, and seminars six days a week. Marble Collegiate is not alone in turning to marketing. To maintain their shrinking flocks, religions institutions have increasingly borrowed marketing tools and tactics from companies selling more worldly goods. Many are tailoring their core product—religion itself—to the needs of specific demographic groups. To get its message out, Marble Collegiate anointed a Madison Avenue advertising agency as its missionary. The agency produced a slick marketing campaign with hip, youth-oriented messages. One ad urges potential parishioners to "Make a friend in a very high place." Exhorts another: "Not crazy about church? You're perfect for ours." All the marketing seems to be working. Marble Collegiate's Web site traffic has increased by 30 percent since its ad campaign launched, and the church has had its highest attendance in more than 30 years.[35]

Similarly, private colleges, facing declining enrollments and rising costs, are using marketing to compete for students and funds. Many performing arts groups—even the Lyric Opera Company of Chicago, which has seasonal sellouts—face huge operating deficits that they must cover by more aggressive donor marketing. Finally, many long-standing not-for-profit organizations—the YMCA, the Salvation Army, the Girl Scouts—have lost members and are now modernizing their missions and "products" to attract more members and donors.[36]

Government agencies have also shown an increased interest in marketing. For example, the U.S. Army has a marketing plan to attract recruits, and various government agencies are now designing *social marketing campaigns* to encourage energy conservation and concern for the environment or to discourage smoking, excessive drinking, and drug use. Even the once stodgy U.S.

Broadening connections: Marble Collegiate Church's advertising agency has produced ads with hip, youth-oriented messages.

Postal Service has developed innovative marketing to sell commemorative stamps, promote its priority mail services against those of its competitors, and lift its image. It invests some $100 million annually in advertising.[37]

Thus, it seems that every type of organization can connect through marketing. The continued growth of not-for-profit and public-sector marketing presents new and exciting challenges for marketing managers.

The New, Connected World of Marketing

So, today, smart marketers of all kinds are taking advantage of new opportunities for connecting with their customers, their marketing partners, and the world around them. Table 1.1 compares the old marketing thinking to the new. The old marketing thinking saw marketing as little more than selling or advertising. It viewed marketing as customer acquisition rather than customer care. It emphasized trying to make a profit on each sale rather than trying to profit by managing customer lifetime value. And it concerned itself with trying to sell products rather than to understand, create, communicate, and deliver real value to customers.

Fortunately, this old marketing thinking is now giving way to newer ways of thinking. Modern marketing companies are improving their customer knowledge and customer connections. They are targeting profitable customers, then finding innovative ways to capture and keep these customers. They are forming more direct connections with customers and building lasting customer relationships. Using more targeted media and integrating their marketing communications, they are delivering meaningful and consistent messages through every customer contact. They are employing more technologies such as videoconferencing, sales automation software, and the Internet, intranets, and extranets. They view their suppliers and distributors as partners, not adversaries. In sum, today's companies are connecting in new ways to deliver superior value to their customers.

We will explore all of these developments in more detail in future pages. For now, we must recognize that marketing will continue to change dramatically as we move into the twenty-first century. The new millennium offers many exciting opportunities for forward-thinking marketers.

TABLE 1.1	MARKETING CONNECTIONS IN TRANSITION
The Old Marketing Thinking	**The New Marketing Thinking**
Connections with Customers	
Be sales and product centered	Be market and customer centered
Practice mass marketing	Target selected market segments or individuals
Focus on products and sales	Focus on customer satisfaction and value
Make sales to customers	Develop customer relationships
Get new customers	Keep old customers
Grow share of market	Grow share of customer
Serve any customer	Serve profitable customers, "fire" losing ones
Communicate through mass media	Connect with customers directly
Make standardized products	Develop customized products
Connections with Marketing Partners	
Leave customer satisfaction and value to sales and marketing	Enlist all departments in the cause of customer satisfaction and value
Go it alone	Partner with other firms
Connections with the World Around Us	
Market locally	Market locally *and* globally
Assume profit responsibility	Assume social and environmental responsibility
Market for profits	Market for nonprofits
Conduct commerce in market*places*	Conduct e-commerce in market*spaces*

LOOKING BACK: REVIEWING THE CONCEPTS

Today's successful companies—whether large or small, for-profit or not-for-profit, domestic or global—share a strong customer focus and a heavy commitment to marketing. Many people think of marketing as only selling or advertising. But marketing combines many activities—marketing research, product development, distribution, pricing, advertising, personal selling, and others—designed to sense, serve, and satisfy consumer needs while meeting the organization's goals. The goal of marketing is to build and manage profitable customer relationships. Marketing seeks to attract new customers by promising superior value and to keep and grow current customers by delivering satisfaction.

Marketing operates within a dynamic global environment. Rapid changes can quickly make yesterday's winning strategies obsolete. In the next century, marketers will face many new challenges and opportunities. To be successful, companies will have to be strongly market focused.

1. Define what marketing is and discuss its core concepts.
Marketing is a social and managerial process whereby individuals and groups obtain what they need and want through creating and exchanging products and value with others. The core concepts of marketing are *needs, wants,* and *demands; marketing offers (products, services, and experiences); value* and *satisfaction; exchange, transactions,* and *relationships;* and *markets. Wants* are the form assumed by human needs when shaped by culture and individual personality. When backed by buying power, wants become *demands.*

Companies address needs by putting forth a *value proposition,* a set of benefits that they promise to consumers to satisfy their needs. The value proposition is fulfilled through a *marketing offer*—some combination of products, services, information, or experiences offered to a market to satisfy a need or want.

2. Define marketing management and compare the five marketing management orientations.
Marketing management is the art and science of choosing target markets and building profitable relationships with them. This involves getting, keeping, and growing customers through creating, delivering, and communicating superior customer value. Marketing management involves more than simply finding enough customers for the company's current output. Marketing is at times also concerned with changing or even reducing demand. Simply put, marketing management is *customer management* and *demand management.*

Marketing management can adopt one of five competing market orientations. The *production concept* holds that consumers favor products that are available and highly affordable; management's task is to improve production efficiency and bring down prices. The *product concept* holds that consumers favor products that offer the most in quality, performance, and innovative features; thus, little promotional effort is required. The *selling concept* holds that consumers will not buy enough of the organization's products unless it undertakes a large-scale selling and promotion effort. The *marketing concept* holds that achieving organizational goals depends on determining the needs and wants of too much target markets and delivering the desired satisfactions more effectively and efficiently than competitors do. The *societal marketing concept* holds that generating customer satisfaction *and* long-run societal well-being are the keys to both achieving the company's goals and fulfilling its responsibilities.

3. Discuss customer relationship management and strategies for building lasting customer relationships.
Narrowly defined, *customer relationship management (CRM)* involves managing detailed information about individual customers and carefully managing customer "touchpoints" in order to

maximize customer loyalty. More broadly, however, customer relationship management is the overall process of building and maintaining profitable customer relationships by delivering superior customer value and satisfaction. The aim of customer relationship management is to produce high *customer equity,* the total combined customer lifetime values of all of the company's customers.

The key to building lasting relationships is the creation of superior *customer value* and *satisfaction,* and companies need to understand the determinants of these important elements. Faced with a growing range of choices of products and services, consumers base their buying decisions on their perceptions of *value. Customer perceived value* is the difference between total customer value and total customer cost. Customers will usually choose the offer that maximizes their perceived value. *Customer satisfaction* results when a company's performance has fulfilled a buyer's expectations. Customers are dissatisfied if performance is below expectations, satisfied if performance equals expectations, and delighted if performance exceeds expectations.

Satisfied customers buy more, are less price sensitive, talk favorably about the company, and remain loyal longer. Companies not only strive to gain customers but, perhaps more importantly, to retain and grow "share of customer." Companies must decide the level at which they want to build relationships with different market segments and individual customers, ranging from basic relationships to full partnerships. Which is best depends on a customer's lifetime value relative to the costs required to attract and keep that customer. Today's marketers use a number of specific marketing tools to develop stronger bonds with customers by adding *financial* and *social benefits* or *structural ties.*

4. Analyze the major challenges facing marketers heading into the new, "connected" millennium.

As we head into the next millennium, dramatic changes in the marketplace are creating many marketing opportunities and challenges. Major marketing developments can be summed up in a single theme: *connecting.* The explosive growth in connecting technologies—computer, information, telecommunications, and transportation technologies—has created an exciting New Economy, filled with new ways for marketers to learn about and serve consumers, in large groups or one-to-one. Marketers are rapidly redefining how they connect with their customers, with their marketing partners, and with the world around them. They are choosing their customers more carefully and developing closer, more direct, and more lasting connections with them. Realizing that going it alone is going out of style, they are connecting more closely with other company departments and with other firms in an integrated effort to bring more value to customers. They are taking a fresh look at the ways in which they connect with the broader world, resulting in increased globalization, growing attention to social and environmental responsibilities, and greater use of marketing by not-for-profit and public-sector organizations. The new, connected millennium offers exciting possibilities for forward-thinking marketers.

REVIEWING THE KEY TERMS

Customer equity 21
Customer lifetime value 16
Customer perceived value 17
Customer relationship
  management 16
Customer satisfaction 17

Demands 6
Demarketing 11
Exchange 9
Internet 24
Market 10
Marketing 5

Marketing concept 12
Marketing management 11
Marketing offer 6
Need 6
Partnership relationship
  management 27

Product concept 12
Production concept 12
Selling concept 12
Societal marketing concept 14
Transaction 9
Want 6

DISCUSSING THE CONCEPTS

1. In your own words, what does the term marketing mean?
2. Marketing is managing profitable customer relationships. Discuss the concept of customer value and how it relates to successful marketing.
3. The value proposition is fulfilled through a marketing offer. Pick a company whose product you've recently purchased. Describe the company's value proposition and a marketing offer.
4. Explain the relationships between customer value, satisfaction, and quality.
5. Briefly discuss the differences between the marketing concept and the production, product, and selling concepts. Which concepts are easier to adopt in the short run? Which concept offers the best chance of long-run success? Why?

6. Highly satisfied customers produce several benefits for a company. List some of these benefits. How do companies *delight* customers? How do companies grow their *share of customer?*
7. Today, most leading companies are developing customer-loyalty-and-retention programs. List and describe three ways marketers can use marketing tools to develop stronger bonds with consumers.
8. The major marketing trends today can be summed up in a single theme: *connecting.* List and discuss three important connections made possible by technology. Give specific examples of companies taking advantage of such connections.

APPLYING THE CONCEPTS

1. Few companies do as much to apply the societal marketing concept and to build relationships with customers as Ben & Jerry's, now a subsidiary of Unilever. One of the early members of the societal marketing movement, today the premium ice cream maker continues its commitment to a wide range of ecological and social causes. The company directs more than 7 percent of its profits to causes that benefit communities all over the world. Although such policies benefit society, do they also build relationships with customers and ultimately benefit Unilever stockholders?
   a. Visit the Ben & Jerry's Web site at www.benjerry.com. What impresses you most about the site? What marketing efforts are evident?

b. What are the company's social and ecological mission statements? What social and ecological causes does the company support?

c. What values does the company communicate? Do these values appear to help or hinder its marketing efforts?

d. How does this company seem to balance profits, consumer wants, and society's interests?

e. Give an example of how Ben & Jerry's uses the relationship building blocks (customer value and satisfaction) to attract and retain customers.

f. How does the company build relationships or "connections" with customers? Which of the three connecting technologies described in Figure 1.6 are compatible with these strategies?

2. More than 50 million people are hooked on eBay, the merchandising giant that began in 1995. The electronic marketplace created by eBay (and its competitors) is the latest trend in e-commerce. Hoards of people dig through their attics and junk drawers looking for things to sell through eBay's virtual yard sales.

As a result, more than half a million items are sold daily on eBay. It's no wonder that the company's business model has critics taking note. As buyers outbid one another to get the goods, the trash-to-treasure approach to retailing has never been so successful. And eBay is cashing in on the auctioning euphoria. Last year alone, the company's profits totaled more than $90 million.

a. Visit the eBay Web site at www.ebay.com. What is eBay's *value proposition*? How does this value proposition translate into a *marketing offer*?

b. Users conduct an estimated 170 million transactions a year on eBay. How are markets identified and formed on eBay?

c. How have those markets generated demand? Is this demand different from that found in traditional marketplaces?

d. How does eBay build "connections" with its customers? How could eBay grow its "share of customer"?

 DIGITAL CONNECTIONS

CONNECTING TECHNOLOGIES THROUGH INVENTION AND ECOLOGICAL RESPONSIBILITY

Inventor Dean Kamen promised the world a new way of thinking about transportation. In 2001 he made good on his promise, introducing the Segway Human Transporter (HT). The Segway HT is a self-balancing personal transportation device that uses gyroscope technology and moves at a maximum of 12.5 miles per hour. With no accelerator and no brakes, the HT responds to the rider's shifting body weight, providing effortless transportation with environmentally friendly electrical power. With this new gadget, Kamen offers a new solution to an enduring need for efficient and effective transportation.

FOR DISCUSSION

1. Go to the Segway Human Transporter Web site at www.segway.com. How has Kamen brought new value to

the marketplace? Does Kamen have a viable and socially responsible solution to the problem of human transportation?

2. How has Kamen created connections with consumers through the Segway Web site? What are your criticisms (if any) of the Web site?

3. Using two columns, list the benefits of Segway to a rider for personal use and for business use. Then match these benefits to potential target markets. Did you generate any benefits not noted on the Web site?

4. Design a statement identifying the Segway HT's target markets, value proposition, and marketing offer. Are the marketing efforts behind the Segway HT more in line with the marketing concept or the societal marketing concept? How does the Segway HT leverage technology to connect with customers?

SatMetrix: Helping to Build Customer Relationships

Outstanding marketing companies go out of their way to keep their customers satisfied. But gauging satisfaction, especially at an individual level, can be difficult. SatMetrix, an Internet-based company, creates and administers e-mail surveys for firms such as eBay, Siebel, eTrade, Hewlett-Packard, and Lucent Technologies. The surveys reveal customer expectations and measure customer satisfaction. The goal? To keep customers happy and loyal. Says Roselie Buonauro, SatMetrix's co-founder and chief customer officer, "Everything in today's economy is about keeping customers. Customer loyalty drives cash flow."

After reviewing the video segment featuring SatMetrix, answer the following questions about customer satisfaction and retention:

1. How might a company, such as eBay or Hewlett-Packard, work with SatMetrix to build customer relationships and encourage customer loyalty?

2. SatMetrix relies on e-mail to gauge customer satisfaction. What are the advantages and disadvantages of obtaining customer feedback through e-mail surveys? How else might a company connect with customers to obtain satisfaction feedback?

3. Think of a time when a product or service failed to meet your expectations. How did the experience affect your relationship with the brand and company? How did you respond? What could the company have done to turn the failure into a positive experience?

Botox: *Almost* Trouble-Free New Faces

In the movie virgule *Face/Off*, John Travolta got a new look by exchanging faces with Nicholas Cage. Unfortunately, he got a lot of trouble along with it. Today, John could receive a much less troublesome new look by using Botox, from Allergan Laboratories in Irvine, California. Not only has Botox smoothed the visages of aging actors, it has also come to the rescue of countless comedians and late-night talk-show hosts. Beyond perhaps doing wonders for their appearance, it's also given them a slew of new jokes as the "next Viagra."

In 1990, Allergan was just a small specialty pharmaceutical firm selling little-known eye and skin drugs and over-the-counter contact lens cleaners. The introduction of Botox wasn't such a big deal initially. After all, typical of Allergan specialty products, it was just another specialty drug aimed at a small market (treatment of cross-eye) supported by little marketing effort.

That was before doctors discovered that injecting Botox around eyes not only eliminated ocular problems, it erased frown lines as well. Once that happened, the buzz was on between doctors and patients. Before long, doctors in most major U.S. cities were giving patients off-label (not approved by the FDA for this use) Botox injections. Even though Allergan could not openly market the product for cosmetic purposes, by 2001 sales of Botox rocketed to $310 million and were growing between 25 percent and 35 percent per year. That translates into over 1.6 million Botox cosmetic procedures performed on roughly 850,000 patients. FDA approval, granted in April 2002, only accelerated this sales bonanza.

The good news for Allergan does not end with wiping out frown lines. Botox also effectively treats migraine headaches, chronic neck and back pain, excessive sweating, and possibly spastic disorders. With all those target markets, Botox could become a blockbuster drug—with more than a billion dollars in sales—bringing Allergan out of the backwaters of the pharmaceutical business.

Botox Cosmetic is botulinum toxin A, a heavily diluted version of the feared botulinum toxin found in spoiled canned soups and vegetables. It contains only 20 units of the toxin compared to the thousands of units found in spoiled food, but it works in the same way—by paralyzing facial muscles to the point where they can no longer contract.

Frown lines are definitely a sign of age, use, and wear. They occur when facial muscles contract, drawing the skin up. When the muscles relax, the lines disappear. As we get older, it becomes more difficult to relax, so that we seldom fully relax our facial muscles.

Although eliminating frown lines sounds great, there is at least one small problem. Totally relaxed forehead muscles leave you incapable of rendering any expression at or above the eyes. For the celebrities and stars that were among the first to use Botox, this resulted in "performance" problems. One TV star commented that when the director kept telling her to show anger, she replied, "I am, I am." Unfortunately, nothing was moving on the upper half of her face. As a consequence, she stopped using Botox except for Emmy awards night!

For others, however, the loss of expression might be a positive. Business people seeking a softer look might want to eliminate frown lines that make them look irritated or impatient. Trial lawyers attempting to establish rapport with juries might want to eliminate expressions of annoyance and anger. And sales representatives might want to appear unperturbed by what their clients and customers are saying. But while some observers think Botox could give us a kinder, gentler-looking America, others think it could turn us into a nation of zombies.

Besides loss of expression, Botox produces additional side effects. When used on the forehead and around the eyes, Botox can cause drooping eyelids (you won't be able to close or open them completely—this could be either a sexy or a dopey look). Used around the mouth, Botox may cause slurred speech, a droopy mouth, and constant drooling. Other possible side effects include nausea, allergic reactions, headaches, respiratory infections, flu symptoms, and redness and swelling around the injections. The redness and swelling usually go away in a couple of days.

Because Botox Cosmetic lasts only three to six months, all side effects are temporary. This also means, however, that Botox treatments must be repeated when the effects wear off. While that is bad news for consumers, it's good news for doctors. The margins on Botox are quite high—around 80 percent. A vial of Botox Cosmetic costs about $400 and can be used for four treatments. Depending on the doctor's pricing scheme, each treatment can be $500 to $1,000. That's quite a nifty profit for a treatment that usually takes less than 15 minutes, and it's quite a bill for the patient, because insurance companies don't pay for Botox Cosmetic treatments.

Botox has become so lucrative and the demand so great that the treatments are sometimes offered in a party atmosphere—sort of like a Tupperware party. Doctors usually ask a current patient to invite 10 to 15 prospective clients to a party at his or her home, where the partygoers are offered such tidbits as chocolates, brie, and champagne. After a brief social period, the doctor gives a short lecture on Botox and invites the partygoers to sign up for treatment. Patients take turns leaving the room, to the applause of other partygoers, and the doctor gives the injections in private. Parties provide a nonclinical atmosphere more conducive to patient receptivity and reduce the time and costs incurred by the doctor. Even good champagne costs less than nurses, receptionists, and rent, and the doctor can give patients a price break—maybe charging only $250 per treatment at a party. Thus, parties are "good" for everyone. Some doctors, however, object to the "party scene" on the basis that this is a medical treatment and not a social gimmick. Therefore, they hold multiple client sessions in their offices in the evening with the same benefits of price breaks for patients and lower costs and less time for themselves.

Resorts have even gotten on the Botox bandwagon. Jamaica's Half Moon Golf, Tennis and Beach Club retains Dr. Z Paul Lorenc on their staff to give customers quick Botox cosmetic treatments. By the time patients return home, any swelling, redness, or other side effects have disappeared.

Once allowed to advertise Botox for cosmetic purposes, Allergan wanted to capitalize on its popularity. It identified the primary market as the approximately 29 million women between the ages of 30 and 64 with household incomes over $50,000. Within that market, the company believed that 7 million women greatly concerned about their appearance were likely to be heavy users. While women constitute the bulk of the market, there are also plenty of guys who want a smoother forehead. Middle-aged men made up 13.8 percent of the market for Botox in 2001, up from 6.1 percent the year before, making males the fastest-growing user segment.

To reach these markets, Allergan began spending $50 million on marketing in 2002. The backbone of this consumer-oriented campaign was advertisements on TV and in 24 magazines such as *People, The New Yorker, Vogue* and *InStyle*. Allergan estimated that 90 percent of the audience would see ads at least 10 times a year. Most of the ads featured models in everyday clothing and wearing wedding bands—a look that communicated the message that Botox is for everyone.

In addition to the consumer campaign, Allergan began an industry outreach campaign directed at doctors and pharmacists. Beginning with the company Web site, health professionals could obtain information about Botox and its use. The company also beefed up its sales force and armed salespeople with promotional materials for distribution to health professionals. Finally, it conducted clinics demonstrating the appropriate use of Botox in treating patients for cosmetic purposes.

All of this was part of CEO David Pyott's plan to move Allergan into position as a major player in the pharmaceuticals industry. When he took office in 1998, he found that Allergan had not changed its strategy in decades. Among his first moves were closing plants, slashing jobs, and cutting overhead. To refocus the company, he selected target industries for growth and started making the moves necessary to achieve that growth. The company increased R&D expenditures by 26 percent and expanded the sales force by 28 percent. As a result, Allergan actually employed more people by the end of 2002 than it had two years earlier. The expanded sales force allowed Allergan to establish relationships with many more doctors and pharmacists, relationships that Pyott believes are the basis for sales growth. After all, patients don't buy treatments directly; doctors buy Botox and use it on patients.

Allergan's major growth opportunity is the ophthalmologic market, where rival Alcon is number one. Allergan believes that it can capture the number one position there within three years.

The second growth target will be dermatology, where Botox gives the company a major advantage and where it can grow by acquiring new formulas or purchasing a license from a foreign producer. Doing that is more cost-effective than developing new products in the R&D laboratory from scratch.

Sales of Botox fuel much of this growth, as Allergan's margins on Botox are about 60 percent. To prevent the competition from developing their own Botox, the formula for making it is one of the most closely held secrets in the world. With the dollars from Botox, Allergan can increase its marketing efforts, add products to its line, and attack competitors. The best news of all is that sales of Botox are not likely to decline unless consumers and movie stars suddenly face up to their age—wrinkles and all.

QUESTIONS FOR DISCUSSION

1. What are the needs, wants, and demands of consumers of Botox products in its different treatment markets? What value does Botox deliver in each market? How does value affect price for Botox?

2. When Allergan sold Botox as a specialty drug for ocular problems, what marketing management orientation was it employing? When it sells Botox as a cosmetic treatment, is it employing the same or a different orientation?

3. When doctors treat patients with Botox in their office, is that an example of a selling concept or a marketing concept? Which concept applies when they hold parties for patients in private homes?

4. Apply the concepts of customer lifetime value and customer equity to Botox. How do doctors and Allergan improve the way they manage customer relationships?

5. How does Allergan connect with its customers (doctors)? How does it connect with final consumers? How does it connect with the world around it? What could it do to improve these connections?

Sources: Richard Corliss, "Smile—You're on Botox," *Time,* February 18, 2002, p. 7; Rafer Guzman, "Takeoffs & Landings," *The Wall Street Journal,* November 23, 2001, p. 11C+; Michael Lemonick, "The Pros and Cons of Botox," *Time,* April 29, 2002, p. 77+; David Noonan and Jerry Adler, "The Botox Boom," *Newsweek,* May 13, 2002, pp. 50–58; Brian O'Reilly, "Facelift in a Bottle," *Fortune,* June 24, 2002, pp. 101–104; Tara Parker-Pope, "Wrinkle-Fighter Botox Is Being Used to Treat a Variety of Ailments," *The Wall Street Journal,* February 22, 2002, p. B1+; Rhonda Rundle, FDA Clears Botox for Cosmetic Use," *The Wall Street Journal,* April 16, 2002, p. D6+; Justin Schack, "Eyes on the Prize," *Institutional Investor,* September 2000, pp. 30–32; and Rachel Zimmerman, "Botox Gives a Special Lift to These Soirees," *The Wall Street Journal,* April 16, 2002, p. B1+.

After studying this chapter you should be able to

1. explain companywide strategic planning and its four steps
2. discuss how to design business portfolios and develop strategies for growth and downsizing
3. assess marketing's role in strategic planning and explain how marketers partner with others inside and outside the firm to build profitable customer relationships
4. describe the marketing process and the forces that influence it
5. list the marketing management functions, including the elements of a marketing plan

Company and Marketing Strategy

PARTNERING TO BUILD CUSTOMER RELATIONSHIPS

LOOKING AHEAD: PREVIEWING THE CONCEPTS

In the first chapter, you learned the core concepts and philosophies of marketing. In this chapter, we'll dig more deeply into marketing's role in the broader organization and into the specifics of the marketing process. First, marketing urges a whole-company philosophy that puts customer relationship at the center. Then, marketers partner with other company departments and with others in the marketing system to design strategies for delivering value to carefully targeted customers. Marketers next develop "marketing mixes"—consisting of product, price, distribution, and promotion tactics—to carry out these strategies profitably. These first two chapters will give you a full introduction to the basics of marketing, the decisions marketing managers make, and where marketing fits into an organization. After that, we'll take a look at the environments in which marketing operates.

Let's look first at the Walt Disney Company. When you hear the name Disney, you probably think of wholesome family entertainment. Most people do. With its theme parks and family films, Disney long ago mastered the concepts of customer relationship building and customer delight that we examined in Chapter 1. For generations, it has woven its special "Disney magic" to create and fulfill fantasies for people around the world. But what you may not know is that the Walt Disney Company has now grown to include much, much more than just theme parks and family films. As you read on, think about the all strategic planning challenges facing Disney's modern-day Magic Kingdom.

When you think of the Walt Disney Company, you probably think first of theme parks and animated films. And no wonder. Since the release of its first Mickey Mouse cartoon 75 years ago, Disney has grown to become the undisputed master of family entertainment. It perfected the art of movie animation. From pioneering films such as *Snow White and the Seven Dwarfs, Fantasia, Pinocchio,* and *Song of the South* to more recent features such as *The Lion King, Toy Story,* and *Monsters, Inc.,* Disney has brought pure magic to the theaters, living rooms, and hearts and minds of audiences around the world.

But perhaps nowhere is the Disney magic more apparent than at the company's premier theme parks. Each year, nearly 40 million people flock to the Disney World Resort alone—15 times more than visit Yellowstone National Park—making it the world's number one tourist attraction. What brings so many people to Walt Disney World? Part of the answer lies in its many attractions. The resort's four major theme parks—Magic Kingdom, Epcot, Disney–MGM Studios, and Disney's Animal Kingdom—brim with such attractions as Cinderella's Castle, Space Mountain, the Tower of Terror, Body Wars, the Kilimanjaro Safari, Big Thunder Mountain Railroad, Typhoon Lagoon, Buzz Lightyear's Space Ranger Spin, and Honey I Shrunk the Audience.

But these attractions reveal only part of the Disney World value proposition. In fact, what visitors like even more, they say, is the park's sparkling cleanliness and the friendliness of Disney World employees. In an increasingly rude, dirty, and mismanaged world, Disney offers warmth, cleanliness, and order. As one observer notes, "In the Magic Kingdom, America still works the way it is supposed to. Everything is clean and safe, quality and service still matter, and the customer is always right."

Thus, the real "Disney Magic" lies in the company's obsessive dedication to its mission to "make people happy" and to "make a dream come true." The company orients all of its people—from the executive in the corner office, to the monorail driver, to the ticket seller at the gate—around the customer's experience. On their first day, all new Disney World employees report for a three-day motivational course at Disney University in Orlando, where they learn about the hard work of making fantasies come true. They learn that they are in the entertainment business—"cast members" in the Disney World "show." The job of each cast member is to enthusiastically serve Disney's "guests."

Before they receive their "theme costumes" and go "on stage," employees take courses titled Traditions I and Traditions II, in which they learn the Disney language, history, and culture. They are taught to be enthusiastic, helpful, and *always* friendly. They learn to do good deeds, such as volunteering to take pictures of guests, so that the whole family can be in the picture. Rumor has it that Disney is so confident that its cast members will charm guests that it forces contact. For example, many items in the park's gift shops bear no price tags, requiring shoppers to ask the price.

Cast members are taught never to say, "It's not my job." When a guest asks a question—whether it's "Where's the nearest restroom?" or "What are the names of Snow White's seven dwarves'?"—they need to know the answer. If they see a piece of trash on the ground, they pick it up. They go to extremes to fulfill guests' expectations and dreams. For example, to keep the Magic Kingdom feeling fresh and clean, five times a year the Main Street painters strip every painted rail in the park down to bare metal and apply a new coat of paint.

Disney's customer-delight mission and marketing have become legendary. Its theme parks are so highly regarded for outstanding customer service that many of America's leading corporations send managers to Disney University to learn find out how Disney does it. However, as it turns out, theme parks are only a small part of a much bigger Disney story. These units make up only a small part of today's Walt Disney Company empire. In recent years, Disney has become a real study in strategic planning. Throughout the 1990s, seeking growth, Disney diversified rapidly, transforming itself into a $25 billion international media and entertainment conglomerate. You might be surprised to learn that, beyond its theme parks, the Walt Disney Company now owns or has a major stake in all of the following:

- A major television and radio network—ABC—along with 10 company-owned television stations, 29 radio stations, and 13 international broadcast channels
- Sixteen cable networks (including the Disney Channel, Toon Disney, SoapNet, ESPN, A&E, the History Channel, Lifetime Television, E! Entertainment, and the ABC Family Channel)

- Four television production companies and eight movie production and distribution companies (including Walt Disney Pictures, Touchstone Pictures, Hollywood Pictures, and Miramax Films)
- Five magazine publishing groups (including Hyperion Books and Miramax Books)
- Five music labels (including Hollywood Records and Mammoth Records)
- Nineteen Internet groups (including Disney Online, Disney's Daily Blast, ABC.com, ESPN Sportzone, Family.com, Toysmart.com, NASCAR.com, NBA.com, and NFL.com)
- Disney Interactive (which develops and markets computer software, video games, and CD-ROMS)
- The Disney Store—660 retail store locations carrying Disney-related merchandise
- Disney Cruise Lines
- Two sports franchises (the Mighty Ducks of Anaheim hockey team and the Anaheim Angels baseball team)

It's an impressive list. However, for Disney, managing this diverse portfolio of businesses has become a real *Monsters, Inc.* Whereas Disney's theme park and family movie operations have been wonderfully successful over the years, the new and more complex Disney has struggled for growth and profitability. For example, during the last half of the 1980s, the smaller, more focused Disney experienced soaring sales and profits—revenues grew at an average rate of 23 percent annually; net income grew at 50 percent a year. In contrast, during the most recent five years, the more diversified Disney's sales have grown at an average rate of only 3 percent annually; net income has *fallen* 23 percent a year.

Thus, for Disney, bigger isn't necessarily better. Many critics assert that Disney has grown too large, too diverse, and too distant from the core strengths that made it so successful over the years. Others, however, believe that such diversification is essential for profitable long-term growth. One thing seems certain—creating just the right blend of businesses to make up the new Magic Kingdom won't be easy. It will take masterful strategic planning—along with some big doses of the famed "Disney magic"—to give the modern Disney story a happy-ever-after ending.[1]

Like Disney, all companies must look ahead and develop long-term strategies to meet the changing conditions in their industries and ensure long-term survival. The hard task of selecting an overall company strategy for long-run survival and growth is called *strategic planning*.

In this chapter, we look first at the organization's overall strategic planning. Next, we discuss how marketers, guided by the strategy plan, work closely with others inside and outside the firm to serve customers. Finally, we examine the marketing management process—how marketers go about choosing target markets and building profitable customer relationships.

Strategic Planning

Strategic planning

The process of developing and maintaining a strategic fit between the organization's goals and capabilities and its changing marketing opportunities. It involves defining a clear company mission, setting supporting objectives, designing a sound business portfolio, and coordinating functional strategies.

Each company must find the game plan that makes the most sense given its specific situation, opportunities, objectives, and resources. This is the focus of **strategic planning**—the process of developing and maintaining a strategic fit between the organization's goals and capabilities and its changing marketing opportunities.

Strategic planning sets the stage for the rest of the planning in the firm. Companies usually prepare annual plans, long range plans, and strategic plans. The annual and long range plans deal with the company's current businesses and how to keep them going. In contrast, the strategic plan involves adapting the firm to take advantage of opportunities in its constantly changing environment.

At the corporate level, the company starts the strategic planning process by defining its overall purpose and mission (see Figure 2.1). This mission then is turned into detailed supporting objectives that guide the whole company. Next, headquarters decides what portfolio of businesses and products is best for the company and how much support to give each one. In turn, each business and product develops detailed marketing and other departmental plans that support the companywide plan. Thus, marketing planning occurs at the business-unit, product, and market levels, supporting company strategic planning with more detailed planning for specific marketing opportunities.[2]

Defining a Market-Oriented Mission

An organization exists to accomplish something. At first, it has a clear purpose or mission, but over time its mission may become unclear as the organization grows, adds new products and markets, or faces new conditions in the environment. When management senses that the organization is drifting, it must renew its search for purpose. It is time to ask: What is our business? Who is the customer? What do consumers value? What should our business be? These simple sounding questions are among the most difficult the company will ever have to answer. Successful companies continuously raise these questions and answer them carefully and completely.

Mission statement

A statement of the organization's purpose—what it wants to accomplish in the larger environment.

Many organizations develop formal mission statements that answer these questions. A **mission statement** is a statement of the organization's purpose—what it wants to accomplish in the larger environment. A clear mission statement acts as an "invisible hand" that guides people in the organization.

Some companies define their missions in product or technology terms ("We make and sell furniture" or "We are a chemical processing firm"). But mission statements should be *market oriented* (see Real Marketing 2.1). Products and technologies eventually become outdated, but basic market needs may last forever.

A market-oriented mission statement defines the business in terms of satisfying basic customer needs. For example, 3M does more than just make adhesives, scientific equipment, and health care products. It solves people's problems by putting innovation to work for them. Charles Schwab isn't just a brokerage firm—it sees itself as the "guardian of our customers' financial dreams." At Hill's Pet Nutrition, "Our mission is to enrich and lengthen the special relationship between you and your pet." Likewise, eBay's mission isn't simply to hold online auctions. Instead, it connects individual buyers and sellers in "the world's online marketplace." Its mission is to be a unique Web community in which people can shop around, have fun, and get to know each other,

FIGURE 2.1

Steps in strategic planning

Company mission: Hill's Pet Nutrition does more than sell pet food. Its mission is "to help enrich and lengthen the special relationships between people and their pets."

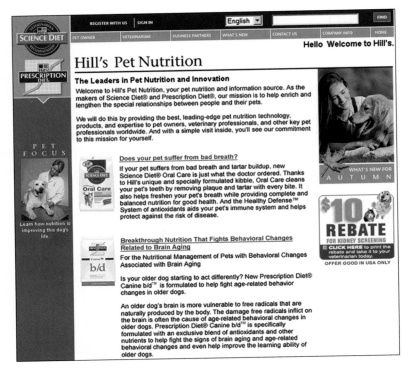

real marketing 2.1

IBM's New Mission: From "Mainframes" to "Customer Solutions"

Only a decade ago, if you'd asked top managers at IBM what business they were in, they might well have answered, "We sell computer hardware and software." Laboring under a pretty bad case of marketing myopia, a heavily product-focused IBM lost sight of its customers' needs. As a result, as customer needs changed, IBM didn't, and its fortunes slipped accordingly. By the early 1990s, "Big Blue's" market share and stock price were falling rapidly.

Since those sadly blue days, however, IBM has undergone a remarkable transformation. The turnaround started in 1993, when new CEO Lou Gerstner brought a renewed customer focus to IBM. As one of his first acts, Gerstner asked all top IBM managers to meet face-to-face with important customers— what he called "bear-hugging customers"— and report back concerning their problems and priorities. Gerstner learned that corporate computing is getting more and more confusing for customers. In this new high-tech, connected age, companies must master a dizzying array of information technologies

to serve not only their customers but also suppliers, distributors, and employees.

In this more complex computing world, customers are buying much more from IBM than just computer hardware and software. They are buying solutions to ever-more-bewildering information technology (IT) problems. This realization led to a fundamental redefinition of IBM's business. Now, if you ask almost any IBM manager to define the business, he or she will tell you, "We deliver *solutions* to customers' information technology problems."

The fact is that most customers don't really care whose hardware or software they buy. For example, Pat Zilvitis, chief information officer at Gillette in Boston and a big IBM customer, claims that it's not IBM's PCs, servers, mainframes, or software that attracts him. "I often don't know if I need hardware or software or services, and I don't care," he says. What draws him to IBM is that Big Blue employs an unmatched breadth of products, people, and services to deliver an IT system that works. "I don't view IBM as a hardware vendor anymore," he says. "I think of them as

an information technology [partner] that can help me in a number of different ways."

The new customer-solutions focus has greatly promoted the role of services relative to hardware and software in the IBM mix. The company now offers an expanded set of IT consulting, total systems management, strategic outsourcing, and e-business services. It helps customers with everything from assessing, planning, designing, implementing, and running their IT systems to bringing them up to speed on e-commerce. Some companies, such as AT&T, Eastman Kodak, and Hertz, have outsourced their entire IT systems to IBM. In such deals, IBM runs the whole IT show—the customer's IT employees work for IBM, and IBM owns the customer's computers, which it then manages.

Services are now IBM's hottest growth area. Its mammoth Global Services division accounts for 40 percent of the company's more than $86 billion in sales and 50 percent of its profits. As one analyst comments, "IBM—International Business Machines—is becoming IBS, where 'S' is for services, software, and

IBM defines its business as delivering customer information technology solutions. It asks, "Who do you need?" The answer: "People who get it. People who get it done."

Internet, intranet, and e-commerce applications.) As more and more companies use the Internet as their primary connecting technology, e-business is growing explosively. IBM wants to be *the* company to turn to for e-business strategies and solutions. During the past few years, the company has introduced dozens of new e-business services, including customer relationship management, business intelligence, supply chain management, and business process management services.

E-business appears to be an ideal setting for IBM's soup-to-nuts menu of IT solutions. Big Blue claims to have 10,000 e-business customers. For some, this means little more than having IBM host their Web sites on one of its servers. For others, however, it means having IBM create and implement a totally new business–customer connection. In its latest initiative, IBM now offers want it calls "e-business on demand," which allows companies to tap into IBM software and supercomputing power via the Web. "Instead of having to constantly buy, maintain, and upgrade the latest technology," says an analyst, "IBM envisions a simpler world in which companies would buy computing power and programs on an as-needed basis, just as they do electricity from power companies." In fact, recent IBM ads promise "introducing e-business on demand—the next utility."

Thus, in a remarkably short time, IBM has transformed itself from a company that "sells computer hardware and software" to one that "delivers customer IT solutions." The marketplace has responded strongly. By the time Gerstner retired in 2002, IBM's market capitalization had grown sixfold; its stock price had soared sevenfold. By defining itself in terms of the customer needs it serves rather than the products it sells, IBM has been transformed from a big blue has-been to a tech-services powerhouse. As one knowledgeable IBM watcher concludes, IBM is now "fantastically positioned for the future."

solutions." In fact, IBM has now become the world's largest supplier of IT services.

To announce its transformation and to counter the out-of-date notion that IBM provides only computer hardware, IBM launched a $75 million global services ad campaign. The campaign profiled specific IBM people—featured in current ads as "People who get it. People who get it done." One ad showcased Nick Simicich, an IBM ethical hacker (unofficial title: "paid professional paranoid") who

purposely invaded customers' critical information systems to see if they were safe from more-hostile hackers. Another featured Patrick McMahon, who helped Prudential reengineer its sales processes, doubling the number of policies sold and raising commissions 153 percent in the pilot program.

In the latest phase of its customer-solutions-makeover, IBM has positioned itself as the "e-business solutions company." (It coined *e-business* as a catch-all term for

Sources: See David Kirkpatrick, "IBM: From Big Blue Dinosaur to E-Business Animal," *Fortune,* April 26, 1999, pp. 116–125; Laura Loro, "IBM Touts Position as No. 1 in IT Services," *Advertising Age's Business Marketing,* April 1999, p. 41; Gary Hamel, "Waking Up IBM," *Harvard Business Review,* July–August 2000, pp. 137–146; Spencer E. Ante, "Big Blues Tech on Tap," *Business Week,* August 27, 2001, pp. 66–69; Spencer E. Ante and Ira Sager, "IBM's New Boss," *Business Week,* February 11, 2002, pp. 66–69; and Spencer E. Ante and David Henry, "Can IBM Keep Earnings Hot?" *Business Week,* April 15, 2002, pp. 58–60.

TABLE 2.1   MARKET-ORIENTED BUSINESS DEFINITIONS

Company	Product-Oriented Definition	Market-Oriented Definition
Amazon.com	We sell books, videos, CDs, toys, consumer electronics, hardware, housewares, and other products.	We make the Internet buying experience fast, easy, and enjoyable—we're the place where you can find and discover anything you want to buy online.
America Online	We provide online services.	We create customer connectivity, anytime, anywhere.
Disney	We run theme parks.	We create fantasies—a place where America still works the way it's supposed to.
eBay	We hold online auctions.	We connect individual buyers and sellers in the world's online marketplace, a unique Web community in which they can shop around, have fun, and get to know each other.
Home Depot	We sell tools and home repair and improvement items.	We provide advice and solutions that transform ham-handed homeowners into Mr. and Mrs. Fixits.
Nike	We sell shoes.	We help people experience the emotion of competition, winning, and crushing competitors.
Revlon	We make cosmetics.	We sell lifestyle and self-expression; success and status; memories, hopes, and dreams.
Ritz-Carlton Hotels	We rent rooms.	We create the Ritz-Carlton experience—one that enlivens the senses, instills well-being, and fulfills even the unexpressed wishes and needs of our guests.
Wal-Mart	We run discount stores.	We deliver low prices, every day.

for example, by chatting at the eBay Cafe.[3] Table 2.1 provides several other examples of product-oriented versus market-oriented business definitions.

Management should avoid making its mission too narrow or too broad. A pencil manufacturer that says it is in the communication equipment business is stating its mission too broadly. Missions should be *realistic*. Singapore Airlines would be deluding itself if it adopted the mission to become the world's largest airline. Missions should also be *specific*. Many mission statements are written for public relations purposes and lack specific, workable guidelines. Too often, companies develop mission statements that look much like this tongue-in-cheek version:

> We are committed to serving the quality of life of cultures and communities everywhere, regardless of sex, age, sexual preference, religion, or disability, whether they be customers, suppliers, employees, or shareholders—we serve the planet—to the highest ethical standards of integrity, best practice, and sustainability, through policies of openness and transparency vetted by our participation in the International Quality Business Global Audit forum, to ensure measurable outcomes worldwide. . . .[4]

Such generic statements sound good but provide little real guidance or inspiration. In contrast, Celestial Seasonings' mission statement is very specific: "Our mission is to grow and dominate the U.S. specialty tea market by exceeding consumer expectations with: The best tasting, 100 percent natural hot and iced teas, packaged with Celestial art and philosophy, creating the most valued tea experience. . . ."[5]

Missions should fit the *market environment*. The Girl Scouts of America would not recruit successfully in today's environment with its former mission: "to prepare young girls for motherhood and wifely duties." The organization should base its mission on its *distinctive competencies*. McDonald's could probably enter the solar energy business, but that would not take advantage of its core competence—providing low cost food and fast service to large groups of customers.

Finally, mission statements should be *motivating*. A company's mission should not be stated as making more sales or profits—profits are only a reward for undertaking a useful activity. A company's employees need to feel that their work is significant and that it contributes to people's

Monsanto defines its mission as one of "food, hope, health"—of helping to feed the world's exploding population while at the same time sustaining the environment. This mission leads to specific business and marketing objectives.

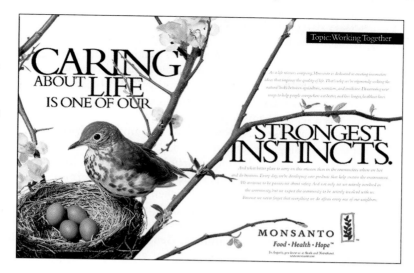

lives. One study found that "visionary companies" set a purpose beyond making money. For example, Walt Disney Company's aim is to "make people happy." But even though profits may not be part of these companies' mission statements, they are the inevitable result. The study showed that 18 visionary companies outperformed other companies in the stock market by more than 6 to 1 over the period from 1926 to 1990.[6]

Setting Company Objectives and Goals

The company's mission needs to be turned into detailed supporting objectives for each level of management. Each manager should have objectives and be responsible for reaching them. For example, Monsanto operates in many businesses, including agriculture, pharmaceuticals, and food products. The company defines its mission as creating "abundant food and a healthy environment." It seeks to help feed the world's exploding population while at the same time sustaining the environment.

This mission leads to a hierarchy of objectives, including business objectives and marketing objectives. Monsanto's overall objective is to create environmentally better products and get them to market faster at lower costs. For its part, the agricultural division's objective is to increase agricultural productivity and reduce chemical pollution by researching new pest- and disease-resistant crops that produce higher yields without chemical spraying. But research is expensive and requires improved profits to plow back into research programs. So improving profits becomes another major Monsanto objective. Profits can be improved by increasing sales or reducing costs. Sales can be increased by improving the company's share of the U.S. market, by entering new foreign markets, or both. These goals then become the company's current marketing objectives.

Marketing strategies must be developed to support these marketing objectives. To increase its U.S. market share, Monsanto might increase its products' availability and promotion. To enter new foreign markets, the company may cut prices and target large farms abroad. These are its broad marketing strategies. Each broad marketing strategy must then be defined in greater detail. For example, increasing the product's promotion may require more salespeople and more advertising; if so, both requirements will have to be spelled out. In this way, the firm's mission is translated into a set of objectives for the current period.

Designing the Business Portfolio

Business portfolio

The collection of businesses and products that make up the company.

Guided by the company's mission statement and objectives, management now must plan its **business portfolio**—the collection of businesses and products that make up the company. The best business portfolio is the one that best fits the company's strengths and weaknesses to opportunities in the environment. Business portfolio planning involves two steps. First, the company must analyze its *current* business portfolio and decide which businesses should receive more, less, or no investment. Second, it must shape the *future* portfolio by developing strategies for growth and downsizing.

Analyzing the Current Business Portfolio

Portfolio analysis
A tool by which management identifies and evaluates the various businesses making up the company.

Strategic business unit (SBU)
A unit of the company that has a separate mission and objectives and that can be planned independently from other company businesses.

The major activity in strategic planning is business **portfolio analysis,** whereby management evaluates the products and businesses making up the company. The company will want to put strong resources into its more profitable businesses and phase down or drop its weaker ones.

Management's first step is to identify the key businesses making up the company. These can be called the strategic business units. A **strategic business unit (SBU)** is a unit of the company that has a separate mission and objectives and that can be planned independently from other company businesses. An SBU can be a company division, a product line within a division, or sometimes a single product or brand.

The next step in business portfolio analysis calls for management to assess the attractiveness of its various SBUs and decide how much support each deserves. Most companies are well advised to "stick to their knitting" when designing their business portfolios. It's usually a good idea to focus on adding products and businesses that fit closely with the firm's core philosophy and competencies. However, some companies have excelled with broad, widely diversified portfolios. An excellent example is General Electric. Through skillful management of its portfolio of businesses, General Electric has grown to be one of the world's largest and most profitable companies. Over the past two decades, GE has shed many low-performing businesses, such as air-conditioning and housewares. It kept only those businesses that could be number one or number two in their industries. At the same time, it has acquired profitable businesses in broadcasting (NBC Television), financial services (Kidder Peabody investment bank), and several other industries. GE now operates 49 business units, selling an incredible variety of products and services—from consumer electronics, financial services, and television broadcasting to aircraft engines, plastics, and a global Internet trading network. Superb management of this diverse portfolio has earned GE shareholders a 29 percent average annual return over the past 10 years. It's also put GE at the top of *Fortune's* Most Admired Companies for five straight years.[7]

The purpose of strategic planning is to find ways in which the company can best use its strengths to take advantage of attractive opportunities in the environment. Thus, most standard portfolio-analysis methods evaluate SBUs on two important dimensions—the attractiveness of the SBU's market or industry and the strength of the SBU's position in that market or industry. The best-known portfolio-planning method was developed by the Boston Consulting Group, a leading management consulting firm.

The business portfolio: Through skillful management of its portfolio of businesses, General Electric has grown to be one of the world's largest and most profitable companies.

FIGURE 2.2
The BCG growth-share
matrix

Growth-share matrix

A portfolio-planning method
that evaluates a company's
strategic business units in
terms of their market growth
rate and relative market
share. SBUs are classified as
stars, cash cows, question
marks, or dogs.

The Boston Consulting Group Approach.   Using the Boston Consulting Group (BCG)
approach, a company classifies all its SBUs according to the **growth-share matrix** shown in
Figure 2.2. On the vertical axis, *market growth rate* provides a measure of market attractiveness.
On the horizontal axis, *relative market share* serves as a measure of company strength in the market. The growth-share matrix defines four types of SBUs:

Stars. Stars are high-growth, high-share businesses or products. They often need heavy
investment to finance their rapid growth. Eventually their growth will slow down, and they will
turn into cash cows.

Cash cows. Cash cows are low-growth, high-share businesses or products. These established
and successful SBUs need less investment to hold their market share. Thus, they produce a lot of
cash that the company uses to pay its bills and to support other SBUs that need investment.

Question marks. Question marks are low-share business units in high-growth markets.
They require a lot of cash to hold their share, let alone increase it. Management has to think hard
about which question marks it should try to build into stars and which should be phased out.

Dogs. Dogs are low-growth, low-share businesses and products. They may generate
enough cash to maintain themselves but do not promise to be large sources of cash.

The ten circles in the growth-share matrix represent a company's ten current SBUs. The company
has two stars, two cash cows, three question marks, and three dogs. The areas of the circles are proportional to the SBU's dollar sales. This company is in fair shape, although not in good shape. It wants to
invest in the more promising question marks to make them stars and to maintain the stars so that they
will become cash cows as their markets mature. Fortunately, it has two good-sized cash cows. Income
from these cash cows will help finance the company's question marks, stars, and dogs. The company
should take some decisive action concerning its dogs and its question marks. The picture would be
worse if the company had no stars, if it had too many dogs, or if it had only one weak cash cow.

Once it has classified its SBUs, the company must determine what role each will play in the future.
One of four strategies can be pursued for each SBU. The company can invest more in the business unit
in order to *build* its share. Or it can invest just enough to *hold* the SBU's share at the current level. It can
harvest the SBU, milking its short term cash flow regardless of the long-term effect. Finally, the company can *divest* the SBU by selling it or phasing it out and using the resources elsewhere.

As time passes, SBUs change their positions in the growth-share matrix. Each SBU has a life
cycle. Many SBUs start out as question marks and move into the star category if they succeed.
They later become cash cows as market growth falls, then finally die off or turn into dogs toward
the end of their life cycle. The company needs to add new products and units continuously so that
some of them will become stars and, eventually, cash cows that will help finance other SBUs.

Problems with Matrix Approaches.   The BCG and other formal methods revolutionized strategic planning. However, such approaches have limitations. They can be difficult, time-consuming,
and costly to implement. Management may find it difficult to define SBUs and measure market
share and growth. In addition, these approaches focus on classifying *current* businesses but provide little advice for *future* planning.

FIGURE 2.3
The product/market
expansion grid

Formal planning approaches can also place too much emphasis on market-share growth or growth through entry into attractive new markets. Using these approaches, many companies plunged into unrelated and new high-growth businesses that they did not know how to manage—with very bad results. At the same time, these companies were often too quick to abandon, sell, or milk to death their healthy mature businesses. As a result, many companies that diversified too broadly in the past now are narrowing their focus and getting back to the basics of serving one or a few industries that they know best.

Because of such problems, many companies have dropped formal matrix methods in favor of more customized approaches that are better suited to their specific situations. Unlike former strategic-planning efforts, which rested mostly in the hands of senior managers at company headquarters, today's strategic planning has been decentralized. Increasingly, companies are placing responsibility for strategic planning in the hands of cross-functional teams of managers who are close to their markets. Some teams even include customers and suppliers in their strategic-planning processes.[8]

Developing Strategies for Growth and Downsizing

Beyond evaluating current businesses, designing the business portfolio involves finding businesses and products the company should consider in the future. Companies need growth if they are to compete more effectively, satisfy their stakeholders, and attract top talent. "Growth is pure oxygen," states one executive. "It creates a vital, enthusiastic corporation where people see genuine opportunity." At the same time, a firm must be careful not to make growth itself an objective. The company's objective must be "profitable growth."

Marketing has the main responsibility for achieving profitable growth for the company. Marketing must identify, evaluate, and select market opportunities and lay down strategies for capturing them. One useful device for identifying growth opportunities is the **product/market expansion grid**,[9] shown in Figure 2.3. We apply it here to Starbucks (see Real Marketing 2.2).

First, Starbucks management might consider whether the company can achieve deeper **market penetration**—making more sales to current customers without changing its products. It might add new stores in current market areas to make it easier for more customers to visit. In fact, Starbucks is adding an average of 27 stores a week, 52 weeks a year. Improvements in advertising, prices, service, menu selection, or store design might encourage customers to stop by more often or to buy more during each visit. For example, Starbucks recently introduced a company debit card, which lets customers prepay for coffee and snacks or give the gift of Starbucks to family and friends. Customers using the card move through stores faster and return more often. Starbucks also began adapting its menu to local tastes around the country.

> In the South, where customers tend to come later in the day and linger for a bit, [such tailoring] meant adding more appealing dessert offerings, as well as designing larger, more comfortable locations. [In Atlanta, Starbucks] opened bigger stores with such amenities as couches and outdoor tables, so that people would feel comfortable hanging out, especially in the evening. . . . Building on its Atlanta experience, Starbucks is tailoring its stores to local tastes around the country. That's why you find café au lait as well as toasted items in New Orleans, neither of which is available elsewhere in the country. (Bagel sales in New Orleans tripled once Starbucks began toasting them.) Or why coffee cake is featured in the Northeast, where it's more popular.[10]

Basically, Starbucks would like to increase patronage by current customers and attract competitors' customers to Starbucks shops.

Second, Starbucks management might consider possibilities for **market development**—identifying and developing new markets for its current products. For instance, managers could review new *demographic markets*. Perhaps new groups—such as senior consumers or ethnic groups—

Product/market expansion grid

A portfolio-planning tool for identifying company growth opportunities through market penetration, market development, product development, or diversification.

Market penetration

A strategy for company growth by increasing sales of current products to current market segments without changing the product.

Market development

A strategy for company growth by identifying and developing new market segments for current company products.

real marketing 2.2

Starbucks Coffee: Where Things Are Really Perking

Back in 1983, Howard Schultz hit on the idea of bringing a European-style coffeehouse to America. People needed to slow down, he believed—to "smell the coffee" and enjoy life a little more. The result was Starbucks, the coffeehouse chain that started the trend in America of enjoying coffee to its fullest. Starbucks doesn't sell just coffee, it sells the "Starbucks experience." As one Starbucks executive puts it, "We're not in the business of filling bellies, we're in the business of filling souls."

Starbucks is now a powerhouse premium brand in a category in which only cheaper commodity products once existed. As the brand has perked, Starbucks's sales and profits have risen like steam off a mug of hot java. Some 20 million customers visit the company's more than 5,500 stores worldwide each week—10 percent of them drop by twice a day. During just the past five years, Starbucks's sales and earnings have both more than tripled.

To maintain its phenomenal growth in an increasingly over-caffeinated marketplace, Starbucks has brewed up an ambitious, multipronged growth strategy.

Starbucks's success, however, has drawn a full litter of copycats, ranging from direct competitors such as Caribou Coffee to fast-food merchants. These days it seems that everyone is peddling its own brand of premium coffee. To maintain its phenomenal growth in an increasingly overcaffeinated marketplace, Starbucks has brewed up an ambitious, multipronged growth strategy. Let's examine the key elements of this strategy:

- *More store growth:* Almost 85 percent of Starbucks's sales comes from its stores. So, not surprisingly, Starbucks is opening new stores at a breakneck pace. Six years ago, Starbucks had just 1,015 stores, total—that's 400 fewer than it built last year alone. Although it may seem that there aren't many places left without a Starbucks, there's still plenty of room to expand. For example, Kansas City has only two Starbucks; the entire state of Indiana has only one; and the states of Alabama, Arkansas, Mississippi, and Tennessee have none at all. Even in crowded markets, such as New York City or San Francisco, the company seems unconcerned about store saturation. Schultz points to Vancouver, Canada, where competing Starbucks stores are located directly across the street from one another. Both stores generate more than $1 million in annual sales, each well above the sales of a typical Starbucks. One three-block stretch in Chicago contains six of the trendy coffee bars.

Beyond opening new shops, Starbucks is expanding each store's food offerings, testing everything from Krispy Kreme doughnuts and Fresh Fields gourmet sandwiches to Greek pasta salads and assorted chips. By offering a beefed-up menu, the company hopes to increase the average customer sales ticket while also boosting lunch and dinner traffic.

- *New retail channels:* The vast majority of coffee in America is bought in stores and sipped at home. To capture this demand, Starbucks is also pushing into America's supermarket aisles. However, rather than going head-to-head with giants such as Procter & Gamble (Folgers) and Kraft (Maxwell House, Sanka), Starbucks struck a co-branding deal with Kraft. Under this deal, Starbucks will continue to roast and package its coffee, while Kraft will market and distribute it. Both companies benefit: Starbucks gains quick entry into 25,000 U.S. supermarkets, supported by the marketing muscle of 3,500 Kraft salespeople. Kraft tops off its coffee line with the best-known premium brand and gains quick entry into the fast-growing premium coffee segment.

Beyond supermarkets, Starbucks has forged an impressive set of new ways to bring its brand to market. Some examples: Host Marriott operates Starbucks kiosks in more than 30 U.S. airports, and several airlines serve Starbucks coffee to their passengers. Westin and Sheraton hotels offer packets of Starbucks brew in their rooms. And Starbucks recently signed a deal with Borders Books to operate coffee shops within the bookshop's superstores. Starbucks also sells gourmet coffee, tea, gifts, and related goods through business and consumer catalogs. And its Web site, Starbucks.com, has become a kind of "lifestyle portal" on which it sells coffee, tea, coffeemaking equipment, compact discs, gifts, and collectibles.

- *New products and store concepts:* Starbucks has partnered with several firms to extend its brand into new categories. For example, it joined with PepsiCo to stamp the Starbucks brand on bottled Frappuccino drinks and a new DoubleShot espresso drink. Starbucks ice cream, marketed in a joint venture with Breyer's, is now the leading brand of coffee ice cream. Starbucks is also examining new store concepts. In Seattle, it's testing Café Starbucks, a European-style family bistro with a menu featuring everything from huckleberry pancakes to oven-roasted seared sirloin and Mediterranean chicken breast on focaccia. In San Francisco, it's testing Circadia—a kind of bohemian coffeehouse concept with tattered rugs, high-speed Internet access, and live music as well as coffee specialties.

- *International growth:* Finally, Starbucks has taken its American-brewed concept global. In 1996, the company had only 11 coffeehouses outside North America. By 2002, the number had grow to more than 1,200 stores in 24 international markets,

(continued)

including more than 350 in Japan, 91 in Taiwan, and 76 in China. Starbucks hopes to have 650 European stores in Europe by the end of 2003. And it's now moving rapidly into Latin and South America, where it plans to build 900 stores by 2005.

Although Starbucks's growth strategy so far has met with great success, some analysts express strong concerns. What's wrong with Starbucks's rapid expansion? Some critics worry that the company may be overextending the Starbucks brand name. "People pay up to $3.15 for a caffe latte because it's supposed to be a premium product," asserts one such critic. "When you see the Starbucks name on what an airline is pouring, you

wonder." Others fear that, by pursuing such a broad-based growth strategy, Starbucks will stretch its resources too thin or lose its focus.

Still others, however, remain true believers. Some even see similarities between Starbucks and a young McDonald's, which rode the humble hamburger to such incredible success. "The similar focus on one product, the overseas opportunities, the rapid emergence as the dominant player in a new niche," says Goldman Sachs analyst Steve Kent, "this all applies to Starbucks, too." Only time will tell whether Starbucks turns out to be the next McDonald's—it all depends how well the company manages growth. For now, things are really perking. But Starbucks has to be careful that it doesn't boil over.

Sources: Quotes from Nelson D. Schwartz, "Still Perking After All These Years," *Fortune,* May 24, 1999, pp. 203–210; Janice Matsumoto, "More than Mocha—Café Starbucks," *Restaurants and Institutions,* October 1, 1998, p. 21; Kelly Barron, "The Cappuccino Conundrum," *Forbes,* February 22, 1999, pp. 54–55; and Stephane Fitch, "Latte Grande, Extra Froth," *Forbes,* March 19, 2001, p. 58. Other information from Richard Papiernik, "Starbucks Still Taking Bows in Long-Running Coffeehouse Show," *Nation's Restaurant News,* February 12, 2001, pp. 11, 78; Jacqueline Doherty, "Make It Decaf," *Barrons,* May 20, 2002, pp. 20–21; and information accessed online at www.starbucks.com, July 2002.

---

could be encouraged to visit Starbucks coffee shops for the first time or to buy more from them. Managers also could review new *geographical markets.* Starbucks is now expanding swiftly into new U.S. markets, especially in the Southeast and Southwest. It is also developing its international markets, with stores popping up rapidly in Asia, Europe, Australia, and Latin and South America.

Product development

A strategy for company growth by offering modified or new products to current market segments.

Third, management could consider **product development**—offering modified or new products to current markets. For example, Starbucks has increased its food offerings in an effort to bring customers into its stores during the lunch and dinner hours and to increase the amount of the average customer's sales ticket. The company has also partnered with other firms to sell coffee in supermarkets and to extend its brand to new products, such as coffee ice cream (with Dreyer's) and bottled coffee drinks (with PepsiCo).

Diversification

A strategy for company growth through starting up or acquiring businesses outside the company's current products and markets.

Fourth, Starbucks might consider **diversification.** It could start up or buy businesses outside of its current products and markets. For example, Starbucks is testing two new restaurant concepts—Café Starbucks and Circadia—in an effort to offer new formats to related but new markets. It has also introduced a Hear Music brand of compilation CDs. In a more extreme diversification, Starbucks might consider leveraging its strong brand name by making and marketing a line of branded casual clothing consistent with the "Starbucks experience." However, this would probably be unwise. Companies that diversify too broadly into unfamiliar products or industries can lose their market focus, something that some critics are already concerned about with Starbucks.

Downsizing

Reducing the business portfolio by eliminating products or business units that are not profitable or that no longer fit the company's overall strategy.

Companies must not only develop strategies for *growing* their business portfolios but also strategies for **downsizing** them. There are many reasons that a firm might want to abandon products or markets. The market environment might change, making some of the company's product or markets less profitable. This might happen during an economic recession or when a strong competitor opens next door. The firm may have grown too fast or entered areas where it lacks experience. This can occur when a firm enters too many foreign markets without the proper research or when a company introduces new products that do not offer superior customer value. Finally, some products or business units just age and die.

When a firm finds products or businesses that no longer fit its overall strategy, it must carefully prune, harvest, or divest them. Weak businesses usually require a disproportionate amount of management attention. Managers should focus on promising growth opportunities, not fritter away energy trying to salvage fading ones.

Strategic Planning and Small Businesses

Many discussions of strategic planning focus on large corporations with many divisions and products. However, small businesses can also benefit from sound strategic planning. Whereas most small ventures start out with extensive business and marketing plans used to attract potential investors, strategic planning often falls by the wayside once the business gets going. Entrepreneurs and presidents of small companies are more likely to spend their time "putting out fires" than planning. But what does a small firm do when it finds that it has taken on too much debt, when its growth is exceeding production capacity, or when it's losing market share to a competitor with lower prices? Strategic planning can help small business managers to anticipate such situations and determine how to prevent or handle them.

King's Medical Company of Hudson, Ohio, provides an example of how one small company has used very simple strategic-planning tools to chart its course every three years. King's Medical owns and manages magnetic-resonance-imaging (MRI) equipment—million-dollar-plus machines that produce X-ray–type pictures. Several years ago, William Patton, then a consultant and the company's "planning guru," pointed to strategic planning as the key to this small company's very rapid growth and high profit margins. Patton claimed, "A lot of literature says there are three critical issues to a small company: cash flow, cash flow, cash flow. I agree those issues are critical, but so are three more: planning, planning, planning." King's Medical's planning process, which hinges on an assessment of the company, its place in the market, and its goals, includes the following steps.[11]

1. Identify the major elements of the business environment in which the organization has operated over the past few years.

2. Describe the mission of the organization in terms of its nature and function for the next two years.

3. Explain the internal and external forces that will impact the mission of the organization.

4. Identify the basic driving force that will direct the organization in the future.

5. Develop a set of long-term objectives that will identify what the organization will become in the future.

6. Outline a general plan of action that defines the logistical, financial, and personnel factors needed to integrate the long-term objectives into the total organization.

Clearly, strategic planning is crucial to a small company's future. Thom Wellington, president of Wellington Environmental Consulting and Construction, Inc., says that it's important to do strategic planning at a site away from the office. An off-site location offers psychologically neutral ground where employees can be "much more candid," and it takes entrepreneurs away from the scene of the fires they spend so much time stamping out.[12]

Planning Marketing: Partnering to Build Customer Relationships

The company's strategic plan establishes what kinds of businesses the company will be in and its objectives for each business. Then, within each business unit, more detailed planning takes place. The major functional departments in each unit—marketing, finance, accounting, purchasing, operations, information systems, human resources, and others—must work together to accomplish strategic objectives.

Marketing plays a key role in the company's strategic planning in several ways. First, marketing provides a guiding *philosophy*—the marketing concept—that suggests that company strategy should revolve around building profitable relationships with important consumer groups. Second, marketing provides *inputs* to strategic planners by helping to identify attractive market opportunities and by assessing the firm's potential to take advantage of them. Finally, within individual business units, marketing designs *strategies* for reaching the unit's objectives. Once the unit's objectives are set, marketing's task is to carry them out profitably.

Customer value and satisfaction are important ingredients in the marketer's formula for success. However, as we noted in Chapter 1, marketers alone cannot produce superior value for customers. Although it plays a leading role, marketing can be only a partner in attracting, keeping, and growing customers. In addition to *customer relationship management*, marketers must also practice **partner relationship management.** They must work closely with partners in other company departments to form an effective *value chain* that serves the customer. Moreover, they must partner effectively with other companies in the marketing system to form a competitively superior *value-delivery network*. We now take a closer look at the concepts of a company value chain and value-delivery network.

Partner relationship management
Working closely with partners in other company departments and outside the company to jointly bring greater value to customers.

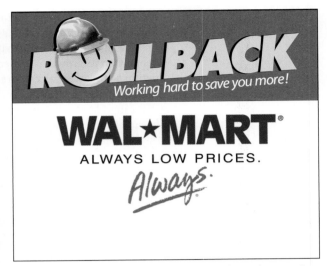

The value chain: Wal-Mart's ability to offer the right products at low prices depends on the contributions from people in all of the company's departments—marketing, purchasing, information systems, and operations.

Partnering with Others in the Company

Value chain

The series of departments that carry out value-creating activities to design, produce, market, deliver, and support a firm's products.

Each company department can be thought of as a link in the company's **value chain**.[13] That is, each department carries out value-creating activities to design, produce, market, deliver, and support the firm's products. The firm's success depends not only on how well each department performs its work but also on how well the activities of various departments are coordinated.

For example, Wal-Mart's goal is to create customer value and satisfaction by providing shoppers with the products they want at the lowest possible prices. Marketers at Wal-Mart play an important role. They learn what customers need and want and aid Wal-Mart merchants as they endeavor to stock the store's shelves with the desired products at unbeatable low prices. Marketers prepare advertising and merchandising programs and assist shoppers with customer service. Through these and other activities, Wal-Mart's marketers help deliver value to customers. However, the marketing department needs help from the company's other departments. Wal-Mart's ability to offer the right products at low prices depends on the purchasing department's skill in tracking down the needed suppliers and buying from them at low cost. Similarly, Wal-Mart's information technology department must provide fast and accurate information about which products are selling in each store. And its operations people must provide effective, low-cost merchandise handling.

A company's value chain is only as strong as its weakest link. Success depends on how well each department performs its work of adding value for customers and on how well the activities of various departments are coordinated. At Wal-Mart, if purchasing can't wring the lowest prices from suppliers or if operations can't distribute merchandise at the lowest costs, then marketing can't deliver on its promise of lowest prices.

Ideally, then, a company's different functions should work in harmony to produce value for consumers. But, in practice, departmental relations are full of conflicts and misunderstandings. The marketing department takes the consumer's point of view. But when marketing tries to develop customer satisfaction, it can cause other departments to do a poorer job *in their terms.* Marketing department actions can increase purchasing costs, disrupt production schedules, increase inventories, and create budget headaches. Thus, the other departments may resist the marketing department's efforts.

Yet marketers must find ways to get all departments to "think consumer" and to develop a smoothly functioning value chain.

Creating value for buyers is much more than a "marketing function"; rather, [it's] analogous to a symphony orchestra in which the contribution of each subgroup is tailored and integrated by a conductor—with a synergistic effect. A seller must draw upon and integrate effectively . . . its entire human and other capital resources. . . . [Creating profitable customer relationships] is the proper focus of the entire business and not merely of a single department in it.[14]

Marketing management can best gain support for its goal of customer satisfaction by working to understand the company's other departments. Marketing managers need to work closely with managers of other functions to develop a system of functional plans under which the different departments can work together to accomplish the company's overall strategic objectives.

Jack Welch, General Electric's highly regarded former CEO, tells his employees: "Companies can't give job security. Only customers can!" He emphasized that all General Electric people, regardless of their department, have an impact on customer satisfaction and retention. His message: "If you are not thinking customer, you are not thinking."[15]

Partnering with Others in the Marketing System

In its quest to create customer value, the firm needs to look beyond its own value chain and into the value chains of its suppliers, distributors, and, ultimately, customers. Consider McDonald's. McDonald's 30,000 restaurants worldwide serve more than 46 million customers daily, capturing a 43 percent share of the burger market.[16] People do not swarm to McDonald's only because they love the chain's hamburgers. In fact, consumers typically rank McDonald's behind Burger King and Wendy's in taste. Consumers flock to the McDonald's *system,* not just to its food products. Throughout the world, McDonald's finely tuned system delivers a high standard of what the company calls QSCV—quality, service, cleanliness, and value. McDonald's is effective only to the extent that it successfully partners with its franchisees, suppliers, and others to jointly deliver exceptionally high customer value.

Value-delivery network

The network made up of the company, suppliers, distributors, and ultimately customers who "partner" with each other to improve the performance of the entire system.

More companies today are partnering with the other members of the supply chain to improve the performance of the customer **value-delivery network.** For example, Honda has designed a program for working closely with its suppliers to help them reduce their costs and improve quality. When Honda chose Donnelly Corporation to supply all of the mirrors for its U.S.-made cars, it sent engineers swarming over Donnelly's plants, looking for ways to improve its products and operations. This helped Donnelly reduce its costs by 2 percent in the first year. As a result of its improved performance, Donnelly's sales to Honda grew from $5 million annually to more than $60 million in less than 10 years. In turn, Honda gained an efficient, low-cost supplier of quality components. And Honda customers received greater value in the form of lower-cost, higher-quality cars.[17]

Increasingly in today's marketplace, competition no longer takes place between individual competitors. Rather, it takes place between the entire value-delivery networks created by these competitors. Thus, Honda's performance against Toyota depends on the quality of Honda's overall value-delivery network versus Toyota's. Even if Honda makes the best cars, it might lose in the marketplace if Toyota's dealer network provides more customer-satisfying sales and service.

The Marketing Process

Marketing process

The process of (1) analyzing marketing opportunities, (2) selecting target markets, (3) developing the marketing mix, and (4) managing the marketing effort.

The strategic plan defines the company's overall mission and objectives. Marketing's role and activities are shown in Figure 2.4, which summarizes the entire **marketing process** and the forces influencing company marketing strategy.

Consumers stand in the center. The goal is to build strong and profitable relationships with customers. As a first step, through market segmentation, targeting, and positioning, the company decides which customers it will serve and how. It identifies the total market, then divides it into smaller segments, selects the most promising segments, and focuses on serving and satisfying these segments. Next, the company designs a marketing mix made up of factors under its control—product, price, place, and promotion. To find the best marketing mix and put it into action, the company engages in marketing analysis, planning, implementation, and control. Through these activities, the company watches and adapts to the actors and forces in the marketing environment. We will now look briefly at each element in the marketing process. In later chapters, we will discuss each element in more depth.

FIGURE 2.4
The marketing process

Relationships with Consumers

To succeed in today's competitive marketplace, companies must be customer centered, winning customers from competitors, then keeping and growing them by delivering greater value. But before it can satisfy consumers, a company must first understand their needs and wants. Thus, sound marketing requires a careful customer analysis.

Companies know that they cannot profitably serve all consumers in a given market—at least not all consumers in the same way. There are too many different kinds of consumers with too many different kinds of needs. And most companies are in a position to serve some segments better than others. Thus, each company must divide up the total market, choose the best segments, and design strategies for profitably serving chosen segments. This process involves three steps: *market segmentation, target marketing,* and *market positioning.*

Market Segmentation

The market consists of many types of customers, products, and needs. The marketer has to determine which segments offer the best opportunity for achieving company objectives. Consumers can be grouped and served in various ways based on geographic, demographic, psychographic, and behavioral factors. The process of dividing a market into distinct groups of buyers who have different needs, characteristics, or behavior and who might require separate products or marketing programs, is called **market segmentation.**

Every market has segments, but not all ways of segmenting a market are equally useful. For example, Tylenol would gain little by distinguishing between male and female users of pain relievers if both respond the same way to marketing efforts. A **market segment** consists of consumers who respond in a similar way to a given set of marketing efforts. In the car market, for example, consumers who choose the biggest, most comfortable car regardless of price make up one market segment. Customers who care mainly about price and operating economy make up another segment. It would be difficult to make one car model that was the first choice of consumers in both segments. Companies are wise to focus their efforts on meeting the distinct needs of individual market segments.

Target Marketing

After a company has defined market segments, it can enter one or many segments of a given market. **Target marketing** involves evaluating each market segment's attractiveness and selecting one or more segments to enter. A company should target segments in which it can generate the greatest customer value profitably and sustain it over time. A company with limited resources might

Market segmentation
Dividing a market into distinct groups of buyers who have distinct needs, characteristics, or behavior and who might require separate products or marketing mixes.

Market segment
A group of consumers who respond in a similar way to a given set of marketing efforts.

Target marketing
The process of evaluating each market segment's attractiveness and selecting one or more segments to enter.

decide to serve only one or a few special segments or "market niches." This strategy limits sales but can be very profitable. Or a company might choose to serve several related segments—perhaps those with different kinds of customers but with the same basic wants. A large company might also decide to offer a complete range of products to serve all market segments.

Most companies enter a new market by serving a single segment, and if this proves successful, they add segments. Large companies eventually seek full market coverage. They want to be the General Motors of their industry. GM says that it makes a car for every "person, purse, and personality." The leading company normally has different products designed to meet the special needs of each segment.

Market Positioning

After a company has decided which market segments to enter, it must decide what positions it wants to occupy in those segments. A product's *position* is the place the product occupies relative to competitors in consumers' minds. Marketers want to develop unique market positions for their products. If a product is perceived to be exactly like others on the market, consumers would have no reason to buy it.

Market positioning

Arranging for a product to occupy a clear, distinctive, and desirable place relative to competing products in the minds of target consumers.

Market positioning is arranging for a product to occupy a clear, distinctive, and desirable place relative to competing products in the minds of target consumers. Thus, marketers plan positions that distinguish their products from competing brands and give them the greatest strategic advantage in their target markets. For example, the Ford Taurus is "built to last"; Chevy Blazer is "like a rock"; Toyota's economical Echo states, "It's not you. It's the car"; and Saturn is "a different kind of company, different kind of car." Lexus avows "the passionate pursuit of excellence," Jaguar is positioned as "the art of performance," and Mercedes says, "In a perfect world, everyone would drive a Mercedes." The luxurious Bentley promises "18 handcrafted feet of shameless luxury." Such deceptively simple statements form the backbone of a product's marketing strategy.

In positioning its product, the company first identifies possible competitive advantages upon which to build the position. To gain competitive advantage, the company must offer greater value to target consumers. It can do this either by charging lower prices than competitors do or by offering more benefits to justify higher prices. But if the company positions the product as *offering* greater value, it must then *deliver* that greater value. Thus, effective positioning begins with actually *differentiating* the company's marketing offer so that it gives consumers more value.

Positioning: Bentley promises "18 handcrafted feet of shameless luxury." In contrast, Toyota promises, "At 41 miles per gallon ... it's not you. It's the car." Such deceptively simple statements form the backbone of a product's marketing strategy.

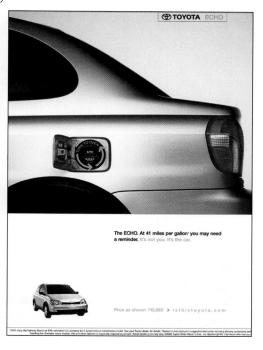

Once the company has chosen a desired position, it must take strong steps to deliver and communicate that position to target consumers. The company's entire marketing program should support the chosen positioning strategy.

Marketing Strategies for Competitive Advantage

To be successful, the company must do a *better job than competitors* of satisfying target consumers. Thus, marketing strategies must be geared to the needs of consumers but also to the strategies of competitors.

Designing competitive marketing strategies begins with thorough competitor analysis. The company constantly compares the value and customer satisfaction delivered by its products, prices, channels, and promotion with those of close competitors. In this way it can discern areas of potential advantage and disadvantage. The company asks: Who are our competitors? What are their objectives and strategies? What are their strengths and weaknesses? And how will they react to different competitive strategies we might use?

The competitive marketing strategy a company adopts depends on its industry position. A firm that dominates a market can adopt one or more of several *market leader* strategies. Well-known leaders include Coca-Cola (soft drinks), Microsoft (computer software), Caterpillar (large construction equipment), IBM (computers and information technology services), Wal-Mart (retailing), Boeing (aircraft), and AOL (Internet and online services). *Market challengers* are runner-up companies that aggressively attack competitors to get more market share. For example, Pepsi challenges Coke, Komatsu challenges Caterpillar, and MSN challenges AOL. The challenger might attack the market leader, other firms its own size, or smaller local and regional competitors.

Some runner-up firms will choose to follow rather than challenge the market leader. *Market followers* seek stable market shares and profits by following competitors' product offers, prices, and marketing programs. Smaller firms in a market, or even larger firms that lack established positions, often adopt *market nicher* strategies. They specialize in serving market niches that major competitors overlook or ignore. For example, Arm & Hammer has a lock on the baking soda corner of most consumer goods categories, including toothpaste, deodorizers, and others. Oshkosh Truck has found its niche as the world's largest producer of airport rescue trucks and frontloading concrete mixers. And Veterinary Pet Insurance provides 82 percent of all health insurance policies for our furry—or feathery—friends (see Real Marketing 2.3). "Nichers" avoid direct confrontations with the majors by specializing along market, customer, product, or marketing-mix lines. Through smart niching, smaller firms in an industry can be as profitable as their larger competitors. We will discuss competitive marketing strategies more fully in Chapter 18.

Developing the Marketing Mix

Marketing mix

The set of controllable tactical marketing tools—product, price, place, and promotion—that the firm blends to produce the response it wants in the target market.

Once the company has decided on its overall competitive marketing strategy, it is ready to begin planning the details of the marketing mix, one of the major concepts in modern marketing. The **marketing mix** is the set of controllable, tactical marketing tools that the firm blends to produce the response it wants in the target market. The marketing mix consists of everything the firm can do to influence the demand for its product. The many possibilities can be collected into four groups of variables known as the "four Ps": *product, price, place,* and *promotion*.[18] Figure 2.5 shows the particular marketing tools under each P.

Product means the goods-and-services combination the company offers to the target market. Thus, a Ford Taurus product consists of nuts and bolts, spark plugs, pistons, headlights, and thousands of other parts. Ford offers several Taurus styles and dozens of optional features. The car comes fully serviced and with a comprehensive warranty that is as much a part of the product as the tailpipe.

Price is the amount of money customers have to pay to obtain the product. Ford calculates suggested retail prices that its dealers might charge for each Taurus. But Ford dealers rarely charge the full sticker price. Instead, they negotiate the price with each customer, offering discounts, trade-in allowances, and credit terms. These actions adjust prices for the current competitive situation and bring them into line with the buyer's perception of the car's value.

Place includes company activities that make the product available to target consumers. Ford partners with a large body of independently owned dealerships that sell the company's many

Niching: Health Insurance for Our Furry—or Feathery—Friends

Health insurance for pets? MetLife, Prudential, Northwestern Mutual, and most other large insurance companies haven't paid much attention to it. But that leaves plenty of

You promised to take care of me.

I don't understand the
"if I can afford it" part.

A wagging tail. A purr of delight. In return for those moments of love, you've promised to take care of your dog or cat.

And whether it's an ear infection, injury or a serious illness, there will come a time when your pet needs medical attention. When that day comes, Veterinary Pet Insurance will help you keep your promise to care.

Besides coverage for accidents and illness, we offer routine care coverage to help pay for an annual veterinary exam, vaccinations—even prescription flea control. And, you can use any veterinarian worldwide. In fact, 9 out of 10 veterinarians who recommend pet insurance recommend VPI. No wonder more and more pet owners depend on Veterinary Pet Insurance, the nation's oldest, largest and number one pet insurance plan.

Veterinary Pet Insurance: We'll help you keep your promise to protect your pet.

Avian and exotic pet coverage available; call for details.

Underwritten by: Veterinary Pet Insurance Co. (CA), Brea, CA; National Casualty Co. (Nat'ls, Madison, WI. ©2002 Veterinary Pet Services Inc.

Protect your best friend.

It's easy, affordable and the benefits can start with your next veterinary visit.

Call 800-USA-PETS
(800-872-7387)
Or go to petinsurance.com

VETERINARY
PET INSURANCE
*Making the miracles of
veterinary medicine affordable*

Nichers: Market nicher VPI is growing faster than a new-born puppy. Its mission is to "make the miracles of veterinary medicine affordable to all pet owners."

knowing that you can heal a sick patient, but the owner lacks the financial resources and instructs you to put the pet down," says Stephens. "I wanted to change that."

Pet insurance is a still-small but fast-growing segment of the insurance business. Insiders think the industry offers huge potential. Currently, there are more than 53 million dogs and 60 million cats in the United States—more than 60 percent of all U.S. households own one or the other or both. Another 4.6 million U.S. households own one or more of about 300 species of birds; 2 million more own pet rabbits. Many people treat their pets as family members—and they buy accordingly. In fact, Americans now spend a whopping $28.5 billion a year on their pets. The average dog owner spends $196 a year on pet medical care alone.

Unlike in Sweden and Britain, where more than half of all pets owners carry pet health insurance, only 1 percent of pet owners in the United States carry such coverage. However, a recent study of pet owners found that nearly 75 percent are willing to go into debt to pay for veterinary care for their furry—or feathery—companions. And for many pet medical procedures, they'd have to! If not diagnosed quickly, even a mundane ear infection in a dog can result in $1,000 worth of medical treatment. A more complicated feline kidney transplant can run as much as $6,500. Cancer treatments, including radiation and chemotherapy, could cost a pet owner more than $10,000. All of this adds up to a lot of potential growth for pet health insurers.

VPI's plans cover more than 6,400 pet medical problems and conditions. The insurance helps pay for office calls, prescriptions, treatments, lab fees, X-rays, surgery, and hospitalization. Like its handful of competitors, VPI issues health insurance policies for dogs and cats. Unlike its competitors, VPI recently expanded its coverage to a menagerie of exotic pets as well. Among other critters, the new Avian and Exotic Pet Plan covers birds, rabbits, ferrets, rats, guinea pigs, snakes (except extra-large ones) and other reptiles, iguanas, possums, turtles, hedgehogs, and pot belly pigs. "There's such a vast array" of pets, says a VPI executive, "and people love them. We have to respect that."

How's VPI doing in its niche? It's growing like a newborn puppy. VPI is by far the largest of the handful of companies that offer pet insurance, providing more than 82 percent of all U.S. pet insurance policies. Since its inception, VPI has issued more than 1 million policies, and it now serves more than 250,000 policyholders. Sales have grown 40 percent in each of the past five years, reaching nearly $52 million last year.

That might not amount to much for the likes of MetLife, Prudential, or Northwestern Mutual, which rack up tens of billions of dollars in yearly revenues. But it's profitable business for nichers like VPI. As importantly, its a real godsend for the company's policyholders.

"Veterinarians and pet owners want to provide their pets with the best medical care possible," says VPI founder Stephens. "But with advances in veterinary medicine keeping pace with those in human medicine, cost often becomes the deciding factor in the level of care owners can provide. We [always will] strive to make the miracles of modern medicine affordable."

Sources: Michelle Desai, "VPI—Twenty Years and Still Going Strong," VPI press release, January 13, 2002; Mary Christine Convey, "Insurers Find Niche in Pet Health Insurance," *National Underwriter,* May 21, 2001, pp. 28–29; Michelle Leder, "How Much Is That $100 Deductible in the Window?" *New York Times,* Jul 22, 2001, p. 3.10; Jane Bennett Clark, "Cover Your Tail," *Kiplinger's Personal Finance,* Jan 2002, pp. 108–112; and information from the Veterinary Health Insurance Web site at www.petinsurance.com, June 2002.

room for more focused nichers, for whom pet health insurance has become a lucrative business. The largest of the small competitors is Veterinary Pet Insurance (VPI). VPI's mission is to "make the miracles of veterinary medicine affordable to all pet owners."

VPI was founded in 1980 by veterinarian Jack Stephens. He never intended to leave his practice, but his life took a dramatic turn when he visited a local grocery store and was identified by a client's daughter as "the man who killed Buffy." Stephens had euthanized the family dog two weeks earlier. He immediately began researching the possibility of creating medical pet insurance. "There is nothing more frustrating for a veterinarian than

FIGURE 2.5
The four *P*s of the
marketing mix

different models. Ford selects its dealers carefully and supports them strongly. The dealers keep an inventory of Ford automobiles, demonstrate them to potential buyers, negotiate prices, close sales, and service the cars after the sale.

Promotion means activities that communicate the merits of the product and persuade target customers to buy it. Ford spends more than $2.3 billion each year on advertising to tell consumers about the company and its many products.[19] Dealership salespeople assist potential buyers and persuade them that Ford is the best car for them. Ford and its dealers offer special promotions—sales, cash rebates, and low financing rates—as added purchase incentives.

An effective marketing program blends all of the marketing-mix elements into a coordinated program designed to achieve the company's marketing objectives by delivering value to consumers. The marketing mix constitutes the company's tactical tool kit for establishing strong positioning in target markets.

Some critics feel that the four *P*s may omit or underemphasize certain important activities. For example, they ask, "Where are services?" Just because they don't start with a *P* doesn't justify omitting them. The answer is that services, such as banking, airline, and retailing services, are products too. We might call them *service products.* "Where is packaging?" the critics might ask. Marketers would answer that they include packaging as just one of many product decisions. All said, as Figure 2.5 suggests, many marketing activities that might appear to be left out of the marketing mix are subsumed under one of the four *P*s. The issue is not whether there should be four, six, or ten *P*s so much as what framework is most helpful in designing marketing programs.

There is another concern, however, that is valid. It holds that the four *P*s concept takes the seller's view of the market, not the buyer's view. From the buyer's viewpoint, in this age of customer relationships, the four *P*s might be better described as the four *C*s:[20]

Four *P*s	**Four *C*s**
Product	Customer solution
Price	Customer cost
Place	Convenience
Promotion	Communication

Thus while marketers see themselves as selling products, customers see themselves as buying value or solutions to their problems. And customers are interested in more than just the price; they are interested in the total costs of obtaining, using, and disposing of a product. Customers want the product and service to be as conveniently available as possible. Finally, they want two-way communication. Marketers would do well to think through the four *C*s first and then build the four *P*s on that platform.

Managing the Marketing Effort

The company wants to design and put into action the marketing mix that will best achieve its objectives in its target markets. Figure 2.6 shows the relationship between the four marketing management functions—*analysis, planning, implementation,* and *control.* The company first develops companywide strategic plans, then translates them into marketing and other plans for each division, product, and brand. Through implementation, the company turns the plans into actions. Control consists of measuring and evaluating the results of marketing activities and taking corrective action where needed. Finally, marketing analysis provides information and evaluations needed for all of the other marketing activities.

Marketing Analysis

Managing the marketing function begins with a complete analysis of the company's situation. The company must analyze its markets and marketing environment to find attractive opportunities and avoid environmental threats. It must analyze company strengths and weaknesses as well as current and possible marketing actions to determine which opportunities it can best pursue. Marketing provides input to each of the other marketing management functions. We discuss marketing analysis more fully in Chapter 5.

Marketing Planning

Through strategic planning, the company decides what it wants to do with each business unit. Marketing planning involves deciding on marketing strategies that will help the company attain its overall strategic objectives. A detailed marketing plan is needed for each business, product, or brand. What does a marketing plan look like? Our discussion focuses on product or brand plans.

Table 2.2 outlines the major sections of a typical product or brand plan. The plan begins with an executive summary, which quickly overviews major assessments, goals, and recommendations. The main section of the plan presents a detailed analysis of the current marketing situation as well as potential threats and opportunities. It next states major objectives for the brand and outlines the specifics of a marketing strategy for achieving them.

Marketing strategy

The marketing logic by which the business unit hopes to achieve its marketing objectives.

A **marketing strategy** is the marketing logic whereby the company hopes to achieve its marketing objectives. It consists of specific strategies for target markets, positioning, the marketing mix, and marketing expenditure levels. In this section, the planner explains how each strategy responds to the threats, opportunities, and critical issues spelled out earlier in the plan. Additional sections of the marketing plan lay out an action program for implementing the marketing strategy along with the details of a supporting *marketing budget.* The last section outlines the controls that will be used to monitor progress and take corrective action.

Marketing implementation

The process that turns marketing strategies and plans into marketing actions in order to accomplish strategic marketing objectives.

Marketing Implementation

Planning good strategies is only a start toward successful marketing. A brilliant marketing strategy counts for little if the company fails to implement it properly. **Marketing implementation** is the process that turns marketing *plans* into marketing *actions* in order to accomplish strategic

FIGURE 2.6

The relationship between analysis, planning, implementation, and control

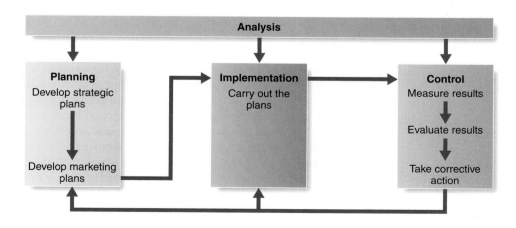

TABLE 2.2   CONTENTS OF A MARKETING PLAN

Section	Purpose
Executive summary	Presents a brief summary of the main goals and recommendations of the plan for management review, helping top management to find the plan's major points quickly. A table of contents should follow the executive summary.
Current marketing situation	Describes the target market and company's position in it, including information about the market, product performance, competition, and distribution. This section includes: • A *market description* that defines the market and major segments, then reviews customer needs and factors in the marketing environment that may affect customer purchasing. • A *product review,* that shows sales, prices, and gross margins of the major products in the product line. • A review of *competition,* which identifies major competitors and assesses their market positions and strategies for product quality, pricing, distribution, and promotion. • A review of *distribution,* which evaluates recent sales trends and other developments in major distribution channels.
Threats and opportunity analysis	Assesses major threats and opportunities that the product might face, helping management to anticipate important positive or negative developments that might have an impact on the firm and its strategies.
Objectives and issues	States the marketing objectives that the company would like to attain during the plan's term and discusses key issues that will affect their attainment. For example, if the goal is to achieve a 15 percent market share, this section looks at how this goal might be achieved.
Marketing strategy	Outlines the broad marketing logic by which the business unit hopes to achieve its marketing objectives and the specifics of target markets, positioning, and marketing expenditure levels. It outlines specific strategies for each marketing-mix element and explains how each responds to the threats, opportunities, and critical issues spelled out earlier in the plan.
Action programs	Spells out how marketing strategies will be turned into specific action programs that answer the following questions: *What* will be done? *When* will it be done? *Who* is responsible for doing it? *How* much will it cost?
Budgets	Details a supporting marketing budget that is essentially a projected profit-and-loss statement. It shows expected revenues (forecasted number of units sold and the average net price) and expected costs (of production, distribution, and marketing). The difference is the projected profit. Once approved by higher management, the budget becomes the basis for materials buying, production scheduling, personnel planning, and marketing operations.
Controls	Outlines the control that will be used to monitor progress and allow higher management to review implementation results and spot products that are not meeting their goals.

marketing objectives. Implementation involves day to day, month to month activities that effectively put the marketing plan to work. Whereas marketing planning addresses the *what* and *why* of marketing activities, implementation addresses the *who, where, when,* and *how.*

Many managers think that "doing things right" (implementation) is as important as, or even more important than, "doing the right things" (strategy). The fact is that both are critical to success.[21] However, companies can gain competitive advantages through effective implementation. One firm can have essentially the same strategy as another, yet win in the marketplace through faster or better execution. Still, implementation is difficult—it is often easier to think up good marketing strategies than it is to carry them out.

In an increasingly connected world, people at all levels of the marketing system must work together to implement marketing plans and strategies. At Black & Decker, for example, marketing implementation for the company's power tool products requires day to day decisions and actions by thousands of people both inside and outside the organization. Marketing managers make decisions about target segments, branding, packaging, pricing, promoting, and distributing. They connect with people elsewhere in the company to get support for their products and programs. They talk with engineering about product design, with manufacturing about production and inventory levels, and with finance about funding and cash flows. They also connect with outside people, such as advertising agencies to plan ad campaigns and the media to obtain publicity support. The sales force urges Home Depot, Wal-Mart, and other retailers to advertise Black & Decker products, provide ample shelf space, and use company displays.

Successful marketing implementation depends on how well the company blends its people, organizational structure, decision and reward systems, and company culture into a cohesive action

Marketers must continually plan their analysis, implementation, and control activities.

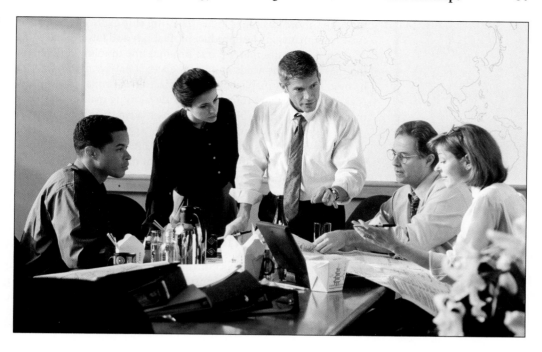

program that supports its strategies. At all levels, the company must be staffed by people who have the needed skills, motivation, and personal characteristics. The company's formal organization structure plays an important role in implementing marketing strategy; so do its decision and reward systems. For example, if a company's compensation system rewards managers for short run profit results, they will have little incentive to work toward long run market-building objectives.

Finally, to be successfully implemented, the firm's marketing strategies must fit with its company culture, the system of values and beliefs shared by people in the organization. A study of America's most successful companies found that these companies have almost cultlike cultures built around strong, market-oriented missions. At companies such as Wal-Mart, Microsoft, Nordstrom, Citicorp, Procter & Gamble, and Walt Disney, "employees share such a strong vision that they know in their hearts what's right for their company."[22]

Marketing Department Organization

The company must design a marketing organization that can carry out marketing strategies and plans. If the company is very small, one person might do all of the research, selling, advertising, customer service, and other marketing work. As the company expands, a marketing department emerges to plan and carry out marketing activities. In large companies, this department contains many specialists. Thus, Black & Decker has product and market managers, sales managers and salespeople, market researchers, advertising experts, and other specialists.

Modern marketing departments can be arranged in several ways. The most common form of marketing organization is the *functional organization,* in which different marketing activities are headed by a functional specialist—a sales manager, advertising manager, marketing research manager, customer service manager, or new-product manager. A company that sells across the country or internationally often uses a *geographic organization,* in which its sales and marketing people are assigned to specific countries, regions, and districts. Geographic organization allows salespeople to settle into a territory, get to know their customers, and work with a minimum of travel time and cost.

Companies with many very different products or brands often create a *product management organization.* Using this approach, a product manager develops and implements a complete strategy and marketing program for a specific product or brand. Product management first appeared at Procter & Gamble in 1929. A new company soap, Camay, was not doing well, and a young P&G executive was assigned to give his exclusive attention to developing and promoting this product. He was successful, and the company soon added other product managers.[23] Since then, many firms, especially consumer products companies, have set up product management organizations. However, recent changes in the marketing environment have caused many companies to rethink the role of the product manager. Many companies are finding that today's marketing environment calls for less brand focus and more customer focus. They are shifting toward *customer equity management*—moving away from managing just product profitability and toward managing *customer* profitability.[24]

For companies that sell one product line to many different types of markets and customers that have different needs and preferences, a *market* or *customer management organization* might be best. A market management organization is similar to the product management organization. Market managers are responsible for developing marketing strategies and plans for their specific markets or customers. This system's main advantage is that the company is organized around the needs of specific customer segments.

Large companies that produce many different products flowing into many different geographic and customer markets usually employ some *combination* of the functional, geographic, product, and market organization forms. This ensures that each function, product, and market receives its share of management attention. However, it can also add costly layers of management and reduce organizational flexibility. Still, the benefits of organizational specialization usually outweigh the drawbacks.

Marketing Control

Marketing control

The process of measuring and evaluating the results of marketing strategies and plans and taking corrective action to ensure that objectives are achieved.

Because many surprises occur during the implementation of marketing plans, the marketing department must practice constant marketing control. **Marketing control** involves evaluating the results of marketing strategies and plans and taking corrective action to ensure that objectives are attained. Figure 2.7 shows that marketing control involves four steps. Management first sets specific marketing goals. It then measures its performance in the marketplace and evaluates the causes of any differences between expected and actual performance. Finally, management takes corrective action to close the gaps between its goals and its performance. This may require changing the action programs or even changing the goals.

Operating control involves checking ongoing performance against the annual plan and taking corrective action when necessary. Its purpose is to ensure that the company achieves the sales, profits, and other goals set out in its annual plan. It also involves determining the profitability of different products, territories, markets, and channels.

Strategic control involves looking at whether the company's basic strategies are well matched to its opportunities. Marketing strategies and programs can quickly become outdated, and each company should periodically reassess its overall approach to the marketplace. A major tool for such strategic control is a **marketing audit.** The marketing audit is a comprehensive, systematic, independent, and periodic examination of a company's environment, objectives, strategies, and activities to determine problem areas and opportunities. The audit provides good input for a plan of action to improve the company's marketing performance.[25]

Marketing audit

A comprehensive, systematic, independent, and periodic examination of a company's environment, objectives, strategies, and activities to determine problem areas and opportunities and to recommend a plan of action to improve the company's marketing performance.

The marketing audit covers *all* major marketing areas of a business, not just a few trouble spots. It assesses the marketing environment, marketing strategy, marketing organization, marketing systems, marketing mix, and marketing productivity and profitability. The audit is normally conducted by an objective and experienced outside party. Table 2.3 shows the kinds of questions the marketing auditor might ask. The findings may come as a surprise—and sometimes as a shock—to management. Management then decides which actions make sense and how and when to implement them.

The Marketing Environment

Managing the marketing function would be hard enough if the marketer had to deal only with the controllable marketing mix variables. But the company operates in a complex marketing environment, consisting of uncontrollable forces to which the company must adapt. The environment produces both threats and opportunities. The company must carefully analyze its environment so that it can avoid the threats and take advantage of the opportunities.

FIGURE 2.7
The control process

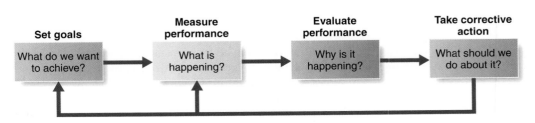

TABLE 2.3	MARKETING AUDIT QUESTIONS

Marketing Environment Audit

1. The *macroenvironment:* What major *demographic, economic, natural, technological, political,* and *cultural* trends pose threats and opportunities for this company?
2. The *task environment:*
   - *Markets and Customers:* What is happening to marketing size, growth, geographic distribution, and profits? What are the major market segments? How do customers make their buying decisions? How do they rate the company on product quality, value, and service?
   - *Other factors* in the marketing system: Who are the company's major *competitors* and what are their strategies, strengths, and weaknesses? How are the company's *channels* performing? What trends are affecting *suppliers?* What key *publics* provide problems or opportunities?

Marketing Strategy Audit

1. *Business mission and marketing objectives:* Is the mission clearly defined and market oriented? Has the company set clear objectives to guide marketing planning and performance?
2. *Marketing strategy:* Does the company have a strong marketing strategy for achieving its objectives?
3. *Budgets:* Has the company budgeted sufficient resources to segments, products, territories, and marketing-mix elements?

Marketing Organization Audit

1. *Formal structure:* Are marketing activities optimally structured along functional, product, market, and territory lines?
2. *Functional efficiency:* Do marketing and sales communicate effectively? Is marketing staff well trained, supervised, motivated, and evaluated?
3. *Cross-functional efficiency:* Do marketing people work well with people in operations, R&D, purchasing, human resources, information technology, and other nonmarketing areas?

Marketing Systems Audit

1. *Marketing information system:* Is the marketing intelligence system providing accurate and timely information? Is the company using marketing research effectively?
2. *Marketing planning system:* Does the company prepare annual, long-term, and strategic plans? Are they used?
3. *Marketing control system:* Are annual plan objectives being achieved? Does management periodically analyze product, market, and channel sales and profitability?
4. *New-product development:* Does the company have an effective new-product development process? Has the company succeeded with new products?

Marketing Productivity Audit

1. *Profitability analysis:* How profitable are the company's different products, markets, territories, and channels? Should the company enter, expand, or withdraw from any business segments?
2. *Cost-effectiveness analysis:* Do any marketing activities have excessive costs? How can costs be reduced?

Marketing Function Audit

1. *Products:* What are the company's product line objectives? Should some current products be phased out or new products be added? Would some products benefit from changes in quality, features, or style?
2. *Price:* Are the company's pricing policies and procedures appropriate? Are prices in line with customers' perceived value?
3. *Distribution:* What are the company's distribution objectives and strategies? Should existing channels be changed or new ones added?
4. *Promotion:* Does the company have well-developed *advertising, sales promotion,* and *public relations* programs? Is the *sales force* large enough and well trained, supervised, and motivated?

The company's marketing environment includes forces close to the company that affect its ability to serve consumers, such as other company departments, channel members, suppliers, competitors, and publics. It also includes broader demographic and economic forces, political and legal forces, technological and ecological forces, and social and cultural forces. In order to connect effectively with consumers, others in the company, external partners, and the world around them, marketers need to consider all of these forces when developing and positioning its offer to the target market. The marketing environment is discussed more fully in Chapter 4.

LOOKING BACK: REVIEWING THE CONCEPTS

All companies must look ahead and find the long-term game plan that makes the most sense given its specific situation, opportunities, objectives, and resources. The hard task of selecting an overall company strategy for long run survival and growth is called *strategic planning*. Strategic planning sets the stage for the rest of the company's planning, including marketing planning.

Guided by the strategic plan, marketers work with others inside and outside the company to design and implement strategies for building profitable relationships with targeted customers.

1. Explain companywide strategic planning and its four steps.

Strategic planning involves developing a strategy for long-run survival and growth. It consists of four steps: defining the company's mission, setting objectives and goals, designing a business portfolio, and developing functional plans. *Defining a clear company mission* begins with drafting a formal mission statement, which should be market oriented, realistic, specific, motivating, and consistent with the market environment. The mission is then transformed into detailed *supporting goals and objectives* to guide the entire company. Based on those goals and objectives, headquarters designs a *business portfolio,* deciding which businesses and products should receive more or fewer resources. In turn, each business and product unit must develop *detailed marketing plans* in line with the companywide plan. Comprehensive and sound marketing plans support company strategic planning by detailing specific opportunities.

2. Discuss how to design business portfolios and develop strategies for growth and downsizing.

Guided by the company's mission statement and objectives, management plans its *business portfolio,* or the collection of businesses and products that make up the company. To produce a business portfolio that best fits the company's strengths and weaknesses to opportunities in the environment, the company must analyze and adjust its *current* business portfolio and develop growth and downsizing strategies for adjusting the *future* portfolio. The company might use a formal portfolio-planning method like the *BCG growth-share matrix.* But many companies are now designing more-customized portfolio-planning approaches that better suit their unique situations. The *product/ market expansion grid* suggests four possible growth paths: market penetration, market development, product development, and diversification.

3. Assess marketing's role in strategic planning and explain how marketers partner with others inside and outside the firm to build profitable customer relationships.

The company's strategic plan establishes what kinds of businesses the company will be in and its objectives for each. Then, within each business unit the major functional departments—marketing, finance, accounting, purchasing, operations, information systems, human resources, and others—must work together to accomplish strategic objectives. Marketing plays a key role in the company's strategic planning by providing a marketing-concept *philosophy* and *inputs* regarding attractive market opportunities. Within individual business units, marketing designs *strategies* for reaching the unit's objectives and helps to carry them out profitably.

Marketers alone cannot produce superior value for customers—it can be only a partner in attracting, keeping, and growing customers. A company's success depends on how well each department performs its customer value-adding activities and how well the departments work together to serve the customer. Thus, marketers must practice *partner relationship management.* They must work closely with partners in other company departments to form an effective *value chain* that serves the customer. And they must partner effectively with other companies in the marketing system to form a competitively superior *value-delivery network.*

4. Describe the marketing process and the forces that influence it.

The *marketing process* matches consumer needs with the company's capabilities and objectives. Consumers are at the center of the marketing process. Through market segmentation, target marketing, and market positioning, the company divides the total market into smaller segments, selects segments it can best serve, and decides how it wants to bring value to target consumers. It then designs a *marketing mix* to produce the response it wants in the target market. The marketing mix consists of product, price, place, and promotion decisions.

5. List the marketing management functions, including the elements of a marketing plan.

To find the best strategy and mix and to put them into action, the company engages in marketing analysis, planning, implementation, and control. The main components of a *marketing plan* are the executive summary, current marketing situation, threats and opportunities, objectives and issues, marketing strategies, action programs, budgets, and controls. To plan good strategies is often easier than to carry them out. To be successful, companies must also be effective at *implementation—* turning marketing strategies into marketing actions.

Much of the responsibility for implementation goes to the company's marketing department. Modern marketing departments can be organized in one or a combination of ways: *functional marketing organization, geographic organization, product management organization,* or *market management organization.* Marketing organizations carry out *marketing control,* both operating control and strategic control. They use *marketing audits* to determine marketing opportunities and problems and to recommend short-run and long-run actions to improve overall marketing performance. Through these activities, the company watches and adapts to the marketing environment.

REVIEWING THE KEY TERMS

DISCUSSING THE CONCEPTS

1. Define strategic planning. List and briefly describe the four steps that lead managers and the firm through the strategic planning process.
2. What is a mission statement? List and briefly discuss the four characteristics of effective mission statements.
3. Examine the Boston Consulting Group's growth-share matrix. Which one of the cells provides the primary revenues for the organization's SBUs? How can an organization use the BCG growth-share matrix to plan its future?
4. Beyond evaluating current businesses, designing the business portfolio involves finding future businesses and products the company should consider. Using the product/market expansion grid, prepare a list of new business and product ideas for one of the following companies: (a) Sony, (b) Fuji film division, (c) Levi Strauss Docker's division, (d) Citibank's senior citizens investment program, or (e) BMW. Be sure to cover all the cells in the grid.
5. Marketing plays a key role in the company's strategic planning by providing a guiding philosophy. What is this philosophy and what impact does it have on the strategic planning process?
6. Partner relationship management (PRM) is increasingly important in meeting the competitive challenges of the twenty-first century. How does PRM use value chains and value-delivery networks to create effective partnerships?
7. Companies must be customer-centered to succeed. What are the three steps in building customer relationships? How does each aid in relationship building?
8. In this age of customer relationships, the four *P*s might be better described as the four *C*s. Comment.

APPLYING THE CONCEPTS

1. Sony has found the right approach for surrounding its customers with electronic wizardry and entertainment. From PlayStation to online games, from movies to TV, DVD and music, Sony is tops in entertainment. But rivals are on the horizon. With hungry competitors such as Disney, Microsoft, Panasonic, and a host of others, Sony must constantly adjust its strategic plans and look for new opportunities. For more general information on Sony and offerings, see www.sony.com.
   a. After considering Sony's approach to the world of electronics and entertainment, identify new and promising product opportunities for Sony.
   b. Choose one of the product opportunities you identified. What makes it distinctive and promising?
   c. What target market would you pursue for this product opportunity?
   d. What marketing mix would be appropriate?
   e. Write a brief marketing plan for this opportunity (see Table 2.2).
   f. Critique your plan. What are its strengths and weaknesses?

2. For more than a decade, several firms have been waging the Sneaker Wars. Notable companies such as Nike, Reebok, Adidas, New Balance, Puma, and Converse have been battling with no holds barred, and the dust is yet to settle! In fact, tough new competitors such as Vans and Skechers have arrived on the scene. Visit these firms at their Web sites: www.nike.com, www.reebok.com, www.adidas.com, www.newbalance.com, www.puma.com, www.converseshoes.com, www.vans.com, and www.skechers.com. As a future marketing strategist, answer the following questions:
   a. Which firm is the market leader? Which firms are market challengers, market followers, and market nichers?
   b. Critique the various Web sites. Are the Web sites consistent with your assessments of the companies' industry positions? Why or why not?
   c. Assume the position of one of the market challengers. Design a strategy for overtaking the market leader.
   d. Assume the position of a market nicher and design a strategy for expanding your business without drawing attacks from your stronger rivals.
   e. Select a market nicher. How might this nicher improve its Web site?

 # DIGITAL CONNECTIONS

CONNECTING WITH OTHERS TO CREATE A VALUE-DELIVERY NETWORK

One of the most stressful events that people encounter is planning a wedding. But a Web services company, The Knot, can help to reduce this stress. It provides links to vendors, fashion consultants, jewelers, and even honeymoon planners. It also provides helpful hints, makeup suggestions, guidance on wedding photography and even an online registry for gifts. In addition to providing value for consumers, The Knot is also good news for suppliers of wedding-related products and services. A true value-delivery network is all about partners working together to solve common customer problems and needs, and then sharing business and profits. The Knot has attracted partners that really understand the wedding and bridal business. See for yourself at www.theknot.com.

FOR DISCUSSION

1. How does The Knot attempt to solve problems for customers? Assume the role of a bride- or groom-to-be and interact with The Knot. Critique your experience.
2. Examine the links to partners. What value chains were created via this Web site? Were you able localize your search?

3. Evaluate the tips and advice provided for the wedding planner. What role does providing information play in building value relationships with consumers? Does The Knot do this effectively?
4. Examine the "My Knot Planning Tools" provided by the Web site. Use these tools to plan your own wedding. Comment and critique.

5. Starting with The Knot and working toward a vendor in your local area, trace a value chain that results in a value-delivery network. From the perspective of the local vendor, how would an affiliation with a service provider such as The Knot be beneficial? What other partnerships should this local vendor consider to expand its business?

NerveWire: Strategic Planning for E-Commerce

NerveWire was founded just as business-to-business e-commerce began its explosive growth and Fortune 500 companies began to move into the online marketplace. The consulting company found success by helping clients create a strategic plan to enter the world of e-commerce. This unique focus earned NerveWire a blue-chip client list, including heavyweights such as Hewlett-Packard, Nokia, UBS Warburg, Merrill Lynch, DuPont, and Cisco. Proclaims one client, "NerveWire's exceptional value is that they can help you think through how to reinvent your business and design the strategy and planning process to help you get there."

After reviewing the NerveWire video, answer the following questions about strategic planning:

1. Why is strategic planning especially important for companies adopting new technologies and preparing to enter the world of e-commerce?
2. NerveWire consultants provide a framework by which marketing managers can redefine their companies. How might IBM have benefited from such consulting services in its effort to redefine its portfolio of services?
3. What is NerveWire's value proposition? What is its marketing strategy?

Trap-Ease America: The Big Cheese of Mousetraps

CONVENTIONAL WISDOM

One April morning, Martha House, president of Trap-Ease America, entered her office in Costa Mesa, California. She paused for a moment to contemplate the Ralph Waldo Emerson quote that she had framed and hung near her desk: "If a man [can] . . . make a better mousetrap than his neighbor . . . the world will make a beaten path to his door." Perhaps, she mused, Emerson knew something that she didn't. She *had* the better mousetrap—Trap-Ease—but the world didn't seem all that excited about it.

Martha had just returned from the National Hardware Show in Chicago. Standing in the trade show display booth for long hours and answering the same questions hundreds of times had been tiring. Yet, all the hard work had paid off. Each year, National Hardware Show officials held a contest to select the best new product introduced at that year's show. The Trap-Ease had won the contest this year, beating out over 300 new products.

Such notoriety was not new for the Trap-Ease mousetrap, however. *People* magazine had run a feature article on the trap,

and the trap had been the subject of numerous talk shows and articles in various popular press and trade publications.

Despite all of this attention, however, the expected demand for the trap had not materialized. Martha hoped that this award might stimulate increased interest and sales.

BACKGROUND

A group of investors had formed Trap-Ease America in January after it had obtained worldwide rights to market the innovative mousetrap. In return for marketing rights, the group agreed to pay the inventor and patent holder, a retired rancher, a royalty fee for each trap sold. The group then hired Martha to serve as president and to develop and manage the Trap-Ease America organization.

Trap-Ease America contracted with a plastics-manufacturing firm to produce the traps. The trap consisted of a square, plastic tube measuring about 6 inches long and 1½ inches in diameter. The tube bent in the middle at a 30-degree angle, so that when the front part of the tube rested on a flat surface, the other end was elevated. The elevated end

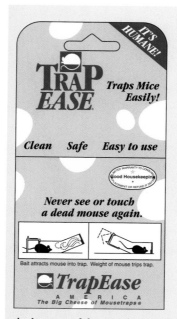

held a removable cap into which the user placed bait (cheese, dog food, or some other aromatic tidbit). The front end of the tube had a hinged door. When the trap was open, this door rested on two narrow "stilts" attached to the two bottom corners of the door. (See Exhibit 1.)

The simple trap worked very efficiently. A mouse, smelling the bait, entered the tube through the open end. As it walked up the angled bottom toward the bait, its weight made the elevated end of the trap drop downward. This action elevated the open end, allowing the hinged door to swing closed, trapping the mouse. Small teeth on the ends of the stilts caught in a groove on the bottom of the trap, locking the door closed. The user could then dispose of the mouse while it was still alive, or the user could leave it alone for a few hours to suffocate in the trap.

Martha believed the trap had many advantages for the consumer when compared with traditional spring-loaded traps or poisons. Consumers could use it safely and easily with no risk of catching their fingers while loading it. It posed no injury or poisoning threat to children or pets. Furthermore, with Trap-Ease, consumers avoided the unpleasant mess they often encountered with the violent spring-loaded traps. The Trap-Ease created no clean-up problem. Finally, the user could reuse the trap or simply throw it away.

Martha's early research suggested that women were the best target market for the Trap-Ease. Men, it seemed, were more willing to buy and use the traditional, spring-loaded trap. The targeted women, however, did not like the traditional trap. These women often stayed at home and took care of their children. Thus, they wanted a means of dealing with the mouse problem that avoided the unpleasantness and risks that the standard trap created in the home.

To reach this target market, Martha decided to distribute Trap-Ease through national grocery, hardware, and drug chains such as Safeway, Kmart, Hechingers, and CB Drug. She sold the trap directly to these large retailers, avoiding any wholesalers or other middlemen.

The traps sold in packages of two, with a suggested retail price of $2.49. Although this price made the Trap-Ease about five to ten times more expensive than smaller, standard traps, consumers appeared to offer little initial price resistance. The manufacturing cost for the Trap-Ease, including freight and packaging costs, was about 31 cents per unit. The company paid an additional 8.2 cents per unit in royalty fees. Martha priced the traps to retailers at 99 cents per unit (two units to a package) and estimated that, after sales and volume discounts, Trap-Ease would produce net revenue from retailers of 75 cents per unit.

To promote the product, Martha had budgeted approximately $60,000 for the first year. She planned to use $50,000 of this amount for travel costs to visit trade shows and to make sales calls on retailers. She planned to use the remaining $10,000 for advertis-

ing. So far, however, because the mousetrap had generated so much publicity, she had not felt that she needed to do much advertising. Still, she had placed advertising in *Good Housekeeping* (after all, the trap had earned the Good Housekeeping Seal of Approval) and in other "home and shelter" magazines. Martha was the company's only salesperson, but she intended to hire more salespeople soon.

Martha had initially forecasted Trap-Ease's first-year sales at five million units. Through April, however, the company had only sold several hundred thousand units. Martha wondered if most new products got off to such a slow start, or if she was doing something wrong. She had detected some problems, although none seemed overly serious. For one, there had not been enough repeat buying. For another, she had noted that many of the retailers upon whom she called kept their sample mousetraps on their desks as conversation pieces—she wanted the traps to be used and demonstrated. Martha wondered if consumers were also buying the traps as novelties rather than as solutions to their mouse problems.

Martha knew that the investor group believed that Trap-Ease America had a "once-in-a-lifetime chance" with its innovative mousetrap, and she sensed the group's impatience with the company's progress so far. She had budgeted approximately $250,000 in administrative and fixed costs for the first year (not including marketing costs). To keep the investors happy, the company needed to sell enough traps to cover those costs and make a reasonable profit.

BACK TO THE DRAWING BOARD

In these first few months, Martha had learned that marketing a new product was not an easy task. Some customers were very demanding. For example, one national retailer had placed a large order with instructions that Trap-Ease America was to deliver the order to the loading dock at one of the retailer's warehouses between 1:00 and 3:00 P.M. on a specified day. When the truck delivering the order arrived after 3:00 P.M., the retailer had refused to accept the shipment. The retailer had told Martha it would be a year before she got another chance.

As Martha sat down at her desk, she realized she needed to rethink her marketing strategy. Perhaps she had missed something or made some mistake that was causing sales to be so slow. Glancing at the quotation again, she thought that perhaps she should send the picky retailer and other customers a copy of Emerson's famous quote.

QUESTIONS FOR DISCUSSION

1. Martha and the Trap-Ease America investors feel they face a once-in-a-lifetime opportunity. What information do they need to evaluate this opportunity? How do you think the group would write its mission statement? How would *you* write it?
2. Has Martha identified the best target market for Trap-Ease? What other market segments might the firm target?
3. How had the company positioned the Trap-Ease relative to the chosen target market? Could it position the product in other ways?
4. Describe the current marketing mix for Trap-Ease. Do you see any problems with this mix?
5. Who is Trap-Ease America's competition?
6. How would you change Trap-Ease's marketing strategy? What kinds of control procedures would you establish for this strategy?

Today not a single one of our Investment Consultants was paid a commission.

There's never been a better time for Charles Schwab.™

At Charles Schwab, our Investment Consultants don't work on individual commissions. Which means the advice you get will be in line with your financial goals — not your broker's.

It's a simple principle that makes us different.

It's called objectivity. Which means we won't peddle hot stock tips. It means we'll help you focus on what is right for you based on your individual needs. Our Investment Consultants are working for you, not a commission. And, of course, their advice is based on the principles of Schwab.

THE PRINCIPLE OF THE INDIVIDUAL INVESTOR

From day one, the individual investor has been at the center of what we do. Every investor is important to us. We're not focused on investment

CHARLES SCHWAB

banking. We represent you, the individual investor.

THE PRINCIPLE OF ADVICE NOT DRIVEN BY COMMISSION

Individual broker commissions can undermine relationships. That may bias the advice you're getting. Our Investment Consultants' compensation is based on their service to you

and assets at Schwab, not commissions. It always has been. And always will be.

THE PRINCIPLE OF OBJECTIVITY

At Schwab, we're not focused on investment banking. For example, we make IPOs available but we don't receive any compensation for their distribution. To us, it's a potential conflict of interest. We always strive to avoid conflicts of interest in everything we do. This is at the heart of our values.

The Schwab Way

charlesSCHWAB

To find out more about Charles Schwab's full range of investment services, call 1-800-4-SCHWAB, and you can also receive our complimentary brochure.

*charles*SCHWAB

| Call | 1-800-4-SCHWAB | Click | schwab.com | Visit | 395 locations nationwide |

After studying this chapter you should be able to

1. identify the major forces shaping the new digital age
2. explain how companies have responded to the Internet and other powerful new technologies with e-business strategies, and how these strategies have resulted in benefits to both buyers and sellers
3. describe the four major e-commerce domains
4. discuss how companies go about conducting e-commerce to profitably deliver more value to customers
5. overview the promise and challenges that e-commerce presents for the future

Marketing in the Digital Age

MAKING NEW CUSTOMER CONNECTIONS

LOOKING AHEAD: PREVIEWING THE CONCEPTS

In the first two chapters, you learned about the basic concepts of marketing, marketing strategies, and the marketing process for building profitable relationships with targeted consumers. However, marketing strategy and practice have undergone dramatic change during the past decade. Major technological advances, including the explosion of the Internet, have had a major impact on buyers and the marketers who serve them. To thrive in this new digital age—even to survive—marketers must rethink their strategies and adapt them to today's new environment.

For starters, consider Charles Schwab Corporation. After at first resisting the Internet, Charles Schwab has transformed itself from a traditional "brick-and-mortar" marketer to a full-fledged "click-and-mortar" marketer. This transformation has propelled the company to leadership in the swiftly changing brokerage industry.

Charles Schwab Corporation began in 1976 as the nation's first discount brokerage. Over the next two decades, Schwab grew and prospered, showing an uncanny ability to adapt to the swiftly changing financial services market. However, when the Internet took off in 1995, several fledgling Web-based brokerages—some offering unlimited trades for a low monthly fee—threatened to beat Schwab at its own value-pricing game. The company faced a difficult decision: Should it stay with the traditional "brick-and-mortar" operations that had made it so successful, or should it embrace the new Internet technology?

Looking back, the decision seems like a no-brainer. Surging Internet usage marked the dawning of a new digital age, to which firms must quickly adapt or risk obsolescence. At the time, however, the idea of offering brokerage services online was downright revolutionary. Tradition dictated that investors needed lots of personal advice and hand-holding—things offered aplenty in Schwab's bustling branches and by its efficient phone reps, but things not readily delivered via the Web. Moreover, by going online, Schwab would cannibalize its existing business. It would be swapping higher commissions on branch and phone transactions for much lower online commissions. Further, going online would put Schwab in direct conflict with its large and profitable network of independent financial advisers and in-house investment specialists.

Staying offline, however, was even riskier than going online. Americans were rapidly discovering the wonders of the Web, and Internet trading offered real price and convenience advantages for customers. If Schwab didn't take advantage of these New Economy opportunities, some competitor would. The company decided that it was better to lead now than follow later. In late 1995, Schwab became the first major U.S. brokerage to go online. It set up a separate division called e.Schwab.

Under the new two-tiered system, Schwab customers had to choose to be either online or offline. E.Schwab offered online customers cheap transactions—$29.95 per trade—but few services. Regular customers continued to place orders over the phone or at a branch, receiving more services but paying about twice the commissions. E.Schwab was a smashing success. By mid-1997, it was claiming an almost 50 percent share of all U.S. online brokerage accounts.

But as e.Schwab sales grew, so did customers' frustrations. Offline customers resented the lower prices given to Web-only customers. At the same time, e.Schwab users wanted access to the same investment advice and other services offered to regular traders. Customers didn't want *either/or*—they wanted *both*. So, once again, Schwab faced a difficult decision: Should it keep e.Schwab separate or merge it back into the company's mainstream services? Integrating the Web services would mean offering everyone the low $29.95 trades, cutting

Schwab's average commission in half and costing the firm an estimate $125 million in lost revenues.

Schwab didn't hesitate. In early 1998, putting customers' interests ahead of its own short-run profit concerns, Schwab integrated e.Schwab, offering low online rates and full offline services to all customers. "There were huge risks," says Charles R. Schwab, the company's founder and co-CEO, "but we thought [it] was better for customers." David Pottruck, Schwab's president and co-CEO, adds, "We needed to focus on our clients and what we wanted to do for them: to make a difference in their lives."

At first, as predicted, sales and profits dropped, and so did Schwab's stock prices. Within a year, however, the gamble was paying off. The lower prices attracted hordes of new customers and ignited trading volume. At the same time, switching transactions to the Web created big productivity gains and reduced costs. For example, by the end of 1998, Schwab was handling five times as many trades on the Web as at its phone centers, producing some $100 million per year in savings. Schwab used the savings to expand investor services and draw even more clients. The results surprised even the most optimistic insiders. By early 1999, only three years after going to the Web, Schwab was capturing more than half of its trading volume online. Its 30 percent Web market share equaled that of its next three online competitors combined.

In melding the Net and non-Net worlds, Schwab created a powerful new "click-and-mortar" model of full-service brokerage—a robust one-stop shop for people's finances. The model recognizes that, most of the time, customers can handle their finances independently, and that they like the convenience and low prices afforded by the Web. Ultimately, however, many want some human contact. "For the vast majority of stock transactions that are fairly straightforward, the Net is a perfect medium," says Pottruck. "But what if you want advice on the right allocation for your portfolio? Then you're dealing with people's trust, and a mouse click isn't enough."

Schwab's click-and-mortar model lets customers design the specific blend of high-tech independence and high-touch service they need. They can log on to Schwab.com, do their own account analysis, conduct investment research, and make trades. At Schwab.com's free online Learning Center, they can hear live audio feeds of lectures or take interactive courses on everything from "Investing Fundamentals" and "How to Place a Stock Order" to "Demystifying the Stock Market" and "The Basics of Bond Investing." Schwab.com also offers more-

advanced features. A "Portfolio Checkup" helps customers do online asset-allocation planning based on their tolerance for risk. A "Sell Analyzer" lets customers evaluate which securities to sell for tax losses, and a "Portfolio Tracker" allows them assess their portfolios against standard indexes.

Customers who want more-personal service or advice can call one of Schwab's round-the-clock call centers or stop by one of Schwab's 365 brick-and-mortar branches, staffed by an army of 7,000 investment advisers. Schwab has installed Web kiosks at its branches so that customers can go online to check their accounts or make a trade while at the same time getting personal help from a service rep on the spot. Branches also provide "Portfolio Consultation" services—for $400 investors can get their existing portfolios analyzed by a broker who offers advice about which stocks or funds to buy and which to drop.

This powerful combination of clicks and bricks presents a menu of options that Schwab's click-only or brick-only competitors simply can't match. Schwab's success with the merged model has competitors on both sides scrambling to catch up. Traditional brick-and-mortar competitors, such as Fidelity and Merrill Lynch, are now clicking along with Web sites of their own. The once arrogant click-only brokerages, such as E*Trade, Datek, and WebStreet, are now building offline shops. Because of the tighter economy, brokerages these days must fight harder than ever to get every possible dollar from their customers. Thus, industry focus is shifting toward customer retention and cross-selling. Than means more services and hand-holding, which in turn mean a return to the good old bricks and mortar. An example of one Web-only firm trying to reinvent itself as a combination of clicks and mortar is E*Trade, which in 2000 began placing branded E*Trade Zone locations inside Target stores.

Just how successful has Schwab been with its click-and-mortar model? By any measure, the company's decision to put customers first has met with stunning success. Schwab now runs the world's largest e-commerce site. From nothing five years ago, Schwab now executes 85 percent of its trades online. It grabs a 21 percent share of all online trading volume, 50 percent more than its nearest competitor. Today, Schwab manages a staggering 37 percent of all online assets. Stockholders have shared richly in this success. Despite recent declines in stock market trading resulting from the nation's economic woes, Charles Schwab stock has yielded a 10-year average annual return of more than 32 percent. Founder Charles R. Schwab hasn't done badly either. His 20 percent stake in the company is now worth more than $6 billion.[1]

In Chapter 1, we discussed sweeping changes in the marketing landscape that are affecting marketing thinking and practice. Recent technological advances, including the widespread use of the Internet, have created what some call a New Economy. Although there has been widespread debate in recent years about the nature of—even the existence of—such a New Economy, few would disagree that the Internet and other powerful new connecting technologies are having a dramatic impact on marketers and buyers. Many standard marketing strategies and practices of the past—mass marketing, product standardization, media advertising, store retailing, and others—were well suited to the so-called Old Economy. These strategies and practices will continue to be important in the New Economy. However, marketers will also have to develop new strategies and practices better suited to today's new environment.

In this chapter, we first describe the key forces shaping the new digital age. Then we examine how marketing strategy and practice are changing to meet the requirements of this new age.

Major Forces Shaping the Internet Age

Many forces are playing a major role in reshaping the world economy, including technology, globalization, environmentalism, and others. Here we discuss four specific forces that underlie the new digital age (see Figure 3.1): digitalization and connectivity, the explosion of the Internet, new types of intermediaries, and customization and customerization.

Digitalization and Connectivity

Many appliances and systems in the past—ranging from telephone systems, wrist watches, and musical recordings to industrial gauges and controls—operated on analog information. Analog information is continuously variable in response to physical stimuli. Today a growing number of appliances and systems operate on *digital information,* which comes as streams of zeros and ones, or *bits.* Text, data, sound, and images can be converted into *bitstreams.* A laptop computer manipulates bits in its thousands of applications. Software consists of digital content for operating systems, games, information storage, and other applications.

For bits to flow from one appliance or location to another requires *connectivity,* a telecommunications network. Much of the world's business today is carried out over networks that connect people and companies. **Intranets** are networks that connect people within a company to each other and to the company network. **Extranets** connect a company with its suppliers, distributors, and other outside partners. And the **Internet,** a vast public web of computer networks, connects users of all types all around the world to each other and to an amazingly large "information repository." The Internet makes up one big "information highway" that can dispatch bits at incredible speeds from one location to another.

The Internet Explosion

With the creation of the World Wide Web and Web browsers in 1990s, the Internet was transformed from a mere communication tool into a certifiably revolutionary technology. During the final decade of the twentieth century, the number of Internet users worldwide grew to almost 400 million. By early 2002, Internet penetration in the United States had reached 66 percent. Although the dot-com crash in 2000 led to cutbacks in technology spending, research suggests that the growth of Internet access among the world's citizens will continue to explode. The number of Web surfers worldwide reached 533 million last year and is expected to approach 1.5 billion by 2007.[2]

Intranet

A network that connects people within a company to each other and to the company network.

Extranet

A network that connects a company with its suppliers and distributors.

Internet

A vast public web of computer networks, which connects users of all types all around the world to each other and to an amazingly large "information repository." The Internet makes up one big "information highway" that can dispatch bits at incredible speeds from one location to another.

FIGURE 3.1
Forces shaping the Internet age

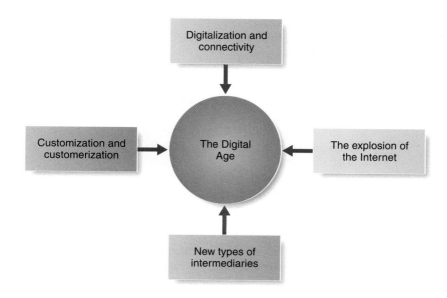

This explosive worldwide growth in Internet usage forms the heart of the so-called New Economy. The Internet has been *the* revolutionary technology of the new millennium, empowering consumers and businesses alike with blessings of connectivity. For nearly every New Economy innovation that has emerged during the past decade, the Internet has played a starring—or at the very least a "best supporting"— role. The Internet enables consumers and companies to access and share huge amounts of information with just a few mouse clicks. Recent studies have shown that consumers are accessing information on the Internet before making major life decisions. One in three consumers relies heavily on the Internet to gather information about choosing a school, buying a car, finding a job, dealing with a major illness, or making investment decisions. As a result, to be competitive in today's new marketplace, companies must adopt Internet technology or risk being left behind.[3]

New Types of Intermediaries

New technologies have led thousands of entrepreneurs to launch Internet companies—the so-called dot-coms—in hopes of striking gold. The amazing success of early Internet-only companies, such as AOL, Amazon.com, Yahoo, eBay, and E*Trade, and dozens of others, struck terror in the hearts of many established manufacturers and retailers. For example, Compaq Computer, which sold its computers only through retailers, worried when Dell Computer grew faster by selling online. Toys "R" Us worried when eToys lured toy buyers to the Web. Established store-based retailers of all kinds—from bookstores, music stores, and florists to travel agents, stockbrokers, and car dealers—began to doubt their futures as competitors sprung up selling their products and services via the Internet. They feared, and rightly so, being *disintermediated* by the new e-tailers—being cut out by this new type of intermediary.

The formation of new types of intermediaries and new forms of channel relationships caused existing firms to reexamine how they served their markets. At first, the established *brick-and-mortar* firms—such as Staples, Barnes & Noble, and Merrill Lynch—dragged their feet hoping that the assaulting *click-only* firms would falter or disappear. Then they wised up and started their own online sales channels, becoming *click-and-mortar* competitors. Ironically, many click-and-mortar competitors have become stronger than the click-only competitors that pushed them reluctantly onto the Internet. Charles Schwab is a good example. In fact, although some click-only competitors are surviving and even prospering in today's marketplace, many once-formidable dot-coms—such as eToys, Pets.com, Garden.com, and Mothernature.com—have failed in the face of poor profitability and plunging stock values.

Customization and Customerization

The Old Economy revolved around *manufacturing companies* that mainly focused on standardizing their production, products, and business processes. They invested large sums in brand building to tout the advantages of their standardized market offerings. Through standardization and branding, manufacturers hoped to grow demand and take advantage of economies of scale. As a key to managing their assets, they set up command-and-control systems that would run their businesses like machines.

In contrast, the New Economy revolves around *information businesses*. Information has the advantages of being easy to differentiate, customize, personalize, and send at incredible speeds over networks. With rapid advances in Internet and other connecting technologies, companies have grown skilled in gathering information about individual customers and business partners (suppliers, distributors, retailers). In turn, they have become more adept at individualizing their products and services, messages, and media.

Dell Computer, for example, lets customers specify exactly what they want in their computers and delivers customer-designed units in only a few days. On its reflect.com Web site, Procter & Gamble allows people to reflect their needs for, say, a shampoo by answering a set of questions. It then formulates a unique shampoo for each person. And cereal maker General Mills is even considering a Web site that lets you design your own cereal:

General Mills is expected to introduce www.mycereal.com, a Web site that allows users to mix and match more than 100 different ingredients to create and name their own breakfast cereals, delivered to their homes in single-serving portions. You want Cheerios to come with

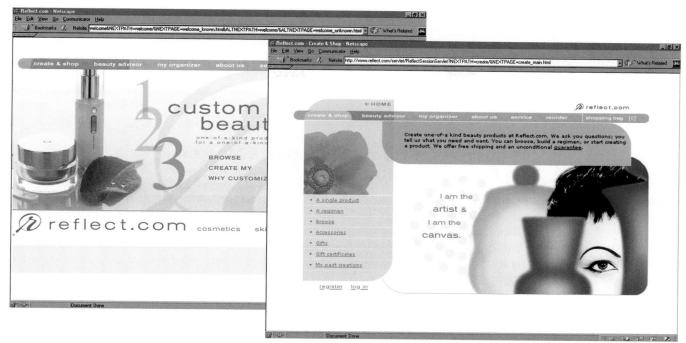

Customerization: At reflect.com, people formulate their own beauty products—it offers "one of a kind products for a one of a kind you." More than 650,000 people visit the site each month.

the marshmallows from Lucky Charms? Done. Mix Cinnamon Toast Crunch with French Toast Crunch? Sure. Wheaties with blueberries, almonds and grains? No problem. Add a tropical touch to your Cocoa Puffs? Have them throw in some coconut shreds and dried mango. Databases connected to the Web site are set up to provide suggestions based on health and nutritional criteria, including cholesterol, blood pressure, and sugar content. For a price of approximately $1 per serving, General Mills will deliver a one- or two-week supply of your personalized cereal mix to your home.[4]

Customerization

Leaving it to individual customers to design the marketing offering—allowing customers to be *prosumers* rather than only consumers.

Customization differs from *customerization*. Customization involves taking the initiative to customize the market offering. For example, a Levi's salesperson takes the person's measurements, and the company customizes the jeans at the factory. In **customerization,** the company leaves it to individual customers to design the offering. For example, jeans customers may take their own measurements and add specific features that they may want in their jeans, such as colorful patches. Such companies have become facilitators and their customers have moved from being consumers to being *prosumers*.[5]

Marketing Strategy in the New Digital Age

Conducting business in the new digital age will call for a new model for marketing strategy and practice. According to one strategist: "Sparked by new technologies, particularly the Internet, the corporation is undergoing a radical transformation that is nothing less than a new industrial revolution. . . . To survive and thrive in this century, managers will need to hard-wire a new set of rules into their brains. The 21st century corporation must adapt itself to management via the Web."[6] Suggests another, the Internet is "revolutionizing the way we think about . . . how to construct relationships with suppliers and customers, how to create value for them, and how to make money in the process; in other words, [it's] revolutionizing marketing."[7]

Some strategists envision a day when all buying and selling will involve direct electronic connections between companies and their customers. The new model will fundamentally change customers' notions of convenience, speed, price, product information, and service. This new consumer thinking will affect every business. Comparing the adoption of the Internet and other new marketing technologies to the early days of the airplane, Amazon.com CEO Jeff Bezos says, "It's the Kitty Hawk era of electronic commerce." Even those offering more cautious predictions agree that the Internet and e-business will have a tremendous impact on future business strategies.

The fact is that today's economy requires a mixture of Old Economy and New Economy thinking and action. Companies need to retain most of the skills and practices that have worked in the past. But they will also need to add major new competencies and practices if they hope to grow and prosper in the new environment. Marketing should play the *lead role* in shaping new company strategy.

E-Business, E-Commerce, and E-Marketing in the New Digital Age

E-business

The use of electronic platforms—intranets, extranets, and the Internet—to conduct a company's business.

E-business involves the use of electronic platforms—intranets, extranets, and the Internet—to conduct a company's business. The Internet and other technologies now help companies carry on their business faster, more accurately, and over a wider range of time and space. Countless companies have set up Web sites to inform about and promote their products and services. They have created intranets to help employees communicate with each other and access information found in the company's computers. They have set up extranets with their major suppliers and distributors to assist information exchange, orders, transactions, and payments. Companies such as Cisco, Microsoft, and Oracle run almost entirely as e-businesses, in which memos, invoices, engineering drawings, sales and marketing information—virtually everything—happens over the Internet instead of on paper.[8]

E-commerce

Buying and selling processes supported by electronic means, primarily the Internet.

E-commerce is more specific than e-business. E-business includes all electronics-based information exchanges within or between companies and customers. In contrast, e commerce involves buying and selling processes supported by electronic means, primarily the Internet. *E-markets* are "market*spaces*," rather than physical market*places*. Sellers use e-markets to offer their products and services online. Buyers use them to search for information, identify what they want, and place orders using credit or other means of electronic payment.

E-marketing

The marketing side of e-commerce—company efforts to communicate about, promote, and sell products and services over the Internet.

E-commerce includes *e-marketing* and *e-purchasing (e-procurement)*. **E-marketing** is the marketing side of e-commerce. It consists of company efforts to communicate about, promote, and sell products and services over the Internet. Thus, Amazon.com, Schwab.com, and Dell.com conduct e-marketing at their Web sites. The flip side of e-marketing is e-purchasing, the buying side of e-commerce. It consists of companies purchasing goods, services, and information from online suppliers.

In business-to-business buying, e marketers and e-purchasers come together in huge e-commerce networks. For example, GE Global eXchange Services (GXS) operates one of the world's largest business-to-business e-commerce networks (www.gegxs.com). More than 100,000 trading partners in 58 countries—including giants such as 3M, DaimlerChrysler, Target, J.C. Penney, Sara Lee, and Kodak—use the GXS network to complete some 1 billion transactions each year, accounting for $1 trillion worth of goods and services.[9]

E-commerce and the Internet bring many benefits to both buyers and sellers. Let's review some of these major benefits.

Benefits to Buyers

Internet buying benefits both final buyers and business buyers in many ways. It can be *convenient*: Customers don't have to battle traffic, find parking spaces, and trek through stores and aisles to find and examine products. They can do comparative shopping by browsing through mail catalogs or surfing Web sites. Direct marketers never close their doors. Buying is *easy* and *private*: Customers encounter fewer buying hassles and don't have to face salespeople or open themselves up to persuasion and emotional pitches. Business buyers can learn about and buy products and services without waiting for and tying up time with salespeople.

In addition, the Internet often provides buyers with greater *product access and selection*. For example, the world's the limit for the Web. Unrestrained by physical boundaries, cybersellers can offer an almost unlimited selection. Compare the incredible selections offered by Web merchants such as Amazon.com or eVineyard to the more meager assortments of their counterparts in the brick-and-mortar world.

Internet buying is easy and private: Final consumers can shop the world from home with few hassles; business buyers can learn about and obtain products and information without tying up time with salespeople.

Beyond a broader selection of sellers and products, e-commerce channels also give buyers access to a wealth of comparative *information,* information about companies, products, and competitors. Good sites often provide more information in more useful forms than even the most solicitous salesperson can. For example, Amazon.com offers top-10 product lists, extensive product descriptions, expert and user product reviews, and recommendations based on customers' previous purchases.

Finally, online buying is *interactive* and *immediate.* Buyers often can interact with the seller's site to create exactly the configuration of information, products, or services they desire, then order or download them on the spot. Moreover, the Internet gives consumers a greater measure of control. Like nothing else before it, the Internet has empowered consumers. For example, 27 percent of car buyers go online before showing up at a dealership, arming themselves with car and cost information. This is the new reality of consumer control.[10]

Benefits to Sellers

E-commerce also yields many benefits to sellers. First, the Internet is a powerful tool for *customer relationship building.* Because of its one-to-one, interactive nature, the Internet is an especially potent marketing tool. Companies can interact online with customers to learn more about specific needs and wants. In turn, online customers can ask questions and volunteer feedback. Based on this ongoing interaction, companies can increase customer value and satisfaction through product and service refinements. One expert concludes: "Contrary to the common view that Web customers are fickle by nature and will flock to the next new idea, the Web is actually a very sticky space in both business-to-consumer and business-to-business spheres. Most of today's online customers exhibit a clear [tendency] toward loyalty."[11]

The Internet and other electronic channels yield additional advantages, such as *reducing costs* and *increasing speed and efficiency.* E-marketers avoid the expense of maintaining a store and the related costs of rent, insurance, and utilities. E-tailers such as Amazon.com reap the advantage of a negative operating cycle: Amazon.com receives cash from credit card companies just one day after customers place an order. Then it can hold on to the money for 46 days until it pays suppliers, book distributors, and publishers.

By using the Internet to link directly to suppliers, factories, distributors, and customers, businesses such as Dell Computer and General Electric are cutting costs and passing savings on to customers. Because customers deal directly with sellers, e-marketing often results in lower costs and improved efficiencies for channel and logistics functions such as order processing, inventory handling, delivery, and trade promotion. Finally, communicating electronically often costs less than communicating on paper through the mail. For instance, a company can produce digital catalogs for much less than the cost of printing and mailing paper ones.

E-marketing also offers greater *flexibility,* allowing the marketer to make ongoing adjustments to its offers and programs. For example, once a paper catalog is mailed to final consumer or business customers, the products, prices, and other catalog features are fixed until the next catalog is sent. However, an online catalog can be adjusted daily or even hourly, adapting product assortments, prices, and promotions to match changing market conditions.

Finally, the Internet is a truly *global* medium that allows buyers and sellers to click from one country to another in seconds. GE's GXS network provides business buyers with immediate access to suppliers in 58 countries, ranging from the United States and the United Kingdom to Hong Kong and the Philippines. A Web surfer from Paris or Istanbul can access an online L.L. Bean catalog as easily as someone living in Freeport, Maine, the direct retailer's hometown. Thus, even small e-marketers find that they have ready access to global markets.

E-Commerce Domains

The four major Internet domains are shown in Figure 3.2 and discussed below. They include B2C (business to consumer), B2B (business to business), C2C (consumer to consumer), and C2B (consumer to business).

B2C (Business to Consumer)

B2C (business-to-consumer) e-commerce
The online selling of goods and services to final consumers.

The popular press has paid the most attention to **B2C (business-to-consumer) e-commerce**—the online selling of goods and services to final consumers. Despite some gloomy predictions, online consumer buying continues to grow at a healthy rate. Last year, consumers spent more than $112 billion online, up 56 percent from the previous year. The largest categories of consumer online spending include travel services; clothing; computer hardware and software; consumer electronics; books; music and video; health and beauty; home and garden; flowers and gifts; sports and fitness equipment; and toys.[12]

Online Consumers

When people envision the typical Internet user, some still mistakenly envision a pasty-faced computer nerd or "cyberhead." Others envision a young, techy, upscale male professional. Such stereotypes are sadly outdated. As more and more people find their way onto the Internet, the cyberspace population is becoming more mainstream and diverse. "The Internet was, at first, an elitist country club reserved only for individuals with select financial abilities and technical skills," says an e-commerce analyst. "Now, nearly every socioeconomic group is aggressively adopting the Web."[13] (See Real Marketing 3.1.)

Thus, increasingly, the Internet provides e-marketers with access to a broad range of demographic segments. For example, home Internet access for blue-collar workers is growing faster than for any other occupational group, surging 52 percent in just the past year. One study of Internet "newbies"— those who started using the Internet in the past year—found that 71 percent had no college degree, 65 percent earn less than $50,000 a year, and only 25 percent were younger than 30.

These days, everybody's logging on. . . . Doral Main, a 51-year-old mother of two and office manager of a low-income property company in Oakland, CA, saves precious time by shopping the Internet for greeting cards and getaways. Her Net-newbie father, Charles, 73, goes online to buy supplies for his wood-carving hobby. Even niece Katrina, 11, finds excitement on the Web, picking gifts she wants from the Disney.com site. "It's addictive," Main says of the Internet. [Indeed,] the Web isn't mostly a hangout for techno-nerds anymore.[14]

FIGURE 3.2
E-marketing domains

	Targeted to consumers	Targeted to businesses
Initiated by business	B2C (business to consumer)	B2B (business to business)
Initiated by consumer	C2C (consumer to consumer)	C2B (consumer to business)

real marketing 3.1

Online America: A Movable Feast for E-marketers

Just a few years ago, when Forrester Research first began classifying North Americans into "technographic" types according to their affinity for technology, the vast majority of Internet users fell predictably into the same group. They were overwhelmingly male, overwhelmingly young, overwhelmingly college educated, and overwhelmingly high-techy. How times have changed. Today, Internet users are found in all of Forrester's segments, even those with downscale, late-adopting, technology-challenged families.

For marketers, the Internet now presents a movable feast of different kinds of people seeking different types of online experiences. Now, in any given month, almost 66 percent of the U.S. population is accessing the Internet, a 30 percent increase over a year earlier. Their average age is 39 years and rising. Their average education—38 percent hold a college degree—is falling. Likewise, their socioeconomic status is sinking, thanks to the fastest-growing segment of Web newbies: Americans over 55 years old with working-class incomes and middlebrow tastes. In a

final blow to the old stereotypes, the number of women online surpassed that of men for the first time in mid-2001.

This mixed portrait is a far cry from the old image of Net users as geeky white guys (GWGs), technophiles who enjoyed hacking their way through chat rooms and bulletin boards. Since those early days, the Web community has exploded. A detailed analysis of wired America reveals an audience of Netizens nearly as diverse—and quirky—as consumers offline. Men and women, rich and poor, old and young—all go their separate ways on the Web.

For example, people from different socioeconomic levels use the Web differently. One study that classified Web users into PRIZM types (a geodemographic segmentation system that segments consumers into lifestyle niches) came up with some surprising results. True, the clusters with the greatest access to the Internet are still those containing early-adopting, upscale Americans. But the clusters whose surfers spend the most time online at home left some analysts agog: Mid-City Mix,

Norma Raeville, and Back Country Folks, characterized by people with lower incomes, modest educations, and blue-collar jobs who like to chat, exchange e-mail, and hang out at entertainment and sweepstakes sites.

Of course, spending more time on the Web doesn't necessarily equate with spending more money there. A kind of e-havioral divide is emerging in how different kinds of Americans use the Internet. The time-pressed consumers, from upscale PRIZM clusters such as Money & Brains (sophisticated urban-fringe couples) and Country Squires (elite exurban families), tend to view the Web as a transactional arena—a place to gather information or buy big-ticket items. They visit news, travel, and financial sites, such as Schwab.com, smartmoney.com, and americanexpress.com. To them, the Internet is just one more tool to help them get information or buy things.

By contrast, Americans at the lower end of the socioeconomic ladder are more likely to view the Internet as a kind of home entertainment center for fun and games. In clusters such as Red, White & Blues (small-town, middle-class families) and Blue Highways (working-class farm families), residents are more likely to surf a variety of entertainment and sweepstakes sites, including icq.com, youwinit.com, and gamesville.com. "Lower-income Americans look to the Internet as a replacement for television," says one analyst.

Along with the socioeconomic differences, many researchers report a growing gender gap on the Internet. Although men and women engage in many activities at roughly equal rates—such as banking and downloading music—the sexes then part company. Men are more likely to go online to buy stocks, get news, compare and buy products, bid at auctions, and visit government Web sites. Women are more likely to send e-mail, play games, score coupons, and get information on health, jobs, and religion. This online gender

For marketers, the Internet now presents a moveable feast of different kinds of people seeking different kinds of online experiences.

(continued)

gap forms early. A study of teenagers by Jupiter Media Metrix found that boys are much more likely to download software and play games online. Girls, by contrast, are more interested in reading online magazines, doing homework, and staying in touch with their e-buddies. Their parents would probably be shocked to find that American teenagers actually spend about 30 percent less time on the Web than adults.

For both sexes, Web behavior shifts with age. For example, women in their twenties and thirties patronize sites offering relationship and parenting information relevant to that life stage. In their forties, they shift to hobby and leisure sites featuring gardening and cooking content. Women in their fifties, meanwhile, turn to Web sites offering advice on financial investments and health care. "It's like holding a mirror to a woman's life," says a measurement analys. "At every stage, her online preferences provide a readable map of her offline interests."

Despite studies showing the Internet gap shrinking between ethnic groups and the general population, differences remain. Asian Americans have been more prevalent online for years and are more likely to invest their money, make purchases, and research products over the Internet than is the general population. Although Hispanics and African Americans have yet to reach the usage levels of other groups online, blacks already top whites in conducting school research, getting sports news, and looking for a job. "African Americans tend to do serious things on the Internet," says one analyst. "Adults see it as an investment for themselves and their children."

In many ways, people behave online much like they do in real life—a pattern that's contrary to early predictions that Web use would be categorically different from day-to-day life. Futurists once maintained that Internet users would form virtual communities to the exclusion of real-world relationships. Well, it hasn't quite turned out that way. Although early research claimed that the Internet contributed to the social isolation of enthusiasts, more recent studies suggest that the opposite might be true. One recent survey found that social relationships are actually strengthened by online use. In another survey, 48 percent of people said that they communicate with their friends and family more often because of the Internet, compared with only 3 percent who said that their contact decreased.

Analysts estimate that the Internet population will reach between 75 percent and 85 percent of all Americans during the next decade. Internet researchers differ in their predictions on how long it will take for the Internet audience to reach its saturation point in the United States. However, they're in remarkable agreement on one point: Say farewell to the geeky white guys. The latest generation of connected Americans looks a lot more like the folks who cruise your local Wal Mart.

Source: Adapted from Michael J. Weiss, "Online America," *American Demographics,* March 2001, pp. 53–60. Also see "A Nation Online: How Americans Are Expanding Their Use of the Internet," Department of Commerce, February 2002; and Robyn Greenspan, "The Web as a Way of Life," May 21, 2002, accessed online at cyberatlas.internet.com.

Growing Internet diversity continues to open new e-commerce targeting opportunities for marketers. For example, the Web now reaches consumers in all age groups. Children and teens are going online more than any other age group. Sixty-five percent of 10- to 13-year-olds and 75 percent of 14- to 17-year-olds now use the Internet.[15] Thus, these "net kids" and teen segments have attracted a host of e-marketers. America Online offers a Kids Only area featuring homework help and online magazines along with the usual games, software, and chat rooms. The Microsoft Network site carries Disney's Daily Blast, which offers kids games, stories, comic strips with old and new Disney characters, and current events tailored to preteens. Nickelodeon (www.nick.com) offers a full slate of games based on favorite Nickelodeon characters.

Although Internet users are still younger on average than the population as a whole, consumers aged 50 and older make up almost 20 percent of the online population. Whereas younger groups are more likely to use the Internet for entertainment and socializing, older Internet surfers go online for more serious matters. For example, 24 percent of people in this age group use the Internet for investment purposes, compared with only 3 percent of those 25 to 29. Thus, older Netizens make an attractive market for Web businesses, ranging from florists and automotive retailers to financial services providers.[16]

To help online marketers to better target their customers, Internet research companies now segment the increasingly diverse Web population by needs and interests. For example, Harris Interactive has tabbed a segment it calls Cyberchondriacs, the roughly 110 million Americans who go online for health care information. Slightly younger, better educated, and more affluent than the general population, typically they or someone else in their family has a medical condition. They view the Internet as a kind of mobile medical library and log on to dig out the latest research and treatments for a specific malady. Pharmaceutical firms such as Pfizer and Johnson & Johnson have launched Web sites to market their prescription drugs directly to these Cyberchondriacs, hoping to spur them to ask their doctors for the medication by brand name. "The Internet is the mother of all customizers," observes a Harris executive. "You can customize a product to a 36-year-old . . . diabetic with red hair. And you can do it in a way that you could never do with traditional media."[17]

Internet consumers differ from traditional offline consumers in their approaches to buying and in their responses to marketing. The exchange process via the Internet has become more customer initiated and customer controlled. People who use the Internet place greater value on information and tend to respond negatively to messages aimed only at selling. Traditional marketing targets a somewhat passive audience. In contrast, e-marketing targets people who actively select which Web sites they will visit and what marketing information they will receive about which products and under what conditions. Thus, the new world of e-commerce requires new marketing approaches.

B2C Web Sites

Consumers can find a Web site for buying almost anything. The Internet is most useful for products and services when the shopper seeks greater ordering convenience or lower costs. The Internet also provides great value to buyers looking for information about differences in product features and value. However, consumers find the Internet less useful when buying products that must be touched or examined in advance. Still, even here there are exceptions. For example, who would have thought that people would order expensive computers from Dell or Gateway without seeing and trying them first?

People now go online to order a wide range of goods—clothing from Gap or L.L. Bean, books or electronics from Amazon.com, furniture from Ethan Allen, major appliances from Sears, flowers from Calyx & Corolla, or even home mortgages from Quicken Loans.

Calyx & Corolla, "The Flower Lover's Flower Company," sells fresh flowers directly to consumers. Customers can order bouquets or plants from a color catalog by phoning 1-800-877-0998 or place orders at the C&C Web site at www.calyxandcorolla.com. Orders go immediately to one of 25 growers in the C&C network, who pick and package the flowers and ship orders via FedEx. When the flowers arrive, they are fresher and last about 10 days longer than flowers ordered from store-based retailers. Calyx and Corolla credits its success to a sophisticated information system and strong alliances with FedEx and the growers.

At Quicken Loans (www.quickenloans.quicken.com), prospective borrowers receive a high-tech, high-touch, one-stop mortgage shopping experience. At the site, customers can research a wide variety of home-financing and refinancing options, apply for a mortgage, and receive quick loan approval—all without leaving the comfort and security of their homes. The site provides useful interactive tools that help borrowers decide how much house they can afford, whether to rent or buy, whether to refinance a current mortgage, the economics of fixing up their current homes rather than moving, and much more. Customers can receive advice by phone or by chatting online with one of 400 loan consultants and sign up for later e-mail rate updates. Quicken Loans originated nearly $3.5 billion in mortgage loans last year.[18]

B2B (Business to Business)

Although the popular press has given the most attention to business-to-consumer (B2C) Web sites, consumer goods sales via the Web are dwarfed by **B2B (business-to-business) e-commerce.** One study estimates that B2B e-commerce will reach $4.3 trillion in 2005, compared with just $282 billion in 2000. Another estimates that by 2005, more than 500,000 enterprises will use e-commerce as buyers, sellers, or both.[19] These firms are using B2B trading networks, auction sites, spot exchanges, online product catalogs, barter sites, and other online resources to reach new customers, serve current customers more effectively, and obtain buying efficiencies and better prices.

Most major business-to-business marketers now offer product information, customer purchasing, and customer support services online. For example, corporate buyers can visit Sun Microsystems' Web site (www.sun.com), select detailed descriptions of Sun's products and solutions, request sales and service information, and interact with staff members. Some major companies conduct almost all of their business on the Web. For example, networking equipment and software maker Cisco Systems takes more than 80 percent of its orders over the Internet.

Much B2B e-commerce takes place in **open trading networks**—huge e-marketspaces in which buyers and sellers find each other online, share information, and complete transactions efficiently. Here are examples of B2B trading network sites:

PlasticsNet.com is an Internet marketplace for the plastic products industry, connecting more than 90,000 monthly visitors with more than 200 suppliers. In addition to facilitating online

---

B2B (business-to-business) e-commerce
Using B2B trading networks, auction sites, spot exchanges, online product catalogs, barter sites, and other online resources to reach new customers, serve current customers more effectively, and obtain buying efficiencies and better prices.

Open trading networks
Huge e-marketspaces in which B2B buyers and sellers find each other online, share information, and complete transactions efficiently.

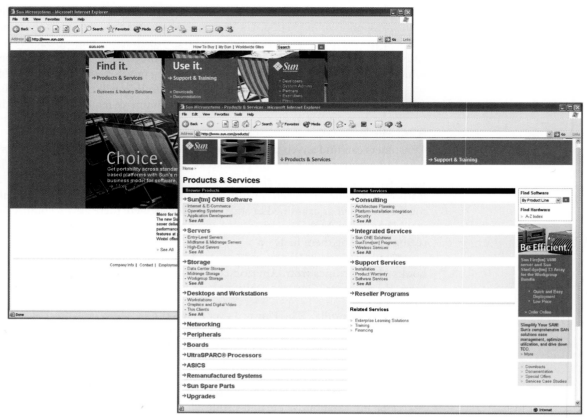

B2B e-commerce: Corporate buyers can visit Sun Microsystems' Web site, learn in detail about Sun's products, request sales and service information, and interact with staff members.

transactions, the site provides a supplier directory, material data sheets, an industry publication, a list of educational programs, and books and seminars relevant to the plastics industry.

The Medical EquipNet serves as a medical equipment e-marketplace. At the site, companies, doctors' offices, and hospitals can buy, sell, or auction off new, used, refurbished, or surplus medical equipment. Members can place classifieds or want ads, place or receive auction bids, or access medical equipment financing, shipping, repair, or installation services. To date, the site has attracted more than 10 million visits.

Covisint is the auto industry's public exchange. Created jointly by the Big Three auto makers—DaimlerChrysler, Ford, and General Motors—the site now connects a total of 11 auto makers with some 5,000 suppliers worldwide. Covisint handled more than $50 billion in auto-parts orders last year. Auto maker purchasing managers submit parts orders to Covisint's auction engineers, who in turn set up special auctions. "These auctions are for millions," says one auction engineer. "We're not messing around here with $10 at a time." In its biggest single auction ever, Covisint conducted a four-day auction in which DaimlerChrysler purchased about $2.6 billion in auto parts. Compare that with eBay, the top consumer auction Web site, which recently reported gross merchandise sales of some $2.4 billion for the entire fourth quarter.[20]

Despite the increasing popularity of such e-marketspaces, one Internet research firm estimates that 93 percent of all B2B e-commerce is conducted through private sites. Increasingly, online sellers are setting up their own **private trading networks (PTNs).** Open trading networks such as PlasticsNet facilitate transactions between a wide range of online buyers and sellers. In contrast, private trading networks link a particular seller with its own trading partners.

Rather than simply completing transactions, PTNs give sellers greater control over product presentation and allow them to build deeper relationships with buyers and sellers by providing value-added services. As an example, take Trane Company, a maker of air-conditioning and heating systems:

Private trading networks (PTNs)

B2B trading networks that link a particular seller with its own trading partners.

Since last autumn, Trane . . . has been red-hot with the business-to-business Internet crowd. Each of the horde of B2B [open trading] exchanges targeting the construction industry wants Trane to join. "Construction.com, MyPlant.com, MyFacility.com—we get up to five calls a week," says James A. Bierkamp, head of Trane's e-business unit. But after some consideration, Bierkamp did not see what any of those [third-party] e-marketplaces could offer that his company couldn't do itself. So in May, Trane rolled out its own private exchange, which allows its 5,000 dealers to browse, buy equipment, schedule deliveries, and process warranties. The site lets Trane operate with greater efficiency and trim processing costs—without losing control of the presentation of its brand name or running the risks of rubbing elbows with competitors in an open exchange. "Why let another party get between us and our customers?'" asks Bierkamp.[21]

C2C (Consumer to Consumer)

C2C (consumer-to-consumer) e-commerce
Online exchanges of goods and information between final consumers.

Much **C2C (consumer-to-consumer) e-commerce** and communication occurs on the Web between interested parties over a wide range of products and subjects. In some cases, the Internet provides an excellent means by which consumers can buy or exchange goods or information directly with one another. For example, eBay, Amazon.com Auctions, and other auction sites offer popular marketspaces for displaying and selling almost anything, from art and antiques, coins and stamps, and jewelry to computers and consumer electronics. EBay's C2C online trading community of more than 42 million registered users worldwide transacted more than $9 billion in trades last year. The company's Web site hosts more than 2 million auctions each month for items in more than 18,000 categories. EBay also maintains auction sites in several foreign countries, including Japan, the United Kingdom, and Germany.[22]

Such C2C sites give people access to much larger audiences than the local flea market or newspaper classifieds (which, by the way, are now also going online). Ask Barbara Dreschsler, a systems engineer in Roanoke, Texas, who began buying and selling Beanie Babies via Internet auction sites such as eBay.com and Amazon.com. What started out as a family hobby rapidly morphed into a part-time business. In the first two months of last year, Dreschsler received 102 orders for Beanie Babies and other toys priced at $10 to $200. "We still call it a hobby, but we would love to do it full time," she says.[23]

C2C e-commerce: Last year, eBay's 42 million members transacted more than $9 billion in trades.

In other cases, C2C involves interchanges of information through forums and Internet newsgroups that appeal to specific special-interest groups. Such activities may be organized for commercial or noncommercial purposes. *Forums* are discussion groups located on commercial online services such as AOL and CompuServe. A forum may take the form of a library, a "chat room" for real-time message exchanges, or even a classified ad directory. For example, AOL boasts some 14,000 chat rooms, which account for a third of its members' online time. It also provides "buddy lists," which alert members when friends are online, allowing them to exchange instant messages.

Newsgroups are the Internet version of forums. However, such groups are limited to people posting and reading messages on a specified topic, rather than managing libraries or conferencing. Internet users can participate in newsgroups without subscribing. There are tens of thousands of newsgroups dealing with every imaginable topic, from healthful eating and caring for your bonsai tree to collecting antique cars or exchanging views on the latest soap opera happenings.

C2C means that online visitors don't just consume product information—increasingly, they create it. They join Internet interest groups to share information, with the result that "word of Web" is joining "word of mouth" as an important buying influence. Word about good companies and products travels fast. Word about bad companies and products travels even faster.

C2B (Consumer to Business)

C2B (consumer-to-business) e-commerce
Online exchanges in which consumers search out sellers, learn about their offers, and initiate purchases, sometimes even driving transaction terms.

The final e-commerce domain is **C2B (consumer-to-business) e-commerce.** Thanks to the Internet, today's consumers are finding it easier to communicate with companies. Most companies now invite prospects and customers to send in suggestions and questions via company Web sites. Beyond this, rather than waiting for an invitation, consumers can search out sellers on the Web, learn about their offers, initiate purchases, and give feedback. Using the Web, consumers can even drive transactions with businesses, rather than the other way around. For example, using Priceline.com, would-be buyers bid for airline tickets, hotel rooms, rental cars, and even home mortgages, leaving the sellers to decide whether to accept their offers.

Consumers can also use Web sites such as PlanetFeedback.com to ask questions, offer suggestions, lodge complaints, or deliver compliments to companies. The site provides letter templates for consumers to use based on their moods and reasons for contacting the company. The site then forwards the letters to the customer service manager at each company and helps to obtain a response. Last year, PlanetFeedback.com forwarded more than 330,000 consumer letters composed on their site. Not all of the letters were complaints. One-quarter of them offered compliments, while another one-fifth made suggestions for product or service improvements.[24]

Conducting E-Commerce

Companies of all types are now engaged in e-commerce. In this section, we first discuss different types of e-marketers shown in Figure 3.3. Then, we examine how companies go about conducting marketing online.

Click-Only Versus Click-and-Mortar E-Marketers

The Internet gave birth to a new species of e-marketers—the *click-only* dot-coms—which operate only online without any brick-and-mortar market presence. In addition, most traditional *brick-and-mortar* companies have now added e-marketing operations, transforming themselves into *click-and-mortar* competitors.

Click-Only Companies

Click-only companies
The so-called dot-coms, which operate only online without any brick-and-mortar market presence.

Click-only companies come in many shapes and sizes. They include *e-tailers,* dot-coms that sell products and services directly to final buyers via the Internet. Familiar e-tailers include Amazon.com, Expedia, and eVineyards. The click-only group also includes *search engines and portals* such as Yahoo, Google, and Excite, which began as search engines and later added services such as news, weather, stock reports, entertainment, and storefronts hoping to become the first port of entry to the Internet.

Internets service providers (ISPs) such as AOL, CompuServe, and Earthlink are click-only companies that provide Internet and Email connections for a fee. *Transaction sites,* such as auc-

FIGURE 3.3
Types of e-marketers

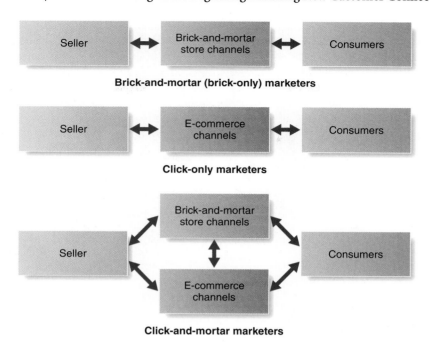

Brick-and-mortar (brick-only) marketers

Click-only marketers

Click-and-mortar marketers

tion site eBay, take commissions for transactions conducted on their sites. Various *content sites,* such as New York Times on the Web (www.nytimes.com), ESPN.com, and Encyclopedia Britannica Online, provide financial, research, and other information. Finally, *enabler sites* provide the hardware and software that enable Internet communication and commerce.

The hype surrounding such click-only Web businesses reached astronomical levels during the "dot-com gold rush" of the late 1990s, when avid investors drove dot-com stock prices to dizzying heights. However, the investing frenzy collapsed in the year 2000, and many high-flying, overvalued dot-coms came crashing back to Earth. Even some of the strongest and most attractive e-tailers—eToys.com, Pets.com, Furniture.com, Mothernature.com, Garden.com, Living.com, ValueAmerica.com—filed for bankruptcy. Survivors such as Amazon.com and Priceline.com saw their stock values plunge. Notes one analyst, "Once teeming with thousands of vibrant new ideas, the consumer Net [began] to look like the mall at midnight."[25]

Dot-coms failed for many reasons. Some rushed into the market without proper research or planning. Often, their primary goal was simply to launch an initial public offering (IPO) while the market was hot. Many relied too heavily on spin and hype instead of developing sound marketing strategies. Flush with investors' cash, the dot-coms spent lavishly offline on mass marketing in an effort to establish brand identities and attract customers to their sites. For example, during the fourth quarter of 1999, the average e-tailer spent an astounding 109 percent of sales on marketing and advertising.[26] As one industry watcher concluded, many dot-coms failed because they "had dumb-as-dirt business models, not because the Internet lacks the power to enchant and delight customers in ways hitherto unimaginable."[27]

The dot-coms tended to devote too much effort to acquiring new customers instead of building loyalty and purchase frequency among current customers. In their rush to cash in, many dot-coms went to market with poorly designed Web sites that were complex, hard to navigate, and unreliable. When orders did arrive, some dot-coms found that they lacked the well-designed distribution systems needed to ship products on time and handle customer inquiries and problems. Finally, the ease with which competitors could enter the Web, and the ease with which customers could switch to Web sites offering better prices, forced many dot-coms to sell at margin-killing low prices.

Pets.com, the now defunct online pet store, provides a good example of how many dot-coms failed to understand their marketplaces.

From the start, Pets.com tried to force its way to online success with unbeatable low prices and heavy marketing hype. In the end, however, neither worked. During its first year of operation, Pets.com lost $61.8 million on a meager $5.8 million in sales. During that time, it paid $13.4 million for the goods it sold for just $5.8 million. Thus, for every dollar that Pets.com paid

Like many other dot-cons, Pets.com never did figure out how to make money on the Web. Following the "dot-com meltdown," the once-bold e-tailer retired its popular Sock Puppet spokesdog and quietly closed its cyberdoors.

suppliers such as Ralston Purina for dog food and United Parcel Service for shipping, it collected only 43 cents from its customers. Moreover, by early spring of 1999, Pets.com had burned more than $21 million on marketing and advertising to create an identity and entice pet owners to its site. Its branding campaign centered on the wildly popular Sock Puppet character, a white dog with black patches. Sock Puppet even made an appearance in Macy's Thanksgiving Day Parade in New York as a 36-foot-high balloon. The singing mascot was also featured in Super Bowl ads that cost Pets.com more than $2 million. At first, investors bought into Pet.com's "landgrab" strategy—investing heavily to stake out an early share, then finding ways later to make a profit. However, even though it attracted 570,000 customers, Pets.com never did figure out how to make money in a low-margin business with high shipping costs. Its stock price slid from a February 1999 high of $14 to a dismal 22 cents by the end of 2000. In early 2001, the once-bold e-tailer retired Sock Puppet and quietly closed its cyberdoors.[28]

At the same time, many click-only dot-coms are surviving and even prospering in today's marketspace. Others are showing losses today but promising profits tomorrow. Consider Earthlink.com:

Earthlink.com is an Internet service provider (ISP) that sells Internet and e-mail connection time for a $20 monthly fee. Customer maintenance expenses amount to only $9 a month, leaving an $11 contribution margin. On average, it costs Earthlink $100 to acquire a new customer. Therefore, it takes 11 months before the company breaks even on a new customer. Fortunately, Earthlink keeps its customers for an average of 31 months. This leaves Earthlink with 20 months of net income from the average customer. At a $9 monthly contribution margin, Earthlink makes $180 (20 months × $9) on the average customer. When Sky Dayton, Earthlink's founder, was asked why Earthlink is still losing money, he answered that Earthlink is acquiring so many new customers that it will take a while for the inflow of contribution margin to cover the $100 customer acquisition.

Thus, for many dot-coms, including Internet giants such as Amazon.com, the Web is still not a moneymaking proposition. Companies engaging in e-commerce need to describe to their investors how they will eventually make profits. They need to define a *revenue and profit model.* Table 3.1 shows that a dot-com's revenues may come from any of several sources.

Click-and-Mortar Companies

Many established companies moved quickly to open Web sites providing information about their companies and products. However, most resisted adding e-commerce to their sites. They felt that

TABLE 3.1   SOURCES OF E-COMMERCE REVENUE

Product and service sales income	Many e-commerce companies draw a good portion of their revenues from markups on goods and services they sell online.
Advertising income	Sales of online ad space can provide a major source of revenue. At one point, Buy.com received so much advertising revenue that it was able to sell products at cost.
Sponsorship income	A dot-com can solicit sponsors for some of its content and collect sponsorship fees to help cover its costs.
Alliance income	Online companies can invite business partners to share costs in setting up a Web site and offer them free advertising on the site.
Membership and subscription income	Web marketers can charge subscription fees for use of their site. Many online newspapers (*Wall Street Journal* and *Financial Times*) require subscription fees for their online services. Auto-By-Tel receives income from selling subscriptions to auto dealers who want to receive hot car buyer leads.
Profile income	Web sites that have built databases containing the profiles of particular target groups may be able to sell these profiles if they get permission first. However, ethical and legal codes govern the use and sale of such customer information.
Transaction commissions and fees	Some dot-coms charge commission fees on transactions between other parties who exchanges goods on their Web sites. For example, eBay puts buyers in touch with sellers and takes from a 1.25 percent to a 5 percent commission on each transaction.
Market research and information fees	Companies can charge for special market information or intelligence. For example, NewsLibrary charges a dollar or two to download copies of archived news stories. LifeQuote provides insurance buyers with price comparisons from approximately 50 different life insurance companies, then collects a commission of 50 percent of the first year's premium from the company chosen by the consumer.
Referral income	Companies can collect revenue by referring customers to others. Edmunds receives a "finder's fee" every time a customer fills out an Auto-By-Tel form at its Edmunds.com Web site, regardless of whether a deal is completed.

this would produce *channel conflict*—that selling their products or services online would be competing with their offline retailers and agents. For example, Compaq Computer feared that its retailers would drop Compaq's computers if the company sold the same computers directly online. Merrill Lynch hesitated to introduce online stock trading to compete with E*Trade, Charles Schwab, and other online brokerages, fearing that its own brokers would rebel. Even store-based bookseller Barnes & Noble delayed opening its online site to challenge Amazon.com.

These companies struggled with the question of how to conduct online sales without cannibalizing the sales of their own stores, resellers, or agents. However, they soon realized that the risks of losing business to online competitors were even greater than the risks of angering channel partners. If they didn't cannibalize these sales, online competitors soon would. Thus, many established brick-and-mortar companies are now prospering as **click-and-mortar companies.**

Click-and-mortar companies

Traditional brick-and-mortar companies that have added e-marketing to their operations.

Consider Staples, the $10.7 billion office-supply retailer. After just two years on the Net, Staples captured annual online sales of $512 million last year. However, it's not robbing from store sales in the process. The average yearly spending of small-business customers jumps from $600 when they shop in stores to $2,800 when they shop online. As a result, although Staples is slowing new store openings to a trickle this year, it plans to spend $50 million on expanding its Net presence. "We're still going whole hog," says CEO Thomas Stemberg. "The payoffs are just very high."[29]

Most click-and-mortar marketers have found ways to resolve the resulting channel conflicts.[30] For example, Gibson Guitars found that although its dealers were outraged when it tried to sell guitars directly to consumers, the dealers didn't object to direct sales of accessories such as guitar strings and parts. Liberty Mutual asks its online customers whether they prefer to buy directly or through a financial adviser. It then refers interested customers and information about their needs to advisers, providing them with a good source of new business. Avon worried that direct online sales might cannibalize the business of its Avon ladies, who had developed close relationships with their customers. Fortunately, Avon's research showed little overlap between existing customers and potential Web customers. Avon shared this finding with the reps and then moved into e-marketing. As an added bonus for the reps, Avon also offered to help them set up their own Web sites.

Despite potential channel-conflict issues, many click-and-mortar companies are now having more online success than their click-only competitors. In fact, in a recent study of the top 50 retail sites, ranked by the number of unique visitors, 56 percent were click-and-mortar retailers, whereas 44 percent were Internet-only retailers.[31]

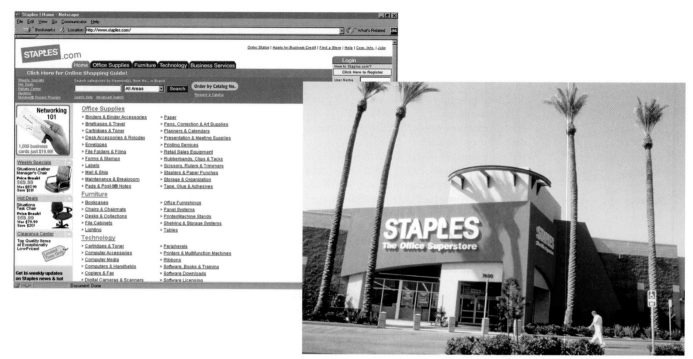

Click-and-mortar: Staples' Web site now supplements its brick-and-mortar operations. After two years on the Net, Staples captured online sales of more than $500 million.

What gives the click-and-mortar companies an advantage? Established companies such as Charles Schwab, Home Depot, Staples, and Gap have known and trusted brand names and greater financial resources. They have large customer bases, deeper industry knowledge and experience, and good relationships with key suppliers. By combining e-marketing and established brick-and-mortar operations, they can offer customers more options. For example, consumers can choose the convenience and assortment of 24-hour-a-day online shopping, the more personal and hands-on experience of in-store shopping, or both. Customers can buy merchandise online, then easily return unwanted goods to a nearby store. For example, those wanting to do business with Fidelity Investments can call a Fidelity agent on the phone, go online to the company's Web site, or visit the local Fidelity branch office. Thus, in its advertising, Fidelity can issue a powerful invitation to "call, click, or visit Fidelity Investments."

Setting Up an E-Marketing Presence

Clearly all companies need to consider moving into e-marketing. Companies can conduct e-marketing in any of the four ways shown in Figure 3.4: creating a Web site, placing ads online, setting up or participating in Web communities, or using online e-mail or Webcasting.

Creating a Web Site

For most companies, the first step in conducting e-marketing is to create a Web site. However, beyond simply creating a Web site, marketers must design attractive sites and find ways to get consumers to visit the site, stay around, and come back often.

Types of Web Sites.   Web sites vary greatly in purpose and content. The most basic type is a **corporate Web site.** These sites are designed to build customer goodwill and to supplement other sales channels, rather than to sell the company's products directly. For example, you can't buy ice cream at benjerrys.com, but you can learn all about Ben & Jerry's company philosophy, products, and locations. Or you can send a free E-card to a friend, subscribe to the Chunk Mail newsletter, or while away time in the Fun Stuff area, playing Scooper Challenge or Virtual Checkers.

Corporate Web sites typically offer a rich variety of information and other features in an effort to answer customer questions, build closer customer relationships, and generate excitement about the company. They generally provide information about the company's history, its

Corporate Web site
A Web site designed to build customer goodwill and to supplement other sales channels, rather than to sell the company's products directly.

FIGURE 3.4

Setting up for e-marketing

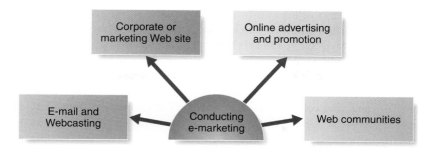

Marketing Web site

A Web site that engages consumers in interactions that will move them closer to a direct purchase or other marketing outcome.

mission and philosophy, and the products and services that it offers. They might also tell about current events, company personnel, financial performance, and employment opportunities. Most corporate Web sites also provide entertainment features to attract and hold visitors. Finally, the site might also provide opportunities for customers to ask questions or make comments through e-mail before leaving the site.

Other companies create a **marketing Web site.** These sites engage consumers in an interaction that will move them closer to a direct purchase or other marketing outcome. Such sites might include a catalog, shopping tips, and promotional features such as coupons, sales events, or contests. For example, visitors to SonyStyle.com can search through dozens of categories of Sony products, review detailed features and specifications lists for specific items, read expert product reviews, and check out the latest hot deals. They can place an order for the desired Sony products online and pay by credit card, all with a few clicks of the mouse button. Companies aggressively promote their marketing Web sites in offline print and broadcast advertising and through "banner-to-site" ads that pop up on other Web sites.

Toyota operates a marketing Web site at www.toyota.com. Once a potential customer clicks in, the carmaker wastes no time trying to turn the inquiry into a sale. The site offers plenty of useful information and a garage full of interactive selling features, such as detailed descriptions of current Toyota models and information on dealer locations and services, complete with maps and dealer Web links. Visitors who want to go further can use the Shop@Toyota feature to choose a Toyota, select equipment, and price it, then contact a dealer and even apply for credit. Or they fill out an online order form (supplying name, address, phone number, and e-mail address) for brochures and a free, interactive CD-ROM that shows off the features of Toyota models. The chances are good that before the CD-ROM arrives, a local dealer will call to invite the prospect in for a test drive. Toyota's Web site has now replaced its 800 number as the number one source of customer leads.

B2B marketers also make good use of marketing Web sites. For example, customers visiting GE Plastics' Web site can draw on more than 1,500 pages of information to get answers about the company's products anytime and from anywhere in the world. FedEx's Web site (www.fedex.com) allows customers to schedule their own shipments, request package pickup, and track their packages in transit.

Designing Attractive Web Sites.   Creating a Web site is one thing; getting people to *visit* the site is another. The key is to create enough value and excitement to get consumers to come to the site, stick around, and come back again.

A recent survey of fervent online surfers shows that people's online expectations have skyrocketed over the last few years. Today's Web users are quick to abandon any Web site that doesn't measure up. "Whether people are online for work reasons or for personal reasons," says the chairman of the firm that ran the survey, "if a Web site doesn't meet their expectations, two-thirds say they don't return—now or ever. They'll visit you and leave and you'll never know. We call it the Internet death penalty."[32]

This means that companies must constantly update their sites to keep them current, fresh, and exciting. Doing so involves time and expense, but the expense is necessary if the e-marketer wishes to cut through the increasing online clutter. In addition, many online marketers spend heavily on good old-fashioned advertising and other offline marketing avenues to attract visitors to their sites. Says one analyst, "The reality today is you can't build a brand simply on the Internet. You have to go offline."[33]

For some types of products, attracting visitors is easy. Consumers buying new cars, computers, or financial services will be open to information and marketing initiatives from sellers.

Marketers of lower-involvement products, however, may face a difficult challenge in attracting Web site visitors. As one veteran notes, "If you're shopping for a computer and you see a banner that says, 'We've ranked the top 12 computers to purchase,' you're going to click on the banner. [But] what kind of banner could encourage any consumer to visit dentalfloss.com?"[34]

For such low-interest products, the company can create a corporate Web site to answer customer questions, build goodwill and excitement, supplement selling efforts through other channels, and collect customer feedback. For example, although Kraft Food's LifeSavers Candystand Web site doesn't sell candy, it does generate a great deal of consumer excitement and sales support:

> The highly entertaining LifeSavers Candystand.com Web site, teeming with free videogames, endless sweepstakes, and sampling offers, has cast a fresh face on a brand that kid consumers once perceived as a stodgy adult confection. Visitors to the site—mostly children and teenagers—are not just passing through. They're clicking the mouse for an average 27-minute stay playing Foul Shot Shootout, Waterpark Pinball, and dozens of other arcade-style games. All the while, they're soaking in a LifeSavers aura swirling with information about products. "Our philosophy is to create an exciting online experience that reflects the fun and quality associated with the LifeSavers brands," says the company's manager of new media. "For the production cost of about two television spots, we have a marketing vehicle that lives 24 hours a day, seven days a week, 365 days a year." While Candystand.com has not directly sold a single roll of candy, the buzz generated by the site makes it an ideal vehicle for offering consumers their first glimpse of a new product, usually with an offer to get free samples by mail. In addition, LifeSavers reps use the site as sales leverage to help seal distribution deals when they talk with retailers. And the site offers LifeSavers an efficient channel for gathering customer feedback. Its "What Do You Think?" feature has generated hundreds of thousands of responses since the site launched five years ago. "It's instant communication that we pass along directly to our brand people," says the manager. Comments collected from the Web site have resulted in improved packaging of one LifeSavers product and the resurrection of the abandoned flavor of another. Candystand is now the number one consumer package-goods Web site, attracting 2.3 million unique visitors a month, more than twice the traffic of the number two site.[35]

A key challenge is designing a Web site that is attractive on first view and interesting enough to encourage repeat visits. The early text-based Web sites have largely been replaced in recent years by graphically sophisticated Web sites that provide text, sound, and animation (for examples, see www.sonystyle.com, www.candyland.com, or www.nike.com). To attract new visitors and to encourage revisits, suggests one expert, e-marketers should pay close attention to the seven *C*s of effective Web site design:[36]

- *Context:* the site's layout and design
- *Content:* the text, pictures, sound, and video that the Web site contains
- *Community:* the ways that the site enables user-to-user communication
- *Customization:* the site's ability to tailor itself to different users or to allow users to personalize the site
- *Communication:* the ways the site enables site-to-user, user-to-site, or two-way communication
- *Connection:* the degree to which the site is linked to other sites
- *Commerce:* the site's capabilities to enable commercial transactions

At the very least, a Web site should be easy to use and physically attractive. Beyond this, however, Web sites must also be interesting, useful, and challenging. Ultimately, it's the value of the site's *content* that will attract visitors, get them to stay longer, and bring them back for more.

Effective Web sites contain deep and useful information, interactive tools that help buyers find and evaluate products of interest, links to other related sites, changing promotional offers, and entertaining features that lend relevant excitement. For example, in addition to convenient online purchasing, Clinique.com offers in-depth information about cosmetics, a library of beauty tips, a computer for determining the buyer's skin type, advice from visiting experts, a bulletin board, a bridal guide, a directory of new products, and pricing information. Burpee.com provides aspiring gardeners with everything they need to make this year's garden the best ever. Besides selling seeds and plants by the thousands, the site offers an incredible wealth of informa-

An effective Web site is full of useful information, useful tools, and entertaining features that lend excitement. Burpee.com provides aspiring gardeners with a wealth of resources, including the Burpee Garden School and a Garden Wizard to help them pick the best plants for specific conditions.

tion resources, including a Garden Wizard (to help new gardeners pick the best plants for specific sun and soil conditions), the Burpee Garden School (online classes about plants and plant care), an archive of relevant service articles, and a chance to subscribe to an e-mail newsletter containing timely tips and gardening secrets.

From time to time, a company needs to reassess its Web site's attractiveness and usefulness. One way is to invite the opinion of site-design experts. But a better way is to have users themselves evaluate what they like and dislike about the site. For example, Otis Elevator Company's Web site serves 20,000 registered customers, among them architects, general contractors, building managers, and others interested in elevators. The site, offered in 52 countries and 26 languages, provides a wealth of helpful information, from modernization, maintenance, and safety information to drawings of various Otis models. Otis uses two sources of information to gauge satisfaction with its complex site. First, in an effort to detect potential problems, it tracks hits, time spent on the site, frequently visited pages, and the sequence of pages the customer visits. Second, it conducts quarterly phone surveys with 200 customers each in half the countries in which Otis does business. Such customer satisfaction tracking has resulted in many site improvements. For example, Otis found that customers in other countries were having trouble linking to the page that would let them buy an elevator online. Now, the link is easier to find. Some customers were finding it hard to locate a local Otis office, so the company added an Office Locator feature.[37]

Placing Ads and Promotions Online

Online advertising

Advertising that appears while consumers are surfing the Web, including banner and ticker ads, interstitials, skyscrapers, and other forms.

E-marketers can use **online advertising** to build their Internet brands or to attract visitors to their Web sites. Here, we discuss forms of online advertising promotion and their future.

Forms of Online Advertising and Promotion.   Online ads pop up while Internet users are surfing online. Such ads include *banner ads* and *tickers* (banners that move across the screen). For example, a Web user or America Online subscriber who is looking up airline schedules or fares might find a flashing banner on the screen exclaiming, "Rent a car from Alamo and get up to 2 days free!" To attract visitors to its own Web site, Toyota sponsors Web banner ads on other sites, ranging from ESPN SportZone (www.espn.com) to Parent Soup (www.parentsoup.com).

New online ad formats include *skyscrapers* (tall, skinny ads at the side of a Web page) and *rectangles* (boxes that are much larger than a banner). *Interstitials* are online ads that pop up between changes on a Web site. Visitors to www.msnbc.com who visit the site's sports area might suddenly be viewing a separate window hawking wireless video cameras. Ads for Johnson & Johnson's Tylenol headache reliever pop up on brokers' Web sites whenever the stock market falls by 100 points or more. Sponsors of *browser ads* pay viewers to watch them. For example, Alladvantage.com downloads a view bar where ads are displayed, to targeted users. Viewers earn 20 cents to $1 per hour in return.

Content sponsorships are another form of Internet promotion. Many companies gain name exposure on the Internet by sponsoring special content on various Web sites, such as news or financial information. For example, Advil sponsors ESPN SportZone's Injury Report and Oldsmobile sponsors AOL's Celebrity Circle. The sponsor pays for showing the content and, in turn, receives recognition as the provider of the particular service on the Web site. Sponsorships are best placed in carefully targeted sites where they can offer relevant information or service to the audience.

E-marketers can also go online with *microsites,* limited areas on the Web managed and paid for by an external company. For example, an insurance company might create a microsite on a car-buying site, offering insurance advice for car buyers and at the same time offering good insurance deals. Internet companies can also develop alliances and affiliate programs in which they work with other online companies to "advertise" each other. For example, AOL has created many successful alliances with other companies and mentions their names on its site. Amazon.com has more than 350,000 affiliates who post Amazon.com banners on their Web sites.

Viral marketing

The Internet version of word-of-mouth marketing—e-mail messages or other marketing events that are so infectious that customers will want to pass them along to friends.

Finally, e-marketers can use **viral marketing,** the Internet version of word-of-mouth marketing. Viral marketing involves creating an e-mail message or other marketing event that is so infectious that customers will want to pass it along to their friends. Because customers pass the message or promotion along to others, viral marketing can be very inexpensive. And when the information comes from a friend, the recipient is much more likely to open and read it. "The idea is to get your customers to do your marketing for you," notes a viral marketing expert. Consider these examples:

Seeking ways to get teenage girls to check out its Clean and Clear skin-care products, Johnson & Johnson created a pop-up microsite from which teens could "send a talking postcard to your friend." The site helped visitors design an e-greeting card, choosing decorations such as animated flowers or messages such as "Best Friends 4ever." Users were also offered a phone number to dictate a short voice message. Friends receiving the e-mail message heard the recording through their computer's speakers. As soon as they played the message, they were invited to click on a button called "Skin analyzer," linking them to Clean and Clear's main Web site.

Gillette used viral marketing to introduce the three-bladed Venus razor for women. To reach college students, Gillette designed a truck that traveled around the Florida spring-break circuit, parking daily near a beach. Women were invited to come in and get some aromatherapy, learn about Venus, enter a "Celebrate the Goddess in You" sweepstakes, and make a digital greeting card with a picture of themselves enjoying the beach. The viral part came when they e-mailed the digital cards to friends. The e-mailed messages automatically included a chance for friends to enter the sweepstakes themselves. If e-mail recipients entered the contest, they saw a pitch for the Venus razor. Some 20 percent of the entries came from the viral-marketing cards, greatly expanding the audience reached by the beach-site promotions.[38]

Viral marketing can also work well for B2B marketers. For example, to improve customer relationships, Hewlett-Packard recently sent tailored e-mail newsletters to customers who registered online. The newsletters contained information about optimizing the performance of H-P products and services. Now that was good, but here's the best part: The newsletters also featured a button that let customers forward the newsletters to friends or colleagues. By clicking the button, customers entered a Web site where they could type in the friend's e-mail address and a comment, then hit Send. The system inserted the message above the newsletter and e-mailed the whole thing to the friend. New recipients were then asked if they'd like to receive future H-P newsletters themselves. In this textbook case of viral marketing, Hewlett-Packard inexpensively met its goal of driving consumers to its Web site and ultimately increasing sales. "For those on our original e-mail list, the click-through rate was 10 to 15 percent," says an H-P executive. "For those who received it from a friend or colleague, it was between 25 and 40 percent."[39]

The Future of Online Advertising.   Online advertising serves a useful purpose, especially as a supplement to other marketing efforts. However, the Internet will not soon rival the major televi-

Gillette used viral marketing to introduce the three-bladed Venus razor for women, greatly expanding the audience reached by its "Celebrate the Goddess in You" truck tour and beach-site promotions.

sion and print media. Many marketers still question the value of Internet advertising as an effective tool. Costs are reasonable compared with those of other advertising media, but Web surfers can easily ignore such advertising and often do. Although many firms are experimenting with Web advertising, it plays only a minor role in most promotion mixes.

As a result, online advertising expenditures still represent only a small fraction of overall advertising media expenditures. Last year, online advertising spending amounted to just $7.2 billion, a mere 3.1 percent of the total spent offline. Moreover, in spite of its early promise, the growth of online advertising spending has slowed recently. According to one account:

> The Internet was supposed to be the ultimate ad medium, the killer app that would eclipse newspapers, magazines, even television. But it's become increasingly clear that the online ad boom was largely a mirage, one created by the unfettered spending of the dot-coms themselves. Those days are over.[40]

Despite the recent setbacks, some industry insiders remain optimistic about the future of online advertising.[41] And some Web sites, such as Google, have been successful in creating effective online advertising processes and environments (see Real Marketing 3.2). Whatever its future, companies are now seeking more effective forms and uses for Web advertising and marketing.

Creating or Participating in Web Communities

Web communities

Web sites upon which members can congregate online and exchange views on issues of common interest.

The popularity of forums and newsgroups has resulted in a rash of commercially sponsored Web sites called **Web communities,** which take advantage of the C2C properties of the Internet. Such sites allow members to congregate online and exchange views on issues of common interest. They are the cyberspace equivalent to a Starbucks coffeehouse, a place where everybody knows your e-mail address.

For example, iVillage.com is a Web community in which women can exchange views and obtain information, support, and solutions on families, food, fitness, relationships, relaxation, home and garden, news and issues, or just about any other topic. The site draws 393 million page views per month, putting it in a league with magazines such as *Cosmopolitan, Glamour,* and *Vogue.* Another example is MyFamily.com, which aspires to be the largest and most active online community in the world for families. It provides free, private family Web sites upon which family members can connect online to hold family discussions, share family news, create online family photo albums, maintain a calendar of family events, share family history information, jointly build

real marketing 3.2

"We Love You, Google Users"—and Advertisers, Too!

When you think back to the early dot-com boom, you probably think of brash, fast-growing startups led by offbeat, young entrepreneurs offering unique work environments to attract creative and talented employees. Google, the Web search services provider, is no different. Founded in September 1998 by Sergey Brin and Larry Page, then 25 and 29 years old, Google got its start in a rented garage, complete with a washer, dryer, and hot tub. Since then, it has grown from three employees to nearly 300. And like many dot-coms, Google offers a relaxed and friendly environment to woo and keep the best employees.

There's no official starting time at Google—or ending time for that matter. It's not about rules here. Far from it. No, workers . . . set their own hours, get backrubs from a company masseuse, even bake bread from scratch if the mood strikes them. When he does arrive, [cofounder] Brin skates into the Googleplex, as headquarters is called—past the undulating red, blue, and yellow lava lamps, the crimson couch, and the self-playing ebony grand piano with Muppet-theme sheet music. . . . At any moment, Yoshka, a 100-plus pound Leonberger (think small Saint Bernard), might come trotting around the corner with his owner.

Although this start-up story mirrors that of previous dot-coms, for Google there is one big difference. Whereas other dot-coms have struggled, Google is growing at a phenomenal rate: some 20 percent a *month*. More than 365 million unique visitors use Google's search engine each month to search 2 billion Web pages. They spend nearly 13 million hours a month searching on Google; second-place Yahoo! logs less than half that figure. Google users make more than 150 million queries each day—2,000 per second during peak hours. Half of the queries originate from outside of the United States, where Google offers search services in 28 different languages. Even more amazing, most of these searches are answered within half a second.

Perhaps more surprising, unlike most other dot-coms, Google turns a profit. In fact, Google is three times more profitable than eBay was at the same stage in its development. What's behind this incredible success? Google's technology is an important part of the equation. Page and Brin started the company to promote their PageRank search technology, which has revolutionized Internet searching. The Google search engine returns results that are usually more reliable and more useful than those of other search engines.

Beyond this revolutionary technology, Google has triumphed because it has focused heavily on helping users search. Unlike Yahoo! and other competitors, Google opted not to offer e-mail, shopping, and other services. Its Web site promises "a laser-like focus on finding the right answer for each and every inquiry." In fact, the name of the company is a play on the word *googol,* a mathematical term for a 1 followed by 100 zeros. It's a very large number. Google chose the name to reflect its mission to organize and make accessible the immense amount of information available on the Web. By focusing only on Internet searching, Google positions itself as "the World's Best Search Engine—accurate and easy to use." Users rave about Google's simple, search-only home page, uncluttered with news reports or banner ads.

The best part is that Google's extraordinary services are free to users. But how, then, does Google make money? About half of Google's revenues come from contracts with corporate partners to provide search services for their own Internet and intranet sites. Today, more than 130 companies in 30 different countries rely on Google's WebSearch and SiteSearch technologies to power the search services on their Web sites. These partners include companies such as Yahoo!, the Washington Post, Cisco, Red Hat, Palm, Nextel, Virgin, Netscape, Sony, and Cingular Wireless.

The other half of Google's revenues come from advertising sales. By attracting the largest online search audience in the world, Google has made itself a very attractive advertising medium. Here's how it works. Through constant data mining, Google determines which search terms are most popular. It then approaches companies who sell in those categories and offers them space for sponsored ad messages and links for a fee. Then, when someone searches Google for a topic related to the sponsor's product or service, a tasteful ad box appears at the top or side of the Google results page, containing a short ad message and links to the sponsor's Web site.

Try it yourself. Go to the Google site (www.google.com), type in a search word or phrase, and see what advertiser messages and links appear. For example, if you search "Disneyland," you'll see ads and links at the top of the search list for online travel services Expedia and Orbitz. The ads promise "Save up to 70% on Disneyland Hotels with Expedia!" and "Incredible deals on Disneyland at Orbitz!" Search "barbeque grills" and you're greeted with "Shop Sears for brand name grills

With the world's largest online search audience, Google has become a very attractive advertising medium. It's highly targeted ads reach users when they are already searching for related information.

and all your barbeque needs" and a link to www.sears.com. Side sponsor boxes link you to a half-dozen other merchants, including GasGrillsDirect.com, grillstuff.com, woodstoves.com, and flaminggrills.com. A search of "outdoor gear" yields "Find the best selection at REI.com" with side boxes for five other outfitters. Search "Rolling Stores" and you'll see ads and links for TicketsNow.com, stagefronttickets.com, ticketcity.com, and primetimetickets.com. You get the idea.

Whereas other forms of online advertising may produce questionable results, advertising on Google delivers. Google's highly targeted ads reach relevant users when they are already searching for information. Moreover, Google's matching process allows advertisers to tailor their ad messages or sites closely to users' search inquiries. As a result, "click-through" rates for the typical ad on Google are four to five times those of traditional banner ads.

Google works hard to make advertising on its site effective. Google's marketers assess each potential advertiser, pinpointing those they think will benefit from advertising on the site and those who won't. It proactively monitors ads to ensure their success. "Especially in a recession, people are looking for results," says a Google marketer. "When you spend money with us, you can actually measure what the return is on investment by measuring the response on our site." Google even lets advertisers know when their ads *aren't* working. One small business owner was shocked when he received an e-mail from Google suggesting that he pull his ads. "Google sent me an e-mail telling me what I was already thinking—that advertising with them was a waste of my money," he says. This unique approach to selling advertising space has resulted in loyalty and satisfaction among the Google clients who do stay. Online advertisers, such as Acura, Expedia, Eddie Bauer, Ernst & Young, and REI, regularly rank Google as their top online advertising choice. This, in turn, has fueled the company's financial success.

Almost from its first day, Google has been something of a cultural phenomenon. Within three months of starting up, it was picked as one of *PC Magazine*'s top 100 Web sites. Google's success stems from its fervent passion to bring value to both the users who flock to its site and the advertisers wanting to reach them. In the company's lobby in Mountain View, California, a six-foot trophy case brims with awards, including a 2000 Webby (the Internet's equivalent of an Oscar), which co-founders Brin and Page accepted wearing hockey uniforms and rollerblades. Their shared acceptance speech was simply, "We love you, Google users." They might have added, "And you, too, Google advertisers."

Sources: Quotes and other information from Betsy Cummings, "Beating the Odds," *Sales and Marketing Management,* March 2002, pp. 24–28; Fred Vogelstein, "Looking for a Dot-Com Winner? Search No Further," *Fortune,* May 27, 2002, pp. 65–68; and information gathered from www.google.com, July 2002.

family trees, and buy gifts for family members quickly and easily. "People talk about forming communities on the Internet," says co-founder Paul Allen. "Well, the oldest community is the family."[42]

Visitors to these Internet neighborhoods develop a strong sense of community. Such communities are attractive to advertisers because they draw consumers with common interests and well-defined demographics. Moreover, cyberhood consumers visit frequently and stay online longer, increasing the chance of meaningful exposure to the advertiser's message. For example, iVillage provides an ideal environment for the Web ads of companies such as Procter & Gamble, Kimberly Clark, Avon, Clairol, Hallmark, and others who target women consumers. And MyFamily.com hosts The Shops@MyFamily, in which such companies as Disney, Kodak, Hallmark, Compaq, Hewlett-Packard, and Microsoft advertise and sell their family-oriented products.

Web communities can be either social or work related. One successful work-related community is @griculture Online. This site offers commodity prices, recent farm news, and chat rooms of all types. Rural surfers can visit the Electronic Coffee Shop and pick up the latest down-on-the-farm joke or join a hot discussion on controlling soybean cyst nematodes. @griculture Online has been highly successful, attracting as many as 5 million hits per month.[43]

Using E-Mail and Webcasting

E-mail has exploded onto the scene as an important e-marketing tool. Jupiter Media Metrix estimates that companies will be spending $7.3 billion annually on e-mail marketing by 2005, up from just $164 million in 1999.[44] To compete effectively in this ever-more-cluttered e-mail environment, marketers are designing "enriched" e-mail messages—animated, interactive, and personalized messages full of streaming audio and video. Then they are targeting these attention-grabbers more carefully to those who want them and will act upon them. (See Real Marketing 3.3.)

E-mail is becoming a mainstay for both B2C and B2B marketers. 3Com Corporation, a B2B marketer of high-tech computer hardware, made good use of e mail to generate and qualify customer leads for its network interface cards. The company used targeted e mail and banner ads on 18 different computer-related Web sites to attract potential buyers to its own Web site featuring a "3Com Classic" sweepstakes, where by filling out the entry form, visitors could register to win a 1959 Corvette. The campaign generated 22,000 leads, which were further qualified using e-mail and telemarketing. "Hot" leads were passed along to 3Com's inside sales force. "[Sales reps] were very skeptical," says a 3Com marketing manager, "but they were blown away by how well the contest did." Of the

Web communities: iVillage.com, a Web community for women, provides an ideal environment for Web ads of companies such as Procter & Gamble, Kimberly Clark, Avon, Hallmark, and others. Here, Redbook magazine advertises its latest issue.

482 leads given to reps, 71 turned into actual sales that totaled $2.5 million. What's more, states the manager, "Now I've got 22,000 names in my e-mail database that I can go back and market to."[45]

Webcasting

The automatic downloading of customized information of interest to recipients' PCs, affording an attractive channel for delivering Internet advertising or other information content.

Companies can also sign on with any of a number of **Webcasting** services, which automatically download customized information to recipients' PCs. An example is Internet Financial Network's Infogate, which sends up-to-date financial news, market data, and real-time stock quotes to subscribers in the financial services industry for a fee. Infogate frames the top and bottom inch of subscribers' computer screens with personalized news and other information tailored to their specific interests. Rather than spending hours scouring the Internet, subscribers can sit back while Infogate automatically delivers information of interest to their desktops.[46] The major commercial online services also offer Webcasting to their members. For example, America Online offers a feature called Driveway that will fetch information, Web pages, and e-mail–based articles on members' preferences and automatically deliver it to their PCs.

Also known as "push" programming, Webcasting affords an attractive channel through which online marketers can deliver their Internet advertising or other information content. For example, via Infogate, advertisers can market their products and services using highly targeted messages to a desirable segment of at-work Internet users.

As with other types of online marketing, companies must be careful that they don't cause resentment among Internet users who are already overloaded with "junk e-mail." E-mail marketers walk a fine line between adding value for consumers and being intrusive. Companies must beware of irritating consumers by sending unwanted e-mail to promote their products. Netiquette, the unwritten rules that guide Internet etiquette, suggests that marketers should ask customers for permission to e-mail marketing pitches. They should also tell recipients how to "opt in" or "opt out" of e-mail promotions at any time. This approach, known as permission-based marketing, has become a standard model for e-mail marketing.

The Promise and Challenges of E-Commerce

E-commerce continues to offer both great promise and many challenges for the future. We now look at both the promises of e-commerce and the "darker side" of the Web.

real marketing 3.3

The New World of E-Mail Marketing

E-mail is *the* hot new marketing medium. In ever-larger numbers, e-mail ads are popping onto our computer screens and filling up our e-mailboxes. What's more, they're no longer just the quiet, plain-text messages of old. The new breed of e-mail ad is designed to command your attention—loaded with glitzy features such as animation, interactive links, color photos, streaming video, and personalized audio messages.

But if you think that you're already getting too much e-mail, hang on to your mouse. Jupiter Media Metrix predicts that the number of commercial e-mail messages sent per year will increase from an already daunting 43 billion in 2000 to an in-box–busting 375 billion by 2005. And no wonder. E-mail allows marketers to send tailored messages to targeted consumers who actually want to receive them, at a cost of only a few cents per contact. Even better, they can target audiences in any country and get responses within 24 hours.

As in any other direct-marketing effort, e-mail success depends on a good customer database. Companies can obtain e-mail addresses from outside list brokers. However, the best way to build an e-mail database easily is simply to ask customers for their e-mail addresses at every point of contact. Marketers can ask for e-mail addresses on their Web sites, in their brick-and-mortar stores, via response cards sent with catalogs, during customer service calls, or even in print ads. Some marketers sponsor sign-up promotions, offering sweepstakes or prizes as incentives for customers who fork over their e-mail addresses. All of these are permission-based methods that allow customers to "opt in" or "opt out," ensuring that e-mails are sent only to customers who ask for them. "That leaves marketers largely immune from the wrath of privacy advocates and spam fighters," states *Business Week* writer Arlene Weintraub.

Another advantage of e-mail ads is that companies can track customer responses—how many people open the message, who clicks through to the Web site, and what they do when they get there. And well-designed e-mail ads really do command attention and get customers to act. ITM Strategies, a sales and marketing research firm, estimates that permission e-mail campaigns typically achieve 10 percent to 15 percent click-through rates. That's pretty good when compared with the .5 percent to 2 percent average response rates for traditional direct mail.

E-mail success stories abound. *Business Week* offers this example:

Zomba Recording, corporate parent of teen band 'N Sync's label Jive Records, cooked up an e-campaign that made other marketers drool. In March, 200,000 fans received a video message about the album *No Strings Attached* that allowed them to hear band members speak and to listen to a snippet of the song "Bye Bye Bye." Fans went wild: 34 percent of the e-mail recipients, whose names had been collected from the 'N Sync Web site, downloaded the video. Of those, 88 percent clicked on one of the links. Thousands forwarded the e-mail to friends. In the world of direct marketing, where a 1 percent response rate is considered acceptable, the numbers were extraordinary. *No Strings Attached* had its debut in April and sold 2.4 million copies in its first week—the biggest opening since SoundScan started tracking sales in 1991. "E-mail is a technology that kids are really into, so it was a great direct-hit way to get to them," says Jeff Dodes, vice-president for new media and Internet operations at Zomba.

Still, even permission-based e-mail can be very annoying. "Even among consumers who opt in to the e-mail barrage, there's a fine line between legitimate marketing and spam," says Weintraub. "As more companies glom onto the trend, there is strong potential for a backlash." Companies crossing that fine line will quickly learn that "opting out" is only a click away for disgruntled customers. According to Weintraub, marketers are aware of the potential for irritation and are taking steps to head it off:

Petopia.com, which mails monthly e-newsletters and personalized pet birthday messages, has set its computer system to automatically limit the number of e-mails any one customer receives in a month. Handheld-computer maker Palm Inc. has been experimenting with the

A new breed of e-mail ads is popping onto our computer screens and filling up our e-mailboxes. They're designed to command your attention—loaded with glitzy features such as animation, interactive links, color photos, streaming video, and personalized audio messages.

(continued)

length of its e-ads, and recently found that a 150-word message produced a better click-through rate than 300 words did. IKEA took an even more drastic step. In April, the furniture retailer promoted its new San Francisco store by e-mailing customers and inviting them to send virtual postcards to friends through its site. A mind-boggling 70,000 postcards were sent in 10 days. But when a handful of recipients cried "spam!," IKEA pulled the campaign. "We only want to communicate with customers in ways that they think are appropriate," says IKEA's manager of new business development.

Still, marketing history is full of examples of effective tactics that were taken too far, and some experts see little reason to expect that e-mail advertising will be any different. A recent study found that more than one out of three messages that hit e-mail inboxes are unwanted. And nearly 40 percent of the e-mail–receiving public deletes even e-mail they've opted in for before they ever read it. E-mail "will be overdone," predicts the president of a firm that creates e-mail campaigns. "Brace your e-mail box for the results," adds Weintraub.

Sources: Quotes and extracts from Arlene Weintraub, "When E-Mail Ads Aren't Spam," *Business Week,* October 16, 2000, pp. 112–114. Also see Chad Kaydo, "As Good As It Gets," *Sales & Marketing Management,* March 2000, pp. 55–60; Eileen P. Gunn, Marketers Are Keen on Enriched E-Mail," *Advertising Age,* October 16, 2000, p. S12; Amy Harmon, "You've Got Mail. Lots of It, and It's Mostly Junk," *New York Times,* December 24, 2001, p. A1; and Christopher Saunders, "Spam, Saturation Plague E-Mail Marketing," *CyberAtlas,* May 16, 2002, accessed online at cyberatlas.internet.com.

The Continuing Promise of E-Commerce

Its most ardent apostles still envision a time when the Internet and e-commerce will replace magazines, newspapers, and even stores as sources for information and buying. However, such "dot-com fever" has cooled recently, and a more realistic view has emerged. "It's time for Act II in the Internet revolution," suggests one analyst. "The first act belonged to dot-coms with big visions and small bank accounts. Now the stages will be taken by big companies that move their factories, warehouses, and customers onto the Web."[47]

To be sure, online marketing will become a successful business model for some companies, Internet firms such as Amazon.com, eBay, Expedia, and Earthlink and direct-marketing companies such as Charles Schwab and Dell Computer. Michael Dell's goal is one day "to have *all* customers conduct *all* transactions on the Internet, globally." And e-business will continue to boom for many B2B marketers, companies such as Cisco Systems, General Electric, and IBM.

However, for most companies, online marketing will remain just one important approach to the marketplace that works alongside other approaches in a fully integrated marketing mix. Eventually, as companies become more adept at integrating e-commerce with their everyday strategy and tactics, the "e" will fall away from e-business or e marketing. "The key question is not whether to deploy Internet technology—companies have no choice if they want to stay competitive—but how to deploy it," says business strategist Michael Porter. He continues: "We need to move away from the rhetoric about 'Internet industries,' 'e-business strategies,' and a 'new economy,' and see the Internet for what it is: . . . a powerful set of tools that can be used, wisely or unwisely, in almost any industry and as part of almost any strategy."[48]

The Web's Darker Side

Along with its considerable promise, there is a "darker side" to Internet marketing. Here we examine two major sets of concerns: Internet profitability and legal and ethical issues.

Internet Profitability

One major concern is profitability, especially for B2C dot-coms. Surprisingly few B2C Internet companies are profitable. Of the 456 Internet companies that went public since 1994, only 11 percent are still in business and profitable. Of those still in business and not acquired by another company, only 25 percent are profitable. One analysts calls this "the Web's pretty little secret."[49]

One problem is that the Internet still offers limited consumer exposure and skewed user demographics. Although expanding rapidly, online marketing still reaches only a limited marketspace. And although the Web audience is becoming more mainstream, online users still tend to be somewhat more upscale and better educated than the general population. This makes the Internet ideal for marketing financial services, travel services, computer hardware and software, and certain other classes of products. However, it makes online marketing less effective for selling

mainstream products. Moreover, in most product categories, users still do more window browsing and product research than actual buying.

Finally, the Internet offers millions of Web sites and a staggering volume of information.
Thus, navigating the Internet can be frustrating, confusing, and time consuming for consumers.
In this chaotic and cluttered environment, many Web ads and sites go unnoticed or unopened.
Even when noticed, marketers will find it difficult to hold consumer attention. One study found
that a site must capture Web surfers' attention within eight seconds or lose them to another site.
That leaves very little time for marketers to promote and sell their goods.

Legal and Ethical Issues

From a broader societal viewpoint, Internet marketing practices have raised a number of ethical
and legal questions. In previous sections, we've touched on some of the negatives associated with
the Internet, such as unwanted e-mail and the annoyance of pop-up ads. Here we examine concerns about consumer online privacy and security and other legal and ethical issues.

Online Privacy and Security.   *Online privacy* is perhaps the number-one e-commerce concern.
Most e marketers have become skilled at collecting and analyzing detailed consumer information. Marketers can easily track Web site visitors, and many consumers who participate in Web
site activities provide extensive personal information. This may leave consumers open to information abuse if companies make unauthorized use of the information in marketing their products or exchanging databases with other companies. Many consumers and policy makers worry
that marketers have stepped over the line and are violating consumers' right to privacy.[50] A recent
survey found that 7 out of 10 consumers are concerned about online privacy.

Many consumers also worry about *online security.* They fear that unscrupulous snoopers will
eavesdrop on their online transactions or intercept their credit card numbers and make unauthorized purchases. In turn, companies doing business online fear that others will use the Internet to
invade their computer systems for the purposes of commercial espionage or even sabotage. There
appears to be an ongoing competition between the technology of Internet security systems and
the sophistication of those seeking to break them.

In response to such online privacy and security concerns, the federal government is considering
legislative actions to regulate how Web operators obtain and use consumer information. Congress is
considering an online privacy bill that would require online service providers and commercial Web
sites to get customers' permission before they disclose important personal information. That would
include financial, medical, ethnic, religious, and political information, along with Social Security data
and sexual orientation. The bill would also direct the Federal Trade Commission to enact rules
imposing similar requirements on both online and offline data collection. "I think this subject of privacy is a ticking time bomb, . . . because people do not want their personally identifiable medical and
financial information spread all over every place," says one senator. "A doctor needs to know what ails
you. But those ailments, your mortgage banker doesn't need to know that."[51]

Of special concern are the privacy rights of children. In 1998, the Federal Trade Commission
surveyed 212 Web sites directed toward children. It found that 89 percent of the sites collected
personal information from children. However, 46 percent of them did not include any disclosure
of their collection and use of such information. As a result, Congress passed the Children's Online
Privacy Protection Act, which requires Web site operators targeting children to post privacy policies on their sites. They must also notify parents about the information they're gathering and
obtain parental consent before collecting personal information from children under age 13.[52]

Many companies have responded to consumer privacy and security concerns with actions of
their own. Companies such as Expedia and E-Loan have conducted voluntary audits of their privacy and security policies. Other companies are going even further.

Royal Bank of Canada (RBC) has used a progressive privacy policy to differentiate itself from
competitors. For the past two years the company has used some 15 different programs to
show consumers that it strives to exceed government-mandated privacy regulations for U.S.
financial service providers. For instance, the company is preparing to give away so-called
personal firewall software to its online banking customers. RBC also delayed the rollout of
wireless banking until it found a Nokia phone with a chip allowing customers to encrypt
passwords and other information. RBC has tried to quantify the effects of its privacy policies,
relying on research suggesting that 7 percent of a customer's buying decision relates to

privacy issues. Using that and other assumptions, RBC's privacy policies were responsible for $700 million worth of consumer banking business.[53]

Still, examples of companies aggressively protecting their customers' personal information are few and far between. The costs of inaction could be great. Jupiter Media Metrix forecasts that in 2006 almost $25 billion in revenues will be lost as a result of consumers' privacy concerns. Moreover, they predict, online sales that year would be as much as 25 percent higher if consumers' concerns were adequately addressed.[54] Finally, if Web marketers don't act to curb privacy abuses, legislators most probably will.

Other Legal and Ethical Issues. Beyond issues of online privacy and security, consumers are also concerned about *Internet fraud,* including identity theft, investment fraud, and financial scams. Last year alone, the federal Internet Fraud Complaint Center (IFCC) received nearly 50,000 complaints related to Internet fraud that resulted in a total consumer loss of more than $17 million. The IFCC reports that nearly 43 percent of reported incidents involve online auctions. Fraudulent activities are most often conducted through Web pages and e-mail, with 70 percent involving e-mail transactions.[55]

There are also concerns about *segmentation and discrimination* on the Internet. Some social critics and policy makers worry about the so-called *Digital Divide*—the gap between those who have access to the latest Internet and information technologies and those who don't. They are concerned that in this information age, not having equal access to information can be an economic and social handicap. The Internet currently serves upscale consumers well. However, poorer consumers still have less access to the Internet, leaving them increasingly less informed about products, services, and prices. Some people consider the Digital Divide to be a national crisis; others see it as an overstated nonissue.[56]

A final Internet marketing concern is that of *access by vulnerable or unauthorized groups.* For example, marketers of adult-oriented materials have found it difficult to restrict access by minors. In a more specific example, sellers using eBay.com, the online auction Web site, recently found themselves the victims of a 13-year-old boy who had bid on and purchased more than $3 million worth of high-priced antiques and rare artworks on the site. eBay has a strict policy against bidding by anyone under age 18 but works largely on the honor system. Unfortunately, this honor system did little to prevent the teenager from taking a cyberspace joyride.[57]

Despite these challenges, companies large and small are quickly integrating online marketing into their marketing strategies and mixes. As it continues to grow, online marketing will prove to be a powerful tool for building customer relationships, improving sales, communicating company and product information, and delivering products and services more efficiently and effectively.

LOOKING BACK: REVIEWING THE CONCEPTS

Recent technological advances have created a new digital age. To thrive in this new environment, marketers will have to add some Internet thinking to their strategies and tactics. This chapter introduces the forces shaping the new Internet environment and discusses the ways in which marketers are adapting. In the next chapter, we'll take a look at other forces and actors affecting the complex and changing marketing environment.

1. Identify the major forces shaping the digital age.
Four major forces underlie the digital age: digitalization and connectivity, the explosion of the Internet, new types of intermediaries, and customization and customerization. Much of today's business operates on digital information, which flows through connected networks. Intranets, extranets, and the Internet now connect people and companies with each other and with important information. The Internet has grown explosively to become *the* revolutionary technology of the new millennium, empowering consumers and businesses alike with the blessings of connectivity.

The Internet and other new technologies have changed the ways that companies serve their markets. New Internet marketers and channel relationships have arisen to replace some types of

traditional marketers. The new technologies are also helping marketers to tailor their offers effectively to targeted customers or even to help customers customerize their own marketing offers. Finally, the New Economy technologies are blurring the boundaries between industries, allowing companies to pursue opportunities that lie at the convergence of two or more industries.

2. Explain how companies have responded to the new Internet and other powerful new technologies with e-business strategies, and how these strategies have resulted in benefits to both buyers and sellers.
Conducting business in the New Economy will call for a new model of marketing strategy and practice. Companies need to retain most of the skills and practices that have worked in the past. However, they must also add major new competencies and practices if they hope to grow and prosper in the New Economy. E-business is the use of electronic platforms to conduct a company's business. E-commerce involves buying and selling processes supported by electronic means, primarily the Internet. It includes e marketing (the selling side of e-commerce) and e-purchasing (the buying side of e-commerce).

E-commerce benefits both buyers and sellers. For buyers, e-commerce makes buying convenient and private, provides greater product access and selection, and makes available a wealth of product and buying information. It is interactive and immediate and gives the consumer a greater measure of control over the buying process. For sellers, e-commerce is a powerful tool for building customer relationships. It also increases the sellers' speed and efficiency, helping to reduce selling costs. E-commerce also offers great flexibility and better access to global markets.

3. Describe the four major e-commerce domains.
Companies can practice e-commerce in any or all of four domains. B2C (business-to-consumer) e-commerce is initiated by businesses and targets final consumers. Despite recent setbacks following the "dot-com gold rush" of the late 1990s, B2C e-commerce continues to grow at a healthy rate. Although online consumers are still somewhat higher in income and more technology oriented than traditional buyers, the cyberspace population is becoming much more mainstream and diverse. This growing diversity opens up new e-commerce targeting opportunities for marketers. Today, consumers can buy almost anything on the Web.

B2B (business-to-business) e-commerce dwarfs B2C e-commerce. Most businesses today operate Web sites or use B2B trading networks, auction sites, spot exchanges, online product catalogs, barter sites, or other online resources to reach new customers, serve current customers more effectively, and obtain buying efficiencies and better prices. Business buyers and sellers meet in huge marketspaces—or open trading networks—to share information and complete transactions efficiently. Or, they set up private trading networks that link them with their own trading partners.

Through C2C (consumer-to-consumer) e-commerce, consumers can buy or exchange goods and information directly from or with one another. Examples include online auction sites, forums, and Internet newsgroups. Finally, through C2B (consumer-to-business) e-commerce, consumers are now finding it easier to search out sellers on the Web, learn about their products and services, and initiate purchases. Using the Web, customers can even drive transactions with business, rather than the other way around.

4. Discuss how companies can go about conducting e-commerce to profitably deliver more value to customers.
Companies of all types are now engaged in e-commerce. The Internet gave birth to the *click-only* dot-coms, which operate only online. In addition, many traditional brick-and-mortar companies have now added e-marketing operations, transforming themselves into *click-and-mortar* competitors. Many click-and-mortar companies are now having more online success than their click-only competitors.

Companies can conduct e-marketing in any of the four ways: creating a Web site, placing ads and promotions online, setting up or participating in Web communities, or using online e-mail or Webcasting. The first step typically is to set up a Web site. Corporate Web sites are designed to build customer goodwill and to supplement other sales channels, rather than to sell the company's products directly. Marketing Web sites engage consumers in an interaction that will move them closer to a direct purchase or other marketing outcome. Beyond simply setting up a site, companies must make their sites engaging, easy to use, and useful in order to attract visitors, hold them, and bring them back again.

E-marketers can use various forms of online advertising to build their Internet brands or to attract visitors to their Web sites. Beyond online advertising, other forms of online marketing include content sponsorships, microsites, and viral marketing, the Internet version of word-of-mouth marketing. Online marketers can also participate in Web communities, which take advantage of the C2C properties of the Web. Finally, e-mail marketing has become a hot new e-marketing tool for both B2C and B2B marketers.

5. Overview the promise and challenges that e-commerce presents for the future.
E-commerce continues to offer great promise for the future. For most companies, online marketing will become an important part of a fully integrated marketing mix. For others, it will be the major means by which they serve the market. Eventually, the "e" will fall away from e-business or e-marketing as companies become more adept at integrating e-commerce with their everyday strategy and tactics. However, e-commerce also faces many challenges. One challenge is Web profitability—surprisingly few companies are using the Web profitably. The other challenge concerns legal and ethical issues—issues of online privacy and security, Internet fraud, and the Digital Divide. Despite these challenges, companies large and small are quickly integrating online marketing into their marketing strategies and mixes.

REVIEWING THE KEY TERMS

B2B (business-to-business) e-commerce 79
B2C (business-to-consumer) e-commerce 76
C2B (consumer-to-consumer) e-commerce 82
C2C (consumer-to-consumer) e-commerce 81

Click-and-mortar companies 85
Click-only companies 82
Corporate Web site 86
Customerization 73
E-business 74
E-commerce 74

E-marketing 74
Extranet 71
Internet 71
Intranet 71
Marketing Web site 87
Online advertising 89

Open trading networks 79
Private trading networks (PTNs) 80
Viral marketing 90
Webcasting 94
Web communities 91

DISCUSSING THE CONCEPTS

1. List and briefly discuss the four major forces that are shaping the Internet age.
2. Assume that you are a newly appointed information services manager for a company that develops customized tours for senior citizens interested in visiting exotic locations. Explain how you could use intranets, extranets, and the Internet to increase your company's contact with its target market and expand its business.
3. Discuss how a traditional retailer or wholesaler can be *disintermediated* by the new e-tailer. Give an example to illustrate.

4. Explain how customization differs from customerization.
5. In New Age marketing, e-commerce and the Internet bring many benefits to both buyers and sellers. Describe these benefits.
6. List and describe each of the four major Internet domains. Which domain is growing fastest? Which domain has the brightest future? Explain.
7. The growth of the Internet has spawned two primary types of e-tailers, click-only and click-and-mortar. Which type of e-marketer do you think will be most successful in the future? Explain.
8. Pick a favorite Web site and write a brief analysis of how the site rates on the seven Cs of effective Web site design. What forms of online advertising and promotion does the Web site employ? How can the site be improved? Be specific.

APPLYING THE CONCEPTS

1. One of the oldest forms of marketing and promotion is word of mouth. On the Internet, word of mouth has become known as viral marketing. To create "buzz," the viral marketer targets a group of carefully chosen trend leaders in a community who can effectively spread the word about the product, event, or service. Viral marketing has worked successfully for a variety of products, including the Doom video game, *The Blair Witch Project,* Harry Potter books, Razor scooters, and Chrysler's PT Cruiser. In addition, viral marketing has revived failing brands such as Lucky Strike cigarettes, Lee jeans, and Vespa scooters.
   a. List three products that you learned about from friends. How did the information offered affect your impression of the product? Did you act based on your friends' recommendations? Why or why not?
   b. Assume you are the marketing manager for a new product to be sold primarily to consumers in their late teens and early twenties. How you would use viral marketing to promote the product? Be specific in describing your plan.
   c. Consider the ethics of viral marketing. What problems might arise with this method? What precautions should an e-marketer consider to prevent such problems?
2. The purchasing department of the future will likely look much different from today's. The New Era purchasing department will most certainly use open and private trading networks and electronic exchanges. These new purchasing methods will result in sizable cost savings. For example, Best Buy saves $16 million annually on purchases of $100 billion of goods and services via electronic exchanges and trading networks. In addition, the huge consumer-electronics retailer can receive as many as 100 bids per hour via electronic networks and receive real-time feedback about potential purchases. In the future, B2B purchasing managers will need to be increasingly "Web smart" to stay even with competitors.
   a. List the advantages and disadvantages of using open and private trading networks and electronic exchanges for purchasing goods and services.
   b. One place that Best Buy "shops" is the Worldwide Retail Exchange (see www.worldwideretailexchange.com). What type of companies found on this site might want to sell to Best Buy? Explain.
   c. Among the first items that firms purchase through trading networks and electronic exchanges are operational supplies and services. Why?
   d. Would open networks be a good place to buy goods that are critical to a company's competitive differentiation? Explain.
   e. When would a handshake with a longtime vendor be more important than an electronic exchange or open trading network?

 # DIGITAL CONNECTIONS

CONNECTING WITH COMPANIES TO ENSURE PRIVACY AND SECURITY

TRUSTe is attempting to do for privacy and security on the Internet what the Good Housekeeping Seal of Approval did for product reliability and the Underwriter's Laboratory Seal did for product safety. As e-commerce companies begin to self-regulate privacy issues and data collection, TRUSTe, a not-for-profit organization, is on a mission to build users' trust and confidence in privacy protection on the Internet. TRUSTe has become a leader in promoting Web site privacy-policy disclosure, informed-user consent, and consumer education. What does all this mean? A company that achieves the TRUSTe "trustmark" has agreed to adhere to TRUSTe-established privacy principles and to comply with TRUSTe oversight and consumer resolution. The "trustmark" assures Web users that a site will openly disclose what personal information is being gathered, where that information is going, how it will be used, and whether the user has the option to control its dissemination. TRUSTe believes it has a solution to the number one concern of most Internet users—privacy and security.

FOR DISCUSSION

1. Visit www.truste.com to learn more about the services TRUSTe provides. What are the advantages for an organization agreeing to self-regulate through TRUSTe? What are the disadvantages? Do the advantages outweigh the disadvantages? Explain.
2. Examine the various Seal programs offered by TRUSTe. Briefly outline the function of each of these. What additional services do you think TRUSTe should offer? Explain.
3. TRUSTe states that consumer education is the number one priority in privacy protection. Do you agree? Explain.
4. Use the Search for Seal Program Participants feature. Pick three of the participants and visit their Web sites. Examine the site's privacy statements. What do these statements have in common? Comment on how these firms are trying to "connect" with their consumers.

FindWhat.com: Searching for Success

Among the Web-browser giants, including Google and Yahoo!, FindWhat.com may seem a relative lightweight, with projected revenues of only about $40 million in 2002. But the company's Pay-For-Performance search model offers an innovative approach to generating advertising revenue and delivering relevant hits for consumers searching the Web. Still, the most important question remains: In the wake of the dot-com meltdown, will the site's unique approach be enough to ensure long-term profitability in the often volatile dot-com market?

After reviewing the video segment featuring FindWhat. com, consider the following questions about online marketing:

1. Visit FindWhat.com and read more about the company. How do FindWhat.com's services to businesses differ from those offered by Google, Yahoo!, or Infoseek? How are its services to consumers similar?
2. What can FindWhat.com do to build consumer loyalty for its search engine? To build loyalty from its business partners?
3. Consider FindWhat.com's business model. How does the approach differ from those of other dot-coms discussed in this chapter? Do you think FindWhat.com's approach to launching and growing its business makes the company more or less likely to succeed in the long run?

eBay: Connecting in China

A RARE SUCCESS

Legend has it that Pierre Omidyar, a young engineer, concocted the idea for eBay in 1995 so that his girlfriend would have an easy way to meet and trade with fellow Pez dispenser collectors. Omidyar envisioned eBay's Internet site as becoming a place where a network of buyers and sellers could connect, forming a community. Bill Cobb, the company's global marketing director, calls eBay a step toward "the first worldwide economic democracy."

eBay is just a step in one sense. The company pales in comparison to, for example, Wal-Mart. Wal-Mart raked in about $220 billion in sales in 2001 from its network of 3,000 stores, 1.3 million workers, and countless warehouses. By comparison, eBay generated only $749 million in revenue from sales fees and advertising on the $9.3 billion in goods sold through 170 million transactions using its system—less than 4 percent of Wal-Mart's sales. However, eBay has no stores or warehouses or inventory and accomplished its results with fewer than 3,000 employees. Further, unlike most of the dot-coms that sprouted in the late 1990s, eBay is profitable, having produced a net profit of $138 million in 2001.

eBay, however, is no flash-in-the-pan. Analysts predict that its revenues will double to about $1.5 billion by the end of 2003 and profits will more than double to about $318 million. Investors seemed to believe the predictions, as eBay's stock was trading at an astounding 113 times earnings at the end of 2001, despite the stock market's depressed condition.

HOW EBAY WORKS

The idea for eBay's business model is simple—and old. Residents in rural and urban communities have for centuries gathered in town squares and marketplaces to buy, sell, and exchange goods and services. The modern-day flea market is a throwback to these markets.

eBay simply took this old idea and removed the need for a physical meeting between buyer and seller. The Internet provided the cyberspace where the marketing exchange could take place. eBay simply created the software programs to enable the transactions. The eBay system, however, improves on the old market system in that the seller can "display" his or her items to a huge number of potential customers at the same time. Given that there may be more than one person interested in the item, the seller can hold a virtual auction, hoping that demand for the item will produce a higher price than a typical market where the number of potential buyers would be more limited or even nonexistent. Obviously, the process also depends on modern transportation and payment systems that allow the buyers and sellers to arrange for the product's physical delivery, as eBay plays no role in closing the transaction.

eBay charges the sellers insertion fees for listing an item, final-value fees upon a sale, and listing-upgrade fees. The following table presents the impact of the final value fee structure at various closing values:

(continued)

Auction's Gross Closing Value	Final Value Fee	Final Value Fee as a Percent of Gross Closing Value
$25	$1.31	5.25%
$50	$2.00	4.00%
$100	$3.38	3.38%
$1,000	$28.13	2.81%
$10,000	$163.13	1.63%

Source: eBay Web site and Merrill Lynch analysis.

In 2001, eBay's transaction fees accounted for all but $84 million of its revenues, with this remainder coming from third-party advertising charges.

Because eBay does not take title to anything sold over its system, it has a gross margin of 82 percent. In 2001, eBay's operating expenses totaled 57.8 percent of revenues, with sales and marketing accounting for 33.8 percent; product development, 10 percent; and general and administrative expenses, 14 percent. Even with eBay's projected growth, analysts predicted that its sales and marketing expense would hold at 30 percent of revenues.

eBay's average auction lasted 6.55 days as of the first quarter of 2002, and the average gross value per auction was $22.50. As of early 2002, the average seller sponsored three auctions and produced $1.72 in net revenue for eBay per auction. eBay classified its offerings into 18,000 categories, with high-priced merchandise, like cars and computers, continuing to grow as a percent of total sales value. In fact, eBay Motors was the company's fastest-growing category in early 2002. Collectibles, like the Pez dispensers, accounted for only about one-third of eBay's items.

eBay's members, or users (never called customers), would tell you that one reason the system has been successful is that they feel like "winners" whenever they are successful at an auction. The members police themselves, providing feedback points to each other so that disreputable buyers and sellers are quickly identified. Members also communicate directly with eBay's staff to point out problems and suggest solutions. In addition, it is very easy for members to use eBay's system.

A NEW CEO

In 1997, eBay recruited Meg Whitman to become the company's CEO. Whitman had worked at Disney and Hasbro, but was not an Internet junkie. She had degrees from Princeton and Harvard and brought with her a marketing background built on a commitment to customer satisfaction. When Whitman took over, the company had only $49 million in merchandise sales. She helped the company go public in 1998.

Whitman has led eBay through many changes. Recently, the company instituted a "buy-it-now" pricing system that lets a seller set a fixed price at which a buyer can purchase the item without going through the traditional auction process. Whitman estimates that this type of purchase will increase from 20 percent to 33 percent of eBay's sales.

Although the company began as a way for individuals to buy and sell, many people have realized that it is a perfect vehicle for their own businesses. As a result, analysts estimate that there are over 200,000 businesses that exist only on eBay.

NEW FRONTIERS

eBay has announced that its goal is to achieve sales of $3 billion by 2005. To reach this lofty target, Whitman realizes that eBay must develop international markets—especially in light of analysts' suggestions that the company's core U.S. market growth rate is slowing and advertising revenues are down due to the economic slowdown.

eBay has already ventured into international markets. It has operations in Australia, Austria, Canada, France, Germany, Ireland, Italy, New Zealand, Switzerland, and the United Kingdom. In the first quarter of 2002, international revenues accounted for 21 percent of eBay's revenues, up from 18 percent in the last quarter of 2001; and its 2001 international revenue reached $115 million, up from $34 million a year earlier.

Despite eBay's progress in international markets, all has not gone well. Yahoo! Japan beat eBay to the punch by offering online auctions in Japan in September 1999. eBay entered Japan five months later, but those five months were critical. eBay charged a fee for each transaction, which Yahoo! did not, and required users to provide a credit card number. Many young Japanese do not use credit cards, preferring to pay by cash or bank draft. Further, although many observers thought online auctions would not work in Japan due to Japanese reluctance to buy used goods from strangers, its economic recession and the emergence of environmental awareness helped to overcome this reluctance. Plus, Yahoo! users could adopt Internet nicknames for their transactions, removing some of the stigma. Then, observers suggested, eBay was slow to adopt local touches, like horoscopes and newsletters, that it needed to attract users. eBay compounded all this by taking a low-key approach to promotion, while Yahoo! bought billboards and opened an Internet café with Starbucks.

All these missteps, analysts argue, resulted in the "network effect." Sellers want to go where there are buyers, and buyers want to go where there is a large selection, i.e., sellers. Once this network reaches critical mass, it becomes very difficult for a competitor to succeed. Sellers and buyers flocked to Yahoo!, and by mid-2001, Yahoo! had captured 95 percent of the $1.6 billion online market—eBay had only 3 percent. By early 2002, eBay threw in the towel and announced its withdrawal from Japan.

Within weeks, however, eBay announced it had purchased 33 percent of a China Internet auction site, EachNet, for $30 million. Two young entrepreneurs who met at Harvard Business School started EachNet in 1999. Shao Yibo and Tan Haiyin studied Internet businesses as part of a class project and decided that the eBay model was the only one that would work in Asia. With support from Asian venture capitalists, they launched their site, which by 2002 had 3.5 million registered users and 50,000 items listed for sale.

Although eBay executives argue that the eBay model has universal application, the company's experience in Japan and China highlight key differences as companies move from one national market to another. In China, for example, EachNet's customers hurried to the site to trade practical items like apparel or cellular phones, not the collectibles that fueled growth in the U.S. market. Rather than use the postal or courier systems to make payment, as one might do in the United States, Chinese traders mostly sell within their own cities. Although transportation systems are improving, they are still creaky by U.S. standards, so shipping items is not easy or reliable. Many Chinese still don't feel comfortable doing business online, especially when they are dealing with other individuals rather than companies. Moreover, e-commerce companies have also been concerned about regulation by the Chinese government. In early 2002, the government blocked access to foreign-based news and information sites.

China represents the world's fifth largest online economy, with 27 million Internet users. Of these, some 32 percent indicate they made purchases online in the past year. Yet 30 percent of users say they rarely visit an e-commerce site. With a population of over 1 billion people, however, there certainly is plenty of room for growth.

Meg Whitman and eBay's other executives know that to meet their sales and revenue targets, they must be successful in international markets—especially in China. eBay is the world's largest person-to-person trading community. Whitman hopes that China, with the world's largest population, will be a perfect fit for eBay's business model.

QUESTIONS FOR DISCUSSION

1. What are the forces shaping the development of Internet businesses like eBay in the United States? How are these forces similar or different in other countries, such as Japan or China?
2. How do the text's terms "customization" and "customerization" apply to eBay's marketing strategy?
3. How does eBay create value for the members of its community?

4. What marketing recommendations would you make to eBay to help it be successful as it enters the Chinese market?

Sources: Jerry Adler, "The eBay Way of Life," *Newsweek,* June 17, 2002, pp. 51–59; Brad Stone, "Meg Gets on the Line," *Newsweek,* June 17, 2002, p. 56; J. Baldauf, "eBay, Inc.," Merrill Lynch Capital Markets, June 6, 2002; H. B. Becker, "eBay, Inc.," Lehman Brothers, Inc., April 24, 2002; "eBay in China," *China E-Business,* April 1, 2002, p. 4; Nick Wingfield and Connie Ling, "Unbowed by Its Failure in Japan, eBay Will Try Its Hand in China," *Wall Street Journal,* March 18, 2002, p. B1; Ina Steiner, "eBay Regroups in Asia: Goodbye Japan, Hello China," www.auctionbytes.com, NewsFlash Number 266, February 27, 2002; Ken Belson, Rob Hoff, and Ben Elgin, "How Yahoo! Japan Beat eBay at Its Own Game, *BusinessWeek Online,* June 4, 2001; Bruce Einhorn, "Can EachNet Become an eBay in China's Image," *BusinessWeek Online,* March 27, 2000; www.ebay.com.

Case Pilot Case for Part 1: Understanding Marketing and Marketing Processes

Advantage Transportation Systems: Understanding Marketing and Marketing Processes

The agenda was full of discussion items for the annual manager's meeting held at Advantage Transportation System's (ATS) national headquarters in Detroit. ATS's president and owner, Victorio Fedeli, wanted his ten territorial marketing managers to devise a plan to improve company net profits, which had averaged 5 percent of sales for the past five years, to the industry average of 8 percent.

The company specialized in transporting small-and medium-sized cars from manufacturers to dealers via transport truck, and had become one of the top six national competitors, capturing nine percent of North America's $450 million per year market. Sales for ATS had increased by an average of 10 percent annually since it started 13 years earlier, and profits had remained stable. Strong financial results were important to Victorio, who was interested in soon arranging an initial public offering (IPO) of ATS shares to help raise funds for expansion. The company was divided into ten different territories, each managed by a regional marketing director who reported directly to Victorio.

Victorio began the meeting by asking for a report on recent marketing financial results and company sales updates. The new West-Coast manager, Alec, indicated that preliminary talks with a large domestic auto manufacturer regarding an exclusive transportation deal for all of their vehicles was promising and could lead to a profitable contract in the future. As a former executive at a car manufacturer, Victorio knew that exclusive contracts in the industry were rare, but ATS's high levels of reliability, customer service, and competitive prices would hopefully help make this deal possible.

Later in the meeting, Lilly, the Mid-West's manager, announced that due to the growing popularity of sport utility vehicles (SUVs), ATS lost one customer to a competitor that could transport larger SUV vehicles on its trucks, while ATS trucks could only handle nor-

mal cars. Lilly went on to say that a national railway company had also recently lowered its rates for transporting vehicles by 10 percent, resulting in ATS losing another contract. This recent news surprised Victorio, and to keep his managers motivated, he quickly reviewed the financial results for the past two months and reinforced that ATS had sufficient financial strength to handle such losses for now.

At the luncheon break, Victorio was approached by Chantelle, the Chief Financial Officer, who commented, "Victorio, I don't think we should take this news too lightly; short-term results are important, but I'm worried because you know we don't have any long-term plans to deal with problems like these." As Victorio sat and reflected on Chantelle's comments, he leafed through ATS's most recent promotional material and wondered what new initiatives could be put into place to best help ATS succeed in the future.

Case Pilot Challenge

Part 1 of the text covered three chapters that discussed how marketing affects our lives, why strategic marketing plans helps businesses, and the various approaches for monitoring an organization's external environment.

In the Advantage Transportation Systems case, above, the manager faces a series of issues that need to be resolved. Try your marketing management skills, visit www.prenhall.com/casepilot/, and see if you can find the answers to the following:

a) What environmental trends are most crucial to the business?

b) Could a strategic marketing plan help the business?

c) What marketing issues should the company address first?

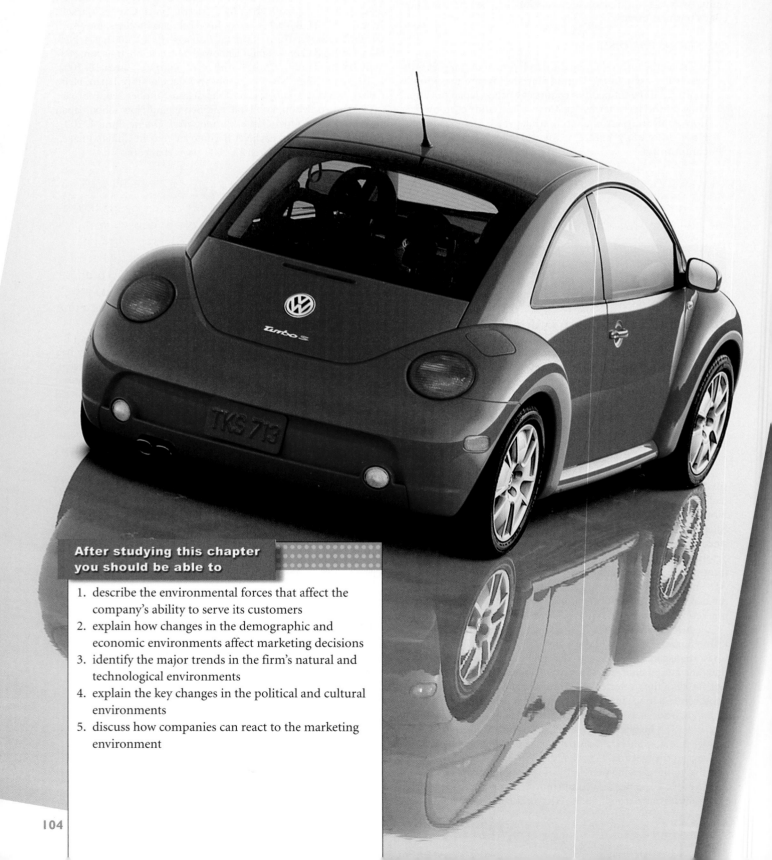

104

After studying this chapter you should be able to

1. describe the environmental forces that affect the company's ability to serve its customers
2. explain how changes in the demographic and economic environments affect marketing decisions
3. identify the major trends in the firm's natural and technological environments
4. explain the key changes in the political and cultural environments
5. discuss how companies can react to the marketing environment

The Marketing Environment

LOOKING AHEAD: PREVIEWING THE CONCEPTS

Now that you've seen how the new Internet age has affected marketing, let's look into other areas of the marketing environment. In this chapter, you'll discover that marketing does not operate in a vacuum but rather in a complex and changing environment. Other *actors* in this environment—suppliers, intermediaries, customers, competitors, publics, and others—may work with or against the company. Major environmental *forces*—demographic, economic, natural, technological, political, and cultural—shape marketing opportunities, pose threats, and affect the company's ability to serve customers and develop lasting relationships with them. To understand marketing, and to develop effective marketing strategies, you must first understand the context in which marketing operates.

First, we'll check out a major development in the marketing environment—millennial fever—and the nostalgia boom that it has produced. Volkswagen responded with the introduction of a born-again New Beetle. As you read on, ask yourself: What has made this little car so right for the times?

As we hurtle into the new millennium, social experts are busier than ever assessing the impact of a host of environmental forces on consumers and the marketers who serve them. "An old year turns into a new one," reflects one such expert, "and the world itself, at least for a moment, seems to turn also. Images of death and rebirth, things ending and beginning, populate . . . and haunt the mind. Multiply this a thousand-fold, and you get 'millennial fever' . . . driving consumer behavior in all sorts of interesting ways."

Such millennial fever has hit the nation's baby boomers, the most commercially influential demographic group in history, especially hard. The oldest boomers, now in their mid-fifties, are resisting the aging process with the vigor they once reserved for antiwar protests. Other factors are also at work. Today, people of all ages seem to feel a bit overworked, overstimulated, overloaded, and technostressed. "Americans are overwhelmed . . . by the breathtaking onrush of the Information Age, with its high-speed modems, cell phones, and pagers," suggests the expert. "While we hail the benefits of these wired [times], at the same time we are buffeted by the rapid pace of change."

The result of this "millennial fever" is a yearning to turn back the clock, to return to simpler times. This yearning has in turn produced a massive nostalgia wave. Marketers of all kinds have responded to these nostalgia pangs by recreating products and images that help take consumers back to "the good old days." Examples are plentiful: Kellogg has revived old Corn Flakes packaging, and carmakers have created retro roadsters such as the Porsche Boxter and Chrysler's PT Cruiser. A Pepsi commercial rocks to the Rolling Stones's "Brown Sugar," James Brown's "I Feel Good" helps sell Senokot laxatives, and Janis Joplin's raspy voice crows, "Oh Lord, won't you buy me a Mercedes-Benz?" Heinz reintroduced its classic glass ketchup bottle, supported by nostalgic "Heinz was there" ads showing two 1950s-era boys eating hot dogs at a ballpark. And the television networks launched what one analyst calls a "retro feeding frenzy" of reunion programs "that revisit the good (*M*A*S*H*, *L.A. Law*, *The Cosby Show*, *The Mary Tyler Moore Show*), the bad (*That's Incredible!*, *Laverne & Shirley*), and the truly ancient (*American Bandstand*, *The Honeymooners*).

Perhaps no company has been more successful in riding the nostalgia wave than Volkswagen. The original Volkswagen Beetle first sputtered into America in 1949. With its simple, buglike design, no-frills engineering, and economical operation, the Beetle was the antithesis of Detroit's chrome-laden gas guzzlers. Although most owners would readily admit that their Beetles were underpowered, noisy, cramped, and freezing in the winter, they saw these as endearing qualities. Overriding these minor inconveniences, the Beetle was cheap to buy and own, dependable, easy to fix, fun to drive, and anything but flashy.

During the 1960s, as young baby boomers by the thousands were buying their first cars, demand exploded and the Beetle blossomed into an unlikely icon. Bursting with personality, the understated Bug came to personify an era of rebellion against conventions. It became the most popular car in American history, with sales peaking at 423,000 in 1968. By the late 1970s, however, the boomers had moved on, Bug mania had faded, and Volkswagen had dropped Beetle production for the United States. Still, decades later, the mere mention of these chugging oddities evokes smiles and strong emotions. Almost everyone over the age of 30, it seems, has a "feel-good" Beetle story to tell.

In an attempt to surf the nostalgia wave, Volkswagen introduced a New Beetle in 1998. Outwardly, the reborn Beetle resembles the original, tapping the strong emotions and memories of times gone by. Beneath the skin, however, the New Beetle is packed with modern features. According to an industry expert, "The Beetle comeback is . . . based on a combination of romance and reason. . . . Built into the dashboard is a bud vase perfect for a daisy plucked straight from the 1960s. But right next to it is a high-tech multi-speaker stereo—and options like power windows, cruise control, and a power sunroof make it a very different car than the rattly old Bug. The new version . . . comes with all the modern features car buyers demand, such as four air bags and power outlets for cell phones. But that's not why . . . folks buy it. With a familiar bubble shape that still makes people smile as it skitters by, the new Beetle offers a pull that is purely emotional."

Initial advertising for the New Beetle played strongly on the nostalgia theme, while at the same time refreshing the old Beetle heritage. "If you sold your soul in the '80s," tweaked one ad, "here's your chance to buy it back." Other ads read, "Less flower, more power," and "Comes with wonderful new features. Like heat." Still another ad declared "0 to 60? Yes."

Volkswagen invested $560 million to bring the New Beetle to market. However, this investment paid big dividends as demand quickly outstripped supply. Even before the first cars reached VW showrooms, dealers across the country had long waiting lists of people who'd paid for the car without ever seeing it, let alone driving it. One California dealer claimed that the New Beetle was such a traffic magnet that he had to remove it from his showroom floor every afternoon at 2 P.M. to discourage gawkers and let his salespeople work with serious prospects.

The New Beetle turned out to be a cross-generational hit, appealing to more than just Woodstock-recovered baby boomers. Even kids too young to remember the original Bug loved this new one. One customer confirms the car's broad appeal: "In 1967, my Dad got me a VW. I loved it. I'm sure the new one will take me back. I'm getting the New Beetle as a surprise for my daughter, but I'm sure I'm going to be stealing it from her all the time."

Volkswagen's first-year sales projections of 50,000 New Beetles in North American proved pessimistic. After only nine months, the company had sold more than 64,000 of the new Bugs in the United States and Canada. The smart little car also garnered numerous distinguished awards, including *Motor Trend*'s 1999 Import Car of the Year, *Time* magazine's The Best of 1998 Design, *Business Week*'s Best New Products, and 1999 North American Car of the Year, awarded by an independent panel of top journalists who cover the auto industry. Sales are still sizzling—the New Beetle now accounts for more than a quarter of Volkswagen's U.S. sales and has helped win VW a fivefold increase in sales since 1993. The car was selected as *Money Magazine*'s Best Car of 2001. To follow up, Volkswagen plans to introduce a reincarnation of its old cult-classic flower-power Microbus in 2005. Although most younger buyers won't remember much about the original Microbus unless they encountered one at a Grateful Dead concert, test models have received rave reviews at auto shows in Japan and Europe.

"Millennial fever" results from the convergence of a wide range of forces in the marketing environment—from technological, economic, and demographic forces to cultural, social, and political ones. Most trend analysts believe that the nostalgia craze will only grow as the baby boomers continue to mature. If so, the New Beetle, so full of the past, has a very bright future. "The Beetle is not just empty nostalgia," says Gerald Celente, publisher of *Trend Journal*. "It is a practical car that is also tied closely to the emotions of a generation." Says another trend analyst, the New Beetle "is our romantic past, reinvented for our hectic here-and-now. Different, yet deeply familiar—a car for the times."[1]

Marketing environment
The actors and forces outside marketing that affect marketing management's ability to build and maintain successful relationships with target customers.

As noted in previous chapters, marketers operate in an increasing connected world. They must be good at *customer relationship management* and *partner relationship management* in order to connect effectively with customers, others in the company, and external partners. However, to do this effectively, marketers must understand the major environmental forces that surround all of these relationships. A company's **marketing environment** consists of the actors and forces outside marketing that affect marketing management's ability to build and maintain successful relationships with target customers. The marketing environment offers both opportunities and threats. Successful companies know the vital importance of constantly watching and adapting to the changing environment.

As we move into the twenty-first century, both consumers and marketers wonder what the future will bring. The environment continues to change at a rapid pace. For example, think about how you buy groceries today. How will your grocery buying change during the next few decades?

What challenges will these changes present for marketers? Here's what two leading futurists envision for the year 2025.

> We won't be shopping in 21-aisle supermarkets in 2025, predicts Gary Wright, corporate demographer for Procter & Gamble in Cincinnati. The growth of e-commerce and the rapid speed of the Internet will lead to online ordering of lower-priced, nonperishable products—everything from peanut butter to coffee filters. Retailers will become "bundlers," combining these orders into large packages of goods for each household and delivering them efficiently to their doorsteps. As a result, we'll see mergers between retailing and home-delivery giants—think Wal-MartExpress, a powerful combo of Wal-Mart and FedEx. Consumers won't waste precious time searching for the best-priced bundle. Online information agents will do it for them, comparing prices among competitors.

> By 2025, computers will essentially be as smart as humans, contends [futurist Ryan Mathews], and consumers will use them to exchange information with on-screen electronic agents that ferret out the best deals online. Thanks to embedded-chip technology in the pantry, products on a CHR (continuous household replenishment) list—such as paper towels and pet food—will sense when they're running low and reorder themselves automatically. If the information agent finds a comparable but cheaper substitute for a CHR product, the item will be switched instantly.[2]

Microenvironment
The actors close to the company that affect its ability to serve its customers—the company, suppliers, marketing intermediaries, customer markets, competitors, and publics.

Macroenvironment
The larger societal forces that affect the microenvironment—demographic, economic, natural, technological, political, and cultural forces.

Such pictures of the future give marketers plenty to think about. More than any other group in the company, marketers must be the trend trackers and opportunity seekers. Although every manager in an organization needs to observe the outside environment, marketers have two special aptitudes. They have disciplined methods—marketing intelligence and marketing research—for collecting information about the marketing environment. They also spend more time in the customer and competitor environments. By carefully studying the environment, marketers can adapt marketing strategies to meet new marketplace challenges and opportunities.

The marketing environment is made up of a *microenvironment* and a *macroenvironment*. The **microenvironment** consists of the actors close to the company that affect its ability to serve its customers—the company, suppliers, marketing intermediaries, customer markets, competitors, and publics. The **macroenvironment** consists of the larger societal forces that affect the microenvironment—demographic, economic, natural, technological, political, and cultural forces. We look first at the company's microenvironment.

The Company's Microenvironment

Marketing management's job is to build relationships with customers by creating customer value and satisfaction. However, marketing managers cannot do this alone. Figure 4.1 shows the major actors in the marketer's microenvironment. Marketing success will require working closely with other company departments, suppliers, marketing intermediaries, customers, competitors, and various publics, which combine to make up the company's value delivery network.

FIGURE 4.1
Actors in the microenvironment

The Company

In designing marketing plans, marketing management takes other company groups into account—groups such as top management, finance, research and development (R&D), purchasing, operations, and accounting. All these interrelated groups form the internal environment. Top management sets the company's mission, objectives, broad strategies, and policies. Marketing managers make decisions within the strategies and plans made by top management.

Marketing managers must also work closely with other company departments. Finance is concerned with finding and using funds to carry out the marketing plan. The R&D department focuses on designing safe and attractive products. Purchasing worries about getting supplies and materials, whereas operations is responsible for producing and distributing the desired quality and quantity of products. Accounting has to measure revenues and costs to help marketing know how well it is achieving its objectives. Together, all of these departments have an impact on the marketing department's plans and actions. Under the marketing concept, all of these functions must "think consumer." They should work in harmony to provide superior customer value and satisfaction.

Suppliers

Suppliers form an important link in the company's overall customer value delivery system. They provide the resources needed by the company to produce its goods and services. Supplier problems can seriously affect marketing. Marketing managers must watch supply availability—supply shortages or delays, labor strikes, and other events can cost sales in the short run and damage customer satisfaction in the long run. Marketing managers also monitor the price trends of their key inputs. Rising supply costs may force price increases that can harm the company's sales volume. Most marketers today treat their suppliers as partners in creating and delivering customer value.

Marketing Intermediaries

Marketing intermediaries

Firms that help the company to promote, sell, and distribute its goods to final buyers; they include resellers, physical distribution firms, marketing service agencies, and financial intermediaries.

Marketing intermediaries help the company to promote, sell, and distribute its goods to final buyers. They include *resellers, physical distribution firms, marketing services agencies,* and *financial intermediaries. Resellers* are distribution channel firms that help the company find customers or make sales to them. These include wholesalers and retailers, who buy and resell merchandise. Selecting and partnering with resellers is not easy. No longer do manufacturers have many small, independent resellers from which to choose. They now face large and growing reseller organizations such as Wal-Mart, Home Depot, and Best Buy. These organizations frequently have enough power to dictate terms or even shut the manufacturer out of large markets.

Physical distribution firms help the company to stock and move goods from their points of origin to their destinations. Working with warehouse and transportation firms, a company must determine the best ways to store and ship goods, balancing factors such as cost, delivery, speed, and safety. *Marketing services agencies* are the marketing research firms, advertising agencies, media firms, and marketing consulting firms that help the company target and promote its products to the right markets. When the company decides to use one of these agencies, it must choose carefully because these firms vary in creativity, quality, service, and price. *Financial intermediaries* include banks, credit companies, insurance companies, and other businesses that help finance transactions or insure against the risks associated with the buying and selling of goods. Most firms and customers depend on financial intermediaries to finance their transactions.

Like suppliers, marketing intermediaries form an important component of the company's overall value delivery system. In its quest to create satisfying customer relationships, the company must do more than just optimize its own performance. It must partner effectively with marketing intermediaries to optimize the performance of the entire system.

Thus, today's marketers recognize the importance of working with their intermediaries as partners rather than simply as channels through which they sell their products. For example, Coca-Cola has a 10-year deal with Wendy's that makes it the fast-food chain's exclusive soft drink provider. In the deal, Coca-Cola provides Wendy's much more than just soft drinks. It also pledges powerful marketing support.

Along with the soft drinks, Wendy's gets a cross-functional team of 50 Coke employees who are dedicated to understanding the finer points of Wendy's business. It also benefits from

Partnering with marketing intermediaries: Coca-Cola provides Wendy's much more than just soft drinks. It also pledges powerful marketing support.

Coke dollars spent in joint marketing campaigns. Bigger still is the staggering amount of consumer research that Coca-Cola provides its partners. Coke provides both analysis of syndicated information and access to Coke's own internal research on consumers' eating-out habits. It goes to great lengths to understand beverage drinkers—and to make sure its partners can use those insights. The company has also analyzed the demographics of every zip code in the country and used the information to create a software program called Solver. By answering questions about their target audience, Wendy's franchise owners can determine which Coke brands are preferred by the customers in their area. Coca-Cola also has even studied the design of drive-through menu boards to better understand which layouts, fonts, letter sizes, colors, and visuals induce consumers to order more food and drink.[3]

Customers

The company needs to study five types of customer markets closely. *Consumer markets* consist of individuals and households that buy goods and services for personal consumption. *Business markets* buy goods and services for further processing or for use in their production process, whereas *reseller markets* buy goods and services to resell at a profit. *Government markets* are made up of government agencies that buy goods and services to produce public services or transfer the goods and services to others who need them. Finally, *international markets* consist of these buyers in other countries, including consumers, producers, resellers, and governments. Each market type has special characteristics that call for careful study by the seller.

Competitors

The marketing concept states that to be successful, a company must provide greater customer value and satisfaction than its competitors do. Thus, marketers must do more than simply adapt to the needs of target consumers. They also must gain strategic advantage by positioning their offerings strongly against competitors' offerings in the minds of consumers.

No single competitive marketing strategy is best for all companies. Each firm should consider its own size and industry position compared to those of its competitors. Large firms with dominant positions in an industry can use certain strategies that smaller firms cannot afford. But being large is not enough. There are winning strategies for large firms, but there are also losing ones. And small firms can develop strategies that give them better rates of return than large firms enjoy. We will look more deeply into competitor analysis and competitive marketing strategies in Chapter 17.

Publics

Public

Any group that has an actual or potential interest in or impact on an organization's ability to achieve its objectives.

The company's marketing environment also includes various publics. A **public** is any group that has an actual or potential interest in or impact on an organization's ability to achieve its objectives. We can identify seven types of publics:

- *Financial publics.* These publics influence the company's ability to obtain funds. Banks, investment houses, and stockholders are the major financial publics.
- *Media publics.* These include newspapers, magazines, and radio and television stations that carry news, features, and editorial opinion.
- *Government publics.* Management must take government developments into account. Marketers must often consult the company's lawyers on issues of product safety, truth in advertising, and other matters.
- *Citizen-action publics.* A company's marketing decisions may be questioned by consumer organizations, environmental groups, minority groups, and others. Its public relations department can help it stay in touch with consumer and citizen groups.
- *Local publics.* These include neighborhood residents and community organizations. Large companies usually appoint a community relations officer to deal with the community, attend meetings, answer questions, and contribute to worthwhile causes.
- *General public.* A company needs to be concerned about the general public's attitude toward its products and activities. The public's image of the company affects its buying.
- *Internal publics.* These include workers, managers, volunteers, and the board of directors. Large companies use newsletters and other means to inform and motivate their internal publics. When employees feel good about their company, this positive attitude spills over to external publics.

Publics: In this ad, Wal-Mart recognizes the importance of both its local and employee publics. Its Good Works scholarship program "is just one of the reasons Wal-Mart associates in Mississippi (such as Tiffany, at lower right), and all over the country, are proud to get involved in the communities they serve."

A company can prepare marketing plans for these major publics as well as for its customer markets. Suppose the company wants a specific response from a particular public, such as goodwill, favorable word of mouth, or donations of time or money. The company would have to design an offer to this public that is attractive enough to produce the desired response.

The Company's Macroenvironment

The company and all of the other actors operate in a larger macroenvironment of forces that shape opportunities and pose threats to the company. Figure 4.2 shows the six major forces in the company's macroenvironment. In the remaining sections of this chapter, we examine these forces and show how they affect marketing plans.

Demographic Environment

Demography

The study of human populations in terms of size, density, location, age, gender, race, occupation, and other statistics.

Demography is the study of human populations in terms of size, density, location, age, gender, race, occupation, and other statistics. The demographic environment is of major interest to marketers because it involves people, and people make up markets.

The world population is growing at an explosive rate. It now totals more than 6.2 billion and will exceed 7.9 billion by the year 2025.[4] The world's large and highly diverse population poses both opportunities and challenges. Think for a few minutes about the world and your place in it. If we reduced the world to a village of 1,000 people representative of the world's population, this would be our reality:[5]

- Our village would have 520 females and 480 males, including 330 children and 60 people over age 65, 10 college graduates, and 335 illiterate adults.

- We'd have 52 North Americans, 55 Russians, 84 Latin Americans, 95 Europeans, 124 Africans, and 584 Asians.

- Communication would be difficult: 165 of us would speak Mandarin, 85 English, 83 Hindi, 64 Spanish, 58 Russian, and 37 Arabic. The other half of us would speak one of more than 5,000 other languages.

- Among us we'd have 329 Christians, 178 Moslems, 32 Hindus, 60 Buddhists, 3 Jews, 167 non-religious, 45 atheists, and 86 others.

- About one-third of our people would have access to clean, safe drinking water. About half of our children would be immunized against infections.

- The woodlands in our village would be decreasing rapidly, and wasteland would be growing. Forty percent of the village's cropland, nourished by 83 percent of our fertilizer, would produce 72 percent of the food to feed its 270 well-fed owners. The remaining 60 percent of the land and 17 percent of the fertilizer would produce 28 percent of the food to feed the other 730 people. Five hundred people in the village would suffer from malnutrition.

- Only 200 of the 1,000 people would control 75 percent of our village's wealth. Another 200 would receive only 2 percent of the wealth. Seventy people would own cars. One would have a computer, and that computer probably would not be connected to the Internet. Only 70 of us would own a car.

FIGURE 4.2
Major forces in the company's macroenvironment

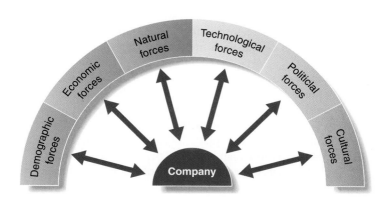

The world population is growing at an explosive rate, presenting both opportunities and challenges for marketers. Think for a few minutes about the world and your place in it.

The explosive world population growth has major implications for business. A growing population means growing human needs to satisfy. Depending on purchasing power, it may also mean growing market opportunities. For example, to curb its skyrocketing population, the Chinese government has passed regulations limiting families to one child each. As a result, Chinese children are spoiled and fussed over as never before. Known in China as "little emperors and empresses," Chinese children are being showered with everything from candy to computers as a result of what's known as the "six-pocket syndrome." As many as six adults—including parents and two sets of doting grandparents—may be indulging the whims of each child. Parents in the average Beijing household now spend about 40 percent of their income on their cherished only child. This trend has encouraged toy companies such as Japan's Bandai Company (known for its Mighty Morphin Power Rangers), Denmark's Lego Group, and Mattel to enter the Chinese market. And McDonald's has triumphed in China in part because it has catered successfully to this pampered generation.[6]

Thus, marketers keep close track of demographic trends and developments in their markets, both at home and abroad. They track changing age and family structures, geographic population shifts, educational characteristics, and population diversity. Here, we discuss the most important demographic trends in the United States.

Changing Age Structure of the Population

The U.S. population stood at more than 287 million in 2002 and may reach 340 million by the year 2025.[7] The single most important demographic trend in the United States is the changing age structure of the population. As shown in Figure 4.3, the U.S. population contains seven generational groups. Here, we discuss the three largest age groups—the baby boomers, Generation X, and Generation Y—and their impact on today's marketing strategies.

Baby boomers

The 78 million people born during the baby boom, following World War II and lasting until the early 1960s.

The Baby Boomers. The post–World War II baby boom produced 78 million **baby boomers,** born between 1946 and 1964. Since then, the baby boomers have become one of the most powerful forces shaping the marketing environment. The boomers have presented a moving target, creating new markets as they grew from infancy to their preadolescent, teenage, young adult, and now middle-age to mature years. Today's baby boomers account for about 28 percent of the population but earn more than half of all personal income.

Baby boomers cut across all walks of life. But marketers typically have paid the most attention to the smaller upper crust of the boomer generation—its more educated, mobile, and

FIGURE 4.3

The seven U.S. generations

Source: Adapted from Alison Stein Wellner, "Generational Divide," *American Demographics,* October 2000, pp. 53–58.

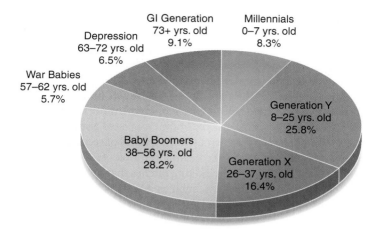

wealthy segments. These segments have gone by many names. In the 1980s, they were called "yuppies" (young urban professionals), "bumpies" (black upwardly mobile professionals), "yummies" (young upwardly mobile mommies), and "DINKs" (dual-income, no-kids couples). In the 1990s, however, yuppies and DINKs gave way to a new breed, with names such as "DEWKs" (dual-earners with kids) and "MOBYs" (mother older, baby younger). Now, to the chagrin of many in this generation, they are acquiring such titles as "WOOFs" (well-off older folks) or even "GRUMPIES" (just what the name suggests).

The youngest boomers are now in their late thirties; the oldest are in their mid-fifties. In fact, somewhere in America, seven boomers will turn 50 every minute from now until 2014. Thus, the boomers have evolved from the "youthquake generation" to the "backache generation." The maturing boomers are experiencing the pangs of midlife and rethinking the purpose and value of their work, responsibilities, and relationships. They are approaching life with a new stability and reasonableness in the way they live, think, eat, and spend. As they continue to age, they will create a large and important seniors market. By 2025, there will be 64 million baby boomers aged 61 to 79, a 90 percent increase in the size of this population from today.[8]

As they mature, the boomers are also reaching their peak earning and spending years. Thus, they constitute a lucrative market for new housing and home remodeling, financial services, travel and entertainment, eating out, health and fitness products, and high-priced cars and other luxuries. It would be a mistake to think of the boomers as aging and staid. Many boomers are rediscovering the excitement of life and have the means to play it out. For example, according to the Travel Industry Association of America, one-half of all U.S. adults took adventure vacations within the past five years. Some 56 percent of these travelers were boomers. And the median age of a Harley-Davidson buyer is 44.6 years old, squarely in the middle of the boomer age range.[9]

The nation's maturing baby boomers constitute a lucrative market for products and services ranging from health and fitness products to financial services, entertainment, and travel. Some 56 percent of the adults who've taken adventure vacations during the past five years have been boomers.

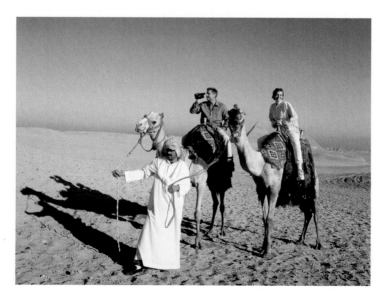

Generation X

The 45 million people born between 1965 and 1976 in the "birth dearth" following the baby boom.

Generation X.   The baby boom was followed by a "birth dearth," creating another generation of 45 million people born between 1965 and 1976. Author Douglas Coupland calls them **Generation X,** because they lie in the shadow of the boomers and lack obvious distinguishing characteristics. Others call them the "baby busters," the "shadow generation," or the "yiffies"—young, individualistic, freedom-minded few.

The Generation Xers are defined as much by their shared experiences as by their age. Increasing divorce rates and higher employment for their mothers made them the first generation of latchkey kids. Whereas the boomers created a sexual revolution, the GenXers have lived in the age of AIDS. Having grown up during times of recession and corporate downsizing, they have developed a more cautious economic outlook. As a result, the GenXers are a more skeptical bunch, cynical of frivolous marketing pitches that promise easy success.

They buy lots of products, such as sweaters, boots, cosmetics, electronics, cars, fast food, computers, and mountain bikes. However, their cynicism makes them more savvy shoppers, and their financial pressures make them more value conscious. They like lower prices and a more functional look. The GenXers respond to honesty in advertising, and they like irreverence and sass and ads that mock the traditional advertising approach. For example, Miller Brewing Company ads appealing to this group have advised, "It's time to embrace your inner idiot," and one featured images of a frenetic, sloppy, hot-dog–eating contest.

GenXers share new cultural concerns. They care about the environment and respond favorably to socially responsible companies. Although they seek success, they are less materialistic; they prize experience, not acquisition. They are cautious romantics who want a better quality of life and are more interested in job satisfaction than in sacrificing personal happiness and growth for promotion.

Once labeled as "the MTV generation" and as body-piercing slackers who whined about "McJobs," the GenXers have now grown up and are beginning to take over. They do surf the Internet more than other groups, but with serious intent. The GenXers are poised to displace the lifestyles, culture, and materialistic values of the baby boomers. And they represent $125 billion in annual purchasing power. By the year 2010, they will have overtaken the baby boomers as a primary market for almost every product category.[10]

Generation Y

The 72 million children of the baby boomers, born between 1977 and 1994.

Generation Y.   Both the baby boomers and GenXers will one day be passing the reins to the latest demographic group, **Generation Y** (or the echo boomers). Born between 1977 and 1994, these children of the baby boomers now number 72 million, dwarfing the GenXers and almost equal in size to the baby boomer segment. Ranging from preteens to mid-twenties, the echo boomer generation is still forming its buying preferences and behaviors.

The echo boom has created large kid and teen markets (see Real Marketing 4.1).[11] After years of bust, markets for kids' and teen's toys and games, clothes, furniture, and food have enjoyed a boom. Designers and retailers have created new lines, new products, and even new stores devoted to children and teens—Tommy Hilfiger, DKNY, Gap, Toys "R" Us, Guess, Talbots, Pottery Barn, and Eddie Bauer, to name just a few. New media appeared that cater specifically to this market: *Time, Sports Illustrated,* and *People* have all started new editions for kids and teens. Banks have offered banking and investment services for kids, including investment camps.

Generation Y oldsters are now graduating from college and beginning careers. Like the trailing edge of the Generation Xers ahead of them, one distinguishing characteristic of Generation Y is their utter fluency and comfort with computer, digital, and Internet technology. For this reason, one analyst has christened them the Net-Gens (or N-Gens). He observes:

> What makes this generation different . . . is not just its demographic muscle, but it is the first to grow up surrounded by digital media. Computers and other digital technologies, such as digital cameras, are commonplace to N-Gen members. They work with them at home, in school, and they use them for entertainment. [They] are so bathed in bits that they are no more intimidated by digital technology than a VCR or a toaster. And it is through their use of the digital media that N-Gen will develop and superimpose its culture on the rest of society. Boomers stand back. Already these kids are learning, playing, communicating, working, and creating communities very differently than did their parents. They are a force for social transformation.[12]

Generation Y represents a complex target for marketers. On average, Gen Ys have access to 62 TV channels, not to mention mobile phones, personal digital assistants (PDAs), and the Internet,

real marketing 4.1

The Teen Market: Youth Will Be Served

Gone are the days when kids saved up their pennies for candy and ice cream at the corner soda fountain. Today's teens are big spenders. The average U.S. teen spends $104

Marketing to teens: Based on focus group research, Wildseed developed cell phones with "smart skins"—replaceable faceplates with computer chips that let teens individualize the phone's functions and appearance to match their personalities.

each week; combined, the nation's 32 million 12-to-19-year-olds spend more than $172 billion a year. What's more, teens influence another $30 billion annually of their parents' spending. With so much cash to spend, teens represent a lucrative market for companies willing to cater to their often fickle, trend-driven tastes.

To tap into this vast market of potential new customers, all kinds of companies are targeting teens with new or modified products. Some of these products are naturals for the teen market, such as action movies, acne creams, teen magazines, cell phones, and 'N Sync. Others are less expected, such as Avon products, cars, and hotels. Here are just a few examples of companies attempting to cash in on the hot teen market:

- *Wildseed:* Software Company Wildseed has spent years conducting research to develop cell phones and intelligent faceplates for teens. For the last two years, the company has regularly summoned teenagers to focus groups, where it pays them $20 to lounge around, eat pizza, play Xbox video games, and give their thumbs-up or thumbs-down on various proposals. The research shows that for teenagers, a desirable cell phone is not about smaller, lighter, sleeker. What teens want from a cell phone ranges from the concrete (music, messaging, and games) to the abstract (style, personality, and individuality). As a result, Wildseed inspired phones will have "Smart Skins™"— replaceable intelligent faceplates with computer chips that allow teens to individualize the phone's functions and appearance to match their personalities. For example, skateboarders can choose graffiti-splattered intelligent faceplates that come with edgy urban ringer tones, gritty icons, screen savers, and games.

- *Teen Vogue:* After years of preliminary market testing, Vogue has announced that, starting in 2003, it will offer a teen version of its popular women's magazine. The publisher, Condé Nast, expects an initial subscription base of more than 450,000 teens.

- *Hot Topic:* Clothing retailer Hot Topic targets the 17 percent of American high school students who consider themselves "alternative teens." Hot Topic's buyers go to rock concerts and raves to check out what performers and fashion-forward fans are wearing. The store carries an assortment of items you just won't find at Abercrombie & Fitch. Rather than khakis

and tank tops, the store stocks fishnets, pink fur pants, blue hair dye, black nail polish, and T-shirts bearing the logos of defunct bands like the Ramones and the Dead Kennedys. Whereas Gap, American Eagle, and other teen retailers have recently reported flat or declining sales, Hot Topic's sales are, well, a hot topic.

- *Avon:* In 2003, Avon plans to roll out a Teen Business unit to target teenage buyers. The new department will employ teens as sales associates who sell to other teens through catalogs, direct selling, and the Internet. Says Avon's chief executive, Andrea Jung, "Marketing to teens is [part] of our stated strategy to extend Avon's brand equity into new customer segments, new distribution channels, and new product categories."

- *Rockport:* When you think of Rockport, you probably think of casual shoes and clothing for the older set. However, in an attempt to build relationships with 12-to-19-year-olds, Rockport recently teamed up with Dubit, a youth-focused company in the United Kingdom, to produce a 3D online store targeting teens (www.dubit.co.uk). Teens roaming Dubit's virtual mall can enter the Rockport store and check out shoes with real youth appeal—such as the Copepoda Crustacean, a sleek "performance sandal with a rubber outsole," or the Tactonic Open Road, a "retro bowling style trainer with a contrast stitching." In the corner of the store, a deejay takes requests and spins digital tracks onto a personalized MP3 player.

- *Ford Motor Company:* One study estimates that 4 million teens will reach driving age every year until 2010. With numbers like those, it's easy to see why car manufacturers market to teens who currently who ride bicycles, mount skateboards, or lace up inline skates. For example, the Ford Focus's marketing campaign includes interactive TV commercials, cinema advertising, and lots of promotional alliances targeting tomorrow's drivers. Most Focus marketing takes place at venues like "Hoop It Up," a national street basketball tour. The car's campaign is really an example of what every automaker is trying to do to reach teenagers.

(continued)

- *The Gorham Hotel:* Hotels and resorts are becoming more and more aware of the impact teens have family vacation decisions. According to one study, 82 percent of parents said they choose vacations based on their kids' input. As a result, many hotels are catering to teens by offering family packages that include access to teen nightclubs, special teen-oriented outings, and computer rooms with unlimited Internet access. At the Gorham Hotel in New York, catering to teens means giving them a little space—in their parents' rooms. Special suites have denlike

rooms with their own doors, pull-out sofas, television, phones, even Nintendo. Downstairs, in the lobby, the Gorham offers 24-hour access to the Internet.

Sources: Examples adapted from those found in Frand Washington, "Aim Young; No, Younger," *Advertising Age,* April 9, 2001; Nancy Keates, "Family Travel: Catering to Kids," *Wall Street Journal,* May 3, 2002, p. W-1; and Jennifer Lee, "Youth Will Be Served, Wirelessly," *New York Times,* May 30, 2002, p. G1. Also see Maureen Tkacik, "Hey Dude, This Sure Isn't the Gap—Pink Fur Pants,

Tongue Rings Draw 'Alternative' Teens to Hot Topic's Mall Stores," *Wall Street Journal,* February 12, 2002, p. B1; "Automakers Agree, Winning Youth Early Key to Future," *Advertising Age,* April 1, 2002, p. S16; Brian Steinberg, "Pop-In Pasta Aims to Lure Teenagers to Drop the Chips," *Wall Street Journal,* April 8, 2002, p. A.21c; "Rockport Opens 3D Shop on Teen Web Site," *Marketing Week,* May 23, 2002, p. 39; and "Debut of Teen Vogue Is Set," *New York Times,* June 7, 2002, p. 2.

offering broad media access. Studies have shown that Gen Y consumers are smart, aware, and fair-minded. They like to be entertained in ads directed at them but don't like ads that make fun of people. They love things that are "green" and they relate well to causes. Making connections now with Gen Ys will pay dividends to marketers beyond capturing their current spending. In future years, as they begin working and their buying power increases, this segment will more than rival the baby boomers in spending and market influence.[13]

Generational Marketing.   Do marketers have to create separate products and marketing programs for each generation? Some experts caution that each generation spans decades of time and many socioeconomic levels. For example, marketers often split the baby boomers into three smaller groups—leading boomers, core boomers, and trailing boomers—each with its own beliefs and behaviors. Similarly, they split Generation Y into Gen Y adults, Gen Y teens, and Gen Y kids. Thus, marketers need to form more precise age-specific segments within each group. More important, defining people by their birth date may be less effective than segmenting them by their lifestyle or life stage.

Others warn that marketers have to be careful about turning off one generation each time they craft a product or message that appeals effectively to another. "The idea is to try to be broadly inclusive and at the same time offer each generation something specifically designed for it," notes one expert. "Tommy Hilfiger has big brand logos on his clothes for teenagers and little pocket polo logos on his shirts for baby boomers. It's a brand that has a more inclusive than exclusive strategy."[14]

The Changing American Family

The "traditional household" consists of a husband, wife, and children (and sometimes grandparents). Yet, the once American ideal of the two child, two car suburban family has lately been losing some of its luster. "Ward and June Cleaver used to represent the typical American household," says one demographer. "Today, marketers would be remiss in not incorporating the likes of Murphy Brown, Ally McBeal, and Will and Grace into their business plans."[15]

In the United States today, married couples with children now make up only about 34 percent the nation's 105 million households, and this percentage is falling. Married couples and people living with other relatives make up 22 percent; single parents comprise another 12 percent. A full 32 percent are nonfamily households—single live-alones or adult live-togethers of one or both sexes.[16] More people are divorcing or separating, choosing not to marry, marrying later, or marrying without intending to have children. Marketers must increasingly consider the special needs of nontraditional households, because they are now growing more rapidly than traditional households. Each group has distinctive needs and buying habits.

The number of working women has also increased greatly, growing from under 30 percent of the U.S. workforce in 1950 to more than 46 percent by the late 1990s.[17] This trend has spawned the child day-care business and increased consumption of convenience foods and services, career-oriented women's clothing, financial services, and many other business opportunities. For example, new niche malls feature customized mixes of specialty shops with extended hours for working women who can find time to shop only before or after work. Stores in these malls feature targeted promotions and phone-in shopping. Busy shoppers can phone ahead with color choices and other preferences while store employees perform a "wardrobe consulting" service. At the same time, more and more workplaces and child-care centers are installing monitoring setups, such as "I See You" equipment from Simplex Knowledge. This system lets working parents see their children at different points throughout the day by viewing photos taken in the child-care center and posted on a secure Web site.[18]

Geographic Shifts in Population

This is a period of great migratory movements between and within countries. Americans, for example, are a mobile people, with about 16 percent of all U.S. residents moving each year.[19] Over the past two decades, the U.S. population has shifted toward the Sunbelt states. The West and South have grown, while the Midwest and Northeast states have lost population. Such population shifts interest marketers because people in different regions buy differently. For example, research shows that people in Seattle buy more toothbrushes per capita than people in any other U.S. city; people in Salt Lake City eat more candy bars; people from New Orleans use more ketchup; and people in Miami drink more prune juice.

Also, for more than a century, Americans have been moving from rural to metropolitan areas. In the 1950s, they made a massive exit from the cities to the suburbs. Today, the migration to the suburbs continues. And more and more Americans are moving to "micropolitan areas," small cities located beyond congested metropolitan areas. These smaller micros offer many of the advantages of metro areas—jobs, restaurants, diversions, community organizations—but without the population crush, traffic jams, high crime rates, and high property taxes often associated with heavily urbanized areas.[20]

The shift in where people live has also caused a shift in where they work. For example, the migration toward micropolitan and suburban areas has resulted in a rapid increase in the number of people who "telecommute"— work at home or in a remote office and conduct their business by phone, fax, modem, or the Internet. This trend, in turn, has created a booming SOHO (small office/home office) market. Nearly 40 million Americans are now working out of their homes with the help of electronic conveniences such as personal computers, cell phones, fax machines, and handheld organizers. Many marketers are actively courting the home office segment of this lucrative SOHO market. One example is Kinko's Copy Centers:

> Founded in the 1970s as a campus photocopying business, Kinko's is now reinventing itself as the well-appointed office outside the home. Where once there were copy machines, Kinko's 902 stores in this country and abroad now feature a uniform mixture of fax machines, ultrafast color

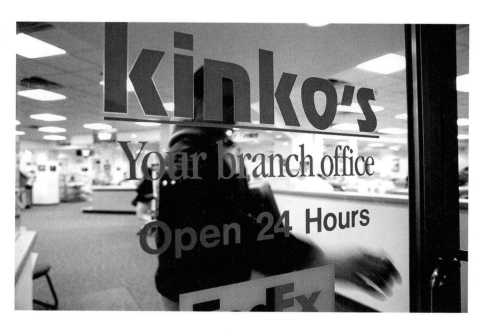

Geographic shifts: The shift in where people live has also caused a shift in where they work, creating a booming SOHO (small office/home office) market.

printers, and networks of computers equipped with popular software programs and high-speed Internet connections. People can come to a Kinko's store to do all their office jobs: They can copy, send and receive faxes, use various programs on the computer, go on the Internet, order stationery and other printed supplies, and even teleconference. As more and more people join the work-at-home trend, Kinko's offers an escape from the isolation of the home office. Besides adding state-of-the-art equipment, the company is talking to Starbucks about opening up coffee shops adjacent to some Kinko's stores. The lettering on the Kinko's door sums up the $1 billion company's new business model: "Your branch office/Open 24 hours."[21]

A Better-Educated and More White-Collar Population

The U.S. population is becoming better educated. For example, in 2000, 84 percent of the U.S. population over age 25 had completed high school and 26 percent had completed college, compared with 69 percent and 17 percent in 1980.[22] The rising number of educated people will lead to an increase in the demand for quality products, books, magazines, travel, personal computers, and Internet services. The workforce also is becoming more white collar. Between 1950 and 1985, the proportion of white collar workers rose from 41 percent to 54 percent, that of blue collar workers declined from 47 percent to 33 percent, and that of service workers increased from 12 percent to 14 percent. These trends have continued into the new millennium.[23]

Increasing Diversity

Countries vary in their ethnic and racial makeup. At one extreme is Japan, where almost everyone is Japanese. At the other extreme is the United States, with people from virtually all nations. The United States has often been called a melting pot—a place where diverse groups from many nations and cultures have melted into a single, more homogenous whole. Instead, the United States seems to have become more of a "salad bowl" in which various groups have mixed together but have maintained their diversity by retaining and valuing important ethnic and cultural differences.

Marketers are facing increasingly diverse markets, both at home and abroad as their operations become more international in scope. In the United States alone, ethnic population growth is 12 times greater than the Caucasian growth rate, and ethnic consumers buy more than $600 billion of goods and services each year. The U.S. population is 71 percent white, with African Americans and Hispanics each making up another 12 percent. The U.S. Asian American population now totals about 4 percent of the population, with the remaining 1 percent made up of American Indian, Eskimo, and Aleut. These ethnic populations are expected to explode during the next 20 years. During that time, the number of African Americans will increase 25 percent, Hispanics about 64 percent, and Asian Americans almost 68 percent. Moreover, there are nearly 26 million people living in the United States—more than 9 percent of the population—who were born in another country.[24]

Most large companies, from Sears, Wal-Mart, and Bank of America to Levi Strauss, Procter & Gamble, and General Mills, now target specially designed products and promotions to one or more of these groups. General Mills targets the African American market with separate campaigns for its Big G cereals—Cheerios, Trix, Honey Nut Cheerios, and Cinnamon Toast Crunch. The campaigns consist of advertising, sponsorships, sampling, and community-based promotions that feature a strong family emphasis. For example, for the past several years, Honey Nut Cheerios has been the title sponsor of the Universal Circus, and for a "Soul Fest" music event that travels to 30 urban markets.

Similarly, Bank of America is quadrupling its multicultural budget this year to $40 million. Based on customer research and careful study of cultural differences, it has developed different advertising messages for Hispanic, Asian, and African American markets.

For Asians, the brand platform is "tangibly committed to the success and growth of all Americans." One commercial shot in China, Korea, and Vietnam—the beginning of an immigrant's journey—flashes back to a boy teaching his younger brother to ride a bike in his homeland. It then draws parallels with the helping hand today of Bank of America with a mortgage. The bike used in the ad is the exact kind an Asian child would learn to ride, not an American kids' bicycle. In contrast, one of the Hispanic spots opens on an exaggerated stack of mortgage-related paperwork the size of a house, and details how Bank of America can reduce it by 80 percent. The ads will run in the appropriate language—Spanish, Chinese, Korean, or Vietnamese—to target consumers who prefer to communicate in their native tongue.[25]

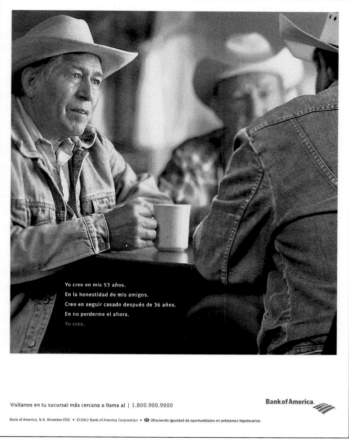

Based on careful study of cultural differences, Bank of America has developed targeted advertising messages for different cultural subgroups, here Asians and Hispanics.

Diversity goes beyond ethnic heritage. For example, many major companies have recently begun to explicitly target gay and lesbian consumers. A Simmons Research study of readers of the National Gay Newspaper Guild's 12 publications found that, compared to the average American, respondents are 12 times more likely to be in professional jobs, almost twice as likely to own a vacation home, times more likely to own a notebook computer, and twice as likely to own individual stocks. They are twice as likely as the general population to have a household income between $60,000 and $250,000, making them a very attractive market segment.

Companies in several industries are now waking up to the needs and potential of the gay and lesbian segment. For example, ad spending to reach gay and lesbian consumers is booming. Gay.com, a Web site that attracts more than 2 million unique visitors each month, has also attracted a diverse set of well-known advertisers, from IBM, eBay, Quicken Mortgage, Saturn, and AT&T to American Airlines and Neiman Marcus. Here are two examples of gay and lesbian marketing efforts:

American Express Financial Advisors launched print ads that depict same-sex couples planning their financial futures. The ads ran in *Out* and *The Advocate,* the two highest-circulation national gay publications. The company's director of segment marketing, Margaret Vergeyle, said, "We're targeting gay audiences with targeted ads and promotions that are relevant to them and say that we understand their specific needs. Often, gay couples are very concerned about issues like Social Security benefits and estate planning, since same-sex marriages often are not recognized under the law."

The British Tourist Authority teamed up with British Airways and the London Tourist Board to target the U.S. gay and lesbian travel market. The group worked with WinMark Concepts, a Washington marketing and advertising firm that specializes in advising mainstream companies on how to target the gay and lesbian market. "We wanted something that was gay-specific (and) fun, but also extremely tasteful," says WinMark's president. "These are educated, savvy consumers." One recent magazine ad shows five young to early-middle-aged men—the target age group is 35 to 50—posing in and around several of London's distinctive red phone booths. The headline reads: "One Call. A rainbow of choices." The campaign has been successful. "The magazine ads got the word out that Britain is gay- and lesbian-friendly and also generated a database of 40,000 names across the country. Now, it's time for a more targeted direct-mail and e-mail campaign to people we know are interested in our offer." Since BTA launched the campaign, both United Airlines and Virgin Airways have signed on to the program, as have the tourist boards of Manchester, Brighton, and Glasgow.[26]

Another attractive segment is the more than 54 million people with disabilities in the United States—a market larger than African Americans or Hispanics—representing almost $1 trillion in annual spending power. People with mobility challenges are an ideal target market for companies such as Peapod (www.peapod.com), which teams up with large supermarket chains in many heavily populated areas to offer online grocery shopping and home delivery. They also represent a growing market for travel, sports, and other leisure-oriented products and services. Consider the following examples:

Julie Perez sees the difference when she goes to the Divi Hotels resort at Flamingo Beach on the Caribbean island of Bonaire. "It's famous for being totally accessible," she says. "The hotel brochures show the wheelchair access. The dive staff are trained and aware, and they really want to take disabled people diving. They're not afraid." Perez, 35, of Ventura, California, is an experienced scuba diver, a travel agent—and a quadriplegic. Before she had children, she made five trips a year to the Caribbean; these days, she gets there only once or twice a year.

Volkswagen targets people with disabilities who want to travel. For example, it recently launched a special marketing campaign for its EuroVan. The campaign touted the EuroVan's extra-wide doors, high ceilings, and overall roominess as features that accommodate most wheelchair lifts and make driving more fun for those traditionally ignored by mainstream automakers. To make the EuroVan even more accessible, Volkswagen offers its Mobility Access Program. Drivers with disabilities who purchase or lease any VW can take advantage of $1,500 in purchase assistance for modifications such as hand controls and wheelchair lifts. Volkswagen even modified its catchy tag line "Drivers Wanted" to appeal to motorists with disabilities, coining the new slogan "All Drivers Wanted." The VW Web site sums up, "We build cars for people who love to drive. Some just happen to use wheelchairs."[27]

Economic Environment

Economic environment
Factors that affect consumer buying power and spending patterns.

Markets require buying power as well as people. The **economic environment** consists of factors that affect consumer purchasing power and spending patterns. Nations vary greatly in their levels and distribution of income. Some countries have *subsistence economies*—they consume most of

Volkswagen targets people with disabilities who want to travel. It offers a Mobility Access Program and has even modified its catchy "Drivers Wanted" tag line to appeal to motorists with disabilities: "All Drivers Wanted."

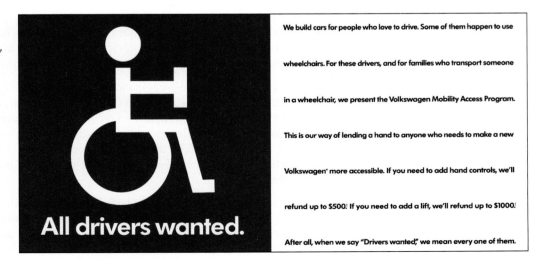

We build cars for people who love to drive. Some of them happen to use

wheelchairs. For these drivers, and for families who transport someone

in a wheelchair, we present the Volkswagen Mobility Access Program.

This is our way of lending a hand to anyone who needs to make a new

Volkswagen® more accessible. If you need to add hand controls, we'll

refund up to $500! If you need to add a lift, we'll refund up to $1000!

After all, when we say "Drivers wanted," we mean every one of them.

All drivers wanted.

their own agricultural and industrial output. These countries offer few market opportunities. At the other extreme are *industrial economies,* which constitute rich markets for many different kinds of goods. Marketers must pay close attention to major trends and consumer spending patterns both across and within their world markets. Following are some of the major economic trends in the United States.

Changes in Income

During the 1980s—tabbed the "roaring eighties" by some—American consumers fell into a consumption frenzy, fueled by income growth, federal tax reductions, rapid increases in housing values, and a boom in borrowing. They bought and bought, seemingly without caution, amassing record levels of debt. "It was fashionable to describe yourself as 'born to shop.' When the going gets tough, it was said, the tough go shopping."[28]

During the 1990s, the baby boom generation moved into its prime wage earning years, and the number of small families headed by dual career couples continued to increase. Thus, many consumers continued to demand quality products and better service, and they were able to pay for them. However, the free spending and high expectations of the 1980s were dashed by a recession in the early 1990s. In fact, the 1990s become the decade of the "squeezed consumer." Along with rising incomes in some segments came increased financial burdens. Consumers faced repaying debts acquired during earlier spending splurges, increased household and family expenses, and saving ahead for college tuition payments and retirement. These financially squeezed consumers sobered up, pulled back, and adjusted to their changing financial situations. They spent more carefully and sought greater value in the products and services they bought. *Value marketing* became the watchword for many marketers.

As we move into the 2000s, consumers continue to spend carefully.[29] Hence, the trend toward value marketing continues. Rather than offering high quality at a high price, or lesser quality at very low prices, marketers are looking for ways to offer today's more financially cautious buyers greater value—just the right combination of product quality and good service at a fair price.

Marketers should pay attention to *income distribution* as well as average income. Income distribution in the United States is still very skewed. At the top are *upper-class* consumers, whose spending patterns are not affected by current economic events and who are a major market for luxury goods. There is a comfortable *middle class* that is somewhat careful about its spending but can still afford the good life some of the time. The *working class* must stick close to the basics of food, clothing, and shelter and must try hard to save. Finally, the *underclass* (persons on welfare and many retirees) must count their pennies when making even the most basic purchases.

Over the past three decades, the rich have grown richer, the middle class has shrunk, and the poor have remained poor. In 1998, the top 5 percent of income-earning households in the United States captured more than 21 percent of aggregate income, up from 17.5 percent in 1967. Meanwhile, the share of income captured by the bottom 20 percent of income-earning households decreased from 4 percent to 3.6 percent.[30] This distribution of income has created a two-tiered market. Many companies are aggressively targeting the affluent:

> Driven by [growing wealth in the affluent segment,] marketers have responded with a ceaseless array of pricey, upscale products aimed at satisfying wealthy Americans' appetite for "the very best": leather-lined SUVs as big as tanks, $1,300 sheets, restaurant-quality appliances, and vast cruise ships offering every form of luxurious coddling. . . . Huge increases in wealth among the very rich have fueled the sales of $17,500 Patek Philippe watches that are sold as family heirlooms (thus justifying the price tag), created the clamor for a $48,000 Lexus (options extra), and resulted in a two-year waiting list for $14,000 Hermes Kelly bags.[31]

Other companies are now tailoring their marketing offers to two different markets—the affluent and the less affluent. For example, Walt Disney Company markets two distinct Winnie-the-Pooh bears:

> The original line-drawn figure appears on fine china, pewter spoons, and pricey kids' stationery found in upscale specialty and department stores such as Nordstrom and Bloomingdale's. The plump, cartoonlike Pooh, clad in a red shirt and a goofy smile, adorns plastic key chains, polyester bed sheets, and animated videos. It sells in Wal-Mart stores and

Income distribution: Walt Disney markets two distinct Pooh bears to match its two-tiered market.

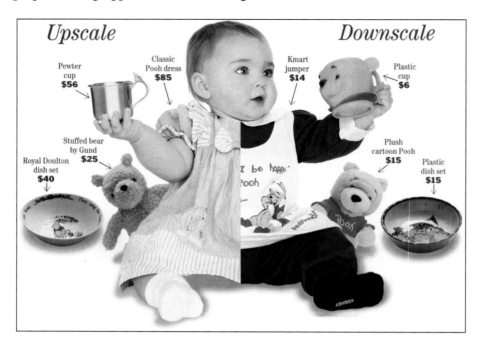

five-and-dime shops. Except at Disney's own stores, the two Poohs do not share the same retail shelf. [Thus, Disney offers both] upstairs and downstairs Poohs, hoping to land customers on both sides of the [income] divide.[32]

Changing Consumer Spending Patterns

Table 4.1 shows the proportion of total expenditures made by U.S. households at different income levels for major categories of goods and services. Food, housing, and transportation use up most household income. However, consumers at different income levels have different spending patterns. Some of these differences were noted over a century ago by Ernst Engel, who studied how people shifted their spending as their income rose. He found that as family income rises, the percentage spent on food declines, the percentage spent on housing remains about constant (except for such utilities as gas, electricity, and public services, which decrease), and both the percentage spent on most other categories and that devoted to savings increase. **Engel's laws** generally have been supported by later studies.

Engel's laws

Differences noted over a century ago by Ernst Engel in how people shift their spending across food, housing, transportation, health care, and other goods and services categories as family income rises.

Changes in major economic variables such as income, cost of living, interest rates, and savings and borrowing patterns have a large impact on the marketplace. Companies watch these

	TABLE 4.1	**CONSUMER SPENDING AT DIFFERENT INCOME LEVELS**	

	Percent of Spending at Different Income Levels		
Expenditure	**$10,000–$15,000**	**$30,000–$40,000**	**$70,000 and Over**
Food	14.8	14.5	11.4
Housing	26.8	24.4	25.6
Utilities	9.3	6.6	4.4
Clothing	4.5	5.4	4.7
Transportation	18.8	19.9	17.4
Health care	8.8	5.6	3.7
Entertainment	4.9	4.8	5.4
Contributions	2.6	3.0	4.3
Insurance	3.0	8.8	15.9

Source: Consumer Expenditure Survey, 1999, U.S. Department of Labor, Bureau of Labor Statistics, accessed online at http://stats.bis.gov/csxstnd.htm#1999, June 2001.

variables by using economic forecasting. Businesses do not have to be wiped out by an economic downturn or caught short in a boom. With adequate warning, they can take advantage of changes in the economic environment.

Natural Environment

Natural environment

Natural resources that are needed as inputs by marketers or that are affected by marketing activities.

The **natural environment** involves the natural resources that are needed as inputs by marketers or that are affected by marketing activities. Environmental concerns have grown steadily during the past three decades. Some trend analysts labeled the 1990s the "Earth Decade," claiming that the natural environment is the major worldwide issue facing business and the public. The Earth Day movement turned 30 in the year 2000. In many cities around the world, air and water pollution have reached dangerous levels. World concern continues to mount about the depletion of the Earth's ozone layer and the resulting "greenhouse effect," a dangerous warming of the Earth. And many environmentalists fear that we soon will be buried in our own trash.

Marketers should be aware of several trends in the natural environment. The first involves growing *shortages of raw materials.* Air and water may seem to be infinite resources, but some groups see long run dangers. Air pollution chokes many of the world's large cities, and water shortages are already a big problem in some parts of the United States and the world. Renewable resources, such as forests and food, also have to be used wisely. Nonrenewable resources, such as oil, coal, and various minerals, pose a serious problem. Firms making products that require these scarce resources face large cost increases, even if the materials do remain available.

A second environmental trend is *increased pollution.* Industry will almost always damage the quality of the natural environment. Consider the disposal of chemical and nuclear wastes, the dangerous mercury levels in the ocean, the quantity of chemical pollutants in the soil and food supply, and the littering of the environment with nonbiodegradable plastic bottles and other packaging materials.

A third trend is *increased government intervention* in natural resource management. The governments of different countries vary in their concern and efforts to promote a clean environment. Some, like the German government, vigorously pursue environmental quality. Others, especially many poorer nations, do little about pollution, largely because they lack the needed funds or political will. Even the richer nations lack the vast funds and political accord needed to mount a worldwide environmental effort. The general hope is that companies around the world will accept more social responsibility, and that less expensive devices can be found to control and reduce pollution.

Environmental responsibility: McDonald's has made a substantial commitment to the so-called "green movement."

In the United States, the Environmental Protection Agency (EPA) was created in 1970 to set and enforce pollution standards and to conduct pollution research. In the future, companies doing business in the United States can expect strong controls from government and pressure groups. Instead of opposing regulation, marketers should help develop solutions to the material and energy problems facing the world.

Concern for the natural environment has spawned the so-called green movement. Today, enlightened companies go beyond what government regulations dictate. They are developing *environmentally sustainable* strategies and practices in an effort to create a world economy that the planet can support indefinitely. They are responding to consumer demands with ecologically safer products, recyclable or biodegradable packaging, better pollution controls, and more energy-efficient operations. 3M runs a Pollution Prevention Pays program that has led to a substantial reduction in pollution and costs. AT&T uses a special software package to choose the least harmful materials, cut hazardous waste, reduce energy use, and improve product recycling in its operations. McDonald's eliminated polystyrene cartons years ago and now uses smaller, recyclable paper wrappings and napkins. Beyond this, the company has a long-standing rainforest policy and a commitment to purchasing recycled products and energy-efficient restaurant construction techniques. Dixon-Ticonderoga, the folks who developed the first pencil made in the United States, developed Prang crayons, which are made from soybeans rather than paraffin wax, a by-product of oil drilling. Soybeans are a renewable resource and produce brighter, richer colors and a smoother texture. More and more, companies are recognizing the link between a healthy economy and a healthy ecology.[33]

Technological Environment

Technological environment
Forces that create new technologies, creating new product and market opportunities.

The **technological environment** is perhaps the most dramatic force now shaping our destiny. Technology has released such wonders as antibiotics, organ transplants, notebook computers, and the Internet. It also has released such horrors as nuclear missiles, chemical weapons, and assault rifles. It has released such mixed blessings as the automobile, television, and credit cards. Our attitude toward technology depends on whether we are more impressed with its wonders or its blunders.

The technological environment changes rapidly. Think of all of today's common products that were not available 100 years ago or even 30 years ago. Abraham Lincoln did not know about automobiles, airplanes, radios, or the electric light. Woodrow Wilson did not know about television, aerosol cans, automatic dishwashers, air conditioners, antibiotics, or computers. Franklin Delano Roosevelt did not know about xerography, synthetic detergents, tape recorders, birth control pills, or Earth satellites. John F. Kennedy did not know about personal computers, CD players, or the World Wide Web.

Technological environment: Technology is perhaps the most dramatic force shaping the marketing environment. Here, a herder makes a call on his cell phone.

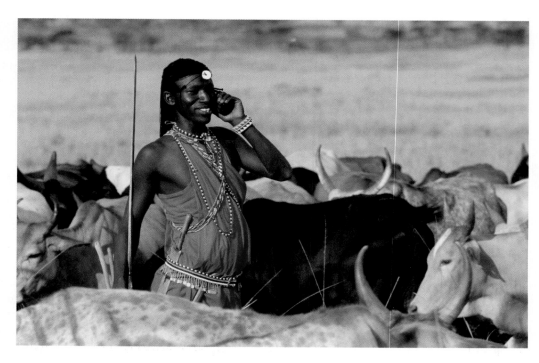

New technologies create new markets and opportunities. However, every new technology replaces an older technology. Transistors hurt the vacuum tube industry, xerography hurt the carbon paper business, the auto hurt the railroads, and compact discs hurt phonograph records. When old industries fought or ignored new technologies, their businesses declined. Thus, marketers should watch the technological environment closely. Companies that do not keep up with technological change soon will find their products outdated. And they will miss new product and market opportunities.

The United States leads the world in research and development spending. Total U.S. R&D spending reached an estimated $285 billion in 2002. The federal government was the largest R&D spender, at $76 billion.[34] Scientists today are researching a wide range of promising new products and services, ranging from practical solar energy, electric cars, and cancer cures to voice-controlled computers and genetically engineered food crops. Today's research usually is carried out by research teams rather than by lone inventors such as Thomas Edison, Samuel Morse, or Alexander Graham Bell. Many companies are adding marketing people to R&D teams to try to obtain a stronger marketing orientation. Scientists also speculate on fantasy products, such as flying cars, three dimensional televisions, and space colonies. The challenge in each case is not only technical but also commercial—to make *practical, affordable* versions of these products.

As products and technology become more complex, the public needs to know that these are safe. Thus, government agencies investigate and ban potentially unsafe products. In the United States, the federal Food and Drug Administration has set up complex regulations for testing new drugs. The Consumer Product Safety Commission sets safety standards for consumer products and penalizes companies that fail to meet them. Such regulations have resulted in much higher research costs and in longer times between new-product ideas and their introduction. Marketers should be aware of these regulations when applying new technologies and developing new products.

Political Environment

Marketing decisions are strongly affected by developments in the political environment. The **political environment** consists of laws, government agencies, and pressure groups that influence or limit various organizations and individuals in a given society.

Legislation Regulating Business

Even the most liberal advocates of free-market economies agree that the system works best with at least some regulation. Well-conceived regulation can encourage competition and ensure fair markets for goods and services. Thus, governments develop *public policy* to guide commerce—sets of laws and regulations that limit business for the good of society as a whole. Almost every marketing activity is subject to a wide range of laws and regulations.

Increasing Legislation.   Legislation affecting business around the world has increased steadily over the years. The United States has many laws covering issues such as competition, fair trade practices, environmental protection, product safety, truth in advertising, consumer privacy, packaging and labeling, pricing, and other important areas (see Table 4.2). The European Commission has been active in establishing a new framework of laws covering competitive behavior, product standards, product liability, and commercial transactions for the nations of the European Union.

Several countries have gone further than the United States in passing strong consumerism legislation. For example, Norway bans several forms of sales promotion—trading stamps, contests, premiums—as being inappropriate or unfair ways of promoting products. Thailand requires food processors selling national brands to market low price brands also, so that low income consumers can find economy brands on the shelves. In India, food companies must obtain special approval to launch brands that duplicate those already existing on the market, such as additional cola drinks or new brands of rice.

Understanding the public policy implications of a particular marketing activity is not a simple matter. For example, in the United States, there are many laws created at the national, state, and local levels, and these regulations often overlap. Aspirins sold in Dallas are governed both by federal labeling laws and by Texas state advertising laws. Moreover, regulations are constantly changing—what was allowed last year may now be prohibited, and what was prohibited may now be allowed. Marketers must work hard to keep up with changes in regulations and their interpretations.

Political environment
Laws, government agencies, and pressure groups that influence and limit various organizations and individuals in a given society.

TABLE 4.2   MAJOR U.S. LEGISLATION AFFECTING MARKETING

Legislation	Purpose
Sherman Antitrust Act (1890)	Prohibits monopolies and activities (price fixing, predatory pricing) that restrain trade or competition in interstate commerce.
Federal Food and Drug Act (1906)	Forbids the manufacture or sale of adulterated or fraudulently labeled foods and drugs. Created the Food and Drug Administration.
Clayton Act (1914)	Supplements the Sherman Act by prohibiting certain types of price discrimination, exclusive dealing, and tying clauses (which require a dealer to take additional products in a seller's line).
Federal Trade Commission Act (1914)	Establishes a commission to monitor and remedy unfair trade methods.
Robinson-Patman Act (1936)	Amends Clayton Act to define price discrimination as unlawful. Empowers FTC to establish limits on quantity discounts, forbid some brokerage allowances, and prohibit promotional allowances except when made available on proportionately equal terms.
Wheeler-Lea Act (1938)	Makes deceptive, misleading, and unfair practices illegal regardless of injury to competition. Places advertising of food and drugs under FTC jurisdiction.
Lanham Trademark Act (1946)	Protects and regulates distinctive brand names and trademarks.
National Traffic and Safety Act (1958)	Provides for the creation of compulsory safety standards for automobiles and tires.
Fair Packaging and Labeling Act (1966)	Provides for the regulation of packaging and labeling of consumer goods. Requires that manufacturers state what the package contains, who made it, and how much it contains.
Child Protection Act (1966)	Bans sale of hazardous toys and articles. Sets standards for child-resistant packaging.
Federal Cigarette Labeling and Advertising Act (1967)	Requires that cigarette packages contain the following statement: "Warning: The Surgeon General Has Determined That Cigarette Smoking Is Dangerous to Your Health."
National Environmental Policy Act (1969)	Establishes a national policy on the environment. The 1970 Reorganization Plan established the Environmental Protection Agency.
Consumer Product Safety Act (1972)	Establishes the Consumer Product Safety Commission and authorizes it to set safety standards for consumer products as well as exact penalties for failure to uphold those standards.
Magnuson-Moss Warranty Act (1975)	Authorizes the FTC to determine rules and regulations for consumer warranties and provides consumer access to redress, such as the class-action suit.
Children's Television Act (1990)	Limits number of commercials aired during children's programs.
Nutrition Labeling and Education Act (1990)	Requires that food product labels provide detailed nutritional information.
Telephone Consumer Protection Act (1991)	Establishes procedures to avoid unwanted telephone solicitations. Limits marketers' use of automatic telephone dialing systems and artificial or prerecorded voices.
Americans with Disabilities Act (1991)	Makes discrimination against people with disabilities illegal in public accommodations, transportation, and telecommunications.
Children's Online Privacy Protection Act (2000)	Prohibits Web sites or online services operators from collecting personal information from children without obtaining consent from a parent and allowing parents to review information collected from their children.

Business legislation has been enacted for a number of reasons. The first is to *protect companies* from each other. Although business executives may praise competition, they sometimes try to neutralize it when it threatens them. So laws are passed to define and prevent unfair competition. In the United States, such laws are enforced by the Federal Trade Commission and the Antitrust Division of the Attorney General's office.

The second purpose of government regulation is to *protect consumers* from unfair business practices. Some firms, if left alone, would make shoddy products, tell lies in their advertising, and deceive consumers through their packaging and pricing. Unfair business practices have been defined and are enforced by various agencies.

The third purpose of government regulation is to *protect the interests of society* against unrestrained business behavior. Profitable business activity does not always create a better quality of life. Regulation arises to ensure that firms take responsibility for the social costs of their production or products.

Changing Government Agency Enforcement.   International marketers will encounter dozens, or even hundreds, of agencies set up to enforce trade policies and regulations. In the United States, Congress has established federal regulatory agencies such as the Federal Trade Commission, the Food and Drug Administration, the Interstate Commerce Commission, the Federal Communications Commission, the Federal Power Commission, the Civil Aeronautics Board, the Consumer Products Safety Commission, the Environmental Protection Agency, and the Office of Consumer Affairs. Because such government agencies have some discretion in enforcing the laws, they can have a major impact on a company's marketing performance. At times, the staffs of these agencies have appeared to be overly eager and unpredictable. Some of the agencies sometimes have been dominated by lawyers and economists who lacked a practical sense of how business and marketing work. In recent years, the Federal Trade Commission has added staff marketing experts, who can better understand complex business issues.

New laws and their enforcement will continue to increase. Business executives must watch these developments when planning their products and marketing programs. Marketers need to know about the major laws protecting competition, consumers, and society. They need to understand these laws at the local, state, national, and international levels.

Increased Emphasis on Ethics and Socially Responsible Actions

Written regulations cannot possibly cover all potential marketing abuses, and existing laws are often difficult to enforce. However, beyond written laws and regulations, business is also governed by social codes and rules of professional ethics. Enlightened companies encourage their managers to look beyond what the regulatory system allows and simply "do the right thing." These socially responsible firms actively seek out ways to protect the long-run interests of their consumers and the environment. More companies are linking themselves to worthwhile causes and using public relations to build more positive images (see Real Marketing 4.2).[35]

The recent rash of business scandals and increased concerns about the environment have created fresh interest in the issues of ethics and social responsibility. Almost every aspect of marketing involves such issues. Unfortunately, because these issues usually involve conflicting interests, well-meaning people can honestly disagree about the right course of action in a given situation. Thus, many industrial and professional trade associations have suggested codes of ethics, and many companies are now developing policies and guidelines to deal with complex social responsibility issues.

The boom in e-commerce and Internet marketing has created a new set of social and ethical issues. Privacy issues are the primary concern. For example, Web site visitors often provide extensive personal information that might leave them open to abuse by unscrupulous marketers. Moreover, both Intel and Microsoft have been accused of covert, high-tech computer chip and software invasions of customers' personal computers to obtain information for marketing purposes.

Throughout the text, we present Real Marketing exhibits that summarize the main public policy and social responsibility issues surrounding major marketing decisions. These exhibits discuss the legal issues that marketers should understand and the common ethical and societal concerns that marketers face. In Chapter 20, we discuss a broad range of societal marketing issues in greater depth.

Cultural Environment

Cultural environment
Institutions and other forces that affect society's basic values, perceptions, preferences, and behaviors.

The **cultural environment** is made up of institutions and other forces that affect a society's basic values, perceptions, preferences, and behaviors. People grow up in a particular society that shapes their basic beliefs and values. They absorb a worldview that defines their relationships with others. The following cultural characteristics can affect marketing decision making.

real marketing 4.2

Cause-Related Marketing: Doing Well by Doing Good

These days, every product seems to be tied to some cause. Buy Purina cat food and help the American Association of Zoological Parks and Aquariums save endangered big-cat species. Drink Tang and earn money for

the early 1980s, when American Express offered to donate one cent to the restoration of the Statue of Liberty for each use of its charge card. American Express ended up having to contribute $1.7 million, but the

The video featured a game-show format that made learning about safety entertaining as well as educational. To promote the campaign, Johnson & Johnson distributed almost 50 million advertising inserts in daily newspapers. It also developed a special information kit for retailers, containing posters, floor displays, and other in-store promotion materials. Started as a program of the Children's National Medical Center, the National SAFE KIDS Campaign has now grown into an independent organization, SAFE KIDS, made up of 300 state and local coalitions across America. Each May, the organization teams with Johnson & Johnson to present National SAFE KIDS week. In addition to providing expertise through partnering, J&J continues to support the organization with millions of dollars in annual grants, public awareness campaigns, corporate advertising, and retail promotions.

In 1996, General Mills launched its Box Tops for Education program. The program offers schools nationwide a chance to earn cash to pay for everything from field trips to computers to playground equipment. Box Tops for Education has really caught on. Today, more than 60 percent of the nation's elementary schools are enrolled. To participate, students and parents clip box tops and labels from any of more than 330 eligible products, including brands like Yoplait, Big G, Lloyd's, and Betty Crocker. General Mills then pays the school 10 cents for every box top redeemed. To date, the company given more than $50 million to local public, private, and parochial schools. Based on that success, General Mills has now teamed up with Visa to offer a Box Tops for Education credit card. Visa donates 1 percent of every purchase made to the cardholder's designated school. In addition, consumers who link to Web sites such as Amazon.com and EddieBauer.com from the Box Tops for Education Web site are guaranteed a

Cause-Related Marketing: The General Mills Box Tops for Education program offers schools nationwide a chance to earn cash to pay for everything from field trips, to computers, to playground equipment. More than 60 percent of the nation's elementary schools are enrolled.

Mothers Against Drunk Driving. Drive a Dollar rental car and help support the Special Olympics. Buy from EddieBauer.com and have a percentage of your purchase go to support your local grade school. Or if you want to help the Leukemia Society of America, buy Helping Hand trash bags or toilet paper. Pay for these purchases with the right charge card and you can support a local cultural arts group or help fight cancer or heart disease.

Cause-related marketing has become a primary form of corporate giving. It lets companies "do well by doing good" by linking purchases of the company's products or services with fund-raising for worthwhile causes or charitable organizations. Cause-related marketing has grown rapidly since

cause-related campaign produced a 28 percent increase in card usage.

Companies now sponsor dozens of cause-related marketing campaigns each year. Many are backed by large budgets and a full complement of marketing activities. Here are other examples:

In 1987 Johnson & Johnson teamed with the Children's Hospital Medical Center and the National Safety Council to sponsor the National SAFE KIDS Campaign. Designed to reduce preventable children's injuries, the leading killer of children, the campaign offered consumers a free SAFE KIDS safety kit for children in exchange for proofs of purchase. Consumers could also buy a Child's Safety Video for $9.95.

donation to their schools amounting to 10 percent of every purchase.

Avon, the world's largest direct seller of cosmetics and beauty items, has for years sponsored programs aimed at raising national and global awareness of breast cancer, a problem afflicting its target audience—women. Avon's Breast Cancer Awareness Crusade in the United States raises money for programs that provide women—especially low-income, minority, and older women—with education and early cancer screening services. The company sells products featuring a pink ribbon (the international symbol of breast cancer) through its 450,000 sales representatives, then donates proceeds to nonprofit and university-based programs. To date, donations from product sales and money raised from events like the Breast Cancer Three-Day walk have exceeded $165 million in the United States alone. Avon publicizes these efforts in its bimonthly sales brochures to 15 million U.S. customers and on its Web site. In addition, the company's famous in-person sales force is fully briefed on the company's efforts, putting a familiar face on the campaign. "The message in the United States and across all of the countries [where Avon does business] is the same: We're looking to position Avon as the company for women, whether that's the place to buy a product, to start your own business, where your health needs are addressed, [or] to function as an advocate on behalf of women's health," says Joanne Mazurki, Avon's director of global cause-related marketing.

Cause-related marketing has stirred some controversy. Critics are concerned that cause-related marketing might eventually undercut traditional "no-strings" corporate giving, as more and more companies grow to expect marketing benefits from their contributions. Critics also worry that cause-related marketing will cause a shift in corporate charitable support toward more visible, popular, and low-risk charities—those with more certain and substantial marketing appeal. For example, MasterCard's "Choose to Make a Difference" campaign raises money for six charities, each selected in part because of its popularity in a consumer poll. Finally, critics worry that cause-related marketing is more a strategy for selling than a strategy for giving—that "cause-related" marketing is really "cause-exploitative" marketing. Thus, companies using cause-related marketing might find themselves walking a fine line between an improved image and charges of exploitation.

However, if handled well, cause-related marketing can greatly benefit both the company and the cause. The company gains an effective marketing tool while building a more positive public image. According to one recent study, 83 percent of consumers have a more positive image of a company that supports a cause they care. Two-thirds say that if price and quality are equal, they are likely to switch to a civic-minded brand or retailer.

Similarly, the charitable organization or cause gains greater visibility and important new sources of funding. This additional funding can be substantial. In total, such campaigns now contribute some $100 million annually to the coffers of charitable organizations Moreover, surveys show that these cause-related contributions usually add to, rather than undercut, direct company contributions. Thus, when cause marketing works, everyone wins.

Sources: See Minette E. Drumwright, "Company Advertising with a Social Dimension: The Role of Noneconomic Criteria," *Journal of Marketing,* October 1996, pp. 71–87; Jerry C. Welsh, "Good Cause, Good Business," *Harvard Business Review,* September–October 1999, pp. 21–24; Alison Fass, "A Campaign by Avon on Breast Cancer," *New York Times,* August 17, 2001, p. C3; Michael Jay Polonsky and Greg Wood, "Can the Overcommercialization of Cause-Related Marketing Harm Society?" *Journal of Macromarketing,* June 2001, pp. 8, 15; Sankar Sen and C. B. Bhattacharya, "Does Doing Good Always Lead to Doing Better? Consumer Reactions to Corporate Social," *Harvard Business Review,* May 2001, pp. 225–243; information from www.avon company.com/women, June 2002; and information from www.boxtops4education. com, June 2002.

Persistence of Cultural Values

People in a given society hold many beliefs and values. Their core beliefs and values have a high degree of persistence. For example, most Americans believe in working, getting married, giving to charity, and being honest. These beliefs shape more-specific attitudes and behaviors found in everyday life. *Core* beliefs and values are passed on from parents to children and are reinforced by schools, churches, business, and government.

Secondary beliefs and values are more open to change. Believing in marriage is a core belief; believing that people should get married early in life is a secondary belief. Marketers have some chance of changing secondary values but little chance of changing core values. For example, family-planning marketers could argue more effectively that people should get married later than that they should not get married at all.

Shifts in Secondary Cultural Values

Although core values are fairly persistent, cultural swings do take place. Consider the impact of popular music groups, movie personalities, and other celebrities on young people's hairstyling, clothing, and sexual norms. Marketers want to predict cultural shifts in order to spot new opportunities or threats. Several firms offer "futures" forecasts in this connection, such as the Yankelovich Monitor, Market Facts' BrainWaves Group, and the Trends Research Institute.

The Yankelovich Monitor has tracked consumer value trends for years. At the dawn of the twenty-first century, it looked back to capture lessons from the past decade that might offer insight into the 2000s. It identified the following eight major consumer themes:[36]

1. *Paradox:* People agree that "life is getting better and worse at the same time."

2. *Trust not:* Confidence in doctors, public schools, TV news, newspapers, federal government, and corporations drops sharply.

3. *Go it alone:* More people agree with the statement "I rely more on my own instincts than on experts."

4. *Smarts really count:* For example, fewer people agree with "It's risky to buy a brand you are not familiar with."

5. *No sacrifices:* For example, many people claim that looks are important but not at any price, that keeping house for show instead of comfort is over, and that giving up taste for nutrition is no longer acceptable.

6. *Stress is hard to beat:* For example, more people claim that they are "concerned about getting enough rest."

7. *Reciprocity is the way to go:* More people agree that "everybody should feel free to do his or her own thing."

8. *Me.2:* For example, people express the need to live in a world that is built by "me," not by you.

Yankelovich maintains that the decade drivers for the 2000s will primarily come from the baby boomers and Generation Xers. The baby boomers will be driven by four factors in the 2000's: "adventure" (fueled by a sense of youthfulness), "smarts" (fueled by a sense of empowerment and willingness to accept change), "intergenerational support" (caring for younger and older, often in nontraditional arrangements), and "retreading" (embracing early retirement with a second career or phase of their work life). Gen Xers will be driven by three factors: "redefining the good life" (being highly motivated to improve their economic well-being and remain in control), "new rituals" (returning to traditional values but with a tolerant mind-set and active lifestyle), and "cutting and pasting" (balancing work, play, sleep, family, and other aspects of their lives).

The major cultural values of a society are expressed in people's views of themselves and others, as well as in their views of organizations, society, nature, and the universe.

People's Views of Themselves.   People vary in their emphasis on serving themselves versus serving others. Some people seek personal pleasure, wanting fun, change, and escape. Others seek self realization through religion, recreation, or the avid pursuit of careers or other life goals. People use products, brands, and services as a means of self-expression, and they buy products and services that match their views of themselves.

In the 1980s, personal ambition and materialism increased dramatically, with significant marketing implications. In a "me society," people buy their "dream cars" and take their "dream vacations." They tended to spend to the limit on self-indulgent goods and services. Today, in contrast, people are adopting more-conservative behaviors and ambitions. As we move into the new millennium, materialism, flashy spending, and self-indulgence have been replaced by more-sensible spending, saving, family concerns, and helping others. The maturing baby boomers are limiting their spending to products and services that improve their lives instead of boosting their images. This suggests a bright future for products and services that serve basic needs and provide real value rather than those relying on glitz and hype.

People's Views of Others.   Recently, observers have noted a shift from a "me society" to a "we society" in which more people want to be with and serve others. Notes one trend tracker, "People want to get out, especially those 48 million people working out of their home and feeling a little cooped up [and] all those shut-ins who feel unfulfilled by the cyberstuff that was supposed to make them feel like never leaving home."[37] This trend suggests a greater demand for "social support" products and services that improve direct communication between people, such as health clubs and family vacations.

People's Views of Organizations.   People vary in their attitudes toward corporations, government agencies, trade unions, universities, and other organizations. By and large, people are will-

American patriotism has been increasing gradually for the past two decades but surged following the September 11 terrorist attacks. Marketers such as Mars, Inc. (the maker of M&Ms) responded with patriotic products and promotions.

ing to work for major organizations and expect them, in turn, to carry out society's work. The late 1980s saw a sharp decrease in confidence in and loyalty toward America's business and political organizations and institutions. In the workplace, there has been an overall decline in organizational loyalty. During the 1990s, waves of company downsizings bred cynicism and distrust. Many people today see work not as a source of satisfaction but as a required chore to earn money to enjoy their nonwork hours. This trend suggests that organizations need to find new ways to win consumer and employee confidence.

People's Views of Society.   People vary in their attitudes toward their society; patriots defend it, reformers want to change it, malcontents want to leave it. People's orientation to their society influences their consumption patterns and attitudes toward the marketplace. American patriotism has been increasing gradually for the past two decades. It surged, however, following the September 11 terrorist attacks. For example, before the attacks, Americans spent some $200 million a year on flags of all sizes and shapes. But in 2001, American flag sales quadrupled. Within the two weeks following the September 11 attacks, K-Mart alone sold more than 662,000 handheld flags nationwide. The swell of national pride initially cleared out stores, with some retailers reporting 12-week backlogs.[38]

Marketers responded with patriotic products and promotions, offering everything from floral bouquets to clothing with patriotic themes. For example, Mars introduced a new limited-edition patriotic package for its M&M brand, featuring red, white, and blue candy pieces. It donated 100 percent of the profits from the sale of those special packages to the American Red Cross. For Christmas, Hallmark offered a card showing a snowman bearing the American flag and reading "God Bless America!" Wal-Mart sold "Little Patriots Diapers" with tiny blue stars. The Heartland Brewery in Times Square even came out with a new beer, DetermiNation Ale. And a heartrending Budweiser Super Bowl ad featured the venerable Budweiser Clydesdales bowing to honor the forever changed Manhattan skyline.[39]

Although most of these marketing efforts were tasteful and well received, waving the red, white, and blue proved tricky for some marketers. Following September 11, consumers quickly became wary of patriotic products and ads. Except in cases where companies tied product sales to charitable contributions, "patriotism as a marketing program was largely unwelcome," says one analyst. They were often "seen by consumers as attempts to cash in on the tragedy." Another expert advises that marketers must take care when responding to such national emotions. Whatever their intentions, they must "be careful not to come across as saying 'Wasn't it awful, now go spend money on our product.'"[40]

People's Views of Nature.   People vary in their attitudes toward the natural world. Some feel ruled by it, others feel in harmony with it, and still others seek to master it. A long term trend has been people's growing mastery over nature through technology and the belief that nature is bountiful. More recently, however, people have recognized that nature is finite and fragile, that it can be destroyed or spoiled by human activities.

Love of nature is leading to more camping, hiking, boating, fishing, and other outdoor activities. Business has responded by offering more products and services catering to these interests. Tour operators are offering more wilderness adventures, and retailers are offering more fitness gear and apparel. Marketing communicators are using appealing natural backgrounds in advertising their products. And food producers have found growing markets for natural and organic foods. Natural and organic products are now a $25 billion industry, growing at a rate of 20 percent annually. Niche marketers, such as Whole Foods Markets, have sprung up to serve this market, and traditional food chains such as Kroger and Safeway have added separate natural and organic food sections.[41]

People's Views of the Universe.   Finally, people vary in their beliefs about the origin of the universe and their place in it. Although most Americans practice religion, religious conviction and practice have been dropping off gradually through the years. Some futurists, however, have noted a renewed interest in spirituality, perhaps as a part of a broader search for a new inner purpose. People have been moving away from materialism and dog-eat-dog ambition to seek more permanent values—family, community, earth, faith—and a more certain grasp of right and wrong.

"Americans are on a spiritual journey," observes one expert, "increasingly concerned with the meaning of life and issues of the soul and spirit. The journey can encompass religion, but it is much more likely to take the form of . . . 'spiritual individualism.'" This new spiritualism affects consumers in everything from the television shows they watch and the books they read to the products and services they buy. "Since consumers don't park their beliefs and values on the bench outside the marketplace," adds the expert, "they are bringing this awareness to the brands they buy. Tapping into this heightened sensitivity presents a unique marketing opportunity for brands."[42]

Responding to the Marketing Environment

Someone once observed, "There are three kinds of companies: those who make things happen, those who watch things happen, and those who wonder what's happened."[43] Many companies view the marketing environment as an uncontrollable element to which they must adapt. They passively accept the marketing environment and do not try to change it. They analyze the environmental forces and design strategies that will help the company avoid the threats and take advantage of the opportunities the environment provides.

Environmental management perspective
A management perspective in which the firm takes aggressive actions to affect the publics and forces in its marketing environment rather than simply watching and reacting to them.

Other companies take an **environmental management perspective.**[44] Rather than simply watching and reacting, these firms take aggressive actions to affect the publics and forces in their marketing environment. Such companies hire lobbyists to influence legislation affecting their industries and stage media events to gain favorable press coverage. They run advertorials (ads expressing editorial points of view) to shape public opinion. They press lawsuits and file complaints with regulators to keep competitors in line, and they form contractual agreements to better control their distribution channels.

Often, companies can find positive ways to overcome seemingly uncontrollable environmental constraints. For example:

Cathay Pacific Airlines . . . determined that many travelers were avoiding Hong Kong because of lengthy delays at immigration. Rather than assuming that this was a problem they could not solve, Cathay's senior staff asked the Hong Kong government how to avoid these immigration delays. After lengthy discussions, the airline agreed to make an annual grant-in-aid to the government to hire more immigration inspectors—but these reinforcements would service primarily the Cathay Pacific gates. The reduced waiting period increased customer value and thus strengthened [Cathay's competitive advantage].[45]

Marketing management cannot always control environmental forces. In many cases, it must settle for simply watching and reacting to the environment. For example, a company would have little success trying to influence geographic population shifts, the economic environment, or major cultural values. But whenever possible, smart marketing managers will take a *proactive* rather than *reactive* approach to the marketing environment (see Real Marketing 4.3).

real marketing 4.3

YourCompanySucks.com

Richard Hatch is one of the few people in this world with a passion for both Harley-Davidson motorcycles and collecting dolls and cute little toys. One day in 1997, the tattooed, 210-pound Hatch got into a shouting match with an employee in his local Wal-Mart and was banned from the store. Hatch claims that his actions didn't warrant his

had a dispute with employees at his local Toys "R" Us store about similar complaints. He was banished from there as well. His response? You guessed it: another sucks.com Web site (www.toysrussucks.com).

An extreme event? Not anymore. As more and more well-intentioned grassroots organizations, consumer watchdog groups, or just plain angry consumers take their gripes to the Web, such "sucks.com" sites are becoming almost commonplace. A search on Yahoo! yields 140 such sites. According to one source, more than half of the Fortune 1000 companies have encountered some type of Web site critical of their businesses. The sites target some highly respected companies with some highly *dis*respectful labels: Microsucks; Gapsucks.org; NonAmazon; Starbucked; BestBuysucks; The I Hate McDonald's Page; Just Do Not Do It (Nike); America Offline; North-Worst Air; Untied Air-

companies is figuring out how far they can go to protect their image without fueling the fire already raging at the sites. One point upon which all experts seem to agree: Don't try to retaliate in kind. "Avoid 'testosterosis'—or the urge to hit someone in the face because they are doing something you don't like," advises one consultant. "It's a free country, and the Web is completely unregulated. Don't get angry and think about doing foolish things."

Some companies have tried to silence the critics through lawsuits, but few have succeeded. For example, McDonald's sued one such site for libel; it spent $16 million on the case and won the suit but received only $94,000 in damages. Wal-Mart's attorneys threatened Hatch with legal action unless he shut down his Wal-Mart sucks Web site. However, Hatch stood up to the $215 billion retailer, and Wal-Mart eventually backed down. As it turns out, a company has legal recourse only when the unauthorized use of its trademarks, brand names, or other intellectual property is apt to be confusing to the public. And no reasonable person is likely to be confused that Wal-Mart maintains and supports a site tagged Walmartsucks.com. Beyond the finer legal points, Wal-Mart also feared that a lawsuit would draw only more attention to the consumer hate site. An industry analyst comments: "Those who operate hate sites adore posting cease-and-desist letters they receive from corporate attorneys. Such letters also validate their fight for the cause, whatever they perceive that to be, and they can use them to cast yet another negative spotlight on the company. They revel in the attention."

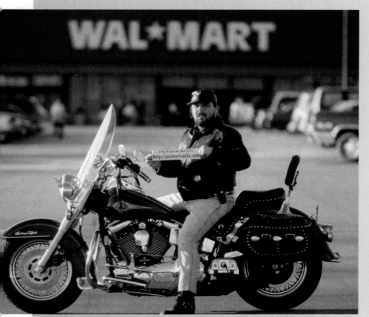

Environmental management: The best strategy for dealing with consumer hate sites is to address complaints directly. "If a company solves my problem, why would I keep up the Web site?"

ousting. He says he'd complained to store managers for months that employees were snapping up the best Hot Wheels and NASCAR collectible toy cars before they hit the shelves.

Wal-Mart didn't budge and the angry Hatch retaliated. He hired a Web designer and created the Wal-Mart Sucks Web site (www.walmartsucks.com). In only a few years, according to one account, the Web site "sprouted beyond Hatch's wildest dreams of revenge. [Thousands] of customers have written in to attack rude store managers, complain about alleged insects in the aisles, offer shoplifting tips, and, from time to time, write romantic odes to cashiers." Hatch, who has amassed some 5,000 Beanie Babies, also

lines: The Most Unfriendly Skies; The Unofficial BMW Lemon Site; AllState Insurancesucks ("Their hands in your pockets"); and Dunkindonuts.org (featuring "unhappy tales about coffee, crullers, and cinnamon buns") to name only a few. Some of these attack sites are little more than a nuisance. Others, however, can draw serious attention and create real headaches. "The same people who used to stand on [the] corner and rail against things to 20 people now can put up a Web site and rail in front of 2 million people," says William Comcowich, whose firm helps companies monitor what's said about them on the Internet.

How should companies react to these attack sites? The real quandary for targeted

Given the difficulties of trying to sue consumer hate sites out of existence, some companies have tried other strategies. For example, most big companies now routinely buy up Web addresses for their firm names preceded by the words "Ihate" or followed by "sucks.com." In general, however, attempts to block, counterattack, or shut down consumer hate sites may be short-sighted. Such sites are often based on real consumer concerns. Hence, the best strategy might be to proactively monitor these sites and respond positively to the concerns they express.

(continued)

Some targeted companies actively listen to concerns posted on hate sites and develop Web presentations to tell their own side of the story. For example, Nike is the target of at least eight different attack sites, mostly criticizing it for alleged unfair labor practices in Southeast Asia. In response, Nike commissioned an independent investigation of labor practices in its Indonesian factories and presented the results on its own Web site (www.Nikebiz.com/social/labor). Monitoring consumer hate sites can yield additional benefits. For example, some sites can actually provide the targeted company with useful information. Walmartsucks.com posts customers' ratings of local stores for cleanliness, prices, and customer service, information that would be costly for Wal-Mart to develop on its own.

According to James Alexander, president of EWatch, an Internet monitoring service, the best strategy for dealing with consumer hate sites is to address their complaints directly. "If a company solves my problem," he says, "why would I keep up the Web site?" Take Dunkin' Donuts, for example:

After a disgruntled customer established dunkindonuts.org, an attack site that appeared on many Internet search engines ahead of the company's own Web page, the company contacted about 25 people who had written in with complaints and offered them coupons for free donuts. "If this was where customers were going to post their comments, we thought it was important for us to go ahead and address them," says spokesperson Jennifer Rosenberg. Now, the company is in negotiations to buy the site from its founder, 25-year-old David Felton, who says he'll sell because "they have been taking complaints and responding."

By proactively responding to a seemingly uncontrollable event in its environment, Dunkin' Donuts has been able to turn a negative into a positive. Dunkinsucks.com is now all smiles.com.

Sources: Quotes and excerpts from Leslie Goff, "<YourCompanyNameHere> sucks.com," *Computerworld,* July 20, 1998, pp. 57–58; and Mike France, "A Site for Soreheads," *Business Week,* April 12, 1999, pp. 86–90. Also see Oscar S. Cisneros, "Legal Tips for Your 'Sucks' Site," accessed online at www.wired.com, August 14, 2000; Hilary Appelman, "I Scream, You Scream: Consumers Vent Over the Net," *New York Times,* March 4, 2001, p. 3.13; and Ronald F. Lopez, "Corporate Strategies for Addressing Internet 'Complaint' Sites," accessed online at www.constructionweblinks.com, June 2002.

LOOKING BACK: REVIEWING THE CONCEPTS

Companies must constantly watch and adapt to the *marketing environment* in order to seek opportunities and ward off threats. The marketing environment comprises all the actors and forces influencing the company's ability to transact business effectively with its target market.

1. Describe the environmental forces that affect the company's ability to serve its customers.

The company's *microenvironment* consists of other actors close to the company that combine to form the company's value delivery network or that affect its ability to serve its customers. It includes the company's *internal environment*—its several departments and management levels—as it influences marketing decision making. *Marketing channel firms*—suppliers and marketing intermediaries, including resellers, physical distribution firms, marketing services agencies, and financial intermediaries—cooperate to create customer value. Five types of customer *markets* include consumer, business, reseller, government, and international markets. *Competitors* vie with the company in an effort to serve customers better. Finally, various *publics* have an actual or potential interest in or impact on the company's ability to meet its objectives.

The *macroenvironment* consists of larger societal forces that affect the entire microenvironment. The six forces making up the company's macroenvironment include demographic, economic, natural, technological, political, and cultural forces. These forces shape opportunities and pose threats to the company.

2. Explain how changes in the demographic and economic environments affect marketing decisions.

Demography is the study of the characteristics of human populations. Today's *demographic environment* shows a changing age structure, shifting family profiles, geographic population shifts, a better-educated and more white-collar population, and increasing diversity. The *economic environment* consists of factors that affect buying power and patterns. The economic environment is characterized by more consumer concern for value and shifting consumer spending patterns. Today's squeezed consumers are seeking greater value—just the right combination of good quality and service at a fair price. The distribution of income also is shifting. The rich have grown richer, the middle class has shrunk, and the poor have remained poor, leading to a two-tiered market. Many companies now tailor their marketing offers to two different markets—the affluent and the less affluent.

3. Identify the major trends in the firm's natural and technological environments.

The *natural environment* shows three major trends: shortages of certain raw materials, higher pollution levels, and more government intervention in natural resource management. Environmental concerns create marketing opportunities for alert companies. The marketer should watch for four major trends in the *technological environment:* the rapid pace of technological change, high R&D budgets, the concentration by companies on minor product improvements, and increased government regulation. Companies that fail to keep up with technological change will miss out on new product and marketing opportunities.

4. Explain the key changes in the political and cultural environments.

The *political environment* consists of laws, agencies, and groups that influence or limit marketing actions. The political environment has undergone three changes that affect marketing worldwide: increasing legislation regulating business, strong government agency enforcement, and greater emphasis on ethics and socially responsible actions. The *cultural environment* is made up of institutions and forces that affect a society's values, perceptions, preferences, and behaviors. The environment shows long-term trends toward a "we society," a lessening trust of institu-

tions, increasing patriotism, greater appreciation for nature, a new spiritualism, and the search for more meaningful and enduring values.

5. Discuss how companies can react to the marketing environment.

Companies can passively accept the marketing environment as an uncontrollable element to which they must adapt, avoiding threats and taking advantage of opportunities as they arise. Or they can take an *environmental management perspective,* proactively working to change the environment rather than simply reacting to it. Whenever possible, companies should try to be proactive rather than reactive.

REVIEWING THE KEY TERMS

Baby boomers 112
Cultural environment 127
Demography 111
Economic environment 120
Engel's laws 122
Environmental management
   perspective 132

Generation X 114
Generation Y 114
Macroenvironment 107
Marketing environment 106
Marketing intermediaries 108

Microenvironment 107
Natural environment 123
Political environment 125
Public 110
Technological environment 124

DISCUSSING THE CONCEPTS

1. Describe "millennial fever" and provide several examples. How are marketers applying this phenomenon in their marketing strategies? What products are you nostalgic about?
2. What is a company's marketing environment? Describe the factors that affect the marketing environment.
3. Identify the seven publics that impact an organization's ability to achieve its objectives. Which of these publics would likely have the greatest impact on the introduction of a new product designed to reduce signs of aging around the eyes? Explain.
4. The single most important demographic trend in the United States may be the changing age structure of the population. Characterize the differences among baby boomers, Generation X, and Generation Y. How might a marketer selling computers target a person in each of these groups? Let's call the next generation Generation D (the *d*igital generation). What preferences and buying patterns might emerge for this group?
5. Americans are becoming more concerned about the natural environment. Explain how this trend might affect a company that markets packaging for (a) candy bars, (b) tires,

(c) gas-powered lawn mowers, and (d) electrical power. Suggest some effective responses to the concerns that consumers might have about these products.
6. Some assert that corporate scandals, the questionable behavior of national accounting firms, and accusations of senior-executive greed are creating an ethical crisis in business. Assume you are on a task force asked to address this crisis. What penalties should exist for unethical behavior? How should the business community respond to this crisis and ensure ethical and social responsibility?
7. The cultural environment is comprised of the values, perceptions, and preferences of the institutions and people in a society. Select a society whose predominant cultural values differ from those of the United States. Compare and contrast the cultural characteristics of the two societies. How might the differing values affect marketing decisions?
8. Companies with an environmental management perspective take aggressive actions to affect the publics and forces in their marketing environments. As a marketing manager, what are some ways that you might proactively influence your marketing environment?

APPLYING THE CONCEPTS

1. With all the attention paid to youth in our society, it may be easy to forget that seniors represent the fastest-growing segment in the United States. The American Association of Retired Persons (AARP), considered a strong voice for

seniors, now has more than 35 million members. The organization raises awareness about senior issues and challenges the stereotypes that have plagued seniors for decades. AARP uses its publications and lobbying efforts to demonstrate and promote senior physical fitness, mental alertness, active lifestyles, and self-pride. The association is expected to gain more momentum as those that came of age in the 1960s join and become active members. AARP offers these new members, infused with political spirit and a desire for change, the opportunity to dramatically alter the view of seniors in the twenty-first century.

Issues such as health care, economic security, long-term care, and independent living are more than just goals for AARP. The association has leveraged these issues to secure major partnerships with airlines, hotels, resorts, insurance companies, retailers, entertainment organizations (such as movie theaters), and automobile firms. To what end? AARP and its members are spending their dollars on businesses that design their activities and products with seniors in mind. Watch for fashions, entertainment, and even the Internet to tap into the significant buying power of this growing segment.

a. Construct a brief profile of seniors in the United States. It may be helpful to examine AARP membership data and other information provided on the AAPR Web site.

b. Does a retailer such as the Gap have to choose between youth and seniors? How could the Gap appeal to both?

c. Think of a specific consumer goods company. How could the company partner with AARP to build relationships with seniors?

d. AARP has shown interest in developing partnerships in several areas. What new partnerships would you recommend for AARP? How might the association's partnerships change in the future?

e. AARP, like any business organization, is interested in expanding its membership and influence. Give three suggestions for how the organization might accomplish this.

2. The Look-Look company studies the youth culture of America. Traditionally, market research has been viewed as a straightforward, somewhat boring field. But research at Look-Look is anything but boring! Co-founders Sharon Lee and DeeDee Gordon have assembled a research team to study the habits and desires of America's youth. Look-Look studies the whole youth culture by focusing on fashion, entertainment, technology, activities, eating and drinking, and health and beauty.

Look-Look specializes in analyzing the youth mindset. Look-Look representatives talk to young people in shopping malls, on the Internet, in clothing stores, eating lunch, or walking down the street. Look-Look researchers take pictures of hairstyles, tattoos, body piercings, makeup, and even T-shirts bought in thrift stores. Look-Look has sources of information beyond just photographs. The company has an active database of over 10,000 trendsetting young people (14–30 years old). The company compiles these photographs, analyzes research results, and projects trends. As a result, Look-Look is on the cutting edge of youth culture. Retailers such as the Limited and Calvin Klein turn to Look-Look as a strong and reliable bridge to the youth culture of America.

a. What is unique about Look-Look's approach to marketing research? Do you think that approach makes the company more or less effective in tracking youth culture?

b. What are some of the current trends for young people? What were some of the predominant trends when you were young?

c. How could Look-Look's analysis help you successfully open a teen fashion-jewelry store in a local mall?

d. What would be the advantages and disadvantages of doing research on the youth market via (1) the Internet and (2) personal interviews in shopping malls?

 DIGITAL CONNECTIONS

CONNECTING COMPANIES WITH CUSTOMERS THROUGH CULTURAL SYMBOLS

What is the hottest-selling brand in the huge urban sportswear market? What brand has been able to successfully bridge the gap between youth fashion and hip-hop music? If you answered FUBU ("For Us By Us"), you answered correctly. FUBU began 10 years ago in the basement of Damon John's home. John, along with partners Carl Brown, Keith Perrin, and Jay Martin, spent long nights sewing hats and creating hip clothing to sell on the streets of Queens, New York. Their goals? To find success in the fashion world and expand African American entrepreneurship. FUBU succeeded where others failed because the company tapped into the cultural heart of inner-city youth. When rap superstar LL Cool J lent his support to the up-and-coming brand, the endorsement brought instant recognition on the streets and in the multimillion-dollar hip-hop music business. Shortly thereafter, electronics giant Samsung backed the company with a lucrative distribution. Today, the NBA, main-stream department stores such as Nordstrom and JC Penney's, and numerous celebrities are all on the FUBU bandwagon, and most experts agree that the company dominates the fashion market in America's inner cities. Now FUBU hopes to ride the wave of hip-hop's popularity into America's suburbs, where 70 percent of hip-hop fans reside.

FOR DISCUSSION

1. Visit FUBU's Web site, www.fubu.com, to learn more about the company. How is FUBU using cultural symbols to market its products? How has FUBU expanded from its original roots in the fashion world?

2. What strategies does FUBU use to connect with its target market?

3. If you were employed as a Web-master for FUBU, how would you improve the site to help the company penetrate the suburban market?

Strike Holdings: Rediscovering the Past

It really does seem that, as this video suggests, "everything old is new again." Much as Volkswagen reinvented the Beetle, Strike Holdings offers an updated version of another old favorite, the local bowling alley. By modifying the decor, adding upscale cuisine, and injecting a hint of technology, the bowling alley now attracts an array of visitors interested in rediscovering the past.

After reviewing the Bowling video, answer the following questions about generational marketing and the marketing environment:

1. Think back to the last time you went bowling. Was the atmosphere designed to appeal to young adults? Baby boomers? Families? Seniors? What elements factor into your thinking? Be specific.
2. How does the reinvention and resurgence of bowling compare to that of the Volkswagen Beetle? How does it differ?
3. List other products or services that are now riding the nostalgia wave. How do those products appeal to you? How do they appeal to your parents?

The Prius: Leading a Wave of Hybrids

There are lots of reasons why Americans might buy a high-tech auto the gives high gas mileage and emits fewer air pollutants. Americans love their cars. The U.S. culture readily adapts to progress—especially progress related to material comfort. It's a culture that worships scientific and technological advances and wants the latest gizmos. Americans rebel against gasoline price increases, even though gasoline is much cheaper in the United States than in many other parts of the world. Finally, surveys consistently show that Americans are "concerned about the environment."

Hoping that all of the above was true, and looking to grab a technological advantage over U.S. automakers, Toyota introduced the hybrid auto, the Prius, to the U.S. market in 2000. The name means "to go before," which may be very prophetic. The Prius and its companion hybrid from Honda, the Insight, are the first in a wave of hybrids coming out ahead of similar vehicles from U.S. automakers and DaimlerChrysler.

At first glance, the Prius seems to have a lot going for it. It combines a 1.5-liter, four-cylinder gas engine and a 33-kilowatt electric motor to deliver 114 horsepower. It comfortably seats five, if the three in the back aren't too tall or too big, and has 12 cubic feet of trunk space. The electric motor starts the car and operates at low speeds, using a nickel metal-hydride battery. At higher speeds, the Prius automatically switches to the gasoline engine. Under normal highway driving conditions, it should get 66 miles per gallon.

The downside is that the Prius is Besides no muscle machine. It also costs about $3,000 more than the Echo, although they are nearly the same car. Of course, getting twice as many miles per gallon of gasoline will help to offset the price differential. Assuming twice the mileage and a typical 2002 gas price of $1.59 per gallon, the Prius owner would have to buy 1,887 gallons of gasoline to offset the price difference. At 66 miles per gallon, that's 124,542 miles, which could take years. Of course, if gasoline prices were to rise drastically, that could change. But even if prices doubled—which is not likely in the United States without a lot of consumer unrest—you'd have to drive more than 60,000 miles to make up the initial price difference.

The picture gets even gloomier when you realize that no one is going to get the estimated gasoline mileage anyway. The EPA has admitted that its testing procedure overstates gasoline mileage by as much as 15 percent. It tests cars on a chassis dynamometer, where the driven wheels turn freely on a set of rotating drums. Does that sound like driving conditions in your part of the United States? In addition, hybrids use regenerative braking to recharge their batteries, with the result that braking during the EPA driving cycle is feeding more energy back into the system, boosting estimated gas mileage.

On the brighter side, Toyota and its competitors believe that costs will decrease once production of hybrids begins to yield economies of scale. The benefits of scale would not stop with the

(continued)

producer. For example, a major part of the cost of the car is the nickel metal-hydride batteries. A company such as Panasonic could reduce the cost of producing batteries through research and development, if the market merited such an investment, and could further reduce the price of batteries through its own economies of scale.

However, realizing that cost reductions are a ways off and that gasoline savings aren't going to be the key to convincing Americans to purchase the Prius, automakers have asked for tax incentives to stimulate purchase of clean-fuel and high-mileage autos. In May 2002, the IRS ruled that owners of hybrid gas-and-electric vehicles can claim a federal income-tax deduction of as much as $2,000 for buying a Prius. Of course, there is a small catch—the actual amount of the deduction depends on the incremental cost of the vehicle's fuel-saving technology. Assuming that you could take the full deduction and are in a 27.5 percent tax bracket, that's a savings of about $500. Coupling that with the gasoline savings, you'd still have to drive the car a lot of miles just to offset the initial price differential.

Why would the U.S. government give hybrid-auto buyers a tax break anyway? The answer lies in emissions regulations, environmental concerns, and politics. At present, the Corporate Average Fuel Economy program (CAFÉ— a government agency) sets emissions standards for automobiles. Environmental interest groups have lobbied the government, and many politicians have run on environmental platform planks requiring reduced auto emissions to enhance air quality. Today, cars and trucks average about 24 miles per gallon, but Senators John Kerry of Massachusetts and Ernest Hollings of South Carolina have aspirations to change that to an average of 36 miles per gallon by 2015. States such as California have considered requiring near-zero emissions standards, while other states such as Arizona, Georgia, Hawaii, Maryland, Virginia, and Utah exempt clean-fuel vehicles from HOV (high-occupancy vehicles) lane restrictions. Clearly many politicians believe that they must appear tough on emissions and gas mileage standards.

Are consumers ready for hybrids? Do improved gas mileage and emissions standards affect their buying decision? A glance at auto sales in the last 10 years would suggest not. The biggest sales growth was in SUVs and trucks, both of which get much poorer gas mileage than standard compacts. After all, we rarely saw Range Rovers 10 years ago; now they're a fairly common sight. Americans, it seems, think it's a good idea for their neighbors to drive "green machines," not themselves.

Actually, when the Prius was introduced, it flew out of dealers' showrooms. Between July and October of 2000, Toyota sold 2,610 Priuses and had difficulty keeping up with demand. By the end of October 2000, the cars were back-ordered through January.

Of course, much of that sales success is attributable to Toyota's clever marketing. Two years before introduction, Toyota began educating consumers about the Prius. The company established a Web site to distribute information and also sent e-brochures to 40,000 likely buyers just before the introduction. Within two weeks, Toyota sold 1,800 cars based on the e-mail message.

In all, Toyota spent $15 million in 2002 touting the Prius. There were print ads in magazines such as *Newsweek* and *Vanity Fair,* but the bulk of the campaign was in television advertising on channels such as Discovery, the History Channel, the Learning Channel, and MSNBC. Ads running before the actual introduction used the tag line "A car that sometimes runs on gas power and sometimes runs on electric power, from a company that always runs on brain power." These ads helped to position Toyota as an "environmentally concerned" company and more subtly stressed the technology aspect of the car. After introduction, the ads appealed more to emotion with tag lines such as "When it sees red, it charges"— a reference to the auto's recharging at stoplights. The headline captured the consumer's attention through ambiguity. Only through focusing on the ad could the consumer learn why the headline was accurate. Again, the appeal is based on the technology of the car. Finally, Toyota took advantage of Earth Day to send out green seed cards shaped like Toyota's logo to prospective buyers, wrapped some Priuses in green, and gave away cars at Earth Day events.

Of course, $15 million is just a drop in the bucket relative to Toyota's overall marketing budget of $190 million for cars and trucks in 2002, but Toyota was satisfied with the effectiveness of the campaign, given the "newness" of the car and the need to explain its technology.

Much of this success can also be attributed to the narrow targeting of the ads. The company expected the first hybrid auto buyers to be "techies" and early adopters (people who are highly likely to buy something new). They were right. Many Prius owners are immersed in the technology. They flood chat rooms with discussion of the car. The Priusenvy.com Web site urges owners to "Kick some gas."

Owners immediately began tinkering with the car's computer system. One owner in Philadelphia was able to add cruise control (an option not offered by Toyota) by wiring in a few switches in the car's computer system. The founder of the Priusenvy Web site figured out how to use the car's dashboard display screen to show files from his laptop, play video games, and view rear-view images from a video camera pointed out the back of the car. One Austrian consumer plans to install a sniffer—a device on the car's computer network that monitors electronic messages. With the sniffer, he will be able to hook up add-ons such as a MiniDisc Player, an MP3 player, a laptop computer, and a TV tuner. Want to know more? Go to www.PriusMod.com. In the past, owners using mechanical skills customized cars with paint, lowered bodies, and souped-up engines. In the future, customization may rely on being computer savvy.

Even though the Internet was a major part of the Prius launch, Toyota does not sell the car from its Web site. Buyers go to prius.toyota.com online to pick a color and decide if they want a CD player and floor mats—the only options from Toyota. After that, the dealers get involved, but it takes specially trained salespeople to explain and promote the Prius. Consequently, only 75 percent of Toyota dealers actually handle the car. Many of them are not happy about the need to train salespeople. And why should they be? Margins are higher on gas-guzzlers, which are also easier to sell.

Given dealer reluctance and consumer resistance from all those SUV and truck owners, you have to wonder why Toyota and Honda have spent so much putting their hybrids on the market. While part of the answer is government regulations, a bigger part of the answer is competition. All automakers concede that they will eventually have to move to hybrids to raise gas mileage and lower emissions, and all of them have plans to do so. Ford, for example, plans to introduce an Escape SUV in 2003 that will get 40 miles per gallon. DaimlerChrysler says that by 2003, 15 percent of its Durangos (about 33,000 SUVs) will be hybrids that will get 20 percent better fuel efficiency than a conventional Durango. General Motors is betting on hybrid buses and trucks.

Toyota hopes, however, that its early entry will be the basis for a system of hybrids from ultracompact "minicars" to luxury sedans, sport-utility vehicles, and even commercial trucks.

The American mass market, however, values space, comfort, and power. Although hybrids may have space and comfort, power would appear to be more elusive. Without greater power, it will be interesting to see if U.S. consumers, who like speed on those open freeways and acceleration on mountain inclines, will settle for a hybrid.

QUESTIONS FOR DISCUSSION

1. What microenvironmental factors affect the introduction and sale of the Toyota Prius? How well has Toyota dealt with these factors?
2. Outline the major macroenvironmental factors—demographic, economic, natural, technological, political, and cultural—that have affected the introduction and sale of the Toyota Prius. How has Toyota dealt with each these factors?
3. Evaluate Toyota's marketing strategy so far. What has Toyota done well? How might it improve its strategy?
4. In your opinion, what are the advantages of Toyota's early entry into the hybrid market? What are the disadvantages? Should Toyota have waited—like Ford, GM and DaimlerChrysler?

Sources: "Hit the Road, Tech," *Fortune,* Winter 2001, pp. 37–38; Jeffrey Ball, "Hybrid Gas-Electric Car Owners Can Get Income-Tax Deductions," *Wall Street Journal,* May 22, 2002, p. D8; Jeff Green, "Attention Techies and Assorted Geniuses: Toyota Prius Wants You," *Brandweek,* May 15, 3000, p. 113; Karl Greenberg, "A Wildflower Grows in Torrance as Toyota Gets Environmentally Aware," *Brandweek,* May 20, 2002, p. 42; Margaret Littman, "Hybrid Engine Cars Do Better with Hybrid Marketing Tactics," *Marketing News,* September 25, 2000, p. 6; John McElroy, "A Long Time Coming," *Ward's Auto World,* July 2001, p. 21; Margot Roosevelt, "Hybrid Power," *Time,* December 11, 2000, pp. 94–95; Norihiko Shirouzu, "Ford Aims to Sell a Gas-Electric SUB That Will Offer Sizable Fuel Efficiency," *Wall Street Journal,* March 7, 2000, p. A2; Sherri Singer, "Toyota Prius," *Machine Design,* January 28, 1989, pp. S52–S53; Emily Thornton, "Enviro-Car: The Race Is On," *Business Week,* February 8, 1999, p. 74; Thomas Weber, "Hacking Your Car: How Auto Buffs Use the Net to Reprogram Vehicles," *Wall Street Journal,* July 2, 2001, p. B1; David Welch, "46 Miles Per Gallon . . . 47 . . . 48," *Business Week,* August 14, 2000, p. 68.

After studying this chapter you should be able to

1. explain the importance of information to the company
2. define the marketing information system and discuss its parts
3. outline the steps in the marketing research process
4. explain how companies analyze and distribute marketing information
5. discuss the special issues some marketing researchers face, including public policy and ethics issues

*M*anaging Marketing Information

LOOKING AHEAD: PREVIEWING THE CONCEPTS

In the last chapter, you learned about the complex and changing marketing environment. In this chapter, we'll look at how companies develop and manage information about important elements of the environment—about their customers, competitors, products, and marketing programs. We'll examine marketing information systems designed to give managers the right information, in the right form, at the right time to help them make better marketing decisions. We'll also take a close look at the marketing research process and at some special marketing research considerations. To succeed in today's marketplace, companies must know how to manage mountains of marketing information effectively.

We'll start by looking at a classic marketing blunder—Coca-Cola's ill-considered decision some years ago to introduce New Coke. The company based its decision on substantial marketing research, yet the new product fizzled badly. As you read on, ask yourself how a large and resourceful marketing company such as Coca-Cola could make such a huge research mistake. The moral: If it can happen to Coca-Cola, it can happen to any company.

In 1985, in what has now become an all-time classic marketing tale, the Coca-Cola Company made a major marketing blunder. After 99 successful years, it set aside its long-standing rule—"Don't mess with Mother Coke"—and dropped its original-formula Coke! In its place came *New* Coke, with a sweeter, smoother taste.

At first, amid the introductory flurry of advertising and publicity, New Coke sold well. But sales soon went flat as a stunned public reacted. Coke began receiving sacks of mail and more than 1,500 phone calls each day from angry consumers. A group called "Old Cola Drinkers" staged protests, handed out T-shirts, and threatened a class-action suit unless Coca-Cola brought back the old formula. After only three months, the Coca-Cola Company brought old Coke back. Now called "Coke Classic," it sold side-by-side with New Coke on supermarket shelves. The company said that New Coke would remain its flagship brand, but consumers had a different idea. By the end of that year, Classic was outselling New Coke in supermarkets by two to one.

Quick reaction saved the company from potential disaster. It stepped up efforts for Coke Classic and slotted New Coke into a supporting role. Coke Classic again became the company's main brand and the country's leading soft drink. New Coke became the company's "attack brand"—its Pepsi stop-per—and ads boldly compared New Coke's taste with Pepsi's. Still, New Coke managed only a 2 percent market share. In the spring of 1990, the company repackaged New Coke and relaunched it as a brand extension with a new name, Coke II. Today, Coke Classic captures almost 17 percent of the U.S. soft drink market; Coke II has quietly disappeared.

Why was New Coke introduced in the first place? What went wrong? Many analysts blame the blunder on poor marketing research.

In the early 1980s, although Coke was still the leading soft drink, it was slowly losing market share to Pepsi. For years, Pepsi had successfully mounted the "Pepsi Challenge," a series of televised taste tests showing that consumers preferred the sweeter taste of Pepsi. By early 1985, although Coke led in the overall market, Pepsi led in share of supermarket sales by 2 percent. (That doesn't sound like much, but 2 percent of today's huge U.S. soft drink market amounts to almost $1.2 billion in retail sales!) Coca-Cola had to do something to stop the loss of its market share, and the solution appeared to be a change in Coke's taste.

Coca-Cola began the largest new-product research project in the company's history. It spent more than two years and $4 million on research before settling on a new formula. It conducted some 200,000 taste tests—30,000 on the final formula alone. In blind tests, 60 percent of consumers chose the new Coke over the old, and 52 percent chose it over Pepsi. Research showed that New Coke would be a winner, and the company introduced it with confidence. So what happened?

Looking back, we can see that Coke defined its marketing research problem too narrowly. The research looked only at taste; it did not explore consumers' feelings about dropping the old Coke and replacing it with a new version. It took no account of the *intangibles*—Coke's name, history, packaging, cultural heritage, and image. However, to many people, Coke stands alongside baseball, hot dogs, and apple pie as an American institution; it represents the very fabric of America. Coke's symbolic meaning turned out to be more important to many consumers than its taste. Research addressing a broader set of issues would have detected these strong emotions.

Coke's managers may also have used poor judgment in interpreting the research and planning strategies around it. For example, they took the finding that 60 percent of consumers preferred New Coke's taste to mean that the new product would win in the marketplace, as when a political candidate wins with 60 percent of the vote. But it also meant that 40 percent still liked the original formula. By dropping the old Coke, the company trampled the taste buds of the large core of loyal Coke drinkers who didn't want a change. The company might have been wiser to leave the old Coke alone and introduce New Coke as a brand extension, as it later did successfully with Cherry Coke.

The Coca-Cola Company has one of the largest, best-managed, and most advanced marketing research operations in America. Good marketing research has kept the company atop the rough-and-tumble soft drink market for decades. But marketing research is far from an exact science. Consumers are full of surprises, and figuring them out can be awfully tough. If Coca-Cola can make a large marketing research mistake, any company can.[1]

In order to produce superior value and satisfaction for customers, companies need information at almost every turn. As the New Coke story highlights, good products and marketing programs begin with a thorough understanding of consumer needs and wants. Companies also need an abundance of information on competitors, resellers, and other actors and forces in the marketplace.

Increasingly, marketers are viewing information not only as an input for making better decisions but also as an important strategic asset and marketing tool. A company's information may prove to be its chief competitive advantage. Competitors can copy each other's equipment, products, and procedures, but they cannot duplicate the company's information and intellectual capital. Several companies have recently recognized this by appointing vice presidents of knowledge, learning, or intellectual capital.[2]

In today's more rapidly changing environments, managers need up-to-date information to make timely, high-quality decisions. In turn, with the recent explosion of information technologies, companies can now generate information in great quantities. In fact, today's managers often receive too much information. One study found that with all the companies offering data, and

Information overload: "In this oh so overwhelming Information age, it's all too easy to be buried, burdened, and burned out by data overload."

FIGURE 5.1
The marketing information system

with all the information now available through supermarket scanners, a packaged-goods brand manager is bombarded with 1 million to 1 *billion* new numbers each week. Another study found that, on average, American office workers spend 60 percent of their time processing information; a typical manager reads about a million words a week. Thus, running out of information is not a problem, but seeing through the "data smog" is. "In this oh-so-overwhelming Information age," comments one observer, "it's all too easy to be buried, burdened, and burned out by data overload.[3]

Despite this data glut, marketers frequently complain that they lack enough information of the *right* kind. One recent study found that managers lose as much as three hours a day looking for the right information, costing U.S. companies more than $2.5 billion annually. Another study found that although half of the managers surveyed said they couldn't cope with the volume of information coming at them, two-thirds wanted even more. The researcher concluded that, "despite the volume, they're still not getting what they want."[4] Thus, most marketing managers don't need *more* information, they need *better* information. Companies must design effective marketing information systems that give managers the right information, in the right form, at the right time to help them make better marketing decisions.

A **marketing information system (MIS)** consists of people, equipment, and procedures to gather, sort, analyze, evaluate, and distribute needed, timely, and accurate information to marketing decision makers. Figure 5.1 shows that the MIS begins and ends with information users—marketing managers, internal and external partners, and others who need marketing information. First, it interacts with these information users to *assess information needs*. Next, it *develops needed information* from internal company databases, marketing intelligence activities, and marketing research. Then it helps users to analyze information to put it in the right form for making marketing decisions and managing customer relationships. Finally, the MIS *distributes* the marketing information and helps managers *use* it in their decision making.

Marketing information system (MIS)

People, equipment, and procedures to gather, sort, analyze, evaluate, and distribute needed, timely, and accurate information to marketing decision makers.

Assessing Marketing Information Needs

The marketing information system primarily serves the company's marketing and other managers. However, it may also provide information to external partners, such as suppliers or marketing services agencies. For example, Wal-Mart might give Procter & Gamble and other key suppliers access to information on customer buying patterns and inventory levels. In addition, important customers may be given limited access to the information system. Dell Computer creates tailored Premium Pages for large customers, giving them access to product design, order status, and product support and service information. FedEx lets customers into its information system to schedule and track shipments. In designing an information system, the company must consider the needs of all of these users.

A good marketing information system balances the information users would *like* to have against what they really *need* and what is *feasible* to offer. The company begins by interviewing managers to find out what information they would like. Some managers will ask for whatever information they can get without thinking carefully about what they really need. Too much information can be as harmful as too little. Other managers may omit things they ought to know or may not know to ask for some types of information they should have. For example, managers might need to know that a competitor plans to introduce a new product during the coming year. Because they do not know about the new product, they do not think to ask about it. The MIS must monitor the marketing environment in order to provide decision makers with information they should have to make key marketing decisions.

Sometimes the company cannot provide the needed information, either because it is not available or because of MIS limitations. For example, a brand manager might want to know how competitors will change their advertising budgets next year and how these changes will affect industry market shares. The information on planned budgets probably is not available. Even if it is, the company's MIS may not be advanced enough to forecast resulting changes in market shares.

Finally, the costs of obtaining, processing, storing, and delivering information can mount quickly. The company must decide whether the benefits of having additional information are worth the costs of providing it, and both value and cost are often hard to assess. By itself, information has no worth; its value comes from its *use*. In many cases, additional information will do little to change or improve a manager's decision, or the costs of the information may exceed the returns from the improved decision. Marketers should not assume that additional information will always be worth obtaining. Rather, they should weigh carefully the costs of additional information against the benefits resulting from it.

Developing Marketing Information

Marketers can obtain the needed information from *internal data, marketing intelligence,* and *marketing research.*

Internal Data

Internal databases
Electronic collections of information obtained from data sources within the company.

Many companies build extensive **internal databases,** electronic collections of information obtained from data sources within the company. Marketing managers can readily access and work with information in the database to identify marketing opportunities and problems, plan programs, and evaluate performance.

Information in the database can come from many sources. The accounting department prepares financial statements and keeps detailed records of sales, costs, and cash flows. Operations reports on production schedules, shipments, and inventories. The sales force reports on reseller reactions and competitor activities. The marketing department furnishes information on customer demographics, psychographics, and buying behavior, and the customer service department keeps records of customer-satisfaction or service problems. Research studies done for one department may provide useful information for several others.

Here is an example of how one company uses its internal database to make better marketing decisions:

USAA, which provides financial services to U.S. military personnel and their families, maintains a customer database built from customer purchasing histories and from information collected directly from customers. USAA uses the database to tailor marketing offers to the specific needs of individual customers. For example, if the family has college-age children, the USAA sends those children information on how to manage their credit

Financial services provider USAA uses its extensive database to tailor marketing offers to the specific needs of individual customers, resulting in greater than 96 percent customer retention.

cards. If the family has younger children, it sends booklets on things like financing a child's education. Or, for customers looking toward retirement, it sends information on estate planning. Through skillful use of its database, USAA serves each customer uniquely, resulting in high levels of customer loyalty—the roughly $65 billion company retains over 96 percent of its customers.[5]

Internal databases usually can be accessed more quickly and cheaply than other information sources, but they also present some problems. Because internal information was collected for other purposes, it may be incomplete or in the wrong form for making marketing decisions. For example, sales and cost data used by the accounting department for preparing financial statements must be adapted for use in evaluating product, sales force, or channel performance. Data ages quickly; keeping the database current requires a major effort. In addition, a large company produces mountains of information, and keeping track of it all is difficult. The database information must be well integrated and readily accessible through user-friendly interfaces so that managers can find it easily and use it effectively.

Marketing Intelligence

Marketing intelligence
The systematic collection and analysis of publicly available information about competitors and developments in the marketing environment.

Marketing intelligence is systematic collection and analysis of publicly available information about competitors and developments in the marketing environment. The goal of marketing intelligence is to improve strategic decision making, assess and track competitors' actions, and provide early warning of opportunities and threats.

Competitive intelligence gathering has grown dramatically as more and more companies are now busily snooping on their competitors. Techniques range from quizzing the company's own employees and benchmarking competitors' products to researching the Internet, lurking around industry trade shows, and rooting through rivals' trash bins.

Much intelligence can be collected from people inside the rival companies—executives, engineers and scientists, purchasing agents, and the sales force. Consider the following examples:

While talking with a Kodak copier salesperson, a Xerox technician learned that the salesperson was being trained to service Xerox products. The Xerox employee reported back to his boss, who in turn passed the news to Xerox's intelligence unit. Using such clues as a classified ad Kodak placed seeking new people with Xerox product experience, Xerox verified Kodak's plan—code-named Ulysses—to service Xerox copiers. To protect its profitable service business, Xerox designed a Total Satisfaction Guarantee, which allowed copier returns for any reason as long as *Xerox* did the servicing. By the time Kodak launched Ulysses, Xerox had been promoting its new program for three months.

Spies don't always enter a rival's lair through the back door. Sometimes they stride in, and are even welcomed by their hosts. Bob Ayling, ex–chief executive of British Airways, accomplished such a mission when he visited the offices of the recently launched EasyJet. . . . Ayling approached the company's founder, Stelios Haji-Ioannou, to ask whether he could visit, claiming to be fascinated as to how the Greek entrepreneur had made the budget airline formula work. Haji-Ioannou not only agreed, but allegedly showed Ayling his business plan. [A year later, British Air] announced the launch of Go. "It was a carbon copy of EasyJet," says . . . EasyGroup's director of corporate affairs. "Same planes, same direct ticket sales, same use of a secondary airport, and same idea to sell on-board refreshments. They succeeded in stealing our business model—it was a highly effective spying job."[6]

The company can also obtain important intelligence information from suppliers, resellers, and key customers. Or it can get good information by observing competitors. It can buy and analyze competitors' products, monitor their sales, check for new patents, and examine various types of physical evidence. For example, one company regularly checks out competitors' parking lots—full lots might indicate plenty of work and prosperity; half-full lots might suggest hard times.[7]

Some companies have even rifled their competitors' garbage, which is legally considered abandoned property once it leaves the premises. In one garbage-snatching incident, Avon hired private detectives to paw through the dumpster of rival Mary Kay Cosmetics to search for revealing documents. An outraged Mary Kay sued to get its garbage back, but the dumpster had been located in a public parking lot and Avon had videotapes to prove it. In another case, Procter & Gamble admitted to "dumpster diving" at rival Unilever's headquarters. The target was Unilever's

Marketing intelligence: Procter & Gamble admitted to "dumpster diving" at rival Unilever's Helene Curtis headquarters. When P&G's top management learned of the questionable practice, it stopped the project, voluntarily informed Unilever, and set up talks to right whatever competitive wrongs had been done.

hair-care products—including Salon Selectives, Finesse, Thermasilk, and Helen Curtis—which competed with P&G's own Pantene, Head & Shoulders, and Pert brands. "Apparently, the operation was a big success," notes an analyst. "P&G got its mitts on just about every iota of info there was to be had about Unilever's brands." However, when news of the questionable tactics reached top P&G managers, they were shocked. They immediately stopped the project, voluntarily informed Unilever, and set up negotiations to right whatever competitive wrongs had been done. Although P&G claims it broke no laws, the company reported that the dumpster raids "violated our strict guidelines regarding our business policies."[8]

Competitors may reveal intelligence information through their annual reports, business publications, trade-show exhibits, press releases, advertisements, and Web pages. The Internet is proving to be a vast new source of competitor-supplied information. Most companies now place volumes of information on their Web sites, providing details to attract customers, partners, suppliers, or franchisees. For example, Allied Signal's Web site provides revenue goals and reveals the company's production-defect rate along with its plans to improve it. Mail Boxes Etc., a chain of mailing services, provides data on its average franchise, including square footage, number of employees, operating hours, and more—all valuable insights for a competitor.

"In today's information age, companies are leaving a paper trail of information online," says an online intelligence expert. Today's managers "don't have to simply rely on old news or intuition when making investment and business decisions."[9] Using Internet search engines, marketers can search specific competitor names, events, or trends and see what turns up. Intelligence seekers can also pore through any of thousands of online databases. Some are free. For example, the U.S. Security and Exchange Commission's database provides a huge stockpile of financial information on public competitors, and the U.S. Patent Office database reveals patents competitors have filed. And for a fee, companies can subscribe to any of more than 3,000 online databases and information search services such as Dialog, DataStar, LEXIS-NEXIS, Dow Jones News Retrieval, UMI ProQuest, and Dun & Bradstreet's Online Access.

Facing determined marketing intelligence efforts by competitors, most companies are now taking countermeasures. For example, Unilever has begun widespread competitive intelligence training. According to a former Unilever staffer, "We were told how to protect information, as well as how to get it from competitors. We were warned to always keep our mouths shut when traveling. . . . We were even warned that spies from competitors could be posing as drivers at the mini-cab company we used." Unilever even performs random checks on internal security. Says the former staffer, "At one [internal marketing] conference, we were set up when an actor was employed to infiltrate the group. The idea was to see who spoke to him, how much they told him, and how long it took to realize that no one knew him. He ended up being there for a long time."[10]

The growing use of marketing intelligence raises a number of ethical issues. Although most of the preceding techniques are legal, and some are considered to be shrewdly competitive, some may involve questionable ethics. Clearly, companies should take advantage of publicly available information. However, they should not stoop to snoop. With all the legitimate intelligence sources now available, a company does not have to break the law or accepted codes of ethics to get good intelligence.[11]

Marketing Research

In addition to information about competitor and environmental happenings, marketers often need formal studies of specific situations. For example, Sears wants to know what appeals will be most effective in its corporate advertising campaign. Or Toshiba wants to know how many and what kinds of people or companies will buy its new superfast notebook computer. In such situations, marketing intelligence will not provide the detailed information needed. Managers will need marketing research.

Marketing research
The systematic design, collection, analysis, and reporting of data relevant to a specific marketing situation facing an organization.

Marketing research is the systematic design, collection, analysis, and reporting of data relevant to a specific marketing situation facing an organization. Companies use marketing research in a wide variety of situations. For example, marketing research can help marketers assess market potential and market share; understand customer satisfaction and purchase behavior; and measure the effectiveness of pricing, product, distribution, and promotion activities.

Some large companies have their own research departments that work with marketing managers on marketing research projects. This is how Kraft, Citigroup, and many other corporate

FIGURE 5.2
The marketing research process

giants handle marketing research. In addition, these companies—like their smaller counterparts—frequently hire outside research specialists to consult with management on specific marketing problems and conduct marketing research studies. Sometimes firms simply purchase data collected by outside firms to aid in their decision making.

The marketing research process (see Figure 5.2) has four steps: *defining the problem and research objectives, developing the research plan, implementing the research plan,* and *interpreting and reporting the findings.*

Defining the Problem and Research Objectives

Marketing managers and researchers must work closely together to define the problem and agree on research objectives. The manager best understands the decision for which information is needed; the researcher best understands marketing research and how to obtain the information.

Defining the problem and research objectives is often the hardest step in the research process. The manager may know that something is wrong, without knowing the specific causes. For example, in the New Coke case, Coca-Cola defined its research problem too narrowly, with disastrous results. In another example, managers of a large discount retail store chain hastily decided that falling sales were caused by poor advertising. As a result, they ordered research to test the company's advertising. When this research showed that current advertising was reaching the right people with the right message, the managers were puzzled. It turned out that the real problem was that the chain was not delivering the prices, products, and service promised in the advertising. Careful problem definition would have avoided the cost and delay of doing advertising research.

After the problem has been defined carefully, the manager and researcher must set the research objectives. A marketing research project might have one of three types of objectives. The objective of **exploratory research** is to gather preliminary information that will help define the problem and suggest hypotheses. The objective of **descriptive research** is to describe things, such as the market potential for a product or the demographics and attitudes of consumers who buy the product. The objective of **causal research** is to test hypotheses about cause-and-effect relationships. For example, would a 10 percent decrease in tuition at a private college result in an enrollment increase sufficient to offset the reduced tuition? Managers often start with exploratory research and later follow with descriptive or causal research.

The statement of the problem and research objectives guides the entire research process. The manager and researcher should put the statement in writing to be certain that they agree on the purpose and expected results of the research.

Developing the Research Plan

Once the research problems and objectives have been defined, researchers must determine the exact information needed, develop a plan for gathering it efficiently, and present the plan to management. The research plan outlines sources of existing data and spells out the specific research approaches, contact methods, sampling plans, and instruments that researchers will use to gather new data.

Research objectives must be translated into specific information needs. For example, suppose Campbell decides to conduct research on how consumers would react to the introduction of new bowl-shaped plastic containers that it has used successfully for a number of its other products. The containers would cost more but would allow consumers to heat the soup in a microwave oven without adding water or milk and to eat it without using dishes. This research might call for the following specific information:

- The demographic, economic, and lifestyle characteristics of current soup users. (Busy working couples might find the convenience of the new packaging worth the price; families with children might want to pay less and wash the pan and bowls.)

Exploratory research

Marketing research to gather preliminary information that will help define problems and suggest hypotheses.

Descriptive research

Marketing research to better describe marketing problems, situations, or markets, such as the market potential for a product or the demographics and attitudes of consumers.

Causal research

Marketing research to test hypotheses about cause-and-effect relationships.

- Consumer-usage patterns for soup: how much soup they eat, where, and when. (The new packaging might be ideal for adults eating lunch on the go, but less convenient for parents feeding lunch to several children.)
- Retailer reactions to the new packaging. (Failure to get retailer support could hurt sales of the new package.)
- Consumer attitudes toward the new packaging. (The red-and-white Campbell can has become an American institution—will consumers accept the new packaging?)
- Forecasts of sales of both new and current packages. (Will the new packaging increase Campbell's profits?)

Campbell managers will need these and many other types of information to decide whether to introduce the new packaging.

The research plan should be presented in a *written proposal*. A written proposal is especially important when the research project is large and complex or when an outside firm carries it out. The proposal should cover the management problems addressed and the research objectives, the information to be obtained, and the way the results will help management decision making. The proposal also should include research costs.

To meet the manager's information needs, the research plan can call for gathering secondary data, primary data, or both. **Secondary data** consist of information that already exists somewhere, having been collected for another purpose. **Primary data** consist of information collected for the specific purpose at hand.

Gathering Secondary Data

Researchers usually start by gathering secondary data. The company's internal database provides a good starting point. However, the company can also tap a wide assortment of external information sources, including commercial data services and government sources (see Table 5.1).

Companies can buy secondary data reports from outside suppliers.[12] For example, Information Resources, Inc., sells supermarket scanner purchase data from a panel of 55,000 households nationally, with measures of trial and repeat purchasing, brand loyalty, and buyer demographics. The *Monitor* service by Yankelovich and Partners sells information on important social and lifestyle trends. These and other firms supply high-quality data to suit a wide variety of marketing information needs.

Using commercial **online databases,** marketing researchers can conduct their own searches of secondary data sources. General database services such as CompuServe, Dialog, and LEXIS-NEXIS put an incredible wealth of information at the keyboards of marketing decision makers. Beyond commercial Web sites offering information for a fee, almost every industry association, government agency, business publication, and news medium offers free information to those tenacious enough to find their Web sites. There are so many Web sites offering data that finding the right ones can become an almost overwhelming task.

Secondary data can usually be obtained more quickly and at a lower cost than primary data. For example, an Internet or online database search might provide all the information Campbell needs on soup usage, quickly and at low cost. A study to collect primary information might take weeks or months and cost thousands of dollars. Also, secondary sources sometimes can provide data an individual company cannot collect on its own—information that either is not directly available or would be too expensive to collect. For example, it would be too expensive for Campbell to conduct a continuing retail store audit to find out about the market shares, prices, and displays of competitors' brands. But it can buy the InfoScan service from Information Resources, Inc., which provides this information from thousands of scanner-equipped supermarkets in dozens of U.S. markets.

Secondary data can also present problems. The needed information may not exist—researchers can rarely obtain all the data they need from secondary sources. For example, Campbell will not find existing information about consumer reactions to new packaging that it has not yet placed on the market. Even when data can be found, they might not be very usable. The researcher must evaluate secondary information carefully to make certain it is *relevant* (fits research project needs), *accurate* (reliably collected and reported), *current* (up-to-date enough for current decisions), and *impartial* (objectively collected and reported).

Secondary data

Information that already exists somewhere, having been collected for another purpose.

Primary data

Information collected for the specific purpose at hand.

Online databases

Computerized collections of information available from online commercial sources or via the Internet.

TABLE 5.1   SELECTED EXTERNAL INFORMATION SOURCES

For business data:

AC Nielsen (www.acnielsen.com) provides supermarket scanner data on sales, market share, and retail prices; data on household purchasing; and data on television audiences.

Information Resources, Inc. (www.infores.com) provides supermarket scanner data for tracking grocery product movement and new product purchasing data.

Arbitron (www.arbitron.com) provides local-market and Internet radio audience and advertising expenditure information, among other media and ad spending data.

NDC Health Information Services (www.simatics.com/index.htm) reports on the movement of drugs, laboratory supplies, animal health products, and personal care products.

Simmons Market Research Bureau (www.smrb.com) provides detailed analysis of consumer patterns in 400 product categories in selected markets.

Dun & Bradstreet (www.dnb.com) maintains a database containing information on more than 50 million individual companies around the globe.

Dialog (http://library.dialog.com) offers access to ABI/INFORM, a database of articles from 800+ publications, and to reports, newsletters, and directories covering dozens of industries.

LEXIS-NEXIS (www.lexis-nexis.com) features articles from business, consumer, and marketing publications plus tracking of firms, industries, trends, and promotion techniques.

CompuServe (www.compuserve.com) provides access to databases of business and consumer demographics, government reports, and patent records, plus articles from newspapers, newsletters, and research reports.

Dow Jones Interactive (http://bis.dowjones.com) specializes in in-depth financial, historical, and operational information on public and private companies.

Hoovers Online (www.hoovers.com) provides business descriptions, financial overviews, and news about major companies around the world.

CNN (www.cnn.com) reports U.S. and global news and covers the markets and news-making companies in detail.

American Demographics (www.americandemographics.com) reports on demographic trends and their significance for businesses.

For government data:

Securities and Exchange Commission Edgar database (www.sec.gov) provides financial data on U.S. public corporations.

Small Business Administration (www.sbaonline.gov) features information and links for small-business owners.

Federal Trade Commission (www.ftc.gov) shows regulations and decisions related to consumer protection and antitrust laws.

Stat-USA (www.stat.usa.gov), a Department of Commerce site, highlights statistics on U.S. business and international trade.

U.S. Census (www.census.gov) provides detailed statistics and trends about the U.S. population.

U.S. Patent and Trademark Office (www.uspto.gov) allows searches to determine who has filed for trademarks and patents.

For Internet data:

CyberAtlas (http://cyberatlas.internet.com) brings together a wealth of information about the Internet and its users, from consumers to e-commerce.

Internet Advertising Bureau (www.iab.net) covers statistics about advertising on the Internet.

Jupiter Media Metrix (www.jmm.com) provides audience measurement and geodemographic analysis of Internet and digital media users around the world.

Primary Data Collection

Secondary data provide a good starting point for research and often help to define problems and research objectives. In most cases, however, the company must also collect primary data. Just as researchers must carefully evaluate the quality of secondary information, they also must take great care when collecting primary data to make sure that it will be relevant, accurate, current, and unbiased. Table 5.2 shows that designing a plan for primary data collection calls for a number of decisions on *research approaches, contact methods, sampling plan,* and *research instruments.*

Online database services such as Dialog put an incredible wealth of information at the keyboards of marketing decision makers. Dialog puts "information to change the world, or your corner of it" at your fingertips.

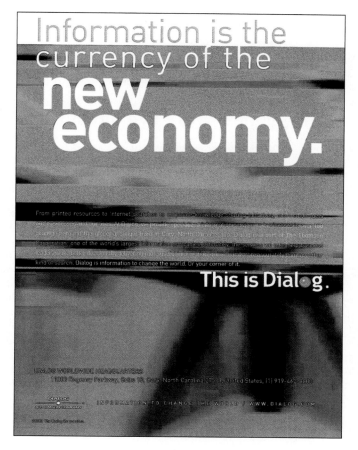

Observational research

The gathering of primary data by observing relevant people, actions, and situations.

Research Approaches. Research approaches for gathering primary data include observation, surveys, and experiments. **Observational research** involves gathering primary data by observing relevant people, actions, and situations. For example, a consumer packaged-goods marketer might visit supermarkets and observe shoppers as they browse the store, pick up products and examine packages, and make actual buying decisions. Or a bank might evaluate possible new branch locations by checking traffic patterns, neighborhood conditions, and the location of competing branches. A wide range of companies now use *ethnographic research*—which combines intensive observation with customer interviews—to gain deep insights into how customers buy and live with their products (see Real Marketing 5.1).

B2B marketers also employ observation in their marketing research. For example, Steelcase used it to help design new office furniture for use by work teams.

TABLE 5.2		PLANNING PRIMARY DATA COLLECTION	
Research Approaches	**Contact Methods**	**Sampling Plan**	**Research Instruments**
Observation	Mail	Sampling unit	Questionnaire
Survey	Telephone	Sample size	Mechanical instruments
Experiment	Personal	Sampling procedure	
	Online		

real marketing 5.1

Ethnographic Research: Keeping a Close Eye on Consumers

What do customers *really* think about your product and what do they say about it to their friends? How do they *really* use it? Will they tell you? *Can* they tell you? These are difficult questions for most marketers. And too often, traditional research simply can't provide accurate answers. To get better

"We beat the s_ out of the front desk and got a terrific room." No, this wasn't an FBI sting operation. Instead, the couple was part of [an ethnographic study in which Best Western International] paid 25 over-55 couples to tape themselves on cross-country journeys. The effort convinced the

delayed its marketing plan in order to weave the insights into its core strategy. Unfortunately for seniors, that means the rooms won't be getting any cheaper.

In today's intensely competitive marketplace, holding on to customers requires more than a superficial understanding of customers' interactions with a product. Companies must have a deep understanding of how customers feel about and interact with products, then adjust their marketing offers and programs accordingly. Ethnographic research helps provide such an understanding. It combines intense observation with customer interviews to get an up-close and personal view of how people actually live with products. Here's another example:

Observing consumers in their "natural environment": Ethnographic researchers video taped consumers pondering "the dreaded sea of red meat" at their local super markets. The conclusion? Confusion. As a result, many grocers' now display beef by cooking method rather than by cuts of meat.

A woman in suburban Baltimore is shopping for her family's meals for the week. She cruises past the poultry section, stopping only momentarily to drop a couple of packages of boneless chicken breasts into her cart. Then, the dreaded sea of red meat looms before her. Tentatively, she picks up a package of beef. "This cut looks good, not too fatty," she says, juggling her two-year-old on her hip. "But I don't know what it is. And I don't know how to cook it," she confesses. She trades it for a small package of sirloin and her regular order of ground beef. Scenes like this play out daily in supermarkets across the country. But this time, it's being captured on videotape, part of a recent ethnographic study of beef consumers for the National Cattlemen's Beef Association (NCBA) and major grocery retailers.

insights, many companies are now turning to an increasingly popular research approach—ethnographic or observational research.

Ethnographic research involves sending trained observers to watch consumers in their "natural environment"—to observe up close the subtleties of how consumers use and feel about products and services.

The 60-ish woman caught on the grainy videotape is sitting on her hotel bed, addressing her husband after a long day spent on the road. "Good job!" she exults.

hotel chain that it didn't need to boost its standard 10 percent senior citizen discount. The tapes showed that seniors who talked the hotel clerk into a better deal didn't need the lower price to afford the room; they were after the thrill of the deal. Instead of attracting new customers, bigger discounts would simply allow the old customers to trade up to a fancier dinner down the street somewhere, doing absolutely nothing for Best Western. . . . Best Western captured such a wealth of customer behavior on tape that it has

Knowing what consumers actually do with beef is vital to the NCBA. Even though sales of ground beef have risen in recent years, other beef products have lost ground. To get a firsthand understanding of what really goes on in consumers' minds as they shop the meat case, NCBA researchers videotaped not only consumers' store behavior but also their preparation habits at home. And they interviewed consumers at each step, asking what they thought about beef, why they did or didn't select particular cuts, their thoughts on meat department layouts, how they prepared the family meal, and the availability of recipes.

The conclusion? Confusion. Although the typical shopper would initially say that she wasn't confused about buying beef, "when we went deeper, we found that she wasn't confused because she always buys the same cuts—ground beef, boneless chicken breast, maybe one steak," says Kevin Yost, NCBA's director of consumer marketing. "When you start to broaden the range [of meat selections], she has no idea what you're talking about." The result? Many grocers' meat cases are now being rearranged to display beef by cooking method, rather than by cuts of meat. Simple, three-step cooking instructions will soon be printed on the packages.

Ethnographic research often yields the kinds of intimate details that just don't emerge from traditional focus groups. For example, focus groups told Best Western that it's the men who decide when to stop for the night and where to stay. The videotapes showed it was usually the women. And by videotaping consumers in the shower, plumbing fixture maker Moen uncovered safety risks that consumers didn't recognize—such as the habit some women had of holding on to one unit's-temperature-control while shaving their legs. Moen would find it almost impossible to dis-

cover such design flaws simply by asking questions.

Procter & Gamble uses ethnographic snooping to try to come up with products that solve problems shoppers didn't even know they had.

Now this is reality TV. But the only one watching is Procter & Gamble. The giant consumer goods marketer now sends ethnographers and video crews into households around the world to capture, on tape, life's daily routines in all their boring glory. P&G thinks such voyeurism will yield a mountain of priceless insights into consumer behavior that more traditional methods might miss. People, it seems, tend to have selective memories when talking to a market researcher. They might say, for example, that they brush their teeth every morning or indulge in just a few potato chips, when in fact they often forget to brush and eat the whole bag. After a subject family agrees to participate, video crews arrive at the home when the alarm clock rings in the morning and stay until bedtime, usually for a four-day stretch.

In a recent case, P&G marketers huddled around a laptop computer in a Cincinnati conference room to watch a mother make breakfast for her baby in a tidy kitchen in Thailand. She rests her baby on a hip with one arm and stirs a pot of noodles with her other hand. Then she brings baby and bowl to a table, sits the baby on her lap, and feeds him while he

grabs for the spoon. Occasionally, she looks at a television set droning the morning news. The P&G managers note several things. She has only one hand to cook with. She isn't using a high chair. There aren't any toys strewn across the floor. "Notice how she glances at the TV while she's feeding the baby," says a P&G director of consumer and marketing knowledge. "You might not have caught some of these things if you had asked her." The behaviors that consumers don't talk about—such as multitasking while feeding a baby—could inspire product and package design in ways that give the company a real edge over rivals.

So, more and more, marketers are keeping a close eye on consumers. "Knowing the individual consumer on an intimate basis has become a necessity," says a research industry consultant, "and ethnography is the intimate connection to the consumer."

Sources: Excerpts adapted from Kendra Parker, "How Do You Like Your Beef?" *American Demographics,* January 2000, pp. 35–37; Gerry Khermouch, "Consumers in the Mist," *Business Week,* February 26, 2001, pp. 92–94; and Emily Nelson, "P&G Checks Out Real Life," *Wall Street Journal,* May 17, 2001, p. B1. For other examples, see Kitty McKinsey, "She Wants to Watch You," *Far Eastern Economic Review,* September 6, 2001, pp. 46–47; and Lawrence Osborne, "Consuming Rights of the Suburban Tribe," *New York Times,* January 13, 2002, p. 6.29.

To learn firsthand how teams actually operate, it set up video cameras at various companies and studied the tapes, looking for motions and behavior patterns that customers themselves might not even notice. It found that teams work best when they can do some work together and some privately. So Steelcase designed highly successful modular office units called Personal Harbor. These units are "rather like telephone booths in size and shape." They can be arranged around a common space where a team works, letting people work together but also alone when necessary. Says a Steelcase executive, "Market data wouldn't necessarily have pointed us that way. It was more important to know how people actually work."[13]

Many companies collect data through *mechanical* observation via machine or computer. For example, the Nielsen Media Research attaches *people meters* to television sets in selected homes to record who watches which programs. Other companies use *checkout scanners* to record shoppers'

"Observational research: Steelcase set up video cameras at various companies to study motions and behavior patterns that customers themselves might not even notice. The result was the highly successful Personal Harbor modular office units."

purchases so that manufacturers and retailers can assess product sales and store performance. And DoubleClick, among other Internet companies, places a *cookie*—a bit of information—on consumers' hard drives to monitor their Web surfing patterns. Similarly, MediaMetrix places special software on consumers' PCs to monitor Web-surfing patterns and produce ratings for top Web sites.

Observational research can obtain information that people are unwilling or unable to provide. In some cases, observation may be the only way to obtain the needed information. In contrast, some things simply cannot be observed, such as feelings, attitudes and motives, or private behavior. Long-term or infrequent behavior is also difficult to observe. Because of these limitations, researchers often use observation along with other data collection methods.

Survey research, the most widely used method for primary data collection, is the approach best suited for gathering *descriptive* information. A company that wants to know about people's knowledge, attitudes, preferences, or buying behavior can often find out by asking them directly.

Some firms provide marketers with a more comprehensive look at buying patterns through **single-source data systems.** These systems start with surveys of huge consumer panels—carefully selected groups of consumers who agree to participate in ongoing research. Then, they electronically monitor survey respondents' purchases and exposure to various marketing activities. Combining the survey and monitoring information gives a better understanding of the link between consumer characteristics, attitudes, and purchase behavior.

The major advantage of survey research is its flexibility—it can be used to obtain many different kinds of information in many different situations. However, survey research also presents some problems. Sometimes people are unable to answer survey questions because they cannot remember or have never thought about what they do and why. People may be unwilling to respond to unknown interviewers or about things they consider private. Respondents may answer survey questions even when they do not know the answer, in order to appear smarter or more informed. Or they may try to help the interviewer by giving pleasing answers. Finally, busy people may not take the time, or they may resent the intrusion into their privacy.

Whereas observation is best suited for exploratory research and surveys for descriptive research, **experimental research** is best suited for gathering *causal* information. Experiments involve selecting matched groups of subjects, giving them different treatments, controlling unrelated factors, and checking for differences in group responses. Thus, experimental research tries to explain cause-and-effect relationships.

For example, before adding a new sandwich to its menu, McDonald's might use experiments to test the effects on sales of two different prices it might charge. It could introduce the new sandwich at one price in one city and at another price in another city. If the cities are similar, and if all

Survey research
The gathering of primary data by asking people questions about their knowledge, attitudes, preferences, and buying behavior.

Single-source data systems
Electronic monitoring systems that link consumers' exposure to television advertising and promotion (measured using television meters) with what they buy in stores (measured using store checkout scanners).

Experimental research
The gathering of primary data by selecting matched groups of subjects, giving them different treatments, controlling related factors, and checking for differences in group responses.

TABLE 5.3	STRENGTHS AND WEAKNESSES OF CONTACT METHODS			
	Mail	**Telephone**	**Personal**	**Online**
Flexibility	Poor	Good	Excellent	Good
Quantity of data that can be collected	Good	Fair	Excellent	Good
Control of interviewer effects	Excellent	Fair	Poor	Fair
Control of sample	Fair	Excellent	Fair	Poor
Speed of data collection	Poor	Excellent	Good	Excellent
Response rate	Fair	Good	Good	Good
Cost	Good	Fair	Poor	Excellent

Source: Adapted with permission from *Marketing Research: Measurement and Method,* 7th ed., by Donald S. Tull and Del I. Hawkins. Copyright 1993 by Macmillan Publishing Company.

other marketing efforts for the sandwich are the same, then differences in sales in the two cities could be related to the price charged.

Contact Methods.   Information can be collected by mail, by telephone, via personal interview, or online. Table 5.3 shows the strengths and weaknesses of each of these contact methods.

Mail questionnaires can be used to collect large amounts of information at a low cost per respondent. Respondents may give more-honest answers to more-personal questions on a mail questionnaire than to an unknown interviewer in person or over the phone. Also, no interviewer is involved to bias the respondent's answers. However, mail questionnaires are not very flexible—all respondents answer the same questions in a fixed order. Mail surveys usually take longer to complete, and the response rate—the number of people returning completed questionnaires—is often very low. Finally, the researcher often has little control over the mail questionnaire sample. Even with a good mailing list, it is hard to control *who* at the mailing address fills out the questionnaire.

Telephone interviewing is the one of the best methods for gathering information quickly, and it provides greater flexibility than mail questionnaires. Interviewers can explain difficult questions and, depending on the answers they receive, skip some questions or probe on others. Response rates tend to be higher than with mail questionnaires, and interviewers can ask to speak to respondents with the desired characteristics or even by name.

However, with telephone interviewing, the cost per respondent is higher than with mail questionnaires. Also, people may not want to discuss personal questions with an interviewer. The method also introduces interviewer bias—the way interviewers talk, how they ask questions, and other differences may affect respondents' answers. Finally, different interviewers may interpret and record responses differently, and under time pressures some interviewers might even cheat by recording answers without asking questions.

Personal interviewing takes two forms—individual and group interviewing. *Individual interviewing* involves talking with people in their homes or offices, on the street, or in shopping malls. Such interviewing is flexible. Trained interviewers can guide interviews, explain difficult questions, and explore issues as the situation requires. They can show subjects actual products, advertisements, or packages and observe reactions and behavior. However, individual personal interviews may cost three to four times as much as telephone interviews.

Group interviewing consists of inviting 6 to 10 people to talk with a trained moderator about a product, service, or organization. Participants normally are paid a small sum for attending. The moderator encourages free and easy discussion, hoping that group interactions will bring out actual feelings and thoughts. At the same time, the moderator "focuses" the discussion—hence the name **focus group interviewing.** The comments are recorded in writing or on videotape for later study.

Focus group interviewing has become one of the major marketing research tools for gaining insight into consumer thoughts and feelings. However, focus group studies usually employ small sample sizes to keep time and costs down, and it may be hard to generalize from the results. Because interviewers have more freedom in personal interviews, the problem of interviewer bias is greater.

Focus group interviewing
Personal interviewing that involves inviting 6 to 10 people to gather for a few hours with a trained interviewer to talk about a product, service, or organization. The interviewer "focuses" the group discussion on important issues.

Today, modern communications technology is changing the way that focus groups are conducted:

> Videoconferencing links, television monitors, remote-control cameras, and digital transmission are boosting the amount of focus group research done over long-distance lines. In a typical videoconferencing system, two cameras focused on the group are controlled by clients who hold a remote keypad. Executives in a far-off boardroom can zoom in on faces and pan the focus group at will. A two-way sound system connects remote viewers to the backroom, focus group room, and directly to the monitor's earpiece. Recently, while testing new product names in one focus group, the client's creative director had an idea and contacted the moderator, who tested the new name on the spot.[14]

Another form of interviewing is *computer-assisted interviewing*, a contact method in which respondents sit at computers, read questions on the screen, and type in their own answers while an interviewer is present. The computers might be located at a research center, trade show, shopping mall, or retail location.

The latest technology to hit marketing research is the Internet. Increasingly, marketing researchers are collecting primary data through **online (Internet) marketing research**—*Internet surveys, experiments,* and *online focus groups*. Online focus groups offer advantages over traditional methods:

> Janice Gjersten, director of marketing for an online entertainment company, wanted to . . . gauge reaction to a new Web site. [She] contacted Cyber Dialogue, which provided focus group respondents drawn from its 10,000-person database. The focus group was held in an online chat room, which Gjersten "looked in on" from her office computer. Gjersten could interrupt the moderator at any time with flash e-mails unseen by the respondents. Although the online focus group lacked voice and body cues, Gjersten says she will never conduct a traditional focus group again. Not only were respondents more honest, but the cost for the online group was one third that of a traditional focus group and a full report came to her in one day, compared to four weeks.[15]

Online (Internet) marketing research

Collecting primary data through Internet surveys and online focus groups.

Online focus groups offer many advantages, including convenience and low cost. Says ActiveGroup about its online research: "No traveling, no scheduling, no problems."

Although online research offers much promise, and some analysts predict that the Internet will soon be the primary marketing research tool, others are more cautious. Real Marketing 5.2 summarizes the advantages, drawbacks, and prospects for conducting marketing research on the Internet.

Sample

A segment of the population selected for marketing research to represent the population as a whole.

Sampling Plan.   Marketing researchers usually draw conclusions about large groups of consumers by studying a small sample of the total consumer population. A **sample** is a segment of the population selected to represent the population as a whole. Ideally, the sample should be representative so that the researcher can make accurate estimates of the thoughts and behaviors of the larger population.

Designing the sample requires three decisions. First, *who* is to be surveyed (what *sampling unit*)? The answer to this question is not always obvious. For example, to study the decision-making process for a family automobile purchase, should the researcher interview the husband, wife, other family members, dealership salespeople, or all of these? The researcher must determine what information is needed and who is most likely to have it.

Second, *how many* people should be surveyed (what *sample size*)? Large samples give more-reliable results than small samples. It is not necessary to sample the entire target market or even a large portion to get reliable results, however. If well chosen, samples of less than 1 percent of a population can often give good reliability.

Third, *how* should the people in the sample be *chosen* (what *sampling procedure*)? Table 5.4 describes different kinds of samples. Using *probability samples,* each population member has a known chance of being included in the sample, and researchers can calculate confidence limits for sampling error. But when probability sampling costs too much or takes too much time, marketing researchers often take *nonprobability samples,* even though their sampling error cannot be measured. These varied ways of drawing samples have different costs and time limitations as well as different accuracy and statistical properties. Which method is best depends on the needs of the research project.

Research Instruments.   In collecting primary data, marketing researchers have a choice of two main research instruments—the *questionnaire* and *mechanical devices.* The *questionnaire* is by far the most common instrument, whether administered in person, by phone, or online.

Questionnaires are very flexible—there are many ways to ask questions. *Closed-ended questions* include all the possible answers, and subjects make choices among them. Examples include multiple-choice questions and scale questions. *Open-ended questions* allow respondents to answer in their own words. In a survey of airline users, Delta might simply ask, "What is your opinion of Delta Airlines?" Or it might ask people to complete a sentence: "When I choose an airline, the most important consideration is . . ." These and other kinds of open-ended questions often reveal more

TABLE 5.4	TYPES OF SAMPLES
Probability Sample	
Simple random sample	Every member of the population has a known and equal chance of selection.
Stratified random sample	The population is divided into mutually exclusive groups (such as age groups), and random samples are drawn from each group.
Cluster (area) sample	The population is divided into mutually exclusive groups (such as blocks), and the researcher draws a sample of the groups to interview.
Nonprobability Sample	
Convenience sample	The researcher selects the easiest population members from which to obtain information.
	The researcher uses his or her judgment to select population members who are good prospects for accurate information.
Judgment sample	The researcher finds and interviews a prescribed number of people in each of several categories.

real marketing 5.2

Online Marketing Research

As more and more consumers connect with the Internet, an increasing number of marketers are moving their research onto the Web. Although online research currently makes up less than 5 percent of all marketing research spending, some industry insiders predict substantial growth. In as little as

matter of days. For example, consider a recent online survey by a soft drink company to test teenager opinions of new packaging ideas. The 10- to 15-minute Internet survey included dozens of questions along with 765 different images of labels, bottle shapes, and such. Some 600 teenagers participated over a three- to four-day period. Detailed analysis from the survey was available just five days after all the responses had come in—lightning quick compared to offline efforts.

Internet research is also relatively low in cost. Participants can dial in for a focus group from anywhere in the world, eliminating travel, lodging, and facility costs. For surveys, the Internet eliminates most of the postage, phone, labor, and printing costs associated with other approaches. "The cost [of Web research] can be anywhere from 10 percent to 80 percent less," says Tod Johnson, head of NPD Group, a firm that conducts online research. Moreover, sample size has little influence on costs. "There's not a huge difference between 10 and 10,000 on the Web," says Johnson.

Online surveys and focus groups are also excellent for reaching the hard-to-reach—the often-elusive teen, single, affluent, and well-educated audiences. "It's very solid for reaching . . . doctors, lawyers, professionals—people you might have difficulty reaching because they are not interested in taking part in surveys," says Paul Jacobson, an executive of Greenfield Online. "It's also a good medium for reaching work-

ing mothers and others who lead busy lives. They can do it in their own space and at their own convenience." The Internet also works well for bringing together people from different parts of the country, especially those in higher-income groups who can't spare the time to travel to a central site.

However, using the Internet to conduct marketing research does have some drawbacks. For one, many consumers still don't have access to the Internet. That makes it difficult to construct research samples that represent a broad cross section of Americans. Still, as Internet usage broadens, many mainstream marketers are now using Web research. General Mills, for example, conducts 60 percent of its consumer research online, reducing costs by 50 percent. And UPS uses online research extensively. "Between 40 percent and 50 percent of our customers are online, so it makes sense," says John Gilbert, UPS marketing research manager. He finds little difference in the results of traditional and online studies, and the online studies are much cheaper and faster.

Another major problem of online research is controlling who's in the sample. Tom Greenbaum, president of Groups Plus, recalls a cartoon in *The New Yorker* in which two dogs are seated at a computer: "'On the Internet, nobody knows you're a dog,' one says to the other. If you can't see a person with whom you are communicating, how do know who they really are?" he says. To overcome such sample and response problems, many online research firms use opt-in communities and respondent panels. For example, Greenfield Online maintains a 1.3-million-member Internet-based respondent panel, recruited through cooperative marketing arrangements with other sites. Because such respondents opt in and can answer questions whenever they are ready, these online surveys yield high response rates. Whereas response rates for telephone surveys have plummeted to less than 14 percent in recent years, online response rates typically reach 40 percent or higher.

Even when you reach the right respondents, online surveys and focus groups can

More and more companies are moving their research onto the Web. According to this Greenfield Online ad, in many ways, it "beats the old-fashioned kind."

five years, some say, it could account for 50 percent of all research spending.

Web research offers some real advantages over traditional surveys and focus groups. The most obvious advantages are speed and low costs. Online focus groups require some advance scheduling, but results are practically instantaneous. Survey researchers routinely complete their online studies in only a lack the dynamics of more personal approaches. "You're missing all of the key things that make a focus group a viable method," says Greenbaum. "You may get people online to talk to each other and play off each other, but it's very different to watch people get excited about a concept." The online world is devoid of the eye contact, body language, and direct personal interactions found in traditional focus group research. And the Internet format—running, typed commentary and online "emoticons" (punctuation marks that express emotion, such as :-) to signify happiness)—greatly restricts respondent expressiveness.

Increasingly, however, advances in technology—such as the integration of animation, streaming audio and video, and virtual environments—will help to overcome these limitations. "In the online survey of the not-so-distant-future," notes an online researcher, "respondents will be able to rotate, zoom in on, and manipulate (like change the color or size of) three-dimensional products. They'll be able to peruse virtual stores, take items off shelves, and see how they function."

Just as the impersonal nature of the Web hinders two-way interactions, it can also provide anonymity. This often yields less-guarded, more-honest responses, especially when discussing topics such as income, medical conditions, lifestyle, or other sensitive issues. "People hiding behind a keyboard get pretty brave," says one researcher. Adds another:

> From those questions that may simply make you squirm a little ("How much money did you lose in the stock market last month?"), to those you most probably don't want to answer to another human being, even if you don't know the person on the other end of the line ("How often do you have sex each week?"), Internet-based surveys tend to draw more honest responses. I once conducted the same survey in a mall and via the Internet. The question was, "How often do you bathe or shower each week?" The average answer, via the mall interview, was 6.2 times per week. The average via the Internet interview was 4.8 times per week, probably a more logical—and honest—response.

Perhaps the most explosive issue facing online researchers concerns consumer privacy. Critics worry that online researchers will spam our e-mail boxes with unsolicited e-mails to recruit respondents. They fear that unethical researchers will use the e-mail addresses and confidential responses gathered through surveys to sell products after the research is completed. They are concerned about the use of electronic agents (called Spambots or Spiders) that collect personal information without the respondents' consent. Failure to address such privacy issues could result in angry, less cooperative consumers and increased government intervention.

Although most researchers agree that online research will never completely replace traditional research, some are wildly optimistic about its prospects. Others, however, are more cautious. "Ten years from now, national telephone surveys will be the subject of research methodology folklore," proclaims one expert. "That's a little too soon," cautions another. "But in 20 years, yes."

Sources: Ian P. Murphy, "Interactive Research," *Marketing News,* January 20, 1997, pp. 1, 17; "NFO Executive Sees Most Research Going to Internet," *Advertising Age,* May 19, 1997, p. 50; Kate Maddox, "Virtual Panels Add Real Insight for Marketers," *Advertising Age,* June 29, 1998, pp. 34, 40; Jon Rubin, "Online Marketing Research Comes of Age," *Brandweek,* October 30, 2000, pp. 26–28; "Web Smart," *Business Week,* May 14, 2001, p. EB56; Noah Shachtman, "Web Enhanced Market Research," *Advertising Age,* June 18, 2001, p. T18; Thomas W. Miller, "Make the Call: Online Results Are a Mixed Bag," *Marketing News,* September 24, 2001, pp. 30–35; David Jamieson, "Online Research Gets Fewer Euro Votes," *Marketing News,* January 21, 2002, p. 15; and Deborah Szynal, "Gaining Steam: Big Bytes," *Marketing News,* March 18, 2002, p. 3.

than closed-ended questions because respondents are not limited in their answers. Open-ended questions are especially useful in exploratory research, when the researcher is trying to find out *what* people think but not measuring *how many* people think in a certain way. Closed-ended questions, on the other hand, provide answers that are easier to interpret and tabulate.

Researchers should also use care in the *wording* and *ordering* of questions. They should use simple, direct, unbiased wording. Questions should be arranged in a logical order. The first question should create interest if possible, and difficult or personal questions should be asked last so that respondents do not become defensive. A carelessly prepared questionnaire usually contains many errors (see Table 5.5).

Although questionnaires are the most common research instrument, researchers also use *mechanical instruments* to monitor consumer behavior, such as supermarket scanners and people meters. Other mechanical devices measure subjects' physical responses. For example, a galvanometer detects the minute degree of sweating that accompanies emotional arousal. It can be used to measure the strength of interest or emotions aroused by a subject's exposure to marketing stimuli such as an ad or product. Eye cameras are used to study respondents' eye movements to determine at what points their eyes focus first and how long they linger on a given item. Here are examples of new technologies that capture information on consumers' emotional and physical responses:

Machine response to facial expressions that indicate emotions will soon be a commercial reality. The technology discovers underlying emotions by capturing an image of a user's

TABLE 5.5	A "QUESTIONABLE QUESTIONNAIRE"

Suppose that a summer camp director had prepared the following questionnaire to use in interviewing the parents of prospective campers. How would you assess each question?

1. What is your income to the nearest hundred dollars? *People don't usually know their income to the nearest hundred dollars, nor do they want to reveal their income that closely. Moreover, a researcher should never open a questionnaire with such a personal question.*
2. Are you a strong or weak supporter of overnight summer camping for your children? *What do "strong" and "weak" mean?*
3. Do your children behave themselves well at a summer camp? Yes () No () *"Behave" is a relative term. Furthermore, are yes and no the best response options for this question? Besides, will people answer this honestly and objectively? Why ask the question in the first place?*
4. How many camps mailed literature to you last year? This year? *Who can remember this?*
5. What are the most salient and determinant attributes in your evaluation of summer camps? *What are salient and determinant attributes? Don't use big words on me!*
6. Do you think it is right to deprive your child of the opportunity to grow into a mature person through the experience of summer camping? *A loaded question. Given the bias, how can any parent answer yes?*

facial features and movements—especially around the eyes and mouth—and comparing the image against facial feature templates in a database. Hence, an elderly man squints at an ATM screen and the font size doubles almost instantly. A woman at a shopping center kiosk smiles at a travel ad, prompting the device to print out a travel discount coupon. Several users at another kiosk frown at a racy ad, leading a store to pull it.

IBM is perfecting an "emotion mouse" that will figure out users' emotional states by measuring pulse, temperature, movement, and galvanic skin response. The company has mapped those measurements for anger, fear, sadness, disgust, happiness, and surprise. The idea is to create a style that fits a user's personality. An Internet marketer, for example, might offer to present a different kind of display if it senses that the user is frustrated.[16]

Implementing the Research Plan

The researcher next puts the marketing research plan into action. This involves collecting, processing, and analyzing the information. Data collection can be carried out by the company's marketing research staff or by outside firms. The data collection phase of the marketing research process is generally the most expensive and the most subject to error. Researchers should watch closely to make sure that the plan is implemented correctly. They must guard against problems with contacting respondents, with respondents who refuse to cooperate or who give biased answers, and with interviewers who make mistakes or take shortcuts.

Researchers must process and analyze the collected data to isolate important information and findings. They need to check data for accuracy and completeness and code it for analysis. The researchers then tabulate the results and compute averages and other statistical measures.

Interpreting and Reporting the Findings

The market researcher must now interpret the findings, draw conclusions, and report them to management. The researcher should not try to overwhelm managers with numbers and fancy statistical techniques. Rather, the researcher should present important findings that are useful in making the major decisions faced by management.

However, interpretation should not be left only to the researchers. They are often experts in research design and statistics, but the marketing manager knows more about the problem and the decisions that must be made. The best research is meaningless if the manager blindly accepts faulty interpretations from the researcher. Similarly, managers may be biased—they might tend to accept research results that show what they expected and to reject those that they did not expect or hope for. In many cases, findings can be interpreted in different ways, and discussions between researchers and managers will help point to the best interpretations. Thus, managers and researchers must work together closely when interpreting research results, and both must share responsibility for the research process and resulting decisions.

Mechanical measures of consumer response: devices are in the works that will allow marketers to measure facial expressions and adjust their offers or communications accordingly.

Analyzing Marketing Informaton

Information gathered in internal databases and through marketing intelligence and marketing research usually requires more analysis. And managers may need help in applying the information to their marketing problems and decisions. This help may include advanced statistical analysis to learn more about both the relationships within a set of data and their statistical reliability. Such analysis allows managers to go beyond means and standard deviations in the data and to answer questions about markets, marketing activities, and outcomes.

Information analysis might also involve a collection of analytical models that will help marketers make better decisions. Each model represents some real system, process, or outcome. These models can help answer the questions of *what if* and *which is best*. Marketing scientists have developed numerous models to help marketing managers make better marketing mix decisions, design sales territories and sales call plans, select sites for retail outlets, develop optimal advertising mixes, and forecast new-product sales.

Customer Relationship Management (CRM)

The question of how best to analyze and use individual customer data presents special problems. Most companies are awash in information about their customers. In fact, smart companies capture information at every possible customer *touch point*. These touch points include customer purchases, sales force contacts, service and support calls, Web site visits, satisfaction surveys, credit and payment interactions, market research studies—every contact between the customer and the company.

The trouble is that this information is usually scattered widely across the organization. It is buried deep in the separate databases, plans, and records of many different company functions and departments. To overcome such problems, many companies are now turning to **customer relationship management (CRM)** to manage detailed information about individual customers and carefully manage customer touch points in order to maximize customer loyalty. In recent years, there has been an explosion in the number of companies using CRM. In fact, one research firm found that 97 percent of all U.S. businesses plan to boost spending on CRM technology within the next two years.[17]

CRM consists of sophisticated software and analytical tools that integrate customer information from all sources, analyze it in depth, and apply the results to build stronger customer relationships. CRM integrates everything that a company's sales, service, and marketing teams know

Customer relationship management (CRM)
Managing detailed information about individual customers and carefully managing customer "touch points" in order to maximize customer loyalty.

Siebel's CRM software integrates individual customer data from every touch point to help build customer relationships. Using CRM, the Siebel customer shown in this ad increased customer satisfaction 86 percent and revenues per customer 20 percent.

about individual customers to provide a 360-degree view of the customer relationship. It pulls together, analyzes, and provides easy access to customer information from all of the various touch points. Companies use CRM analysis to assess the value of individual customers, identify the best ones to target, and customize the company's products and interactions to each customer.

CRM analysts develop *data warehouses* and use sophisticated *data mining* techniques to unearth the riches hidden in customer data. A data warehouse is a companywide electronic storehouse of customer information—a centralized database of finely detailed customer data that needs to be sifted through for gems. The purpose of a data warehouse is not to gather information—many companies have already amassed endless stores of information about their customers. Rather, the purpose is to allow managers to integrate the information the company already has. Then, once the data warehouse brings the data together for analysis, the company uses high-powered data-mining techniques to sift through the mounds of data and dig out interesting relationships and findings about customers.

Companies can gain many benefits from customer relationship management. By understanding customers better, they can provide higher levels of customer service and develop deeper customer relationships. They can use CRM to pinpoint high-value customers, target them more effectively, cross-sell the company's products, and create offers tailored to specific customer requirements. Consider the following examples:[18]

FedEx recently launched a multimillion-dollar CRM system in an effort to cut costs, improve its customer support, and use its existing customer data to cross-sell and up-sell services to potential or existing customers. The new system gives every member of FedEx's 3,300-person sales force a comprehensive view of every customer, detailing each one's needs and suggesting services that might meet those needs. For instance, if a customer who does a lot of international shipping calls to arrange a delivery, a sales rep will see a detailed customer history on his or her computer screen, assess the customer's needs, and determine the most appropriate offering on the spot. Beleaguered sales reps can use such high-tech help. FedEx offers 220 different services—from logistics to transportation to customs brokerage—often making it difficult for salespeople to identify the best fit for customers. The new CRM system will also help FedEx conduct promotions and qualify potential sales leads. The CRM software analyzes market segments, points out market "sweet spots," and calculates how profitable those segments will be to the company and to individual salespeople.

Ping, the golf equipment manufacturer, has used CRM successfully for about two years. Its data warehouse contains customer-specific data about every golf club it has manufactured and sold for the past 15 years. The database, which includes grip size and special assembly instructions, helps Ping design and build golf clubs specifically for each of its customers and allows for easy replacement. If a golfer needs a new nine iron, for example, he can call in the serial number and Ping will ship an exact club to him within two days of receiving the order—a process that used to take two to three weeks. . . . This faster processing of data has given Ping a competitive edge in a market saturated with new products. "We've been up; the golf market has been down," says Steve Bostwick, Ping's marketing manager. Bostwick estimates the golf market to be down about 15 percent, but he says Ping has experienced double-digit growth.

Most experts believe that good customer data, by itself, can give companies a substantial competitive advantage. Just ask American Express. At a secret location in Phoenix, security guards watch over American Express's 500 billion bytes of data on how customers have used its 35 million green, gold, and platinum charge cards. Amex uses the database to design carefully targeted offers in its monthly mailing of millions of customer bills.

CRM benefits don't come without cost or risk, not only in collecting the original customer data but also in maintaining and mining it. U.S. companies will spend an estimated $10 billion to $20 billion this year on CRM software alone from companies such as Siebel Systems, Oracle, and SPSS. Yet more than half of all CRM efforts fail to meet their objectives. The most common cause of CRM failures is that companies mistakenly view CRM only as a technology and software solution.[19] But technology alone cannot build profitable customer relationships. "CRM is not a technology solution—you can't achieve . . . improved customer relationships by simply slapping in some software," says a CRM expert. Instead, CRM is just one part of an effective overall *customer relationship strategy.* "Focus on the *R,*" advises the expert. "Remember, a relationship is what CRM is all about."[20]

When it works, the benefits of CRM can far outweigh the costs and risks. Based on regular polls of its customers, Siebel Systems claims that customers using its CRM software report an average 16 percent increase in revenues and 21 percent increase in customer loyalty and staff efficiency. "No question that companies are getting tremendous value out of this," says a CRM consultant. "Companies [are] looking for ways to bring disparate sources of customer information together, then get it to all the customer touch points." The powerful new CRM techniques can unearth "a wealth of information to target that customer, to hit their hot button."[21]

Distributing and Using Marketing Information

Marketing information has no value until it is used to make better marketing decisions. Thus, the marketing information system must make the information available to the managers and others who make marketing decisions or deal with customers on a day-to-day basis. In some cases, this means providing managers with regular performance reports, intelligence updates, and reports on the results of research studies.

But marketing managers may also need nonroutine information for special situations and on-the-spot decisions. For example, a sales manager having trouble with a large customer may want a summary of the account's sales and profitability over the past year. Or a retail store manager who has run out of a best-selling product may want to know the current inventory levels in the chain's other stores. Increasingly, therefore, information distribution involves entering information into databases and making these available in a user-friendly and timely way.

Many firms use a company *intranet* to facilitate this process. The intranet provides ready access to research information, stored reports, shared work documents, contact information for employees and other stakeholders, and more. For example, iGo, a catalog and Web retailer, integrates incoming customer service calls with up-to-date database information about customers' Web purchases and e-mail inquiries. By accessing this information on the intranet while speaking with the customer, iGo's service representatives can get a well-rounded picture of each customer's purchasing history and previous contacts with the company.

In addition, companies are increasingly allowing key customers and value-network members to access account and product information and other data on demand on *extranets*. Suppliers, customers, and select other network members may access a company's extranet to update their accounts, arrange purchases, and check orders against inventories to improve customer service. For example, one insurance firm allows its 200 independent agents access to a Web-based database of claim information covering 1 million customers. This allows the agents to avoid high-risk customers and to compare claim data with their own customer databases.[22]

Thanks to modern technology, today's marketing managers can gain direct access to the information system at any time and from virtually any location. They can tap into the system while working at a home office, in a hotel room, at an airport—anyplace where they can turn on a laptop computer and link up. Such systems allow managers to get the information they need directly and quickly and to tailor it to their own needs. From just about anywhere, they can obtain information from company or outside data bases, analyze it using statistical software, prepare reports and presentations, and communicate electronically with others in the network.

Other Marketing Information Considerations

This section discusses marketing information in two special contexts: marketing research in small businesses and nonprofit organizations, and international marketing research. Finally, we look at public policy and ethics issues in marketing research.

Marketing Research in Small Businesses and Not-for-Profit Organizations

Just like larger firms, small organizations need market information. Start-up businesses need information about their industries, competitors, potential customers, and reactions to new market offers. Existing small businesses must track changes in customer needs and wants, reactions to new products, and changes in the competitive environment.

Managers of small businesses and not-for-profit organizations often think that marketing research can be done only by experts in large companies with big research budgets. True, large-scale research studies are beyond the budgets of most small businesses. However, many of the marketing research techniques discussed in this chapter also can be used by smaller organizations in a less formal manner and at little or no expense.

Managers of small businesses and not-for-profit organizations can obtain good marketing information simply by *observing* things around them. For example, retailers can evaluate new locations by observing vehicle and pedestrian traffic. They can monitor competitor advertising by collecting ads from local media. They can evaluate their customer mix by recording how many and what kinds of customers shop in the store at different times. In addition, many small-business managers routinely visit their rivals and socialize with competitors to gain insights. Tom Coohill, a chef who owns two Atlanta restaurants, gives managers a food allowance to dine out and bring back ideas. Atlanta jeweler Frank Maier Jr., who often visits out-of-town rivals, spotted and copied a dramatic way of lighting displays.[23]

Managers can conduct informal *surveys* using small convenience samples. The director of an art museum can learn what patrons think about new exhibits by conducting informal focus groups—inviting small groups to lunch and having discussions on topics of interest. Retail salespeople can talk with customers visiting the store; hospital officials can interview patients. Restaurant managers might make random phone calls during slack hours to interview consumers about where they eat out and what they think of various restaurants in the area. Bissell used a small convenience sample to quickly and cheaply test the market for its Steam Gun—a newly developed home-cleaning device that resembled a handheld vacuum cleaner.

Many associations, media, and government agencies provide special help to small organizations. Here the U.S. Small Business Administration offers a Web site that gives advice on topics ranging from starting, financing, and expanding a small business to ordering business cards.

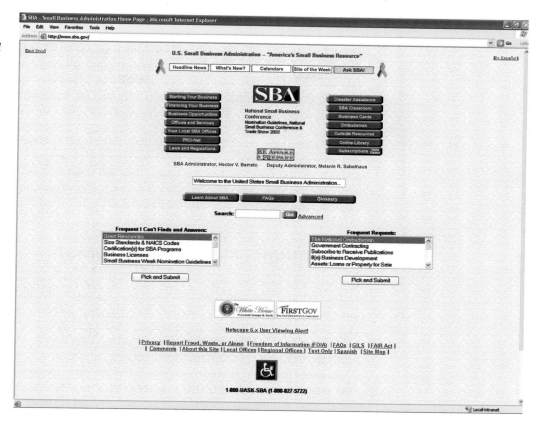

Bissell had only four weeks and a tight budget to get a feel for how consumers would respond to the new product. Aware that women with children often purchase such products, Bissell made a $1,500 donation to a local Parent Teacher Association (PTA) for the opportunity to make a presentation. After the presentation, it gave 20 interested women the Steam Gun to take home, along with journals to record their experiences. Following a two-week trial period, Bissell's marketing research director visited the mothers in their homes to watch them use product. This "research on a shoestring" yielded several interesting discoveries. First, Bissell learned that the women weren't sold on the cleaning ability of hot water used without chemicals. Second, it would have to change the name of the product. When roped into chores, children would arm themselves with the Steam Gun and take aim at their siblings. One child was quoted as saying, "Freeze, or I'll melt your face off!" Finally, Bissell found that the product had special appeal to those who were serious about cleaning. They used it to get into hard to reach places and blast off tough grime. Based on these findings, Bissell changed the name of the product to the Steam 'n Clean and focused on the cleaning power of super hot steam when promoting the product. The Steam 'n Clean was successfully launched through infomercials and in nationwide retail chains.[24]

Managers also can conduct their own simple *experiments*. For example, by changing the themes in regular fund-raising mailings and watching the results, a nonprofit manager can find out much about which marketing strategies work best. By varying newspaper advertisements, a store manager can learn the effects of things such as ad size and position, price coupons, and media used.

Small organizations can obtain most of the secondary data available to large businesses. In addition, many associations, local media, chambers of commerce, and government agencies provide special help to small organizations. The U.S. Small Business Administration offers dozens of free publications and a Web site (www.sbaonline.sba.gov) that give advice on topics ranging from starting, financing, and expanding a small business to ordering business cards. Other excellent Web resources for small businesses include the U.S. Census Bureau (www.census.gov) and the Bureau of Economic Analysis (www.bea.doc.gov).

The business sections at local libraries can also be a good source of information. They often provide access to resources such as *Standard & Poor's, Hoover's Handbooks, The Statistical Abstract of the United States, Dun & Bradstreet, Woods & Poole Economics, Sourcebook America, Claritas, Market Statistics,* and many business periodicals. Local newspapers often provide information on local shoppers and their buying patterns. Finally, small businesses can collect a considerable amount of information at very little cost in the Internet. They can scour competitor and customer Web sites and use Internet search engines to research specific companies and issues.

In summary, secondary data collection, observation, surveys, and experiments can all be used effectively by small organizations with small budgets. Although these informal research methods are less complex and less costly, they still must be conducted carefully. Managers must think carefully about the objectives of the research, formulate questions in advance, recognize the biases introduced by smaller samples and less skilled researchers, and conduct the research systematically.[25]

International Marketing Research

International marketing researchers follow the same steps as domestic researchers, from defining the research problem and developing a research plan to interpreting and reporting the results. However, these researchers often face more and different problems. Whereas domestic researchers deal with fairly homogenous markets within a single country, international researchers deal with differing markets in many different countries. These markets often vary greatly in their levels of economic development, cultures and customs, and buying patterns.

In many foreign markets, the international researcher sometimes has a difficult time finding good secondary data. Whereas U.S. marketing researchers can obtain reliable secondary data from dozens of domestic research services, many countries have almost no research services at all. Some of the largest international research services do operate in many countries. For example, ACNielsen Corporation, the world's largest marketing research company, has offices in more than 100 countries. And 49 percent of the revenues of the world's 25 largest marketing research firms comes from outside their home countries.[26] However, most research firms operate in only a relative handful of countries. Thus, even when secondary information is available, it usually must be obtained from many different sources on a country-by-country basis, making the information difficult to combine or compare.

Because of the scarcity of good secondary data, international researchers often must collect their own primary data. Here again, researchers face problems not found domestically. For example, they may find it difficult simply to develop good samples. U.S. researchers can use current telephone directories, census tract data, and any of several sources of socioeconomic data to construct samples. However, such information is largely lacking in many countries.

Once the sample is drawn, the U.S. researcher usually can reach most respondents easily by telephone, by mail, on the Internet, or in person. Reaching respondents is often not so easy in other parts of the world. Researchers in Mexico cannot rely on telephone and mail data collection—most data collection is door to door and concentrated in three or four of the largest cities. In some countries, few people have phones; for example, there are only 32 phones per thousand people in Argentina. In other countries, the postal system is notoriously unreliable. In Brazil, for instance, an estimated 30 percent of the mail is never delivered. In many developing countries, poor roads and transportation systems make certain areas hard to reach, making personal interviews difficult and expensive. Finally, few people in developing countries are connected to the Internet.[27]

Cultural differences from country to country cause additional problems for international researchers. Language is the most obvious obstacle. For example, questionnaires must be prepared in one language and then translated into the languages of each country researched. Responses then must be translated back into the original language for analysis and interpretation. This adds to research costs and increases the risks of error.

Translating a questionnaire from one language to another is anything but easy. Many idioms, phrases, and statements mean different things in different cultures. For example, a Danish executive noted, "Check this out by having a different translator put back into English what you've translated from English. You'll get the shock of your life. I remember [an example in which] 'out of sight, out of mind' had become 'invisible things are insane.'"[28]

Some of the largest research services operate in many countries: Roper ASW, Inc. provides companies with information resources "from Brazil to Eastern Europe; from Cape Town to Beijing—if you are there, Roper ASW, Inc. is there."

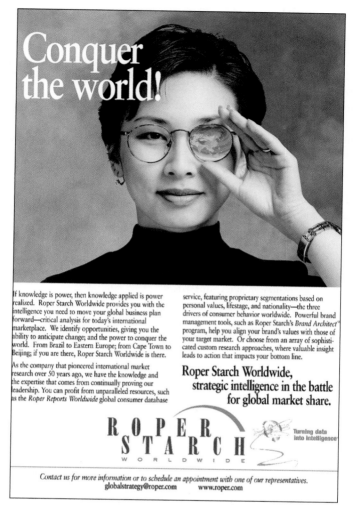

Consumers in different countries also vary in their attitudes toward marketing research. People in one country may be very willing to respond; in other countries, nonresponse can be a major problem. Customs in some countries may prohibit people from talking with strangers. In certain cultures, research questions often are considered too personal. For example, in many Latin American countries, people may feel embarrassed to talk with researchers about their choices of shampoo, deodorant, or other personal care products. Similarly, in most Muslim countries, mixed-gender focus groups are taboo, as is videotaping female-only focus groups.[29]

Even when respondents are *willing* to respond, they may not be *able* to because of high functional-illiteracy rates. And middle-class people in developing countries often make false claims in order to appear well-off. For example, in a study of tea consumption in India, over 70 percent of middle-income respondents claimed that they used one of several national brands. However, the researchers had good reason to doubt these results—more than 60 percent of the tea sold in India is unbranded generic tea.

Despite these problems, the recent growth of international marketing has resulted in a rapid increase in the use of international marketing research. Global companies have little choice but to conduct such research. Although the costs and problems associated with international research may be high, the costs of not doing it—in terms of missed opportunities and mistakes—might be even higher. Once recognized, many of the problems associated with international marketing research can be overcome or avoided.

Public Policy and Ethics in Marketing Research

Most marketing research benefits both the sponsoring company and its consumers. Through marketing research, companies learn more about consumers' needs, resulting in more-satisfying products and services. However, the misuse of marketing research can also harm or annoy consumers. Two major public policy and ethics issues in marketing research are intrusions on consumer privacy and the misuse of research findings.

Intrusions on Consumer Privacy

Many consumers feel positively about marketing research and believe that it serves a useful purpose. Some actually enjoy being interviewed and giving their opinions. However, others strongly resent or even mistrust marketing research. A few consumers fear that researchers might use sophisticated techniques to probe our deepest feelings and then use this knowledge to manipulate our buying. Or they worry that marketers are building huge databases full of personal information about customers.

For example, DoubleClick has profiles on 100 million Web users. Privacy groups have worried that such huge profiling databases could be merged with offline databases and threaten individual privacy. In fact, DoubleClick did integrate its online data with that collected by a consumer panel firm to construct frighteningly accurate consumer profiles. In stirred up much controversy last year when it announced that it would sell about 100,000 of these Web-user profiles to businesses, complete with names and contact information. However, in response to a Federal Trade Commission investigation and to settle federal and state class-action suits, DoubleClick recently adopted sweeping privacy standards.[30]

Others consumers may have been taken in by previous "research surveys" that actually turned out to be attempts to sell them something. Still other consumers confuse legitimate marketing research studies with telemarketing efforts and say "no" before the interviewer can even begin. Most, however, simply resent the intrusion. They dislike mail or telephone surveys that are too long or too personal or that interrupt them at inconvenient times.

Increasing consumer resentment has become a major problem for the research industry. One recent poll found that 82 percent of Americans worry that they lack control over how businesses use their personal information, and 41 percent said that business had invaded their privacy. These concerns have led to lower survey response rates in recent years. One study found that 45 percent of Americans had refused to participate in a survey over the past year, up from 24 percent 15 years ago. Another study found that 59 percent of consumers had refused to give information to a company because they thought it was not really needed or too personal, up from 42 percent five years earlier.[31]

The research industry is considering several options for responding to this problem. One is to expand its "Your Opinion Counts" program to educate consumers about the benefits of marketing research and to distinguish it from telephone selling and database building. Another option is to provide a toll-free number that people can call to verify that a survey is legitimate. The industry also has considered adopting broad standards, perhaps based on Europe's International Code of Marketing and Social Research Practice. This code outlines researchers' responsibilities to respondents and to the general public. For example, it says that researchers should make their names and addresses available to participants, and it bans companies from representing activities such as database compilation or sales and promotional pitches as research.

Many companies—including IBM, AT&T, American Express, DoubleClick, and Microsoft—are now appointing a "chief privacy officer," whose job is to safeguard the privacy of consumers who do business with the company. At least 100 U.S. companies now employ such privacy chiefs, and the number is expected to grow rapidly. The chief privacy officer for Microsoft says that his job is to come up with data policies for the company to follow, make certain that every program the company creates enhances customer privacy, and inform and educate company employees about privacy issues and concerns.[32]

According to Sally Cowan, who runs the privacy operations of American Express, any business that deals with consumers' information has to take privacy issues seriously. "Privacy is not the new hot issue at American Express," she says. The company developed a set of formal privacy principles in 1991, and in 1998 it became one of the first companies to post privacy policies on its Web site. This penchant for customer privacy led American Express to introduce new services that protect consumers' privacy when they use an American Express card to buy items online. American Express views privacy as way to gain competitive advantage—as something that leads consumers to choose one company over another.[33]

In the end, if researchers provide value in exchange for information, customers will gladly supply it. For example, Amazon.com's customers do not mind if the firm builds a database of products they buy in order to make personalized future product recommendations. This saves time and provides value. Similarly, Bizrate users gladly complete surveys rating e-tail sites because they can view the overall ratings of others when making purchase decisions. The best approach is for researchers to ask only for the information they need, to use it responsibly to provide value, and to avoid sharing information without the customer's permission.

Misuse of Research Findings

Research studies can be powerful persuasion tools; companies often use study results as claims in their advertising and promotion. Today, however, many research studies appear to be little more than vehicles for pitching the sponsor's products. In fact, in some cases, the research surveys appear to have been designed just to produce the intended effect. Few advertisers openly rig their research designs or blatantly misrepresent the findings; most abuses tend to be subtle "stretches." Consider the following examples:

A study by Chrysler contends that Americans overwhelmingly prefer Chrysler to Toyota after test-driving both. However, the study included just 100 people in each of two tests. More importantly, none of the people surveyed owned a foreign car, so they appear to be favorably predisposed to U.S. cars.

A Black Flag survey asked: "A roach disk . . . poisons a roach slowly. The dying roach returns to the nest and after it dies is eaten by other roaches. In turn these roaches become poisoned and die. How effective do you think this type of product would be in killing roaches?" Not surprisingly, 79 percent said effective.

A poll sponsored by the disposable diaper industry asked: "It is estimated that disposable diapers account for less than 2 percent of the trash in today's landfills. In contrast, beverage containers, third-class mail, and yard waste are estimated to account for about 21 percent of the trash in landfills. Given this, in your opinion, would it be fair to ban disposable diapers?" Again, not surprisingly, 84 percent said no.[34]

Thus, subtle manipulations of the study's sample or the choice or wording of questions can greatly affect the conclusions reached.

In others cases, so-called independent research studies are actually paid for by companies with an interest in the outcome. Small changes in study assumptions or in how results are interpreted can subtly affect the direction of the results. For example, at least four widely quoted studies compare the environmental effects of using disposable diapers to those of using cloth diapers. The two studies sponsored by the cloth diaper industry conclude that cloth diapers are more environmentally friendly. Not surprisingly, the other two studies, sponsored by the paper diaper industry, conclude just the opposite. Yet both appear to be correct *given* the underlying assumptions used.

Recognizing that surveys can be abused, several associations—including the American Marketing Association, the Council of American Survey Research Organizations, and the Marketing Research Association—have developed codes of research ethics and standards of conduct.[35] In the end, however, unethical or inappropriate actions cannot simply be regulated away. Each company must accept responsibility for policing the conduct and reporting of its own marketing research to protect consumers' best interests and its own.

LOOKING BACK: REVIEWING THE CONCEPTS

In today's complex and rapidly changing environment, marketing managers need more and better information to make effective and timely decisions. This greater need for information has been matched by the explosion of information technologies for supplying information. Using today's new technologies, companies can now handle great quantities of information, sometimes even too much. Yet marketers often complain that they lack enough of the *right* kind of information or have an excess of the *wrong* kind. In response, many companies are now studying their managers' information needs and designing information systems to help managers develop and manage market and customer information.

1. Explain the importance of information to the company.
Good products and marketing programs start with a complete understanding of consumer needs and wants. Thus, the company needs sound information in order to produce superior value and satisfaction for customers. The company also

requires information on competitors, resellers, and other actors and forces in the marketplace. Increasingly, marketers are viewing information not only as an input for making better decisions but also as an important strategic asset and marketing tool.

2. Define the marketing information system and discuss its parts.

The *marketing information system (MIS)* consists of people, equipment, and procedures to gather, sort, analyze, evaluate, and distribute needed, timely, and accurate information to marketing decision makers. A well-designed information system begins and ends with users. The MIS first *assesses information needs*. The marketing information system primarily serves the company's marketing and other managers. However, it may also provide information to external partners, such as suppliers or marketing services agencies. Then, the MIS *develops information* from internal databases, marketing intelligence activities, and marketing research. *Internal databases* provide information on the company's own sales, costs, inventories, cash flows, and accounts receivable and payable. Such data can be obtained quickly and cheaply but often needs to be adapted for marketing decisions. *Marketing intelligence* activities supply everyday information about developments in the external marketing environment. *Market research* consists of collecting information relevant to a specific marketing problem faced by the company. Lastly, the MIS *distributes information* gathered from these sources to the right managers in the right form and at the right time to help them make better marketing decisions.

3. Outline the steps in the marketing research process.

The first step in the marketing research process involves *defining the problem and setting the research objectives,* which may be exploratory, descriptive, or causal research. The second step consists of *developing a research plan* for collecting data from primary and secondary sources. The third step calls for *implementing the marketing research plan* by gathering, processing, and analyzing the information. The fourth step consists of *interpreting and reporting the findings.* Additional information analysis helps marketing managers apply the information and provides them with sophisticated statistical procedures and models from which to develop more rigorous findings.

Both *internal* and *external* secondary data sources often provide information more quickly and at a lower cost than primary data sources, and they can sometimes yield information that a company cannot collect by itself. However, needed information might not exist in secondary sources, and even if data can be found, they might be largely unusable. Researchers

must also evaluate secondary information to ensure that it is *relevant, accurate, current,* and *impartial.* Primary research must also be evaluated for these features. Each primary data collection method—*observational, survey,* and *experimental*—has its own advantages and disadvantages. Each of the various primary research contact methods—mail, telephone, personal interview, and online—also has its own advantages and drawbacks. Similarly, each contact method has its pluses and minuses.

4. Explain how companies analyze and distribute marketing information.

Information gathered in internal databases and through marketing intelligence and marketing research usually requires more analysis. This may include advanced statistical analysis or the application of analytical models that will help marketers make better decisions. In recent years, marketers have paid special attention to the analysis of individual customer data. Many companies have now acquired or developed special software and analysis techniques—called *customer relationship management (CRM)*—that integrate, analyze, and apply the mountains of individual customer data contained in their databases.

Marketing information has no value until it is used to make better marketing decisions. Thus, the marketing information system must make the information available to the managers and others who make marketing decisions or deal with customers. In some cases, this means providing regular reports and updates; in other cases it means making nonroutine information available for special situations and on-the-spot decisions. Many firms use company intranets and extranets to facilitate this process. Thanks to modern technology, today's marketing managers can gain direct access to the information system at any time and from virtually any location.

5. Discuss the special issues some marketing researchers face, including public policy and ethics issues.

Some marketers face special marketing research situations, such as those conducting research in small-business, not-for-profit, or international situations. Marketing research can be conducted effectively by small businesses and not-for-profit organizations with limited budgets. International marketing researchers follow the same steps as domestic researchers but often face more and different problems. All organizations need to respond responsibly to major public policy and ethical issues surrounding marketing research, including issues of intrusions on consumer privacy and misuse of research findings.

REVIEWING THE KEY TERMS

Causal research 148
Customer relationship management (CRM) 161
Descriptive research 148
Experimental research 154
Exploratory research 148
Focus group interviewing 155

Internal databases 144
Marketing information system (MIS) 143
Marketing intelligence 145
Marketing research 147
Observational research 151
Online databases 149

Online (Internet) marketing research 156
Primary data 149
Sample 157
Secondary data 149
Single-source data systems 154
Survey research 154

DISCUSSING THE CONCEPTS

1. Many companies build extensive internal databases so that marketing managers can use them to identify marketing opportunities and problems, plan programs, and evaluate performance. If you were the marketing manager for a large motorcycle manufacturer, what types of information would you like to have available in your company's internal database? Explain.

2. Marketing intelligence has become increasingly important to marketing managers as an aid to formulating strategy. What other benefits are derived from the marketing intelligence function? Assume you have been hired as a consultant to a company that is developing a video/cell phone. What type of intelligence tips would you offer the firm?

3. Imagine that you are the marketing research manager for a small electronics firm that has recently changed management. You are concerned when you receive a memo stating that "marketing research is not really necessary as long as you have a good marketing information system." Write a brief response that outlines the role of marketing research and clarifies how it differs from MIS.

4. Research objectives must be translated into specific information needs. Assume that you are the marketing research director for Apple computer. What specific information might you need in order to pick two new colors for the popular iMac line of computers? List and briefly justify your choices.

5. Name the type of research that would be appropriate in each of the following situations and explain why.

(a) Kellogg wants to investigate the impact of young children on their parents' decisions to buy breakfast foods. (b) Your college bookstore wants to know how students would feel about adding a Starbucks coffee facility to the store's existing services. (c) McDonald's is considering how to market a new line of food products targeting senior citizens. (d) Gillette wants to determine whether a new line of deodorant for teenagers will be profitable.

6. Focus group interviewing is both a widely used and widely criticized research technique in marketing. List the advantages and disadvantages of focus groups. Some experts suggest that the next frontier for focus group research will be the Internet. What are the advantages and disadvantages of using the Internet to conduct focus groups?

7. Assume that your local grocery store has implemented a store service card. The card allows customers to receive special discounts and cash personal checks. Beginning with the registration process for the card and continuing through its use at the checkout stand, discuss all the types of data that could be collected and how the data could be used to build customer relationships.

8. As marketing manager for an emerging cosmetics company, you believe it is time to expand into the global marketplace. The Board of Directors requests an outline of research required to prepare for such an expansion. Prepare a brief report comparing domestic and international marketing research. How might the company change its research approach to gather international data?

APPLYING THE CONCEPTS

1. Companies often conduct marketing research to examine changes in the marketing environment that may affect product design and marketing decisions. Consider the evolution of Barbie, Mattel's most popular doll. Throughout the decades, Barbie has transformed to reflect the changing values and lifestyles of American women. In the 1950s, in keeping with women's predominant roles in society, Barbie was cast as a homemaker. But in the twenty-first century, Barbie reflects the diversity and individuality valued by today's girls. Mattel now offers NASCAR Barbie and veterinarian Barbie. Barbie even has her own Web site where girls can play games, create fashion makeovers, and read interactive books. By reinventing Barbie's image, Mattel has maintained the doll's popularity for more than 40 years and built Barbie into a $1.5 billion brand.

   a. Make a list of the ways Barbie has changed to meet the needs of the contemporary young woman. How do these changes affect female image, self-confidence, and prestige? What kind of research might Mattel conduct to examine these changes? Give examples.

   b. The Barbie Web site allows a young girl to custom-design her own Barbie doll. Go to the Fashion Fun section and try it. What type of information has Mattel just collected about your demographics and preferences? How could this information be used to build "connections" with young women?

   c. You are the marketing manager for a proposed new lifestyle doll for Mattel. Write a brief report outlining the types of research you would conduct to determine the attributes of the new doll. Include which markets and preferences you would collect information on and how you might use the Internet as a research tool.

2. The Internet provides a unique means for targeting minority market segments and gathering information about their preferences. All of the following Web sites are available to assist companies in their minority marketing and research efforts: www.minority.net—a large business-to-business e-commerce mall; www.twmall.com—a large Asian American mall that does business in several languages; www.collardcards.com—this site sells greeting cards and cookbooks featuring upbeat images that target African Americans; and www.demographics.com—a site that explore various demographic segments and the trends that affect them.

   a. What unique features of the above sites might assist marketers wishing to reach minority markets?

   b. Using the American Demographics Web site (www.americandemographics.com), determine the potential size of the African American, Hispanic American, and Asian American Web-user markets. What other information about these important minority markets can you find readily?

   c. How might conducting marketing research on minority markets via the Internet differ from more traditional means of conducting research?

DIGITAL CONNECTIONS

CONNECTING COMPANIES WITH CONSUMERS VIA POLLS

The American consumer is one of the most researched subjects in the world. Millions of dollars are spent annually to find out what you want, when you want it, and how much you will pay for it. Becoming intimate with a consumer is not a luxury; it is a necessity. The desire to get to know the customer has spurred interest in ethnographic research, which combines intensive observation with customer interviews (see Real Marketing 5.1, "Ethnographic Research: Keeping a Close Eye on the Consumer," for more details). However, this form of research can often be an expensive pursuit for a company. Is there a lower-cost alternative? Some people in marketing believe that one of the oldest forms of research—the consumer poll—is the answer. At one time, however, polling was expensive and often seriously inaccurate. But what if the researcher could get the advantages of participatory information results at low cost? Well, the Internet has provided the answer—the online poll. While often not scientifically accurate, the online poll has become a great way to get large amounts of preferential information from an interested audience at a low cost. The Internet provides benefits in addition to cost savings. Ask someone a question in a shopping mall, and then he or she is gone. But on the Internet, this same consumer can be recontacted at a later date with a variety of messages. In fact, many people do not

mind the recontact at all—it is a "connection" they actually desire. Have you been polled lately?

FOR DISCUSSION

Interested in participating in the research process? Visit www.pollingreport.com, www.gallup.com, and www.cnn.com and answer the following questions.

1. Which of the polls or questionnaires seemed most interesting to you?
2. Which of the polls was easiest to complete?
3. Which of the polls could be tied most easily to marketing research? Why?
4. Under what circumstances are you willing to supply information to an online researcher? To a Web site? Explain.
5. The American Consumer Opinion Web site (www.acop.com) maintains a panel of Internet users who agree to complete online surveys. Sign up and see how it works.
6. You are a marketing researcher who has just been hired to establish an online marketing poll. Choose a product or service that interests you. Specify your research objectives, develop questions for your poll, decide whom to poll, whether you will share your results with the people you poll, and, if you do share, how you will get that information to participants. How will conducting the poll help you make connections with your customers?

Unica: Building Better Customer Relationships

A recent study projects that the worldwide market for customer relationship management (CRM) services will reach $45.5 billion in 2006. Although Unica's share of the CRM market is relatively small, the company's success has been built upon the growth of marketing automation, more widely known as customer data mining, data warehousing, and customer relationship management. As Unica CEO Yuchun Lee observes, the software that drives the company's service "enables marketers to gather and analyze knowledge from multiple data sources; identify customer wants and needs; and plan, execute, and manage tailored programs for interactions through multiple touchpoints." Relying on that software, Unica now works with more than 250 companies to turn vast stores of customer data into actionable marketing information. The result: better customer relationships for its clients.

After reviewing the Unica video, answer the following questions about customer data management and CRM:

1. How do Unica's software and consulting services add value for its client companies? How do the services add value for clients' customers?
2. Marketing automation enables marketing managers to more effectively store and use data. How does new data-mining technology leverage traditional marketing research to create stronger customer relationships?

Source: Richard McCausland, "CRM: The Momentum Builds," *Accounting Technology,* June 2002, pp. 36–44.

Enterprise Rent-A-Car: Measuring Service Quality

SURVEYING CUSTOMERS

Kevin Kirkman wheeled his shiny blue BMW coupe into his driveway, put the gearshift into park, set the parking brake, and got out to check his mailbox as he did every day when he returned home. As he flipped through the deluge of catalogs and credit card offers, he noticed a letter from Enterprise Rent-A-Car. He wondered why Enterprise would be writing him.

THE WRECK

Then he remembered. Earlier that month, Kevin had been involved in a wreck. As he was driving to work one rainy morning, another car had been unable to stop on the slick pavement and had plowed into his car as he waited at a stoplight. Thankfully, neither he nor the other driver was hurt, but both cars had sustained considerable damage. In fact, he was not able to drive his car.

Kevin had used his cell phone to call the police, and while he was waiting for the officers to come, he had called his auto insurance agent. The agent had assured Kevin that his policy included coverage to pay for a rental car while he was having his car repaired. He told Kevin to have the car towed to a nearby auto repair shop and gave him the telephone number for the Enterprise Rent-A-Car office that served his area. The agent noted that his company recommended using Enterprise for replacement rentals and that Kevin's policy would cover up to $20 per day of the rental fee.

Once Kevin had checked his car in at the body shop and made the necessary arrangements, he telephoned the Enterprise office. Within 10 minutes, an Enterprise employee had driven to the repair shop and picked him up. They drove back to the Enterprise office, where Kevin completed the paperwork and rented a Ford Taurus. He drove the rental car for 12 days before the repair shop completed work on his car.

"Don't know why Enterprise would be writing me," Kevin thought. "The insurance company paid the $20 per day, and I paid the extra because the Taurus cost more than that. Wonder what the problem could be?"

TRACKING SATISFACTION

Kevin tossed the mail on the passenger's seat and drove up the driveway. Once inside his house, he opened the Enterprise letter to find that it was a survey to determine how satisfied he was with his rental. The survey itself was only one page long and consisted of 13 questions (see Exhibit 1).

Enterprise's executives believed that the company had become the largest rent-a-car company in the U.S. (in terms of number of cars, rental locations, and revenue) because of its laserlike focus on customer satisfaction and because of its concentration on serving the home-city replacement market. It aimed to serve customers like Kevin who were involved in wrecks and suddenly found themselves without a car. While the more well known companies like Hertz and Avis battled for business in the cutthroat airport market, Enterprise quietly built its business by cultivating insurance agents and body-shop managers as referral agents so that when one of their clients or customers needed a replacement vehicle, they would recommend Enterprise. Although such replacement rentals accounted for about 80 percent of the company's business, it also served the discretionary market (leisure/vacation rentals), and the business market (renting cars to businesses for their short-term needs). It had also begun to provide on-site and off-site service at some airports.

Throughout its history, Enterprise had followed founder Jack Taylor's advice. Taylor believed that if the company took care of its customers and employees first, profits would follow. So the company was careful to track customer satisfaction.

About one in 20 randomly selected customers received a letter like Kevin's. An independent company mailed the letter and a postage-paid return envelope to the selected customers. Customers who completed the survey used the envelope to return it to the independent company. That company compiled the results and provided them to Enterprise.

CONTINUOUS IMPROVEMENT

Meanwhile, back at Enterprise's St. Louis headquarters, the company's top managers were interested in taking the next steps in their customer satisfaction program. Enterprise had used the percentage of customers who were completely satisfied to develop its Enterprise Service Quality index (ESQi). It used the survey results to calculate an overall average ESQi score for the company and a score for each individual branch. The company's branch managers believed in and supported the process.

However, top management believed that to really "walk the walk" on customer satisfaction, it needed to make the ESQi a key factor in the promotion process. The company wanted to take the ESQi for the branch or branches a manager supervised into consideration when it evaluated that manager for a promotion. Top management believed that such a process would ensure that its managers and all its employees would focus on satisfying Enterprise's customers.

However, the top managers realized they had two problems in taking the next step. First, they wanted a better survey response rate. Although the company got a 25 percent response rate, which was good for this type of survey, it was concerned that it might still be missing important information. Second, it could take up to two months to get results back, and Enterprise believed it needed a process that would get the customer satisfaction information more quickly, at least on a monthly basis, so its branch

(continued)

SERVICE QUALITY SURVEY

Please mark the box that best reflects your response to each question.

1. Overall, how satisfied were you with your recent car rental from Enterprise on January 1, 2003?

Completely Satisfied	Somewhat Satisfied	Neither Satisfied Nor Dissatisfied	Somewhat Dissatisfied	Completely Dissatisfied
☐	☐	☐	☐	☐

2. What, if anything, could Enterprise have done better? (*Please be specific*) _____

_____

3a. Did you experience any problems during the rental process?   Yes ☐   No ☐

3b. If you mentioned any problems to Enterprise, did they resolve them to your satisfaction?   Yes ☐   No ☐   Did not mention ☐

4. If you personally called Enterprise to reserve a vehicle, how would you rate the telephone reservation process?

Excellent	Good	Fair	Poor	N/A
☐	☐	☐	☐	☐

5. Did you go to the Enterprise office....

Both at start and end of rental	Just at start of rental	Just at end of rental	Neither time
☐	☐	☐	☐

6. Did an Enterprise employee give you a ride to help with your transportation needs....

Both at start and end of rental	Just at start of rental	Just at end of rental	Neither time
☐	☐	☐	☐

7. After you arrived at the Enterprise office, how long did it take you to:

	Less than 5 minutes	5–10 minutes	11–15 minutes	16–20 minutes	21–30 minutes	More than 30 minutes	N/A
◆ pick up your rental car?	☐	☐	☐	☐	☐	☐	☐
◆ return your rental car?	☐	☐	☐	☐	☐	☐	☐

8. How would you rate the...

	Excellent	Good	Fair	Poor	N/A
◆ timeliness with which you were either picked up at the start of the rental or dropped off afterwards?	☐	☐	☐	☐	☐
◆ timeliness with which the rental car was either brought to your location and left with you or picked up from your location afterwards?	☐	☐	☐	☐	☐
◆ Enterprise employee who handled your paperwork... at the START of the rental?	☐	☐	☐	☐	☐
at the END of the rental?	☐	☐	☐	☐	☐
◆ mechanical condition of the car?	☐	☐	☐	☐	☐
◆ cleanliness of the car interior/exterior?	☐	☐	☐	☐	☐

9. If you asked for a specific type or size of vehicle, was Enterprise able to meet your needs?

Yes	No	N/A
☐	☐	☐

10. For what reason did you rent this car?

Car repairs due to accident	All other car repairs/ maintenance	Car was stolen	Business	Leisure/ vacation	Some other reason
☐	☐	☐	☐	☐	☐

11. The next time you need to pick up a rental car in the city or area in which you live, how likely are you to call Enterprise?

Definitely will call	Probably will call	Might or might not call	Probably will not call	Definitely will not call
☐	☐	☐	☐	☐

12. Approximately how many times in total have you rented from Enterprise (including this rental)?

Once—this was first time	2 times	3–5 times	6–10 times	11 or more times
☐	☐	☐	☐	☐

13. Considering *all rental companies*, approximately how many times *within the past year* have you rented a car in the city or area in which you live (including this rental)?

0 times	1 time	2 times	3–5 times	6–10 times	11 or more times
☐	☐	☐	☐	☐	☐

managers could identify and take action on customer service problems quickly and efficiently.

Enterprise's managers wondered how they could improve the customer-satisfaction-tracking process.

QUESTIONS FOR DISCUSSION

1. Analyze Enterprise's Service Quality Survey. What information is it trying to gather? What are its research objectives?
2. What decisions has Enterprise made with regard to primary data collection—research approach, contact methods, sampling plan, and research instruments?
3. In addition to or instead of the mail survey, what other means could Enterprise use to gather customer satisfaction information?
4. What specific recommendations would you make to Enterprise to improve the response rate and the timeliness of feedback from the process?

Source: Officials at Enterprise Rent-A-Car contributed to and supported development of this case. See also Company Case in Chapter 18 for more details on Enterprise Rent-A-Car.

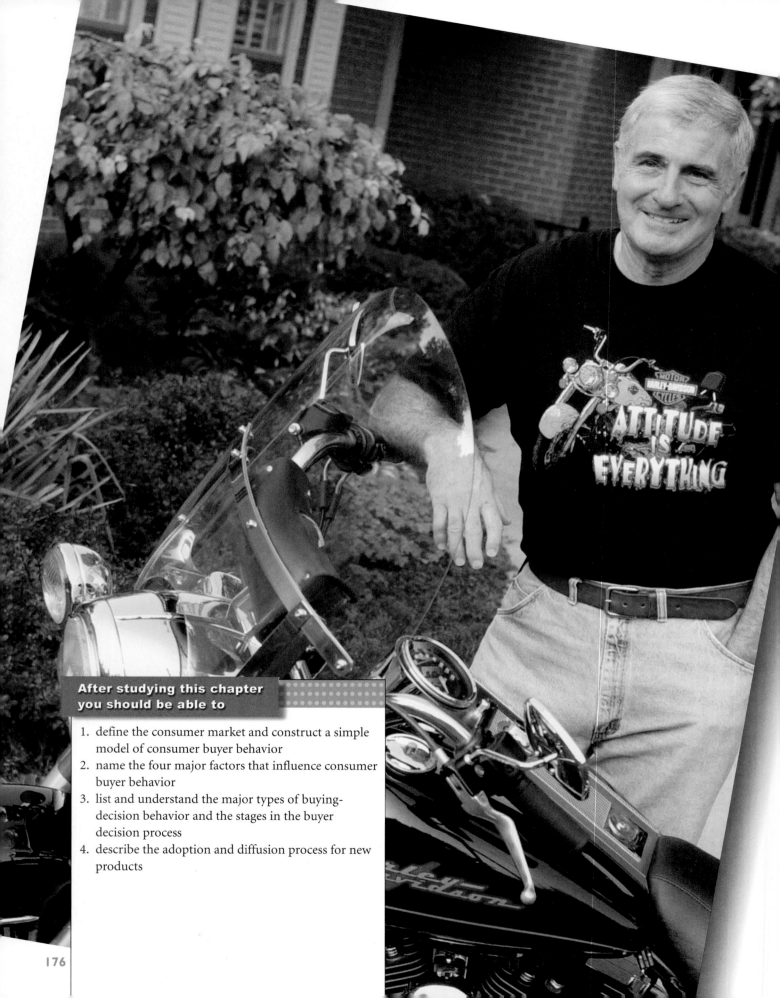

1. define the consumer market and construct a simple model of consumer buyer behavior
2. name the four major factors that influence consumer buyer behavior
3. list and understand the major types of buying-decision behavior and the stages in the buyer decision process
4. describe the adoption and diffusion process for new products

Consumer Markets and Consumer Buyer Behavior

LOOKING AHEAD: PREVIEWING THE CONCEPTS

In the previous chapter, you studied how marketers obtain, analyze, and use information to identify marketing opportunities and to assess marketing programs. In this and the next chapter, we'll continue with a closer look at the most important element of the marketing environment—customers. The aim of marketing is to somehow affect how customers think about and behave toward the organization and its marketing offers. To affect the whats, whens, and hows of buying behavior, marketers must first understand the *whys*. In this chapter, we look at *final consumer* buying influences and processes. In the next chapter, we'll study the buying behavior of *business customers*. You'll see that understanding buying behavior is an essential but very difficult task.

To get a better sense of the importance of understanding consumer behavior, let's look first at Harley-Davidson, maker of the nation's top-selling heavyweight motorcycles. Who rides these big Harley "Hogs"? What moves them to tattoo their bodies with the Harley emblem, abandon home and hearth for the open road, and flock to Harley rallies by the hundreds of thousands? *You* might be surprised, but Harley-Davidson knows *very* well.

Few brands engender such intense loyalty as that found in the hearts of Harley-Davidson owners. "The Harley audience is granitelike" in its devotion, laments the vice president of sales for competitor Yamaha. Observes the publisher of *American Iron*, an industry publication, "You don't see people tattooing *Yamaha* on their bodies." And according to the president of a motorcycle research company, "For a lot of people, it's not that they want a motorcycle; it's that they want a Harley—the brand is that strong." Each year, in early March, more than 400,000 Harley bikers rumble through the streets of Daytona Beach, Florida, to attend Harley-Davidson's Bike Week celebration. Bikers from across the nation lounge on their low-slung Harleys, swap biker tales, and sport T-shirts proclaiming "I'd rather push a Harley than drive a Honda."

Riding such intense emotions, Harley-Davidson has rumbled its way to the top of the fast-growing heavyweight motorcycle market. Harley's "Hogs" capture more than one-fifth of all U.S. bike sales and more than half of the heavyweight segment. Both the segment and Harley's sales are growing rapidly. In fact, for several years running, sales have far outstripped supply, with customer waiting lists of up to two years for popular models and street prices running well above suggested list prices. "We've seen people buy a new Harley and then sell it in the parking lot for $4,000 to $5,000

more," says one dealer. Since its initial public stock offering in 1986, by the year 2000, Harley-Davidson shares had split four times and were up more than 7,100 percent. By 2002, the company had experienced 16 straight years of record sales and income.

Harley-Davidson's marketers spend a great deal of time thinking about customers and their buying behavior. They want to know who their customers are, what they think and how they feel, and why they buy a Harley rather than a Yamaha or a Kawasaki or a big Honda American Classic. What is it that makes Harley buyers so fiercely loyal? These are difficult questions; even Harley owners themselves don't know exactly what motivates their buying. But Harley management puts top priority on understanding customers and what makes them tick.

Who rides a Harley? You might be surprised. It's no longer the Hell's Angels crowd—the burly, black-leather-jacketed rebels and biker chicks who once made up Harley's core clientele. Motorcycles are attracting a new breed of riders—older, more affluent, and better educated. Harley now appeals more to "rubbies" (rich urban bikers) than to rebels. The average Harley customer is a 46-year-old husband with a median household income of $78,300. Harley's big, comfortable cruisers give these new consumers the easy ride, prestige, and twist-of-the-wrist power they want and can afford.

Harley-Davidson makes good bikes, and to keep up with its shifting market, the company has upgraded its showrooms and sales approaches. But Harley customers are buying a lot more than just a quality bike and a smooth sales pitch. To gain a better understanding of customers' deeper motivations, Harley-Davidson conducted focus groups in which it invited bikers to make cut-and-paste collages of pictures that expressed their feelings about Harley-Davidsons. (Can't you just see a bunch of hard-core bikers doing this?) It then mailed out 16,000 surveys containing a typical battery of psychological, sociological, and demographic questions as well as subjective questions such as "Is Harley more typified by a brown bear or a lion?"

The research revealed seven core customer types: adventure-loving traditionalists, sensitive pragmatists, stylish status seekers, laid-back campers, classy capitalists, cool-headed loners, and cocky misfits. However, all owners appreciated their Harleys for the same basic reasons. "It didn't matter if you were the guy who swept the floors of the factory or if you were the CEO at that factory, the attraction to Harley was very similar," says a Harley executive. "Independence, freedom, and power were the universal Harley appeals."

These studies confirm that Harley customers are doing more than just buying motorcycles. They're making a lifestyle statement and displaying an attitude. As one analyst suggests, owning a Harley makes you "the toughest, baddest guy on the block. Never mind that [you're] a dentist or an accountant. You [feel] wicked astride all that power." Your Harley renews your spirits and announces your independence. As the Harley Web site's home page announces, "Thumbing the starter of a Harley-Davidson does a lot more than fire the engine. It fires the imagination." Adds a Harley dealer: "We sell a dream here. Our customers lead hardworking professional or computer-oriented lives. Owning a Harley removes barriers to meeting people on a casual basis, and it gives you maximum self-expression in your own space."

The classic look, the throaty sound, the very idea of a Harley—all contribute to its mystique. Owning this "American legend" makes you a part of something bigger, a member of the Harley family. The fact that you have to wait to get a Harley makes it all that much more satisfying to have one. In fact, the company deliberately restricts its output. "Our goal is to eventually run production at a level that's always one motorcycle short of demand," says Harley-Davidson's chief executive.

Such strong emotions and motivations are captured in a classic Harley-Davidson advertisement. The ad shows a close-up of an arm, the bicep adorned with a Harley-Davidson tattoo. The headline asks, "When was the last time you felt this strongly about anything?" The ad copy outlines the problem and suggests a solution: "Wake up in the morning and life picks up where it left off. You do what has to be done. Use what it takes to get there. And what once seemed exciting has now become part of the numbing routine. It all begins to feel the same. Except when you've got a Harley-Davidson. Something strikes a nerve. The heartfelt thunder rises up, refusing to become part of the background. Suddenly things are different. Clearer. More real. As they should have been all along. The feeling is personal. For some, owning a Harley is a statement of individuality. For others, owning a Harley means being a part of a homegrown legacy that was born in a tiny Milwaukee shed in 1903. . . . To the uninitiated, a Harley-Davidson motorcycle is associated with a certain look, a certain sound. Anyone who owns one will tell you it's much more than that. Riding a Harley changes you from within. The effect is permanent. Maybe it's time you started feeling this strongly. Things are different on a Harley."[1]

The Harley-Davidson example shows that many different factors affect consumer buying behavior. Buying behavior is never simple, yet understanding it is the essential task of marketing management.

This chapter explores the dynamics of the consumer market and final-consumer buyer behavior. **Consumer buyer behavior** refers to the buying behavior of final consumers—individuals and households who buy goods and services for personal consumption. All of these final consumers combine to make up the **consumer market.** The American consumer market consists of more than 287 million people who consume many trillions of dollars' worth of goods and services each year, making it one of the most attractive consumer markets in the world. The world consumer market consists of more than 6.2 *billion* people.[2]

Consumers around the world vary tremendously in age, income, education level, and tastes. They also buy an incredible variety of goods and services. How these diverse consumers connect with each other and with other elements of the world around them impacts their choices among various products, services, and companies. Here we examine the fascinating array of factors that affect consumer behavior.

Consumer buyer behavior
The buying behavior of final consumers—individuals and households who buy goods and services for personal consumption.

Consumer market
All the individuals and households who buy or acquire goods and services for personal consumption.

Model of Consumer Behavior

Consumers make many buying decisions every day. Most large companies research consumer buying decisions in great detail to answer questions about what consumers buy, where they buy, how and how much they buy, when they buy, and why they buy. Marketers can study actual consumer pur-

FIGURE 6.1
Model of buyer behavior

chases to find out what they buy, where, and how much. But learning about the *whys* of consumer buying behavior is not so easy—the answers are often locked deep within the consumer's head.

The central question for marketers is: How do consumers respond to various marketing efforts the company might use? The starting point is the stimulus-response model of buyer behavior shown in Figure 6.1. This figure shows that marketing and other stimuli enter the consumer's "black box" and produce certain responses. Marketers must figure out what is in the buyer's black box.

Marketing stimuli consist of the four *P*s: product, price, place, and promotion. Other stimuli include major forces and events in the buyer's environment: economic, technological, political, and cultural. All these inputs enter the buyer's black box, where they are turned into a set of observable buyer responses: product choice, brand choice, dealer choice, purchase timing, and purchase amount.

The marketer wants to understand how the stimuli are changed into responses inside the consumer's black box, which has two parts. First, the buyer's characteristics influence how he or she perceives and reacts to the stimuli. Second, the buyer's decision process itself affects the buyer's behavior. We look first at buyer characteristics as they affect buying behavior and then discuss the buyer decision process.

Characteristics Affecting Consumer Behavior

Consumer purchases are influenced strongly by cultural, social, personal, and psychological characteristics, shown in Figure 6.2. For the most part, marketers cannot control such factors, but they must take them into account. We illustrate these characteristics for the case of a hypothetical consumer named Anna Flores. Anna is a married college graduate who works as a brand manager in a leading consumer packaged-goods company. She wants to find a new leisure-time activity that will provide some contrast to her working day. This need has led her to consider buying a camera and taking up photography. Many characteristics in her background will affect the way she evaluates cameras and chooses a brand.

Cultural Factors

Cultural factors exert a broad and deep influence on consumer behavior. The marketer needs to understand the role played by the buyer's *culture*, *subculture*, and *social class*.

FIGURE 6.2
Factors influencing consumer behavior

Culture

Culture is the most basic cause of a person's wants and behavior. Human behavior is largely learned. Growing up in a society, a child learns basic values, perceptions, wants, and behaviors from the family and other important institutions. A child in the United States normally learns or is exposed to the following values: achievement and success, activity and involvement, efficiency and practicality, progress, material comfort, individualism, freedom, humanitarianism, youthful-ness, and fitness and health.

Every group or society has a culture, and cultural influences on buying behavior may vary greatly from country to country, or even neighborhood to neighborhood. International differ-ences are most pronounced. Whether or not a company adjusts to such difference can spell the difference between success and failure. For example, different cultures assign different meanings to colors. White is usually associated with purity and cleanliness in Western countries. However, it can signify death in Asian countries. When General Motors was competing for the right to build its cars in China, GM executives gave Chinese officials gifts from Tiffany's jewelers. However, the Americans replaced Tiffany's signature white ribbons with red ones, since red is considered a lucky color in Japan. GM ultimately won approval of its proposal.[3]

In contrast, business representatives of a U.S. community trying to market itself in Taiwan learned a hard cultural lesson. Seeking more foreign trade, they arrived in Taiwan bearing gifts of green baseball caps. It turned out that the trip was scheduled a month before Taiwan elections, and that green was the color of the political opposition party. Worse yet, the visitors learned after the fact that according to Taiwan culture, a man wears green to signify that his wife has been unfaithful. The head of the community delegation later noted, "I don't know what ever happened to those green hats, but the trip gave us an understanding of the extreme differences in our cul-tures." International marketers must understand the culture in each international market and adapt their marketing strategies accordingly.

Anna Flores's cultural background will affect her camera buying decision. Anna's desire to own a camera may result from her being raised in a modern society that has developed camera technology and a whole set of consumer learnings and values.

Marketers are always trying to spot *cultural shifts* in order to discover new products that might be wanted. For example, the cultural shift toward greater concern about health and fitness has created a huge industry for health and fitness services, exercise equipment and clothing, and lower-fat and more-natural foods. The shift toward informality has resulted in more demand for casual clothing and simpler home furnishings.

Subculture

Each culture contains smaller **subcultures,** or groups of people with shared value systems based on common life experiences and situations. Subcultures include nationalities, religions, racial groups, and geographic regions. Many subcultures make up important market segments, and marketers often design products and marketing programs tailored to their needs. Examples of four such important subculture groups include Hispanic, African American, Asian, and mature consumers. As we discuss them, it is important to note that each major subculture is, in turn, made of many smaller subcultures, each with its own preferences and behaviors.

Hispanic Consumers.   The U.S. *Hispanic market*—Americans of Cuban, Mexican, Central American, South American, and Puerto Rican descent—consists of 35 million consumers. Hispanic consumers bought more than $425 billion worth of goods and services each year, up 25 percent from just two years earlier. Expected to grow in number by 64 percent during the next 20 years, Hispanics are easy to reach through the growing selection of Spanish-language broad-cast and print media that cater to them.[4]

Hispanics have long been a target for marketers of food, beverages, and household care prod-ucts. Most marketers now produce products tailored to the Hispanic market and promote them using Spanish-language ads and media. For example, General Mills offers a line of Para su Familia (for your family) cereals for Hispanics, and Colgate's Suavitel fabric softener is the number two brand in the Hispanic segment. Mattel has opened a Spanish-language site for its Barbie dolls—BarbieLatina.com—targeting U.S. Hispanic girls. But as the segment's buying power increases, Hispanics are now emerging as an attractive market for pricier products such as computers, finan-cial services, apparel, large appliances, and automobiles. Hispanic consumers tend to buy more branded, higher-quality products—generics don't sell well to Hispanics. Perhaps more important, Hispanics are very brand loyal, and they favor companies who show special interest in them.[5]

Sears makes a special effort to market to Hispanic American consumers, especially for the 20 percent of its stores that are located in heavily Hispanic neighborhoods:

> Sears currently markets heavily to the attractive Hispanic segment. Last year, it spent some $25 million on advertising to Hispanics—more than any other retailer—and it recently launched a Spanish-language Web site. Sears neighborhoods receive regular visits from a Fiesta Mobile, a colorful Winnebago that plays music, gives out prizes, and promotes the Sears credit card. Sears also sponsors major Hispanic cultural festivals and concerts. One of its most successful marketing efforts is its magazine *Nuestra Gente*—which means Our People—the nation's largest Spanish-language magazine. The magazine features articles about Hispanic celebrities alongside glossy spreads of Sears fashions. As a result of this careful cultivation of Hispanic consumers, although Sears has lost sales in recent years to discount retailers, the Hispanic segment has remained steadfastly loyal.[6]

Targeting Hispanics may also provide an additional benefit. With the passage of the North American Free Trade Agreement (NAFTA)—which reduced trade barriers between the United States, Mexico, and Canada—U.S. and Mexican companies have sought new opportunities to market "pan-American" brands. Companies on both sides of the border see the U.S. Hispanic population as a bridge for spanning U.S. and Latin American markets.

Targeting important subcultures: Hispanic neighborhoods receive regular visits from the Sears Fiesta Mobile, a colorful Winnebago that plays music, gives out prizes, and promotes the Sears credit card.

African American Consumers.   If the U.S. population of 35 million *African Americans* were a separate nation, its buying power of $527 billion annually would rank among the top 15 in the world.[7] The black population in the United States is growing in affluence and sophistication. Although more price conscious than other segments, blacks are also strongly motivated by quality and selection. They place more importance on brand names, are more brand loyal, and do less "shopping around."

In recent years, many companies have developed special products and services, packaging, and appeals to meet the needs of African Americans. Hallmark launched its Afrocentric brand, Mahogany, with only 16 cards in 1987. Today the brand features more than 900 cards designed to celebrate African American culture, heritage, and traditions. Other companies are moving away from creating separate products for African Americans. Instead, they are offering more-inclusive product lines within the same brand that goes out to the general market. For example, Sara Lee discontinued its separate Color-Me-Natural line of L'eggs pantyhose for black women and now offers shades and sheer styles popular among black women as half of the company's general-focus subbrands.[8]

A wide variety of magazines, television channels, and other media now target African American consumers. Marketers are also reaching out to the African American virtual community. Per capita, black consumers spend twice as much as white consumers for online services. African Americans are increasingly turning to Web sites such as The Black World Today (www.tbwt.com), a black *USA Today* on the Internet, that address black culture in ways that network and cable TV rarely do. Other popular sites include Urban Sports Network, NetNoir, Afronet, and Black Voices.[9]

Asian American Consumers.   *Asian Americans,* the fastest-growing and most affluent U.S. demographic segment, now number more than 10 million, with a disposable income of $229 billion annually. Chinese Americans constitute the largest group, followed by Filipinos, Japanese Americans, Asian Indians, and Korean Americans. The U.S. Asian American population is estimated to reach 30 million by 2050.[10] Financial services marketers have long targeted Asian American consumers:

> Discount broker Charles Schwab goes all out to court the large and particularly lucrative Chinese American market. Schwab estimates that the U.S. Chinese community holds as much as $150 billion in investable assets. Schwab has opened 14 Chinese-language offices in such places as New York's and San Francisco's Chinatowns and plans to add many more. Its Chinese-language Web site, launched in 1998, now racks up more than 5 million hits per month. Schwab recently added an online Chinese-language news service, where customers can check market activity, news headlines, and earnings estimates. Although relatively small in number, Chinese Americans have plenty of money. The median Chinese-American household income is $65,000 a year, compared with $40,000 for Americans in general. Even more appealing to brokers is that Chinese American investors pour money into stocks—they trade two and three times as much as other investors, generating a lot of commissions.[11]

Until recently, packaged-goods firms, automobile companies, retailers, and fast-food chains have lagged in this segment. Language and cultural traditions appear to be the biggest barriers. For example, 66 percent of Asian Americans are foreign born, and 56 percent of those five years and older do not speak English fluently. Still, because of the segment's rapidly growing buying power, many firms are now looking seriously at this market. For example, Wal-Mart now caters to this fast-growing market. Today, in one Seattle store, where the Asian American population represents over 13 percent of the population, Wal-Mart stocks a large selection of CDs and videos from Asian artists, Asian-favored health and beauty products, and children's learning videos that feature multiple language tracks.[12]

Mature Consumers.   As the U.S. population ages, *mature consumers* are becoming a very attractive market. Now 75 million strong, the 50-and-older population will swell to 115 million in the next 25 years. The 65-and-over crowd alone numbers 35 million and will swell to 70 million by 2030. Mature consumers are better off financially than are younger consumer groups—the 50-plus group controls 50 percent of all discretionary income, and the median net worth of 65-plussers is more than double that of the national average.[13] Because mature consumers have more time and money, they are an ideal market for exotic travel, restaurants, high-tech home entertainment

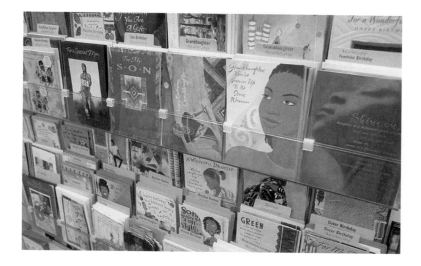

Hallmark launched its Afrocentric brand, Mahogany, with only 16 cards in 1987. Today it offers 800 cards.

products, leisure goods and services, designer furniture and fashions, financial services, and health care services.

Their desire to look as young as they feel also makes more-mature consumers good candidates for cosmetics and personal care products, health foods, fitness products, and other items that combat the effects of aging. The best strategy is to appeal to their active, multidimensional lives. For example, a recent Nike commercial features a senior weight lifter who proudly proclaims, "I'm not strong for my age. I'm strong!" Similarly, Kellogg aired a TV spot for All-Bran cereal in which individuals ranging in age from 53 to 81 are featured playing ice hockey, water skiing, running hurdles, and playing baseball, all to the tune of "Wild Thing." And an Aetna commercial portrays a senior who, after retiring from a career as a lawyer, fulfills a lifelong dream of becoming an archeologist.[14]

Anna Flores's buying behavior will be influenced by her subculture identification. These factors will affect her food preferences, clothing choices, recreation activities, and career goals. Subcultures attach different meanings to picture taking, and this could affect both Anna's interest in cameras and the brand she buys.

Social Class

Social classes

Relatively permanent and ordered divisions in a society whose members share similar values, interests, and behaviors.

Almost every society has some form of social class structure. **Social classes** are society's relatively permanent and ordered divisions whose members share similar values, interests, and behaviors. Social scientists have identified the seven American social classes (see Table 6.1).

Social class is not determined by a single factor, such as income, but is measured as a combination of occupation, income, education, wealth, and other variables. In some social systems, members of different classes are reared for certain roles and cannot change their social positions. In the United States, however, the lines between social classes are not fixed and rigid; people can move to a higher social class or drop into a lower one. Marketers are interested in social class because people within a given social class tend to exhibit similar buying behavior.[15]

Social classes show distinct product and brand preferences in areas such as clothing, home furnishings, leisure activity, and automobiles. Anna Flores's social class may affect her camera decision. If she comes from a higher social class background, her family probably owned an expensive camera and she may have dabbled in photography.

Social Factors

A consumer's behavior also is influenced by social factors, such as the consumer's *small groups, family,* and *social roles* and *status.*

Group

Two or more people who interact to accomplish individual or mutual goals.

Groups

A person's behavior is influenced by many small **groups.** Groups that have a direct influence and to which a person belongs are called *membership groups.* In contrast, *reference groups* serve as direct (face-to-face) or indirect points of comparison or reference in forming a person's attitudes

TABLE 6.1	CHARACTERISTICS OF SEVEN MAJOR AMERICAN SOCIAL CLASSES

Upper uppers (less than 1 percent)
Upper uppers are the social elite who live on inherited wealth and have well-established family backgrounds. They give large sums to charity, own more than one home, and send their children to the finest schools. They are accustomed to wealth and often buy and dress conservatively rather than showing off their wealth.

Lower uppers (about 2 percent)
Lower uppers have earned high income or wealth through exceptional ability in the professions or business. They usually begin in the middle class. They tend to be active in social and civic affairs and buy for themselves and their children the symbols of status, such as expensive homes, educations, and automobiles. They want to be accepted in the upper-upper, stratum, a status more likely to be achieved by their children than by themselves.

Upper middles (12 percent)
Upper middles possess neither family status nor unusual wealth. They have attained positions as professionals; independent businesspersons, and corporate managers. They have a keen interest in attaining the "better things in life." They believe in education and want their children to develop professional or administrative skills. They are joiners and highly civic-minded.

Middle class (32 percent)
The middle class is made up of average-pay white- and blue-collar workers who live on the "the better side of town" and try to "do the proper things." To keep up with the trends, they often buy products that are popular. Most are concerned with fashion, seeking the better brand names. Better living means owning a nice home in a nice neighborhood with good schools.

Working class (38 percent)
The working class consists of those who lead a "working-class lifestyle," whatever their income, school background, or job. They depend heavily on relatives for economic and emotional support, for advice on purchases, and for assistance in times of trouble.

Upper lowers (9 percent)
Upper lowers are working (are not on welfare), although their living standard is just above poverty. Although they strive toward a higher class, they often lack education and perform unskilled work for poor pay.

Lower lowers (7 percent)
Lower lowers are visibly poor. They are often poorly educated and work as unskilled laborers. However, they are often out of work and some depend on public assistance. They tend to live a day-to-day existence.

Sources: See Richard P. Coleman, "The Continuing Significance of Social Class to Marketing," *Journal of Consumer Research,* December 1983, pp. 265–280. © Journal of Consumer Research, Inc., 1983. Also see Leon G. Shiffman and Leslie Lazar Kanuk, *Consumer Behavior,* 6th ed. (Upper Saddle River, N.J.: Prentice Hall, 1997), p. 388; and Linda P. Morton, "Segmenting Publics by Social Class," *Public Relations Quarterly,* Summer 1999, pp. 45–46.

or behavior. People often are influenced by reference groups to which they do not belong. For example, an *aspirational group* is one to which the individual wishes to belong, as when a teenage basketball player hopes to play someday for the Los Angeles Lakers. Marketers try to identify the reference groups of their target markets. Reference groups expose a person to new behaviors and lifestyles, influence the person's attitudes and self-concept, and create pressures to conform that may affect the person's product and brand choices.

Manufacturers of products and brands subjected to strong group influence must figure out how to reach **opinion leaders**—people within a reference group who, because of special skills, knowledge, personality, or other characteristics, exert influence on others.

Many marketers try to identify opinion leaders for their products and direct marketing efforts toward them. For example, the hottest trends in teenage music, language, and fashion start in America's inner cities, then quickly spread to more mainstream youth in the suburbs. Thus, clothing companies who hope to appeal to these fickle and fashion-conscious youth often make a concerted effort to monitor urban opinion leaders' style and behavior. In other cases, marketers may use *buzz marketing* by enlisting or even creating opinion leaders to spread the word about their brands.

Opinion leader
Person within a reference group who, because of special skills, knowledge, personality, or other characteristics, exerts influence on others.

Frequent the right cafes . . . in and around Los Angeles this summer, and you're likely to encounter a gang of sleek, impossibly attractive motorbike riders who seem genuinely interested in getting to know you over an iced latte. Compliment them on their Vespa scooters glinting in the brilliant curbside sunlight, and they'll happily pull out a pad and scribble down an address and phone number—not theirs, but that of the local "boutique" where you can buy your own Vespa, just as (they'll confide) the rap artist Sisqo and the movie queen Sandra Bullock recently did. And that's when the truth hits you: This isn't any spontaneous encounter. Those scooter-riding models are on the Vespa payroll, and they've been hired to generate some favorable word of mouth for the recently reissued European bikes. Welcome to the [new world of buzz marketing. Buzz marketers are now] taking to the streets, as well as cafes, nightclubs, and the Internet, in record numbers. Vespa . . . has its biker gang. Hebrew National is dispatching "mom squads" to grill up its hot dogs in backyard barbecues, while Hasbro Games has deputized hundreds of fourth- and fifth-graders as "secret agents" to tantalize their peers with Hasbro's POX electronic game. Their goal: to seek out the trendsetters in each community and subtly push them into talking up their brand to their friends and admirers.[16]

The importance of group influence varies across products and brands. It tends to be strongest when the product is visible to others whom the buyer respects. Purchases of products that are bought and used privately are not much affected by group influences, because neither the product nor the brand will be noticed by others. If Anna Flores buys a camera, both the product and the brand will be visible to others whom she respects, and her decision to buy the camera and her brand choice may be influenced strongly by some of her groups, such as friends who belong to a photography club.

Family

Family members can strongly influence buyer behavior. The family is the most important consumer buying organization in society, and it has been researched extensively. Marketers are interested in the roles and influence of the husband, wife, and children on the purchase of different products and services.

Husband-wife involvement varies widely by product category and by stage in the buying process. Buying roles change with evolving consumer lifestyles. In the United States, the wife

Family buying influences: Children can exert a strong influence on family buying decisions: Chevrolet actively woos these "back-seat consumers" with carefully targeted advertising and a Chevy Venture Warner Bros. Edition, complete with DVD player.

traditionally has been the main purchasing agent for the family, especially in the areas of food, household products, and clothing. But with 70 percent of women holding jobs outside the home and the willingness of husbands to do more of the family's purchasing, all this is changing. For example, women now make or influence up to 80 percent of car-buying decisions and men account for about 40 percent of food-shopping dollars.[17]

Such changes suggest that marketers who've typically sold their products to only women or only men are now courting the opposite sex. For example, with research revealing that women now account for nearly half of all hardware store purchases, home improvement retailers such as Home Depot and Builders Square have turned what once were intimidating warehouses into female-friendly retail outlets. The new Builders Square II outlets feature decorator design centers at the front of the store. To attract more women, Builders Square runs ads targeting women in *Home, House Beautiful, Woman's Day,* and *Better Homes and Gardens.* Home Depot even offers bridal registries.

Children may also have a strong influence on family buying decisions. For example, children as young as age six may influence the family car purchase decision. "By six, they know the names of cars," says an industry analyst. "They see them on TV." Chevrolet recognizes these influences in marketing its Chevy Venture minivan. For example, it runs ads to woo these "back-seat consumers" in *Sports Illustrated for Kids,* which attracts mostly 8- to 14-year-old boys. "We're kidding ourselves when we think kids aren't aware of brands," says Venture's brand manager, adding that even she was surprised at how often parents told her that kids played a tie-breaking role in deciding which car to buy.[18]

Roles and Status

A person belongs to many groups—family, clubs, organizations. The person's position in each group can be defined in terms of both role and status. With her parents, Anna Flores plays the role of daughter; in her family, she plays the role of wife; in her company, she plays the role of brand manager. A *role* consists of the activities people are expected to perform according to the persons around them. Each of Anna's roles will influence some of her buying behavior. Each role carries a *status* reflecting the general esteem given to it by society. People often choose products that show their status in society. For example, the role of brand manager has more status in our society than does the role of daughter. As a brand manager, Anna will buy the kind of clothing that reflects her role and status.

Personal Factors

A buyer's decisions also are influenced by personal characteristics such as the buyer's *age* and *life-cycle stage, occupation, economic situation, lifestyle,* and *personality* and *self-concept.*

Age and Life-Cycle Stage

People change the goods and services they buy over their lifetimes. Tastes in food, clothes, furniture, and recreation are often age related. Buying is also shaped by the stage of the *family life cycle*—the stages through which families might pass as they mature over time. Marketers often define their target markets in terms of life-cycle stage and develop appropriate products and marketing plans for each stage.

Traditional family life-cycle stages include young singles and married couples with children. Today, however, marketers are increasingly catering to a growing number of alternative, nontraditional stages such as unmarried couples, singles marrying later in life, childless couples, same-sex couples, single parents, extended parents (those with young adult children returning home), and others. For example, more and more companies are now reaching out to serve the fast-growing corps of the recently divorced (see Real Marketing 6.1).

Sony recently overhauled its marketing approach in order to target products and services to consumers based on their life stages. It created a new unit called the Consumer Segment Marketing Division, which has identified seven life-stage segments. They include, among others, Gen Y (under 25), Young Professionals/D.I.N.K.s (double income no kids, 25 to 34), Families (35 to 54), and Zoomers (55 and over). Sony's goal is to create brand loyalty early on and to develop long-term relationships. "The goal is to get closer to consumers," says a Sony marketing executive. [19]

Targeting Nontraditional Life Stages: Just Divorced, Gone Shopping

Divorcees used to be off limits for marketers. Not anymore. Almost half of all marriages now end in divorce, more than four times as many as 30 years ago. As a result, divorcees in the United States now number almost 20 million, representing a distinct market segment in a not-really-so-nontraditional life-cycle stage. Consider these examples:

When [Leila Mesghali] walked out of her marriage of three years, she took only her

Life-stage marketing: Marketers are discovering that when couples split, someone goes shopping. Divorcees, much like newly-weds, restock their homes with everything from pots and pans to televisions.

clothes and some heirloom dishes. . . A few months after she separated from her husband, however, the decorating urge kicked in. Even on a limited budget, she spent $6,000 on a dark teak armoire, sofa, and bedroom set. "I had a lot of motivation to fill my apartment up quickly," she said. "It was an opportunity to do my own thing."

Kim Lombard, a television producer in Toronto, also refurnished from scratch—though not of his own will—after splitting two years ago. "When my wife left me, she took everything," Mr. Lombard said. . . .

[He] quickly spent about $25,000 on a sofa, a good mattress, and a 50-inch television. . . . Consider, too, the suddenly single Wall Street banker who spent $3,000 in an afternoon to outfit a bedroom for his 17-month-old twins, just like the one they already knew. Or the newly separated publisher who visited an Arts and Crafts furniture store to buy a Gustav Stickley headboard and walked out with a recliner, a table, and an armoire as well.

Marketers are discovering that when couples split, someone goes shopping. Divorcees, much like newly-weds, restock their homes with everything from towels to televisions. Notes one consultant, "The divorce rate is keeping the furniture business alive. There's no doubt that life stages are driving consumers. They buy when they get married; they buy when they get divorced." Says Dan Couvrette, publisher of *Divorce Magazine*, "Next year, at least half of the 2.4 million people who will get divorced in the United States and Canada are going to buy new beds. That's over a million people. You can't find a bigger niche."

The recently divorced don't just go shopping out of necessity. It also raises their spirits.

Divorcees don't just buy out of necessity; the shopping cure can ease the pain. People going through a divorce, Couvrette says, "represent a tremendous market potential because they'll spend money to get stuff that makes them feel better." Couvrette [adds] that even those who suffer financial setbacks—often the case with women leaving long-term marriages— try to treat themselves to the best they can afford. . . . [Some] 78 percent of the men bought

new entertainment systems, while 69 percent of the women opted for new bedroom furniture.

Retail stores, such as Crate & Barrel, Sears, and Ikea, are learning to recognize and accommodate the shopper who may be dazed and alone, trailing a long list of household needs. "Our salespeople say they sometimes feel like therapists," [says] Joe Dance, a Crate & Barrel spokesman. "They know they can't be all bubbly around someone who might be upset. It's clearly a situation that demands their most sensitive approach."

National retailers are not alone. One North Carolina furniture maker has trained its salespeople to keep an eye out for customers with such special needs. "We teach our sales associates to look out for that man wandering around. He may have just been kicked out of the house," says one company's owner.

One Ikea spokeswoman, who spent more than five years as a design consultant, estimates that more than 30 percent of the customers she worked with were divorced men. As a result, saleswomen often play the role of surrogate wives. Sharon Klein, a home furnishings consultant with Ikea, regularly assists "gentlemen who want help from someone with a woman's touch in buying just about everything. They come right up to you and say, 'Help!'" And when it comes to their children, she says, "they always want a lot of extras to make their kid's new bedroom more exciting than the one at the other parent's house."

In response to the growing market, advertisers are testing the waters. Sears launched a television featuring a once-loving couple. After separating their washer and dryer in the settlement, they pass each other in the aisles at Sears, smiling awkwardly while shopping for new appliances. "It was a humorous look at a real-life situation," says a Sears marketer. Here's another example.

Some years ago, Ikea ran a television ad that put a positive spin on shopping one's way to a fresh start. It showed a woman driving at night with her daughter asleep in the back seat. She muses

(continued)

aloud about her divorce and embarking on a new life. Flashbacks show her shopping up a storm in the aisles of Ikea.

Many marketers have shunned the divorcee segment as too downbeat. "Divorce is still a niche market with negative connotations," says one analyst. "Historically, advertisers go with more positive images. But that's going to change in keeping with the whole trend to go after more targeted groups." Consider this example:

Montauk Sofas was among the first to run an upbeat breakup ad. A smiling woman cozies up in the embrace of a $1,900 extra-plush armchair. The text begins in bold type: "He left me. Good Riddance." and ends: "Who cares . . . I kept the sofa." The ad has generated such good feelings for Montauk, a Montreal-based furniture manufacturer with seven stores in the United States and Canada, that it has kept running it for five years. "We've gotten an excellent reaction from all walks of life and ages," said Tim Zyto, the owner of Montauk. "Women especially like it. They find it empowering."

Couvrette of *Divorce Magazine* thinks that it's only a matter of time before the once-taboo D-word comes to stand for "divorce registry." "It's not going to be *called* a divorce registry," he predicts, "but everyone's going to know that's what it's for."

Source: Excerpts and quotes from Julie V. Iovine, "Just Divorced, Gone Shopping," *New York Times,* July 12, 2001, p. F1. Also see Pamela Sebastian Ridge, "Tool Sellers Tap Their Feminine Side," *Wall Street Journal,* March 29, 2002, p. B1.

Occupation

A person's occupation affects the goods and services bought. Blue-collar workers tend to buy more rugged work clothes, whereas executives buy more business suits. Marketers try to identify the occupational groups that have an above-average interest in their products and services. A company can even specialize in making products needed by a given occupational group. Thus, computer software companies will design different products for brand managers, accountants, engineers, lawyers, and doctors.

Economic Situation

A person's economic situation will affect product choice. Anna Flores can consider buying an expensive Nikon if she has enough spendable income, savings, or borrowing power. Marketers of income-sensitive goods watch trends in personal income, savings, and interest rates. If economic indicators point to a recession, marketers can take steps to redesign, reposition, and reprice their products closely.

Lifestyle

Lifestyle
A person's pattern of living as expressed in his or her activities, interests, and opinions.

People coming from the same subculture, social class, and occupation may have quite different lifestyles. **Lifestyle** is a person's pattern of living as expressed in his or her *psychographics*. It involves measuring consumers' major *AIO dimensions—activities* (work, hobbies, shopping, sports, social events), *interests* (food, fashion, family, recreation), and *opinions* (about themselves, social issues, business, products). Lifestyle captures something more than the person's social class or personality. It profiles a person's whole pattern of acting and interacting in the world.

Several research firms have developed lifestyle classifications. The most widely used is the SRI Consulting's *Values and Lifestyles (VALS)* typology (see Figure 6.3). VALS classifies people according to how they spend their time and money. It divides consumers into eight groups based on two major dimensions: self-orientation and resources. *Self-orientation* groups include *principle-oriented* consumers who buy based on their views of the world; *status-oriented* buyers who base their purchases on the actions and opinions of others; and *action-oriented* buyers who are driven by their desire for activity, variety, and risk taking.

Consumers within each orientation are further classified into those with *abundant resources* and those with *minimal resources,* depending on whether they have high or low levels of income, education, health, self-confidence, energy, and other factors. Consumers with either very high or very low levels of resources are classified without regard to their self-orientations (actualizers, strugglers). Actualizers are people with so many resources that they can indulge in any or all self-orientations. In contrast, strugglers are people with too few resources to be included in any consumer orientation.

FIGURE 6.3

VALS lifestyle classifications

Source: Reprinted with permission of SRI International, Menlo Park, CA. VALS is a registered trademark of SRI International.

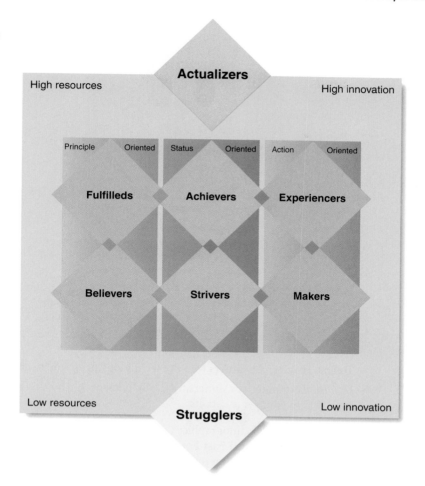

Iron City beer, a well-known brand in Pittsburgh, used VALS to update its image and improve sales. Iron City was losing sales—its aging core users were drinking less beer, and younger men weren't buying the brand. According to VALS research, experiencers drink the most beer, followed by strivers. To assess Iron City's image problems, the company interviewed men in these categories. It gave the men stacks of pictures of different kinds of people and asked them to identify first Iron City brand users and then people most like themselves. The men pictured Iron City drinkers as blue-collar steelworkers stopping off at the local bar. However, they saw themselves as more modern, hardworking, and fun loving. They strongly rejected the outmoded, heavy-industry image of Pittsburgh. Based on this research, Iron City created ads linking its beer to the new self-image of target consumers. The ads mingled images of the old Pittsburgh with those of the new, dynamic city and scenes of young experiencers and strivers having fun and working hard. Within just one month of the start of the campaign, Iron City sales shot up by 26 percent.[20]

Lifestyle segmentation can also be used to understand Internet behavior. Forrester developed its "Technographics" scheme, which segments consumers according to motivation, desire, and ability to invest in technology.[21] The framework splits people into 10 categories, such as:

• *Fast Forwards:* the biggest spenders on computer technology. Fast Forwards are early adopters of new technology for home, office, and personal use.

• *New Age Nurturers:* also big spenders but focused on technology for home uses, such as a family PC.

• *Mouse Potatoes:* consumers who are dedicated to interactive entertainment and willing to spend for the latest in "technotainment."

Lifestyles: The Jeep® brand targets people who want to leave the civilized world behind.

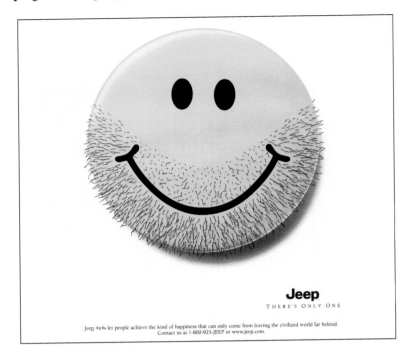

Jeep
THERE'S ONLY ONE

Jeep 4x4s let people achieve the kind of happiness that can only come from leaving the civilized world far behind.
Contact us at 1-800-925-JEEP or www.jeep.com.

- *Techno-Strivers:* consumers who use technology primarily to gain a career edge.
- *Handshakers:* older consumers, typically managers, who don't touch computers at work and leave that to younger assistants.

Delta Airlines used Technographics to better target online ticket sales. It created marketing campaigns for time-strapped Fast Forwards and New Age Nurturers, and eliminated "Technology Pessimists" from its list of targets.

Lifestyle classifications are by no means universal—they can vary significantly from country to country. Advertising agency McCann-Erikson London, for example, found the following British lifestyles: Avant Guardians (interested in change), Pontificators (traditionalists, very British), Chameleons (follow the crowd), and Sleepwalkers (contented underachievers). The agency D'Arcy, Masius, Benton, & Bowles agency identified five categories of Russian consumers: Kuptsi (merchants), Cossacks, Students, Business Executives, and Russian Souls. Cossacks are characterized as ambitious, independent, and status seeking; Russian Souls as passive, fearful of choices, and hopeful. Thus, a typical Cossack might drive a BMW, smoke Dunhill cigarettes, and drink Remy Martin liquor, whereas a Russian Soul would drive a Lada, smoke Marlboros, and drink Smirnoff vodka.[22]

When used carefully, the lifestyle concept can help the marketer understand changing consumer values and how they affect buying behavior. Anna Flores, for example, can choose to live the role of a capable homemaker, a career woman, or a free spirit—or all three. She plays several roles, and the way she blends them expresses her lifestyle. If she becomes a professional photographer, this would change her lifestyle, in turn changing what and how she buys.

Personality and Self-Concept

Personality

A person's distinguishing psychological characteristics that lead to relatively consistent and lasting responses to his or her own environment.

Each person's distinct personality influences his or her buying behavior. **Personality** refers to the unique psychological characteristics that lead to relatively consistent and lasting responses to one's own environment. Personality is usually described in terms of traits such as self-confidence, dominance, sociability, autonomy, defensiveness, adaptability, and aggressiveness. Personality can be useful in analyzing consumer behavior for certain product or brand choices. For example, coffee marketers have discovered that heavy coffee drinkers tend to be high on sociability. Thus, to attract customers, Starbucks and other coffeehouses create environments in which people can relax and socialize over a cup of steaming coffee.

Brand personality

The specific mix of human traits that may be attributed to a particular brand.

The idea is that brands also have personalities, and that consumers are likely to choose brands whose personalities match their own. A **brand personality** is the specific mix of human traits that may be attributed to a particular brand. One researcher identified five brand personality traits:[23]

Heavy coffee drinkers tend to be high on sociability, so to attract customers Starbucks and other coffee-houses create environments in which people can relax and socialize over a cup of steaming coffee.

1. Sincerity (down-to-earth, honest, wholesome, and cheerful)
2. Excitement (daring, spirited, imaginative, and up-to-date)
3. Competence (reliable, intelligent, and successful)
4. Sophistication (upper class and charming)
5. Ruggedness (outdoorsy and tough)

The researcher found that a number of well-known brands tended to be strongly associated with one particular trait: Levi's with "ruggedness," MTV with "excitement," CNN with "competence," and Campbell's with "sincerity." Hence, these brands will attract persons who are high on the same personality traits.

Many marketers use a concept related to personality—a person's *self-concept* (also called *self-image*). The basic self-concept premise is that people's possessions contribute to and reflect their identities; that is, "we are what we have." Thus, in order to understand consumer behavior, the marketer must first understand the relationship between consumer self-concept and possessions. For example, the founder and chief executive of Barnes & Noble, the nation's leading bookseller, notes that people buy books to support their self-images:

> People have the mistaken notion that the thing you do with books is read them. Wrong. . . . People buy books for what the purchase says about them—their taste, their cultivation, their trendiness. Their aim . . . is to connect themselves, or those to whom they give the books as gifts, with all the other refined owners of Edgar Allen Poe collections or sensitive owners of Virginia Woolf collections. . . . [The result is that] you can sell books as consumer products, with seductive displays, flashy posters, an emphasis on the glamour of the book, and the fashionableness of the bestseller and the trendy author.[24]

Psychological Factors

A person's buying choices are further influenced by four major psychological factors: *motivation; perception; learning;* and *beliefs and attitudes.*

Motivation

Motive (drive)
A need that is sufficiently pressing to direct the person to seek satisfaction of the need.

We know that Anna Flores became interested in buying a camera. Why? What is she *really* seeking? What *needs* is she trying to satisfy? A person has many needs at any given time. Some are *biological,* arising from states of tension such as hunger, thirst, or discomfort. Others are *psychological,* arising from the need for recognition, esteem, or belonging. A need becomes a *motive* when it is aroused to a sufficient level of intensity. A **motive** (or *drive*) is a need that is sufficiently pressing to direct the person to seek satisfaction. Psychologists have developed theories of human motivation. Two of the most popular—the theories of Sigmund Freud and Abraham Maslow—have quite different meanings for consumer analysis and marketing.

Sigmund Freud assumed that people are largely unconscious about the real psychological forces shaping their behavior. He saw the person as growing up and repressing many urges. These urges are never eliminated or under perfect control; they emerge in dreams, in slips of the tongue, in neurotic and obsessive behavior, or ultimately in psychoses. Thus, Freud suggested that a person does not fully understand his or her motivation. If Anna Flores wants to purchase an expensive camera, she may describe her motive as wanting a hobby or career. At a deeper level, she may be purchasing the camera to impress others with her creative talent. At a still deeper level, she may be buying the camera to feel young and independent again.

The term *motivation research* refers to qualitative research designed to probe consumers' hidden, subconscious motivations. Motivation researchers collect in-depth information from small samples of consumers to uncover the deeper motives for their product choices. The techniques range from sentence completion, word association, and inkblot or cartoon interpretation tests, to having consumers describe typical brand users or form daydreams and fantasies about brands or buying situations (see Real Marketing 6.2).

Many companies employ teams of psychologists, anthropologists, and other social scientists to carry out motivation research. One agency routinely conducts one-on-one, therapy-like interviews to delve into the inner workings of consumers. Another agency asks consumers to describe their favorite brands as animals or cars (say, Cadillacs versus Chevrolets) in order to assess the prestige associated with various brands. Still another agency has consumers draw figures of typical brand users. In one case, the agency asked 50 participants to sketch likely buyers of two different brands of cake mixes. Consistently, the group portrayed Pillsbury customers as apron-clad, grandmotherly types, whereas they pictured Duncan Hines purchasers as svelte, contemporary women.

Abraham Maslow sought to explain why people are driven by particular needs at particular times. Why does one person spend much time and energy on personal safety and another on gaining the esteem of others? Maslow's answer is that human needs are arranged in a hierarchy, as shown in Figure 6.4, from the most pressing at the bottom to the least pressing at the top. They include *physiological* needs, *safety* needs, *social* needs, *esteem* needs, and *self-actualization* needs.

A person tries to satisfy the most important need first. When that need is satisfied, it will stop being a motivator and the person will then try to satisfy the next most important need. For example, starving people (physiological need) will not take an interest in the latest happenings in the art world (self-actualization needs), nor in how they are seen or esteemed by others (social or esteem needs), nor even in whether they are breathing clean air (safety needs). But as each important need is satisfied, the next most important need will come into play.

What light does Maslow's theory throw on Anna Flores's interest in buying a camera? We can guess that Anna has satisfied her physiological, safety, and social needs; they do not motivate her interest in cameras. Her camera interest might come from a strong need for more esteem. Or it might come from a need for self-actualization—she might want to be a creative person and express herself through photography.

Perception

A motivated person is ready to act. How the person acts is influenced by his or her own perception of the situation. All of us learn by the flow of information through our five senses: sight,

Motivation research: When asked to sketch typical cake mix users, subjects portrayed Pillsbury customers as grandmotherly types and Duncan Hines users as svelte and contemporary.

FIGURE 6.4

Maslow's hierarchy of needs

Source: From *Motivation and Personality* by Abraham H. Maslow. Copyright © 1970 by Abraham H. Maslow. Copyright 1954, 1987 by Harper & Row Publishers, Inc. Reprinted by permission of Addison-Wesley Educational Publishers Inc. Also see Barbara Marx Hubbard, "Seeking Our Future Potentials," *The Futurist,* May 1998, pp. 29–32.

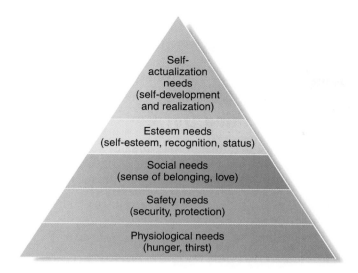

Perception

The process by which people select, organize, and interpret information to form a meaningful picture of the world.

hearing, smell, touch, and taste. However, each of us receives, organizes, and interprets this sensory information in an individual way. **Perception** is the process by which people select, organize, and interpret information to form a meaningful picture of the world.

People can form different perceptions of the same stimulus because of three perceptual processes: selective attention, selective distortion, and selective retention. People are exposed to a great amount of stimuli every day. For example, one analyst estimates that people are exposed to about 5,000 ads every day.[25] It is impossible for a person to pay attention to all these stimuli. *Selective attention*—the tendency for people to screen out most of the information to which they are exposed—means that marketers have to work especially hard to attract the consumer's attention.

Even noted stimuli do not always come across in the intended way. Each person fits incoming information into an existing mind-set. *Selective distortion* describes the tendency of people to interpret information in a way that will support what they already believe. Anna Flores may hear a salesperson mention some good and bad points about a competing camera brand. Because she already has a strong leaning toward Nikon, she is likely to distort those points in order to conclude that Nikon is the better camera. Selective distortion means that marketers must try to understand the mind-sets of consumers and how these will affect interpretations of advertising and sales information.

People also will forget much that they learn. They tend to retain information that supports their attitudes and beliefs. Because of *selective retention,* Anna is likely to remember good points made about the Nikon and to forget good points made about competing cameras. Because of selective exposure, distortion, and retention, marketers have to work hard to get their messages through. This fact explains why marketers use so much drama and repetition in sending messages to their market.

Interestingly, although most marketers worry about whether their offers will be perceived at all, some consumers worry that they will be affected by marketing messages without even knowing it—through *subliminal advertising.* In 1957, a researcher announced that he had flashed the phrases "Eat popcorn" and "Drink Coca-Cola" on a screen in a New Jersey movie theater every five seconds for 1/300th of a second. He reported that although viewers did not consciously recognize these messages, they absorbed them subconsciously and bought 58 percent more popcorn and 18 percent more Coke. Suddenly advertisers and consumer-protection groups became intensely interested in subliminal perception. People voiced fears of being brainwashed, and California and Canada declared the practice illegal. Although the researcher later admitted to making up the data, the issue has not died. Some consumers still fear that they are being manipulated by subliminal messages.

Numerous studies by psychologists and consumer researchers have found no link between subliminal messages and consumer behavior. It appears that subliminal advertising simply doesn't have the power attributed to it by its critics. Most advertisers scoff at the notion of an industry conspiracy to manipulate consumers through "invisible" messages.

real marketing 6.2

"Touchy-Feely" Research: Psyching Out Consumers

Consumers often don't know or can't describe just why they act as they do. Thus, motivation researchers use a variety of probing techniques to uncover underlying emotions and attitudes toward brands and buying situations. These sometimes bizarre

they were your *friends*. Imagine you could talk to your TV dinner. What would he say? And what would you say to him? . . . Now, think of your shampoo as an animal. Go on, don't be shy. Would it be a panda or a lion? A snake

attempt to uncover the real reasons behind a decade-long sales slump:

The manager of corporate advertising for Shell Oil, Sixtus Oeschle, was at his wits' end. For months, he and his team of researchers had pumped the consumer psyche. For months, they'd come up empty. "We tried psychographic memory triggers," he recalls. "We tried dream therapy." All to no avail. At one point, respondents were even given mounds of wet clay and urged to mold figures that expressed their inner feelings about Shell.

It was time, Oeschle decided, to try something radical. To craft a more potent appeal for its brand of gasoline, Shell would have to go deeper—much deeper. Oeschle called in a consumer researcher who specializes in focus groups conducted under hypnosis. The results, Oeschle says, wowed even the skeptics. "I've got to tell you, it was fascinating, fascinating stuff," he says. After dimming the lights, the researcher took respondents back, back—back all the way to their infancy. "He just kept taking them back and back," Oeschle says, "until . . . he's saying, 'Tell me about your first experience in a gas station.' And people were actually having memory flashbacks. I mean, they were going there. They were saying, 'I was three and a half years old. I was in the back of my dad's brand new Chevy.' It was like it was yesterday to them. I was stunned."

The PT Cruiser: The phenomenally successful retro style car that's "part 1920s gangster car, part 1950s hot rod, and part London taxicab"—an actual chrome-and-sheet-metal incarnation of the popular will.

techniques range from free association and inkblot interpretation tests to having consumers form daydreams and fantasies about brands or buying situations. One writer offers the following tongue-in-cheek summary of a motivation research session:

Good morning, ladies and gentlemen. We've called you here today for a little consumer research. Now, lie down on the couch, toss your inhibitions out the window, and let's try a little free association. First, think about brands as if

or a wooly worm? For our final exercise, let's all sit up and pull out our magic markers. Draw a picture of a typical cake-mix user. Would she wear an apron or a negligee? A business suit or a can-can dress?

Such projective techniques seem pretty goofy. But more and more, marketers are using such touchy-feely approaches to dig deeply into consumer psyches and develop better marketing strategies. For example, Shell Oil used motivation research in an

The real breakthrough, however, came after the respondents awoke out of their trance. "When he brought them all back out, he asked them who'd they prefer as a gasoline purveyor," Oeschle says. "What staggered me was that, to a person, it was always linked to that experience in their youth." One woman volunteered that she always made a point of filling up at Texaco. "We asked her why," Oeschle recalls. "And she said, 'I don't know, I guess I just feel good about Texaco.' Well, this was the little three-and-a-half-year-old in the back of her daddy's car speaking."

Shell is now designing new marketing approaches based on the insights gleaned from the groups of mesmerized motorists. Where Shell had gone wrong, it seems, was in reasoning that, since people don't start buying gas until at least age 16, there was no need to target the tiniest consumers. "They weren't even on Shell's radar," Oeschle laments. "It dawned on us . . . that we'd better figure out how to favorably impact people from an early age."

Similarly, DaimlerChrysler used a dose of deep motivation research to create a successful new concept car.

A few years back, DaimlerChrysler set out to find the next "wow car," the "segment buster" that would reach across age and income lines, into the subconscious. That meant doing more than the usual focus group research. So DaimlerChrysler hired psychologist Clothaire Rapaille to probe consumers' innermost feelings. The underlying premise: The products we buy mean something; they form part of a greater whole. "The more we learn about American culture, the more we see how our vehicles fit into our psyche—the more we see how it is that we fit into the overall scheme of living," says David Bostwick, director of market research at Daimler Chrysler.

Rather than convening traditional focus groups, Rapaille used a method known as "archetype research." He had participants lie on soft mats, listen to mood music, and free-associate in the dark.

According to Bostwick, this re-creates the same brain activity you have when you first wake up from a dream. "It's a very special brain activity," he says. "It allows us to actually access some of those unconscious thoughts."

When the lights came back up, Rapaille had learned that Americans are entrepreneurial, individualistic, freedom loving, and inventive—but also juvenile and self-indulgent. More important, he discovered that many suffered nostalgia pangs. In these complex and often unsettling times, car buyers yearned for the good old days—for a time when things seemed simpler and more secure, and when people felt good about themselves. "What that said to us is that people are looking for something that offers protection on the outside, and comfort on the inside," says Bostwick. "We communicated that to our design team."

The result: the PT Cruiser, Daimler Chrysler's phenomenally successful retro-style car. Described by the *Wall Street Journal* as "part 1920s gangster car, part 1950s hot rod, and part London taxicab," the PT Cruiser is what one analyst calls "a focus group on wheels—an actual chrome-and-sheet-metal incarnation of the popular will." Its nostalgic look and protective exterior, combined with a well-appointed and highly functional interior, inspires an emotional reaction from almost everyone. In just two years following its introduction, U.S. consumers snapped up more than 225,000 PT Cruisers. "We didn't set out to create a market," Bostwick says earnestly. "We just tapped into what people had in their heads in the first place. . . . The vehicle takes you back, but not to a particular time in the century. It just takes you back to a time you felt cool."

Some marketers dismiss such motivation research as mumbo jumbo. However, like Shell and DaimlerChrysler, many companies are now delving into the murky depths of the consumer unconscious. "Such tactics have been worshipfully embraced by even the no-nonsense, jut-jawed captains of industry," claims an analyst. "At companies like Kraft, Coca-Cola, Proctor & Gamble, and DaimlerChrysler, the most sought-after consultants hail not from [traditional consulting firms like McKinsey. They come] from brand consultancies with names like Archetype Discoveries, PsychoLogics and Semiotic Solutions."

Sources: Examples adapted from Ruth Shalit, "The Return of the Hidden Persuaders," *Salon Media,* September 27, 1999, accessed online at www.salon.com. Also see Annetta Miller and Dody Tsiantar, "Psyching Out Consumers," *Newsweek,* February 27, 1989, pp. 46–47; Gerry Khermouch, "Consumers in the Mist," *Business Week,* February 26, 2001, pp. 92–94; Alison Stein Wellner, "Research on a Shoestring," *American Demographics,* April 2001, pp. 38–39; Phil Patton, "Car Shrinks," *Fortune,* March 18, 2002, pp. 187–190; and "PT Cruiser," *Journal of Business and Design,* accessed online at the Corporate Design Foundation Web site, www.cdf.org, June 2002.

Learning

Learning

Changes in an individual's behavior arising from experience.

When people act, they learn. **Learning** describes changes in an individual's behavior arising from experience. Learning theorists say that most human behavior is learned. Learning occurs through the interplay of *drives, stimuli, cues, responses,* and *reinforcement.*

We saw that Anna Flores has a drive for self-actualization. A *drive* is a strong internal stimulus that calls for action. Her drive becomes a motive when it is directed toward a particular *stimulus object,* in this case a camera. Anna's response to the idea of buying a camera is conditioned by the surrounding cues. *Cues* are minor stimuli that determine when, where, and how the person responds. Seeing cameras in a shop window, hearing of a special sale price, and receiving her husband's support are all cues that can influence Anna's *response* to her interest in buying a camera.

Suppose Anna buys the Nikon. If the experience is rewarding, she will probably use the camera more and more. Her response to cameras will be *reinforced.* Then the next time she shops for a camera, binoculars, or some similar product, the probability is greater that she will buy a Nikon product. The practical significance of learning theory for marketers is that they can build up demand for a product by associating it with strong drives, using motivating cues, and providing positive reinforcement.

Beliefs and Attitudes

Through doing and learning, people acquire beliefs and attitudes. These, in turn, influence their buying behavior. A **belief** is a descriptive thought that a person has about something. Anna Flores may believe that a Nikon camera takes great pictures, stands up well under hard use, and costs $350. These beliefs may be based on real knowledge, opinion, or faith, and may or may not carry an emotional charge. For example, Anna Flores's belief that a Nikon camera is heavy may or may not matter to her decision.

Marketers are interested in the beliefs that people formulate about specific products and services, because these beliefs make up product and brand images that affect buying behavior. If some of the beliefs are wrong and prevent purchase, the marketer will want to launch a campaign to correct them.

People have attitudes regarding religion, politics, clothes, music, food, and almost everything else. **Attitude** describes a person's relatively consistent evaluations, feelings, and tendencies toward an object or idea. Attitudes put people into a frame of mind of liking or disliking things, of moving toward or away from them. Thus, Anna Flores may hold attitudes such as "Buy the best," "The Japanese make the best products in the world," and "Creativity and self-expression are among the most important things in life." If so, the Nikon camera would fit well into Anna's existing attitudes.

Attitudes are difficult to change. A person's attitudes fit into a pattern, and to change one attitude may require difficult adjustments in many others. Thus, a company should usually try to fit its products into existing attitudes rather than attempt to change attitudes. Of course, there are exceptions in which the great cost of trying to change attitudes may pay off handsomely:

> By 1994, milk consumption had been in decline for 20 years. The general perception was that milk was unhealthy, outdated, just for kids, or good only with cookies and cake. To counter these notions, the National Fluid Milk Processors Education Program (MilkPEP) began an ad campaign featuring milk be-mustached celebrities like Cindy Crawford, Danny DeVito, Patrick Ewing, and Ivana Trump with the tag line "Milk: Where's your mustache?" The campaign has not only been wildly popular, it has been successful as well—not only did it stop the decline, milk consumption actually increased. The campaign is still running. Although

Belief

A descriptive thought that a person holds about something.

Attitude

A person's consistently favorable or unfavorable evaluations, feelings, and tendencies toward an object or idea.

Attitudes are difficult to change, but the National Fluid Milk Processor's wildly popular milk moustache campaign succeeded in changing attitudes toward milk.

Milk isn't just for tadpoles.

Did you know 3 out of 4 adults don't get enough calcium? It takes at least 3 glasses of milk a day. I always keep some at my pad.

got milk?

initially the target market was women in their twenties, the campaign has been expanded to other target markets and has gained cult status with teens, much to their parents' delight. Teens collect the print ads featuring celebrities ranging from music stars Hanson and LeAnn Rimes, supermodel Tyra Banks, Kemit the Frog, and Garfield to sports idols such as Mark McGwire, Jeff Gordon, Pete Sampras, Mia Hamm, and Venus and Serena Williams. Building on this popularity with teens, the industry also promotes milk to them through grass-roots marketing efforts. It recently sponsored a traveling promotion event featuring a 28-foot truck that turns into a backdrop that looks like Manhattan's Times Square. Once recruited, teens can listen to music and do a 15-second "audition" on an artificial set of MTV's "Total Request Live." They can also enter a contest to make an appearance in *Rolling Stone* magazine with a milk mustache of their own. While there, teens are encouraged to drink milk rather than soda. Each is invited to sign a pledge to reduce the national "calcium debt."[26]

We can now appreciate the many forces acting on consumer behavior. The consumer's choice results from the complex interplay of cultural, social, personal, and psychological factors.

Types of Buying-Decision Behavior

Buying behavior differs greatly for a tube of toothpaste, a tennis racket, a digital camera, and a new car. More complex decisions usually involve more buying participants and more buyer deliberation. Figure 6.5 shows types of consumer buying behavior based on the degree of buyer involvement and the degree of differences among brands.[27]

Complex Buying Behavior

Complex buying behavior
Consumer buying behavior in situations characterized by high consumer involvement in a purchase and significant perceived differences among brands.

Consumers undertake **complex buying behavior** when they are highly involved in a purchase and perceive significant differences among brands. Consumers may be highly involved when the product is expensive, risky, purchased infrequently, and highly self-expressive. Typically, the consumer has much to learn about the product category. For example, a personal computer buyer may not know what attributes to consider. Many product features carry no real meaning: a "Pentium chip," "super VGA resolution," or "megs of RAM."

This buyer will pass through a learning process, first developing beliefs about the product, then attitudes, and then making a thoughtful purchase choice. Marketers of high-involvement products must understand the information-gathering and evaluation behavior of high-involvement consumers. They need to help buyers learn about product-class attributes and their relative importance. They need to differentiate their brand's features, perhaps by describing the brand's benefits using print media with long copy. They must motivate store salespeople and the buyer's acquaintances to influence the final brand choice.

Dissonance-reducing buying behavior
Consumer buying behavior in situations characterized by high involvement but few perceived differences among brands.

Dissonance-Reducing Buying Behavior

Dissonance-reducing buying behavior occurs when consumers are highly involved with an expensive, infrequent, or risky purchase, but see little difference among brands. For example, consumers buying carpeting may face a high-involvement decision because carpeting is expen-

FIGURE 6.5
Four types of buying behavior

Source: Adapted from Henry Assael, *Consumer Behavior and Marketing Action* (Boston: Kent Publishing Company, 1987), p. 87. Copyright © 1987 by Wadsworth, Inc. Printed by permission of Kent Publishing Company, a division of Wadsworth, Inc.

sive and self-expressive. Yet buyers may consider most carpet brands in a given price range to be the same. In this case, because perceived brand differences are not large, buyers may shop around to learn what is available, but buy relatively quickly. They may respond primarily to a good price or to purchase convenience.

After the purchase, consumers might experience *postpurchase dissonance* (after-sale discomfort) when they notice certain disadvantages of the purchased carpet brand or hear favorable things about brands not purchased. To counter such dissonance, the marketer's after-sale communications should provide evidence and support to help consumers feel good about their brand choices.

Habitual Buying Behavior

Habitual buying behavior
Consumer buying behavior in situations characterized by low consumer involvement and few significant perceived brand differences.

Habitual buying behavior occurs under conditions of low consumer involvement and little significant brand difference. For example, take salt. Consumers have little involvement in this product category—they simply go to the store and reach for a brand. If they keep reaching for the same brand, it is out of habit rather than strong brand loyalty. Consumers appear to have low involvement with most low-cost, frequently purchased products.

In such cases, consumer behavior does not pass through the usual belief-attitude-behavior sequence. Consumers do not search extensively for information about the brands, evaluate brand characteristics, and make weighty decisions about which brands to buy. Instead, they passively receive information as they watch television or read magazines. Ad repetition creates *brand familiarity* rather than *brand conviction*. Consumers do not form strong attitudes toward a brand; they select the brand because it is familiar. Because they are not highly involved with the product, consumers may not evaluate the choice even after purchase. Thus, the buying process involves brand beliefs formed by passive learning, followed by purchase behavior, which may or may not be followed by evaluation.

Because buyers are not highly committed to any brands, marketers of low-involvement products with few brand differences often use price and sales promotions to stimulate product trial. In advertising for a low-involvement product, ad copy should stress only a few key points. Visual symbols and imagery are important because they can be remembered easily and associated with the brand. Ad campaigns should include high repetition of short-duration messages. Television is usually more effective than print media because it is a low-involvement medium suitable for passive learning. Advertising planning should be based on classical conditioning theory, in which buyers learn to identify a certain product by a symbol repeatedly attached to it.

Variety-Seeking Buying Behavior

Variety-seeking buying behavior
Consumer buying behavior in situations characterized by low consumer involvement but significant perceived brand differences.

Consumers undertake **variety-seeking buying behavior** in situations characterized by low consumer involvement but significant perceived brand differences. In such cases, consumers often do a lot of brand switching. For example, when buying cookies, a consumer may hold some beliefs, choose a cookie brand without much evaluation, then evaluate that brand during consumption. But the next time, the consumer might pick another brand out of boredom or simply to try something different. Brand switching occurs for the sake of variety rather than because of dissatisfaction.

In such product categories, the marketing strategy may differ for the market leader and minor brands. The market leader will try to encourage habitual buying behavior by dominating shelf space, keeping shelves fully stocked, and running frequent reminder advertising. Challenger firms will encourage variety seeking by offering lower prices, special deals, coupons, free samples, and advertising that presents reasons for trying something new.

The Buyer Decision Process

Now that we have looked at the influences that affect buyers, we are ready to look at how consumers make buying decisions. Figure 6.6 shows that the buyer decision process consists of five stages: *need recognition, information search, evaluation of alternatives, purchase decision,* and

FIGURE 6.6
Buyer decision process

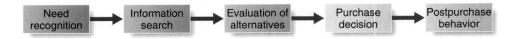

postpurchase behavior. Clearly, the buying process starts long before actual purchase and continues long after. Marketers need to focus on the entire buying process rather than on just the purchase decision.

The figure implies that consumers pass through all five stages with every purchase. But in more routine purchases, consumers often skip or reverse some of these stages. A woman buying her regular brand of toothpaste would recognize the need and go right to the purchase decision, skipping information search and evaluation. However, we use the model in Figure 6.6 because it shows all the considerations that arise when a consumer faces a new and complex purchase situation.

Need Recognition

Need recognition
The first stage of the buyer decision process, in which the consumer recognizes a problem or need.

The buying process starts with **need recognition**—the buyer recognizes a problem or need. The need can be triggered by *internal stimuli* when one of the person's normal needs—hunger, thirst, sex—rises to a level high enough to become a drive. A need can also be triggered by *external stimuli*. Anna Flores might have felt the need for a new hobby when her busy season at work slowed down, and she thought of cameras after talking to a friend about photography or seeing a camera ad. At this stage, the marketer should research consumers to find out what kinds of needs or problems arise, what brought them about, and how they led the consumer to this particular product.

Information Search

Information search
The stage of the buyer decision process in which the consumer is aroused to search for more information; the consumer may simply have heightened attention or may go into active information search.

An interested consumer may or may not search for more information. If the consumer's drive is strong and a satisfying product is near at hand, the consumer is likely to buy it then. If not, the consumer may store the need in memory or undertake an **information search** related to the need. At the least, Anna Flores will probably pay more attention to camera ads, cameras used by friends, and camera conversations. Or Anna may actively look for reading material, phone friends, and gather information in other ways. The amount of searching she does will depend on the strength of her drive, the amount of information she starts with, the ease of obtaining more information, the value she places on additional information, and the satisfaction she gets from searching.

The consumer can obtain information from any of several sources. These include *personal sources* (family, friends, neighbors, acquaintances), *commercial sources* (advertising, salespeople, dealers, packaging, displays), *public sources* (mass media, consumer-rating organizations), and *experiential sources* (handling, examining, using the product). The relative influence of these information sources varies with the product and the buyer. Generally, the consumer receives the most information about a product from commercial sources—those

Need recognition can be triggered by advertising. This ad asks an arresting question that alerts parents to the need for a high-quality bike helmet.

controlled by the marketer. The most effective sources, however, tend to be personal. Commercial sources normally *inform* the buyer, but personal sources *legitimize* or *evaluate* products for the buyer.

People often ask others—friends, relatives, acquaintances, professionals—for recommendations concerning a product or service. Thus, companies have a strong interest in building such *word-of-mouth sources*. These sources have two chief advantages. First, they are convincing: Word of mouth is the only promotion method that is *of* consumers, *by* consumers, and *for* consumers. Having loyal, satisfied customers that brag about doing business with you is the dream of every business owner. Not only are satisfied customers repeat buyers, but they are also walking, talking billboards for your business. Second, the costs are low. Keeping in touch with satisfied customers and turning them into word-of-mouth advocates costs the business relatively little.[28]

As more information is obtained, the consumer's awareness and knowledge of the available brands and features increases. In her information search, Anna Flores learned about the many camera brands available. The information also helped her drop certain brands from consideration. A company must design its marketing mix to make prospects aware of and knowledgeable about its brand. It should carefully identify consumers' sources of information and the importance of each source.

Evaluation of Alternatives

Alternative evaluation
The stage of the buyer decision process in which the consumer uses information to evaluate alternative brands in the choice set.

We have seen how the consumer uses information to arrive at a set of final brand choices. How does the consumer choose among the alternative brands? The marketer needs to know about **alternative evaluation**—that is, how the consumer processes information to arrive at brand choices. Unfortunately, consumers do not use a simple and single evaluation process in all buying situations. Instead, several evaluation processes are at work.

The consumer arrives at attitudes toward different brands through some evaluation procedure. How consumers go about evaluating purchase alternatives depends on the individual consumer and the specific buying situation. In some cases, consumers use careful calculations and logical thinking. At other times, the same consumers do little or no evaluating; instead they buy on impulse and rely on intuition. Sometimes consumers make buying decisions on their own; sometimes they turn to friends, consumer guides, or salespeople for buying advice.

Suppose Anna Flores has narrowed her choices to four cameras. And suppose that she is primarily interested in four attributes—picture quality, ease of use, camera size, and price. Anna has formed beliefs about how each brand rates on each attribute. Clearly, if one camera rated best on all the attributes, we could predict that Anna would choose it. However, the brands vary in appeal. Anna might base her buying decision on only one attribute, and her choice would be easy to predict. If she wants picture quality above everything, she will buy the camera that she thinks has the best picture quality. But most buyers consider several attributes, each with different importance. If we knew the importance weights that Anna assigns to each of the four attributes, we could predict her camera choice more reliably.

Marketers should study buyers to find out how they actually evaluate brand alternatives. If they know what evaluative processes go on, marketers can take steps to influence the buyer's decision.

Purchase Decision

Purchase decision
The buyer's decision about which brand to purchase.

In the evaluation stage, the consumer ranks brands and forms purchase intentions. Generally, the consumer's **purchase decision** will be to buy the most preferred brand, but two factors can come between the purchase *intention* and the purchase *decision*. The first factor is the *attitudes of others*. If Anna Flores's husband feels strongly that Anna should buy the lowest-priced camera, then the chances of Anna's buying a more expensive camera will be reduced.

The second factor is *unexpected situational factors*. The consumer may form a purchase intention based on factors such as expected income, expected price, and expected product benefits. However, unexpected events may change the purchase intention. Anna Flores may lose her job, some other purchase may become more urgent, or a friend may report being disappointed in her preferred camera. Or a close competitor may drop its price. Thus, preferences and even purchase intentions do not always result in actual purchase choice.

Postpurchase Behavior

Postpurchase behavior

The stage of the buyer decision process in which consumers take further action after purchase, based on their satisfaction or dissatisfaction.

The marketer's job does not end when the product is bought. After purchasing the product, the consumer will be satisfied or dissatisfied and will engage in **postpurchase behavior** of interest to the marketer. What determines whether the buyer is satisfied or dissatisfied with a purchase? The answer lies in the relationship between the *consumer's expectations* and the product's *perceived performance*. If the product falls short of expectations, the consumer is disappointed; if it meets expectations, the consumer is satisfied; if it exceeds expectations, the consumer is delighted.

The larger the gap between expectations and performance, the greater the consumer's dissatisfaction. This suggests that sellers should make product claims that faithfully represent the product's performance so that buyers are satisfied. Some sellers might even understate performance levels to boost consumer satisfaction with the product. For example, Boeing's salespeople tend to be conservative when they estimate the potential benefits of their aircraft. They almost always underestimate fuel efficiency—they promise a 5 percent savings that turns out to be 8 percent. Customers are delighted with better-than-expected performance; they buy again and tell other potential customers that Boeing lives up to its promises.

Cognitive dissonance

Buyer discomfort caused by postpurchase conflict.

Almost all major purchases result in **cognitive dissonance,** or discomfort caused by postpurchase conflict. After the purchase, consumers are satisfied with the benefits of the chosen brand and are glad to avoid the drawbacks of the brands not bought. However, every purchase involves compromise. Consumers feel uneasy about acquiring the drawbacks of the chosen brand and about losing the benefits of the brands not purchased. Thus, consumers feel at least some postpurchase dissonance for every purchase.[29]

Why is it so important to satisfy the customer? Such satisfaction is important because a company's sales come from two basic groups—*new customers* and *retained customers.* It usually costs more to attract new customers than to retain current ones. And the best way to retain current customers is to keep them satisfied. Customer satisfaction is a key to building lasting relationships with consumers—to keeping and growing consumers and reaping their customer lifetime value. Satisfied customers buy a product again, talk favorably to others about the product, pay less attention to competing brands and advertising, and buy other products from the company. Many marketers go beyond merely *meeting* the expectations of customers—they aim to *delight* the customer.

A dissatisfied consumer responds differently. Whereas, on average, a satisfied customer tells 3 people about a good product experience, a dissatisfied customer gripes to 11 people. In fact, one study showed that 13 percent of the people who had a problem with an organization complained about the company to more than 20 people.[30] Clearly, bad word of mouth travels farther and faster than good word of mouth and can quickly damage consumer attitudes about a company and its products.

Therefore, a company would be wise to measure customer satisfaction regularly. It cannot simply rely on dissatisfied customers to volunteer their complaints when they are dissatisfied. Some 96 percent of unhappy customers never tell the company about their problem. Companies should set up systems that *encourage* customers to complain (see Real Marketing 6.3). In this way, the company can learn how well it is doing and how it can improve. The 3M Company claims that over two-thirds of its new-product ideas come from listening to customer complaints. But listening is not enough—the company also must respond constructively to the complaints it receives.

By studying the overall buyer decision, marketers may be able to find ways to help consumers move through it. For example, if consumers are not buying a new product because they do not perceive a need for it, marketing might launch advertising messages that trigger the need and show how the product solves customers' problems. If customers know about the product but are not buying because they hold unfavorable attitudes toward it, the marketer must find ways to either change the product or change consumer perceptions.

The Buyer Decision Process for New Products

New product

A good, service, or idea that is perceived by some potential customers as new.

We have looked at the stages buyers go through in trying to satisfy a need. Buyers may pass quickly or slowly through these stages, and some of the stages may even be reversed. Much depends on the nature of the buyer, the product, and the buying situation.

We now look at how buyers approach the purchase of new products. A **new product** is a good, service, or idea that is perceived by some potential customers as new. It may have been around for a while, but our interest is in how consumers learn about products for the first time

real marketing 6.3

Got a Problem? Just Phone, Fax, E-Mail, or Web-Chat with Us!

What should companies do about dissatisfied customers? Everything they can! Unhappy customers not only stop buying but also can quickly damage the company's image by spreading bad word of mouth. Some 68 percent of consumers who defect do so because of bad service. Enlightened companies don't try to hide from dissatisfied customers. They go out of their way to *encourage* customers to complain, then bend over backward to make disgruntled buyers happy again.

At a minimum, most companies offer toll-free numbers to handle complaints, inquiries,

2,400 callers a day. The help line is staffed by English-, French-, and Spanish-speaking operators, and interpreters are available for most other languages. Callers include new parents, day care providers, and even health professionals. They ask a wide variety of questions, from when to feed a baby specific foods to how to babyproof a home. One in five calls to the help line comes from men.

General Electric's Answer Center may be the most extensive 800-number system in the nation. It handles more than 3 million calls a year, only 5 percent of them complaints. At the

people resolve 90 percent of complaints or inquiries on the first call, and complainers often become even more loyal customers. GE has now set up two answer centers online (www.ge.oac and www.geappliances.com/geac/) that help customers obtain product and service information, troubleshoot product problems, locate dealers, and even schedule service appointments.

Companies such as Famous Smoke Shop view their call centers as a tool not just for handling complaints but also for making the most out of each and every customer interaction. For example, whenever cigar enthusiast Cara Biden has called Famous Smoke Shops in search of highly coveted Short Stories cigars, they've been out of stock. Yet, this hasn't stopped Biden from staying loyal. Every time Biden phones Famous, a system known as an ACD (automatic call distributor) immediately kicks in to answer the call and route it to the appropriate contact person. Biden has been impressed with how fast the ACD funnels her to a customer service representative. She also enjoys chatting with the highly knowledgeable rep about alternatives to the tough-to-find cigars. The rep is knowledgeable not only about cigars but also about Biden—whenever she calls, her sales history and previous queries pop up on his computer screen.

Most call centers today are much more than just a bank of phones that receives complaints. They are high-tech, Web-enabled *contact* centers that employ a sophisticated mix of phone, e-mail, fax, and interactive voice and data technologies. Consider the following examples:

It's February 14, and you've just remembered that it's Valentine's Day. There's no time for florist shops, so you jump online to www.1800FLOWERS.com. Then you pause. Red roses? Boxed or in a vase? One dozen or two? Just as your head starts to pound, you notice a button on the Web site. Click on it, and you're connected to a customer service rep at the call center who can help sniff out

Web-enabled customer contact centers: Customers can initiate a chat session with a 1-800-Flowers service representative who answers questions and "pushes" pages to their browsers. In the future, interactive voice and image technology will even let customers see and talk with reps on their computer screens.

and orders. For example, over the past two decades, the Gerber help line (1-800-4-GERBER) has received more than 5 million calls. Help line staffers, most of them mothers or grandmothers themselves, handle customer concerns and provide baby care advice 24 hours a day, 365 days a year to more than

heart of the system is a giant database that provides the center's service reps with instant access to more than 1 million answers concerning 8,500 models in 120 product lines. The center receives some unusual calls, as when a submarine off the Connecticut coast requested help fixing a motor. Still, according to GE, its your options. A chat page opens on your screen, allowing a real-time dialog with the agent. The service rep even "pushes" pages to your browser so you can see different floral arrangements and how much they cost. In minutes, you have placed your order online, with a little hand-holding. Fiction? Not really. Several e-marketers, including 1-800-Flowers, are testing or already offer live interaction with service reps. Some feature real-time chat sessions, others voice-over-Web capabilities. In the future, a "call cam" may even let consumers see an agent on their computer screen.

The idea is to make customers' interactions with companies seamless and uniform, no matter which form of communication they choose. Integrate the telephone with Web technology and you have an extremely powerful means of handling customer questions and concerns. This technology lets a customer browse a Web site on a PC at the same time that a customer service agent browses the site. The two can talk over a separate telephone line or an Internet connection to discuss problems or compare products.

Logistix, a California technology company, uses technology that allows it to synchronize Web screens viewed by the company's agents and customers as they talk. The technology even lets either party draw circles around words or pictures for both to see. This may not seem like a big deal, but when discussing a complex technological device, it really helps if customer and agent are viewing a common diagram. Using the technology, Logistix has turned its call center into a central point of customer contact.

Of course, the best way to keep customers happy is to provide good products and services in the first place. Short of that, however, a company must develop a good system for ferreting out problems and connecting with customers. Such a system is much more than just a necessary evil—customer happiness usually shows up on the company's bottom line. One recent study found that dollars invested in complaint-handling and customer contact systems yield an average return of between 100 percent and 200 percent. Maryanne Rasmussen, vice president of worldwide quality at American Express, offers this formula: "Better complaint handling equals higher customer satisfaction equals higher brand loyalty equals higher performance."

Sources: See "On Mother's Day, Advice Goes a Long Way," *PR Newswire,* Ziff Communications, May 2, 1995; Alessandra Bianchi, "Lines of Fire," *Inc. Technology,* 1998, pp. 36–48; Matt Hamblen, "Call Centers and Web Sites Cozy Up," *Computerworld,* March 2, 1998, p. 1; Ellen Jovin and Jennifer Lach, "Online with the Operator," *American Demographics,* February 1999, pp. 36–39; Bob Wallace and George V. Hulme, "The Modern Call Center," *Informationweek,* April 9, 2001, pp. 38–46; Alice Dragoon, "Put Your Money Where Your Mouthpiece Is," *Darwin,* February 2002, pp. 60–65; and David L. Margulius, "Smarter Call Centers: At Your Service?" *New York Times,* March 14, 2002, p. G1.

Adoption process

The mental process through which an individual passes from first hearing about an innovation to final adoption.

and make decisions on whether to adopt them. We define the **adoption process** as "the mental process through which an individual passes from first learning about an innovation to final adoption," and *adoption* as the decision by an individual to become a regular user of the product.[31]

Stages in the Adoption Process

Consumers go through five stages in the process of adopting a new product:

- *Awareness:* The consumer becomes aware of the new product, but lacks information about it.
- *Interest:* The consumer seeks information about the new product.
- *Evaluation:* The consumer considers whether trying the new product makes sense.
- *Trial:* The consumer tries the new product on a small scale to improve his or her estimate of its value.
- *Adoption:* The consumer decides to make full and regular use of the new product.

This model suggests that the new-product marketer should think about how to help consumers move through these stages. A manufacturer of large-screen televisions may discover that many consumers in the interest stage do not move to the trial stage, because of uncertainty and the large investment. If these same consumers were willing to use a large-screen television on a trial basis for a small fee, the manufacturer should consider offering a trial-use plan with an option to buy.

Individual Differences in Innovativeness

People differ greatly in their readiness to try new products. In each product area, there are "consumption pioneers" and early adopters. Other individuals adopt new products much later. People can be classified into the adopter categories shown in Figure 6.7. After a slow start, an increasing number of people adopt the new product. The number of adopters reaches a peak and

FIGURE 6.7

Adopter categories based on relative time of adoption

Source: Everett M. Rogers, *Diffusion of Innovations,* 4th ed. (New York: Free Press, 1995). Copyright © 1995 by Everett M. Rogers. Copyright © 1962, 1971, 1983 by The Free Press. Reprinted with the permission of The Free Press, a Division of Simon & Schuster.

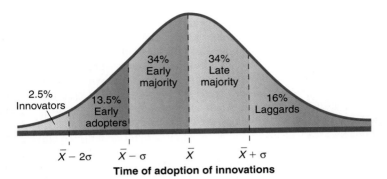

then drops off as fewer nonadopters remain. Innovators are defined as the first 2.5 percent of the buyers to adopt a new idea (those beyond two standard deviations from mean adoption time); the early adopters are the next 13.5 percent (between one and two standard deviations); and so forth.

The five adopter groups have differing values. *Innovators* are venturesome—they try new ideas at some risk. *Early adopters* are guided by respect—they are opinion leaders in their communities and adopt new ideas early but carefully. The *early majority* are deliberate—although they rarely are leaders, they adopt new ideas before the average person. The *late majority* are skeptical—they adopt an innovation only after a majority of people have tried it. Finally, *laggards* are tradition bound—they are suspicious of changes and adopt the innovation only when it has become something of a tradition itself.

This adopter classification suggests that an innovating firm should research the characteristics of innovators and early adopters and should direct marketing efforts toward them. In general, innovators tend to be relatively younger, better educated, and higher in income than later adopters and nonadopters. They are more receptive to unfamiliar things, rely more on their own values and judgment, and are more willing to take risks. They are less brand loyal and more likely to take advantage of special promotions such as discounts, coupons, and samples.

Influence of Product Characteristics on Rate of Adoption

The characteristics of the new product affect its rate of adoption. Some products catch on almost overnight (Beanie Babies), whereas others take a long time to gain acceptance (high-density television, or HDTV). Five characteristics are especially important in influencing an innovation's rate of adoption. For example, consider the characteristics of HDTV in relation to the rate of adoption:

- *Relative advantage:* the degree to which the innovation appears superior to existing products. The greater the perceived relative advantage of using HDTV—say, in picture quality and ease of viewing—the sooner HDTVs will be adopted.
- *Compatibility:* the degree to which the innovation fits the values and experiences of potential consumers. HDTV, for example, is highly compatible with the lifestyles found in upper-middle-class homes. However, it is not very compatible with the programming and broadcasting systems currently available to consumers.
- *Complexity:* the degree to which the innovation is difficult to understand or use. HDTVs are not very complex and, therefore, once programming is available and prices come down, will take less time to penetrate U.S. homes than more complex innovations.
- *Divisibility:* the degree to which the innovation may be tried on a limited basis. HDTVs are still very expensive. To the extent that people can lease them with an option to buy, their rate of adoption will increase.
- *Communicability:* the degree to which the results of using the innovation can be observed or described to others. Because HDTV lends itself to demonstration and description, its use will spread faster among consumers.

Other characteristics influence the rate of adoption, such as initial and ongoing costs, risk and uncertainty, and social approval. The new-product marketer has to research all these factors when developing the new product and its marketing program.

Consumer Behavior Across International Borders

Understanding consumer behavior is difficult enough for companies marketing within the borders of a single country. For companies operating in many countries, however, understanding and serving the needs of consumers can be daunting. Although consumers in different countries may have some things in common, their values, attitudes, and behaviors often vary greatly. International marketers must understand such differences and adjust their products and marketing programs accordingly.

Sometimes the differences are obvious. For example, in the United States, where most people eat cereal regularly for breakfast, Kellogg focuses its marketing on persuading consumers to select a Kellogg brand rather than a competitor's brand. In France, however, where most people prefer croissants and coffee or no breakfast at all, Kellogg advertising simply attempts to convince people that they should eat cereal for breakfast. Its packaging includes step-by-step instructions on how to prepare cereal. In India, where many consumers eat heavy, fried breakfasts and many consumers skip the meal altogether, Kellogg's advertising attempts to convince buyers to switch to a lighter, more nutritious breakfast diet.

Often, differences across international markets are more subtle. They may result from physical differences in consumers and their environments. For example, Remington makes smaller electric shavers to fit the smaller hands of Japanese consumers and battery-powered shavers for the British market, where few bathrooms have electrical outlets. Other differences result from varying customs. In Japan, for example, where humility and deference are considered great virtues, pushy, hard-hitting sales approaches are considered offensive. Failing to understand such differences in customs and behaviors from one country to another can spell disaster for a marketer's international products and programs.

Marketers must decide on the degree to which they will adapt their products and marketing programs to meet the unique cultures and needs of consumers in various markets. On the one hand, they want to standardize their offerings in order to simplify operations and take advantage of cost economies. On the other hand, adapting marketing efforts within each country results in products and programs that better satisfy the needs of local consumers. The question of whether to adapt or standardize the marketing mix across international markets has created a lively debate in recent years.

LOOKING BACK: REVIEWING THE CONCEPTS

The American consumer market consists of more than 287 million people who consume many trillions of dollars worth of goods and services each year, making it one of the most attractive consumer markets in the world. The world consumer market consists of more than 6.2 *billion* people. Consumers around the world vary greatly in age, income, education level, and tastes. Understanding how these differences affect *consumer buying behavior* is one of the biggest challenges marketers face.

1. Define the consumer market and construct a simple model of consumer buyer behavior.

The *consumer market* consists of all the individuals and households who buy or acquire goods and services for personal consumption. The simplest model of consumer buyer behavior is the stimulus-response model. According to this model, marketing stimuli (the four *P*s) and other major forces (economic, technological, political, cultural) enter the consumer's "black box" and produce certain responses. Once in the black box, these inputs produce observable buyer responses, such as product choice, brand choice, purchase timing, and purchase amount.

2. Name the four major factors that influence consumer buyer behavior.

Consumer buyer behavior is influenced by four key sets of buyer characteristics: cultural, social, personal, and psychological. Although many of these factors cannot be influenced by the marketer, they can be useful in identifying interested buyers and in shaping products and appeals to serve consumer needs better. *Culture* is the most basic determinant of a person's wants and behavior. It includes the basic values, perceptions, preferences, and behaviors that a person learns from family and other important institutions. *Subcultures* are "cultures within cultures" that have distinct values and lifestyles and can be based on anything from age to ethnicity. People with different cultural and subcultural characteristics have different product and brand preferences. As a result, marketers may want to focus their marketing programs on the special needs of certain groups.

Social factors also influence a buyer's behavior. A person's *reference groups*—family, friends, social organizations, professional associations—strongly affect product and brand choices. The buyer's age, life-cycle stage, occupation, economic circumstances, lifestyle, personality, and other *personal characteristics* influence his or her buying decisions. Consumer *lifestyles*—the whole pattern of acting and interacting in the world—are also

an important influence on purchase decisions. Finally, consumer buying behavior is influenced by four major *psychological factors*—motivation, perception, learning, and beliefs and attitudes. Each of these factors provides a different perspective for understanding the workings of the buyer's black box.

3. List and understand the major types of buying-decision behavior and stages in the buyer decision process.

Buying behavior may vary greatly across different types of products and buying decisions. Consumers undertake *complex buying behavior* when they are highly involved in a purchase and perceive significant differences among brands. *Dissonance-reducing behavior* occurs when consumers are higher involved but see little difference among brands. *Habitual buying behavior* occurs under conditions of low involvement and little significant brand difference. In situations characterized by low involvement but significant perceived brand differences, consumers engage in *variety-seeking buying behavior*.

When making a purchase, the buyer goes through a decision process consisting of *need recognition, information search, evaluation of alternatives, purchase decision,* and *postpurchase behavior*. The marketer's job is to understand the buyer's behavior at each stage and the influences that are operating. During *need recognition*, the consumer recognizes a problem or need that could be satisfied by a product or service in the market. Once the need is recognized, the consumer is aroused to seek more information and moves into the *information search* stage. With information in hand, the consumer proceeds to *alternative evaluation*, during which the information is used to evaluate brands in the choice set. From there, the consumer makes a *purchase decision* and actually buys the product. In the final stage of the buyer decision process, *postpurchase behavior,* the consumer takes action based on satisfaction or dissatisfaction.

4. Describe the adoption and diffusion process for new products.

The product adoption process is comprised of five stages: awareness, interest, evaluation, trial, and adoption. Initially, the consumer must become aware of the new product. *Awareness* leads to *interest,* and the consumer seeks information about the new product. Once information has been gathered, the consumer enters the *evaluation* stage and considers buying the new product. Next, in the *trial* stage, the consumer tries the product on a small scale to improve his or her estimate of its value. If the consumer is satisfied with the product, he or she enters the *adoption* stage, deciding to use the new product fully and regularly.

With regard to diffusion of new products, consumers respond at different rates, depending on the consumer's characteristics and the product's characteristics. Consumers may be innovators, early adopters, early majority, late majority, or laggards. *Innovators* are willing to try risky new ideas; *early adopters*—often community opinion leaders—accept new ideas early but carefully; the *early majority*—rarely leaders—decide deliberately to try new ideas, doing so before the average person does; the *late majority* try an innovation only after a majority of people have adopted it; whereas *laggards* adopt an innovation only after it has become a tradition itself. Manufacturers try to bring their new products to the attention of potential early adopters, especially those who are opinion leaders.

REVIEWING THE KEY TERMS

Adoption process 203
Alternative evaluation 200
Attitude 196
Belief 196
Brand personality 190
Cognitive dissonance 201
Complex buying behavior 197
Consumer buyer behavior 178
Consumer market 178
Culture 180

Dissonance-reducing buying
　behavior 197
Groups 183
Habitual buying behavior 198
Information search 199
Learning 195
Lifestyle 188
Motive (or drive) 191
Need recognition 199
New product 201

Opinion leaders 184
Perception 193
Personality 190
Postpurchase behavior 201
Purchase decision 200
Social classes 183
Subculture 180
Variety-seeking buying behavior 198

DISCUSSING THE CONCEPTS

1. List several factors that you could add to the model shown in Figure 6.1 to make it a more complete description of consumer behavior. Explain your reasoning.
2. The United States is truly a melting pot of subcultures. Examine the four major subcultures identified in the chapter. Develop a profile of each that indicates the key characteristics that would be of most interest to marketers.
3. In designing the advertising for a bottled water product, which would you find more helpful: information about consumer demographics or consumer lifestyles? Give examples of how you would use each type of information.
4. Many marketers target opinion leaders with marketing messages. Why are opinion leaders important? How might opinion leaders influence buyer behavior? For which products do opinion leaders appear to be most influential? For which are they least influential?
5. Abraham Maslow sought to explain why people are driven by particular needs at particular times. Which of Maslow's needs applies to the following situations: (a) purchasing the newest, fastest personal computer; (b) purchasing food at lunchtime; (c) adjusting your clothing choices to reflect the latest trends; (d) raising funds for effort to save an endangered animal species; and, (e) purchasing a new, advanced form of water filter for your home. Explain the reasons for your choices.
6. Think about a very good or very bad experience you have had with a product. Discuss how the experience shaped your beliefs about the product, the purchasing process, or shopping in stores. How long do you think these beliefs will last? What could change these beliefs?
7. Using the information found in Figure 6.6, trace a recent purchase you have made. Be sure to examine each of the five stages of the buyer decision process, and detail your experiences in each stage. What could the seller have done to make your buying experience better? Did you experience any cognitive dissonance? Explain.
8. Five characteristics are especially important in influencing an innovation's rate of adoption. Indicate how each of these characteristics would affect your adoption of an electric car that travels up to 40 miles per hour, has a battery storage capacity of six hours, and is intended primarily for in-town driving.

APPLYING THE CONCEPTS

1. SRI Consulting has created consumer VALS segments, a typology designed to categorize consumers and their preferences. Companies that market on the Web or in retail stores can use this information to develop their appeals, strategies, and promotions. The concept is that consumer purchases are shaped by the interplay of their psychological, physical, demographic, and material resources. Visit SRI at www.sri-bi.com and follow the links to the VALS questionnaire. Complete the survey to determine your VALS type. Answer the following questions:
   a. What is your VALS type? Do you agree with the assessment? Why or why not?
   b. How can marketers use VALS information to serve consumers better?

c. Name five types of products or services for which VALS information would be particularly useful. Explain.

d. How could advertisers use VALS information to better communicate with consumers? Find three advertising examples from Web sites or current magazines that you believe were designed around VALS segments. Explain your reasoning.

2. When H. J. Heinz needed a boost for sagging ketchup sales, it turned to an old formula for an answer—matching consumer lifestyles with bold innovation. Heinz and competitors had for years incorrectly assumed that ketchup was for grown-ups. When the company realized that Ketchup is also for kids, Heinz discovered a substantial new avenue for growth. Heinz understood that today's kids were brought up on Nickelodeon's green slime, gummy worms, slime pops, and other gross-out products. How could Heinz tap into the market? With Blastin' Green ketchup! Although it tastes the same as traditional ketchup, in addition to the striking color, the new version is packaged in a contoured, kid-friendly bottle complete with a nozzle for writing and drawing with ketchup. As a result, kids are taking the ketchup out of the refrigerator more often and participating in the buying process as never before. The new green ketchup initially boosted Heinz's sales by 5 percent and added 4 points to its market share. The success of Blastin' Green allowed Heinz to roll out Funky Purple and a mystery bottle from which any one of three differently colored ketchups flows. The company is betting that when kids dress up their fries and burgers, they'll reach for red, green, or purple ketchup. Sound gross? That's just what this market segment ordered!

a. How has Heinz has adapted its new products to fit kids' lifestyles? In addition to the contoured bottle, how could Heinz use packaging to enhance the product's appeal to kids? To adults?

b. How can Heinz turn the short-term sales and market share gain into a long-term advantage? What does the company need to know about lifestyles to increase sales in the future?

c. Would you buy green or purple ketchup? Why or why not? If you answered "no," construct a strategy that might change your mind. Consider the sections in the text on attitudes and beliefs as you map out your strategy.

d. Assume that Heinz has hired you to recommend the next color for its line of ketchups. After visiting the EZ Squirt Web site at www.ezsquirt.com describe how you would determine the new color. Whom would you survey? What would you ask? How would you measure the impact of lifestyles and culture on color preferences?

 DIGITAL CONNECTIONS

CONNECTING CONSUMERS WITH WHAT THEY REALLY WANT—FREEDOM OF CHOICE

When asked about their least favorite aspect of TV viewing, most people say it's the commercials. While most consumers understand that commercials support free programming, they are bothered by the growing number of commercial interruptions. One way to avoid all the clutter is to channel-surf and bypass commercials. DVR (digital video recorder) makers offer another solution—skip commercials altogether while still watching your favorite show on your own schedule.

Consumers are discovering DVRs and love the freedom they find through services like TiVo. The service allows consumers to automatically record shows and skip commercials during playback. Statistics show that DVR users watch more TV, channel-surf less, enjoy their DVR almost as much as their cell phone, and move many prime-time week shows to the weekend, when they have more leisure time. Many advertising agencies believe that DVRs will spell the end of commercial dominance and put the consumer in the driver's seat as never before. Will a DVR be in your future? Most advertisers hope not!

FOR DISCUSSION

1. Go to the TiVo (www.tivo.com) and SonicBlue (www.sonicblue.com) Web sites. How do these products or services give consumers more freedom of choice? Is this freedom worth the cost of the product or service? Explain.

2. Movie companies and television networks say DVRs should be declared illegal and have gone to court to prove it. What arguments would support this view? Are DVRs any different from Napster? Explain.

3. How would the elimination of traditional advertising affect the Buyer Decision Process Model shown in Figure 6.6? How would it affect the product adoption process? Explain.

4. Assume you are a marketing manager for a DVR service. Write a brief proposal to settle disputes with the entertainment and television industry while expanding sales of your service.

Zoots: Dry Cleaning—Your Way

Todd Krasnow, a former Staples executive, thought he could do for the $8 billion dry-cleaning industry what national drugstores did for pharmacies: provide more efficient service at a lower price. His concept? Dry-cleaning drive-through service, home pick-up and delivery, and 24-hour access. The idea was so good that his company, Zoots, attracted more than $85 million from investors and the chain has expanded to include 48 stores that service 200 communities in four states. But what is the secret to the company's success? Zoots tapped into key factors that drive consumer behavior.

After viewing the Zoots video, answer the following questions about consumer buyer behavior:

1. In terms of personal factors, what types of consumers will likely choose Zoots for dry-cleaning services? How has Zoots tailored services to appeal specifically to these consumers?
2. How does the addition of Web-based services impact the variety of consumers Zoots appeals to?
3. How might psychological factors influence a consumer's choice in services like dry cleaning? How might cultural factors affect this choice? How does or could Zoots take these factors into account in designing its service?

The Whirlpool Duet: A Soap Opera for Kids?

What part of housework do Americans spend the most time doing but know the least about? Now, think about this for a minute—don't blow it off. When you live away from home, what "housework" takes the biggest chunk of your time?

The answer? Laundry. Americans spend more time each week washing and drying clothes than cleaning house, mowing lawns, or cooking. In fact, the average American "housewife" spends seven to nine hours doing laundry each week.

There are two good reasons. We own more clothes than people in other countries (clothes are cheaper here), and we have a tendency to wash them after only one use. Unfortunately, given that we don't get our clothes very clean when we do wash them (part of the "know the least about" problem), we may *have* to wash them more often.

We don't know much about washing clothes because we tend to do it like Mom did—we haven't just studied the problem very well. In addition, there's a bewildering array of fabric types that we have to take care of, from 100 percent pure cotton to washable silk and even washable, breathable polyester. Rather than learning how to wash each of these, we adopt a sort of middle-of-the-road approach—spray some stain remover on it before throwing it in; maybe pour in some fabric softener; wash it in warm water (Americans seem to be allergic to hot-water washing); rely on the detergent to have a lot of bleaches, color brighteners, and whiteners; give it a cold rinse; and hope for the best.

Unfortunately, that "best," compared to clothes washed in European machines, is noticeably inferior. Why? Whereas Americans use top-loading washing machines, Europeans use front-loading washing machines, and those front loaders do a better job of cleaning clothes. Unlike top loaders that use an agitator that beats clothes as they wash, front-loading machines tumble clothes. The result is that American clothes get old before their time—they wear out faster.

Why do Americans want top loaders? For one thing, they're easier to load. You don't have to stoop over to throw the clothes in or take them out. For another, they can handle larger loads. For a family of four, if you're going to wash everything after it's worn once, the capacity to wash larger loads becomes increasingly important.

Even if we had front-loading machines, we might not get it right. How many of you put in the clothes, the detergent, and extras such as bleach or fabric softener and *then* turn the machine on so that it begins to fill with water? Well, that's all wrong. You should fill the machine, then add the detergent and other concoctions—the clothes go in last.

So, we Americans wash 35 billion loads of laundry the wrong way each year—that's 1,100 loads begun every second. The result is a quarter ton of less-than-pristine clothing generated by each of us each year. What's more, we use 16 or more gallons of water for each load, compared to 4 gallons for a European machine. Aha!—one statistic in our favor: The typical wash cycle in the

(continued)

United States is 35 minutes, compared to 90 minutes in Europe. But maybe that's not good. Perhaps washing clothes more gently for longer gets them cleaner.

Given that old habits (washing clothes like Mom did) die hard, what could an American appliance manufacturer do? Whirlpool decided to build a "global washing machine"—one that used the same "platform" or basic configuration no matter what area of the globe. Then, the basic platform could be modified for different countries and conditions. For example, the tub could be bigger in the United States for people who want to wash larger loads.

However, a global machine had to be a front loader. How did Whirlpool hope to get around American consumers' objections? First, it put the new machine on a pedestal—that eliminated some of the stooping. Then, it put a drawer in the pedestal where cleaning supplies can be stored. To exceed customers' load-size expectations, Whirlpool gave them 3.7 cubic feet of capacity, versus 3.0 cubic feet in the usual U.S. top loader. To accommodate those with limited space, it designed the accompanying dryer to go on top of the washer (try that with a top loader).

Thus were born the new Duet washer and dryer from Whirlpool. The washer is made in Germany, where all of Whirlpool's front-loading machines are made. The Duet washer uses 68 percent less water, and along with less water, less detergent and other cleaners. It has a sanitary cycle that eliminates 99.999 percent of certain bacteria. The Duet removes more water from wet clothes because the tub spins at 900 to 1,100 revolutions per minute, compared to 600 rpm in conventional top-loading machines. Extracting more water also leads to shorter drying times, which also means that the Duet dryer uses 67 percent less electricity. It has "Senseon" computerized technology that heats clothes just enough to reach the proper stage of dryness without overheating them (less wear) and it operates fast enough to dry a load of clothes in the same time that it takes to wash them. Both the washer and dryer exceed Energy Star requirements set by the U.S. Department of Energy and the Environmental Protection Agency.

How does the Duet washer actually work? Its advanced Catalyst washing technology system mixes detergent with a small amount of water and then sprays the foamy lather directly on clothes, which means there's no need for pretreatment. The tumbling action of the machine gently flexes and moves fabrics over three separate baffles that help loosen and remove soil and stains. The water-level control senses the size of the load and introduces only the water needed to clean the load.

Not only is the Duet combo energy and water conscious, it's aesthetically pleasing. The machines are white and come with your choice of two trim colors. Tidal blue is geared to the consumer who wants something that is more expensive looking; Dove Grey is for people who want a product that will blend with their existing surroundings. In a major design competition, Excellence in Design gave the Duet a best overall award for a major appliance. Their evaluative criteria were: (1) aesthetics, (2) ergonomics/human factors and (3) innovative research. It's easy to understand why the Duet won the major award.

What's the catch? The price. The washer retails for $999 to $1,299, the dryer for $799 (electric) or $849 (gas), and the pedestal for $149. Standard agitator washer and dryers sell for about $300 and $400, respectively. Thus, the Duet duo is about three times as expensive, even without the pedestal.

Has that impacted purchase? No. Duet is actually selling at a rate double Whirlpool's original projections. Whirlpool thought that the market for the Duet would be a niche of affluent laundry-doers who would account for only 5 percent of Whirlpool's North American sales. Instead, it's reaping a surprising 10 percent of sales. Even so, any shift to front loaders will be gradual, as washing machines are expected to last 25 years. And obviously, the price would have to come down before the new design can capture mass market demand.

Why have some Americans chosen to buy these very high-priced machines? There are many possible answers. First, there's wealth. Much of the accumulated wealth of the 1990s is still with us, even after the stock market downturn. Second, the savings rate is down, which means households are spending more than they used to. Third, baby boomers are the major market, as many of their kids are out of college and they have more disposable income to spend. Fourth, consumer aspirations have risen. No one wants to be middle class anymore—that was an aspiration for those born in the thirties. Today, people want to be near the top and consider the middle class a starting point, not a goal. Fifth, Duet has provided a new form of entertainment for children—some of whom spend hours watching the clothes go round and round, making the Duet a kind of a "soap opera for kids."

It's also possible that American consumers have gotten wiser about purchasing. Even though the Duet's price is higher, it does offer savings. It should use close to $150 less of water each year, plus offers savings on electricity, detergents, bleaches, and softeners. Thus, the machines should pay for themselves in less than 15 years, maybe even 10 years. That's not including wearing clothes longer because they don't wear out so fast. And some Americans have gotten more quality-conscious and less price-conscious.

There's another phenomenon at work here as well. It's the emerging hourglass effect of income distribution in this country. The middle class is dividing into a lower group focused on low prices and an upscale group looking for quality. In the past, the market was pyramid-shaped with relatively few households at the top willing to pay top dollar for products. Today, however, many middle-class Americans (feeling that wealth from the 1990s are migrating upscale in their purchases. Sales of luxury cars, wines, jeans, jewelry, and electronics and the patronizing of high-priced specialty retailers such as Tiffany's is increasing.

How has Whirlpool marketed the Duet? Initially, TV ads and magazine ads in vehicles such as *House Beautiful* stressed energy efficiency and environmental issues. Finding that their market had an average household income of $50,000 rather than the $75,000 the company first predicted, Whirlpool pulled the original magazine and TV ads in favor of in-store promotions. Its new TV spots feature consumer testimonials stressing the product's practical appeal.

Will all this work? Are Americans shifting to quality products for the long haul? Only time will tell. It will all have to come out in the wash.

QUESTIONS FOR DISCUSSION

1. What sorts of cultural, social, and personal characteristics affect the purchase of a Duet duo?
2. In your opinion, what are the consumer motivations for buying a Duet? How has learning impacted past purchase? How will that change if they buy a Duet washer?
3. What kind of buying decision is the typical purchase of a washer and dryer? Is this different for the purchase of a Duet duo?

4. How will advertising and in-store promotions for the Duet affect the stages of the buyer decision process?

5. Think of the Duet as an innovation. Evaluate it using the product characteristics that affect the rate of adoption. What types of innovators are most likely to purchase a Duet?

6. Are Whirlpool's new marketing efforts well designed to "sell" the Duet? Are they appropriate given that the market is lower in income than Whirlpool expected?

Sources: "Dynamic Duo," *Appliance Manufacturer,* August 2001, p. 62; Paul Dodson, "Benton Harbor, Ind.–Based Whirlpool Creates New Washer, Dryer Appliances," *Knight-Ridder/Tribune Business News,* September 23, 2001; Joe Jancsurak, "Fifteen Annual EID Winners: Designing Outside the Box," *Appliance Manufacturer,* May 2002, p. 19; Emily Nelson, "Wash and Wear: In Doing Laundry, Americans Cling to Outmoded Ways—Machines, Detergents Evolve, but Clothes Still Don't Get as Clean as They Could—Shying Away from Hot Water," *Wall Street Journal,* May 16, 2002, p. A1; Gregory L. White and Shirley Leung, "Stepping Up: Middle Market Shrinks as Americans Migrate Toward the High End—Shifting Consumer Values Create 'Hourglass' Effect; Quality Gets Easier to Sell—Six Air Bags, 22 Towels," *Wall Street Journal,* March 29, 2002, p. A1.

Business Markets and Business Buyer Behavior

LOOKING AHEAD: PREVIEWING THE CONCEPTS

In the previous chapter, you studied *final consumer* buying behavior and factors that influence it. In this chapter, we'll do the same for *business customers*—those that buy goods and services for use in producing their own products and services or for resale to others.

Before moving on, let's look first at Gulfstream Aerospace Corporation, the Rolls-Royce of corporate aircraft makers. In some ways, selling corporate jets to business buyers is like selling cars or household appliances to final consumers. In other ways, however, it's very, very different. For example, think about who might be involved in the purchase decision for an expensive jet and what factors might influence each person's buying behavior. As you'll see, such buying decisions can be pretty complex.

For more than 40 years, Gulfstream Aerospace Corporation has been the Rolls-Royce of corporate aviation. The original Gulfstream model—a twin-engine turboprop introduced in 1958—was the first jet designed expressly for corporate use. Last year, Gulfstream sold more than 100 business jets at an average price tag of $32 million a piece.

Identifying potential buyers isn't a problem. Worldwide, only about 300 to 500 customers—corporations and wealthy individual buyers—have the wherewithal to own and operate multimillion-dollar business aircraft. Customers include Disney, American Express, Coca-Cola, General Motors, IBM, and many others, including Bill Cosby and King Fahd of Saudi Arabia. Gulfstream's more difficult problems involve reaching key decision makers for jet purchases, understanding their complex motivations and decision processes, analyzing what factors will be important in their decisions, and designing marketing approaches.

Gulfstream recognizes the importance of *rational* motives and *objective* factors in buyers' decisions. Customers justify the expense of a corporate jet on utilitarian grounds, such as security, flexibility, responsiveness to customers, and efficient time use. A company buying a jet will evaluate Gulfstream aircraft on quality and performance, prices, operating costs, and service. At times, these "objective" factors may appear to be the only things that drive the buying decision. But having a superior product isn't enough to land the sale: Gulfstream also must consider the more subtle *human factors* that affect the choice of a jet.

The purchase process may be initiated by the chief executive officer (CEO), a board member wishing to increase efficiency or security, the company's chief pilot, or through Gulfstream efforts such as advertising or a sales visit. The CEO will be central in deciding whether to buy the jet, but he or she will be heavily influenced by the company's pilot, financial officer, and members of top management. The involvement of so many people in the purchase decision creates a group dynamic that Gulfstream must factor into its sales planning. Who makes up the buying group? How will the parties interact? Who will dominate and who submit? What priorities do the individuals have?

Each party in the buying process has subtle roles and needs. For example, the salespeople who try to impress both the CEO with depreciation schedules and the chief pilot with minimum runway statistics will almost certainly not sell a plane if they overlook the psychological and emotional components of the buying decision. The chief pilot, as an equipment expert, often has veto power over purchase decisions and may be able to stop the purchase of a certain brand of jet by simply expressing a negative opinion about, say, the plane's bad-weather capabilities. In this sense, the pilot not only influences the decision but also serves as an information "gatekeeper" by advising management on the equipment to select. The users of the jet—middle and upper management of the buying company, important customers, and others—may have at least an indirect role in choosing the equipment.

Although the corporate legal staff will handle the purchase agreement and the purchasing department will acquire the jet, these parties may have little to say about whether or how the plane will be obtained and which type will be selected.

According to one salesperson, in dealing with the CEO, the biggest factor is not the plane's hefty price tag, but its image. You need all the numbers for support, but if you can't find the kid inside the CEO and excite him or her with the raw beauty of the new plane, you'll never sell the equipment. If you sell the excitement, you sell the jet. And Gulfstream has plenty of excitement to sell. As one industry analyst observes, "The sleek, top-of-the line Gulfstream V can zip eight passengers from New York City to Tokyo at 87 percent of the speed of sound in a cabin that looks more like a Manhattan hideaway apartment than an airplane. . . . The most luxurious of these planes come crammed with the toys that keep [even the most discriminating buyers] happy: showers, kitchens, satellite TVs."

Some buying influences may come as a big surprise. Gulfstream may never really know who is behind the purchase of a plane. Although many people inside the customer company can be influential, the most important influence may turn out to be the CEO's spouse. The typical buyer spends about $4

million to outfit the plane's interior. This covers top-of-the-line stereo sound and video systems, a lavish galley, and a bewildering array of custom-made furnishings. To help with such decisions, many CEOs hire designers and bring their spouses along to planning sessions. As one salesperson notes, "Wives are behind the CEO's decisions on a lot of things, not just airplanes. . . . A crucial moment in a deal comes when the CEO's wife takes off her shoes and starts decorating the plane."

In some ways, selling corporate jets to business buyers is like selling cars and kitchen appliances to families. Gulfstream asks the same questions as consumer marketers: Who are the buyers and what are their needs? How do buyers make their buying decisions and what factors influence these decisions? What marketing program will be most effective? But the answers to these questions are usually different for the business buyer. Thus, Gulfstream faces many of the same challenges as consumer marketers—and some additional ones. A solid understanding of the full dynamics of business buyer behavior has Gulfstream flying high these days. The company captures a lion's share of the top-of-the-line segment of the business-jet market and has amassed a $4.1 billion backlog of orders.[1]

In one way or another, most large companies sell to other organizations. Many companies, such as DuPont, Boeing, Cisco Systems, Caterpillar, and countless other firms, sell *most* of their products to other businesses. Even large consumer-products companies, which make products used by final consumers, must first sell their products to other businesses. For example, General Mills makes many familiar consumer products—Cheerios, Betty Crocker cake mixes, Gold Medal flour, and others. But to sell these products to consumers, General Mills must first sell them to the wholesalers and retailers that serve the consumer market.

Business buyer behavior

The buying behavior of the organizations that buy goods and services for use in the production of other products and services or for the purpose of reselling or renting them to others at a profit.

Business buyer behavior refers to the buying behavior of the organizations that buy goods and services for use in the production of other products and services that are sold, rented, or supplied to others. It also includes the behavior of retailing and wholesaling firms that acquire goods for the purpose of reselling or renting them to others at a profit. In the **business buying process,** business buyers determine which products and services their organizations need to purchase, and then find, evaluate, and choose among alternative suppliers and brands. Companies that sell to other business organizations must do their best to understand business markets and business buyer behavior.

Business Markets

Business buying process

The decision process by which business buyers determine which products and services their organizations need to purchase, and then find, evaluate, and choose among alternative suppliers and brands.

The business market is *huge*. In fact, business markets involve far more dollars and items than do consumer markets. For example, think about the large number of business transactions involved in the production and sale of a single set of Goodyear tires. Various suppliers sell Goodyear the rubber, steel, equipment, and other goods that it needs to produce the tires. Goodyear then sells the finished tires to retailers, who in turn sell them to consumers. Thus, many sets of *business* purchases were made for only one set of *consumer* purchases. In addition, Goodyear sells tires as original equipment to manufacturers who install them on new vehicles, and as replacement tires to companies that maintain their own fleets of company cars, trucks, buses, or other vehicles.

Characteristics of Business Markets

In some ways, business markets are similar to consumer markets. Both involve people who assume buying roles and make purchase decisions to satisfy needs. However, business markets

TABLE 7.1 — CHARACTERISTICS OF BUSINESS MARKETS

Marketing Structure and Demand
Business markets contain *fewer but larger buyers.*
Business customers are *more geographically concentrated.*
Business buyer demand is *derived* from final consumer demand.
Demand in many business markets is *more inelastic*—not affected as much in the short run by price changes.
Demand in business markets *fluctuates more,* and more quickly.

Nature of the Buying Unit
Business purchases involve *more buyers.*
Business buying involves a *more professional purchasing effort.*

Types of Decisions and the Decision Process
Business buyers usually face *more complex buying decisions.*
The business buying process is *more formalized.*
In business buying, buyers and sellers work more closely together and build close long-run *relationships.*

differ in many ways from consumer markets. The main differences, shown in Table 7.1 and discussed below, are in *market structure and demand,* the *nature of the buying unit,* and the *types of decisions and the decision process* involved.

Market Structure and Demand

The business marketer normally deals with *far fewer but far larger buyers* than the consumer marketer does. For example, when Goodyear sells replacement tires to final consumers, its potential market includes the owners of the millions of cars currently in use in the United States. But Goodyear's fate in the business market depends on getting orders from one of only a handful of large automakers. Even in large business markets, a few buyers often account for most of the purchasing.

Business markets are also *more geographically concentrated.* More than half the nation's business buyers are concentrated in eight states: California, New York, Ohio, Illinois, Michigan, Texas, Pennsylvania, and New Jersey. Further, business demand is **derived demand**—it ultimately derives from the demand for consumer goods. General Motors buys steel because consumers buy cars. If consumer demand for cars drops, so will the demand for steel and all the other products used to make cars. Therefore, business marketers sometimes promote their products directly to final consumers to increase business demand.

For example, Intel's long-running "Intel Inside" advertising campaign sells personal computer buyers on the virtues of Intel microprocessors. The increased demand for Intel chips boosts demand for the PCs containing them, and both Intel and its business partners win. Similarly, DuPont promotes Teflon directly to final consumers as a key ingredient in many products—from nonstick cookware to stain-repellent, wrinkle-free clothing. You see Teflon Fabric Protector hangtags on clothing lines such as Levi's Dockers, Donna Karan's menswear, and Ralph Lauren denim.[2] By making Teflon familiar and attractive to final buyers, DuPont also makes the products containing it more attractive.

Many business markets have *inelastic demand;* that is, total demand for many business products is not affected much by price changes, especially in the short run. A drop in the price of leather will not cause shoe manufacturers to buy much more leather unless it results in lower shoe prices that, in turn, will increase consumer demand for shoes.

Finally, business markets have more *fluctuating demand.* The demand for many business goods and services tends to change more—and more quickly—than the demand for consumer goods and services does. A small percentage increase in consumer demand can cause large increases in business demand. Sometimes a rise of only 10 percent in consumer demand can cause as much as a 200 percent rise in business demand during the next period.

Nature of the Buying Unit

Compared with consumer purchases, a business purchase usually involves *more decision participants* and a *more professional purchasing effort.* Often, business buying is done by trained purchasing agents who spend their working lives learning how to buy better. The more complex the

Derived demand
Business demand that ultimately comes from (derives from) the demand for consumer goods.

Derived demand: Intel's long-running "Intel Inside" logo advertising campaign boosts demand for Intel chips and for the PCs containing them. Now, most computer markets feature a logo like this one in their ads.

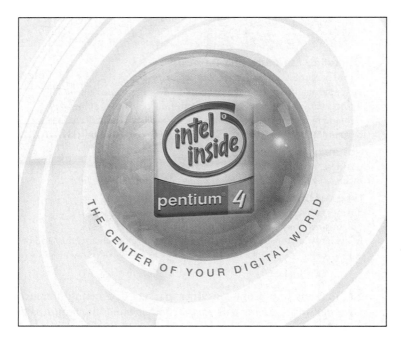

purchase, the more likely that several people will participate in the decision-making process. Buying committees made up of technical experts and top management are common in the buying of major goods. As one observer notes, "It's a scary thought: Your customers may know more about your company and products than you do.... Companies are putting their best and brightest people on procurement patrol."[3] Therefore, business marketers must have well-trained salespeople to deal with well-trained buyers.

Types of Decisions and the Decision Process

Business buyers usually face *more complex* buying decisions than do consumer buyers. Purchases often involve large sums of money, complex technical and economic considerations, and interactions among many people at many levels of the buyer's organization. Because the purchases are more complex, business buyers may take longer to make their decisions. The business buying process also tends to be *more formalized* than the consumer buying process. Large business purchases usually call for detailed product specifications, written purchase orders, careful supplier searches, and formal approval.

Finally, in the business buying process, buyer and seller are often much *more dependent* on each other. Consumer marketers are often at a distance from their customers. In contrast, B2B marketers may roll up their sleeves and work closely with their customers during all stages of the buying process—from helping customers define problems, to finding solutions, to supporting after-sale operation. They often customize their offerings to individual customer needs.

In the short run, sales go to suppliers who meet buyers' immediate product and service needs. However, business marketers also must build close *long-run* partnerships with customers. In recent years, relationships between customers and suppliers have been changing from downright adversarial to close and chummy. In fact, many customer companies are now practicing *supplier relationship management,* developing a core of suppliers and working closely with them. For example, Caterpillar no longer calls its buyers "purchasing agents"—they are managers of "purchasing and supplier development." Says one purchasing expert, "You no longer treat your supplier as a 'supplier' but as an extension of your business." Consider this example:

> Motoman, a leading supplier of industry robotic systems, and Stillwater Technologies, a contract tooling and machinery company and a key supplier to Motoman, are tightly integrated. Not only do they occupy office and manufacturing space in the same facility, they also link their telephone and computer systems and share a common lobby, conference room, and employee cafeteria. Philip Morrison, chairman and CEO of Motoman, says it's like "a joint venture without the paperwork." Short delivery distances are just one benefit of

Business marketers often roll up their sleeves and work closely with their customers throughout the buying and consuming process. In this award-winning business-to-business ad, Fujitsu promises more than just high-tech products: "Our technology helps keep you moving upward. And our people won't let you down."

the unusual partnership. Also key is the fact that employees of both companies have ready access to each other and can share ideas on improving quality and reducing costs. This close relationship has also opened the door to new opportunities. Both companies had been doing work for Honda Motor Company, and Honda suggested that the two work together on systems projects. The symbiotic relationship makes the two bigger and better than they could be individually.[4]

In the long run, business marketers keep a customer's sales by meeting current needs *and* by partnering with customers to help them solve their problems. This is true for marketers in small as well as large businesses. For example, small industrial detergent maker ChemStation does more than simply supply its customers with cleaning chemicals. It works closely with them to custom-design total solutions to their unique cleaning problems. "Our customers . . . oftentimes think of us as more of a partner than a supplier," says the company's newsletter (see Real Marketing 7.1).[5]

A Model of Business Buyer Behavior

At the most basic level, marketers want to know how business buyers will respond to various marketing stimuli. Figure 7.1 shows a model of business buyer behavior. In this model, marketing and other stimuli affect the buying organization and produce certain buyer responses. As with consumer buying, the marketing stimuli for business buying consist of the four *P*s: product, price, place, and promotion. Other stimuli include major forces in the environment: economic, technological, political, cultural, and competitive. These stimuli enter the organization and are turned into buyer responses: product or service choice; supplier choice; order quantities; and delivery, service, and payment terms. In order to design good marketing-mix strategies, the marketer must understand what happens within the organization to turn stimuli into purchase responses.

Within the organization, buying activity consists of two major parts: the buying center, made up of all the people involved in the buying decision, and the buying-decision process. The model shows that the buying center and the buying-decision process are influenced by internal organizational, interpersonal, and individual factors as well as by external environmental factors.

Business Buyer Behavior

The model in Figure 7.1 on page 219 suggests four questions about business buyer behavior: What buying decisions do business buyers make? Who participates in the buying process? What are the major influences on buyers? How do business buyers make their buying decisions?

real
marketing 7.1

ChemStation: More of a Partner than a Supplier

ChemStation sells industrial cleaning chemicals to a wide range of business customers, ranging from car washes to the U.S. Air Force. Whether a customer is washing down a fleet or a factory, a store or a restaurant, a

metic eye makeup containers, yacht-making molds, concrete trucks, oceangoing trawlers, and about anything else you can imagine.

But for most customers, ChemStation is much more than just a cleaning-chemicals

vidual customer to concoct a soap formula specially designed for that customer. Salespeople collect information about the specific customer's cleaning needs and enter it into a customer database called the Tank Management System (TMS). Next, a company chemist develops a special "detergent recipe" for the customer. The recipe is fed into a computer-controlled machine, which mixes up a batch of the special brew. ChemStation delivers the custom-made mixture to a tank installed at the customer's site. It then maintains the tank by monitoring usage and automatically refilling the tank when supplies run low.

Working closely with an individual customer creates a lasting relationship that helps ChemStation to lock out the competition. No one—not even the customer—knows what goes into each formula, making it hard for a customer to jump to competitors. "We tell customers it's a secret," says founder and CEO George Homan. "We're not as protective about our formulas as Coca-Cola, but we're close." Moreover, maintaining the ChemStation tank at the customer's business creates regular customer contact. This regular contact helps ChemStation to detect and smooth out any wrinkles in the customer relationship.

Put it all together and the term *supplier* doesn't really fit ChemStation. Instead, the company is like an extension of each customer's own business. When a customer comes up with a seemingly impossible cleaning challenge, ChemStation is quick to respond, "Yeah, we do that!" As noted in the a recent issue of *Insights,* ChemStation's customer newsletter, "Our customers . . . oftentimes think of us as more of a partner than a supplier."

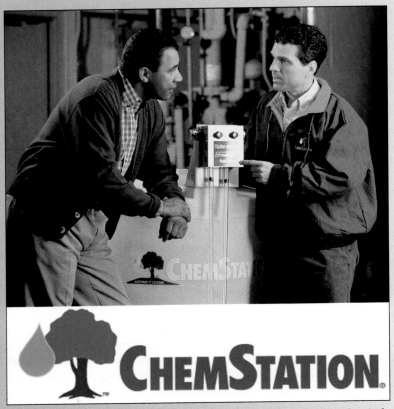

ChemStation does more than simply supply its customers with cleaning chemicals. "Our customers . . . think of us as more of a partner than a supplier."

distillery or an Army base, this small market nicher comes up with the right cleaning solution every time. The company's motto: "Our system is your solution!"

ChemStation will tackle just about any customer cleaning problem. It supplies thousands of products in hundreds of industries. The company has created customized cleaning solutions for all kinds of surfaces: floors, walls, ceilings, machinery, parts, vehicles, and even windows. It has brewed special formulas for cleaning hands, feathers, mufflers, flutes, perfume vats, cos-

supplier. Instead, it makes itself a *partner* in helping customers solve their special cleaning problems. ChemStation starts by learning all it can about customers and their industries. The company's people subscribe to customers' trade journals, attend their industry conferences and trade shows, and even join their trade associations. However, the real partnering takes place at the individual customer level.

What cleans a car won't work to clean an airplane or equipment in a mine shaft. So ChemStation works closely with each indi-

Sources: Sarah Schafer, "Have It Your Way," *Inc,* November 18, 1997; "Keeping Up with Your Industry," *Insights,* February 2000, p. 1; "Common Bond?" *Insights,* February 2001, p. 1; "BJ's Knows . . . Our System Is Their Solution," *Insights,* March 2002, p. 1; and information accessed online at www.chemstation.com, July 2002.

FIGURE 7.1
Model of business buyer behavior

Major Types of Buying Situations

There are three major types of buying situations.[6] At one extreme is the *straight rebuy,* which is a fairly routine decision. At the other extreme is the *new task,* which may call for thorough research. In the middle is the *modified rebuy,* which requires some research.

In a **straight rebuy,** the buyer reorders something without any modifications. It is usually handled on a routine basis by the purchasing department. Based on past buying satisfaction, the buyer simply chooses from the various suppliers on its list. "In" suppliers try to maintain product and service quality. They often propose automatic reordering systems so that the purchasing agent will save reordering time. "Out" suppliers try to offer something new or exploit dissatisfaction so that the buyer will consider them.

In a **modified rebuy,** the buyer wants to modify product specifications, prices, terms, or suppliers. The modified rebuy usually involves more decision participants than does the straight rebuy. The in suppliers may become nervous and feel pressured to put their best foot forward to protect an account. Out suppliers may see the modified rebuy situation as an opportunity to make a better offer and gain new business.

A company buying a product or service for the first time faces a **new-task** situation. In such cases, the greater the cost or risk, the larger the number of decision participants and the greater their efforts to collect information will be. The new-task situation is the marketer's greatest opportunity and challenge. The marketer not only tries to reach as many key buying influences as possible but also provides help and information.

The buyer makes the fewest decisions in the straight rebuy and the most in the new-task decision. In the new-task situation, the buyer must decide on product specifications, suppliers, price limits, payment terms, order quantities, delivery times, and service terms. The order of these decisions varies with each situation, and different decision participants influence each choice.

Many business buyers prefer to buy a packaged solution to a problem from a single seller. Instead of buying and putting all the components together, the buyer may ask sellers to supply the components *and* assemble the package or system. The sale often goes to the firm that provides the most complete system meeting the customer's needs. Thus, **systems selling** is often a key business marketing strategy for winning and holding accounts.

Sellers increasingly have recognized that buyers like this method and have adopted systems selling as a marketing tool. Systems selling is a two-step process. First, the supplier sells a group of interlocking products. For example, the supplier sells not only glue, but also applicators and dryers. Second, the supplier sells a system of production, inventory control, distribution, and other services to meet the buyer's need for a smooth-running operation.

Systems selling is a key business marketing strategy for winning and holding accounts. The contract often goes to the firm that provides the most complete solution to the customer's needs. For example, the Indonesian government requested bids to build a cement factory near Jakarta. An American firm's proposal included choosing the site, designing the cement factory, hiring the construction crews, assembling the materials and equipment, and turning the finished factory over to the Indonesian government. A Japanese firm's proposal included all of these services, plus hiring and training workers to run the factory, exporting the cement through their trading companies, and using the cement to build some needed roads and new office buildings in Jakarta. Although the Japanese firm's proposal cost more, it won the contract. Clearly, the Japanese

---

Straight rebuy

A business buying situation in which the buyer routinely reorders something without any modifications.

Modified rebuy

A business buying situation in which the buyer wants to modify product specifications, prices, terms, or suppliers.

New task

A business buying situation in which the buyer purchases a product or service for the first time.

Systems selling

Buying a packaged solution to a problem from a single seller, thus avoiding all the separate decisions involved in a complex buying situation.

viewed the problem not as just building a cement factory (the narrow view of systems selling) but of running it in a way that would contribute to the country's economy. They took the broadest view of the customer's needs. This is true systems selling.[7]

Participants in the Business Buying Process

Who does the buying of the trillions of dollars' worth of goods and services needed by business organizations? The decision-making unit of a buying organization is called its **buying center:** all the individuals and units that participate in the business decision-making process. The buying center includes all members of the organization who play a role in the purchase decision process. This group includes the actual users of the product or service, those who make the buying decision, those who influence the buying decision, those who do the actual buying, and those who control buying information.

The buying center includes all members of the organization who play any of five roles in the purchase decision process.[8]

- **Users** are members of the organization who will use the product or service. In many cases, users initiate the buying proposal and help define product specifications.
- **Influencers** often help define specifications and also provide information for evaluating alternatives. Technical personnel are particularly important influencers.
- **Buyers** have formal authority to select the supplier and arrange terms of purchase. Buyers may help shape product specifications, but their major role is in selecting vendors and negotiating. In more complex purchases, buyers might include high-level officers participating in the negotiations.
- **Deciders** have formal or informal power to select or approve the final suppliers. In routine buying, the buyers are often the deciders, or at least the approvers.
- **Gatekeepers** control the flow of information to others. For example, purchasing agents often have authority to prevent salespersons from seeing users or deciders. Other gatekeepers include technical personnel and even personal secretaries.

The buying center is not a fixed and formally identified unit within the buying organization. It is a set of buying roles assumed by different people for different purchases. Within the organization, the size and makeup of the buying center will vary for different products and for different buying situations. For some routine purchases, one person—say a purchasing agent—may assume all the buying center roles and serve as the only person involved in the buying decision.

Sidebar (left margin)

Buying center
All the individuals and units that participate in the business buying-decision process.

Users
Members of the buying organization who will actually use the purchased product or service.

Influencers
People in an organization's buying center who affect the buying decision; they often help define specifications and also provide information for evaluating alternatives.

Buyers
The people who make an actual purchase.

Deciders
People in the organization's buying center who have formal or informal power to select or approve the final suppliers.

Gatekeepers
People in the organization's buying center who control the flow of information to others.

Buying center: Allegiance Healthcare Corporation deals with a wide range of buying influences, from purchasing executives and hospital administrators to the surgeons who actually use its products.

For more complex purchases, the buying center may include 20 or 30 people from different levels and departments in the organization.

The buying center concept presents a major marketing challenge. The business marketer must learn who participates in the decision, each participant's relative influence, and what evaluation criteria each decision participant uses. For example, Allegiance Healthcare Corporation, the large health care products and services company, sells disposable surgical gowns to hospitals. It identifies the hospital personnel involved in this buying decision as the vice president of purchasing, the operating room administrator, and the surgeons. Each participant plays a different role. The vice president of purchasing analyzes whether the hospital should buy disposable gowns or reusable gowns. If analysis favors disposable gowns, then the operating room administrator compares competing products and prices and makes a choice. This administrator considers the gown's absorbency, antiseptic quality, design, and cost, and normally buys the brand that meets requirements at the lowest cost. Finally, surgeons affect the decision later by reporting their satisfaction or dissatisfaction with the brand.

The buying center usually includes some obvious participants who are involved formally in the buying decision. For example, the decision to buy a corporate jet will probably involve the company's CEO, chief pilot, a purchasing agent, some legal staff, a member of top management, and others formally charged with the buying decision. It may also involve less-obvious, informal participants, some of whom may actually make or strongly affect the buying decision. Sometimes, even the people in the buying center are not aware of all the buying participants. In the opening Gulfstream example, the decision about which corporate jet to buy may actually be made by a corporate board member who has an interest in flying and who knows a lot about airplanes. This board member may work behind the scenes to sway the decision. Many business buying decisions result from the complex interactions of ever-changing buying center participants.

Major Influences on Business Buyers

Business buyers are subject to many influences when they make their buying decisions. Some marketers assume that the major influences are economic. They think buyers will favor the supplier who offers the lowest price or the best product or the most service. They concentrate on offering strong economic benefits to buyers. However, business buyers actually respond to both economic and personal factors. Far from being cold, calculating, and impersonal, business buyers are human and social as well. They react to both reason and emotion.

Today, most business-to-business marketers recognize that emotion plays an important role in business buying decisions. For example, you might expect that an advertisement promoting large trucks to corporate truck fleet buyers would stress objective technical, performance, and

Emotions play an important role in business buying: This Volvo truck ad mentions objective factors, such as efficiency and ease of maintenance. But it stresses more emotional factors such as the raw beauty of the truck and its comfort and roominess, features that make "drivers a lot more possessive."

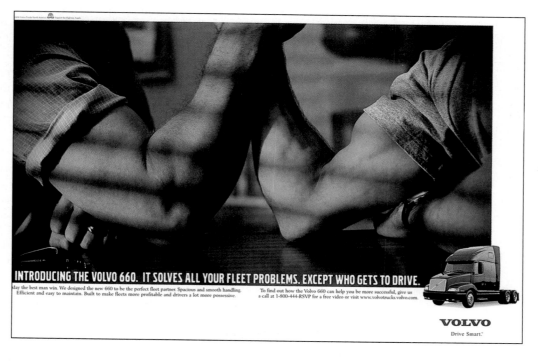

FIGURE 7.2

Major influences on
business buyer behavior

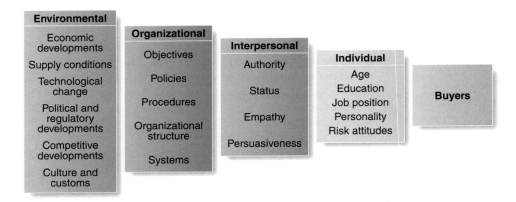

economic factors. However, a recent ad for Volvo heavy-duty trucks shows two drivers arm-wrestling and claims, "It solves all your fleet problems. Except who gets to drive." It turns out that, in the face an industrywide driver shortage, the type of truck a fleet provides can help it to attract qualified drivers. The Volvo ad stresses the raw beauty of the truck and its comfort and roomi-ness, features that make it more appealing to drivers. The ad concludes that Volvo trucks are "built to make fleets more profitable and drivers a lot more possessive."

When suppliers' offers are very similar, business buyers have little basis for strictly rational choice. Because they can meet organizational goals with any supplier, buyers can allow personal factors to play a larger role in their decisions. However, when competing products differ greatly, business buyers are more accountable for their choice and tend to pay more attention to eco-nomic factors. Figure 7.2 lists various groups of influences on business buyers—environmental, organizational, interpersonal, and individual.[9]

Environmental Factors

Business buyers are influenced heavily by factors in the current and expected *economic environ-ment,* such as the level of primary demand, the economic outlook, and the cost of money. As eco-nomic uncertainty rises, business buyers cut back on new investments and attempt to reduce their inventories.

An increasingly important environmental factor is shortages in key materials. Many compa-nies now are more willing to buy and hold larger inventories of scarce materials to ensure ade-quate supply. Business buyers also are affected by technological, political, and competitive devel-opments in the environment. Culture and customs can strongly influence business buyer reactions to the marketer's behavior and strategies, especially in the international marketing envi-ronment (see Real Marketing 7.2). The business marketer must watch these factors, determine how they will affect the buyer, and try to turn these challenges into opportunities.

Organizational Factors

Each buying organization has its own objectives, policies, procedures, structure, and systems, and the business marketer must understand these factors well. Questions such as these arise: How many people are involved in the buying decision? Who are they? What are their evaluative crite-ria? What are the company's policies and limits on its buyers?

Interpersonal Factors

The buying center usually includes many participants who influence each other, so *interpersonal factors* also influence the business buying process. However, it is often difficult to assess such interpersonal factors and group dynamics. As one writer notes, "Managers do not wear tags that say 'decision maker' or 'unimportant person.' The powerful are often invisible, at least to vendor representatives."[10] Nor does the buying center participant with the highest rank always have the most influence. Participants may influence the buying decision because they control rewards and punishments, are well liked, have special expertise, or have a special relationship with other important participants. Interpersonal factors are often very subtle. Whenever possible, business marketers must try to understand these factors and design strategies that take them into account.

real marketing 7.2

International Marketing Manners: When in Rome, Do as the Romans Do

Picture this: Consolidated Amalgamation, Inc., thinks it's time that the rest of the world enjoyed the same fine products it has offered American consumers for two generations. It dispatches Vice President Harry E. Slicksmile

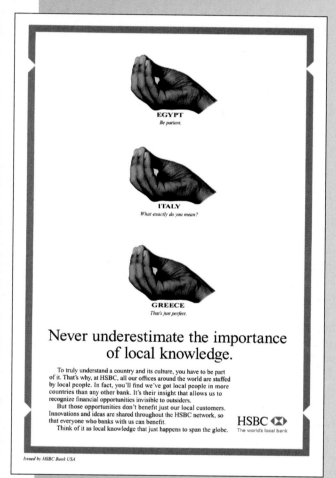

EGYPT
Be patient.

ITALY
What exactly do you mean?

GREECE
That's just perfect.

Never underestimate the importance of local knowledge.

To truly understand a country and its culture, you have to be part of it. That's why, at HSBC, all our offices around the world are staffed by local people. In fact, you'll find we've got local people in more countries than any other bank. It's their insight that allows us to recognize financial opportunities invisible to outsiders.

But those opportunities don't benefit just our local customers. Innovations and ideas are shared throughout the HSBC network, so that everyone who banks with us can benefit.

Think of it as local knowledge that just happens to span the globe.

HSBC
The world's local bank

Issued by HSBC Bank USA

This HSBC ad recognizes the difficulties of doing business globally and understanding international customers, needs, and customs.

to Europe, Africa, and Asia to explore the territory. Mr. Slicksmile stops first in London, where he makes short work of some bankers—he rings them up on the phone. He handles Parisians with similar ease: After securing a table at La Tour d'Argent, he greets his luncheon guest, the director of an industrial engineering firm, with the words, "Just call me Harry, Jacques."

In Germany, Mr. Slicksmile is a power-house. Whisking through a lavish, state-of-the-art marketing presentation, complete with flip charts and audiovisuals, he shows 'em that this Georgia boy *knows* how to make a buck. Heading on to Milan, Harry strikes up a conversation with the Japanese businessman sitting next to him on the plane. He flips his card onto the guy's tray and, when the two say good-bye, shakes hands warmly and clasps the man's right arm. Later, for his appointment with the owner of an Italian packaging design firm, our hero wears his comfy corduroy sport coat, khaki pants, and Topsiders. Everybody knows Italians are zany and laid back.

Mr. Slicksmile next swings through Saudi Arabia, where he coolly presents a potential client with a multimillion-dollar proposal in a classy pigskin binder. His final stop is Beijing, China, where he talks business over lunch with a group of Chinese executives. After completing the meal, he drops his chopsticks into his bowl of rice and presents each guest with an elegant Tiffany's clock as a reminder of his visit.

A great tour, sure to generate a pile of orders, right? Wrong. Six months later, Consolidated Amalgamation has nothing to show for the trip but a stack of bills. Abroad, they weren't wild about Harry.

This hypothetical case has been exaggerated for emphasis. Americans are seldom such dolts. But experts say success in international business has a lot to do with knowing the territory and its people. By learning English and extending themselves in other ways, the world's business leaders have met Americans more than halfway. In contrast, Americans too often do little except assume that others will march to their music. "We want things to be 'American' when we travel. Fast. Convenient. Easy. So we become 'ugly Americans' by demanding that others change," says one American world trade expert. "I think more business would be done if we tried harder."

Poor Harry tried, all right, but in all the wrong ways. The British do not, as a rule, make deals over the phone as much as Americans do. It's not so much a "cultural" difference as a difference in approach. A proper Frenchman neither likes instant familiarity—questions about family, church, or alma mater—nor refers to strangers by their first names. "That poor fellow, Jacques, probably wouldn't show anything, but he'd recoil. He'd *not* be pleased," explains an expert on French business practices. "It's considered poor taste," he continues. "Even after months of business dealings, I'd wait for him or her to make the invitation [to use first names]. . . . You are always right, in Europe, to say 'Mister.'"

Harry's flashy presentation would likely have been a flop with the Germans, who dislike overstatement and ostentatiousness. According to one German expert, however, German businessmen have become accustomed to dealing with Americans. Although differences in body language and customs remain, the past 20 years have softened them. "I hugged an American woman at a business meeting last night," he said. "That would be normal in France, but [older] Germans still have difficulty [with the custom]." He says that calling secretaries by their first names would still be considered rude: "They have a right to be called by their surname. You'd certainly ask—and get—permission first." In Germany, people address each other formally and correctly—someone with two doctorates (which is fairly common) must be referred to as "Herr Doktor Doktor."

When Harry Slicksmile grabbed his new Japanese acquaintance by the arm, the executive probably considered him disrespectful and presumptuous. Japan, like many Asian countries, is a "no-contact culture" in which even shaking hands is a strange experience. Harry made matters

(continued)

worse by tossing his business card. Japanese people revere the business card as an extension of self and as an indicator of rank. They do not *hand* it to people, they *present* it—with both hands. In addition, the Japanese are sticklers about rank. Unlike Americans, they don't heap praise on subordinates in a room; they will praise only the highest-ranking official present.

Hapless Harry also goofed when he assumed that Italians are like Hollywood's stereotypes of them. The flair for design and style that has characterized Italian culture for centuries is embodied in the businesspeople of Milan and Rome. They dress beautifully and admire flair, but they blanch at garishness or impropriety in others' attire.

To the Saudi Arabians, the pigskin binder would have been consider vile. An American salesman who really did present such a binder was unceremoniously tossed out and his company was blacklisted from working with Saudi businesses. In China, Harry's casually dropping his chopsticks could have been misinterpreted as an act of aggression. Stabbing chopsticks into a bowl of rice and leaving them signifies death to the Chinese. The clocks Harry offered as gifts might have confirmed such dark intentions. To "give a clock" in Chinese sounds the same as "seeing someone off to his end."

Thus, to compete successfully in global markets, or even to deal effectively with international firms in their home markets, companies must help their managers to understand the needs, customs, and cultures of international business buyers. The old advice is still good advice: When in Rome, do as the Romans do.

Sources: Adapted from Susan Harte, "When in Rome, You Should Learn to Do What the Romans Do," *Atlanta Journal-Constitution,* January 22, 1990, pp. D1, D6. Additional examples from Terri Morrison, Wayne A. Conway, and Joseph J. Douress, *Dun & Bradstreet's Guide to Doing Business Around the World* (Upper Saddle River, N.J.: Prentice Hall, 2000); Craig S. Smith, "Beware of Green Hats in China and Other Cross-Cultural Faux Pas," *New York Times,* April 30, 2002, p. C11; and James K. Sebenius, "The Hidden Challenge of Cross-Border Negotiations," *Harvard Business Review,* March 2002, pp. 76–85.

Individual Factors

Each participant in the business buying-decision process brings in personal motives, perceptions, and preferences. These individual factors are affected by personal characteristics such as age, income, education, professional identification, personality, and attitudes toward risk. Also, buyers have different buying styles. Some may be technical types who make in-depth analyses of competitive proposals before choosing a supplier. Other buyers may be intuitive negotiators who are adept at pitting the sellers against one another for the best deal.

The Business Buying Process

Figure 7.3 lists the eight stages of the business buying process.[11] Buyers who face a new-task buying situation usually go through all stages of the buying process. Buyers making modified or straight rebuys may skip some of the stages. We will examine these steps for the typical new-task buying situation.

Problem Recognition

Problem recognition
The first stage of the business buying process, in which someone in the company recognizes a problem or need that can be met by acquiring a good or a service.

The buying process begins when someone in the company recognizes a problem or need that can be met by acquiring a specific product or service. **Problem recognition** can result from internal or external stimuli. Internally, the company may decide to launch a new product that requires new production equipment and materials. Or a machine may break down and need new parts. Perhaps a purchasing manager is unhappy with a current supplier's product quality, service, or prices. Externally, the buyer may get some new ideas at a trade show, see an ad, or receive a call

FIGURE 7.3
Stages of the business buying process

from a salesperson who offers a better product or a lower price. In fact, in their advertising, business marketers often alert customers to potential problems and then show how their products provide solutions.

General Need Description

General need description
The stage in the business buying process in which the company describes the general characteristics and quantity of a needed item.

Having recognized a need, the buyer next prepares a **general need description** that describes the characteristics and quantity of the needed item. For standard items, this process presents few problems. For complex items, however, the buyer may have to work with others—engineers, users, consultants—to define the item. The team may want to rank the importance of reliability, durability, price, and other attributes desired in the item. In this phase, the alert business marketer can help the buyers define their needs and provide information about the value of different product characteristics.

Product Specification

Product specification
The stage of the business buying process in which the buying organization decides on and specifies the best technical product characteristics for a needed item.

Value analysis
An approach to cost reduction in which components are studied carefully to determine if they can be redesigned, standardized, or made by less costly methods of production.

The buying organization next develops the item's technical **product specifications,** often with the help of a value analysis engineering team. **Value analysis** is an approach to cost reduction in which components are studied carefully to determine if they can be redesigned, standardized, or made by less costly methods of production. The team decides on the best product characteristics and specifies them accordingly. Sellers, too, can use value analysis as a tool to help secure a new account. By showing buyers a better way to make an object, outside sellers can turn straight rebuy situations into new-task situations that give them a chance to obtain new business.

Supplier Search

Supplier search
The stage of the business buying process in which the buyer tries to find the best vendors.

The buyer now conducts a **supplier search** to find the best vendors. The buyer can compile a small list of qualified suppliers by reviewing trade directories, doing a computer search, or phoning other companies for recommendations. Today, more and more companies are turning to the Internet to find suppliers. For marketers, this has leveled the playing field—the Internet gives smaller suppliers many of the same advantages as larger competitors.

These days, many companies are viewing supplier search more as *supplier development.* These companies want to develop a system of supplier-partners that can help it bring more value to its customers. For example, Wal-Mart has set up a Supplier Development Department which seeks out qualified suppliers and helps them through the complex Wal-Mart buying process. It offers a Supplier Proposal Guide and maintains a Web site offering advice to suppliers wishing to do business with Wal-Mart.

The newer the buying task, and the more complex and costly the item, the greater the amount of time the buyer will spend searching for suppliers. The supplier's task is to get listed in major directories and build a good reputation in the marketplace. Salespeople should watch for companies in the process of searching for suppliers and make certain that their firm is considered.

Proposal Solicitation

Proposal solicitation
The stage of the business buying process in which the buyer invites qualified suppliers to submit proposals.

In the **proposal solicitation** stage of the business buying process, the buyer invites qualified suppliers to submit proposals. In response, some suppliers will send only a catalog or a salesperson. However, when the item is complex or expensive, the buyer will usually require detailed written proposals or formal presentations from each potential supplier.

Business marketers must be skilled in researching, writing, and presenting proposals in response to buyer proposal solicitations. Proposals should be marketing documents, not just technical documents. Presentations should inspire confidence and should make the marketer's company stand out from the competition.

Supplier Selection

Supplier selection
The stage of the business buying process in which the buyer reviews proposals and selects a supplier or suppliers.

The members of the buying center now review the proposals and select a supplier or suppliers. During **supplier selection,** the buying center often will draw up a list of the desired supplier attributes and their relative importance. In one survey, purchasing executives listed the following attributes as most important in influencing the relationship between supplier and customer: quality products and services, on-time delivery, ethical corporate behavior, honest communication, and competitive prices. Other important factors include repair and servicing capabilities,

Supplier development: Wal-Mart's Supplier Development Department offers a Supplier Proposal Guide and maintains a Web site offering advice to suppliers wishing to do business with Wal-Mart.

technical aid and advice, geographic location, performance history, and reputation. The members of the buying center will rate suppliers against these attributes and identify the best suppliers.

Buyers may attempt to negotiate with preferred suppliers for better prices and terms before making the final selections. In the end, they may select a single supplier or a few suppliers. Many buyers prefer multiple sources of supplies to avoid being totally dependent on one supplier and to allow comparisons of prices and performance of several suppliers over time.

Order-Routine Specification

Order-routine specification
The stage of the business buying process in which the buyer writes the final order with the chosen supplier(s), listing the technical specifications, quantity needed, expected time of delivery, return policies, and warranties.

The buyer now prepares an **order-routine specification.** It includes the final order with the chosen supplier or suppliers and lists items such as technical specifications, quantity needed, expected time of delivery, return policies, and warranties. In the case of maintenance, repair, and operating items, buyers may use *blanket contracts* rather than periodic purchase orders. A blanket contract creates a long-term relationship in which the supplier promises to resupply the buyer as needed at agreed prices for a set time period. A blanket order eliminates the expensive process of renegotiating a purchase each time that stock is required. It also allows buyers to write more, but smaller, purchase orders, resulting in lower inventory levels and carrying costs.

Blanket contracting leads to more single-source buying and to buying more items from that source. This practice locks the supplier in tighter with the buyer and makes it difficult for other suppliers to break in unless the buyer becomes dissatisfied with prices or service.

Performance Review

Performance review
The stage of the business buying process in which the buyer rates its satisfaction with suppliers, deciding whether to continue, modify, or drop them.

In this stage, the buyer reviews supplier performance. The buyer may contact users and ask them to rate their satisfaction. The **performance review** may lead the buyer to continue, modify, or drop the arrangement. The seller's job is to monitor the same factors used by the buyer to make sure that the seller is giving the expected satisfaction.

We have described the stages that typically would occur in a new-task buying situation. The eight-stage model provides a simple view of the business buying-decision process. The actual process is usually much more complex. In the modified rebuy or straight rebuy situation, some of these stages would be compressed or bypassed. Each organization buys in its own way, and each buying situation has unique requirements. Different buying center participants may be involved at different stages of the process. Although certain buying-process steps usually do occur, buyers do not always follow them in the same order, and they may add other steps. Often, buyers will repeat certain stages of the process. Finally, a customer relationship might involve many different types of purchases ongoing at a given time, all in different stages of the buying process. The seller must manage the total customer relationship, not just individual purchases.

Business Buying on the Internet

During the past few years, advances in information technology have changed the face of the business-to-business marketing process. Online purchasing, often called *e-procurement*, is growing rapidly. One research firm estimates that the dollar value of materials purchased online will swell from $75 billion in 2000 to more than $3 trillion in 2003.[12] In addition to their own Web pages on the Internet, companies are establishing extranets that link a company's communications and data with its regular suppliers and distributors. Much online purchasing also takes place on public and private online trading exchanges, or through *reverse auctions* in which sellers put their purchasing requests online and invite suppliers to bid for the business.

E-procurement gives buyers access to new suppliers, lowers purchasing costs, and hastens order processing and delivery. In turn, business marketers can connect with customers online to share marketing information, sell products and services, provide customer support services, and maintain ongoing customer relationships.

So far, most of the products bought online are MRO materials—maintenance, repair, and operations. For instance, Los Angeles County purchases everything from chickens to lightbulbs over the Internet. National Semiconductor has automated almost all of the company's 3,500 monthly requisitions to buy materials ranging from the sterile booties worn in its fabrication plants to state-of-the-art software. The actual dollar amount spent on these types of MRO materials pales in comparison to the amount spent for items such as airplane parts, computer systems, and steel tubing. Yet, MRO materials make up 80 percent of all business orders, and the transaction costs for order processing are high. Thus, companies have much to gain by streamlining the MRO buying process on the Web.

General Electric, one of the world's biggest purchasers, plans to be buying *all* of its general operating and industrial supplies online within the next few years. Five years ago, GE set up its Global eXchange Services network—a central Web site through which all GE business units could make their purchases. The site was so successful that GE has now opened it up to other companies, creating a vast electronic e-purchasing clearinghouse.

Business-to-business e-procurement yields many benefits.[13] First, it shaves transaction costs and results in more efficient purchasing for both buyers and suppliers. A Web-powered purchasing program eliminates the paperwork associated with traditional requisition and ordering procedures. On average, companies can trim the costs of purchased goods alone by 15 to 20 percent. For example, Owens Corning estimates that e-procurement has shaved 10 percent off its annual purchasing bill of $3.4 billion.

E-procurement also reduces order processing costs. "The first advantage is clearly the lower prices (about 20 percent) that we are paying," says Hewlett-Packard's vice president of supply-chain services. "But we are now also 20 to 25 percent more efficient." Through online purchasing, Texas Instruments has trimmed its cost of processing a purchase order from $80 to $25. And 3M slashed the price of processing an order from $120 to under $40, while also cutting its error rate dramatically. A more efficient centralized purchasing platform also saves time and money. One key motivation for GE's massive move to online purchasing has been a desire to get rid of overlapping purchasing systems across its many divisions.

E-procurement reduces the time between order and delivery. Time savings are particularly dramatic for companies with many overseas suppliers. Adaptec, a leading supplier of computer storage, used an extranet to tie all of its Taiwanese chip suppliers together in a kind of virtual family. Now messages from Adaptec flow in seconds from its headquarters to its Asian partners, and Adaptec has reduced the time between the order and delivery of its chips from as long as 16 weeks to just 55 days—the same turnaround time for companies that build their own chips.

Finally, beyond the cost and time savings, e-procurement frees purchasing people to focus on more-strategic issues. For many purchasing professionals, going online means reducing drudgery

Online purchasing—or e-procurement: Public trading exchanges like the auto industry's Covisint exchange, offer "a faster, more efficient way to communicate, collaborate, buy, sell, trade, and exchange information—business to business." The exchange handled more than $50 billion in auto-parts orders last year.

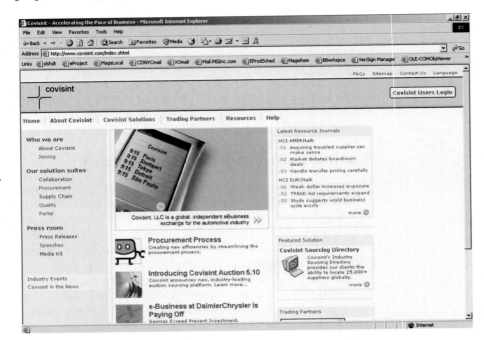

and paperwork and spending more time managing inventory and working creatively with suppliers. "That is the key," says the H-P executive. "You can now focus people on value-added activities. Procurement professionals can now find different sources and work with suppliers to reduce costs and to develop new products."

The rapidly expanding use of e-purchasing, however, also presents some problems. For example, at the same time that the Web makes it possible for suppliers and customers to share business data and even collaborate on product design, it can also erode decades-old customer-supplier relationships. Many firms are using the Web to search for better suppliers. Japan Airlines (JAL) has used the Internet to post orders for in-flight materials such as plastic cups. On its Web site it posts drawings and specifications that will attract proposals from any firm that comes across the site, rather than from just the usual Japanese suppliers.

E-purchasing can also create potential security disasters. More than 80 percent of companies say security is the leading barrier to expanding electronic links with customers and partners. Although e-mail and home banking transactions can be protected through basic encryption, the secure environment that businesses need to carry out confidential interactions is still lacking. Companies are spending millions for research on defensive strategies to keep hackers at bay. Cisco Systems, for example, specifies the types of routers, firewalls, and security procedures that its partners must use to safeguard extranet connections. In fact, the company goes even further—it sends its own security engineers to examine a partner's defenses and holds the partner liable for any security breach that originates from its computer.

Institutional and Government Markets

So far, our discussion of organizational buying has focused largely on the buying behavior of business buyers. Much of this discussion also applies to the buying practices of institutional and government organizations. However, these two nonbusiness markets have additional characteristics and needs. In this final section, we address the special features of institutional and government markets.

Institutional market

Schools, hospitals, nursing homes, prisons, and other institutions that provide goods and services to people in their care.

Institutional Markets

The **institutional market** consists of schools, hospitals, nursing homes, prisons, and other institutions that provide goods and services to people in their care. Institutions differ from one another in their sponsors and in their objectives. For example, Humana hospitals are run for profit, whereas a not-for-profit Sisters of Charity Hospital provides health care to the poor, and a government-run hospital might provide special services to veterans.

Many institutional markets are characterized by low budgets and captive patrons. For example, hospital patients have little choice but to eat whatever food the hospital supplies. A hospital purchasing agent has to decide on the quality of food to buy for patients. Because the food is provided as a part of a total service package, the buying objective is not profit. Nor is strict cost minimization the goal—patients receiving poor-quality food will complain to others and damage the hospital's reputation. Thus, the hospital purchasing agent must search for institutional-food vendors whose quality meets or exceeds a certain minimum standard and whose prices are low.

Many marketers set up separate divisions to meet the special characteristics and needs of institutional buyers. For example, Heinz produces, packages, and prices its ketchup and other products differently to better serve the requirements of hospitals, colleges, and other institutional markets.

Government Markets

Government market
Governmental units—federal, state, and local—that purchase or rent goods and services for carrying out the main functions of government.

The **government market** offers large opportunities for many companies, both big and small. In most countries, government organizations are major buyers of goods and services. In the United States alone, federal, state, and local governments contain more than 82,000 buying units. Government buying and business buying are similar in many ways. But there are also differences that must be understood by companies that wish to sell products and services to governments. To succeed in the government market, sellers must locate key decision makers, identify the factors that affect buyer behavior, and understand the buying-decision process.

Government organizations typically require suppliers to submit bids, and normally they award the contract to the lowest bidder. In some cases, the government unit will make allowance for the supplier's superior quality or reputation for completing contracts on time. Governments will also buy on a negotiated contract basis, primarily in the case of complex projects involving major R&D costs and risks, and in cases where there is little competition.

Government organizations tend to favor domestic suppliers over foreign suppliers. A major complaint of multinationals operating in Europe is that each country shows favoritism toward its nationals in spite of superior offers that are made by foreign firms. The European Economic Commission is gradually removing this bias.

Like consumer and business buyers, government buyers are affected by environmental, organizational, interpersonal, and individual factors. One unique thing about government buying is that it is carefully watched by outside publics, ranging from Congress to a variety of private groups interested in how the government spends taxpayers' money. Because their spending decisions are subject to public review, government organizations require considerable paperwork from suppliers, who often complain about excessive paperwork, bureaucracy, regulations, decision-making delays, and frequent shifts in procurement personnel. Given all the red tape, why would any firm want to do business with the U.S. government? Here's how a consultant who has helped clients obtain more than $30 billion in government contracts answers that question:

> When I hear that question, I tell the story of the businessman who buys a hardware store after moving to a small town. He asks his new employees who the biggest hardware customer in town is. He is surprised to learn that the customer isn't doing business with his store. When the owner asks why not, his employees say the customer is difficult to do business with and requires that a lot of forms be filled out. I point out that the same customer is probably very wealthy, doesn't bounce his checks, and usually does repeat business when satisfied. That's the type of customer the federal government can be.[14]

Most governments provide would-be suppliers with detailed guides describing how to sell to the government. For example, the U.S. Small Business Administration prints a booklet entitled *U.S. Government Purchasing, Specifications, and Sales Directory,* which lists thousands of items most frequently purchased by the government and the specific agencies most frequently buying them. The Government Printing Office issues the *Commerce Business Daily,* which lists major current and planned purchases and recent contract awards, both of which can provide leads to subcontracting markets. The U.S. Commerce Department publishes *Business America,* which provides interpretations of government policies and programs and gives concise information on potential worldwide trade opportunities. In several major cities, the General Services Administration operates *Business*

Service Centers with staffs to provide a complete education on the way government agencies buy, the steps that suppliers should follow, and the procurement opportunities available. Various trade magazines and associations provide information on how to reach schools, hospitals, highway departments, and other government agencies. And almost all of these government organizations and associations maintain Internet sites offering up-to-date information and advice.

Still, suppliers have to master the system and find ways to cut through the red tape. For example, the U.S. government has always been ADI Technology Corporation's most important client—federal contracts account for about 90 percent of its nearly $6 million in annual revenues. Yet managers at this small professional services company often shake their heads at all the work that goes into winning the coveted government contracts. A comprehensive bid proposal will run from 500 to 700 pages because of federal paperwork requirements. And the company's president estimates that the firm has spent as much as $20,000, mostly in worker hours, to prepare a single bid proposal. Fortunately, government buying reforms are being put in place that will simplify contracting procedures and make bidding more attractive, particularly to smaller vendors. These reforms include more emphasis on buying commercial off-the-shelf items instead of items built to the government's specs, online communication with vendors to eliminate the massive paperwork, and a "debriefing" from the appropriate government agency for vendors who lose a bid, enabling them to increase their chances of winning the next time around.[15]

Noneconomic criteria also play a growing role in government buying. Government buyers are asked to favor depressed business firms and areas; small business firms; minority-owned firms; and business firms that avoid race, sex, or age discrimination. Sellers need to keep these factors in mind when deciding to seek government business.

Many companies that sell to the government have not been marketing oriented for a number of reasons. Total government spending is determined by elected officials rather than by any mar-

The Federal government's buying has gone online. The GSA's Advantage! Web site and the DLA's Procurement Gateway allow authorized defense and civilian agencies to buy everything from medical and office supplies to clothing through online purchasing.

keting effort to develop this market. Government buying has emphasized price, making suppliers invest their effort in technology to bring costs down. When the product's characteristics are specified carefully, product differentiation is not a marketing factor. Nor do advertising or personal selling matter much in winning bids on an open-bid basis.

Several companies, however, have established separate government marketing departments. Rockwell, Kodak, and Goodyear are examples. These companies anticipate government needs and projects, participate in the product specification phase, gather competitive intelligence, prepare bids carefully, and produce stronger communications to describe and enhance their companies' reputations. Other companies have set up customized marketing programs for government buyers. For example, Dell Computer has specific business units tailored to meet the needs of federal as well as state and local government buyers. Dell offers its customers tailor-made Web pages that include special pricing, online purchasing, and service and support for each city, state, and federal government entity.[16]

During the past decade, some of the government's buying has gone online. For example, *Commerce Business Daily* is now online with its FedBizOpps/CBD site (http://cbd.cos.com). And the two federal agencies that act as purchasing agents for the rest of government have launched Web sites providing online access to government purchasing activity. The General Services Administration has set up a GSA Advantage! Web site (www.gsa.gov), and the Defense Logistics Agency (www.dla.mil) offers a Procurement Gateway. Such sites allow authorized defense and civilian agencies to buy everything from medical and office supplies to clothing through online purchasing. The GSA and DLA not only sell stocked merchandise through their Web sites but also create direct links between buyers and contract suppliers. For example, the branch of the DSA that sells 160,000 types of medical supplies to military forces transmits orders directly to vendors such as Bristol-Myers. Such Internet systems promise to eliminate much of the hassle sometimes found in dealing with government purchasing.[17]

LOOKING BACK: REVIEWING THE CONCEPTS

Business markets and consumer markets are alike in some key ways. For example, both include people in buying roles who make purchase decisions to satisfy needs. But business markets also differ in many ways from consumer markets. For one thing, the business market is *enormous,* far larger than the consumer market. Within the United States alone, the business market includes organizations that annually purchase trillions of dollars' worth of goods and services.

1. Define the business market and explain how business markets differ from consumer markets.

Business buyer behavior refers to the buying behavior of the organizations that buy goods and services for use in the production of other products and services that are sold, rented, or supplied to others. It also includes the behavior of retailing and wholesaling firms that acquire goods for the purpose of reselling or renting them to others at a profit. As compared to consumer markets, business markets usually have fewer, larger buyers who are more geographically concentrated. Business demand is *derived,* largely *inelastic,* and more *fluctuating.* More buyers are usually involved in the business buying decision, and business buyers are better trained and more professional than are consumer buyers. In general, business purchasing decisions are more complex, and the buying process is more formal than consumer buying.

2. Identify the major factors that influence business buyer behavior.

Business buyers make decisions that vary with the three types of buying situations: *straight rebuys, modified rebuys,* and *new*

tasks. The buying center, which can consist of many different persons playing many different roles, is the decision-making unit of a buying organization. The business marketer needs to know the following: Who are the major participants? In what decisions do they exercise influence? What is their relative degree of influence? What evaluation criteria does each decision participant use? The business marketer also needs to understand the major environmental, organizational, interpersonal, and individual influences on the buying process.

3. List and define the steps in the business buying-decision process.

The business buying-decision process itself can be quite involved, with eight basic stages: (1) *problem recognition,* someone in the company recognizes a problem or need that can be met by acquiring a product or service; (2) *general need description,* the company determines the general characteristics and quantity of the needed item; (3) *product specification,* the buying organization decides on and specifies the best technical product characteristics for the needed item; (4) *supplier search,* the buyer seeks the best vendors; (5) *proposal solicitation,* the buyer invites qualified suppliers to submit proposals; (6) *supplier selection,* the buyer reviews proposals and selects a supplier or suppliers; (7) *order-routine specification,* the buyer writes the final order with the chosen supplier(s), listing the technical specifications, quantity needed, expected time of delivery, return policies, and warranties; and (8) *performance review,* the buyer rates its satisfaction with suppliers, deciding whether to continue, modify, or cancel them.

4. Compare the institutional and government markets and explain how institutional and government buyers make their buying decisions.

The *institutional market* comprises schools, hospitals, prisons, and other institutions that provide goods and services to people in their care. These markets are characterized by low budgets and captive patrons. The *government market,* which is vast, consists of government units—federal, state, and local—that purchase or rent goods and services for carrying out the main functions of government. Government buyers purchase products and services for defense, education, public welfare, and other public needs. Government buying practices are highly specialized and specified, with open bidding or negotiated contracts characterizing most of the buying. Government buyers operate under the watchful eye of Congress and many private watchdog groups. Hence, they tend to require more forms and signatures, and to respond more slowly and deliberately when placing orders.

REVIEWING THE KEY TERMS

Business buyer behavior 214
Business buying process 214
Buyers 220
Buying center 220
Deciders 220
Derived demand 215
Gatekeepers 220
General need description 225

Government market 229
Influencers 220
Institutional market 228
Modified rebuy 219
New task 219
Order-routine specification 226
Performance review 226
Problem recognition 224

Product specification 225
Proposal solicitation 225
Straight rebuy 219
Supplier search 225
Supplier selection 225
Systems selling 219
Users 220
Value analysis 225

DISCUSSING THE CONCEPTS

1. Although business markets are similar in many ways to consumer markets, there are significant differences. What similarities and differences might Staples (www.staples.com) or Office Depot (www.officedepot.com) encounter in selling to the business market versus the consumer market for the following products: (a) a personal computer, (b) paper for a computer or photocopier, (c) a desk chair, and (d) paper clips?

2. Review Table 7.1 and create an example that illustrates the types of decisions facing business buyers and the decision process they use.

3. Compare Figure 6.1 (in the previous chapter) to Figure 7.1. What similarities and differences do you find in inputs and outputs for these two buying models? Comment on them.

4. Which of the major types of buying situations is represented by each of the following: (a) Dell's purchase of the latest Intel chip to increase its PCs processing speed, (b) IBM's purchase of batteries for its line of portable computers, and (c) Hewlett-Packard's purchase of speaker wire for its standard mini-speakers that accompany all of its PCs.

5. Systems selling is a key business marketing strategy for winning and holding accounts. Why?

6. Your company sells standard telephone handsets. You have just been assigned the task of winning the sales account at your former undergraduate university. Although your contacts at the university should make the sale easier, the university relies on a buying center for all major purchases. Considering the roles and needs of the members of a buying center at the university, design a plan for winning the sales account.

7. List and briefly describe the eight stages in the business buying process Create an example that demonstrates how a business buyer might move through this process.

8. Business buying on the Internet has increased dramatically in the past few years. Why? What are the benefits of e-procurement? What are the drawbacks? Give an example of a product that is likely to be offered at a reverse auction.

APPLYING THE CONCEPTS

1. Many companies now use suppliers to produce raw materials or parts instead of producing these components themselves. In the extreme, companies such as Dell Computer own no production facilities and have suppliers make everything to order. This type of company has been nicknamed a "virtual corporation."
   a. Do you think buyers and suppliers are likely to be more cooperative or more adversarial in this type of corporate structure?
   b. List the advantages and disadvantages this sort of supplier relationship has for both the buyer and the supplier.
   c. Explain how the supplier search process might work in the Dell "virtual corporation."
   d. Go to the Dell Web site at www.dell.com and review the information on the company. What can you determine about the sources of "outside" parts contained in a Dell computer—for example, the processor, monitor, or CPU itself? Do buyers know which components are original Dell parts and which are not? Would this be of concern to potential buyers?
   e. Since Dell purchases outside parts for its computers, what do you think would be the most important considerations in supplier selection? Explain.

2. Performance review is one of the most critical stages in a business buying process. Perhaps nowhere is this more important than in the highly competitive aircraft manufacturing business. Whether the planes are large or small, once a purchase is made the buyer enters a long-term relationship with the manufacturer for service and parts requirements. Boeing is working to expand its supplier base. Historically, Boeing has produced parts internally or outsourced domestically. Today, Boeing gets product designs from Moscow, tail sections from central China, aircraft doors from Poland, and fuselage-insulation blankets from Mexico. Although this global outsourcing offers tremendous savings, it can also result in significant problems when not well managed.

a. What complications can occur in the performance review process for foreign suppliers?
b. What problems could Boeing face as it expands its global outsourcing?
c. Besides potential cost advantages, why would Boeing consider global outsourcing?
d. JAL, the huge Japanese airline, represents a substantial account for any aircraft manufacturer. What relationships should Boeing build to secure a long-term contract with JAL? Considering the Japanese affinity for high-class quality control, what role could performance review play in winning the JAL account?

 ## DIGITAL CONNECTIONS

CONNECTING BUSINESS CUSTOMERS WITH VALUABLE INFORMATION

The right knowledge at the right time is a key component of successful business-to-business commerce. Costs of data acquisition are steadily increasing and many companies continue to spend huge sums to secure marketing intelligence and build databases of suppliers and customers. But there are less expensive alternatives. *Business to Business Magazine* provides business buyers with an excellent, inexpensive information resource service. The magazine offers a series links to resource sites and Web service networks. *Business to Business Magazine* offers simplified data acquisition for registered business buyers and suppliers. By registering, users supply company data that expands the magazine's network for future inquiries. This circle of knowledge benefits both the companies and the magazine while addressing the complex problem of information acquisition.

FOR DISCUSSION

1. Go to the *Business to Business Magazine* Web site at www.business2business.on.ca. What services does the magazine offer customers? How might a company searching for suppliers benefit from those services? Which services are free?
2. Follow the Resources link to learn what types of resources are available for the business user. Which of the resource links would be most interesting to the purchasing manager in a firm? To a firm's buying center?
3. Follow the links to the Media Kit/Demographics. How is *Business to Business Magazine* attempting to use the Web to expand the information acquisition process? What do you think of the plan?
4. Pick one of the resource links and research a business-to-business subject. Critique the experience. Suggest ways to improve the process.

Whereoware: Connecting Sellers to Business Buyers

Ben Johns founded Whereoware with the goal of providing a place for businesses in the fragmented home-accents, gifts, and collectibles industry to come together outside of annual trade shows. Today the company administers the leading business-to-business e-commerce site for the industry, offering small retailers access to hundreds of supplier catalogs and more than 165,000 products year round. In addition, the site offers information on recent industry trends. By electronically connecting buyers, sellers, and sales reps, Whereoware streamlines the buying process and reduces order transaction costs by as much as 50 percent.

After reviewing the Whereoware video, answer the following questions about business-to-business marketing:

1. Whereoware caters to the small retailers that represent the majority of the gifts and collectibles industry. How does the Web site offer value to these buyers? Considering the nature of gifts and collectibles merchandise, what drawbacks might be associated with e-procurement?
2. How does Whereoware affect a buyer's supplier search and selection process? How might it affect the long-term buyer–supplier relationships between producer, wholesaler, and retailer?
3. Visit the Whereoware Web site at www.whereoware.com and browse through the information on supplier services. What concerns might a manufacturer selling goods through Whereoware.com have about the services offered? Would the benefits highlighted outweigh those concerns?

company case

Emerson Process Management: Accelerating on the Internet

If you were selling automation products for manufacturing plants, the 1970s were a wonderful time—sales were booming. By 2000, however, the market had changed. Sales had slowed and purchasers were beginning to think of automation products as commodities. So many buyers were using fewer suppliers.

That was the situation that the Fisher-Rosemount division of Emerson Electric faced. How could it attract the interest and attention of industrial purchasers for services that helped buyers optimize their plants and processes? Such decisions are made infrequently and can involve big money, ranging from $25,000 to $25,000,000. How could Fisher-Rosemount demonstrate in an engaging and dynamic way the benefits of reworking processes in customers' existing plants? How could the company *show* what its services could accomplish?

Fisher-Rosemount tackled this situation by first repositioning its services. By looking at the relevant purchase processes from the customer's point of view, it realized that customers were not looking for individual products that they had to assemble themselves, *if* they had the needed in-house expertise. Instead, they were looking for complete *solutions*. Competitors—especially software vendors—had already realized this. Seeking to capitalize on their own expertise, the competitors had assembled product portfolios that included everything from PC-based process control solutions to supply chain management solutions. However, although Fisher-Rosemount's repositioning strategy was similar to that of other industry suppliers, the company had the advantage of being part of a much larger organization.

Emerson Electric was founded in 1890 in St. Louis, Missouri, to manufacture reliable electric motors. By 1892, it was selling the first electric fans in the United States, still one of its major lines. Over the years, however, Emerson Electric has benefited from stable management and consistent growth in its product and service lines. Today, it has over 60 divisions selling a variety of products from fans to process solutions, from to refrigeration and air-conditioning technologies to tools for do-it-yourselfers and professionals, from plastics joining and cleaning compounds to world-class engineering and consulting services. In 2000, Emerson reported sales of $15.5 billion—a 9 percent increase from the previous year. The company also reported increased earnings for the forty-third year and increased dividends for the forty-fourth year in a row. To achieve such an enviable record, Emerson stresses increased growth—particularly in global markets—and innovation.

One way Emerson stays ahead of the competition is through heavy use of the Internet. It has over 115 e-business projects under way. In 2000, it transacted 10 percent of its sales (that's $1.55 billion) online and 70 percent of its 60-plus divisions had Web projects up and running.

The Internet provides a good channel for selling technical products. A survey of industrial users of the Internet indicated that much of the industry (85 percent) has access to the Internet, and that engineers are among early adopters and frequent users of the Net. They use the Internet primarily to gather information, but given the lack of relevant information found there, they spend only up to three hours a week on the Net. Therefore, it appears that supplier companies can best increase the value of the Internet in selling their services by providing more detailed information about products and services.

The folks at Fisher-Rosemount must have seen this report, because they chose to develop an information-packed site called ThePlantWeb (www.plantweb.com). The home page of this Web site provides visitors with information on ThePlantWeb. Right away, visitors learn how they can understand today's technologies better, access information more quickly, reduce costs, and increase revenues. They can do this by taking advantage of PlantWeb University, which provides short business courses on how to improve plant profitability, and engineering courses in which they can explore leading automation technologies. The page also provides short "testimonial-descriptions" of companies that have recently used ThePlantWeb to improve their operations. Visitors who want more information than that provided by the short testimonials can call up longer case studies for information. ThePlantWeb News provides recent examples of new users of ThePlantWeb services and gives a chronological listing for the last five years of successful applications of its services.

What is most interesting, engaging, and unusual about this Web site is a feature called TestDrivePlantWeb. In the test drive, visitors can *see* how much PlantWeb architecture can reduce capital expenditures compared to traditional DCS (Distributed Control Systems) architecture. What does that mean? Assume that you are a manager of a pulp and paper plant. Visit the Web site, go to the TestDrivePlantWeb page, and click on one of the industries listed on the left side of the page. Click on Pulp & Paper, then continue with the test drive, and you'll get a diagram showing all the processes in the pulp and paper industry, from waste treatment through papermaking, recovery, bleaching, and pulping. By using the various buttons, such as Customize Areas and Design Cost Assumptions, you can input data for your plant. All the while, the site provides an estimate of how much you can save using process management from Fisher-Rosemount. In addition to a summary of savings, you'll received information detailing how you would achieve those savings. Can't you just imagine engineers inputting various data to see how much they could save? In fact, the site has proven very effective in attracting new customers. No doubt that's why TestDrivePlantWeb has won several awards.

What is PlantWeb? According to the Web site, it's a revolutionary field-based architecture that changes the economics of process automation. TestDrivePlantWeb allows you to build your own virtual plant to evaluate the economics of process automation. It employs an easy-to-use, drag-and-drop interface that allows users to customize models by adding or deleting process areas, units, or devices or by adjusting variables such as labor rates and average wire run. The effects are shown immediately in the summary. Specific benefits of retrofitting your old plant with automation from Fisher-Rosemount include reduced process variability, increased plant availability, reduced capital and engineering costs, reduced operations and maintenance costs, and streamlined regulatory compliance.

In 2001, as part of its corporate repositioning strategy, Emerson Electric renamed the Fisher-Rosemount division, calling it the Emerson Process Management division. The goal was to enhance the overall corporate brand and to provide insight into the division's services. The repositioning also involved the integration of Fisher-Rosemount with other services in Emerson Electric, such as Emerson Performance Solutions, in order to provide complete solutions to purchasers.

Emerson Process Management does not rely only on the Internet to sell its services. To promote ThePlantWeb, it hired 50 sales reps (dubbed "PlantWeb Champs") and trained them on Internet technology. To support their efforts, it used print advertising and direct marketing to reach prospects that it calls "technical evangelists." The print ads used brilliant colors and images that contrasted old and new technology—for example, a weather vane and a weather satellite. These ads stood out amid the wordy competitor ads surrounding them. Emerson also used the TestDrivePlantWeb site to collect names of prospects and their affiliations. It then sent direct mail to higher-level executives in each organization. The idea was to intrigue the "technical evangelist's" supervisor, who was more likely to be involved in the purchase decision. Perhaps they would meet in the hallway, and the technical evangelist, who was excited from taking a "test drive" on ThePlantWeb, would exchange information with the supervisor who had questions about costs.

Such simple hallway conversations can be the beginning of a process that takes months to complete. During that time, Emerson sends prospects promotional materials and invitations to seminars to keep their interest from flagging. If all of those marketing efforts are not enough, PlantWeb has a guarantee that the purchaser will reduce total installed cost using PlantWeb automation solutions as compared to traditional DCS architectures.

Does this work? You decide. In the first 18 months that TestDrivePlantWeb was up, Emerson identified 65,000 unique visitors to the site, and that translated into 850 installations of ThePlantWeb product.

QUESTIONS FOR DISCUSSION

1. What type of purchase decision is involved in buying solutions to a company's process systems from Emerson Process Management (Fisher-Rosemount)?

2. Who might participate in the buying process? How can ThePlantWeb and the associated marketing campaign impact each of the buying-decision participants?

3. How can ThePlantWeb and the associated marketing campaign affect each stage in the business buying process?

4. What purpose do the testimonials, case studies, and PlantWeb Guarantee serve?

5. Is promotion and selling on the Internet a wise decision for Emerson Process Management? Why or why not? What are the advantages of using the Internet compared with using only personal selling and advertising? The disadvantages?

6. In your opinion, is Emerson wise to reposition itself by branding all of its divisions with the Emerson name? Why would this be beneficial in selling to business markets? How might it be a disadvantage?

Sources: "Briefly Noted," *Mechanical Engineering,* May 1999, p. 24; David Lewis, "Emerson's Web Rollouts to Keep Earnings Rolling Too," *Internet Week,* November 13, 2000, p. 118+; Kevin Parker, "Fisher-Rosemount Out, Solutions Selling In," *Manufacturing Systems,* June 2001, p. 12+; Weld Royal, "Web Marketing's New Wave," *Industry Week,* November 6, 2000, pp. 29–32; George Short, "Information Engineering," *Plant Engineering,* June 1999, p. 54+; plus information from the Emerson and PlantWeb Web sites.

1. define the three steps of target marketing: market segmentation, target marketing, and market positioning
2. list and discuss the major bases for segmenting consumer and business markets
3. explain how companies identify attractive market segments and choose a target marketing strategy
4. discuss how companies position their products for maximum competitive advantage in the marketplace

Segmentation, Targeting, and Positioning

BUILDING THE RIGHT RELATIONSHIPS WITH THE RIGHT CUSTOMERS

LOOKING AHEAD: PREVIEWING THE CONCEPTS

So far, you've learned what marketing is and about the complex environments in which marketing operates. With that as background, you're now ready to delve more deeply into marketing strategy and tactics. This chapter looks further into key marketing strategy decisions—how to divide up markets into meaningful customer groups (market segmentation), choose which customer groups to serve (target marketing), and create marketing offers that best serve targeted customers (positioning). Then, the chapters that follow explore in depth the tactical marketing tools—the *4Ps*—by which marketers bring these strategies to life.

As an opening example of segmentation, targeting, and position at work, let's look first at Procter & Gamble, one of the world's premier consumer goods companies. Some 99 percent of all U.S. households use at least one of P&G's more than 300 brands, and the typical household regularly buys and uses from one to two *dozen* P&G brands. How many P&G products can you name? Why does this superb marketer compete with itself on supermarket shelves by marketing seven different brands of laundry detergent? The P&G story provides a great example of how smart marketers use segmentation, targeting, and positioning.

Procter & Gamble (P&G) sells seven brands of laundry detergent in the United States (Tide, Cheer, Bold, Gain, Era, Dreft, Febreze, and Ivory Snow). It also sells six brands of hand soap (Ivory, Safeguard, Camay, Olay, Zest, and Old Spice); five brands of shampoo (Pantene, Head & Shoulders, Pert, Physique, and Vidal Sassoon); four brands of dishwashing detergent (Dawn, Ivory, Joy, and Cascade); three brands each of tissues and towels (Charmin, Bounty, Puffs), and deodorant (Secret, Sure, and Old Spice); and two brands each of fabric softener (Downy and Bounce), cosmetics (Cover Girl and Max Factor), skin care potions (Olay and Noxema), and disposable diapers (Pampers and Luvs). Moreover, P&G has many additional brands in each category for different international markets. For example, it sells 16 different laundry product brands in Latin America and 19 in Europe, the Middle East, and Africa. (See Procter & Gamble's Web site at www.pg.com for a full glimpse of the company's impressive lineup of familiar brands.)

These P&G brands compete with one another on the same supermarket shelves. But why would P&G introduce several brands in one category instead of concentrating its resources on a single leading brand? The answer lies in the fact that different people want different *mixes of benefits* from the products they buy. Take laundry detergents as an example. People use laundry detergents to get their clothes clean. But they also want other things from their detergents—such as economy, bleaching power, fabric softening, fresh smell, strength or mildness, and lots of suds or only a few. We all want *some* of every one of these benefits from our detergent, but we may have different *priorities* for each benefit. To some people, cleaning and bleaching power are most important; to others, fabric softening matters most; still others want a mild, fresh-scented detergent. Thus, there are groups—or segments—of laundry detergent buyers, and each segment seeks a special combination of benefits.

Procter & Gamble has identified at least seven important laundry detergent segments, along with numerous subsegments, and has developed a different brand designed to meet the special needs of each. The seven brands are positioned for different segments as follows:

- *Tide* provides "fabric cleaning and care at its best." It's the all-purpose family detergent that is "tough on greasy stains."
- *Cheer* is the "color expert." It helps protect against fading, color transfer, and fabric wear, with or without bleach. *Cheer Free* is "dermatologist tested . . . contains no irritating perfume or dye."
- *Bold* is the detergent with built-in fabric softener and pill/fuzz removal.

- *Gain*, originally P&G's "enzyme" detergent, was repositioned as the detergent that gives you clean, fresh-smelling clothes. It "cleans and freshens like sunshine. Great cleaning power and a smell that stays clean."

- *Era* is "the power tool for stain removal and pretreating." It contains advanced enzymes to fight a family's tough stains and help get the whole wash clean. *Era Max* has three types of active enzymes to help fight many stains that active families encounter.

- *Ivory Snow* is "Ninety-nine and forty-four one hundredths percent pure." It provides "mild cleansing benefits for a pure and simple clean."

- *Dreft* also "helps remove tough baby stains . . . for a clean you can trust." It's "pediatrician recommended and the first choice of mothers." It "doesn't remove the flame resistance of children's sleepwear."

Within each segment, Procter & Gamble has identified even *narrower* niches. For example, you can buy regular Tide (in powder or liquid form) or any of several formulations:

- *Tide with Bleach* helps to "keep your whites white and your colors bright." Available in regular or "mountain spring" scents.

- *Tide Liquid with Bleach Alternative* uses active enzymes in pretreating and washing to break down and remove the toughest stains while whitening whites.

- *Tide High Efficiency* "unlocks the cleaning power of high-efficiency top-loading machines"—it prevents oversudsing.

- *Tide Clean Breeze* gives the fresh scent of laundry line-dried in a clean breeze.

- *Tide Mountain Spring* lets you "bring the fresh clean scent of the great outdoors inside—the scent of crisp mountain air and fresh wildflowers."

- *Tide Free* "provides all the stain removal benefits without any dyes or perfumes."

- *Tide Rapid Action Tablets* are portable and powerful. It's Tide "all concentrated into a little blue and white tablet that fits into your pocket."

By segmenting the market and having several detergent brands, Procter & Gamble has an attractive offering for consumers in all important preference groups. As a result, P&G is really cleaning up in the $4 billion U.S. laundry detergent market. Tide, by itself, captures a whopping 38 percent market share. All P&G brands combined take a 57 percent share of the market—three times that of nearest rival Unilever and much more than any single brand could obtain by itself.[1]

Companies today recognize that they cannot appeal to all buyers in the marketplace, or at least not to all buyers in the same way. Buyers are too numerous, too widely scattered, and too varied in their needs and buying practices. Moreover, the companies themselves vary widely in their abilities to serve different segments of the market. Rather than trying to compete in an entire market, sometimes against superior competitors, each company must identify the parts of the market that it can serve best and most profitably.

Thus, most companies are being more choosy about the customers with whom they wish to build relationships. Most have moved away from mass marketing and toward *market segmentation and targeting*—identifying market segments, selecting one or more of them, and developing products and marketing programs tailored to each. Instead of scattering their marketing efforts (the "shotgun" approach), firms are focusing on the buyers who have greater interest in the values they create best (the "rifle" approach).

Companies have not always practiced market segmentation and targeting. For most of the past century, major consumer products companies held fast to *mass marketing*—mass-producing, mass-distributing, and mass-promoting about the same product in about the same way to all consumers. Henry Ford typified this marketing strategy when he offered the Model T Ford to all buyers; they could have the car "in any color as long as it is black." Similarly, Coca-Cola at one time produced only one drink for the whole market, hoping it would appeal to everyone.

These companies argued that mass marketing creates the largest potential market, which leads to the lowest costs. This, in turn, can translate into either lower prices or higher margins. However, many factors now make mass marketing more difficult. For example, the world's mass markets have slowly splintered into a profusion of smaller segments—the baby boomers here, the Gen Xers there; here the Hispanic segment, there the African American segment; here working women, there single parents; here the Sun Belt, there the Rust Belt. Today, marketers find it very hard to create a single product or program that appeals to all of these diverse groups.

The proliferation of distribution channels and advertising media has also made it difficult to practice "one-size-fits-all" marketing. Today's consumers can shop at megamalls, superstores, or specialty shops; through mail catalogs, by telephone, or from online retailers. They are bombarded with messages in media ranging from old standards such as television, radio, magazines,

FIGURE 8.1
Steps in market segmentation, targeting, and positioning

newspapers, and telephone to newcomers such as Web ads, faxes, and e-mails. No wonder some have claimed that mass marketing is dying. Not surprisingly, many companies are retreating from mass marketing and turning to segmented marketing.

Figure 8.1 shows the three major steps in target marketing. The first is **market segmentation**—dividing a market into smaller groups of buyers with distinct needs, characteristics, or behaviors who might require separate products or marketing mixes. The company identifies different ways to segment the market and develops profiles of the resulting market segments. The second step is **target marketing**—evaluating each market segment's attractiveness and selecting one or more of the market segments to enter. The third step is **market positioning**—setting the competitive positioning for the product and creating a detailed marketing mix. We discuss each of these steps in turn.

Market segmentation

Dividing a market into distinct groups with distinct needs, characteristics, or behavior who might require separate products or marketing mixes.

Market Segmentation

Target marketing

The process of evaluating each market segment's attractiveness and selecting one or more segments to enter.

Market positioning

Arranging for a product to occupy a clear, distinctive, and desirable place relative to competing products in the minds of target consumers.

Markets consist of buyers, and buyers differ in one or more ways. They may differ in their wants, resources, locations, buying attitudes, and buying practices. Through market segmentation, companies divide large, heterogeneous markets into smaller segments that can be reached more efficiently and effectively with products and services that match their unique needs. In this section, we discuss four important segmentation topics: segmenting consumer markets, segmenting business markets, segmenting international markets, and requirements for effective segmentation.

Segmenting Consumer Markets

There is no single way to segment a market. A marketer has to try different segmentation variables, alone and in combination, to find the best way to view the market structure. Table 8.1 outlines the major variables that might be used in segmenting consumer markets. Here we look at the major *geographic, demographic, psychographic,* and *behavioral variables*.

Geographic Segmentation

Geographic segmentation

Dividing a market into different geographical units such as nations, states, regions, counties, cities, or neighborhoods.

Geographic segmentation calls for dividing the market into different geographical units such as nations, regions, states, counties, cities, or neighborhoods. A company may decide to operate in one or a few geographical areas, or to operate in all areas but pay attention to geographical differences in needs and wants.

Many companies today are localizing their products, advertising, promotion, and sales efforts to fit the needs of individual regions, cities, and even neighborhoods. For example, Campbell sells Cajun gumbo soup in Louisiana and Mississippi and makes its nacho cheese soup spicier in Texas and California. Starbucks offers more desserts and larger, more comfortable coffee shops in the South, where customers tend to arrive later in the day and stay longer. And Parker Brothers offers localized versions of its popular Monopoly game for several major cities, including Chicago, New York, San Francisco, St. Louis, and Las Vegas. The Las Vegas version features a black board with The Strip rather than Boardwalk, hotel casinos, red Vegas dice, and custom pewter tokens including blackjack cards, a wedding chapel, and a roulette wheel.[2]

Other companies are seeking to cultivate as-yet untapped geographic territory. For example, many large companies are fleeing the fiercely competitive major cities and suburbs to set up shop in small-town America. Hampton Inns has opened a chain of smaller-format motels in towns too small for its standard-size units. For example, Townsend, Tennessee, with a population of only 329, is small even by small-town standards. But looks can be deceiving. Situated on a heavily traveled and picturesque route between Knoxville and the Smoky Mountains, the village serves both business and vacation travelers. Hampton Inns opened a unit in Townsend and

TABLE 8.1	MAJOR SEGMENTATION VARIABLES FOR CONSUMER MARKETS

Geographic

World region or country	North America, Western Europe, Middle East, Pacific Rim, China, India, Canada, Mexico
Country region	Pacific, Mountain, West North Central, West South Central, East North Central, East South Central, South Atlantic, Middle Atlantic, New England
City or metro size	Under 5,000; 5,000–20,000, 20,000–50,000, 50,000–100,000; 100,000–250,000; 250,000–500,000; 500,000–1,000,000; 1,000,000–4,000,000; 4,000,000 or over
Density	Urban, suburban, rural
Climate	Northern, southern

Demographic

Age	Under 6, 6–11, 12–19, 20–34, 35–49, 50–64, 65+
Gender	Male, female
Family size	1–2, 3–4, 5+
Family life-cycle	Young, single; young, married, no children; young, married with children; older, married with children; older, married, no children under 18; older, single; other
Income	Under $10,000; $10,000–$20,000; $20,000–$30,000; $30,000–$50,000; $50,000–$100,000; $100,000 and over
Occupation	Professional and technical; managers, officials, and proprietors; clerical; sales; craftspeople; supervisors; operatives; farmers; retired; students; homemakers; unemployed
Education	Grade school or less; some high school; high school graduate; some college; college graduate
Religion	Catholic, Protestant, Jewish, Muslim, Hindu, other
Race	Asian, Hispanic, black, white
Generation	Baby boomer, Generation X, Generation Y
Nationality	North American, South American, British, French, German, Italian, Japanese

Psychographic

Social class	Lower lowers, upper lowers, working class, middle class, upper middles, lower uppers, upper uppers
Lifestyle	Achievers, strivers, strugglers
Personality	Compulsive, gregarious, authoritarian, ambitious

Behavioral

Occasions	Regular occasion; special occasion
Benefits	Quality, service, economy, convenience, speed
User status	Nonuser, ex-user, potential user, first-time user, regular user
User rates	Light user, medium user, heavy user
Loyalty status	None, medium, strong, absolute
Readiness stage	Unaware, aware, informed, interested, desirous, intending to buy
Attitude toward product	Enthusiastic, positive, indifferent, negative, hostile

plans to open 100 more in small towns. It costs less to operate in these towns, and the company builds smaller units to match lower volume. The Townsend Hampton Inn, for example, has 54 rooms instead of the usual 135.

In contrast, other retailers are developing new store concepts that will give them access to higher-density urban areas. For example, Home Depot is introducing neighborhood stores that look a lot like its traditional stores but at about two-thirds the size. It is placing these stores in high-density markets where full-size stores are impractical. Similarly, Wal-Mart is testing Neighborhood Market grocery stores to complement its supercenters.[3]

Demographic Segmentation

Demographic segmentation
Dividing the market into groups based on demographic variables such as age, gender, family size, family life cycle, income, occupation, education, religion, race, generation, and nationality.

Demographic segmentation divides the market into groups based on variables such as age, gender, family size, family life cycle, income, occupation, education, religion, race, generation, and nationality. Demographic factors are the most popular bases for segmenting customer groups.

One reason is that consumer needs, wants, and usage rates often vary closely with demographic variables. Another is that demographic variables are easier to measure than most other types of variables. Even when market segments are first defined using other bases, such as benefits sought or behavior, their demographic characteristics must be known in order to assess the size of the target market and to reach it efficiently.

Age and life-cycle segmentation

Dividing a market into different age and life-cycle groups.

Age and Life-Cycle Stage. Consumer needs and wants change with age. Some companies use **age and life-cycle segmentation,** offering different products or using different marketing approaches for different age and life-cycle groups. For example, McDonald's targets different age groups—from children and teens to adults and seniors—with different ads and media. Its ads to teens feature dance-beat music, adventure, and fast-paced cutting from scene to scene; ads to seniors are softer and more sentimental. Procter & Gamble boldly targets its Oil of Olay ProVital moisturizing creams and lotions at women over 50 years of age—it helps to improve the elasticity and revitalize the appearance of "maturing skin."[4] And Gap has branched out to target people at different life stages. In addition to its standard line of clothing, the retailer now offers Baby Gap, Gap Kids, and Gap Maternity. Here's another example:

> In several of its stores around the country, clothing retailer Eddie Bauer places large, high-definition video screens in its storefront windows to draw in customers who might otherwise walk on by. The screens allow stores to customize in-store advertising to target different generational segments, depending on the time of day. For example, a store might post images featuring older models during the morning hours when retirees frequently shop, then change the posters to reflect the younger shopping crowd of the evening. In one initial nine-month test, sales at one location rose 56 percent from the previous nine months.[5]

Marketers must be careful to guard against stereotypes when using age and life-cycle segmentation. For example, although some 70-year-olds require wheelchairs, others play tennis. Similarly, whereas some 40-year-old couples are sending their children off to college, others are just beginning new families. Thus, age is often a poor predictor of a person's life cycle, health, work or family status, needs, and buying power. Companies marketing to mature consumers usually employ positive images and appeals. For example, ads for Olay ProVital feature attractive older spokeswomen and uplifting messages. "Many women 50 and older have told us that as they age, they feel more confident, wiser, and freer than ever before," observes Olay's marketing director. "These women are redefining beauty."[6]

Video screens in some Eddie Bauer storefront windows allow stores to customize in-store advertising to target different generational segments, depending on the time of day.

Gender segmentation
Dividing a market into different groups based on gender.

Gender.   **Gender segmentation** has long been used in clothing, cosmetics, toiletries, and magazines. For example, Procter & Gamble was among the first with Secret, a brand specially formulated for a woman's chemistry, packaged and advertised to reinforce the female image. More recently, other marketers have noticed opportunities for gender segmentation. Merrill Lynch offers a *Financial Handbook for Women Investors* for women who want to "shape up their finances." Owens Corning aimed a major advertising campaign for home insulation at women after a study showed that two-thirds of all women were involved in materials installation, with 13 percent doing it themselves. Half the women surveyed compared themselves to Bob Vila, whereas less than half compared themselves to Martha Stewart. Similarly, after its research showed that women make 90 percent of all home improvement decisions, home improvement retailer Lowe's recently launched a family-oriented advertising campaign that reaches out to women buyers.[7]

Even the National Football League and advertisers on the Super Bowl, long the holy day of testosterone, are now targeting women. The 30 million or more women who watch the average Super Bowl make up more than 36 percent of the game's audience. And advertisers know that these women influence 80 percent of all household consumer purchases. Moreover, women now account for almost half of all NFL-licensed merchandise purchases. Anheuser-Busch, the biggest advertiser in the game, actively targets its Super Bowl advertising to both genders. Whereas its competitors are still courting men with big doses of babes and sophomoric humor, A-B is showing a more sensitive side. "Women are a huge part of this audience," says A-B's vice president of brand management. "We've been working hard for five years not to do the typical guy jokes." He continues, "It's been a wonderful eye-opener for us. It's taught us that it's OK to be emotional and have a smile—not always go for the gut-laugh."[8]

A growing number of Web sites also target women. For example, Oxygen Media runs a Web site "designed for women by women" (www.oxygen.com). It appeals 18- to 34-year-old women with fresh and hip information, features, and exchanges on a wide variety of topics—from health and fitness, money and work, and style and home to relationships and self-discovery. The leading women's online community, iVillage (www.iVillage.com), offers "real solutions for real women" and entreats visitors to "join our community of smart, compassionate, real women." Various iVillage channels cover topics ranging from babies, food, fitness, pets, and relationships to

Gender segmentation: After research showed that women make 90 percent of all home improvement decisions, Lowe's launched a family oriented advertising campaign that reaches out to women buyers.

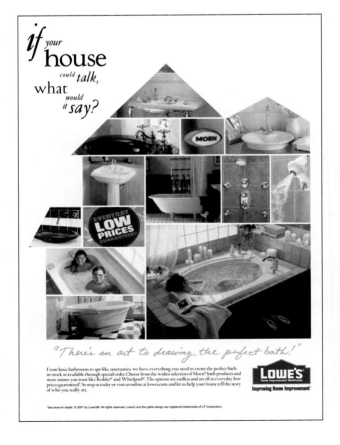

careers, finance, and travel. Cable channels such as Disney's Lifetime network also target women audiences. Lifetime reaches an average of 1.9 million homes per week. [9]

Income.   **Income segmentation** has long been used by the marketers of products and services such as automobiles, boats, clothing, cosmetics, financial services, and travel. Many companies target affluent consumers with luxury goods and convenience services. Stores such as Neiman Marcus pitch everything from expensive jewelry and fine fashions to glazed Australian apricots priced at $20 a pound. To cater to its best customers, Neiman Marcus created its InCircle Rewards program. InCircle members, who must spend $3,000 a year using their Neiman Marcus credit cards to be eligible, earn points with each purchase—one point for each dollar spent. They then cash in points for anything from a snakeskin-patterned Nokia phone cover (10,000 points) or a trip to Los Angeles for a movie premiere with *Instyle* (100,000 points) to a photo shoot with celebrity photographer Annie Liebovitz (1 million points). Car fanatics can trade points for one of six automobiles, from 500,000 points for a Volkswagen Blue Dog Beetle up to 5 million points for a BMW Z8 convertible. InCircle members have an average household income of $568,373 and an average net worth of almost $2.4 million.[10]

However, not all companies that use income segmentation target the affluent. Despite their lower spending power, the nearly one-third of the nation's households that earn less than $25,000 per year offer an attractive market. For example, Greyhound Lines, with its inexpensive nationwide bus network, targets lower-income consumers. Almost half of its revenues come from people with annual incomes under $15,000. Many retailers also target this group, including chains such as Dollar General and Family Dollar stores. When Family Dollar real estate experts scout locations for new stores, they look for lower-middle-class neighborhoods where people wear less

Income segmentation: To thank its very best customers, Neiman Marcus created the InCircle Rewards Program. Members collect a point for each dollar charged on their Neiman Marcus cards. In 2002, members could redeem one million points for a Cadillac CTS. For five million points, they could indulge themselves and 15 friends in the vacation of a lifetime—a six-night Virtuosa-designed itinerary across Europe aboard an Intrav Boeing jet.

expensive shoes and drive old cars that drip a lot of oil. The typical Family Dollar customer's household earns about $25,000 a year, and the average customer spends only about $8 per trip to the store. Similarly, half of Dollar General's customers earn less than $20,000 a year, and about half of its target shoppers do not work. Yet both stores' low-income strategy has put them among the fastest-growing and most profitable discount chains in the country.[11]

Psychographic Segmentation

Psychographic segmentation divides buyers into different groups based on social class, lifestyle, or personality characteristics. People in the same demographic group can have very different psychographic makeups.

In Chapter 6, we discussed how the products people buy reflect their *lifestyles*. As a result, marketers often segment their markets by consumer lifestyles. For example, Duck Head apparel targets a casual student lifestyle, claiming, "You can't get them old until you get them new." One forward-looking grocery store found that segmenting its self-service meat products by lifestyle had a big payoff:

> Walk by the refrigerated self-service meat cases of most grocery stores and you'll usually find the offering grouped by type of meat. Pork is in one case, lamb is another, and chicken is in a third. However, a Nashville, Tennessee, Kroger supermarket decided to experiment and offer groupings of different meats by lifestyle. For instance, the store had a section called "Meals in Minutes," one called "Cookin' Lite," another, filled with prepared products like hot dogs and ready-made hamburger patties, called "Kids Love This Stuff," and one called "I Like to Cook." By focusing on lifestyle needs and not on protein categories, Kroger's test store encouraged habitual beef and pork buyers to consider lamb and veal as well. As a result, the 16-foot service case has seen a substantial improvement in both sales and profits.[12]

Marketers also have used *personality* variables to segment markets. For example, the marketing campaign for Honda's Helix and Elite motor scooters *appears* to target hip and trendy 22-year-olds. But it is *actually* aimed at a much broader personality group. One ad, for example, shows a delighted child bouncing up and down on his bed while the announcer says, "You've been trying to get there all your life." The ad reminds viewers of the euphoric feelings they got when they broke away from authority and did things their parents told them not to do. It suggests that they can feel that way again by riding a Honda scooter. Thus, Honda is appealing to the rebellious, independent kid in all of us. As Honda notes on its Web page, "Fresh air, freedom, and flair—on a Honda scooter, every day is independence day! When it comes to cool, this scooter is off the charts!" In fact, more than half of Honda's scooter sales are to young professionals and older buyers—15 percent are purchased by the over-50 group. Aging baby boomers, now thrill-seeking middle-agers, caused a 26 percent jump in scooter sales last year.[13]

Behavioral Segmentation

Behavioral segmentation divides buyers into groups based on their knowledge, attitudes, uses, or responses to a product. Many marketers believe that behavior variables are the best starting point for building market segments.

Occasions. Buyers can be grouped according to occasions when they get the idea to buy, actually make their purchase, or use the purchased item. **Occasion segmentation** can help firms build up product usage. For example, orange juice is most often consumed at breakfast, but orange growers have promoted drinking orange juice as a cool and refreshing drink at other times of the day. In contrast, Coca-Cola's "Coke in the Morning" advertising campaign attempts to increase Coke consumption by promoting the beverage as an early morning pick-me-up. Some holidays, such as Mother's Day and Father's Day, were originally promoted partly to increase the sale of candy, flowers, cards, and other gifts. And many marketers prepare special offers and ads for holiday occasions. For example, Altoids offers a special "Love Tin," the "curiously strong valentine." Beatrice Foods runs special Thanksgiving and Christmas ads for Reddi-wip during November and December, months that account for 30 percent of all whipped cream sales. Butterball, on the other hand, advertises "Happy Thanksgrilling" during the summer to increase the demand for Turkeys on non-Thanksgiving occasions.

Kodak, Konica, Fuji, and other camera makers use occasion segmentation in designing and marketing their single-use cameras. By mixing lenses, film speeds, and accessories, they have

---

Psychographic segmentation

Dividing a market into different groups based on social class, lifestyle, or personality characteristics.

Behavioral segmentation

Dividing a market into groups based on consumer knowledge, attitude, use, or response to a product.

Occasion segmentation

Dividing the market into groups according to occasions when buyers get the idea to buy, actually make their purchase, or use the purchased item.

Occasion segmentation: Altoids created a special "Love Tin"—a "curiously strong valentine."

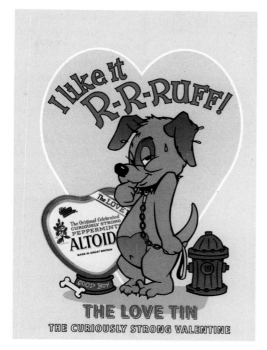

developed special disposable cameras for about any picture-taking occasion, from underwater photography to taking baby pictures.

Standing on the edge of the Grand Canyon? Try Konica's Panoramic, which features a 17 mm lens that takes in nearly 100 degrees horizontally. Going rafting, skiing, or snorkeling? You need Kodak's Max Sport, a rugged camera that can be used underwater to 14 feet. It has big knobs and buttons that let you use it with gloves. Want some pictures of the baby? Kodak offers a model equipped with a short focal-length lens and fast film requiring less light for parents who would like to take snapshots of their darlings without the disturbing flash. Need to check out your golf swing? Just point and shoot the QuickSnap Golf disposable camera, which snaps off eight frames per click showing how your body and club do during the swing. In one Japanese catalog aimed at young women, Kodak sells a package of five pastel-colored cameras, including a version with a fish-eye lens to create a rosy, romantic glow. To make certain that the right cameras are available in the right places, Kodak is rolling out climate-controlled, Internet-connected vending machines in as many as 10,000 locations, including zoos, stadiums, parks, hotels, and resorts.[14]

Benefit segmentation

Dividing the market into groups according to the different benefits that consumers seek from the product.

Benefits Sought.   A powerful form of segmentation is to group buyers according to the different *benefits* that they seek from the product. **Benefit segmentation** requires finding the major benefits people look for in the product class, the kinds of people who look for each benefit, and the major brands that deliver each benefit. For example, our chapter-opening example pointed out that Procter & Gamble has identified several different laundry detergent segments. Each segment seeks a unique combination of benefits, from cleaning and bleaching to economy, fabric softening, fresh smell, strength or mildness, and lots of suds or only a few.

The Champion athletic wear division of Sara Lee Corporation segments its markets according to benefits that different consumers seek from their activewear. For example, "fit and polish" consumers seek a balance between function and style—they exercise for results but want to look good doing it. "Serious sports competitors" exercise heavily and live in and love their activewear—they seek performance and function. By contrast, "value-seeking moms" have low sports interest and low activewear involvement—they buy for the family and seek durability and value. Thus, each segment seeks a different mix of benefits. Champion must target the benefit segment or segments that it can serve best and most profitably using appeals that match each segment's benefit preferences.

User Status.   Markets can be segmented into groups of nonusers, ex-users, potential users, first-time users, and regular users of a product. For example, one study found that blood donors are low in self-esteem, low risk takers, and more highly concerned about their health; nondonors tend to be the opposite on all three dimensions. This suggests that social agencies should use different marketing approaches for keeping current donors and attracting new ones. A company's market position also influences its focus. Market share leaders focus on attracting potential users, whereas smaller firms focus on attracting current users away from the market leader.

Usage Rate.   Markets can also be segmented into light, medium, and heavy product users. Heavy users are often a small percentage of the market but account for a high percentage of total consumption. Marketers usually prefer to attract one heavy user to their product or service rather than several light users. For example, a study of U.S.-branded ice cream buyers showed that heavy users make up only 18 percent of all buyers but consume 55 percent of all the ice cream sold. On average, these heavy users pack away 13 gallons of ice cream per year versus only 2.4 gallons for light users.

Similarly, in the fast-food industry, heavy users make up only 20 percent of patrons but eat up about 60 percent of all the food served. A single heavy user, typically a single male who doesn't know how to cook, might spend as much as $40 in a day at fast-food restaurants and visit them more than 20 times a month. Heavy users "come more often, they spend more money, and that's what makes the cash registers ring," says a Burger King marketing executive. Interestingly, although fast-food companies such as Burger King, McDonald's, and KFC depend a lot on heavy users and do all they can to keep them satisfied with every visit, these companies often target light users with their ads and promotions. The heavy users "are in our restaurants already," says the Burger King marketer. The company's marketing dollars are more often spent trying to convince light users that they want a burger in the first place.[15]

Loyalty Status.   A market can also be segmented by consumer loyalty. Consumers can be loyal to brands (Tide), stores (Wal-Mart), and companies (Ford). Buyers can be divided into groups according to their degree of loyalty. Some consumers are completely loyal—they buy one brand all the time. Others are somewhat loyal—they are loyal to two or three brands of a given product or favor one brand while sometimes buying others. Still other buyers show no loyalty to any brand. They either want something different each time they buy or they buy whatever's on sale.

A company can learn a lot by analyzing loyalty patterns in its market. It should start by studying its own loyal customers. For example, to better understand the needs and behavior of its core soft drink consumers, Pepsi observed them in places where its products are consumed—in homes, in stores, in movie theaters, at sporting events, and at the beach. "We learned that there's a surprising amount of loyalty and passion for Pepsi's products," says Pepsi's director of consumer insights. "One fellow had four or five cases of Pepsi in his basement and he felt he was low on Pepsi and had to go replenish." The company used these and other study findings to pinpoint the Pepsi target market and develop marketing appeals.[16]

By studying its less loyal buyers, the company can detect which brands are most competitive with its own. If many Pepsi buyers also buy Coke, Pepsi can attempt to improve its positioning against Coke, possibly by using direct-comparison advertising. By looking at customers who are shifting away from its brand, the company can learn about its marketing weaknesses. As for non-loyals, the company may attract them by putting its brand on sale.

Using Multiple Segmentation Bases

Marketers rarely limit their segmentation analysis to only one or a few variables. Rather, they are increasingly using multiple segmentation bases in an effort to identify smaller, better-defined target groups. Thus, a bank may not only identify a group of wealthy retired adults but also, within that group, distinguish several segments based on their current income, assets, savings and risk preferences, and lifestyles. Companies often begin by segmenting their markets using a single base, then expand using other bases.

One good example of multivariable segmentation is "geodemographic" segmentation. Several business information services have arisen to help marketing planners link U.S. Census data with lifestyle patterns to better segment their markets down to Zip codes, neighborhoods, and even city blocks. One of the leading lifestyle segmentation systems is PRIZM by Claritas, Inc. (see Real Marketing 8.1).

real marketing 8.1

Blue Blood Estates to Shotguns & Pickups: Segmenting America's Neighborhoods

Using a host of demographic and socioeconomic factors drawn from U.S. Census data, consumer surveys, and its own grass-roots research, Claritas, Inc.'s PRIZM system classifies every one of the more than 260,000 U.S. neighborhoods into one of 62 clusters.

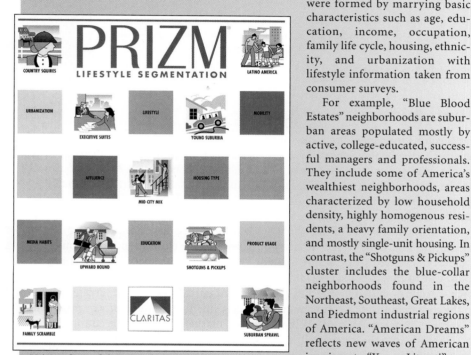

Using a host of demographic and socioeconomic factors drawn from U.S. Census data, Claritas, Inc.'s PRIZM system has classified every one of the more than 260,000 U.S. neighborhoods into one of 62 clusters.

You're 35 years old. The price tag on your suits shows that you're a success. You drive a Volvo. You know your way around the olive oil section of the store, buy fresh-ground coffee, and go on scuba-diving trips. You're living out your own, individual version of the good life in the suburbs. You're unique—not some demographic cliché. Right? Wrong. You're a prime example of [PRIZM's] "Kids & Cul-de-Sacs. . . ." If you consume, you can't hide from . . . Claritas.

The "Kids & Cul-de-Sacs" cluster points to a new migration to the suburbs. Other PRIZM clusters include "Blue Blood Estates," "Money & Brains," "Young Literati," "Shotguns & Pickups," "American Dreams," "New Eco-topias," "Mobility Blues," and "Gray Power." The clusters were formed by marrying basic characteristics such as age, education, income, occupation, family life cycle, housing, ethnicity, and urbanization with lifestyle information taken from consumer surveys.

For example, "Blue Blood Estates" neighborhoods are suburban areas populated mostly by active, college-educated, successful managers and professionals. They include some of America's wealthiest neighborhoods, areas characterized by low household density, highly homogenous residents, a heavy family orientation, and mostly single-unit housing. In contrast, the "Shotguns & Pickups" cluster includes the blue-collar neighborhoods found in the Northeast, Southeast, Great Lakes, and Piedmont industrial regions of America. "American Dreams" reflects new waves of American immigrants, "Young Literati" taps Generation X, and "New Eco-topia" focuses on the country's aging hippies. Each of the other clusters has a unique combination of characteristics.

Companies can combine these PRIZM clusters with other data on product and service usage to get a better picture of specific market areas. For example, the "Shotguns & Pickups" cluster is populated by lower-middle-class, blue-collar consumers who use chain saws and snuff and buy more canning jars, dried soups, and powdered soft drinks. The "Hispanic Mix" cluster prefers high-quality dresses, nonfilter cigarettes, and lip gloss. People in this cluster are highly brand conscious, quality

conscious, and brand loyal. They have a strong family and home orientation.

Such segmentation provides a powerful tool for segmenting markets, refining demand estimates, selecting target markets, and shaping promotion messages. For example, in marketing its Suave shampoo, Unilever's Helene Curtis division uses PRIZM to identify neighborhoods with high concentrations of working women. Such women respond best to advertising messages that Suave is inexpensive yet will make their hair "look like a million." Bookseller Barnes & Noble locates its stores where there are concentrations of "Money & Brains" consumers, because they buy lots of books.

Ohio's Lakewood Public Library used PRIZM to address a low patronage problem. The PRIZM analysis revealed that one of Lakewood's biggest subsets of residents was hardly using the library.

"Many people had a perception of Lakewood as being a city of families and senior citizens," said John Guscott, Lakewood Public Library's manager of electronic services. "Our experiences at the library over the past few years suggested otherwise—that it was fast becoming a city dominated by young, professional singles." PRIZM proved Guscott right. The largest single PRIZM cluster was Urban Achievers, which comprised nearly 26 percent of area residents. These Urban Achievers were characterized as "behaving like middle-class sophisticates" and gravitating toward "specialty shops, ethnic markets, family restaurants, delis, sushi bars, taco joints, Nordstrom, jazz music, Kias, Volkswagens, and Nissans." Their interests also included "multiculturalism, intellectually challenging pursuits, theater, adult education, libraries, public broadcasting, and alternative health." The Lakewood Public Library offered very little of interest to this Gen Xer group. Based on the analysis, the library revamped its collections to cater to its newly discovered target consumers. Today, Lakewood has no problem

(continued)

attracting patrons. The Gen Xer crowd flocks to the library to sample the rich array of programs and the diverse book and CD collections designed just for them. "Our circulation for audio CDs has just flown off the charts," says Guscott.

Similarly, carmaker Hyundai has used PRIZM for everything from targeting direct-marketing efforts to pinpointing prime locations for new dealerships.

The company recently used PRIZM in a campaign to get consumers to test-market its Sonata model. Instead of blanketing entire cities, Hyundai sent carefully targeted test-drive offers to specific PRIZM neighborhoods. Among Hyundai's favorite targets is the "Kids & Cul-de-Sacs" cluster. They are upscale, suburban families with a median household incomes of $68,900 who tend to shop online and visit Disney theme parks. Another major target cluster: "Bohemian Mix," professionals aged 25 to 44, with a median income of $38,500, who are likely to shop at the Gap, watch *Face the Nation,* and read *Elle* magazine. The targeted campaign really paid off for Hyundai. Within weeks in those markets, Hyundai increased its sales as well as the number of people showing up for a test drive. In fact, it cut in half its costs per vehicle sold, an important measure of investment returns. Hyundai has also used PRIZM to track its ever-improving image by asking Claritas to compare its popularity among different clusters. It found that its sales and test drives are growing among more affluent, better-educated groups, such as "Pools & Patios." By studying the shift, the company can adjust its advertising and marketing campaigns from year to year.

Sources: Quotes and extracts from Christina Del Valle, "They Know Where You Live—And How You Buy," *Business Week,* February 7, 1994, p. 89; Evan St. Lifer, "Tapping into the Zen of Marketing," *Library Journal,* May 1, 2001, pp. 44–46; and Amy Merrick, "The 2000 Count: Counting on the Census, *Wall Street Journal,* February 14, 2001, p. B12. Other information accessed online at www.claritas.com, July 2002.

Segmenting Business Markets

Consumer and business marketers use many of the same variables to segment their markets. Business buyers can be segmented geographically, demographically (industry, company size), or by benefits sought, user status, usage rate, and loyalty status. Yet, as Table 8.2 shows, business marketers also use some additional variables, such as customer *operating variables, purchasing approaches, situational factors,* and *personal characteristics.* The table lists major questions that business marketers should ask in determining which customers they want to serve.

By going after segments instead of the whole market, companies have a much better chance to deliver value to consumers and to receive maximum rewards for close attention to consumer needs. Thus, Hewlett-Packard's Computer Systems Division targets specific industries that promise the best growth prospects, such as telecommunications and financial services. Its "red team" sales force specializes in developing and serving major customers in these targeted industries.[17] Within the chosen industry, a company can further segment by *customer size* or *geographic location.* For example, Hewlett-Packard's "blue team" telemarkets to smaller accounts and to those that don't fit neatly into the strategically targeted industries on which HP focuses.

A company might also set up separate systems for dealing with larger or multiple-location customers. For example, Steelcase, a major producer of office furniture, first segments customers into 10 industries, including banking, insurance, and electronics. Next, company salespeople work with independent Steelcase dealers to handle smaller, local, or regional Steelcase customers in each segment. But many national, multiple-location customers, such as Exxon/Mobile or IBM, have special needs that may reach beyond the scope of individual dealers. So Steelcase uses national accounts managers to help its dealer networks handle its national accounts.

Within a given target industry and customer size, the company can segment by purchase approaches and criteria. As in consumer segmentation, many marketers believe that *buying behavior* and *benefits* provide the best basis for segmenting business markets.[18]

Segmenting International Markets

Few companies have either the resources or the will to operate in all, or even most, of the countries that dot the globe. Although some large companies, such as Coca-Cola or Sony, sell products in more than 200 countries, most international firms focus on a smaller set. Operating in many countries presents new challenges. Different countries, even those that are close together, can vary greatly in their economic, cultural, and political makeup. Thus, just as they do within their domestic markets, international firms need to group their world markets into segments with distinct buying needs and behaviors.

TABLE 8.2	MAJOR SEGMENTATION VARIABLES FOR BUSINESS MARKETS

Demographics

Industry: Which industries that buy this product should we focus on?

Company size: What size companies should we focus on?

Location: What geographical areas should we focus on?

Operating Variables

Technology: What customer technologies should we focus on?

User–nonuser status: Should we focus on heavy, medium, or light users or nonusers?

Customer capabilities: Should we focus on customers needing many services or few services?

Purchasing Approaches

Purchasing-function organization: Should we focus on companies with highly centralized or decentralized purchasing?

Power structure: Should we focus on companies that are engineering dominated, financially dominated, or marketing dominated?

Nature of existing relationships: Should we focus on companies with which we already have strong relationships or simply go after the most desirable companies?

General purchase policies: Should we focus on companies that prefer leasing? Service contracts? Systems purchases? Sealed bidding?

Purchasing criteria: Should we focus on companies that are seeking quality? Service? Price?

Situational Factors

Urgency: Should we focus on companies that need quick delivery or service?

Specific application: Should we focus on certain applications of our product rather than all applications?

Size of order: Should we focus on large or small orders?

Personal Characteristics

Buyer–seller similarity: Should we focus on companies whose people and values are similar to ours?

Attitudes toward risk: Should we focus on risk-taking or risk-avoiding customers?

Loyalty: Should we focus on companies that show high loyalty to their suppliers?

Source: Adapted from Thomas V. Bonoma and Benson P. Shapiro, *Segmenting the Industrial Market* (Lexington, Mass.: Lexington Books, 1983). Also see John Berrigan and Carl Finkbeiner, *Segmentation Marketing: New Methods for Capturing Business* (New York: HarperBusiness, 1992).

Companies can segment international markets using one or a combination of several variables. They can segment by *geographic location,* grouping countries by regions such as Western Europe, the Pacific Rim, the Middle East, or Africa. Geographic segmentation assumes that nations close to one another will have many common traits and behaviors. Although this is often the case, there are many exceptions. For example, although the United States and Canada have much in common, both differ culturally and economically from neighboring Mexico. Even within a region, consumers can differ widely. For example, many U.S. marketers think that all Central and South American countries are the same, including their 400 million inhabitants. However, the Dominican Republic is no more like Brazil than Italy is like Sweden. Many Latin Americans don't speak Spanish, including 140 million Portuguese-speaking Brazilians and the millions in other countries who speak a variety of Indian dialects.

World markets can also be segmented on the basis of *economic factors.* For example, countries might be grouped by population income levels or by their overall level of economic development. Some countries, such as the United States, Britain, France, Germany, Japan, Canada, Italy, and Russia, have established, highly industrialized economies. Other countries have newly industrialized or developing economies (Singapore, Taiwan, Korea, Brazil, Mexico). Still others are less developed (China, India). A company's economic structure shapes its population's product and service needs and, therefore, the marketing opportunities it offers.

Countries can be segmented by *political and legal factors* such as the type and stability of government, receptivity to foreign firms, monetary regulations, and the amount of bureaucracy. Such factors can play a crucial role in a company's choice of which countries to enter and how. *Cultural factors* can also be used, grouping markets according to common languages, religions, values and attitudes, customs, and behavioral patterns.

Intermarket segmentation: Teens show surprising similarity no matter where in the world they live. For instance, these two teens could live almost anywhere. Thus, many companies target teenagers with worldwide marketing campaigns.

Intermarket segmentation

Forming segments of consumers who have similar needs and buying behavior even though they are located in different countries.

Segmenting international markets on the basis of geographic, economic, political, cultural, and other factors assumes that segments should consist of clusters of countries. However, many companies use a different approach called **intermarket segmentation.** Using this approach, they form segments of consumers who have similar needs and buying behavior even though they are located in different countries. For example, Mercedes-Benz targets the world's well-to-do, regardless of their country. MTV targets the world's teenagers. One study of more than 6,500 teenagers from 26 countries showed that teens around the world live surprisingly parallel lives. "A group of teenagers chosen randomly from around the world will share many tastes," notes one expert. Says another, "From Rio to Rochester, teens can be found enmeshed in much the same regimen: . . . drinking Coke, . . . dining on Big Macs, and surfin' the Net on their computers."[19] The world's teens have a lot in common: They study, shop, and sleep. They are exposed to many of the same major issues: love, crime, homelessness, ecology, and working parents. In many ways, they have more in common with each other than with their parents. MTV bridges the gap between cultures, appealing to what teens around the world have in common. Sony, Reebok, Nike, Swatch, and Benetton are just a few of many firms that actively target global teens.[20]

Requirements for Effective Segmentation

Clearly, there are many ways to segment a market, but not all segmentations are effective. For example, buyers of table salt could be divided into blond and brunette customers. But hair color obviously does not affect the purchase of salt. Furthermore, if all salt buyers bought the same amount of salt each month, believed that all salt is the same, and wanted to pay the same price, the company would not benefit from segmenting this market.

To be useful, market segments must be

- *Measurable:* The size, purchasing power, and profiles of the segments can be measured. Certain segmentation variables are difficult to measure. For example, there are 32.5 million left-handed people in the United States—almost equaling the entire population of Canada. Yet few products are targeted toward this left-handed segment. The major problem may be that the segment is hard to identify and measure. There are no data on the demographics of lefties, and the U.S. Census Bureau does not keep track of left-handedness in its surveys. Private data companies keep reams of statistics on other demographic segments but not on left-handers.

- *Accessible:* The market segments can be effectively reached and served. Suppose a fragrance company finds that heavy users of its brand are single men and women who stay out late and socialize a lot. Unless this group lives or shops at certain places and is exposed to certain media, its members will be difficult to reach.

- *Substantial:* The market segments are large or profitable enough to serve. A segment should be the largest possible homogenous group worth pursuing with a tailored marketing program. It would not pay, for example, for an automobile manufacturer to develop cars especially for people whose height is less than four feet.
- *Differentiable:* The segments are conceptually distinguishable and respond differently to different marketing mix elements and programs. If married and unmarried women respond similarly to a sale on perfume, they do not constitute separate segments.
- *Actionable:* Effective programs can be designed for attracting and serving the segments. For example, although one small airline identified seven market segments, its staff was too small to develop separate marketing programs for each segment.

Target Marketing

Market segmentation reveals the firm's market segment opportunities. The firm now has to evaluate the various segments and decide how many and which ones to target. We now look at how companies evaluate and select target segments.

Evaluating Market Segments

In evaluating different market segments, a firm must look at three factors: segment size and growth, segment structural attractiveness, and company objectives and resources. The company must first collect and analyze data on current segment sales, growth rates, and expected profitability for various segments. It will be interested in segments that have the right size and growth characteristics. (Appendix 1 discusses approaches for measuring and forecasting market demand.) But "right size and growth" is a relative matter. The largest, fastest-growing segments are not always the most attractive ones for every company. Smaller companies may lack the skills and resources needed to serve the larger segments. Or they may find these segments too competitive. Such companies may select segments that are smaller and less attractive, in an absolute sense, but that are potentially more profitable for them.

The company also needs to examine major structural factors that affect long-run segment attractiveness.[21] For example, a segment is less attractive if it already contains many strong and aggressive *competitors.* The existence of many actual or potential *substitute products* may limit prices and the profits that can be earned in a segment. The relative *power of buyers* also affects segment attractiveness. Buyers with strong bargaining power relative to sellers will try to force prices down, demand more services, and set competitors against one another—all at the expense of seller profitability. Finally, a segment may be less attractive if it contains *powerful suppliers* who can control prices or reduce the quality or quantity of ordered goods and services.

Even if a segment has the right size and growth and is structurally attractive, the company must consider its own objectives and resources in relation to that segment. Some attractive segments could be dismissed quickly because they do not mesh with the company's long-run objectives. The company must consider whether it possesses the skills and resources it needs to succeed in that segment. If the company lacks the strengths needed to compete successfully in a segment and cannot readily obtain them, it should not enter the segment. Even if the company possesses the *required* strengths, it needs to employ skills and resources *superior* to those of the competition in order to really win in a market segment. The company should enter only segments in which it can offer superior value and gain advantages over competitors.

Selecting Target Market Segments

Target market

A set of buyers sharing common needs or characteristics that the company decides to serve.

After evaluating different segments, the company must now decide which and how many segments it will target. A **target market** consists of a set of buyers who share common needs or characteristics that the company decides to serve.

Because buyers have unique needs and wants, a seller could potentially view each buyer as a separate target market. Ideally, then, a seller might design a separate marketing program for each buyer. However, although some companies do attempt to serve buyers individually, most face

FIGURE 8.2
Target marketing strategies

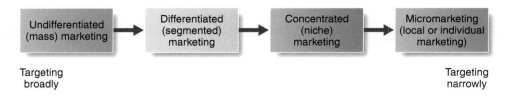

Targeting
broadly

Targeting
narrowly

larger numbers of smaller buyers and do not find individual targeting worthwhile. Instead, they look for broader segments of buyers. More generally, target marketing can be carried out at several different levels. Figure 8.2 shows that companies can target very broadly (undifferentiated marketing), very narrowly (micromarketing), or somewhere in between (differentiated or concentrated marketing).

Undifferentiated Marketing

Undifferentiated (mass) marketing

A market-coverage strategy in which a firm decides to ignore market segment differences and go after the whole market with one offer.

Using an **undifferentiated marketing** (or **mass marketing**) strategy, a firm might decide to ignore market segment differences and target the whole market with one offer. This mass-marketing strategy focuses on what is *common* in the needs of consumers rather than on what is *different*. The company designs a product and a marketing program that will appeal to the largest number of buyers. It relies on mass distribution and mass advertising, and it aims to give the product a superior image in people's minds. As noted earlier in the chapter, most modern marketers have strong doubts about this strategy. Difficulties arise in developing a product or brand that will satisfy all consumers. Moreover, mass marketers often have trouble competing with more-focused firms that do a better job of satisfying the needs of specific segments and niches.

Differentiated Marketing

Differentiated (segmented) marketing

A market-coverage strategy in which a firm decides to target several market segments and designs separate offers for each.

Using a **differentiated marketing** (or **segmented marketing**) strategy, a firm decides to target several market segments and designs separate offers for each. General Motors tries to produce a car for every "purse, purpose, and personality." Nike offers athletic shoes for a dozen or more different sports, from running, fencing, golf, and aerobics to bicycling and baseball. Marriott markets to a variety of segments—business travelers, families, and others—with hotel formats and packages adapted to their varying needs. And American Express offers not only its traditional green cards but also gold cards, corporate cards, and even a black card, called the Centurian, with a $1,000 annual fee aimed at a segment of "superpremium customers."

Estée Lauder offers dozens of different products aimed at carefully defined segments:

> The four best-selling prestige perfumes in the United States belong to Estée Lauder. So do seven of the top ten prestige makeup products and eight of the ten best-selling prestige skin care products. Estée Lauder is an expert in creating differentiated brands that serve the tastes of different market segments. There's the original Estée Lauder brand, which appeals to older, Junior League types. Then there's Clinique, perfect for the middle-aged mom with a GMC Suburban and no time to waste. For the youthful hipster, there's the hip M.A.C. line. And, for the New Age type, there's upscale Aveda, with its aromatherapy line, and earthy Origins, which the company expects will become a $1 billion brand. The company even offers downscale brands, such as Jane by Sassaby, for teens at Wal-Mart and Rite Aid.[22]

By offering product and marketing variations to segments, companies hope for higher sales and a stronger position within each market segment. Developing a stronger position within several segments creates more total sales than undifferentiated marketing across all segments. Procter & Gamble gets more total market share with eight brands of laundry detergent than it could with only one. And Estée Lauder's combined brands give it a much greater market share than any single brand could. The Estée Lauder and Clinique brands alone reap a combined 40 percent share of the prestige cosmetics market.

But differentiated marketing also increases the costs of doing business. A firm usually finds it more expensive to develop and produce, say, 10 units of 10 different products than 100 units of one product. Developing separate marketing plans for the separate segments requires extra marketing research, forecasting, sales analysis, promotion planning, and channel management. And trying to reach different market segments with different advertising increases promotion costs.

Thus, the company must weigh increased sales against increased costs when deciding on a differentiated marketing strategy.

Concentrated Marketing

Concentrated (niche) marketing

A market-coverage strategy in which a firm goes after a large share of one or a few segments or niches.

A third market-coverage strategy, **concentrated marketing** (or **niche marketing**), is especially appealing when company resources are limited. Instead of going after a small share of a large market, the firm goes after a large share of one or a few segments or niches. For example, Oshkosh Truck is the world's largest producer of airport rescue trucks and front-loading concrete mixers. Tetra sells 80 percent of the world's tropical fish food, and Steiner Optical captures 80 percent of the world's military binoculars market.

Whereas segments are fairly large and normally attract several competitors, niches are smaller and may attract only one or a few competitors. Through concentrated marketing, the firm achieves a strong market position because of its greater knowledge of consumer needs in the niches it serves and the special reputation it acquires. It can market more *effectively* by fine-tuning its products, prices, and programs to the needs of carefully defined segments. It can also market more *efficiently,* targeting its products or services, channels, and communications programs toward only consumers that it can serve best and most profitably.

Niching offers smaller companies an opportunity to compete by focusing their limited resources on serving niches that may be unimportant to or overlooked by larger competitors. For example, tiny Vans Inc. specializes in making thick-soled, slip-on sneakers for skateboarders that can absorb the shock of a five-foot leap on wheels. Although it captures only a point or two of market share in the overall athletic shoe market, Vans's small but intensely loyal customer base has made the company more profitable than many of its larger competitors.[23]

Many companies start as nichers to get a foothold against larger, more resourceful competitors, then grow into broader competitors. For example, Southwest Airlines began by concentrating on serving intrastate, no-frills commuters in Texas but is now one of the nation's eight largest airlines. Wal-Mart, which got its start by bringing everyday low prices to small towns and rural areas, is now the world's largest company.

Today, the low cost of setting up shop on the Internet makes it even more profitable to serve seemingly minuscule niches. Small businesses, in particular, are realizing riches from serving small niches on the Web. Here is a "Webpreneur" who achieved astonishing results:

Whereas Internet giants like Amazon.com have yet to even realize a consistent profit, Steve Warrington is earning a six-figure income online selling ostriches—and every product derived from them—online (www.ostrichesonline.com). Launched for next to nothing on

Niche marketing: Tiny Van's Inc. specializes in making thick-soled, slip-on sneakers for skateboarders that can absorb the shock of a five-foot leap on wheels.

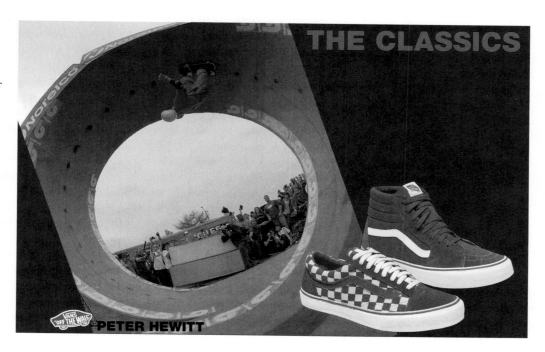

the Web in 1996, Ostrichesonline.com now boasts that it sends newsletters to 29,000 subscribers and sells 17,500 ostrich products to more than 12,000 satisfied clients in more than 100 countries. The site tells visitors everything they ever wanted to know about ostriches and much, much more—it supplies ostrich facts, ostrich pictures, an ostrich farm index, and a huge ostrich database and reference index. Visitors to the site can buy ostrich meat, feathers, leather jackets, videos, eggshells, and skin care products derived from ostrich body oil.[24]

Concentrated marketing can be highly profitable. At the same time, it involves higher-than-normal risks. Companies that rely on one or a few segments for all of their business will suffer greatly if the segment turns sour. Or larger competitors may decide to enter the same segment. For example, California Cooler's early success in the wine cooler segment attracted many large competitors, causing the original owners to sell to a larger company that had more marketing resources. For these reasons, many companies prefer to diversify in several market segments.

Micromarketing

Differentiated and concentrated marketers tailor their offers and marketing programs to meet the needs of various market segments and niches. At the same time, however, they do not customize their offers to each individual customer. **Micromarketing** is the practice of tailoring products and marketing programs to suit the tastes of specific individuals and locations. Micromarketing includes *local marketing* and *individual marketing*.

Local Marketing.   **Local marketing** involves tailoring brands and promotions to the needs and wants of local customer groups—cities, neighborhoods, and even specific stores. Retailers such as Sears and Wal-Mart routinely customize each store's merchandise and promotions to match its specific clientele. Citibank provides different mixes of banking services in its branches, depending on neighborhood demographics. Kraft helps supermarket chains identify the specific cheese assortments and shelf positioning that will optimize cheese sales in low-income, middle-income, and high-income stores and in different ethnic communities.

Local marketing has some drawbacks. It can drive up manufacturing and marketing costs by reducing economies of scale. It can also create logistics problems as companies try to meet the varied requirements of different regional and local markets. Further, a brand's overall image might be diluted if the product and message vary too much in different localities. Still, as companies face increasingly fragmented markets, and as new supporting technologies develop, the advantages of local marketing often outweigh the drawbacks. Local marketing helps a company to market more effectively in the face of pronounced regional and local differences in demographics and lifestyles. It also meets the needs of the company's first-line customers—retailers—who prefer more fine-tuned product assortments for their neighborhoods.

Individual Marketing.   In the extreme, micromarketing becomes **individual marketing**—tailoring products and marketing programs to the needs and preferences of individual customers. Individual marketing has also been labeled *one-to-one marketing, customized marketing,* and *markets-of-one marketing*.[25]

The widespread use of mass marketing has obscured the fact that for centuries consumers were served as individuals: The tailor custom-made the suit, the cobbler designed shoes for the individual, the cabinetmaker made furniture to order. Today, however, new technologies are permitting many companies to return to customized marketing. More-powerful computers, detailed databases, robotic production and flexible manufacturing, and immediate and interactive communication media such as e-mail, fax, and the Internet—all have combined to foster "mass customization." *Mass customization* is the process through which firms interact one-to-one with masses of customers to create customer-unique value by designing products and services tailor-made to individual needs (see Real Marketing 8.2).

Thus, Dell Computer delivers computers to individual customers loaded with customer-specified hardware and software. Peapod, the online grocery shopping and delivery service,

Micromarketing
The practice of tailoring products and marketing programs to the needs and wants of specific individuals and local customer groups— includes *local marketing* and *individual marketing*.

Local marketing
Tailoring brands and promotions to the needs and wants of local customer groups— cities, neighborhoods, and even specific stores.

Individual marketing
Tailoring products and marketing programs to the needs and preferences of individual customers—also labeled "markets-of-one marketing," "customized marketing," and "one-to-one marketing."

real marketing 8.2

Markets of One: Treating Customers as Individuals

Imagine walking into a booth that bathes your body in patterns of white light and, in a matter of seconds, captures your exact three-dimensional form. The digitized data are then imprinted on a credit card, which you use to order customized clothing. No, this isn't a scene from the next *Star Wars* sequel; it's a peek ahead at how you will be able to buy clothing in the not-so-distant future. A consortium of over 100 apparel companies, including Levi-Strauss, has banded together to develop body-scanning technology in the hope of making mass customization commonplace.

Although body-scanning technology and smart cards carrying customer measurements are still in development, many companies are now using existing technologies to tailor products to individual customers. Dell creates custom-configured computers, reflect.com formulates customized beauty products, Ford lets buyers "build a vehicle" from a palette of options, and Golf to Fit crafts custom clubs based on consumer measurements and preferences. Here are some other examples of companies in the forefront of the mass-customization economy:

Levi-Strauss. In 1994, Levi began making measure-to-fit women's jeans under its in-store Personal Pair program. Consumer response was so positive that Levi developed an expanded in-store customization concept called Original Spin, which works a lot like the futuristic sizing scenario described above. Original Spin lets buyers create their own jeans from scratch or modify an existing pair. Customers—both men and women—enter a booth in which a 3-D Body Scanner creates personalized measurements against a backdrop of strobe lights and space-age music. Using the Original Spin terminals, customers can then choose from a range of cuts and styles that represent hundreds of different pairs of jeans available for purchase. Whereas a fully stocked Levi's store carries 130 pairs of ready-to-wear jeans for a given waist and inseam, with Original Spin the number jumps to 750.

Mattel. Since 1998, girls have been able to log on to the "My Design" page of the Barbie Web site (www.barbie.com) and create their very own "friend of Barbie" doll. They choose the doll's skin tone, eye color, hairstyle and hair color, clothes, accessories, and name. They even fill out

Mass customization: Levi's Original Spin lets you create your own Levi jeans from scratch or modify a pair of authentic Levi jeans. Its Web site tells how it works and directs consumers to nearby retail locations.

(continued)

a questionnaire detailing their doll's likes and dislikes. When Barbie's special friend arrives in the mail, the girls find the doll's name on the packaging along with a computer-generated paragraph about her personality.

Nike ID. This Nike Web site (www. NikeID.com) lets customers design their own athletic shoes online. The site leads buyers through a set questions about their preferences for shoe style, base and accent colors, shoe construction, and even personalized IDs of up to 16 characters to be printed on the sole of each shoe. When the customers submit the final design, Nike transmits the order to a specially equipped plant in China or Korea, where the information is fed into a production line that pumps out the customized shoes. Customers pay only an extra $10 for this service.

Consumer goods marketers aren't the only ones going one-to-one. B2B marketers also provide customers with tailor-made goods, often more cheaply and quickly than it used to take to make standardized ones. Particularly for small companies, mass customization provides a way to stand out against larger competitors:

Oshkosh Truck. Oshkosh Truck specializes in making fire, garbage, cement, and military trucks. Oshkosh is small—a tenth the size of larger rivals such as Paccar and Navistar International—and the truck industry is slumping. Yet Oshkosh has doubled its sales and increased its earnings fivefold over the past five years. What's the secret to Oshkosh's success? Mass customization—its ability to personalize its products and services to the needs of individual customers. For example, when firefighters order a truck

from Oshkosh, it's an event. They travel to the plant to watch the vehicle, which may cost as much as $800,000, take shape. The firefighters can choose from 19,000 options. A stripped-down fire truck costs $130,000, but 75 percent of Oshkosh's customers order lots of extras, like hideaway stairs, ladders, special doors, compartments, and firefighting foam systems for those difficult-to-extinguish fires. Some bring along paint chips so they can customize the color of their fleet. Others are content just to admire the vehicles, down to the water tanks and hideaway ladders. "Some chiefs even bring their wives; we encourage it," says the president of Oshkosh's firefighting unit, Pierce Manufacturing. "Buying a fire truck is a very personal thing." Indeed, Pierce customers are in town so often the Holiday Inn renamed its lounge the Hook and Ladder. Through such customization and personalization, smaller Oshkosh has gained a big edge over its languishing larger rivals.

Two trends underlie the growth in one-to-one marketing. First, today's consumers have very high expectations—they expect products and services that meet their individual needs. Yet, it would be too expensive or downright impossible to meet these individual demands if it weren't for another trend: rapid advances in technology. Data warehouses now allow companies to store trillions of bytes of customer information. Computer-controlled factory equipment and industrial robots can now quickly readjust assembly lines. Bar code scanners make it possible to track parts and products. Most important, the Internet ties it all together and makes it easy for a company to interact with customers, learn about their preferences, and respond. Indeed, the Internet

appears to be the ultimate one-to-one medium.

Unlike mass production, which eliminates the need for human interaction, mass customization has made relationships with customers more important than ever. For instance, when Levi's sells made-to-order jeans, the company not only captures consumer data in digitized form but also becomes the customer's "jeans adviser." And Mattel is building a database of information on all the customers of My Design dolls so it can start long-term, one-to-one relationships with each customer.

Just as mass production was the marketing principle of the last century, mass customization is becoming the marketing principle for the twenty-first century. The world appears to be coming full circle—from the good old days when customers were treated as individuals, to mass marketing when nobody knew your name, and back again.

Sources: Erick Schonfeld, "The Customized, Digitized, Have-It-Your-Way Economy," *Fortune,* September 28, 1998, pp. 115–124; Ronald Alsop, "A Special Report on Trends in Industry and Finance," *Wall Street Journal,* April 29, 1999, p. A1; James H. Gilmore and B. Joseph Pine, *Markets of One: Creating Customer-Unique Value Through Mass Customization* (Boston: Harvard Business School Press, 2001); Diane Brady, "Customizing for the Masses," *Business Week,* March 20, 2000, pp. 130B–130F; Mark Tatge, "Red Bodies, Black Ink," *Forbes,* September 18, 2000, p. 114; Paul Zipkin, "The Limits of Mass Customization," *MIT Sloan Management Review,* Spring 2001; and information accessed online at www.us. levi.com, www.Barbie.com, www.NikeID. com, www.chemstation.com, and www. oshkoshtruck.com, July 2002.

lets customers create the virtual supermarket that best fits their individual needs. And Ritz-Carlton Hotels creates custom-designed experiences for its delighted guests:

Check into any Ritz-Carlton hotel around the world, and you'll be amazed at how well the hotel's employees anticipate your slightest need. Without ever asking, they seem to know that you want a nonsmoking room with a king-size bed, a nonallergenic pillow, and breakfast with decaffeinated coffee in your room. How does Ritz-Carlton work this magic? The hotel employs a system that combines information technology and flexible operations to customize the hotel experience. At the heart of the system is a huge customer database, which contains information gathered through the observations of hotel employees. Each day, hotel staffers—from those at the front desk to those in maintenance and housekeeping—discreetly record the unique habits, likes, and dislikes of each guest on small "guest preference pads." These observations are then transferred to a corporatewide "guest preference database." Every morning, a "guest historian" at each hotel reviews the files of all new arrivals who have previously stayed at a Ritz-Carlton and prepares a list of suggested extra touches that might delight each guest. Guests have responded strongly to such markets-of-one service. Since inaugurating the guest-history system in 1992, Ritz-Carlton has boosted guest retention by 23 percent. An amazing 95 percent of departing guests report that their stay has been a truly memorable experience.

Business-to-business marketers are also finding new ways to customize their offerings. For example, Becton-Dickinson, a major medical supplier, offers to customize almost anything for its hospital customers. It offers custom-designed labeling, individual packaging, customized quality control, customized computer software, and customized billing. Motorola salespeople use a hand-held computer to custom-design pagers following individual business customer wishes. The design data are transmitted to the Motorola factory, and production starts within 17 minutes. The customized pagers are ready for shipment within two hours. And John Deere manufactures seeding equipment that can be configured in more than 2 million versions to individual customer specifications. The seeders are produced one at a time, in any sequence, on a single production line.[26]

The move toward individual marketing mirrors the trend in consumer *self-marketing*. Increasingly, individual customers are taking more responsibility for determining which products and brands to buy. Consider two business buyers with two different purchasing styles. The first sees several salespeople, each trying to persuade him to buy his or her product. The second sees no salespeople but rather logs on to the Internet. She searches for information on available products; interacts electronically with various suppliers, users, and product analysts; and then makes up her own mind about the best offer. The second purchasing agent has taken more responsibility for the buying process, and the marketer has had less influence over her buying decision.

As the trend toward more interactive dialogue and less advertising monologue continues, self-marketing will grow in importance. As more buyers look up consumer reports, join Internet product discussion forums, and place orders via phone or online, marketers will have to influence the buying process in new ways. Many companies now practice *customerization*.[27] They combine operationally driven mass customization with customized marketing to empower consumers to design products and services to their own preferences. They involve customers more in all phases of the product development and buying processes, increasing opportunities for buyers to practice self-marketing.

Choosing a Target-Marketing Strategy

Companies need to consider many factors when choosing a target-marketing strategy. Which strategy is best depends on *company resources*. When the firm's resources are limited, concentrated marketing makes the most sense. The best strategy also depends on the degree of *product variability*. Undifferentiated marketing is more suited for uniform products such as grapefruit or steel. Products that can vary in design, such as cameras and automobiles, are more suited to differentiation or concentration.

The *product's life-cycle stage* also must be considered. When a firm introduces a new product, it may be practical to launch only one version, and undifferentiated marketing or concentrated marketing may make the most sense. In the mature stage of the product life cycle, however, differentiated marketing begins to make more sense. Another factor is *market variability*. If most buyers have the same tastes, buy the same amounts, and react the same way to marketing efforts, undifferentiated marketing is appropriate. Finally, *competitors' marketing strategies* are important. When competitors use differentiated or concentrated marketing, undifferentiated marketing can be suicidal. Conversely, when competitors use undifferentiated marketing, a firm can gain an advantage by using differentiated or concentrated marketing.

Socially Responsible Target Marketing

Smart targeting helps companies to be more efficient and effective by focusing on the segments that they can satisfy best and most profitably. Targeting also benefits consumers—companies reach specific groups of consumers with offers carefully tailored to satisfy their needs. However, target marketing sometimes generates controversy and concern. Issues usually involve the targeting of vulnerable or disadvantaged consumers with controversial or potentially harmful products.

For example, over the years, the cereal industry has been heavily criticized for its marketing efforts directed toward children. Critics worry that premium offers and high-powered advertising appeals presented through the mouths of lovable animated characters will overwhelm children's defenses. The marketers of toys and other children's products have been similarly battered, often with good justification.

Other problems arise when the marketing of adult products spills over into the kid segment—intentionally or unintentionally. For example, the Federal Trade Commission and citizen action groups have accused tobacco companies of targeting underage smokers. And a recent FTC study found that 80 percent of R-rated movies and 70 percent of video games with a mature rating were targeted to children under 17.[28] Some critics have even called for a complete ban on advertising to children. To encourage responsible advertising to children, the Children's Advertising Review Unit, the advertising industry's self-regulatory agency, has published extensive children's advertising guidelines that recognize the special needs of child audiences.

Cigarette, beer, and fast-food marketers have also generated much controversy in recent years by their attempts to target inner-city minority consumers. For example, McDonald's and other chains have drawn criticism for pitching their high-fat, salt-laden fare to low-income, inner-city residents who are much more likely than are suburbanites to be heavy consumers. R.J. Reynolds took heavy flak in the early 1990s when it announced plans to market Uptown, a menthol cigarette targeted toward low-income blacks. It quickly dropped the brand in the face of a loud public outcry and heavy pressure from black leaders.

G. Heileman Brewing made a similar mistake with PowerMaster, a potent malt liquor. Because malt liquor had become the drink of choice among many in the inner city, Heileman focused its marketing efforts for PowerMaster on inner-city consumers. However, this group suffers disproportionately from liver diseases brought on by alcohol, and the inner city is already plagued by alcohol-related problems such as crime and violence. Thus, Heileman's targeting decision drew substantial criticism.[29]

The meteoric growth of the Internet and other carefully targeted direct media has raised fresh concerns about potential targeting abuses. The Internet allows increasing refinement of audiences and, in turn, more precise targeting. This might help makers of questionable products or deceptive advertisers to more readily victimize the most vulnerable audiences. As one expert observes, "In theory, an audience member could have tailor-made deceptive messages sent directly to his or her computer screen."[30]

Not all attempts to target children, minorities, or other special segments draw such criticism. In fact, most provide benefits to targeted consumers. For example, Colgate makes a large selection of toothbrushes and toothpaste flavors and packages for children—from Colgate Barbie Sparkling Bubble Fruit, Colgate Barnie Mild Bubble Fruit, and Colgate Looney Tunes Tazmanian Devil Wild Mint toothpastes to Colgate Pokemon and Disney *Monsters, Inc.* character toothbrushes. Such products help make toothbrushing more fun and get children to brush longer and more often.

Golden Ribbon Playthings has developed a highly acclaimed and very successful black character doll named Huggy Bean, which is targeted toward minority consumers. Huggy comes with books and toys that connect her with her African heritage. Nacara Cosmetiques markets cosmetics for "ethnic women who have a thirst for the exotic." The line is specially formulated to complement the darker skin tones of African American women and dark-skinned women of Latin American, Indian, and Caribbean origins. Black-owned ICE theaters noticed that although moviegoing by blacks has surged, there are few inner-city theaters. The chain has opened a the-

Most target marketing benefits both the marketer and the consumer. Nacara Cosmetiques markets cosmetics for "ethnic women who have a thirst for the exotic." Colgate targets children with special flavors, shapes, and packages that help make tooth brushing more fun and get children to brush more often.

ater in Chicago's South Side as well as two other Chicago theaters, and it plans to open in four more cities this year. ICE partners with the black communities in which it operates theaters, using local radio stations to promote films and featuring favorite food items at concession stands.

Thus, in market targeting, the issue is not really *who* is targeted but rather *how* and for *what*. Controversies arise when marketers attempt to profit at the expense of targeted segments—when they unfairly target vulnerable segments or target them with questionable products or tactics. Socially responsible marketing calls for segmentation and targeting that serve not just the interests of the company but also the interests of those targeted.

Positioning for Competitive Advantage

Product position

The way the product is defined by consumers on important attributes—the place the product occupies in consumers' minds relative to competing products.

Beyond deciding which segments of the market it will target, the company must decide what positions it wants to occupy in those segments. A **product's position** is the way the product is *defined by consumers* on important attributes—the place the product occupies in consumers' minds relative to competing products. Positioning involves implanting the brand's unique benefits and differentiation in customers' minds. Tide is positioned as a powerful, all-purpose family detergent; Ivory Snow is positioned as the gentle detergent for fine washables and baby clothes. In the automobile market, the Toyota Echo and Ford Focus are positioned on economy, Mercedes and Cadillac on luxury, and Porsche and BMW on performance. Volvo positions powerfully on safety. At Subway restaurants, you "Eat Fresh." At Olive Garden restaurants, "When You're Here, You're Family."

Consumers are overloaded with information about products and services. They cannot reevaluate products every time they make a buying decision. To simplify the buying process, consumers organize products, services, and companies into categories and "position" them in their minds. A product's position is the complex set of perceptions, impressions, and feelings that consumers have for the product compared with competing products.

Consumers position products with or without the help of marketers. But marketers do not want to leave their products' positions to chance. They must *plan* positions that will give their products the greatest advantage in selected target markets, and they must design marketing mixes to create these planned positions.

Choosing a Positioning Strategy

Some firms find it easy to choose their positioning strategy. For example, a firm well known for quality in certain segments will go for this position in a new segment if there are enough buyers seeking quality. But in many cases, two or more firms will go after the same position. Then, each will have to find other ways to set itself apart. Each firm must differentiate its offer by building a unique bundle of benefits that appeals to a substantial group within the segment.

The positioning task consists of three steps: identifying a set of possible competitive advantages upon which to build a position, choosing the right competitive advantages, and selecting an overall positioning strategy. The company must then effectively communicate and deliver the chosen position to the market.

Identifying Possible Competitive Advantages

Competitive advantage

An advantage over competitors gained by offering consumers greater value, either through lower prices or by providing more benefits that justify higher prices.

The key to winning and keeping target customers is to understand their needs better than competitors do and to deliver more value. To the extent that a company can position itself as providing superior value, it gains **competitive advantage**. But solid positions cannot be built on empty promises. If a company positions its product as *offering* the best quality and service, it must then *deliver* the promised quality and service. Thus, positioning begins with actually *differentiating* the company's marketing offer so that it will give consumers more value than competitors' offers do.

To find points of differentiation, marketers must think through the customer's entire experience with the company's product or service. An alert company can find ways to differentiate itself at every point where it comes in contact with customers.[31] In what specific ways can a company differentiate its offer from those of competitors? A company or market offer can be differentiated along the lines of *product, services, channels, people,* or *image.*

Porsche positions power-fully on performance and the freedom it generates: "The engine launches you forward with its distinctive growl. Any memory of life on a leash evaporates in the wind rushing overhead. It's time to run free."

Product differentiation takes place along a continuum. At one extreme we find physical products that allow little variation: chicken, steel, aspirin. Yet even here some meaningful differentiation is possible. For example, Perdue claims that its branded chickens are better—fresher and more tender—and gets a 10 percent price premium based on this differentiation. At the other extreme are products that can be highly differentiated, such as automobiles, clothing, and furniture. Such products can be differentiated on features, performance, or style and design. Thus, Volvo provides new and better safety features; Whirlpool designs its dishwasher to run more quietly; Bose positions its speakers on their striking design characteristics. Similarly, companies can differentiate their products on such attributes as *consistency, durability, reliability,* or *repairability.*

Beyond differentiating its physical product, a firm can also differentiate the services that accompany the product. Some companies gain *services differentiation* through speedy, convenient, or careful *delivery.* For example, BankOne has opened full-service branches in supermarkets to provide location convenience along with Saturday, Sunday, and weekday-evening hours.

Installation can also differentiate one company from another, as can *repair* services. Many an automobile buyer will gladly pay a little more and travel a little farther to buy a car from a dealer that provides top-notch repair services. Some companies differentiate their offers by providing *customer training service* or *consulting services*—data, information systems, and advising services that buyers need. McKesson Corporation, a major drug wholesaler, consults with its 12,000 independent pharmacists to help them set up accounting, inventory, and computerized ordering systems. By helping its customers compete better, McKesson gains greater customer loyalty and sales.

Firms that practice *channel differentiation* gain competitive advantage through the way they design their channel's coverage, expertise, and performance. Caterpillar's success in the construction-equipment industry is based on superior channels. Its dealers worldwide are renowned for their first-rate service. Amazon.com, Dell Computer, and Avon distinguish themselves by their high-quality direct channels. And Iams pet food achieved success by going against tradition, distributing its products only through veterinarians and pet stores.

Companies can gain a strong competitive advantage through *people differentiation*—hiring and training better people than their competitors do. Thus, Disney people are known to be friendly and upbeat. Singapore Airlines enjoys an excellent reputation largely because of the grace of its flight attendants. IBM offers people who make sure that the solution customers want is the solution they get: "People Who Get It. People Who Get It Done." People differentiation requires that a company select its customer-contact people carefully and train them well. For example, Disney trains its theme park people thoroughly to ensure that they are competent, courteous, and friendly—from the hotel check-in agents, to the monorail drivers, to the ride attendants, to the people who sweep Main Street USA. Each employee understands the importance of understanding customers, communicating with them cheerfully, and responding quickly to their requests and problems. Each is carefully trained to "make people happy."

Even when competing offers look the same, buyers may perceive a difference based on company or brand *image differentiation*. A company or brand image should convey the product's distinctive benefits and positioning. Developing a strong and distinctive image calls for creativity and hard work. A company cannot plant an image in the public's mind overnight using only a few advertisements. If Ritz-Carlton means quality, this image must be supported by everything the company says and does. *Symbols*—such as the McDonald's golden arches, the Prudential rock, the Nike swoosh, the Intel Inside logo, or the Pillsbury doughboy—can provide strong company or brand recognition and image differentiation. The company might build a brand around a famous person, as Nike did with its Air Jordan basketball shoes and Tiger Woods golfing products. Some companies even become associated with colors, such as IBM (blue), Campbell (red and white), or UPS (brown). The chosen symbols, characters, and other image elements must be communicated through advertising that conveys the company's or brand's personality.

Choosing the Right Competitive Advantages

Suppose a company is fortunate enough to discover several potential competitive advantages. It now must choose the ones on which it will build its positioning strategy. It must decide *how many* differences to promote and *which ones.*

How Many Differences to Promote?   Many marketers think that companies should aggressively promote only one benefit to the target market. Ad man Rosser Reeves, for example, said a company should develop a *unique selling proposition* (USP) for each brand and stick to it. Each brand should pick an attribute and tout itself as "number one" on that attribute. Buyers tend to remember number one better, especially in an overcommunicated society. Thus, Crest toothpaste consistently promotes its anticavity protection and Volvo promotes safety. A company that hammers away at one of these positions and consistently delivers on it probably will become best known and remembered for it.

Other marketers think that companies should position themselves on more than one differentiator. This may be necessary if two or more firms are claiming to be best on the same attribute. Today, in a time when the mass market is fragmenting into many small segments, companies are trying to broaden their positioning strategies to appeal to more segments. For example, Unilever introduced the first three-in-one bar soap—Lever 2000—offering cleansing, deodorizing, *and* moisturizing benefits. Clearly, many buyers want all three benefits. The challenge was to convince them that one brand can deliver all three. Judging from Lever 2000's outstanding success, Unilever easily met the challenge. However, as companies increase the number of claims for their brands, they risk disbelief and a loss of clear positioning.

In general, a company needs to avoid three major positioning errors. The first is *underpositioning*—failing ever to really position the company at all. Some companies discover

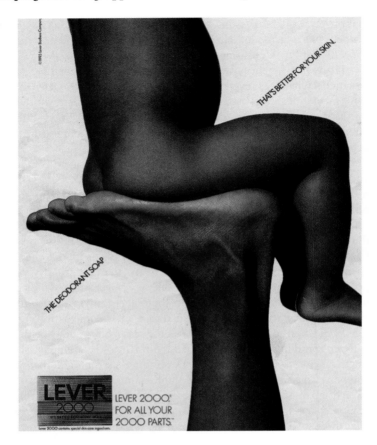

LEVER 2000. FOR ALL YOUR 2000 PARTS.

that buyers have only a vague idea of the company or that they do not really know anything special about it. The second error is *overpositioning*—giving buyers too narrow a picture of the company. Thus, a consumer might think that the Steuben glass company makes only fine glass costing $1,000 and up, when in fact it makes affordable fine glass starting at around $50.

Finally, companies must avoid *confused positioning*—leaving buyers with a confused image of a company. For example, over the past two decades, Burger King has fielded a dozen separate advertising campaigns, with themes ranging from "Herb the nerd doesn't eat here" to "Sometimes you've got to break the rules," "BK Tee Vee," "Got the Urge?" and "Have It Your Way." This barrage of positioning statements has left consumers confused and Burger King with poor sales and profits. Similarly, Kmart has not fared well against more strongly positioned competitors. Wal-Mart positions itself forcefully as offering "Always low prices. Always!" Target has positioned itself as the trendier "upscale discounter." But most consumers have difficulty positioning Kmart favorably on any specific differentiating attributes.

Which Differences to Promote?   Not all brand differences are meaningful or worthwhile; not every difference makes a good differentiator. Each difference has the potential to create company costs as well as customer benefits. Therefore, the company must carefully select the ways in which it will distinguish itself from competitors. A difference is worth establishing to the extent that it satisfies the following criteria:

- *Important:* The difference delivers a highly valued benefit to target buyers.
- *Distinctive:* Competitors do not offer the difference, or the company can offer it in a more distinctive way.
- *Superior:* The difference is superior to other ways that customers might obtain the same benefit.
- *Communicable:* The difference is communicable and visible to buyers.
- *Preemptive:* Competitors cannot easily copy the difference.
- *Affordable:* Buyers can afford to pay for the difference.
- *Profitable:* The company can introduce the difference profitably.

Many companies have introduced differentiations that failed one or more of these tests. The Westin Stamford hotel in Singapore advertises that it is the world's tallest hotel, a distinction that is not important to most tourists—in fact, it turns many off. Polaroid's Polarvision, which produced instantly developed home movies, bombed too. Although Polarvision was distinctive and even preemptive, it was inferior to another way of capturing motion, namely, camcorders. When Pepsi introduced clear Crystal Pepsi some years ago, customers were unimpressed. Although the new drink was distinctive, consumers didn't see "clarity" as an important benefit in a soft drink. Thus, choosing competitive advantages upon which to position a product or service can be difficult, yet such choices may be crucial to success.

Selecting an Overall Positioning Strategy

Value proposition

The full positioning of a brand—the full mix of benefits upon which it is positioned.

Consumers typically choose products and services that give them the greatest value. Thus, marketers want to position their brands on the key benefits that they offer relative to competing brands. The full positioning of a brand is called the brand's **value proposition**—the full mix of benefits upon which the brand is positioned. It is the answer to the customer's question "Why should I buy your brand?" Volvo's value proposition hinges on safety but also includes reliability, roominess, and styling, all for a price that is higher than average but seems fair for this mix of benefits.

Figure 8.3 shows possible value propositions upon which a company might position its products. In the figure, the five green cells represent winning value propositions—positioning that gives the company competitive advantage. The red cells, however, represent losing value propositions. The center yellow cell represents at best a marginal proposition. In the following sections, we discuss the five winning value propositions upon which companies can position their products: more for more, more for the same, the same for less, less for much less, and more for less.[32]

More for More.   "More-for-more" positioning involves providing the most upscale product or service and charging a higher price to cover the higher costs. Ritz-Carlton Hotels, Mont Blanc writing instruments, Mercedes-Benz automobiles—each claims superior quality, craftsmanship, durability, performance, or style and charges a price to match. Not only is the marketing offer high in quality, it also offers prestige to the buyer. It symbolizes status and a loftier lifestyle. Often, the price difference exceeds the actual increment in quality.

Sellers offering "only the best" can be found in every product and service category, from hotels, restaurants, food, and fashion to cars and kitchen appliances. Consumers are sometimes surprised, even delighted, when a new competitor enters a category with an unusually high-priced brand. Starbucks coffee entered as a very expensive brand in a largely commodity category; Häagen-Dazs came in as a premium ice cream brand at a price never before charged.

In general, companies should be on the lookout for opportunities to introduce a "much-more-for-much-more" brand in any underdeveloped product or service category. Yet more-for-more brands can be vulnerable. They often invite imitators who claim the same quality but at a

FIGURE 8.3
Possible value propositions

	Price		
	More	The same	Less
More	More for more	More for the same	More for less
same			The same for less
Less			Less for much less

"Much more for much more" value proposition: Häagen-Dazs offers its superpremium ice cream at a price never before charged.

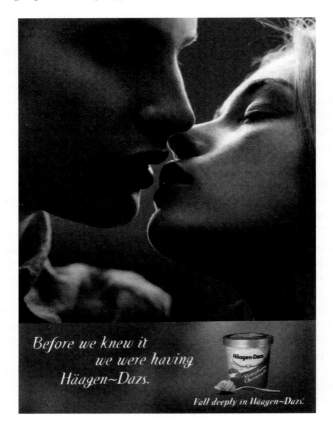

lower price. Luxury goods that sell well during good times may be at risk during economic downturns when buyers become more cautious in their spending.

More for the Same.   Companies can attack a competitor's more-for-more positioning by introducing a brand offering comparable quality but at a lower price. For example, Toyota introduced its Lexus line with a "more-for-the-same" value proposition. Its headline read: "Perhaps the first time in history that trading a $72,000 car for a $36,000 car could be considered trading up." It communicated the high quality of its new Lexus through rave reviews in car magazines, through a widely distributed videotape showing side-by-side comparisons of Lexus and Mercedes automobiles, and through surveys showing that Lexus dealers were providing customers with better sales and service experiences than were Mercedes dealerships. Many Mercedes owners switched to Lexus, and the Lexus repurchase rate has been 60 percent, twice the industry average.

The Same for Less.   Offering "the same for less" can be a powerful value proposition—everyone likes a good deal. For example, Dell Computer offers equivalent quality computers at a lower "price for performance." Discounts stores such as Wal-Mart and "category killers" such as Best Buy, Circuit City, and Sportmart also use this positioning. They don't claim to offer different or better products. Instead, they offer many of the same brands as department stores and specialty stores but at deep discounts based on superior purchasing power and lower-cost operations.

Other companies develop imitative but lower-priced brands in an effort to lure customers away from the market leader. For example, AMD makes less expensive versions of Intel's market-leading microprocessor chips. Many personal computer companies make "IBM clones" and claim to offer the same performance at lower prices.

Less for Much Less.   A market almost always exists for products that offer less and therefore cost less. Few people need, want, or can afford "the very best" in everything they buy. In many cases, consumers will gladly settle for less than optimal performance or give up some of the bells and whistles in exchange for a lower price. For example, many travelers seeking lodgings prefer not to pay for what they consider unnecessary extras, such as a pool, attached restaurant, or mints on the pillow. Motel chains such as Motel 6 suspend some of these amenities and charge less accordingly.

"Less-for-much-less" positioning involves meeting consumers' lower performance or quality requirements at a much lower price. For example, Family Dollar and Dollar General stores offer more affordable goods at very low prices. Sam's Club and Costco warehouse stores offer less merchandise selection and consistency, and much lower levels of service; as a result, they charge rock-bottom prices. Southwest Airlines, the nation's most profitable air carrier, also practices less-for-much-less positioning. It charges incredibly low prices by not serving food, not assigning seats, and not using travel agents.

More for Less.   Of course, the winning value proposition would be to offer "more for less." Many companies claim to do this. For example, Dell Computer claims to have better products *and* lower prices for a given level of performance. Procter & Gamble claims that its laundry detergents provide the best cleaning *and* everyday low prices. In the short run, some companies can actually achieve such lofty positions. For example, when it first opened for business, Home Depot had arguably the best product selection and service *and* the lowest prices compared to local hardware stores and other home improvement chains.

Yet in the long run, companies will find it very difficult to sustain such best-of-both positioning. Offering more usually costs more, making it difficult to deliver on the "for less" promise. Companies that try to deliver both may lose out to more-focused competitors. For example, facing determined competition from Lowe's stores, Home Depot must now decide whether it wants to compete primarily on superior service or on lower prices.

All said, each brand must adopt a positioning strategy designed to serve the needs and wants of its target markets. "More for more" will draw one target market, "less for much less" will draw another, and so on. Thus, in any market, there is usually room for many different companies, each successfully occupying different positions (see Real Marketing 8.3).

The important thing is that each company must develop its own winning positioning strategy, one that makes it special to its target consumers. Offering only "the same for the same" provides no competitive advantage, leaving the firm in the middle of the pack. Companies offering one of the three losing value propositions—"the same for more," "less for more," and "less for the same"—will inevitably fail. Here, customers soon realize that they've been underserved, tell others, and abandon the brand.

Developing a Positioning Statement

Positioning statement

A statement that summarizes company or brand positioning—it takes this form: *To (target segment and need) our (brand) is (concept) that (point-of-difference).*

Company and brand positioning should be summed up in a **positioning statement**. The statement should follow this form: *To (target segment and need) our (brand) is (concept) that (point-of-difference).*[33] For example: "To *busy professionals who need to stay organized,* Palm Pilot is *an electronic organizer* that *allows you to back up files on your PC more easily and reliably than competitive products.*" Sometimes a positioning statement is more detailed:

> To young, active soft-drink consumers who have little time for sleep, Mountain Dew is the soft drink that gives you more energy than any other brand because it has the highest level of caffeine. With Mountain Dew, you can stay alert and keep going even when you haven't been able to get a good night's sleep.[34]

Note that the positioning first states the product's membership in a category (Mountain Dew is a soft drink) and then shows its point of difference from other members of the category (has more caffeine). Placing a brand in a specific category suggests similarities that it might share with other products in the category. But the case for the brand's superiority is made on its points of difference. Sometimes marketers put a brand in a surprisingly different category before indicating the points of difference:

> DiGiorno's is a frozen pizza whose crust rises when the pizza is heated. Instead of putting it in the frozen pizza category, the marketers positioned it in the delivered pizza category. Their ad shows party guests asking which pizza delivery service the host used. But he says, "It's not delivery, its DiGiorno!" This helped highlight DiGiorno's fresh quality and superior taste over the normal frozen pizza.

real marketing 8.3

Airline Positioning: "More for More" or "Less for Much Less"?

Southwest Airlines and Midwest Express Airlines couldn't be more different in their positioning. Southwest offers a classic "less-for-much-less" value proposition. In contrast, Midwest Express offers "more for a tad more." What they have in common, however, is that both have consistently soared above their competitors. In an industry often plagued by huge losses, Southwest has experienced 29 straight years of profits; Midwest Express has turned a profit for 14

Southwest offers a classic "less for much less" value proposition, with lots of zany fun (here, happy-go-lucky CEO Herb Kelleher impersonates Elvis) . . .

of the last 15 years. Both owe their success to strong and clear positioning that serves a well-defined target segment. Here, we compare the alternative positions that have made these airlines so successful.

Southwest Airlines

Southwest Airlines knows its niche. From the start, it has positioned itself firmly as *the*

short-haul, no-frills, low-price airline. Its average flight time is just one hour; its average one-way fare just $84. Southwest's passengers have learned to fly without the amenities. For example, the airline provides no meals—just peanuts. It also offers no first-class section, only three-across seating in all of its planes. There's no such thing as a reserved seat on a Southwest flight. Passengers receive numbered boarding passes—first come, first served—and are herded onto the plane in groups of 30. "Southwest will get you and your luggage where you're going," comments an industry analyst, "but we don't call their planes cattle cars for nothing. It's a mercy that Southwest is a short-haul airline, because you can get pretzelated on their planes p.d.q."

Why, then, do so many passengers love Southwest? Perhaps most importantly, Southwest excels at the basics of getting passengers where they want to go and on time. In 1992, Southwest received the U.S. Department of Transportation's first-ever Triple Crown Award for best on-time service, best baggage handling, *and* best customer service, a feat it repeated for the next five straight years. For more than a decade, Southwest has been an industry leader in on-time performance.

Beyond these basics, however, there are two key elements to Southwest's strong positioning. The analyst sums up Southwest's positioning this way: "It is not luxurious, . . . but it's cheap and it's fun." Southwest is a model of efficiency and low-cost operations. As a result, its prices are shockingly low. In fact, prices are so low that when Southwest enters a new market, it actually increases total air traffic by attracting customers who might otherwise travel by car or bus. For example, when Southwest began its Louisville–Chicago flight at a one-way rate of $49 versus competitors' $250, total weekly air passenger traffic between the two cities increased from 8,000 to 26,000.

No frills and low prices, however, don't mean drudgery. To lighten things up, Southwest adds another key positioning ingredient—lots of good, clean fun. With its happy-go-lucky CEO, Herb Kelleher, leading

the charge, Southwest refuses to take itself seriously. Cheerful employees go out of their way to amuse, surprise, or somehow entertain passengers. According to one account:

Southwest employees are apt to dress as leprechauns on St. Patrick's Day, rabbits on Easter, and almost anything on Halloween. I have heard flight attendants sing the safety lecture as country music, blues, and rap; I have heard them compare the pilot to Rocky Raccoon and insist that passengers introduce themselves to one another, then hug, then kiss, then propose marriage.

Kelleher himself has been known to dress up as Elvis Presley to greet passengers.

During delays at the gate, ticket agents will award prizes to the passenger with the largest hole in his or her sock. Flight attendants have been known to hide in overhead luggage bins and then pop out when passengers start filing on board. Veteran Southwest fliers have learned to listen up to announcements over the intercom. On a recent flight, the pilot suggested, "Flight attendants will please prepare their hair for departure." Later in the flight, he announced, "Good morning, ladies and gentlemen. Those of you who wish to smoke will please file out to our lounge on the wing, where you can enjoy our feature film, *Gone with the Wind*." Safety instructions from the flight attendant included the advice "In the event of a water landing, please remember to paddle, kick, kick, paddle, kick, kick, all the way back."

As a result of its strong positioning, Southwest has grown to become the nation's fourth-largest domestic carrier. The company has successfully beaten off determined challenges from several major competitors who have tried to copy its winning formula, including Continental Lite, Delta Express, and Shuttle by United. Over the past 10 years, Southwest has expanded to serve 58 cities, its revenues have grown 388 percent, its net earnings have soared 1,490 percent, and its stock has yielded an average annual return to investors of 35 percent.

Midwest Express Airlines

Midwest Express Airlines' positioning stands in stark contrast to Southwest's. Whereas Southwest offers no frills, low prices, and zany fun, Midwest Express provides all the creature comforts and calm, refined service at higher but still competitive prices. It targets older, more affluent business travelers—35 percent of Midwest Express fliers earn more than $100,000 per year, and a majority are between the ages of 35 and 54. These

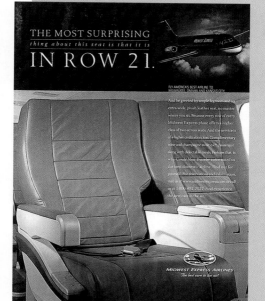

. . . Midwest Express offers a "more for a tad more" value proposition—its calm, refined service provides "the best care in the air."

fliers want more service and Midwest Express delivers it to them.

Flying Midwest Express is a special experience:

You slip into your leather seat. You don't tussle for the armrest with some sweaty stranger in the middle, because there is no middle; everyone sits two by two with loads of legroom. . . . On breakfast flights, the chilled champagne is free. At lunch and dinner, you can choose a quality Merlot or Chardonnay poured from bottles with actual corks. Next comes the hot food on real china. Yes, food—not pretzels or a deli bag, but lobster or salmon, served by certifiably cordial airline employees. You can cover your shirt with a linen napkin. And, in a burst of true genius, the glass you're drinking from is made of . . . glass! This isn't a frequent flier's fantasy; it's a real utopia on a shockingly civilized airline called Midwest Express.

Consistent with its motto, "The Best Care in the Air," Midwest Express provides high-quality, near-first-class service to all passengers. All seats are leather and a full 21 inches wide, compared to the 17- to 18-inch-wide seats of competitors. There are no more than four seats per row, eliminating the dreaded middle seat. Congenial but reserved flight attendants serve hot and elegant meals with complimentary wine or champagne, followed by a helping of the airline's signature chocolate chip cookies, sinfully gooey from being baked right on board. Midwest Express spends about $10 per passenger meal—twice the industry average (Southwest boasts that its average food cost per passenger is about 20¢). In a recent survey rating airline comfort, Midwest Express rated 98 on a scale 100 versus 67 to 74 for the major airlines.

Midwest Express is still a pretty small operation compared with Southwest and other major airlines. Unless you live in Milwaukee, Kansas City, or Omaha, Midwest's primary cities, you've probably never heard of

it. Yet the classy little airline has developed a devout following. Sales are growing steadily and the airline recently posted its fourteenth consecutive year of profitability. Last year, Midwest's revenues were up 13 percent, income increased by 44 percent, and the airline flew a record 2 million passengers. Adding additional luster, three national travel magazines named it the best U.S. airline.

Midwest Express passengers pay more for its first-rate service. The airline's prices are a tad higher than those of competitors, and the company sells very few economy seats. But to those who choose Midwest Express, the extras are well worth the additional costs. As for the future, Midwest Express is constantly on the lookout for new ways to please its already highly satisfied passengers. Says Tim Hoeksema, Midwest's president, "We're already looking for tomorrow's cookie—whatever makes somebody climb aboard [next year] and say, 'Wow.'"

Sources: Quotes from Molly Ivins, "From Texas, with Love and Peanuts," *New York Times,* March 14, 1999, p. 11; Daniel Pedersen, "Cookies and Champagne," *Newsweek,* April 27, 1998, p. 60; and Wendy Zellner, "Southwest: After Kelleher, More Blue Skies," *Business Week,* April 2, 2001, p. 45. Also see Ellen Jovin, "Buckling Up the Business Traveler," *American Demographics,* December 1998, pp. 48–51; Tania D. Panczyk, "Midwest Express Shifts to Spots Touting Service," *Adweek,* April 23, 2001, p. 3; "How Herb Keeps Southwest Hopping," *Money,* June 1999, pp. 61–62; Katrina Brooker, "The Chairman of the Board Looks Back," *Fortune,* May 28, 2001, pp. 63–74; Bill Ellet, "It's So Simple," *T+ D,* March 2002, p. 85; *Southwest Airlines Fact Sheet—June 2002* at www.southwest.com; and information accessed online at www.midwestexpress.com, July 2002.

Communicating and Delivering the Chosen Position

Once it has chosen a position, the company must take strong steps to deliver and communicate the desired position to target consumers. All the company's marketing mix efforts must support the positioning strategy. Positioning the company calls for concrete action, not just talk. If the company decides to build a position on better quality and service, it must first *deliver* that position. Designing the marketing mix—product, price, place, and promotion—involves working out the tactical details of the positioning strategy. Thus, a firm that seizes on a more-for-more position knows that it must produce high-quality products, charge a high price, distribute through high-quality dealers, and advertise in high-quality media. It must hire and train more service people, find retailers who have a good reputation for service, and develop sales and advertising messages that broadcast its superior service. This is the only way to build a consistent and believable more-for-more position.

Companies often find it easier to come up with a good positioning strategy than to implement it. Establishing a position or changing one usually takes a long time. In contrast, positions that have taken years to build can quickly be lost. Once a company has built the desired position, it must take care to maintain the position through consistent performance and communication. It must closely monitor and adapt the position over time to match changes in consumer needs and competitors' strategies. However, the company should avoid abrupt changes that might confuse consumers. Instead, a product's position should evolve gradually as it adapts to the ever-changing marketing environment.

LOOKING BACK: REVIEWING THE CONCEPTS

Marketers know that they cannot appeal to all buyers in their markets, or at least not to all buyers in the same way. Buyers are too numerous, too widely scattered, and too varied in their needs and buying practices. Therefore, most companies today are moving away from mass marketing. Instead, they practice *target marketing*—identifying market segments, selecting one or more of them, and developing products and marketing mixes tailored to each. In this way, sellers can develop the right product for each target market and adjust their prices, distribution channels, and advertising to reach the target market efficiently.

1. Define the three steps of target marketing: market segmentation, target marketing, and market positioning.

Market segmentation is the act of dividing a market into distinct groups of buyers with different needs, characteristics, or behaviors who might require separate products or marketing mixes. Once the groups have been identified, *targeting marketing* evaluates each market segment's attractiveness and suggests one or more segments to enter. *Market positioning* consists of setting the competitive positioning for the product and creating a detailed marketing plan.

2. List and discuss the major bases for segmenting consumer and business markets.

There is no single way to segment a market. Therefore, the marketer tries different variables to see which give the best segmentation opportunities. For consumer marketing, the major segmentation variables are geographic, demographic, psychographic, and behavioral. In *geographic segmentation*, the market is divided into different geographical units such as nations, regions, states, counties, cities, or neighborhoods. In *demographic segmentation,* the market is divided into groups based on demographic variables, including age, gender, family size, family life cycle, income, occupation, education, religion, race, generation, and nationality. In *psychographic segmentation,* the market is divided into different groups based on social class, lifestyle, or personality characteristics. In *behavioral segmentation,* the market is divided into groups based on consumers' knowledge, attitudes, uses, or responses to a product.

Business marketers use many of the same variables to segment their markets. But business markets also can be segmented by business consumer *demographics* (industry, company size), *operating variables, purchasing approaches, situational factors,* and *personal characteristics*. The effectiveness of segmentation

analysis depends on finding segments that are *measurable, accessible, substantial, differentiable,* and *actionable*.

3. Explain how companies identify attractive market segments and choose a target marketing strategy.

To target the best market segments, the company first evaluates each segment's size and growth characteristics, structural attractiveness, and compatibility with company objectives and resources. It then chooses one of four target marketing strategies—ranging from very broad to very narrow targeting. The seller can ignore segment differences and target broadly using *undifferentiated (or mass) marketing*. This involves mass-producing, mass-distributing, and mass-promoting about the same product in about the same way to all consumers. Or the seller can adopt *differentiated marketing*—developing different market offers for several segments. *Concentrated marketing* (or *niche marketing*) involves focusing on only one or a few market segments. Finally, *micromarketing* is the practice of tailoring products and marketing programs to suit the tastes of specific individuals and locations. Micromarketing includes *local marketing* and *individual marketing*. Which targeting strategy is best depends on company resources, product variability, product life-cycle stage, market variablility, and competitive marketing strategies.

4. Discuss how companies can position their products for maximum competitive advantage in the marketplace.

Once a company has decided which segments to enter, it must decide on its *market positioning* strategy—on which positions to occupy in its chosen segments. The positioning task consists of three steps: identifying a set of possible competitive advantages upon which to build a position, choosing the right competitive advantages, and selecting an overall positioning strategy. The brand's full positioning is called its *value proposition*—the full mix of benefits upon which the brand is positioned. In general, companies can choose from one of five winning value propositions upon which to position their products: more for more, more for the same, the same for less, less for much less, or more for less. Company and brand positioning are summarized in positioning statements that state the target segment and need, positioning concept, and specific points of difference. They must then effectively communicate and deliver the chosen position to the market.

REVIEWING THE KEY TERMS

Age and life-cycle segmentation 241
Behavioral segmentation 244
Benefit segmentation 245
Competitive advantage 259
Concentrated (or niche)
   marketing 253
Demographic segmentation 240
Differentiated (or segmented)
   marketing 252

Gender segmentation 242
Geographic segmentation 239
Income segmentation 243
Individual marketing 254
Intermarket segmentation 250
Local marketing 254
Market positioning 239
Market segmentation 239
Micromarketing 254

Occasion segmentation 244
Positioning statement 265
Product position 259
Psychographic segmentation 244
Target market 251
Target marketing 239
Undifferentiated (or mass)
   marketing 252
Value proposition 263

DISCUSSING THE CONCEPTS

1. Figure 8.1 shows three steps in target marketing. Briefly discuss each step.
2. Assume that you are the marketing manager for a cosmetics company that has just developed a new line of male cosmetics. The cosmetics are invisible on the skin, reduce aging lines significantly, and provide some protection from the sun. Using the major segmentation variables found in Table 8.1, construct a brief profile of three market segments that you suspect might be interested in this new product line. Explain your profiling procedure.
3. One approach in segmenting international markets is called intermarket segmentation. Explain this approach and illustrate it with an example.
4. Need help with your financial planning? Intuit's Quicken (financial planning software) and TurboTax (income-tax preparation software) software have secured the company's success in the rapidly growing financial planning and services market. Assuming that the company would like to expand, which of the market coverage strategies shown in Figure 8.2 would you suggest? Explain how the strategy helps Intuit overcome competitive challenges from other software makers, such as Microsoft.
5. Samuel Adams is one of several microbreweries attacking the established brewers' domestic beers. What is micro-

marketing, and how might microbreweries use it to take on larger competitors? How might Samuel Adams use local or individual marketing to advance its products?
6. Socially responsible marketing calls for segmentation and targeting that serve not just the interests of the company but also the interests of those targeted. Do these goals conflict with one another? Provide an example of a company that you believe takes a socially responsible approach to segmentation and targeting. Explain your reasoning.
7. A company or market offer can be differentiated along several lines. Find advertisements for several competitors in a particular industry. Using the advertisements, demonstrate how the companies differentiate themselves with respect to products, services, prices, and image. Which company seems to be more successful in the differentiation attempt? Explain.
8. McDonald's has long been an innovator in the fast-food field. To avoid the flat growth that has recently plagued the fast-food industry, McDonald's plans to experiment with waiter-service diners, McDonuts, Internet access for patrons, Spam breakfast platters, and a Town Center concept where adults can enjoy karaoke while kids go to Playland. Use Figure 8.3 to discuss what value propositions McDonald's would be addressing with these innovations.

APPLYING THE CONCEPTS

1. In 1969, Nissan Motor launched the Datsun 240Z, and for nearly two decades the Z-series ruled the sports car world in the United States. The early "Zs" were stylish Jaguar look-alikes with a budget price tag for the cost-conscious car buyer interested in a sleek sports car. The car's tremendous success inspired competitors to enter the market. Eventually, the sports car market became saturated, and "Z" sales declined. Today, Nissan is again vying for a piece of the budget sports car market with the introduction of the Nissan 350Z, and buyers are taking notice. The 350Z combines the spirit and power of the original model with twenty-first-century styling and technology. There is little question that the 350Z will turn a few heads, but will it generate the same response as its predecessor? Nissan is betting that the answer is yes.
   a. Assume you are the marketing director for the Nissan 350Z. Follow the steps in Figure 8.1 and construct a brief segmentation plan for introducing the car into the U.S. market. For additional product information, visit www.nissandriven.com.

   b. What segmentation, targeting, and positioning strategies would you recommend? Explain.
   c. What competitive advantage would you stress in your marketing campaign? Explain.
   d. What value proposition should be stressed? Why?
2. Have you used a SpinBrush to clean your teeth? If not, you're just the person Procter & Gamble's Crest SpinBrush is seeking. The SpinBrush is a battery-powered toothbrush that is taking the electric toothbrush market by storm. The product is fun, creatively styled (there's even a race car version), great at cleaning your teeth and gums, and attractively priced at only $5 each. Most innovative products begin with a premium pricing strategy. SpinBrush used the opposite approach to secure maximum market penetration and avoid knockoff competitors. The company even skipped the traditional heavy prelaunch advertising campaign in order to keep the product's price down. Instead, it relied on creative packaging that allowed customers to self-demonstrate the product in the store. The SpinBrush's

special "Try Me" feature rocketed sales to 10 million units in its introductory year. Procter & Gamble followed the successful launch by expanding into 35 countries. Competitors have arrived, but they may be too late to take the spin off of SpinBrush's success.

a. For more information on SpinBrush, visit the Procter & Gamble Web site at www.pg.com. Consider the information shown in Table 8.1. Which psychographic and behavioral segmentation variables might have been used by SpinBrush to define its initial market segments? Explain.

b. How could Procter & Gamble encourage consumers of traditional toothbrushes to use SpinBrush? What challenges might P&G marketers face? Explain.

c. What competitive advantage(s) does SpinBrush have?

d. As indicated in the text, not all brand differences are meaningful. Review the product's features on the Proctor & Gamble Web site and explain which characteristics give SpinBrush an advantage over traditional toothbrushes.

 DIGITAL CONNECTIONS

CONNECTING COMPANIES TO THE RIGHT MARKET SEGMENT

Research shows that Tweens—youths aged 8 to 14—are among today's most targeted consumer groups. They spend some $12 million annually to surround themselves with computers, electronic gadgets, music, clothing, magazines, and other gear that expresses their lifestyle. Figuring out how to reach this segment is a challenge to many marketers. But Mountain Dew (Pepsi) and Sprite (Coca-Cola) have had some success. By reorganizing their Web sites and revamping their marketing efforts, these two popular soft drink marketers have struck a chord with Tweens by offering chat rooms, links to music, sporting events, Xtreme challenges, giveaways, games.

FOR DISCUSSION

1. To learn more about marketing to Tweens, visit the following Web sites: Mountain Dew—www.mountaindew.com; Sprite—www.sprite.com; Gap—www.gap.com; Tommy Hilfiger—www.tommy.com; the Limited Too—www.limitedtoo.com; and Nintendo—www.nintendo.com. From what you observe on these sites, construct a brief profile of the Tween market segment.

2. What strategies do these Web sites use to attract Tween interest?

3. What ethical issues might a company encounter when targeting this group? Explain.

4. Assume that you have been hired by Red Bull (an energy drink) to devise a strategy to break into the Tween beverage market. Review the Red Bull Web site (www.redbull.com) and develop a marketing plan. Would you subdivide the Tween market segment? What positioning strategy would be best?

5. Choose a company that currently markets to older youths and young adults. Explain how the company could market its products to Tweens.

SmarterKids.com: Smarter Targeting

Some people assume SmarterKids.com is just another toy e-tailer. But the company offers several unique services. For starters, SmarterKids.com helps parents evaluate their children's skills and choose specific products and services to meet their children's unique educational needs. Each of the nearly 5,000 expert-approved products in SmarterKids.com's database is assigned an astonishing 200 to 300 attributes to describe exactly what it teaches, how it teaches it, and how it might effectively help a child learn. The company rates everything from the Sesame Street Rock & Roll Saxophone to Trivial Pursuit Junior. Richard Secor, SmarterKids.com's CIO, proclaims, "We're so much more than toys."

After reviewing the SmarterKids.com video, answer the following questions about market segmentation, targeting, and positioning:

1. In what ways might SmarterKids.com segment its consumers to do an even better job of individualizing services and recommendations? What segments of consumers are most likely to find value in the Web site's offerings?

2. What consumers does SmarterKids.com target? How does the company's targeting differ from that of other toy sellers such as Toys "Я" Us or Wal-Mart?

3. Visit SmarterKids.com. How has the site strategically positioned itself? What are its competitive advantages?

GM: Downsizing the Hummer

A LITTLE MILITARY HISTORY

Quickly. What is a "High Mobility Multi-Purpose Wheeled Vehicle"? Well, if you've kept up with Arnold Schwarzenegger films or studied the 1991 Gulf War, you may have recognized the formal military description of what soldiers describe using the acronym "Humvee." If you don't really know what a Humvee is, just stand by—General Motors is going to tell you.

This story starts in 1979, when AM General, a specialty vehicle manufacturer, earned a contract from the U.S. Army to design the Humvee. The Army wanted a new vehicle to replace the Jeep, the ever-present multipurpose vehicle that had transported generations of soldiers. The Army believed it needed a more modern, up-to-date vehicle to meet the needs of the modern soldier. AM General produced the big, boxy Humvee, which labored in relative obscurity until the Gulf War in 1991. In that war, the United States and its allies mounted a military operation against Iraq, which had just invaded Kuwait. Television coverage of the military buildup in advance of the short war and live broadcasts of the war itself introduced the public to the workhorse Humvee.

In 1992, AM General, responding to the Humvee's notoriety, decided to introduce the first *civilian* version of the Humvee—the Hummer. Weighing in at 7,100 pounds, the Hummer featured a huge, 6.5-liter V-8, turbo-diesel engine that produced 195 horsepower and propelled the Hummer from 0 to 60 miles per hour in a snail-like 18 seconds. But the Hummer's purpose was not speed. AM General designed it, like its military parent, to take people off the beaten path—way off. The Hummer could plow through water to a depth of 30 inches and climb almost vertical, rocky surfaces. It even had a central tire inflation system that allowed the driver to inflate or deflate the vehicle's tires while on the move.

The advertising tag line dubbed the Hummer "The world's most serious 4 × 4," and ad copy played up the vehicle's off-road capabilities and its military heritage. AM General targeted serious, elite road warriors who were willing to pay more than $100,000 to have the toughest vehicle in the carpool. These were people who also wanted to tell the world that they had been successful. To help buyers learn how to handle the Hummer in extreme off-road situations, AM General even offered a Hummer Driving Academy, where drivers learned to handle 22-inch vertical walls, high water, 40 percent side slopes, and 60 percent inclines.

GM'S MARKET RESEARCH

In 1998, GM was conducting market research using a concept vehicle that it described as rugged and militaristic. When the vehicle bore the GMC brand name (GM's truck division), the company found that consumers had a lukewarm reaction. However, when GM put the Hummer name on the vehicle, researchers found that it had the highest and most widespread appeal of any vehicle GM had *ever* tested. Armed with this insight, GM turned to AM General, which had just abandoned acquisition discussions with Ford Motor Company. In December 1999, GM signed an agreement with AM General giving GM rights to the Hummer brand. AM General also signed a seven-year contract to produce the Hummer H2 sport utility vehicle for GM.

Based on its research, GM believed that the Hummer H2, a smaller version of the Hummer, would appeal to rugged individualists and wealthy baby-boomers who wanted the ability to go off-road and to "successful achievers," thirty- and forty-something wealthy consumers who had jobs in investment banking and the like. GM believed that it could introduce the H2 in the luxury SUV market and compete successfully with brands such as the Lincoln Navigator or GM's own Cadillac Escalade. The company charted production plans that called for AM General to build a new $200 million manufacturing facility in Indiana and for GM to launch the H2 in July 2002 at a base sticker price of about $49,000. It predicted that it could sell 19,000 H2s in 2002 (the 2003 model year) and then ramp up production to sell 40,000 units per year thereafter—a number that would make the H2 the largest seller in the luxury SUV market. Further, GM planned to introduce the H3, a still smaller and more affordable version of the Hummer in 2005. It believed it could sell 80,000 units of the H3 per year. These numbers compared with annual sales of only about 800 Hummers.

SOFTENING UP THE MARKET

During 2000, GM and AM General did not advertise the Hummer, but they mapped out a campaign for the year leading up to the H2's 2002 introduction that would raise awareness of the Hummer brand and serve as a bridge to the introduction. GM hired a marketing firm, Modernista, to develop the estimated $3 million campaign. Modernista found that the Hummer had about a 50 percent awareness level among buyers of full-size SUVs, mainly due to its appearance in movies. AM General had been spending less than $1 million a year on advertising and promotion. Further, 13 to 20 percent of these buyers had considered the Hummer.

In mid-2001, GM launched the Modernista campaign using the tag line "Hummer. Like nothing else." Placements in *The Wall Street Journal*, *Barron's*, *Spin*, *Business Week*, *Cigar Aficionado*, and *Esquire* used four different headlines:

"How did my soul get way out here?"
"What good is the world at your fingertips if you never actually touch it?"
"You can get fresh air lots of places, but this is the really good stuff."
"Out here you're nobody. Perfect."

(continued)

Following each headline was the same copy: "Sometimes you find yourself in the middle of nowhere. And sometimes in the middle of nowhere you find yourself. The legendary H1." One agency official said the ads used journalistic-type photography to make them more believable and to play down the he-man imagery. "Authenticity is probably the most important word when it comes to branding," the official argued. Whereas previous Hummer ads had featured the tough SUV plowing through snow and streams, the new ads featured the Hummer with gorgeous Chilean vistas. The new ads, the agency suggested, were as much about the people who buy Hummers as they were about the vehicle. Hummer owners often believed they got a bum rap as show-offs, the representative suggested, but he argued that the new ads would show the buyer's other side.

THE LAUNCH
Right on schedule in July 2002, GM introduced the 2003 Hummer 2 SUT (Sport Utility Truck). GM and AM General designed and built the H2 in just 16 months, much more quickly than the three-to-four-year time normally required. GM built the H2 on GM's GMT 800 truck platform, and it shared a number of parts with other GM models. The H2 was about the same size as the Chevy Tahoe, five inches narrower than the Hummer and about 700 pounds lighter. However, it was about 1,400 pounds heavier than other SUVs. It had a 316-horsepower engine that slurped a gallon of gasoline every 12 miles. It also featured a nine-speaker Bose stereo system. Buyers could upgrade the base model with a $2,575 luxury package that added heated leather front seats and a six-disc CD changer or with a $2,215 Adventure package that added sir suspension, brush guards, and crossbars for the roof rack.

GM had about 150 dealers who would initially offer the H2. The dealers had to agree to build a special showroom and a test track.

For promotion, GM stayed with the Modernista firm. Late in the summer of 2002, TV ads broke on shows such as *CSI: Miami* and featured a well-dressed woman behind the H2's steering wheel. The Modernista representative indicated that the message was that the H2 is not about blowing things up. Twenty-four print ads showed the H2 not in action but sitting still. Modernista believed that people knew the H2 would be tough—it wanted people to see that the H2 looked good.

THE ON-ROAD TEST
GM targeted buyers with an average age of 42 and annual household incomes above $125,000 versus H1 owners' averages of about 50 years old and household incomes above $200,000. The questions were, could GM position the H2 to appeal to its target market, and was that market large enough to ensure that GM could reach its sales and profitability targets?

One writer who had driven the H2 found it to be comfortable and surprisingly smooth on the highway. However, he criticized the interior and the lack of storage space. He noted that the H2 seated just six people versus eight or nine for other large SUVs.

Analysts argued that GM was pursuing a risky strategy. Would its having borrowed parts from other GM models to keep costs down and speed the time to market damage the H2's image? Would GM be able to justify the H2's high price when it had so much in common with other SUVs that cost thousands less? Would consumers really spend so much for an off-the-road vehicle that, studies showed, only 10 percent of image-conscious buyers would actually take off road? Finally, could GM make the Hummer 2 stand out in an increasingly crowded market? (See Exhibit 1.)

Arnold Schwarzenegger appeared in an H2 promotional video suggesting, "Don't call it the baby Hummer, you'll make it angry." Will the Hummer H2 be a hum-dinger and make GM happy, or will it get stuck in the rocky luxury SUV market?

HUMMER H2'S EXISTING OR COMING COMPETITION

Model/Manufacturer	Base Price
BMW X5 4.6is	$66,845
Mercedes G500	$73,165
Cadillac Escalade EXT	$50,015
Land Rover Range Rover	$69,995
Lincoln Navigator	$48,775
Porsche Cayenne	$45,000–$75,000
Volvo XC 90	$35,000–$45,000
Cadillac SRX	$40,000–$50,000
Infiniti FX 45	$40,000–$50,000

Source: Gregory B. White and Joseph L. White, "Automakers Take One-Up-Manship to New Level with New Extreme SUVs," *Wall Street Journal,* July 19, 2002, p. W1.

QUESTIONS FOR DISCUSSION
1. How has GM used the major segmentation variables for consumer markets in segmenting the SUV market?
2. What target-market decisions has GM made in selecting targets for the Hummer H2? How are those decisions different from AM General's target for the original Hummer?
3. How has GM attempted to position the H2?
4. Why do you think some consumers will pay $40,000 or more for an off-road vehicle that 90 percent of them will never take off road?
5. What segmentation, targeting, and positioning recommendations would you make to GM for the H2?
6. What other marketing recommendations would you make?

Sources: Melanie Well, "Muscle Car," *Forbes,* July 22, 2002, p. 181; David Welch, "More Sport, Less Utility," *Business Week,* July 8, 2002, p. 110; John O'Dell, "GM Sets Price for Hummer H2 SUV," *LATimes.com,* May 29, 2002; Trevor Jensen, "GM Tones Down Macho in New Ads for Hummer," *Adweek Midwest Edition,* August 6, 2001, p. 5; Jean Halliday, "Of Hummers and Zen," *Advertising Age,* August 6, 2001, p. 29; Gregory L. White, "GM's New Baby Hummer Shares Its Toys with Chevy," *Wall Street Journal,* April 10, 2001, p. B1; Rick Kranz, "H2 Baby Hummer Won't Be Far from Concept, GM Says," *Automotive News,* November 20, 2000, p. 6.

Case Pilot Case for Part 2: Developing Marketing Opportunities and Strategies

The Big Wind: Developing Marketing Opportunities and Strategies

Urs Siani, an engineer, had been employed by a large housing construction corporation for nine years and had recently been promoted from project supervisor to company vice-president. Over the past year in her spare time, and because of her passion for energy conservation, she developed a radically new windmill in her garage that she hoped would reduce energy costs for farmers in regions where high winds were common.

Based upon her estimates, two of these windmills, together with a storage battery system, would be capable of supplying the normal electrical energy requirements for an average farm. To date, Urs had received a patent for her "Big Wind" windmill system and had sought some advice of professional colleagues as to the best way to market, make, distribute, and service the windmills for potential customers.

Urs calculated that at a selling price of $16,000, she could net $4,000 per sale after paying for materials and labor for two windmills, a storage battery system, transportation, and installation that would be required for each windmill system sale. An average farmer could expect to save enough on his electricity charges to recover the cost of the equipment within eight years, according to Urs estimates.

Based upon feedback she received while attending a wind-energy conference, Urs believed her windmill could have long-term potential and be made even more efficient with further research and through the use of improved battery systems currently being developed by other companies. Maintenance for the complete system over the eight-year payback period, including battery cell replacement, was estimated to cost about $1,500, which was about half the cost for comparable windmills used in Europe.

Development of the windmills had already cost Urs more than $90,000, which she financed by mortgaging her home. Business colleagues had told Urs that her business idea would need additional funds for marketing, renting equipment and building space, hiring staff, and covering start-up inventory costs. Urs calculated that she would need another $100,000 in order to start the business. Her bank had just confirmed that they would finance another $50,000 using her retirement savings as collateral to secure this new loan. The banker also told Urs that she should decide quickly whether or not to start this business because several utility companies were reported to be developing new less-expensive consumer applications that would be marketed later that year.

Recently, Urs had hired a consulting company to establish potential demand, and using detailed farm locations and weather charts, they estimated that the best markets would be three prairie provinces in Canada (with 11,600 registered farms), and also seven American central states (with 9,700 registered farms) where utility costs were increasing. Another engineer also sent Urs a recent report from Europe where windmills were increasingly used by private homeowners and by smaller businesses to provide most electricity required.

Urs was unsure, however, how to sell windmills to farmers, and which types of farms would be the best to approach first. Finally, she wondered how best to proceed given the many different issues she was trying to juggle and how it might affect her life with her husband and two children.

Case Pilot Challenge

The importance of obtaining and using relevant market research for business and consumer market is the focus of Part 2 of the text. The four chapters in this portion of the book help explain how market research is crucial for marketers so they can successfully segment, target, and position their products and services with this information.

In the Big Wind case, above, Urs has an idea for a new product but needs to conduct market research. Try your marketing management skills, visit www.prenhall.com/casepilot/, and see if you can find the answers to the following:

a) Which market segments holds most promise for this product: Consumer or business market?

b) How could Urs assess the market demand for the windmill?

c) What's the biggest marketing challenge facing the business?

1. define *product* and the major classifications of products and services
2. describe the decisions companies make regarding their individual products and services, product lines, and product mixes
3. discuss branding strategy—the decisions companies make in building and managing their brands
4. identify the four characteristics that affect the marketing of a service and the additional marketing considerations that services require
5. discuss two additional product issues: socially responsible product decisions and international product and services marketing

Product, Services, and Branding Strategies

LOOKING AHEAD: PREVIEWING THE CONCEPTS

Now that you've had a good look at marketing strategy, we'll take a deeper look at the marketing mix—the tactical tools that marketers use to implement their strategies. In this and the next chapter, we'll study how companies develop and manage products and brands. Then, in the chapters that follow, we'll look at pricing, distribution, and marketing communication tools. The product is usually the first and most basic marketing consideration. How well firms manage their individual brands and their overall product and service offerings has a major impact on their success in the marketplace. We'll start with a seemingly simple question: What *is* a product? As it turns out, however, the answer is not so simple.

To start things off, think about cosmetics marketing. Remember that seemingly simple question—what is a product? The following cosmetics industry example shows why there is no easy answer. What, really, *are* cosmetics? Cosmetics makers like Aveda know that when a woman buys cosmetics, she buys much, much more than scented ingredients in fancy bottles.

Each year, cosmetics companies sell billions of dollars' worth of potions, lotions, and fragrances to consumers around the world. In one sense, these products are no more than careful mixtures of oils and chemicals that have nice scents and soothing properties. But the cosmetics companies know that they sell much more than just mixtures of ingredients—they sell the promise of what these concoctions will do for the people who use them.

Of course, in the cosmetics business, like anywhere else, quality and performance contribute to success or failure. For example, perfume marketers agree, "No smell, no sell." However, $180-an-ounce perfume may cost no more than $10 to produce. Thus, to perfume consumers, many things beyond the scent and a few dollars' worth of ingredients add to a perfume's allure. Fragrance names such as Obsession, Passion, Gossip, Wildheart, Opium, Joy, White Linen, Youth Dew, Eternity, and Love suggest that the perfumes will do something more than just make you smell better.

What *is* the promise of cosmetics? The following account by a *New York Times* reporter suggests the extent to which cosmetics take on meaning far beyond their physical makeup.

Last week I bathed in purple water (*I Trust* bubble bath, made by Philosophy) and powdered up with pink powder (*Rebirth*, by 5S,

"to renew the spirit and recharge the soul"). My moisturizer was *Bliss* (Chakra VII by Aveda, for "the joyful enlightenment and soaring of the spirit"); my nail polish was *Spiritual* (by Tony and Tina, "to aid connection with the higher self"). My teeth were clean, my heart was open—however, my bathroom was so crowded with bottles and brochures, the latest tools and totems from the human potential movement, that I could hardly find my third eye. Still, my "Hope in a Jar" package (from Philosophy) pretty well summed it up: "Where there is hope there can be faith. Where there is faith miracles can occur."

If you are looking for enlightenment in all the wrong places, cosmetics companies are eager to help. Because today, feeling good is the new religion. And cosmetics companies are the newest of the new prophets, turning the old notion of hope in a jar on its head.

"Cosmetics are our satellite to the divine!" This is what you'll hear from Tony and Tina, for example. Tony and Tina (Anthony Gillis and Cristina Bornstein) are nice young artists. He's from London, she grew up in New York. Chakra nail polish, which they invented for an installation at the Gershwin Gallery in Manhattan two years ago, was intended as an ironic commentary on the beauty business. But then a friend suggested they get into the beauty business, and now Tony and Tina have a $2 million cosmetics company with a mission statement: "To aid in the evolution of human consciousness." Their products include nail polishes (Vibrational Remedies) in colors meant to do nice things to your chakras, as well as body glitter and hair mascara, lipstick and eyeshadow. You can buy them at Fred Segal, Nordstrom, and Bloomingdale's, where last month they outsold Hard Candy and Urban Decay. "We think color therapy is going to be the new medicine," said Tony.

Rainbows are proliferating as rapidly in the New Age as angels once did. Philosophy, a three-year-old Arizona company, makes a sort of head/heart kit—"a self-help program," the company insists—called the *Rainbow Connection.* You pay $45 for seven bottles of colored bubble bath in a metal box. "Choose your colored bath according to the area of your emotional life that needs attention, i.e. self-love, self-worth," the brochure reads. "My role as I see it," said Christina Carlino, Philosophy's founder, "is to help you stay on your destiny path. It's not about what you look like. Beauty is defined by your deeds."

5S, a new sprout of the Japanese cosmetics company Shiseido, offers a regimen that plays, the company says, on the "fundamental and mythical significance of 5" (Five Pillars of Islam, Five Classics of Confucianism, and so on), and which is organized into emotional rather than physical categories. At the 5S store in SoHo, you don't buy things for dry skin, you buy things that are "energizing" or "nurturing" or "adoring." The company also believes in color therapy. Hence, *Rebirth,* products tinted "nouveau pink" (the color of bubble gum). A customer can achieve rebirth with 5S pink soap, pink powder, and pink toner.

Here are products that are not intended to make you look better, but to make you act better, feel better, and be a better person. You don't need a month's visit to India to find your higher self; you need only buy this bubble bath, that lipstick, this night cream. The beauty business's old come-on (trap your man!) has been swept away in favor of a new pitch. I don't have wrinkles anymore. I've got a chakra blockage.

Of course, who knew about chakras before Aveda? In 1989, the plant-based, eco-friendly cosmetics company Aveda trademarked Chakras I through VII to use as titles for moisturizers and scents. Chakra products were perhaps a little ahead of their time back then. However, the purchase of Aveda [a while] ago by the Estée Lauder Companies, the General Motors of the cosmetics world, suggests that the pendulum of history has finally caught up. "Aveda isn't a marketing idea," says Jeanette Wagner, the vice chairman of Estée Lauder. "It is a passionately held belief. From my point of view, the appeal is first the spirituality, and then the products."

All this might sound like only so much flimflam, but the underlying point is legitimate. The success of such brands affirms that products really are more than just the physical entities. When a woman buys cosmetics, she really does buy much, much more than just oils, chemicals, and fragrances. The cosmetic's image, its promises and positioning, its ingredients, its name and package, the company that makes it, the stores that sell it—all become a part of the total cosmetic product. When Aveda, Philosophy, and 5S sell cosmetics, they sell more than just tangible goods. They sell lifestyle, self-expression, exclusivity, and spirituality; achievement, success, and status; romance, passion, and fantasy; memories, hopes, and dreams.[1]

Clearly, cosmetics are more than just cosmetics when Aveda sells them. This chapter begins with a deceptively simple question: *What is a product?* After answering this question, we look at ways to classify products in consumer and business markets. Then we discuss the important decisions that marketers make regarding individual products, product lines, and product mixes. Next, we look into the critically important issue of how marketers build and manage brands. Finally, we examine the characteristics and marketing requirements of a special form of product—services.

What Is a Product?

Product
Anything that can be offered to a market for attention, acquisition, use, or consumption that might satisfy a want or need.

Service
Any activity or benefit that one party can offer to another that is essentially intangible and does not result in the ownership of anything.

A Sony DVD player, a Ford Taurus, a Costa Rican vacation, a Caffé Mocha at Starbucks, Charles Schwab online investment services, and advice from your family doctor—all are products. We define a **product** as anything that can be offered to a market for attention, acquisition, use, or consumption and that might satisfy a want or need. Products include more than just tangible goods. Broadly defined, products include physical objects, services, events, persons, places, organizations, ideas, or mixes of these entities. Thus, throughout this text, we use the term *product* broadly to include any or all of these entities.

Because of their importance in the world economy, we give special attention to services. **Services** are a form of product that consists of activities, benefits, or satisfactions offered for sale that are essentially intangible and do not result in the ownership of anything. Examples are banking, hotel, airline, retail, tax preparation, and home repair services. We will look at services more closely later in this chapter.

Products, Services, and Experiences

Product is a key element in the *market offering*. Marketing-mix planning begins with formulating an offering that brings value to target customers and satisfies their needs. This offering becomes the basis upon which the company builds profitable relationships with customers.

A company's market offering often includes both tangible goods and services. Each component can be a minor or a major part of the total offer. At one extreme, the offer may consist of a *pure tangible good,* such as soap, toothpaste, or salt—no services accompany the product. At the other extreme are *pure services,* for which the offer consists primarily of a service. Examples include a doctor's exam or financial services. Between these two extremes, however, many goods-and-services combinations are possible.

Today, as products and services become more and more commoditized, many companies are moving to a new level in creating value for their customers. To differentiate their offers, they are developing and delivering total customer *experiences*. Whereas products are tangible and services are intangible, experiences are memorable. Whereas products and services are external, experiences are personal and take place in the minds of individual consumers. Companies that market experiences realize that customers are really buying much more than just products and services. They are buying what those offers will *do* for them (see Real Marketing 9.1).[2]

real
marketing 9.1

Beyond Products and Services: Welcome to the Experience Economy

In their book, *The Experience Economy,* Joseph Pine and James Gilmore argue that, as products and services become less and less differentiated, companies are moving to a new level in creating value for customers. Beyond simply making products and delivering services, companies are staging, marketing, and delivering memorable experiences. Consider the evolution of the birthday cake:

[In an] *agrarian* economy, mothers made birthday cakes from scratch, mixing farm commodities (flour, sugar, butter, and eggs) that together cost mere dimes. As the *goods-based* industrial economy advanced, moms paid a dollar or two to Betty Crocker for premixed ingredients. Later, when the *service* economy took hold, busy parents ordered cakes from the bakery or grocery store, which, at $10 or $15, cost ten times as much as the packaged ingredients. Now, . . . time-starved parents neither make the birthday cake nor even throw the party. Instead, they spend $100 or more to "outsource" the entire event to Chuck E. Cheese's, the Discovery Zone, the Mining Company, or some other business that stages a memorable event for the kids—and often throws in the cake for free.

Welcome to the emerging *experience* economy. . . . From now on, leading-edge companies—whether they sell to consumers or businesses—will find that the next competitive battleground lies in staging experiences.

Experiences are sometimes confused with services, but experiences are as distinct from services as services are distinct from goods. Whereas products and services are external, experiences exist only in the mind of the individual. They are rich with emotional, physical, intellectual, or spiritual sensations created within the consumer. According to Pine and Gilmore:

An experience occurs when a company intentionally uses services as the stage, and goods as props, to engage individual customers in a way that creates a memorable event. . . . To appreciate the difference between services and experiences, recall the episode of the old television show *Taxi* in which Iggy, a usually atrocious (but fun-loving) cab driver, decided to become the best taxi driver in the world. He served sandwiches and drinks, conducted tours of the city, and even sang Frank Sinatra tunes. By engaging passengers in a way that turned an ordinary cab

ride into a memorable event, Iggy created something else entirely—a distinct economic offering. The experience of riding in his cab was more valuable to his customers than the service of being transported by the cab—and in the TV show, at least, Iggy's customers happily responded by giving bigger tips. By asking to go around the block again, one patron even paid more for poorer service just to prolong his enjoyment. The service Iggy provided—taxi transportation—was simply the stage for the experience that he was really selling.

Experiences have always been important in the entertainment industry—Disney has long manufactured memories through its movies and theme parks. Today, however, all kinds of firms are recasting their traditional goods and services to create experiences. For example, restaurants create value well beyond the food they serve. Starbucks patrons are paying for more than just coffee. "Customers at Starbucks are paying for staged experiences," comments one analyst. "The company treats patrons to poetry on its wallpaper and tabletops, jaunty apron-clad performers behind the espresso machine, and an interior ambience that's both cozy and slick, marked by earth tones,

(continued)

brushed steel, and retro music (also for sale). Few people leave without feeling a little more affluent, sophisticated, or jazzed."

Many retailers also stage experiences. Niketown stores create "shoppertainment" by offering interactive displays, engaging activities, and promotional events in a stimu-

Marketing experiences: Sony's Metreon markets an "interactive entertainment experience: four floors and 350,000 square feet jam-packed with ways to entertain and escape into a whole new reality."

lating shopping environment. At stores such as Sharper Image and Brookstone, "people play with the gadgets, listen to miniaturized stereo equipment, sit in massage chairs, and then leave without paying for what they valued, namely, the experience."

In San Francisco, Sony of America has developed Metreon, an "interactive entertainment experience," where visitors can shop, eat, drink, play, or simply soak up the experiences (check it out at www.metreon. com). The huge Metreon complex features 19 theaters, including a Sony IMAX theater, eight restaurants, and several interactive attractions, such as "Where the Wild Things Are" (an interactive playspace inspired by Maurice Sendak's popular children's book) and Moebius's Airtight Garage (an adventure zone featuring original interactive games based on the work of French graphic novelist Jean Giraud). Visitors can also experience any of nine interactive stores, including the flagship Discovery Channel Store: Destination San Francisco (featuring interactive educational exhibits inspired by programming from the Discovery Channel, TLC, and Animal Planet cable networks), Sony Style (a high-touch boutique of Sony products), and microsoftSF (where shoppers can play with the latest computer software and hardware). In all, Metreon offers a dazzling experience that far transcends the goods and services assortment it contains. Sony sums up the experience this way:

Use your eyes, ears, hands, and brain . . . sensory overload to a phenomenal degree. . . . Four floors and 350,000 square feet jam-packed with ways to entertain and escape into a whole new reality. Dazzle a date. Bring wonder to your kids. Shop in amazement. Have fun with your friends. Whenever you want real entertainment, head to Metreon.

The experience economy goes beyond the entertainment and retailing businesses. All companies stage experiences whenever they engage customers in a personal, memorable way:

In the travel business, former British Airways chairman Sir Colin Marshall has noted that the "commodity mind-set" is to "think that a business is merely performing a function—in our case, transporting people from point A to point B on time and at the lowest possible price." What British Airways does, according to Sir Colin, is "to go beyond the function and compete on the basis of providing an experience." The company uses its base service (the travel itself) as the stage for a

distinctive en route experience—one that attempts to transform air travel into a respite from the traveler's normally frenetic life.

Business-to-business marketers also stage experiences for their customers. For example, one Minneapolis computer installation and repair company has found a way to turn its otherwise humdrum service into a memorable encounter. Calling itself the Geek Squad, it sends "special agents" dressed in white shirts with thin black ties and pocket protectors, carrying badges, and driving old cars. Similarly, Silicon Graphics creates an experience as elaborate as any Disney attraction:

[Its] Visionarium Reality Center at corporate headquarters in Mountain View, California, brings customers and engineers together in an environment where they can interact with real-time, three-dimensional product visualizations. Customers can view, hear, and touch—as well as drive, walk, or fly—through myriad product possibilities. [According to one Silicon Graphics executive,] "This is experiential computing at its ultimate, where our customers can know what their products will look like, sound like, and feel like before manufacturing."

Thus, as we move into the twenty-first century, marketers seeking new ways to bring value to customers must look beyond the goods and services they make and sell. They must find ways to turn their offers into total customer experiences. As the experience economy grows, Pine and Gilmore caution, it "threatens to render irrelevant those who relegate themselves to the diminishing world of goods and services."

Sources: Excerpts and quotes from "Welcome to the Experience Economy," *Harvard Business Review,* July–August 1998, pp. 97–105; Wade Roush, "Now Playing: Your Business," *Technology Review,* May–June 1999, p. 96; and Sony's Metreon Web site, www.metreon.com, August 2002. Also see B. Joseph Pine and James H. Gilmore, *The Experience Economy* (New York: Free Press, 1999); Scott Mac Stravic, "Make Impressions Last: Focus on Value," *Marketing News,* October 23, 2000, pp. 44–45; and Stephen E. DeLong, "The Experience Economy," *Upside,* November 2001, p. 28.

FIGURE 9.1
Three levels of product

Levels of Product and Services

Product planners need to think about products and services on three levels (see Figure 9.1). Each level adds more customer value. The most basic level is the *core benefit,* which addresses the question *What is the buyer really buying?* When designing products, marketers must first define the core, problem-solving benefits or services that consumers seek. A woman buying lipstick buys more than lip color. Charles Revson of Revlon saw this early: "In the factory, we make cosmetics; in the store, we sell hope." Charles Schwab does more than sell financial services—it promises to fulfill customers' "financial dreams."

At the second level, product planners must turn the core benefit into an *actual product.* They need to develop product and service features, design, a quality level, a brand name, and packaging. For example, a Sony camcorder is an actual product. Its name, parts, styling, features, packaging, and other attributes have all been combined carefully to deliver the core benefit—a convenient, high-quality way to capture important moments.

Finally, product planners must build an *augmented product* around the core benefit and actual product by offering additional consumer services and benefits. Sony must offer more than

Core, actual, and augmented product: Consumers perceive this Sony camcorder as a complex bundle of tangible and intangible features and services that deliver a core benefit—a convenient, high-quality way to capture important moments.

just a camcorder. It must provide consumers with a complete solution to their picture-taking problems. Thus, when consumers buy a Sony camcorder, Sony and its dealers also might give buyers a warranty on parts and workmanship, instructions on how to use the camcorder, quick repair services when needed, and a toll-free telephone number to call if they have problems or questions.

Consumers see products as complex bundles of benefits that satisfy their needs. When developing products, marketers first must identify the *core* consumer needs the product will satisfy. They must then design the *actual* product and find ways to *augment* it in order to create the bundle of benefits that will provide the most satisfying customer experience.

Product and Service Classifications

Consumer product

Product bought by final consumer for personal consumption.

Convenience product

Consumer product that the customer usually buys frequently, immediately, and with a minimum of comparison and buying effort.

Shopping product

Consumer good that the customer, in the process of selection and purchase, characteristically compares on such bases as suitability, quality, price, and style.

Specialty product

Consumer product with unique characteristics or brand identification for which a significant group of buyers is willing to make a special purchase effort.

Products and services fall into two broad classes based on the types of consumers that use them— *consumer products* and *industrial products*. Broadly defined, products also include other marketable entities such as experiences, organizations, persona, places, and ideas.

Consumer Products

Consumer products are products and services bought by final consumers for personal consumption. Marketers usually classify these products and services further based on how consumers go about buying them. Consumer products include *convenience products, shopping products, specialty products,* and *unsought products.* These products differ in the ways consumers buy them and therefore in how they are marketed (see Table 9.1).

Convenience products are consumer products and services that the customer usually buys frequently, immediately, and with a minimum of comparison and buying effort. Examples include soap, candy, newspapers, and fast food. Convenience products are usually low priced, and marketers place them in many locations to make them readily available when customers need them.

Shopping products are less-frequently-purchased consumer products and services that customers compare carefully on suitability, quality, price, and style. When buying shopping products and services, consumers spend much time and effort in gathering information and making comparisons. Examples include furniture, clothing, used cars, major appliances, and hotel and airline services. Shopping products marketers usually distribute their products through fewer outlets but provide deeper sales support to help customers in their comparison efforts.

Specialty products are consumer products and services with unique characteristics or brand identification for which a significant group of buyers is willing to make a special purchase effort. Examples include specific brands and types of cars, high-priced photographic equipment,

TABLE 9.1   **MARKETING CONSIDERATIONS FOR CONSUMER PRODUCTS**

| Marketing Considerations | Type of Consumer Product | | | |
	Convenience	**Shopping**	**Specialty**	**Unsought**
Customer buying behavior	Frequent purchase, little planning, little comparison or shopping effort, low customer involvement	Less frequent purchase, much planning and shopping effort, comparison of brands on price, quality, style	Strong brand preference and loyalty, special purchase effort, little comparison of brands, low price sensitivity	Little product awareness, knowledge (or, if aware, little or even negative interest)
Price	Low Price	Higher price	High price	Varies
Distribution	Widespread distribution, convenient locations	Selective distribution in fewer outlets	Exclusive distribution in only one or a few outlets per market area	Varies
Promotion	Mass promotion by the producer	Advertising and personal selling by both producer and resellers	More carefully targeted promotion by both producer and resellers	Aggressive advertising and personal selling by producer and resellers
Examples	Toothpaste, magazines, laundry detergent	Major appliances, televisions, furniture, clothing	Luxury goods, such as Rolex watches or fine crystal	Life insurance, Red Cross blood donations

designer clothes, and the services of medical or legal specialists. A Lamborghini automobile, for example, is a specialty product because buyers are usually willing to travel great distances to buy one. Buyers normally do not compare specialty products. They invest only the time needed to reach dealers carrying the wanted products.

Unsought products are consumer products that the consumer either does not know about or knows about but does not normally think of buying. Most major new innovations are unsought until the consumer becomes aware of them through advertising. Classic examples of known but unsought products and services are life insurance, cemetery plots, and blood donations to the Red Cross. By their very nature, unsought products require a lot of advertising, personal selling, and other marketing efforts.

Industrial Products

Industrial products are those purchased for further processing or for use in conducting a business. Thus, the distinction between a consumer product and an industrial product is based on the *purpose* for which the product is bought. If a consumer buys a lawn mower for use around home, the lawn mower is a consumer product. If the same consumer buys the same lawn mower for use in a landscaping business, the lawn mower is an industrial product.

The three groups of industrial products and services include materials and parts, capital items, and supplies and services. *Materials and parts* include raw materials and manufactured materials and parts. Raw materials consist of farm products (wheat, cotton, livestock, fruits, vegetables) and natural products (fish, lumber, crude petroleum, iron ore). Manufactured materials and parts consist of component materials (iron, yarn, cement, wires) and component parts (small motors, tires, castings). Most manufactured materials and parts are sold directly to industrial users. Price and service are the major marketing factors; branding and advertising tend to be less important.

Capital items are industrial products that aid in the buyer's production or operations, including installations and accessory equipment. Installations consist of major purchases such as buildings (factories, offices) and fixed equipment (generators, drill presses, large computer systems, elevators). Accessory equipment includes portable factory equipment and tools (hand tools, lift

Unsought product

Consumer product that the consumer either does not know about or knows about but does not normally think of buying.

Industrial product

Product bought by individuals and organizations for further processing or for use in conducting a business.

Business services: ServiceMaster supplies business services for a wide range of organizations. This advertisement to schools and colleges offers services ranging from custodial, grounds, technology, and energy management services to maintenance and food services.

FOUR GREAT REASONS TO HAVE SERVICEMASTER CARE FOR YOUR FACILITIES:

1. YOU'LL SAVE MONEY.

2. YOU'LL INCREASE QUALITY.

3. YOU'LL IMPROVE MORALE.

4. YOU'LL SAVE TIME.

At ServiceMaster, we offer the most effective way to manage your buildings and grounds while saving you time and money, improving morale and increasing quality. From custodial, grounds, technology and energy management to maintenance and food service, we care for over 500 schools and colleges — top to bottom, inside and out.

Quite simply, we're able to offer so much because we'll work very closely with you and your staff. In fact, we think of it as a partnership. That's because we'll work with *your* budget, *your* employees and *your* existing resources and add to them *our* proven programs and systems.

In other words, we'll help you manage your budget, so you'll get the most for your money. We'll train and manage your employees, so they'll be more productive and efficient. We'll apply our own tried and proven techniques such as Total Quality Management, Customer Support and People Development Programs to get the job done better than you'd ever imagine and to make sure everyone's satisfied with their role in it.

All of this, then, gives you more time to do everything else you were hired to do.

So if you'd like to learn more about contract management services tailor-made for schools and colleges, please give us a call. You've got every reason to.

*Service*MASTER.
Quality Service For Quality Schools
The ServiceMaster Company
One ServiceMaster Way
Downers Grove, Illinois 60515
1-800-SCHOOLS (724-6657)

trucks) and office equipment (computers, fax machines, desks). They have a shorter life than installations and simply aid in the production process.

The final group of business products is *supplies and services.* Supplies include operating supplies (lubricants, coal, paper, pencils) and repair and maintenance items (paint, nails, brooms). Supplies are the convenience products of the industrial field because they are usually purchased with a minimum of effort or comparison. Business services include maintenance and repair services (window cleaning, computer repair) and business advisory services (legal, management consulting, advertising). Such services are usually supplied under contract.

Organizations, Persons, Places, and Ideas

In addition to tangible products and services, in recent years marketers have broadened the concept of a product to include other market offerings—organizations, persons, places, and ideas.

Organizations often carry out activities to "sell" the organization itself. *Organization marketing* consists of activities undertaken to create, maintain, or change the attitudes and behavior of target consumers toward an organization. Both profit and nonprofit organizations practice organization marketing. Business firms sponsor public relations or corporate advertising campaigns to polish their images. *Corporate image advertising* is a major tool companies use to market themselves to various publics. For example, Lucent puts out ads with the tag line "We make the things that make communications work." IBM wants to establish itself as the company to turn to for "e-Business Solutions." And General Electric "brings good things to life." Similarly, not-for-profit organizations, such as churches, colleges, charities, museums, and performing arts groups, market their organizations in order to raise funds and attract members or patrons.

People can also be thought of as products. *Person marketing* consists of activities undertaken to create, maintain, or change attitudes or behavior toward particular people. All kinds of people and organizations practice person marketing. Today's presidents market themselves, their parties, and their platforms to get needed votes and program support. Entertainers and sports figures use marketing to promote their careers and improve their impact and incomes. Professionals such as doctors, lawyers, accountants, and architects market themselves in order to build their reputations and increase business. Businesses, charities, sports teams, fine arts groups, religious groups, and other organizations also use person marketing. Creating or associating with well-known personalities often helps these organizations achieve their goals better. That's why more than a dozen different companies combined—including Nike, Target, Buick, American Express, Disney, and Titleist—pay more than $50 million a year to link themselves with golf superstar Tiger Woods.[3]

Place marketing involves activities undertaken to create, maintain, or change attitudes or behavior toward particular places. Cities, states, regions, and even entire nations compete to attract tourists, new residents, conventions, and company offices and factories. Texas advertises "It's Like a Whole Other Country," and New York State shouts, "I Love New York!"[4] Michigan says "Great Lakes, Great Times" to attract tourists, "Great Lakes, Great Jobs" to attract residents, and "Great Lakes, Great Location" to attract businesses. The Irish Development Agency has attracted more than 1,200 companies to locate their plants in Ireland. At the same time, the Irish Tourist Board has built a flourishing tourism business by advertising "Live a different life: friendly, beautiful, relaxing." And the Irish Export Board has created attractive markets for Irish exports.[5]

Ideas can also be marketed. In one sense, all marketing is the marketing of an idea, whether it be the general idea of brushing your teeth or the specific idea that Crest toothpastes "create smiles every day." Here, however, we narrow our focus to the marketing of *social ideas.* This area has been called **social marketing,** defined by the Social Marketing Institute as the use of commercial marketing concepts and tools in programs designed to influence individuals' behavior to improve their well-being and that of society.[6] Such programs include public health campaigns to reduce smoking, alcoholism, drug abuse, and overeating. Other social marketing efforts include environmental campaigns to promote wilderness protection, clean air, and conservation. Still others address issues such as family planning, human rights, and racial equality.

The Ad Council of America has developed dozens of social advertising campaigns, including classics such as "Smokey Bear," "Keep America Beautiful," "Only You Can Prevent Forest Fires," "Friends Don't Let Friends Drive Drunk," "Say No to Drugs," and "A Mind Is a Terrible Thing to Waste" (see www.adcouncil.org). But social marketing involves much more than just advertising—the Social Marketing Institute encourages the use of a broad range of marketing

Social marketing
The design, implementation, and control of programs seeking to increase the acceptability of a social idea, cause, or practice among a target group.

Social marketing: The Ad Council has developed dozens of social marketing campaigns. This one urges adults to mentor a child. "You don't have to be perfect. You just have to be yourself which, by the way, is pretty good."

tools. "Social marketing goes well beyond the promotional '*P*' of the marketing mix to include every other element to achieve its social change objectives," says the SMI's executive director.[7]

Product and Service Decisions

Marketers make product and services decisions at three levels: individual product decisions, product line decisions, and product mix decisions. We discuss each in turn.

Individual Product and Service Decisions

Figure 9.2 shows the important decisions in the development and marketing of individual products and services. We will focus on decisions about *product attributes, branding, packaging, labeling,* and *product support services.*

Product and Service Attributes

Developing a product or service involves defining the benefits that it will offer. These benefits are communicated and delivered by product attributes such as *quality, features,* and *style and design.*

Product Quality.   **Product quality** is one of the marketer's major positioning tools. Quality has a direct impact on product or service performance; thus, it is closely linked to customer value and

Product quality
The ability of a product to perform its functions; it includes the product's overall durability, reliability, precision, ease of operation and repair, and other valued attributes.

FIGURE 9.2
Individual product and service decisions

Product attributes → Branding → Packaging → Labeling → Product support services satisfaction. In the narrowest sense, quality can be defined as "freedom from defects." But most customer-centered companies go beyond this narrow definition. Instead, they define quality in terms of customer satisfaction. The American Society for Quality defines quality as the characteristics of a product or service that bear on its ability to satisfy stated or implied customer needs. Similarly, Siemans defines quality this way: "Quality is when our customers come back and our products don't."[8] These customer-focused definitions suggest that quality begins with customer needs and ends with customer satisfaction.

Total quality management (TQM) is an approach in which all the company's people are involved in constantly improving the quality of products, services, and business processes. During the past two decades, companies large and small have credited TQM with greatly improving their market shares and profits. Recently, however, the total quality management movement has drawn criticism. Too many companies viewed TQM as a magic cure-all and created token total quality programs that applied quality principles only superficially. Still others became obsessed with narrowly defined TQM principles and lost sight of broader concerns for customer value and satisfaction. As a result, many such programs failed, causing a backlash against TQM.

When applied in the context of creating customer satisfaction, however, total quality principles remain a requirement for success. Although many firms don't use the TQM label anymore, for most top companies customer-driven quality has become a way of doing business. Today, companies are taking a "return on quality" approach, viewing quality as an investment and holding quality efforts accountable for bottom-line results.[9]

Product quality has two dimensions—level and consistency. In developing a product, the marketer must first choose a *quality level* that will support the product's position in the target market. Here, product quality means *performance quality*—the ability of a product to perform its functions. For example, a Rolls-Royce provides higher performance quality than a Chevrolet: It has a smoother ride, handles better, and lasts longer. Companies rarely try to offer the highest possible performance quality level—few customers want or can afford the high levels of quality offered in products such as a Rolls-Royce automobile, a Sub-Zero refrigerator, or a Rolex watch. Instead, companies choose a quality level that matches target market needs and the quality levels of competing products.

Beyond quality level, high quality also can mean high levels of quality *consistency*. Here, product quality means *conformance quality*—freedom from defects and *consistency* in delivering a targeted level of performance. All companies should strive for high levels of conformance quality. In this sense, a Chevrolet can have just as much quality as a Rolls-Royce. Although a Chevy doesn't perform as well as a Rolls, it can as consistently deliver the quality that customers pay for and expect.

Many companies today have turned customer-driven quality into a potent strategic weapon. They create customer satisfaction and value by consistently and profitably meeting customers' needs and preferences for quality.

Product Features.   A product can be offered with varying features. A stripped-down model, one without any extras, is the starting point. The company can create higher-level models by adding more features. Features are a competitive tool for differentiating the company's product from competitors' products. Being the first producer to introduce a needed and valued new feature is one of the most effective ways to compete.

How can a company identify new features and decide which ones to add to its product? The company should periodically survey buyers who have used the product and ask these questions: How do you like the product? Which specific features of the product do you like most? Which features could we add to improve the product? The answers provide the company with a rich list of feature ideas. The company can then assess each feature's *value* to customers versus its *cost* to the company. Features that customers value little in relation to costs should be dropped; those that customers value highly in relation to costs should be added.

Product Style and Design.   Another way to add customer value is through distinctive *product style and design*. Design is a larger concept than style. *Style* simply describes the appearance of a product. Styles can be eye-catching or yawn producing. A sensational style may grab attention and produce pleasing aesthetics, but it does not necessarily make the product *perform* better. Unlike style, *design* is more than skin deep—it goes to the very heart of a product. Good design contributes to a product's usefulness as well as to its looks.

Good style and design can attract attention, improve product performance, cut production costs, and give the product a strong competitive advantage in the target market. Here are two examples:

Product design: The design of the dramatic iMac helped reestablish Apple as a legitimate contender in the PC industry. The innovative Discover 2GO card is a gotta-have-it accessory for people who want to dash off to the gym, the mall, or a restaurant with nothing more than their keys and a credit card.

Who said that computers have to be beige and boxy? Apple's iMac is anything but. The first iMac—which featured a sleek, egg-shaped monitor and hard drive, all in one unit, in a futuristic translucent turquoise casing—redefined the look and feel of the personal computer. There was no clunky tower or desktop hard drive to clutter up your office area. Featuring one-button Internet access, this machine was designed specifically for cruising the Internet (that's what the "i" in "iMac" stands for). The dramatic iMac won raves for design and lured buyers in droves. Within a year, it had sold more than a million units, marking Apple's reemergence in the personal computer industry. Four years later, Apple did it again with a stunning new iMac design—a clean, futuristic machine featuring a flat-panel display that seems to float in the air. Within only three months, Apple-lovers had snapped up nearly one-quarter million of these eye-pleasing yet functional machines.[10]

You turn the flat, kidney-shaped plastic gadget over in your hands, puzzling over what it does. Then you realize that a sliver of red plastic pivots out of the black case like a pocketknife blade. You recognize a familiar strand of embossed numbers, a magnetic stripe, and a signature bar. It's a credit card! To be precise, it's a Discover 2GO card, complete with a key chain, belt clip, and protective case. In consumer terms, the Discover 2GO card is a gotta-have-it accessory for people who want to dash off to the gym, the mall, or a restaurant with nothing more than their keys and a credit card. In industry terms, it's a big design innovation in a business that has rarely thought much outside the 2- by 3-inch box. The new design has drawn praise from card marketing experts. "This is slick. It's different, which is good. And it's functional," says one consultant. "It's the card you'll use when you have your keys in your hand."[11]

Branding

Perhaps the most distinctive skill of professional marketers is their ability to create, maintain, protect, and enhance brands of their products and services. A **brand** is a name, term, sign, symbol, or design, or a combination of these, that identifies the maker or seller of a product or service. Consumers view a brand as an important part of a product, and branding can add value to a product. For example, most consumers would perceive a bottle of White Linen perfume as a high-quality, expensive product. But the same perfume in an unmarked bottle would likely be viewed as lower in quality, even if the fragrance were identical.

Branding has become so strong that today hardly anything goes unbranded. Salt is packaged in branded containers, common nuts and bolts are packaged with a distributor's label, and automobile parts—spark plugs, tires, filters—bear brand names that differ from those of the automakers. Even fruits, vegetables, and poultry are branded—Sunkist oranges, Dole pineapples, Chiquita bananas, Fresh Express salad greens, and Perdue chickens.

Branding helps buyers in many ways. Brand names help consumers identify products that might benefit them. Brands also tell the buyer something about product quality. Buyers who always buy the same brand know that they will get the same features, benefits, and quality each time they buy. Branding also gives the seller several advantages. The brand name becomes the

Brand

A name, term, sign, symbol, or design, or a combination of these, intended to identify the goods or services of one seller or group of sellers and to differentiate them from those of competitors.

Branding has become so strong that hardly anything goes unbranded, even fruits and vegetables.

basis on which a whole story can be built about a product's special qualities. The seller's brand name and trademark provide legal protection for unique product features that otherwise might be copied by competitors. And branding helps the seller to segment markets. For example, General Mills can offer Cheerios, Wheaties, Total, Kix, Lucky Charms, Trix, and many other cereal brands, not just one general product for all consumers.

Building and managing brands is perhaps the marketer's most important task. We will discuss branding strategy in more detail later in the chapter.

Packaging

Packaging
The activities of designing and producing the container or wrapper for a product.

Packaging involves designing and producing the container or wrapper for a product. The package includes a product's primary container (the tube holding Colgate Total toothpaste). It may also include a secondary package that is thrown away when the product is about to be used (the cardboard box containing the tube of Colgate). Finally, it can include a shipping package necessary to store, identify, and ship the product (a corrugated box carrying six dozen tubes of Colgate). Labeling—printed information appearing on or with the package—is also part of packaging.

Traditionally, the primary function of the package was to contain and protect the product. In recent times, however, numerous factors have made packaging an important marketing tool. Increased competition and clutter on retail store shelves means that packages must now perform many sales tasks—from attracting attention, to describing the product, to making the sale.

Companies are realizing the power of good packaging to create instant consumer recognition of the company or brand. For example, in an average supermarket, which stocks 15,000 to 17,000 items, the typical shopper passes by some 300 items per minute, and more than 60 percent of all purchases are made on impulse. In this highly competitive environment, the package may be the seller's last chance to influence buyers. It becomes a "five-second commercial." The Campbell Soup Company estimates that the average shopper sees its familiar red-and-white can 76 times a year, creating the equivalent of $26 million worth of advertising.[12]

Innovative packaging can give a company an advantage over competitors. In contrast, poorly designed packages can cause headaches for consumers and lost sales for the company (see Real Marketing 9.2). For example, a few years ago, Planters Lifesavers Company attempted to use innovative packaging to create an association between fresh-roasted peanuts and fresh-roasted coffee. It packaged its Fresh Roast Salted Peanuts in vacuum-packed "Brik-Pacs," similar to those used for ground coffee. Unfortunately, the coffeelike packaging worked too well: Consumers mistook the peanuts for a new brand of flavored coffee and ran them through supermarket coffee-grinding machines, creating a gooey mess, disappointed customers, and lots of irate store managers.[13]

real marketing 9.2

Those Frustrating, Not-So-Easy-To-Open Packages

Some things, it seems, will never change. This classic letter from an angry consumer to Robert D. Stuart, then chairman of Quaker Oats, beautifully expresses the utter frustration all of us have experienced in dealing with so-called easy-opening packages.

Dear Mr. Stuart:

I am an 86-year-old widow in fairly good health. (You may think of this as advanced

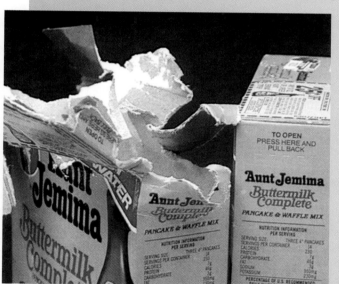

An easy to open package?

age, but for me that description pertains to the years ahead. Nevertheless, if you decide to reply to this letter I wouldn't dawdle, actuarial tables being what they are.)

As I said, my health is fairly good. Feeble and elderly, as one understands these terms, I am not. My two Doberman Pinschers and I take

a brisk 3-mile walk every day. They are two strong and energetic animals and it takes a bit of doing to keep "brisk" closer to a stroll than a mad dash. But I manage because as yet I don't lack the strength. You will shortly see why this fact is relevant.

I am writing to call your attention to the cruel, deceptive, and utterly [false] copy on your Aunt Jemima buttermilk complete pancake and waffle mix. The words on your package read, "to open—press here and pull back."

Mr. Stuart, though I push and press and groan and strive and writhe and curse and sweat and jab and push, poke and ram . . . whew!—I have never once been able to do what the package instructs—to "press here and pull back" the [blankety-blank]. It can't be done! Talk about failing strength! Have you ever tried and succeeded?

My late husband was a gun collector who among other lethal weapons kept a Thompson machine gun in a locked cabinet. It was a good thing that the cabinet was locked. Oh, the number of times I was tempted to give your package a few short bursts.

That lock and a sense of ladylike delicacy kept me from pursuing that vengeful fantasy. Instead, I keep a small cleaver in my pantry for those occasions when I need to open a package of your delicious Aunt Jemima pancakes.

For many years that whacking away with my cleaver served a dual purpose. Not only to open the [blankety-blank] package but also to vent my fury at your sadists who willfully and maliciously did design that torture apparatus that passes for a package.

Sometimes just for the [blank] of it I let myself get carried away. I don't stop after I've lopped off the top. I whack away until the package is utterly destroyed in an outburst of rage, frustration, and vindictiveness. I wind up with a floorful of your delicious Aunt Jemima pancake mix. But that's a small price to pay for blessed release. (Anyway, the Pinschers lap up the mess.)

So many ingenious, considerate (even compassionate) innovations in package closures have been designed since Aunt Jemima first donned her red bandana. Wouldn't you consider the introduction of a more humane package to replace the example of marketing malevolence to which you resolutely cling? Don't you care, Mr. Stuart?

I'm really writing this to be helpful and in that spirit I am sending a copy to Mr. Tucker, president of Container Corp. I'm sure their clever young designers could be of immeasurable help to you in this matter. At least I feel it's worth a try.

Really, Mr. Stuart, I hope you will not regard me as just another cranky old biddy. I am The Public, the source of your fortunes.

Ms. Roberta Pavloff
Malvern, Pa.

Source: This letter was reprinted in "Some Designs Should Just Be Torn Asunder," *Advertising Age,* January 17, 1983, p. M54.

Developing a good package for a new product requires making many decisions. First, the company must establish the *packaging concept,* which states what the package should *be* or *do* for the product. Should it mainly offer product protection, introduce a new dispensing method, suggest certain qualities about the product, or do something else? Decisions then must be made on specific elements of the package, such as size, shape, materials, color, text, and brand mark. These elements must work together to support the product's position and marketing strategy.

Innovative labeling can help to promote a product.

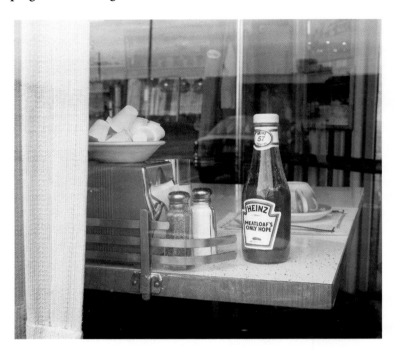

In recent years, product safety has also become a major packaging concern. We have all learned to deal with hard-to-open "childproof" packages. And after the rash of product tampering scares during the 1980s, most drug producers and food makers are now putting their products in tamper-resistant packages. In making packaging decisions, the company also must heed growing environmental concerns. Fortunately, many companies have gone "green" by reducing their packaging and using environmentally responsible packaging materials. For example, SC Johnson repackaged Agree Plus shampoo in a stand-up pouch using 80 percent less plastic. P&G eliminated outer cartons from its Secret and Sure deodorants, saving 3.4 million pounds of paperboard per year.

Labeling

Labels may range from simple tags attached to products to complex graphics that are part of the package. They perform several functions. At the very least, the label *identifies* the product or brand, such as the name Sunkist stamped on oranges. The label might also *describe* several things about the product—who made it, where it was made, when it was made, its contents, how it is to be used, and how to use it safely. Finally, the label might *promote* the product through attractive graphics.

There has been a long history of legal concerns about packaging and labels. The Federal Trade Commission Act of 1914 held that false, misleading, or deceptive labels or packages constitute unfair competition. Labels can mislead customers, fail to describe important ingredients, or fail to include needed safety warnings. As a result, several federal and state laws regulate labeling. The most prominent is the Fair Packaging and Labeling Act of 1966, which set mandatory labeling requirements, encouraged voluntary industry packaging standards, and allowed federal agencies to set packaging regulations in specific industries.

Labeling has been affected in recent times by *unit pricing* (stating the price per unit of standard measure), *open dating* (stating the expected shelf life of the product), and *nutritional labeling* (stating the nutritional values in the product). The Nutritional Labeling and Educational Act of 1990 requires sellers to provide detailed nutritional information on food products, and recent sweeping actions by the Food and Drug Administration regulate the use of health-related terms such as *low-fat, light,* and *high-fiber.* Sellers must ensure that their labels contain all the required information.

Product Support Services

Customer service is another element of product strategy. A company's offer to the marketplace usually includes some support services, which can be a minor or a major part of the total offering. Later in the chapter, we will discuss services as products in themselves. Here, we discuss services that augment actual products.

The first step is to survey customers periodically to assess the value of current services and to obtain ideas for new ones. For example, Cadillac holds regular focus group interviews with owners and carefully watches complaints that come into its dealerships. From this careful monitoring, Cadillac has learned that buyers are very upset by repairs that are not done correctly the first time.

Once the company has assessed the value of various support services to customers, it must next assess the costs of providing these services. It can then develop a package of services that will both delight customers and yield profits to the company. Based on its consumer interviews, Cadillac has set up a system directly linking each dealership with a group of 10 engineers who can help walk mechanics through difficult repairs. Such actions helped Cadillac jump, in one year, from fourteenth to seventh in independent rankings of service.[14]

Many companies are now using the Internet and other modern technologies to provide support services that were not possible before. Using the Web, 24-hour telephone help lines, self-service kiosks, and other digital technologies, these companies are now empowering consumers to tailor their own service and support experiences. For example, Kaiser-Permanente, the nation's largest health maintenance organization (HMO), has rolled out a Web site that lets members register online for office visits and send e-mail questions to nurses and pharmacists (and get responses within 24 hours). Kaiser also plans to give members access to lab results and pharmaceutical refills online.[15]

Product Line Decisions

Product line

A group of products that are closely related because they function in a similar manner, are sold to the same customer groups, are marketed through the same types of outlets, or fall within given price ranges.

Beyond decisions about individual products and services, product strategy also calls for building a product line. A **product line** is a group of products that are closely related because they function in a similar manner, are sold to the same customer groups, are marketed through the same types of outlets, or fall within given price ranges. For example, Nike produces several lines of athletic shoes and apparel, Nokia produces several lines of telecommunications products, and Charles Schwab produces several lines of financial services.

The major product line decision involves *product line length*—the number of items in the product line. The line is too short if the manager can increase profits by adding items; the line is too long if the manager can increase profits by dropping items. The company should manage its product lines carefully. Product lines tend to lengthen over time, and most companies eventually need to prune unnecessary or unprofitable items from their lines to increase overall profitability.

Product line length is influenced by company objectives and resources. For example, one objective might be to allow for upselling. Thus BMW wants to move customers up from it's 3-series models to 5- and 7-series models. Another objective might be to allow cross-selling: Hewlett-Packard sells printers as well as cartridges. Still another objective might be to protect against economic swings: Gap runs several clothing-store chains (Gap, Old Navy, Banana Republic) covering different price points.

A company can lengthen its product line in two ways: by *line stretching* or by *line filling*. *Product line stretching* occurs when a company lengthens its product line beyond its current range. The company can stretch its line downward, upward, or both ways.

Companies located at the upper end of the market can stretch their lines *downward*. A company may stretch downward to plug a market hole that otherwise would attract a new competitor or to respond to a competitor's attack on the upper end. Or it may add low-end products because it finds faster growth taking place in the low-end segments. DaimlerChrysler stretched its Mercedes line downward for all these reasons. Facing a slow-growth luxury car market and attacks by Japanese automakers on its high-end positioning, it successfully introduced its Mercedes C-Class cars. These models sell at less than $30,000 without harming the firm's ability to sell other Mercedes for $100,000 or more. Similarly, Rolex launched its Rolex Tudor watch retailing for about $1,350, compared with a Rolex Submariner, usually priced at $3,875.[16]

Companies at the lower end of a market can stretch their product lines *upward*. Sometimes, companies stretch upward in order to add prestige to their current products. Or they may be attracted by a faster growth rate or higher margins at the higher end. For example, each of the leading Japanese auto companies introduced an upmarket automobile: Toyota launched Lexus, Nissan launched Infinity, and Honda launched Acura. They used entirely new names rather than their own names.

Companies in the middle range of the market may decide to stretch their lines in *both directions*. Marriott did this with its hotel product line. Along with regular Marriott hotels, it added the Renaissance Hotels line to serve the upper end of the market and the TownePlace Suites line to serve the moderate and lower ends. Each branded hotel line is aimed at a different target market. Renaissance aims to attract and please top executives; Marriotts, upper and middle managers;

Two-way stretch: Marriott added the Renaissance Hotels line to serve the upper end of the market and the TownePlace Suites line to serve the moderate and lower ends. Each branded hotel line is aimed at a different target market.

Courtyards, salespeople and other "road warriors"; and Fairfield Inns, vacationers and business travelers on a tight travel budget. ExecuStay by Marriott provides temporary housing for those relocating or away on long-term assignments of 30 days or longer. Marriott's Residence Inn provides a relaxed, residential atmosphere—a home away from home for people who travel for a living. Marriott TownePlace Suites provide a comfortable atmosphere at a moderate price for extended-stay travelers.[17] The major risk with this strategy is that some travelers will trade down after finding that the lower-price hotels in the Marriott chain give them pretty much everything they want. However, Marriott would rather capture its customers who move downward than lose them to competitors.

An alternative to product line stretching is *product line filling*—adding more items within the present range of the line. There are several reasons for product line filling: reaching for extra profits, satisfying dealers, using excess capacity, being the leading full-line company, and plugging holes to keep out competitors. Sony filled its Walkman line by adding solar-powered and waterproof Walkmans, an ultralight model that attaches to a sweatband for exercisers, the MiniDisc Walkman, the CD Walkman, and the Memory Stick Walkman, which enables users to download tracks straight from the Net. However, line filling is overdone if it results in cannibalization and customer confusion. The company should ensure that new items are noticeably different from existing ones.

Product Mix Decisions

Product mix (or product assortment)
The set of all product lines and items that a particular seller offers for sale.

An organization with several product lines has a product mix. A **product mix** (or **product assortment**) consists of all the product lines and items that a particular seller offers for sale. Avon's product mix consists of four major product lines: beauty products, wellness products, jewelry and accessories, and "inspirational" products (gifts, books, music, and home accents). Each product line consists of several sublines. For example, the beauty line breaks down into makeup, skin care, bath and beauty, fragrance, and outdoor protection products. Each line and subline has many individual items. Altogether, Avon's product mix includes 1,300 items. In contrast, a typical Kmart stocks 15,000 items, 3M markets more than 60,000 products, and General Electric manufactures as many as 250,000 items.

A company's product mix has four important dimensions: width, length, depth, and consistency. Product mix *width* refers to the number of different product lines the company carries. Procter & Gamble markets a fairly wide product mix consisting of 250 brands organized into many product lines. These lines include fabric and home care, baby care, feminine care, beauty care, health care, and food and beverage products. Product mix *length* refers to the total number of items the company carries within its product lines. P&G typically carries many brands within each line. For example, it sells seven laundry detergents, six hand soaps, five shampoos, and four dishwashing detergents.

Product line *depth* refers to the number of versions offered of each product in the line. Thus, P&G's Crest toothpaste comes in 13 varieties, ranging from Crest Multicare, Crest Cavity Protection, and Crest Tartar Protection to Crest Sensitivity Protection, Crest Dual Action Whitening, Crest Whitening Plus Scope, Kid's Cavity Protection, and Crest Baking Soda & Peroxide Whitening formulations.[18] (Talk about niche marketing! Remember our Chapter 8 discussion?)

Finally, the *consistency* of the product mix refers to how closely related the various product lines are in end use, production requirements, distribution channels, or some other way. P&G's

product lines are consistent insofar as they are consumer products that go through the same distribution channels. The lines are less consistent insofar as they perform different functions for buyers.

These product mix dimensions provide the handles for defining the company's product strategy. The company can increase its business in four ways. It can add new product lines, thus widening its product mix. In this way, its new lines build on the company's reputation in its other lines. The company can lengthen its existing product lines to become a more full-line company. Or it can add more versions of each product and thus deepen its product mix. Finally, the company can pursue more product line consistency—or less—depending on whether it wants to have a strong reputation in a single field or in several fields.

Branding Strategy: Building Strong Brands

Some analysts see brands as *the* major enduring asset of a company, outlasting the company's specific products and facilities. John Stewart, co-founder of Quaker Oats, once said, "If this business were split up, I would give you the land and bricks and mortar, and I would keep the brands and trademarks, and I would fare better than you." The CEO of McDonald's agrees:

> A McDonald's board member who worked at Coca-Cola once talked to us about the value of our brand. He said if every asset we own, every building, and every piece of equipment were destroyed in a terrible natural disaster, we would be able to borrow all the money to replace it very quickly because of the value of our brand. And he's right. The brand is more valuable than the totality of all these assets.[19]

Thus, brands are powerful assets that must be carefully developed and managed. In this section, we examine the key strategies for building and managing brands.

Brand Equity

Brands are more than just names and symbols. Brands represent consumers' perceptions and feelings about a product and its performance—everything that the product or service *means* to consumers. As one branding expert suggests, "Ultimately, brands reside in the minds of consumers."[20] Thus, the real value of a strong brand is its power to capture consumer preference and loyalty.

A strong brand is a valuable asset. How many familiar brands and brand symbols can you find in this picture?

Brand equity

The positive differential effect that knowing the brand name has on customer response to the product or service.

Brands vary in the amount of power and value they have in the marketplace. A powerful brand has high *brand equity*. **Brand equity** is the positive differential effect that knowing the brand name has on customer response to the product or service. A measure of a brand's equity is the extent to which customers are willing to pay more for the brand. One study found that 72 percent of customers would pay a 20 percent premium for their brand of choice relative to the closest competing brand; 40 percent said they would pay a 50 percent premium.[21] Tide and Heinz lovers are willing to pay a 100 percent premium. Loyal Coke drinkers will pay a 50 percent premium and Volvo users a 40 percent premium.

A brand with strong brand equity is a very valuable asset. *Brand valuation* is the process of estimating the total financial value of a brand. Measuring such value is difficult. However, according to one estimate, the brand value of Coca-Cola is $69 billion, Microsoft is $65 billion, and IBM is $53 billion. Other brands rating among the world's most valuable include General Electric, Nokia, Intel, Disney, Ford, McDonald's, and AT&T.[22] "Brand equity has emerged over the past few years as a key strategic asset," observes a brand consultant. "CEOs in many industries now see their brands as a source of control and a way to build stronger relationships with customers."[23]

High brand equity provides a company with many competitive advantages. A powerful brand enjoys a high level of consumer brand awareness and loyalty. Because consumers expect stores to carry the brand, the company has more leverage in bargaining with resellers. Because the brand name carries high credibility, the company can more easily launch line and brand extensions, as when Coca-Cola leveraged its well-known brand to introduce Diet Coke or when Procter & Gamble introduced Ivory dishwashing detergent. Above all, a powerful brand offers the company some defense against fierce price competition.

Therefore, the fundamental asset underlying brand equity is *customer equity*—the value of the customer relationships that the brand creates. A powerful brand is important, but what it really represents is a set of loyal customers. Thus, the proper focus of marketing is building customer equity, with brand management serving as a major marketing tool.[24]

Building Strong Brands

Branding poses challenging decisions to the marketer. Figure 9.3 shows that the major brand strategy decisions involve brand positioning, brand name selection, brand sponsorship, and brand development.

Brand Positioning

Marketers need to position their brands clearly in target customers' minds. They can position brands at any of three levels.[25] At the lowest level, they can position the brand on *product attributes*. Thus, marketers of Dove soap can talk about the product's attribute of one-quarter cleansing cream. However, attributes are the least desirable level for brand positioning. Competitors can easily copy attributes. More important, customers are not interested in attributes as such; they are interested in what the attributes will do for them.

A brand can be better positioned by associating its name with a desirable *benefit*. Thus, Dove marketers can go beyond the brand's cleansing cream attribute and talk about the resulting benefit of softer skin. Some successful brands positioned on benefits are Volvo (safety), Hallmark (caring), Harley-Davidson (adventure), FedEx (guaranteed overnight delivery), Nike (performance), and Lexus (quality).

The strongest brands go beyond attribute or benefit positioning. They are positioned on strong *beliefs and values*. These brands pack an emotional wallop. Thus, Dove's marketers can talk not just

FIGURE 9.3   Major brand strategy decisions

about cleansing cream attributes and softer skin benefits, but about how these will make you more attractive. Brand expert Marc Gobe argues that successful brands must engage customers on a deeper level, touching a universal emotion.[26] His brand design agency, which has worked on such brands as Starbucks, Victoria's Secret, Godiva, Versace, and Lancome, relies less on a product's tangible attributes and more on creating surprise, passion, and excitement surrounding a brand.

When positioning a brand, the marketer should establish a mission for the brand and a vision of what the brand must be and do. A brand is the company's promise to deliver a specific set of features, benefits, services, and experiences consistently to the buyers. It can be thought of as a contract to the customer regarding how the product or service will deliver value and satisfaction. The brand contract must be simple and honest. Motel 6, for example, offers clean rooms, low prices, and good service but does not promise expensive furniture or large bathrooms. In contrast, Ritz-Carlton offers luxurious rooms and a truly memorable experience but does not promise low prices.

Brand Name Selection

A good name can add greatly to a product's success. However, finding the best brand name is a difficult task. It begins with a careful review of the product and its benefits, the target market, and proposed marketing strategies.

Desirable qualities for a brand name include the following: (1) It should suggest something about the product's benefits and qualities. Examples: Beautyrest, Craftsman, Snuggles, Merrie Maids, OFF! bug spray. (2) It should be easy to pronounce, recognize, and remember. Short names help. Examples: Tide, Crest, Puffs. But longer ones are sometimes effective. Examples: "Love My Carpet" carpet cleaner, "I Can't Believe It's Not Butter" margarine. (3) The brand name should be distinctive. Examples: Taurus, Kodak, Oracle. (4) It should be extendable: Amazon.com began as an online bookseller but chose a name that would allow expansion into other categories. (5) The name should translate easily into foreign languages. Before spending $100 million to change its name to Exxon, Standard Oil of New Jersey tested several names in 54 languages in more than 150 foreign markets. It found that the name Enco referred to a stalled engine when pronounced in Japanese. (6) It should be capable of registration and legal protection. A brand name cannot be registered if it infringes on existing brand names.

Once chosen, the brand name must be protected. Many firms try to build a brand name that will eventually become identified with the product category. Brand names such as Kleenex, Levi's, Jell-O, Scotch Tape, Formica, Ziploc, and Fiberglas have succeeded in this way. However, their very success may threaten the company's rights to the name. Many originally protected brand names—such as cellophane, aspirin, nylon, kerosene, linoleum, yo-yo, trampoline, escalator, thermos, and shredded wheat—are now generic names that any seller can use.

Brand Sponsorship

A manufacturer has four sponsorship options. The product may be launched as a *manufacturer's brand* (or national brand), as when Kellogg and IBM sell their output under their own manufacturer's brand names. Or the manufacturer may sell to resellers who give it a *private brand* (also called a *store brand* or *distributor brand*). Although most manufacturers create their own brand names, others market *licensed brands*. Finally, two companies can join forces and *co-brand* a product.

Manufacturer's Brands Versus Private Brands.   Manufacturers' brands have long dominated the retail scene. In recent times, however, an increasing number of retailers and wholesalers have created their own **private brands** (or *store brands*). For example, Sears has created several names—DieHard batteries, Craftsman tools, Kenmore appliances, Weatherbeater paints. Wal-Mart offers Sam's Choice beverages and food products, Spring Valley nutritional products, Ol' Roy dog food (named for Sam Walton's Irish setter), and White Cloud brand toilet tissue, diapers, detergent, and fabric softener to compete against major national brands. Private brands can be hard to establish and costly to stock and promote. However, they also yield higher profit margins for the reseller. And they give resellers exclusive products that cannot be bought from competitors, resulting in greater store traffic and loyalty.

In the so-called *battle of the brands* between manufacturers' and private brands, retailers have many advantages. They control what products they stock, where they go on the shelf, and which ones they will feature in local circulars. Retailers price their store brands lower than comparable manufacturers' brands, thereby appealing to budget-conscious shoppers, especially in difficult

Private brand (or store brand)

A brand created and owned by a reseller of a product or service.

economic times. And most shoppers believe that store brands are often made by one of the larger manufacturers anyway.

Most retailers also charge manufacturers *slotting fees*—payments demanded by retailers before they will accept new products and find "slots" for them on the shelves. Slotting fees have recently received much scrutiny from the Federal Trade Commission, which worries that they might dampen competition by restricting retail shelf access for smaller manufacturers who can't afford the fees.[27]

As store brands improve in quality and as consumers gain confidence in their store chains, store brands are posing a strong challenge to manufacturers' brands. Consider the case of Loblaws, the Canadian supermarket chain:

> Loblaws's President's Choice Decadent Chocolate Chip Cookies brand is now the leading cookie brand in Canada. Its private label President's Choice cola racks up 50 percent of Loblaws's canned cola sales. Based on this success, the private label powerhouse has expanded into a wide range of food categories. For example, it now offers more than 2,500 items under the President's Choice label, ranging from frozen desserts to paper, prepared foods, and boxed meats. The brand has become so popular that Loblaws now licenses it to retailers across the United States and eight other countries where Loblaws has no stores of its own. President's Choice Decadent Chocolate Chip Cookies are now sold by Jewel Food Stores in Chicago, where they are the number-one seller, beating out even Nabisco's Chips Ahoy brand. The company also offers a Web site where consumers can purchase its branded products directly.[28]

In U.S. supermarkets, taken as a single brand, private-label products are the number-one, -two, or -three brand in over 40 percent of all grocery product categories. In all, they capture more than a 15 percent share of U.S. supermarket sales.[29] To fend off private brands, leading brand marketers will have to invest in R&D to bring out new brands, new features, and continuous quality improvements. They must design strong advertising programs to maintain high awareness and preference. They must find ways to "partner" with major distributors in a search for distribution economies and improved joint performance.

Licensing. Most manufacturers take years and spend millions to create their own brand names. However, some companies license names or symbols previously created by other manufacturers, names of well-known celebrities, or characters from popular movies and books. For a fee, any of these can provide an instant and proven brand name.

Apparel and accessories sellers pay large royalties to adorn their products—from blouses to ties, and linens to luggage—with the names or initials of well-known fashion innovators such as Calvin Klein, Tommy Hilfiger, Gucci, or Armani. Sellers of children's products attach an almost

Store brands: Loblaw's President's Choice brand has become so popular that the company now licenses it to retailers across the United States and in eight other countries where Loblaws has no stores of its own.

endless list of character names to clothing, toys, school supplies, linens, dolls, lunch boxes, cereals, and other items. Licensed character names range from classics such as *Sesame Street,* Disney, Peanuts, Winnie the Pooh, the Muppets, Scooby Doo, and Dr. Seuss characters to the more recent Teletubbies, Pokemon, Powerpuff Girls, Rugrats, Blue's Clues, and Harry Potter characters. Almost half of all retail toy sales come from products based on television shows and movies such as *Scooby Doo, The Rugrats Movie, The Lion King, Batman, Star Trek, Star Wars, Spider-Man,* or *Men in Black.*[30]

Name and character licensing has grown rapidly in recent years. Annual retail sales of licensed products in the United States and Canada has grown from only $4 billion in 1977 to $55 billion in 1987 and more than $71 billion today. Licensing can be a highly profitable business for many companies. For example, Warner Brothers has turned *Looney Tunes* characters into one of the world's most sought-after licenses. More than 225 licensees generate $4 billion in annual retail sales of products sporting Bugs Bunny, Daffy Duck, Foghorn Leghorn, or one of more than 100 other *Looney Tunes* characters. Warner Brothers has yet to tap the full potential of many of its secondary characters. The Tazmanian Devil, for example, initially appeared in only five cartoons. But through cross-licensing agreements with organizations such as Harley-Davidson and the NFL, Taz has become something of a pop icon. Warner Brothers sees similar potential for Michigan Frog or Speedy Gonzales for the Hispanic market.[31]

The fastest-growing licensing category is corporate brand licensing, as more and more for-profit and not-for-profit organizations are licensing their names to generate additional revenues and brand recognition. Coca-Cola, for example, has some 320 licensees in 57 countries producing more than 10,000 products, ranging from baby clothes and boxer shorts to earrings, a Coca-Cola Barbie doll, and even a fishing lure shaped like a tiny Coke can. Last year, licensees sold more than $1 billion worth of licensed Coca-Cola products.[32]

Co-branding

The practice of using the established brand names of two different companies on the same product.

Co-Branding.   Although companies have been **co-branding** products for many years, there has been a recent resurgence in co-branded products. Co-branding occurs when two established brand names of different companies are used on the same product. For example, Nabisco joined forces with Pillsbury to create Pillsbury Oreo Bars baking mix, and Kellogg joined with ConAgra to co-brand Healthy Choice from Kellogg's cereals. Ford and Eddie Bauer co-branded a sport utility vehicle—the Ford Explorer, Eddie Bauer edition. General Electric worked with Culligan to develop its Water by Culligan Profile Performance refrigerator with a built-in Culligan water filtration system. Mattel teamed with Coca-Cola to market Soda Fountain Sweetheart Barbie. In

Character licensing: Warner Brothers has turned Looney Tunes characters into one of the world's most sought-after licenses. More than 225 licensees generate $4 billion in annual retail sales of products sporting one of more than 100 Looney Tunes characters.

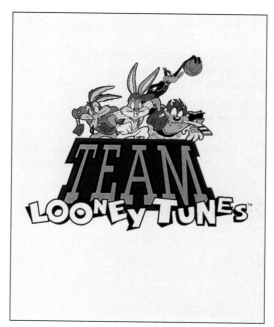

most co-branding situations, one company licenses another company's well-known brand to use in combination with its own.

Co-branding offers many advantages. Because each brand dominates in a different category, the combined brands create broader consumer appeal and greater brand equity. Co-branding also allows a company to expand its existing brand into a category it might otherwise have difficulty entering alone. For example, by licensing its Healthy Choice brand to Kellogg, ConAgra entered the breakfast segment with a solid product. In return, Kellogg could leverage the broad awareness of the Healthy Choice name in the cereal category.

Co-branding also has limitations. Such relationships usually involve complex legal contracts and licenses. Co-branding partners must carefully coordinate their advertising, sales promotion, and other marketing efforts. Finally, when co-branding, each partner must trust the other will take good care of its brand. For example, consider the marriage between Kmart and the Martha Stewart housewares brand. When Kmart declared bankruptcy, it cast a shadow on the Martha Stewart brand. In turn, when Martha Steward was accused of unethical or illegal financial dealings, it created negative associations for Kmart. As one Nabisco manager puts it, "Giving away your brand is a lot like giving away your child—you want to make sure everything is perfect."[33]

Brand Development

A company has four choices when it comes to developing brands (see Figure 9.4). It can introduce *line extensions* (existing brand names extended to new forms, sizes, and flavors of an existing product category), *brand extensions* (existing brand names extended to new product categories), *multibrands* (new brand names introduced in the same product category), or *new brands* (new brand names in new product categories).

Line extension

Using a successful brand name to introduce additional items in a given product category under the same brand name, such as new flavors, forms, colors, added ingredients, or package sizes.

Line Extensions.   **Line extensions** occur when a company introduces additional items in a given product category under the same brand name, such as new flavors, forms, colors, ingredients, or package sizes. Thus, Dannon introduced several line extensions, including seven new yogurt flavors, a fat-free yogurt, and a large, economy-size yogurt. The vast majority of all new-product activity consists of line extensions.

A company might introduce line extensions as a low-cost, low-risk way to introduce new products. Or it might want to meet consumer desires for variety, to utilize excess capacity, or simply to command more shelf space from resellers. However, line extensions involve some risks. An overextended brand name might lose its specific meaning, or heavily extended brands can cause consumer confusion or frustration. For example, a consumer buying cereal at the local supermarket will be confronted by more than 150 brands, including up to 30 different brands, flavors, and sizes of oatmeal alone. By itself, Quaker offers its original Quaker Oats, several flavors of Quaker instant oatmeal, and several dry cereals such as Oatmeal Squares, Toasted Oatmeal, and Toasted Oatmeal-Honey Nut.

Another risk is that sales of an extension may come at the expense of other items in the line. For example, although Fig Newton's cousins Cranberry Newtons, Blueberry Newtons, and Apple Newtons are all doing well for Kraft, the original Fig Newton brand now seems like just another flavor. A line extension works best when it takes sales away from competing brands, not when it "cannibalizes" the company's other items.

Brand extension

Using a successful brand name to launch a new or modified product in a new category.

Brand Extensions.   A **brand extension** involves the use of a successful brand name to launch new or modified products in a new category. Mattel has extended its enduring Barbie Doll brand

FIGURE 9.4
Brand development strategies

into new categories ranging from Barbie home furnishings, Barbie cosmetics, and Barbie electronics to Barbie books, Barbie sporting goods, and even a Barbie band—Beyond Pink. Honda uses its company name to cover different products such as its automobiles, motorcycles, snowblowers, lawn mowers, marine engines, and snowmobiles. This allows Honda to advertise that it can fit "six Hondas in a two-car garage." Swiss Army brand sunglasses, Disney Cruise Lines, Cosmopolitan low-fat dairy products, Century 21 Home Improvements, and Brinks home security systems—all are brand extensions.

A brand extension gives a new product instant recognition and faster acceptance. It also saves the high advertising costs usually required to build a new brand name. At the same time, a brand extension strategy involves some risk. Brand extensions such as Bic pantyhose, Heinz pet food, LifeSavers gum, and Clorox laundry detergent met early deaths. The extension may confuse the image of the main brand. And if a brand extension fails, it may harm consumer attitudes toward the other products carrying the same brand name. Further, a brand name may not be appropriate to a particular new product, even if it is well made and satisfying—would you consider buying Texaco milk or Alpo chili? A brand name may lose its special positioning in the consumer's mind through overuse. Companies that are tempted to transfer a brand name must research how well the brand's associations fit the new product.[34]

Multibrands.   Companies often introduce additional brands in the same category. Thus, P&G markets many different brands in each of its product categories. *Multibranding* offers a way to establish different features and appeal to different buying motives. It also allows a company to lock up more reseller shelf space. Or the company may want to protect its major brand by setting up *flanker* or *fighter brands*. Seiko uses different brand names for its higher-priced watches (Seiko Lasalle) and lower-priced watches (Pulsar) to protect the flanks of its mainstream Seiko brand.

A major drawback of multibranding is that each brand might obtain only a small market share, and none may be very profitable. The company may end up spreading its resources over many brands instead of building a few brands to a highly profitable level. These companies should reduce the number of brands they sell in a given category and set up tighter screening procedures for new brands.

New Brands.   A company may create a new brand name when it enters a new product category for which none of the company's current brand names is appropriate. For example, Honda created the Lexus brand to differentiate its luxury car from the established Honda line. Japan's Matsushita uses separate names for its different families of products: Technics, Panasonic, National, and Quasar. Or, a company might believe that the power of its existing brand name is waning and a new brand name is needed.

As with multibranding, offering too many new brands can result in a company spreading its resources too thin. And in some industries, such as consumer packaged goods, consumers and retailers have become concerned that there are already too many brands, with too few differences between them. Thus, Procter & Gamble, Frito-Lay, and other large consumer-product marketers are now pursuing *megabrand* strategies—weeding out weaker brands and focusing their marketing dollars only on brands that can achieve the number one or number two market share positions in their categories.

Managing Brands

Companies must carefully manage their brands. First, the brand's positioning must be continuously communicated to consumers. Major brand marketers often spend huge amounts on advertising to create brand awareness and to build preference and loyalty. For example, General Motors spends nearly $820 million annually to promote its Chevrolet brands. McDonald's spends more than $660 million.[35]

Such advertising campaigns can help to create name recognition, brand knowledge, and maybe even some brand preference. However, the fact is that brands are not maintained by advertising but by the *brand experience*. Today, customers come to know a brand through a wide range of contacts and touch points. These include advertising, but also personal experience with the brand, word of mouth, personal interactions with company people, telephone interactions, company Web pages, and many others. Any of these experiences can have a positive or negative impact on brand perceptions and feelings. The company must put as much care into managing these touch points as it does into producing its ads.

The brand's positioning will not take hold fully unless everyone in the company lives the brand. Therefore the company needs to train its people to be customer-centered. Even better, the company should build pride in its employees regarding their products and services so that their enthusiasm will spill over to customers. Companies such as Nordstrom, Lexus, Dell, and Harley-Davidson have succeeded in turning all of their employees into enthusiastic brand builders. Companies can carry on internal brand building to help employees to understand, desire, and deliver on the brand promise.[36] Many companies go even further by training and encouraging their distributors and dealers to serve their customers well.

All of this suggests that managing a company's brand assets can no longer be left only to brand managers. Brand managers do not have enough power or scope to do all the things necessary to build and enhance their brands. Moreover, brand managers often pursue short-term results, whereas managing brands as assets calls for longer-term strategy. Thus, some companies are now setting up brand asset management teams to manage their major brands. Canada Dry and Colgate-Palmolive have appointed *brand equity managers* to maintain and protect their brands' images, associations, and quality, and to prevent short-term actions by overeager brand managers from hurting the brand. Similarly, Hewlett-Packard has appointed a senior executive in charge of the customer experience in each of its two divisions, consumer and B2B. Their job is to track, measure, and improve the customer experience with H-P products. They report directly to the presidents of their respective divisions.

Finally, companies need to periodically audit their brands' strengths and weaknesses.[37] They should ask: Does our brand excel at delivering benefits that consumers truly value? Is the brand properly positioned? Do all of our consumer touch points support the brand's positioning? Do the brand's managers understand what the brand means to consumers? Does the brand receive proper, sustained support?

The brand audit may turn up brands that need to be repositioned because of changing customer preferences or new competitors. Some cases may call for completely *rebranding* a product, service, or company. The recent wave of corporate mergers and acquisitions has set off a flurry of corporate rebranding campaigns. A prime example is Verizon Communication, created by the merger of Bell Atlantic and GTE. The company decided that neither of the old names properly positioned the new company. "We needed a master brand to leave all our old names behind," says Verizon's senior vice president of brand management and marketing services. The old names created too much confusion, conjured up an image of old-fashioned phone companies, and "held us back from marketing in new areas of innovation—high-speed Internet and wireless services." The new branding effort appears to have worked. Verizon Wireless is now the leading provider of wireless phone services, with better than a 21 percent market share. Number two is Cingular Wireless, another new brand created through a joint venture between Bell South and SBC Communications.[38]

However, building a new image and re-educating customers can be a huge undertaking. The cost of Verizon's brand overhaul included tens of millions of dollars just for a special four-week advertising campaign to announce the new name, followed by considerable ongoing advertising expenses. And that was only the beginning. The company had to repaint its fleet of 70,000 trucks along with its garages and service centers. The campaign also required relabeling 250,000 pay phones, redesigning 91 million customer billing statements, and producing videos and other in-house employee educational materials.

Services Marketing

Services have grown dramatically in recent years. Services now account for 74 percent of U.S. gross domestic product and nearly 60 percent of personal consumption expenditures. Whereas service jobs accounted for 55 percent of all U.S. jobs in 1970, by 1996 they accounted for 80 percent of total employment. Services are growing even faster in the world economy, making up a quarter of the value of all international trade.[39]

Service industries vary greatly. *Governments* offer services through courts, employment services, hospitals, military services, police and fire departments, postal service, and schools. *Private not-for-profit organizations* offer services through museums, charities, churches, colleges, foundations, and hospitals. A large number of *business organizations* offer services—airlines, banks, hotels, insurance companies, consulting firms, medical and law practices, entertainment companies, real estate firms, advertising and research agencies, and retailers.

FIGURE 9.5
Four service characteristics

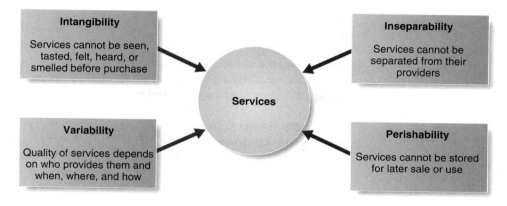

The Nature and Characteristics of a Service

A company must consider four special service characteristics when designing marketing programs: *intangibility, inseparability, variability,* and *perishability* (see Figure 9.5).

Service intangibility means that services cannot be seen, tasted, felt, heard, or smelled before they are bought. For example, people undergoing cosmetic surgery cannot see the result before the purchase. Airline passengers have nothing but a ticket and the promise that they and their luggage will arrive safely at the intended destination, hopefully at the same time. To reduce uncertainty, buyers look for "signals" of service quality. They draw conclusions about quality from the place, people, price, equipment, and communications that they can see. Therefore, the service provider's task is to make the service tangible in one or more ways. Whereas product marketers try to add intangibles to their tangible offers, service marketers try to add tangibles to their intangible offers.

Physical goods are produced, then stored, later sold, and still later consumed. In contrast, services are first sold, then produced and consumed at the same time. **Service inseparability** means that services cannot be separated from their providers, whether the providers are people or machines. If a service employee provides the service, then the employee is a part of the service. Because the customer is also present as the service is produced, *provider–customer interaction* is a special feature of services marketing. Both the provider and the customer affect the service outcome.

Service variability means that the quality of services depends on who provides them as well as when, where, and how they are provided. For example, some hotels—say, Marriott—have reputations for providing better service than others. Still, within a given Marriott hotel, one registration-desk employee may be cheerful and efficient, whereas another standing just a few feet away may be unpleasant and slow. Even the quality of a single Marriott employee's service varies according to his or her energy and frame of mind at the time of each customer encounter.

Service perishability means that services cannot be stored for later sale or use. Some doctors charge patients for missed appointments because the service value existed only at that point and disappeared when the patient did not show up. The perishability of services is not a problem when demand is steady. However, when demand fluctuates, service firms often have difficult problems. For example, because of rush-hour demand, public transportation companies have to own much more equipment than they would if demand were even throughout the day. Thus, service firms often design strategies for producing a better match between demand and supply. Hotels and resorts charge lower prices in the off-season to attract more guests. And restaurants hire part-time employees to serve during peak periods.

Marketing Strategies for Service Firms

Just like manufacturing businesses, good service firms use marketing to position themselves strongly in chosen target markets. Southwest Airlines positions itself as a no-frills, short-haul airline charging very low fares. Wal-Mart promises "Always Low Prices, Always." Ritz-Carlton Hotels positions itself as offering a memorable experience that "enlivens the senses, instills well-being, and fulfills even the unexpressed wishes and needs of our guests." These and other service firms establish their positions through traditional marketing mix activities.

Service intangibility
A major characteristic of services—they cannot be seen, tasted, felt, heard, or smelled before they are bought.

Service inseparability
A major characteristic of services—they are produced and consumed at the same time and cannot be separated from their providers, whether the providers are people or machines.

Service variability
A major characteristic of services—their quality may vary greatly, depending on who provides them and when, where, and how.

Service perishability
A major characteristic of services—they cannot be stored for later sale or use.

However, because services differ from tangible products, they often require additional marketing approaches. In a product business, products are fairly standardized and can sit on shelves waiting for customers. But in a service business, the customer and front-line service employee *interact* to create the service. Thus, service providers must interact effectively with customers to create superior value during service encounters. Effective interaction, in turn, depends on the skills of front-line service employees and on the support processes backing these employees.

The Service-Profit Chain

Service-profit chain

The chain that links service firm profits with employee and customer satisfaction.

Successful service companies focus their attention on *both* their customers and their employees. They understand the **service-profit chain,** which links service firm profits with employee and customer satisfaction. This chain consists of five links:[40]

- *Internal service quality:* superior employee selection and training, a quality work environment, and strong support for those dealing with customers, which results in . . .
- *Satisfied and productive service employees:* more satisfied, loyal, and hardworking employees, which results in . . .
- *Greater service value:* more effective and efficient customer value creation and service delivery, which results in. . .
- *Satisfied and loyal customers:* satisfied customers who remain loyal, repeat purchase, and refer other customers, which results in . . .
- *Healthy service profits and growth:* superior service firm performance.

Therefore, reaching service profits and growth goals begins with taking care of those who take care of customers (see Real Marketing 9.3).

Thus, service marketing requires more than just traditional external marketing using the four *P*s. Figure 9.6 shows that service marketing also requires *internal marketing* and *interactive marketing.* **Internal marketing** means that the service firm must effectively train and motivate its customer-contact employees and supporting service people to work as a *team* to provide customer satisfaction. Marketers must get everyone in the organization to be customer-centered. In fact, internal marketing must *precede* external marketing. Ritz-Carlton orients its employees carefully, instills in them a sense of pride, and motivates them by recognizing and rewarding outstanding service deeds.

Internal marketing

Marketing by a service firm to train and effectively motivate its customer-contact employees and all the supporting service people to work as a team to provide customer satisfaction.

Interactive marketing

Marketing by a service firm that recognizes that perceived service quality depends heavily on the quality of buyer–seller interaction.

Interactive marketing means that service quality depends heavily on the quality of the buyer–seller interaction during the service encounter. In product marketing, product quality often depends little on how the product is obtained. But in services marketing, service quality depends on both the service deliverer and the quality of the delivery. Service marketers, therefore, have to master interactive marketing skills. Thus, Ritz-Carlton selects only "people who care about people" and instructs them carefully in the fine art of interacting with customers to satisfy their every need.

In today's marketplace, companies must know how to deliver interactions that are not only "high-touch" but also "high-tech." For example, customers can log on to the Charles Schwab Web site and access account information, investment research, real-time quotes, after-hours trading, and the Schwab learning center. They can also participate in live online events and chat online with customer service representatives. Customers seeking more-personal interactions can contact service reps by phone or visit a local Schwab branch office. Thus, Schwab has master interactive marketing at all three levels—calls, clicks, *and* visits.[41]

FIGURE 9.6

Three types of marketing in service industries

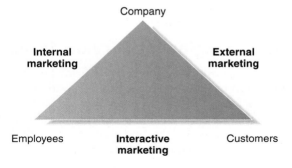

real marketing 9.3

Ritz-Carlton: Taking Care of Those Who Take Care of Customers

Ritz-Carlton, a chain of luxury hotels renowned for outstanding service, caters to the top 5 percent of corporate and leisure travelers. The company's Credo sets high customer service goals: "The Ritz-Carlton Hotel is a place where the genuine care and comfort of our guests is our highest mission. We pledge to provide the finest personal service and facilities for our guests, who will always enjoy a warm, relaxed yet refined ambience. The Ritz-Carlton experience enlivens the senses, instills well-being, and fulfills even the unexpressed wishes and needs of our guests." The company's Web page concludes: "Here a calm settles over you. The world, so recently at your door, is now at your feet."

The Credo is more than just words on paper—Ritz-Carlton delivers on its promises. In surveys of departing guests, some 95 per-

ple's son became sick last year in Naples, the hotel staff brought him hot tea with honey at all hours of the night, she said. When Mr. Heffner had to fly home on business for a day and his return flight was delayed, a driver for the hotel waited in the lobby most of the night.

Such personal, high-quality service has also made The Ritz-Carlton a favorite among conventioneers. "They not only treat us like kings when we hold our top-level meetings in their hotels, but we just never get any complaints," comments one convention planner. "Perhaps the biggest challenge a planner faces when recommending The Ritz-Carlton at Half Moon Bay to the boss, board, and attendees is convincing them that meeting there truly is work," says another. "The . . .

customers return. And despite its hefty room rates, the chain enjoys a 70 percent occupancy rate, almost nine points above the industry average.

Most of the responsibility for keeping guests satisfied falls to Ritz-Carlton's customer-contact employees. Thus, the hotel chain takes great care in selecting its personnel. "We want only people who care about people," notes the company's vice president of quality. Once selected, employees are given intensive training in the art of coddling customers. New employees attend a two-day orientation, in which top management drums into them the "20 Ritz-Carlton Basics." Basic number one: "The Credo will be known, owned, and energized by all employees."

Employees are taught to do everything they can to prevent losing a guest. "There's no negotiating at Ritz-Carlton when it comes to solving customer problems," says the quality executive. Staff learn that *anyone* who receives a customer complaint *owns* that complaint until it's resolved (Ritz-Carlton Basic number eight). They are trained to drop whatever they're doing to help a customer—no matter what they're doing or what their department. Ritz-Carlton employees are empowered to handle problems on the spot, without consulting higher-ups. Each employee can spend up to $2,000 to redress a guest grievance, and each is allowed to break from his or her routine for as long as needed to make a guest happy. "We master customer satisfaction at the individual level," adds the executive. "This is our most sensitive listening post . . . our early warning system." Thus, while competitors are still reading guest comment cards to learn about customer problems, Ritz-Carlton has already resolved them.

Ritz-Carlton instills a sense of pride in its employees. "You serve," they are told, "but you are not servants." The company motto states, "We are ladies and gentlemen serving ladies and gentlemen." Employees understand their role in Ritz-Carlton's success. "We might not be able to afford a hotel like this," says employee Tammy Patton, "but we can make it so people who can afford it will want to keep coming here."

| **THE RITZ-CARLTON®**
CREDO
The Ritz-Carlton Hotel is a place where the genuine care and comfort of our guests is our highest mission.
We pledge to provide the finest personal service and facilities for our guests who will always enjoy a warm, relaxed yet refined ambience.
The Ritz-Carlton experience enlivens the senses, instills well-being, and fulfills even the unexpressed wishes and needs of our guests. | **THREE STEPS**
OF SERVICE
1
A warm and sincere greeting. Use the guest name, if and when possible.
2
Anticipation and compliance with guest needs.
3
Fond farewell. Give them a warm good-bye and use their name, if and when possible. | **THE EMPLOYEE**
PROMISE
At The Ritz-Carlton, our Ladies and Gentlemen are the most important resource in our service commitment to our guests.
By applying the principles of trust, honesty, respect, integrity and commitment, we nurture and maximize talent to the benefit of each individual and the company.
The Ritz-Carlton fosters a work environment where diversity is valued, quality of life is enhanced, individual aspirations are fulfilled, and The Ritz-Carlton mystique is strengthened. | *"We Are Ladies and Gentlemen Serving Ladies and Gentlemen"* |

The Credo and Employee Promise: Ritz-Carlton knows that to take care of customers, you must first take care of those who take care of customers.

cent report that they've had a truly memorable experience. In fact, at Ritz-Carlton, exceptional service encounters have become almost commonplace. Take the experiences of Nancy and Harvey Heffner of Manhattan, who stayed at the Ritz-Carlton Naples, in Naples, Florida (recently rated the best hotel in the United States, fourth best in the world, by *Travel & Leisure* magazine). As reported in the *New York Times:*

"The hotel is elegant and beautiful," Mrs. Heffner said, "but more important is the beauty expressed by the staff. They can't do enough to please you." When the cou-

first-rate catering and service-oriented convention services staff [and] the Ritz-Carlton's ambiance and beauty—the elegant, Grand Dame-style lodge, nestled on a bluff between two championship golf courses overlooking the Pacific Ocean—makes a day's work there seem anything but."

In 1992, Ritz-Carlton became the first hotel company to win the Malcolm Baldrige National Quality Award. Since its incorporation in 1983, the company has received virtually every major award that the hospitality industry bestows. More importantly, service quality has resulted in high customer retention: More than 90 percent of Ritz-Carlton

(continued)

And so they do. When it comes to customer satisfaction, no detail is too small. Customer-contact people are taught to greet guests warmly and sincerely, using guest names when possible. They learn to use the proper language with guests—phrases such as *Good morning, Certainly, I'll be happy to, Welcome back,* and *My pleasure,* never *Hi* or *How's it going?* The Ritz-Carlton Basics urge employees to escort guests to another area of the hotel rather than pointing out directions, to answer the phone within three rings and with a "smile," and to take pride and care in their personal appearance. As the general manager of The Ritz-Carlton Naples puts it, "When you invite guests to your house, you want everything to be perfect."

Ritz-Carlton recognizes and rewards employees who perform feats of outstanding service. Under its 5-Star Awards program, outstanding performers are nominated by peers and managers, and winners receive plaques at dinners celebrating their achievements. For on-the-spot recognition, managers award Gold Standard Coupons, redeemable for items in the gift shop and free weekend stays at the hotel. Ritz-Carlton further rewards and motivates its employees with events such as Super Sports Day, an employee talent show, luncheons celebrating employee anniversaries, a family picnic, and special themes in employee dining rooms. As a result, Ritz-Carlton's employees appear to be just as satisfied as its customers. Employee turnover is less than 30 percent a year, compared with 45 percent at other luxury hotels.

Ritz-Carlton's success is based on a simple philosophy: To take care of customers, you must first take care of those who take care of customers. Satisfied employees deliver high service value, which then creates satisfied customers. Satisfied customers, in turn, create sales and profits for the company.

Sources: Quotes and other information from Edwin McDowell, "Ritz-Carlton's Keys to Good Service," *New York Times,* March 31, 1993, p. D1; Howard Schlossberg, "Measuring Customer Satisfaction Is Easy to Do—Until You Try," *Marketing News,* April 26, 1993, pp. 5, 8; Ginger Conlon, "True Romance," *Sales & Marketing Management,* May 1996, pp. 85–90; "The Ritz-Carlton, Half Moon Bay," *Successful Meetings,* November 2001, p. 40; and the Ritz-Carlton Web site at www.ritzcarlton.com, August 2002. Also see Patricia Sheehan, "Back to Bed: Selling the Perfect Night's Sleep," *Lodging Hospitality,* March 15, 2001, pp. 22–24; and Nicole Harris, "Can't Sleep? Try the Eye Gel in the Minibar—Hotels Roll Out Products to Help Tired Travelers Snooze," *Wall Street Journal,* June 20, 2002, p. D1.

Today, as competition and costs increase, and as productivity and quality decrease, more service marketing sophistication is needed. Service companies face three major marketing tasks: They want to increase their *competitive differentiation, service quality,* and *productivity.*

Managing Service Differentiation

In these days of intense price competition, service marketers often complain about the difficulty of differentiating their services from those of competitors. To the extent that customers view the services of different providers as similar, they care less about the provider than the price.

The solution to price competition is to develop a differentiated offer, delivery, and image. The *offer* can include innovative features that set one company's offer apart from competitors' offers. Some hotels offer car rental, banking, and business center services in their lobbies. Airlines introduced innovations such as in-flight movies, advance seating, air-to-ground telephone service, and frequent flyer award programs to differentiate their offers. British Airways even offers international travelers beds and private "demi-cabins," hot showers, and cooked-to-order breakfasts.

Service companies can differentiate their service *delivery* by having more able and reliable customer-contact people, by developing a superior physical environment in which the service product is delivered, or by designing a superior delivery process. For example, many banks offer their customers Internet banking as a better way to access banking services than having to drive, park, and wait in line.

Finally, service companies also can work on differentiating their *images* through symbols and branding. The Harris Bank of Chicago adopted the lion as its symbol on its stationery, in its advertising, and even as stuffed animals offered to new depositors. The well-known Harris lion confers an image of strength on the bank. Other well-known service symbols include The Travelers' red umbrella, Merrill Lynch's bull, and Allstate's "good hands."

Managing Service Quality

One of the major ways a service firm can differentiate itself is by delivering consistently higher quality than its competitors do. Like manufacturers before them, most service industries have now joined the customer-driven quality movement. And like product marketers, service providers need to identify the expectations of target customers concerning service quality. Unfortunately, service quality is harder to define and judge than is product quality. For instance, it is harder to get agreement on the quality of a haircut than on the quality of a hair dryer.

Service differentiation: British Airways differentiates its offer by providing first-class world travelers private "demi-cabins" and other amenities.

Customer retention is perhaps the best measure of quality—a service firm's ability to hang on to its customers depends on how consistently it delivers value to them.[42]

Top service companies are customer obsessed and set high service quality standards. They do not settle for merely good service; they aim for 100 percent defect-free service. A 98 percent performance standard may sound good, but using this standard, 64,000 FedEx packages would be lost each day, 10 words would be misspelled on each printed page, 400,000 prescriptions would be misfilled daily, and drinking water would be unsafe 8 days a year.[43] Top service firms also *watch service performance closely*, both their own and that of competitors. They communicate their concerns about service quality to employees and provide performance feedback.

Unlike product manufacturers who can adjust their machinery and inputs until everything is perfect, service quality will always vary, depending on the interactions between employees and customers. As hard as they try, even the best companies will have an occasional late delivery, burned steak, or grumpy employee. However, good *service recovery* can turn angry customers into loyal ones. In fact, good recovery can win more customer purchasing and loyalty than if things had gone well in the first place. Therefore, companies should take steps not only to provide good service every time but also to recover from service mistakes when they do occur.[44]

The first step is to *empower* front-line service employees—to give them the authority, responsibility, and incentives they need to recognize, care about, and tend to customer needs. At Marriott, for example, well-trained employees are given the authority to do whatever it takes, on the spot, to keep guests happy. They are also expected to help management ferret out the cause of guests' problems and to inform managers of ways to improve overall hotel service and guests' comfort.

Managing Service Productivity

With their costs rising rapidly, service firms are under great pressure to increase service productivity. They can do so in several ways. The service providers can train current employees better or hire new ones who will work harder or more skillfully. Or they can increase the quantity of their service by giving up some quality. The provider can "industrialize the service" by adding equipment and standardizing production, as in McDonald's assembly-line approach to fast-food retailing. Finally, the service provider can harness the power of technology. Although we often think of technology's power to save time and costs in manufacturing companies, it also has great—and often untapped—potential to make service workers more productive.

However, companies must avoid pushing productivity so hard that doing so reduces quality. Attempts to industrialize a service or to cut costs can make a service company more efficient in the short run. But they can also reduce its longer-run ability to innovate, maintain service quality, or respond to consumer needs and desires. In short, they can take the "service" out of service.

Additional Product Considerations

Here, we discuss two additional product policy considerations: social responsibility in product decisions and issues of international product and service marketing.

Product Decisions and Social Responsibility

Product decisions have attracted much public attention. Marketers should consider carefully a number of public policy issues and regulations involving acquiring or dropping products, patent protection, product quality and safety, and product warranties.

Regarding new products, the government may prevent companies from adding products through acquisitions if the effect threatens to lessen competition. Companies dropping products must be aware that they have legal obligations, written or implied, to their suppliers, dealers, and customers who have a stake in the discontinued product. Companies must also must obey U.S. patent laws when developing new products. A company cannot make its product illegally similar to another company's established product.

Manufacturers must comply with specific laws regarding product quality and safety. The Federal Food, Drug, and Cosmetic Act protects consumers from unsafe and adulterated food, drugs, and cosmetics. Various acts provide for the inspection of sanitary conditions in the meat- and poultry-processing industries. Safety legislation has been passed to regulate fabrics, chemical substances, automobiles, toys, and drugs and poisons. The Consumer Product Safety Act of 1972 established a Consumer Product Safety Commission, which has the authority to ban or seize potentially harmful products and set severe penalties for violation of the law.

If consumers have been injured by a product that has been designed defectively, they can sue manufacturers or dealers. Product liability suits are now occurring in federal and state courts at the rate of almost 110,000 per year, with a median jury award of $1.8 million and individual awards often running into the tens of millions of dollars.[45] This phenomenon has resulted in huge increases in product liability insurance premiums, causing big problems in some industries. Some companies pass these higher rates along to consumers by raising prices. Others are forced to discontinue high-risk product lines. Some companies are now appointing "product stewards," whose job is to protect consumers from harm and the company from liability by proactively ferreting out potential product problems.[46]

Many manufacturers offer written product warranties to convince customers of their products' quality. To protect consumers, Congress passed the Magnuson-Moss Warranty Act in 1975. The act requires that full warranties meet certain minimum standards, including repair "within a reasonable time and without charge" or a replacement or full refund if the product does not work "after a reasonable number of attempts" at repair. Otherwise, the company must make it clear that it is offering only a limited warranty. The law has led several manufacturers to switch from full to limited warranties and others to drop warranties altogether.

International Product and Services Marketing

International product and service marketers face special challenges. First, they must figure out what products and services to introduce and in which countries. Then, they must decide how much to standardize or adapt their products and services for world markets.

On the one hand, companies would like to standardize their offerings. Standardization helps a company to develop a consistent worldwide image. It also lowers manufacturing costs and eliminates duplication of research and development, advertising, and product design efforts. On the other hand, consumers around the world differ in their cultures, attitudes, and buying behaviors. And markets vary in their economic conditions, competition, legal requirements, and physical environments. Companies must usually respond to these differences by adapting their product offerings. Something as simple as an electrical outlet can create big product problems:

> Those who have traveled across Europe know the frustration of electrical plugs, different voltages, and other annoyances of international travel. . . . Philips, the electrical appliance manufacturer, has to produce 12 kinds of irons to serve just its European market. The problem is that Europe does not have a universal [electrical] standard. The ends of irons bristle with different plugs for different countries. Some have three prongs, others two; prongs protrude straight or angled, round or rectangular, fat, thin, and sometimes sheathed. There are circular plug faces, squares, pentagons, and hexagons. Some are perforated and some are notched. One French plug has a niche like a keyhole.[47]

Packaging also presents new challenges for international marketers. Packaging issues can be subtle. For example, names, labels, and colors may not translate easily from one country to another. A firm using yellow flowers in its logo might fare well in the United States but meet with disaster in Mexico, where a yellow flower symbolizes death or disrespect. Similarly, although Nature's Gift might be an appealing name for gourmet mushrooms in America, it would be deadly in Germany, where *gift* means poison. Packaging may also have to be tailored to meet the physical characteristics of consumers in various parts of the world. For instance, soft drinks are sold in smaller cans in Japan to fit the smaller Japanese hand better. Thus, although product and package standardization can produce benefits, companies must usually adapt their offerings to the unique needs of specific international markets.

Service marketers also face special challenges when going global. Some service industries have a long history of international operations. For example, the commercial banking industry was one of the first to grow internationally. Banks had to provide global services in order to meet the foreign exchange and credit needs of their home country clients wanting to sell overseas. In recent years, many banks have become truly global operations. Germany's Deutsche Bank, for example, serves more than 12 million customers in 70 countries. For its clients around the world who wish to grow globally, Deutsche Bank can raise money not only in Frankfurt but also in Zurich, London, Paris, and Tokyo.[48]

Professional and business services industries such as accounting, management consulting, and advertising have only recently globalized. The international growth of these firms followed the globalization of the manufacturing companies they serve. For example, as their client companies began to

Retailers are among the latest service businesses to go global. Here Asian shoppers buy American products in a Dutch-owned Makro store in Kuala Lumpur.

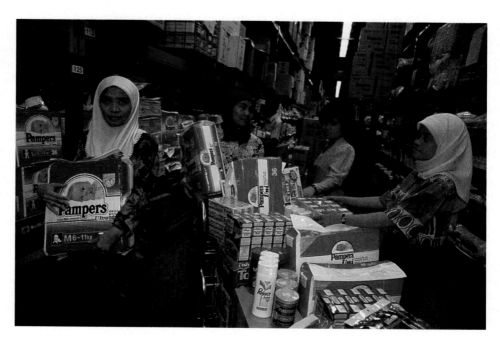

employ global marketing and advertising strategies, advertising agencies and other marketing services firms responded by globalizing their own operations. McCann-Erickson Worldwide, the largest U.S. advertising agency, operates in more than 130 countries, serving international clients such as Coca-Cola, General Motors, ExxonMobile, Microsoft, Johnson & Johnson, and Unilever in markets ranging from the United States and Canada to Korea to Kazakhstan. Moreover, McCann-Erikson is one company in the Interpublic Group of Companies, an immense, worldwide network of commonly owned but autonomous advertising and marketing services companies.[49]

Retailers are among the latest service businesses to go global. As their home markets become saturated, American retailers such as Wal-Mart, Kmart, Toys "R" Us, Office Depot, Saks Fifth Avenue, and Disney are expanding into faster-growing markets abroad. For example, every year since 1995, Wal-Mart has entered a new country; its international division's sales grew 40 percent last year, skyrocketing to more than $32 billion. Foreign retailers are making similar moves. The Japanese retailer Yaohan now operates the largest shopping center in Asia, the 21-story Nextage Shanghai Tower in China, and Carrefour of France is the leading retailer in Brazil and Argentina. Asian shoppers now buy American products in Dutch-owned Makro stores, now Southeast Asia's biggest store group with sales in the region of more than $2 billion.[50]

Service companies wanting to operate in other countries are not always welcomed with open arms. Whereas manufacturers usually face straightforward tariff, quota, or currency restrictions when attempting to sell their products in another country, service providers are likely to face more subtle barriers. In some cases, rules and regulations affecting international service firms reflect the host country's traditions. In others, they appear to protect the country's own fledgling service industries from large global competitors with greater resources. In still other cases, however, the restrictions seem to have little purpose other than to make entry difficult for foreign service firms.

Despite such difficulties, the trend toward growth of global service companies will continue, especially in banking, airlines, telecommunications, and professional services. Today service firms are no longer simply following their manufacturing customers. Instead, they are taking the lead in international expansion.

LOOKING BACK: REVIEWING THE CONCEPTS

A product is more than a simple set of tangible features. Each product or service offered to customers can be viewed on three levels. The *core product* consists of the core problem-solving benefits that consumers seek when they buy a product. The *actual product* exists around the core and includes the quality level, features, design, brand name, and packaging. The *augmented product* is the actual product plus the various services and benefits offered with it, such as warranty, free delivery, installation, and maintenance.

1. Define *product* and the major classifications of products and services.

Broadly defined, a *product* is anything that can be offered to a market for attention, acquisition, use, or consumption that might satisfy a want or need. Products include physical objects but also services, events, persons, places, organizations, ideas, or mixes of these entities. *Services* are products that consist of activities, benefits, or satisfactions offered for sale that are essentially intangible, such as banking, hotel, tax preparation, and home repair services.

Products and services fall into two broad classes based on the types of consumers that use them. *Consumer products*—those bought by final consumers—are usually classified according to consumer shopping habits (convenience products, shopping products, specialty products, and unsought products). *Industrial products*—purchased for further processing or for use in conducting a business—include materials and parts, capital items, and supplies and services. Other marketable entities—

such as organizations, persons, places, and ideas—can also be thought of as products.

2. Describe the decisions companies make regarding their individual products and services, product lines, and product mixes.

Individual product decisions involve product attributes, branding, packaging, labeling, and product support services. *Product attribute* decisions involve product quality, features, and style and design. *Branding* decisions include selecting a brand name and developing a brand strategy. *Packaging* provides many key benefits, such as protection, economy, convenience, and promotion. Package decisions often include designing *labels,* which identify, describe, and possibly promote the product. Companies also develop *product support services* that enhance customer service and satisfaction and safeguard against competitors.

Most companies produce a product line rather than a single product. A *product line* is a group of products that are related in function, customer-purchase needs, or distribution channels. *Line stretching* involves extending a line downward, upward, or in both directions to occupy a gap that might otherwise by filled by a competitor. In contrast, *line filling* involves adding items within the present range of the line. The set of product lines and items offered to customers by a particular seller make up the *product mix.* The mix can be described by four dimensions: width, length, depth, and consistency. These dimensions are the tools for developing the company's product strategy.

3. Discuss branding strategy—the decisions companies make in building and managing their brands.

Some analysts see brands as *the* major enduring asset of a company. Brands are more than just names and symbols—they embody everything that the product or service *means* to consumers. *Brand equity* is the positive differential effect that knowing the brand name has on customer response to the product or service. A brand with strong brand equity is a very valuable asset.

In building brands, companies need to make decisions about brand positioning, brand name selection, brand sponsorship, and brand development. The most powerful *brand positioning* builds around strong consumer beliefs and values. *Brand name selection* involves finding the best brand name based on a careful review of product benefits, the target market, and proposed marketing strategies. A manufacturer has four *brand sponsorship* options: It can launch a *manufacturer's brand* (or national brand), sell to resellers who use a *private brand*, market *licensed brands*, or join forces with another company to *co-brand* a product. A company also has four choices when it comes to developing brands. It can introduce *line extensions*, *brand extensions*, *multibrands*, or *new brands* (new brand names in new product categories).

Companies must build and manage their brands carefully. The brand's positioning must be continuously communicated to consumers. Advertising can help, although brands are not maintained by advertising but by the *brand experience*. Customers come to know a brand through a wide range of contacts and touchpoints. The company must put as much care into managing these touch points as it does into producing its ads. Thus, managing a company's brand assets can no longer be left only to brand managers. Some companies are now setting up brand asset management teams to manage their major brands. Finally, companies must periodically audit their brands' strengths and weaknesses. In some cases, brands may need to be repositioned because of changing customer preferences or new competitors.

Other cases may call for completely *rebranding* a product, service, or company.

4. Identify the four characteristics that affect the marketing of a service and the additional marketing considerations that services require.

Services are characterized by four key characteristics: They are *intangible, inseparable, variable,* and *perishable*. Each characteristic poses problems and marketing requirements. Marketers work to find ways to make the service more tangible, to increase the productivity of providers who are inseparable from their products, to standardize the quality in the face of variability, and to improve demand movements and supply capacities in the face of service perishability.

Good service companies focus attention on *both* customers and employees. They understand the *service-profit chain*, which links service firm profits with employee and customer satisfaction. Services marketing strategy calls not only for external marketing but also for *internal marketing* to motivate employees and *interactive marketing* to create service delivery skills among service providers. To succeed, service marketers must create *competitive differentiation*, offer high *service quality*, and find ways to increase *service productivity*.

5. Discuss two additional product issues: socially responsible product decisions and international product and services marketing.

Marketers must consider two additional product issues. The first is *social responsibility*. These include public policy issues and regulations involving acquiring or dropping products, patent protection, product quality and safety, and product warranties. The second involves the special challenges facing international product and service marketers. International marketers must decide how much to standardize or adapt their offerings for world markets.

REVIEWING THE KEY TERMS

Brand 285
Brand equity 292
Brand extension 296
Co-branding 295
Consumer product 280
Convenience product 280
Industrial product 281
Interactive marketing 300
Internal marketing 300

Line extension 296
Packaging 286
Private brand (or store brand) 293
Product 276
Product line 289
Product mix (or product assortment) 290
Product quality 283
Service 276

Service inseparability 299
Service intangibility 299
Service perishability 299
Service-profit chain 300
Service variability 299
Shopping product 280
Social marketing 282
Specialty product 280
Unsought product 281

DISCUSSING THE CONCEPTS

1. What are the primary differences between products and services? Give illustrations of the differences that you identify. Provide an example of a hybrid offer.
2. List and explain the core, actual, and augmented products for educational experiences that universities offer. How are these products different, if at all, from those offered by junior colleges? Which of these products could be easily moved online? How would such a move affect the educational institution's marketing efforts?
3. List and summarize the characteristics of the four types of consumer products. Provide an example of each.

4. How does an industrial product differ from a consumer product? List and summarize the characteristics of the three major groups of industrial products identified in the text.
5. The text identifies social marketing as the use of commercial marketing concepts and tools in programs designed to influence individuals' behavior in a way that improves their well-being and that of society. Consider a recent social marketing effort, such as Mothers Against Drunk Driving. Identify its intended target market, list the primary objectives of the campaign, suggest how effectiveness could be measured, and document the overall impact of the campaign.

Critique the campaign and comment on what you would do to improve the effort.

6. For many years there was one type of Coca-Cola, one type of Tide, and two types of Crest (mint and regular). Now we find Coke in seven or more varieties; Tide in Ultra, Liquid, and Unscented versions; and Crest Gel with sparkles for kids. List some of the issues these brand extensions raise for manufacturers, retailers, and consumers. Is more always better? How does co-branding affect brand extensions? Suggest a co-branding opportunity that you believe makes sense from a marketing perspective.

7. Explain the types of line stretching and their benefits. Give an example of each. What is line filling? Why would a marketing manager choose line filling over line stretching?

8. Illustrate how a movie theater can deal with the intangibility, inseparability, variability, and perishability of the services it provides. Give specific examples to illustrate your thoughts. How could the movie theater use internal and interactive marketing to enhance its service-profit chain?

APPLYING THE CONCEPTS

1. The core product in the automobile industry is transportation. The problem-solving benefit is getting from one place to another quickly and safely. However, most automobile manufacturers differentiate their products with additional service benefits. These service approaches are almost as varied as are the automobile manufacturers themselves. Examine the Web sites for Ford (www.ford.com), General Motors (www.gm.com), DaimlerChrysler (www.chrysler.com), Honda (www.honda.com), Lexus (www.lexus.com), Mercedes-Benz (www.MBUSA.com), and Toyota (www.toyota.com). Look beyond the automobiles themselves and closely examine the manufacturer's services and service options.

   a. What primary services do the various automobile manufacturers offer? Prepare a grid that compares each company to the others.

   b. What services do the different companies appear to offer in common? What services do they use to differentiate themselves from one another?

   c. Do any of the sites suggest that a company understands the service-profit chain? Explain.

   d. Do any of the companies employ interactive marketing with respect to the service component? Explain.

   e. Visit the Saturn Web site at www.saturn.com. Do you see anything that makes this company different from those you have already visited? What seems to be the company's focus and differential advantage? Suggest ways in which Saturn could use its service component to compete more effectively against its competitors.

2. Which company has the world's strongest brand? Is brand strength determined by sales volume, a global presence, innovation, reputation, amount of advertising, success on the Internet, positive public relations, stock value, or all of these things? Marketing managers know that strong brand equity is the key to entering new markets and successfully penetrating old ones. Strong brands can command premium prices. Brand image also shapes corporate strategy, advertising campaigns, and overall marketing effort. Alliances are made and broken based on brand reputation and confidence. In contrast, loss of confidence in a brand can affect not only the companies involved but also all of the brand's distributors, service providers, and secondary publics. As a result, many consider a strong brand a company's most important asset. So, what is the world's strongest brand? According to recent studies, the Coca-Cola brand tops the list, followed by Microsoft, IBM, and GE. Why do these brands garner so much respect?

   a. What makes a strong brand? How would you go about measuring brand equity?

   b. What makes Coca-Cola the number one brand in the world? What characteristics differentiate the company and brand from its competitors?

   c. With its ongoing legal difficulties, how can Microsoft be considered a strong global brand? Does its international dominance help it overcome public relations and legal problems? Explain.

   d. Examine the Web sites for Coke-Cola (www.cocacola.com), Microsoft (www.microsoft.com), IBM (www.ibm.com), and GE (www.ge.com) for indications of brand strength. Based on your answers to question "a" above, construct a grid that evaluates each of these brands based on the characteristics you listed. Examine the information in your grid. Which company is superior based on your evaluation?

www DIGITAL CONNECTIONS

CONNECTING WITH CONSUMERS VIA THE SERVICE-PROFIT CHAIN

FedEx has been on top of the parcel delivery business for some time. However, United Parcel Service (UPS) has started a "ground war," aiming to overtake number one FedEx. UPS doesn't plan to do it with cheaper rates, better trucks, faster computers, or more manpower. The key is better service. While its rivals average 15 to 20 hours, UPS can move merchandise around the world in a mere 12 hours. The UPS service-profit chain focuses on building long-term relationships with customers. The company finds the cheapest way for a client to ship merchandise and bets that, in the long run, the relationships it builds will yield more business and profits. For example, if a chip maker in Singapore were to use a UPS competitor to ship a box of chips, it might be forced to use expensive overnight air express. Why? Because the method would be the most profitable for the shipping company. In contrast, using its strength in developing long-term relationships, UPS would aid the chip maker in designing its warehouse operation, propose a customized tracking system, counsel on logistics, and find a shipping method profitable for both itself and the client. When UPS integrates the client into its operations, both parties benefit financially in delivering goods and pleasing the ultimate consumer. For these reasons and others, UPS is rapidly overtaking FedEx both domestically and globally as the shipper of preference. UPS also has attracted the attention of the Web generation. The company now handles the majority of all online purchases. The threat has not gone unnoticed by FedEx. The pioneer of both delivering packages overnight and tracking them via computer, FedEx is now planning further innovations in tracking, service, and accountability. Will it be too little too late? The customer will eventually decide.

FOR DISCUSSION

1. How is UPS using a service-profit chain to its advantage? Do either UPS or FedEx appear to employ interactive or integrated marketing? Explain.
2. Match the services provided by these two competitors to the characteristics shown in Figure 9.5. What are the companies' strengths? Weaknesses? Where do opportunities exist for UPS?
3. If you were choosing one of these service providers to deliver a package for you, how would you make your choice? What factors would be important to you?
4. Assume that you are the shipping manager for a company based in Peru that grows and distributes perishable cut flowers. Describe the types of services you might need, how you would evaluate the two companies, and how partnering with the carriers could enhance your business.

Siegelgale: Great Brands Built on a Compelling Promise

For more than 30 years, Siegelgale has helped corporations build and express their brands effectively. The consultancy has worked with companies ranging from Caterpillar, Coca-Cola, and Dell to Kodak, American Express, and the Girl Scouts. Working with the Girl Scouts, Siegelgale transformed the 90-year-old organization associated with cookies and camping into a modern not-for-profit "where girls grow strong." Siegelgale believes that great brands are built on a compelling promise that defines, differentiates, and dramatizes their value.

After viewing the Siegelgale video, answer the following questions about marketing strategy and brand management:

1. Siegelgale helps companies hone their brand messages to deliver a strong, cohesive product image. Select two

brands that you interact with daily. What attributes and values do you associate with those brands? How are those attributes and values communicated through brand messages?

2. Some products, such as Coke, are strongly identified with their packaging. How does packaging affect brand messages? What other products use packaging to differentiate or promote a brand image?

3. Siegelgale works with a variety of companies promoting a range of products and services. How might brand management differ between products such as cell phones and services such as those provided by the Girl Scouts?

Starbucks: Brewing a Worldwide Experience

GROUNDED IN HISTORY

In 1971, entrepreneurs Jerry Baldwin, Gordon Bowker, and Zev Siegl launched the first Starbucks in Seattle's Pike Place Market. At that time, a bitter price war had thrown the American coffee market into turmoil. Trying to maintain profit margins, producers of the major coffee brands had begun using cheaper beans, resulting in what many consumers believed was a dramatic decline in coffee quality.

The Starbucks entrepreneurs brewed the idea of opening a retail store dedicated to selling only the finest coffee-brewing equipment to brew only the highest-quality, whole-bean coffee. They believed that such a store could satisfy the few coffee enthusiasts who had to order coffee from Europe and convert other coffee drinkers to the gourmet coffee experience. To differentiate its coffee from the bland, dishwater-like store brands, Starbucks scoured the globe for arabica beans grown above 10,000 feet in altitude by a carefully selected group of growers in countries like Sumatra, Kenya, Ethopia, and Costa Rica. The company focused on arabica beans, rather than the cheaper robusta beans, because consumers could brew the arabica beans at higher temperatures, thus producing a richer coffee flavor.

Despite early success, Starbucks remained a small-time Seattle operation until the company hired Howard Schultz as its marketing director in 1982. In 1983, Shultz, while traveling in Italy, visited a coffeehouse and realized that Starbucks's future was not in retailing coffee beans and equipment but in serving freshly brewed coffee by the cup in its own coffeehouses. Shultz saw that the coffeehouse strategy would allow Starbucks to differentiate itself from other vendors of beans and equipment that were springing up. Further, although more people were developing tastes for gourmet coffee, many people did not have the time or equipment to brew specialty coffees properly. By brewing the coffee in its coffeehouses, Starbucks could use the proper equipment and well-trained employees to produce the best possible coffee in an environment that enhanced the coffee-drinking experience. And, offering the coffee by the cup made the experience convenient for the busy Seattle businesspeople who were Starbucks's prime customers.

In 1987, Schultz became president of Starbucks and began to reshape its image as a prelude to rapid growth. He updated the company's logo from an earthen brown color to green. He worked to shape Starbucks's coffeehouses to be a blend of Italian elegance and American informality. He carefully designed the store to "enhance the quality of everything the customers see, touch, hear, smell, or taste." He wanted the store to be a "personal treat" for the customers, providing a refreshing break in their day or a place to relax at night. To achieve this goal, Schultz and his managers invested in employee training and a strong employee

benefit program so that they could attract and retain skilled employees who would enhance the customer's experience.

By the late 1990s, Schultz's strategy was paying off handsomely. In 1993, the American coffee market had been worth about $13.5 billion, with specialty coffees, like those Starbucks sold, accounting for only about $1 billion. By 1999, the U.S. coffee market had mushroomed to over $18 billion, with specialty coffees capturing $7.5 billion. In 1996 alone, Starbucks added a store a day and almost matched that by adding 325 in 1997. By the end of 1997, it had added 30,000 employees since Shultz joined the company and was hiring 500 employees a week. Sales had almost doubled from $700 million in just 1996 to over $1.3 billion by 1998. A typical Starbucks customer visited his or her favorite store 18 times a month!

CROSSING CULTURES

Despite Starbucks's success in the U.S. market, Schultz and his team realized that American consumers accounted for only 20 percent of the world coffee market. If Starbucks were going to achieve its goals, it had to venture into foreign markets and prove that a really good cup of coffee was a true global product.

The company first ventured into Japan and Singapore in 1996. In Japan, the company went against the Japanese love of cigarettes and refused to allow smoking in its coffeehouses, as it does in all its markets, arguing that the smoke would overwhelm the coffee aroma. Contrary to some predictions, Japanese women loved the smoke-free stores, and Japanese men followed suit. By early 2000, Starbucks had more than 200 stores in Japan and was profitable two years ahead of schedule.

Then, in 1998, the company looked to Europe. It purchased the Seattle Coffee Company from Scott and Ally Svenson, expatriates who started the Starbucks look-alike in 1990, when they moved to London and couldn't find a good cup of coffee. By 1998, Seattle Coffee had 56 coffee stores in Britain and had begun to make coffee drinking an important part of the British social scene. Whereas England had earned the reputation as a nation of tea drinkers that offered only terrible coffee, by 1998 the country's annual coffee consumption actually topped tea consumption. The Svensons sold the chain to Starbucks for $84 million and stayed to work with the company to help it become a springboard into the European market.

ON TO THE CONTINENT

The major unanswered question was how Starbucks would do when it entered continental Europe, where it would encounter established coffee cultures, anti-American sentiment at times, and, above all, 121,000 existing espresso bars in Italy—the ultimate challenge.

In early 2001, Schultz decided to take the plunge into continental Europe by opening a coffeehouse in Zurich, Switzerland—the first of 650 stores the company said it will open in six neighboring countries by 2003. Schultz knew that continental Europe would be a big challenge, as American coffee had a long-standing bad reputation. He chose Switzerland to develop about 11 stores, seeing the country as a good test market because it mixed French, German, and Italian cultures.

To enter Switzerland, Starbucks followed a strategy it had developed for other international markets. Many of the new stores would be 50-50 partnerships with local business partners who shared its values and wanted to grow aggressively. Partnering allowed Starbucks to utilize the partners' local knowledge and to leverage its capital to expand more rapidly. Before going into a country, Starbucks conducted extensive focus groups and quantitative market research. It would vary its food offerings to meet local tastes, but it would not alter its coffee, like its caramel macchiato. Peter Maslen, president of Starbucks Coffee International, noted, "We want to elicit the same emotional response all over the world." To learn the Starbucks way, new mangers spent 12 weeks in Seattle learning the barista's art and customer service.

Then, in late 2001, Starbucks took its boldest European step to date by opening its first coffeehouse in Vienna, Austria—a stronghold where 1,900 coffee shops catered to persnickety customers, who sometimes visited four times a day to smoke, drink coffee from china cups, and linger while black-jacketed waiters served them. Austria already had one coffeehouse for every 530 people, and the average citizen drank 1,000 cups of coffee a year. Starbucks offered its standard paper cups for to-go orders and counter service. Further, it maintained its no-smoking policy, even as critics noted that 40 percent of Europeans and 60 percent of Italians smoke—about half of Starbucks's potential market. Although it offered some "required" apple strudel and some cakes with poppy seeds, its food fare consisted basically of American-style sweets. The head of Starbucks's Austrian joint venture noted, "We don't want to sell coffee; we want to sell a relaxed 15 minutes."

As of mid-2002, the Austrian experiment was going well. Starbucks had four stores in Vienna serving a mixture of well-to-do tourists and locals in their thirties who spent about $5 per visit, about the same as in other shops. Its total global chain numbered 5,405 stores, with 1,153 of those stores located outside the United States.

In 2002, the company would also enter the Spanish and German markets as it continued its caffeine-laden assault on Europe in preparation for completing the global circle by entering Italy, where Howard Schultz first had his vision for a global frappuccino, and Greece, the site of the 2004 Olympics.

QUESTIONS FOR DISCUSSION

1. What is the core product that Starbucks offers? What are the actual and augmented levels of that product?
2. How would you classify the Starbucks product using the marketing considerations for a consumer product outlined in the chapter? What individual product decisions has Starbucks made?
3. How has Starbucks dealt with issues of brand equity, customer equity, and brand positioning?
4. Is Starbucks a product or a service? How are the concepts of service marketing important to Starbucks?
5. How has Starbucks dealt with the issues it faces in international marketing?
6. What marketing recommendations would you make to Starbucks as it continues its international expansion?

Sources: Steven Erlanger, "An American Coffeehouse (or 4) in Vienna, *The New York Times on the Web,* www.nytimes.com, June 1, 2002; Alwyn Scott, "Starbucks Wins Fans in Europe," *Knight-Ridder/Tribune Business News,* May 19, 2002, item 02139001; Hans Greimel, "Starbucks' Final Frontier Is Winning European Palates," *Detroit News,* March 9, 2001; Mark Pendergrast, "The Starbucks Experience Going Global," *Tea and Coffee Trade Online* 176 (2), February/March, 2002; "Abuzz; Coffee-shop Chains; American Coffee Chains Invade Europe," *The Economist,* May 19, 2001, article A74692901; Dori Jones Yang, "An American (Coffee) in Paris—and Rome," *U.S. News and World Report,* February 19, 2001, p. 47; Steve Ernst, "Starbucks Europe, Asia Next," *Puget Sound Business Journal,* June 2, 2000, p. 33; Chloe Beacham, "Is That to Go?" *The European,* May 11, 1998, p. 25.

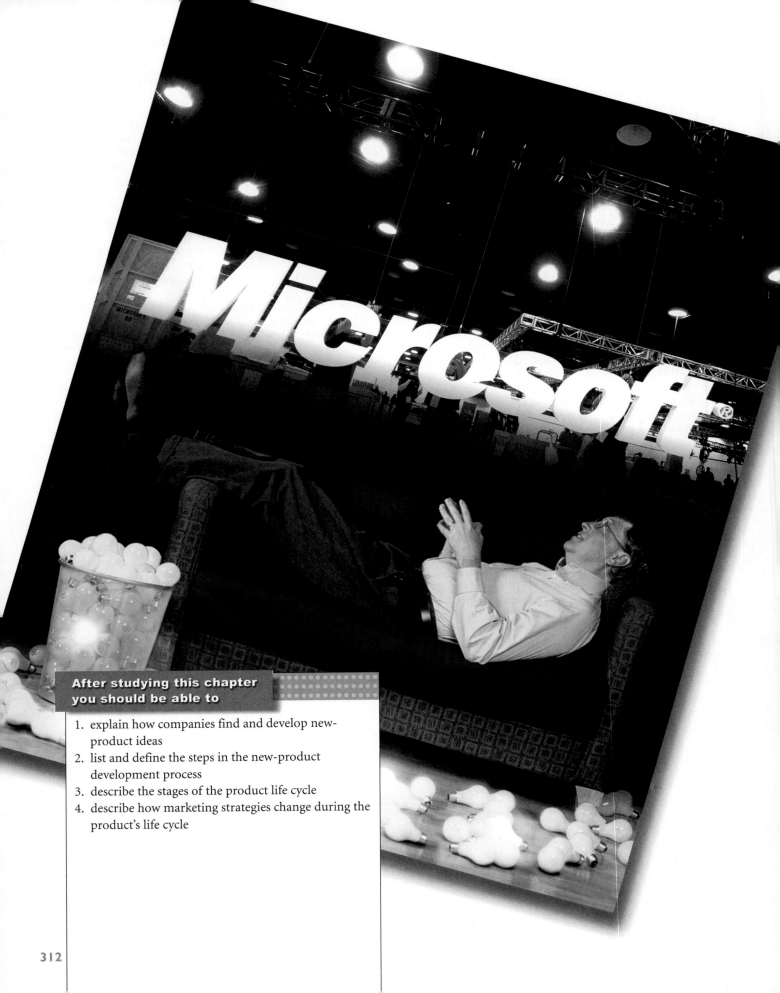

1. explain how companies find and develop new-product ideas
2. list and define the steps in the new-product development process
3. describe the stages of the product life cycle
4. describe how marketing strategies change during the product's life cycle

New-Product Development and Product Life-Cycle Strategies

LOOKING AHEAD: PREVIEWING THE CONCEPTS

In the previous chapter, you learned about decisions that marketers make in managing individual brands and entire product mixes. In this chapter, we'll look into two additional product topics: developing new products and managing products through their life cycles. New products are the lifeblood of an organization. However, new-product development is risky, and many new products fail. So, the first part of this chapter lays out a process for finding and growing successful new products. Once introduced, marketers want their products to enjoy a long and happy life. In the second part of the chapter, you'll see that every product passes through several life-cycle stages and that each stage poses new challenges requiring different marketing strategies and tactics.

For openers, consider Microsoft. The chances are good that you use several Microsoft products and services. Microsoft's Windows software owns a mind-boggling 97 percent share of the PC operating system market, and its Office software captures a 90 percent share! However, this $25 billion company doesn't rest on past performance. As you'll see, it owes much of this success to a passion for innovation, abundant new-product development, and its quest for "the Next Big Thing."

No matter what brand of computer you're using or what you're doing on it, you're almost certain to be using some type of Microsoft product or service. In the world of computer and Internet software and technology, Microsoft dominates.

Microsoft's Windows operating system captures an astonishing 97 percent share of the PC market and a better than 40 percent share in the business server market. Microsoft Office, the company's largest moneymaker, grabs 90 percent of all office applications suite sales. The company's MSN Internet portal (www.msn.com) attracts more than 50 million surfers per month, second only to Yahoo!. Its MSN Internet-access service, with 5 million subscribers, trails only America Online as the most popular way for consumers to get onto the Web. Microsoft's Hotmail is the world's most used free e-mail service, hosting more than 100 million accounts, and its instant messaging service has nearly 30 million users.

These and other successful products and services have made Microsoft incredibly profitable. During its first 27 years, the software giant has racked up more than $50 billion in profits. An investment of $2,800 in 100 shares of Microsoft stock made back when the company went public would by now have mushroomed into 14,400 shares worth a cool

$1 million. All this has made Microsoft co-founder Bill Gates the world's richest man, worth over $47 billion.

A happy ending to a rags-to-riches fairy tale? Not quite. In Microsoft's fast-changing high-tech world, nothing lasts forever—or even for long. Beyond maintaining its core products and businesses, Microsoft knows that its future depends on its ability to conquer new markets with innovative new products.

Microsoft hasn't always been viewed as an innovator. In fact, it has long been regarded as "a big fat copycat." Gates bought the original MS/DOS operating system software upon which he built the company's initial success from a rival programmer for $50,000. Later, Microsoft was accused of copying the user-friendly Macintosh "look and feel." More recently, the company was accused of copying Netscape's Internet browser. It wasn't innovation that made Microsoft, critics claim, but rather its brute-force use of its PC operating-system monopoly to crush competitors and muscle into markets. But no more. The technology giant is now innovating at a breakneck pace.

Thanks to its Windows and Office monopolies, and to Microsoft's legendary cash horde of more than $36 billion, the company has plenty of resources to pump into new products and technologies. This year alone, it will spend $4.2 billion on R&D, more than competitors America Online, Sun Microsystems, and Oracle combined. Along with the cash, Microsoft has a strong, visionary leader in its efforts to innovate—no less than Bill Gates himself. Three years ago, Gates turned the CEO-ship of the company over to longtime number two, Steve Ballmer, and named himself "Chief Software Architect." He now spends most of his time and considerable talents happily attending to the details of Microsoft's new-product and technology development.

At the heart of Gates's innovation strategy is the Internet. "Gates sees a day when Microsoft software will . . . be at nearly every point a consumer or corporation touches the Web, . . . easily connecting people to the Internet wherever they happen to be," says *Business Week* analyst Jay Greene. In this new world, any software application on your computer—or on your cell phone, handheld device, or home electronics device—will tap directly into Internet services that help you manage your work and your life. To prepare for such "anytime, anywhere" computing, Microsoft will transform itself from a software company into an Internet services company. As a part of its Web services, Microsoft will one day rent out the latest versions of its software programs via the Net. "Once that happens," says Greene, "Microsoft hopes to deliver software like a steady flow of electricity, collecting monthly or annual usage fees that will give it a lush, predictable revenue stream."

This vision drives a major new Microsoft innovation initiative—dubbed ".Net My Services."

> .Net My Services is the first of Microsoft's "personal Web services" strategy to upgrade the Internet to be more versatile and interactive. Its initial service, called Passport, provides an online repository for all sorts of personal information and privileges that you can tap into from any computer with a Web browser: contacts, credit card accounts, calendar, file space for documents, . . . an electronic ID card, and more. It will give you access to your important information from anywhere and also simplify online transactions such as purchasing merchandise or airline tickets. Because Passport knows you already, no matter which Web merchant you deal with, it promises to let you transact your business with far fewer clicks and much tighter security and privacy.

Passport members can subscribe to other .Net My Services services, including everything from notifying them of specific events to automatically updating their calendars when they purchase tickets or make an appointment online.

Within this broad strategic framework, Microsoft is now unleashing its biggest-ever new-products assault. "We've never had a year with this many new products," crows Gates. Here are just a few of the new products and technologies that Microsoft has recently launched or will soon introduce (as described in recent *Business Week* and *Fortune* accounts):

- *Dot.Net Services:* technology that lets unrelated Web sites talk with one another and with PC programs. One click can trigger a cascade of actions without the user having to open new programs or visit new Web sites.
- *Stinger:* Microsoft's latest software for cell phones. It will incorporate the functions of a PDA-address book, calendar, audio and video capabilities, and Internet connectivity to give access to .Net My Services services, e-mail, and Web browsing.

- *Natural-language processing:* software that will let computers respond to questions or commands in everyday language, not just computerese or a long series of mouse clicks. Combine that with speech recognition—another area in which Microsoft researchers are plugging away—and one day you'll be able to talk to your computer the same way you do to another person.
- *Face mapping:* using a digital camera to scan a PC user's head into a 3D image. Software then adds a full range of emotions. The point? Microsoft thinks that gamers will want to use their own images in role-playing games.
- *Information agents:* software agents that help you sort the deluge of electronic information. One day, an agent will study what types of messages you read first and know your schedule. Then it will sort e-mail and voice mail, interrupting you with only key messages.
- *Small business technologies:* customer-relationship, human resources, and supply-chain software for small and medium-size businesses. Microsoft also offers bCentral, a Web site and e-commerce hosting service. For a monthly fee, it will host a Web site and provide e-mail services, as well as a shopping-cart setup for e-commerce transactions, credit card clearing, and customer management.
- *The digital home:* next-generation technologies aimed at making the PC the electronic hub of the twenty-first-century digital home. The new technologies will route music, movies, TV programming, e-mail, and news between the Web and PCs, TV set-top boxes, gadgets, and wall-size viewing screens, and sound systems that would make the neighbors call the cops. "Everything in the home will be connected," predicts Gates. And if he gets his way, most of the gizmos will use Microsoft software. Sales from Microsoft's consumer group will account for 18 percent of Microsoft's total business in 2003. The first major Microsoft connected-home product will be a gizmo code-named Mira. It's a flat-panel monitor that detaches from its stand and continues to connect wirelessly to the PC from anywhere in the house. With a stylus tapping icons or scrawling letters on a touch screen, Mom can check e-mail from the kitchen, the kids can chat with online buddies from the couch while watching MTV, and Dad can shop at Amazon.com from the back porch.

So, far from resting on its remarkable past successes, Microsoft is on a quest to discover tomorrow's exciting new technologies. "Even while its latest products are waiting on the launchpad, it continues to pour money into R&D in search of the Next Big Thing," comments Greene. Gates is jazzed about the future. "He gets wound up like a kid over stuff like creating a computer that watches your actions with a small video camera and determines if you're too busy to be interrupted with a phone call or e-mail," says Greene. An excited Gates shares the simple but enduring principle that guides innovation at Microsoft: "The whole idea of valuing the user's time, that's the Holy Grail," he says.[1]

A company has to be good at developing and managing new products. Every product seems to go through a life cycle—it is born, goes through several phases, and eventually dies as newer products come along that better serve consumer needs. This product life cycle presents two major challenges: First, because all products eventually decline, a firm must be good at developing new products to replace aging ones (the problem of *new-product development*). Second, the firm must be good at adapting its marketing strategies in the face of changing tastes, technologies, and competition as products pass through life-cycle stages (the problem of *product life-cycle strategies*). We first look at the problem of finding and developing new products and then at the problem of managing them successfully over their life cycles.

New-Product Development Strategy

New-product development

The development of original products, product improvements, product modifications, and new brands through the firm's own R&D efforts.

Given the rapid changes in consumer tastes, technology, and competition, companies must develop a steady stream of new products and services. A firm can obtain new products in two ways. One is through *acquisition*—by buying a whole company, a patent, or a license to produce someone else's product. The other is through **new-product development** in the company's own research-and-development department. By *new products* we mean original products, product improvements, product modifications, and new brands that the firm develops through its own research-and-development efforts. In this chapter, we concentrate on new-product development.

Innovation can be very risky. Ford lost $350 million on its Edsel automobile; RCA lost $580 million on its SelectaVision videodisc player; and Texas Instruments lost a staggering $660 million before withdrawing from the home computer business. Even these amounts pale in comparison to the failure of the $5 billion Iridium global satellite-based wireless telephone system. Other costly product failures from sophisticated companies include New Coke (Coca-Cola Company), Eagle Snacks (Anheuser-Busch), Zap Mail electronic mail (FedEx), Polarvision instant movies (Polaroid), Premier "smokeless" cigarettes (R.J. Reynolds), Clorox detergent (Clorox Company), and Arch Deluxe sandwiches (McDonald's).[2]

New products continue to fail at a disturbing rate. One source estimates that new consumer packaged goods (consisting mostly of line extensions) fail at a rate of 80 percent. Another study suggested that of the staggering 25,000 new consumer food, beverage, beauty, and health care products to hit the market each year, only 40 percent will be around five years later. Moreover, failure rates for new industrial products may be as high as 30 percent. Still another estimates new-product failures to be as high as 95 percent.[3]

Why do so many new products fail? There are several reasons. Although an idea may be good, the market size may have been overestimated. Perhaps the actual product was not designed as well as it should have been. Or maybe it was incorrectly positioned in the market, priced too high, or advertised poorly. A high-level executive might push a favorite idea despite poor marketing research findings. Sometimes the costs of product development are higher than expected, and sometimes competitors fight back harder than expected.

Because so many new products fail, companies are anxious to learn how to improve their odds of new-product success. One way is to identify successful new products and find out what they have in common. Another is to study new-product failures to see what lessons can be learned (see Real Marketing 10.1). In all, to create successful new products, a company must understand its consumers, markets, and competitors and develop products that deliver superior value to customers.

So companies face a problem—they must develop new products, but the odds weigh heavily against success. The solution lies in strong new-product planning and in setting up a systematic *new-product development process* for finding and growing new products. Figure 10.1 shows the eight major steps in this process.

Idea Generation

Idea generation

The systematic search for new-product ideas.

New-product development starts with **idea generation**—the systematic search for new-product ideas. A company typically has to generate many ideas in order to find a few good ones. According to one well-known management consultant, "For every 1,000 ideas, only 100 will have enough commercial promise to merit a small-scale experiment, only 10 of those will warrant substantial financial commitment, and of those, only a couple will turn out to be unqualified successes." His

FIGURE 10.1

Major stages in new-
product development

conclusion? "If you want to find a few ideas with the power to enthrall customers, foil competitors, and thrill investors, you must first generate hundreds and potentially thousands of unconventional strategic ideas."[4]

Major sources of new-product ideas include internal sources and external sources such as customers, competitors, distributors and suppliers, and others.

Internal Idea Sources

Using *internal sources,* the company can find new ideas through formal research and development. It can pick the brains of its executives, scientists, engineers, manufacturing staff, and salespeople. Some companies have developed successful "intrapreneurial" programs that encourage employees to think up and develop new-product ideas. For example, 3M's well-known "15 percent rule" allows employees to spend 15 percent of their time "bootlegging"—working on projects of personal interest, whether those projects directly benefit the company or not. The spectacularly successful Post-it notes evolved out of this program. Similarly, Texas Instruments's IDEA program provides funds for employees who pursue their own ideas. Among the successful new products to come out of the IDEA program was TI's Speak 'n' Spell, the first children's toy to contain a microchip. Many other speaking toys followed, ultimately generating several hundred million dollars for TI.[5]

External Idea Sources

Good new-product ideas also come from watching and listening to *customers.* The company can analyze customer questions and complaints to find new products that better solve consumer problems. Company engineers or salespeople can meet with and work alongside customers to get suggestions and ideas. The company can conduct surveys or focus groups to learn about consumer needs and wants.

Heinz did just that when its researchers approached children, who consume more than half of the ketchup sold, to find out what would make ketchup more appealing to them. "When we asked them what would make the product more fun," says a Heinz spokesperson, "changing the color was among the top responses." So, Heinz developed and launched EZ Squirt, green ketchup that comes in a soft, squeezable bottle targeted at kids. The new product was a smash hit, so Heinz followed up with an entire rainbow of EZ Squirt colors, including Funky Purple, Passion Pink, Awesome Orange, and Totally Teal. The EZ Squirt bottle's special nozzle also emits a thin ketchup stream, "so tykes can autograph their burgers (or squirt someone across the table, though Heinz neglects to mention that)."[6]

Consumers often create new products and uses on their own, and companies can benefit by finding these products and putting them on the market. For example, Avon capitalized on new uses discovered by consumers for its Skin-So-Soft bath oil and moisturizer. For years, customers have been spreading the word that Skin-So-Soft bath oil is also a terrific bug repellent. Whereas some consumers were content simply to bathe in water scented with the fragrant oil, others carried it in their backpacks to mosquito-infested campsites or kept a bottle on the deck of their beach houses. Now, Avon offers a complete line of Skin-So-Soft Bug Guard products, including

real

marketing 10.1

New Product Failures: What Were They Thinking?

Strolling the aisles at Robert McMath's New Product Showcase and Learning Center or browsing the company's Web site is like finding yourself in some nightmare version of a supermarket. There's Gerber food for adults (pureed sweet-and-sour pork and chicken Madeira), Hot Scoop microwaveable ice cream sundaes, Ben-Gay aspirin, Premier smokeless cigarettes, and Miller Clear Beer. How about Avert Virucidal Tissues, Dr. Care Aerosol Toothpaste, Richard Simmons Dijon Vinaigrette Salad Spray, Look of Buttermilk shampoo, or garlic cake in a jar, parsnip chips, and aerosol mustard? Most of the

80,000 products on display were abject flops. Behind each of them are squandered dollars and hopes, but McMath, the genial curator of this Smithsonian of consumerism, believes that even failure—or perhaps *especially* failure—offers valuable lessons.

The New Product Showcase and Learning Center is a place where product developers pay hundreds of dollars an hour to visit and learn from others' mistakes. McMath's unusual showcase represents $4 billion in product investment. From it he has distilled dozens of lessons for an industry that, by its own admission, has a very short memory.

McMath "draws large audiences and commands a hefty speaking fee by decrying the convoluted thought processes of marketers, package designers, and consumer-opinion pundits who brought these and thousands of other duds-in-the-making to market," comments one analyst. "He gets laughs when he asks, 'What were they thinking?'"

For those who can't make the trip to the center or pay a steep consulting fee, McMath has put his unique insights into a book by that same name, *What Were They Thinking?* Here are a few of the marketing lessons McMath espouses:

The New Product Showcase and Learning Center is like finding yourself in some nightmare version of a supermarket. Each product failure represents squandered dollars and hopes.

(continued)

- *Offer real value.* Many classic flops failed to deliver what customers really wanted. New Coke flopped when Coca-Cola failed to see the real value of the Coke brand to customers—tradition as well as taste. Ford pitched its Edsel as revolutionary; consumers saw it as merely revolting. And consumers quickly snuffed out R.J. Reynolds's Premier smokeless cigarettes. It seemed like a good idea at the time—who could argue against a healthier, nonpolluting cigarette? But Premier didn't deliver what smokers really wanted—smoke. In the first place, in the words of RJR's CEO, the cigarettes "tasted like [expletive]!" Moreover, what is a cigarette without smoke? "It took them a while to figure out that smokers actually like the smoke part of smoking," McMath notes. "The only people who loved the product were nonsmokers, and they somehow aren't the market RJR was trying to reach." Looking back, what was RJR thinking?

- *Cherish thy brand!* The value of a brand is its good name, which it earns over time. People become loyal to it. They trust it to deliver a consistent set of attributes. Don't squander this trust by attaching your good name to something totally out of character. Louis Sherry No Sugar Added Gorgonzola Cheese Dressing was everything that Louis Sherry, known for its rich candies and ice cream, shouldn't be: sugarless, cheese, and salad dressing. Similarly, when you hear the name Ben-Gay, you immediately think of the way that Ben-Gay cream sears and stimulates your skin. Can you imagine swallowing Ben-Gay aspirin? Or how would you feel about quaffing a can of Exxon fruit punch or Kodak quencher? Cracker Jack cereal,

Smucker's premium ketchup, and Fruit of the Loom laundry detergent were other misbegotten attempts to stretch a good name. What *were* they thinking?

- *Be different.* Me-too marketing is the number one killer of new products. Most such attempts fail. The ones that succeed usually require resources and persistence beyond the capabilities of most marketers. Pepsi-Cola led a very precarious existence for decades before establishing itself as the major competitor to Coca-Cola. More to the point, though, Pepsi is one of the few survivors among dozens of other brands that have challenged Coke for more than a century. Ever hear of Toca-Cola? Coco-Cola? Yum-Yum cola? French Wine of Cola? How about King-Cola, "the royal drink"? More recently, Afri Cola failed to attract African American soda drinkers, and Cajun Cola pretty well flopped in the land of gumbo. All things equal, an established product has a distinct advantage over any new product that is not notably different.

- *But don't be* too *different.* Some products are notably different from the products, services, or experiences that consumers normally purchase. *Too* different. They fail because consumers don't relate to them. You can tell that some innovative products are doomed as soon as you hear their names: Toaster Eggs. Cucumber antiperspirant spray. Health-Sea sea sausage. Look of Buttermilk shampoo. Dr. Care Aerosol Toothpaste (many parents questioned the wisdom of arming their kids with something like this!). Other innovative ideas have been victims of a brand's past success. For example, Nabisco's Oreo Little Fudgies, a confectionery product with a chocolate

coating meant to compete with candy, sounds like a natural. But for many years Nabisco has encouraged people to pull apart Oreo cookies and lick out the filling. However, it's very messy to open an Oreo with a chocolate coating. What was *Nabisco* thinking?

- *Accentuate the positive.* Don't be fooled by the success of all the *Dummy's Guide to* . . . books. People usually don't buy products that remind them of their shortcomings. Gillette's For Oily Hair Only shampoo wavered because people did not want to confess that they had greasy hair. People will use products that discreetly say "for oily hair" or "for sensitive skin" in small print on containers that are otherwise identical to the regular product. But they don't want to be hit over the head with reminders that they are overweight, have bad breath, sweat too much, or are elderly. Nor do they wish to advertise their faults and foibles to other people by carrying such products in their grocery carts. Really, what were they thinking?

Sources: Quotes from Gary Slack, "Innovations and Idiocities," *Beverage World,* November 15, 1998, p. 122; and Cliff Edwards, "Where Have All the Edsels Gone?" *Greensboro News Record,* May 24, 1999, p. B6. Bulleted points based on information found in Robert M. McMath and Thom Forbes, *What Were They Thinking? Money-Saving, Time-Saving, Face-Saving Marketing Lessons You Can Learn from Products That Flopped* (New York: Times Business, 1999), various pages; Melissa Master, "Spectacular Failures," *Across the Board,* March–April 2001, p. 24; and information from www.newproductworks.com/product_poll/hm_index.html, July 2002.

Bug Guard Mosquito Repellant Moisturizing Towelettes and Bug Guard Plus, a combination moisturizer, insect repellent, and sunscreen.[7]

Finally, some companies even give customers the tools and resources to design their own products.

Many companies have abandoned their efforts to figure out exactly what products their customers want. Instead, they have equip customers with tools that let them design their own products. The user-friendly tools employ new technologies like computer simulation and rapid prototyping to make product development faster and less expensive. For example, Bush Boake Allen (BBA), a global supplier of specialty flavors to companies like Nestle, provides a tool kit that enables its customers to develop their own flavors, which BBA then manufactures. Similarly, GE Plastics gives customers access to company data sheets, engineering expertise, simulation software, and other Web-based tools for designing better plastics products. Companies like LSI Logic and VLSI Technology provide customers with do-it-yourself

When Heinz asked kids what would make the product more fun, they said "Change the color!" So, Heinz developed and launched EZ Squirt, now in a variety of colors targeted at kids. The EZ Squirt bottle's special nozzle also emits a thin ketchup stream, so tykes can autograph their burgers.

tools that let them design their own specialized chips and customized integrated circuits. Using customers as innovators has become a hot new way to create value.[8]

Companies must be careful not to rely too heavily on customer input when developing new products. For some products, especially highly technical ones, customers may not know what they need. In such cases, "customers should not be trusted to come up with solutions; they aren't expert or informed enough for that part of the innovation process," says the head of an innovation management consultancy. "That's what your R&D team is for. Rather, customers should be asked only for outcomes—that is, what they want a product or service to *do* for them."[9]

Competitors are another good source of new-product ideas. Companies watch competitors' ads and other communications to get clues about their new products. They buy competing new products, take them apart to see how they work, analyze their sales, and decide whether they should bring out a new product of their own. *Distributors and suppliers* can also contribute many good new-product ideas. Resellers are close to the market and can pass along information about consumer problems and new-product possibilities. Suppliers can tell the company about new concepts, techniques, and materials that can be used to develop new products. Other idea sources include trade magazines, shows, and seminars; government agencies; new-product consultants; advertising agencies; marketing research firms; university and commercial laboratories; and inventors.

The search for new-product ideas should be systematic rather than haphazard. Otherwise, few new ideas will surface and many good ideas will sputter and die. Top management can avoid these problems by installing an *idea management system* that directs the flow of new ideas to a central point where they can be collected, reviewed, and evaluated. In setting up such a system, the company can do any or all of the following:[10]

- Appoint a respected senior person to be the company's idea manager.
- Create a cross-functional idea management committee consisting of people from R&D, engineering, purchasing, operations, finance, and sales and marketing to meet regularly and evaluate proposed new product and service ideas.
- Set up a toll-free number or Web site for anyone who wants to send a new idea to the idea manager.
- Encourage all company stakeholders—employees, suppliers, distributors, dealers—to send their ideas to the idea manager.
- Set up formal recognition programs to reward those who contribute the best new ideas.

The idea manager approach yields two favorable outcomes. First, it helps create an innovation-oriented company culture. It shows that top management supports, encourages, and rewards innovation. Second, it will yield a larger number of ideas, among which will be found some especially good ones. As the system matures, ideas will flow more freely. No longer will good ideas wither for the lack of a sounding board or a senior product advocate.

Idea Screening

Idea screening

Screening new-product ideas in order to spot good ideas and drop poor ones as soon as possible.

The purpose of idea generation is to create a large number of ideas. The purpose of the succeeding stages is to *reduce* that number. The first idea-reducing stage is **idea screening,** which helps spot good ideas and drop poor ones as soon as possible. Product development costs rise greatly in later stages, so the company wants to go ahead only with the product ideas that will turn into profitable products. As one marketing executive suggests, "Three executives sitting in a room can get 40 good ideas ricocheting off the wall in minutes. The challenge is getting a steady stream of good ideas out of the labs and creativity campfires, through marketing and manufacturing, and all the way to consumers."[11]

Many companies require their executives to write up new-product ideas on a standard form that can be reviewed by a new-product committee. The write-up describes the product, the target market, and the competition. It makes some rough estimates of market size, product price, development time and costs, manufacturing costs, and rate of return. The committee then evaluates the idea against a set of general criteria. For example, at Kao Company, the large Japanese consumer-products company, the committee asks questions such as these: Is the product truly useful to consumers and society? Is it good for our particular company? Does it mesh well with the company's objectives and strategies? Do we have the people, skills, and resources to make it succeed? Does it deliver more value to customers than do competing products? Is it easy to advertise and distribute? Many companies have well-designed systems for rating and screening new-product ideas.

Concept Development and Testing

Product concept

A detailed version of the new-product idea stated in meaningful consumer terms.

An attractive idea must be developed into a **product concept.** It is important to distinguish between a product idea, a product concept, and a product image. A *product idea* is an idea for a possible product that the company can see itself offering to the market. A *product concept* is a detailed version of the idea stated in meaningful consumer terms. A *product image* is the way consumers perceive an actual or potential product.

Concept Development

DaimlerChrysler is getting ready to commercialize its experimental fuel-cell-powered electric car. This car's nonpolluting fuel-cell system runs directly on methanol, which delivers hydrogen to the fuel cell with only water as a by-product. It is highly fuel efficient (75 percent more efficient than gasoline engines) and gives the new car an environmental advantage over standard internal combustion engine cars or even today's superefficient gasoline-electric hybrid cars.

DaimlerChrysler is currently road-testing its NECAR 5 (New Electric Car) subcompact prototype and plans to deliver the first fuel-cell cars to customers in 2004. Based on the tiny Mercedes A-Class, the car accelerates quickly, reaches speeds of 90 miles per hour, and has a 280-mile driving range, giving it a huge edge over battery-powered electric cars that travel only about 80 miles before needing 3 to 12 hours of recharging.[12]

DaimlerChrysler's task is to develop this new product into alternative product concepts, find out how attractive each concept is to customers, and choose the best one. It might create the following product concepts for the fuel-cell electric car:

Concept 1   A moderately priced subcompact designed as a second family car to be used around town. The car is ideal for running errands and visiting friends.

Concept 2   A medium-cost sporty compact appealing to young people.

Concept 3   An inexpensive subcompact "green" car appealing to environmentally conscious people who want practical transportation and low pollution.

DaimlerChrysler's task is to develop its fuel-cell-powered electric car into alternative product concepts, find out how attractive each is to customers, and choose the best one.

Concept 4   A high-end SUV appealing to those who love the space SUVs provide but lament the poor gas mileage.

Concept Testing

Concept testing

Testing new-product concepts with a group of target consumers to find out if the concepts have strong consumer appeal.

Concept testing calls for testing new-product concepts with groups of target consumers. The concepts may be presented to consumers symbolically or physically. Here, in words, is concept 3:

> An efficient, fun-to-drive, fuel-cell-powered electric subcompact car that seats four. This methanol-powered high-tech wonder provides practical and reliable transportation with virtually no pollution. It goes up to 90 miles per hour and, unlike battery-powered electric cars, it never needs recharging. It's priced, fully equipped, at $20,000.

For some concept tests, a word or picture description might be sufficient. However, a more concrete and physical presentation of the concept will increase the reliability of the concept test. Today, some marketers are finding innovative ways to make product concepts more real to consumer subjects. For example, some are using virtual reality to test product concepts. Virtual reality programs use computers and sensory devices (such as gloves or goggles) to simulate reality. A designer of kitchen cabinets can use a virtual reality program to help a customer "see" how his or her kitchen would look and work if remodeled with the company's products. Hairdressers have used virtual reality for years to show consumers how they might look with a new style. Although virtual reality is still in its infancy, its applications are increasing daily.[13]

After being exposed to the concept, consumers then may be asked to react to it by answering questions such as those in Table 10.1. The answers will help the company decide which concept has the strongest appeal. For example, the last question asks about the consumer's intention to buy. Suppose 10 percent of the consumers said they "definitely" would buy and another 5 percent said "probably." The company could project these figures to the full population in this target group to estimate sales volume. Even then, the estimate is uncertain because people do not always carry out their stated intentions.

Many firms routinely test new-product concepts with consumers before attempting to turn them into actual new products. For example, each month Richard Saunders Inc.'s Acu-Poll research system tests 35 new-product concepts in person on 100 nationally representative grocery store shoppers, rating them as "Pure Gold" or "Fool's Gold" concepts. In past polls, Nabisco's Oreo Chocolate Cones concept received a rare A+ rating, meaning that consumers think it is an outstanding concept that they would try and buy. Glad Ovenware, Reach Whitening Tape dental floss, and Lender's Bake at Home Bagels were also big hits. Other product concepts didn't fare so

TABLE 10.1   QUESTIONS FOR FUEL-CELL ELECTRIC CAR CONCEPT TEST

1. Do you understand the concept of a fuel-cell-powered electric car?
2. Do you believe the claims about the car's performance?
3. What are the major benefits of the fuel-cell-powered electric car compared with a conventional car?
4. What are its advantages compared with a battery-powered electric car?
5. What improvements in the car's features would you suggest?
6. For what uses would you prefer a fuel-cell-powered electric car to a conventional car?
7. What would be a reasonable price to charge for the car?
8. Who would be involved in your decision to buy such a car? Who would drive it?
9. Would you buy such a car? (definitely, probably, probably not, definitely not)

well. Nubrush Anti-Bacterial Toothbrush Spray disinfectant, from Applied Microdontics, received an F. Consumers found Nubrush to be overpriced, and most don't think they have a problem with "infected" toothbrushes. Nor did consumers think much of Excedrin Tension Headache Cooling Pads or Moist Mates premoistened toilet tissues. Another concept that fared poorly was Chef Williams 5 Minute Marinade, which comes with a syringe customers use to inject the marinade into meats. "I can't see that on grocery shelves," comments an Acu-Poll executive. Some consumers might find the thought of injecting something into meat a bit repulsive, and "it's just so politically incorrect to have this syringe on there."[14]

Marketing Strategy Development

Marketing strategy development

Designing an initial marketing strategy for a new product based on the product concept.

Suppose DaimlerChrysler finds that concept 3 for the fuel-cell-powered electric car tests best. The next step is **marketing strategy development,** designing an initial marketing strategy for introducing this car to the market.

The *marketing strategy statement* consists of three parts. The first part describes the target market; the planned product positioning; and the sales, market share, and profit goals for the first few years. Thus:

The target market is younger, well-educated, moderate-to-high-income individuals, couples, or small families seeking practical, environmentally responsible transportation. The car will be positioned as more economical to operate, more fun to drive, and less polluting than today's internal combustion engine or hybrid cars, and as less restricting than battery-powered electric cars, which must be recharged regularly. The company will aim to sell 100,000 cars in the first year, at a loss of not more than $15 million. In the second year, the company will aim for sales of 120,000 cars and a profit of $25 million.

The second part of the marketing strategy statement outlines the product's planned price, distribution, and marketing budget for the first year:

The fuel-cell-powered electric car will be offered in three colors—red, white, and blue—and will have optional air-conditioning and power-drive features. It will sell at a retail price of $20,000—with 15 percent off the list price to dealers. Dealers who sell more than 10 cars per month will get an additional discount of 5 percent on each car sold that month. An advertising budget of $30 million will be split 50-50 between national and local advertising. Advertising will emphasize the car's fun spirit and low emissions. During the first year, $100,000 will be spent on marketing research to find out who is buying the car and their satisfaction levels.

The third part of the marketing strategy statement describes the planned long-run sales, profit goals, and marketing mix strategy:

DaimlerChrysler intends to capture a 3 percent long-run share of the total auto market and realize an after-tax return on investment of 15 percent. To achieve this, product quality will start high and be improved over time. Price will be raised in the second and third years if competition permits. The total advertising budget will be raised each year by about 10 percent. Marketing research will be reduced to $60,000 per year after the first year.

Business Analysis

Business analysis
A review of the sales, costs, and profit projections for a new product to find out whether these factors satisfy the company's objectives.

Once management has decided on its product concept and marketing strategy, it can evaluate the business attractiveness of the proposal. **Business analysis** involves a review of the sales, costs, and profit projections for a new product to find out whether they satisfy the company's objectives. If they do, the product can move to the product development stage.

To estimate sales, the company might look at the sales history of similar products and conduct surveys of market opinion. It can then estimate minimum and maximum sales to assess the range of risk. After preparing the sales forecast, management can estimate the expected costs and profits for the product, including marketing, R&D, operations, accounting, and finance costs. The company then uses the sales and costs figures to analyze the new product's financial attractiveness.

Product Development

Product development
Developing the product concept into a physical product in order to ensure that the product idea can be turned into a workable product.

So far, for many new-product concepts, the product may have existed only as a word description, a drawing, or perhaps a crude mock-up. If the product concept passes the business test, it moves into **product development.** Here, R&D or engineering develops the product concept into a physical product. The product development step, however, now calls for a large jump in investment. It will show whether the product idea can be turned into a workable product.

The R&D department will develop and test one or more physical versions of the product concept. R&D hopes to design a prototype that will satisfy and excite consumers and that can be produced quickly and at budgeted costs. Developing a successful prototype can take days, weeks, months, or even years. Often, products undergo rigorous tests to make sure that they perform safely and effectively, or that consumers will find value in them. Here are some examples of such product tests:[15]

> A scuba-diving Barbie doll must swim and kick for 15 straight hours to satisfy Mattel that she will last at least one year. But because Barbie may find her feet in small owners' mouths rather than in the bathtub, Mattel has devised another, more torturous test: Barbie's feet are clamped by two steel jaws to make sure that her skin doesn't crack—and choke potential owners.

> At Shaw Industries, temps are paid five dollars an hour to pace up and down five long rows of sample carpets for up to eight hours a day, logging an average of 14 miles each. One regular reads three mysteries a week while pacing and shed 40 pounds in two years. Shaw Industries counts walkers' steps and figures that 20,000 steps equal several years of average carpet wear.

> P&G spends $150 million on 4,000 to 5,000 studies a year, testing everything from the ergonomics of picking up a shampoo bottle to how long women can keep their hands in sudsy water. On any given day, subjects meet in focus groups, sell their dirty laundry to researchers, put prototype diapers on their babies' bottoms, and rub mysterious creams on their faces. Last year, one elementary school raised $17,000 by having students and parents take part in P&G product tests. Students tested toothpaste and shampoo and ate brownies, while their mothers watched advertising for Tempo tissue, P&G's paper wipes packaged to fit in a car. This year, P&G is paying the school to have 48 students and parents wear new sneakers that they hand in every month for six months. Half the shoes return cleaned. No one knows what P&G is testing, and the company won't say.

> At Gillette, almost everyone gets involved in new-product testing. Every working day at Gillette, 200 volunteers from various departments come to work unshaven, troop to the second floor of the company's gritty South Boston plant, and enter small booths with a sink and mirror. There they take instructions from technicians on the other side of a small window as to which razor, shaving cream, or aftershave to use. The volunteers evaluate razors for sharpness of blade, smoothness of glide, and ease of handling. In a nearby shower room, women perform the same ritual on their legs, underarms, and what the company delicately refers to as the "bikini area." "We bleed so you'll get a good shave at home," says one Gillette employee.

The prototype must have the required functional features and also convey the intended psychological characteristics. The fuel-cell electric car, for example, should strike consumers as being

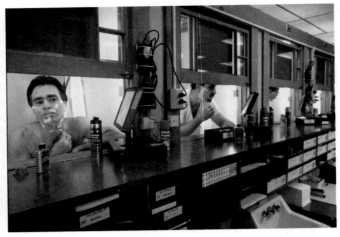

Product testing: Shaw Industries pays temps to pace up and down on sample carpets. Each average about 14 miles a day. Gillette uses employee-volunteers to test new shaving products—"We bleed so you'll get a good shave at home," says one Gillette employee.

well built, comfortable, and safe. Management must learn what makes consumers decide that a car is well built. To some consumers, this means that the car has "solid-sounding" doors. To others, it means that the car is able to withstand heavy impact in crash tests. Consumer tests are conducted in which consumers test-drive the car and rate its attributes.

Test Marketing

Test marketing

The stage of new-product development in which the product and marketing program are tested in more realistic market settings.

If the product passes functional and consumer tests, the next step is **test marketing,** the stage at which the product and marketing program are introduced into more-realistic market settings. Test marketing gives the marketer experience with marketing the product before going to the great expense of full introduction. It lets the company test the product and its entire marketing program—positioning strategy, advertising, distribution, pricing, branding and packaging, and budget levels.

The amount of test marketing needed varies with each new product. Test-marketing costs can be high, and it takes time that may allow competitors to gain advantages. When the costs of developing and introducing the product are low, or when management is already confident about the new product, the company may do little or no test marketing. In fact, test marketing by consumer package-goods firms has been declining in recent years. Companies often do not test-market simple line extensions or copies of successful competitor products. For example, Procter & Gamble introduced its Folger's decaffeinated coffee crystals without test marketing, and Pillsbury rolled out Chewy granola bars and chocolate-covered Granola Dipps with no standard test market.

However, when introducing a new product requires a big investment, or when management is not sure of the product or marketing program, a company may do a lot of test marketing. For instance, Lever USA spent two years testing its highly successful Lever 2000 bar soap in Atlanta before introducing it internationally. Frito-Lay did 18 months of testing in three markets on at least five formulations before introducing its Baked Lays line of low-fat snacks. And both Procter & Gamble and Unilever spent many months testing their new Juvian and MyHome valet laundry and home fabric care services.[16]

Although test-marketing costs can be high, they are often small when compared with the costs of making a major mistake. For example, McDonald's made a costly mistake when it introduced its low-fat burger, the McLean Deluxe, nationally without the chain's normal and lengthy testing process. The new product failed after a big investment but lean results. And Nabisco's launch of one new product without testing had disastrous—and soggy—results:

Nabisco hit a marketing home run with its Teddy Grahams, teddy-bear-shaped graham crackers in several different flavors. So, the company decided to extend Teddy Grahams into a new area. In 1989, it introduced chocolate, cinnamon, and honey versions of Breakfast Bears Graham Cereal. When the product came out, however, consumers didn't like the taste enough, so the product developers went back to the kitchen and modified the formula. But they didn't test it. The result was a disaster. Although the cereal may have tasted better, it no longer stayed crunchy in milk, as the advertising on the box promised. Instead, it left a gooey mess of graham mush on the bottom of cereal bowls. Supermarket managers soon refused to restock the cereal, and Nabisco executives decided it was too late to reformulate the product again. So a promising new product was killed through haste to get it to market.[17]

Still, test marketing doesn't guarantee success. For example, Procter & Gamble tested its new Fit produce rinse for heavily for five years and Olay cosmetics for three years. Although market tests suggested the products would be successful, P&G had to pull the plug on both shortly after their introductions.[18]

When using test marketing, consumer products companies usually choose one of three approaches—standard test markets, controlled test markets, or simulated test markets.

Standard Test Markets

Using standard test markets, the company finds a small number of representative test cities, conducts a full marketing campaign in these cities, and uses store audits, consumer and distributor surveys, and other measures to gauge product performance. The results are used to forecast national sales and profits, discover potential product problems, and fine-tune the marketing program.

Standard test markets have some drawbacks. They can be very costly and they may take a long time—some last as long as three to five years. Moreover, competitors can monitor test-market results or even interfere with them by cutting their prices in test cities, increasing their promotion, or even buying up the product being tested. Finally, test markets give competitors a look at the company's new product well before it is introduced nationally. Thus, competitors may have time to develop defensive strategies, and may even beat the company's product to the market. For example, while Clorox was still test-marketing its new detergent with bleach in selected markets, P&G launched Tide with Bleach nationally. Tide with Bleach quickly became the segment leader; Clorox later withdrew its detergent.

Despite these disadvantages, standard test markets are still the most widely used approach for major in-market testing. However, many companies today are shifting toward quicker and cheaper controlled and simulated test-marketing methods.

Controlled Test Markets

Several research firms keep controlled panels of stores that have agreed to carry new products for a fee. Controlled test marketing systems like ACNielsen's Scantrack and Information Resources Inc.'s (IRI) BehaviorScan track individual behavior from the television set to the checkout counter.

In each BehaviorScan market, IRI maintains a panel of shoppers who report all of their purchases by showing an identification card at check-out in participating stores and by using a hand-held scanner at home to record purchases at non-participating stores.[19] Within test stores, IRI controls such factors as shelf placement, price, and in-store promotions for the product being tested. IRI also measures TV viewing in each panel household and sends special commercials to panel member television sets. Direct mail promotions can also be tested.

Detailed scanner information on each consumer's purchases is fed into a central computer, where it is combined with the consumer's demographic and TV viewing information and reported daily. Thus, BehaviorScan can provide store-by-store, week-by-week reports on the sales of tested products. Such panel purchasing data enables in-depth diagnostics not possible with retail point-of-sale data alone, including repeat purchase analysis, buyer demographics, and earlier, more accurate sales forecasts after just 12 to 24 weeks in market. Most importantly, the system allows companies to evaluate their specific marketing efforts.

Controlled test markets, such as Behaviorscan, usually cost less than standard test markets. Also, because retail distribution is "forced" in the first week of the test, controlled test markets can

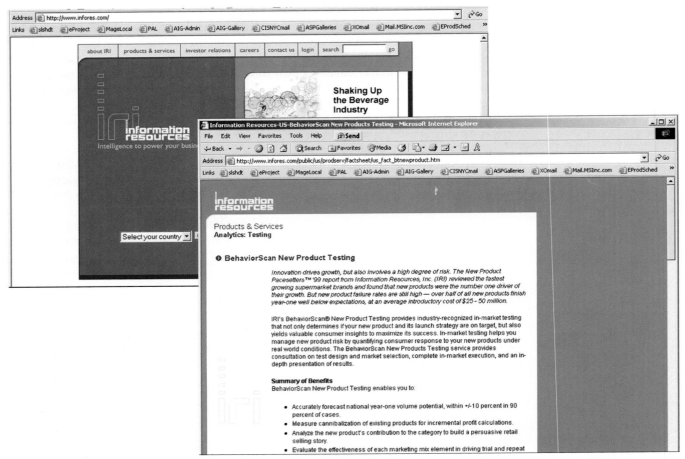

IRI's BehaviorScan provides an in-market laboratory for testing new products and marketing programs under highly controlled yet real-world conditions.

be completed much more quickly than standard test markets. As in standard test markets, controlled test markets allow competitors to get a look at the company's new product. And some companies are concerned that the limited number of controlled test markets used by the research services may not be representative of their products' markets or target consumers. However, the research firms are experienced in projecting test market results to broader markets and can usually account for biases in the test markets used.

Simulated Test Markets

Companies can also test new products in a simulated shopping environment. The company or research firm shows ads and promotions for a variety of products, including the new product being tested, to a sample of consumers. It gives consumers a small amount of money and invites them to a real or laboratory store where they may keep the money or use it to buy items. The researchers note how many consumers buy the new product and competing brands.

This simulation provides a measure of trial and the commercial's effectiveness against competing commercials. The researchers then ask consumers the reasons for their purchase or nonpurchase. Some weeks later, they interview the consumers by phone to determine product attitudes, usage, satisfaction, and repurchase intentions. Using sophisticated computer models, the researchers then project national sales from results of the simulated test market. Recently, some marketers have begun to use interesting new high-tech approaches to simulated-test-market research, such as virtual reality and the Internet.

Simulated test markets overcome some of the disadvantages of standard and controlled test markets. They usually cost much less, can be run in eight weeks, and keep the new product out of competitors' view. Yet, because of their small samples and simulated shopping environments, many marketers do not think that simulated test markets are as accurate or reliable as larger, real-world tests. Still, simulated test markets are used widely, often as "pretest" markets. Because they are fast and inexpensive, they can be run to quickly assess a new product or its marketing program. If the pretest results are strongly positive, the product might be introduced without further testing. If the results are very poor, the product might be dropped or substantially redesigned and retested. If the results are promising but indefinite, the product and marketing program can be tested further in controlled or standard test markets.

Commercialization

Commercialization

Introducing a new product into the market.

Test marketing gives management the information needed to make a final decision about whether to launch the new product. If the company goes ahead with **commercialization**—introducing the new product into the market—it will face high costs. The company will have to build or rent a manufacturing facility. And it may have to spend, in the case of a new consumer packaged good, between $10 million and $200 million for advertising, sales promotion, and other marketing efforts in the first year.

The company launching a new product must first decide on introduction *timing*. If DaimlerChrysler's new fuel-cell electric car will eat into the sales of the company's other cars, its introduction may be delayed. If the car can be improved further, or if the economy is down, the company may wait until the following year to launch it.

Next, the company must decide *where* to launch the new product—in a single location, a region, the national market, or the international market. Few companies have the confidence, capital, and capacity to launch new products into full national or international distribution. They will develop a planned *market rollout* over time. In particular, small companies may enter attractive cities or regions one at a time. Larger companies, however, may quickly introduce new models into several regions or into the full national market.

Companies with international distribution systems may introduce new products through global rollouts. Colgate-Palmolive used to follow a "lead-country" strategy. For example, it launched its Palmolive Optims shampoo and conditioner first in Australia, the Philippines, Hong Kong, and Mexico, then rapidly rolled it out into Europe, Asia, Latin America, and Africa. However, most international companies now introduce their new products in swift global assaults. Recently, in its fastest new-product rollout ever, Colgate introduced its Actibrush battery-powered toothbrush into 50 countries in a year, generating $115 million in sales. Such rapid worldwide expansion solidified the brand's market position before foreign competitors could react.[20]

Sequential product development

A new-product development approach in which one company department works to complete its stage of the process before passing the new product along to the next department and stage.

Organizing for New-Product Development

Many companies organize their new-product development process into the orderly sequence of steps shown in Figure 10.1, starting with idea generation and ending with commercialization. Under this **sequential product development** approach, one company department works individually to complete its stage of the process before passing the new product along to the next department and stage. This orderly, step-by-step process can help bring control to complex and risky projects. But it also can be dangerously slow. In fast-changing, highly competitive markets, such

Colgate introduces new products in swift global assaults, solidifying the brand's market position before foreign competitors can react.

Simultaneous (or team-based) product development

An approach to developing new products in which various company departments work closely together, overlapping the steps in the product-development process to save time and increase effectiveness.

slow-but-sure product development can result in product failures, lost sales and profits, and crumbling market positions. "Speed to market" and reducing new-product development cycle time have become pressing concerns to companies in all industries.

In order to get their new products to market more quickly, many companies are adopting a faster, team-oriented approach called **simultaneous product development** (or teamed-based or collaborative product development). Under this approach, company departments work closely together through cross-functional teams, overlapping the steps in the product development process to save time and increase effectiveness. Instead of passing the new product from department to department, the company assembles a team of people from various departments that stays with the new product from start to finish. Such teams usually include people from the marketing, finance, design, manufacturing, and legal departments, and even supplier and customer companies.

Top management gives the product development team general strategic direction but no clear-cut product idea or work plan. It challenges the team with stiff and seemingly contradictory goals—"turn out carefully planned and superior new products, but do it quickly"—and then gives the team whatever freedom and resources it needs to meet the challenge. In the sequential process, a bottleneck at one phase can seriously slow the entire project. In the simultaneous approach, if one functional area hits snags, it works to resolve them while the team moves on.

The Allen-Bradley Company, a maker of industrial controls, realized tremendous benefits by using simultaneous development. Under its old sequential approach, the company's marketing department handed off a new-product idea to designers, who worked in isolation to prepare concepts that they then passed along to product engineers. The engineers, also working by themselves, developed expensive prototypes and handed them off to manufacturing, which tried to find a way to build the new product. Finally, after many years and dozens of costly design compromises and delays, marketing was asked to sell the new product, which it often found to be too high-priced or sadly out of date. Now, all of Allen-Bradley's departments work together to develop new products. The results have been astonishing. For example, the company recently developed a new electrical control in just two years; under the old system, it would have taken six years.

The simultaneous team-based approach does have some limitations. Superfast product development can be riskier and more costly than the slower, more orderly sequential approach. Moreover, it often creates increased organizational tension and confusion. And the company must take care that rushing a product to market doesn't adversely affect its quality—the objective is not only to create products faster, but to create them *better* and faster.

Despite these drawbacks, in rapidly changing industries facing increasingly shorter product life cycles, the rewards of fast and flexible product development far exceed the risks. Companies that get new and improved products to the market faster than competitors often gain a dramatic competitive edge. They can respond more quickly to emerging consumer tastes and charge higher prices for more-advanced designs. As one auto industry executive states, "What we want to do is get the new car approved, built, and in the consumer's hands in the shortest time possible. . . . Whoever gets there first gets all the marbles."[21]

Thus, new-product success requires more than simply thinking up a few good ideas, turning them into products, and finding customers for them. It requires a systematic approach for finding new ways to create value for target consumers, from generating and screening new-product ideas to creating and rolling out want-satisfying products to customers. More than this, successful new-product development requires a total-company commitment. At companies known for their new-product prowess—such as 3M, Gillette, and Intel—the entire culture encourages, supports, and rewards innovation (see Real Marketing 10.2).

Product Life-Cycle Strategies

After launching the new product, management wants the product to enjoy a long and happy life. Although it does not expect the product to sell forever, the company wants to earn a decent profit to cover all the effort and risk that went into launching it. Management is aware that each product will have a life cycle, although its exact shape and length is not known in advance.

real marketing 10.2

3M: A Culture for Innovation

You see the headline in every 3M ad: "Innovation Working for You." But at 3M, innovation is more than just an advertising pitch. 3M views innovation as its path to growth and new products as its lifeblood. It markets more than 50,000 products. These products range from sandpaper, adhesives,

introduced within the previous four years. More astonishing, it usually succeeds! Each year 3M launches more than 200 new products. And last year, a full third of its $16 billion in sales came from products introduced within the past four years. This legendary emphasis on innovation has con-

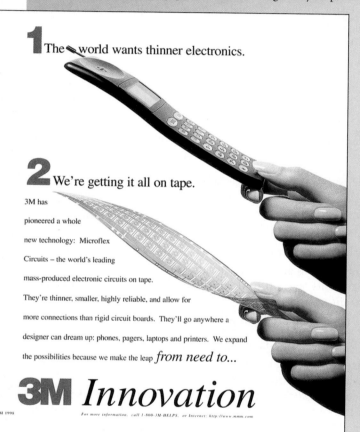

1 The world wants thinner electronics.

2 We're getting it all on tape.

3M has

pioneered a whole

new technology: Microflex

Circuits – the world's leading

mass-produced electronic circuits on tape.

They're thinner, smaller, highly reliable, and allow for

more connections than rigid circuit boards. They'll go anywhere a

designer can dream up: phones, pagers, laptops and printers. We expand

the possibilities because we make the leap *from need to...*

3M *Innovation*

©3M 1998   For more information, call 1-800-3M-HELPS, or Internet: http://www.mmm.com

3M views innovation *as its path to growth and new products as its lifeblood. Its entire culture encourages, supports, and rewards* innovation.

and laser optical disks to contact lenses, heart-lung machines, and futuristic synthetic ligaments; from coatings that sleeken boat hulls to hundreds of sticky tapes—Scotch tape, masking tape, superbonding tape, acid-free photo and document tape, and even refastening-disposable-diaper tape.

3M's goal is to derive an astonishing 30 percent of each year's sales from products

sistently made 3M one of America's most admired companies. In 2002, 3M once again earned the number one spot on *Fortune*'s list of companies most admired for innovation.

At 3M, new products don't just happen. The company works hard to create an environment that supports innovation. Last year, it invested $1 billion, or 6 percent of annual sales, in research and development—almost twice as much as the average company. Its Innovation Task Force seeks out and destroys corporate bureaucracy that might interfere with new-product progress. And hired consultants help 3M find ways to make employees more inventive.

3M encourages everyone to look for new products. The company's renowned "15 percent rule" allows all employees to spend up to 15 percent of their time "bootlegging"—working on projects of personal interest. When a promising idea comes along, 3M forms a venture team made up of the researcher who developed the idea and volunteers from manufacturing, sales, marketing, and legal. The team nurtures the product and protects it from company bureaucracy. Team members stay with the product until it suc-

ceeds or fails and then return to their previous jobs. Some teams have tried three or four times before finally making a success of an idea. Each year, 3M hands out Golden Step Awards to venture teams whose new products earned more than $2 million in U.S. sales, or $4 million in worldwide sales, within three years of introduction.

3M knows that it must try thousands of new-product ideas to hit one big jackpot. One well-worn slogan at 3M is, "You have to kiss a lot of frogs to find a prince." "Kissing frogs" often means making mistakes, but 3M accepts blunders and dead ends as a normal part of creativity and innovation. In fact, its philosophy seems to be, "If you aren't making mistakes, you probably aren't doing anything."

As it turns out, "blunders" have turned into some of 3M's most successful products. Old-timers at 3M love to tell the story about the chemist who accidentally spilled a new chemical on her tennis shoes. Some days later, she noticed that the spots hit by the chemical had not gotten dirty. Eureka! The chemical eventually became Scotchgard fabric protector. They tell about the early 3M scientist who had a deathly fear of shaving with a straight razor. Instead, he invented a very fine, waterproof sandpaper which he used to sand the stubble from his face each morning. Although this invention never caught on as a shaving solution, it became one of 3M's best-selling products—wet-dry sandpaper, now used for a wide variety of commercial and industrial applications.

And then there's the one about 3M scientist Spencer Silver. Silver started out to develop a superstrong adhesive; instead he came up with one that didn't stick very well at all. He sent the apparently useless substance on to other 3M researchers to see whether they could find something to do with it. Nothing happened for several years. Then Arthur Fry, another 3M scientist, had a problem—and an idea. As a choir member in a local church, Mr. Fry was having trouble marking places in his hymnal—the little scraps of paper he used kept falling out. He tried dabbing some of Mr. Silver's

(continued)

weak glue on one of the scraps. It stuck nicely and later peeled off without damaging the hymnal. Thus were born 3M's Post-it Notes, a product that is now one of the top-selling office supply products in the world!

Thus, 3M could easily amend its long-running "Innovation Working for You" ad line to include "and for *3M*." Still, there are limits. Some analysts question whether such a freewheeling, no-questions-asked creative culture is appropriate given the cost-reduction pressures of today's tougher economic times. In fact, 3M's new CEO, Jim McNerney, recently launched a "take-no-prisoners" campaign against inefficiencies. He's cutting costs and slimming down the company's workforce. He is also overhauling the 3M R&D organization and culture, one

in which even 3M old-timers agree that money hasn't always been spent wisely. According to one analyst, McNerney "vows to take an organization of myriad product and research fiefdoms—which happens to be one of the most respected manufacturing concerns in the world—and hammer it into one shared corporate culture." He is carefully examining where R&D dollars are spent and setting uniform performance standards and accountability across the company.

The risk is that the changing culture and organizational restructuring might stifle 3M's hallmark creativity. "The most important thing about 3M—the single most important thing—is you get to do things your own way," says a senior 3M executive and 33-year veteran. McNerney understands

the balancing act: efficiency versus hands-off R&D spending; accountability versus individual creative freedom. "My job is to add scale in a fast-moving, entrepreneurial environment," he says. "If I end up killing that entrepreneurial spirit, I will have failed."

Sources: Quotes from Rick Mullin, "Analysts Rate 3M's New Culture," *Chemical Week,* September 26, 2001, pp. 39–40; and Michael Arndt, "3M: A Lab for Growth," *Business Week,* January 21, 2002, pp. 50–51. Also see William H. Miller, "New Leader, New Era," November 2001, accessed online at www.industryweek.com; "America's Most Admired Companies," *Fortune,* March 4, 2002, p. 75; and information accessed online at www.3m.com, July 2002.

Product life cycle (PLC)
The course of a product's sales and profits over its lifetime. It involves five distinct stages: product development, introduction, growth, maturity, and decline.

Figure 10.2 shows a typical **product life cycle (PLC),** the course that a product's sales and profits take over its lifetime. The product life cycle has five distinct stages:

1. *Product development* begins when the company finds and develops a new-product idea. During product development, sales are zero and the company's investment costs mount.

2. *Introduction* is a period of slow sales growth as the product is introduced in the market. Profits are nonexistent in this stage because of the heavy expenses of product introduction.

3. *Growth* is a period of rapid market acceptance and increasing profits.

4. *Maturity* is a period of slowdown in sales growth because the product has achieved acceptance by most potential buyers. Profits level off or decline because of increased marketing outlays to defend the product against competition.

5. *Decline* is the period when sales fall off and profits drop.

Not all products follow this product life cycle. Some products are introduced and die quickly; others stay in the mature stage for a long, long time. Some enter the decline stage and are then cycled back into the growth stage through strong promotion or repositioning.

The PLC concept can describe a *product class* (gasoline-powered automobiles), a *product form* (SUVs), or a *brand* (the Ford Explorer). The PLC concept applies differently in each case.

FIGURE 10.2
Sales and profits over the product's life from inception to demise

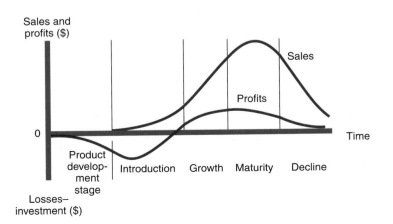

Product life cycles: Companies want their products to enjoy long and happy life cycles. HERSHEY'S Chocolate Bars have been "unchanged" since 1899.

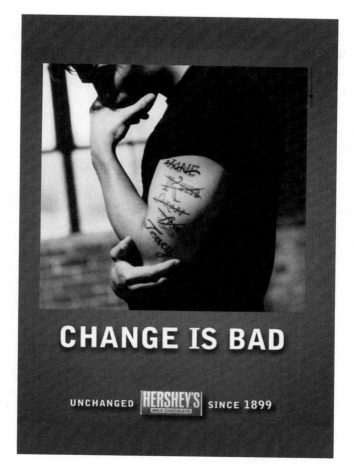

Product classes have the longest life cycles—the sales of many product classes stay in the mature stage for a long time. Product forms, in contrast, tend to have the standard PLC shape. Product forms such as "cream deodorants," "dial telephones," and "cassette tapes" passed through a regular history of introduction, rapid growth, maturity, and decline.

A specific brand's life cycle can change quickly because of changing competitive attacks and responses. For example, although laundry soaps (product class) and powdered detergents (product form) have enjoyed fairly long life cycles, the life cycles of specific brands have tended to be much shorter. Today's leading brands of powdered laundry soap are Tide and Cheer; the leading brands 75 years ago were Fels Naptha, Octagon, and Kirkman.[22]

The PLC concept also can be applied to what are known as styles, fashions, and fads. Their special life cycles are shown in Figure 10.3. A **style** is a basic and distinctive mode of expression. For example, styles appear in homes (colonial, ranch, transitional), clothing (formal, casual), and art (realist, surrealist, abstract). Once a style is invented, it may last for generations, passing in and out of vogue. A style has a cycle showing several periods of renewed interest. A **fashion** is a currently accepted or popular style in a given field. For example, the more formal "business attire"

Style
A basic and distinctive mode of expression.

Fashion
A currently accepted or popular style in a given field.

FIGURE 10.3
Styles, fashions, and fads

Fad
A fashion that enters quickly, is adopted with great zeal, peaks early, and declines very quickly.

look of corporate dress of the 1980s and early 1990s has now given way to the "business casual" look of today. Fashions tend to grow slowly, remain popular for a while, then decline slowly.

Fads are fashions that enter quickly, are adopted with great zeal, peak early, and decline very quickly. They last only a short time and tend to attract only a limited following. "Pet rocks" are a classic example of a fad. Upon hearing his friends complain about how expensive it was to care for their dogs, advertising copywriter Gary Dahl joked about his pet rock and was soon writing a spoof of a dog-training manual for it. Soon Dahl was selling some 1.5 million ordinary beach pebbles at four dollars a pop. Yet the fad, which broke in October 1975, had sunk like a stone by the next February. Dahl's advice to those who want to succeed with a fad: "Enjoy it while it lasts." Other examples of fads include Rubik's Cubes, lava lamps, CB radios, and scooters. Most fads do not survive for long because they normally do not satisfy a strong need or satisfy it well.[23]

The PLC concept can be applied by marketers as a useful framework for describing how products and markets work. But using the PLC concept for forecasting product performance or for developing marketing strategies presents some practical problems. For example, managers may have trouble identifying which stage of the PLC the product is in or pinpointing when the product moves into the next stage. They may also find it hard to determine the factors that affect the product's movement through the stages. In practice, it is difficult to forecast the sales level at each PLC stage, the length of each stage, and the shape of the PLC curve.

Using the PLC concept to develop marketing strategy also can be difficult because strategy is both a cause and a result of the product's life cycle. The product's current PLC position suggests the best marketing strategies, and the resulting marketing strategies affect product performance in later life-cycle stages. Yet, when used carefully, the PLC concept can help in developing good marketing strategies for different stages of the product life cycle.

We looked at the product development stage of the product life cycle in the first part of the chapter. We now look at strategies for each of the other life-cycle stages.

Introduction Stage

Introduction stage
The product life-cycle stage in which the new product is first distributed and made available for purchase.

The **introduction stage** starts when the new product is first launched. Introduction takes time, and sales growth is apt to be slow. Well-known products such as instant coffee, frozen orange juice, and powdered coffee creamers lingered for many years before they entered a stage of rapid growth.

In this stage, as compared to other stages, profits are negative or low because of the low sales and high distribution and promotion expenses. Much money is needed to attract distributors and build their inventories. Promotion spending is relatively high to inform consumers of the new product and get them to try it. Because the market is not generally ready for product refinements at this stage, the company and its few competitors produce basic versions of the product. These firms focus their selling on those buyers who are the most ready to buy.

A company, especially the *market pioneer*, must choose a launch strategy that is consistent with the intended product positioning. It should realize that the initial strategy is just the first step in a grander marketing plan for the product's entire life cycle. If the pioneer chooses its launch strategy to make a "killing," it will be sacrificing long-run revenue for the sake of short-run gain. As the pioneer moves through later stages of the life cycle, it will have to continuously formulate new pricing, promotion, and other marketing strategies. It has the best chance of building and retaining market leadership if it plays its cards correctly from the start.[24]

Growth Stage

Growth stage
The product life-cycle stage in which a product's sales start climbing quickly.

If the new product satisfies the market, it will enter a **growth stage,** in which sales will start climbing quickly. The early adopters will continue to buy, and later buyers will start following their lead, especially if they hear favorable word of mouth. Attracted by the opportunities for profit, new competitors will enter the market. They will introduce new product features, and the market will expand. The increase in competitors leads to an increase in the number of distribution outlets, and sales jump just to build reseller inventories. Prices remain where they are or fall only slightly. Companies keep their promotion spending at the same or a slightly higher level. Educating the market remains a goal, but now the company must also meet the competition.

Profits increase during the growth stage, as promotion costs are spread over a large volume and as unit manufacturing costs fall. The firm uses several strategies to sustain rapid market growth as long as possible. It improves product quality and adds new product features and models. It enters new market segments and new distribution channels. It shifts some advertising from building product awareness to building product conviction and purchase, and it lowers prices at the right time to attract more buyers.

In the growth stage, the firm faces a trade-off between high market share and high current profit. By spending a lot of money on product improvement, promotion, and distribution, the company can capture a dominant position. In doing so, however, it gives up maximum current profit, which it hopes to make up in the next stage.

Maturity Stage

Maturity stage

The stage in the product life cycle in which sales growth slows or levels off.

At some point, a product's sales growth will slow down, and the product will enter a **maturity stage.** This maturity stage normally lasts longer than the previous stages, and it poses strong challenges to marketing management. Most products are in the maturity stage of the life cycle, and therefore most of marketing management deals with the mature product.

The slowdown in sales growth results in many producers with many products to sell. In turn, this overcapacity leads to greater competition. Competitors begin marking down prices, increasing their advertising and sales promotions, and upping their R&D budgets to find better versions of the product. These steps lead to a drop in profit. Some of the weaker competitors start dropping out, and the industry eventually contains only well-established competitors.

Although many products in the mature stage appear to remain unchanged for long periods, most successful ones are actually evolving to meet changing consumer needs (see Real Marketing 10.3). Product managers should do more than simply ride along with or defend their mature products—a good offense is the best defense. They should consider modifying the market, product, and marketing mix.

In *modifying the market,* the company tries to increase the consumption of the current product. It looks for new users and market segments, as when Johnson & Johnson targeted the adult market with its baby powder and shampoo. The manager also looks for ways to increase usage among present customers. Campbell does this by offering recipes and convincing consumers that "soup is good food." Amazon.com sends permission-based e-mails to regular customers letting them know when their favorite authors or performers publish new books or CDs. Or the company may want to reposition the brand to appeal to a larger or faster-growing segment, as Verizon did when it expanded into high-speed Internet and wireless services.

The company might also try *modifying the product*—changing characteristics such as quality, features, or style to attract new users and to inspire more usage. It might improve the product's quality and performance—its durability, reliability, speed, taste. It can improve the product's styling and attractiveness. Thus, car manufacturers restyle their cars to attract buyers who want a new look. The makers of consumer food and household products introduce new flavors, colors, ingredients, or packages to revitalize consumer buying.

Or the company might add new features that expand the product's usefulness, safety, or convenience. For example, Sony keeps adding new styles and features to its Walkman and Discman lines, and Volvo adds new safety features to its cars. Kimberly-Clark is adding a new twist to revitalize the product life cycle of an old standby, toilet tissue:

Almost without exception, every American family knows what the paper roll next to the toilet is for, knows how to use it, and purchases it faithfully. Selling an omnipresent household item requires a vital brand that stands out at the supermarket, but how do you make toilet tissue new and exciting? Kimberly-Clark, the maker of Cottonelle and Kleenex, has the answer with an unprecedented innovation: a premoistened toilet paper called Cottonelle Rollwipes, "the breakthrough product that is changing the toilet paper category." Like baby wipes on a roll, the product is designed to complement traditional toilet tissue. "In this category, your growth has to come from significant product innovations," says a marketing director for Cottonelle. Another marketing executive agrees: "Without new products, old brands become older brands. In categories where there's basic satisfaction with the products, you still have to provide new benefits . . . to build brand share."[25]

real marketing 10.3

Age-Defying Products or Just Skillful PLC Management?

Some products are born and die quickly. Others, however, seem to defy the product life cycle, enduring for decades, or even generations, with little or no apparent change in their makeup or marketing. Look deeper, however, and you'll find that such products are far from unchanging. Rather, skillful product life-cycle management keeps them fresh, relevant, and appealing to customers. Here are examples of three products that might have been only fads but instead were

tle animals, and the company couldn't get them onto store shelves fast enough.

Yet Ty quickly realized that scarcity would be the key to keeping the Beanie Babies craze going—and going and going. The company became adept at maintaining consumer demand by limiting distribution and keeping the character lineup fresh. Ty adds to the hype by regularly retiring old characters and replacing them with many new ones. Retired models fetch as much as $1,000 from hard-core collectors.

had planned all along to continue Beanies Babies—at the time of the announcement, it had recently expanded its factories and held several trademarks for new Beanies. Whatever the explanation, long after the experts would have predicted the demise of these cute little critters, avid collectors are still lining up to get their hands on new styles. A recent Google search turned up more than 800 Web sites featuring Beanie Babies.

Barbie

Talk about age-defying products. Although Mattel's Barbie turned 44 this year, Mattel has kept Barbie both timeless and trendy. Since her creation in 1959, Barbie has mirrored girls' dreams of what they'd like to be when they grow up. As such, Barbie has changed as girls' dreams have changed. Her aspirations have evolved from jobs such as stewardess, fashion model, and nurse to astronaut, rock singer, surgeon, and presidential candidate. These days, Barbie hardly notices her age—she's too busy being a WNBA basketball player, Olympic skater, and NASCAR race car driver.

Some products seem to defy the product life-cycle: Over the years, Crayola has lived a colorful life cycle, adding a steady stream of new colors, forms, and packages.

turned into long-term market winners with plenty of staying power.

Beanie Babies

When Ty Inc. unleashed Beanie Babies in 1993, most experts saw them as just a passing fad. Priced under five dollars, the tiny bean-filled creatures were designed as a back-to-basics toy that kids could buy with their own allowance money. Soon, however, adults began compulsively collecting the floppy lit-

In early 2000, Ty stunned collectors when it announced its intention to stop making Beanie Babies altogether. After receiving stacks of letters from children, teachers, hospitals, clinics, and charities around the world, Ty reconsidered. It conducted a worldwide vote by telephone and the Internet to let consumers decide whether it should continue to make the little animals. More than 200,000 people responded; 91 percent favored continued production. Skeptics suspected that Ty

Pursuing its mission to "engage, enchant, and empower girls," Mattel introduces new Barbie dolls every year in order to keep up with the latest definitions of achievement, glamour, romance, adventure, and nurturing. Barbie also reflects America's diverse and changing population. Mattel has produced African American Barbie dolls since 1968 and has since introduced Hispanic and Asian dolls as well. In recent years, Mattel has introduced Crystal Barbie (a gorgeous glamour doll), Puerto Rican Barbie (part of its "dolls of the world" collection), Great Shape Barbie (to tie into the fitness craze), Flight Time Barbie (a pilot), Soccer Barbie (to tie in with the recent boom in girls' soccer), and Children's Doctor Barbie (the first in the "I Can Be" Career Series Barbies). Barbie herself has received several makeovers. The most recent one gave her a wider face, her first belly button, slightly less prominent breasts, and a more athletic body.

As a result of Mattel's adept product life-cycle handling, Barbie has kept her market allure as well as her youth. Available in 150 countries, Barbie now sells at a rate of two each second worldwide and racks up sales of more than $1.5 billion a year. If you placed head to foot every doll ever sold, Barbie and her friends would circle the globe 72 times.

Crayola Crayons

Over the past 100 years or so, Binney & Smith's Crayola crayons have become a household staple in more than 80 countries around the world. Few people can forget their first pack of "64s"—64 beauties neatly arranged in the familiar green and yellow flip-top box with a sharpener on the back. The aroma of a freshly opened Crayola box still drives kids into a frenzy and takes members of the older generation back to some of their fondest childhood memories.

In some ways, Crayola crayons haven't changed much since 1903, when they were sold in an eight-pack for a nickel. But a closer look reveals that Binney & Smith has made many adjustments to keep the brand out of decline. The company has added a steady stream of new colors, shapes, sizes, and packages. It has gradually increased the number of colors from the original eight in 1903 (red, yellow, blue, green, orange, black, brown, and white) to 120 in 2002. Binney & Smith has also extended the Crayola brand to new markets such as Crayola Markers, scissors, watercolor paints, gel pens, themed stamps and stickers, and activity kits. The company has

licensed the Crayola brand for use on everything from camera outfits, backpacks, and bookends to cartoon cups and mousepads. Finally, the company has added several programs and services to help strengthen its relationships with Crayola customers. Its *Crayola Kids* magazine and Crayola Web site offer features for children along with interactive art and suggestions for parents and educators on helping develop reading skills and creativity.

Not all of Binney & Smith's life-cycle adjustments have been greeted favorably by consumers. For example, in 1990, to make room for more modern colors, it retired eight colors from the time-honored box of 64—raw umber, lemon yellow, maize, blue grey, orange yellow, orange red, green blue, and violet blue—into the Crayola Hall of Fame. The move unleashed a groundswell of protest from loyal Crayola users, who formed such organizations as the RUMPS—the Raw Umber and Maize Preservation Society—and the National Committee to Save Lemon Yellow. Company executives were flabbergasted—"We were aware of the loyalty and nostalgia surrounding Crayola crayons," a spokesperson says, "but we didn't know we [would] hit such a nerve." The company reissued the old standards in a special collector's tin—it sold all of the 2.5 million tins made.

Thus, Crayola continues its long and colorful life cycle. Through smart product life-

cycle management, Binney & Smith, now a subsidiary of Hallmark, has dominated the crayon market for almost a century. The company now makes nearly 3 billion crayons a year, enough to circle the world six times. Sixty-five percent of all American children between the ages of two and seven pick up a crayon at least once a day and color for an average of 28 minutes. Nearly 80 percent of the time, they pick up a Crayola crayon.

Sources: See Carole Schmidt and Lynn Kaladjian, "Ty Connects Hot-Property Dots," *Brandweek,* June 16, 1997, p. 26; "Consumers Vote for More Beanie Babies," *New York Times,* January 3, 2000, C2; information access online at www.ty.com, August 2002; "Hue and Cry over Crayola May Revive Old Colors," *Wall Street Journal,* June 14, 1991, p. B1; Margaret O. Kirk, "Coloring Our Children's World Since '03," *Chicago Tribune,* October 29, 1986, sec. 5, p. 1; "Crayola Trivia," accessed online at www.crayola.com, July 2002; Alice Cuneo and Laura Petrecca, "Barbie Has to Work Harder to Help Out Sagging Mattel," *Advertising Age,* March 6, 2000, p. 4; Christopher Palmeri, "Mattel: Up the Hill Minus Jill," *Business Week,* April 9, 2001, pp. 53–54; Alexandria Peers, "Art Journal: Goodbye Dolly!" *Wall Street Journal,* January 4, 2002, p. W1; and www.barbie.com, August 2002.

Finally, the company can try *modifying the marketing mix*—improving sales by changing one or more marketing mix elements. It can cut prices to attract new users and competitors' customers. It can launch a better advertising campaign or use aggressive sales promotions—trade deals, cents-off, premiums, and contests. The company can also move into larger market channels, using mass merchandisers, if these channels are growing. Finally, the company can offer new or improved services to buyers.

Decline Stage

Decline stage

The product life-cycle stage in which a product's sales decline.

The sales of most product forms and brands eventually dip. The decline may be slow, as in the case of oatmeal cereal, or rapid, as in the case of phonograph records. Sales may plunge to zero, or they may drop to a low level where they continue for many years. This is the **decline stage.**

Sales decline for many reasons, including technological advances, shifts in consumer tastes, and increased competition. As sales and profits decline, some firms withdraw from the market. Those remaining may prune their product offerings. They may drop smaller market segments and marginal trade channels, or they may cut the promotion budget and reduce their prices further.

Carrying a weak product can be very costly to a firm, and not just in profit terms. There are many hidden costs. A weak product may take up too much of management's time. It often requires frequent price and inventory adjustments. It requires advertising and sales force attention that might be better used to make "healthy" products more profitable. A product's failing reputation can cause customer concerns about the company and its other products. The biggest

Back into the growth stage: When this timeless brand was running out of time, Frito-Lay reconnected it with a new generation of kids. Sales more than doubled during the two years following the acquisition.

cost may well lie in the future. Keeping weak products delays the search for replacements, creates a lopsided product mix, hurts current profits, and weakens the company's foothold on the future.

For these reasons, companies need to pay more attention to their aging products. The firm's first task is to identify those products in the decline stage by regularly reviewing sales, market shares, costs, and profit trends. Then, management must decide whether to maintain, harvest, or drop each of these declining products.

Management may decide to *maintain* its brand without change in the hope that competitors will leave the industry. For example, Procter & Gamble made good profits by remaining in the declining liquid soap business as others withdrew. Or management may decide to reposition or reformulate the brand in hopes of moving it back into the growth stage of the product life cycle. Frito-Lay did this with the classic Cracker Jack brand:

> When Cracker Jack passed the 100-year-old mark, it seemed that the timeless brand was running out of time. By the time Frito-Lay acquired the classic snack-food brand from Borden Foods in 1997, sales and profits had been declining for five straight years. Frito-Lay set out to reconnect the box of candy-coated popcorn, peanuts, and a prize with a new generation of kids. "We made the popcorn bigger and fluffier with more peanuts and bigger prizes, and we put it in bags, as well as boxes," says Chris Neugent, VP-marketing for wholesome snacks for Frito-Lay. New promotional programs shared a connection with baseball and fun for kids, featuring baseball star Mark McGwire, Rawlings Sporting Goods trading cards, F.A.O. Schwarz, and Pokemon and Scooby Doo characters. The revitalized marketing pulled Cracker Jack out of decline. Sales more than doubled during the two years following the acquisition and the brand has posted double-digit increases each year since.[26]

Management may decide to *harvest* the product, which means reducing various costs (plant and equipment, maintenance, R&D, advertising, sales force) and hoping that sales hold up. If successful, harvesting will increase the company's profits in the short run. Or management may decide to *drop* the product from the line. It can sell it to another firm or simply liquidate it at salvage value. If the company plans to find a buyer, it will not want to run down the product through harvesting.

Table 10.2 summarizes the key characteristics of each stage of the product life cycle. The table also lists the marketing objectives and strategies for each stage.[27]

TABLE 10.2   SUMMARY OF PRODUCT LIFE-CYCLE CHARACTERISTICS, OBJECTIVES, AND STRATEGIES

Characteristics	Introduction	Growth	Maturity	Decline
Sales	Low sales	Rapidly rising sales	Peak sales	Declining sales
Costs	High cost per customer	Average cost per customer	Low cost per customer	Low cost per customer
Profits	Negative	Rising profits	High profits	Declining profits
Customers	Innovators	Early adopters	Middle majority	Laggards
Competitors	Few	Growing number	Stable number beginning to decline	Declining number
Marketing Objectives	Create product awareness and trial	Maximize market share	Maximize profit while defending market share	Reduce expenditure and milk the brand
Strategies				
Product	Offer a basic product	Offer product extensions, service, warranty	Diversify brand and models	Phase out weak items
Price	Use cost-plus	Price to penetrate market	Price to match or beat competitors	Cut price
Distribution	Build selective distribution	Build intensive distribution	Build more intensive distribution	Go selective: phase out unprofitable outlets
Advertising	Build product awareness among early adopters and dealers	Build awareness and interest in the mass market	Stress brand differences and benefits	Reduce to level needed to retain hard-core loyals
Sales Promotion	Use heavy sales promotion to entice trial	Reduce to take advantage of heavy consumer demand	Increase to encourage brand switching	Reduce to minimal level

Source: Philip Kotler, *Marketing Management,* 11th ed. (Upper Saddle River, N.J.: Prentice Hall, 2003), p. 340.

LOOKING BACK: REVIEWING THE CONCEPTS

A company's current products face limited life spans and must be replaced by newer products. But new products can fail—the risks of innovation are as great as the rewards. The key to successful innovation lies in a total-company effort, strong planning, and a systematic *new-product development* process.

1. Explain how companies find and develop new-product ideas.

Companies find and develop new-product ideas from a variety of sources. Many new-product ideas stem from *internal sources.* Companies conduct formal research and development, pick the brains of their employees, and brainstorm at executive meetings. By conducting surveys and focus groups and analyzing *customer* questions and complaints, companies can generate new-product ideas that will meet specific consumer needs. Companies track *competitors'* offerings and inspect new products, dismantling them, analyzing their performance, and deciding whether to introduce a similar or improved product. *Distributors and suppliers* are close to the market and can pass along information about consumer problems and new-product possibilities.

2. List and define the steps in the new-product development process.

The new-product development process consists of eight sequential stages. The process starts with *idea generation.* Next comes *idea screening,* which reduces the number of ideas based on the company's own criteria. Ideas that pass the screening stage continue through *product concept development,* in which a detailed version of the new-product idea is stated in meaningful consumer terms. In the next stage, *concept testing,* new-product concepts are tested with a group of target consumers to determine whether the concepts have strong consumer appeal. Strong concepts proceed to *marketing strategy development,* in which an initial marketing strategy for the new product is developed from the product concept. In the *business analysis* stage, a review of the sales, costs, and profit projections for a new product is conducted to determine whether the new product is likely to satisfy the company's objectives. With positive results here, the ideas become more concrete through *product development* and *test marketing* and finally are launched during *commercialization.*

3. Describe the stages of the product life cycle.

Each product has a *life cycle* marked by a changing set of problems and opportunities. The sales of the typical product follow an S-shaped curve made up of five stages. The cycle begins with the *product development stage* when the company finds and develops a new-product idea. The *introduction stage* is marked by slow growth and low profits as the product is distributed to the market. If successful, the product enters a *growth stage,* which offers rapid sales growth and increasing profits. Next comes a *maturity stage* when sales growth slows down and profits stabilize. Finally, the product enters a *decline stage* in which sales and profits dwindle. The company's task during this stage is to recognize the decline and to decide whether it should maintain, harvest, or drop the product.

4. Describe how marketing strategies change during the product's life cycle.

In the *introduction stage,* the company must choose a launch strategy consistent with its intended product positioning. Much money is needed to attract distributors and build their inventories and to inform consumers of the new product and achieve trial. In the *growth stage,* companies continue to educate poten-tial consumers and distributors. In addition, the company works to stay ahead of the competition and sustain rapid market growth by improving product quality, adding new product features and models, entering new market segments and distribution channels, shifting advertising from building product awareness to building product conviction and purchase, and lowering prices at the right time to attract new buyers. In the *maturity stage,* companies continue to invest in maturing products and consider modifying the market, the product, and the marketing mix. When *modifying the market,* the company attempts to increase the consumption of the current product. When *modifying the product,* the company changes some of the product's characteristics—such as quality, features, or style—to attract new users or inspire more usage. When *modifying the marketing mix,* the company works to improve sales by changing one or more of the marketing mix elements. Once the company recognizes that a product has entered the *decline stage,* management must decide whether to *maintain* the brand without change, hoping that competitors will drop out of the market; *harvest* the product, reducing costs and trying to maintain sales; or *drop* the product, selling it to another firm or liquidating it at salvage value.

REVIEWING THE KEY TERMS

Business analysis 323
Commercialization 327
Concept testing 321
Decline stage 335
Fad 332
Fashion 331
Growth stage 332

Idea generation 315
Idea screening 320
Introduction stage 332
Marketing strategy development 322
Maturity stage 333
New-product development 315
Product concept 320

Product development 323
Product life cycle (PLC) 330
Sequential product development 327
Simultaneous (or team-based) product development 328
Style 331
Test marketing 324

DISCUSSING THE CONCEPTS

1. Pick a familiar company and assume you are responsible for generating new-product ideas. How would you structure your new-product development process? What sources of new ideas would be most valuable? How would you stimulate the development of new ideas in the organization?

2. One of the challenges faced by today's new-product development manager is how to use the Internet to get innovative ideas from customers and competitors. Propose three ways to form relationships with consumers that encourage the generation of new ideas. Propose three ways to observe competitors to gain insight into their new-product ventures.

3. America is currently undergoing a health craze that is affecting the way consumers eat. Assume you have been hired by Burger King to develop and test a new sandwich that would appeal to vegetarians. Develop three alternative product concepts for the new sandwich. Think carefully about how to test each of these concepts. What testing method(s) would you suggest? Which of your three concepts do you think has the greatest potential? Why?

4. Your company has just developed a revolutionary new skiing product. Grasskis allow the user to ski on hill slopes when there is no snow. Not only will this product allow the novice and professional to practice snow-skiing skills during summer months, Grasskis may eventually lead to an entirely new summer sport. Construct a marketing strategy statement to present to potential investors. Construct sales forecasts based on your confidence in this new product.

5. Crayola has just developed a new product aimed at the young adult market. Tattoo Pens allow users to draw tattoos that fade in about two weeks. Initial consumer tests have been positive. However, the company would like to ensure a positive reception before beginning full commercialization. Which of the three test marketing methods suggested in the text would be best for this new product? Support your findings.

6. Pick a soft drink, car, fashion, food product, or electronic gadget and trace the product's life cycle. Explain how you separated the stages of the product's development.

7. Discuss the differences between a fad, a fashion, and a style. Find a contemporary illustration for each. List three ways a fad might be extended by a creative marketing planner.

8. Which product life-cycle stage, if any, is the most important? Which stage is the riskiest? Which stage offers the greatest profit potential? Which stage seems to need the greatest amount of "hands-on" management? Explain the thinking behind each of your answers.

APPLYING THE CONCEPTS

1. "Danger, Will Robinson! Danger!" might be one of the most memorable phrases ever uttered by a robot. However, today the phrase would more likely be "Buy Me! Take Me Home!" Who will offer the first practical, affordable home robot? NASA? Intel? Sony? Lego? Did you say "Lego"? Yes, the same company that developed those great plastic building blocks has now developed several models of home robots (such as the R2D2 model from the *Star Wars* series) that sell for as little as $220. The Lego model kits contain Lego pieces, light sensors, touch sensors, gears, and a mini-computer brick that forms the core of the system. The small, efficient robots already perform many hard-to-believe tasks (without complaining), and Lego is making daily upgrades. Copycat competitors have begun a frenzy of activity that will one day produce an amazing array of domesticated robots.

   a. Who might be the first customers to buy a Lego robot? Explain.

   b. Project the life cycle for this new product. Explain your thinking.

   c. Outline a strategy for positioning this product as a "personal electronic device" rather than a toy. What is the most important aspect of your strategy?

   d. What headline would you select for the first Lego robot ad appearing in *USA Today*? In *Business Week*?

   e. Visit www.lego.com. What other new products has Lego produced to complement its robot line? How could Lego extend the robot concept into other products?

2. What is the hottest new trend in shoes for teens? Is it Air Jordans, soccer shoes, combat boots, or retro tennis shoes? If you answered, "None of the above," you're right. Heelys are the newest fad to hit teen footwear. They may look like thick-soled sneakers, but Heelys have a hidden feature. The shoes include a detachable wheel in each heel, enabling wearers to switch from walking to skating simply by shifting their weight. Texas-based Heeling Sports, Ltd., which produces these unique shoes, has venture capitalists lined up to support the new product. Why? Because teens are lined up to buy the shoes. Heeling has kept the shoes out of mainstream stores like Target, focusing instead on skate shops, surf shops, and mall chains such as Gadzooks—stores that target teens and offer higher price margins. The response has been tremendous. Heeling expects to ship more than a million pairs this year. If the success continues, you may soon see someone on campus "heeling" to class.

   a. After visiting the Heelys Web site at www.heelys.com, comment on the strategy devised by the company to reach its target market. What improvements in the strategy would you recommend?

   b. What stage of the product life cycle is the product currently experiencing? Using the information found in Table 10.2, comment on what the company must do to move forward to the next stage. How can Heeling Sports turn its fad into a long-term trend?

   c. How has the company used the Internet to expand sales? Comment.

   d. What other target markets should the company be considering? What other distribution outlets should be employed? How could the company expand into new markets and outlets but remain true to its core following?

   e. As the new-product development manager for Heeling Sports, Ltd., what new product would you advise for next year's shoe market? Explain your thinking and outline a plan for developing, testing, and introducing this product.

WWW DIGITAL CONNECTIONS

CONNECTING CUSTOMERS WITH LIFELONG SATISFACTION AND VALUE

As you register for next semester's classes, will any of you consider attending Silly Putty U? Probably not, but the American toy classic Silly Putty has been around for 50 years and is still going strong. From Binney & Smith, maker of Crayola crayons, Silly Putty connects with new and old customers through its online Silly Putty U. Consumers (students) learn through History 101 that Silly Putty has produced over 300 million eggs (the package for Silly Putty) since 1950—selling more than 4,500 tons of putty. Fans also find out that, although the original Silly Putty was pink, the substance now comes in 16 vibrant colors, including glow-in-the dark. Silly Putty users can log on to suggest zany uses, like making a boat for your pet hampster, or more common uses like cleaning a computer keyboard, fixing a wobbly table leg, and reproducing images.

The site may be the most tangible effort by Binney & Smith to extend Silly Putty's life cycle. The company is betting that the newest generation of cyber-surfers will find its Web site fun, informative, and a great way to extend or begin a relationship with the product. Is the company's strategy a good one? See for yourself.

FOR DISCUSSION

1. To learn more about Silly Putty, visit www.sillyputty.com. How does Binney & Smith use the Web site to connect with consumers? What consumer segments does the site target? Be specific.

2. In what stage of the life cycle is Silly Putty positioned? How can the Internet affect the life cycle of this product?

3. What innovations or product extensions would you suggest to Binney & Smith to increase sales of Silly Putty?

4. Would you call Silly Putty a fad, fashion, or style? Explain your thinking.

5. Beyond the company's current plans, what strategies would you suggest to attract new Silly Putty buyers? As the marketing manager for Silly Putty, how would you market the product globally?

SensAble Technologies: Designing Products Digitally

SensAble Technologies hopes to forever change the way companies design and develop new products. Using its FreeForm modeling system, product engineers digitally interact with prototypes using the sense of touch. Researchers at Michelin use the technology to develop new tire treads. Hasbro used FreeForm to create several new dinosaur toys for the new Jurassic Park Junior line. Other mega-marketers, including Adidas, Motorola, PlayMobil, Nokia, and Spaulding, also rely on the technology to streamline and coordinate the new-product design process.

After viewing the SensAble video, answer the following questions about new-product development and product life cycles:

1. SensAble's FreeForm technology enables designers to digitally interact with product concepts and transform them into marketable products. What products are particularly well suited to such technology? What products are not well suited?
2. In addition to product development, what other stages of the new-product development process might benefit from the use of the FreeForm modeling system?
3. How do product design and time to market affect the length of the product life cycle?

Red Bull: Waking a New Market

IN THE BEGINNING
Little did Austrian businessman Dietrich Mateschitz suspect when he visited Bankok, Thailand, in the early 1980s that his trip would launch not only a new product but also a new product category. Mateschitz, international marketing director for Blendax, a German toothpaste producer, encountered Krating Daeng, a "tonic syrup" that Red Bull Beverage Company had been marketing in Thailand for years. Mateschitz discovered that one glass of the product eliminated his jet lag.

Returning to Austria, Mateschitz began a three-year product development process that included developing the drink's image, packaging, and marketing strategy. In 1987, he obtained the marketing rights to Red Bull (the translated Thai name) from the Thai company and launched his marketing strategy.

THE PRODUCT
Although marketers credit Red Bull with creating the "energy drink" category, the pursuit of drinks to enhance performance and well-being is not new. Back in 1886, some folks in Atlanta introduced a product they called "Coca-Cola" that had extracts from cola nuts and coca leaves and advertised it as an "esteemed brain tonic and intellectual beverage."

Red Bull is a lightly carbonated energy drink that comes in a slender aluminum can that holds 8.3 ounces. The label indicates that it has 110 calories, 0 grams of fat, 200 milligrams of sodium, 28 grams of carbohydrates, 27 grams of sugar, and less than one gram of protein. Ingredients include sucrose, glucose, sodium citrate, taurine, glucurono-lactone, caffeine, inositol, niacinamide, calcium-pantothenate, pyridoxine HCL, vitamin B_{12}, and artificial flavors and colors, all mixed in carbonated water.

Sounds delicious, don't you think? Well, that is part of the problem. Each of an energy drink's ingredients has a specific purpose—but each also has it own taste, and in some cases, an aftertaste. It's no easy matter to blend the ingredients to get not only the correct benefits for the consumer but also something the consumer will drink voluntarily.

Energy drinks have a number of different types of ingredients. The body takes *carbohydrates* and metabolizes them into glucose (sugar). Simple sugars produce a rapid rise in blood sugar, while complex carbohydrates produce a slower rise. By combining different types of sugars, a drink can produce glycemic responses at different times.

Energy drinks sometimes include *amino acids* that are protein building blocks. Taurine, for example, is an important aid in the release of insulin and can prevent abnormal blood clotting. Because researchers have cited a deficiency of *vitamins and minerals* as being associated with a lack of energy, beverage makers often include them in energy drinks. Niacin (vitamin B_3) works with other vitamins to metabolize carbohydrates. Riboflavin (vitamin B_{12}) helps combat anemia and fatigue by helping to manufacture red blood cells.

Some drinks include *botanicals* such as gingko biloba, guarana, and ginseng. Ginkgo biloba is purported to provide mental energy and "sharpness" by stimulating blood flow to the brain. Finally, most energy drinks contain *caffeine,* an alkaloid stimulant that the body absorbs and circulates to all body tissues. Caffeine affects the central nervous system, the digestive tract, and the body's metabolism, boosting adrenaline levels to increase blood pressure and heart rate. Typical energy drinks, like Red Bull, contain about the same amount of caffeine as a cup of coffee.

Packaging is also important. Some fruity energy beverages come in glass bottles, but many energy drinks that contain light-sensitive vitamins, like B_{12}, come in slender metal cans to prevent the vitamins from breaking down.

THE MARKETING STRATEGY

Mateschitz designed an unusual marketing strategy. "We don't bring the product to the people," he argues, "we bring people to the product." Initially, when Red Bull entered the U.S. market in Santa Monica, California, it used traditional beverage distributors. But as the product gained popularity, the company began to pursue a more focused distribution strategy. Red Bull sales representatives now approach a beverage distributor and insist that he or she sell only Red Bull and no other energy drink. If the distributor will not agree, Red Bull hires young people to load the product in vans and distribute it themselves.

The company divided the United States into eight territories, with sales teams in each area responsible for developing distribution and targeted marketing plans. The local team seeks to determine where people aged 16 to 29 are hanging out and what they find interesting. First, the sales team calls on trendy clubs and bars that will offer the drink on-premise. As incentives, the team offers Red Bull coolers and other promotional items. Red Bull works with individual accounts rather than large chains because it has found that the process goes much faster due to the lack of bureaucracy. It has also found that young people in local hot spots are open to trying new things and help generate a "buzz" about Red Bull. However, the company does not endorse all the new things people try, like mixing the product with vodka or tequila, and it has a FAQ section on its Web site, www.redbull.com, to counter the many rumors that have developed around the product.

Second, the sales team also opens off-premise accounts such as gyms, health-food stores, and convenience stores near colleges. The product sells for about $2.00 in convenience stores. In addition, "consumer educators" roam local streets and hand out free samples. The company has encouraged students to drive around with big Red Bull cans strapped to the tops of their cars and to throw Red Bull parties focused on weird themes.

Contrary to traditional promotion practice, Red Bull starts traditional advertising only *after* it believes a local market is maturing. The company's philosophy is that media can reinforce but not introduce a brand. Thus, it builds demand even before it introduces the product at retail. Only about 19 percent of the $100 million the brand spent on promotion in 2000 was for measured media. Red Bull spends about 35 percent of sales on promotion. The company has also begun sponsoring extreme sporting events and extreme athletes.

UNCANNY RESULTS

Does all this grass-roots marketing work? Well, in 2001, Red Bull sold 1.6 billion cans in 62 countries, up 80 percent over 2000. In the United States, Red Bull entered the list of the top 10 carbonated beverage distributors with a mere 0.1 percent market share—but its case volume grew 118 percent over 2000 to 10.5 million cases. Red Bull is the number one product in Store24 and had similar results at 7-Eleven. It now captures a 70 to 90 percent share of the energy drink market.

With results like that, it did not take long for competitors to jump in. Pepsi bought South Beach Beverage Company (makers of the SoBe brand) and developed an energy drink it calls "Adrenaline Rush." Coca-Cola jumped in with KMX. Even Anheuser-Busch, of Budweiser fame, joined in with a product it calls "180" to denote that it turns your energy around 180 degrees. In early 2002, another Thai company, Otsotspa, entered the fray with its own energy drink, called "Shark."

Mateschitz does not seem concerned about competition. He knows Red Bull has a tremendous head start and strong local marketing teams. He already has plans to enter Brazil and South Africa.

However, Mateschitz does have one concern. "It makes no sense to build a company on one product," he argues. So far, he has put the Red Bull brand on only one other product. LunAqua is a still water that the company claims it bottles only 13 times per year, during each full moon when the moon reaches its full energy level. There is also a variety of LunAqua that contains caffeine. But Mateschitz knows that it will take more than just moon power to stay ahead of the competition in the energy drink market. You can bet he will be up all night, sipping Red Bull and developing new product ideas.

QUESTIONS FOR DISCUSSION

1. Based on the information in the case, evaluate Red Bull's product development process. What process would you recommend as it considers developing new products?
2. At what stage of the product life cycle are energy drinks as a category? What does this position imply for category competitors?
3. Do you believe there is a long-term market for functional foods and beverages like energy drinks? Why or why not?
4. Using the "product-market expansion grid" presented in Chapter 2 (see Figure 2.3), recommend specific ideas for Red Bull in the areas of market penetration, product development, and market development.

Sources: David Jago, "Global Trends: Hitting the Shelves," *Prepared Foods,* June 2002, p. 9; "Selling Energy Face Value," *The Economist,* May 11, 2002; "Sales of Red Bull Beverage in United States Grow to 10.5 Million Cases," *Knight-Ridder/Tribune Business News* March 14, 2002, from the *Bankok Post;* "Shark UK Launch to Challenge Red Bull's Dominance," *Marketing,* February 28, 2002, p. 6; Kenneth Hein, "A Bull's Market," *Brandweek,* May 28, 2001, p. 21; David Noonan, "Red Bull's Good Buzz," *Newsweek,* May 14, 2001, p. 39; Laura A. Brandt, "Energizing Elixirs!" *Prepared Foods,* April 2001, p. 55; Jeff Cioletti, "Boosting Beverages," *Supermarket Business,* January 15, 2001, p. 31; and www.RedBull.com.

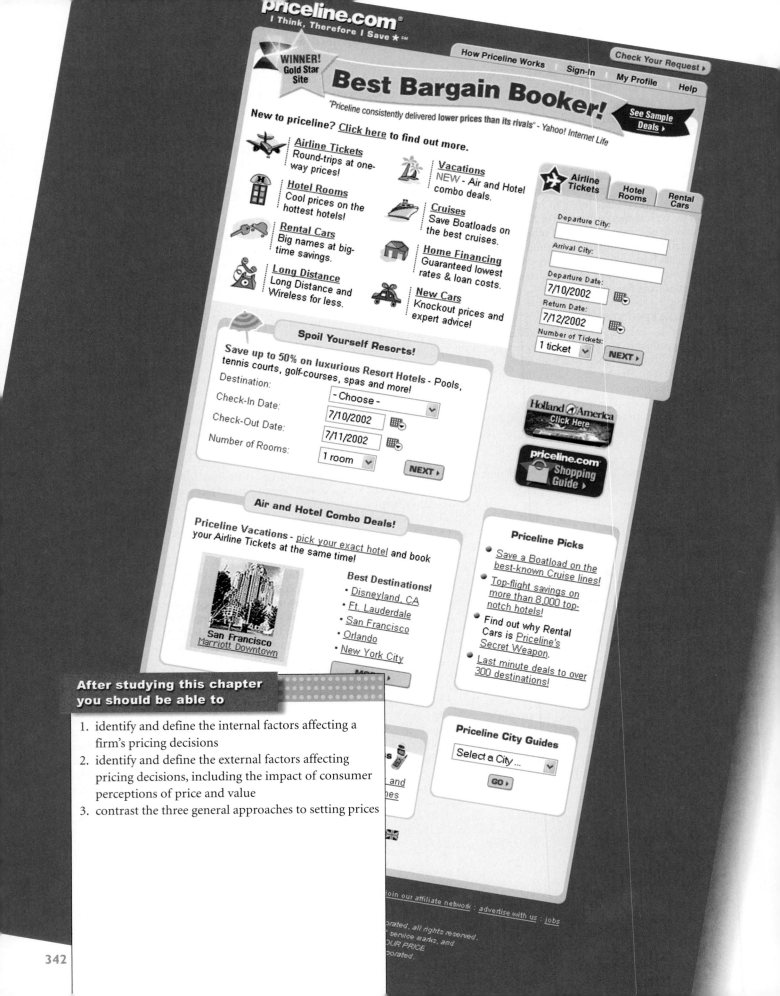

1. identify and define the internal factors affecting a firm's pricing decisions
2. identify and define the external factors affecting pricing decisions, including the impact of consumer perceptions of price and value
3. contrast the three general approaches to setting prices

Pricing Considerations and Approaches

LOOKING AHEAD: PREVIEWING THE CONCEPTS

Next, we look at a second major marketing mix tool—pricing. According to one pricing expert, pricing involves "harvesting your profit potential."[1] If effective product development, promotion, and distribution sow the seeds of business success, effective pricing is the harvest. Firms successful at creating customer value with the other marketing mix activities must still capture some of this value in the prices they earn. Yet, despite its importance, many firms do not handle pricing well. In this chapter, we'll examine internal and external factors that affect pricing decisions and three general pricing approaches. In the next chapter, we dig into pricing strategies.

To start off, let's look at one of the most dramatic new developments in the fast-changing world of pricing—the impact of the Internet. Five years ago, Priceline.com burst onto the Web with a simple but compelling new pricing concept—let consumers name their own prices! This radical new idea caught on, making Priceline one of today's few profitable dot-coms. Sound too good to be true? It could only happen on the Internet.

The headlines scream: *Name your own price! Top-flight savings on more than 8,000 top-notch hotels! Last-minute deals to more than 300 destinations! Save a boatload on best-known cruise lines! Big savings on long-distance calling!* Just the usual come-ons from fly-by-night operators? Too good to be true? Not at Priceline.com, at least not according to *Yahoo! Internet Life Magazine,* which recently proclaimed Priceline as the "Best Bargain Booker" on the Web. Priceline's byline: "I Think. Therefore I Save."

In 1998, founder Jay Walker launched Priceline as a radical new Internet service. It was based on an ingeniously simple concept—empower consumers to name their own prices, then dangle their offers in front of sellers and see who bites. Such transactions, he reasoned, benefited both buyers and sellers—buyers got lower prices; sellers turned excess inventory into profits. Although simple in concept, however, such "buyer-driven commerce" represented a dramatic departure from long-held pricing practices in which sellers—not buyers—set prices. Still, the idea caught on. Priceline has now grown to become the leading name-your-own-price Internet service and one of the few profitable dot-coms.

Priceline deals primarily in travel-related products—plane tickets, hotel rooms, rental cars, cruises, and vacation packages. Here's how it works—say, for a hotel room. First, you select your destination and desired dates. If it's a big city, you can scan Priceline's maps to narrow down the area in which you'd like to stay. You can also select the types of hotels you're willing to stay in—from one-star ("economy hotels that provide comfort with no frills") to five-star ("the best that money can buy"). Give Priceline the usual billing information and a credit card number—and decide how much you'd like to bid. Click on "Buy My Hotel Room," then sit back and wait for Priceline to broker the deal. Within 15 minutes, Priceline e-mails you with the news. If no suitable hotel is willing to accept your price, you can bid again later. If Priceline finds a taker, it immediately charges your credit card—no refunds, changes, or cancellations allowed—and lets you know where you'll be staying.

The concept of setting your own prices over the Internet has real appeal to consumers. It starts with a good value proposition—getting really low prices. Beyond that, "name-your-price is a great hook," say a Priceline marketing executive. "If you get it, it's like 'I won!'" As a result, Priceline is attracting more and more customers. Its customer base has grown to 13.5 million users, and as many as 9 million people visit the Priceline site monthly. Through strategic partnerships forged with companies such as eBay, AOL, and LowestFare.com, over the past year Priceline has extended its online audience by 810 percent, now reaching more than 85 million unique Web users. Since it opened for business in 1998, Priceline has sold more than 12 million airline tickets, 6 million hotel room nights, and 6 million rental car days.

Despite accepting fire-sale prices, sellers also benefit from Priceline's services. It's especially attractive to those who sell products that have "time sensitivity." "If airlines or hotels don't sell seats on particular flights or rooms for certain nights, those assets become worthless," comments an analyst. "Such businesses are a natural fit for Priceline." Moreover, notes the analyst, "by requiring customers to commit to payment up front with their credit card, retailers face little risk in dumping excess inventory. It's particularly attractive in markets that have huge fixed costs from creating capacity and relatively small marginal costs, like air travel, cruise ships, and automobiles."

Priceline makes its money by buying up unsold rooms, seats, or vacation packages at heavily discounted rates, marking them up, and selling them to consumers for as much as a 12 percent return. So, on a $215 plane ticket, Priceline makes about $35, compared to the $10 gross profit made by a traditional travel agent.

Along with the successes and its recent profitability, however, Priceline has encountered some formidable obstacles. For example, not all products lend themselves to Priceline's quirky business model, and the company has met with uneven success in attempts to grow beyond travel services. Although it currently takes bids in three other categories—New Cars, Long Distance, and Home Financing (home mortgages, refinancing, and home equity loans)—selling products and services that aren't time sensitive has proven difficult. Last year's efforts to expand into gasoline blew up. Priceline had no trouble lining up customers interested in buying gas over the Internet. Unfortunately, however, gas and oil companies had no incentive to dump excess inventories because gas is not a perishable good. And, as one analyst points out, "oil companies that spend millions building brands are loath to sell gasoline via a site that puts price before brand." As a result, after only eight months but millions of dollars in loses, Priceline closed its virtual gas pumps.

Moreover, not all customers are thrilled with their Priceline experiences. Forcing customers to commit to purchases before they know the details—such as which hotel or airline, flight times, and hotel locations—can leave some customers feeling cheated. One frustrated user recently summed up his Priceline experience this way: "You don't get what you think you're gonna get."

But for every disappointed customer, Priceline has hundreds or thousands of happy ones. Some 64 percent of those who now visit Priceline to name their own prices are repeat customers. You don't have to go far to get positive testimonials such as these:

> Using Priceline.com has worked out great! I remember the first time I used it. I'm not very technically savvy, but after navigating around the site, I set what I thought was a lowball price. It turns out that my offer was accepted and I saved more than 50 percent off the normal room rate. The hotel was great. In fact, I usually stay there when traveling, so I also knew I was getting it for a great price.

> I discovered Priceline.com and decided to try it out to visit my college roommate. She's in Albuquerque, New Mexico, and I'm in Hanover, Germany. The best price from the airlines was too high. After reading about Priceline.com, I decided I had nothing to lose by trying it to get a better deal. I offered a low price but was sure I wouldn't stand the slightest chance of an acceptance. To my amazement, within 20 minutes of logging in, I received a happy "congratulations" e-mail from Priceline. The visit was wonderful, my friend was amazed, and I've been telling everyone (lots of seasoned travelers who didn't believe my story at first) from Germany to the United States about this spectacular new way to travel.

More than just changing how people pay for travel services, Priceline is perhaps the best example of how the Internet is changing today's pricing practices. "Only through the Web could you match millions of bids with millions of products, all without a fixed price," says one analyst. "In the offline world, this would be a strange market indeed," says another. Try to imagine a real-world situation in which "buyers attach money to a board, along with a note stating what they want to buy for the sum. Later, sellers come along and have a look. If they like an offer, they take the money and deliver the goods." It couldn't happen anywhere but on the Web.[2]

Companies today face a fierce and fast-changing pricing environment. The recent economic downturn has put many companies in a "pricing vise." One analyst sums it up this way: "They have virtually no pricing power. It's impossible to raise prices, and often, the pressure to slash them continues unabated. The pricing pinch is affecting business across the spectrum of manufacturing and services—everything from chemicals and autos to hoteliers and phone services."[3] It seems that almost every company is slashing prices, and that is hurting their profits.

Yet, cutting prices is often not the best answer. Reducing prices unnecessarily can lead to lost profits and damaging price wars. It can signal to customers that price is more important than brand. Instead, companies should "sell value, not price."[4] They should persuade customers that paying a higher price for the company's brand is justified by the greater value it delivers. Most customers will gladly pay a fair price in exchange for real value. The challenge is to find the price that will let the company make a fair profit by harvesting the customer value it creates.

In this chapter and the next, we focus on the process of setting prices. This chapter defines prices, looks at the factors marketers must consider when setting prices, and examines general pricing approaches. In the next chapter, we look at pricing strategies for new-product pricing, product mix pricing, price adjustments for buyer and situational factors, and price changes.

What Is a Price?

All profit organizations and many not-for-profit organizations must set prices on their products or services. *Price* goes by many names:

> Price is all around us. You pay *rent* for your apartment, *tuition* for your education, and a *fee* to your physician or dentist. The airline, railway, taxi, and bus companies charge you a *fare,* the local utilities call their price a *rate,* and the local bank charges you *interest* for the money you borrow. The price for driving your car on Florida's Sunshine Parkway is a *toll,* and the company that insures your car charges you a *premium.* The guest lecturer charges an *honorarium* to tell you about a government official who took a *bribe* to help a shady character steal *dues* collected by a trade association. Clubs or societies to which you belong may make a special *assessment* to pay unusual expenses. Your regular lawyer may ask for a *retainer* to cover her services. The "price" of an executive is a *salary,* the price of a salesperson may be a *commission,* and the price of a worker is a *wage.* Finally, although economists would disagree, many of us feel that *income taxes* are the price we pay for the privilege of making money.[5]

Price

The amount of money charged for a product or service, or the sum of the values that consumers exchange for the benefits of having or using the product or service.

In the narrowest sense, **price** is the amount of money charged for a product or service. More broadly, price is the sum of all the values that consumers exchange for the benefits of having or using the product or service. Historically, price has been the major factor affecting buyer choice. This is still true in poorer nations, among poorer groups, and with commodity products. However, nonprice factors have become more important in buyer-choice behavior in recent decades.

Throughout most of history, prices were set by negotiation between buyers and sellers. *Fixed price* policies—setting one price for all buyers—is a relatively modern idea that arose with the development of large-scale retailing at the end of the nineteenth century. Now, some one hundred years later, the Internet promises to reverse the fixed pricing trend and take us back to an era of **dynamic pricing**—charging different prices depending on individual customers and situations (see Real Marketing 11.1). The Internet, corporate networks, and wireless communications are connecting sellers and buyers as never before. Web sites such as Compare.Net and PriceSCAN.com allow buyers to compare products and prices quickly and easily. Online auction sites such as eBay.com and Amazon.com Auctions make it easy for buyers and sellers to negotiate prices on thousands of items—from refurbished computers to antique tin trains. Sites like Priceline even let customers set their own prices. At the same time, new technologies allow sellers to collect detailed data about customers' buying habits, preferences, and even spending limits, so they can tailor their products and prices.[6]

Dynamic pricing

Charging different prices depending on individual customers and situations.

Price is the only element in the marketing mix that produces revenue; all other elements represent costs. Price is also one of the most flexible elements of the marketing mix. Unlike product features and channel commitments, price can be changed quickly. At the same time, pricing and price competition is the number one problem facing many marketing executives. Yet, many companies do not handle pricing well. One frequent problem is that companies are too quick to reduce prices in order to get a sale rather than convincing buyers that their products are worth a higher price. Other common mistakes include pricing that is too cost oriented rather than customer-value oriented, prices that are not revised often enough to reflect market changes, pricing that does not take the rest of the marketing mix into account, and prices that are not varied enough for different products, market segments, and purchase occasions.

real marketing 11.1

Back to the Future: Dynamic Pricing on the Web

The Internet is more than simply a new "marketspace"—it's actually changing the rules of commerce. Take pricing, for example. From the mostly fixed pricing practices of the past century, the Web seems now to be taking us back—into a new age of fluid pricing. "Potentially, [the Internet] could push aside sticker prices and usher in an era of dynamic pricing," says *Business Week* writer Robert Hof, "in which a wide range of goods would be priced according to what the market will bear—instantly, constantly." Here's how the Internet is changing the rules of pricing for both sellers and buyers.

Sellers Can . . .

- *charge lower prices, reap higher margins.* Web buying and selling can result in drastically lower costs, allowing online sellers to charge lower prices and still make higher margins. "Thanks to their Internet connections, buyers and sellers around the world can connect at almost no cost—making instant bargaining [economically feasible]," observes Hof. Reduced inventory and distribution costs add to the savings. For example, by selling made-to-order computers online, Dell Computer greatly reduces inventory costs and eliminates retail markups. It shares the savings with buyers in the form of the "lowest price per performance."

- *monitor customer behavior and tailor offers to individuals.* With the help of new technologies, Web merchants can now target special prices to specific customers. For example, Internet sellers such as Amazon.com can mine their databases to gauge a specific shopper's desires, measure his or her means, instantaneously tailor products to fit that shopper's behavior, and price products accordingly. However, companies must be careful in how they apply dynamic pricing. When it recently came to light that Amazon.com had been charging different prices to different customers for the same DVDs, many customers were angry. Amazon.com claims that the pricing variations were a "pure and simple price test" and stopped the practice as soon as complaints began coming in. Despite these difficulties, Amazon still employs dynamic pricing by offering individualized suggestions to customers each time they log in. By doing so, it gives customers better value while also depleting unwanted inventory.

- *change prices on the fly according to changes in demand or costs.* Just ask online catalog retailers such as Lands' End, Spiegel, or Fingerhut. With printed catalogs, a price is a price, at least until the next catalog is printed. Online sellers, however, can change prices for specific items on a day-by-day or even hour-by-hour basis, adjusting quickly to changing costs and merchandise movement. Many B2B marketers monitor inventories, costs, and demand at any given moment and adjust prices instantly. For example, IBM automatically adjusts prices on its servers based on customer demand and product life-cycle factors. As a result, customers will find that prices change dynamically when they visit the IBM Web site on any given day. Dell also uses dynamic online pricing. "If the price of memory or processors decreases, we pass those savings along to the customer almost in real time," says a Dell spokesperson.

Both Sellers and Buyers Can . . .

- *negotiate prices in online auctions and exchanges.* Suddenly the centuries-old art of haggling is back in vogue. Want to sell that antique pickle jar that's been collecting dust for generations? Post it on eBay, the world's biggest online flea market. Want to purchase vintage baseball cards at a bargain price? Go to Boekhout's Collectibles Mall at www.azww.com/mall/. Want to dump that excess

The Internet is ushering in a new era of fluid pricing. mySimon is an independent site that provides product comparisons and guides and searches all merchant sites for the best prices.

inventory? Try adding an auction feature to your own Web site—Sharper Image claims it's getting 40 percent of retail for excess goods sold via its online auction site, compared with only 20 percent from liquidators.

Of the dozens of Internet auction sites, eBay and Amazon.com Auctions are the largest. eBay, which began when its owner used the Web to find a market for his girl-friend's vintage Pez dispenser collection, hosts more than 2 million auctions each month for items in more than 18,000 cate-gories, generating more than $9 billion in trades annually. Buyers like auctions because, quite simply, they like the bar-gains they find. Sellers like auctions because, over the Internet, the cost per transaction drops dramatically. Thus, it becomes practical—even profitable—to auction an item for mere dollars rather than thousands of dollars. For example, the seller can program its computers to accept the 3,000 best bids higher than $2.10 for 3,000 pieces of costume jewelry. Business marketers, whose transactions account for 68 percent of online auction sales, also use auctions to offer time-sensitive deals and gauge interest on possible price points for new products.

Buyers Can . . .

- *get instant price comparisons from thou-sands of vendors.* The Internet gives con-sumers access to reams of data about products and prices. Online compari-son guides—such as CompareNet and PriceSCAN—give product and price com-parisons at the click of a mouse. Other sites offer intelligent shopping agents—such as mySimon—that seek out products, prices, and reviews. MySimon (www.mySimon.

com), for instance, takes a buyer's criteria for a PC, camcorder, or collectible Barbie, then roots through top sellers' sites to find the best match at the best price.

- *find and negotiate lower prices.* With mar-ket information and access come buyer power. In addition to simply finding the vendor with the best price, customers armed with price information can often negotiate lower prices. Here are examples of both consumers and industrial buyers exercising this newfound power:

In search of the best possible deal on a Palm organizer, Stephen Manes first checked PriceSCAN.com, where he learned that buysoware.com had the high-tech gadget for only $358. Buy-soware, however, was "out of stock," as was the second-lowest-priced vendor, mcglen.com. Undaunted, Stephen skipped to the other end of the list, where he found that PC Zone was offering the device for $449, and it was in stock. "Time to haggle," said Stephen. "I picked up the phone. In seconds, an eager salesperson quoted me the official price. 'I saw it at buy. com for $358,' I said, omitting men-tion of the word[s 'out of stock']. 'I don't know if I can match buy.com,' came the response. 'But we can do it for $375.'" Stephen snapped up the offer, saving himself a bundle off the store price.

Business buyers have also learned the price advantages of shopping the Web. For example, hoping to save some money, United Technologies Corporation tried something new last year. Instead of the usual haggling

with dozens of individual vendors to secure printed circuit boards for vari-ous subsidiaries worldwide, UTC put the contract out on FreeMarkets, an online marketplace for industrial goods. To the company's delight, bids poured in from 39 suppliers, saving UTC a cool $10 million off its initial $24 million estimate. Says a UTC executive, "The technology drives the lowest price in a hurry."

Will dynamic pricing sweep the market-ing world? "Not entirely," says Hof. "It takes a lot of work to haggle—which is why fixed prices happened in the first place." However, he continues, "Pandora's E-box is now open, and pricing will never be the same. For many . . . products, millions of buyers figure a little haggling is a small price to pay for a sweet deal."

Sources: Quotes, extracts, and other informa-tion from Robert D. Hof, "Going, Going, Gone," *Business Week,* April 12, 1999, pp. 30–32; Hof, "The Buyer Always Wins," *Business Week,* March 22, 1999, pp. EB26–EB28; Stephen Manes, "Off-Web Dickering," *Forbes,* April 5, 1999, p. 134; Michael Vizard, Ed Scannell, and Dan Neel, "Suppliers Toy with Dynamic Pricing," *InfoWorld,* May 14, 2001, p. 28; and eBay annual reports and other information accessed at www.ebay.com, July 2002. Also see David Streitfeld, "On the Web, Price Tags Blur, *Washington Post,* September 27, 2000, p. A1; Walter Baker, Mike Marn, and Craig Zawada, "Price Smarter on the Net," *Harvard Business Review,* February 2001, pp. 122–127; and Ajit Kambil, H. James Wilson III, and Vipul Agrawal, "Are You Leaving Money on the Table?" *Journal of Business Strategy,* January–February 2002, pp. 40–43.

Factors to Consider When Setting Prices

A company's pricing decisions are affected by both internal company factors and external envi-ronmental factors (see Figure 11.1).[7]

Internal Factors Affecting Pricing Decisions

Internal factors affecting pricing include the company's marketing objectives, marketing mix strategy, costs, and organizational considerations.

Marketing Objectives

Before setting a price, the company must decide on its strategy for the product. If the company has selected its target market and positioning carefully, then its marketing mix strategy, including price, will be fairly straightforward. For example, when Honda and Toyota decided to develop

FIGURE 11.1
Factors affecting price
decisions

their Acura and Lexus brands to compete with European luxury-performance cars in the higher-income segment, this required charging a high price. In contrast, Motel 6, Econo Lodge, and Red Roof Inn have positioned themselves as motels that provide economical rooms for budget-minded travelers; this position requires charging a low price. Thus, pricing strategy is largely determined by decisions on market positioning.

At the same time, the company may seek additional objectives. Common objectives include *survival, current profit maximization, market share leadership,* and *product quality leadership.* Companies set *survival* as their major objective if they are troubled by too much capacity, heavy competition, or changing consumer wants. To keep a plant going, a company may set a low price, hoping to increase demand. In the long run, however, the firm must learn how to add value that consumers will pay for or face extinction.

Many companies use *current profit maximization* as their pricing goal. They estimate what demand and costs will be at different prices and choose the price that will produce the maximum current profit, cash flow, or return on investment. Other companies want to obtain *market share leadership.* To become the market share leader, these firms set prices as low as possible.

A company might decide that it wants to achieve *product quality leadership.* This normally calls for charging a high price to cover higher performance quality and the high cost of R&D. For example, Caterpillar charges 20 percent to 30 percent more than competitors for its heavy construction equipment based on superior product and service quality. Gillette's product superiority lets it price its Mach3 razor cartridges at a 50 percent premium over its own SensorExcel and competitors' cartridges. And A. T. Cross doesn't sell just ballpoint pens—you can get those from Bic. Instead, it sells "fine writing instruments" in models bearing names like Classic Century, Ion, Morph, Matrix, ATX, and Radiance, selling for prices as high as $400.

A company might also use price to attain other, more specific objectives. It can set prices low to prevent competition from entering the market or set prices at competitors' levels to stabilize the market. Prices can be set to keep the loyalty and support of resellers or to avoid government intervention. Prices can be reduced temporarily to create excitement for a product or to draw more customers into a retail store. One product may be priced to help the sales of other products in the company's line. Thus, pricing may play an important role in helping to accomplish the company's objectives at many levels.

Not-for-profit and public organizations may adopt a number of other pricing objectives. A university aims for *partial cost recovery,* knowing that it must rely on private gifts and public grants to cover the remaining costs. A not-for-profit hospital may aim for *full cost recovery* in its pricing. A not-for-profit theater company may price its productions to fill the maximum number of theater seats. A social service agency may set a *social price* geared to the varying income situations of different clients.

Marketing Mix Strategy

Price is only one of the marketing mix tools that a company uses to achieve its marketing objectives. Price decisions must be coordinated with product design, distribution, and promotion decisions to form a consistent and effective marketing program. Decisions made for other marketing mix variables may affect pricing decisions. For example, producers using many resellers who are expected to support and promote their products may have to build larger reseller margins into their prices. The decision to position the product on high-performance quality will mean that the seller must charge a higher price to cover higher costs.

Companies often position their products on price and then tailor other marketing mix decisions to the prices they want to charge. Here, price is a crucial product-positioning factor that defines the product's market, competition, and design. Many firms support such price-positioning strategies with a technique called **target costing,** a potent strategic weapon. Target

Target costing
Pricing that starts with an ideal selling price, then targets costs that will ensure that the price is met.

Product quality leadership: Four Seasons starts with very high quality service—"we await you with the perfect sanctuary." It then charges a price to match.

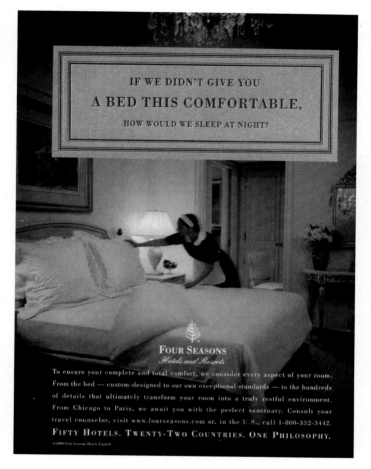

costing reverses the usual process of first designing a new product, determining its cost, and then asking, "Can we sell it for that?" Instead, it starts with an ideal selling price based on customer considerations, then targets costs that will ensure that the price is met.

The original Swatch watch provides a good example of target costing. Rather than starting with its own costs, Swatch surveyed the market and identified an unserved segment of watch buyers who wanted "a low-cost fashion accessory that also keeps time." Swatch set out to give consumers in this segment the watch they wanted at a price they were willing to pay, and it managed the new product's costs accordingly. Like most watch buyers, targeted consumers were concerned about precision, reliability, and durability. However, they were also concerned about fashion and affordability. To keep costs down, Swatch designed fashionable but simpler watches that contained fewer parts and that were constructed from high-tech but less expensive materials. It then developed a revolutionary automated process for mass-producing the new watches and exercised strict cost controls throughout the manufacturing process. By managing costs carefully, Swatch created a watch that offered just the right blend of fashion and function at a price consumers were willing to pay. As a result, the company sold more than 2 million watches in its first two years. Based on this initial success, consumers have placed increasing value on Swatch products, allowing the company to introduce successively higher-priced designs.[8]

Other companies deemphasize price and use other marketing mix tools to create *nonprice* positions. Often, the best strategy is not to charge the lowest price, but rather to differentiate the marketing offer to make it worth a higher price. For example, for years Johnson Controls, a producer of climate-control systems for office buildings, used initial price as its primary competitive tool. However, research showed that customers were more concerned about the total cost of installing and maintaining a system than about its initial price.

Repairing broken systems was expensive, time-consuming, and risky. Customers had to shut down the heat or air-conditioning in the whole building, disconnect a lot of wires, and face the dangers of electrocution. So Johnson designed an entirely new system called "Metasys."

Target costing: By managing costs carefully, Swatch was able to create a watch that offered just the right blend of fashion and function at a price consumers were willing to pay.

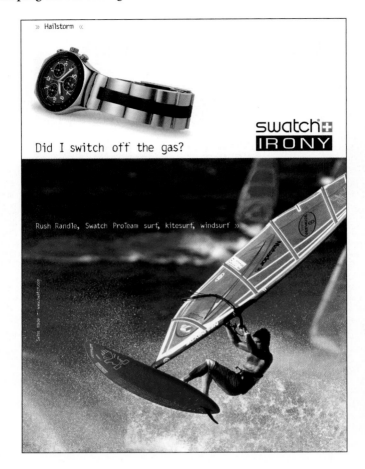

To repair the new system, customers need only pull out an old plastic module and slip in a new one—no tools required. Metasys costs more to make than the old system, and customers pay a higher initial price, but it costs less to install and maintain. Despite its higher asking price, the new Metasys system brought in $500 million in revenues in its first year. More than 15,000 systems are now installed around the world in markets including education, health care, hospitality, commercial office, telecommunications, government, pharmaceutical, retail, and industrial.[9]

Thus, marketers must consider the total marketing mix when setting prices. If the product is positioned on nonprice factors, then decisions about quality, promotion, and distribution will strongly affect price. If price is a crucial positioning factor, then price will strongly affect decisions made about the other marketing mix elements. But even when featuring price, marketers need to remember that customers rarely buy on price alone. Instead, they seek products that give them the best value in terms of benefits received for the price paid.

Costs

Costs set the floor for the price that the company can charge. The company wants to charge a price that both covers all its costs for producing, distributing, and selling the product and delivers a fair rate of return for its effort and risk. A company's costs may be an important element in its pricing strategy. Many companies, such as Southwest Airlines, Wal-Mart, and Union Carbide, work to become the "low-cost producers" in their industries. Companies with lower costs can set lower prices that result in greater sales and profits.

Fixed costs

Costs that do not vary with production or sales level.

Variable costs

Costs that vary directly with the level of production.

Types of Costs.   A company's costs take two forms, fixed and variable. **Fixed costs** (also known as overhead) are costs that do not vary with production or sales level. For example, a company must pay each month's bills for rent, heat, interest, and executive salaries, whatever the company's output. **Variable costs** vary directly with the level of production. Each personal computer produced by Compaq involves the cost of computer chips, wires, plastic, packaging, and other inputs. These costs tend to be the same for each unit produced. They are called variable because their total varies with the number of units produced. **Total costs** are the sum of the fixed and variable costs for any given level of production. Management wants to charge a price that will at least cover the total production costs at a given level of production. The company must watch its costs carefully. If it costs the company more than competitors to produce and sell its product, the company will have to charge a higher price or make less profit, putting it at a competitive disadvantage.

Total costs

The sum of the fixed and variable costs for any given level of production.

Costs at Different Levels of Production. To price wisely, management needs to know how its costs vary with different levels of production. For example, suppose Texas Instruments (TI) has built a plant to produce 1,000 calculators per day. Figure 11.2A shows the typical short-run average cost curve (SRAC). It shows that the cost per calculator is high if TI's factory produces only a few per day. But as production moves up to 1,000 calculators per day, average cost falls. This is because fixed costs are spread over more units, with each one bearing a smaller share of the fixed cost. TI can try to produce more than 1,000 calculators per day, but average costs will increase because the plant becomes inefficient. Workers have to wait for machines, the machines break down more often, and workers get in each other's way.

If TI believed it could sell 2,000 calculators a day, it should consider building a larger plant. The plant would use more efficient machinery and work arrangements. Also, the unit cost of producing 2,000 calculators per day would be lower than the unit cost of producing 1,000 units per day, as shown in the long-run average cost (LRAC) curve (Figure 11.2B). In fact, a 3,000-capacity plant would even be more efficient, according to Figure 11.2B. But a 4,000-daily production plant would be less efficient because of increasing diseconomies of scale—too many workers to manage, paperwork slowing things down, and so on. Figure 11.2B shows that a 3,000-daily production plant is the best size to build if demand is strong enough to support this level of production.

Costs as a Function of Production Experience. Suppose TI runs a plant that produces 3,000 calculators per day. As TI gains experience in producing calculators, it learns how to do it better. Workers learn shortcuts and become more familiar with their equipment. With practice, the work becomes better organized, and TI finds better equipment and production processes. With higher volume, TI becomes more efficient and gains economies of scale. As a result, average cost tends to fall with accumulated production experience. This is shown in Figure 11.3.[10] Thus, the average cost of producing the first 100,000 calculators is $10 per calculator. When the company has produced the first 200,000 calculators, the average cost has fallen to $9. After its accumulated production experience doubles again to 400,000, the average cost is $7. This drop in the average cost with accumulated production experience is called the **experience curve** (or the **learning curve**).

If a downward-sloping experience curve exists, this is highly significant for the company. Not only will the company's unit production cost fall, but it will fall faster if the company makes and sells more during a given time period. But the market has to stand ready to buy the higher output. And to take advantage of the experience curve, TI must get a large market share early in the product's life cycle. This suggests the following pricing strategy: TI should price its calculators low; its sales will then increase, and its costs will decrease through gaining more experience, and then it can lower its prices further.

Experience curve (learning curve)

The drop in the average per-unit production cost that comes with accumulated production experience.

FIGURE 11.2

Cost per unit at different levels of production per period

A. Cost behavior in a fixed-size plant

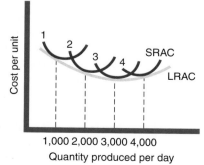

B. Cost behavior over different-size plants

FIGURE 11.3

Cost per unit as a function of accumulated production: The experience curve

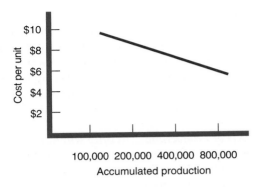

Some companies have built successful strategies around the experience curve. For example, Bausch & Lomb solidified its position in the soft contact lens market by using computerized lens design and steadily expanding its one Soflens plant. As a result, its market share climbed steadily to 65 percent. However, a single-minded focus on reducing costs and exploiting the experience curve will not always work. Experience-curve pricing carries some major risks. The aggressive pricing might give the product a cheap image. The strategy also assumes that competitors are weak and not willing to fight it out by meeting the company's price cuts. Finally, while the company is building volume under one technology, a competitor may find a lower-cost technology that lets it start at prices lower than the market leader's, who still operates on the old experience curve.

Organizational Considerations

Management must decide who within the organization should set prices. Companies handle pricing in a variety of ways. In small companies, prices are often set by top management rather than by the marketing or sales departments. In large companies, pricing is typically handled by divisional or product line managers. In industrial markets, salespeople may be allowed to negotiate with customers within certain price ranges. Even so, top management sets the pricing objectives and policies, and it often approves the prices proposed by lower-level management or salespeople.

In industries in which pricing is a key factor (aerospace, steel, railroads, oil companies), companies often have a pricing department to set the best prices or help others in setting them. This department reports to the marketing department or top management. Others who have an influence on pricing include sales managers, production managers, finance managers, and accountants.

External Factors Affecting Pricing Decisions

External factors that affect pricing decisions include the nature of the market and demand, competition, and other environmental elements.

The Market and Demand

Whereas costs set the lower limit of prices, the market and demand set the upper limit. Both consumer and industrial buyers balance the price of a product or service against the benefits of owning it. Thus, before setting prices, the marketer must understand the relationship between price and demand for its product. In this section, we explain how the price–demand relationship varies for different types of markets and how buyer perceptions of price affect the pricing decision. We then discuss methods for measuring the price–demand relationship.

Pricing in Different Types of Markets.   The seller's pricing freedom varies with different types of markets. Economists recognize four types of markets, each presenting a different pricing challenge.

Under *pure competition*, the market consists of many buyers and sellers trading in a uniform commodity such as wheat, copper, or financial securities. No single buyer or seller has much effect on the going market price. A seller cannot charge more than the going price, because buyers can obtain as much as they need at the going price. Nor would sellers charge less than the market price, because they can sell all they want at this price. If price and profits rise, new sellers can easily enter the market. In a purely competitive market, marketing research, product development, pricing, advertising, and sales promotion play little or no role. Thus, sellers in these markets do not spend much time on marketing strategy.

Under *monopolistic competition*, the market consists of many buyers and sellers who trade over a range of prices rather than a single market price. A range of prices occurs because sellers can differentiate their offers to buyers. Either the physical product can be varied in quality, features, or style, or the accompanying services can be varied. Buyers see differences in sellers' products and will pay different prices for them. Sellers try to develop differentiated offers for different customer segments and, in addition to price, freely use branding, advertising, and personal selling to set their offers apart. Thus, Kinko's differentiates its offer through strong branding and advertising, reducing the impact of price. Because there are many competitors in such markets, each firm is less affected by competitors' marketing pricing strategies than in oligopolistic markets.

Under *oligopolistic competition*, the market consists of a few sellers who are highly sensitive to each other's pricing and marketing strategies. The product can be uniform (steel, aluminum) or nonuniform (cars, computers). There are few sellers because it is difficult for new sellers to enter the market. Each seller is alert to competitors' strategies and moves. If a steel company slashes its price by 10 percent, buyers will quickly switch to this supplier. The other steelmakers must respond by lowering their prices or increasing their services. An oligopolist is never sure that it will gain anything permanent through a price cut. In contrast, if an oligopolist raises its price, its competitors might not follow this lead. The oligopolist then would have to retract its price increase or risk losing customers to competitors.

In a *pure monopoly*, the market consists of one seller. The seller may be a government monopoly (the U.S. Postal Service), a private regulated monopoly (a power company), or a private nonregulated monopoly (DuPont when it introduced nylon). Pricing is handled differently in each case. A government monopoly can pursue a variety of pricing objectives. It might set a price below cost because the product is important to buyers who cannot afford to pay full cost. Or the price might be set either to cover costs or to produce good revenue. It can even be set quite high to slow down consumption.

In a regulated monopoly, the government permits the company to set rates that will yield a "fair return," one that will let the company maintain and expand its operations as needed. Nonregulated monopolies are free to price at what the market will bear. However, they do not always charge the full price for a number of reasons: a desire not to attract competition, a desire to penetrate the market faster with a low price, or a fear of government regulation.

Monopolistic competition: Canadian pickle marketer Bick's sets its pickles apart from dozens of other brands using both price and nonprice factors.

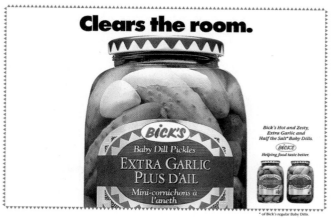

Consumer Perceptions of Price and Value.   In the end, the consumer will decide whether a product's price is right. Pricing decisions, like other marketing mix decisions, must be buyer oriented. When consumers buy a product, they exchange something of value (the price) to get something of value (the benefits of having or using the product). Effective, buyer-oriented pricing involves understanding how much value consumers place on the benefits they receive from the product and setting a price that fits this value.

A company often finds it hard to measure the values customers will attach to its product. For example, calculating the cost of ingredients in a meal at a fancy restaurant is relatively easy. But assigning a value to other satisfactions such as taste, environment, relaxation, conversation, and status is very hard. And these values will vary both for different consumers and in different situations. Still, consumers will use these values to evaluate a product's price. If customers perceive that the price is greater than the product's value, they will not buy the product. If consumers perceive that the price is below the product's value, they will buy it, but the seller loses profit opportunities.

Analyzing the Price–Demand Relationship.   Each price the company might charge will lead to a different level of demand. The relationship between the price charged and the resulting demand level is shown in the **demand curve** in Figure 11.4. The demand curve shows the number of units the market will buy in a given time period at different prices that might be charged. In the normal case, demand and price are inversely related; that is, the higher the price, the lower the demand. Thus, the company would sell less if it raised its price from P_1 to P_2. In short, consumers with limited budgets probably will buy less of something if its price is too high.

In the case of prestige goods, the demand curve sometimes slopes upward. Consumers think that higher prices mean more quality. For example, Gibson Guitar Corporation recently toyed with the idea of lowering its prices to compete more effectively with Japanese rivals such as Yamaha and Ibanez. To its surprise, Gibson found that its instruments didn't sell as well at lower prices. "We had an inverse [price-demand relationship]," noted Gibson's chief executive officer. "The more we charged, the more product we sold." At a time when other guitar manufacturers have chosen to build their instruments more quickly, cheaply, and in greater numbers, Gibson still promises guitars that "are made one-at-a-time, by hand. No shortcuts. No substitutions." It turns out that low prices simply aren't consistent with "Gibson's century-old tradition of creating investment-quality instruments that represent the highest standards of imaginative design and masterful craftsmanship."[11] Still, if the company charges too high a price, the level of demand will be lower.

Most companies try to measure their demand curves by estimating demand at different prices. The type of market makes a difference. In a monopoly, the demand curve shows the total market demand resulting from different prices. If the company faces competition, its demand at different prices will depend on whether competitors' prices stay constant or change with the company's own prices.

In measuring the price–demand relationship, the market researcher must not allow other factors affecting demand to vary. For example, if Sony increased its advertising at the same time that it lowered its television prices, we would not know how much of the increased demand was due to the lower prices and how much was due to the increased advertising. The same problem

Demand curve

A curve that shows the number of units the market will buy in a given time period, at different prices that might be charged.

FIGURE 11.4
Demand curves

A. Inelastic demand   B. Elastic demand

The demand curve some-times slopes upward: Gibson was surprised to learn that its high-quality instruments didn't sell as well at lower prices.

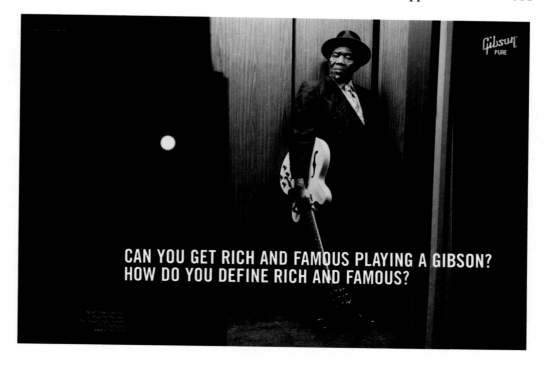

arises if a holiday weekend occurs when the lower price is set—more gift giving over the holidays causes people to buy more televisions. Economists show the impact of nonprice factors on demand through shifts in the demand curve rather than movements along it.

Price elasticity

A measure of the sensitivity of demand to changes in price.

Price Elasticity of Demand.   Marketers also need to know **price elasticity**—how responsive demand will be to a change in price. Consider the two demand curves in Figure 11.4. In Figure 11.4A, a price increase from P_1 to P_2 leads to a relatively small drop in demand from Q'_1 to Q'_2. In Figure 11.4B, however, the same price increase leads to a large drop in demand from Q'_1 to Q'_2. If demand hardly changes with a small change in price, we say the demand is *inelastic*. If demand changes greatly, we say the demand is *elastic*. The price elasticity of demand is given by the following formula:

$$\text{Price Elasticity of Demand} = \frac{\text{\% Change in Quantity Demanded}}{\text{\% Change in Price}}$$

Suppose demand falls by 10 percent when a seller raises its price by 2 percent. Price elasticity of demand is therefore −5 (the minus sign confirms the inverse relation between price and demand) and demand is elastic. If demand falls by 2 percent with a 2 percent increase in price, then elasticity is −1. In this case, the seller's total revenue stays the same: The seller sells fewer items but at a higher price that preserves the same total revenue. If demand falls by 1 percent when price is increased by 2 percent, then elasticity is −1/2 and demand is inelastic. The less elastic the demand, the more it pays for the seller to raise the price.

What determines the price elasticity of demand? Buyers are less price sensitive when the product they are buying is unique or when it is high in quality, prestige, or exclusiveness. They are also less price sensitive when substitute products are hard to find or when they cannot easily compare the quality of substitutes. Finally, buyers are less price sensitive when the total expenditure for a product is low relative to their income or when the cost is shared by another party.[12]

If demand is elastic rather than inelastic, sellers will consider lowering their price. A lower price will produce more total revenue. This practice makes sense as long as the extra costs of producing and selling more do not exceed the extra revenue. At the same time, most firms want to avoid pricing that turns their products into commodities. In recent years, forces such as deregulation and the instant price comparisons afforded by the Internet and other technologies have increased consumer price sensitivity, turning products ranging from telephones and computers to new automobiles into commodities in consumers' eyes. Marketers need to work harder than ever to differentiate their offerings when a dozen competitors are selling virtually the same product at a comparable or lower price. More than ever, companies need to understand the price sensitivity of their customers and prospects and the trade-offs people are willing to make between price and product characteristics. In the words of marketing consultant Kevin Clancy, those who target only the price sensitive are "leaving money on the table."

Even in the energy marketplace, where you would think that a kilowatt is a kilowatt is a kilowatt, some utility companies are beginning to wake up to this fact. They are differentiating their power, branding it, and marketing it, even if it means higher prices. For example, Green Mountain Energy (GME) targets consumers who are not only concerned with the environment but are also willing to support their attitudes with dollars. Offering electricity made from cleaner sources such as water, wind, and natural gas, GME positions itself as "the nation's leading brand of cleaner energy." By providing energy from clean, renewable sources and developing products and services that help consumers protect the environment, GME completes successfully against "cheaper" brands that focus on more price-sensitive consumers. "Is helping to clean the air worth the price of a movie?" the company asks. "That's about how much extra it costs each month when you choose cleaner, Green Mountain Energy electricity."[13]

Competitors' Costs, Prices, and Offers

Another external factor affecting the company's pricing decisions is competitors' costs and prices and possible competitor reactions to the company's own pricing moves. A consumer who is considering the purchase of a Canon camera will evaluate Canon's price and value against the prices and values of comparable products made by Nikon, Minolta, Pentax, and others. In addition, the company's pricing strategy may affect the nature of the competition it faces. If Canon follows a high-price, high-margin strategy, it may attract competition. A low-price, low-margin strategy, however, may stop competitors or drive them out of the market.

Canon needs to benchmark its costs against its competitors' costs to learn whether it is operating at a cost advantage or disadvantage. It also needs to learn the price and quality of each com-

By pledging leadership in providing clean, renewable energy sources and helping consumers protect the environment, GME completes successfully against "cheaper" brands that focused on more price-sensitive consumers.

petitor's offer. Once Canon is aware of competitors' prices and offers, it can use them as a starting point for its own pricing. If Canon's cameras are similar to Nikon's, it will have to price close to Nikon or lose sales. If Canon's cameras are not as good as Nikon's, the firm will not be able to charge as much. If Canon's products are better than Nikon's, it can charge more. Basically, Canon will use price to position its offer relative to the competition.

Other External Factors

When setting prices, the company also must consider other factors in its external environment. *Economic conditions* can have a strong impact on the firm's pricing strategies. Economic factors such as boom or recession, inflation, and interest rates affect pricing decisions because they affect both the costs of producing a product and consumer perceptions of the product's price and value. The company must also consider what impact its prices will have on other parties in its environment. How will *resellers* react to various prices? The company should set prices that give resellers a fair profit, encourage their support, and help them to sell the product effectively. The *government* is another important external influence on pricing decisions. Finally, *social concerns* may have to be taken into account. In setting prices, a company's short-term sales, market share, and profit goals may have to be tempered by broader societal considerations.

General Pricing Approaches

The price the company charges will be somewhere between one that is too low to produce a profit and one that is too high to produce any demand. Figure 11.5 summarizes the major considerations in setting price. Product costs set a floor to the price; consumer perceptions of the product's value set the ceiling. The company must consider competitors' prices and other external and internal factors to find the best price between these two extremes.

Companies set prices by selecting a general pricing approach that includes one or more of these three sets of factors. We will examine the following approaches: the *cost-based approach* (cost-plus pricing, break-even analysis, and target profit pricing), the *buyer-based approach* (value-based pricing), and the *competition-based approach* (going-rate and sealed-bid pricing).

Cost-Based Pricing

Cost-plus pricing
Adding a standard markup to the cost of the product.

The simplest pricing method is **cost-plus pricing**—adding a standard markup to the cost of the product. Construction companies, for example, submit job bids by estimating the total project cost and adding a standard markup for profit. Lawyers, accountants, and other professionals typically price by adding a standard markup to their costs. Some sellers tell their customers they will charge cost plus a specified markup; for example, aerospace companies price this way to the government.

To illustrate markup pricing, suppose a toaster manufacturer had the following costs and expected sales:

Variable cost	$10
Fixed costs	$300,000
Expected unit sales	50,000

FIGURE 11.5

Major considerations in setting price

Then the manufacturer's cost per toaster is given by:

$$\text{Unit Cost} = \text{Variable Cost} + \frac{\text{Fixed Costs}}{\text{Unit Sales}} = \$10 + \frac{\$300,000}{50,000} = \$16$$

Now suppose the manufacturer wants to earn a 20 percent markup on sales. The manufacturer's markup price is given by:[14]

$$\text{Markup Price} = \frac{\text{Unit Cost}}{1 - \text{Desired Return on Sales}} = \frac{\$16}{1 - .2} = \$20$$

The manufacturer would charge dealers $20 a toaster and make a profit of $4 per unit. The dealers, in turn, will mark up the toaster. If dealers want to earn 50 percent on sales price, they will mark up the toaster to $40 ($20 + 50% of $40). This number is equivalent to a *markup on cost* of 100 percent ($20/$20).

Does using standard markups to set prices make sense? Generally, no. Any pricing method that ignores demand and competitor prices is not likely to lead to the best price. Suppose the toaster manufacturer charged $20 but sold only 30,000 toasters instead of 50,000. Then the unit cost would have been higher because the fixed costs are spread over fewer units, and the realized percentage markup on sales would have been lower. Markup pricing works only if that price actually brings in the expected level of sales.

Still, markup pricing remains popular for many reasons. First, sellers are more certain about costs than about demand. By tying the price to cost, sellers simplify pricing—they do not have to make frequent adjustments as demand changes. Second, when all firms in the industry use this pricing method, prices tend to be similar and price competition is thus minimized. Third, many people feel that cost-plus pricing is fairer to both buyers and sellers. Sellers earn a fair return on their investment but do not take advantage of buyers when buyers' demand becomes great.

Break-Even Analysis and Target Profit Pricing

Break-even pricing (target profit pricing)

Setting price to break even on the costs of making and marketing a product; or setting price to make a target profit.

Another cost-oriented pricing approach is **break-even pricing,** or a variation called **target profit pricing.** The firm tries to determine the price at which it will break even or make the target profit it is seeking. Such pricing is used by General Motors, which prices its automobiles to achieve a 15 to 20 percent profit on its investment. This pricing method is also used by public utilities, which are constrained to make a fair return on their investment.

Target pricing uses the concept of a *break-even chart,* which shows the total cost and total revenue expected at different sales volume levels. Figure 11.6 shows a break-even chart for the toaster manufacturer discussed here. Fixed costs are $300,000 regardless of sales volume. Variable costs are added to fixed costs to form total costs, which rise with volume. The total revenue curve starts at zero and rises with each unit sold. The slope of the total revenue curve reflects the price of $20 per unit.

FIGURE 11.6
Break-even chart for determining target price

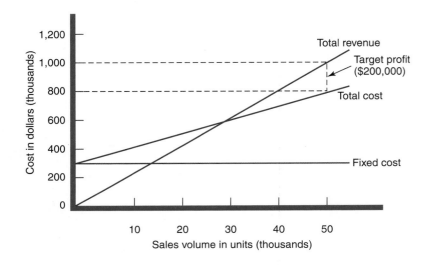

The total revenue and total cost curves cross at 30,000 units. This is the *break-even volume*. At $20, the company must sell at least 30,000 units to break even; that is, for total revenue to cover total cost. Break-even volume can be calculated using the following formula:

$$\text{Break-Even Volume} = \frac{\text{Fixed Cost}}{\text{Price} - \text{Variable Cost}} = \frac{\$300,000}{\$20 - \$10} = \$30,000$$

If the company wants to make a target profit, it must sell more than 30,000 units at $20 each. Suppose the toaster manufacturer has invested $1,000,000 in the business and wants to set price to earn a 20 percent return, or $200,000. In that case, it must sell at least 50,000 units at $20 each. If the company charges a higher price, it will not need to sell as many toasters to achieve its target return. But the market may not buy even this lower volume at the higher price. Much depends on the price elasticity and competitors' prices.

The manufacturer should consider different prices and estimate break-even volumes, probable demand, and profits for each. This is done in Table 11.1. The table shows that as price increases, break-even volume drops (column 2). But as price increases, demand for the toasters also falls off (column 3). At the $14 price, because the manufacturer clears only $4 per toaster ($14 less $10 in variable costs), it must sell a very high volume to break even. Even though the low price attracts many buyers, demand still falls below the high break-even point, and the manufacturer loses money. At the other extreme, with a $22 price, the manufacturer clears $12 per toaster and must sell only 25,000 units to break even. But at this high price, consumers buy too few toasters, and profits are negative. The table shows that a price of $18 yields the highest profits. Note that none of the prices produce the manufacturer's target profit of $200,000. To achieve this target return, the manufacturer will have to search for ways to lower fixed or variable costs, thus lowering the break-even volume.

Value-Based Pricing

An increasing number of companies are basing their prices on the product's perceived value. **Value-based pricing** uses buyers' perceptions of value, not the seller's cost, as the key to pricing. Value-based pricing means that the marketer cannot design a product and marketing program and then set the price. Price is considered along with the other marketing mix variables *before* the marketing program is set.

Figure 11.7 compares cost-based pricing with value-based pricing. Cost-based pricing is product driven. The company designs what it considers to be a good product, totals the costs of making the product, and sets a price that covers costs plus a target profit. Marketing must then convince buyers that the product's value at that price justifies its purchase. If the price turns out to be too high, the company must settle for lower markups or lower sales, both resulting in disappointing profits.

Value-based pricing reverses this process. The company sets its target price based on customer perceptions of the product value. The targeted value and price then drive decisions about product design and what costs can be incurred. As a result, pricing begins with analyzing consumer needs and value perceptions, and price is set to match consumers' perceived value. It's important to remember that "good value" is not the same as "low price." For example, Parker sells

Value-based pricing
Setting price based on buyers' perceptions of value rather than on the seller's cost.

TABLE 11.1		**BREAK-EVEN VOLUME AND PROFITS AT DIFFERENT PRICES**			
(1) Price	**(2)** Unit Demand Needed to Break Even	**(3)** Expected Unit Demand at Given Price	**(4)** Total Revenue (1) × (3)	**(5)** Total Costs*	**(6)** Profit (4) − (5)
$14	75,000	71,000	$ 994,000	$1,010,000	−$ 16,000
16	50,000	67,000	1,072,000	970,000	102,000
18	37,500	60,000	1,080,000	900,000	180,000
20	30,000	42,000	840,000	720,000	120,000
22	25,000	23,000	506,000	530,000	−24,000

* Assumes fixed costs of $300,000 and constant unit variable costs of $10.

FIGURE 11.7

Cost-based versus value-based pricing

Source: Thomas T. Nagle and Reed K. Holden, *The Strategy and Tactics of Pricing,* 3rd ed. (Upper Saddle River, N.J.: Prentice Hall, 2002), p. 4.

pens priced as high as $3,500. A less expensive pen might write as well, but some consumers place great value on the intangibles they receive from a fine writing instrument.

A company using value-based pricing must find out what value buyers assign to different competitive offers. However, measuring perceived value can be difficult. Sometimes, companies ask consumers how much they would pay for a basic product and for each benefit added to the offer. Or a company might conduct experiments to test the perceived value of different product offers. If the seller charges more than the buyers' perceived value, the company's sales will suffer. Many companies overprice their products, and their products sell poorly. Other companies underprice. Underpriced products sell very well, but they produce less revenue than they would have if price were raised to the perceived-value level.

During the past decade, marketers have noted a fundamental shift in consumer attitudes toward price and quality. Many companies have changed their pricing approaches to bring them into line with changing economic conditions and consumer price perceptions. According to Jack Welch, former CEO of General Electric, "The value decade is upon us. If you can't sell a top-quality product at the world's best price, you're going to be out of the game. . . . The best way to hold your customers is to constantly figure out how to give them more for less."[15]

Perceived value: A less-expensive pen might write as well, but some consumers will pay much more for the intangibles. This Parker model runs $185. Others are priced as high as $3,500.

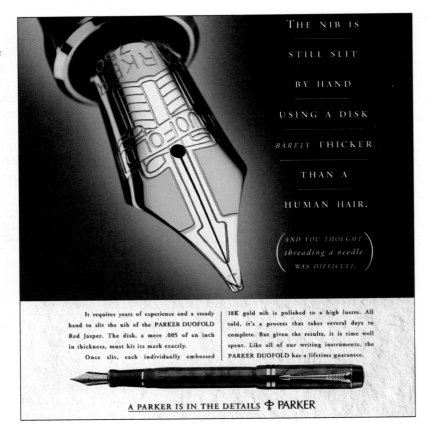

Value pricing

Offering just the right combination of quality and good service at a fair price.

Thus, more and more, marketers have adopted **value pricing** strategies—offering just the right combination of quality and good service at a fair price. In many cases, this has involved the introduction of less expensive versions of established, brand name products. Campbell introduced its Great Starts Budget frozen-food line, Holiday Inn opened several Holiday Express budget hotels, Revlon's Charles of the Ritz offered the Express Bar collection of affordable cosmetics, and fast-food restaurants such as Taco Bell and McDonald's offered "value menus." In other cases, value pricing has involved redesigning existing brands in order to offer more quality for a given price or the same quality for less.

In many business-to-business marketing situations, the pricing challenge is to find ways to maintain the company's *pricing power*—its power to maintain or even raise prices without losing market share. To retain pricing power—to escape price competition and to justify higher prices and margins—a firm must retain or build the value of its marketing offer. This is especially true for suppliers of commodity products, which are characterized by little differentiation and intense price competition. In such cases, many companies adopt *value-added* strategies. Rather than cutting prices to match competitors, they attach value-added services to differentiate their offers and thus support higher margins (see Real Marketing 11.2). "Even in today's economic environment, it's not about price," says a pricing expert. "It's about keeping customers loyal by providing service they can't find anywhere else."[16]

An important type of value pricing at the retail level is *everyday low pricing (EDLP)*. EDLP involves charging a constant, everyday low price with few or no temporary price discounts. In contrast, *high–low pricing* involves charging higher prices on an everyday basis but running frequent promotions to lower prices temporarily on selected items below the EDLP level. In recent years, high–low pricing has given way to EDLP in retail settings ranging from Saturn car dealerships to upscale department stores such as Nordstrom.

Retailers adopt EDLP for many reasons, the most important of which is that constant sales and promotions are costly and have eroded consumer confidence in the credibility of everyday shelf prices. Consumers also have less time and patience for such time-honored traditions as watching for supermarket specials and clipping coupons.

The king of EDLP is Wal-Mart, which practically defined the concept. Except for a few sale items every month, Wal-Mart promises everyday low prices on everything it sells. In contrast, Kmart's recent attempts to match Wal-Mart's EDLP strategy failed. To offer everyday low prices, a company must first have everyday low costs. Wal-Mart's EDLP strategy works well because its expenses are only 15 percent of sales. However, because Kmart's costs are much higher, it could not make money at the lower prices and quickly abandoned the attempt.[17]

Competition-Based Pricing

Competition-based pricing

Setting prices based on the prices that competitors charge for similar products.

Consumers will base their judgments of a product's value on the prices that competitors charge for similar products. One form of **competition-based pricing** is *going-rate pricing*, in which a firm bases its price largely on competitors' prices, with less attention paid to its own costs or to demand. The firm might charge the same as, more than, or less than its major competitors. In oligopolistic industries that sell a commodity such as steel, paper, or fertilizer, firms normally charge the same price. The smaller firms follow the leader: They change their prices when the market leader's prices change, rather than when their own demand or costs change. Some firms may charge a bit more or less, but they hold the amount of difference constant. Thus, minor gasoline retailers usually charge a few cents less than the major oil companies, without letting the difference increase or decrease.

Going-rate pricing is quite popular. When demand elasticity is hard to measure, firms feel that the going price represents the collective wisdom of the industry concerning the price that will yield a fair return. They also feel that holding to the going price will prevent harmful price wars.

Competition-based pricing is also used when firms *bid* for jobs. Using *sealed-bid pricing*, a firm bases its price on how it thinks competitors will price rather than on its own costs or on the demand. The firm wants to win a contract, and winning the contract requires pricing less than other firms. Yet the firm cannot set its price below a certain level. It cannot price below cost without harming its position. In contrast, the higher the company sets its price above its costs, the lower its chance of getting the contract.

real marketing 11.2

Pricing Power: The Value of Value Added

When a company finds its major competitors offering a similar product at a lower price, the natural tendency is to try to match or beat that price. Although the idea of undercutting competitor's prices and watching customers flock to you is tempting, there are dangers. Successive rounds of price-cutting can lead to price wars that erode the profit margins of all competitors in an industry. Or worse, discounting a product can cheapen it in the minds of customers, greatly reducing the seller's power to maintain profitable prices in the long term. "It ends up being a losing battle," notes one marketing executive. "You focus away from quality, service, prestige—the things brands are all about."

So, how can a company keep its pricing power when a competitor undercuts its price? Often, the best strategy is not to price

But what if the company is operating in a "commodity" business, in which the products of all competitors seem pretty much alike? In such cases, the company must find ways to "decommoditize" its products—to create superior value for customers. It can do this by developing value-added features and services that differentiate its offer and justify higher prices and margins. Here are some examples of how suppliers are using value-added features and services to give them a competitive edge:

- *Caterpillar:* Caterpillar is a master at charging premium prices for its heavy construction and mining equipment and convincing customers that its products and service justify every additional cent— or, rather, the extra tens of thousands of dollars. Caterpillar typically reaps a 20 to

dealer explains that, even at the higher price, Cat offers the best value. Caterpillar equipment is designed with modular componentry that can be removed and repaired quickly, minimizing machine downtime. Caterpillar dealers carry an extensive parts inventory and guarantee delivery within 48 hours anywhere in the world, again minimizing downtime. Cat's products are designed to be rebuilt, providing a "second life" that competitors cannot match. As a result, Caterpillar used-equipment prices are often 20 percent to 30 percent higher. In all, the dealer explains, even at the higher initial price, Caterpillar equipment delivers the lowest total cost per cubic yard of earth moved, ton of coal uncovered, or mile of road graded over the life of the product—guaranteed! Most customers seem to agree with Caterpillar's value proposition—the company dominates its markets, with a more than 40 percent worldwide market share.

- *Pioneer Hi-Bred International:* A major supplier of corn seed and other agricultural products often thought of as commodities, DuPont subsidiary Pioneer Hi-Bred hardly acts like a commodity supplier. Its patented hybrid seeds yield 10 percent more corn than competitors' seeds. Beyond producing a superior product, Pioneer Hi-Bred provides a bundle of value-added services. For example, it equips its sales representatives with notebook computers that allow them to provide farmers with customized information and advice. The rep can plug in the type of hybrid that a farmer is using, along with information about pricing, acreage, and yield characteristics, then advise the farmer on how to do a better job of farm management. The reps can also supply farmers with everything from agricultural research reports to assistance in comparison shopping. Pioneer Hi-Bred also offers farmers crop insurance, financing, and marketing services. Backing its claim "We believe in customer success" with superior products and value-added services gives Pioneer Hi-Bred plenty of pricing power. Despite charging a signifi-

Value added: Caterpillar offers its dealers a wide range of value-added services—from guaranteed parts delivery to investment management advice and equipment training. Such added value supports a higher price.

below the competitor, but rather to price above and convince customers that the product is worth it. The company should ask, "What is the value of the product to the customer?" then stand up for what the product is worth. In this way, the company shifts the focus from price to value.

30 percent price premium over competitors—that can amount to an extra $200,000 or more on one of those huge yellow million-dollar dump trucks. When a large potential customer says, "I can get it for less from a competitor," rather than discounting the price, the Caterpillar

cant price premium—or perhaps because of it—the company's share of the North American corn market has grown from 35 percent during the mid-1980s to its current level of 44 percent.

- *Jefferson Smurfit Corporation:* When General Electric expanded a no-frost refrigerator line in 1990, it needed more shipping boxes, and fast. Jefferson Smurfit Corporation, a $4.5 billion packaging supplier, assigned a coordinator to juggle production from three of its plants—and sometimes even divert product intended for other customers—to keep GE's Decatur plant humming. This kind of value-added hustling helped Jefferson Smurfit win the GE appliance unit's "Distinguished Supplier Award." It has also sheltered Smurfit from the bruising struggle of competing only on price. "Today, it's not just getting the best price but getting the best value—and there are a lot of pieces to value," says a vice president for procurement at Emerson Electric Company, a major Smurfit customer that has cut its supplier count by 65 percent.

- *Microsystems Engineering Company:* "The way we sell on value is by differentiating ourselves," says Mark Beckman, director of sales for Microsystems, a software company. "My product is twice as much as my nearest competitor's, but we sell as much as—if not more than—our competition." Rather than getting into price wars, Microsystems adds value to its products by adding new components and services. "[Customers] get more for their money," says Beckman. "We get the price because we understand what people want." When customers see the extra value, price becomes secondary. Ultimately, Beckman asserts, "let the customer decide whether the price you're charging is worth all the things they're getting." What if the answer is no? Beckman would suggest that dropping price is the last thing you want to do. Instead, look to the value of value added.

Sources: Jim Morgan, "Value Added: From Cliché to the Real Thing," *Purchasing,* April 3, 1997, pp. 59–61; James E. Ellis, "There's Even a Science to Selling Boxes," *Business Week,* August 3, 1992, pp. 51–52; John Jesitus, "Close Connections," *Industry Week,* October 6, 1997, pp. 28–34; James C. Anderson and James A. Narus, "Business Marketing: Understand What Customers Value," *Harvard Business Review,* November–December 1998, pp. 53–65; Tom Nagle, "How to Pull It Off," *Across the Board,* March 1999, pp. 53–56; Robert B. Tucker, "Adding Value Profitably," *American Salesman,* April 2001, pp. 17–20; Erin Stout, "Keep Them Coming Back for More," *Sales & Marketing Management,* February 2002, pp. 51–52; and information accessed online at www.pioneer.com, July 2002.

LOOKING BACK: REVIEWING THE CONCEPTS

Price can be defined narrowly as the amount of money charged for a product or service, or more broadly, as the sum of the values that consumers exchange for the benefits of having and using the product or service. Despite the increased role of nonprice factors in the modern marketing process, price remains an important element in the marketing mix. It is the only element in the marketing mix that produces revenue; all other elements represent costs. Price is also one of the most flexible elements of the marketing mix. Unlike product features and channel commitments, price can be raised or lowered quickly. Even so, many companies are not good at handling pricing—pricing decisions and price competition are major problems for many marketing executives. Pricing problems often arise because prices are too cost oriented, not revised frequently enough to reflect market changes, not consistent with the rest of the marketing mix, or not varied enough for differing products, market segments, and purchase occasions.

1. Identify and define the internal factors affecting a firm's pricing decisions.

Many internal factors influence the company's pricing decisions, including the firm's *marketing objectives, marketing mix strategy, costs,* and *organization for pricing.* The pricing strategy is largely determined by the company's *target market* and *positioning objectives.* Pricing decisions affect and are affected by product design, distribution, and promotion decisions. Therefore, pricing strategies must be carefully coordinated with the other marketing mix variables when designing the marketing program.

Costs set the floor for the company's price—the price must cover all the costs of making and selling the product, plus a fair rate of return. Common pricing objectives include survival, current profit maximization, market share leadership, and product quality leadership.

In order to coordinate pricing goals and decisions, management must decide who within the organization is responsible for setting price. In large companies, some pricing authority may be delegated to lower-level managers and salespeople, but top management usually sets pricing policies and approves proposed prices. Production, finance, and accounting managers also influence pricing decisions.

2. Identify and define the external factors affecting pricing decisions, including the impact of consumer perceptions of price and value.

External factors that influence pricing decisions include the nature of the *market and demand; competitors' prices and offers;* and factors such as the *economy, reseller needs,* and *government actions.* The seller's pricing freedom varies with different types of markets. Pricing is especially challenging in markets characterized by monopolistic competition or oligopoly.

Ultimately, the consumer decides whether the company has set the right price. The consumer weighs the price against the perceived values of using the product—if the price exceeds the sum of the values, consumers will not buy the product. The more *inelastic* the demand, the higher the company can set its price. Therefore, *demand* and *consumer value perceptions* set the ceiling for prices. Consumers differ in the values they assign to different product features, and marketers often vary their pricing strategies for different price segments. When assessing the market and demand, the company estimates the demand curve, which shows the probable quantity purchased per period at alternative price levels. Consumers also compare a product's price to the prices of *competitors*' products. As a result, a company must learn the price and quality of competitors' offers and use them as a starting point for its own pricing.

3. Contrast the three general approaches to setting prices.
A company can select one or a combination of three general pricing approaches: the *cost-based approach* (cost-plus pricing, break-even analysis, and target profit pricing), the *value-based approach,* and the *competition-based approach.* Cost-based pricing sets prices based on the seller's cost structure, whereas value-based pricing relies on consumer perceptions of value to drive pricing decisions. Competition-based pricing has two major variations: In *going-rate pricing,* the firm sets prices based on what competitors are charging. *Sealed-bid pricing* forces the company to set prices based on what they think the competition will charge.

REVIEWING THE KEY TERMS

Break-even pricing (target profit pricing) 358
Competition-based pricing 361
Cost-plus pricing 357
Demand curve 354
Dynamic pricing 345

Experience curve (learning curve) 351
Fixed costs 350
Price 345
Price elasticity 355
Target costing 348

Total costs 351
Value-based pricing 359
Value pricing 361
Variable costs 350

DISCUSSING THE CONCEPTS

1. Explain the concept of dynamic pricing. How is dynamic pricing used on the Internet?
2. Assume you are the vice president for financial affairs at a major college or university. For the past three years, enrollments have declined steadily, at a rate of about 10 percent per year. You are under great pressure to raise tuition to compensate for the falling revenues. However, you suspect that raising tuition might only make matters worse. What internal and external pricing factors should you consider before you make your decision? Explain.
3. List the typical pricing objectives, outlined in the chapter. Which of these objectives do you believe (a) is the most commonly used; (b) is the most difficult to achieve; (c) has the greatest potential for long-term growth of the organization; and (d) is most likely to be employed by an e-commerce company? Explain.
4. Explain the concept of an experience curve (or learning curve) as it applies to pricing (a) a Texas Instruments

calculator (www.ti.com) (b) a Toyota Camry automobile (www.toyota.com) and (c) Papa John's home pizza-delivery service (www.papajohns.com).
5. The seller's pricing freedom varies with the type of market. Identify the four types of markets economists generally recognize and characterize the pricing challenges facing each one.
6. List and briefly discuss the external factors affecting pricing decisions.
7. As a newly appointed director of marketing for a small sports car manufacturing firm, you believe it is time to change the firm's pricing philosophy. In the past, the company used what might be described as cost-based pricing. You believe that a value-based pricing approach is superior. Write a short memo making the case for value-based pricing.
8. Describe competition-based pricing. Why is it popular? Under what circumstances is it used?

APPLYING THE CONCEPTS

1. Conduct a pricing survey of several gasoline stations in your area. Check prices at stations near exit ramps off a major highway, at a local commercial strip, at a convenience store, and at a truck stop. Record the brand of gasoline, prices of regular and premium grades, type of location, distance to the nearest competitor, and whether the station is multipurpose (includes a food store or fast-food facility).
   a. What patterns do you detect for the pricing of gasoline at the various outlets?
   b. Do these stations appear to be using cost-based, buyer-based, or competition-based pricing? What internal and external factors are important to consider when choosing a pricing strategy in this industry?
   c. Talk to several of the station operators. What factors do they think usually trigger a price war? How much control do the station operators have over pricing?

2. Wal-Mart is the king of everyday low pricing (EDLP). EDLP has allowed Wal-Mart and other value-oriented retailers to maintain steady growth even in a down economy. In fact, EDLP is overtaking high-low pricing as the pricing strategy of choice. And the spectrum of companies embracing EDLP is growing. For example, car dealerships such as Saturn and upscale department stores such as Nordstrom use EDLP to attract and keep customers. (For more details on EDLP, see www.walmart.com, www.saturn.com, and www.nordstrom.com).
   a. After reviewing material in the chapter, explain the EDLP pricing strategy. What are the advantages of the strategy? What are the disadvantages?
   b. Why is EDLP classified as a value-pricing strategy? Does EDLP make sense for every retailer? List some types of retailers that might not benefit from the strategy.

DIGITAL CONNECTIONS

PRICING CONNECTIONS BY FOCUSING ON THE ELASTICITY OF DEMAND

Airline tickets are a price-driven market for most customers. Many people will trade off nonstop flights, preferred travel times, and choice of airline to get the lowest possible price. To achieve economies of scale, airlines offer advance purchase discounts to make sure they fill as many seats as possible. Demand tends to be very elastic, as evidenced by high ticket sales during fare wars. In this exercise we are going to plan a flight online in order to observe the price elasticity in this industry.

Using Expedia (www.expedia.com) or Travelocity (www.travelocity.com), a consumer can book flights, reserve hotel rooms, and rent cars online. These sites specialize in aiding the consumer in finding and then obtaining low-price travel and hotel accommodations. Register a new account with either service; it's free. Price a round-trip flight from New York (any airport) to San Francisco (any airport), traveling coach class,

departing tomorrow, and returning the day after you arrive. Record the results of your search in the table below. Then search again, altering the criteria to complete the table. Then answer the following questions.

FOR DISCUSSION

1. What can you conclude from this exercise about the elasticity of demand for coach fares? For first-class fares?
2. Do you think the higher price for a first-class seat is justified by higher costs incurred in servicing the first-class traveler?
3. How do the prices differ from one-day versus one-week trips? How can you explain this?
4. For first class, do the prices differ for trips departing tomorrow versus next month? Why or why not?
5. Which of the pricing approach(es) mentioned in this chapter might the airlines be using? Explain your answer.

Class	Departing	Returning After	Airline and Departure Flight	Price
Coach	Tomorrow	1 day		
Coach	Tomorrow	1 week		
Coach	Next month	1 day		
Coach	Next month	1 week		
First	Tomorrow	1 day		
First	Tomorrow	1 week		
First	Next month	1 day		
First	Next month	1 week		

Metreo: Automating Pricing?

Marketers are always looking for ways to hone the pricing process and avoid leaving money on the table. Metreo's software helps companies increase profit margins by setting prices, evaluating customer sales requests, and ensuring that every deal is in line with marketing objectives. Compaq uses the software to enable representatives at its call centers to quickly respond to purchase requests from small businesses interested in Compaq's products. Metreo also works with DHL, the worldwide leader in air express service, to integrate customer information into the company's pricing process. But can the pricing process be fully automated? Should it be?

After viewing the Metreo video, visit the Metreo Web site (www.metreo.com) to learn more about Metreo's software.

Then answer the following questions about product pricing approaches:

1. Does Metreo's software encourage a cost-based or value-based pricing approach? What internal and external factors does the software take into account when assessing offers and analyzing prices?
2. In what ways does Metreo's approach mimic dynamic pricing? In what ways does the approach differ?
3. Can the pricing process be fully automated? How can Metreo's software improve the pricing process? What limitations does automation present?

DVDs: Lieberfarbian Economics?

Here's a challenge: Let's compare prices for DVDs at Target, Wal-Mart, Best Buy, and Blockbuster. What are you likely to find?

Target: Carries the most limited selection of DVDs in two price ranges, $9.44 and $14.44. The $9.44 price range contains older movies (1950s) and more recent but not so popular ones such as *Snow White* (not the Disney version), *Requiem, Flatliners,* and *Crouching Tiger, Hidden Dragon.* The $14.44 price range includes popular movies and recent movies such as *Coming to America, Big Daddy, RunAway Bride,* and *Thin Red Line.*

Wal-Mart: Carries a much wider selection and wider range of prices. The least expensive are $9.44 and include old action films such as *A Fist Full of Dollars* and *The Great Escape.* There are some more recent movies in that price range, such as *Stigmata* and *HeartBreakers,* movies that weren't too popular at the box office or that Wal-Mart thinks are moving too slowly. For $13.72, you can buy movies such as *The Patriot, A Knight's Tale,* and *Men of Honor.* At $14.88, you can get *The Yards, The Horse Whisperer,* and *The Hand That Rocks the Cradle.* For $18.44, you could buy *A Bug's Life, Original Sin, Ocean's 11, Interview with the Vampire,* and *Crouching Tiger, Hidden Dragon.* At a price of $19.95 comes *Training Day, John Q,* or *Vanilla Sky* (very recent movies). The disc of *Tarzan and Jane* is $19.95, whereas the fancy boxed set of *Pearl Harbor* is $28.88.

Best Buy: Carries the largest selection and widest range of prices. At the bottom of the range are DVDs for $5.99, which include *Home Fries, The Bachelor, Drop Dead Gorgeous,* and *Fort Apache, The Bronx.* At $9.99 you get *Above the Law;* $14.99 would purchase the long version of the old John Wayne movie *The Alamo* or *Anaconda* or *The Art of War.* For $19.99 (their widest selection), you could buy *Harry Potter, The Mothman Prophecies, From Hell, The Others, Shallow Hal,* or *Ocean's 11,* among others. The fancy boxed set of *Pearl Harbor* is $29.99, while *Apocalypse Now* is $26.99. The 60th Anniversary Set of *Pearl Harbor* is $39.99 and the plain two-disc set is $22.99. For *Buffy, the Vampire Slayer* fans, there is a six-disc set (maybe all the Buffy episodes?) for $43.99.

Blockbuster: Carries a selection smaller that Wal-Mart's but bigger than Target's. The most popular price range is $19.99 and includes popular, fairly recent movies such as *Ocean's 11, Chocolat, Pay It Forward, Harry Potter, The Others,* and *Proof of Life.* At $24.99, you can buy *Notting Hill* or one of my favorites, *Jay and Silent Bob Strike Back.* Moderately old movies such as *Rising Sun* and *Thelma and Louise* are $9.99. Goldies such as *Casablanca* are $16.99, and more recent popular movies such as *Corelli's Mandolin* are $21.99. Older movies (by a couple of years), such as *Original Sin* and *Cast Away,* are $22.99.

Why such a wide range of assortments and prices? The answer is a tangled web of corporate pricing strategies, the speed of technological product life cycles, and consumer motivations.

The various companies involved in producing and distributing movies have different pricing objectives. Usually, production studios want to maintain prices by controlling distribution. That's why VHS tapes were usually rented out first, with purchase occurring later. The studios wanted to maximize revenue for distribution to theaters, then for rentals, and finally for home purchase. Rental companies, such as Blockbuster, found that customers sometimes made five trips to the store and still failed to rent "hot" movies, because studios allowed each rental store to stock only a few copies of the VHS tapes. To motivate studios to give them more copies of the tapes, rental companies initiated a revenue-sharing plan, giving the studios part of the rental revenue along with the purchase price paid by firms such as Blockbuster. When VHS tapes were released for sale to the public, they initially were priced high, then the price declined slowly to mass-market levels.

Thus, when DVDs hit the market, many in the industry expected the same pricing approach for DVDs as for VHS tapes. In the meantime, however, Blockbuster had grown to the point of capturing 40 percent of the rental market and was unwilling to give revenue sharing on DVDs. As a result, studios had to think in terms of maximizing revenue on DVD sales to retailers and final consumers.

Discount stores such as Target, Wal-Mart, and Best Buy were eager to capitalize on this opportunity. Why? Target and Wal-Mart want to offer a wide range of movies (VHS and DVD) to consumers to *prevent* them from going to electronics stores. In contrast, electronics stores such as Best Buy want a wide range of movies to attract customers who will then buy more expensive, higher-margin merchandise such as telephones or computers. By buying DVDs cheaper and reselling them at low prices, the discount stores could compete among themselves and counter the competition from rental companies such as Blockbuster.

This led to closer relations between the studios and the discounters. For example, DreamWorks produced a video for Wal-Mart in which the characters from *Shrek* did the famous Wal-Mart cheer (Give me a *W*, Give me an *A* . . .). Although originally intended to pump up Wal-Mart personnel, the video was so well received that Wal-Mart began showing it in their stores. Sales of the *Shrek* DVD skyrocketed.

Into this already hectic situation stepped Warren Lieberfarb, head of Warner Home Video. Like most large, old-line studios, Warner could use two-tiered pricing, in which it rereleased old movies from its huge inventory in DVD format at low prices while at the same time releasing recent movies at higher prices. Although ideal for large studios, such two-tiered pricing does not work well for small, newer studios such as DreamWorks that have a smaller assortment of mostly recent movies. Sensing an opportunity to gain an advantage over other studios and to outcompete Blockbuster, Lieberfarb decided to price *all* releases for the mass market. That would give Warner widespread distribution in the discount stores and, to some extent, force the smaller studios to also lower their prices. Recently dubbed "Lieberfarbian" economics, this move caused major concern among studio executives who had planned to "milk" sales of DVDs as they had with VHS tapes.

How are consumers responding to DVD technology? DVDs were introduced in 1997, and their sales increased rapidly during the next five years. By 2002, DVD player sales were expected to top those of VCRs, even though VCR prices had dropped as low as $70. In 2001, 14.1 million DVD players were sold along with 14.9 million VCRs; in 2002, sales of DVD players were estimated to be 15.5 million and sales of VCRs to be 13.2 million. That meant that 35 percent of American homes would have DVD players, while 90 percent had VCRs. Rentals of DVDs increased by more than 120 percent in 2001.

Consumers obviously appreciate the advantages of DVD—better picture quality, no rewinding, and extras such as outtakes. The only drawback is the inability to record DVDs, but companies expect to solve that problem quickly. Another problem, initially, was the higher price of DVD players, but Best Buy attacked that issue by sending out a request for a company to produce a $299 player by Christmas of 1999. Toshiba responded and prices of DVD players have been coming down ever since, increasing buyers' willingness to purchase DVDs at mass-market prices.

Why would the studios seemingly cut their own pricing throats? The answer is VOD, video on demand. They expect that before long, consumers will be watching movies at home on TV with all the advantages of digital technology. Digital TV is already available and VOD is already established in some communities. With VOD, consumers can watch whatever they want whenever they want to. They can fast-forward, pause, and rewind movies, and they don't have to go to stores, check availability of tapes or discs, and then store large numbers of tapes or discs at home. With the ability to record discs, consumers might even make their own DVDs at home. When VOD is successful, the studios will still be selling movies in digital format for home viewing, but Wal-Mart, Target, and Best Buy may have to find new floor-traffic builders.

But what about Blockbuster? Is it going to take all this quietly? The answer is *no*. In an effort to reduce its reliance on major studios, Blockbuster has begun to buy up independent films and even to finance the making of some movies. By mid-2002, 10 percent of all its new titles were its own movies. Although many of these are action-adventure, horror, and even R-rated movies, Blockbuster

occasionally produced an "art house" film, such as *How to Kill Your Neighbor's Dog*, starring Kenneth Branagh and Robin Wright Penn. While teens stand in line at night to see "made-for-teens" Hollywood movies, parents are at Blockbuster—sometimes just looking for something interesting.

How long will it take before VOD arrives in the mass market? Will consumers continue to patronize Blockbuster in the face of VOD? Will they quickly adopt VOD or stick to DVD? The answers to these questions depend on how consumers respond, and Warren Lieberfarb is betting that lowering prices is the way to mold consumer response.

QUESTIONS FOR DISCUSSION
1. What kind of pricing strategy was used for VHS tapes?
2. What are the differences in costs for old movies (from the 1940s and 1950s) and movies released to theaters within the last six months?
3. From the perspective of the studios, what external factors affect the pricing of DVDs? From the perspective the discount stores? For a rental company such as Blockbuster?
4. What kind of pricing strategies were the discount stores using for DVDs?
5. Is Lieberfarbian pricing appropriate for an oligopolistic industry such as movies? What kind of pricing strategy is it?
6. The studios expect VOD to replace both VHS tapes and DVDs. What factors might inhibit the growth of VOD? What factors will accelerate sales of VOD?

Sources: Shelly Emling, "DVD Era Dawns, but VHS Won't Be Obsolete for Years," *Greensboro News and Record,* July 15, 2002, p. F1; Bruce Orwell, Martin Peers, and Ann Zimmerman, "Disc Jockeying: DVD Gains on Tape, but Economics Have Hollywood in a Tizzy—As Format's Sales Surge, How Do You Keep Wal-Mart, Blockbuster Both Happy?—Warner's Low-Price Crusade," *Wall Street Journal,* February 5, 2002, p. A1; Martin Peers, "Blockbuster Breaks Away—Reducing Reliance on Studios, Video Chain Acquires Titles, Even Produces Its Own Films," *Wall Street Journal,* April 22, 2002, p. B1; Vito J. Racanelli, "Blockbusters?" *Barron's,* August 27, 2001, pp. 17–19; Evan Ramstad, "As Prices Tumble, Sales of DVD Players Explode for the Holidays," *Wall Street Journal,* December 9, 1999, pp. B1–B2.

1. describe the major strategies for pricing imitative and new products
2. explain how companies find a set of prices that maximizes the profits from the total product mix
3. discuss how companies adjust their prices to take into account different types of customers and situations
4. discuss the key issues related to initiating and responding to price changes

Pricing Strategies

LOOKING AHEAD: PREVIEWING THE CONCEPTS

In the last chapter, you explored the many internal and external factors that affect a firm's pricing decisions and examined three general approaches to setting prices. In this chapter, we'll look at pricing strategies available to marketers—new-product pricing strategies, product mix pricing strategies, price adjustment strategies, and price reaction strategies.

When you think "pricing strategy" these days, you often think "low price." But good pricing can also mean differentiating a product or service so that it offers greater value that commands a *higher* price. For openers, consider AT&T Wireless's "mLife" campaign. AT&T and its competitors are now mired in an ugly price war that has sapped everyone's profits. With mLife, AT&T Wireless hopes to break away from the pricing pack. It wants to build meaningful bonds with consumers based on the value of its services rather than low, low prices. But it won't be easy, and it won't happen fast.

What is *mLife*? How do you get one? AT&T Wireless has been asking and answering these questions in an advertising mega-campaign that began with a blockbuster Super Bowl ad three years ago. The ads show a montage of happy people enjoying mLife (short for *mobile life*) and talking about how it helps them to live freely but stay connected at the same time. From AT&T Wireless's viewpoint, however, mLife is much more than just an advertising campaign. It's a massive brand-building effort designed to distance AT&T Wireless from the pricing and "deal-of-the-day" promotions so popular among competitors. By building stronger bonds with customers based on the value of its services rather than price, AT&T hopes to escape the wireless war that's squeezing everyone's profits.

When you bought a cell phone and calling plan, chances are you focused on price. If so, you're not alone—almost one-quarter of all cell phone users list price as their as their number one criterion when selecting a wireless service provider. Only 3 percent base their decision on the brand or company reputation. The wireless companies share much of the blame for this consumer price focus. Following deregulation of the telecommunications industry, AT&T and other major competitors rushed in to lure consumers and grab market share. But rather than emphasizing brand value and customer relationships, they competed almost entirely on cutthroat pricing. This strategy plunged the wireless world into an ugly price war that still rages today.

"The U.S. wireless industry is every customer's dream these days—and every wireless company's nightmare," comments an industry analyst. Customers reap all the benefits of wide-open competition—lots of good-quality service providers, plenty of plans and equipment from which to choose, and "humdinger prices." All the options that cost extra on a home phone—call waiting, voice mail, long distance, and caller ID—are free to cell phone users. And it all just keeps getting cheaper—prices for wireless service have dropped 25 percent over the past three years.

But this consumer heaven is a wireless service provider's hell. "The wireless sector is sick," says the analyst. "Prices are in a free fall." Price competition is so intense that only two companies—Verizon and Cingular—managed to make any money last year. And it all just keeps getting worse. U.S. subscriber growth is slowing—to a predicted 6 percent a year through 2005 compared with 30 percent per year during the past decade—making it even more difficult to reap profits in a price-focused environment. Worse yet, cell phones have become near-commodities. All the major competitors offer much the same products and services for about the same cut-rate prices. When one provider introduces a new offer, others almost immediately follow suit.

It's against this dismal industry backdrop that AT&T wireless is staging its mLife branding campaign. The goal is to get wireless customers to think less about prices for minutes, roaming charges, calling plans, upgrades, and free phones, and more about how AT&T Wireless services can bring more value to their lives. mLife is "more than a slogan," says Neve Savage, AT&T Wireless's VP of marketing communications. "It's an overall positioning for the brand, a . . . vision for the company, [and a] broad platform that redefines the customer experience." Instead of pitching price, price, price, it "champions the freedom and flexibility wireless services can add to users' lives."

The massive nonprice positioning effort is a bold move in an industry strewn with price and promotional offers. "AT&T is trying to change the basis of competition . . . and move toward competing on the warm fuzzies," says telecommunications analyst Jeff Kagan. "You can't compete on price; you have to change the rules of the game and terms of the debate."

Last year's ad campaign got mLife off to a good start. It started with a blast of teaser ads that asked the "What is mLife?" question. AT&T's highly successful Super Bowl ad provided the answer. Loaded with warmth, humor, and sentimentality, the ad featured belly buttons, all kinds of belly buttons. It ended with an ultimate act of independence—the cutting of a baby's umbilical cord—and concluded, "We are meant to lead a wireless life. Now we truly can. Welcome to mLife." The Super Bowl ad connected enormously with consumers. Traffic to the mLife Web site (www.mLife.com) jumped by an astounding 1,900 percent, with more than 681,000 unique visitors on the day the ad aired. Of those, more than one-third registered to get more information about the new mLife services.

"We wanted to emphasize that AT&T Wireless's services enable people to cut the cord; to cut all of the connections that tie them down," says an AT&T Wireless spokesperson. "There has been too much effort on pricing and promotions in our industry, and we are getting back to the basics." Those basics for AT&T Wireless include packaging services in a way that consumers can see and feel the value they offer. Says John Zeglis, AT&T Wireless chairman and chief executive, "With this new brand campaign, we are making a bold break from our industry's obsession with plans, prices, promotions, and patter about esoteric technology issues. Instead, we are reaffirming the real power of wireless communication to keep human beings connected—to the people, information, and things that are important to them—while letting them be free of the limitations inherent in wired communication."

In the first several months following the premier of mLife, AT&T Wireless added as many as 150,000 customers beyond what analysts had predicted. That's a start. But it remains to be seen just how successful AT&T Wireless will be over the longer haul in its attempts to break away from the industry's price addiction. Creating a new value bond with customers will take persistence and time. Cautions one analyst, "Launching [mLife] isn't going to change things overnight."

Most important, AT&T Wireless must back up its mLife promise by actually differentiating its services from those of competitors. The company has already introduced new text-messaging and data products under the mLife umbrella, along with new calling plans. Mohan Gyani, president of AT&T's mobility services business, promises one thing: AT&T Wireless "will change the way it creates and introduces new service offers, with primary emphasis on how the offer helps the customer lead his or her mLife. Price will not be the star of this new movie."[1]

Pricing decisions are subject to an incredibly complex array of environmental and competitive forces. A company sets not a single price, but rather a *pricing structure* that covers different items in its line. This pricing structure changes over time as products move through their life cycles. The company adjusts product prices to reflect changes in costs and demand and to account for variations in buyers and situations. As the competitive environment changes, the company considers when to initiate price changes and when to respond to them.

This chapter examines the major dynamic pricing strategies available to marketers. In turn, we look at *new-product pricing strategies* for products in the introductory stage of the product life cycle, *product mix pricing strategies* for related products in the product mix, *price adjustment strategies* that account for customer differences and changing situations, and strategies for initiating and responding to *price changes*.[2]

New-Product Pricing Strategies

Pricing strategies usually change as the product passes through its life cycle. The introductory stage is especially challenging. Companies bringing out a new product face the challenge of setting prices for the first time. They can choose between two broad strategies: *market-skimming pricing* and *market-penetration pricing*.

Market-Skimming Pricing

Market-skimming pricing

Setting a high price for a new product to skim maximum revenues layer by layer from the segments willing to pay the high price; the company makes fewer but more profitable sales.

Many companies that invent new products initially set high prices to "skim" revenues layer by layer from the market. Sony frequently uses this strategy, called **market-skimming pricing.** When Sony introduced the world's first high-definition television (HDTV) to the Japanese market in 1990, the high-tech sets cost $43,000. These televisions were purchased only by customers who could afford to pay a high price for the new technology. Sony rapidly reduced the price over the next several years to attract new buyers. By 1993 a 28-inch HDTV cost a Japanese buyer just over $6,000. In 2001, a Japanese consumer could buy a 40-inch HDTV for about $2,000, a price that many more customers could afford. HDTV sets now sell for about $3,000 in the United States, and "HDTV-ready" sets sell for about $1,500. In this way, Sony skimmed the maximum amount of revenue from the various segments of the market.[3]

Market skimming makes sense only under certain conditions. First, the product's quality and image must support its higher price, and enough buyers must want the product at that price. Second, the costs of producing a smaller volume cannot be so high that they cancel the advantage of charging more. Finally, competitors should not be able to enter the market easily and undercut the high price.

Market-Penetration Pricing

Market-penetration pricing

Setting a low price for a new product in order to attract a large number of buyers and a large market share.

Rather than setting a high initial price to *skim* off small but profitable market segments, some companies use **market-penetration pricing.** They set a low initial price in order to *penetrate* the market quickly and deeply—to attract a large number of buyers quickly and win a large market share. The high sales volume results in falling costs, allowing the company to cut its price even further. For example, Dell used penetration pricing to enter the personal computer market, selling high-quality computer products through lower-cost direct channels. Its sales soared when IBM, Apple, and other competitors selling through retail stores could not match its prices. Wal-Mart and other discount retailers also use penetration pricing.

Market penetration: Dell used penetration pricing to enter the personal computer market, selling high-quality computer products through lower-cost direct channels.

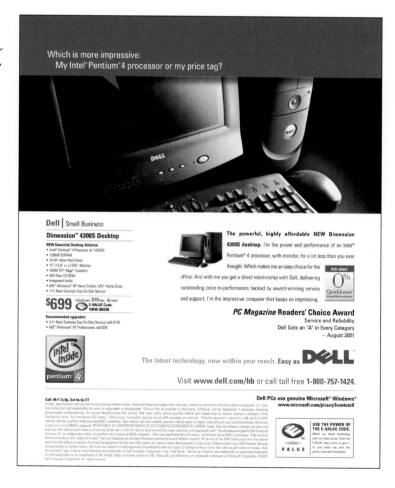

Several conditions must be met for this low-price strategy to work. First, the market must be highly price sensitive so that a low price produces more market growth. Second, production and distribution costs must fall as sales volume increases. Finally, the low price must help keep out the competition, and the penetration pricer must maintain its low-price position—otherwise, the price advantage may be only temporary. For example, Dell faced difficult times when IBM and other competitors established their own direct distribution channels. However, through its dedication to low production and distribution costs, Dell has retained its price advantage and established itself as the industry's number one personal computer maker.

Product Mix Pricing Strategies

The strategy for setting a product's price often has to be changed when the product is part of a product mix. In this case, the firm looks for a set of prices that maximizes the profits on the total product mix. Pricing is difficult because the various products have related demand and costs and face different degrees of competition. We now take a closer look at five product mix pricing situations summarized in Table 12.1: *product line pricing, optional-product pricing, captive-product pricing, by-product pricing,* and *product bundle pricing.*

Product Line Pricing

Product line pricing

Setting the price steps between various products in a product line based on cost differences between the products, customer evaluations of different features, and competitors' prices.

Companies usually develop product lines rather than single products. For example, Snapper makes many different lawn mowers, ranging from simple walk-behind versions priced at $259.95, $299.95, and $399.95, to elaborate "Yard Cruisers" and lawn tractors priced at $1,000 or more. Each successive lawn mower in the line offers more features. Sony offers not just one type of television, but several lines of televisions, each containing many models. It offers everything from Watchman portable color TVs starting at $99.99, to flat-screen Trinitrons ranging from $200 to $1,500, to its top-of-the-line plasma WEGA flat-panel sets running from $6,000 to $8,000. In **product line pricing,** management must decide on the price steps to set between the various products in a line.

The price steps should take into account cost differences between the products in the line, customer evaluations of their different features, and competitors' prices. In many industries, sellers use well-established *price points* for the products in their line. Thus, men's clothing stores might carry men's suits at three price levels: $185, $325, and $495. The customer will probably associate low-, average-, and high-quality suits with the three price points. Even if the three prices are raised a little, men normally will buy suits at their own preferred price points. The seller's task is to establish perceived quality differences that support the price differences.

Optional-Product Pricing

Optional-product pricing

The pricing of optional or accessory products along with a main product.

Many companies use **optional-product pricing**—offering to sell optional or accessory products along with their main product. For example, a car buyer may choose to order power windows, cruise control, and a CD changer. Refrigerators come with optional ice makers.

Pricing these options is a sticky problem. Automobile companies have to decide which items to include in the base price and which to offer as options. Until recent years, General Motors'

TABLE 12.1	PRODUCT MIX PRICING STRATEGIES
Strategy	**Description**
Product line pricing	Setting price steps between product line items
Optional-product pricing	Pricing optional or accessory products sold with the main product
Captive-product pricing	Pricing products that must be used with the main product
By-product pricing	Pricing low-value by-products to get rid of them
Product bundle pricing	Pricing bundles of products sold together

normal pricing strategy was to advertise a stripped-down model at a base price to pull people into showrooms and then to devote most of the showroom space to showing option-loaded cars at higher prices. The economy model was stripped of so many comforts and conveniences that most buyers rejected it. Then, GM and other U.S. carmakers followed the example of the Japanese and German automakers and included in the sticker price many useful items previously sold only as options. Most advertised prices today represent a well-equipped car. However, during the recent economic downturn, the auto companies are beginning to move certain features back into the "options" category in order to reduce the prices of standard models.

Captive-Product Pricing

Captive-product pricing

Setting a price for products that must be used along with a main product, such as blades for a razor and film for a camera.

Companies that make products that must be used along with a main product are using **captive-product pricing.** Examples of captive products are razor blades, camera film, video games, and printer cartridges. Producers of the main products (razors, cameras, video game consoles, and printers) often price them low and set high markups on the supplies. Thus, Gillette sells low-priced razors but makes money on the replacement cartridges. U-Haul rents out trucks at low rates but commands high margins on accessories such as boxes, pads, insurance, and storage space rental. H-P makes very low margins on its printers but very high margins on printer cartridges and other supplies.

Nintendo sells its game consoles at low prices and makes money on video game titles. In fact, whereas Nintendo's margins on its consoles run a mere 1 percent to 5 percent, margins on its game cartridges run close to 45 percent. Video game sales contribute more than half the company's profits. Similarly, Sony and Microsoft recently dropped the prices of their PlayStation 2 and Xbox game consoles by one-third despite the fact that the original prices were already set below cost. Despite losses on the game console, Sony makes more than 60 percent of its operating profit from the sale of PlayStation 2 and its accompanying games.[4]

In the case of services, this strategy is called *two-part pricing.* The price of the service is broken into a *fixed fee* plus a *variable usage rate.* Thus, a telephone company charges a monthly

Captive-product pricing: Nintendo sells game consoles at reasonable prices and makes money on video game titles.

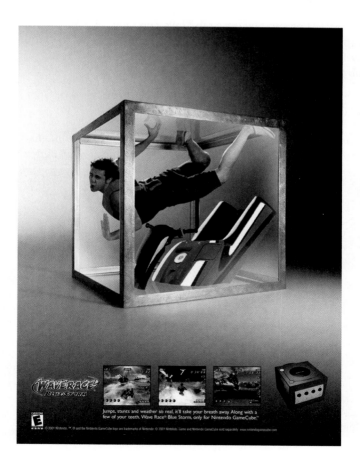

rate—the fixed fee—plus charges for calls beyond some minimum number—the variable usage rate. Amusement parks charge admission plus fees for food, midway attractions, and rides over a minimum. Theaters charge admission, then generate additional revenues from concessions. The service firm must decide how much to charge for the basic service and how much for the variable usage. The fixed amount should be low enough to induce usage of the service; profit can be made on the variable fees.

By-Product Pricing

By-product pricing

Setting a price for by-products in order to make the main product's price more competitive.

In producing processed meats, petroleum products, chemicals, and other products, there are often by-products. If the by-products have no value and if getting rid of them is costly, this will affect the pricing of the main product. Using **by-product pricing,** the manufacturer will seek a market for these by-products and should accept any price that covers more than the cost of storing and delivering them. This practice allows the seller to reduce the main product's price to make it more competitive. By-products can even turn out to be profitable. For example, many lumber mills have begun to sell bark chips and sawdust profitably as decorative mulch for home and commercial landscaping. EcoStrat, a consulting firm in Canada, takes the idea further. The firm partnered with WoodworkingSite.com to give wood product companies a place to sell their chips, shavings, dust, and other by-products. To find buyers, a manufacturer can log on to WoodworkingSite.com, answer a few questions, and hit Send. EcoStrat does the rest.[5]

Sometimes, companies don't realize how valuable their by-products are. For example, most zoos don't realize that one of their by-products—their occupants' manure—can be an excellent source of additional revenue. But the Zoo Doo Compost Company has helped many zoos understand the costs and opportunities involved with these by-products. Zoo Doo licenses its name to zoos and receives royalties on manure sales. "Many zoos don't even know how much manure they are producing or the cost of disposing of it," explains president and founder Pierce Ledbetter. They are often so pleased with any savings they can find on disposal that they don't think to move into active by-product sales.

However, sales of the fragrant by-product can be substantial. So far, novelty sales have been the largest, with tiny containers of Zoo Doo (and even "Love, Love Me Doo" valentines) available in 160 zoo stores and 700 additional retail outlets. You can also buy Zoo Doo products online ("the easiest way to buy our crap," says Zoo Doo) or even send a friend (or perhaps a foe) a free Poopy Greeting via e-mail. For the long-term market, Zoo Doo looks to organic gardeners who buy 15 to 70 pounds of manure at a time. Zoo Doo is already planning a "Dung-of-the-Month" club to reach this lucrative by-products market.[6]

By-product pricing: Zoo Doo sells tiny containers of zoo "by-products"—even "Love me Doo" valentines—through 160 zoo stores and 700 additional retail outlets.

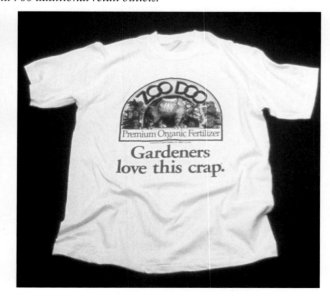

Product Bundle Pricing

Product bundle pricing

Combining several products and offering the bundle at a reduced price.

Using **product bundle pricing,** sellers often combine several of their products and offer the bundle at a reduced price. Thus, theaters and sports teams sell season tickets at less than the cost of single tickets; hotels sell specially priced packages that include room, meals, and entertainment; computer makers include attractive software packages with their personal computers; and Internet service providers sell packages that include Web access, Web hosting, e-mail, and an Internet search program. Price bundling can promote the sales of products consumers might not otherwise buy, but the combined price must be low enough to get them to buy the bundle.[7]

Price Adjustment Strategies

Companies usually adjust their basic prices to account for various customer differences and changing situations. Here we examine the six price adjustment strategies summarized in Table 12.2: *discount and allowance pricing, segmented pricing, psychological pricing, promotional pricing, geographical pricing,* and *international pricing.*

Discount and Allowance Pricing

Most companies adjust their basic price to reward customers for certain responses, such as early payment of bills, volume purchases, and off-season buying. These price adjustments—called *discounts* and *allowances*—can take many forms.

Discount

A straight reduction in price on purchases during a stated period of time.

The many forms of **discounts** include a *cash discount,* a price reduction to buyers who pay their bills promptly. A typical example is "2/10, net 30," which means that although payment is due within 30 days, the buyer can deduct 2 percent if the bill is paid within 10 days. The discount must be granted to all buyers meeting these terms. Such discounts are customary in many industries and help to improve the sellers' cash situation and reduce bad debts and credit-collection costs.

A *quantity discount* is a price reduction to buyers who buy large volumes. A typical example might be "$10 per unit for less than 100 units, $9 per unit for 100 or more units." By law, quantity discounts must be offered equally to all customers and must not exceed the seller's cost savings associated with selling large quantities. These savings include lower selling, inventory, and transportation expenses. Discounts provide an incentive to the customer to buy more from one given seller, rather than from many different sources.

A *functional discount* (also called a *trade discount*) is offered by the seller to trade-channel members who perform certain functions, such as selling, storing, and record keeping. Manufacturers may offer different functional discounts to different trade channels because of the varying services they perform, but manufacturers must offer the same functional discounts within each trade channel.

A *seasonal discount* is a price reduction to buyers who buy merchandise or services out of season. For example, lawn and garden equipment manufacturers offer seasonal discounts to retailers during the fall and winter months to encourage early ordering in anticipation of the heavy spring

TABLE 12.2   **PRICE ADJUSTMENT STRATEGIES**

Strategy	Description
Discount and allowance pricing	Reducing prices to reward customer responses such as paying early or promoting the product
Segmented pricing	Adjusting prices to allow for differences in customers, products, or locations
Psychological pricing	Adjusting prices for psychological effect
Promotional pricing	Temporarily reducing prices to increase short-run sales
Geographical pricing	Adjusting prices to account for the geographic location of customers
International pricing	Adjusting prices for international markets

and summer selling seasons. Hotels, motels, and airlines will offer seasonal discounts in their slower selling periods. Seasonal discounts allow the seller to keep production steady during an entire year.

Allowance

Promotional money paid by manufacturers to retailers in return for an agreement to feature the manufacturer's products in some way.

Allowances are another type of reduction from the list price. For example, *trade-in allowances* are price reductions given for turning in an old item when buying a new one. Trade-in allowances are most common in the automobile industry but are also given for other durable goods. *Promotional allowances* are payments or price reductions to reward dealers for participating in advertising and sales support programs.

Segmented Pricing

Segmented pricing

Selling a product or service at two or more prices, where the difference in prices is not based on differences in costs.

Companies will often adjust their basic prices to allow for differences in customers, products, and locations. In **segmented pricing,** the company sells a product or service at two or more prices, even though the difference in prices is not based on differences in costs.

Segmented pricing takes several forms. Under *customer-segment* pricing, different customers pay different prices for the same product or service. Museums, for example, will charge a lower admission for students and senior citizens. Under *product-form pricing,* different versions of the product are priced differently but not according to differences in their costs. For instance, Black & Decker prices its most expensive iron at $54.98, which is $12 more than the price of its next most expensive iron. The top model has a self-cleaning feature, yet this extra feature costs only a few more dollars to make.

Using *location pricing,* a company charges different prices for different locations, even though the cost of offering each location is the same. For instance, theaters vary their seat prices because of audience preferences for certain locations, and state universities charge higher tuition for out-of-state students. Finally, using *time pricing,* a firm varies its price by the season, the month, the day, and even the hour. Public utilities vary their prices to commercial users by time of day and weekend versus weekday. The telephone company offers lower off-peak charges, and resorts give seasonal discounts.

Segmented pricing goes by many names. Robert Cross, a longtime consultant to the airlines, calls it *revenue management.* According to Cross, the practice ensures that "companies will sell the right product to the right consumer at the right time for the right price." Airlines, hotels, and restaurants call it *yield management* and practice it religiously. The airlines, for example, routinely set prices on an hour-by-hour—even minute-by-minute—basis, depending on seat availability and demand. "A business traveler who shells out $1,700 for a coach seat bought at the last minute is well aware that the passenger in the next seat might have paid $300 for a ticket booked weeks in advance, while another passenger across the aisle may have scored a seat through a discount broker for, perhaps, $129," observes an industry analyst.[8]

Segmented pricing and yield management aren't really new ideas. For instance, Marriott Corporation used seat-of-the-pants yield-management approaches long before it installed its current sophisticated system.

Back when Bill Marriott was a young man working at the family's first hotel, the Twin Bridges in Washington, D.C., he sold rooms from a drive-up window. As Bill tells it, the hotel charged a flat rate for a single occupant, with an extra charge for each additional person staying in the room. When room availability got tight on some nights, Bill would lean out the drive-up window and assess the cars waiting in line. If some of the cars were filled with passengers, Bill would turn away vehicles with just a single passenger to sell his last rooms to those farther back in line who would be paying for multiple occupants. He might have accomplished the same result by charging a higher rate at peak times, regardless of the number of room occupants.[9]

For segmented pricing to be an effective strategy, certain conditions must exist. The market must be segmentable, and the segments must show different degrees of demand. Members of the segment paying the lower price should not be able to turn around and resell the product to the segment paying the higher price. Competitors should not be able to undersell the firm in the segment being charged the higher price. Nor should the costs of segmenting and watching the market exceed the extra revenue obtained from the price difference. Of course, the segmented pricing must also be legal. Most importantly, segmented prices should reflect real differences in customers' perceived value. Otherwise, in the long run, the practice will lead to customer resentment and ill will.

Psychological Pricing

Price says something about the product. For example, many consumers use price to judge quality. A $100 bottle of perfume may contain only $3 worth of scent, but some people are willing to pay the $100 because this price indicates something special.

In using **psychological pricing,** sellers consider the psychology of prices and not simply the economics. For example, consumers usually perceive higher-priced products as having higher quality. When they can judge the quality of a product by examining it or by calling on past experience with it, they use price less to judge quality. But when they cannot judge quality because they lack the information or skill, price becomes an important quality signal:

> Heublein produces Smirnoff, America's leading vodka brand. Some years ago, Smirnoff was attacked by another brand. Wolfschmidt, priced at one dollar less per bottle, claimed to have the same quality as Smirnoff. To hold on to market share, Heublein considered either lowering Smirnoff's price by one dollar or holding Smirnoff's price but increasing advertising and promotion expenditures. Either strategy would lead to lower profits and it seemed that Heublein faced a no-win situation. At this point, however, Heublein's marketers thought of a third strategy. They *raised* the price of Smirnoff by one dollar! Heublein then introduced a new brand, Relska, to compete with Wolfschmidt. Moreover, it introduced yet another brand, Popov, priced even *lower* than Wolfschmidt. This clever strategy positioned Smirnoff as the elite brand and Wolfschmidt as an ordinary brand, producing a large increase in Heublein's overall profits. The irony is that Heublein's three brands are pretty much the same in taste and manufacturing costs. Heublein knew that a product's price signals its quality. Using price as a signal, Heublein sells roughly the same product at three different quality positions.

Another aspect of psychological pricing is **reference prices**—prices that buyers carry in their minds and refer to when looking at a given product. The reference price might be formed by noting current prices, remembering past prices, or assessing the buying situation. Sellers can influence or use these consumers' reference prices when setting price. For example, a company could display its product next to more expensive ones in order to imply that it belongs in the same class. Department stores often sell women's clothing in separate departments differentiated by price: Clothing found in the more expensive department is assumed to be of better quality. Companies can also influence consumers' reference prices by stating high manufacturer's suggested prices, by indicating that the product was originally priced much higher, or by pointing to a competitor's higher price.

Psychological pricing

A pricing approach that considers the psychology of prices and not simply the economics; the price is used to say something about the product.

Reference prices

Prices that buyers carry in their minds and refer to when they look at a given product.

Psychological pricing: What do the prices marked on this tag suggest about the product and buying situation?

Even small differences in price can suggest product differences. Consider a stereo priced at $300 compared to one priced at $299.95. The actual price difference is only 5 cents, but the psychological difference can be much greater. For example, some consumers will see the $299.95 as a price in the $200 range rather than the $300 range. The $299.95 will more likely be seen as a bargain price, whereas the $300 price suggests more quality. Some psychologists argue that each digit has symbolic and visual qualities that should be considered in pricing. Thus, 8 is round and even and creates a soothing effect, whereas 7 is angular and creates a jarring effect.[10]

Promotional Pricing

Promotional pricing

Temporarily pricing products below the list price, and sometimes even below cost, to increase short-run sales.

With **promotional pricing,** companies will temporarily price their products below list price and sometimes even below cost to create buying excitement and urgency. Promotional pricing takes several forms. Supermarkets and department stores will price a few products as *loss leaders* to attract customers to the store in the hope that they will buy other items at normal markups. For example, supermarkets often sell disposable diapers at less than cost in order to attract family buyers who make larger average purchases per trip. Sellers will also use *special-event pricing* in certain seasons to draw more customers. Thus, linens are promotionally priced every January to attract weary Christmas shoppers back into stores.

Manufacturers will sometimes offer *cash rebates* to consumers who buy the product from dealers within a specified time; the manufacturer sends the rebate directly to the customer. Rebates have been popular with automakers and producers of durable goods and small appliances, but they are also used with consumer packaged goods. Some manufacturers offer *low-interest financing, longer warranties,* or *free maintenance* to reduce the consumer's "price." This practice has recently become a favorite of the auto industry. Or, the seller may simply offer *discounts* from normal prices to increase sales and reduce inventories.

Promotional pricing, however, can have adverse effects. Used too frequently and copied by competitors, price promotions can create "deal-prone" customers who wait until brands go on sale before buying them. Or, constantly reduced prices can erode a brand's value in the eyes of customers. Marketers sometimes use price promotions as a quick fix instead of sweating through the difficult process of developing effective longer-term strategies for building their brands. In fact, one observer notes that price promotions can be downright addicting to both the company and the customer: "Price promotions are the brand equivalent of heroin: easy to get into but hard to get out of. Once the brand and its customers are addicted to the short-term high of a price cut it is hard to wean them away to real brand building. . . . But continue and the brand dies by 1,000 cuts."[11]

The frequent use of promotional pricing can also lead to industry price wars. Such price wars usually play into the hands of only one or a few competitors—those with the most efficient operations. For example, until recently, the computer industry avoided price wars. Computer companies, including IBM, Hewlett-Packard, Compaq, and Gateway, showed strong profits as their new technologies were snapped up by eager consumers. When the market cooled, however, many competitors began to unload PCs at discounted prices. In response, Dell, the industry's undisputed low-cost leader, started a price war that only it could win.

In mid-2000, Dell declared a brutal price war just as the industry slipped into its worst slump ever. The result was nothing short of a rout. While Dell chalked up $361 million in profits the following year, the rest of the industry logged $1.1 billion in losses. Dell's edge starts with its direct-selling approach. By taking orders straight from customers and building machines to order, Dell avoids paying retailer markups, getting stuck with unsold PCs, and keeping costly inventories. For example, at any given moment, Dell's warehouses hold just four days of stock, compared with 24 days for competitors. That gives it a gigantic edge in a market where the price of chips, drives, and other parts typically falls 1 percent a week. Moreover, Dell has mastered supply chain management. Last year, it required suppliers to use sophisticated software that wires them straight into Dell's factory floor, allowing Dell's plants to replenish supplies only as needed throughout the day. That software alone saved Dell $50 million in the first six months of use. Since launching the price war, the price of a Dell computer has dropped more than 18 percent, leaving competitors with few effective weapons. IBM has responded by outsourcing its PC production and sales. And H-P and Compaq merged in hopes of finding strength in num-

Promotional pricing: Companies offer promotional prices to create buying excitement and urgency.

bers. Says Michael Dell, "When we sell these products, we make money. When our competitors sell them, they lose money."[12]

By contrast, Kmart's mishandling of promotional pricing started a price war that the struggling discount retailer could never win, plunging the firm into bankruptcy (see Real Marketing 12.1). The point is that promotional pricing can be an effective means of generating sales in certain circumstances but can be damaging if taken as a steady diet.

Geographical Pricing

A company also must decide how to price its products for customers located in different parts of the country or world. Should the company risk losing the business of more-distant customers by charging them higher prices to cover the higher shipping costs? Or should the company charge all customers the same prices regardless of location? We will look at five geographical pricing strategies for the following hypothetical situation:

The Peerless Paper Company is located in Atlanta, Georgia, and sells paper products to customers all over the United States. The cost of freight is high and affects the companies from whom customers buy their paper. Peerless wants to establish a geographical pricing policy. It is trying to determine how to price a $100 order to three specific customers: Customer A (Atlanta), Customer B (Bloomington, Indiana), and Customer C (Compton, California).

real marketing 12.1

BlueLight Specials Mean "Lights Out" for Kmart

Kmart was once the top discount retailer in the United States, with more stores and sales than any other chain in the country. Then came Wal-Mart. With its low-cost operations, efficient distribution, and "Always Low Prices, Always" positioning, Wal-Mart quickly left Kmart in its wake. Consumers soon learned that, day in and day out, without a doubt, Wal-Mart is the low-price leader—always. Throughout the 1980s and 1990s, Kmart struggled as Wal-Mart grew.

Then, in the 1990s, shoppers seeking a slightly classier store environment but unwilling to pay for it found Target, which offers an alternative to the bare-bones Wal-Mart

could find no meaningful way to differentiate itself. So in early 2001, a desperate Kmart launched a repositioning campaign. It targeted family buyers and set out to establish itself as the place for moms to find great values every day on items ranging from clothing to cereal. However, rather than building the Kmart brand on value, the repositioning effort quickly degenerated into a focus on price. It hinged on a seemingly contradictory combination of everyday low prices—to make Kmart more price-competitive with Wal-Mart—and promotional pricing—to lend new excitement and pull in shoppers.

an industrious store manager, for many consumers the BlueLight Specials still symbolize Kmart's early success.

In December 1965, Earl Bartell, a 24-year-old Kmart store manager in Fort Wayne, Indiana, was having a problem getting rid of some holiday wrapping paper he had put on sale. Frankly, people were having trouble finding it. After thinking it over, he went to the sporting goods section and picked up a flashing lantern. He taped the lantern to the end of a two-by-four, which in turn he taped to a little stock cart. He rolled the cart to the sale aisle, turned on the flashing light, and made another announcement. This time, everyone went to the right place. Bartell continued to use this gimmick to feature other discounted items, and after watching sales steadily improve, he sent a short report back to the home office. Within six months, the flashing lights were part of the landscape of every Kmart store in the country. The presence of BlueLight Specials in Kmart stores continued for more than 20 years. But the retail scene was changing dramatically, and by 1984 Wal-Mart had overtaken Kmart as the number one discount department store chain. By the late 1980s, Kmart was close to bankruptcy, and a typical BlueLight Special had devolved into mismatched socks or two left shoes. In 1991, after 26 years, Kmart officially killed the BlueLight Special in an effort to turn the chain around by cleaning house and getting rid of every reminder of the past. To this day, however, when many consumers think back to the good old days at Kmart, they remember those BlueLight Specials.

Blue lights out for Kmart: BlueLight Specials and Dare to Compare campaigns kicked off a price war that Kmart had no chance of winning.

atmosphere. Target positions itself strongly as the "upscale discounter." With its promise of "Expect More, Pay Less," Target delivers value with an upscale feel for those who are price conscious but not price obsessed.

The emergence of Wal-Mart and Target left Kmart in a positioning no-man's-land. With its prices higher than Wal-Mart's, and its stores less chic than Target's, Kmart

For starters, Kmart slashed its everyday prices on more than 50,000 items in stores around the country to bring them within 2 percent of Wal-Mart's prices, as compared to 9 percent before the campaign. On top of this, Kmart resurrected an old promotional pricing ploy. As the centerpiece of its new positioning, Kmart rekindled its age-old BlueLight Specials. First offered years ago by

To kick off the repositioning campaign, Kmart launched a series of television ads featuring hip, animated blue spotlights dancing to Motown tunes and lowering everyday prices across the store. And, with hopes running high, Kmart introduced a new and improved version of its BlueLight Specials. The new program involved daylong discounts on certain items brought out in a cart every hour, flagged by sirens and a flashing blue light.

Despite the high hopes, the flashing blue lights signaled little more than "lights out" for Kmart. On the everyday-low-price front, Kmart simply could not outprice Wal-Mart. Its purchasing, distribution, and operating costs averaged 15 percent to 20 percent higher than Wal-Mart's. So in order to match Wal-Mart's prices, or even to come close, Kmart had to drop prices below cost.

To make matters worse, Kmart also failed to deliver consistently on the featured BlueLight Specials promotional pricing program. As a result of disorganization and poor management, some stores carried the signage but didn't offer the specials. Accounts like the following were all too common:

At one Chicago Kmart recently, a banner proclaims, "You are now entering the BlueLight Zone. Remain calm." Everyone does, because there is no BlueLight Special to be seen. A manager said one would be broadcast that day; pressed further, he promised it would happen within the hour. It didn't.

In addition, in too many cases, shoppers never had a chance to take advantage of BlueLight Always items, those supposedly offered at everyday low prices. Customers drawn to Kmart stores for advertised items often encountered only empty shelves.

At the height of the madness, Kmart launched a "Dare to Compare" campaign, in which it directly compared Kmart prices on specific products with those of other discounters, including Target and Wal-Mart. The campaign turned out to be a disaster. Kmart often got the comparisons wrong. In some cases, it quoted outdated or incorrect prices; in others, it compared products that other stores didn't even carry. One study, commissioned by Target, found that of the 622 displays it surveyed, nearly three-quarters of those mentioning Target had at least one error. For almost one-third of the comparisons, the nearest Target store didn't stock the item. And when the Target stores did carry the item, the price quoted by Kmart was wrong more than 50 percent of the time. Target took Kmart to court, forcing the company to stop the promotions.

In the end, the BlueLight Specials and Dare to Compare campaigns kicked off a price war that Kmart had no chance of winning. Wal-Mart, the undisputed king of the discounters, responded in its usual ruthless way—by buckling down and cutting prices further. For Kmart, the results were disastrous—its losses mounted to more than $2.4 billion for the year. In early 2002, the once-dominant discount chain was forced into bankruptcy, closing 283 of its stores and letting go more than 22,000 employees. Kmart's stock dropped by 68 percent in just three weeks. During that same time, sales at Target and Wal-Mart rose 8 percent. Asserts one retail consultant, "To go head-to-head with a 10,000-pound gorilla is nonsense. It's like Switzerland declaring war on the United States. That, of course, doesn't work. Wal-Mart ate Kmart's lunch."

Sources: Excerpts adapted from Ann Zimmerman and Amy Merrick, "Kmart Rivals Appear to Benefit from BlueLight," *Wall Street Journal*, September 7, 2001, p. B1; and Mark Danzig, "By Design: The BlueLight Brand Story," *Design Management Journal*, Winter 2002, pp. 26–32. Also see Amy Merrick, "Target Sues Kmart Claiming Ads Misstate Prices in Comparisons," *Wall Street Journal*, August 22, 2001, p. B8; Debbie Howell, "Kmart's New Ad Campaign Puts Spotlight on EDLP," *DSN Retailing Today*, September 17, 2001, pp. 1, 67; Alice Z. Cuneo, "Ailing Kmart Surrenders in Price War," *Advertising Age*, January 21, 200, pp. 1, 43; Keith Naughton, "Crisis at Kmart: Not a Good Thing," *Newsweek*, January 28, 2002, p. 38; and Constance L. Hays, "Kmart Reports $2.42 Billion Annual Loss," *New York Times*, May 16, 2002, p. C1.

FOB-origin pricing

A geographical pricing strategy in which goods are placed free on board a carrier; the customer pays the freight from the factory to the destination.

Uniform-delivered pricing

A geographical pricing strategy in which the company charges the same price plus freight to all customers, regardless of their location.

Zone pricing

A geographical pricing strategy in which the company sets up two or more zones. All customers within a zone pay the same total price; the more distant the zone, the higher the price.

One option is for Peerless to ask each customer to pay the shipping cost from the Atlanta factory to the customer's location. All three customers would pay the same factory price of $100, with Customer A paying, say, $10 for shipping; Customer B, $15; and Customer C, $25. Called **FOB-origin pricing,** this practice means that the goods are placed *free on board* (hence, *FOB*) a carrier. At that point the title and responsibility pass to the customer, who pays the freight from the factory to the destination. Because each customer picks up its own cost, supporters of FOB pricing feel that this is the fairest way to assess freight charges. The disadvantage, however, is that Peerless will be a high-cost firm to distant customers.

Uniform-delivered pricing is the opposite of FOB pricing. Here, the company charges the same price plus freight to all customers, regardless of their location. The freight charge is set at the average freight cost. Suppose this is $15. Uniform-delivered pricing therefore results in a higher charge to the Atlanta customer (who pays $15 freight instead of $10) and a lower charge to the Compton customer (who pays $15 instead of $25). Although the Atlanta customer would prefer to buy paper from another local paper company that uses FOB-origin pricing, Peerless has a better chance of winning over the California customer. Other advantages of uniform-delivered pricing are that it is fairly easy to administer and it lets the firm advertise its price nationally.

Zone pricing falls between FOB-origin pricing and uniform-delivered pricing. The company sets up two or more zones. All customers within a given zone pay a single total price; the more distant the zone, the higher the price. For example, Peerless might set up an East Zone and charge $10 freight to all customers in this zone, a Midwest Zone in which it charges $15, and a West Zone in which it charges $25. In this way, the customers within a given price zone receive no price advantage from the company. For example, customers in Atlanta and Boston pay the same total price to Peerless. The complaint, however, is that the Atlanta customer is paying part of the Boston customer's freight cost.

Basing-point pricing

A geographical pricing strategy in which the seller designates some city as a basing point and charges all customers the freight cost from that city to the customer.

Using **basing-point pricing,** the seller selects a given city as a "basing point" and charges all customers the freight cost from that city to the customer location, regardless of the city from which the goods are actually shipped. For example, Peerless might set Chicago as the basing point and charge all customers $100 plus the freight from Chicago to their locations. This means that an Atlanta customer pays the freight cost from Chicago to Atlanta, even though the goods may be shipped from Atlanta. If all sellers used the same basing-point city, delivered prices would be the same for all customers and price competition would be eliminated. Industries such as sugar, cement, steel, and automobiles used basing-point pricing for years, but this method has become less popular today. Some companies set up multiple basing points to create more flexibility: They quote freight charges from the basing-point city nearest to the customer.

Freight-absorption pricing

A geographical pricing strategy in which the seller absorbs all or part of the freight charges in order to get the desired business.

Finally, the seller who is anxious to do business with a certain customer or geographical area might use **freight-absorption pricing.** Using this strategy, the seller absorbs all or part of the actual freight charges in order to get the desired business. The seller might reason that if it can get more business, its average costs will fall and more than compensate for its extra freight cost. Freight-absorption pricing is used for market penetration and to hold on to increasingly competitive markets.

International Pricing

Companies that market their products internationally must decide what prices to charge in the different countries in which they operate. In some cases, a company can set a uniform worldwide price. For example, Boeing sells its jetliners at about the same price everywhere, whether in the United States, Europe, or a third-world country. However, most companies adjust their prices to reflect local market conditions and cost considerations.

The price that a company should charge in a specific country depends on many factors, including economic conditions, competitive situations, laws and regulations, and development of the wholesaling and retailing system. Consumer perceptions and preferences also may vary from country to country, calling for different prices. Or the company may have different marketing objectives in various world markets, which require changes in pricing strategy. For example, Panasonic might introduce a new product into mature markets in highly developed countries with the goal of quickly gaining mass-market share—this would call for a penetration-pricing strategy. In contrast, it might enter a less developed market by targeting smaller, less price-sensitive segments; in this case, market-skimming pricing makes sense.

Costs play an important role in setting international prices. Travelers abroad are often surprised to find that goods that are relatively inexpensive at home may carry outrageously higher

Companies that market products internationally must decide what prices to charge in the different countries.

price tags in other countries. A pair of Levi's selling for $30 in the United States goes for about $63 in Tokyo and $88 in Paris. A McDonald's Big Mac selling for a modest $2.25 here costs $5.75 in Moscow, and an Oral-B toothbrush selling for $2.49 at home costs $10 in China. Conversely, a Gucci handbag going for only $60 in Milan, Italy, fetches $240 in the United States. In some cases, such *price escalation* may result from differences in selling strategies or market conditions. In most instances, however, it is simply a result of the higher costs of selling in another country—the additional costs of product modifications, shipping and insurance, import tariffs and taxes, exchange-rate fluctuations, and physical distribution.

For example, Campbell found that distribution in the United Kingdom cost 30 percent more than in the United States. U.S. retailers typically purchase soup in large quantities—48-can cases of a single soup by the dozens, hundreds, or carloads. In contrast, English grocers purchase soup in small quantities—typically in 24-can cases of *assorted* soups. Each case must be hand-packed for shipment. To handle these small orders, Campbell had to add a costly extra wholesale level to its European channel. The smaller orders also mean that English retailers order two or three times as often as their U.S. counterparts, bumping up billing and order costs. These and other factors caused Campbell to charge much higher prices for its soups in the United Kingdom.[13]

Thus, international pricing presents some special problems and complexities. We discuss international pricing issues in more detail in Chapter 19.

Price Changes

After developing their pricing structures and strategies, companies often face situations in which they must initiate price changes or respond to price changes by competitors.

Initiating Price Changes

In some cases, the company may find it desirable to initiate either a price cut or a price increase. In both cases, it must anticipate possible buyer and competitor reactions.

Initiating Price Cuts

Several situations may lead a firm to consider cutting its price. One such circumstance is excess capacity. In this case, the firm needs more business and cannot get it through increased sales effort, product improvement, or other measures. It may drop its "follow-the-leader pricing"—charging about the same price as its leading competitor—and aggressively cut prices to boost sales. But as the airline, construction equipment, fast-food, and other industries have learned in recent years, cutting prices in an industry loaded with excess capacity may lead to price wars as competitors try to hold on to market share.

Another situation leading to price changes is falling market share in the face of strong price competition. Several American industries—automobiles, consumer electronics, cameras, watches, and steel, for example—lost market share to Japanese competitors whose high-quality products carried lower prices than did their American counterparts. In response, American companies resorted to more-aggressive pricing action.

A company may also cut prices in a drive to dominate the market through lower costs. Either the company starts with lower costs than its competitors, or it cuts prices in the hope of gaining market share that will further cut costs through larger volume. Bausch & Lomb used an aggressive low-cost, low-price strategy to become an early leader in the competitive soft contact lens market.

Initiating Price Increases

A successful price increase can greatly increase profits. For example, if the company's profit margin is 3 percent of sales, a 1 percent price increase will increase profits by 33 percent if sales volume is unaffected. A major factor in price increases is cost inflation. Rising costs squeeze profit margins and lead companies to pass cost increases along to customers. Another factor leading to price increases is overdemand: When a company cannot supply all its customers' needs, it can raise its prices, ration products to customers, or both.

Companies can increase their prices in a number of ways to keep up with rising costs. Prices can be raised almost invisibly by dropping discounts and adding higher-priced units to the line. Or prices can be pushed up openly. In passing price increases on to customers, the company must avoid being perceived as a price gouger. Companies also need to think of who will bear the brunt of increased prices. Customer memories are long, and they will eventually turn away from companies or even whole industries that they perceive as charging excessive prices.

This happened to the cereal industry in the 1990s. Industry leader Kellogg covered rising costs and preserved profits by steadily raising prices without also increasing customer value. Eventually, frustrated consumers retaliated with a quiet fury by shifting away from branded cereals toward cheaper private-label brands. Worse, many consumers switched to less expensive, more portable handheld breakfast foods, such as bagels, muffins, and breakfast bars. As a result, total American cereal sales began falling off by 3 to 4 percent a year. Thus, customers paid the price in the short run but Kellogg paid the price in the long run.[14]

There are some techniques for avoiding this problem. One is to maintain a sense of fairness surrounding any price increase. Price increases should be supported with a company communication program telling customers why prices are being increased. When possible, customers should be given advance notice so they can do forward buying or shop around. Making low-visibility price moves first is also a good technique: Eliminating discounts, increasing minimum order sizes, and curtailing production of low-margin products are some examples. Contracts or bids for long-term projects should contain escalator clauses based on such factors as increases in recognized national price indexes. The company sales force should help business customers find ways to economize.

Wherever possible, the company should consider ways to meet higher costs or demand without raising prices. For example, it can consider more cost-effective ways to produce or distribute its products. It can shrink the product instead of raising the price, as candy bar manufacturers often do. It can substitute less expensive ingredients or remove certain product features, packaging, or services. Or it can "unbundle" its products and services, removing and separately pricing elements that were formerly part of the offer. IBM, for example, now offers training and consulting as separately priced services.

Buyer Reactions to Price Changes

Whether the price is raised or lowered, the action will affect buyers, competitors, distributors, and suppliers and may interest government as well. Customers do not always interpret prices in a straightforward way. They may view a price *cut* in several ways. For example, what would you think if Joy perfume, "the costliest frangrance in the world," were to cut its price in half? Or what if IBM suddenly to cut its personal computer prices drastically? You might think that the computers are about to be replaced by newer models or that they have some fault and are not selling well. You might think that IBM is abandoning the computer business and may not stay in this business long enough to supply future parts. You might believe that quality has been reduced. Or you might think that the price will come down even further and that it will pay to wait and see.

Similarly, a price *increase*, which would normally lower sales, may have some positive meanings for buyers. What would you think if IBM *raised* the price of its latest personal computer model? On the one hand, you might think that the item is very "hot" and may be unobtainable unless you buy it soon. Or you might think that the computer is an unusually good value. On the other hand, you might think that IBM is greedy and charging what the traffic will bear.

Competitor Reactions to Price Changes

A firm considering a price change has to worry about the reactions of its competitors as well as those of its customers. Competitors are most likely to react when the number of firms involved is small, when the product is uniform, and when the buyers are well informed.

How can the firm anticipate the likely reactions of its competitors? If the firm faces one large competitor, and if the competitor tends to react in a set way to price changes, that reaction can easily be anticipated. But if the competitor treats each price change as a fresh challenge and reacts according to its self-interest, the company will have to figure out just what makes up the competitor's self-interest at the time.

Buyer reactions to price changes: What would you think if the price of Joy was suddenly cut in half?

The problem is complex because, like the customer, the competitor can interpret a company price cut in many ways. It might think the company is trying to grab a larger market share, that the company is doing poorly and trying to boost its sales, or that the company wants the whole industry to cut prices to increase total demand.

When there are several competitors, the company must guess each competitor's likely reaction. If all competitors behave alike, this amounts to analyzing only a typical competitor. In contrast, if the competitors do not behave alike—perhaps because of differences in size, market shares, or policies—then separate analyses are necessary. However, if some competitors will match the price change, there is good reason to expect that the rest will also match it.

Responding to Price Changes

Here we reverse the question and ask how a firm should respond to a price change by a competitor. The firm needs to consider several issues: Why did the competitor change the price? Was it to take more market share, to use excess capacity, to meet changing cost conditions, or to lead an industrywide price change? Is the price change temporary or permanent? What will happen to the company's market share and profits if it does not respond? Are other companies going to respond? And what are the competitor's and other firms' responses to each possible reaction likely to be?

Besides these issues, the company must make a broader analysis. It has to consider its own product's stage in the life cycle, the product's importance in the company's product mix, the intentions and resources of the competitor, and the possible consumer reactions to price changes. The company cannot always make an extended analysis of its alternatives at the time of a price change, however. The competitor may have spent much time preparing this decision, but the company may have to react within hours or days. About the only way to cut down reaction time is to plan ahead for both possible competitor's price changes and possible responses.

Figure 12.1 shows the ways a company might assess and respond to a competitor's price cut. Once the company has determined that the competitor has cut its price and that this price reduction is likely to harm company sales and profits, it might simply decide to hold its current price and profit margin. The company might believe that it will not lose too much market share, or that it would lose too much profit if it reduced its own price. It might decide that it should wait and respond when it has more information on the effects of the competitor's price

FIGURE 12.1

Assessing and responding to competitor's price changes

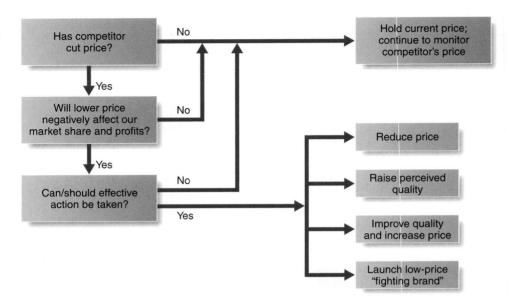

change. For now, it might be willing to hold on to good customers, while giving up the poorer ones to the competitor. The argument against this holding strategy, however, is that the competitor may get stronger and more confident as its sales increase and that the company might wait too long to act.

If the company decides that effective action can and should be taken, it might make any of four responses. First, it could *reduce its price* to match the competitor's price. It may decide that the market is price sensitive and that it would lose too much market share to the lower-priced competitor. Or it might worry that recapturing lost market share later would be too hard. Cutting the price will reduce the company's profits in the short run. Some companies might also reduce their product quality, services, and marketing communications to retain profit margins, but this will ultimately hurt long-run market share. The company should try to maintain its quality as it cuts prices.

Alternatively, the company might maintain its price but *raise the perceived quality* of its offer. It could improve its communications, stressing the relative quality of its product over that of the lower-price competitor. The firm may find it cheaper to maintain price and spend money to improve its perceived value than to cut price and operate at a lower margin.

Or, the company might *improve quality and increase price,* moving its brand into a higher-price position. The higher quality justifies the higher price, which in turn preserves the company's higher margins. Or the company can hold price on the current product and introduce a new brand at a higher-price position.

Finally, the company might *launch a low-price "fighting brand"*—adding a lower-price item to the line or creating a separate lower-price brand. This is necessary if the particular market segment being lost is price sensitive and will not respond to arguments of higher quality. Thus, when challenged on price by store brands and other low-price entrants, Procter & Gamble turned a number of its brands into fighting brands, including Luvs disposable diapers, Joy dishwashing detergent, and Camay beauty soap. In turn, P&G competitor Kimberly-Clark offers its value-priced Scott Towels brand as "the Bounty killer." It scores well on customer satisfaction measures but sells for a lower price than P&G's Bounty brand.[15]

Public Policy and Pricing

Price competition is a core element of our free-market economy. In setting prices, companies are not usually free to charge whatever prices they wish. Many federal, state, and even local laws govern the rules of fair play in pricing. In addition, companies must consider broader societal pric-

Fighting brands: Kimberly Clark offers its value-priced Scott Towels brand as "the Bounty killer." It scores well on customer satisfaction but sells for a lower price than P&G's Bounty.

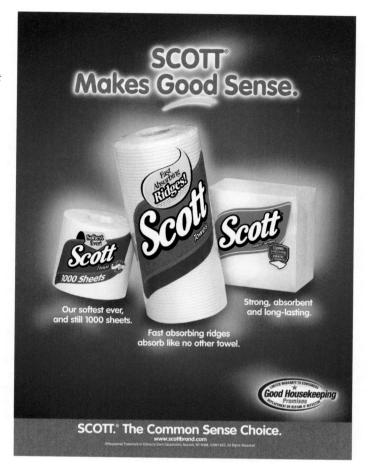

ing concerns (see Real Marketing 12.2). The most important pieces of legislation affecting pricing are the Sherman, Clayton, and Robinson-Patman acts, initially adopted to curb the formation of monopolies and to regulate business practices that might unfairly restrain trade. Because these federal statutes can be applied only to interstate commerce, some states have adopted similar provisions for companies that operate locally.

Figure 12.2 shows the major public policy issues in pricing. These include potentially damaging pricing practices within a given level of the channel (price-fixing and predatory pricing) and across levels of the channel (retail price maintenance, discriminatory pricing, and deceptive pricing).[16]

Pricing Within Channel Levels

Federal legislation on *price-fixing* states that sellers must set prices without talking to competitors. Otherwise, price collusion is suspected. Price-fixing is illegal per se—that is, the government does not accept any excuses for price-fixing. Companies found guilty of such practices can receive heavy fines. For example, when the U.S. Justice Department found that Archer Daniels Midland Company and three of its competitors had met regularly in the early 1990s to illegally fix prices, the four companies paid more than $100 million to settle the charges. Similarly, Sotheby's and Christie's, two auction houses that for years have dominated the market for high-end sales, were recently convicted of collusion and price-fixing. The collusion reportedly saved the companies in excess of $33 million a year, but they ended paying more than $512 million in fines and settlements.[17] Recently, governments at the state and national levels have been aggressively enforcing price-fixing regulations in industries ranging from tobacco, gasoline, and newsprint to vitamins and compact discs.[18]

Even a simple conversation between competitors can have serious consequences. For example, during the early 1980s, American Airlines and Braniff were immersed in a price war

real marketing 12.2

Pricing Pharmaceutical Products: More Than Sales and Profits

The U.S. pharmaceutical industry has historically been one of the nation's most profitable industries. However, critics claim that this success has come at the expense of consumers. The U.S. population spent more than $154 billion on prescription medications last year, and prescription prices have risen rapidly over the years. For example, last year, the prices of the 50 most prescribed drugs for older Americans rose, on average, at almost triple the overall inflation rate.

The critics claim that competitive forces do not operate well in the pharmaceutical market, allowing companies to charge excessive prices. Unlike purchases of other consumer products, drug purchases cannot be postponed. Consumers don't usually shop for the best deal on medicines—they simply take what the doctor orders. Because physicians who write the prescriptions don't pay for the medicines they recommend, they have little incentive to be price conscious. Moreover, because of patents and FDA approvals, few competing brands exist to force lower prices, and existing brands don't go on sale. Finally, expensive advertising and promotional efforts dictate higher prices at the same time that they build demand for more-expensive remedies. These market factors leave pharmaceutical companies free to practice monopoly pricing, the critics claim, resulting in seemingly outlandish cases of price gouging.

One classic case involved the drug levamisole. Forty years ago, Johnson & Johnson introduced levamisole as a drug used to deworm sheep. When farmers using the drug noticed that dewormed sheep also suffered fewer cases of shipping fever, researchers began investigating the drug for human use. They found that levamisole, in combination with another drug, proved effective for patients with advanced colon cancer, reducing recurrence of the disease by 40 percent and cutting deaths by a third.

The FDA quickly approved levamisole for human use, and the Janssen division of Johnson & Johnson introduced the drug under the brand name Ergamisol. All went well until an Illinois farm woman noticed that her cancer pills contained the same active ingredient as the medicine she used to deworm her sheep. It wasn't the fact that both humans and sheep were using the drug that disturbed her. What really rankled her was that the sheep medicine sold for pennies a pill, whereas the human medicine sold for $5 to $6 per tablet. In a year's time, humans had to spend $1,250 to $3,000 for Ergamisol; the cost for treating sheep was only about $14.95.

The price discrepancy caused quite a stir. One consumer even filed suit against Janssen, claiming that he was forced to pay "an outrageous, unconscionable, and extortionate price for a lifesaving drug" that is sold at a fraction of the cost for treating sheep. Janssen replied that the price reflected decades of costly research and testing conducted to determine if levamisole could be used to treat humans. The company said it had conducted over 1,400 studies with 40,000 subjects. Critics disagreed, claiming that the National Cancer Institute, funded by the American taxpayer, had sponsored the levamisole studies. Further, they asserted, Janssen had had 25 years to recoup its investment before it ever sold the drug to humans.

The levamisole case may be extreme, but at one time or another we've all gulped at the prices we've had to pay for prescription drugs. The average price of a prescription last year was nearly $50, up 10 percent from the previous year. Even when doctors or pharmacists recommend less expensive generic drugs, consumers may pay substantial markups. Pharmacies may look like good guys when they encourage the use of generics to save consumers money, but they also pocket a handsome profit. One recent study found that drugstores and pharmacies are marking up the price of some generics by more than 1,000 percent. For their part, pharmacies argue that the high gross margins for generics don't tell the whole story. Just as a patient who visits a doctor and gets handed a Band-Aid is not billed for just the Band-Aid, a pharmacy customer has to pay for the pharmacist's time and other expenses of maintaining a pharmacy department.

These examples highlight many important drug-pricing issues. Most consumers appreciate the steady stream of beneficial drugs produced by the U.S. pharmaceutical industry. And there is no question that developing new drugs is a risky endeavor, involving legions of scientists, expensive technology, and often years of effort with no certainty of success. However, there is much concern that the industry may be taking advantage of its monopoly-pricing power. Perhaps the most serious concern is that high drug prices may have life-and-death consequences. Without

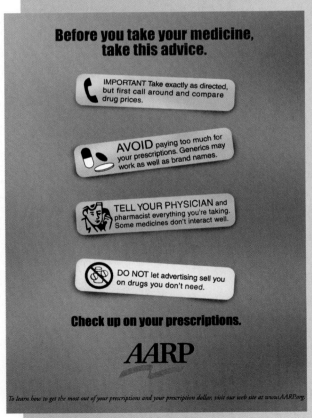

Before you take your medicine, take this advice.

IMPORTANT Take exactly as directed, but first call around and compare drug prices.

AVOID paying too much for your prescriptions. Generics may work as well as brand names.

TELL YOUR PHYSICIAN and pharmacist everything you're taking. Some medicines don't interact well.

DO NOT let advertising sell you on drugs you don't need.

Check up on your prescriptions.

AARP

To learn how to get the most out of your prescriptions and your prescription dollar, visit our web site at www.AARP.org.

The critics claim that the lack of competitive forces in the pharmaceutical market lets companies charge excessive prices. Here, the AARP advises, "Avoid paying too much for your prescriptions" and "don't let advertising sell you drugs you don't need."

levamisole, for example, many of the 22,000 patients diagnosed with advanced colon cancer each year would die. Thus, some critics claim that drug company profits may come at the expense of human life.

As a result, the industry is facing ever-greater pressure from the federal government, insurance companies, managed-care providers, and consumer advocates to exercise restraint in setting prices. Legislation has been passed to curb drug pricing and more is pending. Rather than waiting for tougher legislation on prices—or simply because it's the right thing to do—some forward-thinking drug companies have taken action on their own by agreeing to keep their average price hikes at or below inflation. Others have voluntarily provided discounts to agencies such as the U.S. Public Health Service and to federally funded drug- and alcohol-treatment centers. Still other companies make drugs available free or at low prices to people who cannot afford them. Consider the following example:

Abbott Laboratories CEO Miles White returned from a recent eye-opening visit to Tanzania—where the HIV/AIDS epidemic rages almost unabated—with a new mission for his company. Among other things, he learned firsthand that

when local doctors decide whether or not to use a drug, the biggest consideration is its price, not whether it is the right drug. "I found out how much the price of drugs matters," says White. As a result, within days, he decided to reduce the price of Abbott's AIDS drugs to below cost for poor African nations. White also learned that the cost of the company's "rapid" AIDS detection test was the main reason it wasn't being used as a crucial tool in helping prevent the spread of the virus from infected pregnant women to their unborn children. Once detected, virus transmission can be blocked with the one-time use of a drug being given away by a competitor. But without an easy-to-use detection test, many expectant mothers are unaware they are infected. White now plans to give away 20 million test kits during the next five years. Asked how he can explain taking money out of the company coffers to fund such price cuts and give-aways, he says he'll tell shareholders that Abbott is doing "our part because we can." But, in a refreshing bit of honesty, he adds, "There is a practical business reason. If we don't lower prices and provide other help, we'll find governments altering patent laws."

Thus, Abbott and other companies recognize that in setting prices, their short-term sales, market share, and profit goals must be tempered by broader societal considerations. They know that in the long run, socially responsible pricing will benefit both the consumer and the company.

Sources: Abbott example adapted from Michael Waldholz, "Abbott Labs Improves Its Effort to Combat AIDS in Africa," *Wall Street Journal,* June 27, 2002. p. D4. Also see Marilyn Chase, "Doctor Assails J&J Price Tag on Cancer Drug," *Wall Street Journal,* May 20, 1992, p. B1; "Cancer Patient Sues Johnson & Johnson over Drug Pricing," *Wall Street Journal,* August 13, 1992, p. B6; Mike King, "Colon Cancer Drug: 5 Cents for an Animal, $5 for Humans," *Atlanta Constitution,* March 11, 1991, p. E1; John Carry and Amy Barrett, "Drug Prices: What's Fair?" *Business Week,* December 10, 2001, pp. 61–68; Robert M. Goldberg, "A Better Prescription for Medicare," *Wall Street Journal,* May 7, 2002, p. A26; "Prescription Volume Causes Continued Rise in Drug Costs," *Best's Review,* May 2002, p. 18; and "Drug Prices Surging," *Raleigh News and Observer,* June 25, 2002, p. D1.

in the Texas market. In the heat of the battle, American's CEO, Robert Crandall, called the president of Braniff and said, "Raise your . . . fares 20 percent. I'll raise mine the next morning. You'll make more money and I will, too." Fortunately for Crandall, the Braniff president warned him off, saying, "We can't talk about pricing!" As it turns out, the phone conversation had been recorded, and the U.S. Justice Department began action against Crandall and American for price-fixing. The charges were eventually dropped—the courts ruled that because Braniff had rejected Crandall's proposal, no actual collusion had occurred and that a proposal to fix prices was not an actual violation of the law. Still, as part of the settlement, for two years Crandall was required to keep a detailed log of his conversations with fellow airline

FIGURE 12.2 Public policy issues in pricing

Source: Adapted from Dhruv Grewel and Larry D. Compeau, "Pricing and Public Policy: A Research Agenda and Overview of Special Issue," *Journal of Marketing and Public Policy,* Spring 1999, pp. 3–10.

chiefs.[19] Such cases have made most executives very reluctant to discuss prices in any way with competitors.

Sellers are also prohibited from using *predatory pricing*—selling below cost with the intention of punishing a competitor or gaining higher long-run profits by putting competitors out of business. This protects small sellers from larger ones who might sell items below cost temporarily or in a specific locale to drive them out of business. The biggest problem is determining just what constitutes predatory pricing behavior. Selling below cost to sell off excess inventory is not considered predatory; selling below cost to drive out competitors is. Thus, the same action may or may not be predatory depending on intent, and intent can be very difficult to determine or prove.

In recent years, several large and powerful companies have been accused of this practice. For example, Wal-Mart has been sued by dozens of small competitors charging that it lowered prices in their specific areas to drive them out of business. In another recent case, the Justice Department sued American Airlines for allegedly using predatory pricing to muscle three small competitors—Vanguard Airlines, Sun Jet, and Western Pacific—out of its huge Dallas–Fort Worth hub.

> Every time a fledgling airline tried to get a toehold in the Dallas market, for example, American met its fares and added flights. As soon as the rival retreated, American jacked fares back up. Between Dallas and Kansas City, for instance, American's average one-way ticket was $108 before low-cost startup Vanguard Airlines entered the market. That prompted American to cut fares to $80 and almost double the number of daily flights, to 14. When Vanguard gave up [less than a year later], American jacked up prices to $147 and scaled back the number of flights. Justice lawyers even had memos from American execs plotting the upstarts' demise.

Despite such evidence, the case against American was dismissed. American had consistently priced flights higher than variable costs, thus avoiding predatory pricing. American won by arguing that it was just being a tough competitor.[20]

Giant Microsoft has also been a Justice Department target:

> When Microsoft targets a market for domination, it frequently wins over customers with an irresistible offer: free products. In 1996, Microsoft started giving away Internet Explorer, its Web browser—and in some cases arguably even "paid" people to use it by offering free software and marketing assistance. The strategy was crucial in wrestling market dominance from Netscape Communications Corporation. Netscape constantly revised its pricing structure but "better than free" is not the most appealing sales pitch. Most of Microsoft's giveaways were offered as part of its effort to gain share in the interactive corporate computing market. For instance, the company offered free Web-server software to customers who purchase the Windows NT network operating system. Netscape was selling a higher-powered version of the same software for $4,100. Although such pricing and promotion strategies might be viewed as shrewd marketing by some, competitors saw them as purely predatory. They noted that in the past, once Microsoft had use these tactics to gain a lion's share of the market, it had tended to raise prices *above* market levels. For example, the wholesale price it charged PC makers for its Windows operating system (in which is bundled the Internet Explorer) had doubled during the past seven years.[21]

Pricing Across Channel Levels

The Robinson-Patman Act seeks to prevent unfair *price discrimination* by ensuring that sellers offer the same price terms to customers at a given level of trade. For example, every retailer is entitled to the same price terms from a given manufacturer, whether the retailer is Sears or the local bicycle shop. However, price discrimination is allowed if the seller can prove that its costs are different when selling to different retailers—for example, that it costs less per unit to sell a large volume of bicycles to Sears than to sell a few bicycles to a local dealer. Or the seller can discriminate in its pricing if the seller manufactures different qualities of the same product for different retailers. The seller has to prove that these differences are proportional. Price differentials may also be used to "match competition" in "good faith," provided the price discrimination is temporary, localized, and defensive rather than offensive.

Retail price maintenance is also prohibited—a manufacturer cannot require dealers to charge a specified retail price for its product. Although the seller can propose a manufacturer's *suggested* retail price to dealers, it cannot refuse to sell to a dealer who takes independent pricing action, nor can it punish the dealer by shipping late or denying advertising allowances. For example, in 1996 the Federal Trade Commission (FTC) charged that New Balance had engaged in fixing retail prices for its athletic shoes. Its agreements with retailers required that the retailers raise the price of New Balance products, maintain prices at levels set by New Balance, and not discount the products.

Deceptive pricing occurs when a seller states prices or price savings that mislead consumers or are not actually available to consumers. This might involve bogus reference or comparison prices, as when a retailer sets artificially high "regular" prices then announces "sale" prices close to its previous everyday prices. Such comparison pricing is widespread:

Open any Sunday newspaper and find hundreds of such promotions being offered by a variety of retailers, such as supermarkets, office supply stores, furniture stores, computer stores, appliance stores, pharmacies and drugstores, car dealers, department stores, and others. Surf the Internet and see similar price promotions. Watch the shopping channels on television and find more of the same. It seems that, today, selling prices rarely stand alone. Instead retailers are using an advertised reference price (e.g., regular price, original price, manufacturer's suggested price) to suggest that buyers will save money if they take advantage of the "deal" being offered.[22]

Such claims are legal if they are truthful. However, the FTC's *Guides Against Deceptive Pricing* warns sellers not to advertise a price reduction unless it is a saving from the usual retail price, not to advertise "factory" or "wholesale" prices unless such prices are what they are claimed to be, and not to advertise comparable value prices on imperfect goods.

Other deceptive pricing issues include *scanner fraud* and price confusion. The widespread use of scanner-based computer checkouts has led to increasing complaints of retailers overcharging their customers. Most of these overcharges result from poor management—from a failure to enter current or sale prices into the system. Other cases, however, involve intentional overcharges. *Price confusion* results when firms employ pricing methods that make it difficult for consumers to understand just what price they are really paying. For example, consumers are sometimes misled regarding the real price of a home mortgage or car leasing agreement. In other cases, important pricing details may be buried in the "fine print."

Many federal and state statutes regulate against deceptive pricing practices. For example, the Automobile Information Disclosure Act requires automakers to attach a statement to new-car windows stating the manufacturer's suggested retail price, the prices of optional equipment, and the dealer's transportation charges. However, reputable sellers go beyond what is required by law. Treating customers fairly and making certain that they fully understand prices and pricing terms is an important part of building strong and lasting customer relationships.[23]

LOOKING BACK: REVIEWING THE CONCEPTS

Pricing decisions are subject to an incredibly complex array of environmental and competitive forces. A company sets not a single price, but rather a *pricing structure* that covers different items in its line. This pricing structure changes over time as products move through their life cycles. The company adjusts product prices to reflect changes in costs and demand and to account for variations in buyers and situations. As the competitive environment changes, the company considers when to initiate price changes and when to respond to them.

1. Describe the major strategies for pricing imitative and new products.

Pricing is a dynamic process. Companies design a *pricing structure* that covers all their products. They change this structure over time and adjust it to account for different customers and situations. Pricing strategies usually change as a product passes through its life cycle. The company can decide on one of several price–quality strategies for introducing an imitative product, including premium pricing, economy pricing, good value, or overcharging. In pricing innovative new products, it can follow a *skimming policy* by initially setting high prices to "skim" the maximum amount of revenue from various segments of the market. Or it can use *penetration pricing* by setting a low initial price to penetrate the market deeply and win a large market share.

2. Explain how companies find a set of prices that maximizes the profits from the total product mix.

When the product is part of a product mix, the firm searches for a set of prices that will maximize the profits from the total mix. In *product line pricing*, the company decides on price steps for the entire set of products it offers. In addition, the company must set prices for *optional products* (optional or accessory products included with the main product), *captive products*

(products that are required for use of the main product), *by-products* (waste or residual products produced when making the main product), and *product bundles* (combinations of products at a reduced price).

3. Discuss how companies adjust their prices to take into account different types of customers and situations.

Companies apply a variety of *price adjustment strategies* to account for differences in consumer segments and situations. One is *discount and allowance pricing*, whereby the company establishes cash, quantity, functional, or seasonal discounts, or varying types of allowances. A second strategy is *segmented pricing*, where the company sells a product at two or more prices to accommodate different customers, product forms, locations, or times. Sometimes companies consider more than economics in their pricing decisions, using *psychological pricing* to better communicate a product's intended position. In *promotional pricing*, a company offers discounts or temporarily sells a product below list price as a special event, sometimes even selling below cost as a loss leader. Another approach is *geographical pricing*, whereby the company decides how to price to distant customers, choosing from such alternatives as FOB pricing, uniform-delivered

pricing, zone pricing, basing-point pricing, and freight-absorption pricing. Finally, *international pricing* means that the company adjusts its price to meet different conditions and expectations in different world markets.

4. Discuss the key issues related to initiating and responding to price changes.

When a firm considers initiating a *price change*, it must consider customers' and competitors' reactions. There are different implications to *initiating price cuts* and *initiating price increases*. Buyer reactions to price changes are influenced by the meaning customers see in the price change. Competitors' reactions flow from a set reaction policy or a fresh analysis of each situation.

There are also many factors to consider in responding to a competitor's price changes. The company that faces a price change initiated by a competitor must try to understand the competitor's intent as well as the likely duration and impact of the change. If a swift reaction is desirable, the firm should preplan its reactions to different possible price actions by competitors. When facing a competitor's price change, the company might sit tight, reduce its own price, raise perceived quality, improve quality and raise price, or launch a fighting brand.

REVIEWING THE KEY TERMS

Allowances 376
Basing-point pricing 382
By-product pricing 374
Captive-product pricing 373
Discounts 375
FOB-origin pricing 381

Freight-absorption pricing 382
Market-penetration pricing 371
Market-skimming pricing 371
Optional-product pricing 372
Product bundle pricing 375
Product line pricing 372

Promotional pricing 378
Psychological pricing 377
Reference prices 377
Segmented pricing 376
Uniform-delivered pricing 381
Zone pricing 381

DISCUSSING THE CONCEPTS

1. Which pricing strategy—market skimming or market penetration—does each of the following companies use? (a) McDonald's, (b) Sony (television and other home electronics), (c) Bic (pens, lighters, razors, and related products), and (d) IBM (personal computers). Are these the right strategies for each company? Explain.

2. A clothing store sells men's suits at three price levels: $180, $250, and $340. If shoppers use these price points as reference prices in comparing different suits, what would be the effect of adding a new line of suits priced at $280? Would you expect sales of the $250 suits to increase, decrease, or stay the same? What would be the effect of adding a line of suits priced at $450?

3. Which of the five product-mix pricing strategies found in Table 12.1 apply to the following examples? (a) Ben & Jerry's sells the residue or sludge produced in the ice cream manufacturing process to farmers for use as animal feed. (b) RCA sells its latest 32-inch color television set with six additional speakers to enhance DVD sound. (c) Sega's video game system will play only Sega games. (d) At many of its popular resorts, Marriott offers a weekend package that includes a two-night stay, a complementary breakfast, valet parking, and two tickets to a local theme park.

4. Matt Hollingshead recently opened a new lumberyard. He realizes that to succeed in this industry, he and his staff will have to work very hard to compete against industry giant

Home Depot. Design a plan for using discounts as a way to attract and keep customers. Is stressing price the best way for Matt to compete?

5. Companies will often adjust their basic prices to allow for differences in customers, products, and locations. List and briefly describe the different forms of segmented pricing. Provide an example (other than those provided in the text) of each of these forms. Which forms might be used in pricing products on the Internet? Explain.

6. Explain the concepts of psychological pricing and reference prices. Create an example (other than those provided in the text) for each of these concepts.

7. Since becoming an assistant manager of a local J.C. Penney store, you are amazed by the number of promotional pricing techniques used by the chain. While you realize the value of promotional pricing, you also understand the problems associated with the strategy. Prepare a short report that outlines the advantages and disadvantages of promotional pricing for J.C. Penney.

8. Assume that you have just been appointed manager of children's wear at a local department store. Formulate rules that govern (a) initiating a price cut, (b) initiating a price increase, (c) a negative reaction on the part of buyers to a price change by your company, (d) a competitor's response to your price change, and (e) your response to a competitor's price change. State the assumptions underlying your proposed rules.

APPLYING THE CONCEPTS

1. The computer printer industry is intensively competitive with respect to pricing. Only a few years ago, consumers were often shocked to find that a good printer could account for as much as half the cost of an entire home computer setup. No more! Recently, such companies as Epson, Hewlett-Packard, Canon, Tektronix, and Xerox have introduced expanded lines of technologically advanced but less expensive printer models. Despite dramatic improvements in speed, quality, color, and optional features, today's printers sell at much lower prices than their predecessors.

   a. What role does pricing play in a consumer's selection of a home printer? An office printer? A portable printer to take on business trips?

   b. What pricing strategies are Epson, Hewlett-Packard, Canon, Tektronix, Xerox, and other companies using to sell printers to the consumer and business markets? (Visit each Web site to get additional information.) Which companies appear to have the most effective pricing strategies? Explain.

   c. Assume that you are the marketing manager of a company introducing a new line of color printers and seeking quick entry into the small color-printer market. Your products are comparable to those of primary competitors, and you have the funds necessary to compete with industry leaders. Design a pricing strategy for capturing business in the home computer, home office, and mobile office markets. What factors would be critical to your product's success? How would you combat competitive reaction to your entry?

2. What weighs 16 tons, is 40 feet long, costs $350,000, and has the mysterious name "Intrigue"? If you guessed the "big daddy" of all motor homes, you're right. Country Coach accurately predicted several years ago that bigger would be better for aging baby boomers who increasingly want to head out on the highway. In response to this demand, Country Coach makes huge motor homes for those people who enjoy roomy, luxurious transportation. Is this a narrow market niche? Hardly. Despite the hefty price tag, the company sells about 250,000 large motor homes per year. Whether an Intrigue owner uses the giant motor home for vacations or as a home on wheels, it certainly gets the attention of passing motorists.

   Visit the Country Coach Web site at www.countrycoach.com. Then answer the following questions:

   a. Which pricing strategy does Country Coach appear to be using for its motor homes? What are the advantages and disadvantages of this pricing strategy? In your opinion, is the company justified in using this strategy? Explain.

   b. How might the pricing strategies change if Country Coach targeted Generation X?

   c. You have been hired as a consultant for Country Coach to review the pricing strategies of the company. After your review, you determine that the company could increase sales (without damaging profits) by implementing a price adjustment strategy. Review Table 12.2. Then suggest strategies for adjusting the price of the Intrigue.

 DIGITAL CONNECTIONS

CONNECTING CUSTOMERS TO PRICING INFORMATION VIA INTERACTIVE TECHNOLOGY

"Gallery Furniture Saves You Money!" is an advertising slogan heard many times a day in the Houston, Texas, market. This dynamic furniture outlet uses many types of advertising media to spread its consistent message to cost-conscious consumers. Gallery Furniture sells from its vast showroom and warehouse facility and also promotes its products via an elaborate Web site (see www.galleryfurniture.com). When visiting the Web site, consumers can see showroom furniture in "real time" via robotic cameras that pan the entire store (see Mobile Cam or PhotoLog features). This feature allows customers to see what is currently on the showroom floor and how much the item costs (including the specials of the day). This remote form of shopping saves local customers time and money because they can avoid traffic in one of America's largest cities, and it gives distant customers a virtual in-store experience. By using the robotic-camera feature, Gallery Furniture can constantly update its prices without having to manually update its Web site. Locally, Gallery Furniture boasts, "Buy it today, receive it tonight!" As an extension of this pledge, the company recently declared that one of its new goals was to expand statewide (and eventually nationwide) with its aggressive pricing policies. Would you shop for furniture from Houston if it could be delivered promptly and at a cost comparable with local competitors? Gallery Furniture is exploring the possibility that you (and thousands of others) will.

FOR DISCUSSION

1. Which general pricing strategy does Gallery Furniture use?

2. If Gallery Furniture expands into state and national markets, which geographical pricing method would you recommend?

3. Considering what you learned in the previous chapter, what internal and external factors might affect Gallery Furniture's decision to expand?

4. Which product-mix pricing strategies could benefit Gallery Furniture? Explain.

5. Would psychological pricing make sense for this organization? Explain.

6. Visit Gallery Furniture's Web site and familiarize yourself with the organization's approach to pricing and selling furniture. Now assume that you are the marketing manager of a rival furniture organization. After carefully considering the information found in this chapter, outline a plan for competing against Gallery Furniture. What role would your Web site play in this strategy?

Site 59: Adding Value for Customers Through Pricing

Although little known, Site 59-has received "best of Web" awards from *Forbes,* CNN, the *Wall Street Journal,* the *Today* show, *Reader's Digest, PC Magazine, USA Today,* and the *Washington Post.* Why? Site 59's technology has revolutionized the last-minute travel market. The site's systems automate and assemble excess inventory from more than 2,600 industry suppliers, including major airlines, hotel companies, car rental companies, and hundreds of specialty providers worldwide in real time. The company then assembles and prices travel packages for consumers interested in last-minute getaways. Site 59's technology is so well designed that Travelocity, Orbitz, Yahoo! Travel, aavacations.com, Northwest's nwa.com, Bestfares.com, and Lowestfare.com rely on it to power their last-minute offers.

After viewing the Site 59 video, answer the following questions about pricing strategies:

1. How do Site 59's pricing strategies differ from those of Priceline as discussed in Chapter 11? How does the company segment its markets? How does it differentiate itself and add value for customers through its pricing strategies?
2. The airline industry has been plagued by price wars and consumer confusion over dynamic pricing systems that constantly change prices based on shifts in demand and costs. How might Site 59 alter the pricing strategies of companies in the travel industry?
3. The Internet has had a tremendous impact on pricing strategies. Select two of the price-adjustment strategies covered in this chapter and discuss how e-commerce has changed the application of those approaches.

Southeast Bank: Free Checking?

CHECKING INTO CHECKING

Kelly James, director of strategic planning at Southeast Bank,* looked up from her conference table as Bonnie Summers, manager of retail deposits, and Paul Bridges, retail product manager, knocked at her office door.

"Come on in," Kelly exclaimed as she waved them in. "I'm ready to hear what you've determined on the issue of whether we should start offering free checking. I know there are a lot of pros and cons, and the issue's generated a lot of heated discussion around the bank. As you know, the Executive Committee's asked me to look into the issue and make a recommendation."

"Well, I've found some interesting information from a recent national study," Bonnie began. "Every six months, researchers at Bankrate.com conduct a national survey of checking accounts, looking at things like fees, minimum balances, service charges, and so on. It recently reported the results of its Fall 2001 survey that included 1,276 different accounts at 350 institutions.

"The survey found that the interest rate paid on checking account balances fell from a 1.17 percent annual rate to 0.97 percent. The average minimum balance required to open an account and earn interest was $695, a 6 percent increase in just one year. On the other hand, to open a non-interest-bearing checking account required just $76.30 on average, an amount that's barely changed in three years.

"To avoid monthly service fees on an interest-bearing account, you need an average minimum balance of $2,434.50, up 5.6 per-

cent since 1998. The average minimum balance in non-interest-bearing accounts is just $408.16. If you don't want to keep a high balance in an interest-bearing account, the average monthly service fee is $10.85, up 4 percent per year for the last three years. The average monthly fee on non-interest-bearing accounts actually dropped to $6.19.

"About one-fourth of the checking accounts also charge per-item fees for various transactions, like check writing or deposits. The average interest-paying account allows 17 "freebies," while the average non-interest-paying account allows 12 before fees kick in. I also found that ATM fees for noncustomers who use a bank's ATM system have become almost universal and now average about $1.32 per transaction."

"Are there any true free checking accounts with no minimum balance, no monthly service charges, and no per-item fees?" Kelly asked.

"The study showed that about 7.5 percent of the accounts surveyed were free, as you describe it, an all-time high," Bonnie answered. "I also found that the number of banks offering free non-interest checking accounts jumped more than 15 percentage points to 45.3 percent. This move was especially true among large banks, like Southeast."

"What about insufficient funds charges (NSFs)?" Paul asked.

"The survey showed that they were at an all-time high, also, Paul, averaging $24.85," Bonnie noted. "So, it's very expensive to bounce a check. Many banks offer overdraft protection—often for a fee, of course. Some banks charge an annual fee, such as $10, for overdraft protection and then add a $5 charge each time the customer uses the service."

SOUTHEAST'S SITUATION

"That's very helpful, Bonnie. Paul, how would you summarize our situation?" Kelly asked.

"Competitors have not yet offered completely free checking in our markets, although some are promoting no-fee checking accounts that require that the account holder use direct deposit of payroll checks. These accounts often limit access to tellers. Some banks have used free checking as their number one weapon in entering new markets and as a result have enjoyed significant gains in demand-deposit accounts (DDAs). These banks promote their free checking on an ongoing basis.

"From a defensive standpoint, we should be prepared for a competitor to launch a completely free checking product in our markets. From an offensive standpoint, we have the opportunity to be the first in our markets with our own free-checking product. I believe we could realize significant DDA share gains if we advertised the product."

"What experience have we had with these products?" Kelly asked.

"Well, we've acquired some small banks that had no-fee products, and we've experimented with some limited promotional campaigns in limited market areas," Paul replied. Our free accounts have typically required a minimum balance of $500 or there was a $9.95-per-month fee. The account holder also had to pay $.35 per item for all checks or debits in excess of 20 per month."

"Are these accounts profitable for the bank?" Kelly asked.

"Profitability depends on several variables," Paul answered. "First, there's the account's cash balance during the month. Then, we earn income through fees like NSF charges and ATM fees. We give certain credits to the branch that opened the account, which we treat as revenue. Then, there are allocated expenses, non-interest expenses we allocate to every account. If, however, the account has direct deposit, the allocated expenses are about 25 percent lower, as it is less expensive for us to handle direct deposits. That is why so many free-checking products require direct deposits. The savings help offset the lost fees.

"Given all that, our study shows that the free-checking accounts we have experimented with had average balances of $1,262. Our annual revenue per account from all sources was about $274, and our fully allocated expenses were about $237, giving us an annual profit of about $37. The average account had about four NSF or overdraft charges a year, producing the largest source of account revenue."

"I should add," Bonnie interjected, "that for our 10 different types of checking accounts, including accounts for students and seniors, the lower the average balance, the greater the number of NSF charges, except for our student accounts. Students averaged only about half of the bank's overall NSF average."

"Okay, what's the bottom line in terms of the impact on our revenue if we offered a free-checking product just in our home state?" Kelly asked.

"Our analysis focused on just our home state and estimated that varying percentages of customers from each type of checking account would move to the new product," Paul began. "If we offered the account in all 282 branches in the state for all 522,000 accounts, and if our switching estimates are correct, we could lose

about $4.5 million in various fees (revenue) per year that those accounts are now paying. That is, we would lose this money as our current customers switched from fee-paying accounts to the free accounts. But, of course, we would hope that the new product would draw in new customers to offset those losses, and that those customers would also use other bank products, like home equity loans or car loans."

"Speaking of 'drawing in,' what'll it cost us to promote this program?" Kelly asked.

"Our best estimate for an eight-week promotional program is about $127,000," Paul answered.

WHAT TO DO?

"Thanks for your good work," Kelly responded. "This information is helpful. I've got to decide what to recommend to the Executive Committee.

"I know that free checking is the 'in' thing now in banking, with people believing that free checking gets people in the door. I also know that we make money on lower-income customers' accounts due to fee income and on higher-income customers' accounts due to higher balances. Further, although our total dollar balance in our checking accounts has been growing, our total number of accounts has been declining somewhat.

"One concern I have is whether or not free checking fits the bank's positioning. We've tried to position ourselves as a relationship bank, differentiating ourselves based on service versus price. We build and value long-term customer relationships. For that reason, we've not tried to pay the highest interest rates or charge the lowest fees because we didn't want customers who were focused only on price. I'm not sure free checking fits our image. Further, we've not traditionally advertised products. Rather, we've used corporate advertising that focused on the bank's relationships with its customers.

"This certainly isn't as easy a decision as it might appear," Bonnie noted.

"You can say that again!" Kelly responded. "I'll just have to ponder all this information and decide what to recommend. Thanks for your help."

QUESTIONS FOR DISCUSSION

1. What type of new-product pricing strategy would be involved in considering a new free-checking product for the bank?
2. What types of product-mix pricing considerations do you see in bank's pricing for checking accounts?
3. What types of price adjustment considerations do you see in the pricing strategies for checking accounts?
4. What strategy would you recommend that Southeast Bank pursue on the free-checking account issue? What options does it have? How can break-even analysis (presented in Chapter 11) assist you in your analysis of the various options?

---

*The name of the bank and the names of people in this case have been disguised. Certain data on the bank's operations have also been adjusted but are indicative of reality.

Sources: Officials at Southeast Bank cooperated in development of this case. See also: Tim Henderson, "More ATM Fees, Free Checking," *American Banker,* June 17, 2002, p. 24; Laura Bruce, "Checking Accounts Keep Climbing in Price," Bankrate.com, posted September 28, 2001.

1. explain why companies use distribution channels and discuss the functions these channels perform
2. discuss how channel members interact and how they organize to perform the work of the channel
3. identify the major channel alternatives open to a company
4. explain how companies select, motivate, and evaluate channel members
5. discuss the nature and importance of marketing logistics and integrated supply chain management

Marketing Channels and Supply Chain Management

LOOKING AHEAD: PREVIEWING THE CONCEPTS

We will now examine the third marketing-mix tool—distribution. Firms rarely work alone in bringing value to customers. Instead, most are only a single link in a larger supply chain or distribution channel. As such, an individual firm's success depends not only on how well *it* performs but also on how well its *entire marketing channel* competes with competitors' channels. For example, Ford can make the world's best cars but still not do well if its dealers perform poorly in sales and service against the dealers of Toyota, GM, Chrysler, or Honda. Ford must choose its channel partners carefully and practice sound partner relationship management. The first part of this chapter explores the nature of distribution channels and the marketer's channel design and management decisions. We then examine physical distribution—or logistics—an area that is growing dramatically in importance and sophistication. In the next chapter, we'll look more closely at two major channel intermediaries—retailers and wholesalers.

First, we'll take a look at Caterpillar. You might think that Caterpillar's success, and its ability to charge premium prices, rests on the quality of the construction and mining equipment that it produces. But Caterpillar's former chairman and CEO sees things differently. The company's dominance, he claims, results from its unparalleled distribution and customer support system—from the strong and caring partnerships that it has built with independent Caterpillar dealers. Read on and see why.

For more than half a century, Caterpillar has dominated the world's markets for heavy construction and mining equipment. Its familiar yellow tractors, crawlers, loaders, bulldozers, and trucks are a common sight at any construction area. Caterpillar sells more than 300 products in nearly 200 companies, generating sales of more than $20 billion annually. It captures 27 percent of the worldwide construction-equipment business, more than double that of number two Komatsu. It's share of the North American market is more than twice that of competitors Komatsu and Deere combined.

Many factors contribute to Caterpillar's enduring success—high-quality products, flexible and efficient manufacturing, a steady stream of innovative new products, and a lean organization that is responsive to customer needs. Although Caterpillar charges premium prices for its equipment, its high-quality and trouble-free operation provide greater long-term value. Yet these are not the most important reasons for Caterpillar's dominance. Instead, Caterpillar credits its focus on customers and its corps of 220 outstanding independent dealers worldwide, who do a superb job of taking care of

every customer need. According to former Caterpillar CEO Donald Fites:

> After the product leaves our door, the dealers take over. They are the ones on the front line. They're the ones who live with the product for its lifetime. They're the ones customers see. Although we offer financing and insurance, they arrange those deals for customers. They're out there making sure that when a machine is delivered, it's in the condition it's supposed to be in. They're out there training a customer's operators. They service a product frequently throughout its life, carefully monitoring a machine's health and scheduling repairs to prevent costly downtime. The customer . . . knows that there is a $20-billion-plus company called Caterpillar. But the dealers create the image of a company that doesn't just stand *behind* its products but *with* its products, anywhere in the world. Our dealers are the reason that our motto—Buy the Iron, Get the Company—is not an empty slogan.

Caterpillar's dealers build strong customer relationships in their communities. "Our independent dealer in Novi, Michigan, or in Bangkok, Thailand, knows so much more about the requirements of customers in those locations than a huge corporation like Caterpillar could," says Fites. Competitors often bypass their dealers and sell directly to big customers to cut costs or make more profits for themselves. However, Caterpillar wouldn't think of going around its dealers. "The knowledge of the local market and the close relations with customers that our dealers provide are worth every penny," he asserts with passion. "We'd rather cut off our right arm than sell directly to customers and bypass our dealers."

Caterpillar and its dealers work in close harmony to find better ways to bring value to customers. The entire system is linked by a single worldwide computer network. For example, working at their desktop computers, Caterpillar managers can check to see how many Cat machines in the world are waiting for parts. Closely linked dealers play a vital role in almost every aspect of Caterpillar's operations, from product design and delivery, to product service and support, to market intelligence and customer feedback.

In the heavy-equipment industry, in which equipment downtime can mean big losses, Caterpillar's exceptional service gives it a huge advantage in winning and keeping customers. Consider Freeport-McMoRan, a Cat customer that operates one of the world's largest copper and gold mines, 24 hours a day, 365 days a year. High in the mountains of Indonesia, the mine is accessible only by aerial cableway or helicopter. Freeport-McMoRan relies on more than 500 pieces of Caterpillar mining and construction equipment—worth several hundred million dollars—including loaders, tractors, and mammoth 240-ton, 2,000-plus-horsepower trucks. Many of these machines cost well over $1 million apiece. When equipment breaks down, Freeport-McMoRan loses money fast. Freeport-McMoRan gladly pays a premium price for machines and service it can count on. It knows that it can count on Caterpillar and its outstanding distribution network for superb support.

The close working relationship between Caterpillar and its dealers comes down to more than just formal contracts and business agreements. The powerful partnership rests on a handful of basic principles and practices:

- *Dealer profitability:* Caterpillar's rule: "Share the gain as well as the pain." When times are good, Caterpillar shares the bounty with its dealers rather than trying to grab all the riches for itself. When times are bad, Caterpillar protects its dealers. In the mid-1980s, facing a depressed global construction-equipment market and cutthroat competition, Caterpillar sheltered its dealers by absorbing much of the economic damage. It lost almost $1 billion dollars in just three years but didn't lose a single dealer. In contrast, competitors' dealers struggled and many failed. As a result, Caterpillar emerged with its distribution system intact and its competitive position stronger than ever.

- *Extraordinary dealer support:* Nowhere is this support more apparent than in the company's parts delivery system, the fastest and most reliable in the industry.

Caterpillar maintains 36 distribution centers and 1,500 service facilities around the world, which stock 320,000 different parts and ship 84,000 items per day, every day of the year. In turn, dealers have made huge investments in inventory, warehouses, fleets of trucks, service bays, diagnostic and service equipment, and information technology. Together, Caterpillar and its dealers guarantee parts delivery within 48 hours anywhere in the world. The company ships 80 percent of parts orders immediately and 99 percent on the same day the order is received. In contrast, it's not unusual for competitors' customers to wait four or five days for a part.

- *Communications:* Caterpillar communicates with its dealers—fully, frequently, and honestly. According to Fites, "There are no secrets between us and our dealers. We have the financial statements and key operating data of every dealer in the world. . . . In addition, virtually all Caterpillar and dealer employees have real-time access to continually updated databases of service information, sales trends and forecasts, customer satisfaction surveys, and other critical data. . . . [Moreover,] virtually everyone from the youngest design engineer to the CEO now has direct contact with somebody in our dealer organizations."

- *Dealer performance:* Caterpillar does all it can to ensure that its dealerships are run well. It closely monitors each dealership's sales, market position, service capability, financial situation, and other performance measures. It genuinely wants each dealer to succeed, and when it sees a problem, it jumps in to help. As a result, Caterpillar dealerships, many of which are family businesses, tend to be stable and profitable. The average Caterpillar dealership has remained in the hands of the same family for more than 50 years. Some actually predate the 1925 merger that created Caterpillar.

- *Personal relationships:* In addition to more formal business ties, Cat forms close personal ties with its dealers in a kind of family relationship. Fites relates the following example: "When I see Chappy Chapman, a retired executive vice-president . . . , out on the golf course, he always asks about particular dealers or about their children, who may be running the business now. And every time I see those dealers, they inquire, 'How's Chappy?' That's the sort of relationship we have. . . . I consider the majority of dealers personal friends."

Thus, Caterpillar's superb distribution system serves as a major source of competitive advantage. The system is built on a firm base of mutual trust and shared dreams. Caterpillar and its dealers feel a deep pride in what they are accomplishing together. As Fites puts it, "There's a camaraderie among our dealers around the world that really makes it more than just a financial arrangement. They feel that what they're doing is good for the world because they are part of an organization that makes, sells, and tends to the machines that make the world work."[1]

Most firms cannot bring value to customers by themselves. Instead, they must work closely with other firms in a larger value delivery network.

Supply Chains and the Value Delivery Network

Producing a product or service and making it available to buyers requires building relationships not just with customers, but also with key suppliers and resellers in the company's *supply chain*. This supply chain consists of upstream and downstream partners, including suppliers, intermediaries, and even intermediary's customers.

Upstream from the manufacturer or service provider is the set of firms that supply the raw materials, components, parts, information, finances, and expertise needed to create a product or service. Marketers, however, have traditionally focused on the "downstream" side of the supply chain—on the *marketing channels* or *distribution channels* that look forward toward the customer. Marketing channel partners such as wholesalers and retailers form a vital connection between the firm and its target consumers.

Both upstream and downstream partners may also be part of other firms' supply chains. But it is the unique design of each company's supply chain that enables it to deliver superior value to customers. An individual firm's success depends not only on how well *it* performs but also on how well its entire supply chain and marketing channel competes with competitors' channels.

The term *supply chain* may be too limited—it takes a *make-and-sell* view of the business. It suggests that raw materials, productive inputs, and factory capacity should serve as the starting point for market planning. A better term would be *demand chain* because it suggests a *sense-and-respond* view of the market. Under this view, planning starts with the needs of target customers, to which the company responds by organizing resources with the goal of building profitable customer relationships.

Even a demand-chain view of a business may be too limited, because it takes a step-by-step linear view of purchase-production-consumption activities. With the advent of the Internet, however, companies are forming more numerous and complex relationships with other firms. For example, Ford manages numerous supply chains. It also sponsors or transacts on many B2B Web sites and online purchasing exchanges as needs arise. Like Ford, most large companies today are engaged in building and managing a continuously evolving *value delivery network*.

Value delivery network

The network made up of the company, suppliers, distributors, and ultimately customers who "partner" with each other to improve the performance of the entire system.

Companies today are increasingly taking a full-value-delivery-network view of their businesses. As defined in Chapter 2, a **value delivery network** is made up of the company, suppliers, distributors, and ultimately customers who "partner" with each other to improve the performance of the entire system. For example, Palm, the leading manufacturer of handheld devices, manages a whole community of suppliers and assemblers of semiconductor components, plastic cases, LCD displays, and accessories; of offline and online resellers; and of 45,000 complementors who have created over 5,000 applications for the Palm operating systems. All of these diverse partners must work effectively together to bring superior value to Palm's customers.

This chapter focuses on marketing channels—on the downstream side of the value delivery network. However, it is important to remember that this is only part of the full value network. To bring value to customers, companies need upstream supplier partners just as the need downstream channel partners. To provide banking services, for example, Citibank buys equipment and supplies such as automated teller machines (ATMs), printed deposit slips, and computers. To make its services available to customers and obtain information about customer transactions, the bank maintains a distribution channel consisting of company-owned bank branches and Web sites as well as thousands of ATMs owned by other banks. Increasingly, marketers are participating in and influencing their company's upstream activities as well as its downstream activities. More than marketing channel managers, they are becoming full network managers.

The chapter examines four major questions concerning marketing channels: What is the nature of marketing channels and why are they important? How do channel firms interact and organize to do the work of the channel? What problems do companies face in designing and

Value delivery network: Palm manages a whole community of suppliers, assemblers, resellers, and complementors who must work effectively together to make life easier for Palm's customers.

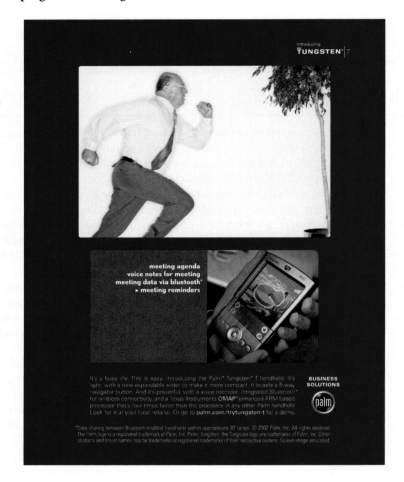

managing their channels? What role do physical distribution and supply chain management play in attracting and satisfying customers? In Chapter 14, we will look at marketing channel issues from the viewpoint of retailers and wholesalers.

The Nature and Importance of Marketing Channels

Marketing channel (distribution channel)

A set of interdependent organizations involved in the process of making a product or service available for use or consumption by the consumer or business user.

Few producers sell their goods directly to the final users. Instead, most use intermediaries to bring their products to market. They try to forge a **marketing channel** (or **distribution channel**)—a set of interdependent organizations involved in the process of making a product or service available for use or consumption by the consumer or business user.[2]

A company's channel decisions directly affect every other marketing decision. The company's pricing depends on whether it works with national discount chains, uses high-quality specialty stores, or sells directly to consumers via the Web. The firm's sales force and communications decisions depend on how much persuasion, training, motivation, and support its channel partners need. Whether a company develops or acquires certain new products may depend on how well those products fit the capabilities of its channel members.

Companies often pay too little attention to their distribution channels, however, sometimes with damaging results. In contrast, many companies have used imaginative distribution systems to *gain* a competitive advantage. The creative and imposing distribution system of FedEx made it a leader in the transportation industry. Dell Computer revolutionized its industry by selling personal computers directly to consumers rather than through retail stores. And Charles Schwab & Company pioneered the delivery of financial services via the Internet.

Distribution channel decisions often involve long-term commitments to other firms. For example, companies such as Ford, IBM, or McDonald's can easily change their advertising, pricing, or promotion programs. They can scrap old products and introduce new ones as market tastes demand. But when they set up distribution channels through contracts with franchisees,

FedEx's creative and imposing distribution system made it a leader in the small-package delivery industry.

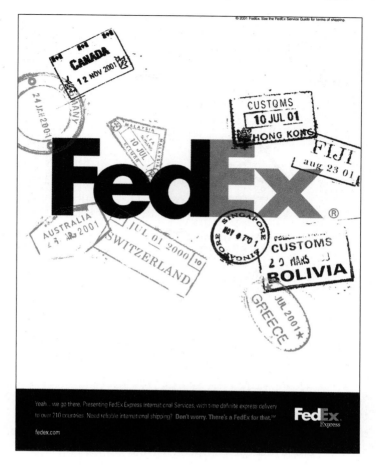

independent dealers, or large retailers, they cannot readily replace these channels with company-owned stores or Web sites if conditions change. Therefore, management must design its channels carefully, with an eye on tomorrow's likely selling environment as well as today's.

How Channel Members Add Value

Why do producers give some of the selling job to channel partners? After all, doing so means giving up some control over how and to whom the products are sold. The use of intermediaries results from their greater efficiency in making goods available to target markets. Through their contacts, experience, specialization, and scale of operation, intermediaries usually offer the firm more than it can achieve on its own.

Figure 13.1 shows how using intermediaries can provide economies. Figure 13.1A shows three manufacturers, each using direct marketing to reach three customers. This system requires nine different contacts. Figure 13.1B shows the three manufacturers working through one distributor, which contacts the three customers. This system requires only six contacts. In this way, intermediaries reduce the amount of work that must be done by both producers and consumers.

From the economic system's point of view, the role of marketing intermediaries is to transform the assortments of products made by producers into the assortments wanted by consumers. Producers make narrow assortments of products in large quantities, but consumers want broad assortments of products in small quantities. In the marketing channels, intermediaries buy large quantities from many producers and break them down into the smaller quantities and broader assortments wanted by consumers. Thus, intermediaries play an important role in matching supply and demand.

In making products and services available to consumers, channel members add value by bridging the major time, place, and possession gaps that separate goods and services from those who would use them. Members of the marketing channel perform many key functions. Some help to complete transactions:

FIGURE 13.1

How a marketing intermediary reduces the number of channel transactions

A. Number of contacts without a distributor
$M \times C = 3 \times 3 = 9$

B. Number of contacts with a distributor
$M + C = 3 + 3 = 6$

= Manufacturer   = Customer   = Distributor

- *Information:* Gathering and distributing marketing research and intelligence information about actors and forces in the marketing environment needed for planning and aiding exchange.
- *Promotion:* Developing and spreading persuasive communications about an offer.
- *Contact:* Finding and communicating with prospective buyers.
- *Matching:* Shaping and fitting the offer to the buyer's needs, including activities such as manufacturing, grading, assembling, and packaging.
- *Negotiation:* Reaching an agreement on price and other terms of the offer so that ownership or possession can be transferred.

Others help to fulfill the completed transactions:

- *Physical distribution:* Transporting and storing goods.
- *Financing:* Acquiring and using funds to cover the costs of the channel work.
- *Risk taking:* Assuming the risks of carrying out the channel work.

The question is not *whether* these functions need to be performed—they must be—but rather *who* will perform them. To the extent that the manufacturer performs these functions, its costs go up and its prices have to be higher. When some of these functions are shifted to intermediaries, the producer's costs and prices may be lower, but the intermediaries must charge more to cover the costs of their work. In dividing the work of the channel, the various functions should be assigned to the channel members who can add the most value for the cost.

Channel level

A layer of intermediaries that performs some work in bringing the product and its ownership closer to the final buyer.

Direct marketing channel

A marketing channel that has no intermediary levels.

Indirect marketing channel

Channel containing one or more intermediary levels.

Number of Channel Levels

Companies can design their distribution channels to make products and services available to customers in different ways. Each layer of marketing intermediaries that performs some work in bringing the product and its ownership closer to the final buyer is a **channel level.** Because the producer and the final consumer both perform some work, they are part of every channel.

The *number of intermediary levels* indicates the *length* of a channel. Figure 13.2A shows several consumer distribution channels of different lengths. Channel 1, called a **direct marketing channel,** has no intermediary levels; the company sells directly to consumers. For example, Avon, Amway, and Tupperware sell their products door-to-door, through home and office sales parties, and on the Web; L.L. Bean sells clothing direct through mail catalogs, by telephone, and online; and a university sells education on its campus or through distance learning. The remaining channels in Figure 13.2A are **indirect marketing channels,** containing one or more intermediaries.

FIGURE 13.2
Consumer and business marketing channels

A. Consumer marketing channels

B. Business marketing channels

Figure 13.2B shows some common business distribution channels. The business marketer can use its own sales force to sell directly to business customers. Or it can sell to various types of intermediaries, who in turn sell to these customers. Consumer and business marketing channels with even more levels are sometimes found, but less often. From the producer's point of view, a greater number of levels means less control and greater channel complexity. Moreover, all of the institutions in the channel are connected by several types of *flows*. These include the *physical flow* of products, the *flow of ownership,* the *payment flow,* the *information flow,* and the *promotion flow.* These flows can make even channels with only one or a few levels very complex.

Channel Behavior and Organization

Distribution channels are more than simple collections of firms tied together by various flows. They are complex behavioral systems in which people and companies interact to accomplish individual, company, and channel goals. Some channel systems consist only of informal interactions among loosely organized firms; others consist of formal interactions guided by strong organizational structures. Moreover, channel systems do not stand still—new types of intermediaries emerge and whole new channel systems evolve. Here we look at channel behavior and at how members organize to do the work of the channel.

Channel Behavior

A marketing channel consists of firms that have banded together for their common good. Each channel member depends on the others. For example, a Ford dealer depends on Ford to design cars that meet consumer needs. In turn, Ford depends on the dealer to attract consumers, persuade them to buy Ford cars, and service cars after the sale. The Ford dealer also depends on other dealers to provide good sales and service that will uphold the brand's reputation. In fact, the success of individual Ford dealers depends on how well the entire Ford marketing channel competes with the channels of other auto manufacturers.

Each channel member plays a specialized role in the channel. For example, Sony's role is to produce personal consumer electronics products that consumers will like and to create demand

Direct marketing channels: L. L. Bean sells direct through mail catalogs, the telephone, and the Internet.

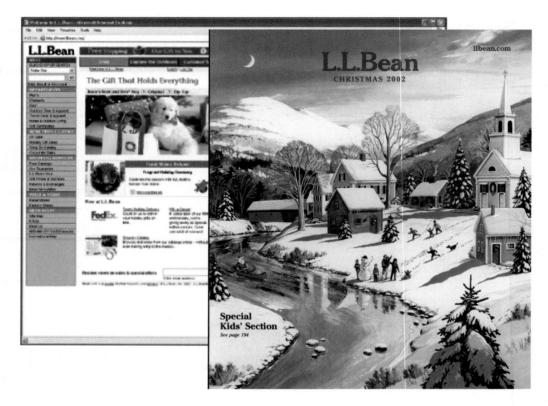

through national advertising. Best Buy's role is to display these Sony products in convenient locations, to answer buyers' questions, and to close sales. The channel will be most effective when each member is assigned the tasks it can do best.

Ideally, because the success of individual channel members depends on overall channel success, all channel firms should work together smoothly. They should understand and accept their roles, coordinate their activities, and cooperate to attain overall channel goals. However, individual channel members rarely take such a broad view. Cooperating to achieve overall channel goals sometimes means giving up individual company goals. Although channel members depend on one another, they often act alone in their own short-run best interests. They often disagree on who should do what and for what rewards. Such disagreements over goals, roles, and rewards generate **channel conflict.**

Horizontal conflict occurs among firms at the same level of the channel. For instance, some Ford dealers in Chicago might complain the other dealers in the city steal sales from them by pricing too low or by selling outside their assigned territories. Or Holiday Inn franchisees might complain about other Holiday Inn operators overcharging guests or giving poor service, hurting the overall Holiday Inn image.

Vertical conflict, conflicts between different levels of the same channel, is even more common. For example, H&R Block franchisees complained when the parent company began using the Internet to deal directly with customers. Similarly, McDonald's created conflict with some of its California dealers when it placed new stores in areas that took business from existing locations. And office furniture maker Herman Miller created conflict with its dealers when it opened an online store—www.hmstore.com—and began selling its products directly to customers. Although Herman Miller believed that the Web site was reaching only smaller customers who weren't being served by current channels, dealers complained loudly. As a result, the company closed down its online sales operations.[3]

Some conflict in the channel takes the form of healthy competition. Such competition can be good for the channel—without it, the channel could become passive and noninnovative. But severe or prolonged conflict can disrupt channel effectiveness and cause lasting harm to channel relationships. Companies should manage channel conflict to keep it from getting out of hand. Here's an example:

P&G recently moved to manage channel conflict stemming from its change to multichannel distribution for Iams pet products. Traditionally, Iams had been distributed through special-

Channel conflict

Disagreement among marketing channel members on goals and roles—who should do what and for what rewards.

ized pet stores and veterinary offices. After studies showed that 70 percent of pet-food buyers never visit pet stores, P&G decided to add 25,000 grocery stores and mass retailers to its channel. To head off conflict with traditional channels, P&G's president wrote to the specialty stores and veterinarians, explaining that the new arrangements would increase brand awareness and not hurt brand equity. Although some pet stores stopped carrying Iams, most continued on, helping Iams boost sales and market share for all of its dealer.[4]

Vertical Marketing Systems

For the channel as a whole to perform well, each channel member's role must be specified and channel conflict must be managed. The channel will perform better if it includes a firm, agency, or mechanism that provides leadership and has the power to assign roles and manage conflict.

Historically, *conventional distribution channels* have lacked such leadership and power, often resulting in damaging conflict and poor performance. One of the biggest channel developments over the years has been the emergence of *vertical marketing systems* that provide channel leadership. Figure 13.3 contrasts the two types of channel arrangements.

A **conventional distribution channel** consists of one or more independent producers, wholesalers, and retailers. Each is a separate business seeking to maximize its own profits, even at the expense of the system as a whole. No channel member has much control over the other members, and no formal means exists for assigning roles and resolving channel conflict. In contrast, a **vertical marketing system (VMS)** consists of producers, wholesalers, and retailers acting as a unified system. One channel member owns the others, has contracts with them, or wields so much power that they must all cooperate. The VMS can be dominated by the producer, wholesaler, or retailer.

We look now at three major types of VMSs: *corporate, contractual,* and *administered.* Each uses a different means for setting up leadership and power in the channel.

Corporate VMS

A **corporate VMS** integrates successive stages of production and distribution under single ownership. Coordination and conflict management are attained through regular organizational channels. For example, Sears obtains more than 50 percent of its goods from companies that it partly or wholly owns. Giant Food Stores operates an ice-making facility, a soft drink bottling operation, an ice cream plant, and a bakery that supplies Giant stores with everything from bagels to birthday cakes. And little-known Italian eyewear maker Luxottica sells its many famous eyewear brands—including Giorgio, Armani, Yves Saint Laurent, and Ray-Ban—through the world's largest optical chain, LensCrafters, which it also owns.[5]

Conventional distribution channel

A channel consisting of one or more independent producers, wholesalers, and retailers, each a separate business seeking to maximize its own profits, even at the expense of profits for the system as a whole.

Vertical marketing system (VMS)

A distribution channel structure in which producers, wholesalers, and retailers act as a unified system. One channel member owns the others, has contracts with them, or has so much power that they all cooperate.

Corporate VMS

A vertical marketing system that combines successive stages of production and distribution under single ownership—channel leadership is established through common ownership.

FIGURE 13.3
A conventional marketing channel versus a vertical marketing system

Controlling the entire distribution chain has turned Spanish clothing chain Zara into the world's fastest-growing fashion retailer.

The secret to Zara's success is its control over almost every aspect of the supply chain, from design and production to its own worldwide distribution network. Zara makes 40 percent of its own fabrics and produces more than half of its own clothes, rather than relying on a hodgepodge of slow-moving suppliers. New styles take shape in Zara's own design centers, supported by real-time sales data. New designs feed into Zara manufacturing centers, which ship finished products directly to 450 Zara stores in 30 countries, saving time, eliminating the need for warehouses, and keeping inventories low. Effective vertical integration makes Zara faster, more flexible, and more efficient than international competitors such as Gap, Benetton, and Sweden's H&M. Zara can make a new line from start to finish in just three weeks, so a look seen on MTV can be in Zara stores within a month, versus an industry average of nine months. And Zara's low costs let it offer midmarket chic at downmarket prices. The company's stylish but affordable offerings have attracted a cult following, and the company's sales have more than doubled to $2.3 billion in the past five years.[6]

Contractual VMS

Contractual VMS

A vertical marketing system in which independent firms at different levels of production and distribution join together through contracts to obtain more economies or sales impact than they could achieve alone.

Franchise organization

A contractual vertical marketing system in which a channel member, called a franchiser, links several stages in the production-distribution process.

A **contractual VMS** consists of independent firms at different levels of production and distribution who join together through contracts to obtain more economies or sales impact than each could achieve alone. Coordination and conflict management are attained through contractual agreements among channel members. The **franchise organization** is the most common type of contractual relationship—a channel member called a *franchiser* links several stages in the production-distribution process. An estimated 2,000 franchised U.S. companies with over 320,000 outlets account for some $1 trillion in annual sales. Industry analysts estimate the a new franchise outlet opens somewhere in the United States every eight minutes and that about one out of every 12 retail business establishments outlets is a franchised business.[7] Almost every kind of business has been franchised—from motels and fast-food restaurants to dental centers and dating services, from wedding consultants and maid services to funeral homes and fitness centers.

There are three type of franchises. The first type is the *manufacturer-sponsored retailer franchise system*—for example, Ford and its network of independent franchised dealers. The second type is the *manufacturer-sponsored wholesaler franchise system*—Coca-Cola licenses bottlers (wholesalers) in various markets who buy Coca-Cola syrup concentrate and then bottle and sell the finished product

Contractual VMS: An estimated 2,000 franchised U.S. companies with over 320,000 outlets account for some $1 trillion in annual sales.

to retailers in local markets. The third type is the *service-firm-sponsored retailer franchise system*—examples are found in the auto-rental business (Hertz, Avis), the fast-food service business (McDonald's, Burger King), and the motel business (Holiday Inn, Ramada Inn).

The fact that most consumers cannot tell the difference between contractual and corporate VMSs shows how successfully the contractual organizations compete with corporate chains. Chapter 14 presents a fuller discussion of the various contractual VMSs.

Administered VMS

Administered VMS

A vertical marketing system that coordinates successive stages of production and distribution, not through common ownership or contractual ties, but through the size and power of one of the parties.

In an **administered VMS,** leadership is assumed not through common ownership or contractual ties but through the size and power of one or a few dominant channel members. Manufacturers of a top brand can obtain strong trade cooperation and support from resellers. For example, General Electric, Procter & Gamble, and Kraft can command unusual cooperation from resellers regarding displays, shelf space, promotions, and price policies. Large retailers such as Wal-Mart, Home Depot, and Barnes & Noble can exert strong influence on the manufacturers that supply the products they sell.

Horizontal Marketing Systems

Horizontal marketing system

A channel arrangement in which two or more companies at one level join together to follow a new marketing opportunity.

Another channel development is the **horizontal marketing system,** in which two or more companies at one level join together to follow a new marketing opportunity. By working together, companies can combine their financial, production, or marketing resources to accomplish more than any one company could alone.

Companies might join forces with competitors or noncompetitors. They might work with each other on a temporary or permanent basis, or they may create a separate company. For example, the Lamar Savings Bank of Texas arranged to locate its savings offices and automated teller machines in Safeway stores. Lamar gained quicker market entry at a low cost, and Safeway was able to offer in-store banking convenience to its customers. Similarly, McDonald's now places "express" versions of its restaurants in Wal-Mart stores. McDonald's benefits from Wal-Mart's considerable store traffic, while Wal-Mart keeps hungry shoppers from having to go elsewhere to eat.

Such channel arrangements also work well globally. For example, because of its excellent coverage of international markets, Nestlé jointly sells General Mills's cereal brands in markets outside North America. Coca-Cola and Nestlé formed a joint venture to market ready-to-drink coffee and tea worldwide. Coke provides worldwide experience in marketing and distributing beverages, and Nestlé contributes two established brand names—Nescafé and Nestea. Seiko Watch's distribution partner in Japan, K. Hattori, markets Schick's razors there, giving Schick the leading market share in Japan, despite Gillette's overall strength in many other markets.

Horizontal marketing systems: Nestlé jointly sells General Mills cereal brands in markets outside North America.

FIGURE 13.4
Multichannel distribution
system

Multichannel Distribution Systems

Multichannel distribution system

A distribution system in which a single firm sets up two or more marketing channels to reach one or more customer segments.

In the past, many companies used a single channel to sell to a single market or market segment. Today, with the proliferation of customer segments and channel possibilities, more and more companies have adopted **multichannel distribution systems**—often called *hybrid marketing channels.* Such multichannel marketing occurs when a single firm sets up two or more marketing channels to reach one or more customer segments. The use of multichannel systems has increased greatly in recent years.

Figure 13.4 shows a hybrid channel. In the figure, the producer sells directly to consumer segment 1 using direct-mail catalogs, telemarketing, and the Internet and reaches consumer segment 2 through retailers. It sells indirectly to business segment 1 through distributors and dealers and to business segment 2 through its own sales force.

These days, almost every large company and many small ones distribute through multiple channels. Charles Schwab reaches customers through its branch offices, by telephone, and over the Internet. Staples markets through its traditional retail outlets, a direct-response Internet site, virtual malls, and 30,000 links on affiliated sites. And IBM uses multiple channels to serve dozens of segments and niches, ranging from large corporate buyers to small businesses to home office buyers. In addition to selling through its vaunted sales force, IBM also sells through a full network of distributors and value-added resellers, which sell IBM computers, systems, and services to a variety of special business segments. Final consumers can buy IBM personal computers from specialty computer stores or any of several large retailers. IBM uses telemarketing to service the needs of small and medium-size business. And both business and final consumers can buy online from the company's Web site (www.ibm.com).

Multichannel distribution systems offer many advantages to companies facing large and complex markets. With each new channel, the company expands its sales and market coverage and gains opportunities to tailor its products and services to the specific needs of diverse customer segments. But such multichannel channel systems are harder to control, and they generate conflict as more channels compete for customers and sales. For example, when IBM began selling directly to customers through catalogs, telemarketing, and its own Web site, many of its retail dealers cried "unfair competition" and threatened to drop the IBM line or to give it less emphasis. Many outside salespeople felt that they were being undercut by the new "inside channels."

Changing Channel Organization

Disintermediation

The displacement of traditional resellers from a marketing channel by radically new types of intermediaries.

Changes in technology and the explosive growth of direct and online marketing are having a profound impact on the nature and design of marketing channels. One major trend is toward **disintermediation**—a big term with a clear message and important consequences. Disintermediation means that more and more, product and service producers are bypassing intermediaries and going directly to final buyers, or that radically new types of channel intermediaries are emerging to displace traditional ones.

Thus, in many industries, traditional intermediaries are dropping by the wayside. For example, companies such as Dell Computer and American Airlines are selling directly to final buyers, eliminating retailers from their marketing channels. E-commerce is growing rapidly, taking business from traditional brick-and-mortar retailers. Consumers can buy Flowers from 1-800-Flowers.com; books, videos, CDs, toys, consumer electronics, and other goods from Amazon.com; and clothes from landsend.com or gap.com, all without ever visiting a store.

Disintermediation presents problems and opportunities for both producers and intermediaries (see Real Marketing 13.1). To avoid being swept aside, traditional intermediaries must find new ways to add value in the supply chain. To remain competitive, product and service producers must develop new channel opportunities, such as the Internet and other direct channels. However, developing these new channels often brings them into direct competition with their established channels, resulting in conflict.

To ease this problem, companies often look for ways to make going direct a plus for both the company and its channel partners. For example, to trim costs and add business, Hewlett-Packard opened three direct-sales Web sites—Shopping Village (for consumers), H-P Commerce Center (for businesses buying from authorized resellers), and Electronic Solutions Now (for existing contract customers). However, to avoid conflicts with its established reseller channels, HP forwards all its Web orders to resellers, who complete the orders, ship the products, and get the commissions. In this way, H-P gains the advantages of direct selling but also boosts business for resellers.

Channel Design Decisions

We now look at several channel decisions manufacturers face. In designing marketing channels, manufacturers struggle between what is ideal and what is practical. A new firm with limited capital usually starts by selling in a limited market area. Deciding on the *best* channels might not be a problem: The problem might simply be how to convince one or a few good intermediaries to handle the line.

If successful, the new firm might branch out to new markets through the existing intermediaries. In smaller markets, the firm might sell directly to retailers; in larger markets, it might sell through distributors. In one part of the country, it might grant exclusive franchises; in another, it might sell through all available outlets. Then, it might add a Web store that sells directly to hard-to-reach customers. In this way, channel systems often evolve to meet market opportunities and conditions.

For maximum effectiveness, however, channel analysis and decision making should be more purposeful. Designing a channel system calls for analyzing consumer needs, setting channel objectives, identifying major channel alternatives, and evaluating them.

Analyzing Consumer Needs

As noted previously, marketing channels are part of the overall *customer value delivery network*. Each channel member adds value for the customer. Thus, designing the marketing channel starts with finding out what target consumers want from the channel. Do consumers want to buy from nearby locations or are they willing to travel to more distant centralized locations? Would they rather buy in person, over the phone, through the mail, or via the Internet? Do they value breadth of assortment or do they prefer specialization? Do consumers want many add-on services (delivery, credit, repairs, installation), or will they obtain these elsewhere? The faster the delivery, the greater the assortment provided, and the more add-on services supplied, the greater the channel's service level.

Providing the fastest delivery, greatest assortment, and most services may not be possible or practical. The company and its channel members may not have the resources or skills needed to provide all the desired services. Also, providing higher levels of service results in higher costs for the channel and higher prices for consumers. The company must balance consumer needs not only against the feasibility and costs of meeting these needs but also against customer price preferences. The success of discount retailing—on and off the Web—shows that consumers will often accept lower service levels in exchange for lower prices.

real marketing 13.1

Disintermediation: A Fancy Word but a Clear Message

Sunflower Travel of Wichita, Kansas, typifies the kind of business most threatened by the advent of new marketing channels, particularly the surge in Internet selling. Like other traditional travel agencies, Sunflower faces some scary new-age competitors. In recent years, it's seen a flurry of online competitors—ranging from giant travel supersites such as

number of U.S. travel agents dropped by 18 percent, and some studies suggest that another 25 percent will go out of business during the next few years.

Resellers in dozens of industries face similar situations as new channel forms threaten to make them obsolete. There's even a fancy 17-letter word to describe this

costs and inefficiencies from the traditional computer supply chain.

More broadly, disintermediation includes not only the elimination of channel levels through direct marketing but also the displacement of traditional resellers by radically new types of intermediaries. For example, the publishing industry had for decades assumed that book buyers wanted to purchase their books from small, intimate, neighborhood bookshops. Then along came the book superstores—Barnes & Noble and Borders—with their huge inventories and low prices. Disintermediation occurred as the new intermediaries rapidly displaced traditional independent booksellers. Then online bookseller Amazon.com emerged to threaten the category killers. Amazon.com doesn't eliminate the retail channel—it's actually a new type of retailer that increases consumers' channel choices rather than reducing them. Still, disintermediation has occurred as Amazon.com and the superstores' own Web sites are displacing traditional brick-and-mortar retailers.

Disintermediation is often associated with the surge in online selling. And, in fact, the Internet is a major disintermediating force. By facilitating direct contact between buyers and sellers, the Internet is displacing channels in industries ranging from books, apparel, and consumer electronics to travel, stock brokerage, and real estate services. However, disintermediation can involve almost any new form of channel competition. For example, Dell bypassed retailers through telephone and mail-order selling long before it took to the Internet.

Disintermediation works only when a new channel form succeeds in bringing greater value to consumers. Thus, if Amazon.com weren't giving buyers greater convenience, selection, and value, it wouldn't be able to lure customers away from traditional retailers. If Dell's direct channel weren't more efficient and effective in serving the needs of computer buyers, traditional retail channels would have little to fear. However, the success of these new channels suggests that they *are* bringing greater value to significant segments of consumers.

From a producer's viewpoint, although eliminating unneeded intermediaries makes

Top avoid "disintermediation," Sunflower Travel now adds value in ways that online travel merchants can't—by getting to know consumers and specializing in market niches. It's even turned the Web from foe to friend.

Expedia, Travelocity, Priceline, and Orbitz to newcomers like Trip.com and Hotwire.com—that let consumers surf the Web for rockbottom travel deals. To make matters worse, the airlines themselves now sell more half of their own tickets online and no longer pay travel agencies commissions on ticket sales.

These new channels give consumers more choices, but they threaten the very existence of Sunflower Travel and other traditional travel agents. During the 1990s, the

phenomenon: *disintermediation*. Strictly speaking, disintermediation means the elimination of a layer of intermediaries from a marketing channel. For example, for years personal computer makers assumed that customers needed hands-on buying experience, with lots of point-of-sale inventory and hand-holding sales assistance from retailers. Then, along came Dell Computer with its direct model. By eliminating retailers, Dell eliminated many sense, disintermediation can be very difficult. One analyst summarizes it this way:

> You thought e-commerce would bring nothing but good news. Here at last, you reasoned, is a way to add customers, boost market share, and cut sales costs. All manufacturers have to do is set up an electronic conduit between themselves and their customers and voilà, instant sales channel. There's just one little hitch. Those same thoughts terrify the retailers, distributors, and resellers that account for up to 90 percent of manufacturers' revenues. They fear that their role between company and customer will be rendered obsolete by the virtual marketplace. And that puts manufacturers in a bind. Either they surrender to the seductions of e-commerce and risk a mutiny from those valuable partners, or they do nothing and risk the wrath of [successful e-commerce competitors].

Thus, although bypassing channel intermediaries can help a company compete, it also may create conflict with the established channel partners that most companies count on for the bulk of their sales.

Still, most producers know that when more-effective channels come along, they have no choice but to change. Despite the risks, most companies are more afraid of being late to the party than of angering their channel partners. The major question often is not whether to move to a new, high-growth channel but how quickly to do it and what to do with the established channel. One answer is to join forces with channel partners so that both benefit from new channel opportunities. For example, consider Maytag:

> Appliance giant Maytag wanted to leverage its powerful brand name and great quality reputation by selling appliances on the Web. Maytag's goal was to sell to customers without forcing them to travel to a dealer, where they might be seduced by other brands. However, Maytag didn't want to damage its relationships with the thousands of dealers around the country that sell the bulk of its appliances. The solution was to help *dealers* close sales online. The company created My Maytag, a feature on its main Web site, by which customers could learn about and purchase Maytag products. But rather than filling the orders directly, the company handed them off to dealers. With My Maytag, everyone wins: Online consumers get a convenient and seamless shopping experience, dealers get the sales, and Maytag avoids channel conflict and boosts its business.

What about traditional resellers? How can they avoid being "Delled" or "Amazoned"? The answer lies in continually looking for new ways to create real customer value. For example, Sunflower Travel now works at adding value in ways that online computers can't—by getting to know consumers and specializing in market niches. It's even turned the Web from foe to friend by using it as a tool for ferreting out new customers and serving them better.

To meet the Internet threat, Sunflower began focusing on packaged tours in the South Pacific, an area that owner Barbara Hansen loves and has traveled to extensively. She established a strong business relationship with a wholesaler who works in Australia and New Zealand, and began promoting packaged tours. In addition to her Sunflower Web site, she launched a new one: ANZtours.com. She made certain that the New Zealand Tourist Office in New York had a link to her site. To put together tour groups, Hansen began scouring Web sites for wine stores, sending them information about food and wine tours through Australia. She's been in touch with garden clubs and florists, and is selling a package tour to Canberra, Australia's "Floriade," a horticultural show in Canberra, Australia. She knows the music director for a local chamber group who hails from New Zealand, and is making him part of a tour of musical performances Down Under. "The Internet is so neat," she says. "You can go and search for these groups, and let them know what you are doing." The lesson: New technologies can put entire industries out of business. But the same technologies open doors, too, for entrepreneurs with the courage to walk through them.

Discount brokerage Charles Schwab also proves the value point. Facing a horde of price-cutting e-commerce competitors who got there first—including E*Trade and Ameritrade—Schwab jumped into the Internet with both feet (remember our Chapter 3 discussion?). However, instead of becoming just another no-frills Internet trading operation, Schwab did competitors one better. It plied customers with a wealth of tools and information for managing their accounts, assuming the role of an investment adviser. Rather than dragging its feet or fighting the change, Schwab embraced the new channel as a competitive opportunity.

Thus, disintermediation is a big word but the meaning is clear. Those who continually seek new ways to add real value for customers have little to fear. However, those who fall behind in adding value risk being swept aside by their customers and channel partners.

Sources: Extracts adapted from Rochelle Garner, "Mad as Hell," *Sales & Marketing Management,* June 1999, pp. 55–61; Maricris G. Briones, "What Technology Wrought: Distribution Channel in Flux," *Marketing News,* February 1, 1999, pp. 3, 15; Barb Gomolski, "No Channel Conflict," *InfoWorld,* July 9, 2001, p. 10; and Paulette Thomas, "Case Study: Travel Agency Meets Technology's Threats," *Wall Street Journal,* May 21, 2002, p. B4. Also see Ted Kemp, "Beware the Pitfalls of Bypassing the Channel," *B to B,* February 11, 2002, pp. 1, 28; Jeff Bailey, "Enterprise: Web Sites Force Middlemen to Redefine Markets," *Wall Street Journal,* June 11, 2002, p. B4; and Everett Potter, "Helping Hand: Yes, the Internet Is Nice, but Some People Still Won't Leave Home Without Their Travel Agent," *Wall Street Journal,* June 24, 2002, p. R6.

Setting Channel Objectives

Companies should state their marketing channel objectives in terms of targeted levels of customer service. Usually, a company can identify several segments wanting different levels of service. The company should decide which segments to serve and the best channels to use in each case. In each segment, the company wants to minimize the total channel cost of meeting customer service requirements.

The company's channel objectives are also influenced by the nature of the company, its products, its marketing intermediaries, its competitors, and the environment. For example, the company's size

Channel objectives: GEICO markets auto insurance via the telephone and Web for those looking to save money and do business directly with the company.

and financial situation determine which marketing functions it can handle itself and which it must give to intermediaries. Companies selling perishable products may require more-direct marketing to avoid delays and too much handling.

In some cases, a company may want to compete in or near the same outlets that carry competitors' products. In other cases, producers may avoid the channels used by competitors. Avon, for example, uses door-to-door selling rather than going head-to-head with other cosmetics makers for scarce positions in retail stores. And GEICO Direct markets auto and homeowner's insurance directly to consumers via the telephone and Web rather than through agents. Finally, environmental factors such as economic conditions and legal constraints may affect channel objectives and design. For example, in a depressed economy, producers want to distribute their goods in the most economical way, using shorter channels and dropping unneeded services that add to the final price of the goods.

Identifying Major Alternatives

When the company has defined its channel objectives, it should next identify its major channel alternatives in terms of *types* of intermediaries, the *number* of intermediaries, and the *responsibilities* of each channel member.

Types of Intermediaries

A firm should identify the types of channel members available to carry out its channel work. For example, suppose a manufacturer of test equipment has developed an audio device that detects poor mechanical connections in machines with moving parts. Company executives think this product would have a market in all industries in which electric, combustion, or steam engines are made or used. The company's current sales force is small, and the problem is how best to reach these different industries. The following channel alternatives might emerge from management discussion:

Company sales force: Expand the company's direct sales force. Assign outside salespeople to territories and have them contact all prospects in the area or develop separate company sales forces for different industries. Or, add an inside telesales operation in which telephone salespeople handle small or midsize companies.

Manufacturer's agency: Hire manufacturer's agents—independent firms whose sales forces handle related products from many companies—in different regions or industries to sell the new test equipment.

Industrial distributors: Find distributors in the different regions or industries who will buy and carry the new line. Give them exclusive distribution, good margins, product training, and promotional support.

Number of Marketing Intermediaries

Companies must also determine the number of channel members to use at each level. Three strategies are available: intensive distribution, exclusive distribution, and selective distribution. Producers of convenience products and common raw materials typically seek **intensive distribution**—a strategy in which they stock their products in as many outlets as possible. These goods must be available where and when consumers want them. For example, toothpaste, candy, and other similar items are sold in millions of outlets to provide maximum brand exposure and consumer convenience. Kraft, Coca-Cola, Kimberly-Clark, and other consumer goods companies distribute their products in this way.

By contrast, some producers purposely limit the number of intermediaries handling their products. The extreme form of this practice is **exclusive distribution,** in which the producer gives only a limited number of dealers the exclusive right to distribute its products in their territories. Exclusive distribution is often found in the distribution of new automobiles and prestige women's clothing. For example, Bentley dealers are few and far between—even large cities may have only one dealer. By granting exclusive distribution, Bentley gains stronger distributor selling support and more control over dealer prices, promotion, credit, and services. Exclusive distribution also enhances the car's image and allows for higher markups.

Between intensive and exclusive distribution lies **selective distribution**—the use of more than one, but fewer than all, of the intermediaries who are willing to carry a company's products. Most television, furniture, and small-appliance brands are distributed in this manner. For example, KitchenAid, Maytag, Whirlpool, and General Electric sell their major appliances through

Intensive distribution
Stocking the product in as many outlets as possible.

Exclusive distribution
Giving a limited number of dealers the exclusive right to distribute the company's products in their territories.

Selective distribution
The use of more than one, but fewer than all, of the intermediaries who are willing to carry the company's products.

Exclusive distribution: Luxury car makers sell exclusively through a limited number of dealerships. Such limited distribution enhances the car's image and generates stronger dealer support.

dealer networks and selected large retailers. By using selective distribution, they do not have to spread their efforts over many outlets, including many marginal ones. They can develop good working relationships with selected channel members and expect a better-than-average selling effort. Selective distribution gives producers good market coverage with more control and less cost than does intensive distribution.

Responsibilities of Channel Members

The producer and intermediaries need to agree on the terms and responsibilities of each channel member. They should agree on price policies, conditions of sale, territorial rights, and specific services to be performed by each party. The producer should establish a list price and a fair set of discounts for intermediaries. It must define each channel member's territory, and it should be careful about where it places new resellers.

Mutual services and duties need to be spelled out carefully, especially in franchise and exclusive distribution channels. For example, McDonald's provides franchisees with promotional support, a record-keeping system, training at Hamburger University, and general management assistance. In turn, franchisees must meet company standards for physical facilities, cooperate with new promotion programs, provide requested information, and buy specified food products.

Evaluating the Major Alternatives

Suppose a company has identified several channel alternatives and wants to select the one that will best satisfy its long-run objectives. Each alternative should be evaluated against economic, control, and adaptive criteria.

Using *economic criteria,* a company compares the likely sales, costs, and profitability of different channel alternatives. The company must also consider *control issues.* Using intermediaries usually means giving them some control over the marketing of the product, and some intermediaries take more control than others. Other things being equal, the company prefers to keep as much control as possible. Finally, the company must apply *adaptive criteria.* Channels often involve long-term commitments, yet the company wants to keep the channel flexible so that it can adapt to environmental changes. Thus, to be considered, a channel involving long-term commitments should be greatly superior on economic and control grounds.

Designing International Distribution Channels

International marketers face many additional complexities in designing their channels. Each country has its own unique distribution system that has evolved over time and changes very slowly. These channel systems can vary widely from country to country. Thus, global marketers must usually adapt their channel strategies to the existing structures within each country.

In some markets, the distribution system is complex and hard to penetrate, consisting of many layers and large numbers of intermediaries. Consider Japan:

> The Japanese distribution system stems from the early seventeenth century, when cottage industries and a [quickly growing] urban population spawned a merchant class. . . . Despite Japan's economic achievements, the distribution system has remained remarkably faithful to its antique pattern. . . . [It] encompasses a wide range of wholesalers and other agents, brokers, and retailers, differing more in number than in function from their American counterparts. There are myriad tiny retail shops. An even greater number of whole-salers supplies goods to them, layered tier upon tier, many more than most U.S. executives would think necessary. For example, soap may move through three wholesalers plus a sales company after it leaves the manufacturer before it ever reaches the retail outlet. A steak goes from rancher to consumers in a process that often involves a dozen middle agents. . . . The distribution network . . . reflects the traditionally close ties among many Japanese companies . . . [and places] much greater emphasis on personal relationships with users. . . . Although [these channels appear] inefficient and cumbersome, they seem to serve the Japanese customer well. . . . Lacking much storage space in their small homes, most Japanese homemakers shop several times a week and prefer convenient [and more personal] neighborhood shops.[8]

The Japanese distribution system has remained remarkably traditional. A profusion of tiny retail shops are supplied by an even greater number of small wholesalers.

Many Western firms have had great difficulty breaking into the closely knit, tradition-bound Japanese distribution network.

At the other extreme, distribution systems in developing countries may be scattered and inefficient, or altogether lacking. For example, China and India would appear to be huge markets, each with populations over 1 billion. In reality, however, these markets are much smaller than the population numbers suggest. Because of inadequate distribution systems in both countries, most companies can profitably access only a small portion of the population located in each country's most affluent cities.[9]

Thus, international marketers face a wide range of channel alternatives. Designing efficient and effective channel systems between and within various country markets poses a difficult challenge. We discuss international distribution decisions further in Chapter 19.

Channel Management Decisions

Once the company has reviewed its channel alternatives and decided on the best channel design, it must implement and manage the chosen channel. Channel management calls for selecting, managing, and motivating individual channel members and evaluating their performance over time.

Selecting Channel Members

Producers vary in their ability to attract qualified marketing intermediaries. Some producers have no trouble signing up channel members. For example, when Toyota first introduced its Lexus line in the United States, it had no trouble attracting new dealers. In fact, it had to turn down many would-be resellers. In some cases, the promise of exclusive or selective distribution for a desirable product will draw plenty of applicants.

At the other extreme are producers who have to work hard to line up enough qualified intermediaries. When Polaroid started, for example, it could not get photography stores to carry its new cameras, and it had to go to mass-merchandising outlets. Similarly, when the U.S. Time Company first tried to sell its inexpensive Timex watches through regular jewelry stores, most jewelry stores refused to carry them. The company then managed to get its watches into mass-merchandise outlets. This turned out to be a wise decision because of the rapid growth of mass merchandising.

When selecting intermediaries, the company should determine what characteristics distinguish the better ones. It will want to evaluate each channel member's years in business, other lines carried, growth and profit record, cooperativeness, and reputation. If the intermediaries are sales agents, the company will want to evaluate the number and character of other lines carried and the size and quality of the sales force. If the intermediary is a retail store that wants exclusive or selective distribution, the company will want to evaluate the store's customers, location, and future growth potential.

Managing and Motivating Channel Members

Once selected, channel members must be continuously managed and motivated to do their best. The company must sell not only *through* the intermediaries but *to* and *with* them. Most companies see their intermediaries as first-line customers and partners. They practice strong *partner relationship management (PRM)* to forge long-term partnerships with channel members. This creates a marketing system that meets the needs of both the company *and* its partners. (See Real Marketing 13.2.)

In managing its channels, a company must convince distributors that they can succeed better by working together as a part of a cohesive value delivery system.[10] Thus, Procter & Gamble and Wal-Mart work together to create superior value for final consumers. They jointly plan merchandising goals and strategies, inventory levels, and advertising and promotion plans. Similarly, GE Appliances has created an alternative distribution system called CustomerNet to coordinate, support, and motivate its dealers.

> GE CustomerNet gives dealers instant online access to GE Appliances' distribution and order-processing system, 24 hours a day, seven days a week. By logging on to the GE CustomerNet Web site, dealers can obtain product specifications, photos, feature lists, and side-by-side model comparisons for hundreds of GE appliance models. They can check on product availability and prices, place orders, and review order status. They can even create custom brochures, order point-of-purchase materials, or download "advertising slicks"—professionally prepared GE appliance ads ready for insertion in local media. GE promises next-day delivery on most appliance models, so dealers need carry only display models in their stores. This greatly reduces inventory costs, making even small dealers more price competitive. GE CustomerNet also helps dealers to sell GE appliances more easily and effectively. A dealer can put a computer terminal on the showroom floor, where salespeople and customers together can use the system to dig through detailed product specifications and check availability for GE's entire line of appliances. Perhaps the biggest benefit to GE Appliances, however, is that the system builds strong bonds between the company and its dealers and motivates dealers to put more push behind the company's products.[11]

Creating dealer satisfaction and profitability: Using GE's CustomerNet system, dealers have instant online access to GE Appliances' distribution system, 24 hours a day, 7 days a week to check on product availability and prices, place orders, and review order status. Simply put, it's an electronic one-stop shopping breakthrough that can help you sell.

real marketing 13.2

Partner Relationship Management: Hewlett Packard's No-Fly Zone

Hewlett Packard has a long history of working *with* its channel partners, rather than *through* them or *against* them. It understands the great value that these partners add, both for HP and for customers. "Partners are core to HP's business go-to-market strategy," says Webb McKinney. "[Only by working closely] with our channel

tomers, HP had to decide whether it would do the same. Not only could direct selling reduce costs and increase profits, but some customers actually prefer to deal directly with HP. Says HP CEO Carly Fiorina, "The reality is there are some customers who prefer to order through a direct distribution capability *à la* Dell, and we have to satisfy

their distributors through direct sales to even the smallest customers, HP has "drawn a line in the sand," Gilroy says. Its direct sales program, sometimes referred to as the "hard deck" program, clearly limits which accounts the company will target with direct selling.

"Hard deck" refers to an aviation term that defines a boundary under which there is a "no-fly zone." For HP, it means that the company will sell direct only to potential customers that exceed a set of established specifications. To date, that includes about 1,000 large accounts. Customers falling below the specifications—those in the "no-fly zone"—are off limits to HP for direct sales. Such an arrangement allows HP to concentrate its direct sales force on the largest national and international companies that expect dedicated supplier service. At the same time, it creates a market for channel partners, below the hard deck, that is completely free from direct selling competition.

In addition to establishing the no-fly zone, HP goes out of its way to ensure that its partners find success in selling the company's products and services. When HP sales reps get leads on accounts in the no-fly zone, they pass the information along to HP distributors, who make the sale and provide service and support. In addition, HP dedicates sales and technical resources to help channel members find the best customer solutions.

The day-to-day management of relationships with more than 20,000 channel partners selling everything from computer networks to pocket calculators presents an immense challenge. Something as simple as distributing sales leads collected through various HP marketing campaigns—everything from business cards dropped in fishbowls at trade shows to requests for product information from HP's Internet site—can be a daunting task. To manage these tasks, HP set up an integrating partner relationship management (PRM) system, which links HP directly with its channel partners and helps coordinate channelwide marketing efforts. Using a secure Web site, channel partners can log on at any time to obtain leads that have been generated for them. While at the Web site, they can also order literature and sales support materials, check product specifications, and obtain pricing information. In

Partner relationship management: To support its channel partners and avoid conflict, HP's "hard deck" guideline clearly outlines "which accounts the channel leads and which accounts HP leads."

partners [can we] meet the diverse needs of our customers." Channel partners extend HP's reach far beyond its own capacity. They have a clear understanding of customers' needs and possess the resources necessary to build customer relationships and provide hands-on support. Managing channel relationships is one of the most important things HP does. "Put simply, it's a partnering world," adds Kevin Gilroy, general manager for HP's channel program.

A few years back, however, HP faced a difficult decision. Given competitor Dell's incredible success at selling direct to cus-

those customers." So HP really had no choice—it had to go direct. The problem? By selling direct, HP would be putting itself into direct competition with its traditional distribution channel partners. This, in turn, posed a threat to HP's prized relationships with its distributors.

Thus, HP had to find a way to both sell direct to customers *and* build support and trust among its traditional partners. To solve the problem, the company has developed a direct sales program carefully designed to avoid infringing on its partners' turf. Whereas HP's competitors were taking business from

(continued)

addition, HP communicates with channel members regularly, offering training seminars and promotional materials to support sales. In fact, many partners receive one or two e-mails a day offering information, resources, and support.

The PRM system not only provides strong support for channel partners, it improves their collective effectiveness and provides assessment feedback to HP. Under the old system, says an HP manager, "we would generate a mass-mailing campaign, send it off to who knows where, out it would go, and we'd hope it would work. Now we can generate a targeted campaign, see when the opportunities start coming back, and . . . the channel partner tells us what happened. . . . It's changing the way we do campaigns."

The results of HP's partner relationship marketing efforts speak for themselves. HP has won multiple awards for its support of and relationships with channel members. Most recently, HP swept almost every category it was eligible for in this year's Channel Champions awards sponsored by *Crn,* a technology-focused trade journal. In surveys administered to determine the winners, one channel member offered that "you won't find a support network out there that's better. Overall, HP is a step above the rest." Referring to the support HP reps provide to channel partners, another distributor commented, "We treat our HP reps more like our sales managers. HP has high integrity. In a gray area, HP will always default to its partners."

Sources: Pat Curry, "Channel Changes," *Industry Week,* April 2, 2001, pp. 45–48; "Reinventing Partnership: Kevin Gilroy Answers Questions from the Channel," accessed online at http://partner.americas. HP.com/partner/harddeck.pdf, July 2002; Craig Zarley, "Making the Call," *Crn,* February 11, 2002, pp. 14–17; Joseph F. Kovar, "Channel Champions 2002: HP Software Decisive," *Crn,* March 18, 2002, p. 52; Jennifer Hagendorf Follett, "Channel Champions 2002: HP's Hard Deck Is Aces," *Crn,* March 18, 2002, p. 66; Mike Cruz, "Channel Champions 2002: HP Takes All in Printers," *Crn,* March 18, 2002, p. 84; and information gathered from the Hewlett Packard Web site at http://partner. americas. HP.com/partner/harddeck.pdf, July 2002.

Many companies are now installing integrated high-tech partner relationship management systems to coordinate their whole-channel marketing efforts. Just as they use customer relationship management (CRM) software systems to help manage relationships with important customers, companies can now use PRM software to help recruit, train, organize, manage, motivate, and evaluate relationships with channel partners.[12]

Evaluating Channel Members

The producer must regularly check channel member performance against standards such as sales quotas, average inventory levels, customer delivery time, treatment of damaged and lost goods, cooperation in company promotion and training programs, and services to the customer. The company should recognize and reward intermediaries who are performing well and adding good value for consumers. Those who are performing poorly should be assisted or, as a last resort, replaced. A company may periodically "requalify" its intermediaries and prune the weaker ones.

Finally, manufacturers need to be sensitive to their dealers. Those who treat their dealers poorly risk not only losing dealer support but also causing some legal problems. The next section describes various rights and duties pertaining to manufacturers and their channel members.

Public Policy and Distribution Decisions

For the most part, companies are legally free to develop whatever channel arrangements suit them. In fact, the laws affecting channels seek to prevent the exclusionary tactics of some companies that might keep another company from using a desired channel. Most channel law deals with the mutual rights and duties of the channel members once they have formed a relationship.

Many producers and wholesalers like to develop exclusive channels for their products. When the seller allows only certain outlets to carry its products, this strategy is called *exclusive distribution.* When the seller requires that these dealers not handle competitors' products, its strategy is called *exclusive dealing.* Both parties can benefit from exclusive arrangements: The seller obtains more loyal and dependable outlets, and the dealers obtain a steady source of supply and stronger seller support. But exclusive arrangements also exclude other producers from selling to these dealers. This situation brings exclusive dealing contracts under the scope of the Clayton Act of 1914. They are legal as long as they do not substantially lessen competition or tend to create a monopoly and as long as both parties enter into the agreement voluntarily.

Exclusive dealing often includes *exclusive territorial agreements*. The producer may agree not to sell to other dealers in a given area, or the buyer may agree to sell only in its own territory. The first practice is normal under franchise systems as a way to increase dealer enthusiasm and commitment. It is also perfectly legal—a seller has no legal obligation to sell through more outlets than it wishes. The second practice, whereby the producer tries to keep a dealer from selling outside its territory, has become a major legal issue.

Producers of a strong brand sometimes sell it to dealers only if the dealers will take some or all of the rest of the line. This is called full-line forcing. Such *tying agreements* are not necessarily illegal, but they do violate the Clayton Act if they tend to lessen competition substantially. The practice may prevent consumers from freely choosing among competing suppliers of these other brands.

Finally, producers are free to select their dealers, but their right to terminate dealers is somewhat restricted. In general, sellers can drop dealers "for cause." However, they cannot drop dealers if, for example, the dealers refuse to cooperate in a doubtful legal arrangement, such as exclusive dealing or tying agreements.[13]

Marketing Logistics and Supply Chain Management

In today's global marketplace, selling a product is sometimes easier than getting it to customers. Companies must decide on the best way to store, handle, and move their products and services so that they are available to customers in the right assortments, at the right time, and in the right place. Physical distribution and logistics effectiveness has a major impact on both customer satisfaction and company costs. Here we consider the *nature and importance of logistics management in the supply chain, goals of the logistics system, major logistics functions,* and the need for *integrated supply chain management.*

The Nature and Importance of Marketing Logistics

Marketing logistics (physical distribution)

The tasks involved in planning, implementing, and controlling the physical flow of materials, final goods, and related information from points of origin to points of consumption to meet customer requirements at a profit.

Supply chain management

Managing upstream and downstream value-added flows of materials, final goods, and related information among suppliers, the company, resellers, and final consumers.

To some managers, marketing logistics means only trucks and warehouses. But modern logistics is much more than this. **Marketing logistics**—also called **physical distribution**—involves planning, implementing, and controlling the physical flow of goods, services, and related information from points of origin to points of consumption to meet customer requirements at a profit. In short, it involves getting the right product to the right customer in the right place at the right time.

In the past, physical distribution typically started with products at the plant and then tried to find low-cost solutions to get them to customers. However, today's marketers prefer customer-centered logistics thinking, which starts with the marketplace and works backward to the factory, or even to sources of supply. Marketing logistics addresses not only *outbound distribution* (moving products from the factory to resellers and ultimately to customers) but also *inbound distribution* (moving products and materials from suppliers to the factory) and *reverse distribution* (moving broken, unwanted, or excess products returned by consumers or resellers). That is, it involves entire **supply chain management**—managing upstream and downstream value-added flows of materials, final goods, and related information among suppliers, the company, resellers, and final consumers, as shown in Figure 13.5.

Thus, the logistics manager's task is to coordinate activities of suppliers, purchasing agents, marketers, channel members, and customers. These activities include forecasting, information systems, purchasing, production planning, order processing, inventory, warehousing, and transportation planning.

Companies today are placing greater emphasis on logistics for several reasons. First, companies can gain a powerful competitive advantage by using improved logistics to give customers better service or lower prices. Second, improved logistics can yield tremendous cost savings to both the company and its customers. About 15 percent of an average product's price is accounted for by shipping and transport alone. Last year, American companies spent more than

FIGURE 13.5
Supply chain management

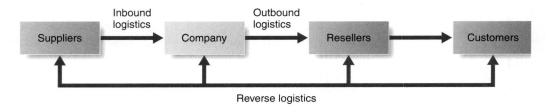

$900 billion—close to 10 percent of gross domestic product—to wrap, bundle, load, unload, sort, reload, and transport goods. By itself, Ford has more than 500 million tons of finished vehicles, production parts, and aftermarket parts in transit at any given time, running up an annual logistics bill of around $4 billion.[14] Shaving off even a small fraction of these costs can mean substantial savings.

Third, the explosion in product variety has created a need for improved logistics management. For example, in 1911 the typical A&P grocery store carried only 270 items. The store manager could keep track of this inventory on about 10 pages of notebook paper stuffed in a shirt pocket. Today, the average A&P carries a bewildering stock of more than 16,700 items. A Wal-Mart Supercenter stores carry more than 100,000 products.[15] Ordering, shipping, stocking, and controlling such a variety of products presents a sizable logistics challenge.

Finally, improvements in information technology have created opportunities for major gains in distribution efficiency. Using sophisticated supply chain management software, Web-based logistics systems, point-of-sale scanners, uniform product codes, satellite tracking, and electronic transfer of order and payment data, companies can quickly and efficiently manage the flow of goods, information, and finances through the supply chain.

Goals of the Logistics System

Some companies state their logistics objective as providing maximum customer service at the least cost. Unfortunately, no logistics system can *both* maximize customer service *and* minimize distribution costs. Maximum customer service implies rapid delivery, large inventories, flexible assortments, liberal returns policies, and other services—all of which raise distribution costs. In contrast, minimum distribution costs imply slower delivery, smaller inventories, and larger shipping lots—which represent a lower level of overall customer service.

The goal of marketing logistics should be to provide a *targeted* level of customer service at the least cost. A company must first research the importance of various distribution services to customers and then set desired service levels for each segment. The objective is to maximize *profits*, not sales. Therefore, the company must weigh the benefits of providing higher levels of service against the costs. Some companies offer less service than their competitors and charge a lower price. Other companies offer more service and charge higher prices to cover higher costs.

Major Logistics Functions

Given a set of logistics objectives, the company is ready to design a logistics system that will minimize the cost of attaining these objectives. The major logistics functions include *warehousing, inventory management, transportation,* and *logistics information management.*

Warehousing

Distribution center

A large, highly automated warehouse designed to receive goods from various plants and suppliers, take orders, fill them efficiently, and deliver goods to customers as quickly as possible.

Production and consumption cycles rarely match. So most companies must store their tangible goods while they wait to be sold. For example, Snapper, Toro, and other lawn mower manufacturers run their factories all year long and store up products for the heavy spring and summer buying seasons. The storage function overcomes differences in needed quantities and timing, ensuring that products are available when customers are ready to buy them.

A company must decide on *how many* and *what types* of warehouses it needs and *where* they will be located. The company might use either *storage warehouses* or *distribution centers.* Storage warehouses store goods for moderate to long periods. **Distribution centers** are designed to move goods rather than just store them. They are large and highly automated warehouses designed to receive goods from various plants and suppliers, take orders, fill them efficiently, and deliver goods to customers as quickly as possible.

For example, Wal-Mart operates a network of 78 huge U.S. distribution centers and another 37 around the globe. Almost 84 percent of the merchandise shipped to Wal-Mart stores is routed through one of its own distribution centers, giving Wal-Mart tremendous control over inventory management. One center, which might serve the daily needs of 165 Wal-Mart stores, typically contains more than a million square feet of space (about 24 football fields) under a single roof. Laser scanners route as many as 190,000 cases of goods per day along 11 miles of conveyer belts, and the center's 1,000 workers load or unload some 500 trucks daily. Wal-Mart's Monroe, Georgia, distribution center contains a 127,000-square-foot freezer that can hold 10,000 pallets—room enough for 58 million Popsicles.[16]

Like almost everything else these days, warehousing has seen dramatic changes in technology in recent years. Older, multistoried warehouses with outdated materials-handling methods are steadily being replaced by newer, single-storied *automated warehouses* with advanced, computer-controlled materials-handling systems requiring few employees. Computers and scanners read orders and direct lift trucks, electric hoists, or robots to gather goods, move them to loading docks, and issue invoices.

Inventory Management

Inventory management also affects customer satisfaction. Here, managers must maintain the delicate balance between carrying too little inventory and carrying too much. With too little stock, the firm risks not having products when customers want to buy. To remedy this, the firm may need costly emergency shipments or production. Carrying too much inventory results in higher-than-necessary inventory-carrying costs and stock obsolescence. Thus, in managing inventory, firms must balance the costs of carrying larger inventories against resulting sales and profits.

Many companies have greatly reduced their inventories and related costs through *just-in-time* logistics systems. With such systems, producers and retailers carry only small inventories of parts or merchandise, often only enough for a few days of operations. For example, Dell Computer, a master just-in-time producer, carries just 5 days of inventory, whereas competitors might carry 40 days or even 60.[17] New stock arrives exactly when needed, rather than being stored in inventory until being used. Just-in-time systems require accurate forecasting along with fast, frequent, and flexible delivery so that new supplies will be available when needed. However, these systems result in substantial savings in inventory-carrying and handling costs.

Marketers are always looking for new ways to make inventory management more efficient. In the not-too-distant future, handling inventory might even become fully automated.[18]

Imagine knowing, at any time, exactly where a product—no matter how large or small—is located physically within the supply chain. Or imagine "smart shelves" that not only tell you when it's time to reorder, but also place the order automatically with your supplier. Welcome to the wonderful world of Auto-ID, an exciting new information technology application that could revolutionize distribution as we know it. MIT's Auto-ID center is now developing "smart tag" technology, which might soon be used to embed intelligence, identity, and Internet connectivity into millions of everyday products. Think about what that means. Physical objects would have the ability to communicate with each other and with retailers, suppliers, and consumers through the Internet. The entire global supply chain becomes a seamless network of direct, real-time supply and demand. "Smart" products could make the entire supply chain—which accounts for nearly 75 percent of a product's cost—intelligent and automated. Products from anywhere on Earth could be linked to the Internet, where manufacturers and retailers could access information ranging from consumer trends to theft alerts. This, in turn, would let companies effectively meet consumer demands while at the same time saving billions of dollars.

Transportation

The choice of transportation carriers affects the pricing of products, delivery performance, and condition of the goods when they arrive—all of which will affect customer satisfaction. In shipping goods to its warehouses, dealers, and customers, the company can choose among five main transportation modes: truck, rail, water, pipeline, and air, along with an alternative mode for digital products: the Internet.

Roadway and other trucking firms have added many services in recent years, such as satellite tracking of shipments and sleeper tractors that keep freight moving around the clock.

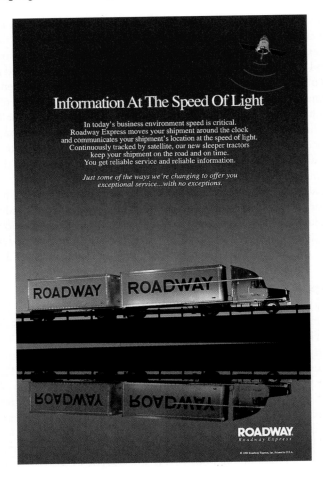

Trucks have increased their share of transportation steadily and now account for 39 percent of total cargo ton-miles (more than 69 percent of actual tonnage).[19] They account for the largest portion of transportation *within* cities as opposed to *between* cities. Each year in the United States, trucks travel more than 600 billion miles—equal to nearly 1.3 million round trips to the moon—carrying 7.7 billion tons of freight. Trucks are highly flexible in their routing and time schedules, and they can usually offer faster service than railroads. They are efficient for short hauls of high-value merchandise. Trucking firms have added many services in recent years. For example, Roadway Express and most other major carriers now offer satellite tracking of shipments and sleeper tractors that move freight around the clock.

Railroads account for 38 percent of total cargo ton-miles moved. They are one of the most cost-effective modes for shipping large amounts of bulk products—coal, sand, minerals, and farm and forest products—over long distances. In recent years, railroads have increased their customer services by designing new equipment to handle special categories of goods, providing flat-cars for carrying truck trailers by rail (piggyback), and providing in-transit services such as the diversion of shipped goods to other destinations en route and the processing of goods en route.

Water carriers, which account for about 10 percent of cargo ton-miles, transport large amounts of goods by ships and barges on U.S. coastal and inland waterways. Although the cost of water transportation is very low for shipping bulky, low-value, nonperishable products such as sand, coal, grain, oil, and metallic ores, water transportation is the slowest mode and may be affected by the weather. *Pipelines* are a specialized means of shipping petroleum, natural gas, and chemicals from sources to markets. Most pipelines are used by their owners to ship their own products.

Although *air* carriers transport less than 1 percent of the nation's goods, they are an important transportation mode. Airfreight rates are much higher than rail or truck rates, but airfreight is ideal when speed is needed or distant markets have to be reached. Among the most frequently airfreighted products are perishables (fresh fish, cut flowers) and high-value, low-bulk items (technical instruments, jewelry). Companies find that airfreight also reduces inventory levels, packaging costs, and the number of warehouses needed.

The *Internet* carries digital products from producer to customer via satellite, cable modem, or telephone wire. Software firms, the media, music companies, and education all make use of the Internet to transport digital products. While these firms primarily use traditional transportation to distribute CDs, newspapers, and more, the Internet holds the potential for lower product distribution costs. One FedEx executive notes, "Planes and trucks move packages, and digital technology moves bits."[20]

Intermodal transportation

Combining two or more modes of transportation.

Shippers increasingly are using **intermodal transportation**—combining two or more modes of transportation. *Piggyback* describes the use of rail and trucks; *fishyback,* water and trucks; *trainship,* water and rail; and *airtruck,* air and trucks. Combining modes provides advantages that no single mode can deliver. Each combination offers advantages to the shipper. For example, not only is piggyback cheaper than trucking alone but it also provides flexibility and convenience.

In choosing a transportation mode for a product, shippers must balance many considerations: speed, dependability, availability, cost, and others. Thus, if a shipper needs speed, air and truck are the prime choices. If the goal is low cost, then water or pipeline might be best.

Logistics Information Management

Companies manage their supply chains through information. Channel partners often link up to share information and to make better joint logistics decisions. From a logistics perspective, information flows such as customer orders, billing, inventory levels, and even customer data are closely linked channel performance.

Information can be shared and managed in many ways—by mail or telephone, through salespeople, via the Internet, or through *electronic data interchange (EDI)*, the computerized exchange of data between organizations. Wal-Mart, for example, maintains EDI links with 20 percent of its 91,000 suppliers.[21] The company wants to design a simple, accessible, fast, and accurate process for capturing, processing, and sharing channel information.

In some cases, suppliers might actually be asked to generate orders and arrange deliveries for their customers. Many large retailers—such as Wal-Mart and Home Depot—work closely with major suppliers such as Procter & Gamble or Black & Decker to set up *vendor-managed inventory* (VMI) systems or *continuous inventory replenishment* systems.[22] Using VMI, the customer shares real-time data on sales and current inventory levels with the supplier. The supplier then takes full responsibility for managing inventories and deliveries. Some retailers even go so far as to shift inventory and delivery costs to the supplier. Such systems require close cooperation between the buyer and seller.

Here is an example of how two channel partners—Sara Lee and Target Corporation—share information and coordinate their logistics functions:

> The Branded Apparel division of giant Sara Lee Corporation says that retailer Target Corporation's willingness to share information with suppliers separates this company from its competitors. Target's Global Merchandising System (GMS), its supply chain management system, consists of more than 60 applications, including forecasting, ordering, and trend analysis. Target stores can use GMS to order a certain number of sweatshirts from Sara Lee Branded Apparel without specifying more than style. As the delivery date draws near, Target analyzes trends for colors and sizes. Based on those forecasts, Sara Lee makes trial lots and Target starts to sell them. If customers buy more navy sweatshirts than initially predicted, Target adjusts its order. The result: Both Sara Lee and Target have fewer goods in inventory while at the same time doing a better job of meeting customer preferences, which in turn results in fewer markdowns.[23]

Integrated logistics management

The logistics concept that emphasizes teamwork, both inside the company and among all the marketing channel organizations, to maximize the performance of the entire distribution system.

Integrated Logistics Management

Today, more and more companies are adopting the concept of **integrated logistics management.** This concept recognizes that providing better customer service and trimming distribution costs requires *teamwork,* both inside the company and among all the marketing channel organizations. Inside, the company's various functional departments must work closely together to maximize the company's own logistics performance. Outside, the company must integrate its logistics system with those of its suppliers and customers to maximize the performance of the entire distribution system.

Cross-Functional Teamwork Inside the Company

In most companies, responsibility for various logistics activities is assigned to many different functional units—marketing, sales, finance, manufacturing, purchasing. Too often, each function tries to optimize its own logistics performance without regard for the activities of the other functions. However, transportation, inventory, warehousing, and order-processing activities interact, often in an inverse way. Lower inventory levels reduce inventory-carrying costs. But they may also reduce customer service and increase costs from stock outs, back orders, special production runs, and costly fast-freight shipments. Because distribution activities involve strong trade-offs, decisions by different functions must be coordinated to achieve superior overall logistics performance.

The goal of integrated supply chain management is to harmonize all of the company's logistics decisions. Close working relationships among functions can be achieved in several ways. Some companies have created permanent logistics committees made up of managers responsible for different physical distribution activities. Companies can also create management positions that link the logistics activities of functional areas. For example, Procter & Gamble has created supply managers, who manage all of the supply chain activities for each of its product categories. Many companies have a vice president of logistics with cross-functional authority. Finally, companies can employ sophisticated, systemwide supply chain management software, now available from Oracle and other software providers.[24] The important thing is that the company coordinate its logistics and marketing activities to create high market satisfaction at a reasonable cost.

Building Logistics Partnerships

Companies must do more than improve their own logistics. They must also work with other channel members to improve whole-channel distribution. The members of a distribution channel are linked closely in delivering customer satisfaction and value. One company's distribution system is another company's supply system. The success of each channel member depends on the performance of the entire supply chain. For example, Wal-Mart can charge the lowest prices at retail only if its entire supply chain—consisting of thousands of merchandise suppliers, transport companies, warehouses, and service providers—operates at maximum efficiency.

Supply chain management: many companies can use sophisticated, system-wide supply chain management software, such as that available from Oracle and other software providers.

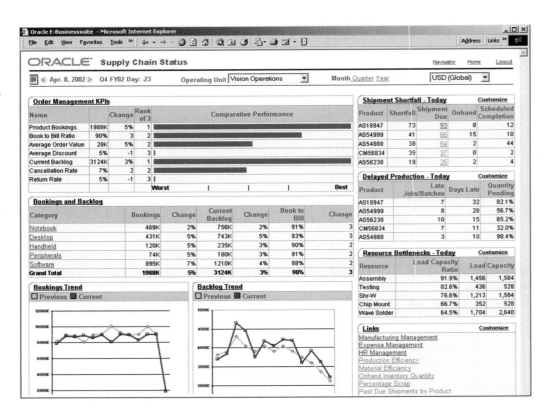

Smart companies coordinate their logistics strategies and forge strong partnerships with suppliers and customers to improve customer service and reduce channel costs. Many companies have created *cross-functional, cross-company teams.* For example, Procter & Gamble has a team of almost 100 people working in Bentonville, Arkansas, home of Wal-Mart. The P&Gers work jointly with their counterparts at Wal-Mart to find ways to squeeze costs out of their distribution system. Working together benefits not only P&G and Wal-Mart but also their final consumers.

Other companies partner through *shared projects.* For example, many larger retailers are working closely with suppliers on in-store programs. Home Depot allows key suppliers to use its stores as a testing ground for new merchandising programs. The suppliers spend time at Home Depot stores watching how their product sells and how customers relate to it. They then create programs specially tailored to Home Depot and its customers. Western Publishing Group, publisher of "Little Golden Books" for children, formed a similar partnership with Toys "R" Us. Western and the giant toy retailer coordinated their marketing strategies to create mini-bookstore sections—called Books "R" Us—within each Toys "R" Us store. Toys "R" Us provides the locations, space, and customers; Western serves as distributor, consolidator, and servicer for the Books "R" Us program.[25] Clearly, both the supplier and the customer benefit from such partnerships.

The point is that all supply chain members must work together in the cause of serving final consumers. "The functions that customers value deserve close, creative attention from all supply chain participants," says one expert. "Together, component suppliers, manufacturers, wholesalers, and retailers must . . . differentiate the way they provide and package these [values] to the ultimate customer."[26]

Third-Party Logistics

Third-party logistics (3PL) provider

An independent logistics provider that performs any or all of the functions required to get its client's product to market.

Most businesses perform their own logistics functions. However, a growing number of firms now outsource some or all of their logistics to **third-party logistics (3PL) providers** such as Ryder Systems, UPS Worldwide Logistics, FedEx Logistics, Roadway Logistics Services, or Emory Global Logistics (see Real Marketing 13.3). Such integrated logistics companies perform any or all of the functions required to get their clients' product to market.

Western Publishing Group partners with Toys "R" Us to create mini-bookstore sections—called Books "R" Us—within each store. Toys "R" Us provides the space and customers: Western serves as distributor and servicer for the Books "R" Us sections.

real marketing 13.3

Go Ryder, and Leave the Delivering to Us

Most big companies love to make and sell their products. But many loathe the associated logistics "grunt work"—the bundling, loading, unloading, sorting, storing, reloading, transporting, and tracking required to supply their factories and to get products out to customers. They hate it so much that

get products to customers more quickly and reliably. Below are some examples:

Ford: Ford uses an international logistics partner to move Ford products between continents. In North America, it uses third-party logistics partner UPS Autogistics to

cent. The result: lower costs *and* better customer service.

Cisco Systems: This vendor of computer networking equipment and network management software ships tons of routers to Europe daily. It needs to know where each box is at any given time and may have to reroute orders on short notice to fill urgent customer requests. Moreover, Cisco's customers need to know exactly when orders will arrive. When Cisco handled its own logistics, deliveries took up to three weeks. Now, the company contracts its complex distribution process to UPS Worldwide Logistics. Leveraging its knowledge of international plane, train, and trucking schedules, UPS Worldwide can speed routers to European customers in less than four days. Such superfast delivery saves Cisco Systems a bundle on inventories.

Cisco reaps some additional advantages from the logistics partnership. For example, UPS Worldwide has extensive knowledge of local customs laws and import duties. It recently arranged with Dutch customs to aggregate Cisco's import duties into a monthly bill, paid once customers receive shipments instead of each time the routers land at the airport. The result: even more savings in time and paperwork.

National Semiconductor: In the early 1990s, National Semiconductor—whose chips end up inside everything from cars and computers to telecommunications gear—faced a logistics nightmare. National produced and assembled chips at 13 plants located in the United States, Britain, Israel, and Southeast Asia. Finished products were then shipped to an array of large customers—IBM, Toshiba, Ford, Siemens—each with factories scattered around the globe. On their way to customers, chips traveled any of 20,000 direct routes, mostly in the cargo holds of planes flown by 12 airlines, stopping along the way at 10 different warehouses. National's logistics performance left much to be desired: 95 percent of its products were delivered within 45 days of the order. The other 5 percent took as long as 90 days. Because customers never knew which 5 percent would be late, they demanded 90 days' worth of inventory in everything. "We had buffer stocks all along the line," comments a

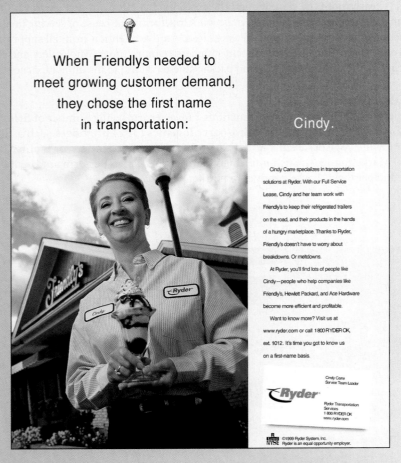

When Friendlys needed to meet growing customer demand, they chose the first name in transportation: Cindy.

Cindy Carre specializes in transportation solutions at Ryder. With our Full Service Lease, Cindy and her team work with Friendlys to keep their refrigerated trailers on the road, and their products in the hands of a hungry marketplace. Thanks to Ryder, Friendly's doesn't have to worry about breakdowns. Or meltdowns.

At Ryder, you'll find lots of people like Cindy—people who help companies like Friendly's, Hewlett Packard, and Ace Hardware become more efficient and profitable.

Want to know more? Visit us at www.ryder.com or call 1 800 RYDER OK ext. 1012. It's time you got to know us on a first-name basis.

Cindy Carre
Service Team Leader

Ryder
Ryder Transportation Services
1 800 RYDER OK
www.ryder.com

©1999 Ryder System, Inc. Ryder is an equal opportunity employer.

Third-party logistics: Many companies are now outsourcing logistics tasks to companies like Ryder Integrated Logistics. Here, Ryder describes a system it designed to keep Friendly's refrigerated trucks on the road. "Thanks to Ryder, Friendly's doesn't have to worry about breakdowns. Or meltdowns."

nearly three-quarters of the nation's largest manufacturing companies now outsource some or all of these functions, nearly double the percentage a decade ago.

Increasingly, companies are handing over their logistics to suppliers that specialize in helping them tighten up sluggish, over-stuffed supply chains, slash inventories, and

coordinate shipments from its 21 assembly plants, four rail centers, and 55 destination ramps to its 6,000-plus North American dealer network. That arrangement, in its first year alone, reduced Ford inventories by $1 billion, trimmed inventory carrying costs by $125 million, and decreased delivery time to dealers by four days, or 26 per-

National executive. "The whole system was awash in inventory."

National's management set out to overhaul its global logistics network. However, whereas National knew a lot about making chips, it knew little about how to fix its logistics. "To do that," says the executive, "we would have had to make our company into FedEx." Instead, National *hired* FedEx to handle its global distribution. FedEx Logistics now runs National's distribution center in Singapore, conducting all storage, sorting, and shipping activities. The results have been startling. Within two years, National's distribution costs fell 27 percent. At the same time, sales jumped by $584 million and delivery performance improved dramatically. National can now move products from the factory to customers in an average of four days or less, and it's well on its way toward its goal of a 72-hour turnaround.

Sony: Sony knows logistics. In fact, the company considers logistics to be one of its competitive advantages. So you might wonder why an industry leader would outsource half of its distribution requirements in Mexico to Redwood Systems, a third-party logistics (3PL) provider with headquarters in Atlanta. It turns out that even a logistics leader needs help some of the time. The reasons are growth and speed to market. "In Mexico, logistics is challenging because of a lack of infrastructure," says Carlos Rojas, logistics division manager for Sony Electronicas, Mexico. "Given those limitations, we couldn't take

advantage of a growing market without a 3PL partner who could quickly expand our operations. By relying on Redwood to manage the day-to-day details of our Mexico-based distribution, we can concentrate on marketing and sales instead of logistics, and do it without adding to our head count." Today, Redwood manages over 500 different products and another 15,000 different parts for Sony. Product is received into the facility from all over the world, and in quantities ranging from parcel shipments to full containers. The 3PL supplier ships an estimated 200 orders per day, with an average of 10 line items per order.

Saturn: Saturn's just-in-time production system allows for almost no parts inventory at the plant. Instead, it relies on a world-class logistics system to keep parts flowing into the factory at precisely the times they're needed. Saturn is so good in managing its supply chain that in four years it has had to halt production just once—for only 18 minutes—because the right part failed to arrive at the right time. Most of the credit, however, goes to Ryder Integrated Logistics. Ryder, best known for renting trucks, manages Saturn's far-ranging supply chain, moving the automaker's materials, parts, and products efficiently and reliably from supplier to factory to dealer showroom.

To keep Saturn's assembly lines humming, Ryder transports thousands of preinspected and presorted parts—more than 2,200 receiving-dock transactions every day—hitting delivery windows as narrow as

five minutes. Ryder keeps its parts, people, and trucks in a nearly constant blur of high-tech motion. For example, according to one account, when delivering service parts to Saturn dealerships, Ryder's longhaul drivers "plug a plastic key, loaded with electronic data, into an onboard computer. The screen tells them exactly where to go, which route to take, and how much time to spend getting there." Ryder's effective supply chain management results in lower costs, improved operations, more productive dealers, and—in the end—more satisfied customers.

Sources: Quotes and other information from Ronald Henkoff, "Delivering the Goods," *Fortune,* November 28, 1994, pp. 64–77; Lisa H. Harrington, "Special Report on Contract Logistics," *Transportation & Distribution,* September 1996, pp. A–N; Scott Woolley, "Replacing Inventory with Information," *Forbes,* March 24, 1997, pp. 54–58; Allen Allnoch, "Third-Party Logistics Industry Poised for Growth in U.S. and Abroad," *IIE Solutions,* January 1998, p. 10; Martha Celestino, "Choosing a Third-Party Logistics Provider," *World Trade,* July 1999, pp. 54–56; "Even a Logistics Leader Needs Help Some of the Time," *Modern Materials Handling,* December 2000, p. S15; "3PLs on the Rise," *Modern Materials Handling,* December 2001, p. 15; and Mike Verespej, "Logistics' New Look? Now It's Service," *Frontline Solutions,* June 2002, pp. 24–33.

For example, Emory's Global Logistics unit provides clients with coordinated, single-source logistics services including supply chain management, customized information technology, inventory control, warehousing, transportation management, customer service and fulfillment, and freight auditing and control. "From sourcing raw materials to delivering finished products to stores," proclaims the Emory Web site, "our experts work with you to streamline and manage your entire supply chain and to keep you in control." Last year, U.S. manufacturers and distributors spent more than $61 billion on third-party logistics (also called *3PL, outsourced logistics,* or *contract logistics*) services, and the market has been growing by 20 percent per year.[27]

Companies use third-party logistics providers for several reasons. First, because getting the product to market is their main focus, these providers can often do it more efficiently and at lower cost. According to one study, outsourcing typically results in 15 percent to 30 percent cost savings.[28] Second, outsourcing logistics frees a company to focus more intensely on its core business. Finally, integrated logistics companies understand increasingly complex logistics environments. This can be especially helpful to companies attempting to expand their global market coverage. For example, companies distributing their products across Europe face a bewildering array of environmental restrictions that affect logistics, including packaging standards, truck size and weight limits, and noise and emissions pollution controls. By outsourcing its logistics, a company can gain a complete pan-European distribution system without incurring the costs, delays, and risks associated with setting up its own system.

LOOKING BACK: REVIEWING THE CONCEPTS

Producing a product or service and making it available to buyers requires building relationships not just with customers, but also with key suppliers and resellers in the company's *supply chain*. Marketers have traditionally focused on the "downstream" side of the supply chain—on the *marketing channels* or *distribution channels* that look forward toward the customer.

Marketing channel decisions are among the most important decisions that management faces. A company's channel decisions directly affect every other marketing decision. Each channel system creates a different level of revenues and costs and reaches a different segment of target consumers. Management must make channel decisions carefully, incorporating today's needs with tomorrow's likely selling environment. Some companies pay too little attention to their distribution channels, but others have used imaginative distribution systems to gain competitive advantage.

1. Explain why companies use distribution channels and discuss the functions these channels perform.

Most producers use intermediaries to bring their products to market. They try to forge a *marketing channel*—a set of interdependent organizations involved in the process of making a product or service available for use or consumption by the consumer or business user. Through their contacts, experience, specialization, and scale of operation, intermediaries usually offer the firm more than it can achieve on its own. Distribution channels perform many key functions. Some help *complete* transactions by gathering and distributing *information* needed for planning and aiding exchange; by developing and spreading persuasive *communications* about an offer; by performing *contact* work—finding and communicating with prospective buyers; by *matching*—shaping and fitting the offer to the buyer's needs; and by entering into *negotiation* to reach an agreement on price and other terms of the offer so that ownership can be transferred. Other functions help to *fulfill* the completed transactions by offering *physical distribution*—transporting and storing goods; *financing*—acquiring and using funds to cover the costs of the channel work; and *risk taking*—assuming the risks of carrying out the channel work.

2. Discuss how channel members interact and how they organize to perform the work of the channel.

The channel will be most effective when each member is assigned the tasks it can do best. Ideally, because the success of individual channel members depends on overall channel success, all channel firms should work together smoothly. They should understand and accept their roles, coordinate their goals and activities, and cooperate to attain overall channel goals. By cooperating, they can more effectively sense, serve, and satisfy the target market. In a large company, the formal organization structure assigns roles and provides needed leadership. But in a distribution channel made up of independent firms, leadership and power are not formally set. Traditionally, distribution channels have lacked the leadership needed to assign roles and man-

age conflict. In recent years, however, new types of channel organizations have appeared that provide stronger leadership and improved performance.

3. Identify the major channel alternatives open to a company.

Each firm identifies alternative ways to reach its market. Available means vary from direct selling to using one, two, three, or more intermediary *channel levels*. Marketing channels face continuous and sometimes dramatic change. Three of the most important trends are the growth of *vertical, horizontal,* and *multichannel distribution systems*. These trends affect channel cooperation, conflict, and competition. *Channel design* begins with assessing customer channel service needs and company channel objectives and constraints. The company then identifies the major channel alternatives in terms of the *types* of intermediaries, the *number* of intermediaries, and the *channel responsibilities* of each. Each channel alternative must be evaluated according to economic, control, and adaptive criteria. Channel management calls for selecting qualified intermediaries and motivating them. Individual channel members must be evaluated regularly.

4. Explain how companies select, motivate, and evaluate channel members.

Producers vary in their ability to attract qualified marketing intermediaries. Some producers have no trouble signing up channel members. Others have to work hard to line up enough qualified intermediaries. When selecting intermediaries, the company should evaluate each channel member's qualifications and select those who best fit its channel objectives. Once selected, channel members must be continuously motivated to do their best. The company must sell not only *through* the intermediaries but *to* and *with* them. It should work to forge long-term partnerships with their channel partners to create a marketing system that meets the needs of both the manufacturer *and* the partners. The company must also regularly check channel member performance against established performance standards, rewarding intermediaries who are performing well and assisting or replacing weaker ones.

5. Discuss the nature and importance of marketing logistics and integrated supply chain management.

Just as firms are giving the marketing concept increased recognition, more business firms are paying attention to *marketing logistics* (or *physical distribution*). Logistics is an area of potentially high cost savings and improved customer satisfaction. Marketing logistics addresses not only *outbound distribution* but also *inbound distribution* and *reverse distribution*. That is, it involves entire *supply chain management*—managing value-added flows between suppliers, the company, resellers, and final users. No logistics system can both maximize customer service and minimize distribution costs. Instead, the goal of logistics management is to provide a *targeted* level of service at the least cost. The major logistics functions include *warehousing, inventory management, transportation,* and *logistics information management*.

The *integrated logistics management* concept recognizes that improved logistics requires teamwork in the form of close working relationships across functional areas inside the company and across various organizations in the supply chain. Companies can achieve logistics harmony among functions by creating cross-functional logistics teams, integrative supply manager positions, and senior-level logistics executives with cross-functional authority. Channel partnerships can take the form of cross-company teams, shared projects, and information-sharing systems. Today, some companies are outsourcing their logistics functions to third-party logistics providers to save costs, increase efficiency, and gain faster and more effective access to global markets.

REVIEWING THE KEY TERMS

Administered VMS 407
Channel conflict 404
Channel level 402
Contractual VMS 406
Conventional distribution channel 405
Corporate VMS 405
Direct marketing channel 402
Disintermediation 408
Distribution center 420

Exclusive distribution 413
Franchise organization 406
Horizontal marketing system 407
Indirect marketing channel 402
Integrated logistics management 423
Intensive distribution 413
Intermodal transportation 423
Marketing channel (distribution channel) 400

Marketing logistics (physical distribution) 419
Multichannel distribution system 408
Selective distribution 413
Supply chain management 419
Third-party logistics (3PL) provider 425
Value delivery network 399
Vertical marketing system (VMS) 405

DISCUSSING THE CONCEPTS

1. Explain the purpose of a company's supply chain. Why may the term "supply chain" be too limited for today's business activities? What is a value delivery network, and how is it different from a supply chain?
2. Discuss the nature and importance of marketing channels. Define a marketing channel (distribution channel) and list its important characteristics.
3. List and briefly discuss the marketing channel functions that are involved in completing and fulfilling transactions. Which function applies most in each of the following situations? (a) A retailer puts in a rush reorder for a needed Christmas item that is in short supply. (b) An Internet marketer seeks ways to identify and contact its market. (c) A small retailer wants to expand its order size but does not currently have funds needed to pay for the expanded order. (d) A business buyer attends a large trade show wanting to buy higher quality products on a limited budget.
4. Describe the horizontal and vertical channel conflicts that might occur in one of the following: (a) the personal computer industry, (b) the automobile industry, (c) the music industry, or (d) the clothing industry. How would you remedy the problems you have just described?
5. Give an example of each of the three major forms of vertical marketing systems described in the chapter. What advantages do such systems have over traditional channel organizations?
6. What is disintermediation? Give an example other than those discussed in the chapter. What opportunities and problems does disintermediation present for traditional retailers? Explain.
7. Describe which distribution strategy—intensive, selective, or exclusive—is used for each of the following products: (a) Piaget watches, (b) Acura automobiles, (c) Snickers candy bars.
8. Regarding outsourcing: (a) Why would a company choose to outsource its distribution function? (b) What major factors contribute to a successful outsourcing relationship? What are the potential dangers of such a relationship? (c) Give an example of a company that could benefit from outsourcing its logistics, and suggest some practical outsourcing alternatives for the company. (For more information on outsourcing, see the Outsourcing Institute's Web site at www.outsourcing.com.)

APPLYING THE CONCEPTS

1. You know about the Internet, but have you ever heard of the "extranet"? A company creates an "extranet" when it opens its own internal network (or intranet) to trusted suppliers, distributors, and other selected business partners. Via the extranet, a company can communicate quickly and efficiently with its partners, complete transactions, and share data. A supplier might analyze the company's inventory needs. (Boeing booked $100 million in spare parts from airline customers in one year.) Partners might swap customer lists for interrelated products and services or share purchasing systems to gain savings through more efficient purchasing. (General Electric claims that $500 million in purchasing costs can be saved using an extranet.) Imagine the strategic advantages created when

virtual partners communicate in nanoseconds about shifting supply-and-demand situations, customer requests and opportunities, and just-in-time inventory needs. Purchase-processing times can be reduced from weeks to minutes at enormous cost savings that can be passed along to consumers.

   a. What role will extranets play in distribution decisions for retailers, wholesalers, and manufacturers?

   b. Discuss the potential dangers and benefits of an extranet system. How do those benefits differ for business partners?

   c. How does the extranet concept work with outsourcing (if at all)?

   d. Write a short position paper that outlines your thoughts on the advantages and disadvantages of extranets and their future in marketing commerce.

2. Although strong partnerships benefit both the supplier and the buyer, retailers often have difficulty forging strong ties with suppliers. Why? Differing marketing objectives, profit expectations, and business relationships with competitors can result in poor retailer–supplier partnerships. One organization that overcame these difficulties is Ralph Lauren's Polo brand (see www.polo.com). To improve its customer relationship management system with retailers, Polo found new ways to bring value to the retail operation while reducing the retailer's costs. The company now offers its clients a variety of merchandise purchase options. First, retailers can purchase Polo products in the traditional way—through inventory acquisition. For retailers uninterested in carrying expensive inventory loads, Polo offers a second option—the leased department. Under this agreement, Polo leases floor space, provides its own merchandise, staffs the department with its own employees, and promotes the department in conjunction with the retailer. Though the majority of profits go to Polo, the retailer benefits from having a prestige line in its store without having the burden of inventory. Polo has found that this method not only forges a better working relationship with retailers but often results in the retailer taking over the Polo lease and operating the department on its own, creating value for both the suppliers and retailers.

   a. How has Polo forged a value delivery system with retailers?

   b. What are the advantages of partner relationship management? (For additional information, see Real Marketing 13.2).

   c. What conflicts between retailer and supplier might Polo avoid by using the leased department method? What conflicts might be heightened by the leasing approach?

   d. Construct a short list of criteria that a retailer might use to evaluate its relationship with Polo.

   e. Polo recently decided to open free-standing retail stores in selected cities. What would be the advantages and disadvantages of this strategy with respect to Polo's customer relationship management process? Do the advantages outweigh the disadvantages? Explain your reasoning.

 # DIGITAL CONNECTIONS

CONNECTIONS VIA MULTICHANNEL DISTRIBUTION ALTERNATIVES

Marketers in many industries are constantly on the lookout for new ways to put their products into the hands of consumers. Such is the case in the music industry. Multichannel distribution alternatives include retail stores of many types (department stores, specialty stores, discount stores), catalog merchants, mail-order clubs, and Internet Web sites (both for the music company and for those that carry the company's products). Music is one of the easiest and most popular items to buy on the Web. In fact, it has become the major channel choice for many young buyers (the chief market for the industry). Buyers have learned that they can often obtain better prices from Web retailers than from music stores, even after paying shipping and handling. Examine the following Web sites for more information on purchasing music via the Web: (a) Amazon.com at www.Amazon.com, (b) CD Now at www.cdnow.com, (c) Compact Disc Connection at www.cdconnection.com, and (d) Columbia House at www.columbiahouse.com.

FOR DISCUSSION

1. What are the primary advantages of ordering CDs via the Internet? What are the disadvantages?

2. How will Web music retailing affect the more traditional channels such as music stores and book-music combination stores?

3. How can music producers handle the channel conflicts that arise when using multichannel distribution alternatives?

4. Rank the following factors in terms of importance in purchasing a CD: price, location, selection, personal service, and immediacy of possession? Companies selling through the Internet are betting that price and selection (especially for those hard-to-find titles) will rank higher than location (such as a mall) or immediate possession. Is this true for you? How might those preferences differ for baby boomers?

5. After visiting each of the noted Web sites, compare the marketing and distribution strategies of each. Prepare a grid that compares the sites on important attributes. Which site ranks highest in your comparison? Which site would you be most likely to use?

Celarix: Web-Based Logistics Management

Distribution and logistics management have grown into a $1 billion industry worldwide. But despite its size, until recently, the industry's varied services were fractured and difficult to navigate. Celarix is trying to change the way distribution and logistics tasks are managed. The company's Web-based solution connects a company's suppliers, factories, consolidators, carriers, and transportation service providers to provide real-time information about the movement of goods. The site also allows companies to search for alternate logistics suppliers. Now, customers ranging from Agilent Technologies and Sharp Electronics to Abercrombie & Fitch and Lowe's rely on Celarix services.

After viewing the Celarix video, answer the following questions about distribution and logistics management:

1. Celarix dramatically alters a market's access to information about distribution options. How does that information impact channel design decisions? Be specific.
2. What benefits do third-party logistics providers offer that Celarix does not? Why might a company choose third-party logistics over in-house logistics management?
3. How might physical distribution decisions enhance relationships with channel partners? How might such decisions erode those relationships?

Staples, Inc.: Revising the Strategy

TAKING OVER

In January 2002, Ronald Sargent assumed the reins of office supply superstore Staples from founder Thomas Stemberg. Sargent and Staples faced many challenges. The office supply market seemed to be maturing—industry sales in 2001 actually shrank 3 percent after years of double-digit growth. Further, although Staples had significantly more stores than its two major competitors—Office Depot and OfficeMax—it trailed Office Depot in sales revenue (see Exhibit 1).

There were bright spots for Staples—whereas both Office Depot's and OfficeMax's sales had declined by 5.6 percent and 9.7 percent, respectively, in 2001, Staples's sales had inched up by 0.7 percent, and its profits had soared from just $59.7 million in 2000 to $265 million in 2001. Yet, analysts noted that Staples's return on net assets (RONA) was below its weighted-average cost of capital (WACC) and argued that the firm needed to improve its profitability. Sargent knew he had his work cut out for him.

EXHIBIT 1: OFFICE SUPPLY DATA FOR FISCAL 2001

Company	Number of Stores	Sales Revenue ($B)	Net Income ($M)	Revenue per Store ($M)*	Employees
Staples	1,400	$10.74	$265	$5.7	53,000
Office Depot	859	$11.15	$201	$6.7	48,000
OfficeMax	1,000	$4.64	($296)	$4.6	30,000

*Revenue per store does not include revenue from Internet or catalog sales.
Source: Westchester County Business Journal, April 1, 2002, p. 14.

(continued)

TAKING STOCK

Sargent began by questioning one of the company's basic strategic assumptions—build a store with lots of inventory and the lowest prices in town and customers will beat a path to your door. Under this philosophy, Staples operated 400 more stores than OfficeMax and 541 more than Office Depot. Staples's stores were typically stocked from floor to ceiling, warehouse style, with all sorts of products. Yet, Staples's sales revenue per store was well below Office Depot's.

Sargent therefore decided to slow the company's store expansion. He also closed 32 under-performing stores, the largest store closing in the company's 16-year history. And the company planned to open only 115 new stores in 2002, down from 160 in 2001. It would also open most of these new stores in existing markets rather than new market areas in order to take advantage of operating efficiencies.

Further, focus groups with Staples's target market of small-business customers indicated that those customers did not like the warehouse look. Customers wanted to be able to see across a store and to determine quickly from signage where items were located. Staples responded by experimenting with a smaller store (20,000 square feet versus about 24,000) with lower shelving and a more open atmosphere. This meant that it had to reduce inventory. As a result, the company removed many items that it found were not really necessary, such as child-oriented computer games and educational software. Based on customer feedback, it also stopped offering some business services, like health insurance or prepaid legal services, so that it could focus on consumable products. Customers, it found, did not want to shop at Staples for these services.

The results with this new store format proved promising, with sales increasing by up to 10 percent with about 10 percent less inventory. Sargent noted that "we're doing the same sales volume with two printers selling for more than $100 than we did selling five printers at the different price points." As a result, Sargent decided to roll out the new format and reconfigure 280 stores in 2002 in hopes of improving both sales and inventory turnover. Staples's inventory turnover ratio was about 5.1 times as compared with Office Depot's 6.3 times.

As a second part of his strategy, Sargent turned to what the company calls its "North American Delivery" segment. This segment includes the company's Internet, catalog, and corporate contracts operations—all of its operations that *bypass* its stores. In 2001, this segment accounted for 28 percent of sales and 40 percent of profits. Competitor Office Depot got 34 percent of its sales and 33 percent of its profits from similar operations. In a Home Furnishing Network survey of Web site traffic for the first four months of 2002, Office Depot had the highest number of unique Web site visits, over 24 million, of the top 20 retail Web sites, ahead of Best Buy, Wal-Mart, Target, and others. Staples's site, www.staples.com, came in seventh with just under 14 million visits, while OfficeMax finished tenth with just under 10 million visits. *Forbes* magazine named Staples's site as the "Best of the Web Pick for Entrepreneurs" for the third year in a row, based on its ability to assist smaller businesses to run as smoothly as larger organizations.

To handle its catalog operations, Staples has a subsidiary, Quill.com. A survey ranked Quill.com as highest in terms of its online sales conversion rate of 30.3 percent versus the average site's rate of 8 percent or lower. Quill.com offered 35 percent of its products as private-label brands as compared to 7 percent for Staples. Sargent saw this as an opportunity for Staples to offer more of it own private-label brands that carried higher margins.

Although Staples had built its business by targeting small businesses, while OfficeMax had targeted household consumers, it also developed programs for businesses with more than 100 employees. Its StaplesLink program allowed companies to link their internal procurement systems with Staples's computer systems. This allowed users to place their orders directly with Staples, which then prepared the order and delivered it to the business the next day.

For both its catalog and contract businesses, Sargent believed that Staples should beat a path to customers' doors. He ordered the doubling, to 400, of Staples's special sales force, which worked with customers to get them to order through its catalog or its Web site. He also added 100 staff members to the 600-person sales force that worked exclusively with corporate and small-business accounts.

To find a away to get more small-business customers into the stores, Staples entered a test with FleetBoston Financial Corp. to opening 10 offices in select Staples stores in the Northeast. These 150-foot, in-store offices would have two Fleet staff members who would work with business owners to open specially designed business checking accounts, get debit cards, and make small-business loan applications. The offices would not dispense cash or take deposits and would be open six or seven days a week. Fleet already had more than 100 nontraditional branches, mostly in supermarkets.

Next, Sargent planned to continue Staples's international expansion. The retailer already operated 180 stores in the United Kingdom, Germany, the Netherlands, and Portugal. It planned to add 20 new stores in Europe and to expand into one more country. European operations accounted for about $796 million of 2001's sales.

Finally, Sargent focused on customer retention. He understood that getting a customer was expensive. The company estimated that a customer doing business for three years was 4.5 times more profitable than a new customer. Staples's managers estimated that the company had a 30 percent share of their customers' office supply purchases, and they wanted to increase that share.

TAKING THE CHALLENGE

Sargent knew Staples's 53,000 employees would have to execute all of these strategic moves for the company to reach its target of $12 billion in sales and $440 million in net income by 2003. And he knew that competition was only going to intensify. The struggling OfficeMax was trying to capture more of Staples's small-business customers. These customers were often willing to buy higher-margin items, thus leading to Staples's higher-than-average margins. In an industry with lots of stores, catalogs, and Internet sites offering similar merchandise at similar prices, maintaining a competitive advantage would not be easy. Further, Sargent worried about offering the same products and services to the same customers through multiple channels. Would this strategy generate channel conflict within the company?

QUESTIONS FOR DISCUSSION

1. How are store, catalog, and Internet-based distribution channels alike or different in terms of the channel functions they perform?

2. Do you see any potential for conflict among Staples's different channels? Why or why not?

3. Is the Staples/FleetBoston horizontal marketing effort a good idea? Why or why not?

4. What are the advantages of more intensive development of individual market areas versus the advantages of putting more stores in new markets?

5. How can Staples develop a competitive advantage in a commodity market? What marketing recommendations would you make to Staples?

Sources: "Staples, Inc.," Corporate Technology Information Services, Inc., July 3, 2002; W. Julian, "Staples, Inc.," Salomon Smith Barney, June 21, 2002; Alissa Swchmelkin, "Fleet to Open Offices in Staples," *American Banker,* July 11, 2002, p. 20; "Staples' eProcurement System Integration Available On-Line," *Office Products International,* May 2002, p. 13; Alex Philippidis, "Whither the Warehouse Look: Can Staples, OfficeMax Raise Profits by Lowering Shelves," *Westchester County Business Journal,* April 1, 2002, p. 14; "Staples Reports Strong Q4," *Office Products International,* April 2002, p. 14; Joseph Pereira, "Staples Inc. Pulls Back on Its Store-Expansion Plans, *Wall Street Journal,* March 13, 2002, p. B4; A. H. Rubinson, "Staples," UBS Warburg, December 10, 2001.

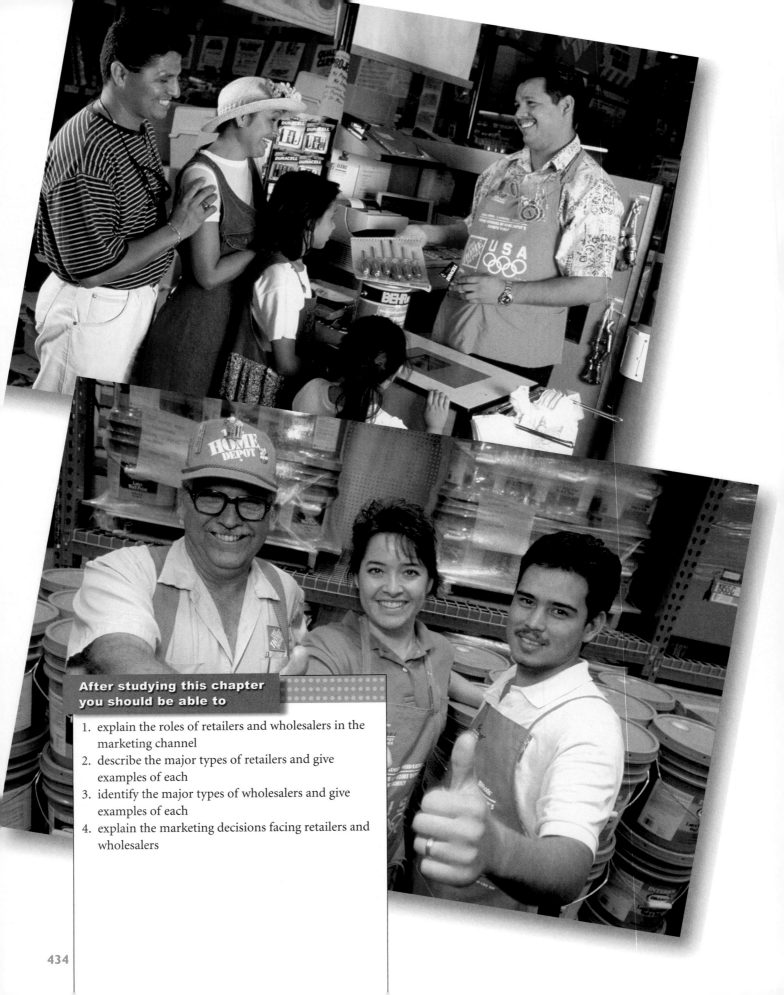

After studying this chapter you should be able to

1. explain the roles of retailers and wholesalers in the marketing channel
2. describe the major types of retailers and give examples of each
3. identify the major types of wholesalers and give examples of each
4. explain the marketing decisions facing retailers and wholesalers

Retailing and Wholesaling

LOOKING AHEAD: PREVIEWING THE CONCEPTS

In the previous chapter, you learned the basics of marketing channel design and channel partner relationship management. Now, we'll look more deeply into the two major intermediary channel functions, retailing and wholesaling. You already know something about retailing—you're served every day by retailers of all shapes and sizes. However, you probably know much less about the hoard of wholesalers that work behind the scenes. In this chapter, we'll investigate the characteristics of different kinds of retailers and wholesalers, the marketing decisions they make, and trends for the future. You'll see that the retailing and wholesaling landscapes are changing rapidly to match explosive changes in markets and technology.

To start, we'll look in on Home Depot, the highly successful home improvement retailer. This "category killer's" success has resulted not from a focus on sales but from an obsession with building customer relationships. However, to take care of customers, Home Depot must first take care of those who take care of customers.

Home Depot, the giant do-it-yourself home improvement retail chain, is one of the world's hottest retailers. At first glance, a cavernous Home Depot store doesn't look like much. With its cement floors and drafty, warehouselike interior, the store offers all the atmosphere of an airplane hangar. But the chances are good that you'll find exactly what you're looking for, priced to make it a real value. Home Depot carries a huge assortment of some 40,000 to 50,000 items—anything and everything related to home improvement. Its prices run 20 to 30 percent below those of local hardware stores.

Home Depot provides more than the right products at the right prices, however. Perhaps the best part of shopping at Home Depot is the high quality of its customer service. Home Depot is more than just customer driven—it's customer *obsessed*. In the words of co-founder Bernie Marcus, "All of our people understand what the Holy Grail is. It's not the bottom line. It's an almost blind, passionate commitment to taking care of customers."

Bernie Marcus and Arthur Blank founded Home Depot with the simple mission of helping customers solve their home improvement problems. Their goal: "To take ham-handed homeowners who lack the confidence to do more than screw in a lightbulb and transform them into Mr. and Ms. Fixits." Accomplishing this mission takes more than simply peddling the store's products and taking the customers' money. It means building lasting customer relationships.

Bernie and Arthur understand the importance of customer satisfaction. They calculate that a satisfied customer is worth more than $25,000 in customer lifetime value ($38 per store visit, times 30 visits per year, times about 22 years of patronage). Customer satisfaction, in turn, results from interactions with well-trained, highly motivated employees who consistently provide good value and high-quality service. "The most important part of our formula," says Arthur, "is the quality of caring that takes place in our stores between the employee and the customer." Thus, at Home Depot, taking care of customers begins with taking care of employees. Says a senior Home Depot executive, "Take care of your people and they will take care of your company. I know it is a cliché, but it is so true."

Home Depot attracts the best salespeople by paying above-average salaries; then it trains them thoroughly. All employees take regular "product knowledge" classes to gain hands-on experience with problems customers will face. When it comes to creating customer value and satisfaction, Home Depot treats its employees as partners. All full-time employees receive at least 7 percent of their annual salary in company stock. As a result, Home Depot employees take ownership in the business of serving customers. Each employee wears a bright orange apron labeled, "Hello, I'm _____, a Home Depot stockholder. Let me help you."

Home Depot avoids the high-pressure sales techniques used by some retailers. Instead, it encourages salespeople to build long-term relationships with customers—to spend whatever time it takes, visit after visit, to solve customer problems. Home Depot pays employees a straight salary so that they can spend as much time as necessary with customers without worrying about making the sale. Bernie Marcus once declared, "The day I'm dead with an apple in my mouth is the day we'll pay commissions." In fact, rather than pushing customers to *overspend*, employees are trained to help customers spend *less* than they expected. "I love it when shoppers tell me they were prepared to spend $150 and our people showed them how to do the job for four or five bucks," says Bernie.

Home Depot has also extended its high-grade relationship-building efforts to the Internet. In addition to selling goods online, the company's Web site also offers plenty of how-to tips for household projects: how to fix it, build it, grow it, decorate it, or install it. It provides useful tools, such as calculators for figuring out how much paint or wallpaper is needed to cover a given amount of space. Home Depot also sends e-mail to regular site users alerting them to how-to workshops or other events at nearby stores.

Taking care of customers has made Home Depot one of today's most successful retailers. Founded in 1978, in less than 25 years it has grown explosively to 1,400 stores and $54 billion in sales, nearly two and one-half times that of nearest competitor Lowe's. That makes Home Depot the nation's largest do-it-yourself chain, the second-largest retailer behind Wal-Mart, and the youngest retailer ever to break the $50 billion mark in annual sales. Through the 1990s, its sales grew by an average 25 percent annually; profits grew by 31 percent. One hundred shares of Home Depot stock purchased in 1982 would be worth $1.6 million today.

Still, the larger Home Depot gets, and the more saturated its markets become, the tougher it will be for the retailer to remain a go-go growth company. Home Depot can't rest on its lofty past achievements. "Being number one," says new CEO Bob Nardelli, "it's easy to get complacent." But one thing's for certain: Continued success will depend on the passionate pursuit of customer satisfaction. Home Depot's new management would be wise to heed the six pieces of advice that Arthur Blank, Home Depot's co-founder, once offered to all new store managers: "Serve the customer, serve the customer, serve the customer, serve the customer, serve the customer. And number 6, kick [butt]."[1]

The Home Depot story provides many insights into the workings of one of today's most successful retailers. This chapter looks at *retailing* and *wholesaling*. In the first section, we look at the nature and importance of retailing, major types of store and nonstore retailers, the decisions retailers make, and the future of retailing. In the second section, we discuss these same topics as they relate to wholesalers.

Retailing

Retailing

All activities involved in selling goods or services directly to final consumers for their personal, nonbusiness use.

Retailer

Business whose sales come *primarily* from retailing.

What is retailing? We all know that Wal-Mart, Home, and Target are retailers, but so are Avon representatives, Amazon.com, the local Holiday Inn, and a doctor seeing patients. **Retailing** includes all the activities involved in selling products or services directly to final consumers for their personal, nonbusiness use. Many institutions—manufacturers, wholesalers, and retailers—do retailing. But most retailing is done by **retailers:** businesses whose sales come *primarily* from retailing.

Although most retailing is done in retail stores, in recent years *nonstore retailing* has been growing much faster than has store retailing. Nonstore retailing includes selling to final consumers through direct mail, catalogs, telephone, the Internet, TV home shopping shows, home and office parties, door-to-door contact, vending machines, and other direct-selling approaches. We discuss such direct-marketing approaches in detail in Chapter 17. In this chapter, we focus on store retailing.

Types of Retailers

Retail stores come in all shapes and sizes, and new retail types keep emerging. The most important types of retail stores are described in Table 14.1 and discussed in the following sections. They can be classified in terms of several characteristics, including the *amount of service* they offer, the breadth and depth of their *product lines*, the *relative prices* they charge, and how they are *organized*.

TABLE 14.1   MAJOR STORE RETAILER TYPES

Specialty Stores: Carry a narrow product line with a deep assortment, such as apparel stores, sporting-goods stores, furniture stores, florists, and bookstores. A clothing store would be a *single-line* store, a men's clothing store would be a *limited-line store,* and a men's custom-shirt store would be a *superspecialty* store. Examples: The Body Shop, Gap, The Athlete's Foot.

Department Stores: Carry several product lines—typically clothing, home furnishings, and household goods—with each line operated as a separate department managed by specialist buyers or merchandisers. Examples: Sears, Macy's, Marshall Field's.

Supermarkets: A relatively large, low-cost, low-margin, high-volume, self-service operation designed to serve the consumer's total needs for food and household products. Examples: Kroger, Vons, A&P, Food Lion.

Convenience Stores: Relatively small stores located near residential areas, open long hours seven days a week, and carrying a limited line of high-turnover convenience products at slightly higher prices. Examples: 7-Eleven, Stop-N-Go, Circle K.

Discount Stores: Carry standard merchandise sold at lower prices with lower margins and higher volumes. Examples: General—Wal-Mart, Target, Kmart, Specialty—Circuit City.

Off-Price Retailers: Sell merchandise bought at less-than-regular wholesale prices and sold at less than retail: often leftover goods, overruns, and irregulars obtained at reduced prices from manufacturers or other retailers. These include *factory outlets* owned and operated by manufacturers (example: Mikasa); *independent off-price retailers* owned and run by entrepreneurs or by divisions of larger retail corporations (example: TJ Maxx); and *warehouse (or wholesale) clubs* selling a limited selection of brand-name groceries, appliances, clothing, other goods at deep discounts to consumers who pay membership fees (examples: Costco, Sam's, BJ's Wholesale Club).

Superstores: Very large stores traditionally aimed at meeting consumers' total needs for routinely purchased food and nonfood items. Includes *category killers*, which carry a deep assortment in a particular category and have a knowledgeable staff (examples: Circuit City, Petsmart, Staples); *supercenters,* combined supermarket and discount stores (examples: Wal-Mart Supercenters, SuperTarget, Super Kmart Center); and *hypermarkets* with up to 220,000 square feet of space combining supermarket, discount, and warehouse retailing (examples: Carrefour [France], Pyrca [Spain]).

Amount of Service

Different products require different amounts of service, and customer service preferences vary. Retailers may offer one of three levels of service—self-service, limited service, and full service.

Self-service retailers serve customers who are willing to perform their own "locate-compare-select" process to save money. Self-service is the basis of all discount operations and is typically used by sellers of convenience goods (such as supermarkets) and nationally branded, fast-moving shopping goods (such as Best Buy).

Limited-service retailers, such as Sears or J.C. Penney, provide more sales assistance because they carry more shopping goods about which customers need information. Their increased operating costs result in higher prices. In *full-service retailers,* such as specialty stores and first-class department stores, salespeople assist customers in every phase of the shopping process. Full-service stores usually carry more specialty goods for which customers like to be "waited on." They provide more services, resulting in much higher operating costs, which are passed along to customers as higher prices.

Product Line

Specialty store

A retail store that carries a narrow product line with a deep assortment within that line.

Department store

A retail organization that carries a wide variety of product lines—typically clothing, home furnishings, and household goods; each line is operated as a separate department managed by specialist buyers or merchandisers.

Retailers also can be classified by the length and breadth of their product assortments. Some retailers, such as **specialty stores,** carry narrow product lines with deep assortments within those lines. Today, specialty stores are flourishing. The increasing use of market segmentation, market targeting, and product specialization has resulted in a greater need for stores that focus on specific products and segments.

In contrast, **department stores** carry a wide variety of product lines. In recent years, department stores have been squeezed between more focused and flexible specialty stores on the one hand, and more efficient, lower-priced discounters on the other. In response, many have added promotional pricing to meet the discount threat. Others have stepped up the use of store brands and single-brand "designer shops" to compete with specialty stores. Still others are trying mail-order, telephone, and Web selling. Service remains the key differentiating factor. Department stores such as Nordstrom, Saks, Neiman Marcus, and other high-end department stores are doing well by emphasizing high-quality service.

Supermarket

Large, low-cost, low-margin, high-volume, self-service store that carries a wide variety of food, laundry, and household products.

Convenience store

A small store, located near a residential area, that is open long hours seven days a week and carries a limited line of high-turnover convenience goods.

Superstore

A store much larger than a regular supermarket that carries a large assortment of routinely purchased food and nonfood items and offers services such as dry cleaning, post offices, photo finishing, check cashing, bill paying, lunch counters, car care, and pet care.

Category killer

Giant specialty store that carries a very deep assortment of a particular line and is staffed by knowledgeable employees.

Discount store

A retail institution that sells standard merchandise at lower prices by accepting lower margins and selling at higher volume.

Supermarkets are the most frequently shopped type of retail store. Today, however, they are facing slow sales growth because of slower population growth and an increase in competition from convenience stores, discount food stores, and superstores. Supermarkets also have been hit hard by the rapid growth of out-of-home eating.

Thus, most supermarkets are making improvements to attract more customers. In the battle for "share of stomachs," many large supermarkets have moved upscale, providing from-scratch bakeries, gourmet deli counters, and fresh seafood departments. Others are cutting costs, establishing more efficient operations, and lowering prices in order to compete more effectively with food discounters. Finally, a few have added Web-based sales. Forrester Research estimates that 18 percent of the nation's household will be good prospects for online grocery buying and that the number buying online will increase from 4.5 million households last year to more that 14 million by 2006.[2]

Convenience stores are small stores that carry a limited line of high-turnover convenience goods. Some 125,000 U.S. convenience stores posted sales last year of $283 billion. More than 60 percent of convenience store revenues come from sales of gasoline; more the 50 percent of in-store revenues are from cigarette and beverage sales.[3]

In recent years, the convenience store industry has suffered from overcapacity as its primary market of young, blue-collar men has shrunk. As a result, many chains are redesigning their stores to attract female shoppers. They are shedding the image of a "truck stop" where men go to buy beer, cigarettes, and magazines, and instead offer fresh prepared foods and cleaner, safer environments. Many are also applying micromarketing—tailoring each store's merchandise to the specific needs of its surrounding neighborhood. For example, a Stop-N-Go in an affluent neighborhood carries fresh produce, gourmet pasta sauces, chilled Evian water, and expensive wines. Stop-N-Go stores in Hispanic neighborhoods carry Spanish-language magazines and other goods catering to the specific needs of Hispanic consumers.

Superstores are much larger than regular supermarkets and offer a large assortment of routinely purchased food products, nonfood items, and services. Wal-Mart, Kmart, Target, and other discount retailers offer *supercenters,* combination food and discount stores that emphasize cross-merchandising. Toasters are above the fresh-baked bread, kitchen gadgets are across from produce, and infant centers carry everything from baby food to clothing. Supercenters are growing in the United States at an annual rate of 25 percent, compared with a supermarket industry growth rate of only 1 percent. Wal-Mart, which opened its first supercenter in 1988, now has more than 1,100, capturing more than 70 percent of all supercenter volume.[4]

Recent years have also seen the explosive growth of superstores that are actually giant specialty stores, the so-called **category killers.** They feature stores the size of airplane hangars and carry a very deep assortment of a particular line with a knowledgeable staff. Category killers are prevalent in a wide range of categories, including books, baby gear, toys, electronics, home improvement products, linens and towels, party goods, sporting goods, even pet supplies. Another superstore variation, the *hypermarket,* is a huge superstore, perhaps as large as *six* football fields. Although hypermarkets have been very successful in Europe and other world markets, they have met with little success in the United States.

Finally, for some retailers, the product line is actually a service. Service retailers include hotels and motels, banks, airlines, colleges, hospitals, movie theaters, tennis clubs, bowling alleys, restaurants, repair services, hair care shops, and dry cleaners. Service retailers in the United States are growing faster than product retailers.

Relative Prices

Retailers can also be classified according to the prices they charge (see Table 14.1). Most retailers charge regular prices and offer normal-quality goods and customer service. Others offer higher-quality goods and service at higher prices. The retailers that feature low prices are discount stores and "off-price" retailers.

Discount Stores.   A **discount store** sells standard merchandise at lower prices by accepting lower margins and selling higher volume. The early discount stores cut expenses by offering few services and operating in warehouselike facilities in low-rent, heavily traveled districts. In recent years, facing intense competition from other discounters and department stores, many

Category killers: Best Buy has stores the size of airplane hangars that carry a deep assortment of consumer electronics, personal computers, entertainment software, and appliances.

discount retailers have "traded up." They have improved décor, added new lines and services, and expanding regionally and nationally, leading to higher costs and prices.

Off-Price Retailers.   When the major discount stores traded up, a new wave of **off-price retailers** moved in to fill the low-price, high-volume gap. Ordinary discounters buy at regular wholesale prices and accept lower margins to keep prices down. In contrast, off-price retailers buy at less-than-regular wholesale prices and charge consumers less than retail. Off-price retailers can be found in all areas, from food, clothing, and electronics to no-frills banking and discount brokerages.

The three main types of off-price retailers are *independents, factory outlets,* and *warehouse clubs.* **Independent off-price retailers** either are owned and run by entrepreneurs or are divisions of larger retail corporations. Although many off-price operations are run by smaller independents, most large off-price retailer operations are owned by bigger retail chains. Examples include store retailers such as TJ Maxx and Marshall's, owned by TJX Companies, and Web sellers such as RetailExchange.com, Redtag.com, and CloseOutNow.com.

Factory outlets—such as the Manhattan's Brand Name Fashion Outlet and the factory outlets of Liz Claiborne, Carters, Levi Strauss, and other manufacturers—sometimes group together in *factory outlet malls* and *value-retail centers,* where dozens of outlet stores offer prices as low as 50 percent below retail on a wide range of items. Whereas outlet malls consist primarily of manufacturers' outlets, value-retail centers combine manufacturers' outlets with off-price retail stores and department store clearance outlets. Factory outlet malls have become one of the hottest growth areas in retailing.

The malls now are moving upscale—and even dropping "factory" from their descriptions—narrowing the gap between factory outlet and more traditional forms of retailers. As the gap narrows, the discounts offered by outlets are getting smaller. However, a growing number of outlet malls now feature brands such as Coach, Polo Ralph Lauren, Dolce & Gabbana, Giorgio Armani, Gucci, and Versace, causing department stores to protest to the manufacturers of these brands. Given their higher costs, the department stores have to charge more than the off-price outlets. Manufacturers counter that they send last year's merchandise and seconds to the factory outlet malls, not the new merchandise that they supply to the department stores. The malls are also located far from urban areas, making travel to them more difficult. Still, the department stores are concerned about the growing number of shoppers willing to make weekend trips to stock up on branded merchandise at substantial savings.[5]

Warehouse clubs (or *wholesale clubs* or *membership warehouses*), such as Sam's Club, Costco, and BJ's, operate in huge, drafty, warehouselike facilities and offer few frills. Customers themselves must wrestle furniture, heavy appliances, and other large items to the checkout line. Such clubs make no home deliveries and often accept no credit cards. However, they do offer ultralow

Off-price retailer

Retailer that buys at less-than-regular wholesale prices and sells at less than retail. Examples are factory outlets, independents, and warehouse clubs.

Independent off-price retailer

Off-price retailer that is either owned and run by entrepreneurs or is a division of a larger retail corporation.

Factory outlet

Off-price retailing operation that is owned and operated by a manufacturer and that normally carries the manufacturer's surplus, discontinued, or irregular goods.

Warehouse club

Off-price retailer that sells a limited selection of brand-name grocery items, appliances, clothing, and a hodgepodge of other goods at deep discounts to members who pay annual membership fees.

Factory outlet malls and value-retail centers have blossomed in recent years, making them one of retailing's hottest growth areas.

prices and surprise deals on selected branded merchandise. Whereas a weakening economy has slowed the growth of many traditional retailers, warehouse club sales have soared recently. These days, "consumers are laser-beam-focused on finding the best value," says an industry analyst, "and the absolute best value is at a club."[6]

Organizational Approach

Although many retail stores are independently owned, an increasing number are banding together under some form of corporate or contractual organization. The major types of retail organizations—*corporate chains, voluntary chains, retailer cooperatives, franchise organizations,* and *merchandising conglomerates*—are described in Table 14.2.

Chain stores are two or more outlets that are commonly owned and controlled. They have many advantages over independents. Their size allows them to buy in large quantities at lower prices and gain promotional economies. They can hire specialists to deal with areas such as pricing, promotion, merchandising, inventory control, and sales forecasting.

The great success of corporate chains caused many independents to band together in one of two forms of contractual associations. One is the *voluntary chain*—a wholesaler-sponsored group of independent retailers that engages in group buying and common merchandising—which we discussed in Chapter 11. Examples include Western Auto and Do it Best hardwares. The other form of contractual association is the *retailer cooperative*—a group of independent retailers that bands together to set up a jointly owned, central wholesale operation and conducts joint merchandising and promotion efforts. Examples are Associated Grocers and Ace Hardware. These organizations give independents the buying and promotion economies they need to meet the prices of corporate chains.

Another form of contractual retail organization is a **franchise.** The main difference between franchise organizations and other contractual systems (voluntary chains and retail cooperatives) is that franchise systems are normally based on some unique product or service; on a method of doing business; or on the trade name, goodwill, or patent that the franchiser has developed. Franchising has been prominent in fast foods, video stores, health and fitness centers, haircutting, auto rentals, motels, travel agencies, real estate, and dozens of other product and service areas.

Once considered upstarts among independent businesses, franchises now command 35 percent of all retail sales in the United States. These days, it's nearly impossible to stroll down a city block or drive on a suburban street without seeing a McDonald's, Subway, Jiffy Lube, or Holiday Inn. One of the best-known and most successful franchisers, McDonald's, now has 30,000 stores in

Chain stores

Two or more outlets that are owned and controlled in common, have central buying and merchandising, and sell similar lines of merchandise.

Franchise

A contractual association between a manufacturer, wholesaler, or service organization (a franchiser) and independent businesspeople (franchisees) who buy the right to own and operate one or more units in the franchise system.

TABLE 14.2 MAJOR TYPES OF RETAIL ORGANIZATIONS

Type	Description	Examples
Corporate chain stores	Two or more outlets that are commonly owned and controlled, employ central buying and merchandising, and sell similar lines of merchandise. Corporate chains appear in all types of retailing, but they are strongest in department stores, variety stores, food stores, drugstores, shoe stores, and women's clothing stores.	Tower Records, Fayva (shoes), Pottery Barn (dinnerware and home furnishings)
Voluntary chains	Wholesaler-sponsored groups of independent retailers engaged in bulk buying and common merchandising.	Independent Grocers Alliance (IGA), Sentry Hardwares, Western Auto, True Value
Retailer cooperatives	Groups of independent retailers who set up a central buying organization and conduct joint promotion efforts.	Associated Grocers (groceries), Ace (hardware)
Franchise organizations	Contractual association between a *franchiser* (a manufacturer, wholesales, or service organization) and *franchisees* (independent businesspeople who buy the right to own and operate one or more units in the franchise system). Franchise organizations are normally based on some unique product, service, or method of doing business, or on a trade name or patent, or on goodwill that the franchiser had developed.	McDonald's, Subway, Pizza Hut, Jiffy Lube, Meineke Mufflers, 7-Eleven
Merchandising conglomerates	A free-form corporation that combines several diversified retailing lines and forms under central ownership, along with some integration of their distribution and management functions.	Target Corporation

120 countries serving more than 46 million customers a day and racking up more than $40 billion in systemwide sales. More than 70 percent of McDonald's restaurants worldwide are owned and operated by franchisees. Gaining fast is Subway Sandwiches and Salads, one of the fastest-growing franchises, with more than 16,000 shops in 74 countries, including some 13,250 in the United States. Franchising is even moving into new areas such as education. For example, LearnRight Corporation franchises its methods for teaching students thinking skills.[7]

Finally, *merchandising conglomerates* are corporations that combine several different retailing forms under central ownership. An example is Target Corporation, which operates Marshall Fields (upscale department stores), Target (upscale discount stores), Mervyn's (middle-market apparel and home soft goods), and Target.direct (online retailing and direct marketing). Diversified retailing, similar to a multibranding strategy, provides superior management systems and economies that benefit all the separate retail operations, and is likely to increase.

Retailer Marketing Decisions

Retailers are always searching for new marketing strategies to attract and hold customers. In the past, retailers attracted customers with unique products, more or better services than their competitors offered, or credit cards. Today, national-brand manufacturers, in their drive for volume, have placed their branded goods everywhere. National brands are found not only in department stores but also in mass-merchandise discount stores, off-price discount stores, and on the Web. As a result, retail assortments are looking more and more alike.

Service differentiation among retailers has also eroded. Many department stores have trimmed their services, whereas discounters have increased theirs. Customers have become smarter and more price sensitive. They see no reason to pay more for identical brands, especially when service differences are shrinking. For all these reasons, many retailers today are rethinking their marketing strategies.

As shown in Figure 14.1, retailers face major marketing decisions about their *target market and positioning, product assortment and services, price, promotion,* and *place.*

FIGURE 14.1
Retailer marketing decisions

Target Market and Positioning Decision

Retailers first must define their target markets and then decide how they will position themselves in these markets. Should the store focus on upscale, midscale, or downscale shoppers? Do target shoppers want variety, depth of assortment, convenience, or low prices? Until they define and profile their markets, retailers cannot make consistent decisions about product assortment, services, pricing, advertising, store décor, or any of the other decisions that must support their positions.

Too many retailers fail to define their target markets and positions clearly. They try to have "something for everyone" and end up satisfying no market well. In contrast, successful retailers define their target markets well and position themselves strongly. Even large stores such as Wal-Mart, Sears, and Target must define their major target markets in order to design effective marketing strategies. In fact, in recent years, thanks to strong targeting and positioning, Wal-Mart has become not just the world's largest retailer, but the world's largest *company* (see Real Marketing 14.1).

Wal-Mart: The World's Largest Retailer

In 1962, Sam Walton and his brother opened the first Wal-Mart discount store in small-town Rogers, Arkansas. It was a big, flat, warehouselike store that sold everything from apparel to automotive supplies to small appliances at very low prices. Experts gave the fledgling retailer little chance—conventional wisdom suggested that discount stores could succeed only in large cities.

Yet, from these modest beginnings, the chain exploded onto the national retailing scene. Incredibly, Wal-Mart's annual sales now approach $220 billion—more than those of Sears, Kmart, Target, J.C. Penney, and French giant Carrefour combined—making it the world's largest company. Each year in the United States, Wal-Mart sells one out of every four quarts of motor oil, one out of every five deodorants, and one out of every four replacement toilet seats. It sells a

Timex watch every 7.4 seconds and a Barbie Doll every 2 seconds. One out of every 220 men, women, and children in the United States is a Wal-Mart associate.

Wal-Mart's phenomenal growth shows few signs of slowing. The company is now well established in larger cities and is expanding rapidly into international markets. Within only a few years of entering the grocery business with its supercenters—and more recently with its smaller Neighborhood Market stores—Wal-Mart is now the nation's largest grocery retailer, with more than one and one-half times the food sales of number two Kroger. And many industry experts believe that Wal-Mart will one day dominate Internet marketspaces in the same way that it now dominants the physical marketplace. "At the end of the next four years," predicts one retail-

ing industry consultant, "Wal-Mart will be number one on land and online."

What are the secrets behind this spectacular success? First and foremost, Wal-Mart is passionately dedicated to its value proposition of "Always Low Prices, Always!" To deliver on this promise, it listens to and takes care of its customers, treats employees as partners, and keeps a tight rein on costs.

Listening to and Taking Care of Customers

Wal-Mart positioned itself strongly in a well-chosen target market. Initially, Sam Walton focused on value-conscious consumers in small-town America. The chain built a strong everyday low-price position long before it became fashionable in retailing. It grew rapidly by bringing the lowest possible prices to towns ignored by national discounters—towns such as Van Buren, Arkansas, and Idabel, Oklahoma.

Wal-Mart knows its customers well and takes good care of them. As one analyst puts it, "The company gospel . . . is relatively simple: Be an agent for customers, find out what they want, and sell it to them for the lowest possible price." The company stays close to customers—for example, each top Wal-Mart executive spends at least two days a week visiting stores, talking directly with customers and getting a firsthand look at operations. Then, Wal-Mart delivers what customers want: a broad selection of carefully selected goods at unbeatable prices.

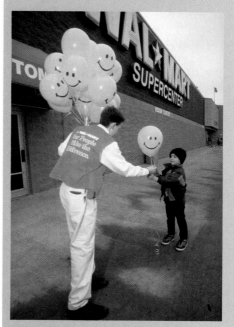

Thanks to strong targeting and positioning, Wal-Mart has become not just the world's largest retailer, but the world's largest company.

Concludes Wal-Mart's current president and chief executive, "We're obsessed with delivering value to customers."

But the right merchandise at the right price isn't the only key to Wal-Mart's success. Compared with other discounters, Wal-Mart also provides the kind of service that keeps customers satisfied. A sign reading "Satisfaction Guaranteed" hangs prominently at each store's entrance. Another sign inside the store reads, "At Wal-Mart, our goal is: You're always next in line!" Customers are often welcomed by "people greeters" eager to lend a helping hand or just to be friendly. And, sure enough, the store opens extra checkout counters to keep waiting lines short.

Treating Employees as Partners

Wal-Mart believes that, in the final accounting, the company's people are what really make it better. Thus, it works hard to show employees that it cares about them. Wal-Mart was first to call employees "associates," a practice now widely copied by competitors. The associates work as partners, become deeply involved in operations, and share rewards for good performance.

> Everyone at Wal-Mart [is] an associate—from [the CEO] . . . to a cashier named Janet at the Wal-Mart on Highway 50 in Ocoee, Florida. "We," "us," and "our" are the operative words. Wal-Mart department heads, hourly associates who look after one of more of 30-some departments ranging from sporting goods to electronics, see figures that many companies never show general managers: costs, freight charges, profit margins. The company sets a profit margin for each store, and if the store exceeds it, then the hourly associates share part of the additional profit.

The partnership concept is deeply rooted in the Wal-Mart corporate culture. The only discount retailer to make the list, Wal-Mart has been named one of *Fortune* magazine's "100 Best Companies to Work For" in four of the last five years. Wal-Mart's concern for its employees translates into high employee satisfaction, which in turn translates into greater customer satisfaction.

Keeping a Tight Rein on Costs

Wal-Mart is a lean, mean, distribution machine—it has the lowest cost structure in the industry. This lets Wal-Mart charge lower prices but still reap higher profits. Wal-Mart's lower prices attract more shoppers, producing more sales, making the company more efficient, and enabling it to lower prices even more.

Wal-Mart's low costs result in part from superior management and more sophisticated technology. Its Bentonville, Arkansas, headquarters contains a computer communications system that the Defense Department would envy, giving managers around the country instant access to sales and operating information. And its huge, fully automated distribution centers employ the latest technology to supply stores efficiently. Wal-Mart also spends less than competitors on advertising as a percentage of sales. Because Wal-Mart has what customers want at the prices they'll pay, its reputation has spread

rapidly by word of mouth. It has not needed more advertising.

Finally, Wal-Mart keeps costs down through good old "tough buying." Whereas the company is known for the warm way it treats customers, it is equally well known for the cold, calculated way it wrings low prices from suppliers. The following passage describes a visit to Wal-Mart's buying offices:

> Don't expect a greeter and don't expect friendly. . . . Once you are ushered into one of the spartan little buyers' rooms, expect a steely eye across the table and be prepared to cut your price. "They are very, very focused people, and they use their buying power more forcefully than anyone else in America," says the marketing vice president of a major vendor. "All the normal mating rituals are [forbidden]. Their highest priority is making sure everyone at all times in all cases knows who's in charge, and it's Wal-Mart. They talk softly, but they have piranha hearts, and if you aren't totally prepared when you go in there, you'll have your [head] handed to you."

Some observers wonder whether Wal-Mart can be so big and still retain its focus and positioning. They wonder if an ever-larger Wal-Mart can stay close to its customers and employees. The company's managers are betting on it. No matter where it operates, Wal-Mart's announced policy is to take care of customers "one store at a time." Says one top executive: "We'll be fine as long as we never lose our responsiveness to the consumer."

Sources: Quotes and other information from material from Bill Saporito, "Is Wal-Mart Unstoppable?" *Fortune,* May 6, 1991, pp. 50–59; John Huey, "Wal-Mart: Will It Take Over the World?" *Fortune,* January 30, 1998, pp. 52–61; Carol J. Loomis, "Sam Would Be Proud," *Fortune,* April 17, 2001, pp. 131–144; and Stephanie Thompson, "Wal-Mart Tops List for New Food Lines," *Advertising Age,* April 29, 2002, pp. 4, 61. Also see Mike Troy, "The Super Growth Leaders—Wal-Mart: Global Dominance Puts Half Trillion in Sight," *DSN Retailing Today,* December 10, 2001, pp. 17–18+; Cait Murphy, "Introduction: Wal-Mart Rules," *Fortune,* April 15, 2002, pp. 94–98; and *Wal-Mart Annual Report 2002,* accessed online at www.walmartstores.com.

How can any discounter hope to compete with the likes of huge and dominating Wal-Mart? Again, the answer is good targeting and positioning. For example, rather than facing Wal-Mart head-on, Target aims for a seemingly oxymoronic niche—the "upscale discount" segment.

Target—or Tar-*zhay* as many fans call it—has developed its own distinct targeting and positioning. "Going to Target is a cool experience, and everybody now considers it cool to save money," says one retailing consultant. "On the other hand, is it cool to save at Kmart, at Wal-Mart? I don't think so." Target isn't Wal-Mart, the giant that wooed suburbia with its acres of guns and gummy bears. And it definitely isn't Kmart, which still seems downscale despite its Martha Stewart tea-towel sets. Target's aim is more subtle: Stick to low prices, of course, but rise above the discount fray with upmarket style and design and higher-grade service. Target's ability to position itself as an upscale alternative really separates it from its mass-merchant peers. "We have a very clear strategy and a very clear brand," says Target vice chairman Jerry Storch. And it's all based on a clearly defined customer. Target's "expect more, pay less" positioning appeals to more-affluent consumers. Its average customer is typically female, 40, and college educated, with a household income approaching $50,000. On average, Target customers spend $40 a visit, almost twice that of other mass merchants. "The higher-income, better educated guest is in our stores," says Storch. "As your income rises, you love Target more and more." Target's upscale discount niche has helped insulate it from giant competitor Wal-Mart. "Wal-Mart is the greatest retailer that ever was," says Storch. "Very few have been able to compete with them and survive." Now 1,100 stores strong, more than survive, Target has thrived. "People used to say, 'Ooh, a Nordstrom's coming to town,'" says the consultant. "Those same people now say, 'Ooh, we're getting a Target!'"[8]

Product Assortment and Services Decision

Retailers must decide on three major product variables: *product assortment, services mix,* and *store atmosphere.*

The retailer's *product assortment* should differentiate the retailer while matching target shoppers' expectations. One strategy is to offer merchandise that no other competitor carries, such as private brands or national brands on which it holds exclusives. For example, Saks gets exclusive rights to carry a well-known designer's labels. The retailer can feature blockbuster merchandising events—Bloomingdale's is known for running spectacular shows featuring goods from a certain country, such as India or China. Or the retailer can offer surprise merchandise, as when Costco offers surprise assortments of seconds, overstocks, and closeouts. Finally, the retailer can differentiate itself by offering a highly targeted product assortment—Lane Bryant carries goods in larger sizes; Brookstone offers an unusual assortment of gadgets in what amounts to an adult toy store.

The *services mix* can also help set one retailer apart from another. For example, some retailers invite customers to ask questions or consult service representatives in person or via phone or keyboard. Home Depot offers a diverse mix of services to do-it-yourselfers, from "how-to" classes to a proprietary credit card.

The *store's atmosphere* is another element in the reseller's product arsenal. Every store has a physical layout that makes moving around in it either hard or easy. Each store has a "feel"; one store is cluttered, another cheerful, a third plush, a fourth somber. The store must plan an atmosphere that suits the target market and moves customers to buy. For example, outdoor equipment retailer REI practices "experiential retailing": Consumers can try out climbing equipment on a huge wall in the store, and they can test Gore-Tex raincoats by going under a simulated rain shower. And many retailers add fragrances in their stores to stimulate certain moods in shoppers. London's Heathrow Airport sprays the scent of pine needles because it evokes the sense of holidays and weekend walks. Automobile dealers will spray a "leather" scent in used cars to make them smell "new."

Increasingly, retailers are turning their stores into theaters that transport customers into unusual, exciting shopping environments. For example, Barnes & Noble uses atmospherics to turn shopping for books into entertainment. It has found that "to consumers, shopping is a social activity. They do it to mingle with others in a prosperous-feeling crowd, to see what's new, to enjoy the theatrical dazzle of the display, to treat themselves to something interesting or

Target—or Tar-zhay as many fans call it—has developed its own distinct positioning as an "upscale discounter." As this ad suggests, Target is not your usual discount store.

unexpected." Thus, Barnes & Noble stores are designed with "enough woody, traditional, soft-colored library to please book lovers; enough sophisticated modern architecture and graphics, sweeping vistas, and stylish displays to satisfy fans of the theater of consumption. And for everyone, plenty of space, where they can meet other people and feel at home. . . . [Customers can sip a cup of Starbucks coffee and] settle in at heavy chairs and tables to browse through piles of books; they fill the cafes [designed] to increase the festivities. . . ." As one Barnes & Noble executive notes: "The feel-good part of the store, the quality-of-life contribution, is a big part of the success."[9]

Perhaps the most dramatic conversion of stores into theater is the Mall of America near Minneapolis. Containing more than 520 specialty stores and 49 restaurants, the mall is a veritable playground. Under a single roof, it shelters a seven-acre Camp Snoopy amusement park featuring 25 rides and attractions, an ice-skating rink, an Underwater World featuring hundreds of marine specimens and a dolphin show, and a two-story miniature golf course. One of the stores, Oshman Supersports USA, features a basketball court, a boxing gym, a baseball batting cage, a 50-foot archery range, and a simulated ski slope.[10]

All of this confirms that retail stores are much more than simply assortments of goods. They are environments to be experienced by the people who shop in them. Store atmospheres offer a powerful tool by which retailers can differentiate their stores from those of competitors.

Bijan's boutique on Rodeo Drive in Beverly Hills sells $375 silk ties and $19,000 ostrich-skin vests. Its "by appointment only" policy makes wealthy, high-profile clients comfortable with these prices.

Price Decision

A retailer's price policy must fit its target market and positioning, product and service assortment, and competition. All retailers would like to charge high markups and achieve high volume, but the two seldom go together. Most retailers seek *either* high markups on lower volume (most specialty stores) *or* low markups on higher volume (mass merchandisers and discount stores).

Thus, Bijan's boutique on Rodeo Drive in Beverly Hills sells $375 silk ties and $19,000 ostrich-skin vests. Its "by appointment only" policy is designed to make its wealthy, high-profile clients comfortable with these prices. (Says Mr. Bijan, "If a man is going to spend $400,000 on his visit, don't you think it's only fair that he have my full attention?")[11] Bijan's sells a low volume but makes hefty profits on each sale. At the other extreme, T.J. Maxx sells brand-name clothing at discount prices, settling for a lower margin on each sale but selling at a much higher volume.

Promotion Decision

Retailers use any or all of the promotion tools—advertising, personal selling, sales promotion, public relations, and direct marketing—to reach consumers. They advertise in newspapers, magazines, radio, television, and on the Internet. Advertising may be supported by newspaper inserts and direct mail. Personal selling requires careful training of salespeople in how to greet customers, meet their needs, and handle their complaints. Sales promotions may include in-store demonstrations, displays, contests, and visiting celebrities. Public relations activities, such as press conferences and speeches, store openings, special events, newsletters, magazines, and public service activities, are always available to retailers. Most retailers have also set up Web sites, offering customers information and other features and often selling merchandise directly.

Place Decision

Retailers often point to three critical factors in retailing success: *location, location,* and *location!* It's very important that retailers select locations that are accessible to the target market in areas that are consistent with the retailer's positioning. Small retailers may have to settle for whatever locations they can find or afford. Large retailers, however, usually employ specialists who select locations using advanced methods.

Two of the savviest location experts in recent years have been the off-price retailer TJ Maxx and toy-store giant Toys "R" Us. Both put the majority of their new locations in rapidly growing areas where the population closely matches their customer base. The undisputed winner in the "place race" has been Wal-Mart, whose strategy of being the first mass merchandiser to locate in small and rural markets was one of the key factors in its phenomenal early success.

Most stores today cluster together to increase their customer pulling power and to give consumers the convenience of one-stop shopping. *Central business districts* were the main form of retail cluster until the 1950s. Every large city and town had a central business district with department stores, specialty stores, banks, and movie theaters. When people began to move to the suburbs, however, these central business districts, with their traffic, parking, and crime problems, began to lose business. Downtown merchants opened branches in suburban shopping centers, and the decline of the central business districts continued. In recent years, many cities have joined with merchants to try to revive downtown shopping areas by building malls and providing underground parking.

Shopping center

A group of retail businesses planned, developed, owned, and managed as a unit.

A **shopping center** is a group of retail businesses planned, developed, owned, and managed as a unit. A *regional shopping center,* or *regional shopping mall,* the largest and most dramatic shopping center, contains from 40 to over 200 stores. It is like a covered mini-downtown and attracts customers from a wide area. A *community shopping center* contains between 15 and 40 retail stores. It normally contains a branch of a department store or variety store, a supermarket, specialty stores, professional offices, and sometimes a bank. Most shopping centers are *neighborhood shopping centers* or *strip malls* that generally contain between 5 and 15 stores. They are close and convenient for consumers. They usually contain a supermarket, perhaps a discount store, and several service stores—dry cleaner, self-service laundry, drugstore, video-rental outlet, barber or beauty shop, hardware store, or other stores.

A recent addition to the shopping center scene is the so-called *power center.* These huge unenclosed shopping centers consist of a long strip of retail stores, including large, freestanding anchors such as Wal-Mart, Home Depot, Best Buy, Michaels, OfficeMax, and CompUSA. Each store has its own entrance with parking directly in front for shoppers who wish to visit only one store. Power centers have increased rapidly during the past few years to challenge traditional indoor malls.

Combined, all shopping centers now account for about one-third of all retail sales. The average American makes 3.2 trips to the mall per month, shopping for an average of 75 minutes per trip and spending about $71. However, many experts suggest that America is now "over-malled." There are now 20 square feet of retail space per person in the United States, up from 15 square feet in 1986. During the 1990s, shopping space grew at about twice the rate of population growth. As a result, as many as 20 percent of America's regional malls are in danger of going out of business. There "is a glut of retail space," says one retail analyst. "There's going to have to be a shakeout," concludes another.[12]

Thus, despite the recent development of many new "megamalls," such as the spectacular Mall of America, the current trend is toward value-oriented outlet malls and power centers on the one hand, and smaller malls on the other. Many shoppers now prefer to shop at "lifestyle centers," smaller malls with upscale stores, convenient locations, and expensive atmospheres. "Think of lifestyle centers as part Main Street and part Fifth Avenue," comments one industry observer. "The idea is to combine the hominess and community of an old-time village square with the cachet of fashionable urban stores; the smell and feel of a neighborhood park with the brute convenience of a strip center."[13]

The Future of Retailing

Retailers operate in a harsh and fast-changing environment, which offers threats as well as opportunities. For example, the industry suffers from chronic overcapacity, resulting in fierce competition for customer dollars. Consumer demographics, lifestyles, and shopping patterns are changing rapidly, as are retailing technologies. To be successful, then, retailers will have to choose target segments carefully and position themselves strongly. They will have to take the following retailing developments into account as they plan and execute their competitive strategies.

New Retail Forms and Shortening Retail Life Cycles

New retail forms continue to emerge to meet new situations and consumer needs, but the life cycle of new retail forms is getting shorter. Department stores took about 100 years to reach the mature

Shopping centers: The spectacular Mall of America contains more than 520 specialty stores, 49 restaurants, a 7-acre indoor theme park, an Underwater World featuring hundreds of marine specimens and a dolphin show, and a two-story miniature golf course.

stage of the life cycle; more recent forms, such as warehouse stores, reached maturity in about 10 years. In such an environment, seemingly solid retail positions can crumble quickly. Of the top 10 discount retailers in 1962 (the year that Wal-Mart and Kmart began), not one still exists today.

Consider the Price Club, the original warehouse store chain. When Sol Price opened his first warehouse store outside San Diego in 1976, he launched a retailing revolution. Selling everything from tires and office supplies to five-pound tubs of peanut butter at superlow prices, his store chain was generating $2.6 billion a year in sales within 10 years. But Price refused to expand beyond its California base. And as the industry quickly matured, Price ran headlong into wholesale clubs run by such retail giants as Wal-Mart and Kmart. Only 17 years later, in a stunning reversal of fortune, a faltering Price sold out to competitor Costco. Price's rapid rise and fall "serves as a stark reminder to mass-market retailers that past success means little in a fiercely competitive and rapidly changing industry."[14] Thus, retailers can no longer sit back with a successful formula. To remain successful, they must keep adapting.

Many retailing innovations are partially explained by the **wheel-of-retailing concept**.[15] According to this concept, many new types of retailing forms begin as low-margin, low-price, low-status operations. They challenge established retailers that have become "fat" by letting their costs and margins increase. The new retailers' success leads them to upgrade their facilities and offer more services. In turn, their costs increase, forcing them to increase their prices. Eventually, the new retailers become like the conventional retailers they replaced. The cycle begins again when still newer types of retailers evolve with lower costs and prices. The wheel-of-retailing concept seems to explain the initial success and later troubles of department stores, supermarkets, and discount stores, and the recent success of off-price retailers.

Wheel-of-retailing concept
A concept of retailing that states that new types of retailers usually begin as low-margin, low-price, low-status operations but later evolve into higher-priced, higher-service operations, eventually becoming like the conventional retailers they replaced.

Growth of Nonstore Retailing

Although most retailing still takes place the old-fashioned way across countertops in stores, consumers now have an array of alternatives, including mail-order, television, phone, and online shopping (see Real Marketing 14.2). Americans are increasingly avoiding the hassles and crowds at malls by doing more of their shopping by phone or computer. Although such retailing advances may threaten some traditional retailers, they offer exciting opportunities for others. Most store retailers have now developed direct retailing channels. In fact, more online retailing is conducted by "click-and-brick" retailers than by "click-only" retailers. For example, office-supply retailer Office Depot is now the world's biggest online retailer after Amazon.com.[16]

real marketing 14.2

E-Tailing: Still Alive, Well, and Growing

Most of us still make most of our purchases the old-fashioned way: We go to the store, find what we want, wait patiently in line to plunk down our cash or credit card, and bring home the goods. However, a growing number of retailers now provide an attractive alternative—one that lets us browse, select, order, and pay with little more effort than it takes to apply an index finger to a mouse button. They sell a rich variety of goods ranging from books, CDs, flowers, and food to stereo equipment, kitchen appliances, airplane tickets, auto parts, home mortgages, and bags of cement.

Only a few years ago, prospects for online retailing were soaring. Many experts predicted that as more and more consumers flocked to the Web, a new breed of fast-moving e-tailers would quickly surpass stodgy, "old economy" store retailers. Some even saw a day when we'd be doing almost all of our shopping via the Internet. However, the dot-com meltdown of 2000 dashed these overblown expectations. Many once-brash Web sellers such as eToys.com, Pets.com, Webvan.com, and Garden.com crashed and burned. In fact, after the shakeout of 2000, expectations reversed almost overnight. The experts began to predict that no Web-only retailer could survive and that e-tailing was destined to be little more than a tag-on to in-store retailing.

Such doom-and-gloom scenarios, however, don't reflect the current state of Internet retailing. Although the pace has slowed and the playing ground is shifting, today's e-tailing is alive, well, and growing. With today's easier-to-use Web sites, improved online service, and the demise of so many early competitors, business is booming for the survivors. In fact, online buying is growing at a much brisker pace than retail buying as a whole. Online retail sales grew 21 percent in 2001 and were expected to jump another 41 percent in 2002 to $72 billion. By 2006, online retailing is expected to rival catalogs, capturing some 5 percent of total retail sales.

Although the dramatic dot-com collapses grabbed most of the headlines, some click-only retailers are now making it big on the Web. Heading this group is online auction site eBay, which has been consistently profitable since its inception—click-only competitors such as eBay and Amazon.com Auctions account for a lion's share of the online auctions business. Click-only e-tailers account for a majority of online sales in several other categories as well, including books, music and video; foods and beverages; and collectibles.

Business is also booming for online travel companies such as Travelocity.com and Expedia, which use the Web to sell airline tickets, hotel rooms, and discount travel packages to consumers. Thanks to these sites, online travel bookings are expected to capture more than one-fifth of U.S. travel revenue by 2006. In many ways, selling air travel on the Internet is a natural. Most air travel sold online uses e-tickets and e-confirmations, so no products need to be stored or shipped. "There are a bunch of businesses that don't make sense on the Internet," says a Wall Street analyst. "Travel is the quintessential one that does."

Still, much of the anticipated growth in online sales will go to multichannel retailers— the click-and-brick marketers who can successfully merge the virtual and physical worlds. Such retailers accounted for 67 percent of total online sales last year. Toys "R" Us executive Ray Arthur points out that Toysrus.com's initial online competitors, click-only operations such as eToys.com and Toysmart.com, have now shuttered their cyberdoors. In their place is a new lineup of click-and-brick competitors such as Walmart.com and Kbkids.com. In other categories as well, the true winners these days appear to be established brick-and-mortar

Online retailing: Today's e-tailing is alive, well, and growing, especially for click-and-brick competitors such as Office Depot. Last year, the company's Internet sales grew 40 percent, accounting for 14 percent of overall sales. Business is also booming for click-only e-tailers such as Travelocity.

(continued)

companies that have added Web selling. It seems that almost every established retailer is now hanging out a shingle in Webland. Examples include Charles Schwab and Fidelity Investments (financial services), Dell and IBM (computers), Lands' End and L.L. Bean (apparel), and Staples and Office Depot (office supplies), to name just a few.

Consider retailer Office Depot's burgeoning Web business:

Since the early 1990s, Bank of America executives have been letting employees order supplies from their desktop computers, but they were using an old-fashioned system that was expensive and difficult to operate. The bankers knew that there had to be a better way, but they couldn't figure it out on their own. That's when Monica Luechtefeld, Office Depot's chief of e-commerce, came calling. She explained how the office-supply retailer could easily plug its online store into Bank of America's internal network. Bank of America would be able to set it up to recognize who had clearance to buy an executive chair or a box of pencils. And Luechtefeld offered rebates for online purchases. It was a winning pitch. Today, Bank of America orders 85 percent of it supplies online through Office Depot and is saving millions of dollars a year.

Now, 40 percent of Office Depot's major customers are using the online network to buy everything from paper clips to cherry conference-room tables. Last year, the company's Internet sales grew 40 percent to $1.5 billion, almost 14 percent of overall sales. That makes Office Depot the biggest online retailer after Amazon.com. Better yet, Office Depot's online unit was profitable from day one. How has Office Depot succeeded online where so many dot-coms have failed? "Office Depot gets it," says an e-commerce consultant. "It used the Net to build deeper relationships with customers."

So, despite some serious setbacks and uncertainties, online retailing is anything but dead. As one analyst says about the recent successes of online retailers like Travelocity.com and Expedia: "None of this guarantees that online travel won't crash someday like the rest of the dot-coms. But as the market takes off, these skies are looking downright friendly."

Sources: Home Depot example adapted from Charles Haddad, "Office Depot's E-Diva," *Business Week,* August 6, 2001, pp. EB22–EB24; and Meryl Davids Landau, "Sweet Revenge," *Chief Executive,* May 2002, pp. 58–62. Other information from Dennis K. Berman and Heather Green, "Cliff-Hanger Christmas," *Business Week,* October 23, 2000, pp. EB30–EB38; Molly Prior, "E-Commerce Alive and Well in the New Economy," *DSN Retailing Today,* June 4, 2001, p. 10; Wendy Zellner, "Where the Net Delivers: Travel," *Business Week,* June 11, 2001, pp. 142–144; Lewis Braham, "E-Tailers Are Clicking," *Business Week,* July 23, 2001, p. 73; Heather Green and Robert D. Hof, "Lessons of the Cyber Survivors," *Business Week,* April 22, 2002, p. 42; and Nick Wingfield, "Online Retailing Still Growing Despite Some Losses Last Year," *Wall Street Journal,* June 12, 2002, p. B4.

Retail Convergence

Today's retailers are increasingly selling the same products at the same prices to the same consumers in competition with a wider variety of other retailers. For example, any consumer can buy CDs at about the same price from any or all of a dozen different types of retailers—specialty music stores, discount music stores, electronics superstores, general merchandise discount stores, video-rental outlets, and any of dozens of Web sites. You can buy books at outlets ranging from independent local bookstores to discount stores such as Wal-Mart, superstores such as Barnes & Noble or Borders, or Web sites such as Amazon.com. And when it comes to brand-name appliances, department stores, discount stores, off-price retailers, electronics superstores, and a slew of Web sites all compete for the same customers.

This merging of consumers, products, prices, and retailers is called *retail convergence*:

Retail convergence is the coming together of shoppers, goods, and prices. Customers of all income levels are shopping at the same stores, often for the same goods. Old distinctions such as discount store, specialty store, and department store are losing significance: The successful store must match a host of rivals on selection, service, and price.

The American consumer's road map for where products can be found has shifted from a segmented approach to a consolidation that is almost a throwback to the 1800s, when a general store was the place to shop for everything from coffee to a coffeepot. In the 1900s, shoppers migrated from the Sears catalog to the department store, and then to the shopping mall and specialty stores. A few years ago, the coffeepot customer may have gone to Williams-Sonoma or even Starbucks. Today, it could be Target or Wal-Mart.

Where you go for what you want—that has created the biggest challenge facing retailers. Consider fashion. Once the exclusive domain of the wealthy, fashion now moves quickly from the runways of New York and Paris to retailers at all levels. Ralph Lauren sells in department stores and in the Marshall's at the strip mall. Designer Stephen Sprouse, fresh off a limited edition of Louis Vuitton handbags and luggage, has designed a summer line of clothing and other products for Target.[17]

Such convergence means greater competition for retailers and greater difficulty in differentiating offerings. The competition between chain superstores and smaller, independently owned stores has become particularly heated. Because of their bulk-buying power and high sales volume, chains can buy at lower costs and thrive on smaller margins. The arrival of a superstore can quickly force nearby independents out of business. For example, the decision by electronics superstore Best Buy to sell CDs as loss leaders at rock-bottom prices pushed a number of specialty record store chains into bankruptcy. And Wal-Mart has been accused of destroying independents in countless small towns around the country.

Yet the news is not all bad for smaller companies. Many small, independent retailers are thriving. They are finding that sheer size and marketing muscle are often no match for the personal touch small stores can provide or the specialty niches that small stores fill for a devoted customer base.

The Rise of Megaretailers

The rise of huge mass merchandisers and specialty superstores, the formation of vertical marketing systems and buying alliances, and a rash of retail mergers and acquisitions have created a core of superpower megaretailers. Through their superior information systems and buying power, these giant retailers are able to offer better merchandise selections, good service, and strong price savings to consumers. As a result, they grow even larger by squeezing out their smaller, weaker competitors.

The megaretailers are also shifting the balance of power between retailers and producers. A relative handful of retailers now controls access to enormous numbers of consumers, giving them the upper hand in their dealings with manufacturers. For example, in the United States, Wal-Mart's revenues are more than five times those of Procter & Gamble, and Wal-Mart generates more than 20 percent of P&G's revenues. Wal-Mart can, and often does, use this power to wring concessions from P&G and other suppliers.[18]

The Growing Importance of Retail Technology

Retail technologies are becoming critically important as competitive tools. Progressive retailers are using advanced information technology and software systems to produce better forecasts, control inventory costs, order electronically from suppliers, send e-mail between stores, and even sell to customers within stores. They are adopting checkout scanning systems, online transaction processing, electronic funds transfer, electronic data interchange, in-store television, and improved merchandise-handling systems.

Perhaps the most startling advances in retailing technology concern the ways in which today's retailers are connecting with customers:

In the past, life was simple. Retailers connected with their customers through stores, through their salespeople, through the brands and packages they sold, and through direct mail and advertising in the mass media. But today, life is more complex. There are dozens of new ways to attract and engage consumers. . . . Indeed, even if one omits the obvious—the Web—retailers are still surrounded by technical innovations that promise to redefine the way they and manufacturers interact with customers. Consider, as just a sampling, touch-screen kiosks, electronic shelf labels and signs, handheld shopping assistants, smart cards, self-scanning systems, virtual reality displays, and intelligent agents. So, if we ask the question, Will technology change the way [retailers] interface with customers in the future? the answer has got to be yes.[19]

Global Expansion of Major Retailers

Retailers with unique formats and strong brand positioning are increasingly moving into other countries. Many are expanding internationally to escape mature and saturated home markets. Over the years, several giant U.S. retailers—McDonald's, Gap, Toys "R" Us—have become globally prominent as a result of their great marketing prowess. Others, such as Wal-Mart and Kmart, are rapidly establishing a global presence. Wal-Mart, which now operates more than 1,200 stores in nine countries abroad, sees exciting global potential. Its international division last year racked up sales of more than $35 billion, an increase of 11 percent over the previous year. Here's what happened when it opened two new stores in Shenzhen, China:

[Customers came] by the hundreds of thousands—up to 175,000 on Saturdays alone—to China's first Wal-Mart Supercenter and Sam's Club. They broke the display glass to snatch out chickens at one store and carted off all the big-screen TVs before the other store had been open an hour. The two outlets . . . were packed on Day One and have been bustling ever since.[20]

However, U.S retailers are still significantly behind Europe and Asia when it comes to global expansion. Only 18 percent of the top U.S. retailers operate globally, compared to 40 percent of European retailers and 31 percent of Asian retailers. Among foreign retailers that have gone global are France's Carrefour, Britain's Marks and Spencer, Italy's Benetton, Sweden's IKEA home furnishings stores, and Japan's Yaohan supermarkets.[21]

Marks and Spencer, which started out as a penny bazaar in 1884, grew into a chain of variety stores over the decades and now has a thriving string of 150 franchised stores around the world, which sell mainly its private-label clothes, including Brooks Brothers. It also runs a major food business. IKEA's well-constructed but fairly inexpensive furniture has proven very popular in the United States, where shoppers often spend an entire day in an IKEA store. And French discount retailer Carrefour, the world's second largest retailer after Wal-Mart, has embarked on an aggressive mission to extend its role as a leading international retailer:

> Carrefour now operates more than 5,300 discount stores in 30 countries in Europe, Asia, and the Americas, including 657 hypermarkets. By purchasing or merging with a variety of retailers, Carrefour has accelerated its hold over the European market, where it now claims retail dominance in four leading markets: France, Spain, Belgium, and Greece; it's the number two retailer in Italy. But one of the retailer's greatest strengths is its market position outside of France and Europe. In South America, for instance, Carrefour is the market leader in Brazil and Argentina, where it operates more than 300 stores. By comparison, Wal-Mart has only 25 units in those two countries. In China, the land of more than a billion consumers, Carrefour operates 22 hypermarkets to Wal-Mart's five supercenters and one Sam's Club. In the Pacific Rim, excluding China, Carrefour operates 33 hypermarkets in five countries to Wal-Mart's five units in South Korea alone. Carrefour is also on track to beat the competition into the Japanese market, the world's second largest nation in terms of consumption. In the all-important emerging markets of China, South America, and the Pacific Rim, Carrefour outpaces Wal-Mart five-to-one in actual revenue. In short, Carrefour is bounding ahead of Wal-Mart in most markets outside North America. The only question: Can the French titan hold its lead? While no one retailer can rightly claim to be in the same league with Wal-Mart as an overall retail presence, Carrefour stands a better chance than most to dominate global retailing.[22]

Retail Stores as "Communities" or "Hangouts"

With the rise in the number of people living alone, working at home, or living in isolated and sprawling suburbs, there has been a resurgence of establishments that, regardless of the product or service they offer, also provide a place for people to get together. These places include cafes, tea shops, juice bars, bookshops, superstores, children's play spaces, brew pubs, and urban greenmarkets. Brew pubs such as New York's Zip City Brewing and Seattle's Trolleyman Pub (run by Red Hook Brewery) offer tastings and a place to pass the time. And today's bookstores have become part bookstore, part library, and part living room.

> Welcome to today's bookstore. The one featuring not only shelves and cash registers but also cushy chairs and coffee bars. It's where backpack-toting high school students come to do homework, where retirees thumb through the gardening books, and parents read aloud to their toddlers. If no one actually buys books, that's just fine, say bookstore owners and managers. They're offering something grander than ink and paper, anyway. They're selling comfort, relaxation, community.[23]

Brick-and-mortar retailers are not the only ones creating community. Others have also built virtual communities on the Internet.

> Sony Computer Entertainment America (SCEA) actively builds community among its Playstation®2 customers. Its recent Playstation.com campaign created message boards where its game players could post messages to one another. The boards are incredibly active, discussing techie topics but also providing the opportunity for members, fiercely competitive and opinionated, to vote on lifestyle issues, such as music and personal taste, no matter how trivial. Although SCEA is laissez-faire about the boards and does not feed them messages, the company sees the value in having its customers' adamant conversations occur directly on its site. "Our customers are our evangelists. They are a very vocal and loyal fan base," says an SCEA spokesperson. "There are things we can learn from them."[24]

Retailer communities: Sony Computer Entertainment America's Playstation.com Web site builds community among its customers. The site's message boards are incredibly active, discussing techie topics but also lifestyle issues, such as music and personal taste.

Wholesaling

Wholesaling

All activities involved in selling goods and services to those buying for resale or business use.

Wholesaler

A firm engaged *primarily* in wholesaling activity.

Wholesaling includes all activities involved in selling goods and services to those buying for resale or business use. We call **wholesalers** those firms engaged *primarily* in wholesaling activity.

Wholesalers buy mostly from producers and sell mostly to retailers, industrial consumers, and other wholesalers. As a result, many of the nation's largest and most important wholesalers are largely unknown to final consumers. For example, you may never have heard of SuperValu, even though it's a $20 billion company and the nation's largest food wholesaler. Or how about Grainger, the leading wholesaler of maintenance, repair, and operating (MRO) supplies? (See Real Marketing 14.3.)

But why are wholesalers used at all? For example, why would a producer use wholesalers rather than selling directly to retailers or consumers? Quite simply, wholesalers add value by performing one or more of the following channel functions:

- *Selling and promoting:* Wholesalers' sales forces help manufacturers reach many small customers at a low cost. The wholesaler has more contacts and is often more trusted by the buyer than the distant manufacturer.

- *Buying and assortment building:* Wholesalers can select items and build assortments needed by their customers, thereby saving the consumers much work.

- *Bulk-breaking:* Wholesalers save their customers money by buying in carload lots and breaking bulk (breaking large lots into small quantities).

- *Warehousing:* Wholesalers hold inventories, thereby reducing the inventory costs and risks of suppliers and customers.

- *Transportation:* Wholesalers can provide quicker delivery to buyers because they are closer than the producers.

real marketing 14.3

Grainger: The Biggest Market Leader You've Never Heard Of?

It's a 4.8 billion business that offers more than 500,000 products and parts to more than 1.3 million customers. Its 600 North American branches, more than 15,000 employees, and innovative Web site handle more than 100,000 transactions a day. Grainger's customers include businesses ranging from factories, garages, and grocers to military bases and schools. Most American businesses are located within 20 minutes of a Grainger branch. Customers include notables such as Abbott Laboratories, General

Although you may never have heard it, Grainger is by far the world's leading wholesaler of maintenance, repair, and operating supplies.

Motors, Campbell Soup, American Airlines, Mercedes-Benz, and the U.S. Postal Service. Grainger also operates one of the highest-volume B2B sites on the Web.

So, how come you've never heard of Grainger? Most likely it's because Grainger is a wholesaler. And like most wholesalers, it operates behind the scenes, selling only to other businesses. Moreover, Grainger operates in the not-so-glamorous world of maintenance, repair, and operating (MRO) supplies.

But whereas you might know little about Grainger, to its customers the company is very well known and much valued. Through its branch network, service centers, sales reps, catalog, and Web site, Grainger links customers with the supplies they need to keep their facilities running smoothly—everything from lightbulbs, cleaners, and display cases to nuts and bolts, motors, valves, power tools, and test equipment. Grainger is by far the nation's largest MRO wholesaler. Notes one industry reporter, "If industrial America is an engine, Grainger is its lubricant."

Grainger serves as an important link between thousands of MRO supplies manufacturers on one side and millions of industrial and commercial customers on the other. It operates on a simple value proposition: to make it easier and less costly for customers to find and buy MRO supplies. It starts by acting as a one-stop shop for anything and everything MRO related. Most customers will tell you that Grainger sells everything—*everything*—from the ordinary to the out-of-the-ordinary. For example, it stocks thousands of lightbulbs—about every lightbulb known to mankind. If you don't believe it, go to www.grainger.com and search "lightbulbs"! As for the not-so-ordinary:

Grainger sells 19 different models of floor-cleaning machines, has 49 catalog pages of socket wrenches, and offers nine different sizes of hydraulic service jacks, an assortment of NFL-licensed hard hats bearing team logos, and item No. 6AV22, a $36.90 dispenser rack for two 1-gallon containers of Gatorade. According to corporate legend, Grainger is the only place that workers on the Alaskan Pipeline have been able to find repellent to cope with arctic bears during their mating season.

Beyond making it easier for customers to find the products they need, Grainger also helps them to streamline their acquisition processes. For most companies, acquiring MRO supplies is a very costly process. In fact, 40 percent of the cost of MRO supplies stems from the purchase process, including finding a supplier, negotiating the best deal, placing the order, receiving the order, and paying the invoice. Grainger constantly seeks ways to reduce the costs associated with MRO supplies acquisition, both internally and externally. Says one analyst, "Grainger will reduce your search and your process costs for items, instead of your having to order 10 things from 10 different companies, and you'll get one invoice. That's pretty powerful."

One company found that working with Grainger cut MRO requisition time by more than 60 percent; lead times went from days to hours. Its supply chain dropped from 12,000 suppliers to 560—significantly reducing expenses. Similarly, a large timber and paper-products company, has come to appreciate the value of Grainger's selection and streamlined ordering process. It orders two-thirds of its supplies from Grainger's Web site at an annual acquisition cost of only $300,000. By comparison, for the remainder of its needs, this company deals with more than 1,300 small distributors at an acquisition cost of $2.4 million each year—eight times the cost of dealing with Grainger for half of the volume. As a result, the company is now looking for ways to buy all of its MRO supplies from Grainger.

You might think that helping customers find what they need easily and efficiently would be enough to keep Grainger atop of the MRO mountain. But Grainger goes even further. On a broader level, it builds lasting relationships with customers by helping them find *solutions* to their overall MRO problems. Acting as consultants, Grainger sales reps help buyers with everything from improving their supply chain management to reducing inventories and streamlining warehousing operations.

Branches . . . serve as the base for Grainger territory managers who provide on-site help to big facilities. . . . [Reps can] tour a factory or an office complex or even a hotel and suggest to its managers exactly what supplies they really need to keep the place up to snuff, right down to how many gallons of carpet cleaner they'll require each week. That's how Grainger knows, for example, that one Biltmore Hotel has 7,000 lightbulbs. . . . "Our reps can pretty much stand outside a building and get a general feel for what kinds of products the customer needs," [says James Ryan, Grainger's executive vice president of marketing, sales, and service].

Grainger has launched a series of programs designed to add value to its commodity business. For example, through its "Click & Sell" program, Grainger uses information collected about customers, such as industry data and purchase histories, to help sales reps find solutions for customer needs. If, for example, a customer places an order for a pump to use with caustic chemicals, the Grainger rep might also suggest gloves and safety glasses. If an item is unavailable, the database identifies alternative products to get the job done.

Grainger also offers value to customers through its links to and clout with suppliers.

Jason Eastin is facilities operations director for JRV Management, a . . . company that runs community and private sports facilities in metropolitan Detroit. He relies on Grainger in part because of its clout with factory reps. When his company was opening up its newest complex, he asked Chris Clemons, a Grainger territory manager, for help figuring out the number and kinds of fixtures that would be required. Clemens summoned a rep from Rubbermaid, the household-products maker, who showed up with a laptop and a software program that churned out a reasonable supply chain within 20 minutes. Similarly, Clemens worked with a General Electric salesperson who figured out how Eastin could stretch out "relamping" his facilities to every two years, instead of annually, and cut costs significantly as well by switching to a different kind of metal-halide bulb as the primary kind of illumination for his ice arenas. "To have General Electric provide that service to me at no charge would never happen," Eastin says. "But Grainger has that buying-power structure. They open up those kinds of opportunities to me."

So now you've heard of Grainger, a wholesaler that succeeds by making life eas-

ier and more efficient for commercial and industrial buyers and sellers. Although a market leader, Grainger still captures only 4 percent of the highly fragmented U.S. market for MRO goods. That leaves a lot of room for growth. But to take advantage of the opportunities, Grainger must continue to find innovative ways to add value. "Our system makes our business partners and suppliers more efficient," says Fred Loepp, vice president of product management at Grainger, "and that benefits the entire supply chain." Says Theresa Dubiel, branch manager at Grainger's Romulus, Michigan branch, "If we don't save [customers] time and money every time they come [to us], they won't come back."

Sources: Excerpts from Dale Buss, "The New Deal," *Sales & Marketing Management,* June 2002, pp. 25–30; and Colleen Gourley, "Redefining Distribution," *Warehousing Management,* October 2000, pp. 28–30. Also see Leslie Langnau, "B2B E-Commerce: A Look at What Works," *Material Handling Management,* February 2002, p. 42; Steve Konicki and Eileen Colkin, "Attitude Adjustment," *Informationweek,* March 25, 2002, pp. 20–22; and information accessed at www.grainger.com, December 2002.

- *Financing:* Wholesalers finance their customers by giving credit, and they finance their suppliers by ordering early and paying bills on time.
- *Risk bearing:* Wholesalers absorb risk by taking title and bearing the cost of theft, damage, spoilage, and obsolescence.
- *Market information:* Wholesalers give information to suppliers and customers about competitors, new products, and price developments.
- *Management services and advice:* Wholesalers often help retailers train their salesclerks, improve store layouts and displays, and set up accounting and inventory control systems.

Types of Wholesalers

Merchant wholesaler
Independently owned business that takes title to the merchandise it handles.

Broker
A wholesaler who does not take title to goods and whose function is to bring buyers and sellers together and assist in negotiation.

Agent
A wholesaler who represents buyers or sellers on a relatively permanent basis, performs only a few functions, and does not take title to goods.

Wholesalers fall into three major groups (see Table 14.3): *merchant wholesalers; agents and brokers;* and *manufacturers' sales branches and offices.* **Merchant wholesalers** are the largest single group of wholesalers, accounting for roughly 50 percent of all wholesaling. Merchant wholesalers include two broad types: full-service wholesalers and limited-service wholesalers. *Full-service wholesalers* provide a full set of services, whereas the various *limited-service wholesalers* offer fewer services to their suppliers and customers. The several different types of limited-service wholesalers perform varied specialized functions in the distribution channel.

Brokers and *agents* differ from merchant wholesalers in two ways: They do not take title to goods, and they perform only a few functions. Like merchant wholesalers, they generally specialize by product line or customer type. A **broker** brings buyers and sellers together and assists in negotiation. **Agents** represent buyers or sellers on a more permanent basis. *Manufacturers' agents* (also called manufacturers' representatives) are the most common type of agent wholesaler. The third

TABLE 14.3   MAJOR TYPES OF WHOLESALERS

Type	Description
Merchant wholesalers	Independently owned businesses that take title to the merchandise they handle. In different trades they are called *jobbers, distributors,* or *mill supply houses.* Include full-service wholesalers and limited-service wholesalers:
Full-service wholesalers	Provide a full line of services: carrying stock, maintaining a sales force, offering credit, making deliveries, and providing management assistance. There are two types:
Wholesale merchants	Sell primarily to retailers and provide a full range of services. *General merchandise wholesalers* carry several merchandise lines, whereas *general line wholesalers* carry one or two lines in great depth. *Specialty wholesalers* specialize in carrying only part of a line. Examples: health food wholesalers, seafood wholesalers.
Industrial distributors	Sell to manufacturers rather than to retailers. Provide several services, such as carrying stock, offering credit, and providing delivery. May carry a broad range of merchandise, a general line, or a specialty line.
Limited-service wholesalers	Offer fewer services than full-service wholesalers. Limited-service wholesalers are of several types:
Cash-and-carry wholesalers	Carry a limited line of fast-moving goods and sell to small retailers for cash. Normally do not deliver. Example: A small fish store retailer may drive to a cash-and-carry fish wholesaler, buy fish for cash, and bring the merchandise back to the store.
Truck wholesalers (or truck jobbers)	Perform primarily a selling and delivery function. Carry limited line of semiperishable merchandise (such as milk, bread, snack foods), which they sell for cash as they make their rounds to supermarkets, small groceries, hospitals, restaurants, factory cafeterias, and hotels.
Drop shippers	Do not carry inventory or handle the product. On receiving an order, they select a manufacturer, who ships the merchandise directly to the customer. The drop shipper assumes title and risk from the time the order is accepted to its delivery to the customer. They operate in bulk industries, such as coal, lumber, and heavy equipment.
Rack jobbers	Serve grocery and drug retailers, mostly in nonfood items. They send delivery trucks to stores, where the delivery people set up toys, paperbacks, hardware items, health and beauty aids, or other items. They price the goods, keep them fresh, set up point-of-purchase displays, and keep inventory records. Rack jobbers retain title to the goods and bill the retailers only for the goods sold to consumers.
Producers' cooperatives	Are owned by farmer members and assemble farm produce to sell in local markets. The co-op's profits are distributed to members at the end of the year. They often attempt to improve product quality and promote a co-op brand name, such as Sun Maid raisins, Sunkist oranges, or Diamond walnuts.
Mail-order wholesalers	Send catalogs to retail, industrial, and institutional customers featuring jewelry, cosmetics, specialty foods, and other small items. Maintain no outside sales, force. Main customers are businesses in small outlying areas. Orders are filled and sent by mail, truck, or other transportation.
Brokers and agents	Do not take title to goods. Main function is to facilitate buying and selling, for which they earn a commission on the selling price. Generally specialize by product line or customer type.
Brokers	Chief function is bringing buyers and sellers together and assisting in negotiation. They are paid by the party who hired them and do not carry inventory, get involved in financing, or assume risk. Examples: food brokers, real estate brokers, insurance brokers, and security brokers.
Agents	Represent either buyers or sellers on a more permanent basis than brokers do. There are several types:
Manufacturers' agents	Represent two or more manufacturers of complementary lines. A formal written agreement with each manufacturer covers pricing, territories, order-handling, delivery service and warranties, and commission rates. Often used in such lines as apparel, furniture and electrical goods. Most manufacturers' agents are small businesses, with only a few skilled salespeople as employees. They are hired by small manufacturers who cannot afford their own field sales forces and by large manufacturers who use agents to open new territories or to cover territories that cannot support full-time salespeople.
Selling agents	Have contractual authority to sell a manufacturer's entire output. The manufacturer either is not interested in the selling function or feels unqualified. The selling agent serves as a sales department and has significant influence over prices, terms, and conditions of sale. Found in product areas such as textiles, industrial machinery and equipment, coal and coke, chemicals, and metals.
Purchasing agents	Generally have a long-term relationship with buyers and make purchases for them, often receiving, inspecting, warehousing, and shipping the merchandise to the buyers. They provide helpful market information to clients and help them obtain the best goods and prices available.

Type	Description
Commission merchants	Take physical possession of products and negotiate sales. Normally, they are not employed on a long-term basis. Used most often in agricultural marketing by farmers who do not want to sell their own output and do not belong to producers' cooperatives. The commission merchant takes a truckload of commodities to a central market, sells it for the best price, deducts a commission and expenses, and remits the balance to the producers.
Manufacturers' and retailers' branches and offices	Wholesaling operations conducted by sellers or buyers themselves rather than through independent wholesalers. Separate branches and offices can be dedicated to either sales or purchasing.
Sales branches and offices	Set up by manufacturers to improve inventory control, selling, and promotion. *Sales branches* carry inventory and are found in industries such as lumber and automotive equipment and parts. *Sales offices* do not carry inventory and are most prominent in dry-goods and notions industries.
Purchasing officers	Perform a role similar to that of brokers or agents but are part of the buyer's organization. Many retailers set up purchasing offices in major market centers such as New York and Chicago.

Manufacturers' sales branches and offices
Wholesaling by sellers or buyers themselves rather than through independent wholesalers.

major type of wholesaling is that done in **manufacturers' sales branches and offices** by sellers or buyers themselves rather than through independent wholesalers.

Wholesaler Marketing Decisions

Wholesalers now face growing competitive pressures, more-demanding customers, new technologies, and more direct-buying programs on the part of large industrial, institutional, and retail buyers. As a result, they have had to take a fresh look at the marketing strategies. As with retailers, their marketing decisions include choices of target markets, positioning, and the marketing mix—product assortments and services, price, promotion, and place (see Figure 14.2).

Target Market and Positioning Decision

Like retailers, wholesalers must define their target markets and position themselves effectively—they cannot serve everyone. They can choose a target group by size of customer (only large retailers), type

Merchant wholesalers: A typical Fleming Companies, Inc., wholesale food distribution center. The average Fleming warehouse contains 500,000 square feet of floor space (with a 30-foot-high ceiling), carries 16,000 different food items, and serves 150 to 200 retailers within a 500-mile radius.

FIGURE 14.2
Wholesaler marketing
decisions

of customer (convenience stores only), need for service (customers who need credit), or other factors. Within the target group, they can identify the more profitable customers, design stronger offers, and build better relationships with them. They can propose automatic reordering systems, set up management-training and advising systems, or even sponsor a voluntary chain. They can discourage less profitable customers by requiring larger orders or adding service charges to smaller ones.

Marketing-Mix Decisions

Like retailers, wholesalers must decide on product assortment and services, prices, promotion, and place. The wholesaler's "product" is the assortment of *products and services* that it offers. Wholesalers are under great pressure to carry a full line and to stock enough for immediate delivery. But this practice can damage profits. Wholesalers today are cutting down on the number of lines they carry, choosing to carry only the more profitable ones. Wholesalers are also rethinking which services count most in building strong customer relationships and which should be dropped or charged for. The key is to find the mix of services most valued by their target customers.

Price is also an important wholesaler decision. Wholesalers usually mark up the cost of goods by a standard percentage—say, 20 percent. Expenses may run 17 percent of the gross margin, leaving a profit margin of 3 percent. In grocery wholesaling, the average profit margin is often less than 2 percent. Wholesalers are trying new pricing approaches. They may cut their margin on some lines in order to win important new customers. They may ask suppliers for special price breaks when they can turn them into an increase in the supplier's sales.

Although *promotion* can be critical to wholesaler success, most wholesalers are not promotion minded. Their use of trade advertising, sales promotion, personal selling, and public relations is largely scattered and unplanned. Many are behind the times in personal selling—they still see selling as a single salesperson talking to a single customer instead of as a team effort to sell, build, and service major accounts. Wholesalers also need to adopt some of the nonpersonal promotion techniques used by retailers. They need to develop an overall promotion strategy and to make greater use of supplier promotion materials and programs.

Finally, *place* is important—wholesalers must choose their locations, facilities, and Web locations carefully. Wholesalers typically locate in low-rent, low-tax areas and tend to invest little money in their buildings, equipment, and systems. As a result, their materials-handling and order-processing systems are often outdated. In recent years, however, large and progressive wholesalers are reacting to rising costs by investing in automated warehouses and online ordering systems. Orders are fed from the retailer's system directly into the wholesaler's computer, and the items are picked up by mechanical devices and automatically taken to a shipping platform where they are assembled. Most large wholesalers are using technology to carry out accounting, billing, inventory control, and forecasting. Modern wholesalers are adapting their services to the needs of target customers and finding cost-reducing methods of doing business.

Trends in Wholesaling

As the wholesaling industry moves into the twenty-first century, it faces considerable challenges. The industry remains vulnerable to one of the most enduring trends of the last decade—fierce resistance to price increases and the winnowing out of suppliers who are not adding value based on cost and quality. Progressive wholesalers constantly watch for better ways to meet the changing needs of their suppliers and target customers. They recognize that, in the long run, their only reason for existence comes from adding value by increasing the efficiency and effectiveness of the entire marketing channel. To achieve this goal, they must constantly improve their services and reduce their costs.

To improve efficiency and service, McKesson offers retail pharmacists a wide range of online resources, including supply management assistance, catalog searches, real-time order tracking, and an account management system. Retailers can even use the McKesson system to maintain medical profiles on their customers.

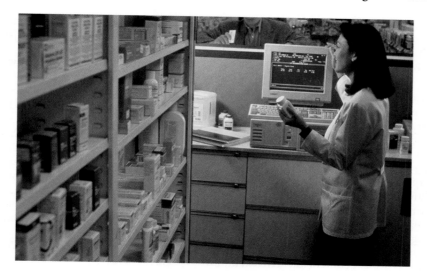

McKesson HBOC, the nation's leading wholesaler of pharmaceuticals, health and beauty care, and home health care products, provides an example of progressive wholesaling. To survive, McKesson HBOC has to remain more cost-effective than manufacturers' sales branches. Thus, the company has built efficient automated warehouses, established direct computer links with drug manufacturers, and set up extensive online supply management and accounts-receivable systems for customers. It offers retail pharmacists a wide range of online resources, including supply management assistance, catalog searches, real-time order tracking, and account management system. Retailers can even use the McKesson system to maintain medical profiles on their customers. McKesson's medical-surgical supply and equipment customers receive a rich assortment of online solutions and supply management tools, including an online order-management system and real-time information on products and pricing, inventory availability, and order status. According to McKesson, it adds value in the channel by "delivering unique supply and information management solutions that reduce costs and improve quality for health care customers."[25]

The distinction between large retailers and large wholesalers continues to blur. Many retailers now operate formats such as wholesale clubs and hypermarkets that perform many wholesale functions. In return, many large wholesalers are setting up their own retailing operations. SuperValu and Fleming, both leading food wholesalers, now operate their own retailing operations. For example, SuperValu, the nation's largest food wholesaling company, is also the country's eleventh largest food retailer. Almost 45 percent of the company's $20 billion in sales comes from its Bigg's, Cub Foods, Save-A-Lot, Farm Fresh, Hornbacher's, Laneco, Metro, Scott's Foods, Shop 'n Save, and Shoppers Food Warehouse stores.[26]

Wholesalers will continue to increase the services they provide to retailers—retail pricing, cooperative advertising, marketing and management information reports, accounting services, online transactions, and others. Rising costs on the one hand, and the demand for increased services on the other, will put the squeeze on wholesaler profits. Wholesalers who do not find efficient ways to deliver value to their customers will soon drop by the wayside. However, the increased use of computerized, automated, and Web-based systems will help wholesalers to contain the costs of ordering, shipping, and inventory holding, boosting their productivity.

Finally, facing slow growth in their domestic markets and such developments as the North American Free Trade Agreement, many large wholesalers are now going global. For example, in 1991, McKesson bought out its Canadian partner, Provigo. The company now receives about 3 percent of its total revenues from Canada.

LOOKING BACK: REVIEWING THE CONCEPTS

This chapter digs more deeply into the two major channel functions—retailing and wholesaling. Today's retailers face a rapidly changing environment, characterized by overcapacity, new kinds of competitors, and retail convergence. As a result, to prosper or even to survive, they must sharpen their marketing strategies. Wholesalers, too, have experienced recent environmental changes, most notably mounting competitive pressures. They have faced new sources of competition, more-demanding customers, new technologies, and more direct-buying programs on the part of large industrial, institutional, and retail buyers.

1. Explain the roles of retailers and wholesalers in the marketing channel.
Retailing and wholesaling consist of many organizations bringing goods and services from the point of production to the point of use. *Retailing* includes all activities involved in selling goods or services directly to final consumers for their personal, nonbusiness use. *Wholesaling* includes all the activities involved in selling goods or services to those who are buying for the purpose of resale or for business use. Wholesalers perform many functions, including selling and promoting, buying and assortment building, bulk-breaking, warehousing, transporting, financing, risk bearing, supplying market information, and providing management services and advice.

2. Describe the major types of retailers and give examples of each.
Retailers can be classified as *store retailers* and *nonstore retailers*. Although most goods and services are sold through stores, nonstore retailing has been growing much faster than has store retailing. Store retailers can be further classified by the *amount of service* they provide (self-service, limited service, or full service), *product line sold* (specialty stores, department stores, supermarkets, convenience stores, superstores, and service businesses), and *relative prices* (discount stores and off-price retailers). Today, many retailers are banding together in corporate and contractual *retail organizations* (corporate chains, voluntary chains and retailer cooperatives, franchise organizations, and merchandising conglomerates).

3. Identify the major types of wholesalers and give examples of each.
Wholesalers fall into three groups. First, *merchant wholesalers* take possession of the goods. They include *full-service wholesalers* (wholesale merchants, industrial distributors) and *limited-service wholesalers* (cash-and-carry wholesalers, truck wholesalers, drop shippers, rack jobbers, producers' cooperatives, and mail-order wholesalers). Second, *brokers* and *agents* do not take possession of the goods but are paid a commission for aiding buying and selling. Finally, *manufacturers' sales branches and offices* are wholesaling operations conducted by nonwholesalers to bypass the wholesalers.

4. Explain the marketing decisions facing retailers and wholesalers.
Each retailer must make decisions about its target markets and positioning, product assortment and services, price, promotion, and place. Retailers need to choose target markets carefully and position themselves strongly. Today, wholesaling is holding its own in the economy. Progressive wholesalers are adapting their services to the needs of target customers and are seeking cost-reducing methods of doing business. Faced with slow growth in their domestic markets and developments such as the North American Free Trade Association, many large wholesalers are also now going global.

REVIEWING THE KEY TERMS

Agent 455
Broker 455
Category killer 438
Chain stores 440
Convenience store 438
Department store 437
Discount store 438
Factory outlet 439

Franchise 440
Independent off-price retailer 439
Manufacturers' sales branches and offices 457
Merchant wholesaler 455
Off-price retailer 439
Retailer 436
Retailing 436

Shopping center 447
Specialty store 437
Supermarket 438
Superstore 438
Warehouse club 439
Wheel-of-retailing concept 448
Wholesaler 453
Wholesaling 453

DISCUSSING THE CONCEPTS

1. Describe the similarities and differences between retailing and wholesaling. Can a company be a retailer and a wholesaler at the same time? Explain.
2. Giant superstores called category killers are an emerging trend. How is a category killer different from other types of retailers? Why has this form of retailing grown so rapidly? What types of retailers are most threatened by category killers? Why? How will online retailing affect category killers? Give an example of a category killer that has been affected by online marketing.
3. How has the growth of other types of large retailers affected the willingness of manufacturers to sell their goods at or below regular wholesale rates to off-price retailers?

   What policy should Sony set for selling the following products to off-price retailers: (a) HDTV televisions, (b) big-screen televisions, (c) regular televisions, (d) Walkman cassette players. Explain.

4. List and characterize the major types of retail organizations. Which of these organizational forms seems to be growing in popularity? Which are declining in popularity? Why?
5. Retailers are always searching for new marketing strategies to attract and retain customers. List and briefly describe the strategies retailers use to differentiate themselves from competitors.
6. Use the "wheel of retailing" to assess the emergence and evolution of outlet malls. What do you predict will be the future of outlet malls? Explain.
7. List and describe each of the channel functions that have been traditionally assigned to wholesalers. How will wholesalers have to change to meet the threat of increasing competition from large retailers? What type of wholesaler is best equipped to compete and evolve in the next decade? Explain.
8. Nature's Foods is a food market that will be opening soon in your local community. Nature's Foods carries only

organically grown fruits and vegetables. No red meat products or products with high amounts of chemical additives or preservatives will be stocked. The store hopes to appeal to the health-conscious consumer and the vegetarian looking for an alternative to the traditional grocery store. As a specialty store, Nature's Foods has relatively few available suppliers and a limited purchasing budget. Examine the major types of wholesalers described in Table 14.3. Which category of wholesaler(s) should Nature's Foods pursue? Explain your reasoning.

APPLYING THE CONCEPTS

1. As American consumers demand more and more service and customization, virtual retailing seems to have an ever-brighter future. Through virtual retailing, a seller can come directly into your home, at your convenience, and allow you to participate in designing your own personalized product and shopping experience. This sounds great—no more ill-fitting bathing suits or greeting cards that seem like they were written for someone else, no high-pressure salespeople, and no congested parking lots. At virtual retail sites, you can spend as much or as little time as you need to make up your mind. Virtual retailing has made mass customization a reality. All you have to do is point and click. Take a look at the following Web sites for more on customizing clothing, eyeglasses, and shoes: Interactive Custom Clothes (www.ic3d.com), Lands' End (www.landsend.com), Eyeglasses.com (www.eyeglasses.com), and Nike (www.nike.com).
   a. How does virtual retailing compare with more traditional shopping formats? What are the primary advantages and disadvantages for consumers?
   b. What target markets would be most interested in virtual retailing? Do the Web sites you just visited appear to be appealing to those segments? Explain.
   c. Compare the marketing strategies of the various Web retailers you have just visited. Which company most appeals to you? Why?
   d. Pick one of the Web sites and design your own product. Discuss the pros and cons of your experience. How was this experience different from buying in a retail store? Would you be willing to purchase the item you designed?

2. When Wal-Mart flexes its cybermuscles, everyone pays attention. After several years of careful study, Wal-Mart finally jumped into cyberspace. Its beefed-up Web site sells everything from prescriptions to apparel to consumer electronics. Long-range plans call for Wal-Mart's Web site to rival its brick-and-mortar stores. Wal-Mart has worked with order-processing expert Fingerhut Business Services to get the kinks out of its logistics. In addition, with a multitude of partners, such as Books-A-Million, the retailing giant has added depth to its cyberline. These moves have already brought the giant retailer into direct competition with such Web-only merchants as Amazon.com. Wal-Mart believes that customers have spoken, and they're saying, "Move to the Web." When the customer speaks, Wal-Mart listens.
   a. Compare Wal-Mart's Web site (www.walmart.com) with the Web site of rival Target (www.target.com). What are each site's the strengths and weaknesses with respect to cybermarketing?
   b. Are the markets for Wal-Mart's brick-and-mortar stores different from the markets for its cyberstore? How?
   c. What opportunities do you see for Wal-Mart on the Web? What difficulties?

DIGITAL CONNECTIONS

CONNECTIONS WITH PARTNERS AND NEW MARKETS SPUR GROWTH IN RETAILING

If someone told you a few years ago that you would willingly stand in line to pay two dollars for a cup of coffee, you might have strongly disagreed. Not so anymore. Consumers do it every day at the coffee counters of the thousands of Starbucks locations across the country. For millions of Americans, a daily espresso has become an expensive necessity. But Starbucks's success may be short-lived if the company fails to stay abreast of its changing market. The company's phenomenal growth has inspired a long list of competitors, from coffee shops to grocery stores (and their sophisticated coffee aisles) to ice cream distributors, and even to restaurants. With a wealth of new competition, Starbucks is looking for new ways to maintain its phenomenal 40 percent annual earnings growth rate. Current strategies include developing new products (juices, teas, and frozen drinks), rejuvenating past product stars (Frappuccino—a cold blended drink), and driving joint ventures (partnering with PepsiCo for bottling Frappuccino and with Dreyers Grand Ice Cream for packaging coffee ice cream). Additionally, Starbucks is expanding its traditional retail endeavors by opening several Café Starbucks restaurants and entering international markets.

FOR DISCUSSION

1. Assess Starbucks's retail strategy. What are the major strengths and weaknesses of the strategy? Why has the chain been so successful? (See www.starbucks.com for additional information.)
2. Do you see potential problems with the company's aggressive expansion plans? Will cannibalization among stores and formats be a problem?
3. How might other fast-growing franchises that offer coffee products threaten Starbucks? How should Starbucks deal with these challenges?
4. Assume you are the marketing manager for Starbucks. Design a growth strategy for this company for the next two years. How will you avoid cannibalizing existing sales? What partnerships, alliances, and new product alternatives best fit with the company's image and current offerings? What forms of new competition do you think will emerge? How are competitors likely to react to your plan?

Accordia: Balancing Traditional and Online Retailing

With the new emphasis on cyber-retailing, what's a traditional brick-and-mortar retailer to do? Hire a consultant! The consultants at Online Retail Partners (ORP), recently renamed Accordia, work with traditional retailers to create an online presence that builds customer relationships, promotes products and services, and enhances sales. In addition to providing Web technology expertise, ORP educates clients about how to use existing brick-and-mortar resources to drive new customers to the online retail marketplace.

After viewing the Online Retail Partners video, answer the following questions about retailing and wholesaling:

1. Executives at ZanyBrainy assert that it's important to maintain a balance between online and traditional retailing. How do the two channels interact and support one another? How might building an online presence influence the place decision for retailers? How might it influence other marketing decisions?
2. Should Online Retail Partners consider expanding its services to wholesalers? How would the services required by wholesalers interested in building an online presence differ from those required by retailers? Which types of wholesalers are most likely to find success online?
3. How does the growth of e-commerce affect or interact with the retailing trends discussed in the chapter?

dELiA's: Searching for the Right Way to Connect with Teens

Finding the right target market is a first step toward success; maintaining connection and community with the market comes next. Consider the case of Christopher Edgar and Steve Kahn, two college roommates who started a catalog targeting college girls—specifically, sorority sisters. Sales were at best ho-hum until the guys realized that it was the college girls' little sisters who were actually buying the merchandise. Sensing an opportunity, in 1994 they shifted targets and aimed at the 12-to-17-year-old market with a catalog named dELiA's. Since that decision, dELiA's has become *the* shopping place for teens.

How did dELiA's connect with teens? Initially, part of the connection was its edgy image. There were lots of fresh-faced, wide-eyed models with whipped-up hair that was sometimes green and sometimes blue. The catalog featured styles such as wide-legged pants, clunky shoes, baby-doll dresses, ankle-length skirts, striped T-shirts, and the like—all very hip and high-spirited. Lately, however, dELiA's has softened its image. The latest look from dELiA's is called desert rose, a hippie-bohemian-gypsy look that includes drawstring peasant tops in small floral prints and jeans with lace-up trims.

As part of its connecting to teens, dELiA's signed a contract with Shakira, Latin America's answer to Madonna, who was just becoming popular in the United States. Shakira appeared on the cover of the catalog, wearing clothes she chose from dELiA's inventory. The Web site featured contests in which cus-

tomers could win one of 500 autographed CDs, an autographed guitar, and a $500 shopping spree. It also offered a Q & A with Shakira, along with video and audio clips and editorial features. Shakira described her thing as mostly pants, boots, belts, and studs, making her an ideal hip spokesperson for the dELiA's spring 2002 look. The goal was to communicate that both were super-cool.

In another effort to connect with teens, dELiA's turned cataloging into a two-way street. They hired high school and college girls to answer telephones, chat, answer questions, and provide shoppers with fashion tips while also finding out what was on the market's mind. Teenage girls responded by sending the catalogers photos of themselves, letters, critiques of the clothes, suggestions for new merchandise, and tons of e-mail. Then, specially designated employees answered all those letters and e-mails. The result was a major investment in relationship building with what is often a very fickle market. When selling to teens, constant communication becomes crucial to understanding what will sell.

Initially, dELiA's catalog was passed around from hand to hand. But by the late 1990s, it had developed a stable mailing list, which has become one of dELiA's key strengths. Over the years, the company has compiled the list from telephone requests (sometimes 5,000 a day). By 2002, dELiA's had a database of 13 million names that included 6 million actual buyers. To maintain the loyalty of its customers, dELiA's does not sell or share the list, and it keeps communications with customers private and confidential.

Once the catalog was well established, Steve and Chris employed two strategies to maintain growth. In the first strategy, they moved into bricks-and-mortar retailing by acquiring TSI Soccer Corp., a soccer apparel and equipment retailer, and Screeem!, which operated 11 stores under that name and 15 under the name Jeans Country. These two purchases expanded dELiA's geographic retail coverage to include the entire East Coast. Then, in February 1999, the company opened the first of many dELiA's stores, in the Westchester Mall in White Plains, New York. By mid-2002, it had opened 54 dELiA's stores, with another 13 planned for late 2002 and 30 more in 2003.

In dELiA's stores, the merchandise assortment includes not only clothing but also cosmetics, bath products, posters, candy, novelty home accessories, and underwear. It looks like a three-dimensional version of the catalog, with the dELiA's logo featured throughout the brightly lit store. Initially, merchandise flew off the shelves.

The second strategy took dELiA's online. It started a Web site, dELiA's.com, which was mostly informational and entertaining, although later it began to sell merchandise. That site was so successful that the company added other Web sites, such as gURL.com, aimed at teen-age girls; dotdotdash.com, aimed at girls age 7–11; Droog.com, a site aimed at teenage boys; and contentsonline.com, which was a home furnishings site. The latter two sites were paired with their own catalogs. To manage all the sites and the connections between them, the management of dELiA's set up a subsidiary, named ITurf.

Such rapid expansion came at a high price, along with losses in every quarter in 2001. Several factors can explain this. First, direct selling and store retailing differ in operating-capital requirements. Stores are much more capital intensive than direct sales. Investments in leases, furnishings, inventory, and sales help are required up front. A catalog with slow-selling merchandise can be quickly replaced, but a store with slow-selling merchandise suffers from sales and markdowns to move inventory. Beginning in the first quarter of 1999, the conversion of the Screeem! stores led to a $13.7 million first-quarter after-tax charge and necessitated many markdowns and additional promotions to move merchandise.

Second, Internet operations were another drain on resources. The ITurf subsidiary required building an expensive infrastructure. Unfortunately, this effort did not yield the third *C* of Internet operations—commerce. Internet sales were a disappointing 3 percent to 4 percent in 1999 and 2000.

As the losses continued to mount, dELiA's spun off the ITurf subsidiary in 1999, liquidated the Droog catalog of boys apparel in 2000, sold TSI Soccer in 2001, and sold off the assets of gURL.com. In a turnaround, it re-merged with ITurf in November of 2000.

What does this mean for dELiA's future? Clearly, the company no longer sees itself as a cataloger. Instead, it is aiming for multichannel mastery, like Coldwater Creek or J. Jill Group. Chairman-CEO Steve Kahn believes that dELiA's can expand to 250-plus stores *if* it can leverage its opportunities quickly and profitably.

Industry observers believe that moving from cataloging to bricks-and-mortar is easier than moving from retail stores to cataloging. Retailers can respond much more quickly to changes in trends by changing floor displays, and displays can be used along with the Web to test trends before they are put into the catalog. Retail stores and catalogs both utilize dELiA's big database. Retailers can use the database for direct mailings promoting stores, and catalogs can be directed to teens according to their level of purchases. To keep the database growing—especially to build databases for local stores—dELiA's retailers capture customer information such as zip codes and dollar amount of sales in stores.

dELiA's faces obstacles to future success. One of these is the fickleness of its target market. Teens can turn on a retailer in an instant, and keeping up with the market is very difficult. Second, many teens don't like to order over the Internet: After they select items to purchase, they often need to get permission and a credit card number from Mom or Dad—a screening that may not always result in sales. Third, increasing postage and delivery costs coupled with mailbox glut are having a negative impact on direct selling. Fourth, there's heavy competition for any mall's floor traffic—can dELiA's brand withstand that competition?

The key to multichannel selling is to build a unified brand across channels. dELiA's has done well at building its dELiA's Web site and paginating its catalog, but it has yet to perfect the physical layout of its stores, not to mention making sure that all three retailing venues project the same image.

QUESTIONS FOR DISCUSSION

1. Check out the dELiA's Web site. Is it attractive? Is it easy to use? In your opinion, would it appeal to teens? Why?
2. Is Shakira a good spokesperson for dELiA's? Why or why not?
3. The 3 *C*s of the Internet retailing are community, content, and commerce. Evaluate the dELiA's Web site on these criteria.
4. If you have a dELiA's store close by, visit it and compare it to the Web site and catalog. Do they present a unified image? Why or why not?
5. What are the advantages and disadvantages of catalogs, retail stores, and the Internet? How can the advantages of one be used to overcome the disadvantages of the others?
6. In your opinion, is dELiA's likely to succeed in all three channels? Why or why not?

Sources: "ITurf IPO Lifts dELiA's Profits," *WWD,* June 10, 1999, p. 9; "DELiA's 2nd Quarter Loss Deepens," *WWD,* September 2, 1999, p. 5; "dELiA's Screeem! and Jean Country Acquisition a Done Deal," *Daily News Record,* August 3, 1998, p. 8; "Business Brief—dELiA's Corp.: Web Site Closings Are Cited as Wider Loss Is Recorded," *Wall Street Journal,* August 30, 2001; "DELiA's Sees Profitable Quarter," *WWD,* June 10, 2002, p. 12; Mark Del Franco, "dELiA's Growth Strategy, Take Two," *Catalog Age,* September 2001, pp. 5, 16; Yolanda Gault, "Marketer Drops as DELiA's Shops, but Analysts Stand by Cataloger: Marketer to Teens Makes Move to Stores," *Crain's New York Business,* June 8, 1998, p. 23; Karen Parr, "New Catalogs Target Gen Y," *WWD,* July 24, 1997, p. 12; Cynthia Redecker, "dELiA's Opens First Retail Unit," *WWD,* February 25, 1999, p. 11; Kristin Young, "dELiA's New Diva: Shakira Signs On," *WWW,* December 21, 2001, p. 10.

Giving your customers better service means letting th
know when they'll receive what you promised. Brown c
do that. With UPS E-mail Ship Notification, your custome
not only get confirmation that their orders are on the wa
Brown lets them track those orders themselves. So you'
have time to pursue future sales instead of past shipments. And you
thought we just delivered packages. **WHAT CAN BROWN DO FOR YOU?**

BROWM

and the Customer Service Manager

**After studying this chapter
you should be able to**

1. name and define the tools of the marketing
   communications mix
2. discuss the process and advantages of integrated
   marketing communications
3. outline the steps in developing effective marketing
   communications
4. explain the methods for setting the promotion
   budget and factors that affect the design of the
   promotion mix

Integrated Marketing Communication Strategy

LOOKING AHEAD: PREVIEWING THE CONCEPTS

In this and the next two chapters, we'll examine the last of the marketing mix tools—promotion. You'll find that promotion is not a single tool but rather a mix of several tools. Ideally, under the concept of *integrated marketing communications,* the company will carefully coordinate these promotion elements to deliver a clear, consistent, and compelling message about the organization and its products. We'll begin by introducing you to the various promotion mix tools, the importance of integrated marketing communications, the steps in developing marketing communication, and the promotion-budgeting process. In the next two chapters, we'll visit the specific marketing communications tools.

To start, let's look at UPS. You probably know UPS as a small-package delivery company. In recent years, however, the company has grown rapidly into a corporate giant offering a broad range of supply chain management services. Its challenge: How can it communicate the "new UPS" to customers large and small while at the same time building on the rich heritage we've come to associate with the old UPS? The answer comes in the form of a question: "What Can Brown Do for You?"

When you think about UPS, you probably envision one of those familiar brown trucks with a friendly driver who hustles around your neighborhood dropping off important parcels. And no wonder. The company's 88,000 delivery fleet (package cars, vans, tractors, and motorcycles) and 80,000 brown-clad drivers deliver more than 3.4 billion packages annually, an average of 13.6 million each day.

For most of us, seeing a brown UPS truck evokes fond memories of past packages delivered. And the drivers give UPS a friendly, local face. Stories abound of UPS delivery men and women who've gone to extremes to deliver a package or serve a customer. Former UPS CEO Jim Kelly relates the following example:

Right before Christmas, while delivering packages on a sprawling military base, driver Rene D'Augustino discovered an overnight letter bearing only a name with no specific address. Rather than giving up, Rene obtained permission to open the letter and look for clues as to the recipient's whereabouts. Inside, she found a handwritten note and a money order. The note read: "Make me happy. Come home for Christmas. Love, Mom." Rene knew she had to keep trying. After much searching, Rene finally located the young soldier sitting on a couch, surrounded by a big pile of movie rentals intended to get him through a lonely Christmas. The surprised soldier read the note, saw the money order, grinned, and jumped up to hug his

UPS driver. As he ran for the door, letter in hand, he turned back to Rene and asked her one more favor. Could she return all those movies to the Rec Center rental counter for him?

In some cases, dedicated UPS drivers have even become local heroes. In one such case, driver Kevin Brophy saved a mother and child from a flash flood in Pennsylvania. "In an era increasingly defined by the self-absorbed and the superficial, it's refreshing to know that the Kevin Brophy's of the world still exist," wrote the woman. "The world needs more heroes. One of ours is dressed in brown." Such bonds between drivers and customers strengthen the image of UPS as a community-based business serving local consumers.

In recent years, however, UPS has grown to become much more than a neighborhood small-package delivery service. It is now a $30.3 billion corporate giant offering a broad range of services to customers of all types and sizes—everything from transportation and package delivery to third-party logistics, inventory management, financing, and global customer clearance services. UPS now moves an astounding 6 percent of the gross domestic product in the United States, links 1.6 million sellers with 7 million buyers every day, and processes more than 460 million electronic transactions every week. It serves 90 percent of the world population and 99 percent of businesses in the Fortune 1000.

Rapid growth and diversification presents many opportunities for UPS; it also presents challenges. Perhaps the biggest challenge: communicating with all of UPS's many customers about the capabilities of UPS. The company's old communications theme—"We run the tightest ship in the shipping business"—presented UPS narrowly as a shipping company rather than an agile supply chain solutions provider. It was also myopic, focusing on the company's efficient operations rather than on what those efficiencies meant to and did for customers. UPS needed a new marketing communications campaign, one that positioned the company as an agile logistics solutions provider, while at the same time building on the rich values that customers have come to associate with UPS over the past 95 years.

The search for a new corporate communications theme began with customers. UPS conducted focus groups and market tests with customers at every level, from residential package shippers to mail room managers to corporate CEOs—anyone and everyone who could influence the decision to use UPS. It also held interviews with UPS insiders. The question? How could UPS simplify the complicated story about its diverse portfolio of services and all of the things for which UPS stands? When they'd run the numbers on the research, UPS's marketers came up with an obvious answer: Brown! That's right, Brown. Dale Hayes, UPS vice president of brand management and customer communications, explains:

> We needed to become more aggressive in communicating to our customers without losing one of our core values . . . humility. We're a roll-up-your-sleeves, get-it-done kind of company; people love our drivers, they love our brown trucks, they love everything we do. We found that there was tremendous strength in the color brown. So we built our new campaign on the idea of telling our story through the customers' eyes by talking about what brown could do for them. [The color brown held deep meaning for UPS employees as well.] We have said for years that "we are brown" to the core, our blood runs brown. . . . We've been referred to for years as Big Brown. . . . But we had never found the voice to embrace brown publicly and to let brown speak for us.

Thus was born the "What Can Brown Do for You?" theme that now unifies UPS's communications efforts. To introduce the new theme, UPS launched its largest-ever national media campaign during the 2002 Winter Olympics. The campaign uses warm, humorous ads featuring a variety of professionals discussing how UPS's broad range of services can make their jobs easier. Says John Beystehner, senior vice president of worldwide sales and marketing at UPS, "Instead of trying to convey our capabilities from *our* point of view, we are putting ourselves in the shoes of our customers and literally having them ask themselves: 'What Can Brown Do for You?'"

The corporate advertising campaign is just the tip of the UPS marketing communications effort. The ad promise has little meaning if it's not reinforced by the full mix of UPS's communications activities. "The campaign is an initial step to . . . help [our audiences] start thinking beyond their current perceptions of UPS, but it is just a first step," says Beystehner. "The next step is to continue to align our organization behind the brand [promise]." Says former UPS CEO Jim Kelly, "It's important to note . . . that a brand can be very hollow and lifeless . . . if the people and the organization . . . are not 100 percent dedicated to [communicating and] living out the brand promise every day."

To deliver the "What Can Brown Do for You?" message every day in a more personal way, UPS is realigning its sales and marketing organization. Rather than having departments and reps that focus on one set of services, UPS is combining all of its sales, marketing, and operations units into a single team. The move will provide a single face to each customer that can bring all of Brown's capabilities to bear on providing total supply chain solutions to customers, regardless of their needs.

In addition to relying on its sales and marketing people to deliver the new message personally, UPS also communicates with customers through several Web sites. At www.ups.com, consumers can check shipping rates, track packages, order supplies, and schedule pick-ups. At www.upslogistics.com, corporate customers can learn more about UPS's business-to-business services, including supply chain management and technology solutions. Potential clients can browse through success stories of UPS's Fortune 500 customers. At www.capital.ups.com, corporate clients can establish lines of credit, apply for financing, lease equipment, and learn about UPS's insurance services.

Communicating the new "What Can Brown Do for You" theme and giving it life will be no easy task. It will take more than just advertising and friendly drivers. UPS must communicate the new positioning at every customer touch-point: It must integrate all of its communications—from advertising and personal contact to sales promotion, public relations, direct marketing, and its multiple Web sites—to deliver a seamless message about what Brown can do for its customers.[1]

Modern marketing calls for more than just developing a good product, pricing it attractively, and making it available to target customers. Companies must also *communicate* with current and prospective customers, and what they communicate should not be left to chance. All of their communications efforts must be blended into a consistent and coordinated communications program. Just as good communication is important in building and maintaining any kind of relationship, it is a crucial element in a company's efforts to build customer relationships.

The Marketing Communications Mix

Marketing communications mix (promotion mix)
The specific mix of advertising, personal selling, sales promotion, and public relations a company uses to pursue its advertising and marketing objectives.

Advertising
Any paid form of nonpersonal presentation and promotion of ideas, goods, or services by an identified sponsor.

Sales promotion
Short-term incentives to encourage the purchase or sale of a product or service.

Public relations
Building good relations with the company's various publics by obtaining favorable publicity, building up a good "corporate image," and handling or heading off unfavorable rumors, stories, and events.

Personal selling
Personal presentation by the firm's sales force for the purpose of making sales and building customer relationships.

Direct marketing
Direct connections with carefully targeted individual consumers to both obtain an immediate response and cultivate lasting customer relationships.

A company's total **marketing communications mix**—also called its **promotion mix**—consists of the specific blend of advertising, sales promotion, public relations, personal selling, and direct-marketing tools that the company uses to pursue its advertising and marketing objectives. Definitions of the five major promotion tools follow:[2]

Advertising: Any paid form of nonpersonal presentation and promotion of ideas, goods, or services by an identified sponsor.

Sales promotion: Short-term incentives to encourage the purchase or sale of a product or service.

Public relations: Building good relations with the company's various publics by obtaining favorable publicity, building up a good corporate image, and handling or heading off unfavorable rumors, stories, and events.

Personal selling: Personal presentation by the firm's sales force for the purpose of making sales and building customer relationships.

Direct marketing: Direct connections with carefully targeted individual consumers to both obtain an immediate response and cultivate lasting customer relationships—the use of telephone, mail, fax, e-mail, the Internet, and other tools to communicate directly with specific consumers.

Each category involves specific tools. For example, advertising includes print, broadcast, outdoor, and other forms. Sales promotion includes point-of-purchase displays, premiums, discounts, coupons, specialty advertising, and demonstrations. Public relations includes press releases and special events. Personal selling includes sales presentations, trade shows, and incentive programs. Direct marketing includes catalogs, telephone marketing, kiosks, the Internet, and more. Thanks to technological breakthroughs, people can now communicate through traditional media (newspapers, radio, telephone, television) as well as through newer media forms (fax, cell phones, and computers).

At the same time, communication goes beyond these specific promotion tools. The product's design, its price, the shape and color of its package, and the stores that sell it—*all* communicate something to buyers. Thus, although the promotion mix is the company's primary communication activity, the entire marketing mix—promotion *and* product, price, and place—must be coordinated for greatest communication impact.

In this chapter, we begin by examining the rapidly changing marketing communications environment, the concept of integrated marketing communications, and the marketing communication process. Next, we discuss the factors that marketing communicators must consider in shaping an overall communication mix. Finally, we summarize the legal, ethical, and social responsibility issues in marketing communications. In Chapter 16, we look at *mass-communication tools*—advertising, sales promotion, and public relations. Chapter 17 examines the *sales force* and *direct marketing* as communication and promotion tools.

Integrated Marketing Communications

During the past several decades, companies around the world have perfected the art of mass marketing—selling highly standardized products to masses of customers. In the process, they have developed effective mass-media advertising techniques to support their mass-marketing strategies. These companies routinely invest millions of dollars in the mass media, reaching tens of millions of customers with a single ad. However, as we move into the twenty-first century, marketing managers face some new marketing communications realities.

The Changing Communications Environment

Two major factors are changing the face of today's marketing communications. First, as mass markets have fragmented, marketers are shifting away from mass marketing. More and more, they are developing focused marketing programs designed to build closer relationships with customers in more narrowly defined micromarkets. Second, vast improvements in information technology are speeding the movement toward segmented marketing. Today's information technology helps marketers to keep closer track of customer needs—more information about consumers at the individual and household levels is available than ever before. New technologies also provide new communications avenues for reaching smaller customer segments with more-tailored messages.

The shift from mass marketing to segmented marketing has had a dramatic impact on marketing communications. Just as mass marketing gave rise to a new generation of mass-media communications, the shift toward one-to-one marketing is spawning a new generation of more specialized and highly targeted communications efforts.

Given this new communications environment, marketers must rethink the roles of various media and promotion mix tools. Mass-media advertising has long dominated the promotion mixes of consumer product companies. However, although television, magazines, and other mass media remain very important, their dominance is now declining. *Market* fragmentation has resulted in *media* fragmentation—in an explosion of more-focused media that better match today's targeting strategies. Beyond the traditional mass-media channels, advertisers are making increased use of new, highly targeted media, ranging from highly focused specialty magazines and cable television channels, to CD catalogs and Web coupon promotions, to airport kiosks and floor decals in supermarket aisles. In all, companies are doing less *broadcasting* and more *narrowcasting*.

The Need for Integrated Marketing Communications

The shift from mass marketing to targeted marketing, and the corresponding use of a larger, richer mix of communication channels and promotion tools, poses a problem for marketers. Customers don't distinguish between message sources the way marketers do. In the consumer's mind, advertising messages from different media and different promotional approaches all become part of a single message about the company. Conflicting messages from these different sources can result in confused company images and brand positions.

The new media environment: The relatively few mass magazines of past decades have been replaced today by thousands of magazines targeting special-interest audiences. HFM alone publishes more than 20 specialty magazines—ranging from Women's Day and Elle to Car & Driver, Road & Track, Cycle World, and Popular Photography. Courtesy of Hachette Filipacchi Media U.S., Inc.

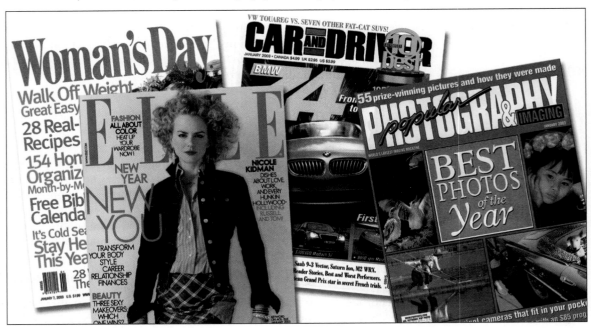

All too often, companies fail to integrate their various communications channels. The result is a hodgepodge of communications to consumers. Mass-media advertisements say one thing, a price promotion sends a different signal, a product label creates still another message, company sales literature says something altogether different, and the company's Web site seems out of sync with everything else.

The problem is that these communications often come from different company sources. Advertising messages are planned and implemented by the advertising department or advertising agency. Personal selling communications are developed by sales management. Other functional specialists are responsible for public relations, sales promotion, direct marketing, online sites, and other forms of marketing communications.

Recently, such functional separation has been a major problem for many companies and their Internet communications. Many companies first organized their new Web communications operations into separate groups or divisions, isolating them from mainstream marketing activities. However, whereas some companies have compartmentalized the new communications tools, customers won't. According to one IMC expert:

> The truth is, most [consumers] won't compartmentalize their use of the new systems. They won't say, "Hey, I'm going off to do a bit of Web surfing. Burn my TV, throw out all my radios, cancel all my magazine subscriptions and, by the way, take out my telephone and don't deliver any mail anymore." It's not that kind of world for consumers, and it shouldn't be that kind of world for marketers either.[3]

To be sure, the Internet promises exciting marketing communications potential. However, marketers trying to use the Web alone to build brands face many challenges. One limitation is that the Internet doesn't build mass brand awareness. Instead, it's like having millions of private conversations. The Web simply can't match the impact of the Super Bowl, where tens of millions of people see the same 30-second Nike or Hallmark ad at the same time. Using the Internet, it's hard to establish the universal meanings—such as "Just Do It!" or "When you care enough to send the very best"—that are at the heart of brand recognition and brand value.

Thus, if treated as a special case, the Internet—or any other marketing communication tool—can be a *dis*integrating force in marketing communications. Instead, all the communication tools must be carefully integrated into the broader marketing communications mix. Today, the best bet is to wed the emotional pitch and impact of traditional brand marketing with the interactivity and real service offered online. For example, television ads for Saturn still offer the same old-fashioned humorous appeal. But now they point viewers to the company's Web site, which offers lots of help and very little hype. The site helps serious car buyers select a model, calculate payments, and find a retailer online.

Even marketers that can't really sell their goods via the Web are using the Internet as an effective customer communication and relationship enhancer. For example, Harpo Enterprises, the company that oversees *The Oprah Winfrey Show,* also maintains a Web site (www.oprah.com) that offers in-depth information on show topics, access to footage taped after the live show ends, and a sneek peek at the content of upcoming issues of *O* magazine. The Web site, show, and magazine are all consistently designed. Says one analyst, the "consistency in design and tone makes the brand stronger because the consumer immediately recognizes the image, which engenders emotion and brand loyalty."[4]

In the past, no one person or department was responsible for thinking through the communication roles of the various promotion tools and coordinating the promotion mix. Today, however, more companies are adopting the concept of **integrated marketing communications (IMC)**. Under this concept, as illustrated in Figure 15.1, the company carefully integrates and coordinates its many communications channels to deliver a clear, consistent, and compelling message about the organization and its products.[5]

As one marketing executive puts it, "IMC builds a strong brand identity in the marketplace by tying together and reinforcing all your images and messages. IMC means that all your corporate messages, positioning and images, and identity are coordinated across all [marketing communications] venues. It means that your PR materials say the same thing as your direct-mail campaign, and your advertising has the same 'look and feel' as your Web site."[6]

IMC calls for recognizing all contact points where the customer may encounter the company, its products, and its brands. Each *brand contact* will deliver a message, whether good, bad, or indifferent. The company must strive to deliver a consistent and positive message at all contact points.

Integrated marketing communications (IMC)

The concept under which a company carefully integrates and coordinates its many communications channels to deliver a clear, consistent, and compelling message about the organization and its products.

Today, all the marketing communication tools must be carefully integrated. For example, Saturn's television and print ads help build brand appeal while the company's Web site helps serious car buyers select a model, calculate payments, and find a dealer online.

To help implement integrated marketing communications, some companies appoint a marketing communications director—or *marcom manager*—who has overall responsibility for the company's communications efforts. Integrated marketing communications produces better communications consistency and greater sales impact. It places the responsibility in someone's hands—where none existed before—to unify the company's image as it is shaped by thousands of company activities. It leads to a total marketing communication strategy aimed at showing how the company and its products can help customers solve their problems.

FIGURE 15.1
Integrated marketing communications

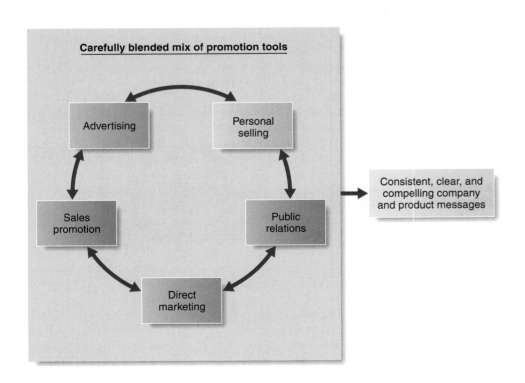

A View of the Communication Process

Integrated marketing communications involves identifying the target audience and shaping a well-coordinated promotional program to elicit the desired audience response. Too often, marketing communications focus on overcoming immediate awareness, image, or preference problems in the target market. But this approach to communication is too shortsighted. Today, marketers are moving toward viewing communications as *managing the customer relationship over time*. Because customers differ, communications programs need to be developed for specific segments, niches, and even individuals. And, given the new interactive communications technologies, companies must ask not only, "How can we reach our customers?" but also, "How can we find ways to let our customers reach us?"

Thus, the communications process should start with an audit of all the potential contacts target customers may have with the company and its brands. For example, someone purchasing a new computer may talk to others, see television ads, read articles and ads in newspapers and magazines, visit various Web sites, and try out computers in one or more stores. The marketer needs to assess what influence each of these communications experiences will have at different stages of the buying process. This understanding will help marketers allocate their communication dollars more efficiently and effectively.

To communicate effectively, marketers need to understand how communication works. Communication involves the nine elements shown in Figure 15.2. Two of these elements are the major parties in a communication—the *sender* and the *receiver*. Another two are the major communication tools—the *message* and the *media*. Four more are major communication functions—*encoding, decoding, response,* and *feedback*. The last element is *noise* in the system. Definitions of these elements follow and are applied to an ad for Hewlett-Packard (HP) color copiers.

- *Sender:* The *party sending the message* to another party—here, HP.
- *Encoding:* The process of *putting thought into symbolic form*—HP's advertising agency assembles words and illustrations into an advertisement that will convey the intended message.
- *Message:* The *set of symbols* that the sender transmits—the actual HP copier ad.
- *Media:* The *communication channels* through which the message moves from sender to receiver—in this case, the specific magazines that HP selects.
- *Decoding:* The process by which the receiver *assigns meaning to the symbols* encoded by the sender—a consumer reads the HP copier ad and interprets the words and illustrations it contains.
- *Receiver:* The *party receiving the message* sent by another party—the home office or business customer who reads the HP copier ad.

FIGURE 15.2
Elements in the communication process

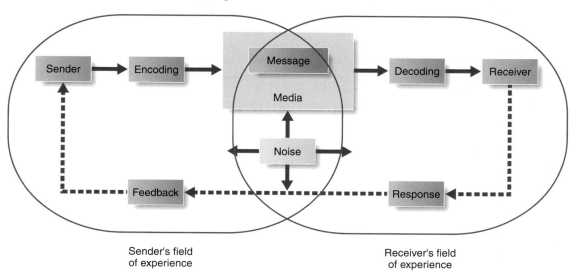

Sender's field
of experience

Receiver's field
of experience

- *Response:* The *reactions of the receiver* after being exposed to the message—any of hundreds of possible responses, such as the consumer is more aware of the attributes of HP copiers, actually buys an HP copier, or does nothing.
- *Feedback:* The part of the *receiver's response communicated back to the sender*—HP research shows that consumers are struck by and remember the ad, or consumers write or call HP praising or criticizing the ad or HP's products.
- *Noise:* The *unplanned static or distortion* during the communication process, which results in the receiver's getting a different message than the one the sender sent—the consumer is distracted while reading the magazine and misses the HP ad or its key points.

For a message to be effective, the sender's encoding process must mesh with the receiver's decoding process. Thus, the best messages consist of words and other symbols that are familiar to the receiver. The more the sender's field of experience overlaps with that of the receiver, the more effective the message is likely to be. Marketing communicators may not always *share* their consumer's field of experience. For example, an advertising copywriter from one social stratum might create ads for consumers from another stratum—say, blue-collar workers or wealthy business owners. However, to communicate effectively, the marketing communicator must *understand* the consumer's field of experience.

This model points out several key factors in good communication. Senders need to know what audiences they wish to reach and what responses they want. They must be good at encoding messages that take into account how the target audience decodes them. They must send messages through media that reach target audiences, and they must develop feedback channels so that they can assess the audience's response to the message.

Steps in Developing Effective Communication

We now examine the steps in developing an effective integrated communications and promotion program. The marketing communicator must do the following: identify the target audience, determine the communication objectives, design a message, choose the media through which to send the message, select the message source, and collect feedback.

Identifying the Target Audience

A marketing communicator starts with a clear target audience in mind. The audience may be potential buyers or current users, those who make the buying decision or those who influence it. The audience may be individuals, groups, special publics, or the general public. The target audience will heavily affect the communicator's decisions on *what* will be said, *how* it will be said, *when* it will be said, *where* it will be said, and *who* will say it.

Determining the Communication Objectives

Buyer-readiness stages

The stages consumers normally pass through on their way to purchase, including awareness, knowledge, liking, preference, conviction, and purchase.

Once the target audience has been defined, the marketing communicator must decide what response is sought. Of course, in many cases, the final response is *purchase.* But purchase is the result of a long process of consumer decision making. The marketing communicator needs to know where the target audience now stands and to what stage it needs to be moved. The target audience may be in any of six **buyer-readiness stages,** the stages consumers normally pass through on their way to making a purchase. These stages include *awareness, knowledge, liking, preference, conviction,* and *purchase* (see Figure 15.3).

FIGURE 15.3
Buyer-readiness stages

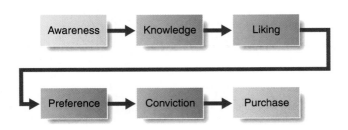

The marketing communicator's target market may be totally unaware of the product, know only its name, or know one or a few things about it. The communicator must first build *awareness* and *knowledge.* For example, when Nissan introduced its Infiniti automobile line, it began with an extensive "teaser" advertising campaign to create name familiarity. Initial ads for the Infiniti created curiosity and awareness by showing the car's name but not the car. Later ads created knowledge by informing potential buyers of the car's high quality and its many innovative features.

Assuming target consumers *know* the product, how do they *feel* about it? Once potential buyers knew about the Infiniti, Nissan's marketers wanted to move them through successively stronger stages of feelings toward the car. These stages included *liking* (feeling favorable about the Infiniti), *preference* (preferring Infiniti to other car brands), and *conviction* (believing that Infiniti is the best car for them). Infiniti marketers used a combination of the promotion mix tools to create positive feelings and conviction. Advertising extolled the Infiniti's advantages over competing brands and established its "Accelerating the Future" positioning. Press releases and other public relations activities stressed the car's innovative features and performance. Dealer salespeople told buyers about options, value for the price, and after-sale service.

Finally, some members of the target market might be convinced about the product, but not quite get around to making the *purchase.* Potential Infiniti buyers might have decided to wait for more information or for the economy to improve. The communicator must lead these consumers to take the final step. Actions might include offering special promotional prices, rebates, or premiums. Salespeople might call or write to selected customers, inviting them to visit the dealership for a special showing. The Infiniti Web site (www.infiniti.com) allows potential buyers to virtually build their own car, explains various financing options, and invites them to visit the local dealer's showroom.

Of course, marketing communications alone cannot create positive feelings and purchases for Infiniti. The car itself must provide superior value for the customer. In fact, outstanding marketing communications can actually speed the demise of a poor product. The more quickly potential buyers learn about the poor product, the more quickly they become aware of its faults. Thus, good marketing communication calls for "good deeds followed by good words."

Designing a Message

Having defined the desired audience response, the communicator turns to developing an effective message. Ideally, the message should get *Attention,* hold *Interest,* arouse *Desire,* and obtain *Action* (a framework known as the *AIDA model*). In practice, few messages take the consumer all the way from awareness to purchase, but the AIDA framework suggests the desirable qualities of a good message.

In putting the message together, the marketing communicator must decide what to say (*message content*) and how to say it (*message structure* and *format*).

Message Content

The communicator has to figure out an appeal or theme that will produce the desired response. There are three types of appeals: rational, emotional, and moral. *Rational appeals* relate to the audience's self-interest. They show that the product will produce the desired benefits. Examples are messages showing a product's quality, economy, value, or performance. Thus, in its ads, Mercedes offers automobiles that are "engineered like no other car in the world," stressing engineering design, performance, and safety.

Emotional appeals attempt to stir up either negative or positive emotions that can motivate purchase. Communicators may use positive emotional appeals such as love, pride, joy, and humor. For example, advocates for humorous messages claim that they attract more attention and create more liking and belief in the sponsor. In a recent RoperASW survey, Americans picked humor as their favorite ad approach, with 85 percent saying they like ads with humorous themes. These days, it seems as though almost every company is using humor in its advertising, from consumer product firms such as Anheuser-Busch and Levi-Strauss, to high tech product and service marketers such as Dell and Computer Associates, to the scholarly American Heritage Dictionary. Other favorite emotional themes in the post–September 11, 2001, era include such reassuring

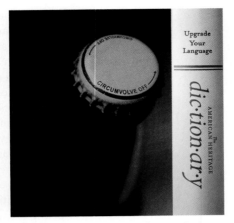

Humor in advertising: These days, it seems as though almost every company is using humor in its advertising, even the scholarly American Heritage Dictionary.

ones as "safety and security" (77 percent), "family closeness" (76 percent), "giving to others" (74 percent), "patriotism" (74 percent), and "optimism" (64 percent).[7]

Advertising in recent Super Bowls appears to reflect consumers' preferences for humor. E*Trade provides a great example:

> E*Trade has set itself apart from competitors and attracted traders by using humorous high-profile advertising. The star of the show: a chimpanzee! During the 2000 Super Bowl, E*Trade sponsored the halftime show and debuted a television spot that featured little more than the chimpanzee dancing on an oil drum and the tag line "We just wasted two million bucks. What are you doing with your money?" That year, E*Trade spent $522 million on marketing—or nearly 40 percent of revenues—and generated 1.7 million new accounts. The company followed the first Super Bowl success with another ad during the 2001 Super Bowl, starring the chimp on horseback, that poked fun at dot-com excesses and companies, such as Pets.com, that hadn't survived the bursting bubble. The ad earned high marks from critics and was selected by *Wall Street Journal online* users as the best Super Bowl ad. In 2002, E*Trade spent $10 million more on the Super Bowl, including a very funny ad in which the chimp was "fired" for the poor performance of an imaginary Super Sunday musical extravaganza to promote the fact that company was now more than just online trading. The ad walked away with *Advertising Age*'s Best Ad of the Year award for financial services for the second year running.[8]

Properly used, humor can capture attention, make people feel good, and give a brand personality. However, the advertiser must be careful when using humor. Used poorly, it can detract from comprehension, wear out its welcome fast, overshadow the product, or even irritate consumers. Take this example:

> Recent Domino's pizza ads featured a character named Bad Andy, a blue critter who looked like a cross between a monkey and a rat. Bad Andy was shown to live in the back of a Domino's Pizza store, and his voracious appetite muddled up the store's operations. Unfortunately, the attempt at humor sputtered. Despite the comic possibilities, the ads did little to highlight the quality of Domino's pizza or service, and Bad Andy's cavorting was more irritating than endearing. Bad Andy was annoying. He was obnoxious. "Bad Andy got some of the highest dislikability ratings of any spokescharacter in the history of advertising," admits a Domino's marketing executive. "Sales didn't respond." Besides, the notion of a squirrel-like animal being holed up in the back of a pizza joint was unappetizing to say the least.[9]

Communicators can also use negative emotional appeals, such as fear, guilt, and shame in order to get people to do things they should (brush their teeth, buy new tires) or to stop doing things they shouldn't (smoke, drink too much, eat fatty foods). For example, a Crest ad invokes mild fear when it claims, "There are some things you just can't afford to gamble with" (cavities). Etonic ads ask, "What would you do if you couldn't run?" They go on to note that Etonic athletic shoes are designed to avoid injuries—they're "built so you can last." The American Academy of Dermatology advertises, "One in every five Americans will develop skin cancer. Don't be the one."

Moral appeals are directed to the audience's sense of what is "right" and "proper." They are often used to urge people to support social causes such as a cleaner environment, better race relations, equal rights for women, and aid to the disadvantaged. An example of a moral appeal is the March of Dimes appeal "God made you whole. Give to help those He didn't."

Message Structure

The communicator must also decide how to handle three message-structure issues. The first is whether to draw a conclusion or leave it to the audience. Early research showed that drawing a conclusion was usually more effective. More recent research, however, suggests that in many cases the advertiser is better off asking questions and letting buyers come to their own conclusions. The second message-structure issue is whether to present a one-sided argument (mentioning only the product's strengths) or a two-sided argument (touting the product's strengths while also admitting its shortcomings). Usually, a one-sided argument is more effective in sales presentations—except when audiences are highly educated or likely to hear opposing claims, or when the communicator has a negative association to overcome. In this spirit, Heinz ran the message "Heinz Ketchup is slow good" and Listerine ran the message "Listerine tastes bad twice a day." In such cases, two-sided messages can enhance the advertiser's credibility and make buyers more resistant to competitor attacks. The third message-structure issue is whether to present the strongest arguments first or last. Presenting them first gets strong attention but may lead to an anticlimactic ending.

Message Format

The marketing communicator also needs a strong *format* for the message. In a print ad, the communicator has to decide on the headline, copy, illustration, and color. To attract attention, advertisers can use novelty and contrast; eye-catching pictures and headlines; distinctive formats; message size and position; and color, shape, and movement. If the message is to be carried over the radio, the communicator has to choose words, sounds, and voices. The "sound" of an announcer promoting banking services should be different from one promoting quality furniture.

If the message is to be carried on television or in person, then all these elements plus body language have to be planned. Presenters plan their facial expressions, gestures, dress, posture, and hairstyle. If the message is carried on the product or its package, the communicator has to watch texture, scent, color, size, and shape. For example, age and other demographics affect the way in which consumers perceive and react to color. Here are examples:

How do you sell margarine—stodgy, wholesome margarine—to today's kids? One answer: color. "We knew we wanted to introduce a color product. It's been a big trend with kids since the blue M&M," says a Parkay spokesperson. So Parkay tried out margarine in blue, pink, green, and purple. "When we tested four different colors in focus groups, kids had a blast." Electric blue and shocking pink margarine emerged as clear favorites. Similarly, when Landor Associates remade Yoo-Hoo a few years back, color proved to be the way to win teen boys. The brand, packaged in a clear glass bottle with a yellow wraparound label, was languishing. To give it a jump start, the company reworked the package completely, introducing an oversized logo and coloring the bottle itself with a punched-up yellow. "When the whole bottle went yellow, they loved it," says a Yoo-Hoo marketer. Finally, as we get older, our eyes mature and our vision takes on a yellow cast. Color looks less bright to older people, so they gravitate to white and other bright tones. A recent survey found 10 percent of people 55 years and older want the brightness of a white car, compared with 4 percent of 21-to-34-year-olds and 2 percent of teens. Lexus, which skews toward older buyers, makes sure that 60 percent of its cars are light in color.[10]

Thus, in designing effective marketing communications, marketers must consider color and other seemingly unimportant details carefully.

Message format: To attract attention, advertisers can use distinctive formats, novelty, and eye-catching pictures, as in this award-winning Volkswagen ad.

Drivers wanted. VW

Choosing Media

The communicator now must select *channels of communication*. There are two broad types of communication channels—*personal* and *nonpersonal*.

Personal Communication Channels

Personal communication channels

Channels through which two or more people communicate directly with each other, including face to face, person to audience, over the telephone, or through the mail.

Word-of-mouth influence

Personal communication about a product between target buyers and neighbors, friends, family members, and associates.

Buzz marketing

Cultivating opinion leaders and getting them to spread information about a product or service to others in their communities.

In **personal communication channels,** two or more people communicate directly with each other. They might communicate face-to-face, over the telephone, through the mail, or even through an Internet "chat." Personal communication channels are effective because they allow for personal addressing and feedback.

Some personal communication channels are controlled directly by the company. For example, company salespeople contact buyers in the target market. But other personal communications about the product may reach buyers through channels not directly controlled by the company. These might include independent experts—consumer advocates, consumer buying guides, and others—making statements to target buyers. Or they might be neighbors, friends, family members, and associates talking to target buyers. This last channel, known as **word-of-mouth influence,** has considerable effect in many product areas.

Personal influence carries great weight for products that are expensive, risky, or highly visible. For example, buyers of automobiles and major appliances often go beyond mass-media sources to seek the opinions of knowledgeable people.

Companies can take steps to put personal communication channels to work for them. For example, they can create *opinion leaders*—people whose opinions are sought by others—by supplying influential people with the product on attractive terms. **Buzz marketing** involves cultivating opinion leaders and getting them to spread information about a product or service to others in their communities (see Real Marketing 15.1). BMW used buzz marketing to kick-start demand for its new retro-style Mini Cooper sedan:

The Mini USA unit of BMW of North America is bucking car-advertising tradition by using unconventional tactics to create a buzz for its retro-looking Mini Cooper. To launch the return of the diminutive British-made sedan, "we wanted to be as different as we could

real marketing 15.1

Buzz Marketing: A Powerful New Way to Spread the Word

These days, buzz marketing is all the rage. Buzz marketing involves cultivating opinion leaders and getting them to spread information about a product or service to others in their communities. "In a successful buzz-marketing campaign, each carefully cultivated recipient of the brand message becomes a powerful carrier, spreading the word to yet more carriers, much as a virus rampages through a given population," says one expert. "Firms don't 'do' [buzz] marketing: It's done to you," says another. Companies of all kinds—from Procter & Gamble, Hebrew National, and Hasbro Games to Ford, Vespa, and IBM—are now using buzz marketing as a new way to connect with hard-to-reach consumers.

Why the new trend? For starters, buzz marketing is cheap. It's a great way to extend brand exposure without blowing out the marketing budget. Buzz marketing's increasing popularity can also be attributed to bur-

roots opinion leaders who are far removed from corporate America.

Perhaps the single most important reason that marketers are employing buzz marketing is that it really works. Consider the following examples.

Lee Dungarees: In recent years, Lee had managed to reenergize the image of its stodgy Lee jeans brand among younger target consumers—mostly young males 17 to 22. But it needed to do more to convert that cooler image into sales at teen-toxic retailers like J.C. Penney and Sears Roebuck, its biggest outlets. So Lee came up with one of the most freewheeling and influential buzz-marketing campaigns to date. The campaign played on target consumers' weakness for video games and computers. First, Lee developed a list of 200,000 "influential" guys from a list of Web surfers. It then zapped them a trio of grainy video clips that were hilarious in their appar-

actually were abetting in a marketing campaign orchestrated by Lee. According to Lee research, the "stupid little films" were so intriguing that, on average, recipients forwarded them to six friends apiece. Despite virtually no advertising, some 100,000 visitors stormed the fictional filmmakers' Web sites the week they went live, crashing the server. The marketing connection only became clear a few months later, after a TV and radio ad blitz finally revealed the three characters to be fictional antagonists developed as part of an online computer game. And that was a key to the program: To play the game at an advanced level, participants had to snag the product identification numbers—the "secret code"—off Lee items, which of course required a visit to a store. Ultimately, the effort drove thousands of kids age 17 to 22 into the stores and helped propel Lee sales upward by 20 percent last year.

Listerine PocketPaks: Pfizer Consumer Healthcare recently launched the $20 million TV ad portion of its marketing effort behind Listerine PocketPaks. But that wasn't what turned Karen Tennant into a consumer of the tiny, portable mouthwash strips that melt on your tongue. Her middle-school-age daughter had already heard about them from a friend. The friend had heard about them from her dad, owner of an independent pharmacy. The dad had received a case of trial-size PocketPaks he'd never ordered, along with a bill. Intrigued, he put the packs on display. They sold out almost immediately, generating a voluntary reorder. That's just one of dozens of ways Pfizer generated buzz about Listerine PocketPaks, even before the big TV push and a parallel online media effort. Pfizer used an elaborate array of buzz-building efforts, including professional marketing through dentists, sampling through college campus welcome packs, publicity efforts, prominent placement on such retailer Web sites as Kroger.com and RiteAid.com, and an online game at PocketPaks.com. The Listerine PocketPaks "Germinator" game includes a pass-along feature that's part of the buzz-marketing effort, encouraging players to e-mail scores to friends to get them to play. Pfizer estimates that PocketPak sales will exceed $100 million in the first 12 months.

Pfizer used an elaborate array of buzz-building efforts for Listerine Pocketpaks. It's "Germinator" game includes a pass-along feature that encourages players to e-mail scores to friends to get them to play.

geoning Internet usage. Marketers can now use the Web to reach large numbers of consumers, particularly trend leaders, quickly and easily. Finally, buzz marketing provides a nonadvertising alternative for reaching the growing ranks of skeptical consumers—such as twenty-somethings—who are notoriously disdainful of mass-media advertising. Instead of the usual ad pitches, buzz marketing spreads the word through grass-

ent stupidity. The videos appeared to be ultra-low-budget flicks meant to draw visitors to the Web game sites of amateur filmmakers, such as open-shirted Curry, a 23-year-old race car driver. To the young Web surfers who received them, the clips seemed like delicious examples of the oddball digital debris that litters the Web. So not many of the recipients who eagerly forwarded the flicks to their friends would have guessed that they

(continued)

Ford Focus: Building a successful buzz campaign hinges on finding the right message carriers—influencers who are obsessed with staying one step ahead of their peers. That was Ford's strategy last year when it set out to turn a new generation of buyers on to its new $13,000 subcompact, the Ford Focus. Ford marketers figured a word-of-mouth foray might position the Focus as a hip, young person's car and help it win the "buzz war" against the small-car-market leader, the Honda Civic. To kick-start the buzz, Ford tapped New York youth marketing boutique Fusion Five to help it identify 120 influential young consumers in five key markets: New York, Miami, Los Angeles, Chicago, and San Francisco. Each of the 120 people was given a Focus to drive for six months. The ploy worked on Joe Regner, a 21-year-old operations engineer in Miami. Regner spotted a yellow Focus in the parking lot as he cruised by hip-hop radio station WEDR 99 Jamz. He pulled over to get a closer look. It turned out to be a loaner to Jill Tracey, one of Regner's favorite deejays. "It was so cool, I took pictures and really checked it out," he says. While waiting to order a special, high-performance version of the Focus called the SVT that's due out this fall, Regner persuaded his girlfriend, Eli Dominguez, a legal assistant, to scrap her plans to buy a Civic in favor of a

Focus ZX3. With enthusiasts like Regner as an unpaid sales force, Ford was able to get the Focus off to a brisk start, selling 286,166 units in its first full year—even outselling the Civic in some months.

Not all companies have had such success with buzz marketing. In fact, the practice can be risky. If consumers catch on or get the wrong impression, the results can be disastrous.

Sony Pictures Entertainment generated the kind of publicity you'd like to avoid when a couple of recent buzz strategies backfired. First, it turned out that Sony had fabricated quotes from a fictitious film critic praising movies such as *Vertical Limit* and *The Animal.* Soon after, two supposed moviegoers who gushed about *The Patriot* in Sony commercials were unmasked as studio employees. Rather than delighting or surprising, the ham-handed efforts merely confirmed consumers' worst suspicions about marketers. "It can turn into a horrible public-relations nightmare if it turns out you're deceiving people," says one research analyst.

Still, when done correctly, buzz marketing can generate amazing results. For

products that meet real needs with innovative or stylish designs, the positive word travels fast. Notes one global marketing executive, "Finding a revolutionary new way to market an established brand doesn't work unless it's grounded in the product truth. . . . Great marketing is simply a megaphone for the truth, and when the 'buzz' is true it delivers unconventional messages very effectively to unconventional audiences."

Sources: Excerpts adapted from Gerry Khermouch and Jeff Green, "Buzz Marketing, *Business Week,* July 30, 2001, pp. 50–56; Jack Neff, "Building the Buzz for PocketPaks," *Advertising Age,* December 3, 2001, pp. 4, 42; and Micheline Maynard, "Even Cars Need to Make a Good First Impression," *New York Times,* March 8, 2002, p. F1. Also see James C. Schroer, "The Ultimate Buzz," *Marketing Management,* September–October 2001, p. 56; John Brandt, "Beware of Bad Buzz," *Chief Executive,* November 2001, p. 12; Laura Mazur, "Firms Can't 'Do' Viral Marketing: It Is Done to You," *Marketing,* June 27, 2002, p. 16; and Kathryn Shattuck, "Mouthwash Without a Bottle," *New York Times,* July 2002, p. 3.2.

because the car is so different from anything out there," says a Mini marketer. As a result, there is no national television advertising. Instead, BMW has generated buzz for the Mini in less conventional ways. For example, the "Mini Ride" display touring the United States, which includes an actual Mini, looks like a children's ride. "Rides $16,850. Quarters only," the sign says. The car is also being promoted on the Internet, in ads painted on city buildings, and on baseball-type cards handed out at auto shows. To intrigue passersby, BMW put Minis on top of sport utilities and drove them around 24 cities. In addition, BMW is selling unusual Mini-brand items—including remote-control cars, watches, and cuckoo clocks—on its Web site. The nation's 70 dealers—top BMW dealers who agreed to build separate Mini showrooms—have been deluged with orders, practically assuring that the 20,000 cars available in the United States will quickly be sold. More than 50,000 people have expressed interest in buying the car by registering at www.miniusa.com. And that interest was built from the ground up through buzz marketing. Only three years ago, only 2 percent of Americans had ever even heard of the original Mini.[11]

Nonpersonal Communication Channels

Nonpersonal communication channels
Media that carry messages without personal contact or feedback, including major media, atmospheres, and events.

Nonpersonal communication channels are media that carry messages without personal contact or feedback. They include major media, atmospheres, and events. Major *media* include print media (newspapers, magazines, direct mail), broadcast media (radio, television), display media (billboards, signs, posters), and online media (online services, Web sites). *Atmospheres* are designed environments that create or reinforce the buyer's leanings toward buying a product. Thus, lawyers' offices and banks are designed to communicate confidence and other qualities that might be valued by their clients. *Events* are staged occurrences that communicate messages to target audiences. For example, public relations departments arrange press conferences, grand openings, shows and exhibits, public tours, and other events.

Marketers hire celebrity endorsers to deliver their messages. Mia Hamm and Tiger Woods speak for Nike. NASCAR superstar Jeff Gordon pitches everything from Ray-Ban sun glasses to Pepsi and Edy's ice cream.

Nonpersonal communication affects buyers directly. In addition, using mass media often affects buyers indirectly by causing more personal communication. Communications first flow from television, magazines, and other mass media to opinion leaders and then from these opinion leaders to others. Thus, opinion leaders step between the mass media and their audiences and carry messages to people who are less exposed to media. This suggests that mass communicators should aim their messages directly at opinion leaders, letting them carry the message to others.

Selecting the Message Source

In either personal or nonpersonal communication, the message's impact on the target audience is also affected by how the audience views the communicator. Messages delivered by highly credible sources are more persuasive. Thus, many food companies promote to doctors, dentists, and other health care providers to motivate these professionals to recommend their products to patients. And marketers hire celebrity endorsers—well-known athletes, actors, and even cartoon characters—to deliver their messages. Tiger Woods speaks for Nike, Buick, and a dozen other brands. NASCAR superstar Jeff Gordon pitches everything from Ray-Ban sun glasses to Pepsi and Edy's ice cream. And soccer star Mia Hamm stands behind Gatorade, Nike, Disney, and Wheaties.

But companies must be careful when selecting celebrities to represent their brands. Picking the wrong spokesperson can result in embarrassment and a tarnished image. Hertz found this out when it entrusted its good name to the care of O.J. Simpson. Pepsi and Kodak faced similar embarrassment when their spokesperson, boxer Mike Tyson, was accused of beating his wife and was later jailed for rape. More recently, NBA star Allen Iverson was arrested for breaking into an apartment while brandishing a gun, forcing Reebok to reconsider ads featuring the basketball star.

Collecting Feedback

After sending the message, the communicator must research its effect on the target audience. This involves asking the target audience members whether they remember the message, how many times they saw it, what points they recall, how they felt about the message, and their past and present attitudes toward the product and company. The communicator would also like to measure behavior resulting from the message—how many people bought a product, talked to others about it, or visited the store.

Feedback on marketing communications may suggest changes in the promotion program or in the product offer itself. For example, American Airlines uses television and newspaper advertising to inform area consumers about the airline, its routes, and its fares. Suppose feedback research shows that 80 percent of all fliers in an area recall seeing the airline's ads and are aware of its flights and prices. Sixty percent of these aware fliers have flown American, but only 20 percent of those who tried it were satisfied. These results suggest that although promotion is creating *awareness,* the airline isn't giving consumers the *satisfaction* they expect. Therefore, American needs to improve its service while staying with the successful communication program. In contrast, suppose the research shows that only 40 percent of area consumers are aware of the airline, only 30 percent of those aware have tried it, but 80 percent of those who have tried it return. In this case, American needs to strengthen its promotion program to take advantage of its power to create customer satisfaction.

Setting the Total Promotion Budget and Mix

We have looked at the steps in planning and sending communications to a target audience. But how does the company decide on the total *promotion budget* and its division among the major promotional tools to create the *promotion mix?* By what process does it blend the tools to create integrated marketing communications? We now look at these questions.

Setting the Total Promotion Budget

One of the hardest marketing decisions facing a company is how much to spend on promotion. John Wanamaker, the department store magnate, once said, "I know that half of my advertising is wasted, but I don't know which half. I spent $2 million for advertising, and I don't know if that is half enough or twice too much." Thus, it is not surprising that industries and companies vary widely in how much they spend on promotion. Promotion spending may be 20 to 30 percent of sales in the cosmetics industry and only 2 or 3 percent in the industrial machinery industry. Within a given industry, both low and high spenders can be found.[12]

How does a company decide on its promotion budget? We look at four common methods used to set the total budget for advertising: the *affordable method,* the *percentage-of-sales method,* the *competitive-parity method,* and the *objective-and-task method.*[13]

Affordable Method

Affordable method

Setting the promotion budget at the level management thinks the company can afford.

Some companies use the **affordable method:** They set the promotion budget at the level they think the company can afford. Small businesses often use this method, reasoning that the company cannot spend more on advertising than it has. They start with total revenues, deduct operating expenses and capital outlays, and then devote some portion of the remaining funds to advertising.

Unfortunately, this method of setting budgets completely ignores the effects of promotion on sales. It tends to place advertising last among spending priorities, even in situations in which advertising is critical to the firm's success. It leads to an uncertain annual promotion budget, which makes long-range market planning difficult. Although the affordable method can result in overspending on advertising, it more often results in underspending.

Percentage-of-Sales Method

Percentage-of-sales method

Setting the promotion budget at a certain percentage of current or forecasted sales or as a percentage of the unit sales price.

Other companies use the **percentage-of-sales method,** setting their promotion budget at a certain percentage of current or forecasted sales. Or they budget a percentage of the unit sales price. The percentage-of-sales method has advantages. It is simple to use and helps management think about the relationships between promotion spending, selling price, and profit per unit.

Despite these claimed advantages, however, the percentage-of-sales method has little to justify it. It wrongly views sales as the *cause* of promotion rather than as the *result.* "A study in this area found good correlation between investments in advertising and the strength of the brands concerned—but it turned out to be effect and cause, not cause and effect. . . . The strongest brands had the highest sales and could afford the biggest investments in advertising!"[14] Thus, the percentage-of-sales budget is based on availability of funds rather than on opportunities. It may prevent the increased spending sometimes needed to turn around falling sales. Because the budget varies with year-to-year sales, long-range planning is difficult. Finally, the method does not provide any basis for choosing a *specific* percentage, except what has been done in the past or what competitors are doing.

Competitive-Parity Method

Competitive-parity method
Setting the promotion budget to match competitors' outlays.

Still other companies use the **competitive-parity method,** setting their promotion budgets to match competitors' outlays. They monitor competitors' advertising or get industry promotion spending estimates from publications or trade associations, and then set their budgets based on the industry average.

Two arguments support this method. First, competitors' budgets represent the collective wisdom of the industry. Second, spending what competitors spend helps prevent promotion wars. Unfortunately, neither argument is valid. There are no grounds for believing that the competition has a better idea of what a company should be spending on promotion than does the company itself. Companies differ greatly, and each has its own special promotion needs. Finally, there is no evidence that budgets based on competitive parity prevent promotion wars.

Objective-and-Task Method

Objective-and-task method
Developing the promotion budget by (1) defining specific objectives; (2) determining the tasks that must be performed to achieve these objectives; and (3) estimating the costs of performing these tasks. The sum of these costs is the proposed promotion budget.

The most logical budget-setting method is the **objective-and-task method,** whereby the company sets its promotion budget based on what it wants to accomplish with promotion. This budgeting method entails (1) defining specific promotion objectives, (2) determining the tasks needed to achieve these objectives, and (3) estimating the costs of performing these tasks. The sum of these costs is the proposed promotion budget.

The objective-and-task method forces management to spell out its assumptions about the relationship between dollars spent and promotion results. But it is also the most difficult method to use. Often, it is hard to figure out which specific tasks will achieve specific objectives. For example, suppose Sony wants 95 percent awareness for its latest camcorder model during the six-month introductory period. What specific advertising messages and media schedules should Sony use to attain this objective? How much would these messages and media schedules cost? Sony management must consider such questions, even though they are hard to answer.

Setting the Overall Promotion Mix

The concept of integrated marketing communications suggests that the company must blend the promotion tools carefully into a coordinated *promotion mix.* But how does the company determine what mix of promotion tools it will use? Companies within the same industry differ greatly in the design of their promotion mixes. For example, Avon spends most of its promotion funds on personal selling and direct marketing, whereas Revlon spends heavily on consumer advertising. Hewlett-Packard relies on advertising and promotion to retailers when marketing personal computers, whereas Dell Computer uses only direct marketing. We now look at factors that influence the marketer's choice of promotion tools.

Promotion mix: Companies within the same industry may use different mixes. Avon relies heavily on personal selling and direct marketing; Revlon devotes significant resources to advertising.

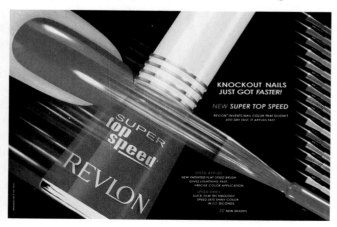

The Nature of Each Promotion Tool

Each promotion tool has unique characteristics and costs. Marketers must understand these characteristics in selecting their mix of tools.

Advertising.   Advertising can reach masses of geographically dispersed buyers at a low cost per exposure, and it enables the seller to repeat a message many times. For example, television advertising can reach huge audiences. An estimated 120 million to 130 million Americans tuned in to at least part of the most recent Super Bowl, more than 72 million people watched at least part of the last Academy Awards broadcast, and nearly 52 million watched the final episode of the first *Survivor* series. "If you want to get to the mass audience," says a media services executive, "broadcast TV is where you have to be." He adds, "For anybody introducing anything who has to lasso audience in a hurry—a new product, a new campaign, a new movie—the networks are still the biggest show in town."[15]

Beyond its reach, large-scale advertising says something positive about the seller's size, popularity, and success. Because of advertising's public nature, consumers tend to view advertised products as more legitimate. Advertising is also very expressive—it allows the company to dramatize its products through the artful use of visuals, print, sound, and color. On the one hand, advertising can be used to build up a long-term image for a product (such as Coca-Cola ads). On the other hand, advertising can trigger quick sales (as when Sears advertises a weekend sale).

Advertising also has some shortcomings. Although it reaches many people quickly, advertising is impersonal and cannot be as directly persuasive as can company salespeople. For the most part, advertising can carry on only a one-way communication with the audience, and the audience does not feel that it has to pay attention or respond. In addition, advertising can be very costly. Although some advertising forms, such as newspaper and radio advertising, can be done on smaller budgets, other forms, such as network TV advertising, require very large budgets.

Personal Selling.   Personal selling is the most effective tool at certain stages of the buying process, particularly in building up buyers' preferences, convictions, and actions. It involves personal interaction between two or more people, so each person can observe the other's needs and characteristics and make quick adjustments. Personal selling also allows all kinds of relationships to spring up, ranging from a matter-of-fact selling relationship to personal friendship. The effective salesperson keeps the customer's interests at heart in order to build a long-term relationship. Finally, with personal selling, the buyer usually feels a greater need to listen and respond, even if the response is a polite "No thank you."

These unique qualities come at a cost, however. A sales force requires a longer-term commitment than does advertising—advertising can be turned on and off, but sales force size is harder to change. Personal selling is also the company's most expensive promotion tool, costing companies $170 on average per sales call.[16] U.S. firms spend up to three times as much on personal selling as they do on advertising.

Sales Promotion.   Sales promotion includes a wide assortment of tools—coupons, contests, cents-off deals, premiums, and others—all of which have many unique qualities. They attract consumer attention, offer strong incentives to purchase, and can be used to dramatize product offers and to boost sagging sales. Sales promotions invite and reward quick response—whereas advertising says, "Buy our product," sales promotion says, "Buy it now." Sales promotion effects are often short-lived, however, and often are not as effective as advertising or personal selling in building long-run brand preference.

Public Relations.   Public relations is very believable—news stories, features, sponsorships, and events seem more real and believable to readers than ads do. Public relations can also reach many prospects who avoid salespeople and advertisements—the message gets to the buyers as "news" rather than as a sales-directed communication. And, as with advertising, public relations can dramatize a company or product. Marketers tend to underuse public relations or to use it as an afterthought. Yet a well-thought-out public relations campaign used with other promotion mix elements can be very effective and economical.

Direct Marketing.   Although there are many forms of direct marketing—telephone marketing, direct mail, online marketing, and others—they all share four distinctive characteristics. Direct

FIGURE 15.4
Push versus pull promotion strategy

marketing is *nonpublic:* The message is normally directed to a specific person. Direct marketing is *immediate* and *customized:* Messages can be prepared very quickly and can be tailored to appeal to specific consumers. Finally, direct marketing is *interactive:* It allows a dialogue between the marketing team and the consumer, and messages can be altered depending on the consumer's response. Thus, direct marketing is well suited to highly targeted marketing efforts and to building one-to-one customer relationships.

Promotion Mix Strategies

Marketers can choose from two basic promotion mix strategies—*push* promotion or *pull* promotion. Figure 15.4 contrasts the two strategies. The relative emphasis on the specific promotion tools differs for push and pull strategies. A **push strategy** involves "pushing" the product through distribution channels to final consumers. The producer directs its marketing activities (primarily personal selling and trade promotion) toward channel members to induce them to carry the product and to promote it to final consumers. Using a **pull strategy,** the producer directs its marketing activities (primarily advertising and consumer promotion) toward final consumers to induce them to buy the product. If the pull strategy is effective, consumers will then demand the product from channel members, who will in turn demand it from producers. Thus, under a pull strategy, consumer demand "pulls" the product through the channels.

Some industrial goods companies use only push strategies; some direct-marketing companies use only pull. However, most large companies use some combination of both. For example, Kraft uses mass-media advertising and consumer promotions to pull its products and a large sales force and trade promotions to push its products through the channels. In recent years, consumer goods companies have been decreasing the pull portions of their mixes in favor of more push. This has caused concern that they may be driving short-run sales at the expense of long-term brand equity (see Real Marketing 15.2).

Companies consider many factors when designing their promotion mix strategies, including *type of product/market* and the *product life-cycle stage.* For example, the importance of different promotion tools varies between consumer and business markets. B2C companies usually "pull" more, putting more of their funds into advertising, followed by sales promotion, personal selling, and then public relations. In contrast, B2B marketers tend to "push" more, putting more of their funds into personal selling, followed by sales promotion, advertising, and public relations. In general, personal selling is used more heavily with expensive and risky goods and in markets with fewer and larger sellers.

The effects of different promotion tools also vary with stages of the product life cycle. In the introduction stage, advertising and public relations are good for producing high awareness, and sales promotion is useful in promoting early trial. Personal selling must be used to get the trade to carry the product. In the growth stage, advertising and public relations

Push strategy

A promotion strategy that calls for using the sales force and trade promotion to push the product through channels. The producer promotes the product to wholesalers, the wholesalers promote to retailers, and the retailers promote to consumers.

Pull strategy

A promotion strategy that calls for spending a lot on advertising and consumer promotion to build up consumer demand. If the strategy is successful, consumers will ask their retailers for the product, the retailers will ask the wholesalers, and the wholesalers will ask the producers.

real marketing 15.2

Are Consumer Goods Companies Getting Too Pushy?

Consumer packaged-goods companies such as Kraft, Procter & Gamble, Kellogg, General Mills, and Gillette grew into giants by using mostly pull promotion strategies. They used massive doses of national advertising to differentiate their products, gain market share, and build brand equity and customer loyalty. But during the past few decades, these companies have gotten more "pushy," deem-

Today's food marketers are using more and more push promotion, including consumer price promotions. But they must be careful that they don't win the battle for short-run sales at the expense of long-run brand equity.

phasizing national advertising and putting more of their marketing budgets into trade and consumer sales promotions.

General trade promotions (trade allowances, displays, cooperative advertising, slotting fees) now account for 49 percent of total marketing spending by consumer product companies. Another 10 percent of the marketing budget goes to the trade in the form of "account-specific" marketing expenditures—promotional spending personalized to the

local needs of a specific retail chain that backs both the brand and the retailer. The total of 59 percent represents a seven-percentage-point increase in trade spending in just the past five years. Consumer promotions (coupons, cents-off deals, premiums) account for another 17 percent of the typical marketing budget. That leaves less than 24 percent of total marketing spending for mass-media advertising, down from 42 percent 20 years ago.

Why have these companies shifted so heavily toward push strategies? One reason is that mass-media campaigns have become more expensive and less effective in recent years. Network television costs have risen sharply while audiences have fallen off, making national advertising less cost-effective. Companies have also increased their market segmentation efforts and are now tailoring their marketing programs more narrowly, making national advertising less suitable than localized retailer promotions. And in these days of brand extensions and me-too products, companies sometimes have trouble finding meaningful product differences to feature in advertising. So they have differentiated their products through price reductions, premium offers, coupons, and other push techniques.

Another factor speeding the shift from pull to push has been the growing strength of retailers. Today's retailers are larger and have more access to product sales-and-profit information. Retail giants such as Kroger, Safeway, A&P, and Wal-Mart now have the power to demand and get what they want—

and what they want is more push. Whereas national advertising bypasses them on its way to the masses, push promotion benefits them directly. Consumer promotions give retailers an immediate sales boost, and cash from trade allowances and other trade promotions pads retailer profits. Thus, producers must often use push just to obtain good shelf space and advertising support from important retailers.

However, many marketers are concerned that the reckless use of push will lead to fierce price competition and a never-ending spiral of price slashing and deal making. This situation would mean lower margins, and companies would have less money to invest in the research and development, packaging, and advertising needed to improve products and maintain long-run consumer preference and loyalty.

If used improperly, push promotion can mortgage a brand's future for short-term gains. Sales promotion buys short-run reseller support and consumer sales, but advertising builds long-run brand equity and consumer preference. By robbing the media advertising budget to pay for more sales promotion, companies might win the battle for short-run earnings but lose the war for long-run brand equity, consumer loyalty, and market share. In fact, some analysts blame the shift away from advertising dollars for a recent two-decade-long drop in the percentage of consumers who buy only well-known brands.

Of special concern is the overuse of price promotions. The regular use of price as a selling tool can destroy brand equity by encouraging consumers to seek value though price rather than through the benefits of the brand. Many marketers are too quick to drive short-term sales by reducing prices rather than building long-term brand equity through advertising. In cases where price is a key part of the brand's positioning, featuring price makes sense. But for brands where price does not underlie value, "price promotions are really desperate acts by brands that have their backs against the wall," says one marketing executive. "Generally speaking, it is better to stick to your guns with price and invest in advertising to drive sales."

Jack Trout, a well-known marketing consultant, cautions that some categories tend to self-destruct by always being on sale. Discount pricing has become routine for a surprising number of companies. Furniture, automobile tires, and many other categories of goods are rarely sold at anything near list price, and when automakers get rebate happy, the market just sits back and waits for a deal. Even Coca-Cola and Pepsi, two of the world's most popular brands, engage in regular price wars that ultimately tarnish their brand equity. Trout offers several "Commandments of Discounting," such as "Thou shalt not offer discounts because everyone else does," "Thou shalt be creative with your discounting," "Thou shalt put time limits on the deal," and "Thou shalt stop discounting as soon as you can."

Many consumer companies now are rethinking their promotion strategies and reversing the trend by shifting their promotion budgets back toward advertising. Many have realized that it's not a question of sales promotion versus advertising, or of push versus pull. Success lies in finding the best mix of the two: consistent advertising to build long-run brand value and consumer preference, and sales promotion to create short-run trade support and consumer excitement. The company needs to blend both push and pull elements into an integrated promotion program that meets immediate consumer and retailer needs as well as long-run strategic needs.

Sources: Promotion spending statistics from *2002 Trade Promotion Spending & Merchandising Industry Study,* Cannondale Associates, Wilton, Conn., May 2002, p. 13. Other information from Jack Trout, "Prices: Simple Guidelines to Get Them Right," *Journal of Business Strategy,* November–December 1998, pp. 13–16; Tim Ambler, "Kicking Price Promotion Habit Is Like Getting Off Heroin—Hard," *Marketing,* May 27, 1999, p. 24; "Study: Trade Dollars Up," *Frozen Food Age,* September 2001, p. 14; and Robert Gray, "Driving Sales at Any Price," *Marketing,* April 11, 2002, pp. 24–25.

continue to be powerful influences, whereas sales promotion can be reduced because fewer incentives are needed. In the mature stage, sales promotion again becomes important relative to advertising. Buyers know the brands, and advertising is needed only to remind them of the product. In the decline stage, advertising is kept at a reminder level, public relations is dropped, and salespeople give the product only a little attention. Sales promotion, however, might continue strong.

Integrating the Promotion Mix

Having set the promotion budget and mix, the company must now take steps to see that all of the promotion mix elements are smoothly integrated. Here is a checklist for integrating the firm's marketing communications.[17]

- *Analyze trends—internal and external—that can affect your company's ability to do business.* Look for areas where communications can help the most. Determine the strengths and weaknesses of each communications function. Develop a combination of promotional tactics based on these strengths and weaknesses.

- *Audit the pockets of communications spending throughout the organization.* Itemize the communications budgets and tasks and consolidate these into a single budgeting process. Reassess all communications expenditures by product, promotional tool, stage of the life cycle, and observed effect.

- *Identify all contact points for the company and its brands.* Work to ensure that communications at each point are consistent with your overall communications strategy and that your communications efforts are occurring when, where, and how your *customers* want them.

- *Team up in communications planning.* Engage all communications functions in joint planning. Include customers, suppliers, and other stakeholders at every stage of communications planning.

- *Create compatible themes, tones, and quality across all communications media.* Make sure each element carries your unique primary messages and selling points. This consistency achieves greater impact and prevents the unnecessary duplication of work across functions.

- *Create performance measures that are shared by all communications elements.* Develop systems to evaluate the combined impact of all communications activities.

- *Appoint a director responsible for the company's persuasive communications efforts.* This move encourages efficiency by centralizing planning and creating shared performance measures.

Socially Responsible Marketing Communication

In shaping its promotion mix, a company must be aware of the large body of legal and ethical issues surrounding marketing communications. Most marketers work hard to communicate openly and honestly with consumers and resellers. Still, abuses may occur, and public policy makers have developed a substantial body of laws and regulations to govern advertising, sales promotion, personal selling, and direct-marketing activities. In this section, we discuss issues regarding advertising, sales promotion, and personal selling. Issues regarding direct marketing are addressed in Chapter 17.

Advertising and Sales Promotion

By law, companies must avoid false or deceptive advertising. Advertisers must not make false claims, such as suggesting that a product cures something when it does not. They must avoid ads that have the capacity to deceive, even though no one actually may be deceived. An automobile cannot be advertised as getting 32 miles per gallon unless it does so under typical conditions, and a diet bread cannot be advertised as having fewer calories simply because its slices are thinner.

Sellers must avoid bait-and-switch advertising that attracts buyers under false pretenses. For example, a large retailer advertised a sewing machine at $179. However, when consumers tried to buy the advertised machine, the seller downplayed its features, placed faulty machines on showroom floors, understated the machine's performance, and took other actions in an attempt to switch buyers to a more expensive machine. Such actions are both unethical and illegal.

A company's trade promotion activities also are closely regulated. For example, under the Robinson-Patman Act, sellers cannot favor certain customers through their use of trade promotions. They must make promotional allowances and services available to all resellers on proportionately equal terms.

Beyond simply avoiding legal pitfalls, such as deceptive or bait-and-switch advertising, companies can use advertising to encourage and promote socially responsible programs and actions. For example, State Farm has joined with the National Council for Social Studies, the National Science Teachers Association, and other national teachers' organizations to create a Good Neighbor Teacher Award to recognize primary and secondary teachers for innovation, leadership, and involvement in their profession. State Farm promotes the award through a series of print advertisements in magazines such as *Smithsonian, Parents, Reader's Digest, American Heritage, Family Fun, Business Today, Forbes,* and *National Geographic.* Similarly, Caterpillar is one of several companies and environmental groups forming the Tropical Forest Foundation, which is working to save the great Amazon rain forest. It uses advertising to promote the cause and its involvement.[18]

Personal Selling

A company's salespeople must follow the rules of "fair competition." Most states have enacted deceptive sales acts that spell out what is not allowed. For example, salespeople may not lie to consumers or mislead them about the advantages of buying a product. To avoid bait-and-switch practices, salespeople's statements must match advertising claims.

Different rules apply to consumers who are called on at home versus those who go to a store in search of a product. Because people called on at home may be taken by surprise and may be especially vulnerable to high-pressure selling techniques, the Federal Trade Commission (FTC) has adopted a *three-day cooling-off rule* to give special protection to customers who are not seeking products. Under this rule, customers who agree in their own homes to buy something costing more than $25 have 72 hours in which to cancel a contract or return merchandise and get their money back, no questions asked.

Much personal selling involves business-to-business trade. In selling to businesses, salespeople may not offer bribes to purchasing agents or to others who can influence a sale. They may not obtain or use technical or trade secrets of competitors through bribery or industrial espionage. Finally, salespeople must not disparage competitors or competing products by suggesting things that are not true.[19]

State Farm uses advertising to promote socially responsible programs and actions—here its Good Neighbor Teacher Award.

LOOKING BACK: REVIEWING THE CONCEPTS

Modern marketing calls for more than just developing a good product, pricing it attractively, and making it available to target customers. Companies also must *communicate* with current and prospective customers, and what they communicate should not be left to chance. For most companies, the question is not *whether* to communicate, but *how much to spend* and *in what ways.*

1. Name and define the tools of the marketing communications mix.

A company's total *marketing communications mix*—also called its *promotion mix*—consists of the specific blend of *advertising, personal selling, sales promotion, public relations,* and *direct-marketing tools* that the company uses to pursue its advertising and marketing objectives. Advertising includes any paid form of nonpersonal presentation and promotion of ideas, goods, or services by an identified sponsor. Personal selling is any form of personal presentation by the firm's sales force for the purpose of making sales and building customer relationships. Firms use sales promotion to provide short-term incentives to encourage the purchase or sale of a product or service. Public relations focuses on building good relations with the company's various publics by obtaining favorable unpaid publicity. Finally, firms seeking immediate response

from targeted individual customers use nonpersonal direct-marketing tools to communicate with customers.

2. Discuss the process and advantages of integrated marketing communications.

Recent shifts in marketing strategy from mass marketing to targeted or one-on-one marketing, coupled with advances in information technology, have had a dramatic impact on marketing communications. Although still important, the mass media are giving way to a profusion of smaller, more focused media. Companies are doing less *broadcasting* and more *narrowcasting.* As marketing communicators adopt richer but more fragmented media and promotion mixes to reach their diverse markets, they risk creating a communications hodgepodge for consumers. To prevent this, more companies are adopting the concept of *integrated marketing communications,* which calls for carefully integrating all sources of company communication to deliver a clear and consistent message to target markets.

To integrate its external communications effectively, the company must first integrate its internal communications activities. The company then works out the roles that the various promotional tools will play and the extent to which each will be used. It carefully coordinates the promotional activities and the timing of when major campaigns take place. Finally, to help implement its integrated marketing strategy, the company appoints a marketing communications director who has overall responsibility for the company's communications efforts.

3. Outline the steps in developing effective marketing communications.

In preparing marketing communications, the communicator's first task is to *identify the target audience* and its characteristics. Next, the communicator has to determine the *communication objectives* and define the response sought, whether it be *awareness, knowledge, liking, preference, conviction,* or *purchase.* Then a *message* should be constructed with an effective content and structure. *Media* must be selected, both for personal and nonpersonal communication. The communicator must find highly credible sources to deliver messages. Finally, the communicator must collect *feedback* by watching how much of the market becomes aware, tries the product, and is satisfied in the process.

4. Explain the methods for setting the promotion budget and factors that affect the design of the promotion mix.

The company has to decide how much to spend for promotion. The most popular approaches are to spend what the company can afford, to use a percentage of sales, to base promotion on competitors' spending, or to base it on an analysis and costing of the communication objectives and tasks.

The company has to divide the *promotion budget* among the major tools to create the *promotion mix.* Companies can pursue a *push* or a *pull* promotional strategy, or a combination of the two. The best specific blend of promotion tools depends on the type of product/market, the buyer's readiness stage, and the product life-cycle stage.

People at all levels of the organization must be aware of the many legal and ethical issues surrounding marketing communications. Companies must work hard and proactively at communicating openly, honestly, and agreeably with their customers and resellers.

REVIEWING THE KEY TERMS

Advertising 467
Affordable method 480
Buyer-readiness stages 472
Buzz marketing 476
Competitive-parity method 481
Direct marketing 467
Integrated marketing communications (IMC) 469

Marketing communications mix (promotion mix) 467
Nonpersonal communication channels 478
Objective-and-task method 481
Percentage-of-sales method 480
Personal communication channels 476
Personal selling 467

Public relations 467
Pull strategy 483
Push strategy 483
Sales promotion 467
Word-of-mouth influence 476

DISCUSSING THE CONCEPTS

1. A company's total marketing communications mix (promotion mix) is a blend of five major promotion tools. List and describe each of these promotional tools.
2. The shift from mass marketing to targeted marketing, and the corresponding use of a richer mixture of promotion tools and communication channels, poses problems for many marketers. Using all of the promotion mix elements suggested in the chapter, propose a plan for integrating marketing communications at *one* of the following: (a) your university or college, (b) Wendy's restaurants (www.wendys.com), (c) Burton Snowboards (www.burton.com), or (d) a local zoo, museum, theater, or civic event.
3. The Internet promises exciting marketing communications potential. However, when mismanaged, the Internet can also serve as a disintegrating force in marketing communications. Explain. How can disintegration be avoided?
4. Using Figure 15.2, describe the communications process for (a) a local newspaper ad for new cars, (b) a phone call from a representative of Sprint requesting service sign-up, (c) a salesperson in Sears attempting to sell you a television set, and (d) Microsoft's interactive Web page (www.microsoft.com).

5. List and briefly describe each of the six buyer-readiness stages consumers pass through on their way to making a purchase. Provide an example to illustrate how a consumer passes through these stages.
6. The marketing communicator can use one or more types of appeals or themes to produce a desired response. What are the three types of appeals and when should each be used? Provide an example of each of the three appeals using three different magazine ads.
7. Decide which of the promotional budget models described in the text would be most appropriate for (a) a small retail gift store, (b) an office-supply company that has had a predictable sales and promotion pattern in each of the past five years, (c) a grocery store that has faced intense competition from three competitors in its immediate market area, and (d) an electronics manufacturer seeking to expand its market base and national appeal.
8. Marketers select from two basic promotion mix strategies: push and pull. Compare and contrast these strategies. It is possible to balance these two strategies? Provide an example of a company that effectively employs both strategies.

APPLYING THE CONCEPTS

1. The manufacturers of today's highly complicated computer products face a difficult task in determining how to promote their products effectively. Consumers do not respond well to the detailed descriptions that are often needed to explain complex technological features and differences. As the personal computer and handheld computer markets continue to grow, the computer industry faces an interesting communication problem—how to tell consumers in plain terms what they need to know about new generations of products without boring them. The answer may be as close as the computer company's Web site. Experts predict that more and more consumers will be "surfing" for their product information and will rely less and less on traditional information sources. Examine the following Web sites for more information on new PC products: Sharp (www.sharpelectronics.com), IBM (www.ibm.com), Dell (www.dell.com), Casio (www.casio.com), Apple (www.apple.com), and Sony (www.sony.com).

   a. How are the marketing communications at these Web sites different from those found in traditional advertising media? Which is more effective? Explain.

   b. After reviewing each of the sites, pick a product that you might like to own (such as a laptop or handheld computer). Based solely on the information provided at the Web sites, which company and product most grabs your attention and purchasing interest? Critique your information-gathering experience: What information was most useful? How could the communications be improved? Would you be willing to purchase the product via the Internet? Why or why not?

2. McDonald's is one of the most powerful brands in the world. In addition to its product mix, wide distribution of restaurants, and value pricing, McDonald's has extremely effective communications with important audiences. The concept of integrated marketing communications recognizes that customers are only one group a firm wants to reach with persuasive information. In addition to targeting kids and their parents, McDonald's communicates with stockholders, potential franchisees, potential employees, and communities in which the restaurants operate.

   a. Visit McDonald's online (www.mcdonalds.com) and browse the various Web pages. How does McDonald's target its message to different customer groups (such as kids, senior citizens, adults, office workers, and so on) and to its publics (such as stockholders, potential franchisees, potential employees, and the community at large)? Why do you think McDonald's wants to communicate with each of the noncustomer groups?

   b. Although the specific messages may differ, is the overall appeal of McDonald's messages consistent to all audiences? What is the overall message you get from visiting the site? Is that message consistent with those you've seen on TV and elsewhere?

   c. Assume McDonald's has hired you to review marketing communications transmitted via its Web site. Write a short report that critiques the site. Where does the Web site need improvement? What would you suggest?

 DIGITAL CONNECTIONS

CONNECTIONS THROUGH COMMUNICATION TO PROTECT A BRAND NAME

Have you gone "rollerblading" recently? Benetton Sportsystems, maker of Rollerblades, prefers that you call it in-line skating. The company spends thousands of dollars each year to protect the Rollerblade brand name and differentiate it from the activity of in-line skating. Beginning in the early 1980s, Rollerblade developed a series of products that propelled in-line skating into the forefront of outdoor recreation. However, along with increasing sales of its popular high-quality products came increasing problems with brand-name dilution and copycat manufacturers. Understanding the value of its trademark, Benetton Sportsystems stepped up its efforts to keep Rollerblade from becoming a generic description for in-line skating. The organization's aggressive efforts to protect its brand name helped it maintain its trademark distinction. So the next time you go in-line skating, think of Rollerblade as a product, not as a sport!

FOR DISCUSSION

1. Visit the Rollerblade Web site at www.rollerblade.com. As a pioneer of in-line skating, what problems did Rollerblade face with trademark protection? Examine the "Why It's Important to Use Trademarks Properly" section of the Web site. Critique Rollerblade's effort to differentiate the brand.

2. Do you think that Rollerblade's approach to trademark protection has hurt the company's overall sales or image? In what way?

3. Design a tag to attach to each pair of new Rollerblades that explains the company's concerns about trademark protection. Do you think a tag is an effective way to communicate with consumers? What other forms of marketing communications could the company use to protect the Rollerblade brand?

Schwartz Communications: Spreading the Word through Public Relations

In a world full of marketing messages, how can a marketer with a limited budget get the word out about new products and services? Companies, large and small, are increasingly turning to public relations to communicate with overwhelmed consumers. Schwartz Communications, an award-winning public relations firm focused on high-tech companies, works with clients to encourage news coverage and arrange product placements that support the company's marketing goals. But is public relations the most important component of the marketing communications mix?

After viewing the Schwartz Communications video, answer the following questions about integrated marketing communications:

1. Marketers face increasing clutter in traditional mass-communication media. Schwartz Communications specializes in using public relations to reach consumers. Is such a singular focus the answer to effective marketing communications? What are PR's unique advantages? What are its shortcomings?
2. How can marketers break through the clutter using other promotion tools in the communications mix? Be specific.
3. Select a company that communicates with consumers through multiple media and outline its various communications efforts. Does the company send a consistent message? How could the company better integrate its marketing communications efforts?

Procter & Gamble: Feeling the Heat

APPLYING PRESSURE

Consumer products giant Procter & Gamble has felt pressure in recent years as shareholders expressed their concerns over what they saw as the company's sometimes lackluster performance. Shareholders and stock-market analysts pressed the company to develop new products to beef up its stable of long-term successes like Pampers, Tide, and Crest, which were competing in mature, saturated markets.

The company responded with a wave of new products. Some, like Dryel, a home dry-cleaning product, and Fit, a rinse for fruit and vegetables, failed to register with consumers. Others, however, like Crest Whitestrips, a tooth-whitening system launched in 2000, reached the company's new-product goal of $200 million in first-year sales. Such successes are not enough, however—P&G has to keep the new products coming if it is to reach its goals of 4 to 6 percent annual sales growth and double-digit earnings growth.

PAIN RELIEF

To meet its ambitious growth goals, P&G developed a new-ventures unit, staffed with employees whose job was to develop new-product ideas and then pass them on to the appropriate business unit for development. The new-ventures unit examined the $3.3 billion pain-relief market to see if the company had any skills that it might apply to that market. It already knew much about this market due to its previous marketing of Aleve pain reliever (since sold to Bayer). Further, from its work on Pampers, Charmin, and Bounty, the company also had excellent knowledge in paper technology.

Merging these two capabilities, P&G's researchers developed the idea of the "external analgesic"—a product that consumers could use externally to provide long-lasting warmth to specific areas of the body where they experienced pain. After seven years of consumer and scientific testing, in early 2002 P&G announced that it would launch ThermaCare HeatWraps.

P&G designed ThermaCare for the temporary relief of minor muscle and joint aches and pain associated with overexertion, overuse, strains, sprains, and arthritis. Women could also use the product for temporary relief of minor menstrual cramping and associated back pain. The HeatWraps were portable, air-activated, disposable (single-use), self-heating devices that provided a continuous low-level therapeutic heat (104°F or 40°C) for up to eight hours.

The HeatWrap was a small pad that resembled a very thin diaper and came in shapes designed for the lower or upper back, the neck or arm, and the abdomen. When the consumer opened the package, the HeatWrap was exposed to air. Inside the wrap were a series of oval-shaped heat discs that contained a mixture of natural heat-generating materials: iron, carbon sodium chloride, sodium thiosulfate, and water. The air penetrated a perforated film that controlled oxygen permeability. The iron in the heat discs began to oxidize, and the chemical process generated the heat. The process was basically the same one that manufacturers of hand warmers had used for years. However, P&G had found a way to use its paper technology to sustain and control the heat-generating reaction.

Doctors and pharmacists recommended that people who experienced muscle pain due to exercising should first apply ice packs for up to 20 minutes at a time, three to four times per day for one to two days, accompanied with a pain reliever, such as aspirin or aspirinlike products. Then, they recommended that the patient should use heat therapy.

P&G recommended that consumers wear the HeatWrap for at least three hours and up to eight hours, repeating the process each day for up to seven days. Users could wear the HeatWraps under their clothing and go about their normal routines. Consumers were warned that they should not use the HeatWraps with other externally applied medications like lotions or ointments due to the risk of a skin reaction.

When finished with the HeatWrap, consumers could dispose of it in the household trash, as all materials in the product were environmentally compatible.

WRAPPING IT UP

P&G's marketers were excited about what they saw as a breakthrough product. The company planned to price the product at $6.99 per box at retail, producing a 25 percent profit margin for retailers, well above the margin for other pain-relief products. The package contained either two wraps in the back size or three wraps in the neck, arm, or abdomen sizes.

The company planned to concentrate on U.S. sales during the first year. It decided to allocate up to $90 million for an integrated promotional campaign to introduce ThermaCare. To design the campaign, P&G hired D'Arcy Masius Benton & Bowles, an advertising agency it had used for many years.

The agency knew that for a breakthrough product, it needed a breakthrough promotion program. After all, P&G was offering a unique product that presented consumers with many new concepts at the same time. Consumers would not be familiar with the product or how it worked. How could the advertising and promotion keep consumers from just shrugging and taking another pain pill? How could it educate consumers about what ThermaCare was, what it did, and how it was different from other pain-relief strategies? How could it help P&G make ThermaCare the next Tide?

QUESTIONS FOR DISCUSSION

1. What are possible target audiences for ThermaCare? In what buyer-readiness stages will these target audiences be?
2. What issues will the advertising agency face in designing messages for the selected target audiences? What message "theme" or "headline" summarizes the positioning that you'd recommend for ThermaCare?
3. What recommendations would you make to P&G and D'Arcy to help them develop an integrated promotion strategy for ThermaCare? Be sure to deal with the issues of setting the overall promotion mix, selecting a message source, and collecting feedback.

Sources: Stuart Elliott, "Things Heat Up for P&G," *NYTimes.com,* February 12, 2002, p. 1; "Procter and Gamble," *Drug Store News,* September 10, 2001, p. 19; Cliff Peale, "P&G Hopes ThermaCare Is a Blockbuster," *Cincinnati Enquirer,* Cincinnati.com, July 22, 2001; "ThermaCare Therapeutic HeatWraps," New Product Bulletin, American Pharmaceutical Association, 2001; www. ThermaCare.com, August 2002.

1. define the roles of advertising, sales promotion, and public relations in the promotion mix
2. describe the major decisions involved in developing an advertising program
3. explain how sales promotion campaigns are developed and implemented
4. explain how companies use public relations to communicate with their publics

Advertising, Sales Promotion, and Public Relations

LOOKING AHEAD: PREVIEWING THE CONCEPTS

Now that we've looked at overall integrated marketing communications planning, let's dig more deeply into the specific marketing communications tools. In this chapter, we'll explore the mass-communications tools—advertising, sales promotion, and public relations.

For starters, let's look closely at a highly successful advertising campaign that features an improbable spokesperson—er, spokes*duck*. As you read along, ask yourself, Just what is it that makes this such an effective campaign?

Quick, name a supplemental insurance company! The chances are good that you thought of AFLAC, even if you're not entirely certain what supplemental insurance is. The highly successful $9.7 billion insurer is now by far the best-known firm in the supplemental insurance industry, which offers policies that kick in to pay expenses not covered by the standard health, life, and disability policies provided by most employers.

But AFLAC hasn't always enjoyed such high levels of recognition. Until recently, about the only people who'd ever heard of AFLAC lived either in Columbus, Georgia (where the company was founded) or in Japan (where it does more than 75 percent of its business, commands 85 percent of the supplemental insurance market, and serves 95 percent of the companies listed on the Tokyo Stock Exchange). Just a few years ago, only 13 percent of Americans even recognized the company's name. But now, thanks to an unorthodox advertising campaign—featuring an improbable squawking white duck—practically every American knows about AFLAC.

AFLAC's ads used to look just like every other insurance company's ads. They were what one analyst describes as "warm and fuzzy, with happy family members looking at one another lovingly." And while they were no better or worse than the competitors' efforts, these run-of-the-mill ads were seriously overshadowed by the smart and funny ads of companies in other industries. "We realized we are competing for the attention of viewers who are not only watching [other] insurance ads, but [are also seeing] entertaining commercials for other products," says Kathelen Spencer, AFLAC's director of corporate communications.

So, in 1999, AFLAC began looking for a better way to build brand awareness and deliver its message to consumers. The company needed something radically different—ads that would break through today's unending advertising clutter. "We were at a point to try something new, and we were willing to take a risk," says Spencer.

The new brand-building effort presented challenges. According to the analyst, "Research showed that people didn't recognize the name, and coming up with a memory device was difficult, because the company's name is an acronym, not a word." (AFLAC stands for American Family Life Assurance Company.) However, someone on the creative team at AFLAC's advertising agency pointed out that "AFLAC" sounds like a duck squawk, and the rest is history. The idea gave birth to an American icon—an adenoidal white duck with a bright yellow beak and a blue bib that has made its "Aaaaaa-flaaack!" squawk a part of the American popular culture. The web-footer jolted AFLAC out of obscurity, raising the company's profile to soaring heights.

The campaign was risky. Some critics wondered whether the oddball spokesduck was suitable for the serious business of earning customer trust and selling insurance. But these fears proved unfounded—consumers love the duck. "He's the underduck," Spencer says. "We can rant and rave against policies and institutions, but as one person, we never feel as if we're heard. That's the role of the duck. He'll go on a roller coaster to tell the world about supplemental insurance."

Despite its humorous approach, the campaign delivers a serious message:

AFLAC's campaign still hammers home the importance of making sure that family members are protected by having its duck pop up . . . to quack "Aaaaaa-flaaack!" in situations and at times when people seem likely to need supplemental insurance. For instance, in a spot set in an airport, a passenger trips over his luggage, prompting a couple of flight attendants to talk about a friend who was hurt on the job and lacked supplemental insurance. The duck, passing by on a people-mover, squawks "AFLAC!" . . . Another spot features a couple in the front car of a roller coaster, and the duck is in the car behind them to reassure them of their insurance coverage should the coaster jump the tracks.

The duck campaign has been incredibly successful in lifting both AFLAC's image and its sales. The company's name recognition jumped from 13 percent to 91 percent in the two years following the start of the campaign. More impressive, 4 out of 10 people in the United States not only recognize the name, they can identify AFLAC as a supplemental insurer. AFLAC experienced more sales leads in just the first two weeks following the start of the duck campaign than it had in the previous two years combined. As a result, despite flat industry performance, AFLAC's sales have grown almost 30 percent each year since the ads began running.

"We never dreamed it would be this successful," says Daniel Amos, CEO of AFLAC. "When you call on a person selling insurance, a wall goes up. . . . But people ask us about the AFLAC duck constantly, and when they do, that wall falls down. . . . It's hard to think what things would be like without the duck." The quirky duck has become so popular that AFLAC now sells a stuffed toy duck and other "duck gear"—ranging from T-shirts and baseball caps to golf club covers—on its Web site. Proceeds go to support the AFLAC Cancer Center and Blood Disorder Center at Children's Healthcare of Atlanta.

What is it that makes the AFLAC campaign so successful? First, it presents an important message about a worthwhile product. But as important, the duck ads break through the clutter and present the brand message in a very memorable way. "They stick in the mind," says one advertising critic. "You can remember [the duck] and the name of the company." And, says an AFLAC spokeswoman, "People enjoy the humor; they like the duck's attitude. The AFLAC duck also has helped consumers understand our business."

"You have to zig when everybody's zagging," concludes an executive from AFLAC's ad agency. "Emotion is the lightning rod, the trigger, to make a purchase," she adds. "A baby evokes a very warm response. A little duck waddling around with an attitude is funny." And a walking, talking duck sells.[1]

Companies must do more than make good products—they must inform consumers about product benefits and carefully position products in consumers' minds. To do this, they must skillfully use the mass-promotion tools of *advertising, sales promotion,* and *public relations.* In this chapter, we take a closer look at each of these tools.

Advertising

Advertising
Any paid form of nonpersonal presentation and promotion of ideas, goods, or services by an identified sponsor.

Advertising can be traced back to the very beginnings of recorded history. Archaeologists working in the countries around the Mediterranean Sea have dug up signs announcing various events and offers. The Romans painted walls to announce gladiator fights, and the Phoenicians painted pictures promoting their wares on large rocks along parade routes. Modern advertising, however, is a far cry from these early efforts. U.S. advertisers now run up an estimated annual advertising bill of more than $231 billion; worldwide ad spending approaches an estimated $500 billion. General Motors, the nation's largest advertiser, last year spent more than $3.3 billion on U.S. advertising.[2]

Although advertising is used mostly by business firms, it also is used by a wide range of not-for-profit organizations, professionals, and social agencies that advertise their causes to various target publics. In fact, the twenty-fourth largest advertising spender is a not-for-profit organization—the U.S. government. Advertising is a good way to inform and persuade, whether the purpose is to sell Coca-Cola worldwide or to get consumers in a developing nation to use birth control.

Marketing management must make four important decisions when developing an advertising program (see Figure 16.1): *setting advertising objectives, setting the advertising budget, developing advertising strategy (message decisions* and *media decisions),* and *evaluating advertising campaigns.*

Setting Advertising Objectives

The first step is to set *advertising objectives.* These objectives should be based on past decisions about the target market, positioning, and marketing mix, which define the job that advertising must do in the total marketing program.

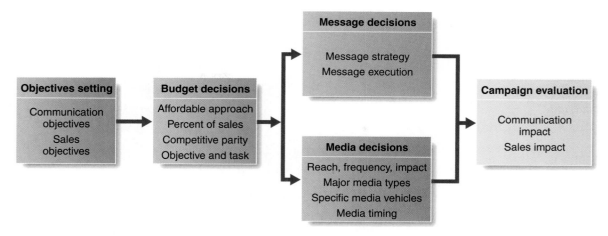

FIGURE 16.1 Major advertising decisions

Advertising objective

A specific communication *task* to be accomplished with a specific *target* audience during a specific period of *time*.

An **advertising objective** is a specific communication *task* to be accomplished with a specific *target* audience during a specific period of *time*. Advertising objectives can be classified by primary purpose—whether the aim is to *inform, persuade,* or *remind.* Table 16.1 lists examples of each of these objectives.

Informative advertising is used heavily when introducing a new product category. In this case, the objective is to build primary demand. Thus, producers of DVD players must first inform consumers of the image quality and convenience benefits of the new product. *Persuasive advertising* becomes more important as competition increases. Here, the company's objective is to build selective demand. For example, once DVD players are established, Sony begins trying to persuade consumers that *its* brand offered the best quality for their money.

Some persuasive advertising has become *comparative advertising,* in which a company directly or indirectly compares its brand with one or more other brands. Comparative advertising has been used for products ranging from soft drinks and computers to batteries, pain relievers, car rentals, and credit cards. For example, in its classic comparative campaign, Avis positioned itself against market-leading Hertz by claiming, "We're number two, so we try harder."

More recently, Progresso ran ads showing side-by-side comparisons of its soups versus Campbell's condensed soups, inviting consumers to "Enjoy a better soup . . . with a more adult taste." In its long-running comparative campaign, Visa has advertised, "American Express is offering

TABLE 16.1	POSSIBLE ADVERTISING OBJECTIVES
Informative Advertising	
Telling the market about a new product	Describing available services
Suggesting new uses for a product	Correcting false impressions
Informing the market of a price change	Reducing consumers' fears
Explaining how the product works	Building a company image
Persuasive Advertising	
Building brand preference	Persuading customer to purchase now
Encouraging switching to your brand	Persuading customer to receive a sales call
Changing customer's perception of product attributes	
Reminder Advertising	
Reminding consumer that the product may be needed in the near future	Keeping it in customer's mind during off-seasons
Reminding consumer where to buy it	Maintaining its top-of-mind awareness

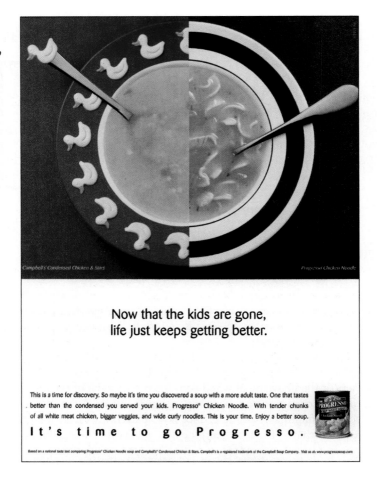

you a new credit card, but you don't have to accept it. Heck, 7 million merchants don't." American Express has responded with ads bashing Visa, noting that AmEx's cards offer benefits not available with Visa's regular card, such as rapid replacement of lost cards and higher credit limits. As often happens with comparative advertising, both sides complain that the other's ads are misleading.

Reminder advertising is important for mature products—it keeps consumers thinking about the product. Expensive Coca-Cola television ads primarily remind people about Coca-Cola rather than informing or persuading them.

Setting the Advertising Budget

After determining its advertising objectives, the company next sets its *advertising budget* for each product. Four commonly used methods for setting promotion budgets are discussed in Chapter 15. Here we discuss some specific factors that should be considered when setting the advertising budget.

A brand's advertising budget often depends on its *stage in the product life cycle*. For example, new products typically need large advertising budgets to build awareness and to persuade consumer's to try the products. In contrast, mature brands usually require lower budgets as a ratio to sales. *Market share* also impacts the amount advertising needed: Because building the market or taking share from competitors requires larger advertising spending than does simply maintaining current share, low-share brands usually need more advertising spending as a percentage of sales. Also, brands in a market with many competitors and high advertising clutter must be advertised more heavily to be noticed above the noise in the market. Undifferentiated brands—those that closely resemble other brands in their product class (beer, soft drinks, laundry detergents)—may require heavy advertising to set them apart. When the product differs greatly from competitors, advertising can be used to point out the differences to consumers.

No matter what method is used, setting the advertising budget is no easy task. How does a company know if it is spending the right amount? Some critics charge that large consumer packaged-goods firms tend to spend too much on advertising and business-to-business marketers generally underspend on advertising. They claim that, on the one hand, the large consumer companies use lots of image advertising without really knowing its effects. They overspend as a form of "insurance" against not spending enough. On the other hand, business advertisers tend to rely too heavily on their sales forces to bring in orders. They underestimate the power of company and product image in preselling industrial customers. Thus, they do not spend enough on advertising to build customer awareness and knowledge.

Companies such as Coca-Cola and Kraft have built sophisticated statistical models to determine the relationship between promotional spending and brand sales, and to help determine the "optimal investment" across various media. Still, because so many factors affect advertising effectiveness, some controllable and others not, measuring the results of advertising spending remains an inexact science. In most cases, managers must rely on large doses of judgment along with more-quantitative analysis when setting advertising budgets.[3]

Developing Advertising Strategy

Advertising strategy consists of two major elements: creating advertising *messages* and selecting advertising *media*. In the past, companies often viewed media planning as secondary to the message-creation process. The creative department first created good advertisements, then the media department selected the best media for carrying these advertisements to desired target audiences. This often caused friction between "creatives" and media planners.

Today, however, media fragmentation, soaring media costs, and more-focused target marketing strategies have promoted the importance of the media-planning function. More and more, advertisers are orchestrating a closer harmony between their messages and the media that deliver them. In some cases, an advertising campaign might start with a great message idea, followed by the choice of appropriate media. In other cases, however, a campaign might begin with a good media opportunity, followed by advertisements designed to take advantage of that opportunity. Among the more noteworthy ad campaigns based on tight media-creative partnerships is the pioneering campaign for Absolut vodka, marketed by The Absolut Spirits Company, Inc.

> The Absolut team and its ad agency meet regularly with a slew of magazines to set Absolut's media schedule. The team first goes through the 800 produced ads, which all run frequently in a copy rotation, and, if needed, they agency's creative department then creates media-specific ads. The result is a wonderful assortment of very creative ads for Absolut, tightly targeted to audiences of the media in which they appear. For example, an "Absolut Bravo" ad in playbills has roses adorning a clear bottle, while business magazines contain an "Absolut Merger" foldout. In Chicago, the windy city, ads show an Absolut bottle with the letters on the label blown askew. An "Absolut Primary" ad run during the political season featured the well-known bottle spattered with mud. In some cases, the creatives even developed ads for magazines not yet on the schedule, such as a clever "Absolut Centerfold" ad for *Playboy* magazine. The ad portrayed a clear, unadorned "Playmate" bottle ("11-inch bust, 11-inch waist, 11-inch hips"). In all, Absolut has developed more than 800 ads for the almost two-decades-old campaign. At a time of soaring media costs and cluttered communication channels, a closer cooperation between creative and media people has paid off handsomely for Absolut. Largely as a result of its breakthrough advertising, in the United States, Absolut now sells 4.5 million 9-liter cases each year in the United States and captures a 63 percent share of the imported vodka market.[4] (Please note: used with permission by V & S Vin & Spirit AB. Absolut country of Sweden Vodka and logo, Absolut, Absolut bottle design, and Absolut calligraphy are trademarks owned by V & S Vin & Spirit AB. © 2003 V & S Vin & Spirit AB.)

Creating the Advertising Message

No matter how big the budget, advertising can succeed only if commercials gain attention and communicate well. Good advertising messages are especially important in today's costly and cluttered advertising environment. The average number of television channels beamed into U.S. homes has skyrocketed from 3 in 1950 to more than 50 today, and consumers have more than 17,700 magazines from which to choose.[5] Add the countless radio stations and a continuous barrage of catalogs, direct-mail and e-mail ads, and out-of-home media, and consumers are being

Media planners for Absolut vodka work with creatives to design ads targeted to specific media audiences. "Absolut Bravo" appears in theater playbills. "Absolut Chicago" targets the Windy City.

bombarded with ads at home, at work, and at all points in between. One expert estimates that the average person in the United States is exposed to about 5,000 ads a day.[6]

If all this advertising clutter bothers some consumers, it also causes big problems for advertisers. Take the situation facing network television advertisers. They regularly pay $200,000 or more for 30 seconds of advertising time during a popular prime-time program, even more if it's an especially popular program such as *ER* ($445,000 per 30-second spot), *Friends* ($354,000), *Will & Grace* ($320,000 per spot), or a mega-event such as the Super Bowl (more than $2 million!).[7] Then, their ads are sandwiched in with a clutter of some 60 other commercials, announcements, and network promotions per hour.

Until recently, television viewers were pretty much a captive audience for advertisers. Viewers had only a few channels from which to choose. But with the growth in cable and satellite TV, VCRs, and remote-control units, today's viewers have many more options. They can avoid ads by watching commercial-free cable channels. They can "zap" commercials by pushing the fast-forward button during taped programs. With remote control, they can instantly turn off the sound during a commercial or "zip" around the channels to see what else is on. A recent study found that half of all television viewers now switch channels when the commercial break starts. And the new wave of personal video recorders (PVRs) and personal television services—such as TiVo, ReplayTV, and Microsoft's UltimateTV—have armed viewers with an arsenal of new-age zipping and zapping weapons. A recent study of TiVo and other personal video recorder system users found that these users skip commercials 72 percent of the time, a much higher rate than for those watching live television or using VCRs.[8]

Just to gain and hold attention, today's advertising messages must be better planned, more imaginative, more entertaining, and more rewarding to consumers. "Today we have to entertain and not just sell, because if you try to sell directly and come off as boring or obnoxious, people are going to press the remote on you," points out one advertising executive. "When most TV viewers are armed with remote channel switchers, a commercial has to cut through the clutter and seize the viewers in one to three seconds, or they're gone," comments another.[9] Some advertisers even create intentionally controversial ads to break through the clutter and gain attention for their products (see Real Marketing 16.1).

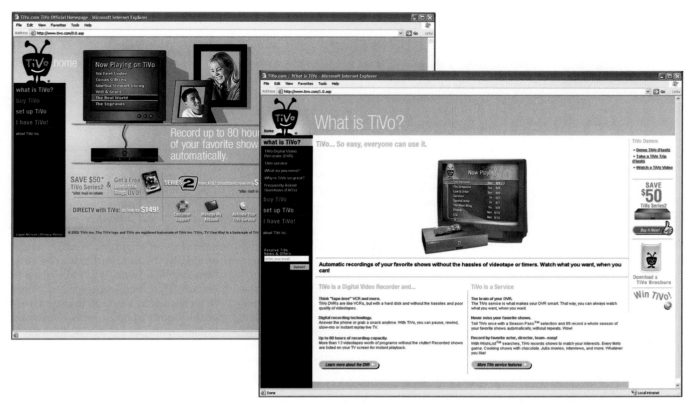

A new advertising challenge: The new wave of personal video recorders, such as TiVo, has armed viewers with an arsenal of new-age zipping and zapping weapons.

Message Strategy.   The first step in creating effective advertising messages is to decide what general message will be communicated to consumers—to plan a *message strategy.* The purpose of advertising is to get consumers to think about or react to the product or company in a certain way. People will react only if they believe that they will benefit from doing so. Thus, developing an effective message strategy begins with identifying customer *benefits* that can be used as advertising appeals. Ideally, advertising message strategy will follow directly from the company's broader positioning strategy.

Message strategy statements tend to be plain, straightforward outlines of benefits and positioning points that the advertiser wants to stress. The advertiser must next develop a compelling *creative concept*—or *"big idea"*—that will bring the message strategy to life in a distinctive and memorable way. At this stage, simple message ideas become great ad campaigns. Usually, a copywriter and art director will team up to generate many creative concepts, hoping that one of these concepts will turn out to be the big idea. The creative concept may emerge as a visualization, a phrase, or a combination of the two.

The creative concept will guide the choice of specific appeals to be used in an advertising campaign. *Advertising appeals* should have three characteristics: First, they should be *meaningful,* pointing out benefits that make the product more desirable or interesting to consumers. Second, appeals must be *believable*—consumers must believe that the product or service will deliver the promised benefits. However, the most meaningful and believable benefits may not be the best ones to feature. Appeals should also be *distinctive*—they should tell how the product is better than the competing brands. For example, the most meaningful benefit of owning a wristwatch is that it keeps accurate time, yet few watch ads feature this benefit. Instead, based on the distinctive benefits they offer, watch advertisers might select any of a number of advertising themes. For years, Timex has been the affordable watch that "Takes a lickin' and keeps on tickin.'" In contrast, Swatch has featured style and fashion, whereas Rolex stresses luxury and status.

Message Execution.   The advertiser now has to turn the big idea into an actual ad execution that will capture the target market's attention and interest. The creative people must find the best

real marketing 16.1

Advertising on the Edge: You Either Hate 'Em or Love 'Em

You may remember the ad. It opens with a calm, deep-voiced announcer sitting comfortably in a leather chair in a library setting. The spot cuts to a concrete wall with "Outpost.com" emblazoned on it. "Hello," he intones, "we want you to remember our name—Outpost.com." To the shock of some viewers and to the surprised delight of others, he continues, "That's why we've decided to fire gerbils out of this cannon through the 'O' in 'Outpost.'" He gives a nod, and his assistant fires a nearby cannon. *Boom!* The cannon hurls a gerbil toward the hole. *Splat!* A near miss—the gerbil hits the wall, then falls to the ground and scurries away. "Cute little guy," says the announcer, smiling warmly. "Again," he instructs. *Boom!* This time, a gerbil sails high over the wall. *Boom! Splat! Boom! Splat!* "So close," affirms the announcer. Finally, the cannon blasts a gerbil cleanly through the "O," setting off a fanfare of sirens, buzzers, and flashing lights. The ad closes with an invitation to viewers to "send complaints to Outpost.com—the cool place to buy computer stuff online."

It was all pretend, of course, but complain people did. These ads by Outpost.com—the Internet company that sells computer technology products and consumer electronics online—set off a flurry of controversy on Madison Avenue and among animal-protection groups. But the ads did draw attention—Outpost.com rocketed from near obscurity into the national spotlight in a matter of weeks.

Outpost.com's commercials were in the vanguard of a new genre of irreverent, cutting-edge advertising: commercials that intentionally create controversy, even if it means turning off some potential customers. In today's cluttered advertising environment, such ads go to extremes to get attention—you either love 'em or hate 'em. "It's the age-old question of breaking through the clutter," says the creative director of the ad agency that developed the Outpost.com ads. You turn to "anything you can to get noticed," he says.

Other controversial ads abound. While flipping through your favorite magazine, you might encounter a Toyota ad targeting Gen Ys with the headline "Attention nose pickers . . . " On the next page is a boundary-pushing ad from Candies, featuring company spokes-model Jenny McCarthy sitting on a toilet with her pants around her calves, wearing little more than her bright orange Candies shoes. Next comes an Altoids ad in which a man peers down the front of his boxer shorts: "Shrinkage may occur," proclaims the ad's headline. "The curiously strong mints." Other Altoids ads feature a woman in a seductively devilish outfit, complete with horns, and headlines such as "Hot and bothered?" "Frigid?" and "Taste like hell!"

On television, a Fox Sports television ad shows an able-bodied young guy, engrossed in his Fox Sports Web site, casually ignoring an old man just a few feet away struggling to get a jar down from a shelf. An Orange Slice "twisted taste" commercial opens with the camera panning across a row of squeamish students in a science class, frog legs dangling from their dissection trays. As the teacher drones on about ruptured spleens and green discharges, one kid lunches on his lab project.

For pure gross-out value, few ads top the "Blind Date" spot from SmartBeep, the retail paging-services provider. The spot, which generated enormous response, was part of a wacky five-part campaign that contrasted smart versus not-so-smart behavior to promote SmartBeep's free pagers and low rates on paging services. In it, a woman climbs into the front seat of her blind date's car. While he's crossing around to the other side, thinking she is alone, she leans to one side and lets rip a frat-house blast of gas. When her date hops in the car, she hesitates then turns red with embarrassment as he introduces her to another couple in the back seat. "You guys meet? Gregg, Janice?" he asks, to which Janice in the back seat responds, "We sure did." The announcer concludes, "That was stupid. . . . This is smart. A beeper service for just $1.99 a month." The ad closes: "We've got chemistry here. You feel it?" says the blind-date guy. "I felt it!" says Janice from the back seat. The ad became an immediate Internet cult item.

Outpost.com's ads—three in all—themselves rated pretty high on the irreverence meter. The gerbils ad wasn't the only one

SHRINKAGE MAY OCCUR
THE CURIOUSLY STRONG MINTS

CURIOUS?

WWW.TOOHOT.COM

To be truly cutting-edge, advertising must do more than just capture attention. Altoids' irreverent ads fit the brand's "curious, strong, original" positioning and appeal to its cutting-edge target customers.

to set fur flying. In a second ad, a tattoo artist attempted to make the Outpost.com name more memorable by inscribing it on the foreheads of six-year-old kids at a day care center, reducing them to tears. In a third, a high school marching band spelling out the company's name on a football field is attacked by "a pack of ravenous wolves," who jump on band members, tearing at their limbs. "Ha, ha, ha," said the announcer, "that's good stuff."

Outpost.com's marketers knew that the ads would be controversial—that was the point. "Our intent was to create memorable ads that would force people to remember our name," said an Outpost.com spokesperson. The agency creative director adds, "We told the people at Outpost.com that we didn't know if these ads were good or bad. What we told them was that they were memorable—they'll get people to your Web site."

Mission accomplished. Site traffic doubled and Outpost.com signed 15,000 new customers in the two weeks after the commercials first aired, 30,000 new customers by the end of the campaign. Moreover, as a testament to its cutting-edge creativity, the campaign amassed more than a dozen of the ad industry's highest awards and spawned many competitors.

However, while the outrageous ads grabbed attention and awards, they did little

to position Outpost.com or to tell people what it had to sell. Although Outpost.com's name was all over the place, nobody knew why he or she should visit the site. The ads mentioned "computer stuff," laments the company's former CEO, but "the ads were so dominating that people missed that. They didn't know that we sold computers. They thought that we sold clothes or didn't sell anything. We had a lot of visitors—but no buyers."

A year after the first ads ran, Outpost.com shifted to a more serious campaign chock full of information and positioning the company on its products and free overnight delivery policy. The new campaign resulted in a 40 percent increase in site visitors, and people who visited the site were also buying. However, it may have been too little, too late. Recently acquired by electronics retailer Fry's Electronics, Outpost.com is still struggling to turn its first profits.

So, it appears that to be truly cutting edge, advertising must do more than just capture attention. It must support and enhance the brand and its positioning. If used properly, cutting edge humor can help do that, as proved by Altoids and its "Curiously Strong" campaign. In these ads, the irreverence fits the brand's "curious, strong, original" positioning. It also appeals

to the tastes as well as the taste buds of Altoids' cutting-edge target consumers. As a result, in only two years, the small-budget but high-impact ad campaign has propelled Altoids past longtime strong-mint market leader Tic Tac. "Altoids is now—improbably—the boss of the mint world," says an analyst. What's the power behind this cheeky campaign? The analyst confirms that "everything links back to [the brand's] 'curiously strong' and 'original' [positioning]."

Sources: Melanie Wells, "Wanted: Television Ad Complaints," *USA Today,* January 11, 1999, p. 4B; Dottie Enrico, "Creature Feature," *TV Guide,* January 23, 1999, p. 13; Hank Kim, "Creature Feature," *Adweek,* November 23, 1998, p. 20; Tom Kurtz, "Unsettling TV Commercials: And Now, a Gross-Out from Our Sponsor," *New York Times,* July 25, 1999, p. 7; Anne Marie Borrego, "Wild Ads Make Web Stars," *Inc,* February 2000, p. 66; Verne Gay, "Best Use of Out-of-Home: Stargate Worldwide," *Adweek,* June 19, 2000; pp. M6–M10; Laurie J. Flynn, "As Cyberian Outpost Plunges Toward the Abyss, Two Suitors Wait Patiently to Pick Up the Pieces," *New York Times,* July 24, 2001, p. C10; and information accessed online at About Altoids at www.altoids.com, August 2002.

style, tone, words, and format for executing the message. Any message can be presented in different *execution styles,* such as the following:

- *Slice of life:* This style shows one or more "typical" people using the product in a normal setting. For example, two mothers at a picnic discuss the nutritional benefits of Jif peanut butter.

- *Lifestyle:* This style shows how a product fits in with a particular lifestyle. For example, an ad for Mongoose mountain bikes shows a serious biker traversing remote and rugged but beautiful terrain and states, "There are places that are so awesome and so killer that you'd like to tell the whole world about them. But please, *don't.*"

- *Fantasy:* This style creates a fantasy around the product or its use. For instance, many ads are built around dream themes. Gap even introduced a perfume named Dream. Ads show a woman sleeping blissfully and suggests that the scent is "the stuff that clouds are made of."

- *Mood or image:* This style builds a mood or image around the product, such as beauty, love, or serenity. No claim is made about the product except through suggestion. Bermuda tourism ads create such moods.

- *Musical:* This style shows one or more people or cartoon characters singing about the product. For example, one of the most famous ads in history was a Coca-Cola ad built around the song "I'd Like to Teach the World to Sing."

- *Personality symbol:* This style creates a character that represents the product. The character might be *animated* (the Jolly Green Giant, Cap'n Crunch, Garfield the Cat) or *real* (the Marlboro man, Ol' Lonely the Maytag repairman, Morris the 9-Lives Cat, or the AFLAC duck).

- *Technical expertise:* This style shows the company's expertise in making the product. Thus, Maxwell House shows one of its buyers carefully selecting coffee beans, and Gallo tells about its many years of wine-making experience.
- *Scientific evidence:* This style presents survey or scientific evidence that the brand is better or better liked than one or more other brands. For years, Crest toothpaste has used scientific evidence to convince buyers that Crest is better than other brands at fighting cavities.
- *Testimonial evidence or endorsement:* This style features a highly believable or likable source endorsing the product. It could be ordinary people saying how much they like a given product or a celebrity presenting the product. For example, Apple recently ran ads featuring real people who'd recently switched from Microsoft Windows–based PCs to Macs. And many companies use actors or sports celebrities as product endorsers.

The advertiser also must choose a *tone* for the ad. Procter & Gamble always uses a positive tone: Its ads say something very positive about its products. P&G usually avoids humor that might take attention away from the message. In contrast, many advertisers now use edgy humor to break through the commercial clutter.

The advertiser must use memorable and attention-getting *words* in the ad. For example, rather than claiming simply that "a BMW is a well-engineered automobile," BMW uses more creative and higher-impact phrasing: "The ultimate driving machine." Instead of stating plainly that Hanes socks last longer than less expensive ones, Hanes suggests, "Buy cheap socks and you'll pay through the toes." It's not Häagen-Dazs is "a good-tasting luxury ice cream," it's "Our passport to indulgence: passion in a touch, perfection in a cup, summer in a spoon, one perfect moment."

Finally, *format* elements make a difference in an ad's impact as well as in its cost. A small change in ad design can make a big difference in its effect. The *illustration* is the first thing the reader notices—it must be strong enough to draw attention. Next, the *headline* must effectively entice the right people to read the copy. Finally, the *copy*—the main block of text in the ad—must be simple but strong and convincing. Moreover, these three elements must effectively work *together*.

Selecting Advertising Media

The major steps in media selection are (1) deciding on *reach, frequency,* and *impact;* (2) choosing among major *media types;* (3) selecting specific *media vehicles;* and (4) deciding on *media timing.*

Testimonials: Apple recently ran ads featuring real people who'd recently switched from Microsoft Windows-based PCs to Macs. "Janie Porche got her first Apple in January after she'd finally had enough of her PC's temperamental behavior."

"My PC wasn't Plug-n-Play. It was Plug-n-Get-Mad."

Janie Porche got her first Apple computer after she finally had enough of her PC's temperamental behavior. To learn how easy it is for you to switch to a reliable Mac, visit apple.com/switch.

Deciding on Reach, Frequency, and Impact.   To select media, the advertiser must decide what reach and frequency are needed to achieve advertising objectives. *Reach* is a measure of the *percentage* of people in the target market who are exposed to the ad campaign during a given period of time. For example, the advertiser might try to reach 70 percent of the target market during the first three months of the campaign. *Frequency* is a measure of how many *times* the average person in the target market is exposed to the message. For example, the advertiser might want an average exposure frequency of three.

The advertiser also must decide on the desired *media impact*—the *qualitative value* of a message exposure through a given medium. For example, for products that need to be demonstrated, messages on television may have more impact than messages on radio because television uses sight *and* sound. The same message in one magazine (say, *Newsweek*) may be more believable than in another (say, *The National Enquirer*). In general, the more reach, frequency, and impact the advertiser seeks, the higher the advertising budget will have to be.

Choosing Among Major Media Types.   The media planner has to know the reach, frequency, and impact of each of the major media types. As summarized in Table 16.2, the major media types are newspapers, television, direct mail, radio, magazines, outdoor, and the Internet. Each medium has advantages and limitations.

Media planners consider many factors when making their media choices. The *media habits of target consumers* will affect media choice—advertisers look for media that reach target consumers effectively. So will the *nature of the product*—for example, fashions are best advertised in color magazines, and automobile performance is best demonstrated on television. Different *types of messages* may require different media. A message announcing a major sale tomorrow will require radio or newspapers; a message with a lot of technical data might require magazines, direct mailings, or an online ad and Web site. *Cost* is another major factor in media choice. For example, network television is very expensive, whereas newspaper or radio advertising costs much less but also reaches fewer consumers. The media planner looks both at the total cost of using a medium and at the cost per thousand exposures—the cost of reaching 1,000 people using the medium.

Media impact and cost must be reexamined regularly. For a long time, television and magazines have dominated in the media mixes of national advertisers, with other media often

TABLE 16.2	**PROFILES OF MAJOR MEDIA TYPES**	
Medium	**Advantages**	**Limitations**
Newspapers	Flexibility; timeliness; good local market coverage; broad acceptability; high believability	Short life; poor reproduction quality; small pass-along audience
Television	Good mass-market coverage; low cost per exposure; combines sight, sound, and motion; appealing to the senses	High absolute costs; high clutter; fleeting exposure; less audience selectivity
Direct mail	High audience selectivity; flexibility; no ad competition within the same medium; allows personalization	Relatively high cost per exposure, "junk mail" image
Radio	Good local acceptance; high geographic and demographic selectivity; low cost	Audio only, fleeting exposure; low attention ("the half-heard" medium); fragmented audiences
Magazines	High geographic and demographic selectivity; credibility and prestige; high-quality reproduction; long life and good pass-along readership	Long ad purchase lead time; high cost; no guarantee of position
Outdoor	Flexibility; high repeat exposure; low cost; low message competition; good positional selectivity	Little audience selectivity; creative limitations
Internet	High selectivity; low cost; immediacy; interactive capabilities	Small, demographically skewed audience; relatively low impact; audience controls exposure

neglected. Recently, however, as network television costs soar and audiences shrink, many advertisers are looking for new ways to reach consumers. The move toward micromarketing strategies, focused more narrowly on specific consumer groups, has also fueled the search for new media to replace or supplement network television. As a result, advertisers are increasingly shifting larger portions of their budgets to media that cost less and target more effectively.

Three media benefiting greatly from the shift are outdoor advertising, cable television, and digital satellite television systems. Billboards have undergone a resurgence in recent years. Gone are the ugly eyesores of the past; in their place we now see cleverly designed, colorful attention grabbers. Outdoor advertising provides an excellent way to reach important local consumer segments at a fraction of the cost per exposure of other major media. Cable television and digital satellite systems are also booming. Such systems allow narrow programming formats such as all sports, all news, nutrition, arts, gardening, cooking, travel, history, and others that target select groups. Advertisers can take advantage of such "narrowcasting" to "rifle in" on special market segments rather than use the "shotgun" approach offered by network broadcasting.

Outdoor, cable, and satellite media seem to make good sense. But, increasingly, ads are popping up in far less likely places. In their efforts to find less costly and more highly targeted ways to reach consumers, advertisers have discovered a dazzling collection of "alternative media" (see Real Marketing 16.2).

Selecting Specific Media Vehicles.   The media planner now must choose the best *media vehicles*—specific media within each general media type. For example, television vehicles include *ER* and *ABC World News Tonight*. Magazine vehicles include *Newsweek, People, In Style,* and *Sports Illustrated.*

Media planners must compute the cost per thousand persons reached by a vehicle. For example, if a full-page, four-color advertisement in *Newsweek* costs $183,000 and *Newsweek*'s readership is 3.1 million people, the cost of reaching each group of 1,000 persons is about $59. The same advertisement in *Business Week* may cost only $95,000 but reach only 970,000 persons—at a cost per thousand of about $98. The media planner ranks each magazine by cost per thousand and favors those magazines with the lower cost per thousand for reaching target consumers.[10]

The media planner must also consider the costs of producing ads for different media. Whereas newspaper ads may cost very little to produce, flashy television ads may cost millions. On average, U.S. advertisers pay $332,000 to produce a single 30-second television commercial. A few years ago, Nike paid a cool $2 million to make a single ad called "The Wall."[11]

In selecting media vehicles, the media planner must balance media cost measures against several media impact factors. First, the planner should balance costs against the media vehicle's *audience quality.* For a baby lotion advertisement, for example, *New Parents* magazine would have a high exposure value; *Gentlemen's Quarterly* would have a low exposure value. Second, the media planner should consider *audience attention.* Readers of *Vogue,* for example, typically pay more attention to ads than do *Newsweek* readers. Third, the planner should assess the vehicle's *editorial quality*—*Time* and the *Wall Street Journal* are more believable and prestigious than *The National Enquirer.*

Deciding on Media Timing.   The advertiser must also decide how to schedule the advertising over the course of a year. Suppose sales of a product peak in December and drop in March. The firm can vary its advertising to follow the seasonal pattern, to oppose the seasonal pattern, or to be the same all year. Most firms do some seasonal advertising. Some do *only* seasonal advertising: For example, Hallmark advertises its greeting cards only before major holidays. Beatrice Foods runs special Thanksgiving and Christmas ads for Reddi-wip during November and December, months that account for 30 percent of all whipped cream sales.

Finally, the advertiser has to choose the pattern of the ads. *Continuity* means scheduling ads evenly within a given period. *Pulsing* means scheduling ads unevenly over a given time period. Thus, 52 ads could either be scheduled at one per week during the year or pulsed in several bursts. The idea behind pulsing is to advertise heavily for a short period to build awareness that carries over to the next advertising period. Those who favor pulsing feel that it can be used to achieve the same impact as a steady schedule but at a much lower cost. However, some media planners believe that although pulsing achieves minimal awareness, it sacrifices depth of advertising communications.

Recent advances in technology have had a substantial impact on the media planning and buying functions. Today, for example, computer software applications called *media optimizers*

real marketing 16.2

Advertisers Seek Alternative Media

As consumers, we're used to ads on television, in magazines and newspapers, on the radio, and along the roadways. But these days, no matter where you go or what you do, you probably will run into some new form of advertising.

Tiny billboards attached to shopping carts, ads on shopping bags, and even advertising decals on supermarket floors urge you to buy Jell-O Pudding Pops or Pampers. Signs atop parking meters hawk everything from Jeeps to Minolta cameras to Recipe dog food. A city bus rolls by, fully wrapped for Trix cereal. You escape to the ballpark, only to find billboard-size video screens running Budweiser ads while a blimp with an electronic message board circles lazily overhead. How about a quiet trip in the country? Sorry—you find an enterprising farmer using his milk cows as four-legged billboards mounted with ads for Ben & Jerry's ice cream.

You pay to see a movie at your local theater, only to learn that the movie is full of not-so-subtle promotional plugs for Pepsi, Domino's Pizza, MasterCard, Fritos, Mercedes, Ray-Ban sunglasses, Rockport

shoes, or any of a dozen other products. You head home for a little TV to find your favorite sitcom full of "virtual placements" of Coca-Cola, Sony, or M&M/Mars products digitally inserted into the program.

At the local rail station, it's the Commuter Channel; at the airport, you're treated to the CNN Airport Network. Shortly after your plane lifts off the runway, you look out the window and spot a 500-foot-diameter crop circle carved into a farmer's field depicting Monster.com's mascot and corporate logo. As you wait to pick up your luggage, ads for Kenneth Cole baggage roll by on the luggage carousel conveyor belt.

These days, you're likely to find ads—well, anywhere. Boats cruise along public beaches flashing advertising messages for Sundown Sunscreen as sunbathers spread their towels over ads for Snapple pressed into the sand. Ad space is being sold on video cases, parking-lot tickets, golf scorecards, delivery trucks, gas pumps, ATMs, and municipal garbage cans. Even church bulletins carry ads for Campbell's soup.

The following accounts takes a humorous look ahead at what might be in store for the future:

Tomorrow your alarm clock will buzz at 6 A.M., as usual. Then the digital readout will morph into an ad for Burger King's breakfast special. Hungry for a Croissan'wich, you settle for a bagel that you plop into the toaster. The coils burn a Toastmaster brand onto the sides. Biting into your embossed bread, you pour a cup of coffee as the familiar green-and-white Starbucks logo forms on the side. Sipping the brew, you slide on your Nikes to go grab the newspaper. The pressure-sensitive shoes leave a temporary trail of swooshes behind them wherever you step. Walking outside, you pick up the *Times* and gaze at your lawn, where the fertilizer you put down last month time-releases ads for Scotts Turf Builder, Toro lawn mowers, Weber grills. . . .

Even some of the current alternative media seem a bit far-fetched, and they sometimes irritate consumers who resent it all as

Marketers have discovered a dazzling array of "alternative media."

(continued)

"ad nauseam." But for many marketers, these media can save money and provide a way to hit selected consumers where they live, shop, work, and play. "We like to call it the captive pause," says an executive of an alternative-media firm, where consumers "really have nothing else to do but either look at the person in front of them or look at some engaging content as well as 15-second commercials"—the average person waits in line about 30 minutes a day.

Of course, this may leave you wondering if there are any commercial-free havens remaining for ad-weary consumers. The back seat of a taxi, perhaps, or public elevators, or stalls in a public restroom? Forget it! Each has already been invaded by innovative marketers.

Sources: See Cara Beardi, "From Elevators to Gas Stations, Ads Multiplying," *Advertising Age,* November 13, 2000, pp. 40–42; Charles

Pappas, "Ad Nauseam," *Advertising Age,* July 10, 2000, pp. 16–18; Beardi, "Airport Powerhouses Make Connection," *Advertising Age,* October 2, 2000, p. 8; Wayne Friedman, "Eagle-Eye Marketers Find Right Spot," *Advertising Age,* January 22, 2001, pp. S2–S3; Jean Halliday, "Mercedes Ties Car to 'Men in Black II,'" *Advertising Age,* May 27, 2002, p. 4; and Cara Griffin, "Rockport, Ray-Ban Back in Black," *Sporting Goods Business,* April 2002, p. 14.

allow media planners to evaluate vast combinations of television programs and prices. Such programs help advertisers to make better decisions about which mix of networks, programs, and hours of the day will yield the highest reach per ad dollar.

Evaluating Advertising

The advertising program should evaluate both the communication effects and the sales effects of advertising regularly. Measuring the *communication effects* of an ad—*copy testing*—tells whether the ad is communicating well. Copy testing can be done before or after an ad is printed or broadcast. Before the ad is placed, the advertiser can show it to consumers, ask how they like it, and measure recall or attitude changes resulting from it. After the ad is run, the advertiser can measure how the ad affected consumer recall or product awareness, knowledge, and preference.

But what *sales* are caused by an ad that increases brand awareness by 20 percent and brand preference by 10 percent? The *sales effects* of advertising are often harder to measure than the

Media timing: Beatrice Foods runs special Thanksgiving and Christmas ads for Reddi-wip during November and December, months that account for 30 percent of all whipped cream sales.

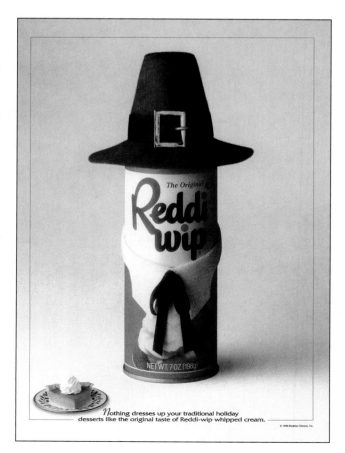

communication effects. Sales are affected by many factors besides advertising—such as product features, price, and availability.

One way to measure the sales effect of advertising is to compare past sales with past advertising expenditures. Another way is through experiments. For example, to test the effects of different advertising spending levels, Coca-Cola could vary the amount it spends on advertising in different market areas and measure the differences in the resulting sales levels. It could spend the normal amount in one market area, half the normal amount in another area, and twice the normal amount in a third area. If the three market areas are similar, and if all other marketing efforts in the area are the same, then differences in sales in the three areas could be related to advertising level. More complex experiments could be designed to include other variables, such as difference in the ads or media used.

Other Advertising Considerations

In developing advertising strategies and programs, the company must address two additional questions. First, how will the company organize its advertising function—who will perform which advertising tasks? Second, how will the company adapt its advertising strategies and programs to the complexities of international markets?

Organizing for Advertising

Different companies organize in different ways to handle advertising. In small companies, advertising might be handled by someone in the sales department. Large companies set up advertising departments whose job it is to set the advertising budget, work with the ad agency, and handle other advertising not done by the agency. Most large companies use outside advertising agencies because they offer several advantages.

Advertising agency

A marketing services firm that assists companies in planning, preparing, implementing, and evaluating all or portions of their advertising programs.

How does an **advertising agency** work? Advertising agencies were started in the mid-to-late 1800s by salespeople and brokers who worked for the media and received a commission for selling advertising space to companies. As time passed, the salespeople began to help customers prepare their ads. Eventually, they formed agencies and grew closer to the advertisers than to the media. Today's agencies employ specialists who can often perform advertising tasks better than can the company's own staff. Agencies also bring an outside point of view to solving the company's problems, along with lots of experience from working with different clients and situations. Thus, today, even companies with strong advertising departments of their own use advertising agencies.

Some ad agencies are huge—the largest U.S. agency, McCann-Erickson Worldwide, has a worldwide annual gross income of nearly $1.9 billion on billings (the dollar amount of advertising placed for clients) of almost $18 billion. In recent years, many agencies have grown by gobbling up other agencies, thus creating huge agency holding companies. The largest of these agency "megagroups," WPP Group, includes several large advertising, public relations, and promotion agencies and has a combined worldwide gross income of $8 billion on billings exceeding $75 billion.[12]

Most large advertising agencies have the staff and resources to handle all phases of an advertising campaign for their clients, from creating a marketing plan to developing ad campaigns and preparing, placing, and evaluating ads. Agencies usually have four departments: *creative*, which develops and produces ads; *media*, which selects media and places ads; *research*, which studies audience characteristics and wants; and *business*, which handles the agency's business activities. Each account is supervised by an account executive, and people in each department are usually assigned to work on one or more accounts.

Ad agencies traditionally have been paid through commissions and fees. In the past, the agency typically received 15 percent of the media cost as a rebate. For example, suppose the agency bought $60,000 of magazine space for a client. The magazine would bill the advertising agency for $51,000 ($60,000 less 15 percent), and the agency would then bill the client for $60,000, keeping the $9,000 commission. If the client bought space directly from the magazine, it would have paid $60,000 because commissions are paid only to recognized advertising agencies.

However, both advertisers and agencies have become more and more unhappy with the commission system. Larger advertisers complain that they pay more for the same services received by smaller ones simply because they place more advertising. Advertisers also believe that the commission system drives agencies away from low-cost media and short advertising campaigns. Another factor is vast changes in how ad agencies reach consumers, using methods that go way beyond network TV or magazine advertising.

"The commission formula tends to encourage costly media buys and has been criticized for overlooking important emerging mediums such as the Internet," say one advertising analyst. Therefore, she continues, "the 15 percent commission on media spending that . . . was once standard in the advertising business . . . is about as dead as the three-martini lunch." New agency payment methods may include anything from fixed retainers or straight hourly fees for labor to incentives keyed to performance of the agencies' ad campaigns, or some combination of these.[13]

Another trend is affecting the advertising agency business: Many agencies have sought growth by diversifying into related marketing services. These new diversified agencies offer a complete list of integrated marketing and promotion services under one roof, including advertising, sales promotion, marketing research, public relations, and direct and online marketing. Some have even added marketing consulting, television production, and sales training units in an effort to become full "marketing partners" to their clients.

However, agencies are finding that most advertisers don't want much more from them than traditional media advertising services plus direct marketing, sales promotion, and sometimes public relations. Thus, many agencies have recently limited their diversification efforts in order to focus more on traditional services. Some have even started their own "creative boutiques," smaller and more independent agencies that can develop creative campaigns for clients free of large-agency bureaucracy.

International Advertising Decisions

International advertisers face many complexities not encountered by domestic advertisers. The most basic issue concerns the degree to which global advertising should be adapted to the unique characteristics of various country markets. Some large advertisers have attempted to support their global brands with highly standardized worldwide advertising, with campaigns that work as well in Bangkok as they do in Baltimore. For example, Jeep has created a worldwide brand image of ruggedness and reliability; Coca-Cola's Sprite brand uses standardized appeals to target the world's youth. Gillette's ads for its Sensor Excel for Women are almost identical worldwide, with only minor adjustments to suit the local culture. Ericsson, the Swedish telecommunications giant, spent $100 million on a standardized global television campaign with the tag line "Make yourself heard," which features Agent 007, James Bond.

Standardization produces many benefits—lower advertising costs, greater global advertising coordination, and a more consistent worldwide image. But it also has drawbacks. Most importantly, it ignores the fact that country markets differ greatly in their cultures, demographics, and economic conditions. Thus, most international advertisers "think globally but act locally." They develop global advertising *strategies* that make their worldwide advertising efforts more efficient and consistent. Then they adapt their advertising *programs* to make them more responsive to consumer needs and expectations within local markets. For example, Coca-Cola has a pool of different commercials that can be used in or adapted to several different international markets. Some can be used with only minor changes—such as language—in several different countries. Local and regional managers decide which commercials work best for which markets.

Global advertisers face several special problems. For instance, advertising media costs and availability differ vastly from country to country. Countries also differ in the extent to which they regulate advertising practices. Many countries have extensive systems of laws restricting how much a company can spend on advertising, the media used, the nature of advertising claims, and other aspects of the advertising program. Such restrictions often require advertisers to adapt their campaigns from country to country.

For example, alcoholic products cannot be advertised or sold in Muslim countries. In many countries, Norway and Sweden, for example, no TV ads may be directed at children under 12. Moreover, Sweden is lobbying to extend that ban to all European Union member countries. To play it safe, McDonald's advertises itself as a family restaurant in Sweden. Comparative ads, while acceptable and even common in the United States and Canada, are less commonly used in the United Kingdom, unacceptable in Japan, and illegal in India and Brazil. China has restrictive censorship rules for TV and radio advertising; for example, the words *the best* are banned, as are ads that "violate social customs" or present women in "improper ways."

DaimlerChrysler creates a worldwide brand image of ruggedness and reliability for its Jeep brand. Here, its Thai, German, and U.S. Web sites contain only minor adjustments in messages to suit local languages and cultures.

Coca-Cola's Indian subsidiary was forced to end a promotion that offered prizes, such as a trip to Hollywood, because it violated India's established trade practices by encouraging customers to buy in order to "gamble."[14]

Thus, although advertisers may develop global strategies to guide their overall advertising efforts, specific advertising programs must usually be adapted to meet local cultures and customs, media characteristics, and advertising regulations.

Sales Promotion

Sales promotion

Short term incentives to encourage the purchase or sale of a product or service.

Advertising and personal selling often work closely with another promotion tool, sales promotion. **Sales promotion** consists of short-term incentives to encourage purchase or sales of a product or service. Whereas advertising and personal selling offer reasons to buy a product or service, sales promotion offers reasons to buy *now*.

Examples of sales promotions are found everywhere. A freestanding insert in the Sunday newspaper contains a coupon offering $1 off Folgers coffee. An e-mail from Amazon.com offers free shipping on your next purchase over $35. The end-of-the-aisle display in the local supermarket tempts impulse buyers with a wall of Coke cartons. An executive who buys a new Sony laptop gets a free carrying case, or a family buys a new Taurus and receives a rebate check for $500. A hardware store chain receives a 10 percent discount on selected Black & Decker portable power tools if it agrees to advertise them in local newspapers. Sales promotion includes a wide variety of promotion tools designed to stimulate earlier or stronger market response.

Rapid Growth of Sales Promotion

Sales promotion tools are used by most organizations, including manufacturers, distributors, retailers, trade associations, and not-for-profit institutions. They are targeted toward final buyers (*consumer promotions*), retailers and wholesalers (*trade promotions*), business customers (*business promotions*), and members of the sales force (*sales force promotions*). Today, in the average consumer packaged-goods company, sales promotion accounts for 76 percent of all marketing expenditures.[15]

Several factors have contributed to the rapid growth of sales promotion, particularly in consumer markets. First, inside the company, product managers face greater pressures to increase their current sales, and promotion is viewed as an effective short-run sales tool. Second, externally, the company faces more competition and competing brands are less differentiated. Increasingly, competitors are using sales promotion to help differentiate their offers. Third, advertising efficiency has declined because of rising costs, media clutter, and legal restraints. Finally, consumers have become more deal oriented, and ever-larger retailers are demanding more deals from manufacturers.

The growing use of sales promotion has resulted in *promotion clutter,* similar to advertising clutter. Consumers are increasingly tuning out promotions, weakening their ability to trigger immediate purchase. Manufacturers are now searching for ways to rise above the clutter, such as offering larger coupon values or creating more dramatic point-of-purchase displays.

In developing a sales promotion program, a company must first set sales promotion objectives and then select the best tools for accomplishing these objectives.

Sales Promotion Objectives

Sales promotion objectives vary widely. Sellers may use *consumer promotions* to increase short-term sales or to help build long-term market share. Objectives for *trade promotions* include getting retailers to carry new items and more inventory, getting them to advertise the product and give it more shelf space, and getting them to buy ahead. For the *sales force,* objectives include getting more sales force support for current or new products or getting salespeople to sign up new accounts. Sales promotions are usually used together with advertising, personal selling, or other promotion mix tools. Consumer promotions must usually be advertised and can add excitement and pulling power to ads. Trade and sales force promotions support the firm's personal selling process.

In general, rather than creating only short-term sales or temporary brand switching, sales promotions should help to reinforce the product's position and build long-term *customer relationships.* Increasingly, marketers are avoiding "quick fix," price-only promotions in favor of promotions designed to build brand equity.

Even price promotions can be designed to help build customer relationships. Examples include all of the "frequency marketing programs" and clubs that have mushroomed in recent years. For example, Waldenbooks sponsors a Preferred Reader Program, which has attracted more than 4 million members, each paying $5 to receive mailings about new books, a 10 percent discount on book purchases, toll-free ordering, and many other services. American Express's Custom Extras program automatically awards customers deals and discounts based on frequency of purchases at participating retailers. Norwegian Cruise Lines sponsors a loyalty program called Latitudes, a co-branding effort with Visa. Latitudes members receive exclusive deals and promotions, and up to $200 on-board credit, the services of a special person assigned to answer their questions at sea, savings on future sailings, invitations to an exclusive captain's reception and escorted tours of the ship's bridge and galley, and *Latitudes* magazine, which contains special articles on NCL's fleet and ports. If properly designed, every sales promotion tool has the potential to build consumer relationships.

Major Sales Promotion Tools

Many tools can be used to accomplish sales promotion objectives. Descriptions of the main consumer, trade, and business promotion tools follow.

Customer relationship-building promotions: "Frequent marketing programs" and clubs have mushroomed in recent years. Lladro's Collectors Society members receive a subscription to Expressions magazine, a bisque plaque, free enrollment in the Lladro Museum of New York, and other relationship-building benefits.

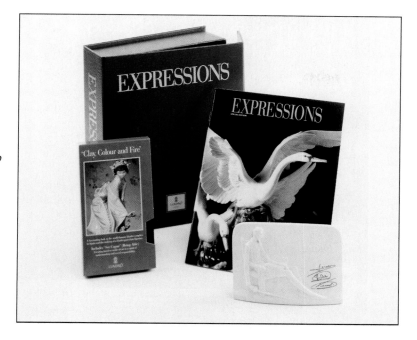

Consumer Promotion Tools

The main *consumer promotion tools* include samples, coupons, cash refunds, price packs, premiums, advertising specialties, patronage rewards, point-of-purchase displays and demonstrations, and contests, sweepstakes, and games.

Sample

A small amount of a product offered to consumers for trial.

Samples are offers of a trial amount of a product. Sampling is the most effective—but most expensive—way to introduce a new product. About 84 percent of consumer packaged-goods marketers use sampling as a part of their promotion strategy. For example, to launch Vanilla Coke, Coca-Cola distributed more than 1.3 million samples of the beverage. But the soft drink marketer didn't just hand out the samples. Instead, Coke staffers stopped targeted teen consumers at hangouts like malls, skate parks, concerts, and fairs, then delivered live commercials with messages like "Satisfy your curiosity, try a free Vanilla Coke." Says the president of Coca Cola's promotion agency, "We wanted to get Vanilla Coke's target audience with a memorable live experience for the brand."[16]

Some samples are free; for others, the company charges a small amount to offset its cost. The sample might be delivered door-to-door, sent by mail, handed out in a store, attached to another product, or featured in an ad. Sometimes, samples are combined into sample packs, which can then be used to promote other products and services. Procter & Gamble has even distributed samples via the Internet:

> When Procter & Gamble decided to relaunch Pert Plus shampoo, it extended its $20 million ad campaign by constructing a new Web site (www.pertplus.com). P&G had three objectives for the Web site: to create awareness for reformulated Pert Plus, get consumers to try the product, and gather data about Web users. The site's first page invites visitors to place their heads against the computer screen in a mock attempt to measure the cleanliness of their hair. After "tabulating the results," the site tells visitors that they "need immediate help." The solution: "How about a free sample of new Pert Plus?" Visitors obtain the sample by filling out a short demographic form. The site offers other interesting features as well. For example, clicking "get a friend in a lather" produces a template that will send an e-mail to a friend with an invitation to visit the site and receive a free sample. How did the sampling promotion work out? Even P&G was shocked by the turnout. Within just two months of launching the site, 170,000 people visited and 83,000 requested samples. More surprising, given that the site is only 10 pages deep, the average person visited the site 1.9 times and spent a total of 7.5 minutes each visit.[17]

Coupon

Certificate that gives buyers a saving when they purchase a specified product.

Coupons are certificates that give buyers a saving when they purchase specified products. Most consumers love coupons: They clip some 4.8 billion of them each year with an average face

Point-of-sale couponing: Using Checkout Direct technology, marketers can dispense personalized coupons to carefully targeted buyers at the checkout counter. This avoids the waste of poorly targeted coupons delivered through FSIs (coupon pages inserted into newspapers).

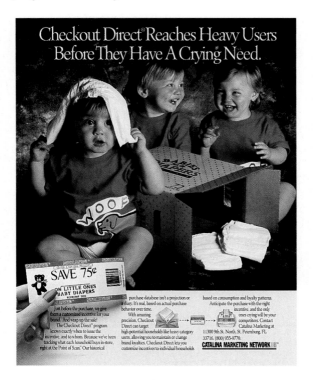

value of 70 cents, for a total savings of $3.4 billion.[18] Coupons can stimulate sales of a mature brand or promote early trial of a new brand. However, as a result of coupon clutter, redemption rates have been declining in recent years. Thus, most major consumer goods companies are issuing fewer coupons and targeting them more carefully.

They are also cultivating new outlets for distributing coupons, such as supermarket shelf dispensers, electronic point-of-sale coupon printers, or "paperless coupon systems." An example is Catalina Marketing Network's Checkout Direct system, which dispenses personalized discounts to targeted buyers at the checkout counter in stores. Some companies also offer coupons on their Web sites or through online coupon services such as coolsavings.com, valupage.com, hotcoupons.com, and directcoupons.com.[19]

Cash refund offer (rebate)
Offer to refund part of the purchase price of a product to consumers who send a "proof of purchase" to the manufacturer.

Cash refund offers (or **rebates**) are like coupons except that the price reduction occurs after the purchase rather than at the retail outlet. The consumer sends a "proof of purchase" to the manufacturer, who then refunds part of the purchase price by mail. For example, Toro ran a clever preseason promotion on some of its snowblower models, offering a rebate if the snowfall in the buyer's market area turned out to be below average. Competitors were not able to match this offer on such short notice, and the promotion was very successful.

Price pack (cents off deal)
Reduced price that is marked by the producer directly on the label or package.

Price packs (also called **cents-off deals**) offer consumers savings off the regular price of a product. The reduced prices are marked by the producer directly on the label or package. Price packs can be single packages sold at a reduced price (such as two for the price of one), or two related products banded together (such as a toothbrush and toothpaste). Price packs are very effective—even more so than coupons—in stimulating short-term sales.

Premium
Good offered either free or at low cost as an incentive to buy a product.

Premiums are goods offered either free or at low cost as an incentive to buy a product, ranging from toys included with kids' products to phone cards and CDs. A premium may come inside the package (in-pack), outside the package (on-pack), or through the mail. In its "Treasure Hunt" promotion, for example, Quaker Oats inserted $5 million worth of gold and silver coins in Ken-L Ration dog food packages. Cutty Sark offered a brass tray with the purchase of one bottle of its scotch and a desk lamp with the purchase of two. United Airlines rewarded Chicago-area 75,000 Mileage Plus frequent-flier club members with a custom CD. The 10-song, Chicago-themed compilation disk, entitled "Chicago—Our Kind of Town," was widely played on local radio stations. It became so popular that United ended up selling it at record stores. The airline plans similar custom-designed premiums for four other major cities it serves.[20]

Advertising specialty
Useful article imprinted with an advertiser's name, given as a gift to consumers.

Advertising specialties are useful articles imprinted with an advertiser's name that are given as gifts to consumers. Typical items include pens, calendars, key rings, matches, shopping bags, T-shirts, caps, nail files, and coffee mugs. Such items can be very effective. In a recent study, 63 percent of all consumers surveyed were either carrying or wearing an ad specialty item. More than three-quarters of those who had an item could recall the advertiser's name or message before showing the item to the interviewer.[21]

Patronage reward
Cash or other award for the regular use of a certain company's products or services.

Patronage rewards are cash or other awards offered for the regular use of a certain company's products or services. For example, airlines offer frequent-flier plans, awarding points for miles traveled that can be turned in for free airline trips. Hotels have adopted honored-guest plans that award points to users of their hotels. And supermarkets issue frequent-shopper cards that dole out a wealth of discounts at the checkout. Baskin-Robbins offers frequent-purchase awards—for every 10 purchases, customers receive a free quart of ice cream.

Point-of-purchase (POP) promotion
Display and demonstration that takes place at the point of purchase or sale.

Point-of-purchase (POP) promotions include displays and demonstrations that take place at the point of purchase or sale. An example is a five-foot-high cardboard display of Cap'n Crunch next to Cap'n Crunch cereal boxes. Unfortunately, many retailers do not like to handle the hundreds of displays, signs, and posters they receive from manufacturers each year. Manufacturers have responded by offering better POP materials, tying them in with television or print messages, and offering to set them up.

Contests, sweepstakes, games
Promotional events that give consumers the chance to win something—such as cash, trips, or goods—by luck or through extra effort.

Contests, sweepstakes, and **games** give consumers the chance to win something, such as cash, trips, or goods, by luck or through extra effort. A *contest* calls for consumers to submit an entry—a jingle, guess, suggestion—to be judged by a panel that will select the best entries. A *sweepstakes* calls for consumers to submit their names for a drawing. A *game* presents consumers with something—bingo numbers, missing letters—every time they buy, which may or may not help them win a prize. A sales contest urges dealers or the sales force to increase their efforts, with prizes going to the top performers.

Trade Promotion Tools

Manufacturers direct more sales promotion dollars toward retailers and wholesalers (78 percent) than to consumers (22 percent). Trade promotion can persuade resellers to carry a brand, give it shelf space, promote it in advertising, and push it to consumers. Shelf space is so scarce these days that manufacturers often have to offer discounts, allowances, buy-back guarantees, or free goods to retailers and wholesalers to get products on the shelf and, once there, to stay on it.

Discount
A straight reduction in price on purchases during a stated period of time.

Manufacturers use several trade promotion tools. Many of the tools used for consumer promotions—contests, premiums, displays—can also be used as trade promotions. Or the manufacturer may offer a straight **discount** off the list price on each case purchased during a stated period of time (also called a *price-off, off-invoice,* or *off-list*). Manufacturers also may offer an **allowance** (usually so much off per case) in return for the retailer's agreement to feature the manufacturer's products in some way. An *advertising allowance* compensates retailers for advertising the product. A *display allowance* compensates them for using special displays.

Allowance
Promotional money paid by manufacturers to retailers in return for an agreement to feature the manufacturer's products in some way.

Manufacturers may offer *free goods,* which are extra cases of merchandise, to resellers who buy a certain quantity or who feature a certain flavor or size. They may offer *push money*—cash or gifts to dealers or their sales forces to "push" the manufacturer's goods. Manufacturers may give retailers free *specialty advertising items* that carry the company's name, such as pens, pencils, calendars, paperweights, matchbooks, memo pads, and yardsticks.

Business Promotion Tools

Companies spend billions of dollars each year on promotion to industrial customers. These *business promotion tools* are used to generate business leads, stimulate purchases, reward customers, and motivate salespeople. Business promotion includes many of the same tools used for consumer or trade promotions. Here, we focus on two additional major business promotion tools—conventions and trade shows, and sales contests.

Many companies and trade associations organize *conventions and trade shows* to promote their products. Firms selling to the industry show their products at the trade show. More than 4,300 trade shows take place every year, drawing as many as 85 million people. Vendors receive many benefits, such as opportunities to find new sales leads, contact customers, introduce new products, meet new customers, sell more to present customers, and educate customers with publications and audiovisual materials. Trade shows also help companies reach many prospects not

More than 4,300 trade shows take place every year, drawing as many as 85 million people, giving sellers chances to introduce new products and meet new customers. At this consumer electronics trade show, 2,000 exhibitors attracted more than 91,000 professional visitors.

reached through their sales forces. About 90 percent of a trade show's visitors see a company's salespeople for the first time at the show. Business marketers may spend as much as 35 percent of their annual promotion budgets on trade shows.[22]

A *sales contest* is a contest for salespeople or dealers to motivate them to increase their sales performance over a given period. Sales contests motivate and recognize good company performers, who may receive trips, cash prizes, or other gifts. Some companies award points for performance, which the receiver can turn in for any of a variety of prizes. Sales contests work best when they are tied to measurable and achievable sales objectives (such as finding new accounts, reviving old accounts, or increasing account profitability).

Developing the Sales Promotion Program

The marketer must make several other decisions in order to define the full sales promotion program. First, the marketer must decide on the *size of the incentive*. A certain minimum incentive is necessary if the promotion is to succeed; a larger incentive will produce more sales response. The marketer also must set *conditions for participation*. Incentives might be offered to everyone or only to select groups.

The marketer must then decide how to *promote and distribute the promotion program* itself. A 50-cents-off coupon could be given out in a package, at the store, by mail, or in an advertisement. Each distribution method involves a different level of reach and cost. Increasingly, marketers are blending several media into a total campaign concept. The *length of the promotion* is also important. If the sales promotion period is too short, many prospects (who may not be buying during that time) will miss it. If the promotion runs too long, the deal will lose some of its "act now" force.

Evaluation is also very important. Yet many companies fail to evaluate their sales promotion programs, and others evaluate them only superficially. The most common evaluation method is to compare sales before, during, and after a promotion. Suppose a company has a 6 percent market share before the promotion, which jumps to 10 percent during the promotion, falls to 5 percent right after, and rises to 7 percent later on. The promotion seems to have attracted new "triers" and stimulated more buying by current customers. After the promotion, sales fell as consumers used up their inventories. The long-run rise to 7 percent means that the company gained some new users. If the brand's share had returned to the old level, then the promotion would have changed only the *timing* of demand rather than the *total* demand.

Consumer research would also show the kinds of people who responded to the promotion and what they did after it ended. *Surveys* can provide information on how many consumers recall the promotion, what they thought of it, how many took advantage of it, and how it affected their buying. Sales promotions also can be evaluated through *experiments* that vary factors such as incentive value, length, and distribution method.

Clearly, sales promotion plays an important role in the total promotion mix. To use it well, the marketer must define the sales promotion objectives, select the best tools, design the sales promotion program, implement the program, and evaluate the results. Moreover, sales promotion must be coordinated carefully with other promotion mix elements within the integrated marketing communications program.

Public Relations

Public relations

Building good relations with the company's various publics by obtaining favorable publicity, building up a good corporate image, and handling or heading off unfavorable rumors, stories, and events.

Another major mass-promotion tool is **public relations**—building good relations with the company's various publics by obtaining favorable publicity, building up a good corporate image, and handling or heading off unfavorable rumors, stories, and events. Public relations departments may perform any or all of the following functions:[23]

- *Press relations or press agentry:* Creating and placing newsworthy information in the news media to attract attention to a person, product, or service.
- *Product publicity:* Publicizing specific products.
- *Public affairs:* Building and maintaining national or local community relations.
- *Lobbying:* Building and maintaining relations with legislators and government officials to influence legislation and regulation.
- *Investor relations:* Maintaining relationships with shareholders and others in the financial community.
- *Development:* Public relations with donors or members of nonprofit organizations to gain financial or volunteer support.

Public relations is used to promote products, people, places, ideas, activities, organizations, and even nations. Trade associations have used public relations to rebuild interest in declining commodities such as eggs, apples, milk, and potatoes. New York City turned its image around

Public relations involves many functions beyond product publicity, including public affairs, lobbying, and investor relations. For example, most company Web sites feature special sections for current and potential investors—like this one for Nike.

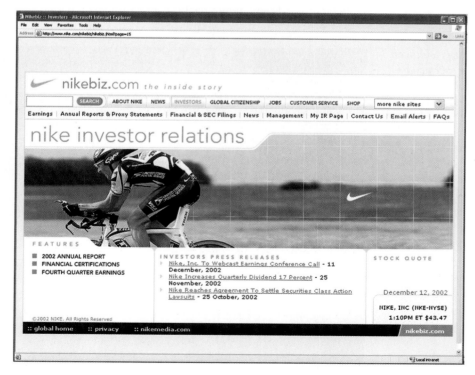

when its "I ♥ New York!" campaign took root, bringing millions more tourists to the city. Johnson & Johnson's masterly use of public relations played a major role in saving Tylenol from extinction after its product-tampering scare. Nations have used public relations to attract more tourists, foreign investment, and international support.

The Role and Impact of Public Relations

Public relations can have a strong impact on public awareness at a much lower cost than advertising can. The company does not pay for the space or time in the media. Rather, it pays for a staff to develop and circulate information and to manage events. If the company develops an interesting story, it could be picked up by several different media, having the same effect as advertising that would cost millions of dollars. And it would have more credibility than advertising.

Public relations results can sometimes be spectacular. Here's how publisher Scholastic, Inc., used public relations to turn a simple new book introduction into a major international event, all on a very small budget:

> Secret codes. A fiercely guarded text. Huddled masses lined up in funny hats at the witching hour. Welcome to one of the biggest and oddest literary events in history. As the clock crept past midnight, kids worldwide rushed to buy the fourth installment of the Harry Potter series. It was the fastest-shrinking book pile in history—with nearly 3 million copies selling in 48 hours in the United States alone. The spellbinding plots, written by Scottish welfare-mom-turned-millionaire J. K. Rowling, captivated kids everywhere, but the hidden hand of [public relations] played a role, too. With contests, theme parties, and giveaways, conditions were hot for Harry. How do you whip up a consumer frenzy with a mere $1.8 million promotion budget? Scholastic mixed in-store promotions with a few carefully placed ads [and a heap of public relations hype] to create a sense of celebration. It heightened the tension by keeping the title and book jacket under wraps almost until the last minute, even forcing booksellers to sign secrecy agreements.[24]

Despite its potential strengths, public relations is often described as a marketing stepchild because of its limited and scattered use. The public relations department is usually located at corporate headquarters. Its staff is so busy dealing with various publics—stockholders, employees, legislators, city officials—that public relations programs to support product marketing objectives may be ignored. Marketing managers and public relations practitioners do not always talk the same language. Many public relations practitioners see their job as simply communicating. In

Public relations results can sometimes be spectacular. Scholastic sponsored low-cost sleepovers, games, and costume contests to whip up consumer frenzy for the fourth installment of its Harry Potter series.

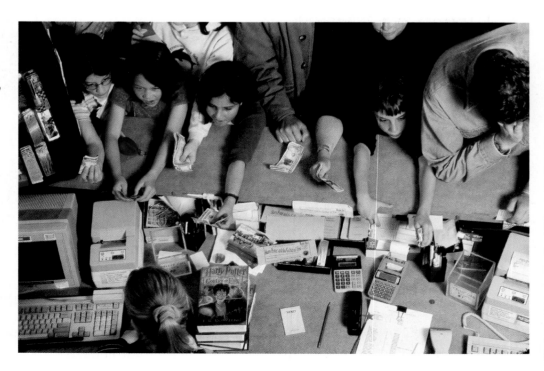

contrast, marketing managers tend to be much more interested in how advertising and public relations affect brand building, sales, and profits.

This situation is changing, however. Although public relations still captures only a small portion of the overall marketing budgets of most firms, PR is playing an increasingly important brand-building role. For example, when Gillette launched its Mach 3 men's razor, it relied on PR, including a full-length feature in *The New Yorker,* to generate more than 1.6 billion consumer impressions.[25] When Heinz launched EZ Squirt ketchup, the value of the free media space it received based on the product's unique green color amounted to more than three times what the company spent on traditional advertising. And when Proctor & Gamble launched its highly successful White Strips, prelaunch efforts generated $23 million in sales prior to retail availability. Of those sales, one-third were directly linked to public relations.

Segway supported the debut of its self-balancing human transporter with a heavily orchestrated public relations push. It unveiled the device on ABC's *Good Morning America.* The show's co-hosts, Diane Sawyer and Charlie Gibson, smiled and laughed as they rode around Bryant Park on their Segway human transporters. Articles in major papers followed, along with a lengthy story in *Time* magazine, which featured a picture of Osama bin Laden making his escape on a Segway HT. Next, the television character Niles, on NBC's *Frasier,* scooted about on a Segway HT for a full episode. In only one month, Segway's publicity onslaught generated 758 million impressions, equivalent to the impact of some $70 million to $80 million worth of advertising. All of this resulted in high levels of product awareness—at low cost and with no advertising—well before the device was available for retail purchase. Moreover, it helped to convince the U.S. Postal Service to outfit many of its carriers with transporters to increase efficiency on their routes.

Thus, good public relations can be a powerful brand-building tool. In fact, two well-known marketing consultants have concluded that advertising doesn't build brands, PR does. They provide the following advice, which points to the potential power of public relations as a first step in brand building:

> Just because a heavy dose of advertising is associated with most major brands doesn't necessarily mean that advertising built the brands in the first place. The birth of a brand is usually accomplished with [public relations], not advertising. Our general rule is [PR] first, advertising second. [Public relations] is the nail, advertising the hammer. [PR] creates the credentials that provide the credibility for advertising. . . . Anita Roddick built the Body Shop into a major brand with no advertising at all. Instead, she traveled the world on a relentless quest for publicity. . . . Until recently Starbucks Coffee Co. didn't spend a hill of beans on advertising, either. In 10 years, the company spent less than $10 million on advertising, a trivial amount for a brand that delivers annual sales of $1.3 billion. Wal-Mart Stores became the world's largest retailer . . . with very little advertising. . . . In the toy field, Furby, Beanie Babies, and Tickle Me Elmo became highly successful . . . and on the Internet, Yahoo!, Amazon.com, and Excite became powerhouse brands, [all] with virtually no advertising.[26]

In their book *The Fall of Advertising and the Rise of PR,* the consultants assert that the era of advertising is over, and that public relations is quietly becoming the most powerful marketing communications tools. Although most marketers don't go this far, the point is a good one. Advertising and public relations should work hand in hand to build and maintain brands.

Major Public Relations Tools

Public relations professionals use several tools. One of the major tools is *news.* PR professionals find or create favorable news about the company and its products or people. Sometimes news stories occur naturally, and sometimes the PR person can suggest events or activities that would create news. *Speeches* can also create product and company publicity. Increasingly, company executives must field questions from the media or give talks at trade associations or sales meetings, and these events can either build or hurt the company's image.

Another common PR tool is *special events,* ranging from news conferences, press tours, grand openings, and fireworks displays to laser shows, hot air balloon releases, multimedia presentations and star-studded spectaculars, and educational programs designed to reach and interest target

A company's Web site can be a good public relations vehicle. Butterball's site, which features cooking and carving tips, received 550,000 visits in one day during Thanksgiving week last year.

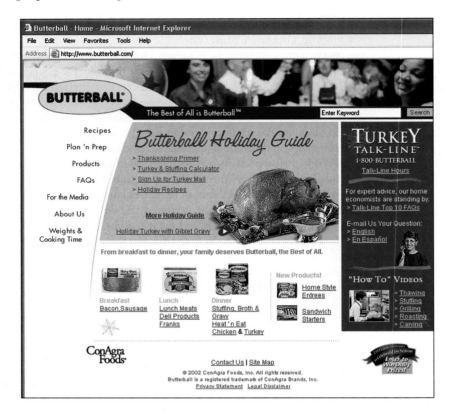

publics. Recently, *mobile marketing*—traveling promotional tours that bring the brand to consumers—has emerged as an effective way to build one-to-one relationships with targeted consumers.

These days, it seems that almost every company is putting its show on the road, with a record number of marketers launching nationwide tours. Not only are such tours relatively cheap, they offer an irresistible opportunity to build brands while attracting additional sponsorship dollars and promotional relationships with retailers and trade marketing partners. Home Depot recently brought do-it-yourself home project workshops and demonstrations to 26 NASCAR racetracks. Court TV launched a tour that visited malls in 20 cities, challenging consumers to solve a crime by visiting six "forensic labs" and interviewing a computerized virtual witness. Mattel's Matchbox Toys launched its first-ever tour last year, hitting store parking lots in 25 cities over six months to celebrate Matchbox's 50th anniversary. Events included interactive games, historic displays, free gifts, and an obstacle course for kids riding battery-powered vehicles. And Krispy Kreme recently unveiled a 53-foot-long, fully functioning store on wheels at an event in Winston-Salem, North Carolina, the chain's headquarters. It takes a day to set up the shop—which sells doughnuts, coffee, and logoed merchandise—so the company is targeting planned festivals, fairs, and events around the country. The mobile unit is scheduled to be on the road approximately 250 days during the next year, visiting cities that are new to the company along with more established markets.[27]

Public relations people also prepare *written materials* to reach and influence their target markets. These materials include annual reports, brochures, articles, and company newsletters and magazines. *Audiovisual materials,* such as films, slide-and-sound programs, and video- and audio-cassettes, are being used increasingly as communication tools. *Corporate identity materials* can also help create a corporate identity that the public immediately recognizes. Logos, stationery, brochures, signs, business forms, business cards, buildings, uniforms, and company cars and trucks—all become marketing tools when they are attractive, distinctive, and memorable. Finally, companies can improve public goodwill by contributing money and time to *public service activities.*

A company's Web site can be a good public relations vehicle. Consumers and members of other publics can visit the site for information and entertainment. Such sites can be extremely popular. For example, Butterball's site (www.butterball.com), which features cooking and carving tips, received

550,000 visitors in one day during Thanksgiving week last year. Web sites can also be ideal for handling crisis situations. For example, when several bottles of Odwalla apple juice sold on the West Coast were found to contain *E. coli* bacteria, Odwalla initiated a massive product recall. Within only three hours, it set up a Web site laden with information about the crisis and Odwalla's response. Company staffers also combed the Internet looking for newsgroups discussing Odwalla and posted links to the site. In another example, American Home Products quickly set up a Web site to distribute accurate information and advice after a model died reportedly after inhaling its Primatene Mist. The Primatene site, up less than 12 hours after the crisis broke, remains in place today (www.primatene.com). In all, notes one analyst, "Today, public relations is reshaping the Internet, and the Internet, in turn, is redefining the practice of public relations." Says another, "People look to the Net for information, not salesmanship, and that's the real opportunity for public relations."[28]

As with the other promotion tools, in considering when and how to use product public relations, management should set PR objectives, choose the PR messages and vehicles, implement the PR plan, and evaluate the results. The firm's public relations should be blended smoothly with other promotion activities within the company's overall integrated marketing communications effort.

LOOKING BACK: REVIEWING THE CONCEPTS

Companies must do more than make good products—they have to inform consumers about product benefits and carefully position products in consumers' minds. To do this, they must skillfully employ three mass-promotion tools in addition to personal selling, which targets specific buyers: *advertising, sales promotion,* and *public relations.*

1. Define the roles of advertising, sales promotion, and public relations in the promotion mix.

Advertising—the use of paid media by a seller to inform, persuade, and remind about its products or organization—is a strong promotion tool. American marketers spend more than $150 billion each year on advertising, and it takes many forms and has many uses. *Sales promotion* covers a wide variety of short-term incentive tools—coupons, premiums, contests, buying allowances—designed to stimulate final and business consumers, the trade, and the company's own sales force. Sales-promotion spending has been growing faster than advertising spending in recent years. *Public relations*—gaining favorable publicity and creating a favorable company image—is the least used of the major promotion tools, although it has great potential for building consumer awareness and preference.

2. Describe the major decisions involved in developing an advertising program.

Advertising decision making involves decisions about the objectives, the budget, the message, the media, and, finally, the evaluation of results. Advertisers should set clear *objectives* as to whether the advertising is supposed to inform, persuade, or remind buyers. The advertising *budget* can be based on sales, on competitors' spending, or on the objectives and tasks. The

message decision calls for planning a message strategy and executing it effectively. The *media decision* involves defining reach, frequency, and impact goals; choosing major media types; selecting media vehicles; and deciding on media timing. Message and media decisions must be closely coordinated for maximum campaign effectiveness. Finally, *evaluation* calls for evaluating the communication and sales effects of advertising before, during, and after the advertising is placed.

3. Explain how sales promotion campaigns are developed and implemented.

Sales promotion campaigns call for setting sales promotions objectives (in general, sales promotions should be *consumer relationship building*); selecting tools; developing and implementing the sales promotion program by using trade promotion tools (*discounts, allowances, free goods, push money*) and business promotion tools (*conventions, trade shows, sales contests*) as well as deciding on such things as the size of the incentive, the conditions for participation, how to promote and distribute the promotion package, and the length of the promotion. After this process is completed, the company evaluates the results.

4. Explain how companies use public relations to communicate with their publics.

Companies use public relations to communicate with their publics by setting PR objectives, choosing PR messages and vehicles, implementing the PR plan, and evaluating PR results. To accomplish these goals, public relations professionals use several tools, such as *news, speeches,* and *special events.* They also prepare *written, audiovisual,* and *corporate identity materials* and contribute money and time to *public service activities.*

REVIEWING THE KEY TERMS

Advertising 494
Advertising agency 507
Advertising objective 495
Advertising specialty 513
Allowance 513
Cash refund offer (rebate) 512

Contests, sweepstakes, games 513
Coupon 511
Discount 513
Patronage reward 513
Point-of-purchase (POP) promotion 513

Premium 512
Price pack (cents-off deal) 512
Public relations 515
Sales promotion 509
Sample 511

DISCUSSING THE CONCEPTS

1. Marketing managers make four important decisions when developing an advertising program. List and briefly describe these decisions.

2. Advertising objectives can be classified by primary purpose: to inform, persuade, or remind. Using your local newspaper, find examples of ads that address each of these objectives. Using Table 16.1, discuss why your examples fit the chosen objectives.

3. Until recently, television viewers were considered a captive audience for advertisers. How has this changed? How do you think the changes in consumer television viewing habits will impact advertising? What actions should advertisers consider to regain the consumer audience?

4. Advertisers must develop compelling creative concepts—or "big ideas"—that will bring their message strategies to life in a distinctive way. The creative concept, then, will guide the choice of specific appeals to be used in an advertising campaign. Find what you perceive to be a compelling creative concept in a magazine advertisement. Identify the specific appeals being used, and comment on what you think the advertiser is trying to accomplish with the ad.

5. The chapter lists nine different execution styles that advertisers often use to meet advertising objectives. Which of these styles do you think is most commonly used? Select three styles and find an example of each. Critique each example on its content, effectiveness, and match to the selected target market.

6. A bicycle shop owner in a suburban college town wants to target both serious cyclists and college students. Her limited annual advertising budget totals $8,000. She has already constructed a Web site, which includes pictures of products found in the store. Review Table 16.2 and build a media mix to help the owner target the intended audience on her limited budget.

7. Which of the sales promotional tools described in the chapter would be best for stimulating sales of the following products and services: (a) a dry cleaner wishing to emphasize low prices on washed and pressed dress shirts, (b) Gummy Bears' new Sun Burst Orange flavor, (c) Procter & Gamble's efforts to bundle laundry detergent and fabric softener together in a combined marketing effort, (d) an online merchant trying to engage customers in the development of a new advertising jingle, and (e) Outpost.com's effort to increase name recognition and traffic at its Web site.

8. The Internet is the latest public relations frontier. Web users now routinely share their experiences and problems with a company's products, service, prices, and warranties on electronic bulletin boards and in chat rooms. What kinds of special public relations problems and opportunities does the Internet present to today's marketers? How can companies use their own Web sites to address these problems and opportunities? Find an example of a company that uses its Web site as a proactive public relations tool.

APPLYING THE CONCEPTS

1. Beginning with a thrilling chase scene in the 1996 hit movie *The Rock,* Hummer all-terrain vehicles have been all the rage among "Xtreme" drivers. The Hummer comes in two basic versions—the H1 and the H2. Both vehicles can scale a 20-inch vertical wall, ford 20 inches of water, climb a 60 percent incline, and traverse a 40 percent side slope. Despite these amazing characteristics, Hummer has a problem—it has sold itself to the "Xtreme" crowd too well. As a result, the car is no longer seen as a practical choice for the average driver. In an attempt to reposition the vehicle, Hummer is shifting the emphasis of its advertising to promote the vehicle's safety features and luxury interiors. Will the company succeed in its attempt at an image makeover? Hummer has yet to approach a barrier it cannot overcome!

   a. Visit www.hummer.com for more information on the Hummer. Does either the H1 or the H2 appeal to you? Would either appeal to your parents?

   b. Based on your visit to the company's Web site, how is Hummer trying to position its brand? Does the information presented on the Web site effectively reinforce the repositioning of the brand?

   c. Design a magazine advertisement for Hummer to appear in *Sports Illustrated, Business Week,* and *TV Guide* magazines. Construct a "rough" of an ad that would have as its primary purpose the repositioning of the Hummer brand to a more consumer-friendly vehicle. Be sure to add a headline or theme line that indicates the new direction Hummer is pursuing.

2. Philip Morris Company is the world's largest tobacco company. It's also one of the most controversial. Philip Morris is full of apparent contradictions. For example, it recently spent $100 million to persuade children not to smoke. It contributes $60 million in cash and $15 million in food each year to fight hunger, combat domestic violence, and support the arts. And it has paid billions of dollars to reimburse states for the costs of treating smoking-related illnesses. Even its employees have given more than $5 million to charities. So why is Philip Morris on every social crusader's hit list? The answer: the tobacco culture that engulfs the organization. For years, Philip Morris operated under a siege mentality, closing itself off from the questions and criticism coming from the outside world. Recently, this culture has begun to change. The company is now renewing its efforts to change its image. But being a responsible corporate citizen and changing the company's culture, products, and image won't be easy.

   a. What public relations issues does Philip Morris face?

   b. On its Web site (www.philipmorris.com), Philip Morris admits that "cigarette smoking is addictive." What kind of public relations advantages does this admission create? What problems?

   c. Visit the Web sites of other Philip Morris companies. What public relations synergies do you see? What problems might these synergies create?

   d. Outline a public relations program for gaining public trust and shareholder interest.

e. The use of tobacco products has been under attack in the United States for several years. However, this adversarial environment does not exist in all markets. In Europe, Africa, and Asia (especially China and Japan), smoking is a popular and growing habit. Considering the social and public relations approach Philip Morris is using in the United States, outline a global public relations strategy for the company. What role do advertising, sales promotion, and the company's Web site play in your strategy?

 DIGITAL CONNECTIONS

COMMUNICATION CONNECTIONS VIA ONLINE ADVERTISING

Is online advertising a boom or a bust? Even most critics still believe that advertising on the Internet has a bright future as long as its unique features are expanded and exploited. Online advertising is unique and has its own set of strengths and weaknesses. Banners, pop-ups, sponsorships, vertical and horizontal space usage, and the ability to target unique (and interested) audiences are the strengths that new and dynamic online communication strategies are built on. How is the medium doing? With more than $7 billion in sales annually at the beginning of the twenty-first century, it has already surpassed outdoor advertising in it usage. While Web-based advertising is not designed to broadcast messages to the masses in the same way television advertising does, it does focus on particular target markets, making it attractive to many marketers. Today most large advertising agencies now have online advertising divisions to ensure that this media form is used effectively. The new challenge in online advertising will be to determine not only how many times a consumer views an ad but what action he or she takes as a result. Although it may take a while, the Internet may yet achieve advertising superstar status.

FOR DISCUSSION

1. DoubleClick, one of the largest online advertising firms, specializes in targeted advertising. Visit the Web site at www.doubleclick.com. Read the information for potential advertisers, then describe how DoubleClick targets ads using audience psychographics and buying behavior.
2. When compared to television and magazine advertising, what are the advantages and disadvantages of online advertising?
3. How does online advertising monitor consumers' behavior and capture data about them? What other media forms capture consumer data?
4. Assume you are the advertising manager for a large toy manufacturer considering a significant expenditure in online advertising for the upcoming Christmas season. Visit NetRatings (www.netratings.com) to examine statistics on the top banner ads currently online. Then design a banner ad you think would be most effective for your company. Explain any assumptions you made about your company and its products when you designed your ad.

Potty Perfection: Creating a Customer Experience

In recent years, Procter & Gamble has set out to change "the public restroom experience from the bottom up." The consumer goods giant has "Charmin-ized" restrooms at 15 different state and county fairs across the country, adding greenery, hiring bathroom attendants, putting up curtains, and replacing the usual scratchy one-ply tissue with Charmin Ultra. The result? "People love it," says a P&G spokesperson. Close to 350,000 people visited the Charmin-ized facilities at the Ohio State Fair alone.

After viewing the "Potty Perfection" video, featuring the Charmin Fair Tour, answer the following questions about advertising and public relations:

1. P&G's approach to promoting Charmin at state and county fairs represents a unique approach to brand promotion. How might this sponsorship affect consumers differently from traditional mass-media advertising?
2. Think back to the last public event you attended—a sporting event, fair, arts festival, or other event. Did you notice any interesting sponsorships or advertisements? How did those promotions affect your interest in the product or service promoted?
3. Select one of your favorite brands. What forms of alternative media might a marketer employ to promote that brand or product? Are there event sponsorships that fit naturally with the brand's image or functionality?

Source: Additional information gathered from Laura Pulfer, "Charmin Exhibit: Changing Bathroom's Bottom Line," *Cincinnati Enquirer,* August 5, 2001, accessed online at http://enquirer.com/editions/2001/08/05/loc_1pulfer_charmin.html.

Pepsi: Promoting Nothing

WATER WARS

Everyone's familiar with the cola wars—the epic battles between Pepsi Cola and Coca-Cola in the soft drink market. The war has featured numerous taste tests and mostly friendly, but sometimes not-so-friendly, television ads featuring Pepsi and Coke delivery-truck drivers, each trying to outdo the other.

The major problem that Pepsi and Coke face is that the cola market is mature and not growing very rapidly. Thus, to generate new sales and new customers, the companies have to look for new fronts.

In the early 1990s, the bottled-water market was just a drop in the huge U.S. beverage market bucket. The Evian and Perrier brands dominated the tiny niche and helped establish bottled spring water's clean, healthy image. Pepsi took an early interest in the water market. It tried several different ways to attack this market, with both spring water and sparkling water, but each failed. Then it hit on the idea of taking advantage of a built-in resource—its existing bottlers.

Pepsi's bottlers already had their own water treatment facilities to further purify the municipal tap water used in making soft drinks. All municipal tap water must be pure enough to pass constant monitoring and rigorous quarterly EPA prescribed tests. Still, cola bottlers filtered it again before using it in the production process.

Pepsi decided that it would *really* filter the tap water. It experimented with a reverse osmosis process, pushing already-filtered tap water at high pressure through fiberglass membranes to remove even the tiniest particles. Then, carbon filters removed chlorine and any other particles that might give the water any taste or smell. All this filtering removed even good particles that killed bacteria, so Pepsi had to add ozone to the water to keep bacteria from growing. The result? Aquafina—a water with no taste or odor—that Pepsi believed could compete with the spring waters already on the market. Further, Pepsi could license its bottlers to use the Aquafina name and sell them the filtration equipment. Because the process used tap water that was relatively inexpensive, Pepsi's Aquafina would also compete well on price with the spring waters.

The marketing strategy was relatively simple. Whereas Evian and the other early entrants targeted women and high-end consumers, Pepsi wanted consumers to see Aquafina as a "unisex, mainstream" water with an everyday price. When the company launched the product in 1994, it was content just to build distribution using its established system and spend very little money on promotion. Pepsi believed that soft drink advertising should be for soft drinks, not water.

COME ON IN—THE WATER'S FINE

By 1999, what had been a minor trickle in the beverage market had turned into a geyser—bottled water had become the fastest-growing beverage category, and Pepsi had a big head start. Coca-Cola decided it was time to take the plunge. Like Pepsi, Coca-Cola realized its bottlers were already set up to handle a filtered-water process. Unlike Pepsi, however, rather than taking everything out of the tap water, it wanted to put something in.

Coca-Cola's researchers analyzed tap waters and bottled waters and concocted a combination of minerals they believed would give filtered tap water a fresh, clean taste. The formula included magnesium sulfate, potassium chloride, and salt. Coca-Cola guarded the new water formula just as it had the original Coke recipe. Thus, it could sell the formula to its bottlers, as it does Coke concentrate, and let them make the water.

Like Pepsi, Coca-Cola was content initially just to get its water, which it called Dasani, into distribution.

HOW TO PROMOTE WATER

By 2001, however, the bottled-water category had over 800 competitors and had grown to $3.53 billion in U.S. sales. Analysts predicted bottled water would become the second largest beverage category by 2004. Nestlé's Perrier Group (Perrier, Poland Spring, and others) held 37.4 percent of the market, followed by Pepsi with 13.8 percent, Coca-Cola with 12 percent, Group Danone (Evian and others) with 11.8 percent, and all others with 25 percent.

Given the rapid market growth rate and all the competition, Pepsi and Coca-Cola decided they had better promote their products, just as they did their soft drinks. In 2001, Pepsi launched a $14 million campaign showing real people and how water was part of their lives. Coca-Cola countered with a $20 million campaign that targeted women and used the tag line "Treat yourself well. Everyday."

Not to be outdone, Pepsi responded by more than doubling its promotion budget to $40 million in 2002. Included in the advertising was a spot featuring *'Friends'* star Lisa Kudrow. Lisa described how refreshing and mouthwatering Aquafina was—emphasizing that it made no promises it couldn't keep. She described Aquafina as "Pure nothing." The ads featured the tag line "We promise nothing."

So, Pepsi and Coca-Cola had drawn new battle lines—this time for the water wars. Could Pepsi convince consumers to prefer a water that offered nothing versus Coca-Cola's water that offered something—although both products were colorless, odorless, and tasteless? Further, what would Pepsi and Coca-Cola do in response to the pressure on them to launch "aquaceuticals"—water that was *enhanced* with calcium and fluoride or perhaps even (are you ready for this?) *flavors*? What impact would such products have on Pepsi's advertising strategy?

QUESTIONS FOR DISCUSSION

1. What markets should Pepsi target for Aquafina?
2. What advertising objectives should Pepsi set for Aquafina?

3. What message strategy and message execution recommendations would you make for Aquafina?
4. What advertising media recommendations would you make for Aquafina, and how would you evaluate the effectiveness of those media and your advertising?
5. What sales promotion and public relations recommendations would you make for Aquafina?
6. If Pepsi launches an "aquaceutical," should it use the Aquafina brand name?

Sources: "Non-Alcoholic Beverages: Aquafina," *Advertising Age,* May 6, 2002, p. S10; Betsy McKay, "In a Water Fight, Coke and Pepsi Try Opposite Tacks," *Wall Street Journal,* April 18, 2002, p. A1; Hillary Chura, "Dasani: Kellam Graitcer," *Advertising Age,* October 8, 2001, p. S14; Bob Garfield, "The Product Is Questionable, but Aquafina's Ads Hold Water," *Advertising Age,* July 9, 2001, p. 39; Kenneth Hein, "Coke, Pepsi Mull Jump into 'Aquaceuticals,'" *Brandweek,* June 25, 2001, p. 8; Betsy McKay, "Coke and Pepsi Escalate Their Water Fight, *Wall Street Journal,* May 18, 2001, p. B8.

1. discuss the role of a company's salespeople in creating value for customers and building customer relationships
2. identify and explain the six major sales force management steps
3. discuss the personal selling process, distinguishing between transaction-oriented marketing and relationship marketing
4. define direct marketing and discuss its benefits to customers and companies
5. identify and discuss the major forms of direct marketing

LEAR CORPORATION

Personal Selling and Direct Marketing

LOOKING AHEAD: PREVIEWING THE CONCEPTS

In the previous two chapters, you learned about integrated marketing communication (IMC) and three specific elements of the marketing communications mix—advertising, sales promotion, and publicity. In this chapter, we'll learn about the final two IMC elements—personal selling and direct marketing. Personal selling is the interpersonal arm of marketing communications in which the sales force interacts with customers and prospects to make sales and build relationships. Direct marketing consists of direct connections with carefully targeted consumers to both obtain an immediate response and cultivate lasting customer relationships. Actually, direct marketing can be viewed as more than just a communications tool. In many ways, it constitutes an overall marketing *approach*—a blend of communications and distribution channels all rolled into one. As you read on, remember that although this chapter examines personal selling and direct marketing as separate tools, they must be carefully integrated with other elements of the marketing communications mix.

We'll begin with a look at Lear Corporation's sales force. Although you may never have heard of Lear (it's not the company that makes Lear jets), the chances are good that you've spent lots of time in one or more of the car interiors that it supplies to the world's major automotive manufacturers. Before you read on, close your eyes for a moment and envision a typical salesperson. If what you see is a stereotypical glad-hander out to lighten your wallet or purse by selling you something that you don't really need, you might be in for a surprise.

When someone says "salesperson," what image comes to mind? Perhaps it's the stereotypical "traveling salesman"—the fast-talking, ever-smiling peddler who travels his territory foisting his wares on reluctant customers. Such stereotypes, however, are sadly out of date. Today, most professional salespeople are well-educated, well-trained men and women who work to build long-term, value-producing relationships with their customers. They succeed not by taking customers in but by helping them out—by assessing customer needs and solving customer problems.

Consider Lear Corporation, one of the largest, fastest-growing, and most successful automotive suppliers in the world. Each year, Lear produces more than $14 billion worth of automotive interiors—seat systems, instrument panels, door panels, floor and acoustic systems, overhead systems, and electronic and electrical distribution systems. Its customers include most of the world's leading automotive companies, from Ford, DaimlerChrysler, General Motors, Fiat, Toyota, and Volvo to BMW, Ferrari, Rolls-Royce, and more than a dozen others. Lear now operates more than 300 facilities in 33 countries around the globe. During the past few years, Lear has achieved record-breaking sales and earnings growth. Lear's sales during the past five years have more than doubled, and its "average content per car" in North America has increased more than fourfold since 1990. It owns about a 30 percent share of the North American interior components market.

Lear Corporation owes its success to many factors, including a strong customer orientation and a commitment to continuous improvement, teamwork, and customer value. But perhaps more than any other part of the organization, it's Lear's outstanding 145-person sales force that makes the company's credo, "Consumer driven. Customer focused," ring true. Lear's sales force was recently rated by *Sales & Marketing Management* magazine as one of "America's Best Sales Forces." What makes this an outstanding sales force? Lear knows that good selling these days takes much more than just a sales rep covering a territory and convincing customers to buy the product. It takes teamwork, relationship building, and doing what's best for the customer. Lear's sales force excels at these tasks.

Lear's sales depend completely on the success of its customers. If the automakers don't sell cars, Lear doesn't sell interiors. So the Lear sales force strives to create not just sales, but customer success. In fact, Lear salespeople aren't "sales reps," they're "account managers" who function more as consultants than as order getters. "Our salespeople don't really close deals," notes a senior marketing executive. "They consult and work with customers to learn exactly what's needed and when."

To more fully match up with customers' needs, Lear has diversified its product line to become a kind of "one-stop shopping" source. Until a few years ago, Lear supplied only seats; now it sells almost everything for a car's interior. Providing complete interior solutions for customers also benefits Lear. "It used to be that we'd build a partnership and then get only a limited amount of revenue from it," the executive says. "Now we can get as much as possible out of our customer relationships."

Lear is heavily customer focused, so much so that it's broken up into separate divisions dedicated to specific customers. For example, there's a Ford division and a General Motors division, and each operates as its own profit center. Within each division, high-level "platform teams"—made up of salespeople, engineers, and program managers—work closely with their customer counterparts. These platform teams are closely supported by divisional manufacturing, finance, quality, and advanced technology groups. Lear's limited customer base, consisting of only a few dozen customers in all, allows Lear's sales teams to get very close to their customers. "Our teams don't call on purchasers; they're linked to customer operations at all levels," the marketer notes. "We try to put a system in place that creates continuous contact with customers." In fact, Lear often locates its sales offices in customers' plants. For example, the team that handles GM's light truck division works at GM's truck operation campus. "We can't just be there to give quotes and ask for orders," says the marketing executive. "We need to be involved with customers every step of the way—from vehicle concept through launch."

Lear's largest customers are worth billions of dollars in annual sales to the company. Maintaining profitable relationships with such large customers takes much more than a nice smile and a firm handshake. And certainly there's no place for the "smoke and mirrors" or "flimflam" sometimes mistakenly associated with personal selling. Success in such a selling environment requires careful teamwork among well-trained, dedicated sales professionals who are bent on profitably taking care of their customers.[1]

In this chapter, we examine two more marketing communication and promotion tools—*personal selling* and *direct marketing*. Both involve direct connections with customers aimed toward building customer-unique value and lasting relationships.

Personal Selling

Robert Louis Stevenson once noted that "everyone lives by selling something." We are all familiar with the sales forces used by business organizations to sell products and services to customers around the world. But sales forces are also found in many other kinds of organizations. For example, colleges use recruiters to attract new students, and churches use membership committees to attract new members. Hospitals and museums use fund-raisers to contact donors and raise money. Even governments use sales forces. The U.S. Postal Service, for instance, uses a sales force to sell Express Mail and other services to corporate customers. In the first part of this chapter, we examine the role of personal selling in the organization, sales force management decisions, and the personal selling process.

The Nature of Personal Selling

Selling is one of the oldest professions in the world. The people who do the selling go by many names: *salespeople, sales representatives, account executives, sales consultants, sales engineers, agents, district managers, marketing representatives,* and *account development reps,* to name just a few.

People hold many stereotypes of salespeople—including some unfavorable ones. "Salesman" may bring to mind the image of Arthur Miller's pitiable Willy Loman in *Death of a Salesman.* Or you might think of Meredith Willson's cigar-smoking, backslapping, joke-telling Harold Hill in *The Music Man.* Both examples depict salespeople as loners, traveling their territories, trying to foist their wares on unsuspecting or unwilling buyers.

However, modern salespeople are a far cry from these unfortunate stereotypes. Today, most salespeople are well-educated, well-trained professionals who work to build and maintain long-term customer relationships by listening to their customers, assessing customer needs, and organizing the company's efforts to solve customer problems. Consider Boeing, the aerospace giant

The term salesperson covers a wide range of positions, from the clerk selling in a retail store to the engineering salesperson who consults with client companies.

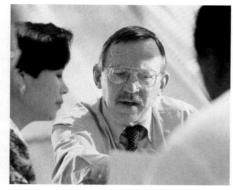

competing in the rough-and-tumble worldwide commercial aircraft market. It takes more than a warm smile to sell expensive airplanes:

> Selling high-tech aircraft at $70 million or more a copy is complex and challenging. A single big sale can easily run into billions of dollars. Boeing salespeople head up an extensive team of company specialists—sales and service technicians, financial analysts, planners, engineers—all dedicated to finding ways to satisfy airline customer needs. The salespeople begin by becoming experts on the airlines, much like Wall Street analysts would. They find out where each airline wants to grow, when it wants to replace planes, and details of its financial situation. The team runs Boeing and competing planes through computer systems, simulating the airline's routes, cost per seat, and other factors to show that their planes are most efficient. Then the high-level negotiations begin. The selling process is nerve-rackingly slow—it can take two or three years from the first sales presentation to the day the sale is announced. Sometimes top executives from both the airline and Boeing are brought in to close the deal. After getting the order, salespeople then must stay in almost constant touch to keep track of the account's equipment needs and to make certain the customer stays satisfied. Success depends on building solid, long-term relationships with customers, based on performance and trust. "When you buy an airplane, it is like getting married," says the head of Boeing's commercial airplane division. "It is a long-term relationship."[2]

Salesperson

An individual acting for a company by performing one or more of the following activities: prospecting, communicating, servicing, and information gathering.

The term **salesperson** covers a wide range of positions. At one extreme, a salesperson might be largely an *order taker,* such as the department store salesperson standing behind the counter. At the other extreme are *order getters,* whose positions demand the *creative selling* of products and services ranging from appliances, industrial equipment, and airplanes to insurance, advertising, and information technology services. Here, we focus on the more creative types of selling and on the process of building and managing an effective sales force.

The Role of the Sales Force

Personal selling is the interpersonal arm of the promotion mix. Advertising consists of one-way, nonpersonal communication with target consumer groups. In contrast, personal selling involves two-way, personal communication between salespeople and individual customers—whether face-to-face, by telephone, through video or Web conferences, or by other means. Personal selling can be more effective than advertising in more complex selling situations. Salespeople can probe customers to learn more about their problems, then adjust the marketing offer to fit the special needs of each customer and negotiate terms of sale. They can build long-term personal relationships with key decision makers.

The role of personal selling varies from company to company. Some firms have no salespeople at all—for example, companies that sell only through mail-order catalogs or companies that sell through manufacturer's reps, sales agents, or brokers. In most firms, however, the sales force plays a major role. In companies that sell business products and services, such as Xerox, Cisco Systems, and DuPont, the company's salespeople work directly with customers. In consumer product companies such as Procter & Gamble and Nike, which sell through intermediaries, final consumers rarely meet salespeople or even know about them. Still, the sales force plays an important behind-the-scenes role. It works with wholesalers and retailers to gain their support and to help them be more effective in selling the company's products.

The sales force serves as a critical link between a company and its customers. In many cases, salespeople serve both masters—the seller and the buyer. First, they *represent the company to customers.* They find and develop new customers and communicate information about the company's products and services. They sell products by approaching customers, presenting their products, answering objections, negotiating prices and terms, and closing sales. In addition, salespeople provide customer service and carry out market research and intelligence work.

At the same time, salespeople *represent customers to the company,* acting inside the firm as "champions" of customers' interests and managing the buyer–seller relationship. Salespeople relay customer concerns about company products and actions back inside to those who can handle them. They learn about customer needs and work with other marketing and nonmarketing people in the company to develop greater customer value. The old view was that salespeople should worry about sales and the company should worry about profit. However, the current view holds that salespeople should be concerned with more than just producing *sales*—they should work with others in the company to produce *customer satisfaction* and *company profit.*

Managing the Sales Force

Sales force management

The analysis, planning, implementation, and control of sales force activities. It includes setting and designing sales force strategy and recruiting, selecting, training, supervising, compensating, and evaluating the firm's salespeople.

We define **sales force management** as the analysis, planning, implementation, and control of sales force activities. It includes designing sales force strategy and structure and recruiting, selecting, training, compensating, supervising, and evaluating the firm's salespeople. These major sales force management decisions are shown in Figure 17.1 and are discussed in the following sections.

Designing Sales Force Strategy and Structure

Marketing managers face several sales force strategy and design questions. How should salespeople and their tasks be structured? How big should the sales force be? Should salespeople sell alone or work in teams with other people in the company? Should they sell in the field or by telephone? We address these issues below.

Sales Force Structure

A company can divide up sales responsibilities along any of several lines. The decision is simple if the company sells only one product line to one industry with customers in many locations. In that case the company would use a *territorial sales force structure.* However, if the company sells many products to many types of customers, it might need either a *product sales force structure,* a *customer sales force structure,* or a combination of the two.

Territorial sales force structure

A sales force organization that assigns each salesperson to an exclusive geographic territory in which that salesperson sells the company's full line.

Territorial Sales Force Structure.   In the **territorial sales force structure,** each salesperson is assigned to an exclusive geographic area and sells the company's full line of products or services to all customers in that territory. This organization clearly defines each salesperson's job and fixes accountability. It also increases the salesperson's desire to build local business relationships that, in turn, improve selling effectiveness. Finally, because each salesperson travels within a limited geographic area, travel expenses are relatively small.

A territorial sales organization is often supported by many levels of sales management positions. For example, Campbell Soup uses a territorial structure in which each salesperson is responsible for selling all Campbell Soup products. Starting at the bottom of the organization, *sales merchandisers* report to *sales representatives,* who report to *retail supervisors,* who report to *directors of retail sales operations,* who report to 1 of 22 *regional sales managers.* Regional sales

FIGURE 17.1 Major steps in sales force management

managers, in turn, report to 1 of 4 *general sales managers* (West, Central, South, and East), who report to a *vice president* and *general sales manager*.

Product Sales Force Structure.   Salespeople must know their products—especially when the products are numerous and complex. This need, together with the growth of product management, has led many companies to adopt a **product sales force structure,** in which the sales force sells along product lines. For example, Kodak uses different sales forces for its film products than for its industrial products. The film products sales force deals with simple products that are distributed intensively, whereas the industrial products sales force deals with complex products that require technical understanding.

The product structure can lead to problems, however, if a single large customer buys many different company products. For example, Allegiance Healthcare Corporation, the large health care products and services company, has several product divisions, each with a separate sales force. Several Allegiance salespeople might end up calling on the same hospital on the same day. This means that they travel over the same routes and wait to see the same customer's purchasing agents. These extra costs must be compared with the benefits of better product knowledge and attention to individual products.

Product sales force structure

A sales force organization under which salespeople specialize in selling only a portion of the company's products or lines.

Customer Sales Force Structure.   More and more companies are now using a **customer sales force structure,** in which they organize the sales force along customer or industry lines. Separate sales forces may be set up for different industries, for serving current customers versus finding new ones, and for major accounts versus regular accounts.

Organizing the sales force around customers can help a company to become more customer focused and build closer relationships with important customers. For example, IBM shifted from a product-based structure to a customer-based one. Before the shift, droves of salespeople representing different IBM software, hardware, and services divisions might call on a single large client, creating confusion and frustration. Such large customers wanted a "single face," one point of contact for all of IBM's vast array of products and services. Following the restructuring, a single IBM "client executive" works with each large customer and manages a team of IBMers—product reps, systems engineers, consultants, and others—who work with the customer. The client executive becomes an expert in the customer's industry. Greg Buseman, a client executive in the distribution industry who spends most of his time working with a major consumer packaged-goods customer, describes his role this way: "I am the owner of the business relationship with the client. If the client has a problem, I'm the one who pulls together software or hardware specialists or consultants. At the customer I work most closely with, we usually have 15 to 20 projects going at once, and I have to manage them."[3] Such an intense focus on customers is widely credited for IBM's dramatic turnaround in recent years.

Customer sales force structure

A sales force organization under which salespeople specialize in selling only to certain customers or industries.

Complex Sales Force Structures.   When a company sells a wide variety of products to many types of customers over a broad geographic area, it often combines several types of sales force structures. Salespeople can be specialized by customer and territory, by product and territory, by product and customer, or by territory, product, and customer. No single structure is best for all companies and situations. Each company should select a sales force structure that best serves the needs of its customers and fits its overall marketing strategy.

Sales Force Size

Once the company has set its structure, it is ready to consider *sales force size*. Salespeople constitute one of the company's most productive—and most expensive—assets. Therefore, increasing their number will increase both sales and costs.

Many companies use some form of *workload approach* to set sales force size. Using this approach, a company first groups accounts into different classes according to size, account status, or other factors related to the amount of effort required to maintain them. It then determines the number of salespeople needed to call on each class of accounts the desired number of times. The company might think as follows: Suppose we have 1,000 Type-A accounts and 2,000 Type-B accounts. Type-A accounts require 36 calls a year and Type-B accounts require 12 calls a year. In this case, the sales force's *workload*—the number of calls it must make per year—is 60,000 calls $[(1,000 \times 36) + (2,000 \times 12) = 36,000 + 24,000 = 60,000]$. Suppose our average salesperson can make 1,000 calls a year. Thus, the company needs 60 salespeople $(60,000 \div 1,000)$.

Other Sales Force Strategy and Structure Issues

Sales management must also decide who will be involved in the selling effort and how various sales and sales support people will work together.

Outside sales force (or field sales force)

Outside salespeople who travel to call on customers.

Inside sales force

Inside salespeople who conduct business from their offices via telephone or visits from prospective buyers.

Outside and Inside Sales Forces.   The company may have an **outside sales force** (or *field sales force*), an **inside sales force,** or both. Outside salespeople travel to call on customers. Inside salespeople conduct business from their offices via telephone or visits from prospective buyers.

To reduce time demands on their outside sales forces, many companies have increased the size of their inside sales forces. Inside salespeople include technical support people, sales assistants, and telemarketers. *Technical support people* provide technical information and answers to customers' questions. *Sales assistants* provide clerical backup for outside salespeople. They call ahead and confirm appointments, conduct credit checks, follow up on deliveries, and answer customers' questions when outside salespeople cannot be reached. *Telemarketers* use the phone to find new leads and qualify prospects for the field sales force, or to sell and service accounts directly.

The inside sales force frees outside salespeople to spend more time selling to major accounts and finding major new prospects. Depending on the complexity of the product and customer, a telemarketer can make from 20 to 33 decision-maker contacts a day, compared to the average of 4 that an outside salesperson can make. And for many types of products and selling situations, telemarketing can be as effective as a personal call but much less expensive. Whereas the average personal sale call costs about $170, a routine industrial telemarketing call costs only about $5 and a complex call about $20.[4] Notes a DuPont telemarketer: "I'm more effective on the phone. [When you're in the field], if some guy's not in his office, you lose an hour. On the phone, you lose 15 seconds. . . . Through my phone calls, I'm in the field as much as the rep is." There are other advantages. "Customers can't throw things at you," quips the rep, "and you don't have to outrun dogs."[5]

Telephone marketing can be used successfully by both large and small companies:

IBM's traditional image has long been symbolized by the salesman in the blue suit, crisp white shirt, and red tie—an imposing fellow far more comfortable in corporate America's plush executive suites than in the cramped quarters of some fledgling entrepreneur. Small businesses were often ignored. Now, to sell its e-business solutions to small businesses, IBM is boosting emphasis on its telemarketing effort. Stroll through the IBM call center in suburban Atlanta, with its sea of cubicles, and a new image of the IBM salesperson emerges: men and women, many recent college grads, sporting golf shirts and khakis or—gasp!—blue jeans. They wear headsets and talk on the phone with customers they'll likely never meet in person. IBM's roughly 1,200 phone reps now generate 30 percent of IBM's revenues from small and midsize businesses. The reps focus on specific industries and each calls on as many as 300 accounts. They nurture client relationships, pitch IBM solutions, and, when needed, refer customers to product and service specialists within the call center or to resellers in their region.[6]

Climax Portable Machine Tools has proven that a small company can use telemarketing to save money and still lavish attention on buyers. Under the old system, Climax sales engineers spent one-third of their time on the road, training distributor salespeople and accompanying them on calls. They could make about 4 contacts a day. Now, each of 5 sales engineers on Climax's telemarketing team calls about 30 prospects a day, following up on leads generated by ads and direct mail. Because it takes about 5 calls to close a sale, the sales engineers update a prospect's computer file after each contact, noting the degree of commitment, requirements, next call date, and personal comments. "If anyone mentions he's going on a fishing trip, our sales engineer enters that in the computer and uses it to personalize the next phone call," says Climax's president, noting that's just one way to build good relations. Another is that the first mailing to a prospect includes the sales engineer's business card with his or her picture on it. Of course, it takes more than friendliness to sell $15,000 machine tools over the phone (special orders may run $200,000), but the telemarketing approach is working well. When Climax customers were asked, "Do you see the sales engineer often enough?" the response was overwhelmingly positive. Obviously, many people didn't realize that the only contact they'd had with Climax had been on the phone.[7]

Just as telemarketing is changing the way that many companies go to market, the Internet offers explosive potential for restructuring sales forces and conducting sales operations. More

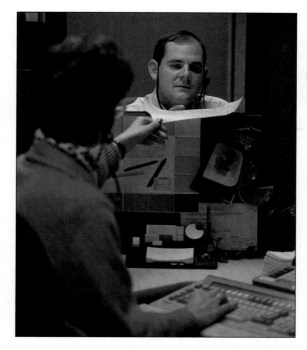

Experienced telemarketers sell complex chemical products by telephone at DuPont's Customer Telecontact Center. Quips one, "I'm more effective on the phone . . . and you don't have to outrun dogs."

and more companies are now using the Internet to support their personal selling efforts—not just for selling, but for everything from training salespeople to conducting sales meetings and servicing accounts (see Real Marketing 17.1).

Team Selling.   As products become more complex, and as customers grow larger and more demanding, a single salesperson simply can't handle all of a large customer's needs. Instead, most companies now are using **team selling** to service large, complex accounts. Companies are finding that sales teams can unearth problems, solutions, and sales opportunities that no individual salesperson could. Such teams might include experts from any area or level of the selling firm—sales, marketing, technical and support services, R&D, engineering, operations, finance, and others. In team selling situations, the salesperson shifts from "soloist" to "orchestrator."

Team selling

Using teams of people from sales, marketing, engineering, finance, technical support, and even upper management to service large, complex accounts.

In many cases, the move to team selling mirrors similar changes in customers' buying organizations. According to a recent study by *Purchasing* magazine, nearly 70 percent companies polled are using or are extremely interested in using multifunctional buying teams. Says the director of sales education at Dow Chemical, to sell effectively to such buying teams, "our sellers . . . have to captain selling teams. There are no more lone wolves."[8]

Some companies, such as IBM, Xerox, and Procter & Gamble, have used teams for a long time. P&G sales reps are organized into "customer business development (CBD) teams." Each CBD team is assigned to a major P&G customer. Teams consist of a customer business development manager, several account executives (each responsible for a specific category of P&G products), and specialists in marketing strategy, operations, information systems, logistics, and finance. This organization places the focus on serving the complete needs of each important customer.

Other companies have only recently reorganized to adopt the team concept. For example, Cutler-Hammer, which supplies circuit breakers, motor starters, and other electrical equipment to heavy industrial manufacturers such as Ford, recently developed "pods" of salespeople that focus on a specific geographical region, industry, or market. Each pod member contributes unique expertise and knowledge about a product or service that salespeople can leverage when selling to increasingly sophisticated buying teams.[9]

Team selling does have some pitfalls. For example, selling teams can confuse or overwhelm customers who are used to working with only one salesperson. Salespeople who are used to having customers all to themselves may have trouble learning to work with and trust others on a team. Finally, difficulties in evaluating individual contributions to the team selling effort can create some sticky compensation issues.

real marketing 17.1

Point, Click, and Sell: Welcome to the Web-Based Sales Force

There are few rules at Fisher Scientific International's sales training sessions. The chemical company's salespeople are allowed to show up for new workshops in their pajamas. And no one flinches if they stroll in at midnight for their first class, take a dozen breaks to call clients, or invite the family cat to sleep in their laps while they take an exam. Sound unorthodox? It would be if Fisher's salespeople were trained in a regular classroom. But for the past year and a half, the company has been using the Internet to teach the majority of its salespeople in the privacy of their homes, cars, hotel rooms, or wherever else they bring their laptops.

In the past few years sales organizations around the world have begun saving money and time by using a host of new Web approaches to train reps, hold sales meetings, and even conduct live sales presentations. "Web-based technologies are becoming really hot in sales because they save salespeople's time," says technology consultant Tim Sloane. Web-based technologies help companies save time and travel costs while keeping reps up to speed on their company's new products and sales strategies. Fisher Scientific's reps can dial up the Web site at their leisure, and whereas newer reps might spend hours online going through

Training is only one of the ways sales organizations are using the Internet. Many companies are using the Web to make sales presentations and service accounts. For example, Digital Equipment Corporation's salespeople used to spend a great deal of time traveling to the offices of clients and prospects. But since 1997 the company (now a division of Compaq) has been delivering sales pitches by combining teleconferences with Web presentations. For example, when Digital's account team in Connecticut needed to see what marketing manager Joe Batista and his team in Massachusetts had prepared for a client, Batista input his ideas into a Powerpoint presentation and uploaded it using Internet Conference Center, Web-based software provided by Contigo Software. The account team joined Batista via teleconference and used their own computers to log on to the Web site Batista specified.

Once everyone was logged on, Batista was able to take control of the browsers and lead the reps through the presentation in real time, highlighting and pointing out specific items as he went. The account reps added their comments, based on their more detailed knowledge of the client, and the revised presentation was then shown online to the client. The beauty of the whole process? It's so fast. "The use of [the Web] clearly helps shorten our sales cycle," Batista says. Presentations are created and delivered in less time—sometimes weeks less than the process would take face-to-face—and salespeople are able to close deals more quickly.

Other companies are using Web-based sales presentations to find new prospects. Oracle Corporation, the $8 billion software and information technology services company, conducts online, live product seminars for prospective clients. Prospects can scan the high-tech company's Web site to see which seminars they might want to attend, then dial in via modem and telephone at the appropriate time (Oracle pays for the cost of the phone call). The seminars, which usually consist of a live lecture describing the product's applications followed by a question-and-answer session, average about 125 prospective clients apiece. Once a seminar is completed, prospects are directed to another part of Oracle's Web site, from which they

Internet selling support: Sales organizations around the world are now using a host of new Web approaches to train reps, hold sales meetings, and even conducts live sales presentations.

To get updates on Fisher's pricing or refresh themselves on one of the company's highly technical products, all salespeople have to do is log on to the Web site and select from the lengthy index. Any time of the day or night, they can get information on a new product, take an exam, or post messages for product experts—all without ever entering a corporate classroom. Welcome to the new world of the Web-based sales force.

each session in order, more seasoned sellers might just log on for a quick refresher on a specific product before a sales call. "It allows them to manage their time better, because they're only getting training when they need it, in the doses they need it in," says John Pavlik, director of the company's training department. If salespeople are spending less time on training, Pavlik says, they're able to spend more time on what they do best: selling.

can order products. "It costs our clients nothing but time," says Oracle's manager of Internet marketing programs, "and we're reaching a much wider audience than we would if we were doing in-person seminars."

The Internet can also be a handy way to hold sales strategy meetings. Consider Cisco Systems, which provides networking solutions for the Internet. Sales meetings used to take an enormous bite out of Cisco's travel budget. Now the company saves about $1 million per month by conducting many of those sessions on the Web using PlaceWare virtual conference center software. Whenever Cisco introduces a new product, it holds a Web meeting to update salespeople, in groups of 100 or more, on the product's marketing and sales strategy.

Usually led by the product manager or a vice president of sales, the meetings typically begin with a 10-minute slide presentation that spells out the planned strategy. Then, salespeople spend the next 50 or so minutes asking questions via teleconference. The meeting's leader can direct attendees' browsers to competitors' Web sites or ask them to vote on certain issues by using the software's instant polling feature. "Our salespeople are actually meeting more online then they ever were face-to-face," says Mike Mitchell, Cisco's distance learning manager, adding that some salespeople who used to meet with other reps and managers only a few times a quarter are meeting online nearly every day. "That's very empowering for the sales force, because they're able to make suggestions at every step of the way about where we're going with our sales and marketing strategies."

Thus, Web-based technologies can produce big organizational benefits for sales forces. They help conserve salespeople's valuable time, save travel dollars, and give salespeople a new vehicle for selling and servicing accounts. But the technologies also have some drawbacks. For starters, they're not cheap. Setting up a Web-based system can cost up to several hundred thousand dollars. And such systems can intimidate low-tech salespeople or clients. "You must have a culture that is comfortable using computers," says one marketing communications manager. "As simple as it is, if your salespeople or clients aren't comfortable using the Web, you're wasting your money." Also, Web tools are susceptible to server crashes and other network difficulties, not a happy event when you're in the midst of an important sales meeting or presentation.

For these reasons, some high-tech experts recommend that sales executives use Web technologies for training, sales meetings, and preliminary client sales presentations, but resort to old-fashioned, face-to-face meetings when the time draws near to close the deal. "When push comes to shove, if you've got an account worth closing, you're still going to get on that plane and see the client in person," says sales consultant Sloane. "Your client is going to want to look you in the eye before buying anything from you, and that's still one thing you just can't do online."

Source: Portions adapted from Melinda Ligos, "Point, Click, and Sell," *Sales & Marketing Management,* May 1999, pp. 51–55. Also see Chad Kaydo, "You've Got Sales," *Sales & Marketing Management,* October 1999, pp. 29–39; Ginger Conlon, "Ride the Wave," *Sales & Marketing Management,* December 2000, pp. 67–74; and Tom Reilly, "Technology and the Salesperson," *Industrial Distribution,* January 2001, p. 88.

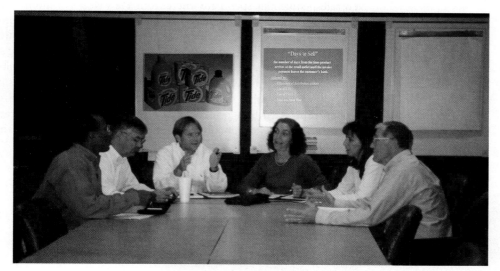

This Procter & Gamble "customer business development team" serves a major southeastern grocery retailer. It consists of a customer business development manager and five accounts executives (shown here), along with specialists from other functional areas.

Recruiting and Selecting Salespeople

At the heart of any successful sales force operation is the recruitment and selection of good salespeople. The performance difference between an average salesperson and a top salesperson can be substantial. In a typical sales force, the top 30 percent of the salespeople might bring in 60 percent of the sales. Thus, careful salesperson selection can greatly increase overall sales force performance. Beyond the differences in sales performance, poor selection results in costly turnover. When a salesperson quits, the costs of finding and training a new salesperson—plus the costs of lost sales—can be very high. Also, a sales force with many new people is less productive.

What traits spell surefire sales success? One survey suggests that good salespeople have a lot of enthusiasm, persistence, initiative, self-confidence, and job commitment. They are committed to sales as a way of life and have a strong customer orientation. Another study suggests that good salespeople are independent and self-motivated and are excellent listeners. Still another study advises that salespeople should be a friend to the customer as well as persistent, enthusiastic, attentive, and—above all—honest. They must be internally motivated, disciplined, hardworking, and able to build strong relationships with customers. Finally, studies show that good salespeople are team players rather than loners (see Real Marketing 17.2).[10]

When recruiting, companies should analyze the sales job itself and the characteristics of its most successful salespeople to identify the traits needed by a successful salesperson in their industry. Does the job require a lot of planning and paperwork? Does it call for much travel? Will the salesperson face a lot of rejections? Will the salesperson be working with high-level buyers? The successful salesperson should be suited to these duties.

After management has decided on needed traits, it must *recruit* salespeople. The human resources department looks for applicants by getting names from current salespeople, using employment agencies, placing classified ads, searching the Web, and contacting college students. Another source is to attract top salespeople from other companies. Proven salespeople need less training and can be immediately productive.

Recruiting will attract many applicants from whom the company must select the best. The selection procedure can vary from a single informal interview to lengthy testing and interviewing. Many companies give formal tests to sales applicants. Tests typically measure sales aptitude, analytical and organizational skills, personality traits, and other characteristics. Test results count heavily in companies such as IBM, Prudential, Procter & Gamble, and Gillette. Gillette claims that tests have reduced turnover by 42 percent and that test scores have correlated well with the later performance of new salespeople. But test scores provide only one piece of information in a set that includes personal characteristics, references, past employment history, and interviewer reactions.[11]

Training Salespeople

New salespeople may spend anywhere from a few weeks or months to a year or more in training. The average initial training period is four months. Then, most companies provide continuing sales training via seminars, sales meetings, and the Web throughout the salesperson's career. In all, U.S. companies spend more than $7 billion annually on training salespeople. Although training can be expensive, it can also yield dramatic returns on the training investment. For example, Nabisco did an extensive analysis of the return on investment of its two-day Professional Selling Program, which teaches sales reps how to plan for and make professional presentations to their retail customers. Although it cost about $1,000 to put each sales rep through the program, the training resulted in additional sales of more than $122,000 per rep and yielded almost $21,000 of additional profit per rep.[12]

Great Salespeople—Drive, Discipline, and Relationship-Building Skills

What sets great salespeople apart from all the rest? What separates the masterful from the merely mediocre? In an effort to profile top sales performers, Gallup Management Consulting Group, a division of the well-known Gallup polling organization, has inter-

viewed as many as half a million salespeople. Its research suggests that the best salespeople possess four key talents: intrinsic motivation, disciplined work style, the ability to close a sale, and perhaps most important, the ability to build relationships with customers.

Intrinsic Motivation

"Different things drive different people— pride, happiness, money, you name it," says one expert. "But all great salespeople have one thing in common: an unrelenting drive to excel." This strong internal drive can be shaped and molded, but it can't be taught. The source of the motivation varies—some are driven by money, some by hunger for recognition, some by a yearning to build relationships.

The Gallup research revealed four general personality types, all high performers, but all with different sources of motivation. *Competitors* are people who not only want to win but also crave the satisfaction of beating specific rivals—other companies *and* their fellow salespeople. They'll come right out and say to a colleague, "With all due respect, I know you're salesperson of the year, but I'm going after your title." The *ego driven* are salespeople who just want to experience the glory of winning. They want to be recognized as being the best, regardless of the competition. *Achievers* are a rare breed who are almost completely self-motivated. They like accomplishment and routinely set goals that are higher than what is expected of them. They often make the best sales managers because they don't mind seeing other people succeed, as long as the organization's goals are met. Finally, *service-oriented* salespeople are

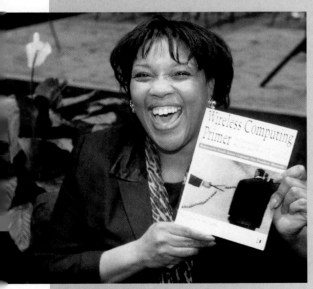

Great salespeople: The best salespeople possess intrinsic motivation, disciplined work style, the ability to close a sale, and perhaps most important, the ability to build relationships with customers.

those whose strength lies in their ability to build and cultivate relationships. They are generous, caring, and empathetic. "These people are golden," says the national training manager of Minolta Corporation's business equipment division. "We need salespeople who will take the time to follow up on the 10

questions a customer might have, salespeople who love to stay in touch."

No one is purely a competitor, an achiever, ego driven, or service driven. There's at least some of each in most top performers. "A *competitor* with a strong sense of *service* will probably bring in a lot of business while doing a great job of taking care of customers," observes the managing director of the Gallup Management Consulting Group. "Who could ask for anything more?"

Disciplined Work Style

Whatever their motivation, if salespeople aren't organized and focused, and if they don't work hard, they can't meet the ever-increasing demands customers are making these days. Great salespeople are tenacious about laying out detailed, organized plans, then following through in a timely, disciplined way. There's no magic here, just solid organization and hard work. "Our best sales reps never let loose ends dangle," says the president of a small business equipment firm. "If they say they're going to make a follow-up call on a customer in six months, you can be sure that they'll be on the doorstep in six months." Top sellers rely on hard work, not luck or gimmicks. "Some people say it's all technique or luck," notes one sales trainer. "But luck happens to the best salespeople when they get up early, work late, stay up till two in the morning working on a proposal, or keep making calls when everyone is leaving at the end of the day."

The Ability to Close a Sale

Other skills mean little if a seller can't ask for the sale. No close, no sale. Period. So what makes for a great closer? For one thing, an unyielding persistence, say managers and sales consultants. Claims one, "Great closers are like great athletes. They're not afraid to fail, and they don't give up until they close." Here's a classic example:

The great [salespeople] have all been undaunted by rejection and failure. Farm equipment vendor Cyrus McCormick, for example, sold only two McCormick Harvesters in his first three years of trying. He sold seven in the fourth year, and sold enough of them to make a living in the fifth year. (The point here is he was still trying in that fifth year.) McCormick eventually achieved great suc-

cess. His company, once known as the International Harvester Company, is still around today under the name Navistar International.

Part of what makes the failure rate tolerable for top performers is their deep-seated belief in themselves and what they are selling. Great closers have a high level of self-confidence and believe that they are doing the right thing. And they've got a burning need to make the sale happen—to do whatever it takes within legal and ethical standards to get the business.

The Ability to Build Relationships

Perhaps most important in today's relationship-marketing environment, top salespeople are customer problem solvers and relationship builders. They have an instinctive understanding of their customers' needs. Talk to sales executives and they'll describe top performers in these terms: Empathetic. Patient. Caring. Responsive. Good listeners. Even *honest.* Top sellers can put themselves on the buyer's side of the desk and see the world through their customers' eyes. Today, customers are looking for business partners, not golf partners. "At the root of it all," says a Dallas sales consultant, "is an integrity of intent. High performers don't just want to be liked, they want to add value." High-performing salespeople, he adds, are "always thinking about the big picture, where the customer's organization is going, and how they can help them get there." Concludes one top performer, "The relationship you build with your prospects and customers is more important than the close."

Sources: Adapted from Geoffrey Brewer, "Mind Reading: What Drives Top Salespeople to Greatness?" *Sales & Marketing Management,* May 1994, pp. 82–88, with excerpt from Larry Blaine, "Sales Fundamentals," *American Salesman,* May 2002, pp. 14–17. Also see Roberta Maynard, "Finding the Essence of Good Salespeople," *Nation's Business,* February 1998, p. 10; Jeanie Casison, "Closest Thing to Cloning," *Incentive,* June 1999, p. 7; Erika Rasmusson, "The 10 Traits of Top Salespeople," *Sales & Marketing Management,* August 1999, pp. 34–37; Kevin Dobbs, Jack Gordon, Kim Kiser, and David Stamps, "The Seven Secrets of Great Salespeople," *Training,* January 2000, p. 14; Andy Cohen, "The Traits of Great Sales Forces," *Sales & Marketing Management,* October 2000, pp. 67–72; and Edwin Richard Rigsbee, "The Relationship You Build with Your Prospects and Customers Is More Important than the Close," *Cost Engineering,* February 2002, pp. 40–41.

Training programs have several goals. Salespeople need to know and identify with the company, so most training programs begin by describing the company's history and objectives, its organization, its financial structure and facilities, and its chief products and markets. Salespeople also need to know the company's products, so sales trainees are shown how products are produced and how they work. They also need to know customers' and competitors' characteristics, so the training program teaches them about competitors' strategies and about different types of customers and their needs, buying motives, and buying habits. Because salespeople must know how to make effective presentations, they are trained in the principles of selling. Finally, salespeople need to understand field procedures and responsibilities. They learn how to divide time between active and potential accounts and how to use an expense account, prepare reports, and route communications effectively.

Today, many companies are adding Web-based training to their sales training programs. Such training may range from simple text-based product information to Internet-based sales exercises that build sales skills to sophisticated simulations that re-create the dynamics of real-life sales calls. Networking equipment and software maker Cisco Systems has learned that using the Internet to train salespeople offers many advantages.

> Two years ago, Cisco changed its training strategy dramatically by launching its Field E-Learning Connection, an internal learning portal for Cisco's sales force. Today, the company has more than 9,000 learning resources online. Under the new system, online learning involves the blending of audio and video, live broadcasts of classes, and straight content. Cisco makes online training as convenient as possible: Online content can be turned into an MP3 file, viewed on-screen, downloaded to the computer, even printed out in magazine form. Existing content is updated twice yearly, and new content is created in response to surveys of those out in the field. When new salespeople come on board, they immediately log on to FAST (Field, Acculturation, and Sales Training), which familiarizes them with Cisco's objectives and expectations. "We used to fly people to a central location and put them through a week of death-by-PowerPoint," says a Cisco training executive. The change has saved Cisco "several hundred thousand dollars," and the company has cut training-associated travel by 60 percent. Its innovative approach to training earned Cisco recognition as last year's *Sales & Marketing Management* magazine's Best Trained Sales Force. "The company's overall culture is focused on having the best-trained sales force," says an industry analyst. "They don't necessarily have the best products, but they have the best sales team to push those products."[13]

Sales training: Cisco's Field E-Learning Connection, an online learning portal for Cisco's sales force, blends audio and video, which can be turned into an MP3 file, viewed on-screen, downloaded to the computer, or even printed out in magazine form.

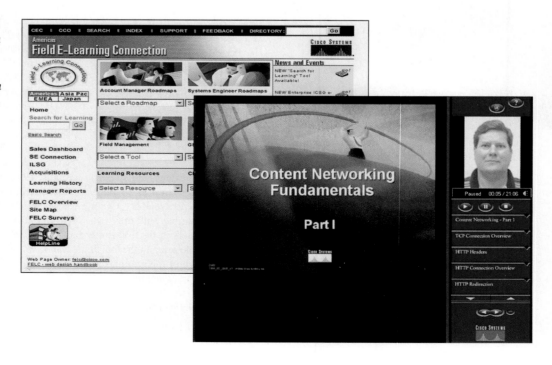

Compensating Salespeople

To attract salespeople, a company must have an appealing compensation plan. Compensation is made up of several elements—a fixed amount, a variable amount, expenses, and fringe benefits. The fixed amount, usually a salary, gives the salesperson some stable income. The variable amount, which might be commissions or bonuses based on sales performance, rewards the salesperson for greater effort. Expense allowances, which repay salespeople for job-related expenses, let salespeople undertake needed and desirable selling efforts. Fringe benefits, such as paid vacations, sickness or accident benefits, pensions, and life insurance, provide job security and satisfaction.

Management must decide what *mix* of these compensation elements makes the most sense for each sales job. Different combinations of fixed and variable compensation give rise to four basic types of compensation plans—straight salary, straight commission, salary plus bonus, and salary plus commission. A study of sales force compensation plans showed that 70 percent of all companies surveyed use a combination of base salary and incentives. The average plan consisted of about 60 percent salary and 40 percent incentive pay.[14]

The sales force compensation plan can both motivate salespeople and direct their activities. Compensation should direct the sales force toward activities that are consistent with overall marketing objectives. Table 17.1 illustrates how a company's compensation plan should reflect its overall marketing strategy. For example, if the strategy is to grow rapidly and gain market share, the compensation plan might include a larger commission component coupled with a new-account bonus to encourage high sales performance and new-account development. In contrast, if the goal is to maximize current account profitability, the compensation plan might contain a larger base-salary component with additional incentives for current account sales or customer satisfaction. In fact, more and more companies are moving away from high-commission plans that may drive salespeople to make short-term grabs for business. Notes one sales force expert, "The last thing you want is to have someone ruin a customer relationship because they're pushing too hard to close a deal." Instead, companies are designing compensation plans that reward salespeople for building customer relationships and growing the long-run value of each customer.[15]

Supervising Salespeople

New salespeople need more than a territory, compensation, and training—they need *supervision*. Through supervision, the company *directs* and *motivates* the sales force to do a better job.

Companies vary in how closely they supervise their salespeople. Many help their salespeople in identifying customer targets and setting call norms. Some may also specify how much time the sales forces should spend prospecting for new accounts and set other time management

TABLE 17.1	**THE RELATIONSHIP BETWEEN OVERALL MARKETING STRATEGY AND SALES FORCE COMPENSATION**		
	Strategic Goal		
	To Gain Market Share Rapidly	*To Solidify Market Leadership*	*To Maximize Profitability*
Ideal salesperson	• An independent self-starter	• A competitive problem solver	• A team player • A relationship manager
Sales focus	• Deal making • Sustained high effort	• Consultative selling	• Account penetration
Compensation role	• To capture accounts • To reward high performance	• To reward new and existing account sales	• To manage the product mix • To encourage team selling • To reward account management

Source: Adapted from Sam T. Johnson, "Sales Compensation: In Search of a Better Solution," *Compensation & Benefits Review,* November–December 1993, pp. 53–60. Copyright © 1998 American Management Association, NY, www.amanet.org. All rights reserved, used with permission.

FIGURE 17.2

How salespeople spend
their time

Source: Dartnell Corporation;
*30th Sales Force Compensation
Survey.* © 1999 Dartnell
Corporation.

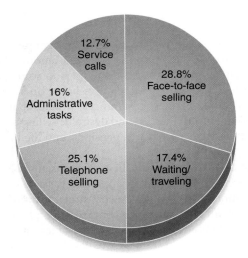

priorities. One tool is the *annual call plan* that shows which customers and prospects to call on in which months and which activities to carry out. Activities include taking part in trade shows, attending sales meetings, and carrying out marketing research. Another tool is *time-and-duty analysis.* In addition to time spent selling, the salesperson spends time traveling, waiting, eating, taking breaks, and doing administrative chores.

Figure 17.2 shows how salespeople spend their time. On average, actual face-to-face selling time accounts for less than 30 percent of total working time! If selling time could be raised from 30 percent to 40 percent, this would be a 33 percent increase in the time spent selling. Companies always are looking for ways to save time—using phones instead of traveling, simplifying record-keeping forms, finding better call and routing plans, and supplying more and better customer information.

Many firms have adopted *sales force automation systems,* computerized sales force operations for more efficient order-entry transactions, improved customer service, and better salesperson decision-making support. Salespeople use laptops, handheld computing devices, and Web technologies, coupled with customer-contact software and customer relationship management (CRM) software, to profile customers and prospects, analyze and forecast sales, manage account relationships, schedule sales calls, make presentations, enter orders, check inventories and order status, prepare sales and expense reports, process correspondence, and carry out many other activities. Sales force automation not only lowers sales force costs and improves productivity, it also improves the quality of sales management decisions. Here is an example of successful sales force automation:

Owens-Corning has put its sales force online with FSA—its Field Sales Advantage system. FSA gives Owens-Corning salespeople a constant supply of information about their company and the people they're dealing with. Using laptop computers, each salesperson can access three types of programs. First, FSA gives them a set of *generic tools,* everything from word processing to fax and e-mail transmission to creating presentations online. Second, it provides *product information*—tech bulletins, customer specifications, pricing information, and other data that can help close a sale. Finally, it offers up a wealth of *customer information*—buying history, types of products ordered, and preferred payment terms. Before FSA, reps stored such information in loose-leaf books, calendars, and account cards. Now, FSA makes working directly with customers easier than ever. Salespeople can prime themselves on backgrounds of clients; call up prewritten sales letters; transmit orders and resolve customer-service issues on the spot during customer calls; and have samples, pamphlets, brochures, and other materials sent to clients with a few keystrokes. With FSA, "salespeople automatically become more empowered," says Charley Causey, regional general manager. "They become the real managers of their own business and their own territories."[16]

Perhaps the fastest-growing sales force technology tool is the Internet. In a survey by Dartnell Corporation of 1,000 salespeople, 61 percent reported using the Internet regularly in their daily selling activities. The most common uses include gathering competitive information,

Owens-Corning's Field Sales Advantage system gives salespeople a constant supply of information about their company and the people with whom they're dealing.

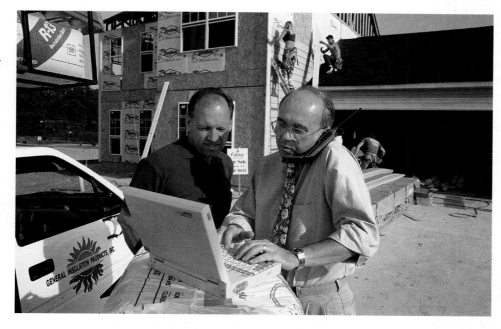

monitoring customer Web sites, and researching industries and specific customers. As more and more companies provide their salespeople with Web access, experts expect continued growth in sales force Internet usage.[17]

Beyond directing salespeople, sales managers must also motivate them. Some salespeople will do their best without any special urging from management. To them, selling may be the most fascinating job in the world. But selling can also be frustrating. Salespeople often work alone and they must sometimes travel away from home. They may face aggressive competing salespeople and difficult customers. Therefore, salespeople often need special encouragement to do their best.

Management can boost sales force morale and performance through its organizational climate, sales quotas, and positive incentives. *Organizational climate* describes the feeling that salespeople have about their opportunities, value, and rewards for a good performance. Some companies treat salespeople as if they are not very important, and performance suffers accordingly. Other companies treat their salespeople as valued contributors and allow virtually unlimited opportunity for income and promotion. Not surprisingly, these companies enjoy higher sales force performance and less turnover.

Sales quota

A standard that states the amount a salesperson should sell and how sales should be divided among the company's products.

Many companies motivate their salespeople by setting **sales quotas**—standards stating the amount they should sell and how sales should be divided among the company's products. Compensation is often related to how well salespeople meet their quotas. Companies also use various *positive incentives* to increase sales force effort. *Sales meetings* provide social occasions, breaks from routine, chances to meet and talk with "company brass," and opportunities to air feelings and to identify with a larger group. Companies also sponsor *sales contests* to spur the sales force to make a selling effort above what would normally be expected. Other incentives include honors, merchandise and cash awards, trips, and profit-sharing plans. In all, American companies spend some $27 billion a year on incentives to motivate and reward sales-force performance.[18]

Evaluating Salespeople

We have thus far described how management communicates what salespeople should be doing and how it motivates them to do it. This process requires good feedback. And good feedback means getting regular information about salespeople to evaluate their performance.

Management gets information about its salespeople in several ways. The most important source is *sales reports*, including weekly or monthly work plans and longer-term territory marketing plans. Salespeople also write up their completed activities on *call reports* and turn in *expense reports* for which they are partly or wholly repaid. Additional information comes from personal observation, customer surveys, and talks with other salespeople.

Sales force incentives: Many companies offer cash, trips, or merchandise as incentives. American Express suggests that companies reward outstanding sales performers with high-tech Persona Select cards—electronically prepaid reward cards that allow recipients to purchase whatever they want most.

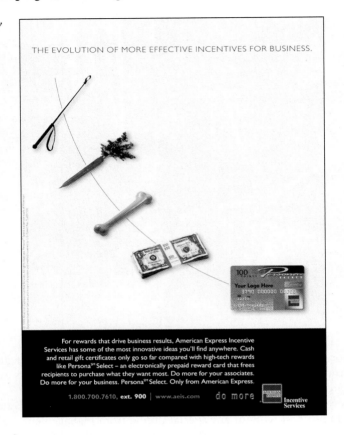

THE EVOLUTION OF MORE EFFECTIVE INCENTIVES FOR BUSINESS.

For rewards that drive business results, American Express Incentive Services has some of the most innovative ideas you'll find anywhere. Cash and retail gift certificates only go so far compared with high-tech rewards like Persona℠ Select – an electronically prepaid reward card that frees recipients to purchase what they want most. Do more for your associates. Do more for your business. Persona℠ Select. Only from American Express.

1.800.700.7610, **ext. 900** | www.aeis.com   do more Incentive Services

Using various sales force reports and other information, sales management evaluates members of the sales force. It evaluates salespeople on their ability to "plan their work and work their plan." Formal evaluation forces management to develop and communicate clear standards for judging performance. It also provides salespeople with constructive feedback and motivates them to perform well.

The Personal Selling Process

Selling process

The steps that the salesperson follows when selling, which include prospecting and qualifying, preapproach, approach, presentation and demonstration, handling objections, closing, and follow-up.

We now turn from designing and managing a sales force to the actual personal selling process. The **selling process** consists of several steps that the salesperson must master. These steps focus on the goal of getting new customers and obtaining orders from them. However, most salespeople spend much of their time maintaining existing accounts and building long-term customer *relationships*. We discuss the relationship aspect of the personal selling process in a later section.

Steps in the Selling Process

As shown in Figure 17.3, the selling process consists of seven steps: Prospecting and qualifying, preapproach, approach, presentation and demonstration, handling objections, closing, and follow-up.

FIGURE 17.3

Major steps in effective selling

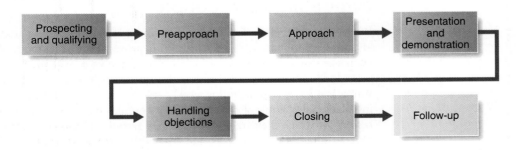

Prospecting and qualifying → Preapproach → Approach → Presentation and demonstration → Handling objections → Closing → Follow-up

Prospecting and Qualifying

Prospecting

The step in the selling process in which the salesperson identifies qualified potential customers.

The first step in the selling process is **prospecting**—identifying qualified potential customers. Approaching the right potential customers is crucial to selling success. As one expert puts it: "If the sales force starts chasing anyone who is breathing and seems to have a budget, you risk accumulating a roster of expensive-to-serve, hard-to-satisfy customers who never respond to whatever value proposition you have." He continues, "The solution to this isn't rocket science. [You must] train salespeople to actively scout the right prospects. If necessary, create an incentive program to reward proper scouting."[19]

The salesperson must often approach many prospects to get just a few sales. Although the company supplies some leads, salespeople need skill in finding their own. They can ask current customers for referrals. They can cultivate referral sources, such as suppliers, dealers, noncompeting salespeople, and bankers. They can search for prospects in directories or on the Web and track down leads using the telephone and direct mail. Or they can drop in unannounced on various offices (a practice known as "cold calling").

Salespeople also need to know how to *qualify* leads—that is, how to identify the good ones and screen out the poor ones. Prospects can be qualified by looking at their financial ability, volume of business, special needs, location, and possibilities for growth.

Preapproach

Preapproach

The step in the selling process in which the salesperson learns as much as possible about a prospective customer before making a sales call.

Before calling on a prospect, the salesperson should learn as much as possible about the organization (what it needs, who is involved in the buying) and its buyers (their characteristics and buying styles). This step is known as the **preapproach.** The salesperson can consult standard industry and online sources, acquaintances, and others to learn about the company. The salesperson should set *call objectives,* which may be to qualify the prospect, to gather information, or to make an immediate sale. Another task is to decide on the best approach, which might be a personal visit, a phone call, or a letter. The best timing should be considered carefully because many prospects are busiest at certain times. Finally, the salesperson should give thought to an overall sales strategy for the account.

Approach

Approach

The step in the selling process in which the salesperson meets the customer for the first time.

During the **approach** step, the salesperson should know how to meet and greet the buyer and get the relationship off to a good start. This step involves the salesperson's appearance, opening lines, and the follow-up remarks. The opening lines should be positive to build goodwill from the beginning of the relationship. This opening might be followed by some key questions to learn more about the customer's needs or by showing a display or sample to attract the buyer's attention and curiosity. As in all stages of the selling process, listening to the customer is crucial.

Presentation and Demonstration

Presentation

The step in the selling process in which the salesperson tells the "product story" to the buyer, highlighting customer benefits.

During the **presentation** step of the selling process, the salesperson tells the product "story" to the buyer, presenting customer benefits and showing how the product solves the customer's problems. The problem-solver salesperson fits better with today's marketing concept than does a hard-sell salesperson or the glad-handing extrovert. Buyers today want solutions, not smiles; results, not razzle-dazzle. They want salespeople who listen to their concerns, understand their needs, and respond with the right products and services.

This *need-satisfaction approach* calls for good listening and problem-solving skills. "I think of myself more as a . . . well, psychologist," notes one experienced salesperson. "I listen to customers. I listen to their wishes and needs and problems, and I try to figure out a solution. If you're not a good listener, you're not going to get the order." Another salesperson suggests, "It's no longer enough to have a good relationship with a client. You have to understand their problems. You have to feel their pain."[20] The qualities that buyers *dislike most* in salespeople include being pushy, late, deceitful, and unprepared or disorganized. The qualities they *value most* include empathy, good listening, honesty, dependability, thoroughness, and follow-through. Great salespeople know how to sell, but more importantly they know how to listen and to build strong customer relationships.[21]

Today, advanced presentation technologies allow for full multimedia presentations to only one or a few people. Audio- and videocassettes, CDs, laptop computers with presentation software, and online presentation technologies have replaced the flip chart. Advanced

New sales presentation technologies: Advanced Sterilization Products, a Johnson & Johnson Company, provides its sales force with a presentation in which prospects don a helmet for a virtual reality tour of the inner workings of the STERRAD Sterilization System for medical devices and surgical instruments.

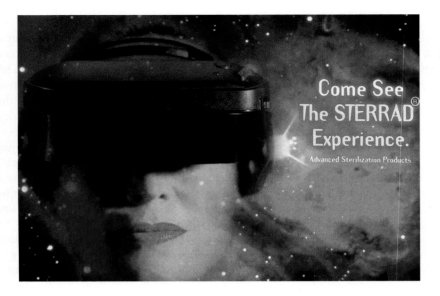

Sterilization Products (ASP), a Johnson & Johnson company, even provides its sales force with a virtual reality presentation, called the STERRAD Experience. Originally designed for use at conferences, the presentation equipment has been redesigned for sales calls and consists of a small video player with five headsets, all easily transported in an ordinary-sized briefcase. Prospects don a helmet for a virtual reality tour of the inner workings of the STERRAD Sterilization System for medical devices and surgical instruments. The presentation provides more information in a more engaging way than could be done by displaying the actual machinery. For customers with less time, ASP salespeople can introduce the STERRAD system using online demonstration videos.[22]

Handling Objections

Customers almost always have objections during the presentation or when asked to place an order. The problem can be either logical or psychological, and objections are often unspoken. In **handling objections,** the salesperson should use a positive approach, seek out hidden objections, ask the buyer to clarify any objections, take objections as opportunities to provide more information, and turn the objections into reasons for buying. Every salesperson needs training in the skills of handling objections.

Closing

After handling the prospect's objections, the salesperson now tries to close the sale. Some salespeople do not get around to **closing** or do not handle it well. They may lack confidence, feel guilty about asking for the order, or fail to recognize the right moment to close the sale. Salespeople should know how to recognize closing signals from the buyer, including physical actions, comments, and questions. For example, the customer might sit forward and nod approvingly or ask about prices and credit terms. Salespeople can use one of several closing techniques. They can ask for the order, review points of agreement, offer to help write up the order, ask whether the buyer wants this model or that one, or note that the buyer will lose out if the order is not placed now. The salesperson may offer the buyer special reasons to close, such as a lower price or an extra quantity at no charge.

Follow-Up

The last step in the selling process—**follow-up**—is necessary if the salesperson wants to ensure customer satisfaction and repeat business. Right after closing, the salesperson should complete any details on delivery time, purchase terms, and other matters. The salesperson then should schedule a follow-up call when the initial order is received, to make sure there is proper installation, instruction, and servicing. This visit would reveal any problems, assure the buyer of the salesperson's interest, and reduce any buyer concerns that might have arisen since the sale.

Handling objections
The step in the selling process in which the salesperson seeks out, clarifies, and overcomes customer objections to buying.

Closing
The step in the selling process in which the salesperson asks the customer for an order.

Follow-up
The last step in the selling process, in which the salesperson follows up after the sale to ensure customer satisfaction and repeat business.

Personal Selling and Customer Relationship Management

The principles of personal selling as just described are *transaction oriented*—their aim is to help salespeople close a specific sale with a customer. But in many cases, the company is not seeking simply a sale: It has targeted a major customer that it would like to win and keep. The company would like to show that it has the capabilities to serve the customer over the long haul in a mutually profitable *relationship*. The sales force usually plays an important role in building and managing long-term customer relationships.

Today's large customers favor suppliers who can sell and deliver a coordinated set of products and services to many locations, and who can work closely with customer teams to improve products and processes. For these customers, the first sale is only the beginning of the relationship. Unfortunately, some companies ignore these new realities. They sell their products through separate sales forces, each working independently to close sales. Their technical people may not be willing to lend time to educate a customer. Their engineering, design, and manufacturing people may have the attitude that "it's our job to make good products and the salesperson's to sell them to customers." Other companies, however, recognize that winning and keeping accounts requires more than making good products and directing the sales force to close lots of sales. It requires a carefully coordinated whole-company effort to create value-laden, satisfying relationships with important customers.

Direct Marketing

Many of the marketing and promotion tools that we've examined in previous chapters were developed in the context of *mass marketing:* targeting broad markets with standardized messages and offers distributed through intermediaries. Today, however, with the trend toward more narrowly targeted or one-to-one marketing, many companies are adopting *direct marketing,* either as a primary marketing approach or as a supplement to other approaches. Increasingly, companies are using direct marketing to reach carefully targeted customers more efficiently and to build stronger, more personal, one-to-one relationships with them. In this section, we explore the exploding world of direct marketing.

Direct marketing

Direct communications with carefully targeted individual consumers to obtain an immediate response.

Direct marketing consists of direct connections with carefully targeted individual consumers to both obtain an immediate response and cultivate lasting customer relationships. Direct marketers communicate directly with customers, often on a one-to-one, interactive basis. Using detailed databases, they tailor their marketing offers and communications to the needs of narrowly defined segments or even individual buyers. Beyond brand and image building, they usually seek a direct, immediate, and measurable consumer response. For example, Dell Computer interacts directly with customers, by telephone or through its Web site, to design built-to-order systems that meet customers' individual needs. Buyers order directly from Dell, and Dell quickly and efficiently delivers the new computers to their homes or offices.

The New Direct-Marketing Model

Early direct marketers—catalog companies, direct mailers, and telemarketers—gathered customer names and sold goods mainly by mail and telephone. Today, however, fired by rapid advances in database technologies and new marketing media—especially the Internet—direct marketing has undergone a dramatic transformation.

In previous chapters, we've discussed direct marketing as direct distribution—as marketing channels that contain no intermediaries. We also include direct marketing as one element of the marketing communications mix—as an approach for communicating directly with consumers. In actuality, direct marketing is both these things.

Most companies still use direct marketing as a supplementary channel or medium for marketing their goods. Thus, Lexus markets mostly through mass-media advertising and its high-quality dealer network but also supplements these channels with direct marketing. Its direct marketing includes promotional videos and other materials mailed directly to prospective buyers and a Web page (www.lexus.com) that provides consumers with information about various models, competitive comparisons, financing, and dealer locations. Similarly, office supply retailer Staples conducts most of its business through brick-and-mortar stores but also markets directly through its Web site. And most department stores sell the majority of their merchandise off their store shelves but also mail out catalogs.

However, for many companies today, direct marketing is more than just a supplementary channel or medium. For these companies, direct marketing—especially in its newest transformation, Internet marketing and e-commerce—constitutes a new and complete model for doing business. More than just another marketing channel or advertising medium, this new *direct model* is rapidly changing the way companies think about building relationships with customers.

Whereas most companies use direct marketing and the Internet as supplemental approaches, firms employing the direct model use it as the *only* approach. Some of these companies, such as Dell Computer, Amazon.com, and eBay, began as only direct marketers. Other companies—such as Cisco Systems, Charles Schwab, IBM, and many others—are rapidly transforming themselves into direct-marketing superstars. The company that perhaps best exemplifies this new direct-marketing model is Dell Computer (see Real Marketing 17.3). Dell has built its entire approach to the marketplace around direct marketing. This direct model has proved highly successful, not just for Dell, but for the fast-growing number of other companies that employ it. Many strategists have hailed direct marketing as the new marketing model of the next millennium.

Benefits and Growth of Direct Marketing

Whether employed as a complete business model or as a supplement to a broader integrated marketing mix, direct marketing brings many benefits to both buyers and sellers. As a result, direct marketing is growing very rapidly.

For buyers, direct marketing is convenient, easy to use, and private. From the comfort of their homes or offices, they can browse mail catalogs or company Web sites at any time of the day or night. Direct marketing gives buyers ready access to a wealth of products and information, at home and around the globe. Finally, direct marketing is immediate and interactive—buyers can interact with sellers by phone or on the seller's Web site to create exactly the configuration of information, products, or services they desire, then order them on the spot.

For sellers, direct marketing is a powerful tool for building customer relationships. Using database marketing, today's marketers can target small groups or individual consumers, tailor offers to individual needs, and promote these offers through personalized communications. Direct marketing can also be timed to reach prospects at just the right moment. Because of its one-to-one, interactive nature, the Internet is an especially potent direct-marketing tool. Direct marketing also gives sellers access to buyers that they could not reach through other channels. For example, the Internet provides access to *global* markets that might otherwise be out of reach.

Finally, direct marketing can offer sellers a low-cost, efficient alternative for reaching their markets. For example, direct marketing has grown rapidly in B2B marketing, partly in response to the ever-increasing costs of marketing through the sales force. When personal sales calls cost $170 per contact, they should be made only when necessary and to high-potential customers and prospects. Lower cost-per-contact media—such as telemarketing, direct mail, and company Web sites—often prove more cost-effective in reaching and selling to more prospects and customers.

As a result of these advantages to both buyers and sellers, direct marketing has become the fastest-growing form of marketing. Sales through traditional direct-marketing channels (telephone marketing, direct mail, catalogs, direct-response television, and others) have been growing rapidly. Direct sales to consumers and businesses in the United States last year reached an estimated $1.86 trillion, nearly 9 percent of the economy. Moreover, whereas total U.S. sales over the next five years will grow at an estimated 5 percent annually, direct-marketing sales will grow at an estimated 8 percent annually. According to the Direct Marketing Association, total U.S. spending on direct marketing exceeded $197 billion last year, or more than 55 percent of total U.S. advertising expenditures.[23]

Customer database

An organized collection of comprehensive data about individual customers or prospects, including geographic, demographic, psychographic, and behavioral data.

Customer Databases and Direct Marketing

Effective direct marketing begins with a good customer database. A **customer database** is an organized collection of comprehensive data about individual customers or prospects, including geographic, demographic, psychographic, and behavioral data. The database can be used to

real marketing 17.3

Dell: Be Direct!

When 19-year-old Michael Dell began selling personal computers out of his college dorm room in 1984, competitors and industry insiders scoffed at the concept of mail-order computer marketing. PC buyers, they contended, needed the kind of advice and handholding that only full-service channels could provide. Yet young Michael Dell has proved the skeptics wrong—way wrong. In less than two decades, he has turned his dorm-room mail-order business into a burgeoning, $32 billion computer empire.

Dell Computer is now the world's largest direct marketer of computer systems and the number one PC maker worldwide. In the United States, Dell is number one in desktop PC sales, number one in laptops, and number one in servers. Over the past 10 years, despite the recent tech slump, Dell's sales have grown at an average annual rate of over 40 percent, and Dell's stock has delivered a dazzling 59 percent average annual return to shareholders. Dell's stock was the number one performer of the 1990s, yielding an incredible 97 percent average annual return. Once-skeptical competitors are now scrambling to build their own direct-marketing systems. Last year, while all of Dell's competitors lost market share, Dell's share of the U.S. PC market climbed 31 percent.

What's the secret to Dell's stunning success? Anyone at Dell can tell you without hesitation: It's the company's radically different business model—the *direct model*. "We have a tremendously clear business model," says Michael Dell, the 37-year-old founder. "There's no confusion about what the value proposition is, what the company offers, and why it's great for customers. That's a very simple thing, but it has tremendous power and appeal." An industry analyst agrees: "There's no better way to make, sell, and deliver PCs than the way Dell does it, and nobody executes that model better than Dell."

Dell's direct-marketing approach delivers greater customer value through an unbeatable combination of product customization, low prices, fast delivery, and award-winning customer service. A customer can talk by phone with a Dell representative or log on to www.dell.com on Monday morning; order a fully customized, state-of-the-art PC to suit his or her special needs; and have the machine delivered to his or her doorstep or desktop by Wednesday—all at a price that's 10 to 15 percent below competitors' prices for a comparably performing PC. Dell backs its products with high-quality service and support. As a result, Dell consistently ranks among the industry leaders in product reliability and service, and its customers are routinely among the industry's most satisfied.

Dell customers get exactly the machines they need. Michael Dell's initial idea was to serve individual buyers by letting them customize machines with the special features they wanted at low prices. However, this one-to-one approach also appeals strongly to corporate buyers, because Dell can so easily preconfigure each computer to precise requirements. Dell routinely preloads machines with a company's own software and even undertakes tedious tasks such as pasting inventory tags onto each machine so that computers can be delivered directly to a given employee's desk. As a result, nearly two-thirds of Dell's sales now come from large corporate, government, and educational buyers.

Direct selling results in more efficient selling and lower costs, which translate into lower prices for customers. Because Dell builds machines to order, it carries barely any inventory—less than five days' worth by some

The Dell Direct Model: Dell's direct-marketing approach delivers greater customer value through an unbeatable combination of product customization, low prices, fast delivery, and award-winning customer service.

(continued)

accounts. Dealing one-to-one with customers helps the company react immediately to shifts in demand, so Dell doesn't get stuck with PCs no one wants. Finally, by selling directly, Dell has no dealers to pay. As a result, on average, Dell's costs are 12 percent lower than those of its leading PC competitor.

Dell knows that time is money, and the company is obsessed with "speed." For example, Dell has long been a model of just-in-time manufacturing and efficient supply chain management. Dell has also mastered the intricacies of today's lightning-fast electronic commerce. According to one account, "Dell calls it 'velocity'—squeezing time out of every step in the process—from the moment an order is taken to collecting the cash. [By selling direct, manufacturing to order, and] tapping credit cards and electronic payment, Dell converts the average sale to cash in less than 24 hours. By contrast, [competitors selling through dealers might take 35 days or longer.] Even mail-order rival Gateway takes 16.4 days."

Such blazing speed results in more satisfied customers and still lower costs. For example, customers are often delighted to find their new computers arriving within as few as 36 hours of placing an order. And because Dell doesn't order parts until an order is booked, it can take advantage of ever-falling component costs. On average, its parts are 60 days newer than those in competing machines, and, hence, 60 days farther down the price curve. This gives Dell a 6 percent profit advantage from parts costs alone. It also gives Dell what one analysts calls a

"negative cash conversion cycle." Says the analyst, "Because it keeps only five days of inventories, manages receivables to 30 days, and pushes payables out to 59 days, the Dell model will generate cash even if the company were to report no profit whatsoever."

The Internet is a perfect extension of Dell's direct-marketing model. Customers who are already comfortable buying direct from Dell now have an even more powerful way to do so. Now, by simply clicking the "Buy a Dell" icon at Dell's Web site, customers can design and price customized computer systems electronically. Then, with a click on the "Purchase" button, they can submit an order, choosing from online payment options that include a credit card, company purchase order, or corporate lease. Dell dashes out a digital confirmation to customers within five minutes of receiving the order. After receiving confirmation, customers can check the status of the order online at any time. "The Internet," says Michael Dell, "is the ultimate direct model. . . . [Customers] like the immediacy, convenience, savings, and personal touches that the [Internet] experience provides. Not only are some sales done online, but people who call on the phone after having visited Dell.com are twice as likely to buy."

The direct-marketing pioneer now sells more than $43 million worth of computers daily from its more than 80 country-specific Web sites, accounting for more than 50 percent of revenues. Buyers range from individuals purchasing home computers to large business users buying high-end $30,000

servers. "The Internet is like a booster rocket on our sales and growth," proclaims Dell. "Our vision is to have *all* customers conduct *all* transactions on the Internet, globally."

As you might imagine, competitors are no longer scoffing at Michael Dell's vision of the future. In fact, competing and noncompeting companies alike are studying the Dell model closely. "Somehow Dell has been able to take flexibility and speed and build it into their DNA. It's almost like drinking water," says the CEO of another Fortune 500 company, who visited recently to absorb some of the Dell magic to apply to his own company. "I'm trying to drink as much water here as I can."

It's hard to argue with success, and Michael Dell has been very successful. By following his hunches, at the tender age of 37 he has built one of the world's hottest companies. In the process, he's amassed a personal fortune exceeding $17 billion.

Sources: Quotes, performance statistics, and other information from Gary McWilliams, "Whirlwind on the Web," *Business Week,* April 7, 1997, pp. 132–136; "The InternetWeek Interview—Michael Dell," *InternetWeek,* April 13, 1999, p. 8; J. William Gurley, "Why Dell's World Isn't Dumb," *Fortune,* July 9, 2001, pp. 134–136; "America's 40 Richest Under 40," *Fortune,* September 17, 2001, p. 193; Andy Serwer, "Dell Does Domination," *Fortune,* January 21, 2002, pp. 71–75; Daniel Fisher, "The Best Little Factory in Texas," *Forbes,* June 10, 2002, p. 110; and www.dell.com/us/en/gen/corporate/vision_directmodel.htm, August 2002.

locate good potential customers, tailor products and services to the special needs of targeted consumers, and maintain long-term customer relationships.

Many companies confuse a customer mailing list with a customer database. A customer mailing list is simply a set of names, addresses, and telephone numbers. A customer database contains much more information. In B2B marketing, the salesperson's customer profile might contain the products and services the customer has bought; past volumes and prices; key contacts (and their ages, birthdays, hobbies, and favorite foods); competitive suppliers; status of current contracts; estimated customer spending for the next few years; and assessments of competitive strengths and weaknesses in selling and servicing the account.

In consumer marketing, the customer database might contain a customer's demographics (age, income, family members, birthdays), psychographics (activities, interests, and opinions), buying behavior (past purchases, buying preferences), and other relevant information. Some of these databases are huge. For example, Ritz-Carlton's database holds more than 500,000 individual customer preferences. Pizza Hut's database lets it track the purchases of more than 50 million customers. Internet portal Yahoo! records every click made by every visitor, adding some 400 billion bytes of data per day to its database—the equivalent of 800,000 books. And Wal-Mart's database contains more than 100 terabytes of data—that's 100 trillion bytes, equivalent to 16,000 bytes for every one of the world's 6 billion people.[24]

Armed with the information in their databases, these companies can identify small groups of customers to receive fine-tuned marketing offers and communications. Kraft Foods has amassed a list of more than 30 million users of its products who have responded to coupons or other Kraft promotions. Based on their interests, the company sends these customers tips on issues such as nutrition and exercise, as well as recipes and coupons for specific Kraft brands. FedEx uses its sophisticated database to create 100 highly targeted, customized direct-mail and telemarketing campaigns each year to its nearly 5 million customers shipping to 212 countries. By analyzing customers carefully and reaching the right customers at the right time with the right promotions, FedEx achieves response rates of 20 to 25 percent and earns an 8-to-1 return on its direct-marketing dollars.[25]

Nordstrom manages customer data on a more personal, one-to-one basis. Its Personal Touch program provides a good example:

> [Nordstrom] knows that a person can extrapolate from past choices to current styles much more reliably than a computer, so it uses Personal Touch shoppers—fashion consultants seeking long-term customer relationships. The company trains the personal shoppers in color use, current fashions, and the matching of products to a customer's appearance, taste, and lifestyle. The personal shoppers record customer likes, dislikes, lifestyle, and apparel needs, ascertained through telephone contacts or face-to-face conversations. Then they apply their fashion expertise to sell the customers entire ensembles, not just individual items. The personal shoppers can also access a customer's purchasing history to gain insight into a customer's tastes or to suggest items that might complement a prior purchase.[26]

Companies use their databases in many ways. They can use a database to identify prospects and generate sales leads by advertising products or offers. Or they can use the database to profile customers based on previous purchasing and to decide which customers should receive particular offers. Databases can help the company to deepen customer loyalty—companies can build customers' interest and enthusiasm by remembering buyer preferences and by sending appropriate information, gifts, or other materials.

In Germany, Mars has compiled a database containing information on virtually every German family that owns a cat. To build lasting relationships with cat owners, it sends a birthday card to each cat in Germany each year, along with samples and coupons.

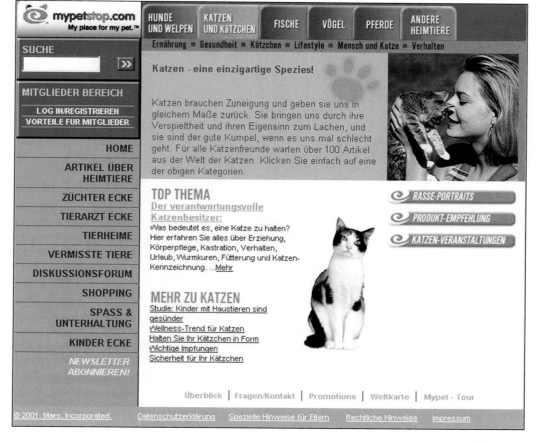

For example, Mars, a market leader in pet food as well as candy, maintains an exhaustive pet database. In Germany, the company has compiled the names of virtually every German family that owns a cat. It has obtained these names by contacting veterinarians, via its mypetstop.com Web site, and by offering the public a free booklet titled "How to Take Care of Your Cat." People who request the booklet fill out a questionnaire, providing their cat's name, age, birthday, and other information. Mars then sends a birthday card to each cat in Germany each year, along with a cat food sample and money-saving coupons for Mars brands. The result is a lasting relationship with the cat's owner.

The database can help a company make attractive offers of product replacements, upgrades, or complementary products, just when customers might be ready to act. For example, a General Electric appliance customer database contains each customer's demographic and psychographic characteristics along with an appliance-purchasing history. Using this database, GE marketers assess how long specific customers have owned their current appliances and which past customers might be ready to purchase again. They can determine which customers need a new GE range, refrigerator, clothes washer, or something else to go with other recently purchased products. Or they can identify the best past GE purchasers and send them gift certificates or other promotions to apply against their next GE purchases. A rich customer database allows GE to build profitable new business by locating good prospects, anticipating customer needs, cross-selling products and services, and rewarding loyal customers.

Like many other marketing tools, database marketing requires a special investment. Companies must invest in computer hardware, database software, analytical programs, communication links, and skilled personnel. The database system must be user-friendly and available to various marketing groups, including those in product and brand management, new-product development, advertising and promotion, direct mail, telemarketing, Web marketing, field sales, order fulfillment, and customer service. A well-managed database should lead to sales gains that will more than cover its costs.

Forms of Direct Marketing

The major forms of direct marketing—as shown in Figure 17.4—include *personal selling, telephone marketing, direct-mail marketing, catalog marketing, direct-response television marketing, kiosk marketing,* and *online marketing.* We examined personal selling in depth earlier in this chapter and looked closely at online marketing in Chapter 3. Here, we examine the other direct-marketing forms.

FIGURE 17.4
Forms of direct marketing

Marketers use Inbound toll-free 800 numbers to receive orders from television and print ads, direct mail, or catalogs. Here, the Carolina Cookie Company urges, "Don't wait another day. Call now to place an order or request a catalog."

Telephone Marketing

Telephone marketing
Using the telephone to sell directly to customers.

Telephone marketing—using the telephone to sell directly to consumers—has become the major direct-marketing communication tool. Telephone marketing now accounts for more than 38 percent of all direct-marketing media expenditures and 36 percent of direct-marketing sales. We're all familiar with telephone marketing directed toward consumers, but B2B marketers also use telephone marketing extensively, accounting for 58 percent of all telephone marketing sales.[27]

Marketers use *outbound* telephone marketing to sell directly to consumers and businesses. *Inbound* toll-free 800 numbers are used to receive orders from television and print ads, direct mail, or catalogs. The use of 800 numbers has taken off in recent years as more and more companies have begun using them, and as current users have added new features such as toll-free fax numbers. Residential use has also grown. To accommodate this rapid growth, new toll-free area codes (888, 877, 866) have been added. After the 800 area code was established in 1967, it took almost 30 years before its 8 million numbers were used up. In contrast, 888 area code numbers, established in 1996, were used up in only 2 years.[28]

Properly designed and targeted telemarketing provides many benefits, including purchasing convenience and increased product and service information. However, the recent explosion in unsolicited telephone marketing has annoyed many consumers, who object to the almost daily "junk phone calls" that pull them away from the dinner table or fill the answering machine. Lawmakers around the country are responding with legislation ranging from banning unsolicited telemarketing calls during certain hours to letting households sign up for "Do Not Call" lists. Most telemarketers support some action against random and poorly targeted telemarketing. As a Direct Marketing Association executive notes, "We want to target people who want to be targeted."[29]

Direct-Mail Marketing

Direct-mail marketing
Direct marketing through single mailings that include letters, ads, samples, foldouts, and other "salespeople with wings" sent to prospects on mailing lists.

Direct-mail marketing involves sending an offer, announcement, reminder, or other item to a person at a particular address. Using highly selective mailing lists, direct marketers send out millions of mail pieces each year—letters, ads, brochures, samples, video- and audiotapes, CDs, and other "salespeople with wings." Direct mail accounts for more than 23 percent of all direct-marketing media expenditures and 31 percent of direct-marketing sales. Together, telemarketing and direct-mail marketing account for more than 60 percent of direct-marketing expenditures and 66 percent of direct-marketing sales.[30]

Direct mail is well suited to direct, one-to-one communication. It permits high target-market selectivity, can be personalized, is flexible, and allows easy measurement of results. Although the cost per thousand people reached is higher than with mass media such as television or magazines, the people who are reached are much better prospects. Direct mail has proved successful in promoting all kinds of products, from books, magazine subscriptions, and insurance to gift items, clothing, gourmet foods, and industrial products. Direct mail is also used heavily by charities to raise billions of dollars each year.

The direct-mail industry constantly seeks new methods and approaches. For example, America Online has mailed out CDs by the hundreds of millions in one of the most successful direct-mail campaigns in history. Now other marketers, especially those in technology or e-commerce, are using CDs in their direct-mail offers. Used in conjunction with the Internet, CDs offer an affordable way to drive traffic to Web pages personalized for a specific market segment or a specific promotion. They can also be used to demonstrate computer-related products. For example, Sony sent out a CD that allowed PC users to demo its VAIO portable notebook on their own computers.[31]

Until recently, all mail was paper based and handled by the U.S. Post Office or delivery services such as FedEx, DHL, or Airborne Express. Recently, however, three new forms of mail delivery have become popular:

- *Fax mail:* Marketers now routinely send fax mail announcing special offers, sales, and other events to prospects and customers with fax machines. Fax mail messages can be sent and received almost instantaneously. However, some prospects and customers resent receiving unsolicited fax mail, which ties up their machines and consumes their paper.

- *E-mail:* Many marketers now send sales announcements, offers, product information, and other messages to e-mail addresses—sometimes to a few individuals, sometimes to large groups. As discussed in Chapter 3, today's e-mail messages have moved far beyond the drab text-only messages of old. The new breed of e-mail ad uses glitzy features such as animation, interactive links, streaming video, and personalized audio messages to reach out and grab attention. However, as people receive more and more e-mail, they resent the intrusion of unrequested messages. Smart marketers are using permission-based programs, sending e-mail ads only to those who want to receive them.

- *Voice mail:* Some marketers have set up automated programs that exclusively target voice-mail mailboxes and answering machines with prerecorded messages. These systems target homes between 10 A.M. and 4 P.M. and businesses between 7 P.M. and 9 P.M., when people are least likely to answer. If the automated dialer hears a live voice, it disconnects. Such systems thwart hang-ups by annoyed potential customers. However, they can also create substantial ill will.

These new forms deliver direct mail at incredible speeds compared to the post office's "snail mail" pace. Yet, much like mail delivered through traditional channels, they may be resented as "junk mail" if sent to people who have no interest in them. For this reason, marketers must carefully identify appropriate targets so as not waste their money and recipients' time (see Real Marketing 17.4).

Catalog Marketing

Catalog marketing

Direct marketing through print, video, or electronic catalogs that are mailed to select customers, made available in stores, or presented online.

Advances in technology, along with the move toward personalized, one-to-one marketing, have resulted in exciting changes in **catalog marketing.** *Catalog Age* magazine used to define a *catalog* as "a printed, bound piece of at least eight pages, selling multiple products, and offering a direct ordering mechanism." Today, only a few years later, this definition is sadly out of date. With the stampede to the Internet, more and more catalogs are going electronic. Many traditional print catalogers have added Web-based catalogs to their marketing mixes, and a variety of new Web-only catalogers have emerged. However, the Internet has not yet killed off printed catalogs—far from it. Web catalogs currently generate only about 13 percent of all catalog sales. Printed catalogs remain the primary medium, and many former Web-only companies have created printed catalogs to expand their business.[32]

real marketing 17.4

Misdirected Marketing: My Dead Dog May Already Be a Winner!

Poor database management and wrongly targeted direct marketing not only aggravates consumers, it costs companies millions of dollars each year and sometimes makes them look downright foolish. Take the following account, written by Lee Coppola, the bemused recipient of some of this misdirected mania:

Ever wonder what happens when a pet takes on a persona? Ashley could have told you, if he could have talked. Ashley was the family mutt, an SPCA special, part beagle and part spaniel. For years, most of them after he died, he also served as the family's representative in the local telephone book. He was picked for the role quite haphazardly one day when I tried to keep my number out of the book to avoid getting business calls at home. When I balked at the $60-a-year fee, the cheery telephone company representative suggested I list the number in one of my children's names.

I was munching on a sandwich at the time and Ashley followed me around the kitchen waiting for a crumb to fall. "Can I put the phone in any name?" I asked the rep as I sidestepped Ashley. "Certainly," she answered, and therein gave birth to 10 years of telephone calls and mail to a dog.

"A remarkable new book about the Coppolas since the Civil War is about to make history—and you, Ashley Coppola, are in it," touted one letter asking Ashley to send $10 right away for "this one-time offer." Ashley received hundreds of pieces of mail, the bulk soliciting his money.

The most ironic pitches for cash were from the SPCA and the Buffalo Zoo, a kind of animal-helping-animal scenario. And we wondered how the chief executive of a local cemetery might react if he knew he was asking a canine to buy a plot

to give his family "peace of mind." Or a local lawn service's thoughts about asking a dog who daily messed the grass, "Is your lawn as attractive as it could be?" Then there was the letter offering Ashley "reliable electronic security to protect your home." One of the kids asked if that wasn't Ashley's job.

The kids soon got into the swing of having their dog receive mail and telephone calls. "He's sleeping under the dining room table," one would tell telemarketers. "He's out in the backyard taking a whiz," was the favorite reply of another. My wife would have nothing of that frivolity, preferring to simply reply, "He's deceased."

But that tack backfired on her one day when our youngest child took an almost pleading call from a survey-company employee looking for Ashley. "I'm Ashley," the 17-year-old politely replied, taking pity on the caller. He dutifully gave his age and answered a few questions before he realized he was late for an appointment and hurriedly cut short the conversation. "Can I call you again?" the surveyor asked. "OK," our son said as he hung up.

Sure enough, the surveyor called again the next day and asked for Ashley. But this time Mom answered and gave her standard reply. "Oh, my God," exclaimed the caller. "I'm so, so sorry." The surveyor's horrified grief puzzled my wife until our son explained how he had been a healthy teenage Ashley the day before.

Sometimes we worried about our dog's fate. You see, he broke several chain letters urging him to copy and send 20 others or risk some calamity. After all, Ashley was warned, didn't one person die nine days after throwing out the letter?

Did I mention credit cards? Ashley paid his bills on time, judging from the $5,000 lines-of-credit for which he "automatically" qualified. Made us wonder about the scrutiny of the nation's credit-card industry.

Of course, Ashley was no ordinary dog. He was an Italian dog. How else to explain the solicitation to Mr. Coppola Ashley that came all the way from Altamura, Italy, and sought donations to an orphanage? Then there was the offer to obtain his family's cherished crest, "fashioned hundreds of years ago in Italy," and purchase the Coppola family registry that listed him along with all the other Coppolas in America.

Is there some message to all this? Think of the saplings that were sacrificed to try to squeeze money from a canine. Or the time, energy, and money that were wasted each time a postage or bulk-mail stamp was affixed to an envelope being sent to a mutt. We did feel sheepish about the deception when the mail came from the self-employed trying to make a buck. We wondered if a local dentist really would have given Ashley a "complete initial consultation, exam, and bitewing X-rays for ONLY THREE DOLLARS." And what might have been the expression on the saleswoman's face if Ashley had shown up for his complimentary Mary Kay facial?

Ashley did appreciate, however, the coupon for dog food.

Source: Lee Coppola, "My Dead Dog May Already Be a Winner!" *Newsweek,* July 5, 1999, p. 11. Also, see Louella Miles, "Should DM Still Be Missing Its Mark?" *Marketing,* June 14, 2001, pp. 29–31.

Catalog marketing has grown explosively during the past 25 years. Some 10,000 companies now produce 14,000 unique catalog titles in the United States.

Catalog marketing has grown explosively during the past 25 years. Annual catalog sales (both print and electronic) are expected to grow from $69 billion in 1996 to more than $160 billion by 2006.[33] Some huge general-merchandise retailers—such as J.C. Penney and Spiegel—sell a full line of merchandise through catalogs. In recent years, these giants have been challenged by thousands of specialty catalogs that serve highly specialized market niches. According to one study, some 10,000 companies now produce 14,000 unique catalog titles in the United States.[34]

Consumers can buy just about anything from a catalog. Sharper Image sells $2,400 jet-propelled surfboards. The Banana Republic Travel and Safari Clothing Company features everything you would need to go hiking in the Sahara or the rain forest. And each year Lillian Vernon sends out 37 editions of its 8 catalogs with total circulation of 162 million copies to its 20-million-person database, selling everything from shoes to decorative lawn birds and monogrammed oven mitts.[35] Specialty department stores, such as Neiman Marcus, Bloomingdale's, and Saks Fifth Avenue, use catalogs to cultivate upper-middle-class markets for high-priced, often exotic, merchandise. Several major corporations have also developed or acquired catalog divisions. For example, Avon now issues 10 women's fashion catalogs along with catalogs for children's and men's clothes. Walt Disney Company mails out over 6 million catalogs each year featuring videos, stuffed animals, and other Disney items.

More than 90 percent of all catalog companies now present merchandise and take orders over the Internet. For example, the Lands' End Web site, which debuted in 1995, greeted 28 million visitors last year. Its Web-based sales have more than doubled in the past two years, now accounting for 16 percent of total sales. During the hectic Christmas season, the site handled a record of 15,000 visitors in just one hour.[36] Here's another example that illustrates this dramatic shift in catalog marketing:

> When novelty gifts marketer Archie McPhee launched its Web site in September 1995, response was underwhelming. But when the company added a shopping basket ordering feature in 1997, the site roared to life. According to Mark Pahlow, president of the catalog company, the site now has 35,000 unique visitors each month, generating 55 percent of the cataloger's total sales. The Web numbers are so positive that Archie McPhee has slashed circulation of its print catalog from 1 million to less than 300,000, and reduced the frequency from five issues a year to three. The Web site has saved the company more than 50 percent in the costs of producing, printing, and mailing its color catalog, which had been as high as $700,000 annually. The site can also offer much more merchandise. "A 48-page catalog would show fewer than 200 items, whereas the Web site offers more than 500," Pahlow notes. Another benefit is the site's real-time inventory feature. "The day a new product arrives, it is shown on the site. The moment we run out of an item, we pull it

off. We are also able to show items we have small quantities of as Web-only specials." As an added benefit, the Web site also lets the cataloger build dynamic customer relationships using interactive features, such as "The Nerd Test" and a fortune-telling ball. Customers can elect to join the "Cult of McPhee" e-mail list and receive free monthly e-mails announcing the direct marketer's upcoming events, contests, and specials. Cult members also get advance notice of our new products and qualify for special members-only deals.[37]

Along with the benefits, however, Web-based catalogs also present challenges. Whereas a print catalog is intrusive and creates its own attention, Web catalogs are passive and must be marketed. "Attracting new customers is much more difficult to do with a Web catalog," says an industry consultant. "You have to use advertising, linkage, and other means to drive traffic to it." Thus, even catalogers who are sold on the Web are not likely to abandon their print catalogs completely. For example, Archie McPhee relies on its print catalogs to promote its site. "I think we will always produce at least one catalog a year," Pahlow says.

Direct-Response Television Marketing

Direct-response television marketing

Direct marketing via television, including direct-response television advertising and home shopping channels.

Direct-response television marketing takes one of two major forms. The first is *direct-response advertising.* Direct marketers air television spots, often 60 or 120 seconds long, that persuasively describe a product and give customers a toll-free number for ordering. Television viewers often encounter 30-minute advertising programs, or *infomercials,* for a single product.

Some successful direct-response ads run for years and become classics. For example, Dial Media's ads for Ginsu knives ran for seven years and sold almost 3 million sets of knives worth more than $40 million in sales; its Armourcote cookware ads generated more than twice that much. And over the past 40 years, infomercial czar Ron Popeil's company, Ronco, has sold more than $1 billion worth of TV-marketed gadgets, including the original Veg-O-Matic, the Pocket Fisherman, Mr. Microphone, the Giant Food Dehydrator and Beef Jerky Machine, and the Showtime Rotisserie & BBQ.[38] The current infomercial champ?

> It's three o'clock in the morning. Plagued with insomnia, you grab the remote and flip around until a grinning blonde in an apron catches your attention: "I'm going to show you something you won't believe! Juicy meals in minutes! Something else you won't believe . . . George Foreman!" The studio roars, and boxing's elder statesman, in a red apron, shows off his Lean Mean Fat-Reducing Grilling Machine and highlights the grease caught in the pan below. "Eew!" the audience screams. It can be yours for three easy payments of $19.95 (plus shipping and handling). Don't laugh. Such infomercials helped the Foreman grills product line notch almost $400 million in sales last year.[39]

For years, infomercials have been associated with somewhat questionable pitches for juicers and other kitchen gadgets, get-rich-quick schemes, and nifty ways to stay in shape without working very hard at it. In recent years, however, a number of large companies—GTE, Johnson & Johnson, MCA Universal, Sears, Procter & Gamble, Revlon, IBM, Cadillac, Volvo, Land Rover, Anheuser-Busch, even the U.S. Navy—have begun using infomercials to sell their wares over the phone, refer customers to retailers, send out coupons and product information, or attract buyers to their Web sites. Direct response TV commercials are usually cheaper to make and the media purchase is less costly. Moreover, results are easily measured. "Unlike branding campaigns, direct-response ads always include a 1-800 number of Web address, making it easier for marketers to gauge whether consumers are paying attention to their pitches," says an industry analyst.[40]

Home shopping channels, another form of direct-response television marketing, are television programs or entire channels dedicated to selling goods and services. Some home shopping channels, such as Home Shopping Network (HSN), the Quality Value Channel (QVC), and ValueVision, broadcast 24 hours a day. On HSN, the program's hosts offer bargain prices on products ranging from jewelry, lamps, collectible dolls, and clothing to power tools and consumer electronics—usually obtained by the home shopping channel at closeout prices. Viewers call a toll-free number to order goods. At the other end of the operation, 400 operators handle more than 1,200 incoming lines, entering orders directly into computer terminals.

With widespread distribution on cable and satellite television, the top three shopping networks combined now reach 248 million homes worldwide, selling more than $4 billion of goods each year. They are now combining direct-response television marketing with online selling. For

The current infomercial champ? Direct-response TV ads helped George Foreman's Lean Mean Fat-Reducing Machines notch $400 million in sales last year.

example, QVC recently launched a feature called "61st Minute," in which QVC viewers are urged to go online immediately after a given product showcase. Once there, viewers find a Webcast continuation of the product pitch.[41]

Kiosk Marketing

Some companies place information and ordering machines—called *kiosks* (in contrast to vending machines, which dispense actual products)—in stores, airports, and other locations. Hallmark and American Greetings use kiosks to help customers create and purchase personalized greeting cards. Tower Records has listening kiosks that let customers listen to the music before purchase. Kiosks in the do-it-yourself ceramics stores of California-based Color Me Mine Inc. contain clip-art images that customers can use to decorate the ceramics pieces they purchase in the store. At Car Max, the used-car superstore, customers use a kiosk with a touch-screen computer to get information about its vast inventory of as many as 1,000 cars and trucks. Customers can choose a handful and print out photos, prices, features, and location on the store's lot. The use of such kiosks is expected to increase fivefold during the next three years.[42]

Business marketers also use kiosks. For example, Dow Plastics places kiosks at trade shows to collect sales leads and to provide information on its 700 products. The kiosk system reads customer data from encoded registration badges and produces technical data sheets that can be printed at the kiosk or faxed or mailed to the customer. The system has resulted in a 400 percent increase in qualified sales leads.[43]

Like about everything else these days, kiosks are also going online, as many companies merge the powers of the real and virtual worlds. For example, in some Levi Strauss stores, you can plug your measurements into a Web kiosk and have custom-made jeans delivered to your home within two weeks. At the local Disney Store, kiosk guests can buy merchandise online, purchase theme-park passes, and learn more about Disney vacations and entertainment products. Gap has installed interactive kiosks, called Web lounges, in some of its stores that provide gift ideas or let customers match up outfits without trying them in dressing rooms. Outdoor equipment retailer REI recently outfitted its stores with kiosks that provide customers with product information and let them place orders online.[44]

Integrated Direct Marketing

Too often, a company's individual direct-marketing efforts are not well integrated with one another or with other elements of its marketing and promotion mixes. For example, a firm's

FIGURE 17.5
An integrated direct-marketing campaign

media advertising may be handled by the advertising department working with a traditional advertising agency. Meanwhile, its direct-mail and catalog business may be handled by direct-marketing specialists, while its Web site is developed and operated by an outside Internet firm. Even within a given direct-marketing campaign, too many companies use only a "one-shot" effort to reach and sell a prospect or a single vehicle in multiple stages to trigger purchases.

Integrated direct marketing

Direct-marketing campaigns that use multiple vehicles and multiple stages to improve response rates and profits.

A more powerful approach is **integrated direct marketing,** which involves using carefully coordinated multiple-media, multiple-stage campaigns. Such campaigns can greatly improve response. Whereas a direct-mail piece alone might generate a 2 percent response, adding a Web site and toll-free phone number might raise the response rate by 50 percent. Then, a well-designed outbound telemarketing effort might lift response by an additional 500 percent. Suddenly, a 2 percent response has grown to 15 percent or more by adding interactive marketing channels to a regular mailing.

More elaborate integrated direct-marketing campaigns can be used. Consider the multimedia, multistage campaign shown in Figure 17.5. Here, the paid ad creates product awareness and stimulates phone, mail, or Web inquiries. The company immediately sends direct mail or e-mail responses to those who inquire. Within a few days, the company follows up with a phone call seeking an order. Some prospects will order by phone or the company's Web site; others might request a face-to-face sales call. In such a campaign, the marketer seeks to improve response rates and profits by adding media and stages that contribute more to additional sales than to additional costs.

Public Policy and Ethical Issues in Direct Marketing

Direct marketers and their customers usually enjoy mutually rewarding relationships. Occasionally, however, a darker side emerges. The aggressive and sometimes shady tactics of a few direct marketers can bother or harm consumers, giving the entire industry a black eye. Abuses range from simple excesses that irritate consumers to instances of unfair practices or even outright deception and fraud. The direct-marketing industry has also faced growing concerns about invasion-of-privacy issues.

Irritation, Unfairness, Deception, and Fraud

Direct-marketing excesses sometimes annoy or offend consumers. Most of us dislike direct-response TV commercials that are too loud, too long, and too insistent. Especially bothersome are dinnertime or late-night phone calls. Beyond irritating consumers, some direct marketers have been accused of taking unfair advantage of impulsive or less sophisticated buyers. TV shopping shows and program-long "infomercials" seem to be the worst culprits. They feature smooth-talking hosts, elaborately staged demonstrations, claims of drastic price reductions, "while they last" time limitations, and unequaled ease of purchase to inflame buyers who have low sales resistance.

Worse yet, so-called heat merchants design mailers and write copy intended to mislead buyers. Even well-known direct mailers have been accused of deceiving consumers. Sweepstakes promoter Publishers Clearing House recently paid $52 million to settle accusations that its high-pressure mailings confused or misled consumers, especially the elderly, into believing that they had won prizes or would win if they bought the company's magazines.[45]

Other direct marketers pretend to be conducting research surveys when they are actually asking leading questions to screen or persuade consumers. Fraudulent schemes, such as investment scams or phony collections for charity, have also multiplied in recent years. Crooked direct marketers can be hard to catch: Direct-marketing customers often respond quickly, do not interact personally with the seller, and usually expect to wait for delivery. By the time buyers realize that they have been bilked, the thieves are usually somewhere else plotting new schemes.

Invasion of Privacy

Invasion of privacy is perhaps the toughest public policy issue now confronting the direct-marketing industry. These days, it seems that almost every time consumers enter a sweepstakes, apply for a

The DMA recently developed its "Privacy Promise to American Consumers," which attempts to build customer confidence by requiring that all DMA members adhere to certain carefully developed consumer privacy rules.

credit card, take out a magazine subscription, or order products by mail, telephone, or the Internet, their names are entered into some company's already bulging database. Using sophisticated computer technologies, direct marketers can use these databases to "microtarget" their selling efforts.

Consumers often benefit from such database marketing—they receive more offers that are closely matched to their interests. However, many critics worry that marketers may know *too* much about consumers' lives and that they may use this knowledge to take unfair advantage of consumers. At some point, they claim, the extensive use of databases intrudes on consumer privacy.

For example, they ask, should AT&T be allowed to sell marketers the names of customers who frequently call the 800 numbers of catalog companies? Should a company such as American Express be allowed to make data on its 175 million American cardholders available to merchants who accept AmEx cards? Is it right for credit bureaus to compile and sell lists of people who have recently applied for credit cards—people who are considered prime direct-marketing targets because of their spending behavior? Or is it right for states to sell the names and addresses of driver's license holders, along with height, weight, and gender information, allowing apparel retailers to target tall or overweight people with special clothing offers?

In their drives to build databases, companies sometimes get carried away. For example, when first introduced, Intel's Pentium III chip contained an embedded serial number that allowed the company to trace users' equipment. When privacy advocates screamed, Intel disabled the feature. Similarly, Microsoft caused substantial privacy concerns when it introduced its Windows 95 software. It used a "Registration Wizard," which allowed users to register their new software online. However, when users went online to register, without their knowledge, Microsoft "read" the configurations of their PCs to learn about the major software products running on each customer's system. When users learned of this invasion, they protested loudly and Microsoft abandoned the practice.

These days, it's not only the large companies that can access such private information. The explosion of information technology has put these capabilities into the hands almost any business. For example, one bar owner discovered the power of information technology after he acquired a simple, inexpensive device to check IDs.

About 10,000 people a week go to The Rack, a bar in Boston. . . . One by one, they hand over their driver's licenses to a doorman, who swipes them through a sleek black machine. If a license is valid and its holder is over 21, a red light blinks and the patron is waved through. But most of the customers are not aware that it also pulls up the name, address, birth date, and other personal details from a data strip on the back of the license. Even height, eye color, and sometimes Social Security number are registered. "You swipe the license, and all of a sudden someone's whole life as we know it pops up in front of you," said Paul Barclay, the bar's owner. "It's almost voyeuristic." Mr. Barclay bought the machine to keep out underage drinkers who use fake IDs. But he soon found that he could build a database of personal information, providing an intimate perspective on his clientele that can be useful in marketing. "It's not just an ID check," he said. "It's a tool." Now, for any given night or hour, he can break down his clientele by sex, age, ZIP code, or other characteristics. If he wanted to, he could find out how many blond women named Karen over 5 feet 2 inches came in over a weekend, or how many of his customers have the middle initial M. More practically, he can build mailing lists based on all that data—and keep track of who comes back.[46]

Such access to and use of information has caused much concern and debate among companies, consumers, and public policy makers. Consumer privacy has become a major regulatory issue. For example, in 2001 alone, more than 250 pieces of privacy legislation were put before Congress. [47]

The direct-marketing industry is addressing issues of ethics and public policy. For example, in an effort to build consumer confidence in direct shopping, the Direct Marketing Association (DMA)—the largest association for businesses practicing interactive and database marketing, with more than 4,600 member companies—launched a "Privacy Promise to American Consumers." The Privacy Promise requires that all DMA members adhere to a carefully developed set of consumer privacy rules. Members must agree to notify customers if any personal information is rented, sold, or exchanged with others. They must also honor consumer requests to "opt out" of information exchanges with other marketers or not to receive mail, telephone, or other solicitations again. Finally, they must abide by the DMA's Mail Preference Service (www.the-dma.org/consumers/offmailinglist.html), Telephone Preference Service (www.the-dms.org/consumers/offtelephonelist.html), and e-mail preference services, three national services to remove the names of consumers from direct-mail and telemarketing lists.

Direct marketers know that, left untended, such problems will lead to increasingly negative consumer attitudes, lower response rates, and calls for more restrictive state and federal legislation. "Privacy and customer permission have become the cornerstones of customer trust, [and] trust has become the cornerstone to a continuing relationship," says one expert. Companies must "become the custodians of customer trust and protect the privacy of their customers."[48]

Most direct marketers want the same things that consumers want: honest and well-designed marketing offers targeted only toward consumers who will appreciate and respond to them. Direct marketing is just too expensive to waste on consumers who don't want it.

LOOKING BACK: REVIEWING THE CONCEPTS

Personal selling and direct marketing are both direct tools for communicating with and persuading current and prospective customers. Selling is the interpersonal arm of the communications mix. To be successful in personal selling, a company must first build and then manage an effective sales force. Firms must also be good at direct marketing, the process of forming one-to-one connections with customers. Today, many companies are turning to direct marketing in an effort to reach carefully targeted customers more efficiently and to build stronger, more personal, one-to-one relationships with them.

1. Discuss the role of a company's salespeople in creating value for customers and building customer relationships.

Most companies use salespeople, and many companies assign them an important role in the marketing mix. For companies selling business products, the firm's salespeople work directly with customers. Often, the sales force is the customer's only direct contact with the company and therefore may be viewed by customers as representing the company itself. In contrast, for consumer product companies that sell through intermediaries, consumers usually do not meet salespeople or even know about them. The sales force works behind the scenes, dealing with wholesalers and retailers to obtain their support and helping them become effective in selling the firm's products.

As an element of the promotion mix, the sales force is very effective in achieving certain marketing objectives and carrying out such activities as prospecting, communicating, selling and servicing, and information gathering. But with companies becoming more market oriented, a market-focused sales force also works to produce both *customer satisfaction* and *company profit*. To accomplish these goals, the sales force needs skills in marketing analysis and planning in addition to the traditional selling skills.

2. Identify and explain the six major sales force management steps.

High sales force costs necessitate an effective *sales management process* consisting of six steps: *designing sales force strategy and structure, recruiting and selecting, training, compensating, supervising,* and *evaluating* salespeople.

In designing a sales force, sales management must address issues such as what type of sales force structure will work best (territorial, product, customer, or complex structure); how large the sales force should be; who will be involved in the selling effort; and how its various sales and sales support people will work together (inside or outside sales forces and team selling).

To hold down the high costs of hiring the wrong people, salespeople must be *recruited* and *selected* carefully. In recruiting salespeople, a company may look to job duties and the characteristics of its most successful salespeople to suggest the traits it wants in its salespeople and then look for applicants through recommendations of current salespeople, employment agencies, classified ads, and the Internet and by contacting college students. In the selection process, the procedure can vary from a single informal interview to lengthy testing and interviewing. After the selection process is complete, *training* programs familiarize new salespeople not only with the art of selling but also with the company's history, its products and policies, and the characteristics of its market and competitors.

The sales force *compensation* system helps to reward, motivate, and direct salespeople. In compensating salespeople, companies try to have an appealing plan, usually close to the going rate for the type of sales job and needed skills. In addition to compensation, all salespeople need *supervision,* and many need continuous encouragement because they must make many decisions and face many frustrations. Periodically, the company must *evaluate* their performance to help them do a better job. In evaluating salespeople, the company relies on getting regular information gathered through sales reports, personal observations, customers' letters and complaints, customer surveys, and conversations with other salespeople.

3. Discuss the personal selling process, distinguishing between transaction-oriented marketing and relationship marketing.

The art of selling involves a seven-step *selling process: prospecting and qualifying, preapproach, approach, presentation and demonstration, handling objections, closing,* and *follow-up.* These steps help marketers close a specific sale and as such are *transaction oriented.* However, a seller's dealings with customers should be guided by the larger concept of *relationship marketing.* The company's sales force should help to orchestrate a whole-company effort to develop profitable long-term relationships with key customers based on superior customer value and satisfaction.

4. Define direct marketing and discuss its benefits to customers and companies.

Direct marketing consists of direct connections with carefully targeted individual consumers to both obtain an immediate response and cultivate lasting customer relationships. Using detailed databases, direct marketers tailor their offers and communications to the needs of narrowly defined segments or even individual buyers.

For buyers, direct marketing is convenient, easy to use, and private. It gives them ready access to a wealth of products and information, at home and around the globe. Direct marketing is also immediate and interactive, allowing buyers to create exactly the configuration of information, products, or services they desire, then order them on the spot. For sellers, direct marketing is a powerful tool for building customer relationships. Using database marketing, today's marketers can target small groups or individual consumers, tailor offers to individual needs, and promote these offers through personalized communications. It also offers them a low-cost, efficient alternative for reaching their markets. As a result of these advantages to both buyers and sellers, direct marketing has become the fastest growing form of marketing.

5. Identify and discuss the major forms of direct marketing.

The main forms of direct marketing include *personal selling, telephone marketing, direct-mail marketing, catalog marketing, direct-response television marketing, kiosk marketing,* and *online marketing.* We discuss personal selling in the first part of this chapter and examined online marketing in detail in Chapter 3. *Telephone marketing* consists of using the telephone to sell directly to consumers. *Direct-mail marketing* consists of the company sending an offer, announcement, reminder, or other item to a person at a specific address. Recently, three new forms of mail delivery have become popular—*fax mail, e-mail,* and *voice mail.* Some marketers rely on *catalog marketing,* or selling through catalogs mailed to a select list of customers or made available in stores. *Direct-response television marketing* has two forms: *direct-response advertising* and *home shopping channels. Kiosks* are information and ordering machines that direct marketers place in stores, airports, and other locations. *Online marketing,* discussed in Chapter 3, involves online channels and e-commerce, which electronically link consumers with sellers.

REVIEWING THE KEY TERMS

DISCUSSING THE CONCEPTS

1. What did Robert Louis Stevenson mean when he said that "everyone lives by selling something"? Describe the various roles the modern salesperson plays.

2. The term *salesperson* covers a wide range of positions. List and briefly describe those positions and provide an example of each. State your career ambition. How might you be involved in selling?

3. One of the most pressing issues that sales managers face is how to structure the sales force and their tasks. Evaluate the methods described in the text. For each method, provide (a) a brief description of its chief characteristics, (b) an example of how it's used, and (c) a critique of its effectiveness.

4. What is team selling, and what are its advantages and disadvantages? How would recruiting and training for a sales team differ from recruiting and training for individual selling?

5. Many people think that they do not have the attributes and abilities required for successful selling. What role does training play in helping a person develop selling skills?

6. List and briefly describe the steps in personal selling. Which step do you think is the most difficult for the average salesperson? Which step is the most critical to successful selling? Which step is usually done correctly?

7. The chapter suggests that a new direct-marketing model has been created. What is direct marketing? How does it differ from other forms of marketing? How will the new direct-marketing model affect the emerging electronic marketplace?

8. List and briefly describe each of the major forms of direct marketing. Pick one of the following companies and demonstrate how it could use each form of direct marketing to sell its products and services: (a) Microsoft, (b) General Motors, or (c) the Gap.

APPLYING THE CONCEPTS

1. Being a stockbroker can be an exciting and challenging occupation. In years past, broker trainees received extensive training on the technical workings of the stock market and the characteristics of potential clients. One of the most difficult tasks for new brokers was finding and developing clients. This involved long and often discouraging hours of telephone "prospecting" and "cold-calling" potential clients. Today, however, things are changing. The rapid expansion of investment and information alternatives has made a broker's job more challenging. Most major investment brokerages are now online and brokers can help information-hungry investors in ways that would have been unimaginable only a few years ago. Visit the following Web sites: E*TRADE (www.etrade.com), Harris Direct (www.harrisdirect.com), Charles Schwab (www.schwab.com), Datek (www.datek.com), and Waterhouse (www.waterhouse.com).

   a. Which Web site is the most "user friendly"? Why? Which of the sites makes it easy to get in touch with a broker in your local area? How could a broker in your local area find out that you had been using his or her company's online service?

   b. Prepare an analysis grid that compares the above sites on sales stimulation, information services, cost, graphic design, responsiveness, security, and relationship marketing. Which site is best? Why?

   c. How have such sites changed the brokerage business? How is the selling function in the brokerage business changing?

2. Jonathan Ellermann is excited about his new job as a personal communication consultant for Nokia (www.nokia.com), the giant phone producer that captures a quarter of the global market. Rivals such as Ericsson (www.ericsson.com), Vodafone (www.vodaphone.com), Panasonic (www.panasonic.com), and Motorola (www.motorola.com) have vowed to make things much tougher for Nokia in the coming year. They have developed new designs, communications applications, and strategic alliances between hardware and software makers in an effort to lure fickle consumers away from Nokia.

   a. Ellermann is seeking to sell Nokia's latest-model personal communication device to Shell Oil's Houston branch (approximately 5,000 phones). What sales strategy should Ellermann recommend to Nokia? In your answer, consider the advantages and disadvantages of Nokia's product.

   b. Would you recommend that Nokia employ individual selling or team selling? Explain.

   c. Which step of the sales process do you think will be most critical to Ellermann's success?

   d. What could Ellermann do to establish a strong relationship with local Shell representatives?

DIGITAL CONNECTIONS

**COMMUNICATION CONNECTIONS
FOR PROSPECTING ONLINE**

The Herman Miller Company is a leading global provider of office furniture, producing about $2 billion in revenues annually. The company's presence extends to more than 40 countries through licenses, sales offices, dealerships, and the Web. Herman Miller has long been an innovator in design and customer relationship management. For example, Herman Miller designers were among the first to recognize the impact of ergonomic work stations on employee productivity. To build relationships, the company surveys customers, examines responses, and designs products that appeal to consumers and enhance efficiency. Solving real problems (with respect to the office work environment) for real companies is a Herman Miller trait.

To add to the traditional sales leads derived from customers and standard promotion avenues, Herman Miller has turned its attention to the Web. The first step in building prospect lists is to examine the links other companies have to your company's

Web site. Alta Vista, an online search engine found at **www.altavista.com**, provides a feature that automatically constructs a list of links. In the Alta Vista search box, type "link:www.hermanmiller.com" to find out which Web sites are linked to Herman Miller's home page. You have just begun the first step in constructing a prospect list.

FOR DISCUSSION

1. How many Web addresses (contact points) did the Alta Vista search produce? Select four Web sites generated by the search that might be good prospects and explain why you chose them. Would these companies constitute good prospects for Herman Miller?
2. What is the next step after building the prospect list?
3. How could Herman Miller identify prospects through its own Web site?
4. How could Herman Miller use e-mail to move prospects closer to purchase?

MarketSoft: Turning Prospects into Customers

What is the key to closing a business deal? It could be as simple as following a lead. MarketSoft helps clients automate the communication between marketers and sales representatives to ensure that hot leads are passed along quickly and effectively. Leveraging technology, the company offers software that analyzes the information available on a lead, determines the best salesperson to handle the potential sale, and delivers the contact information through e-mails, cell phones, faxes, and pagers. The result? For companies like Cisco Systems, IBM, American Express, MetLife, and Allstate, prospects become customers.

After viewing the MarketSoft video, answer the following questions about personal selling and direct marketing:

1. Are leads the key to successful sales? How important are the other components of the selling process? How might the software that MarketSoft markets alter or reinforce the role of the sales force?
2. How could companies use the MarketSoft software to evaluate marketing efforts? To evaluate salespeople?
3. The video mentions that MarketSoft plans to expand its software and services. What expansions do you think might be most successful? Should MarketSoft consider expanding its services to direct marketers? What additional features would direct marketers require?

Jefferson-Pilot Financial: Growing the Sales Force

AFTER THE MEETING

On a hot Friday afternoon in July 2002, Bob Powell and John Knowles walked across a parking lot towards Bob's car. They had just finished a two-day strategic planning meeting with other members of Jefferson-Pilot Financial's (JPF) Independent Marketing channel at the Grandover Resort and Conference Hotel just outside Greensboro, North Carolina. The group had gathered to develop the sales goals it wanted to achieve by the end of 2005, to identify strategic projects it needed to accomplish to meet those goals, and to assign responsibility for each project.

"Wow, it's going to be hot in your car," John noted. John served as vice president for Independent Marketing and Bob was senior vice president.

"Especially after sitting in that air-conditioned room for two days," Bob responded. "But I'm glad we're riding together. This'll give us a few minutes to talk about the sales force strategy project the group assigned us."

JEFFERSON-PILOT FINANCIAL

Jefferson-Pilot Corporation (JP), a holding company, was one of the nation's largest shareholder-owned life insurance companies. Jefferson-Pilot's life insurance and annuity businesses, known collectively as Jefferson-Pilot Financial, included Jefferson-Pilot Life Insurance Company, Jefferson-Pilot Financial Insurance Company, and Jefferson-Pilot Life America Insurance Company. JPF offered full lines of individual and group life insurance products as well as annuity and investment products. Jefferson-Pilot Communications Company, which operated three network television stations and 17 radio stations, produced and syndicated sports programming.

In 2001, the company amassed $3.33 billion in revenues and $513 million in net income. JP's insurance and investment products produced about 84 percent of its net income. JP took pride in its excellent financial ratings, having earned the highest possible financial ratings from A.M. Best, Standard and Poors, and Fitch.

Historically, the company generated its individual life insurance sales using a career sales force. The company employed managers to recruit and train life insurance agents, paying the managers commissions based on the insurance premiums their agents generated and an expense allowance to cover their overhead costs. The agents became "captive" Jefferson-Pilot employees who sold *only* JP's policies.

Like most life insurance companies, the company paid agents on a commission-only basis. The agent earned a commission of 50 percent of the *first-year* premium paid by the policyholder plus the potential for up to 20 percent more based on achieving certain annual premium sales goals. In the following years, the agent earned a much lower commission on annual renewal premiums, usually in the range of 3 percent. In addition to paying commission, the company provided the career agents with a full range of

fringe benefits, such as health insurance, vacation, and sick leave. The individual agent had to pay his or her own business expenses.

A NEW STRATEGY

In 1993, JP was a conservative, well-run company. However, the board of directors wanted the company to grow more rapidly. The board brought in a new top-management team and charged the team with speeding up the company's growth. The new team immediately examined the company's sales force strategy. It concluded that although the career sales force had been a valuable asset, the company was not capable of meeting its growth goals using only a career force. It simply took too long to hire and train new agents and bring them up to the necessary productivity levels. Further, industry wide, only about one of every seven or eight recruits actually succeeded in the insurance business.

In addition to career agents, JPF had used some independent agents all along. Independent agents worked for themselves or for independent companies. They, like captive agents, sold life insurance, but they could sell policies offered by a variety of companies. JPF decided to expand it sales force by focusing on the independent agents. It began to recruit these established, experienced independent salespeople, licensing them to sell JPF's policies and encouraging them to do so. Because the agents remained independent, JPF did not have to provide them with typical employee benefits. However, because the independent agents still had to cover these expenses, the company had to pay a higher percentage of first-year premium, usually about 85 percent. The average first-year premium in the independent channel was about $5,000. Because there were independent agents located throughout the United States, the company was able to expand more rapidly outside of its traditional southeastern market area and have agents offering its policies nationwide.

The new focus was extremely successful, and by 1999, the independent channels had become JPF's primary distribution channel, although the company still retained its career agents. In 1999, JPF hired Bob Powell to head the Independent Marketing channel.

JPF had begun to recruit not only individual independent agents but also so-called independent marketing organizations (IMOs). An IMO was in the business of serving life insurance agents. IMOs did not produce or "manufacture" life insurance policies; they just served independent life insurance agents. Thus, the insurance company was the "manufacturer," the IMO an independent "wholesaler," and the independent agent the "retailer." The IMO represented multiple insurance companies and often had a large staff that helped agents develop customized policies to serve special customer needs.

IMOs dealt with the insurance companies, talked with underwriters and medical directors, and helped secure the needed life

(continued)

insurance on behalf of the agent's client. This allowed the agents to sell policies without having to worry about the massive amounts of paperwork and administrative details that someone had to perform after an agent made a sale. As a result, the IMO earned an additional fee from the insurance company on policies sold by the agents who worked through it. The insurance company was able to pay this additional fee because the IMOs performed some functions that the insurance company would have to perform if it were supporting the agent directly.

By recruiting IMOs, JPF was able to expand its distributive capacity by bringing on more agents more rapidly than it could by having to recruit individual agents either by itself or solely through its career channel. There were also some IMOs that were "recruiting only," that is, they recruited agents but did not provide any of the administrative support for the agents.

Powell and Knowles realized that there was no way JPF could recruit and serve the thousands of IMOs in the United States from the Greensboro home office. Thus, they began to put together a field sales team. They divided the country into five multistate regions and, with the help of an executive search firm, recruited a sales vice president (SVP) for each region.

The SVPs JPF recruited had many years of industry experience with other insurance companies, and several had held similar sales positions with other companies. The SVPs typically spent several days a week traveling to recruit new IMOs or to provide training and support for IMOs with whom JPF had a relationship. They also worked with the IMOs to resolve policy issuance or customer service problems the IMOs might have with the home office. The SVPs were relationship builders. They saw themselves as "premium gatherers" who wanted to get more "shelf space" for JPF's products with each IMO. They wanted to get the IMOs, their staff, and agents into the JPF "culture," make them comfortable doing business with JPF (versus other competitor companys the IMO also represented), and make it convenient to do so.

Like the career agents, the SVPs were JPF employees to whom it paid a small percentage of all the first-year premium dollars generated by JPF policies sold in their territory. Even though the percentage was small, because of the size of their territories, SVPs could earn a substantial income.

Because the SVPs put more "feet on the street" for JPF, and because JPF had very competitive products, policy sales had taken off in 2001. By mid-2002, the Independent Marketing channel was well ahead of its annual sales targets.

BACK IN THE CAR

"The problem we have," Bob Powell noted, "is that we are too successful. We are way ahead of 2002's targets and you know top management is going to want us to exceed what we do this year in 2003. And all of us are working as hard as we can. We can't do more by working any harder. You know that means we will have to add more SVPs."

"That's right," John Knowles observed, "but you saw in the meeting how the five SVPs reacted when we brought this up. They want to protect and keep all of their territory."

"Yes, but we all know that an SVP can't possibly cover 8 to 12 states and develop the kinds of IMO relationships we need," Bob answered. "I don't think an SVP can work with more than 30 or so IMOs. What are we going to do when an SVP gets a full client load? How do we bring on more SVPs without upsetting the apple cart?"

"Well," John said, "that brings up the additional issue of productivity. We have three salaried marketing coordinators now based in Greensboro who work with the five SVPs. However, we don't have a formal job description for them, and the SVPs are unhappy that they don't each have their own coordinator. If we add more SVPs, we will be even that much further behind in supporting their needs. And you know that in these economic times the company's reluctant to add more people, more overhead."

"I can see that some of our discussions may get as hot as this July weather," Bob said, laughing.

"When I get home," John said, "I'm going to dig out the old Kotler/Armstrong marketing textbook I had at Auburn and look back over the chapter on personal selling to see if it'll remind me of any issues we ought to be considering."

"We have a September 30 deadline for our sales force strategy proposals, so we'd better get to work," Bob concluded.

QUESTIONS FOR DISCUSSION

1. What are the advantages and disadvantages of using a career sales force versus an independent sales force?
2. What are the advantages and disadvantages of commission-only compensation versus salary-only compensation?
3. What problems do you see with JPF's sales force strategy and structure decisions?
4. What recommendations would you make to JPF to help it deal with these problems?

Source: Officials at Jefferson-Pilot Financial cooperated in development of this case.

Case Pilot Case Part 3: Developing the Marketing Mix

Yumm Yummeries: Developing the Marketing Mix

After four decades of restaurant experience, Edith started Yumm Yummeries eight years ago to produce and retail premium-priced handmade chocolates and candies sold from a quaint cottage-style store. She made all of the high-quality products herself and supervised a staff of three part-time students who primarily worked during the busy summers in their resort town.

Due to overwhelming popularity of her products, two years ago Edith doubled the size of her store, legally incorporated her business, and spent $50,000 to expand the capacity of her equipment. A typical candy purchase averaged $18.00 per person, with monthly store sales ranging from $33,000 in the slow months to $62,000 in the busy tourist months (May through October). The average gross margin for all products was approximately 31 percent, and net profits after taxes were stable at nine percent. Over the past few years, sales and profits had seemed to reach their maximum, and Edith now wondered what other options there were for her business.

Marketing had initially been done exclusively by Edith, but last year she hired a local marketing firm, AdMad, recommended by another successful business person, to take care of the Yumm Yummeries's advertising and promotional campaigns. Edith was surprised by the odd AdMad promotions and that many clients hadn't seen or heard the ads, but mostly that there had been little change in sales despite the $25,000 marketing fees that AdMad had billed her.

Edith was regularly testing new products and she had recently developed a new product called Gummy Yumms that could be produced with Yumm Yummeries's current machinery and inventory. Although the product used high-priced, premium ingredients and was very time consuming to produce, Edith priced Gummy Yumms to compete with a similar product at a nearby competitor that specialized in lower-priced confections.

While leafing through a restaurant industry magazine, Edith read an article stating that franchising was a growing trend throughout North America that could lead to significant profit increases for the franchiser. After learning more about franchising from contacting several business friends, Edith advertised her wish to franchise Yumm Yummeries in numerous newspapers. After one week, she received a visit from the owner of the Travel Unlimited Resort Group (TURG), who was interested in purchasing one Yumm Yummeries franchise for each of its 24 ocean-side locations. Edith was unprepared for such a quick response and was surprised when TURG offered her a franchise payment of $20,000 per store, plus two percent of all sales for five years in return for Edith agreeing to train the staff of the new stores.

While watching the evening TV news that night, Edith discovered that a truck driver strike had been planned that would result in all deliveries to area businesses being cancelled until the dispute was resolved. As the busy tourist season was about to start, Edith wondered what impact the possible strike might have on her business and the TURG franchise deal, and thus decided to seek advice as to her best plan of action.

Case Pilot Challenge

Part 3 of the text details one of the most important and well-known cornerstones of marketing: The marketing mix. The nine chapters in this section reinforce how product, pricing, promotion, and distribution decisions are all interrelated. Most importantly, we learn that the marketing mix is pivotal in traditional and Internet marketing and is used in both not-for-profit organizations (e.g., museums) and for-profit businesses.

In the Yum Yummeries case above, Edith has several issues that she needs to address. Try your marketing management skills, visit www.prenhall.com/casepilot/, and see if you can find the answers to the following:

a) How should Edith proceed with the franchise offer?

b) How effective has AdMad been?

c) What is one option Edith may have for dealing with the strike?

1. discuss the need to understand competitors as well as customers through competitor analysis
2. explain the fundamentals of competitive marketing strategies based on creating value for customers
3. illustrate the need for balancing customer and competitor orientations in becoming a truly market-centered organization

Creating Competitive Advantage

LOOKING AHEAD: PREVIEWING THE CONCEPTS

In previous chapters, you explored the basics of marketing. You learned that good marketing companies win, keep, and grow customers by building relationships with them based on superior customer value and satisfaction. In this chapter, we pull all of these basics together. Understanding customers is an important first step in developing strong customer relationships, but it's not enough. To gain competitive advantage, companies must use this understanding to design market offers that deliver more value than the offers of *competitors* seeking to win over the same customers. Thus, beyond understanding consumers, firms must also understand their competitors. In this chapter, we look first at competitor analysis, the process companies use to identify and analyze competitors. Then, we examine competitive marketing strategies by which companies position themselves against competitors to gain the greatest possible competitive advantage.

First let's examine Intel, a company that flat-out dominates the microprocessor industry. As you read about Intel, ask yourself: Just what *is* it about this company's marketing strategy that has earned it a better than 80 percent share of the worldwide microprocessor market? What has Intel done so right? How will the company have to adapt its marketing strategy in future years to stay on top in its fast-changing high-tech marketplace?

For more than 30 years, Intel has dominated the microprocessor market. How's this for eye-popping market performance: In the 20 years or so since IBM introduced its first PCs based on Intel's 8088 microprocessor, the chip giant's sales have jumped 25-fold to more than $26 billion. Intel's share of the worldwide microprocessor market tops 80 percent, and 88 percent of the world's servers say "Intel Inside." Through the decade of the 1990s, Intel's annual return to investors averaged an astounding 38 percent.

Intel's stunning success has resulted from its relentless dedication to a simple competitive marketing strategy: provide the most value and satisfaction to customers through product leadership. Some companies deliver superior value through convenience and low prices; others by coddling their customers and tailoring products to meet the special needs of precisely defined market niches. In contrast, Intel delivers superior value by creating a continuous stream of leading-edge products. The result is intense customer loyalty and preference from final and business buyers who want their technology to do ever-more-cool things. The company invests heavily to develop state-of-the-art products and bring them quickly to market—in the last two years alone it spent a whopping $20.7 billion on R&D and capital spending. The result has been a rapid succession of better and better technologies and products.

Intel's microprocessors are true wonders of modern technology. Intel's very first microprocessor held only 2,300 transistors. Early PC users were dazzled by Intel's i386 chips, which contained one-quarter million transistors and ran at clock speeds approaching 20 megahertz. Just 15 years later, current buyers yawn over Intel's Pentium 4 microprocessors, which contain more than 55 million transistors and run at speeds exceeding 2 *giga*hertz. Incredibly, the Intel microprocessors of 2009 will pack a cool *1 billion* transistors and will blaze along at clock speeds of 300 gigahertz. In fact, Intel has innovated at such a torrid pace that its microprocessors have sometimes outpaced market needs and capabilities. To help things along, Intel has invested heavily in market development, creating new applications that can take full advantage of the latest Intel-powered equipment.

Intel's marketing strategy goes beyond innovative products and market development. It also includes innovative advertising. In mid-1991, Intel launched its groundbreaking "Intel Inside" advertising campaign to build relationships with final computer buyers—Intel's customers' customers. Traditionally, chip companies like Intel had marketed only to the manufacturers who buy chips directly. But as long as microprocessors remained anonymous little lumps hidden inside a user's computer, Intel remained at the mercy of the clone makers and other competitors. The brand-awareness ads created brand personality and convinced PC and server buyers that Intel microprocessors really were superior. Intel also subsidizes ads by computer manufacturers that include the "Intel Inside" logo. Over the years, the hundreds of millions of dollars invested by Intel and its partners in the "Intel Inside" campaign have created strong brand preference for Intel chips among final buyers, in turn making Intel's chips more attractive to computer manufacturers.

Intel's strategy of innovation has brought it amazing success. However, no company can afford to rest on it laurels. Even the best marketing strategy requires constant adaptation and refinement—sometimes even radical transformation. During the past two decades, Intel's success has gone hand in hand with the explosive growth of personal computer sales. Entering the twenty-first century, as the personal computer industry has matured, Intel has faced some difficult challenges. After two decades of 35 percent average annual growth, sales in 2001 grew only 5 percent and earnings declined for the first time in a decade. In 2002, Intel's stock price plunged. "The biggest culprit in Intel's slowdown was a changing PC landscape," explains an industry analyst. "PCs were losing some of their luster. Instead of clamoring for more power to run fatter software programs, many customers just wanted cheap PCs to get online. Low-cost PCs meant low-cost chips." Falling PC prices, coupled with stronger competition from new rivals, cut into Intel's sales, market share, and profit margins.

To meet this challenge, Intel has had to adapt its strategy and find new ways to grow. Of course, microprocessors are still the heart of Intel's business. To cement its dominance and sell more chips in the increasingly competitive PC market, Intel continues to invest heavily to develop the expected stream of new microprocessors needed to run the next-generation applications. But given the falloff in PC sales growth, Intel knows that it must move in new directions if it is to achieve the 20 percent annual growth it seeks. For starters, Intel has introduced a bevy of new non-PC microprocessors, including

chips for everything from mobile phones to consumer electronics products.

But Intel's strategy is undergoing a more sweeping transformation. The company has taken its passion for innovation in an exciting new direction—the Internet. "The PC was the dominant force in the last decade," says Intel president and CEO Craig Barrett. "The Internet is clearly the dominant force in the forthcoming decade. So we're hitching to that star and riding it as fast as we can." Our mission "for years was to be the building-block supplier to the computer industry," he says. Now, Intel must become "an integral part of the hearts and brains of the new Internet economy."

This new Internet mission takes Intel in some dramatically different directions. It's pushing rapidly into areas such as business networking and wireless communications. Such new ventures are putting some strain on management and a culture that have long focused on a single product. When it comes to these new businesses, notes an industry analyst, "Intel is a gawky adolescent."

Most experts agree that Intel has the skills, clout, and resources to build or buy its way into these new markets. To speed the transformation, for example, Intel is spending lavishly to acquire existing technology companies. Over the past few years, it's spent billions to snap up companies such as Dialogic, which makes Internet telephony hardware; Ipivot, an e-commerce system vendor; and DSP Communications, a developer of mobile wireless chip technology. Intel has also established an investment fund, called Intel Capital, which invests in small technology start-up firms from which the company can draw insights and energy. "Our goal is to expose the company to every facet of the Internet economy," says the fund's manager. "It has already led to an opening of minds."

Looking ahead, Intel must plan its competitive marketing strategy carefully. The driving force remains constant—innovate or fall by the wayside. As one analyst puts it: "Intel's identity is inseparable from innovation." Intel's top executives don't foresee any slowing of the pace. Says Barrett, "We picture ourselves going down the road at 120 miles an hour. Somewhere there's going to be a brick wall, . . . but our view is that it's better to run into the wall than to anticipate it and fall short."[1]

Today's companies face their toughest competition ever. In previous chapters, we argued that to succeed in today's fiercely competitive marketplace, companies will have to move from a product-and-selling philosophy to a customer-and-marketing philosophy. John Chambers, CEO of Cisco Systems, put it well: "Make your customer the center of your culture."

Competitive advantage

An advantage over competitors gained by offering consumers greater value than competitors offer.

This chapter spells out in more detail how companies can go about outperforming competitors in order to win, keep, and grow customers. To win in today's marketplace, companies must become adept not just in *managing products,* but in *managing customer relationships* in the face of determined competition. Understanding customers is crucial, but it's not enough. Building profitable customer relationships and gaining **competitive advantage** requires delivering *more* value and satisfaction to target consumers than *competitors* do.

Competitor analysis
The process of identifying key competitors; assessing their objectives, strategies, strengths and weaknesses, and reaction patterns; and selecting which competitors to attack or avoid.

In this chapter, we examine *competitive marketing strategies*—how companies analyze their competitors and develop successful, value-based strategies for building and maintaining profitable customer relationships. The first step is **competitor analysis,** the process of identifying, assessing, and selecting key competitors. The second step is developing **competitive marketing strategies** that strongly position the company against competitors and give it the greatest possible competitive advantage.

Competitor Analysis

Competitive marketing strategies
Strategies that strongly position the company against competitors and that give the company the strongest possible strategic advantage.

To plan effective marketing strategies, the company needs to find out all it can about its competitors. It must constantly compare its products, prices, channels, and promotion with those of close competitors. In this way the company can find areas of potential competitive advantage and disadvantage. As shown in Figure 18.1, competitor analysis involves first identifying and assessing competitors and then selecting which competitors to attack or avoid.

Identifying Competitors

Normally, identifying competitors would seem a simple task. At the narrowest level, a company can define its competitors as other companies offering similar products and services to the same customers at similar prices. Thus, Coca-Cola might view Pepsi as a major competitor, but not Budweiser or Kool-Aid. Bookseller Barnes & Noble might see Borders as a major competitor, but not Wal-Mart or Costco. Buick might see Ford as a major competitor, but not Mercedes or Hyundai.

But companies actually face a much wider range of competitors. The company might define competitors as all firms making the same product or class of products. Thus, Buick would see itself as competing against all other automobile makers. Even more broadly, competitors might include all companies making products that supply the same service. Here Buick would see itself competing not only against other automobile makers but also against companies that make trucks, motorcycles, or even bicycles. Finally, and still more broadly, competitors might include all companies that compete for the same consumer dollars. Here Buick would see itself competing with companies that sell major consumer durables, new homes, or vacations abroad.

Companies must avoid "competitor myopia." A company is more likely to be "buried" by its latent competitors than its current ones. For example, for many years, Kodak held a comfortable lead in the photographic film business. It saw Fuji as its major competitor in this market. However, in recent years, Kodak's major new competition has not come from Fuji and other film producers. It has come from Sony, Canon, and other makers of digital cameras, which don't even use film. Because of its myopic focus on film, Kodak was late to enter the digital camera market. And even though Kodak is now the market share leader in the digital segment, its digital camera business still isn't profitable.[2]

Similarly, 230-year-old Encyclopaedia Britannica viewed itself as competing with other publishers of printed encyclopedia sets selling for as much as $2,200 per set. However, in the mid-1990s it learned a hard lesson. It seems that computer-savvy kids were now most often finding information online or on CD-ROMs such as Microsoft's Encarta, which sold for only $50. In 1996, the company dismissed its entire 2,300-person door-to-door sales force and introduced its own CD-ROM and online versions. However, Britannica is still struggling to regain profitability. Sales of its print edition dropped 80 percent during the 1990s, and revenues from the CD-ROM and online versions have not made up the difference. Thus, Encyclopaedia Britannica's real competitors were the computer and the Internet.[3]

Companies can identify their competitors from the *industry* point of view. They might see themselves as being in the oil industry, the pharmaceutical industry, or the beverage industry. A company must understand the competitive patterns in its industry if it hopes to be an effective "player" in that industry. Companies can also identify competitors from a *market* point of view.

FIGURE 18.1
Steps in analyzing competitors

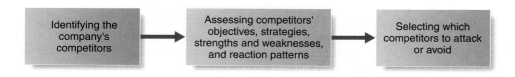

Identifying competitors: 230-year old Encyclopedia Britannica viewed itself as competing with other publishers of printed encyclopedias. It's real competitors were the computer and the Internet.

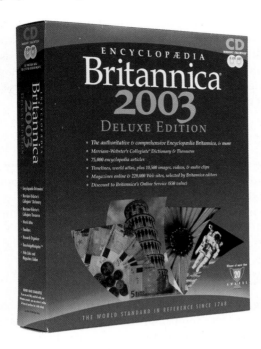

Here they define competitors as companies that are trying to satisfy the same customer need or build relationships with the same customer group.

From an industry point of view, Coca-Cola might see its competition as Pepsi, Dr Pepper, 7UP, and other soft drink makers. From a market point of view, however, the customer really wants "thirst quenching." This need can be satisfied by iced tea, fruit juice, bottled water, or many other fluids. Similarly, Hallmark's Binney & Smith, maker of Crayola crayons, might define its competitors as other makers of crayons and children's drawing supplies. But from a market point of view, it would include all firms making recreational products for children.

In general, the market concept of competition opens the company's eyes to a broader set of actual and potential competitors. One approach is to profile the company's direct and indirect competitors by mapping the steps buyers take in obtaining and using the product. Figure 18.2 illustrates their *competitor map* of Eastman Kodak in the film business.[4] In the center is a list of consumer activities: buying a camera, buying film, taking pictures, and others. The first outer ring lists Kodak's main competitors with respect to each consumer activity: Olympus for buying a camera, Fuji for purchasing film, and so on. The second outer ring lists indirect competitors—HP, cameraworks.com, and others—who may become direct competitors. This type of analysis highlights both the competitive opportunities and the challenges a company faces.

Assessing Competitors

Having identified the main competitors, marketing management now asks: What are competitors' objectives—what does each seek in the marketplace? What is each competitor's strategy? What are various competitors' strengths and weaknesses, and how will each react to actions the company might take?

Determining Competitors' Objectives

Each competitor has a mix of objectives. The company wants to know the relative importance that a competitor places on current profitability, market share growth, cash flow, technological leadership, service leadership, and other goals. Knowing a competitor's mix of objectives reveals whether the competitor is satisfied with its current situation and how it might react to different competitive actions. For example, a company that pursues low-cost leadership will react much more strongly to a competitor's cost-reducing manufacturing breakthrough than to the same competitor's advertising increase.

FIGURE 18.2

Competitor map

Source: Jeffrey F. Rayport and Bernard J. Jaworski, *e-Commerce* (New York: McGraw-Hill, 2001), p. 53.

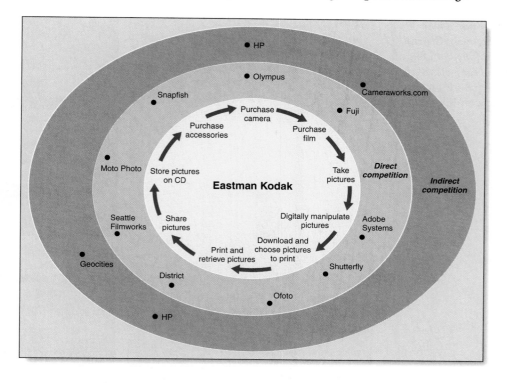

A company also must monitor its competitors' objectives for various segments. If the company finds that a competitor has discovered a new segment, this might be an opportunity. If it finds that competitors plan new moves into segments now served by the company, it will be forewarned and, hopefully, forearmed.

Identifying Competitors' Strategies

The more that one firm's strategy resembles another firm's strategy, the more the two firms compete. In most industries, the competitors can be sorted into groups that pursue different strategies. A **strategic group** is a group of firms in an industry following the same or a similar strategy in a given target market. For example, in the major appliance industry, General Electric, Whirlpool, and Maytag all belong to the same strategic group. Each produces a full line of medium-price appliances supported by good service. In contrast, Sub-Zero and Viking belong to a different strategic group. They produce a narrower line of higher-quality appliances, offer a higher level of service, and charge a premium price.

Some important insights emerge from identifying strategic groups. For example, if a company enters one of the groups, the members of that group become its key competitors. Thus, if the company enters the first group, against General Electric, Whirlpool, and Maytag, it can succeed only if it develops strategic advantages over these competitors.

Although competition is most intense within a strategic group, there is also rivalry among groups. First, some of the strategic groups may appeal to overlapping customer segments. For example, no matter what their strategy, all major appliance manufacturers will go after the apartment and home builders segment. Second, the customers may not see much difference in the offers of different groups—they may see little difference in quality between Whirlpool and Viking. Finally, members of one strategic group might expand into new strategy segments. Thus, General Electric's Monogram line of appliances competes in the premium-quality, premium-price line with Viking and Sub-Zero.

The company needs to look at all of the dimensions that identify strategic groups within the industry. It needs to know each competitor's product quality, features, and mix; customer services; pricing policy; distribution coverage; sales force strategy; and advertising and sales promotion programs. And it must study the details of each competitor's R&D, manufacturing, purchasing, financial, and other strategies.

Strategic group

A group of firms in an industry following the same or a similar strategy.

Expanding into a new strategy segment: General Electric's Monogram line of appliances competes in the premium quality, premium price line with Viking and SubZero.

Assessing Competitors' Strengths and Weaknesses

Marketers need to assess each competitor's strengths and weaknesses carefully in order to answer the critical question: What *can* our competitors do? As a first step, companies can gather data on each competitor's goals, strategies, and performance over the last few years. Admittedly, some of this information will be hard to obtain. For example, B2B marketers find it hard to estimate competitors' market shares because they do not have the same syndicated data services that are available to consumer packaged-goods companies.

Companies normally learn about their competitors' strengths and weaknesses through secondary data, personal experience, and word of mouth. They also can conduct primary marketing research with customers, suppliers, and dealers. Or they can **benchmark** themselves against other firms, comparing the company's products and processes to those of competitors or leading firms in other industries to find ways to improve quality and performance. Benchmarking has become a powerful tool for increasing a company's competitiveness.

Benchmarking

The process of comparing the company's products and processes to those of competitors or leading firms in other industries to find ways to improve quality and performance.

Estimating Competitors' Reactions

Next, the company wants to know: What *will* our competitors do? A competitor's objectives, strategies, and strengths and weaknesses go a long way toward explaining its likely actions. They also suggest its likely reactions to company moves such as price cuts, promotion increases, or new-product introductions. In addition, each competitor has a certain philosophy of doing business, a certain internal culture and guiding beliefs. Marketing managers need a deep understanding of a given competitor's mentality if they want to anticipate how the competitor will act or react.

Each competitor reacts differently. Some do not react quickly or strongly to a competitor's move. They may feel their customers are loyal; they may be slow in noticing the move; they may lack the funds to react. Some competitors react only to certain types of moves and not to others. Other competitors react swiftly and strongly to any action. Thus, Procter & Gamble does not let a new detergent come easily into the market. Many firms avoid direct competition with P&G and look for easier prey, knowing that P&G will react fiercely if challenged.

In some industries, competitors live in relative harmony; in others, they fight constantly. Knowing how major competitors react gives the company clues on how best to attack competitors or how best to defend the company's current positions.

Selecting Competitors to Attack and Avoid

A company has already largely selected its major competitors through prior decisions on customer targets, distribution channels, and marketing-mix strategy. Management now must decide which competitors to compete against most vigorously.

Strong or Weak Competitors

The company can focus on one of several classes of competitors. Most companies prefer to compete against *weak competitors*. This requires fewer resources and less time. But in the process, the firm may gain little. You could argue that the firm also should compete with *strong competitors* in order to sharpen its abilities. Moreover, even strong competitors have some weaknesses, and succeeding against them often provides greater returns.

Customer value analysis

Analysis conducted to determine what benefits target customers value and how they rate the relative value of various competitors' offers.

A useful tool for assessing competitor strengths and weaknesses is **customer value analysis.** The aim of customer value analysis is to determine the benefits that target customers value and how customers rate the relative value of various competitors' offers. In conducting a customer value analysis, the company first identifies the major attributes that customers value and the importance customers place on these attributes. Next, it assesses the company's and competitors' performance on the valued attributes. The key to gaining competitive advantage is to take each customer segment and examine how the company's offer compares to that of its major competitor. If the company's offer exceeds the competitor's offer on all important attributes, the company can charge a higher price and earn higher profits, or it can charge the same price and gain more market share. But if the company is seen as performing at a lower level than its major competitor on some important attributes, it must invest in strengthening those attributes or finding other important attributes where it can build a lead on the competitor.

Close or Distant Competitors

Most companies will compete with *close competitors*—those that resemble them most—rather than *distant competitors*. Thus, Chevrolet competes more against Ford than against Lexus. And Target competes with Wal-Mart and Kmart rather than against Neiman Marcus or Marshall Field's.

At the same time, the company may want to avoid trying to "destroy" a close competitor. For example, in the late 1970s, Bausch & Lomb moved aggressively against other soft lens manufacturers with great success. However, this forced weak competitors to sell out to larger firms such as Schering-Plough and Johnson & Johnson. As a result, Bausch & Lomb now faced much larger competitors—and it suffered the consequences. Johnson & Johnson acquired Vistakon, a small nicher with only $20 million in annual sales. Backed by Johnson & Johnson's deep pockets, however, the small but nimble Vistakon developed and introduced its innovative Acuvue disposable lenses. With Vistakon leading the way, Johnson & Johnson is now the top U.S. contact lens maker, while Bausch & Lomb is struggling.[5] In this case, success in hurting a close rival brought in tougher competitors.

"Good" or "Bad" Competitors

A company really needs and benefits from competitors. The existence of competitors results in several strategic benefits. Competitors may help increase total demand. They may share the costs of market and product development and help to legitimize new technologies. They may serve less-attractive segments or lead to more product differentiation. Finally, they lower the antitrust risk and improve bargaining power versus labor or regulators. For example, Intel's recent aggressive pricing on low-end computer chips has sent smaller rivals like AMD and 3Com reeling. However, Intel may want to be careful not to knock these competitors completely out. "If for no other reason than to keep the feds at bay," notes one analyst, "Intel needs AMD, 3Com, and other rivals to stick around." Says another: "Intel may have put the squeeze on a little too hard. If AMD collapsed, the FTC would surely react."[6]

After driving smaller competitors from the market, Bausch & Lomb faces larger, more resourceful ones, such as Johnson & Johnson's Vistakon division. With Vistakon's Acuvue lenses leading the way, J & J is now the top U.S. contact lens maker.

However, a company may not view all of its competitors as beneficial. An industry often contains *"good"* competitors and *"bad"* competitors.[7] Good competitors play by the rules of the industry. Bad competitors, in contrast, break the rules. They try to buy share rather than earn it, take large risks, and in general shake up the industry. For example, American Airlines finds Delta and United to be good competitors because they play by the rules and attempt to set their fares sensibly. But American finds Continental and America West bad competitors because they destabilize the airline industry through continual heavy price discounting and wild promotional schemes.

The implication is that "good" companies would like to shape an industry that consists of only well-behaved competitors. A company might be smart to support good competitors, aiming its attacks at bad competitors. Thus, some analysts claim that American Airlines has from time to time used huge fare discounts intentionally designed to teach disruptive airlines a lesson or to drive them out of business altogether.

Designing a Competitive Intelligence System

We have described the main types of information that companies need about their competitors. This information must be collected, interpreted, distributed, and used. The cost in money and time of gathering competitive intelligence is high, and the company must design its competitive intelligence system in a cost-effective way.

The competitive intelligence system first identifies the vital types of competitive information and the best sources of this information. Then, the system continuously collects information from the field (sales force, channels, suppliers, market research firms, trade associations, Web sites) and from published data (government publications, speeches, articles). Next the system checks the information for validity and reliability, interprets it, and organizes it in an appropriate way. Finally, it sends key information to relevant decision makers and responds to inquiries from managers about competitors.

With this system, company managers will receive timely information about competitors in the form of phone calls, e-mails, bulletins, newsletters, and reports. In addition, managers can connect with the system when they need an interpretation of a competitor's sudden move, or when they want to know a competitor's weaknesses and strengths, or when they need to know how a competitor will respond to a planned company move.

Smaller companies that cannot afford to set up formal competitive intelligence offices can assign specific executives to watch specific competitors. Thus, a manager who used to work for a competitor might follow that competitor closely; he or she would be the "in-house expert" on that competitor. Any manager needing to know the thinking of a given competitor could contact the assigned in-house expert.[8]

Competitive Strategies

Having identified and evaluated its major competitors, the company now must design broad competitive marketing strategies by which it can gain competitive advantage by offering superior customer value. But what broad marketing strategies might the company use? Which ones are best for a particular company, or for the company's different divisions and products?

Approaches to Marketing Strategy

No one strategy is best for all companies. Each company must determine what makes the most sense given its position in the industry and its objectives, opportunities, and resources. Even within a company, different strategies may be required for different businesses or products. Johnson & Johnson uses one marketing strategy for its leading brands in stable consumer markets and a different marketing strategy for its new high-tech health care businesses and products.

Companies also differ in how they approach the strategy-planning process. Many large firms develop formal competitive marketing strategies and implement them religiously. However, other companies develop strategy in a less formal and orderly fashion. A recent book, *Radical Marketing,* praises companies such as Harley-Davidson, Virgin Atlantic Airways, and Boston Beer for succeeding by breaking many of the "rules" of marketing strategy.[9] Such companies don't operate large marketing departments, conduct expensive marketing research, spell out formal and elaborate competitive strategies, and spend huge sums on advertising and selling. Instead, they sketch out strategies on the fly, stretch their limited resources, live close to their customers, and create more-satisfying solutions to customer needs. They form buyer's clubs, use buzz marketing, and focus on delivering high product quality and winning long-term customer loyalty. It seems that not all marketing must follow in the footsteps of marketing giants such as IBM and Procter & Gamble.

In fact, approaches to marketing strategy and practice often pass through three stages: entrepreneurial marketing, formulated marketing, and intrepreneurial marketing.

- *Entrepreneurial marketing:* Most companies are started by individuals who live by their wits. They visualize an opportunity, construct flexible strategies on the backs of envelopes, and knock on every door to gain attention. Jim Koch, founder of Boston Beer Company, whose Samuel Adams beer has become a top-selling microbrewery beer, started out in 1984 carrying bottles of Samuel Adams from bar to bar to persuade bartenders to carry it. He would coax them into adding Samuel Adams beer to their menus. For 10 years, he couldn't afford advertising; he sold his beer through direct selling and grassroots public relations. Today, however, his business pulls in nearly $200 million, making it the leader over more than 1000 competitors in the microbrewery market.

- *Formulated marketing:* As small companies achieve success, they inevitably move toward more-formulated marketing. They develop formal marketing strategies and adhere to them closely. Boston Beer now employs more than 175 salespeople and has a marketing department that carries out market research and plans strategy. Although Boston Beer is far less formal and sophisticated in its strategy than archcompetitor Anheuser-Busch, it has adopted some of the tools used in professionally run marketing companies.

- *Intrepreneurial marketing.* Many large and mature companies get stuck in formulated marketing. They pore over the latest Nielsen numbers, scan market research reports, and try to fine-tune their competitive strategies and programs. These companies sometimes lose the marketing creativity and passion that they had at the start. They now need to reestablish within their companies the entrepreneurial spirit and actions that made them successful in the first place. They need to encourage more initiative and "intrepreneurship" at the local level. They need to refresh their marketing strategies and try new approaches. Their brand and product managers need to get out of the office, start living with their customers, and visualize new and creative ways to add value to their customers' lives.

The bottom line is that there are many approaches to developing effective competitive marketing strategy. There will be a constant tension between the formulated side of marketing and the creative side. It is easier to learn the formulated side of marketing, which has occupied most of our attention in this book. But we have also seen how marketing creativity and passion in the strategies of many of the company's we've studied—whether small or large, new or mature—have helped to build and maintain success in the marketplace. With this in mind, we now look at broad competitive marketing strategies companies can use.

Basic Competitive Strategies

More than two decades ago, Michael Porter suggested four basic competitive positioning strategies that companies can follow—three winning strategies and one losing one.[10] The three winning strategies include:

Overall cost leadership: Here the company works hard to achieve the lowest production and distribution costs. Low costs let it price lower than its competitors and win a large market share. Texas Instruments, Dell Computer, and Wal-Mart are leading practitioners of this strategy.

Differentiation: Here the company concentrates on creating a highly differentiated product line and marketing program so that it comes across as the class leader in the industry. Most customers would prefer to own this brand if its price is not too high. IBM and Caterpillar follow this strategy in information technology products and services and heavy construction equipment, respectively.

Focus: Here the company focuses its effort on serving a few market segments well rather than going after the whole market. For example, Ritz-Carlton focuses on the top 5 percent of corporate and leisure travelers. Glassmaker AFG Industries focuses on users of tempered and colored glass. It makes 70 percent of the glass for microwave oven doors and 75 percent of the glass for shower doors and patio tabletops. Similarly, Hohner owns a stunning 85 percent of the harmonica market.

Companies that pursue a clear strategy—one of the above—will likely perform well. The firm that carries out that strategy best will make the most profits. But firms that do not pursue a clear strategy—*middle-of-the-roaders*—do the worst. Sears, Holiday Inn, and Kmart encountered difficult times because they did not stand out as the lowest in cost, highest in perceived value, or best in serving some market segment. Middle-of-the-roaders try to be good on all strategic counts, but end up being not very good at anything.

More recently, two marketing consultants, Michael Treacy and Fred Wiersema, offered a new classification of competitive marketing strategies.[11] They suggest that companies gain leadership positions by delivering superior value to their customers. Companies can pursue any of three strategies—called *value disciplines*—for delivering superior customer value. These are:

Operational excellence: The company provides superior value by leading its industry in price and convenience. It works to reduce costs and to create a lean and efficient value delivery system. It serves customers who want reliable, good-quality products or services, but who want them cheaply and easily. Examples include Wal-Mart, Southwest Airlines, and Dell Computer.

Focus: Small but profitable Hohner owns a stunning 85 percent of the harmonica market.

Customer intimacy: The company provides superior value by precisely segmenting its markets and tailoring its products or services to match exactly the needs of targeted customers. It specializes in satisfying unique customer needs through a close relationship with and intimate knowledge of the customer. It builds detailed customer databases for segmenting and targeting, and empowers its marketing people to respond quickly to customer needs. Customer-intimate companies serve customers who are willing to pay a premium to get precisely what they want. They will do almost anything to build long-term customer loyalty and to capture customer lifetime value. Examples include Nordstrom, Sony, Lexus, American Express, and British Airways (see Real Marketing 18.1).

Product leadership: The company provides superior value by offering a continuous stream of leading-edge products or services. It aims to make its own and competing products obsolete. Product leaders are open to new ideas, relentlessly pursue new solutions, and work to get new products to market quickly. They serve customers who want state-of-the-art products and services, regardless of the costs in terms of price or inconvenience. Examples include Intel, Motorola, and Microsoft.

Some companies successfully pursue more than one value discipline at the same time. For example, FedEx excels at both operational excellence and customer intimacy. However, such companies are rare—few firms can be the best at more than one of these disciplines. By trying to be *good at all* of the value disciplines, a company usually ends up being *best at none*.

Treacy and Wiersema have found that leading companies focus on and excel at a single value discipline, while meeting industry standards on the other two. Such companies design their entire value delivery network to single-mindedly support the chosen discipline. For example, Wal-Mart knows that customer intimacy and product leadership are important. Compared with other discounters, such as Kmart, it offers very good customer service and an excellent product assortment. Still, it offers less customer service and less product depth than do Nordstrom, Eddie Bauer,

Marketing Upscale: Creating Customer Intimacy

Some companies go to extremes to coddle their customers, particularly when those customers are big spenders. These days, building relationships with high-end consumers often means providing extraordinary service. From department stores like Nordstrom, to carmakers like Lexus and BMW, to hotels like Ritz-Carlton and Four Seasons, customer-intimate companies give their customers exactly what they need—and even more.

For example, concierge services are no longer the sole province of five-star hotels and fancy credit cards. They are starting to show up at airlines, retailers, and even electronic-goods makers. Sony Electronics, for instance, offers a service for its richest customers, called Cierge, that provides a free personal shopper and early access to new gadgets, as well as "white-glove" help with the installation. (Translation: They will send someone over to set up the new gear.) Here are two more examples:

Customer intimacy: British Airways' At Your Service program—there's almost nothing that the service won't do for members.

British Airways: A new British Airways program, "At Your Service," really takes care of the company's best customers. There's almost nothing that the service won't do for members—tracking down hard-to-get Wimbledon tickets, for example, or running errands around town, sitting in a member's home to wait for the plumber or cable guy, or even planning your wedding, right down to the cake. But At Your Service isn't available to just anyone: Only British Airways frequent-fliers with Gold member status have access, and

then only when the airline handpicks them. The program includes only a fraction of BA's Gold-level elite.

Where does BA's At Your Service concierge service draw the line on what it will do for its exclusive membership? Member Roderick Stevens has yet to find the limit. The Chicago resident recently asked if BA would help plan his wedding in a castle in the United Kingdom. To his surprise, the airline readily agreed. "I thought it would be too big," says Stevens, a 36-year-old information technology consultant. He found the castle himself but the airline is handling the hotel accommodations. More, the At Your Service concierge in charge of his account, Emily Brodsky, has also made suggestions about wedding cakes, flowers, and other details. Of course, there is a payoff for BA: The airline will also make the travel arrangements for Mr. Stevens's 100 guests, who will be flying in from Australia, Germany, the United States, and elsewhere.

American Express: Long known for its premium services, American Express recently debuted its most elite card to date: the Centurion Card, better known as "the Black Card." The card comes dripping with perks, from a personal travel agent to a fleet of concierges on call 24 hours a day. Want that hard-to-get Mombasa handbag? They'll track one down and ship it to your suite at the Four Seasons (room upgrade courtesy of the Black Card). First-class seats on some airlines are also part of the deal. If the flight is to Europe, they'll even throw in a loaner cell phone.

For frequent travelers, the benefits of the Black Card can sometimes pay for themselves in travel perks. Besides the better rooms at the Four Seasons and Ritz-Carlton, the card offers bonus miles on Continental, Delta, and US Airways, plus enrollment in the elite level of the frequent-guest programs at Hilton, Hyatt, Inter-Continental, and Starwood.

The elusive plastic, with its elegant matte finish, is coveted by big spenders. But the card's success stems from its exclusivity.

Although American Express won't say how many are in circulation, analysts estimate roughly 5,000 people in the United States have them. (American Express describes the card as "invitation only" but denies the rumor that people calling to request one are automatically rejected.) Although American Express is discreet about the requirements, it confirms the basics: $150,000 in annual spending on an existing Amex card, plus a $2,500 annual fee. Also, it can't hurt to have a large balance in an account managed by an American Express financial planner.

Byron Watson was so desperate to get a Black Card that he rounded up friends to run up his bill so that he could hit the spending target. He simply asked the company to issue additional cards on his existing Platinum account, and then handed them out. "I paid their annual fees, and they got the benefits that come from having the Platinum card," says Watson, a Denver executive. "Everyone thinks I'm crazy." But it worked—he finally qualified.

Then there's Richard Mannion, of Swindon, England. He discovered that the domain name www.amexcenturion.co.uk was available. So he set up a Web site there and posted everything he knew about the qualification requirements. "I did it to annoy them, just because they were giving me the runaround," he says. He finally got a Centurion card, after charging up a storm while working as a consultant for a large technology company. Now, his site automatically redirects people to the official Amex Centurion page. Still, he receives at least five e-mails each week from people wanting to know how he pulled it off. "Sometimes, I get very shocked reactions when I use it," says the 21-year-old consultant. "People think I've stolen it."

Sources: Examples adapted from Ron Lieber, "The Credit Card That You Can't Get—Invitation-Only 'Black Card' Offers Concierge, Hotel Suites; But Is It Worth a $1,000 Fee?" *Wall Street Journal,* April 9, 2002, p. D1; and Eleena de Lisser, "How to Get an Airline to Wait for Your Plumber—In Battle for Biggest Spenders, British Airways, Sony Roll Out Hotel-Style 'Concierge' Service," *Wall Street Journal,* July 2, 2002, p. D1.

FIGURE 18.3
Hypothetical market
structure

or The Sharper Image, which pursue customer intimacy. Instead, Wal-Mart focuses obsessively on operational excellence—on reducing costs and streamlining its order-to-delivery process in order to make it convenient for customers to buy just the right products at the lowest prices.

Classifying competitive strategies as value disciplines is appealing. It defines marketing strategy in terms of the single-minded pursuit of delivering superior value to customers. Each value discipline defines a specific way to build lasting customer relationships.

Competitive Positions

Firms competing in a given target market, at any point in time, differ in their objectives and resources. Some firms are large, others small. Some have many resources, others are strapped for funds. Some are old and established, others new and fresh. Some strive for rapid market share growth, others for long-term profits. And the firms occupy different competitive positions in the target market.

We now examine competitive strategies based on the roles firms play in the target market—leader, challenger, follower, or nicher. Suppose that an industry contains the firms shown in Figure 18.3. Forty percent of the market is in the hands of the **market leader,** the firm with the largest market share. Another 30 percent is in the hands of **market challengers,** runner-up firms that are fighting hard to increase their market share. Another 20 percent is in the hands of **market followers,** other runner-up firms that want to hold their share without rocking the boat. The remaining 10 percent is in the hands of **market nichers,** firms that serve small segments not being pursued by other firms.

Table 18.1 shows specific marketing strategies that are available to market leaders, challengers, followers, and nichers.[12] Remember, however, that these classifications often do not apply to a whole company, but only to its position in a specific industry. Large companies such as IBM, Microsoft, Procter & Gamble, or Disney might be leaders in some markets and nichers in others. For example, Procter & Gamble leads in many segments, such as dishwashing and laundry detergents, disposable diapers, and shampoo. But it challenges Lever in the hand soaps and Kimberly-Clark in facial tissues. Such companies often use different strategies for different business units or products, depending on the competitive situations of each.

Market Leader Strategies

Most industries contain an acknowledged market leader. The leader has the largest market share and usually leads the other firms in price changes, new-product introductions, distribution coverage, and promotion spending. The leader may or may not be admired or respected, but other firms concede its dominance. Competitors focus on the leader as a company to challenge, imitate, or avoid. Some of the best-known market leaders are Wal-Mart (retailing), General Motors (autos), IBM (computers and information technology services), Caterpillar (earth-moving

Market leader

The firm with the largest market share in an industry.

Market challenger

A runner-up firm that is fighting hard to increase its market share in an industry.

Market follower

A runner-up firm that wants to hold its share in an industry without rocking the boat.

Market nicher

A firm that serves small segments that the other firms in its industry overlook or ignore.

TABLE 18.1	STRATEGIES FOR MARKET LEADERS, CHALLENGERS, FOLLOWERS, AND NICHERS		
Market Leader Strategies	**Market Challenger Strategies**	**Market Follower Strategies**	**Market Nicher Strategies**
Expand total market	Full frontal attack	Follow closely	By customer, market, quality–price, service
Protect market share	Indirect attack	Follow at a distance	Multiple niching
Expand market share			

equipment), Coca-Cola (soft drinks), McDonald's (fast food), Nike (athletic footwear), and Gillette (razors and blades).

A leader's life is not easy. It must maintain a constant watch. Other firms keep challenging its strengths or trying to take advantage of its weaknesses. The market leader can easily miss a turn in the market and plunge into second or third place. A product innovation may come along and hurt the leader (as when Nokia's and Ericsson's digital phones took the lead from Motorola's analog models). The leader might grow arrogant or complacent and misjudge the competition (as when Sears lost its lead to Wal-Mart). Or the leader might look old-fashioned against new and peppier rivals (as when Levi's lost serious ground to more current or stylish brands like Gap, Tommy Hilfiger, DKNY, or Guess).

To remain number one, leading firms can take any of three actions. First, they can find ways to expand total demand. Second, they can protect their current market share through good defensive and offensive actions. Third, they can try to expand their market share further, even if market size remains constant.

Expanding the Total Demand

The leading firm normally gains the most when the total market expands. If Americans take more pictures, Kodak stands to gain the most because it sells more than 80 percent of this country's film. If Kodak can convince more Americans to take pictures, or to take pictures on more occasions, or to take more pictures on each occasion, it will benefit greatly.

Market leaders can expand the market by developing new users, new uses, and more usage of its products. They usually can find *new users* in many places. For example, Revlon might find new perfume users in its current markets by convincing women who do not use perfume to try it. It might find users in new demographic segments, such as by producing fragrances for men. Or it might expand into new geographic segments, perhaps by selling its fragrances in other countries.

Marketers can expand markets by discovering and promoting *new uses* for the product. For example, Intel invests heavily to develop new PC, networking, and telecommunications applications, which in turn increases the demand for microprocessors. It knows that it will get a large share of the new microprocessor business. Another example of new-use expansion is Arm & Hammer baking soda, whose sales had flattened after 125 years. Then the company discovered that consumers were using baking soda as a refrigerator deodorizer. It launched a heavy advertising and publicity campaign focusing on this use and persuaded consumers in half of America's homes to place an open box of baking soda in their refrigerators and to replace it every few months. Today, its Web site (www.armandhammer.com) regularly features new uses, from removing residue left behind by hair-styling products and sweetening garbage disposals, laundry hampers, refrigerators, and trash cans to creating a home spa in your bathroom. Similarly, The WD-40 Company collected user suggestions and sponsored contests to uncover new uses for its all-purpose lubricant, making WD-40 one of the truly essential survival items in most American homes. (See Real Marketing 18.2.)

Finally, market leaders can encourage *more usage* by convincing people to use the product more often or to use more per occasion. For example, Campbell urges people to eat soup more often by running ads containing new recipes. It also offers a toll-free hot line (1-888-MM-MM-GOOD), staffed by live "recipe representatives" who offer recipes to last-minute cooks at a loss for meal ideas. And the Campbell's Kitchen section of the company's Web site (www.cambellsoup.com) lets visitors search for or exchange recipes, set up their own personal recipe box, and even sign up for a daily or weekly Meal Mail program.

Protecting Market Share

While trying to expand total market size, the leading firm also must protect its current business against competitors' attacks. Coca-Cola must also constantly guard against Pepsi; Gillette against Bic; Wal-Mart against Target; and McDonald's against Wendy's.

What can the market leader do to protect its position? First, it must prevent or fix weaknesses that provide opportunities for competitors. It must always fulfill its value promise. Its prices must remain consistent with the value that customers see in the brand. It must work tirelessly to keep strong relationships with valued customers. The leader should "plug holes" so that competitors

real marketing 18.2

WD-40: Slick Ways to Create New Uses

Along with duct tape and the trusty hammer, WD-40 has become one of the truly essential survival items in most American homes. Originally developed in 1953 to prevent rust and corrosion on Atlas missiles, it takes its name from the fortieth and final attempt at creating a *water displacement* formula. Over the past 40 years, WD-40 has achieved a kind of "cult" status—it's now found in more than 80 percent of American households. As Garry Ridge, CEO of the WD-40 Company points out, "More people use WD-40 than dental floss."

The WD-40 Company's knack for finding new uses has made this popular substance one of the truly essential survival items in most American homes.

The WD-40 Company has shown a real knack for expanding the market by finding new uses for its popular substance. In 2000, the company launched a search to uncover 2,000 unique uses for WD-40. After receiving 300,000 individual submissions, it narrowed the list to the best 2,000 and posted it on the company's Web site.

Many new uses come from WD-40 Fan Club members, who enthusiastically write to suggest new applications for the slippery stuff. Only one year old, the fan club already has 40,000 members. At the fan club Web site, members can share their favorite WD-40 stories or browse through thousands of uses suggested by others. They can also download a fan club certificate and membership card, sign up to receive an e-tip of the day, and pass time playing the WD-40 spray game.

Some consumers suggest simple and practical uses. One teacher uses WD-40 to clean old chalkboards in her classroom. "Amazingly, the boards started coming to life again," she reports. "Not only were they restored, but years of masking and Scotch tape residue came off as well." Others, however, report some pretty unusual applications. One man uses WD-40 to polish his glass eye; another uses it to remove a prosthetic leg. In another case, a California woman's parakeet, "Cookie," fell off her shoulder and landed on sticky mousetrap paper. When she tried to free the bird, she got both her hands stuck. The vet used good old WD-40 to free both victims. Still other claims seem highly improbable—one fan reported that after spraying his Frisbee with WD-40, it flew out of sight, never to be seen again.

By now, almost everyone has discovered that WD-40 comes in handy for lubricating machinery, protecting tools from rust, loosening nuts and bolts, quieting squeaky hinges, and freeing stuck doors, drawers, windows, and zippers. And many fans know that you can use WD-40 to remove sticky-back labels from glassware, plastic, and metal items; bubble gum from hair and carpets; scuff marks from vinyl floors; and crayon marks from just about anywhere. Whether it be crayon or bubble gum on walls or in hair, WD-40 is a lifesaver for the parents of precocious mess-makers. For example, when one user's two-year-old daughter took crayons in hand to create a colorful rainbow on the living room wall, a few squirts of WD-40 took care of the problem.

Such common uses make good sense, but did you hear about the nude burglary suspect who had wedged himself in a vent at a cafe in Denver? The fire department extracted him with a large dose of WD-40. Or how about the Mississippi naval officer who used WD-40 to repel an angry bear? Then there's the college student who wrote to say that a friend's nightly amorous activities in the next room were causing everyone in his dorm to lose sleep—he solved the problem by treating the squeaky bedsprings with WD-40.

Others report using WD-40 to clean paintbrushes, keep snow from sticking to snow shovels, and clean hard-water stains and soap scum off shower doors and bathroom tiles. One inventive cemetery grounds keeper even uses WD-40 to clean and polish headstones. Many fishermen report that spraying a little WD-40 on bait helps them catch more fish. Some recreational users claim that spraying their golf clubs, golf balls, or bowling balls has greatly improved their games.

WD-40 has been used to unstick just about everything, including a repairman's finger from a toilet fitting, a little boy's head from his potty-training seat, and a cow's head from a fence. Reports the farmer, "We just sprayed a little WD-40 on his head, and he slipped right out." Ranchers and racehorse trainers say they use WD-40 to untangle manes and tails and to repel mud from hooves. And then there's the Florida man who found an entirely different way to use the product. When modern-day pirates boarded his boat, he hit one of the would-be hijackers over the head with a can of WD-40, which knocked him off the boat and saved the day.

Sources: Numerous WD-40 Company press releases created by Philips-Ramsey Advertising & Public Relations, San Diego, Calif. Also see John Hahn, "A Little Squirt Comes to the Rescue," *Seattle Post-Intelligencer,* September 2, 1994, p. C2; "World-Famous Lubricant Uncovers 2,000 Uses in 2000," February 22, 2001, accessed online at www.wd40.com/ PressRoom; Jay Palmer, "The Cult of WD-40," *Barron's,* December 3, 2001, pp. 19–20; and information accessed online at http://fanclub. wd40.com, September 2002.

do not jump in. But the best defense is a good offense, and the best response is *continuous innovation*. The leader refuses to be content with the way things are and leads the industry in new products, customer services, distribution effectiveness, and cost cutting. It keeps increasing its competitive effectiveness and value to customers.

For example, International Game Technology (IGT) manufactures slot machines and video poker machines for casinos around the world. It has achieved the daunting 75 percent market share in its mature market. Unlike the people who use its products, IGT doesn't rely on luck. Instead, it has formed partnerships with both casino operators and competitive gaming manufacturers to develop innovative new equipment to replace the old. IGT spends aggressively on R&D, allocating $31 million annually to create new games. "We know months, years, in advance what our customers want," says Robert Shay, a sales director for IGT. In this way, IGT takes the offensive, sets the pace, and exploits competitors' weaknesses.[13]

Expanding Market Share.   Market leaders also can grow by increasing their market shares further. In many markets, small market share increases mean very large sales increases. For example, in the coffee market, a 1 percent increase in market share is worth $48 million; in soft drinks, $500 million!

Studies have shown that, on average, profitability rises with increasing market share. Because of these findings, many companies have sought expanded market shares to improve profitability. General Electric, for example, declared that it wants to be at least number one or two in each of its markets or else get out. GE shed its computer, air-conditioning, small-appliances, and television businesses because it could not achieve top-dog position in these industries.

However, some studies have found that many industries contain one or a few highly profitable large firms, several profitable and more focused firms, and a large number of medium-sized firms with poorer profit performance. It appears that profitability increases as a business gains share relative to competitors in its *served market*. For example, Lexus holds only a small share of the total car market, but it earns high profit because it is a high-share company in its luxury-performance car segment. And it has achieved this high share in its served market because it does other things right, such as producing high quality, giving good service, and building close customer relationships.

Companies must not think, however, that gaining increased market share will improve profitability automatically. Much depends on their strategy for gaining increased share. There are many high-share companies with low profitability and many low-share companies with high profitability. The cost of buying higher market share may far exceed the returns. Higher shares tend to produce higher profits only when unit costs fall with increased market share, or when the company offers a superior-quality product and charges a premium price that more than covers the cost of offering higher quality.

Market Challenger Strategies

Firms that are second, third, or lower in an industry are sometimes quite large, such as Colgate, Ford, Target, Avis, and Pepsi. These runner-up firms can adopt one of two competitive strategies: They can challenge the leader and other competitors in an aggressive bid for more market share (market challengers). Or they can play along with competitors and not rock the boat (market followers).

A market challenger must first define which competitors to challenge and its strategic objective. The challenger can attack the market leader. This is a high-risk but potentially high-gain strategy that makes good sense if the leader is not serving the market well. To succeed with such an attack, a company must have some sustainable competitive advantage over the leader. This might be a cost advantage leading to lower prices or the ability to provide better value at a premium price. If the company goes after the market leader, its objective may be to wrest a certain market share. Bic knows that it can't topple Gillette in the razor market—it simply wants a larger share. Or the challenger's goal might be to take over market leadership. Wal-Mart began as a nicher in small towns in the Southwest, grew rapidly to challenge market leader Sears, and finally assumed market leadership, all within a span of less than 25 years.

Alternatively, the challenger can avoid the leader and instead challenge firms its own size, or smaller local and regional firms. These smaller firms may be underfinanced and not serving their customers well. Several of the major beer companies grew to their present size not by challenging large competitors, but by gobbling up small local or regional competitors. If the company goes after a small local company, its objective may be to put that company out of business. The impor-

Market challengers: Pepsi aggressively challenges market leader Coca-Cola in the soft drink market.

tant point remains: The challenger must choose its opponents carefully and have a clearly defined and attainable objective.

How can the market challenger best attack the chosen competitor and achieve its strategic objectives? It may launch a full *frontal attack,* matching the competitor's product, advertising, price, and distribution efforts. It attacks the competitor's strengths rather than its weaknesses. The outcome depends on who has the greater strength and endurance. If the market challenger has fewer resources than the competitor, a frontal attack makes little sense. For example, the runner-up razor-blade manufacturer in Brazil attacked Gillette, the market leader. The attacker was asked if it offered the consumer a better razor blade. "No," was the reply. "A lower price?" "No." "A better package?" "No." "A clever advertising campaign?" "No." "Better allowances to the trade?" "No." "Then how do you expect to take share away from Gillette?" "Sheer determination" was the reply. Needless to say, the offensive failed. Even great size and strength may not be enough to challenge a firmly entrenched, resourceful competitor successfully.

Rather than challenging head-on, the challenger can make an *indirect attack* on the competitor's weaknesses or on gaps in the competitor's market coverage. For example, Dell Computer found a foothold against giant IBM in the personal computer market by selling directly to consumers. Southwest Airlines challenged American and other large carriers by serving the overlooked short-haul, no-frills commuter segment. Such indirect challenges make good sense when the company has fewer resources than the competitor.

Market Follower Strategies

Not all runner-up companies want to challenge the market leader. Challenges are never taken lightly by the leader. If the challenger's lure is lower prices, improved service, or additional product features, the leader can quickly match these to defuse the attack. The leader probably has more staying power in an all-out battle for customers. For example, Kmart recently launched a renewed low-price "BlueLight Special" campaign challenging Wal-Mart's everyday low prices. However, given its lower costs and greater resources, Wal-Mart had little trouble fending off Kmart's challenge, leaving Kmart worse off for the attempt. Thus, many firms prefer to follow rather than challenge the leader.

Similarly, after years of challenging Procter & Gamble unsuccessfully in the U.S. laundry detergent market, Unilever recently decided to throw in the towel and become a follower instead. P&G, which captures a 57 percent share of the market versus Unilever's 17 percent share, has outmuscled competitors on every front. For example, it spends more than $100 million a year on advertising for Tide alone, and has battered competitors with a relentless stream of new and improved products. Unilever is now cutting prices and promotion on its detergents to focus on profit rather than market share.[14]

A follower can gain many advantages. The market leader often bears the huge expenses of developing new products and markets, expanding distribution, and educating the market. By contrast, the market follower can learn from the leader's experience. It can copy or improve on

Dial Corporation, maker of such well-know brands as Dial, Purex, Renuzit, and Armour, follows in the slip-stream of giant rivals— and does very well in its markets.

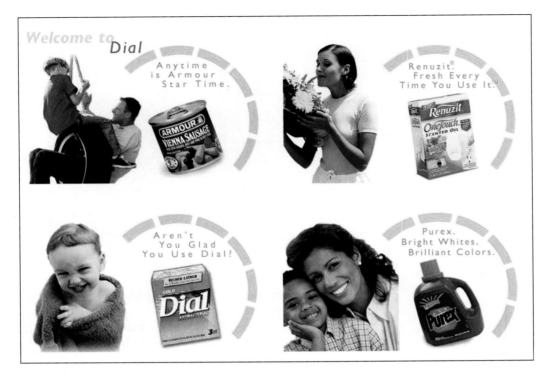

the leader's products and programs, usually with much less investment. Although the follower will probably not overtake the leader, it often can be as profitable. A good example of a follower is Dial Corporation, maker of such well-known brands as Dial, Tone, and Pure&Natural hand soaps, Armour Star canned meats, Purex laundry products, and Renuzit air fresheners. Throughout the 1990s, Dial pursued a "fast follow" strategy:

> Flashy it isn't. "We want to be the dullest story in America," declares Dial's CEO. . . . Dial doesn't spend zillions to make its offerings household names across the nation. Instead, Dial prefers to coast in the slipstream of giant rivals, such as Procter & Gamble. . . . Instead of spending big on research and development or marketing, Dial leaves it to others. . . . And Dial lets other companies educate consumers about new products. P&G, for instance, introduced concentrated powder detergents in 1990. Dial followed over a year later with its own concentrated version, Purex— priced as much as one-third lower than P&G's Tide. Despite this low profile, the company does well in its markets. For example, Dial soap is America's number one antibacterial soap, and Purex has staked out a leadership position in the value segment of the laundry detergent market. Renuzit is the nation's number two air freshener brand, and Amour Star is number two in canned meats.[15]

Following is not the same as being passive or a carbon copy of the leader. For example, in recent years, follower Dial's has focused on being "first, fresh, and fast to market" with innovative new brand extensions such as Dial Complete and Renuzit Super Odor Neutralizer. A market follower must know how to hold current customers and win a fair share of new ones. It must find the right balance between following closely enough to win customers from the market leader but following at enough of a distance to avoid retaliation. Each follower tries to bring distinctive advantages to its target market—location, services, financing. The follower is often a major target of attack by challengers. Therefore, the market follower must keep its manufacturing costs low and its product quality and services high. It must also enter new markets as they open up.

Market Nicher Strategies

Almost every industry includes firms that specialize in serving market niches. Instead of pursuing the whole market, or even large segments, these firms target subsegments. Nichers are often smaller firms with limited resources. But smaller divisions of larger firms also may pursue niching strategies. Firms with low shares of the total market can be highly profitable through smart niching. For example, you've probably never heard of McDonald's competitor Jollibee. In terms of global market share, Jollibee is a mouse among the elephants. But in its niche, the Philippines, Jollibee captures a 75 percent share of hamburger market and 53 percent of the fast-food market as a whole (see Real Marketing 18.3).

Why is niching profitable? The main reason is that the market nicher ends up knowing the target customer group so well that it meets their needs better than other firms that casually sell to this niche. As a result, the nicher can charge a substantial markup over costs because of the added value. Whereas the mass marketer achieves *high volume,* the nicher achieves *high margins.*

Nichers try to find one or more market niches that are safe and profitable. An ideal market niche is big enough to be profitable and has growth potential. It is one that the firm can serve effectively. Perhaps most importantly, the niche is of little interest to major competitors. And the firm can build the skills and customer goodwill to defend itself against a major competitor as the niche grows and becomes more attractive. Here are just a few examples of profitable nichers:

Logitech has become a $944 million global success story by focusing on human interface devices—computer mice, game controllers, keyboards, PC video cameras, and others. It makes every variation of computer mouse imaginable. Logitech turns out mice for left- and right-handed people, wireless mice, mice shaped like real mice for children, and 3-D mice that let the user appear to move behind screen objects. Breeding computer mice has been so successful that Logitech dominates the world market, with Microsoft as its runner-up. This year, Logitech had its best year ever. Revenues were up 28 percent and profits soared 66 percent.[16]

The First Commerce Bank in Charlotte, North Carolina, opened its doors in 1996 with a laser focus on serving the banking needs of small- to mid-size businesses. It offered extended business hours, Internet banking for cash management, and a courier service for daily pick-up of noncash deposits from small-business clients, most of whom have few employees and prefer to remain in the office. Early ads focused on First Commerce's small size and more personalized service, building on the insecurities that small-business owners have in dealing with large banks. One ad showed a huge tower with a headline that read, "Your loan application is in there somewhere." In just five years, First Commerce Bank grew from $1 million to $131 million in assets with three branches, no small accomplishment in a city filled with large national banks. The U.S. Small Business Administration recently named First Commerce the top community bank in North Carolina. "The big banks in Charlotte were so focused on [bigger game] that we've picked up some of their business," says CEO Wes Sturges. "Their crumbs are tasty morsels for us."[17]

The key idea in niching is specialization. A market nicher can specialize along any of several market, customer, product, or marketing mix lines. For example, it can specialize in serving one type of *end user,* as when a law firm specializes in the criminal, civil, or business law markets. The nicher can specialize in serving a given *customer-size* group. Many nichers, such as First Commerce Bank, specialize in serving small customers who are neglected by the majors.

Some nichers focus on one or a few *specific customers,* selling their entire output to a single company, such as Wal-Mart or General Motors. Still other nichers specialize by *geographic market,* selling only in a certain locality, region, or area of the world. *Quality–price* nichers operate at the low or high end of the market. For example, Hewlett-Packard specializes in the high-quality, high-price end of the hand-calculator market. Finally, *service nichers* offer services not available from other firms. An example is a bank that takes loan requests over the phone and hand-delivers the money to the customer.

Niching carries some major risks. For example, the market niche may dry up, or it might grow to the point that it attracts larger competitors. That is why many companies practice *multiple niching.* By developing two or more niches, a company increases its chances for survival. Even some large firms prefer a multiple niche strategy to serving the total market. For example, Alberto Culver is a $2.5 billion company that has used a multiple niching strategy to grow profitably without incurring the wrath of the market leader. CEO Howard Bernick explains the Alberto Culver philosophy this way: "We know who we are and, perhaps more importantly, we know who we are not. We know that if we try to out-Procter Procter, we will fall flat on our face." Instead, the company known mainly for its Alberto VO5 hair products has focused its marketing muscle on

Jollibee vs. McDonald's: Small Can Be Beautiful

When someone says "fast-food restaurant," what's the first name that comes to mind? Chances are it's McDonald's, the world's largest food service organization. McDonald's holds a 43 percent share of the U.S. fast-food burger market, many times the share of nearest competitor Burger King. Ask the same question in the Philippines, however, and the first name uttered will likely be Jollibee. That's right, Jollibee. In the grand scheme of global commerce, Jollibee Foods Corporation isn't

Market nicher Jollibee is king of the burger market in the Philippines. The Jollibee burger is similar to "what a Filipino mother would cook at home."

exactly a household name. But in its niche, the Philippines, it's king of the burger market. "If McDonald's is the Goliath of fast food," notes one industry analysis, "Jollibee is its Filipino David."

At first glance, the rivalry between Jollibee and McDonald's looks like no contest. McDonald's has some 30,000 outlets in 121 countries, more than 3,000 of them in Asia alone, and more than $40 billion in annual systemwide sales. By comparison, Jollibee has only about 400 restaurants contributing about $480 million in annual revenues. Its sales equal only a fraction of the $1.3 billion or more that McDonald's spends annually just on U.S. advertising. When in 1981 the first golden arches went up in Manila, everyone

assumed that McDonald's would dominate in the Philippines as it has everywhere else.

But despite these lopsided numbers, in the Philippines, small Jollibee has humbled the invading global giant. Jollibee captures a 75 percent share of the Philippines' hamburger market and 53 percent of the fast-food market as a whole. Its sales are growing rapidly and profitably. What's Jollibee's secret? Smart niching. Whereas McDonald's exports largely standardized fare to consumers around the world, Jollibee is relentlessly local—it concentrates on serving the unique tastes of Filipino consumers.

In many ways, Jollibee's operations mirror those of McDonald's: Both offer cleanliness, fast service, and convenient locations. Jollibee's Champ burger competes with the Big Mac, and its peach-mango pie replicates McDonald's apple version. However, in contrast to the fairly bland fare that McDonald's serves so successfully worldwide, Jollibee's menu and flavors are specially suited to Filipino tastes. The local chain cooks up sweet, spicy burgers and serves seasoned chicken and spaghetti with sweet sauce, the way Filipinos like it. It serves these meals with rice or noodles, not french fries. "We've designed these products, which are really all-American delights, to suit the Filipino palate," says Jollibee's marketing vice president. Some items, however, are uniquely Filipino. For example, Jollibee's Palabok Fiesta meal, featuring noodles with fish and shrimp, is very popular in the Philippines. Most Americans wouldn't like it because it smells of fish.

Beyond its special understanding of the Filipino palate, Jollibee has also mastered the country's culture and lifestyle. "What happens in the normal Filipino family is that weekends are especially for children," notes a Philippine business analyst, "and parents try to ask their children where they want to eat." Jollibee lures kids with in-store play activities and a cast of captivating characters. Its hamburger-headed Champ, complete with boxing gloves, goes head-to-head with McDonald's Hamburglar. And its massive orange-jacketed Jolly Bee character and a blonde spaghetti-haired girl named Hetti are better known and loved in the Philippines than Ronald McDonald.

The well-known Jolly Bee character epitomizes the Filipino spirit of lighthearted, everyday happiness. Like Filipino working people, explains Jollibee CEO Tony Tan, "the bee hops around and produces sweet things for life, and is happy even though it is busy." Indeed, the company's "jolliness is infectious," says the analyst. It's "as much a part of [the chain's] success as its recipes. Jollibee's staff outsmile McDonald's by a huge stretch. [They recently] started greeting customers with a gesture adopted from the sign language of the deaf—a vertical stroke for 'bee' and hands shoveling towards the heart for 'happy'— which kids have now started using on playgrounds. Jollibee staff call customers and one another 'sir' and 'mom,' which is at once casual and respectful in the Philippines. . . . everyone at Jollibee projects fun."

Jollibee has some additional advantages in this seemingly unfair rivalry. Although much smaller in global terms than McDonald's, Jollibee concentrates most of its limited resources within the Philippines, where its restaurants outnumber McDonald's two to one. It also receives a measure of protection through government regulations that limit McDonald's and other foreign competitors. But its primary advantage comes from simply doing a better job of giving Filipino consumers what they want. Notes the analyst, "The Jollibee burger is similar to what a Filipino mother would cook at home." Small can be beautiful, and Jollibee has shown that through smart niching small players can compete effectively against industry giants.

Sources: See "Happy Meals for McDonald's Rival," *Business Week,* July 29, 1996, p. 77; Cris Prystay and Sanjay Kumar, "Asia Bites Back," *Asian Business,* January 1997, pp. 58–60; Dominic Jones and Nicholas Bradbury, "Blue Chips of the Future," *Euromoney,* December 1998, pp. 99–102; Rene Mallari, "Jolly Good Show," *Asian Business,* pp. 33+; "Business: a Busy Bee in the Hamburger Hive," *The Economist,* March 2, 2002, p. 62; and "Our Company: The Jollibee Phenomenon," accessed online at www.jollibee.com.ph/corporate/phenomenon.htm, August 2002.

Nichers: First Commerce Bank of Charlotte, NC, keeps a laser focus on serving the banking needs of small- to mid-size businesses. As for its bigger rivals: "Their crumbs are tasty morsels for us."

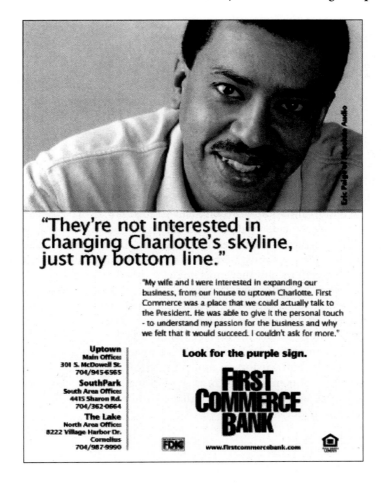

"They're not interested in changing Charlotte's skyline, just my bottom line."

"My wife and I were interested in expanding our business, from our house to uptown Charlotte. First Commerce was a place that we could actually talk to the President. He was able to give it the personal touch - to understand my passion for the business and why we felt that it would succeed. I couldn't ask for more."

Uptown
Main Offices
301 S. McDowell St.
704/945-6565
SouthPark
South Area Offices
4415 Sharon Rd.
704/362-0664
The Lake
North Area Offices
8222 Village Harbor Dr.
Cornelius
704/987-9990

Look for the purple sign.

FIRST COMMERCE BANK

FDIC   www.firstcommercebank.com

acquiring a stable of smaller niche brands. Its other items include flavor enhancers Molly McButter and Mrs. Dash, static-cling fighter Static Guard, and Consort men's hairspray. Each of these brands is number one in its niche.[18]

Balancing Customer and Competitor Orientations

Whether a company is a market leader, challenger, follower, or nicher, it must watch its competitors closely and find the competitive marketing strategy that positions it most effectively. And it must continually adapt its strategies to the fast-changing competitive environment. This question now arises: Can the company spend too much time and energy tracking competitors, damaging its customer orientation? The answer is yes! A company can become so competitor centered that it loses its even more important focus on maintaining profitable customer relationships.

Competitor-centered company

A company whose moves are mainly based on competitors' actions and reactions.

A **competitor-centered company** is one that spends most of its time tracking competitors' moves and market shares and trying to find strategies to counter them. This approach has some pluses and minuses. On the positive side, the company develops a fighter orientation. It trains its marketers to be on a constant alert, watching for weaknesses in their own position and searching out competitors' weaknesses. On the negative side, the company becomes too reactive. Rather than carrying out its own customer relationship strategy, it bases its own moves on competitors' moves. As a result, because so much depends on what the competitors do, the company does not move in a planned direction toward a goal. And it may end up simply matching or extending industry practices rather than seeking innovative new ways to bring more value to customers.

FIGURE 18.4
Evolving company orientations

Market-centered company

A company that pays balanced attention to both customers and competitors in designing its marketing strategies.

Customer-centered company

A company that focuses on customer developments in designing its marketing strategies and on delivering superior value to its target customers.

A **customer-centered company,** by contrast, focuses more on customer developments in designing its strategies. Clearly, the customer-centered company is in a better position to identify new opportunities and set long-run strategies that make sense. By watching customer needs evolve, it can decide what customer groups and what emerging needs are the most important to serve, then concentrate its resources on delivering superior value to target customers. In practice, today's companies must be **market-centered companies,** watching both their customers and their competitors. But they must not let competitor watching blind them to customer focusing.

Figure 18.4 shows that companies have moved through four orientations over the years. In the first stage, they were product oriented, paying little attention to either customers or competitors. In the second stage, they became customer oriented and started to pay attention to customers. In the third stage, when they started to pay attention to competitors, they became competitor oriented. Today, companies need to be market oriented, paying balanced attention to both customers and competitors. Rather than simply watching competitors and trying to beat them on current ways of doing business, they need to watch customers and find innovative ways to build profitable customer relationships by delivering more value than competitors do.

LOOKING BACK: REVIEWING THE CONCEPTS

Today's companies face their toughest competition ever. Understanding customers is an important first step in developing strong customer relationships, but it's not enough. To gain competitive advantage, companies must use this understanding to design market offers that deliver more value than the offers of *competitors* seeking to win over the same customers. This chapter examines how firms analyze their competitors and design effective competitive marketing strategies.

1. Discuss the need to understand competitors as well as customers through competitor analysis.

In order to prepare an effective marketing strategy, a company must consider its competitors as well as its customers. Building profitable customer relationships requires satisfying target consumer needs *better than competitors do.* A company must continuously analyze competitors and develop *competitive marketing strategies* that position it effectively against competitors and give it the strongest possible *competitive advantage.*

Competitor analysis first involves identifying the company's major competitors, using both an industry-based and a market-based analysis. The company then gathers information on competitors' objectives, strategies, strengths and weaknesses, and reaction patterns. With this information in hand, it can select competitors to attack or avoid. Competitive intelligence must be collected, interpreted, and distributed continuously. Company marketing managers should be able to obtain full and reliable information about any competitor affecting their decisions.

2. Explain the fundamentals of competitive marketing strategies based on creating value for customers.

Which *competitive marketing strategy* makes the most sense depends on the company's industry, and on whether it is a market leader, challenger, follower, or nicher. A *market leader* has to mount strategies to expand the total market, protect market share, and expand market share. A *market challenger* is a firm that tries aggressively to expand its market share by attacking the leader, other runner-up companies, or smaller firms in the industry. The challenger can select from a variety of direct or indirect attack strategies. A *market follower* is a runner-up firm that chooses not to rock the boat, usually from fear that it stands to lose more than it might gain. But the follower is not without a strategy and seeks to use its particular skills to gain market growth. Some followers enjoy a higher rate of return than the leaders in their industry. A *market nicher* is a smaller firm that is unlikely to attract the attention of larger firms. Market nichers often become specialists in some end use, customer size, specific customer, geographic area, or service.

3. Illustrate the need for balancing customer and competitor orientations in becoming a truly market-centered organization.

A competitive orientation is important in today's markets, but companies should not overdo their focus on competitors. Companies are more likely to be hurt by emerging consumer needs and new competitors than by existing competitors. *Market-centered companies* that balance consumer and competitor considerations are practicing a true market orientation.

REVIEWING THE KEY TERMS

Benchmarking 570
Competitive advantage 566
Competitive marketing strategy 567
Competitor analysis 567
Competitor-centered company 585

Customer-centered company 586
Customer value analysis 571
Market-centered company 586
Market challenger 577
Market follower 577

Market leader 577
Market nicher 577
Strategic group 569

DISCUSSING THE CONCEPTS

1. Explain competitor myopia. Provide an example of an organization that appears to be competitively myopic and an organization that is not. How do your examples relate to Michael Porter's four basic competitive strategies?

2. Once a company has identified its main competitors, it must assess them. Describe the four-step process used to make this assessment.

3. Customer value analysis is a useful tool for assessing competitor strengths and weaknesses. List and briefly describe the steps for conducting customer value analysis. What is the ultimate goal of the analysis?

4. You have been hired as a strategic consultant for a paper products company that manufactures and distributes lined writing paper and tablets for school-aged children. Write a brief memo to the CEO of the company outlining the structure and importance of an intelligence system as part of a competitive strategy.

5. Marketing strategy and practice often pass through three stages. List and briefly discuss these stages.

6. Compare and contrast the basic competitive strategies outlined by Michael Porter with those of Michael Treacy and Fred Wiersema. Which of these approaches is most relevant to the situations today's marketers face?

7. The chapter describes competitive strategies for firms playing the role of market leader, challenger, follower, or nicher. Answer the following questions for either the personal computer, cellular phone, automobile, *or* beer industry: (a) Which firms in the industry assume each of the roles listed above? (b) What general competitive strategy does each of the major competitors use? (c) What are the general strengths and weaknesses of each competitor?

8. The company's goal under the marketing concept is to satisfy customer wants and needs. What is the goal of a firm adopting a competitor orientation? Do the marketing concept and a competitor orientation conflict?

APPLYING THE CONCEPTS

1. With product brands including Nestlé candies, Nescafé coffees, and Friskies pet foods, Nestlé is a packaged-foods global dynamo. For years, Nestlé has been gaining on rivals Kraft and General Mills. Recently, Nestlé acquired Chef America (Stouffer's brand), Dreyer's Grand Ice Cream (which compares favorably with its own Häagen-Dazs brand), and Ralston Purina (which makes Nestle the number one U.S. pet-food maker). Though Nestlé seems to be going in the right direction, there may be clouds on the horizon. To minimize risk, Nestlé considers each move carefully to avoid mergers and acquisitions that raise concerns about unfair competition.

   a. Visit the Nestlé Web site at www.nestle.com. List all the various brands under the Nestlé corporate umbrella. Are there natural synergies between any of the brands? Which ones?

   b. Visit the Web sites of rivals Kraft (www.kraft.com) and General Mills (www.generalmills.com). How do these competitors' brands compare with Nestlé's brands? What similarities and differences do you observer between the brand portfolios?

   c. Based on the information found in the chapter, should Nestlé attack or avoid competition with Kraft and General Mills?

   d. Should Nestlé consider adding Hershey Foods to its corporate portfolio? Visit the Hershey Web site at

www.hersheys.com and make a case for or against acquisition.

2. The directionally impaired may soon be saved by technology. What would you think about a car navigation system that would offer step-by-step directions to your destination and even book a room for you before you arrive? Sound too good to be true? OnStar's on-board concierge system combines cutting-edge technology with attentive personal service to provide travelers with safety, security, and convenience. Using global positioning satellites, OnStar maps your location and provides remote system diagnostics (such as engine performance), remote door unlock, stolen-vehicle tracking, roadside assistance, accident assistance, and many other services. In the future, a motorist's best friend may be the friendly voice from OnStar that says, "May I be of assistance?"

   a. Visit www.onstar.com to learn more about OnStar's services. What appears to be OnStar's overall competitive strategy?

   b. Which consumers should OnStar target? What is the best way to reach these markets?

   c. Who are OnStar's competitors? Is OnStar well positioned to compete with these services?

   d. Is OnStar a customer-centered company or a competitor-centered company? Why?

DIGITAL CONNECTIONS

MAKING CONNECTIONS THROUGH CUSTOMER INTIMACY

In the highly competitive world of Internet content providers, customer satisfaction is key. Therefore, content providers must continually innovate to meet or exceed customer expectations to remain competitive. Portals such as Yahoo! have added numerous services to their portfolios—many of them free—in an effort to build lasting customer relationships and enhance intimacy with clients. Visit Yahoo! and record five of its services that you would consider using.

FOR DISCUSSION

1. There is no charge for many Yahoo! services. What benefits does Yahoo! realize from providing these services?
2. For each of the services that you have chosen, find a Yahoo! competitor providing the same service and compare the strengths and weaknesses. Which company provides the better service in each instance?
3. Is it important for Yahoo! to be the market leader in each service area? Why or why not?

Telephia: Keeping an Eye on the Competition

With six national companies in the wireless industry, the competition is fierce. The result? Wireless customers have an astounding number of choices at very competitive prices. Although such a market is prime for consumers, wireless companies are struggling to survive. Telephia provides information about consumer usage and competitor strategies to help wireless companies effectively attract, retain, and serve customers. Says one client, "We use Telephia market intelligence to keep our wireless offerings competitive [and to] show us how our competitors are positioning, pricing, and marketing their products."

After viewing the Telephia video, answer the following questions about creating competitive advantage:

1. How does information about competitor plans and promotions help a company attract and retain customers? What types of information would be particularly useful in the wireless industry?
2. How could the information that Telephia provides benefit a market leader? Would the information be more helpful for a market challenger? For a market nicher?
3. Is competitive intelligence essential for companies, like American Express, that are building customer intimacy? How can such companies use market information to build better customer relationships?

Source: Information gathered online at www.telephia.com, August, 2002.

Enterprise Rent-A-Car: Selling the Dream

IN THE FAST LANE

Early on a bright August 2002 morning, Anne Cain pulled her Pontiac Grand Prix into a parking place at the Sacramento, California, International Airport. Anne, an Area Manager for Enterprise Rent-A-Car, walked briskly into the airport's consolidated car-rental center. She smiled as she walked past competitors' rental counters toward the green-and-white Enterprise location. Most Enterprise locations were in neighborhood facilities, but several years ago the company had begun to move into the airport market and now had a number of on-airport locations like hers. She liked being able to see the competition and watch them work. She believed it kept her on her toes and always looking for ways to satisfy Enterprises' customers better than the other companies.

Anne also smiled because she realized how far she had come—and how fast. She had grown up in Turlock, California, and graduated from California State University at Stanislaus with a major in English and a minor in psychology. Anne had put herself through school, sometimes working several jobs at a time. One job had been with an insurance company, and in that role she had met Enterprise employees who often called on the insurance company to encourage it to use Enterprise's cars for its customers who needed replacement rentals. She did not know much about Enterprise, but she saw that the employees were sharp, well trained, and clearly liked their jobs. One had suggested that she consider interviewing with Enterprise when she graduated. "Me? I'm an English major. And, a rental car company?" she remembered thinking. But she had gone for the interview, liked what she heard, and a week later decided to take the job.

Enterprise had told Anne that it would give her all the training and tools she would need to be successful and that she would be able to chart her own career. She completed the manager training program in 10 months, served as an assistant manager in a branch for 10 months, and then earned promotion to branch manager. In four years, she had become an Area Manager, responsible for six branches, 30 full-time employees, millions of dollars in annual revenue, and millions of dollars' worth of rental vehicles. Her pay when she started had been about equal to her classmates who had taken other jobs, but since then it had doubled and tripled based on Enterprise's philosophy of sharing branch and area profits with employees. Now, Enterprise had asked her to be the Area Manager with responsibility for establishing and running the new airport location.

Anne sat down at her desk and began to review her work plans for the day. She paused and smiled again as she thought about her success. Her job really was a dream come true. Where else could someone her age have so much responsibility, so much fun at work, such high earnings, and such a feeling of empowerment?

COMPANY AND INDUSTRY BACKGROUND

Anne's good fortune mirrored that of Enterprise itself. The company's founder, Jack Taylor, had started Enterprise as a leasing company in 1957 and then entered the rent-a-car business in 1962 with a single location and 17 cars in St. Louis, Missouri. Since then, Enterprise had grown dramatically to become the nation's largest rent-a-car company. By 2002, Enterprise had 5,000 offices in five countries, including 400 offices in Canada, the United Kingdom, Germany, and Ireland. Worldwide sales had reached nearly $7 billion. The company had more than 600,000 vehicles in its fleet and 50,000 employees.

Auto Rental News, an industry trade publication, estimated that the entire U.S. rent-a-car market, including the local (home) market and the airport market, was about $18.7 billion in 2001 revenues (see Exhibit 1). *Auto Rental News* divided the local market into replacement rentals, business rentals, service/maintenance rentals, and leisure rentals. It divided the airport market into business and leisure segments.

A WINNING STRATEGY

Analysts attributed Enterprise's success to several factors. First, cars had become a more important part in people's lives. They just couldn't do without their cars, even for a day or two. And, as less and less families included a stay-at-home spouse, there was often no one in the family who could pick people up when they had car problems. Tied in to this, the courts ruled in the 1970s that insurance companies had to offer replacement coverage so that insured motorists would be covered for a replacement rental car if they lost the use of their car.

Beyond theses environmental factors, the company's success resulted from its focus on one segment of the rent-a-car market. Instead of following Hertz, Avis, and other rent-a-car companies by setting up branches at airports to serve national travelers, Enterprise built an extensive network of neighborhood locations serving the "home-city" market—people who needed rental cars as replacements when their cars were wrecked or in the shop being repaired. Because these customers often needed a ride from a body shop or repair garage and had no easy way to get to a rental office, Enterprise offered to pick them up.

However, Enterprise's first customer in the replacement market was often the referral source—the insurance agent or auto body shop employee who recommended Enterprise to the stranded customer. Few of Enterprise's customers got up in the morning thinking they'd need to rent a car—but then they were involved in a wreck. So employees visited the referral sources frequently, often taking them doughnuts or pizza as a way of thanking them for their business. The company also developed an online product that allowed insurance companies to reserve and pay for replacement rentals online. Some analysts estimated that

(continued)

the company served the majority of the insurance replacement market, partly because its rental rates in the replacement market tended to be lower than rates for comparable rentals at airport-based companies—some analysts estimated up to 20 percent lower. A focus on efficient operations helped it keep rates lower.

Enterprise also began to serve a second home-city market segment, the "discretionary" or "leisure/vacation" segment. Many people found that their car just wouldn't do for all occasions. Friends or relatives might visit and need a car, or the family might decide to take a vacation and believe that the family car was really not as dependable as they would like. More and more people were renting for trips just to keep the extra miles off the family car.

Finally, Enterprise was also developing the local corporate market. Many small businesses and some large ones had found that it was less expensive and easier for them to rent their fleets from Enterprise rather than trying to maintain their own fleets. Some businesses preferred that their employees rent a car for business trips rather than drive their own and get reimbursed.

Enterprise's success in the home-city market attracted competition. Although it had the largest share of that market, a handful of major regional competitors, when combined, captured a large market share. The airport-rental companies, such as Hertz, Avis, Budget, Thrifty, and Alamo, got only a small portion of the home-city business. Hertz, a wholly owned subsidiary of Ford Motor Company, had started "Hertz Local Edition," which had neighborhood locations that operated in a fashion similar to Enterprise's locations, including offering the pick-up service. Also, there was a wide range of smaller, regionally based rental companies, that served the remainder of the market.

Enterprise grew very quietly, depending on its referral sources and word-of-mouth promotion. It wasn't until 1989 that the company did its first national advertising. At that time, marketing research indicated that if you showed people a list of company names and asked them to identify the rent-a-car companies, only about 20 percent knew Enterprise. The company started advertising nationally, but still kept its ads low key. By 1997, it had more than quadrupled its annual advertising and promotion spending, using the theme "Pick Enterprise. We'll pick you up." By 2001, the company's research showed that 80 percent of consumers were aware of the company and 60 percent associated the brand with the "pick-you-up" attribute. In late 2001, *Advertising Age* reported that Enterprise had initiated a $30 million ad campaign encouraging drivers to rent its cars, trucks, and vans for special purposes, like carrying building materials or the neighborhood softball team. *AdAge.com* reported that in 2000 the average auto rental/leasing company spent about 2.6 percent of sales on advertising.

THE IMPORTANCE OF CULTURE

Company founder Jack Taylor's philosophy drove the company's strategy. Taylor believed that the employees' and the company's first job was to serve the customer. From the beginning, Taylor urged his employees to do whatever they had to do in order to make the customer happy.

Taylor believed that to satisfy customers, a company had to have satisfied, challenged employees who worked as a team. So he set up the company so that all of Enterprise's branch employees, from assistant manager on up, earned a substantial portion of their pay based on branch profitability. In addition, the company had a profit-sharing plan for all employees. Enterprise

hired primarily college-educated employees and promoted from within. Ninety-nine percent of its senior managers started as management trainees at the branch level, so they understood the customer-oriented culture. As important, they understood their local markets and the needs of customers in those markets. Thus, Enterprise was really a collection of small, independent businesses, with the corporation providing capital and logistical support.

Finally, Taylor believed that if the company took care of its customers and employees, profits would follow. And sure enough, Enterprise had consistently been profitable in an industry where many firms had not. In 2001, Enterprise was the only one of the top seven rent-a-car companies to report an increase in revenue over 2000.

In fact, in late 2001, ANC Rental Corporation, owner of the Alamo and National brands, filed for Chapter 11 bankruptcy protection. Then, in July 2002, Budget Group filed for bankruptcy protection, and Cendent Corporation, the owner of Avis, purchased the company. This created the nation's second largest car-rental company, behind Enterprise. The September 11, 2001, terrorist attack badly hurt the pure-airport rent-a-car companies due to reduced business and leisure travel.

WHAT'S NEXT?

The question is, how can Enterprise continue to grow and prosper in the face of growing competition and market uncertainty?

First, it must continue to attract and retain college-educated employees. The company needs to hire more than 5,000 management trainees a year, making it one of the largest recruiters of college graduates. Yet many college grads, like Anne Cain, may know little or nothing about Enterprise and may have negative feelings about working for a rent-a-car company. Further, Enterprise is committed to having a diverse workforce that reflects the racial and ethnic make up of its local markets. The company's workforce is about 20 percent African American and 30 percent minority. How can Enterprise continue to recruit college graduates, especially members of racial and ethnic minorities and women?

Second, Enterprise must continue to examine its marketing strategy. Despite its focus on the local market, it also began to venture into the airport market in the late 1990s as its customers asked it to take its brand of customer service and value pricing to that market. The company responded by opening some on-airport locations. These operations served the local market as well as targeting the "infrequent" air travelers and budget-conscious business travelers who would appreciate its personal service and lower rates. By 2002, Enterprise served more than 100 of the top 150 U.S. airports and had plans to add 22 more. J. D. Power and Associates found that Enterprise had the number one customer-satisfaction rating among airport customers for four years in a row.

As Enterprise considers its growth options, it must decide which markets it should target. How should it position itself in those markets? Are there new services it could offer that would make sense given its current strategy? How can it do a better job of increasing Enterprise's awareness among targeted customers? And how should it respond as new competitors, including the airport-based firms like Hertz, attack the home-city and leisure travel markets?

Perhaps the most important question is, how can Enterprise continue to grow without losing its focus and without losing the corporate culture that has been so important in helping it and its employees, like Anne Cain, realize their dreams?

QUESTIONS FOR DISCUSSION

1. How does Enterprise create value for its customers?
2. Who are Enterprise's competitors, and what is the nature of competition in its markets?
3. Which of Porter's and Treacy and Wiersema's competitive strategies has Enterprise pursued? What is its competitive position?
4. What marketing recommendations would you make to Enterprise to help it improve its recruiting?
5. What marketing recommendations would you make to Enterprise to improve its marketing strategy?
6. Will Enterprise's strategy work in international markets?

Sources: Enterprise Rent-A-Car supported development of this case. *Auto Rental News* also provided information. Also see Kortney Stringer, "Industry Turmoil Sparks a New Car-Rental Game," *Wall Street Journal*," July 31, 2002, p. D1; Kortney Stringer, "Budget Group's Bankruptcy Filing Could Lead to Sale to Competitor," *Wall Street Journal,* July 30, 2002, p. D5; Eric Berkman, "How to Stay Ahead of the Curve," *CIO,* February 1, 2002, p. 72; Luisa Kroll, "Hard Drive," *Forbes,* November 26, 2001, p. 160; Jean Halliday, "Enterprising Angle: New Auto-Rental Effort Plays to Everyday Renters," *Advertising Age,* September 10, 2001, p. 4; and www.enterprise.com.

1. discuss how the international trade system, economic, political-legal, and cultural environments affect a company's international marketing decisions
2. describe three key approaches to entering international markets
3. explain how companies adapt their marketing mixes for international markets
4. identify the three major forms of international marketing organization

The Global Marketplace

LOOKING AHEAD: PREVIEWING THE CONCEPTS

You've now learned the fundamentals of how companies develop competitive marketing strategies and marketing mixes to build lasting customer relationships by creating superior customer value. In the final two chapters, we'll extend these fundamentals to two special areas—global marketing, and social responsibility and marketing ethics. Although we visited these topics regularly in each previous chapter, because of their special importance, we will focus exclusively on them here. We'll look first at special considerations in global marketing. As we move into the twenty-first century, advances in communication, transportation, and other technologies have made the world a much smaller place. Today, almost every firm, large or small, faces international marketing issues. In this chapter, we will examine six major decisions marketers make in going global.

Our first stop is Coca-Cola—America's soft drink. Or *is* it just America's brand? Read on and see how finding the right balance between global standardization and local adaptation has made Coca-Cola the number one brand worldwide.

What could be more American than Coca-Cola—right? The brand is as American as baseball and apple pie. Coke got its start in an Atlanta pharmacy in 1893, where it sold for five cents a glass. From there, the company's first president, savvy businessman Asa Candler, set out to convince America that Coca-Cola really was "the pause that refreshes." He printed coupons offering complimentary first tastes of Coca-Cola and outfitted pharmacists who distributed the brand with clocks, calendars, scales, and trays bearing the now-so-familiar red-and-white Coca-Cola logo. The beverage quickly became an all-American phenomenon; by 1895, the company had set up syrup plants in Chicago, Dallas, and Los Angeles.

But from the get-go, Coke was destined to be more than just America's soft drink. By 1900, Coca-Cola had already ventured beyond America's borders into numerous countries, including Cuba, Puerto Rico, and France. By the 1920s, Coca-Cola was slapping its logo on everything from dogsleds in Canada to the walls of bullfighting arenas in Spain. During World War II, Coca-Cola built bottling plants in Europe and Asia to supply American soldiers in the field.

As the years passed, Coca-Cola's persuasive and plentiful advertising cemented the brand at home as the all-American beverage. At the same time, strong marketing abroad fueled Coke's popularity throughout the world. In 1971, the company ran its legendary "I'd like to buy the world a Coke" television spot, in which a crowd of children sang the song from atop a hill in Italy. More recently, Coca-Cola's increased focus on emerging markets such as China, India, and Indonesia—home to 2.4 billion people, half the world's population—has bolstered the brand's global success. Coca-Cola is now arguably the best-known and most admired brand in the world.

Coca-Cola's worldwide success results from a skillful balancing of global standardization and brand building with local adaptation. For years, the company has adhered to the mantra "Think globally, act locally." Coca-Cola spends lavishly on global Coke advertising—some $900 million a year—to create a consistent overall positioning for the brand across the 200 countries it serves. In addition, Coke's taste and packaging are largely standardized around the world—the bottle of Coke you'd drink in New York or Philadelphia looks and tastes much the same as one you might order in Paris, Hong Kong, Moscow, Sidney, or Abu Dhabi. As one ad agency executive asserts, "There are about two products that lend themselves to global marketing—and one of them is Coca-Cola."

Although Coke's taste and positioning are fairly consistent worldwide, in other ways Coca-Cola's marketing is relentlessly local. The company carefully adapts its mix of brands and flavors, promotions, price, and distribution to local customs and preferences in each market. For example, beyond its core Coca-Cola brand, the company makes nearly 300 different beverage brands, created especially for the taste buds of local consumers. It sells a pear-flavored drink in Turkey, a berry-flavored Fanta for Germany, a honey-flavored green tea in China, and a sports drink called Aquarius in Belgium and the Netherlands.

Consistent with this local focus, within the framework of its broader global positioning, Coca-Cola adapts specific ads to individual country markets. For example, a localized Chinese New Year television ad features a dragon in a holiday parade, adorned from head to tail with red Coke cans. The spot concludes, "For many centuries, the color red has been the color for good luck and prosperity. Who are we to argue with ancient wisdom?" Coke's now classic "Mean Joe" Green TV ad from the United States—in which the weary football star reluctantly accepts a Coke from an admiring young fan and then tosses the awed kid his jersey in appreciation—was replicated in several different regions using the same format but substituting famous local athletes (ads in South America used Argentine soccer star Maradona; those in Asia used Thai soccer star Niat).

More recently, Coke launched local ads to support its sponsorship of the 2002 World Cup. Based on careful research on local attitudes toward the event, ads were tailored to each country's experience with the competition. An Italian ad featured a bustling Roman marketplace. An emotional Turkish TV ad shows two kids stringing red and white lightbulbs throughout Ankara, which light up the city in the team's colors. "There's even a special World Cup TV ad for the Netherlands—which scandalously failed to reach the tournament this time around," notes a global advertising analyst, "showing Dutch star Ruud Van Nistelroy quietly mowing his lawn while the drama unfolds in Japan and South Korea."

In India, Coca-Cola uses local promotions to aggressively cultivate a local image. It claimed official sponsorship for World Cup cricket, a favorite national sport, and used Indian cricket fans rather than actors to promote Coke products. Coca-Cola markets effectively in India to both retailers and imbibers. Observes one Coke watcher, "The company hosts massive gatherings of up to 15,000 retailers to showcase everything from the latest coolers and refrigerators, which Coke has for loan, to advertising displays. And its salespeople go house-to-house in their quest for new customers. In New Delhi alone, workers handed out more than 100,000 free bottles of Coke and Fanta last year."

Nothing better illustrates Coca-Cola's skill in balancing standardized global brand building with local adaptation than the explosive global growth of Sprite. Sprite's advertising uniformly targets the world's young people with the tag line "Image is nothing. Thirst is everything. Obey your thirst." The campaign taps into the rebellious side of teenagers and into their need to form individual identities. According to Sprite's director of brand marketing, "The meaning of [Sprite] and what we stand for is exactly the same globally. Teens tell us it's incredibly relevant in nearly every market we go into." However, as always, Coca-Cola tailors its message to local consumers. In China, for example, the campaign was given a softer edge: "You can't be irreverent in China, because it's not acceptable in that society. It's all about being relevant [to the specific audience]," notes the marketer. As a result of such smart targeting and powerful positioning, Sprite's worldwide sales surged 35 percent within three years of the start of the campaign, making it the world's number-four soft drink brand.

As a result of its international marketing prowess, Coca-Cola dominates the global soft drink market. More than 70 percent of the company's sales come from abroad. In the United States Coca-Cola captures an impressive 44 percent market share versus Pepsi's 31 percent. Overseas, however, it outsells Pepsi 2.5 to 1 and boasts four of the world's six leading soft drink brands: Coca-Cola, Diet Coke, Sprite, and Fanta.

Thus, Coca-Cola is truly an all-world brand. No matter where in the world you are, you'll find Coke "within an arm's length of desire." Yet, Coca-Cola also has a very personal meaning to consumers in different parts of the globe. Coca-Cola *is* as American as baseball and apple pie. But it's also as English as Big Ben and afternoon tea, as German as bratwurst and beer, as Japanese as sumo and sushi, and as Chinese as Ping-Pong and the Great Wall. Consumers in more than 200 countries think of Coke as *their* beverage. In Spain, Coke has been used as a mixer with wine; in Italy, Coke is served with meals in place of wine or cappuccino; in China, the beverage is served at special government occasions.

Says the company's Web site, "Our local strategy enables us to listen to all the voices around the world asking for beverages that span the entire spectrum of tastes and occasions. What people want in a beverage is a reflection of who they are, where they live, how they work and play, and how they relax and recharge. Whether you're a student in the United States enjoying a refreshing Coca-Cola, a woman in Italy taking a tea break, a child in Peru asking for a juice drink, or a couple in Korea buying bottled water after a run together, we're there for you. . . . It's a special thing to have billions of friends around the world, and we never forget it."[1]

In the past, U.S. companies paid little attention to international trade. If they could pick up some extra sales through exporting, that was fine. But the big market was at home, and it teemed with opportunities. The home market was also much safer. Managers did not need to learn other languages, deal with strange and changing currencies, face political and legal uncertainties, or adapt their products to different customer needs and expectations. Today, however, the situation is much different.

Global Marketing into the Twenty-First Century

The world is shrinking rapidly with the advent of faster communication, transportation, and financial flows. Products developed in one country—Gucci purses, Mont Blanc pens, McDonald's hamburgers, Japanese sushi, German BMWs—are finding enthusiastic acceptance in other countries. We would not be surprised to hear about a German businessman wearing an Italian suit meeting an English friend at a Japanese restaurant who later returns home to drink Russian vodka and watch *Frasier* on TV.

International trade is booming. Since 1969, the number of multinational corporations in the world's 14 richest countries has more than tripled, from 7,000 to 24,000. Imports of goods and services now account for 24 percent of gross domestic product worldwide, twice the level of 40 years ago. International trade now accounts for a quarter of the United States's GDP, and between 1996 and 2006, U.S. exports are expected to increase 51 percent. World trade now accounts for 29 percent of world GDP, a 10 percent increase from 1990.[2]

Many U.S. companies have long been successful at international marketing: Coca-Cola, McDonald's, IBM, Xerox, Corning, Gillette, Colgate, General Electric, Caterpillar, Ford, Kodak, 3M, Boeing, Motorola, and dozens of other American firms have made the world their market. And in the United States, names such as Sony, Toyota, Nestlé, Norelco, Nokia, Mercedes, Panasonic, and Prudential have become household words. Other products and services that appear to be American are in fact produced or owned by foreign companies: Bantam books, Baskin-Robbins ice cream, GE and RCA televisions, Carnation milk, Pillsbury food products, Universal Studios, and Motel 6, to name just a few. "Already two-thirds of all industry either operates globally or is in the process of doing so," notes one analyst. "Michelin, the oh-so-French tire manufacturer, now makes 35 percent of its money in the United States, while Johnson & Johnson does 43 percent of its business abroad. . . . The scope of every manager is the world."[3]

But today global competition is intensifying. Foreign firms are expanding aggressively into new international markets, and home markets are no longer as rich in opportunity. Few industries are now safe from foreign competition. Although some companies would like to stem the tide of foreign imports through protectionism, in the long run this would only raise the cost of living and protect inefficient domestic firms. The better way for companies to compete is to continuously improve their products at home and expand into foreign markets.

Companies that delay taking steps toward internationalizing risk being shut out of growing markets in Western Europe, Eastern Europe, the Pacific Rim, and elsewhere. Firms that stay at home to play it safe not only might lose their chances to enter other markets but also risk losing

Many American companies have made the world their market.

FIGURE 19.1
Major decisions in international marketing

their home markets. Domestic companies that never thought about foreign competitors suddenly find these competitors in their own backyards.

Ironically, although the need for companies to go abroad is greater today than in the past, so are the risks. Companies that go global confront several major problems. High debt, inflation, and unemployment in many countries have resulted in highly unstable governments and currencies, which limit trade and expose U.S. firms to many risks. Governments are placing more regulations on foreign firms, such as requiring joint ownership with domestic partners, mandating the hiring of nationals, and limiting profits that can be taken from the country. Moreover, foreign governments often impose high tariffs or trade barriers in order to protect their own industries. Finally, corruption is an increasing problem—officials in several countries often award business not to the best bidder but to the highest briber.

Still, companies selling in global industries have no choice but to internationalize their operations. A *global industry* is one in which the competitive positions of firms in given local or national markets are affected by their global positions. A **global firm** is one that, by operating in more than one country, gains marketing, production, R&D, and financial advantages that are not available to purely domestic competitors.

> **Global firm**
> A firm that, by operating in more than one country, gains R&D, production, marketing, and financial advantages in its costs and reputation that are not available to purely domestic competitors.

The global company sees the world as one market. It minimizes the importance of national boundaries and raises capital, obtains materials and components, and manufactures and markets its goods wherever it can do the best job. For example, Ford's "world truck" sports a cab made in Europe and a chassis built in North America. It is assembled in Brazil and imported to the United States for sale. Otis Elevator gets its elevators' door systems from France, small geared parts from Spain, electronics from Germany, and special motor drives from Japan. It uses the United States only for systems integration. Thus, global firms gain advantages by planning, operating, and coordinating their activities on a worldwide basis.

This does not mean that small and medium-size firms must operate in a dozen countries to succeed. These firms can practice global niching. In fact, companies marketing on the Internet may find themselves going global whether they intend it or not (see Real Marketing 19.1). But the world is becoming smaller, and every company operating in a global industry—whether large or small—must assess and establish its place in world markets.

The rapid move toward globalization means that all companies will have to answer some basic questions: What market position should we try to establish in our country, in our economic region, and globally? Who will our global competitors be, and what are their strategies and resources? Where should we produce or source our products? What strategic alliances should we form with other firms around the world?

As shown in Figure 19.1, a company faces six major decisions in international marketing. Each decision will be discussed in detail in this chapter.

Looking at the Global Marketing Environment

Before deciding whether to operate internationally, a company must thoroughly understand the international marketing environment. That environment has changed a great deal in the last two decades, creating both new opportunities and new problems. The world economy has globalized. World trade and investment have grown rapidly, with many attractive markets opening up in Western and Eastern Europe, China and the Pacific Rim, Russia, and elsewhere. There has been a growth of global brands in automobiles, food, clothing, electronics, computers and software, and many other categories. The number of global companies has grown dramatically.

real marketing 19.1

www.TheWorldIsYourOyster.com: The Ins and Outs of Global E-Commerce

Companies large and small are now taking advantage of cyberspace's vanishing national boundaries. Major marketers doing global e-commerce range from automakers (General Motors and Toyota) to computer makers (Dell and IBM) to direct-mail companies (L.L. Bean) to Internet superstars such as Amazon.com and Yahoo!

For some companies, global Web marketing has been a hit-or-miss affair. They put their Web site content in English for the American market, and if any international users stumble across it and end up buying something, so much the better. Such orders can be gravy for U.S.-focused marketers.

Other marketers have made a more strategic decision to dive into the global marketspace. They're using the Web and online services to reach new customers outside their home countries, support existing customers who live abroad, source from international suppliers, and build global brand awareness. Most international companies have adapted their Web sites to provide country-specific content and services to their best potential international markets, often in the local language.

Many marketers are taking advantage of the Internet's global reach. For example, Dell Computer offers dozens of different Web site choices tailored to the languages and situations of specific countries, here Hungary and France.

Go to www.nike.com and Nike's home Web page first asks which site you want: North America, Europe, Asia Pacific, or Latin America. The European option lists five language choices: English, Deutsch, Français, Espagnol, and Italiano. Similarly, Dell Computer offers dozens of country-specific, local-language Web sites for markets, from France, Germany, China, and Japan to Belgium and Brunei. And Texas Instruments uses tailored "TI & Me" sites to sell and support its signal processors, logic devices, and other chips in B2B markets across Europe, Asia, and South America.

Before expanding their Web presences internationally, companies need to find the countries or regions with the largest potential online populations. The biggest growth area today is the Asia-Pacific region. By 2004, the number of Asia-Pacific Internet users is expected to swell to 188 million, thanks to declines in Internet access costs, increases in local-language content, and infrastructure improvements. In China alone, the number of Internet subscriptions is growing by 6 percent each month. Europe is another hot spot for Internet growth. Europe has typically lagged about four years behind the United States but is now catching up quickly. European Internet penetration, which stood at 19 percent in 1999, reached 38 percent in 2002. By 2003, the five countries with the highest European penetration levels—Germany, France, the Netherlands, the United Kingdom, and Sweden—will have online populations totaling 60 million, up from 34 million in 1999.

Despite these encouraging global e-commerce developments in Asia and Europe, Internet marketers sometimes overstate global opportunities. Developed countries offer many choices for Internet access—Hong Kong alone has more than 240 registered Internet service providers (ISPs). However, less developed countries in Central and South America or Africa have fewer or none at all, forcing users to make international calls to go online. As of 2000, only 6 percent of the world's population had Internet access. Even with adequate phone lines and PC penetration, high connection costs sharply restrict Internet use. In Asia, ISP subscriptions can run up to $60 a month, more than triple the average U.S. rate.

In addition, global marketers may run up against governmental or cultural restrictions. France, for instance, has laws against providing encrypted content. In Germany, a vendor can't accept payment via credit card until two weeks after an order has been sent. German law also prevents companies from

(continued)

using certain marketing techniques, such as unconditional lifetime guarantees. This affects companies with international Web sites, such as Lands' End, which prominently features its lifetime guarantee on its network of Web sites. On a wider scale, the issue of who pays sales taxes and duties on global e-commerce is murkier still.

Businesses need to realize that the Web does not offer complete solutions for transacting global business—and it probably never will. Most companies will always find it difficult to complete a big business-to-business deal via e-mail. The Internet will not surmount customs red tape or local regulations regarding import or export of certain goods. The Web also can't guarantee that goods will arrive in perfect condition.

What the Web can do is give companies access to markets they could never serve otherwise. The Web certainly has done that for Lands' End. The direct clothing retailer now has online stores in the United Kingdom, Ireland, France, Italy, Germany, and Japan,

markets it would have great difficulty developing through its traditional catalog channels. According to Sam Taylor, vice president of international operations at Lands' End:

The challenge in launching a catalog business is customer acquisition. When you're starting out, you have to rent lists of names, . . . it's so expensive to print and mail those catalogs, and the conversion rate is very low. So the cost to acquire a customer is very high. Now, the Internet has changed all that. All of a sudden, we've got a French Web site. We do some PR, we do some limited online advertising, we get word of mouth, and the business starts to build. We're not overinvesting in upfront marketing. At some point in the future, once the business is big enough, we will launch a paper catalog [in France], but not before the business is ready. That's one of the good things about the Internet. It has totally turned businesses upside down and changed how we do business.

However, Lands' End is landing right-side up in the international arena. The company now ships products to 185 countries, and international Web sales now contribute about 14 percent of all Lands' End's revenues.

Sources: "One In Three Europeans Will Embrace a Digital Lifestyle by 2003, According to Forrester," *Business Wire,* December 6, 2000; Brandon Mitchener, "E-Commerce: Border Crossings," *Wall Street Journal,* November 22, 1999; Janet Purdy Levaux, "Adapting Products and Services for Global E-Commerce," *World Trade,* January 2001, pp. 52–54; Carol Sliwa, "Clothing Retailer Finds Worldwide Business on the Web," *Computerworld,* April 30, 2001, p. 40; "Nielsen/NetRatings Find China Has the World's Second Largest At-Home Internet Population," April 22, 2002, accessed online at www.nielsen-netratings.com; and "Internet Penetration in Europe Plateaus," accessed online at www.europemedia.net, July 2002.

The International Trade System

Tariff
A tax levied by a government against certain imported products.

Quota
A limit on the amount of goods that an importing country will accept in certain product categories.

Embargo
A ban on the import of a certain product.

Exchange controls
Government limits on the amount of foreign exchange with other countries and on the exchange rate against other currencies.

Nontariff trade barriers
Nonmonetary barriers to foreign products, such as biases against a foreign company's bids, or product standards that go against a foreign company's product features.

The U.S. company looking abroad must start by understanding the international *trade system.* When selling to another country, the U.S. firm faces various trade restrictions. The most common is the **tariff,** which is a tax levied by a foreign government against certain imported products. The tariff may be designed either to raise revenue or to protect domestic firms. The exporter also may face a **quota,** which sets limits on the amount of goods the importing country will accept in certain product categories. The purpose of the quota is to conserve on foreign exchange and to protect local industry and employment. An **embargo,** or boycott, which totally bans some kinds of imports, is the strongest form of quota.

American firms may face **exchange controls** that limit the amount of foreign exchange and the exchange rate against other currencies. The company also may face **nontariff trade barriers,** such as biases against U.S. company bids or restrictive product standards or other rules that go against American product features:

One of the cleverest ways the Japanese have found to keep foreign manufacturers out of their domestic market is to plead "uniqueness." Japanese skin is different, the government argues, so foreign cosmetics companies must test their products in Japan before selling there. The Japanese say their stomachs are small and have room for only the *mikan,* the local tangerine, so imports of U.S. oranges are limited. Now the Japanese have come up with what may be the flakiest argument yet: Their snow is different, so ski equipment should be too.[4]

At the same time, certain forces *help* trade between nations. Examples include the General Agreement on Tariffs and Trade and various regional free trade agreements.

The World Trade Organization and GATT

The General Agreement on Tariffs and Trade (GATT) is a 55-year-old treaty designed to promote world trade by reducing tariffs and other international trade barriers. Since the treaty's inception in 1948, member nations (currently numbering 144) have met in eight rounds of GATT negotiations to reassess trade barriers and set new rules for international trade. The first seven rounds of negotiations reduced the average worldwide tariffs on manufactured goods from 45 percent to just 5 percent.

The most recently completed GATT negotiations, dubbed the Uruguay Round, dragged on for seven long years before concluding in 1993. The benefits of the Uruguay Round will be felt for many years as the accord promotes long-term global trade growth. It reduced the world's remaining merchandise tariffs by 30 percent, boosting global merchandise trade by as much as 10 percent, or $270 billion in current dollars, by 2002. The new agreement also extended GATT to cover trade in agriculture and a wide range of services, and it toughened international protection of copyrights, patents, trademarks, and other intellectual property.[5]

Beyond reducing trade barriers and setting international standards for trade, the Uruguay Round established the World Trade Organization (WTO) to enforce GATT rules. One of the WTO's first major tasks was to host negotiations on the General Agreement on Trade in Services, which deals with worldwide trade in banking, securities, and insurance services. In general, the WTO acts as an umbrella organization, overseeing GATT, the General Agreement on Trade in Services, and a similar agreement governing intellectual property. In addition, the WTO mediates global disputes and imposes trade sanctions, authorities that the previous GATT organization never possessed. Top decision makers from the WTO meet once every two years to discuss matters pertaining to all WTO agreements. The most recent meetings took place in Doha, Qatar, in late 2001.

Regional Free Trade Zones

Economic community

A group of nations organized to work toward common goals in the regulation of international trade.

Certain countries have formed *free trade zones* or **economic communities**—groups of nations organized to work toward common goals in the regulation of international trade. One such community is the *European Union (EU)*. Formed in 1957, the European Union—then called the Common Market—set out to create a single European market by reducing barriers to the free flow of products, services, finances, and labor among member countries and developing policies on trade with nonmember nations. Today, the European Union represents one of the world's single largest markets. Its current 15 member countries contain more than 374 million consumers and account for 20 percent of the world's exports, and it is preparing for the accession of 13 new eastern and southern European members. During the next decade, as more European nations gain admission, the EU could contain as many as 450 million people in 28 countries.[6]

European unification offers tremendous trade opportunities for U.S. and other non-European firms. However, it also poses threats. As a result of increased unification, European companies will grow bigger and more competitive. Perhaps an even bigger concern, however, is that lower barriers *inside* Europe will create only thicker *outside* walls. Some observers envision a "Fortress Europe" that heaps favors on firms from EU countries but hinders outsiders by imposing obstacles such as stiffer import quotas, local content requirements, and other nontariff barriers.

Progress toward European unification has been slow—many doubt that complete unification will ever be achieved. However, on January 1, 1999, 11 of the 15 member nations took a significant step toward unification by adopting the euro as a common currency. In January 2001, Greece became the twelfth member nation to adopt the euro. Currencies of the individual countries were phased out gradually until January 1, 2002, when the euro became the only currency. Adoption of the euro will decrease much of the currency risk associated with doing business in Europe, making member countries with previously weak currencies more attractive markets. In addition, by removing currency conversion hurdles, the switch will likely increase cross-border trade and highlight differences in pricing and marketing from country to country.[7]

Even with the adoption of the euro as a standard currency, from a marketing viewpoint, creating an economic community will not create a homogenous market. With 15 different languages and distinctive national customs, it is unlikely that the EU will ever go against 2,000 years of tradition and become the "United States of Europe." Although economic and political boundaries may fall, social and cultural differences will remain, and companies marketing in Europe will face a daunting mass of local rules. Still, even if only partly successful, European unification will make a more efficient and competitive Europe a global force with which to reckon.[8]

In North America, the United States and Canada phased out trade barriers in 1989. In January 1994, the *North American Free Trade Agreement (NAFTA)* established a free trade zone among the United States, Mexico, and Canada. The agreement created a single market of 360 million people who produce and consume $6.7 trillion worth of goods and services. As it is implemented over a 15-year period, NAFTA will eliminate all trade barriers and investment restrictions among the three countries.

Thus far, the agreement has allowed trade between the countries to flourish. Each day the United States exchanges more than $1 billion in goods and services with Canada, its largest

Wal-Mart and other companies are expanding rapidly in Mexico and Canada to take advantage of the many opportunities presented by NAFTA. The trade agreement establishes a single market of 360 million people in Mexico, Canada, and the United States.

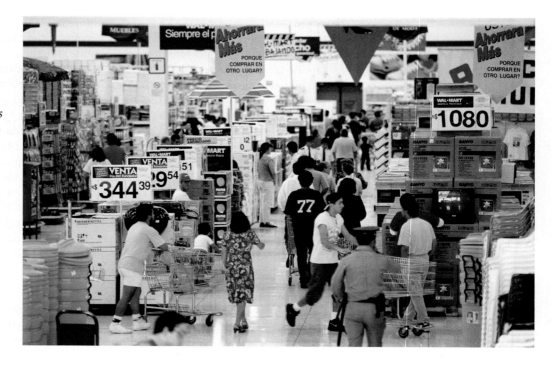

trading partner. Since the agreement was signed in 1993, U.S. merchandise exports to Mexico are up 170 percent, while Mexican exports to the United States grew some 241 percent. In 1998, Mexico passed Japan to become America's second largest trading partner. Given the apparent success of NAFTA, talks are now under way to investigate establishing a Free Trade Area of the Americas (FTAA). This mammoth free trade zone would include 34 countries stretching from the Bering Strait to Cape Horn, with a population of 800 million and a combined gross domestic product of more than $11 trillion.[9]

Other free trade areas have formed in Latin America and South America. For example, MERCOSUR now links six members, including full members Argentina, Brazil, Paraguay, and Uruguay and associate members Bolivia and Chile. With a population of more than 200 million and a combined economy of more than $1 trillion a year, these countries make up the largest trading bloc after NAFTA and the European Union. There is talk of a free trade agreement between the EU and MERCOSUR, and MERCOSUR's member countries are considering adopting a common currency, the merco.[10]

Although the recent trend toward free trade zones has caused great excitement and new market opportunities, this trend also raises some concerns. For example, in the United States, unions fear that NAFTA will lead to the further exodus of manufacturing jobs to Mexico, where wage rates are much lower. Environmentalists worry that companies that are unwilling to play by the strict rules of the U.S. Environmental Protection Agency will relocate in Mexico, where pollution regulation has been lax.

Each nation has unique features that must be understood. A nation's readiness for different products and services and its attractiveness as a market to foreign firms depend on its economic, political-legal, and cultural environments.

Economic Environment

The international marketer must study each country's economy. Two economic factors reflect the country's attractiveness as a market: the country's industrial structure and its income distribution.

The country's *industrial structure* shapes its product and service needs, income levels, and employment levels. The four types of industrial structures are as follows:

- *Subsistence economies:* In a subsistence economy, the vast majority of people engage in simple agriculture. They consume most of their output and barter the rest for simple goods and services. They offer few market opportunities.

- *Raw material exporting economies:* These economies are rich in one or more natural resources but poor in other ways. Much of their revenue comes from exporting these resources. Examples are Chile (tin and copper), Zaire (copper, cobalt, and coffee), and Saudi Arabia (oil). These countries are good markets for large equipment, tools and supplies, and trucks. If there are many foreign residents and a wealthy upper class, they are also a market for luxury goods.

- *Industrializing economies:* In an industrializing economy, manufacturing accounts for 10 to 20 percent of the country's economy. Examples include Egypt, the Philippines, India, and Brazil. As manufacturing increases, the country needs more imports of raw textile materials, steel, and heavy machinery, and fewer imports of finished textiles, paper products, and automobiles. Industrialization typically creates a new rich class and a small but growing middle class, both demanding new types of imported goods.

- *Industrial economies:* Industrial economies are major exporters of manufactured goods and investment funds. They trade goods among themselves and also export them to other types of economies for raw materials and semifinished goods. The varied manufacturing activities of these industrial nations and their large middle class make them rich markets for all sorts of goods.

The second economic factor is the country's *income distribution.* Countries with subsistence economies may consist mostly of households with very low family incomes. In contrast, industrialized nations may have low-, medium-, and high-income households. Still other countries may have households with only either very low or very high incomes. However, in many cases, poorer countries may have small but wealthy segments of upper-income consumers. Also, even in low-income and developing economies, people may find ways to buy products that are important to them:

> Philosophy professor Nina Gladziuk thinks carefully before shelling out her hard-earned zlotys for Poland's dazzling array of consumer goods. But spend she certainly does. Although she earns just $550 a month from two academic jobs, Gladziuk, 41, enjoys making purchases: They are changing her lifestyle after years of deprivation under communism. In the past year, she has furnished a new apartment in a popular neighborhood near Warsaw's Kabaty Forest, splurged on foreign-made beauty products, and spent a weekend in Paris before attending a seminar financed by her university. . . . Meet Central Europe's fast-rising consumer class. From white-collar workers like Gladziuk to factory workers in Budapest to hip young professionals in Prague, incomes are rising and confidence surging as a result of four years of economic growth. In the region's leading economies—the Czech Republic, Hungary, and Poland—the new class of buyers is growing not only in numbers but also in sophistication. . . . In Hungary, ad agency Young & Rubicam labels 11 percent of the country as "aspirers," with dreams of the good life and buying habits to match. Nearly one-third of all Czechs, Hungarians, and Poles—some 17 million people—are under 30 years old, eager to snap up everything from the latest fashions to compact disks.[11]

Thus, international marketers face many challenges in understanding how the economic environment will affect decisions about which global markets to enter and how.

Political-Legal Environment

Nations differ greatly in their political-legal environments. At least four political-legal factors should be considered in deciding whether to do business in a given country: attitudes toward international buying, government bureaucracy, political stability, and monetary regulations.

In their *attitudes toward international buying,* some nations are quite receptive to foreign firms and others are quite hostile. For example, India has bothered foreign businesses with import quotas, currency restrictions, and limits on the percentage of the management team that can be nonnationals. As a result, many U.S. companies left India. In contrast, neighboring Asian countries such as Singapore, Thailand, Malaysia, and the Philippines court foreign investors and shower them with incentives and favorable operating conditions.[12]

A second factor is *government bureaucracy*—the extent to which the host government runs an efficient system for helping foreign companies: efficient customs handling, good market information, and other factors that aid in doing business. A common shock to Americans is how quickly barriers to trade disappear in some countries if a suitable payment (bribe) is made to some official.

Developing economies: In Central Europe, companies are catering to the new class of buyers with dreams of the good life and buying habits to match who are eager to snap up everything from western consumer goods to high fashions and the latest cell phones.

Political stability is another issue. Governments change hands, sometimes violently. Even without a change, a government may decide to respond to new popular feelings. The foreign company's property may be taken, its currency holdings may be blocked, or import quotas or new duties may be set. International marketers may find it profitable to do business in an unstable country, but the unstable situation will affect how they handle business and financial matters.

Finally, companies must also consider a country's *monetary regulations.* Sellers want to take their profits in a currency of value to them. Ideally, the buyer can pay in the seller's currency or in other world currencies. Short of this, sellers might accept a blocked currency—one whose removal from the country is restricted by the buyer's government—if they can buy other goods in that country that they need themselves or can sell elsewhere for a needed currency. Besides currency limits, a changing exchange rate also creates high risks for the seller.

Countertrade
International trade involving the direct or indirect exchange of goods for other goods instead of cash.

Most international trade involves cash transactions. Yet many nations have too little hard currency to pay for their purchases from other countries. They may want to pay with other items instead of cash, which has led to a growing practice called **countertrade.** Countertrade makes up an estimated 20 percent of all world trade.[13] It takes several forms: *Barter* involves the direct exchange of goods or services, as when Australian cattlemen swapped beef on the hoof for Indonesian goods including beer, palm oil, and cement. Another form is *compensation* (or *buyback*), whereby the seller sells a plant, equipment, or technology to another country and agrees to take payment in the resulting products. Thus, Goodyear provided China with materials and training for a printing plant in exchange for finished labels. Another form is *counterpurchase,* in which the seller receives full payment in cash but agrees to spend some portion of the money in the other country within a stated time period. For example, Pepsi sells its cola syrup to Russia for rubles and agrees to buy Russian-made Stolichnaya vodka for sale in the United States.

Countertrade deals can be very complex. For example, a few years back, DaimlerChrysler agreed to sell 30 trucks to Romania in exchange for 150 Romanian jeeps, which it then sold to Ecuador for bananas, which were in turn sold to a German supermarket chain for German currency. Through this roundabout process, DaimlerChrysler finally obtained payment in German money.[14]

Cultural Environment

Each country has its own folkways, norms, and taboos. When designing global marketing strategies, companies must understand how culture affects consumer reactions in each of its world markets. In turn, they must also understand how their strategies affect local cultures.

The Impact of Culture on Marketing Strategy

The seller must examine the ways consumers in different countries think about and use certain products before planning a marketing program. There are often surprises. For example, the aver-

Overlooking cultural differences can result in embarrassing mistakes. When Nike learned that this stylized "Air" logo resembled "Allah" in Arabic script, it apologized and pulled the shoes from distribution.

age French man uses almost twice as many cosmetics and beauty aids as his wife. The Germans and the French eat more packaged, branded spaghetti than do Italians. Italian children like to eat chocolate bars between slices of bread as a snack. Women in Tanzania will not give their children eggs for fear of making them bald or impotent.

Companies that ignore such differences can make some very expensive and embarrassing mistakes. Here's an example:

> McDonald's and Coca-Cola managed to offend the entire Muslim world by putting the Saudi Arabian flag on their packaging. The flag's design includes a passage from the Koran (the sacred text of Islam), and Muslims feel very strongly that their Holy Writ should never be wadded up and tossed in the garbage. Nike faced a similar situation in Arab countries when Muslims objected to a stylized "Air" logo on its shoes, which resembled "Allah" in Arabic script. Nike apologized for the mistake and pulled the shoes from distribution.[15]

Business norms and behavior also vary from country to country. American business executives need to be briefed on these factors before conducting business in another country. Here are some examples of different global business behavior:[16]

- South Americans like to sit or stand very close to each other when they talk business—in fact, almost nose-to-nose. The American business executive tends to keep backing away as the South American moves closer. Both may end up being offended.

- Fast and tough bargaining, which works well in other parts of the world, is often inappropriate in Japan and other Asian countries. Moreover, in face-to-face communications, Japanese business executives rarely say no. Thus, Americans tend to become impatient with having to spend time in polite conversation about the weather or other such topics before getting down to business. And they become frustrated when they don't know where they stand. However, when Americans come to the point quickly, Japanese business executives may find this behavior offensive.

- In France, wholesalers don't want to promote a product. They ask their retailers what they want and deliver it. If an American company builds its strategy around the French wholesaler's cooperation in promotions, it is likely to fail.

- When American executives exchange business cards, each usually gives the other's card a cursory glance and stuffs it in a pocket for later reference. In Japan, however, executives dutifully study each other's cards during a greeting, carefully noting company affiliation and rank. They show a business card the same respect they show a person. Also, they hand their card to the most important person first.

By the same token, companies that understand cultural nuances can use them to advantage when positioning products internationally. Consider the following example:

A television ad running these days in India shows a mother lapsing into a daydream: Her young daughter is in a beauty contest dressed as Snow White, dancing on a stage. Her flowing gown is an immaculate white. The garments of other contestants, who dance in the background, are a tad gray. Snow White, no surprise, wins the blue ribbon. The mother awakes to the laughter of her adoring family—and glances proudly at her Whirlpool White Magic washing machine. The TV spot is the product of 14 months of research by Whirlpool into the psyche of the Indian consumer. Among other things, [Whirlpool] learned that Indian homemakers prize hygiene and purity, which they associate with white. The trouble is, white garments often get discolored after frequent machine washing in local water. Besides appealing to this love of purity in its ads, Whirlpool custom-designed machines that are especially good with white fabrics. Whirlpool hasn't stopped there. It uses generous incentives to get thousands of Indian retailers to stock its goods. To reach every cranny of the vast nation, it uses local contractors conversant in India's 18 languages to collect payments in cash and deliver appliances by truck, bicycles, even oxcart. Since 1996, Whirlpool's sales in India have leapt 80 percent—and should hit $200 million this year. Whirlpool now is the leading brand in India's fast-growing market for fully automatic washing machines.[17]

Thus, understanding cultural traditions, preferences, and behaviors can help companies not only to avoid embarrassing mistakes but also to take advantage of cross-cultural opportunities.

The Impact of Marketing Strategy on Cultures

Whereas marketers worry about the impact of culture on their global marketing strategies, other may worry about the impact of marketing strategies on global cultures. For example, some critics argue that "globalization" really means "Americanization." They worry that the more people around the world are exposed to the American culture and lifestyle in the food they eat, the stores they shop, and television shows and movies they watch, the more they will lose their individual cultural identities.

These critics contend that exposure to American values and products erodes other cultures and westernizes the world. They point out that teens in India watch MTV and ask their parents for more westernized clothes and other symbols of American pop culture and values. Grandmothers in small villas in northern Italy no longer spend each morning visiting local meat, bread, and produce markets to gather the ingredients for dinner. Instead, they now they shop at Wal-Mart Supercenters. Women in Saudi Arabia see American films and question their societal roles. In China, most people never drank coffee before Starbucks entered the market. Now Chinese consumers rush to Starbucks stores "because it's a symbol of a new kind of lifestyle." Similarly, in China, where McDonald's operates 80 restaurants in Beijing alone, nearly half of all children identify the chain as a domestic brand.[18]

An American reporter writing from Japan claimed:

[It will] only be a matter of time before an Asian family [will] take cash from their corner U.S. bank, "drive off to Wal-Mart and fill the trunk of their Ford with the likes of Fritos and Snickers," then stop at the American-owned movie theater to see the latest Disney film before returning home to check their U.S. mutual fund accounts and America Online (on their IBM computer with Microsoft software). Asians see this as no less than the U.S. "desire to bury Asian values," and they are not pleased.[19]

Recently, such concerns have led to a backlash against American globalization. For example, as a symbol of American capitalism, McDonald's has been singled out by antiglobalization protestors all over the world. Its restaurants are also targeted when anti-American sentiment peaks. For example, almost immediately after U.S. armed forces unleashed their attack on Afghanistan following the September 11, 2001, terrorist attacks, McDonald's stores in Pakistan, India, and elsewhere around the world came under attack. Local protestors burned American flags outside the restaurants and vandalized McDonald's storefronts.

Some critics worry that world exposure to American culture and lifestyle will result in the "Americanization" of other cultures. Nearly half of all Chinese children identify McDonald's as a domestic brand. Chinese consumers rush to Starbucks stores "because it's a symbol of a new kind of lifestyle."

Despite the concerns, most studies reveal that, although globalization may bridge culture gaps, it does not eliminate them. Instead, the cultural exchange goes both ways.

African consumers are more apt to be fans of Hindi musicals than MTV. And even American childhood has increasingly been shaped by Asian cultural imports. Most parents now know about the Power Rangers, Tamagotchi and Pokemon, Sega and Nintendo. For the moment, English remains cyberspace's dominant language, and having Web access often means that Third World youth have greater exposure to American popular culture. Yet these same technologies enable Balkan students studying in the United States to hear Webcast news and music from Serbia or Bosnia. Thanks to broadband communication, foreign media producers will distribute films and television programs directly to American consumers without having to pass by U.S. gatekeepers.[20]

Moreover, American companies have learned that to succeed abroad they must adapt to local cultural values and traditions rather than trying to force their own. CEO Jack Greenberg notes that McDonald's is "a decentralized entrepreneurial network of locally owned stores that is very flexible and adapts very well to local conditions. We offer an opportunity to entrepreneurs to run a local business with local people supplied by a local infrastructure." This concept is echoed on the McDonald's Web site and throughout its corporate culture. The company encourages franchisees to introduce menu items that reflect local tastes, including the Maharaja Mac (made of mutton) in India, the Tatsuta Burger in Japan, the McPork Burger with Thai Basil in Thailand, and the McTempeh Burger (made from fermented soybeans) in Indonesia. In fact, McDonald's restaurants in Bombay and Delhi feature a menu that is more than 75 percent locally developed.[21]

Similarly, Disneyland Paris flopped at first because it failed to take local cultural values and behaviors into account. Says Euro Disney Chief Executive Jay Rasulo, "When we first launched, there was the belief that it was enough to be Disney. Now we realize that our guests need to be welcomed on the basis of their own culture and travel habits." That realization, and the changes it spawned, has made Disneyland Paris the number one tourist attraction in Europe—even more popular than the Eiffel Tower. The park now attracts more the 12 million visitors each year. And Disney recently introduced a new movie-themed park to accompany the revitalized Paris attraction. The new park blends Disney entertainment and attractions with the history and culture of European film. A show celebrating the history of animation features Disney characters speaking six different languages. Rides are narrated by foreign-born stars, including Jeremy Irons, Isabella Rossellini, and Nastassja Kinski, speaking in their native tongues.[22]

Deciding Whether to Go International

Not all companies need to venture into international markets to survive. For example, most local businesses need to market well only in the local marketplace. Operating domestically is easier and safer. Managers need not learn another country's language and laws, deal with volatile currencies, face political and legal uncertainties, or redesign their products to suit different customer needs and expectations. However, companies that operate in global industries, where their strategic positions in specific markets are affected strongly by their overall global positions, must compete on a worldwide basis to succeed.

Any of several factors might draw a company into the international arena. Global competitors might attack the company's domestic market by offering better products or lower prices. The company might want to counterattack these competitors in their home markets to tie up their resources. Or the company might discover foreign markets that present higher profit opportunities than the domestic market does. The company's domestic market might be stagnant or shrinking, or the company might need an enlarged customer base in order to achieve economies of scale. The company might want to reduce its dependence on any one market so as to reduce its risk. Finally, the company's customers might be expanding abroad and require international servicing.

Before going abroad, the company must weigh several risks and answer many questions about its ability to operate globally. Can the company learn to understand the preferences and buyer behavior of consumers in other countries? Can it offer competitively attractive products? Will it be able to adapt to other countries' business cultures and deal effectively with foreign nationals? Do the company's managers have the necessary international experience? Has management considered the impact of regulations and the political environments of other countries?

Because of the risks and difficulties of entering international markets, most companies do not act until some situation or event thrusts them into the global arena. Someone—a domestic exporter, a foreign importer, a foreign government—may ask the company to sell abroad. Or the company may be saddled with overcapacity and need to find additional markets for its goods.

Deciding Which Markets to Enter

Before going abroad, the company should try to define its international *marketing objectives and policies*. It should decide what *volume* of foreign sales it wants. Most companies start small when they go abroad. Some plan to stay small, seeing international sales as a small part of their business. Other companies have bigger plans, seeing international business as equal to or even more important than their domestic business.

The company also needs to choose *how many* countries it wants to market in. Companies must be careful not to spread themselves too thin or to expand beyond their capabilities by operating in too many countries too soon. For example, although consumer products company Amway is now breaking into markets at a furious pace, it is doing so only after decades of gradually building up its overseas presence. Known for its neighbor-to-neighbor direct-selling networks, Amway expanded into Australia in 1971, a country far away but similar to the U.S. market. In the 1980s, Amway expanded into 10 more countries, and the pace increased rapidly from then on. By 1994, Amway was firmly established in 60 countries, including Hungary, Poland, and the Czech Republic. Following substantial success in Japan, China, and other Asian countries, the company entered India in 1998. Today, Amway sells its products in 90 countries and international proceeds contribute more than 70 percent of the company's overall revenues.[23]

Next, the company needs to decide on the *types* of countries to enter. A country's attractiveness depends on the product, geographical factors, income and population, political climate, and other factors. The seller may prefer certain country groups or parts of the world. In recent years, many major new markets have emerged, offering both substantial opportunities and daunting challenges (see Real Marketing 19.2).

real
marketing 19.2

Emerging Markets: China and Russia

As Eastern Europe and Asia reform their markets, and as the United States continues to dismantle its trade barriers, U.S. companies are eagerly anticipating the profits that await them. Here are "snapshots" of the opportunities and challenges that marketers face in two emerging markets: China and Russia.

China: 1.3 Billion Consumers

In Guangdong province, Chinese "yuppies" walk department store aisles to buy $95 Nike or Reebok sneakers and think nothing of spending $4 on a jar of Skippy peanut butter in the supermarket section. Although the average annual income amounts to only $360 per person, China's ever-growing pool of elite consumers still has plenty of spending money because of subsidized housing and health care and lots of savings under the mattress.

The prevalence of wide-screen televisions, fancy stereos, and home-karaoke

Emerging markets: Contemporary Russia—with its young, well-educated, cultured population and a booming, younger middle class— looks like a nifty place for American marketers. However, the newfound middle class is still fragile, fearing the next national economic calamity.

machines in Shanghai apartments suggests that this new upper middle class has more money than it admits to. . . . Among urban households, fewer than one in five households had a color television in 1985; today the average such home has more than one. Then, 7 percent had a refrigera-

tor; now 73 percent do. Cameras are four times more common. Among richer urban households, more than half now have a VCR, a pager, air conditioner, and shower, and nearly a third of households also own a mobile phone.

In Shenzen, Guangdong's second-largest city, consumers have the highest disposable income in all of China—$3,900 annually. With purchasing power like this, a population of 1.3 billion, and the fastest-growing economy in the world, China is encouraging companies from around the planet to set up shop there. Instead of the communist propaganda of yore, modern Chinese billboards exclaim, "Give China a chance." To further encourage foreign development, in December 2001 China joined the World Trade Organization and committed to lowering the barriers to entering the Chinese market.

Yet for all the market potential, there are many hurdles to clear in establishing businesses in China and marketing to the Chinese. For one, China is not one market but many, and regional governments may discriminate against certain goods. Distribution channels are undeveloped, consisting of thousands of tiny mom-and-pop stores that can afford to stock only a few bottles or packages at a time. And China's dismal infrastructure can turn a rail shipment traveling from Guanzhou to Beijing into a monthlong odyssey. Smart firms, such as Allied Signal and Kodak, try to jump these hurdles by partnering with Chinese government bodies or acquiring Chinese business partners who can help penetrate distribution channels and hire experienced personnel.

A major concern to some U.S. businesses has been China's distressing human rights record. Levi Strauss has turned its back on China's vast market for blue jeans because of such concerns. But other U.S. firms counter that industry can be part of the solution. "Supporting the business sector will result in

economic and political freedoms for the Chinese people," says a 3M spokesperson.

Russia: Many Opportunities, Many Pitfalls

Contemporary Russia certainly looks like a nifty place for American marketers: 150 million people; gross domestic product (GDP) growth of 7.2 percent last year; a young, well-educated, cultured population; a booming, younger middle class, many members of which are starting their own businesses.

Irina Lyakhnovskaya is a go-getter. Her hometown of Samara in central Russia straddles the Volga River and is surrounded by miles of fertile grassland and the Zhigulevskiye Mountains. Five years ago, she started a tourist company, with seed capital supplied by herself and three friends, that specializes in arranging hunting and fishing trips for visitors from Finland and Norway. She drives a Russian-made Lada that she purchased new for $3,500 two years ago, and she spends weekends at a country dacha that has an apple orchard she harvests to make her own wine. Last year she took vacations in Hungary and Romania, and this year she plans to get to Britain. In a country where the average factory worker is lucky to make $150 a month, she makes as much as $500. Lyakhnovskaya, 38, embodies a major shift in Russia's economic landscape. Boosted by a resurgent national economy and by its own bootstraps, a middle class is taking root in the former land of the proletariat. Analysts estimate 12 million to 30 million Russians, some 8 percent to 20 percent of the nation's 150 million population, qualify as middle class.

On the one hand, demographics and the economy—on the rebound from the 1998 crash—are converging to make Russia one of the more attractive emerging markets on the globe. Compared to other emerging markets, its population is more literate. Moreover, it's a population that embraces technology: Television penetration is high in Russia, the number of Internet users is rising 50 percent each year, and although industries such as two-way telecommunications are in their infancy, that's changing quickly.

(continued)

Still, Russia is not all sunshine and roses for American marketers. This fast-growing market also presents rampant corruption, a widespread lack of basic business controls, a barely liquid currency, and a business culture that, while increasingly capitalist, is definitely not American. Moreover, the new-found middle class is still fragile, fearing the prospect of a fresh national economic calamity. It's happened before. A fledgling middle class began to grow during the chaotic rein of Boris Yeltsin, only to see their fortunes wiped out by the economic crisis of 1998. "One new crisis, everything I have will be wiped out," says Lyakhnovskaya. All of this makes Russia an attractive but still tricky market in which to do business.

Russia is currently experiencing a retail invasion, especially in Moscow, where much of the country's population and wealth are concentrated. Moscow's population exceeds that of Belgium and Bulgaria combined, and Muscovites spend some $10 billion a year shopping for food and home furnishings, a third of the country's total spending in those categories. Muscovites are now filling their shopping carts to the brim with everything from futons to Camembert at the new stores.

Food companies have done especially well in Russia. McDonald's opened its first Russian restaurant in 1990 and now has 58 outlets there—the McDonald's in Moscow's Pushkin Square is the world's busiest. Companies in other industries are also making a push into this promising but chancy market. The world's auto companies see huge potential. By 2005, some analysts expect, Russia will become one of the world's largest automotive markets. Indeed, between 1991 and 1998, with the growth of the country's middle class, Russian auto sales skyrocketed 60 percent.

Leisure pursuits, once considered a luxury, have also trickled down to the middle class. Gold's Gym, which operates 560 gyms worldwide, opened one in Moscow in 1993 that now is one of the chain's solid performers. The Moscow facility has about 3,000 members, matching the company's average worldwide. The Moscow gym looks much like those in the United States, except that the signs are in Cyrillic. "If I were to show you a video of the Moscow gym, you'd think it was New York or Los Angeles," says a Gold's executive. "The women are gorgeous, and people are in good shape."

Although U.S. businesspeople may feel more at home in Russia now than at any time in that country's history, they still face the typical challenges of an emerging market. Beyond corruption and difficult currency, differences in culture and social habits can affect how business is done. For instance, Russians place much more value on hospitality than Americans. "They tend to be touchy-feely; there's lots of hugging," says a Russian trade expert. Eating and drinking with business prospects is also important, although Americans can sometimes get into trouble trying to match Russians drink for drink. (The solution? "Say up front that you can't drink for medical reasons," advises the trade expert.)

Sources: Portions of the Russian example adapted from Lisa Bertagnoli, "To Russia with . . . Reservations," *Marketing News,* April 9, 2001, pp. 1, 11. Quotes and other information in both examples from "Business: Not Quite a Billion," *The Economist,* January 2, 1999, p. 56; Paul Starobin, "Russia's Middle Class," *Business Week,* October 16, 2000, pp. 78–85; Sabrina Tavernise, "Moscow Is Getting a Taste of the Mall," *New York Times,* August 10, 2001, p. W1; Lisa Bertagnoli, "Red Square Rising," *Marketing News,* December 3, 2001, pp. 12–13; and Dexter Roberts and Alysha Webb, "Motor Nation," *Business Week,* June 17, 2002, pp. 44–45.

After listing possible international markets, the company must screen and rank each one. Consider the following example:

Many mass marketers dream of selling to China's more than 1.3 billion people. For example, Colgate is waging a pitched battle in China, seeking control of the world's largest toothpaste market. Yet, this country of infrequent brushers offers great potential. Only 20 percent of China's rural dwellers brush daily, so Colgate and its competitors are aggressively pursuing promotional and educational programs, from massive ad campaigns to visits to local schools to sponsoring oral care research. Through such efforts, in this $350 million market, Colgate has expanded its market share from 7 percent in 1995 to 35 percent today, despite competing with a state-owned brand managed by Unilever and P&G's Crest.[24]

Colgate's decision to enter the Chinese market seems fairly simple and straightforward: China is a huge market without established competition. Given the low rate of brushing, this already huge market can grow even larger. Yet we still can question whether market size *alone* is reason enough for selecting China. Colgate also must consider other factors: Will the Chinese government remain stable and supportive? Does China provide for the production and distribution technologies needed to produce and market Colgate's products profitably? Will Colgate be able to overcome cultural barriers and convince Chinese consumers to brush their teeth regularly? Can Colgate continue to compete effectively with dozens of local competitors? Colgate's current success in China suggests that it could answer yes to all of these questions. Still, the company's future in China is filled with uncertainties.

Possible global markets should be ranked on several factors, including market size, market growth, cost of doing business, competitive advantage, and risk level. The goal is to determine the potential of each market, using indicators such as those shown in Table 19.1. Then the marketer must decide which markets offer the greatest long-run return on investment.

TABLE 19.1	INDICATORS OF MARKET POTENTIAL

1. Demographic Characteristics	**4. Technological Factors**
Size of population	Level of technological skills
Rate of population growth	Existing production technology
Degree of urbanization	Existing consumption technology
Population density	Education levels
Age structure and composition of the population	
2. Geographic Characteristics	**5. Sociocultural Factors**
Physical size of a country	Dominant values
Topographical characteristics	Lifestyle patterns
Climate conditions	Ethnic groups
	Linguistic fragmentation
3. Economic Factors	**6. National Goals and Plans**
GDP per capita	Industry priorities
Income distribution	Infrastructure investment plans
Rate of growth of GNP	
Ratio of investment to GNP	

Source: Susan P. Douglas, C. Samuel Craig, and Warren Keegan, "Approaches to Assessing International Marketing Opportunities for Small- and Medium-Sized Businesses," *Columbia Journal of World Business,* Fall 1982, pp. 26–32. Copyright 1982, 1999, *Columbia Journal of World Business.* Reprinted with permission. Also see Pankaj Ghemawat, "Distance Still Matters," *Harvard Business Review,* September 2001, pp. 137–147.

Deciding How to Enter the Market

Once a company has decided to sell in a foreign country, it must determine the best mode of entry. Its choices are *exporting, joint venturing,* and *direct investment.* Figure 19.2 shows three market entry strategies, along with the options each one offers. As the figure shows, each succeeding strategy involves more commitment and risk, but also more control and potential profits.

Exporting

Exporting
Entering a foreign market by selling goods produced in the company's home country, often with little modification.

The simplest way to enter a foreign market is through **exporting.** The company may passively export its surpluses from time to time, or it may make an active commitment to expand exports to a particular market. In either case, the company produces all its goods in its home country. It may or may not modify them for the export market. Exporting involves the least change in the company's product lines, organization, investments, or mission.

Companies typically start with *indirect exporting,* working through independent international marketing intermediaries. Indirect exporting involves less investment because the firm does not require an overseas sales force or set of contacts. It also involves less risk. International marketing intermediaries—domestic-based export merchants or agents, cooperative organizations, and

FIGURE 19.2
Market entry strategies

export-management companies—bring know-how and services to the relationship, so the seller normally makes fewer mistakes.

Sellers may eventually move into *direct exporting*, whereby they handle their own exports. The investment and risk are somewhat greater in this strategy, but so is the potential return. A company can conduct direct exporting in several ways: It can set up a domestic export department that carries out export activities. It can set up an overseas sales branch that handles sales, distribution, and perhaps promotion. The sales branch gives the seller more presence and program control in the foreign market and often serves as a display center and customer service center. The company can also send home-based salespeople abroad at certain times in order to find business. Finally, the company can do its exporting either through foreign-based distributors who buy and own the goods or through foreign-based agents who sell the goods on behalf of the company.

Joint Venturing

Joint venturing

Entering foreign markets by joining with foreign companies to produce or market a product or service.

A second method of entering a foreign market is **joint venturing**—joining with foreign companies to produce or market products or services. Joint venturing differs from exporting in that the company joins with a host country partner to sell or market abroad. It differs from direct investment in that an association is formed with someone in the foreign country. There are four types of joint ventures: licensing, contract manufacturing, management contracting, and joint ownership.

Licensing

Licensing

A method of entering a foreign market in which the company enters into an agreement with a licensee in the foreign market, offering the right to use a manufacturing process, trademark, patent, trade secret, or other item of value for a fee or royalty.

Licensing is a simple way for a manufacturer to enter international marketing. The company enters into an agreement with a licensee in the foreign market. For a fee or royalty, the licensee buys the right to use the company's manufacturing process, trademark, patent, trade secret, or other item of value. The company thus gains entry into the market at little risk; the licensee gains production expertise or a well-known product or name without having to start from scratch.

Coca-Cola markets internationally by licensing bottlers around the world and supplying them with the syrup needed to produce the product. In Japan, Budweiser beer flows from Kirin breweries, Lady Borden ice cream is churned out at Meiji Milk Products dairies, and Marlboro cigarettes roll off production lines at Japan Tobacco, Inc. Online brokerage E*TRADE has set up E*TRADE-branded Web sites under licensing agreements in Canada, Australia/New Zealand, and France. And Tokyo Disneyland is owned and operated by Oriental Land Company under license from the Walt Disney Company. The 45-year license

Licensing: Tokyo Disneyland is owned and operated by the Oriental Land Co., Ltd. (a Japanese development company), under license from Walt Disney Company.

gives Disney licensing fees plus 10 percent of admissions and 5 percent of food and merchandise sales.[25]

Licensing has potential disadvantages, however. The firm has less control over the licensee than it would over its own production facilities. Furthermore, if the licensee is very successful, the firm has given up these profits, and if and when the contract ends, it may find it has created a competitor.

Contract Manufacturing

Contract manufacturing

A joint venture in which a company contracts with manufacturers in a foreign market to produce its product or provide its service.

Another option is **contract manufacturing**—the company contracts with manufacturers in the foreign market to produce its product or provide its service. Sears used this method in opening up department stores in Mexico and Spain, where it found qualified local manufacturers to produce many of the products it sells. The drawbacks of contract manufacturing are decreased control over the manufacturing process and loss of potential profits on manufacturing. The benefits are the chance to start faster, with less risk, and the later opportunity either to form a partnership with or to buy out the local manufacturer.

Management Contracting

Management contracting

A joint venture in which the domestic firm supplies the management know-how to a foreign company that supplies the capital; the domestic firm exports management services rather than products.

Under **management contracting,** the domestic firm supplies management know-how to a foreign company that supplies the capital. The domestic firm exports management services rather than products. Hilton uses this arrangement in managing hotels around the world.

Management contracting is a low-risk method of getting into a foreign market, and it yields income from the beginning. The arrangement is even more attractive if the contracting firm has an option to buy some share in the managed company later on. The arrangement is not sensible, however, if the company can put its scarce management talent to better uses or if it can make greater profits by undertaking the whole venture. Management contracting also prevents the company from setting up its own operations for a period of time.

Joint Ownership

Joint ownership

A joint venture in which a company joins investors in a foreign market to create a local business in which the company shares joint ownership and control.

Joint ownership ventures consist of one company joining forces with foreign investors to create a local business in which they share joint ownership and control. A company may buy an interest in a local firm, or the two parties may form a new business venture. Joint ownership may be needed for economic or political reasons. The firm may lack the financial, physical, or managerial resources to undertake the venture alone. Or a foreign government may require joint ownership as a condition for entry.

KFC entered Japan through a joint ownership venture with Japanese conglomerate Mitsubishi. KFC sought a good way to enter the large but difficult Japanese fast-food market. In turn, Mitsubishi, one of Japan's largest poultry producers, understood the Japanese culture and had money to invest. Together, they helped KFC succeed in the semiclosed Japanese market.

Joint ownership: KFC entered Japan through a joint ownership venture with Japanese conglomerate Matsushita.

Surprisingly, with Mitsubishi's guidance, KFC developed decidedly un-Japanese positioning for its Japanese restaurants:

> While its initial reception in Japan was great, KFC still had a number of obstacles to overcome. The Japanese were uncomfortable with the idea of fast food and franchising. They saw fast food as artificial, made by mechanical means, and unhealthy. KFC Japan knew that it had to build trust in the KFC brand and flew to Kentucky to do it. There it filmed the most authentic version of Colonel Sanders's beginnings possible. To show the philosophy of KFC—the southern hospitality, old American tradition, and authentic home cooking—the agency first created the quintessential southern mother. With "My Old Kentucky Home" by Stephen Foster playing in the background, the commercial showed Colonel Sanders's mother making and feeding her grandchildren KFC chicken made with 11 secret spices. It conjured up scenes of good home cookin' from the American South, positioning KFC as wholesome, aristocratic food. In the end, the Japanese people could not get enough of this special American chicken. The campaign was hugely successful, and in less than eight years KFC expanded its presence from 400 locations to more than 1,000. Most Japanese now know "My Old Kentucky Home" by heart.[26]

Joint ownership has certain drawbacks. The partners may disagree over investment, marketing, or other policies. Whereas many U.S. firms like to reinvest earnings for growth, local firms often prefer to take out these earnings; and whereas U.S. firms emphasize the role of marketing, local investors may rely on selling.

Direct Investment

Direct investment
Entering a foreign market by developing foreign-based assembly or manufacturing facilities.

The biggest involvement in a foreign market comes through **direct investment**—the development of foreign-based assembly or manufacturing facilities. If a company has gained experience in exporting and if the foreign market is large enough, foreign production facilities offer many advantages. The firm may have lower costs in the form of cheaper labor or raw materials, foreign government investment incentives, and freight savings. The firm may improve its image in the host country because it creates jobs. Generally, a firm develops a deeper relationship with government, customers, local suppliers, and distributors, allowing it to adapt its products to the local market better. Finally, the firm keeps full control over the investment and therefore can develop manufacturing and marketing policies that serve its long-term international objectives.

The main disadvantage of direct investment is that the firm faces many risks, such as restricted or devalued currencies, falling markets, or government changes. In some cases, a firm has no choice but to accept these risks if it wants to operate in the host country.

Deciding on the Global Marketing Program

Standardized marketing mix
An international marketing strategy for using basically the same product, advertising, distribution channels, and other elements of the marketing mix in all the company's international markets.

Adapted marketing mix
An international marketing strategy for adjusting the marketing-mix elements to each international target market, bearing more costs but hoping for a larger market share and return.

Companies that operate in one or more foreign markets must decide how much, if at all, to adapt their marketing mixes to local conditions. At one extreme are global companies that use a **standardized marketing mix,** selling largely the same products and using the same marketing approaches worldwide. At the other extreme is an **adapted marketing mix.** In this case, the producer adjusts the marketing mix elements to each target market, bearing more costs but hoping for a larger market share and return.

The question of whether to adapt or standardize the marketing mix has been much debated in recent years. The marketing concept holds that marketing programs will be more effective if tailored to the unique needs of each targeted customer group. If this concept applies within a country, it should apply even more in international markets. Consumers in different countries have widely varied cultural backgrounds, needs and wants, spending power, product preferences, and shopping patterns. Because these differences are hard to change, most marketers adapt their products, prices, channels, and promotions to fit consumer desires in each country.

However, global standardization is not an all-or-nothing proposition but rather a matter of degree. Companies should look for ways to standardize to help keep down costs and prices and to build greater global brand power. But they must not replace long-run marketing thinking with

Marketing mix adaptation: In India, McDonald's serves chicken, fish, vegetable burgers, and the Maharaja Mac—two all-mutton patties, special sauce, lettuce, cheese, pickles, onions, on a sesame-seed bun.

short-run financial thinking. Although standardization saves money, marketers must make certain that they offer what consumers in each country want.[27]

Many possibilities exist between the extremes of standardization and complete adaptation. For example, although Whirlpool ovens, refrigerators, clothes washers, and other major appliances share the same interiors worldwide, their outer styling and features are designed to meet the preferences of consumers in different countries. Coca-Cola sells virtually the same Coca-Cola Classic beverage worldwide, positioned to have broad cross-cultural appeal. However, Coca-Cola is less sweet or less carbonated in certain countries. The company also sells a wide variety of other beverages created specifically for local markets and modifies its distribution channels according to local conditions.

Similarly, McDonald's uses the same basic operating formula in its restaurants around the world but adapts its menu to local tastes. For example, it uses chili sauce instead of ketchup on its hamburgers in Mexico. In Vienna, its restaurants include "McCafes," which offer coffee blended to local tastes, and in Korea, it sells roast pork on a bun with a garlicky soy sauce. In India, where cows are considered sacred, McDonald's serves chicken, fish, vegetable burgers, and the Maharaja Mac—two all-mutton patties, special sauce, lettuce, cheese, pickles, onions on a sesame-seed bun.[28]

Some international marketers suggest that companies should "think globally but act locally." They advocate a "glocal" strategy in which the firm standardizes certain core marketing elements and localizes others. The corporate level gives strategic direction; local units focus on the individual consumer differences. They conclude: global marketing, yes; global standardization, not necessarily.

Product

Five strategies allow for adapting product and promotion to a global market (see Figure 19.3).[29] We first discuss the three product strategies and then turn to the two promotion strategies.

Straight product extension
Marketing a product in a foreign market without any change.

Straight product extension means marketing a product in a foreign market without any change. Top management tells its marketing people, "Take the product as is and find customers for it." The first step, however, should be to find out whether foreign consumers use that product and what form they prefer.

Straight extension has been successful in some cases and disastrous in others. Kellogg cereals, Gillette razors, IBM computer services, Heineken beer, and Black & Decker tools are all sold successfully in about the same form around the world. But General Foods introduced its standard powdered Jell-O in the British market only to find that British consumers prefer a solid wafer or

FIGURE 19.3

Five international product
and promotion strategies

cake form. Likewise, Philips began to make a profit in Japan only after it reduced the size of its coffeemakers to fit into smaller Japanese kitchens and its shavers to fit smaller Japanese hands. Straight extension is tempting because it involves no additional product development costs, manufacturing changes, or new promotion. But it can be costly in the long run if products fail to satisfy foreign consumers.

Product adaptation

Adapting a product to meet local conditions or wants in foreign markets.

   Product adaptation involves changing the product to meet local conditions or wants. For example, Procter & Gamble's Vidal Sassoon shampoos contain a single fragrance worldwide, but the amount of scent varies by country: less in Japan, where subtle scents are preferred, and more in Europe. General Foods blends different coffees for the British (who drink their coffee with milk), the French (who drink their coffee black), and Latin Americans (who prefer a chicory taste). Gerber serves the Japanese baby food fare that might turn the stomachs of many Western consumers—local favorites include flounder and spinach stew, cod roe spaghetti, mugwort casserole, and sardines ground up in white radish sauce. Finnish cellular phone maker Nokia customized its 6100 series phone for every major market. Developers built in rudimentary voice recognition for Asia where keyboards are a problem and raised the ring volume so the phone could be heard on crowded Asian streets.

   Even MTV, with its largely global programming, has retrenched along more local lines:

   Pummeled by dozens of local music channels in Europe, such as Germany's Viva, Holland's The Music Factory, and Scandinavia's ZTV, MTV Europe has had to drop its pan-European programming, which featured a large amount of American and British pop along with local European favorites. In its place, the division created regional channels broadcast by four separate MTV stations—MTV: U.K. & Ireland, MTV: Northern Europe, MTV: Central Europe, and MTV: Southern Europe. Each of the four channels shows programs tailored to the musical tastes of its local market, along with more traditional pan-European pop selections. Within each region, MTV further subdivides its programming. For example, within the U.K., MTV offers sister stations M2 and VH-1, along with three new digital channels: MTV Extra, MTV Base, and VH-1 Classic. Says the head of MTV Europe, "We hope to offer every MTV fan something he or she will like to watch any time of the day."[30]

   In some instances, products must also be adapted to local customs or spiritual beliefs. In Asia, the spiritual world often relates directly to sales. Hyatt Hotels' experience with the concept of *feng shui* is a good example:

   A practice widely followed in China, Hong Kong, and Singapore (and which has spread to Japan, Vietnam, and Korea), *feng shui* means "wind and water." Practitioners of *feng shui,* or geomancers, will recommend the most favorable conditions for any venture, particularly the placement of office buildings and the arrangement of desks, doors, and other items within. To have good *feng shui,* a building should face the water and be flanked by mountains. However, it should not block the view of the mountain spirits. The Hyatt Hotel in Singapore was designed without *feng shui* in mind, and as a result had to be redesigned to boost business. Originally the front desk was parallel to the doors and road, and this was thought to lead to wealth flowing out. Furthermore, the doors were facing northwest, which easily let undesirable spirits in. The geomancer recommended design alterations so that wealth could be retained and undesirable spirits kept out. Western businesses, from hotel chains, restaurants, and grocery retailers to Las Vegas casinos that serve many Asian visitors, are now incorporating *feng shui* principles into their facilities' designs.[31]

Product invention

Creating new products or services for foreign markets.

Product invention consists of creating something new for the foreign market. This strategy can take two forms. It might mean reintroducing earlier product forms that happen to be well adapted to the needs of a given country. The National Cash Register Company reintroduced its crank-operated cash register at half the price of a modern cash register and sold large numbers in Asia, Latin America, and Spain. Or a company might create a new product to meet a need in another country. For example, an enormous need exists for low-cost, high-protein foods in less developed countries. Companies such as Quaker Oats, Swift, Monsanto, and Archer Daniels Midland are researching the nutrition needs of these countries, creating new foods, and developing advertising campaigns to gain product trial and acceptance. Product invention can be costly but the payoffs are worthwhile.

Promotion

Companies can either adopt the same promotion strategy they used in the home market or change it for each local market. Consider advertising messages. Some global companies use a standardized advertising theme around the world. For example, to help communicate its global reach, IBM Global Services ran virtually identical "People Who Think. People Who Do. People Who Get It" ads in dozens of countries around the world. Of course, even in highly standardized promotion campaigns, some small changes might be required to adjust for language and minor cultural differences. For example, Guy Laroche uses virtually the same ads for its Drakkar Noir fragrances in Europe as in Arab countries. However, it subtly tones down the Arab versions to meet cultural differences in attitudes toward sensuality.

Colors also are changed sometimes to avoid taboos in other countries. Purple is associated with death in most of Latin America, white is a mourning color in Japan, and green is associated with jungle sickness in Malaysia. Even names must be changed. In Sweden, Helene Curtis changed the name of its Every Night Shampoo to Every Day because Swedes usually wash their hair in the morning. Kellogg also had to rename Bran Buds cereal in Sweden, where the name roughly translates as "burned farmer." (See Real Marketing 19.3 for more on language blunders in international marketing.)

Communication adaptation

A global communication strategy of fully adapting advertising messages to local markets.

Other companies follow a strategy of **communication adaptation,** fully adapting their advertising messages to local markets. Kellogg ads in the United States promote the taste and nutrition of Kellogg's cereals versus competitors' brands. In France, where consumers drink little milk and eat little for breakfast, Kellogg's ads must convince consumers that cereals are a tasty and

Some companies standardize their advertising around the world, adapting only to meet cultural differences. Guy LaRoche uses similar ads in Europe (left) and Arab countries (right), but tones down the sensuality in the Arab version—the man is clothed and the woman barely touches him.

real marketing 19.3

Watch Your Language!

Many global companies have had difficulty crossing the language barrier, with results ranging from mild embarrassment to outright failure. Seemingly innocuous brand names and advertising phrases can take on unintended or hidden meanings when translated into other languages. Careless translations can make a marketer look downright foolish to foreign consumers.

We've all run across examples when buying products from other countries. Here's one from a firm in Taiwan attempting to instruct children on how to install a ramp on a garage for toy cars: "Before you play with, fix waiting plate by yourself as per below diagram. But after you once fixed it, you can play with as is and no necessary to fix off again." Many U.S. firms are guilty of such atrocities when marketing abroad.

The classic language blunders involve standardized brand names that do not translate well. When Coca-Cola first marketed Coke in China in the 1920s, it developed a group of Chinese characters that, when pronounced, sounded like the product name. Unfortunately, the characters actually translated to mean "bite the wax tadpole." Now, the characters on Chinese Coke bottles translate as "happiness in the mouth."

Several U.S. carmakers have had similar problems when their brand names crashed into the language barrier. Chevy's Nova translated into Spanish as *no va*—"it doesn't go." GM changed the name to Caribe and sales increased. Ford introduced its Fiera truck only to discover that the name means "ugly old woman" in Spanish. And Rolls-Royce avoided the name Silver Mist in German markets, where *mist* means "manure." Sunbeam, however, entered the German market with its Mist Stick hair curling iron. As should have been expected, the

Germans had little use for a "manure wand." A similar fate awaited Colgate when it introduced a toothpaste in France called Cue, the name of a notorious porno magazine.

One well-intentioned firm sold its shampoo in Brazil under the name Evitol. It soon realized it was claiming to sell a "dandruff contraceptive." An American company reportedly had trouble marketing Pet milk in French-speaking areas. It seems that the word *pet* in French means, among other things, "to break wind." Hunt-Wesson introduced its Big John products in Quebec as Gros Jos before learning that it means "big breasts" in French. This gaffe had no apparent effect on sales. Interbrand of London, the firm that created household names such as Prozac and Acura, recently developed a brand-name "hall of shame" list, which contained these and other foreign brand names you're never likely to see inside the local A&P: Krapp toilet paper (Denmark), Crapsy Fruit cereal (France), Happy End toilet paper (Germany), Mukk yogurt (Italy), Zit lemonade (Germany), Poo curry powder (Argentina), and Pschitt lemonade (France).

Travelers often encounter well-intentioned advice from service firms that takes on meanings very different from those intended. The menu in one Swiss restaurant proudly stated, "Our wines leave you nothing to hope for." Signs in a Japanese hotel pronounced, "You are invited to take advantage of the chambermaid." At a laundry in Rome, it was, "Ladies, leave your clothes here and spend the afternoon having a good time." The brochure at a Tokyo car rental offered this sage advice: "When passenger of foot heave in sight, tootle the horn. Trumpet him melodiously at first, but if he still obstacles your passage, tootle him with vigor."

Advertising themes often lose—or gain—something in the translation. The Coors beer slogan "get loose with Coors" in Spanish came out as "get the runs with Coors." Coca-Cola's "Coke adds life" theme in Japanese translated into "Coke brings your ancestors back from the dead." The milk industry learned too late that its American advertising question "Got Milk?" translated in Mexico as a more provocative "Are you lactating?" In Chinese, the KFC slogan "finger-lickin' good" came out as "eat your fingers off." And Frank Perdue's classic line, "It takes a tough man to make a tender chicken," took on added meaning in Spanish: "It takes an aroused man to make a chicken affectionate." Even when the language is the same, word usage may differ from country to country. Thus, the British ad line for Electrolux vacuum cleaners— "Nothing sucks like an Electrolux"—would capture few customers in the United States.

Sources: See David A. Ricks, "Perspectives: Translation Blunders in International Business," *Journal of Language for International Business,* 7:2, 1996, pp. 50–55; David W. Helin, "When Slogans Go Wrong," *American Demographics,* February 1992, p. 14; "But Will It Sell in Tulsa?" *Newsweek,* March 17, 1997, p. 8; "What You Didn't Learn in Marketing 101," *Sales & Marketing Management,* May 1997, p. 20; Ken Friedenreich, "The Lingua Too Franca," *World Trade,* April 1998, p. 98; Richard P. Carpenter, "What They Meant to Say Was . . . ," *Boston Globe,* August 2, 1998, p. M6; Thomas T. Sermon, "Cutting Corners in Language Risky Business," *Marketing News,* April 23, 2001, p. 9; and Lara L Sowinski, "Ubersetzung, Traduzione, or Traduccion," *World Trade,* February 2002, pp. 48–49.

---

healthful breakfast. In India, where many consumers eat heavy, fried breakfasts, Kellogg's advertising convinces buyers to switch to a lighter, more nutritious breakfast diet. Similarly, Coca-Cola sells its low-calorie beverage as Diet Coke in North America, the United Kingdom, and the Middle and Far East but as Light elsewhere. According to Diet Coke's global brand manager, in Spanish-speaking countries Coke Light ads "position the soft drink as an object of desire, rather than as a way to feel good about yourself, as Diet Coke is positioned in the United States." This "desire positioning" plays off research showing that "Coca-Cola Light is seen in other parts of world as a vibrant brand that exudes a sexy confidence."[32]

Media also need to be adapted internationally because media availability varies from country to country. TV advertising time is very limited in Europe, for instance, ranging from four hours a day in France to none in Scandinavian countries. Advertisers must buy time months in advance, and they have little control over airtimes. Magazines also vary in effectiveness. For example, magazines are a major medium in Italy and a minor one in Austria. Newspapers are national in the United Kingdom but are only local in Spain.[33]

Price

Companies also face many problems in setting their international prices. For example, how might Black & Decker price its power tools globally? It could set a uniform price all around the world, but this amount would be too high a price in poor countries and not high enough in rich ones. It could charge what consumers in each country would bear, but this strategy ignores differences in the actual costs from country to country. Finally, the company could use a standard markup of its costs everywhere, but this approach might price Black & Decker out of the market in some countries where costs are high.

Regardless of how companies go about pricing their products, their foreign prices probably will be higher than their domestic prices. A Gucci handbag may sell for $60 in Italy and $240 in the United States. Why? Gucci faces a *price escalation* problem. It must add the cost of transportation, tariffs, importer margin, wholesaler margin, and retailer margin to its factory price. Depending on these added costs, the product may have to sell for two to five times as much in another country to make the same profit. For example, a pair of Levi's jeans that sells for $30 in the United States typically fetches $63 in Tokyo and $88 in Paris. A computer that sells for $1,000 in New York may cost £1,000 in the United Kingdom. A DaimlerChrysler automobile priced at $10,000 in the United States sells for more than $47,000 in South Korea.

Another problem involves setting a price for goods that a company ships to its foreign subsidiaries. If the company charges a foreign subsidiary too much, it may end up paying

International pricing: Twelve European Union countries have adopted the euro as a common currency, creating "pricing transparency" and forcing companies harmonize their prices throughout Europe.

higher tariff duties even while paying lower income taxes in that country. If the company charges its subsidiary too little, it can be charged with *dumping*. Dumping occurs when a company either charges less than its costs or less than it charges in its home market. Thus, Harley-Davidson accused Honda and Kawasaki of dumping motorcycles on the U.S. market. The U.S. International Trade Commission agreed and responded with a special five-year tariff on Japanese heavy motorcycles, starting at 45 percent in 1983 and gradually dropping to 10 percent by 1988. Various governments are always watching for dumping abuses, and they often force companies to set the price charged by other competitors for the same or similar products.[34]

Recent economic and technological forces have had an impact on global pricing. For example, in the European Union, the transition to the euro is reducing the amount of price differentiation. As consumers recognize price differentiation by country, companies are being forced to harmonize prices throughout the countries that have adopted the single currency. Companies and marketers that offer the most unique or necessary products or services will be least affected by such "price transparency."

> For Marie-Claude Lang, a 72-year-old retired Belgian postal worker, the euro is the best thing since bottled water—or French country sausage. Always on the prowl for bargains, Ms. Lang is now stalking the wide aisles of an Auchan hypermarket in Roncq, France, a 15-minute drive from her Wervick home. . . . Ms. Lang has been coming to France every other week for years to stock up on bottled water, milk, and yogurt. But the launch of the euro . . . has opened her eyes to many more products that she now sees cost less across the border. Today she sees that "saucisse de campagne," is cheaper "by about five euro cents," a savings she didn't notice when she had to calculate the difference between Belgian and French francs. At Europe's borders, the euro is turning into the coupon clipper's delight. Sure, price-conscious Europeans have long crossed into foreign territory to find everything from cheaper television sets to bargain bottles of Coca-Cola. But the new transparency is making comparisons a whole lot easier.[35]

The Internet will also make global price differences more obvious. When firms sell their wares over the Internet, customers can to see how much products sell for in different countries. They might even be able to order a given product directly from the company location or dealer offering the lowest price. This will force companies toward more standardized international pricing.

Distribution Channels

Whole-channel view

Designing international channels that take into account all the necessary links in distributing the seller's products to final buyers, including the seller's headquarters organization, channels among nations, and channels within nations.

The international company must take a **whole-channel view** of the problem of distributing products to final consumers. Figure 19.4 shows the three major links between the seller and the final buyer. The first link, the *seller's headquarters organization*, supervises the channels and is part of the channel itself. The second link, *channels between nations*, moves the products to the borders of the foreign nations. The third link, *channels within nations*, moves the products from their foreign entry point to the final consumers. Some U.S. manufacturers may think their job is done once the product leaves their hands, but they would do well to pay more attention to its handling within foreign countries.

Channels of distribution within countries vary greatly from nation to nation. First, there are the large differences in the *numbers and types of intermediaries* serving each foreign market. For example, a U.S. company marketing in China must operate through a frustrating maze of state-controlled wholesalers and retailers. Chinese distributors often carry competitors' products and frequently refuse to share even basic sales and marketing information with their suppliers.

FIGURE 19.4

Whole-channel concept for international marketing

A "neighborhood committee" member sells Coke in Shanghai.

Hustling for sales is an alien concept to Chinese distributors, who are used to selling all they can obtain. Working with or getting around this system sometimes requires substantial time and investment.

When Coke first entered China, for example, customers bicycled up to bottling plants to get their soft drinks. Many shopkeepers still don't have enough electricity to run soft drink coolers. Now, Coca-Cola has set up direct-distribution channels, investing heavily in refrigerators and trucks, and upgrading wiring so that more retailers can install coolers. Still, most of its products in China are sold through large state-owned sugar, tobacco, and wine enterprises or through former state-owned wholesale distributors that have now been privatized.[36] Moreover, Coke is always on the lookout for innovative distribution approaches:

> Stroll through any residential area in a Chinese city and sooner or later you'll encounter a senior citizen with a red armband eyeing strangers suspiciously. These are the pensioners who staff the neighborhood committees, which act as street-level watchdogs for the ruling Communist Party. In Shanghai, however, some of these socialist guardians have been signed up by the ultimate symbol of American capitalism, Coca-Cola. As part of its strategy to get the product to the customer, Coke approached 14 neighborhood committees . . . with a proposal. The head of Coke's Shanghai division outlines the deal: "We told them, 'You have some old people who aren't doing much. Why don't we stock our product in your office? Then you can sell it, earn some commission, and raise a bit of cash.'" Done. So . . . how are the party snoops adapting to the market? Not badly, reports the manager. "We use the neighborhood committees as a sales force," he says. Sales aren't spectacular, but because the committees supervise housing projects with up to 200 families, they have proved to be useful vehicles for building brand awareness.[37]

Another difference lies in the *size and character of retail units* abroad. Whereas large-scale retail chains dominate the U.S. scene, much retailing in other countries is done by many small, independent retailers. In India, millions of retailers operate tiny shops or sell in open markets. Their markups are high, but the actual price is lowered through haggling. Supermarkets could offer lower prices, but supermarkets are difficult to build and open because of many economic and cultural barriers. Incomes are low, and people prefer to shop daily for small amounts rather than weekly for large amounts. They also lack storage and refrigeration to keep food for several days. Packaging is not well developed because it would add too much to the cost. These factors have kept large-scale retailing from spreading rapidly in developing countries.

Deciding on the Global Marketing Organization

Companies manage their international marketing activities in at least three different ways: Most companies first organize an export department, then create an international division, and finally become a global organization.

A firm normally gets into international marketing by simply shipping out its goods. If its international sales expand, the company organizes an *export department* with a sales manager and a few assistants. As sales increase, the export department can expand to include various marketing services so that it can actively go after business. If the firm moves into joint ventures or direct investment, the export department will no longer be adequate.

Many companies get involved in several international markets and ventures. A company may export to one country, license to another, have a joint ownership venture in a third, and own a subsidiary in a fourth. Sooner or later it will create an *international division* or subsidiary to handle all its international activity.

International divisions are organized in a variety of ways. The international division's corporate staff consists of marketing, manufacturing, research, finance, planning, and personnel specialists. They plan for and provide services to various operating units, which can be organized in one of three ways. They can be *geographical organizations,* with country managers who are responsible for salespeople, sales branches, distributors, and licensees in their respective countries. Or the operating units can be *world product groups,* each responsible for worldwide sales of different product groups. Finally, operating units can be *international subsidiaries,* each responsible for its own sales and profits.

Many firms have passed beyond the international division stage and become truly *global organizations.* They stop thinking of themselves as national marketers who sell abroad and start thinking of themselves as global marketers. The top corporate management and staff plan worldwide manufacturing facilities, marketing policies, financial flows, and logistical systems. The global operating units report directly to the chief executive or executive committee of the organization, not to the head of an international division. Executives are trained in worldwide operations, not just domestic *or* international. The company recruits management from many countries, buys components and supplies where they cost the least, and invests where the expected returns are greatest.

Moving into the twenty-first century, major companies must become more global if they hope to compete. As foreign companies successfully invade their domestic markets, companies must move more aggressively into foreign markets. They will have to change from companies that treat their international operations as secondary, to companies that view the entire world as a single borderless market.

LOOKING BACK: REVIEWING THE CONCEPTS

It's time to stop and think back about the global marketing concepts you've covered in this chapter. In the past, U.S. companies paid little attention to international trade. If they could pick up some extra sales through exporting, that was fine. But the big market was at home, and it teemed with opportunities. Companies today can no longer afford to pay attention only to their domestic market, regardless of its size. Many industries are global industries, and firms that operate globally achieve lower costs and higher brand awareness. At the same time, *global marketing* is risky because of variable exchange rates, unstable governments, protectionist tariffs and trade barriers, and several

other factors. Given the potential gains and risks of international marketing, companies need a systematic way to make their global marketing decisions.

1. Discuss how the international trade system, economic, political-legal, and cultural environments affect a company's international marketing decisions.

A company must understand the *global marketing environment,* especially the international trade system. It must assess each foreign market's *economic, political-legal,* and *cultural characteristics.* The company must then decide whether it wants to go abroad and consider the potential risks and benefits. It must decide on the volume of international sales it wants, how many countries it wants to market in, and which specific markets it wants to enter. This decision calls for weighing the probable rate of return on investment against the level of risk.

2. Describe three key approaches to entering international markets.

The company must decide how to enter each chosen market—whether through *exporting, joint venturing,* or *direct investment.* Many companies start as exporters, move to joint ventures, and finally make a direct investment in foreign markets. In *exporting,* the company enters a foreign market by sending and selling products through international marketing intermediaries (indirect exporting) or the company's own department, branch, or sales representative or agents (direct exporting). When establishing a *joint venture,* a company enters foreign markets by joining with foreign companies to produce or market a product or service. In *direct investment,* the company enters a foreign market by developing foreign-based assembly or manufacturing facilities.

3. Explain how companies adapt their marketing mixes for international markets.

Companies must also decide how much their products, promotion, price, and channels should be adapted for each foreign market. At one extreme, global companies use a *standardized marketing mix* worldwide. Others use an *adapted marketing mix,* in which they adjust the marketing mix to each target market, bearing more costs but hoping for a larger market share and return.

4. Identify the three major forms of international marketing organization.

The company must develop an effective organization for international marketing. Most firms start with an *export department* and graduate to an *international division.* A few become *global organizations,* with worldwide marketing planned and managed by the top officers of the company. Global organizations view the entire world as a single, borderless market.

REVIEWING THE KEY TERMS

Adapted marketing mix 612
Communication adaptation 615
Contract manufacturing 611
Countertrade 602
Direct investment 612
Economic community 599
Embargo 598
Exchange controls 598

Exporting 609
Global firm 596
Joint ownership 611
Joint venturing 610
Licensing 610
Management contracting 611
Nontariff trade barriers 598
Product adaptation 614

Product invention 615
Quota 598
Standardized marketing mix 612
Straight product extension 613
Tariff 598
Whole-channel view 618

DISCUSSING THE CONCEPTS

1. The world is shrinking rapidly with the advent of faster communication, transportation, and financial flows. The terms *global industry* and *global firm* are becoming more common. Define these terms and provide an example of each.

2. When exporting goods to a foreign country, a marketer may be faced with various trade restrictions. Discuss the effects that each of these restrictions might have on an exporter's marketing mix: (a) tariffs, (b) quotas, and (c) embargoes.

3. What is a free trade zone? What benefits and drawbacks does NAFTA offer to each of its member nations? Why have U.S. trade unions traditionally lobbied against NAFTA?

4. A country's industrial structure shapes its product and service needs, income levels, and employment levels. Briefly describe the four major types of industrial structures.

5. Countertrade makes up an estimated 20 percent of world trade. Describe countertrade and its various forms. What are the advantages and disadvantages of countertrade in its various forms?

6. Before going abroad, a company should try to define its international marketing objectives, policies, and modes of entry. Assume that you are a product manager for Nike soccer products. Outline a brief plan for expanding your sales and marketing efforts into the country of South Africa.

7. Once a company has decided to sell in a foreign country, it must determine the best mode of entry. Assume you are the marketing manager for Mountain Dew, and devise a plan for marketing your product in China. Pick a mode of entry, explain your marketing strategy, and comment on the possible difficulties you might encounter.

8. Which type of international marketing organization would you suggest for the following companies: (a) Ty, which intends to open a new division to sell its Beanie Babies globally, (b) a European perfume firm that plans to expand into the United States, and (c) DaimlerChrysler, which plans to sell its full line of products in the Middle East.

APPLYING THE CONCEPTS

1. What area of the United States has the highest concentration of tuberculosis? Where in the United States is the population increasing at twice the national average? Where is the largest Wal-Mart in the United States located? The answer to all these questions: along the border between the United States and Mexico. This huge and often desolate part of America stretches from San Diego, California, in the west to Brownsville, Texas, in the east. It is a complicated maze of contradictions: poverty, a high incidence of drug trafficking, and an immigration problem of staggering proportions on the one hand; merging cultures, wealth, and great manufacturing and trade opportunities on the other hand. Wal-Mart read the border facts correctly and built its largest domestic store in boarder town Laredo, Texas, where both U.S. and Mexican cultures trade in profitable harmony. Marketers have found that moving goods and services across the border can be highly profitable and benefit the economies of both countries. Good jobs, cheap labor, quality products, affordable products, and the spirit of cooperation are all discussed by the two countries' leaders in trade talks that occur on an increasingly frequent basis. To learn more about the problems and challenges of the "border market," examine the following Web sites: (a) Center for International Business Education and Research—Michigan State University (http://ciber.bus.msu.edu/busres.htm), (b) International Trade Association (www.ita.doc.gov), (c) The 2001 World Fact Book—a CIA publication (www.odci.gov/cia/publications/factbook/index.html), (d) The World Bank (www.worldbank.org), (e) the World Trade Organization (www.wto.org), and (f) Cyberatlas (www.cyberatlas.internet.com).

    a. How could a manager seeking information about the Mexico–United States international market use the above reference sites to find needed data?

    b. What were the most interesting facts you learned about the United States–Mexico border market?

    c. How could the information you discovered at the Web sites be converted into opportunities for market expansion?

2. Nowhere is international competition more apparent than in the digital camera market. Overnight, the advent of digital cameras changed the way photographers view their craft. Digital cameras offer opportunities for reproduction and Internet viewing unmatched by more traditional models. However, the market is uncharted, chaotic, and increasingly crowded with more than 20 manufacturers competing worldwide. The latest entrant is film giant Fuji (www.fujifilm.com). As the world's number two film producer, Fuji now plans to meet or beat Kodak (www.kodak.com), Sony (www.sony.com), Olympus (www.olympus.com), and Konica (www.konica.com) in digital camera products. Fuji introduced its first digital cameras in its own backyard—Japan—which is also a Sony stronghold. One factor motivating the move into digital cameras was Fuji's inability to erode Kodak's worldwide share of the film market. If the wave of the future in cameras turns out to be digital, Fuji plans to ride the wave's crest for as long as it can.

    a. Analyze Fuji's strategy to enter the digital camera market. What challenges will the company face? How might Fuji's traditional strengths in film aid its efforts in the new market?

    b. What world markets should Fuji consider after Japan?

    c. If you were the marketing manager of Fuji, what advertising strategy would you recommend for the new venture? What distribution strategy? What role will price play in the success of the strategy?

    d. What actions might Kodak, Sony, Olympus, and Konica take to counter Fuji's entry?

 DIGITAL CONNECTIONS

BRINGING VALUE TO THE GLOBAL CONSUMER

Technology lovers have long looked to Japan for the next big innovation. The latest high-growth product to come from Japan is "i-mode," NTT DoCoMo's multimedia service that has over 34 million subscribers after only three years of operation. The i-mode service provides cell phone users with a variety of services including e-mail, information search and news distribution services, and games. The company believes it has transformed the way Japanese customers use mobile phone services and personal communication devices. Having successfully penetrated the Japanese market, the company is looking to Europe for its future success. Are you ready to i-mode?

FOR DISCUSSION

1. Visit NTT DoCoMo's Web site at www.nttdocomo.com. Briefly summarize the services provided by i-mode technology.

2. What international partnerships did NTT DoCoMo use to bring i-mode to Europe? How did those partnerships impact the company's success and add value for consumers?

3. As a marketing manager with AT&T (www.att.com), you believe that i-mode technology might help the company compete against Sprint's (www.sprint.com) new PCS Vision phone system. Write a brief memo to your superior outlining why i-mode is worth investigating. Be sure to point out advantages and disadvantages with respect to Sprint's new product. Close the memo by indicating how i-mode would bring value to your customers.

Idiom: Translating Culture in Cyberspace

Some assume that going global is as simple as setting up a Web site. But companies are finding that keeping up with multiple sites that target international markets can be troublesome. That's where Idiom steps in. Idiom's WorldServer software manages the content of international Web sites. The software translates changes made to a central Web site and applies the changes to multinational sites, keeping content consistent while taking into account differences in languages, local regulations, currencies, and cultures. The goal is to ensure that customers around the world have consistently high-quality experiences with companies like Xerox, Lycos, MasterCard, Staples, Oracle, and Charles Schwab. But can software translate culture?

After viewing the Idiom video, visit Idiom's Web site at www.idiom.com. Then answer the following questions about global marketing:

1. WorldServer software translates new content by relying on a series of rules set by the user. What are the benefits of using such software? What are the drawbacks? Can software reliably translate language and culture?
2. How might Idiom's services alter the way a company decides which markets to enter and how to enter them?
3. Is e-commerce the best way to reach out to global markets? What are the benefits of approaching globalization through e-commerce? What are the limitations?

Wal-Mart: *The Global Retailer*

Wal-Mart is the world's largest retailer. In fact, it's the world's largest *company,* with sales last year totaling nearly $220 billion. Of that total, $35.5 billion were from the fast-growing Wal-Mart International Division. Wal-Mart is growing at an incredible clip, both at home and abroad. In the early 1990s, its sales were a little less than $85 billion; it had 2,200 stores and no international division. Today, it has over 3,200 stores, with about 1,100 of them outside the United States. Even though Wal-Mart continues to open stores in the United States, the biggest opportunity for future growth lies in international expansion.

Wal-Mart first "went abroad" to Canada when it purchased 122 Canadian Woolco stores in 1993. By mid-2002, it had 196 stores in Canada, where it was ranked the best retailer and the ninth best company for which to work. Following its move north, the retailing giant turned south into Mexico, using joint ventures and sometimes buying companies outright. Wal-Mart opened its first Mexican store in 1991. By mid-2002, it had opened 66 supercenters, 47 Sam's Clubs, 454 Superama supermarkets, 51 Suburbia Apparel outlets, 245 restaurants under the Vips division, and 110 Bodego units carrying a limited assortment of discount merchandise. In the first half of 2002, sales in Mexico

totaled $4.9 billion, and the company announced plans to add 60 new stores in Mexico by the end of 2003. Obviously, Mexico has been a big success for Wal-Mart.

From Mexico, Wal-Mart moved to another Latin market, Puerto Rico. During the next 10 years, Wal-Mart opened 11 more Puerto Rican stores. In 2002 it announced that it would buy Supermercados Amigo, Puerto Rico's second largest grocery retailer. After the purchase, Wal-Mart would have 47 stores and an estimated $1.5 billion in Puerto Rican sales. Sensing a good market, Wal-Mart intended to invest $400 million more in Puerto Rico in the next five years.

Next, it was on to South America. In late 1995, Wal-Mart established stores in Brazil and Argentina. These have been Wal-Mart's most disappointing ventures in the western hemisphere. For one thing, the Argentinean economy is troubled; Argentina's presidency seems to be a revolving door, and inflation is spiraling upward. There's not much Wal-Mart can do about these environmental factors, but it has maintained 11 stores there in the hopes that the economic picture will eventually turn around. The picture in Brazil is a little brighter. There, Wal-Mart has 12 supercenters, 8 Sam's Clubs, and 2 small-format stores called "Todo

(continued)

Dia." Future investment in Brazil may follow the Todo Dia format of 45,000-square-foot stores selling general merchandise. These smaller stores enable Wal-Mart to enter crowded Brazilian neighborhoods where they could never locate a supercenter.

From Latin America, Wal-Mart moved into Asia. Wal-Mart's first stop in Southeast Asia was Hong Kong, where it entered a joint venture with Ek Chor Distribution System Co. Ltd. to establish Value Clubs. Because Ek Chor is actually owned by C. P. Pokphand of Bangkok, Wal-Mart was then able to locate in Thailand and Indonesia. Hong Kong was also a stepping stone to the world's most populous country, China. Wal-Mart opened its first Chinese store in 2000, operated 19 stores there by 2002, and plans to open 10 more there in 2003. It also operated 9 stores in South Korea (up from 4 in 1998), although growth potential there is not as good.

Wal-Mart has not overlooked Europe. In 1998, it bought the 21-unit Wertkauf chain in Germany; in 1999, it snapped up the 74-unit Interspar hypermarket chain from Spar Handel. Germany looked especially attractive because it is the third largest retail market in the world, behind the United States and Japan. From the start, however, Germany presented problems. Some of these involved real estate: strict zoning laws, scarcity of land, and high real estate prices. Another problem was well-entrenched unions, which were unlikely to allow their members to gather in the morning to respond to Wal-Mart's traditional "Give me a *W*; Give me an *A* . . ." motivational sessions. Another issue: retailing in Germany is dominated by a few large chains, generating intense competition. Finally, German consumers are among the most demanding in the world. Although not as price sensitive as consumers in some other countries, they are very quality conscious. This last point begs the question, Is Germany a good market for a discounter?

In fact, Germany has yet to work for Wal-Mart. By early 2002, the company was still experiencing losses across its 95 stores. In the summer of 2002, the retailer announced that it would close a store in Ingolstadt and merge two stores in Wilhelmshaven. Wal-Mart admits that it pursued too many initiatives too quickly in Germany and lost too many talented managers when the headquarters of acquired firms closed. But it will not give up on Germany and is tentatively eyeing more expansion possibilities there.

From Germany, Wal-Mart moved across the channel to the United Kingdom, where it bought the third largest U.K. grocery chain, ASDA. Why? Margins in the U.K. are among the highest in Europe, at 5 percent to 7 percent. The expansion into the U.K. has worked brilliantly—Wal-Mart now has 260 ASDA stores, which are its International Division's largest profit contributor. ASDA sales in 2001 contributed $15.3 billion of the company's $35.5 billion in international sales. With such strong growth, Wal-Mart plans to add 12 more U.K. stores in 2003.

What's in store for the future? Wal-Mart recently agreed to acquire 66.7 percent of Seiyu, Japan's fourth largest retail group. Ten years earlier, Wal-Mart had tried selling its private label cookies in Japanese stores, and consumers had grabbed them off the shelves. But they did not repeat their purchases because the cookies were too sweet and 30 to 40 percent of them were broken. Japan, like Germany, is a land of finicky shoppers.

Having learned this lesson in Germany, Wal-Mart is moving more slowly in Japan, meticulously studying consumer habits and preferences. However, Wal-Mart will face some serious challenges. Japanese consumers differ from the typical Wal-Mart shopper in other parts of the world. They want local merchandise, look for very fresh produce and fish, and are very detail oriented and want a lot of information about products. They want name brands, buy in small quantities—just a couple of days' worth of food at one time—and want items individually wrapped.

After Japan, there's Russia. In 2002, Wal-Mart began talks with ZAO Promyshlenno-Finanovaya Kompaniya BIN, which has 31 supermarkets across Russia with forecasted sales of $170 million. Wal-Mart would acquire 75 percent of the company's stock.

In all, what has Wal-Mart learned in its international ventures? It has learned a lot about store design. For example, not all locations or markets can accommodate large supercenters. However, the Neighborhood Market concept, first used in densely populated areas in Mexico, has been successfully transplanted elsewhere. For instance, the first Neighborhood Market in China was in Shenzhen. It was 27,000 square feet and located underground. Customers reach it by escalators from the busy street above.

Another lesson for Wal-Mart was in global sourcing. Global sourcing at Wal-Mart is not the same as global procurement—Wal-Mart has its own definition. There, global sourcing does not mean buying things. Instead, managers in Wal-Mart's global sourcing unit focus on categories of goods or items where there is an opportunity to improve quality, lower price, or gain efficiencies on a worldwide or regional basis. First, they identify basic products that people use all over the world, and then they look for opportunities to improve supply. Next, they work with producers to improve quality or lower price. Afterwards, the improved product is made available to all managers around the world. It is the managers who make the purchase decision.

An example of successful global sourcing is Wal-Mart's success with copy paper. It first worked with a supplier to improve value to the customer through better-quality paper. As a result, sales of copy paper increased by 46 percent in the U.K., 94 percent in Germany, 38 percent in Canada, and 25 percent in the United States. In the end, Wal-Mart wound up with only one supplier of copy paper, but that isn't always the case. When global sourcing managers investigated sources of bananas, they reduced the number of suppliers to three, not just one.

Global sourcing does not always mean lost sales for some suppliers. Sometimes it can mean almost instant global sales. Take the case of Oxyclean, a household cleaner. Originally sold only in the United States, it was later offered to stores elsewhere. By the end of the year, it was being sold in virtually every country where Wal-Mart operates. This is why suppliers are so keen to work with Wal-Mart. They might have to shave their costs, but the return in global sales can be enormous. What's more, Wal-Mart picks up the distribution tab.

Recently, Wal-Mart created an "in-country global sourcing champion" program. Designated in-country sourcing champions locate new items and promote them to Wal-Mart. Once that happens, Wal-Mart brings merchants from around the world to a summit meeting where they can learn about new products. The company gets the managers' buy-in and feedback so that, once they leave, they become champions of new products. In addition to ensuring that merchants are on board with new products, the summits also foster communication and the study of best practices. A recent summit featured food managers from ASDA because ASDA is a superior retailer of food. The ASDA people shared their ideas, which could then be used in other countries to enhance food retailing.

Innovative management practices, such as global sourcing and the constant sharing of ideas, have helped to make the Wal-Mart the largest worldwide retailer—and also the best.

QUESTIONS FOR DISCUSSION

1. Does Wal-Mart standardize or adapt its marketing strategy around the globe? How does the global sourcing initiative support its marketing strategy?
2. Strictly defined, a global firm is one that looks at its operations from a worldwide perspective rather than from the perspective of its country of origin. In your opinion, is Wal-Mart a truly global firm?
3. In which countries has Wal-Mart done well? Can you identify any common traits across these countries that might account for Wal-Mart's success?
4. Wal-Mart has not been successful in Germany. If you were a consultant to Wal-Mart, what recommendations would you make for the retailer's German operations?
5. In your opinion, will Wal-Mart be successful in Japan and Russia? Why or why not?
6. To what countries should Wal-Mart expand next? What factors are important in making this decision? Be prepared to defend the countries that you choose.

Sources: "Mexico: Wal-Mart Mexico Earnings Rise 9 Percent," *IPR Strategic Business Information Database,* July 17, 2002; "Wal-Mart Set to Take on Russian Chain," *Grocer,* June 22, 2002, p. 16; "Wal-Mart to Buy Stakes in Japanese Chain," *Home Textiles Today,* May 27, 2002, p. 2; "Japan Company: Wal-Mart Develops a Taste for Japan," *Country ViewsWire,* May 3, 2002; "DJ: Wal-Mart January Sales," *FWN Select,* February, 7, 2002; Laura Heller, "Latin Market Never Looked So Bueno," *DSN Retailing Today,* June 10, 2002, p. 125+; Laura Heller, "Southern Hemisphere Woes Persist," *DSN Retailing Today,* June 10, 2002, p. 126; Victor Homola, "Germany: Wal-Mart Closings," *New York Times,* July 11, 2002, p. 1; Mike Troy, "Global Reach Gets Broader Every Day," *DSN Retailing Today,* June 10, 2002, p. 117+; Mike Troy, "Foothold in the Orient Keeps Growing," *DSN Retailing Today,* June 10, p. 121; and Mike Troy, "Continental Divide: U.K. OK, but Germany Still Ailing," *DSN Retailing Today,* June 10, 2002, p. 118.

1. identify the major social criticisms of marketing
2. define *consumerism* and *environmentalism* and explain how they affect marketing strategies
3. describe the principles of socially responsible marketing
4. explain the role of ethics in marketing

Marketing and Society

SOCIAL RESPONSIBILITY AND MARKETING ETHICS

LOOKING AHEAD: PREVIEWING THE CONCEPTS

In this final chapter, we'll focus on marketing as a social institution. First, we'll look at some common criticisms of marketing as it impacts individual consumers, other businesses, and society as a whole. Then, we'll examine consumerism, environmentalism, and other citizen and public actions to keep marketing in check. Finally, we'll see how companies themselves can benefit from proactively pursuing socially responsible and ethical practices. You'll see that social responsibility and ethical actions are more than just the right thing to do; they're also good for business.

Before moving on, let's visit the concept of social responsibility in business. Over the past 25 years, companies such as Ben & Jerry's and The Body Shop have pioneered the idea of "values-led business" or "caring capitalism"—putting "principles ahead of profits." But *can* a company dedicated to doing good still do well? *Can* it successfully serve a "double bottom line"—values *and* profits?

Chances are, when you hear the term *socially responsible business*, a handful of companies—and their founders—leap to mind, companies such as Ben & Jerry's Homemade (Ben Cohen, Jerry Greenfield) and The Body Shop International (Anita Roddick). Such social revolutionaries pioneered the concept of "values-led business" or "caring capitalism." Their mission: Use business to make the world a better place.

Ben Cohen and Jerry Greenfield founded Ben & Jerry's Homemade in 1978 as a company that cared deeply about its social and environmental responsibilities. It bought only hormone-free milk and cream and used only organic fruits and nuts to make its ice cream, which it sold in environmentally friendly containers. It went to great lengths to buy from minority and disadvantaged suppliers. From its early Rainforest Crunch to its most recent One Sweet Whirled flavors and awareness campaigns, Ben & Jerry's has championed a host of social and environmental causes over the years. From the start, Ben & Jerry's donated a whopping 7.5 percent of pre-tax profits to support projects that exhibited "creative problem solving and hopefulness . . . relating to children and families, disadvantaged groups, and the environment." By the mid-1990s, Ben & Jerry's had become the nation's number two superpremium ice cream brand.

Anita Roddick opened The Body Shop in 1976 with a similar mission: "to dedicate our business to the pursuit of social and environmental change." The company manufactured and retailed natural-ingredient-based cosmetics in simple and appealing recyclable packaging. All products were formulated without any animal testing, and supplies were often sourced from developing countries. Roddick became a vocal advocate for putting "passion before profits," and The Body Shop, which now operates nearly 1,850 stores in 47 countries, donates a percentage of profits each year to animal-rights groups, homeless shelters, Amnesty International, Save the Rain Forest, and other social causes.

Both companies set up shop in the late 1970s and grew fast and furiously through the 1980s and early 1990s. However, as competitors not shackled by their "principles before profits" missions invaded their markets, growth and profits flattened. In recent years, both Ben & Jerry's and The Body Shop have struggled. In 2000, after several years of less than stellar financial returns, Ben & Jerry's was acquired by giant food producer Unilever. And Anita Roddick recently handed over The Body Shop's reins to a more business-savvy turnaround team, taking the role of consultant.

What happened to the founders' lofty ideals of caring capitalism? Looking back, both companies may have focused on social issues at the expense of sound business management. Neither Ben Cohen nor Anita Roddick really wanted to be businesspeople. In fact, according to one analyst, Cohen and Roddick "saw businesspeople as tools of the military-industrial complex and profits as a dirty word." Cohen once commented, "There came a time [when I had to admit] 'I'm a businessman.'

And I had a hard time mouthing those words." Likewise, Roddick admitted, "A lot of us would have slit our wrists if we ever thought we'd be part of corporate America or England. Big business was alien to me."

Having a "double bottom line" of values and profits is no easy proposition. In the words of one especially harsh critic, "Ben and Jerry want to use ice cream to solve the world's problems. They call it running a values-led business; I call it a mess. Operating a business is tough enough. Once you add social goals to the demands of serving customers, making a profit, and returning value to shareholders, you tie yourself up in knots." For sure, it's often difficult to take good intentions to the bank.

The experiences of the 1980s revolutionaries taught the socially responsible business movement some hard lessons. The result is a new generation of activist entrepreneurs—not social activists with big hearts who hate capitalism, but well-trained business managers and company builders with a passion for a cause. According to a recent *Inc* article, here are some of the lessons:

- *What you sell is important:* The product or service, not just the mission, must be socially responsible. Hence, Honest Tea Inc. markets barely sweetened iced tea and totally biodegradable tea bags; WorldWise Inc. offers garden, home, and pet products made from recycled or organic materials; Sustainable Harvest Inc. sells organic, shade-grown coffee with a guaranteed base price for growers; CitySoft Inc. does Web development using urban workers; Wild Planet Toys Inc. creates nonsexist, nonviolent toys; and Village Real Estate Services revitalizes communities and neighborhoods.

- *Be proud to be in business:* Unlike the 1980s revolutionaries, the new young founders are businesspeople—and proud of it—and all appreciate solid business training. Honest Tea founder Seth Goldman won a business-plan competition as a student at the Yale School of Management and later started the company with one of his professors. Wild Planet CEO Daniel Grossman has an MBA from the Stanford Business School. Sustainable Harvest's David Griswold hires business school graduates because he believes that success "really depends on competing, using the rules of business. Good deeds alone don't work."

- *Make a solid commitment to change:* Cohen and Greenfield stumbled into making ice cream to make ends meet; Roddick owned a small hotel in England before opening her first store. By contrast the new social entrepreneurs' companies are a natural outgrowth of their long-held values. For example, Wild Planet's Grossman served for eight years in the U.S. Foreign Service. David Griswold co-founded and ran Aztec Harvest, a sales-and-marketing outfit for farmer-owned Mexican coffee cooperatives. And CitySoft CEO Nick Gleason was a community and labor organizer in Oakland, California, and ran his own urban-development consulting company, serving nonprofits, foundations, school districts, and governments.

- *Focus on two bottom lines:* Today's social entrepreneurs are just as dedicated to building a viable, profitable business as to shaping a mission. WorldWise's Lamstein comments, "You can't be successful if you can't do both." Lamstein's strategy for getting WorldWise up and running, built around the concept of environmentally responsible products, illustrates such double-bottom-line thinking. "Our whole concept was that our products had to work as well as or better than others, look as good or finer, cost the same or less, and be better for the environment," says Lamstein. Honest Tea's Goldman agrees: "A commitment to socially responsible business cannot be used as an excuse to make poor business decisions. If we were to accept lower margins, then we'd be doing the . . . socially responsible business movement a disservice, because we wouldn't be as competitive or as attractive to investors."

- *Forget the hype:* For these socially responsible companies, it's not about marketing and image. They go about doing their good deeds quietly. Village Real Estate Services concentrates primarily on marketing its services, not on publicizing the company's Village Fund, which funds the revitalization of urban neighborhoods. Honest Tea buys the peppermint leaves for its First Nation tea from I'tchik Herbal Tea, a small woman-owned company on the Crow Reservation in Montana. I'tchik gets royalties from the sales of the tea, as does a Native American organization called Pretty Shield Foundation, which includes foster care among its activities. However, "when we first brought out our peppermint tea, our label didn't mention that we were sharing the revenues with the Crow Nation," says Goldman. "We didn't want people to think that was a gimmick."

It remains to be seen how these new socially responsible companies will fare down the road. Many are less than five years old and post sales from $2 million to $10 million. Ben & Jerry's, by contrast, has sales of some $150 million (down from more than $350 million at its peak), and cash registers in The Body Shop stores rang up nearly $1 billion in sales last year. Still, this much is clear: Social responsibility for the recent crop of company founders—at least at this early date—seems to be not about them nor even about their companies. It's about the mission.[1]

Responsible marketers discover what consumers want and respond with marketing offers that give satisfaction and value to buyers and profit to the producer. The *marketing concept* is a philosophy of customer satisfaction and mutual gain. Its practice leads the economy by an invisible hand to satisfy the many and changing needs of millions of consumers.

Not all marketers follow the marketing concept, however. In fact, some companies use questionable marketing practices, and some marketing actions that seem innocent in themselves strongly affect the larger society. Consider the sale of cigarettes. On the face of it, companies should be free to sell cigarettes and smokers should be free to buy them. But this transaction affects the public interest. First, the smokers are harming their health and may be shortening their own lives. Second, smoking places a financial burden on the smoker's family and on society at large. Third, other people around smokers may suffer discomfort and harm from secondhand smoke. Finally, marketing cigarettes to adults might also influence young people to begin smoking. Thus, the marketing of tobacco products has sparked substantial debate and negotiation in recent years.[2] This example shows that private transactions may involve larger questions of public policy.

This chapter examines the social effects of private marketing practices. We examine several questions: What are the most frequent social criticisms of marketing? What steps have private citizens taken to curb marketing ills? What steps have legislators and government agencies taken to curb marketing ills? What steps have enlightened companies taken to carry out socially responsible and ethical marketing? We examine how marketing affects and is affected by each of these issues.

Social Criticisms of Marketing

Marketing receives much criticism. Some of this criticism is justified; much is not. Social critics claim that certain marketing practices hurt individual consumers, society as a whole, and other business firms.

Marketing's Impact on Individual Consumers

Consumers have many concerns about how well the American marketing system serves their interests. Surveys usually show that consumers hold mixed or even slightly unfavorable attitudes toward marketing practices. Consumers, consumer advocates, government agencies, and other critics have accused marketing of harming consumers through high prices, deceptive practices, high-pressure selling, shoddy or unsafe products, planned obsolescence, and poor service to disadvantaged consumers.

High Prices

Many critics charge that the American marketing system causes prices to be higher than they would be under more "sensible" systems. They point to three factors—*high costs of distribution, high advertising and promotion costs,* and *excessive markups.*

High Costs of Distribution. A long-standing charge is that greedy intermediaries mark up prices beyond the value of their services. Critics charge that there are too many intermediaries, that intermediaries are inefficient and poorly run, or that they provide unnecessary or duplicate services. As a result, distribution costs too much, and consumers pay for these excessive costs in the form of higher prices.

How do resellers answer these charges? They argue that intermediaries do work that would otherwise have to be done by manufacturers or consumers. Markups reflect services that consumers themselves want—more convenience, larger stores and assortment, longer store hours, return privileges, and others. Moreover, the costs of operating stores keep rising, forcing retailers to raise their prices. In fact, they argue, retail competition is so intense that margins are actually quite low. For example, after taxes, supermarket chains are typically left with barely 1 percent profit on their sales. If some resellers try to charge too much relative to the value they add, other resellers will step in with lower prices. Low-price stores such as Wal-Mart, Best Buy, and other discounters pressure their competitors to operate efficiently and keep their prices down.

High Advertising and Promotion Costs. Modern marketing is also accused of pushing up prices to finance heavy advertising and sales promotion. For example, a dozen tablets of a heavily promoted brand of aspirin sell for the same price as 100 tablets of less promoted brands. Differentiated products—cosmetics, detergents, toiletries—include promotion and packaging costs that can amount to 40 percent or more of the manufacturer's price to the retailer. Critics charge that much of the packaging and promotion adds only psychological value to the product

A heavily promoted brand of antacid sells for much more than a virtually identical non-branded or store-branded product. Critics charge that promotion adds only psychological value to the product rather than functional value.

rather than functional value. Retailers use additional promotion—advertising, displays, and sweepstakes—that adds several cents more to retail prices.

Marketers respond that consumers can usually buy functional versions of products at lower prices. However, they *want* and are willing to pay more for products that also provide psychological benefits—that make them feel wealthy, attractive, or special. Brand name products may cost more, but branding gives buyers assurances of consistent quality. Heavy advertising adds to product costs but adds value by informing millions of potential buyers of the availability and merits of a brand. If consumers want to know what is available on the market, they must expect manufacturers to spend large sums of money on advertising. Also, heavy advertising and promotion may be necessary for a firm to match competitors' efforts—the business would lose "share of mind" if it did not match competitive spending. At the same time, companies are cost-conscious about promotion and try to spend their money wisely.

Excessive Markups.   Critics also charge that some companies mark up goods excessively. They point to the drug industry, where a pill costing 5 cents to make may cost the consumer $2 to buy. They point to the pricing tactics of funeral homes that prey on the confused emotions of bereaved relatives and to the high charges for television repair and auto repair.

Marketers respond that most businesses try to deal fairly with consumers because they want repeat business. Most consumer abuses are unintentional. When shady marketers do take advantage of consumers, they should be reported to Better Business Bureaus and to state and federal agencies. Marketers also respond that consumers often don't understand the reasons for high markups. For example, pharmaceutical markups must cover the costs of purchasing, promoting, and distributing existing medicines plus the high research and development costs of formulating and testing new medicines.

Deceptive Practices

Marketers are sometimes accused of deceptive practices that lead consumers to believe they will get more value than they actually do. Deceptive practices fall into three groups: deceptive pricing, promotion, and packaging. *Deceptive pricing* includes practices such as falsely advertising "factory" or "wholesale" prices or a large price reduction from a phony high retail list price. *Deceptive promotion* includes practices such as overstating the product's features or performance, luring the customer to the store for a bargain that is out of stock, or running rigged contests. *Deceptive packaging* includes exaggerating package contents through subtle design, not filling the package to the top, using misleading labeling, or describing size in misleading terms.

Questionable marketing practices: Sweepstakes promoter Publishers Clearing House recently paid heavily to settle claims that its high-pressure tactics had misled consumers into believing that they had won prizes when they hadn't.

To be sure, questionable marketing practices do occur. For example, at one time or another, we've all gotten an envelope in the mail screaming something like "You have won $10,000,000!" or a pop-up Web screen promising free goods or discounted prices. In recent years, sweepstakes companies have come under the gun for their deceptive communication practices. Sweepstakes promoter Publishers Clearing House recently paid heavily to settle claims that its high-pressure tactics had misled consumers into believing that they had won prizes when they hadn't. The Wisconsin Attorney General asserts that "there are older consumers who send [sweepstakes companies] checks and money orders on a weekly basis with a note that says they were very upset that the prize patrol did not come."[3]

Deceptive practices have led to legislation and other consumer protection actions. For example, in 1938 Congress reacted to such blatant deceptions as Fleischmann's Yeast's claim to straighten crooked teeth by enacting the Wheeler-Lea Act giving the Federal Trade Commission (FTC) power to regulate "unfair or deceptive acts or practices." The FTC has published several guidelines listing deceptive practices. The toughest problem is defining what is "deceptive." For example, Palm recently agreed to settle Federal Trade Commission accusations that ads for the company's handheld computers were deceptive. The ads claimed the Palm's devices provide built-in wireless access to the Internet. Now this was true, but only for some models. Many Palm models did not provide such access without separate wireless modems and additional software. What's more, the ads failed to tell buyers that one model providing wireless Internet and e-mail access requires that users pay monthly subscription fees to the company's Palm.Net Internet service. Thus, although the information in the ads was technically true, omissions left some consumers with the wrong impressions. The FTC ordered Palm to "disclose, clearly and conspicuously, when consumers have to buy add-ons in order to perform advertised functions.[4]

Marketers argue that most companies avoid deceptive practices because such practices harm their business in the long run. If consumers do not get what they expect, they will switch to more reliable products. In addition, consumers usually protect themselves from deception. Most consumers recognize a marketer's selling intent and are careful when they buy, sometimes to the point of not believing completely true product claims.

One noted marketing thinker, Theodore Levitt, claims that some advertising puffery is bound to occur—and that it may even be desirable: "There is hardly a company that would not go down in ruin if it refused to provide fluff, because nobody will buy pure functionality. . . . Worse, it denies . . . people's honest needs and values. Without distortion, embellishment, and elaboration, life would be drab, dull, anguished, and at its existential worst."[5]

High-Pressure Selling

Salespeople are sometimes accused of high-pressure selling that persuades people to buy goods they had no thought of buying. It is often said that insurance, real estate, and cars are *sold*, not *bought*. Salespeople are trained to deliver smooth, canned talks to entice purchase. They sell hard because sales contests promise big prizes to those who sell the most.

Marketers know that buyers often can be talked into buying unwanted or unneeded things. Laws require door-to-door and telephone salespeople to announce that they are selling a product. Buyers also have a "three-day cooling-off period" in which they can cancel a contract after rethinking it. In addition, consumers can complain to Better Business Bureaus or to state consumer protection agencies when they feel that undue selling pressure has been applied.

But in most cases, marketers have little to gain from high-pressure selling. Such tactics may work in one-time selling situations for short-term gain. However, most selling involves building long-term relationships with valued customers. High-pressure or deceptive selling can do serious damage to such relationships. For example, imagine a Procter & Gamble account manager trying to pressure a Wal-Mart buyer, or an IBM salesperson trying to browbeat a General Electric information technology manager. It simply wouldn't work.

Shoddy or Unsafe Products

Another criticism is that products lack the quality they should have. One complaint is that many products are not made well and many services are not performed well. A second complaint is that many products deliver little benefit. For example, some consumers are surprised to learn that many of the "healthy" foods being marketed today, such as cholesterol-free salad dressings, low-fat frozen dinners, and high-fiber bran cereals, may have little nutritional value. In fact, they may even be harmful.

> [Despite] sincere efforts on the part of most marketers to provide healthier products, . . . many promises emblazoned on packages and used as ad slogans continue to confuse nutritionally uninformed consumers and . . . may actually be harmful to that group. . . . [Many consumers] incorrectly assume the product is "safe" and eat greater amounts than are good for them. . . . For example, General Foods USA's new Entenmann's "low-cholesterol, low-calorie" cherry coffee cake . . . may confuse some consumers who shouldn't eat much of it. While each serving is only 90 calories, not everyone realizes that the suggested serving is tiny [one-thirteenth of the small cake]. Although eating half an Entenmann's cake may be better than eating half a dozen Dunkin Donuts, . . . neither should be eaten in great amounts by people on restrictive diets.[6]

A third complaint concerns product safety. Product safety has been a problem for several reasons, including manufacturer indifference, increased production complexity, poorly trained labor, and poor quality control. For years, Consumers Union—the nonprofit testing and information organization that publishes the *Consumer Reports* magazine and Web site—has reported various hazards in tested products: electrical dangers in appliances, carbon monoxide poisoning from room heaters, injury risks from lawn mowers, and faulty automobile design, among many others. The organization's testing and other activities have helped consumers make better buying decisions and encouraged businesses to eliminate product flaws (see Real Marketing 20.1).

However, most manufacturers *want* to produce quality goods. The way a company deals with product quality and safety problems can damage or help its reputation. Companies selling poor-quality or unsafe products risk damaging conflicts with consumer groups and regulators. Moreover, unsafe products can result in product liability suits and large awards for damages. More fundamentally, consumers who are unhappy with a firm's products may avoid future purchases and talk other consumers into doing the same. Consider what happened to Bridgestone/Firestone following its recent recall of 6.5 million flawed Firestone tires. Product liability and safety concerns have driven the company to the edge of backruptcy:

> Profits have disappeared, and both customers and tire dealers alike are fleeing the Firestone make. Ford, the tire maker's biggest customer, recently announced plans to replace another 13 million

real marketing 20.1

When *Consumer Reports* Talks, Buyers Listen

For more than 65 years, *Consumer Reports* has given buyers the lowdown on everything from sports cars to luggage to lawn sprinklers. Published by Consumers Union, the nonprofit product-testing organization, the magazine's mission can be summed up by CU's motto: Test, Inform, Protect. With more than 4 million subscribers and several times that many borrowers, as dog-eared library copies will attest, *Consumer Reports* is one of the nation's most-read magazines. Its companion Web site, Consumer Reports Online (www.consumerreports.org), established in 1997, is the Web's largest paid-subscriber site, with 350,000 users.

Beyond being one of the most-read publications, *Consumer Reports* is also one of the most influential. In 1988, when its car testers rated Suzuki's topple-prone Samurai as "not acceptable"—meaning don't even take one as a gift—sales plunged 70 percent the following month. More recently, when it raved about Saucony's Jazz 3000 sneaker, sales doubled, leading to nationwide shortages.

Although some may view *Consumer Reports* as a deadly dull shopper's guide to major household appliances, it does a lot more than rate cars and refrigerators. It has looked at almost anything consumable—from mutual funds, home mortgages, and public health policies to retirement communities and prostate surgery. When a recent Consumers Union study found that that less than one-third of consumers trust e-commerce Web sites, the organization launched Consumer WebWatch (www.consumerwebwatch.org). The project's mission is "to investigate, inform, and improve the credibility of information published on the World Wide Web." The site gives ratings on everything from the disclosure of transaction fees and business partnerships to the publication of privacy policies and the labeling of pop-up ads.

In the 1930s, Consumers Union was one of the first organizations to urge a boycott of products imported from Nazi Germany, and it's been calling for nationalized health care since 1937. In the 1950s, it warned the nation that fallout from nuclear tests was contaminating milk supplies. In the 1960s and 1970s, it prodded carmakers to install seat belts, then air bags.

Yet the magazine is rarely harsh or loud. Instead, it's usually understated, and it can even be funny. The very first issue, in 1936, noted that Lifebuoy soap was itself so smelly that it simply overwhelmed your B.O. with L.O. And what reader didn't delight to find in a 1990 survey of soaps that the most expensive bar, Eau de Gucci at 31 cents per handwashing, wound up dead last in a blind test.

Consumer Reports users clearly appreciate CU, its magazine, and its Web sites. It is unlikely that any other organization in the world could have raised $17 million toward a new building simply by asking users for donations. To avoid even the appearance of bias, CU has a strict no-ads, no-freebies policy. It buys all of its product samples on the open market and anonymously. CU's steadfast editorial independence has made *Consumer Reports* the bible of consumerism. "We're very single-minded about who we serve," says Rhoda Karpatkin, CU's recently retired president. "We serve the consumer."

A visit to CU's maze of labs confirms the thoroughness with which CU's testers carry out their mission. A chemist performs a cholesterol extraction test on a small white blob in a beaker: a ground-up piece of Turkey enchilada, you are told. Elsewhere you find

Consumers Union carries out its testing mission: Suitcases bang into one another inside the huge "mechanical gorilla," and a staffer coats the interiors of self-cleaning ovens with a crusty concoction called "monster mash."

(continued)

the remains of a piston-driven machine called Fingers that added 1 + 1 on pocket calculators hundreds of thousands of times or until the calculators failed, whichever came first. You watch suitcases bang into one another inside a huge contraption—affectionately dubbed the "Mechanical Gorilla"—that looks like an eight-foot-wide clothes dryer.

Down the hall in the appliance department, a pair of "food soilers" will soon load 20 dishwashers with identical sets of dirty dishes. A sample dinner plate is marked off with scientific precision into eight wedge-shaped sections, each with something different caked on it—dried spaghetti, spinach, chipped beef, or something else equally difficult to clean. Next door, self-cleaning ovens are being tested, their interiors coated with a crusty substance—called "Monster Mash" by staffers—that suggests month-old chili sauce. The recipe includes tapioca, cheese, lard, grape jelly, tomato sauce, and cherry pie filling—mixed well and baked one hour at 425 degrees. If an oven's self-cleaning cycle doesn't render the resulting residue into harmless-looking ash, 4 million readers will be so informed.

Some of the tests that CU runs are standard tests, but many are not. Several years ago, in a triumph of low-tech creativity, CU's engineers stretched paper towels across embroidery hoops, moistened the center of each with exactly 10 drops of water, then poured lead shot into the middle. The winner held seven pounds of shot; the loser, less than one. Who could argue with that? There is an obvious logic to such tests, and the results are plainly quantifiable.

From the start, *Consumer Reports* has generated controversy. The second issue dismissed the Good Housekeeping Seal of Approval as nothing more than a fraudulent ploy by publisher William Randolph Hearst to reward loyal advertisers. *Good Housekeeping* responded by accusing CU of prolonging the Depression. To the business community, *Consumer Reports* was at first viewed as a clear threat to the American way of doing business. During its early years, more than 60 advertising-dependent publications, including the *New York Times, Newsweek,* and the *New Yorker,* refused to accept *Consumer Reports'* subscription ads.

In 1939, in a move that would seem ludicrous today, Congress's new House UnAmerican Activities Committee (then known as the Dies Committee) branded CU a subversive organization. However, the controversy has more often helped than hurt subscriptions. And through the years, only 13 makers of panned products have filed suit against CU challenging findings unfavorable to their products. To this day Consumers Union has never lost or settled a libel suit.

Sources: Portions adapted from Doug Stewart, "To Buy or Not to Buy, That Is the Question at *Consumer Reports,*" *Smithsonian,* September 1993, pp. 34–43. Other quotes and information from Robin Finn, "Still Top Dog, Consumers' Pitt Bull to Retire," *New York Times,* October 5, 2000, p. B2; Barbara Quint, "Consumers Union Launches Consumer WebWatch," *Information Today,* June 2002, p. 48; and the Consumers Union Web site at www.consumersunion.org and the Consumer Reports Online site at www.consumerreports.org, August 2002.

Firestone tires that it believes are unsafe. "You have a serious risk of the Firestone brand imploding," warns an industry analyst. How bad will the financial hit get? Cutting ties with Ford will cost the company 4 percent of its $7.5 billion in revenues—about 40 percent of its sales to car companies. Mounting damages awards from rollover suits and legal bills could easily top the company's $463 million legal reserve. And if the National Highway Traffic and Safety Administration supports Ford's latest recall, Firestone could find itself liable for much of the $3 billion cost.[7]

Thus, quality missteps can have severe consequences. Today's marketers know that customer-driven quality results in customer satisfaction, which in turn creates profitable customer relationships.

Planned Obsolescence

Critics also have charged that some producers follow a program of planned obsolescence, causing their products to become obsolete before they actually should need replacement. For example, critics charge that some producers continually change consumer concepts of acceptable styles to encourage more and earlier buying. An obvious example is constantly changing clothing fashions.

Other producers are accused of holding back attractive functional features, then introducing them later to make older models obsolete. Critics claim that this occurs in the consumer electronics and computer industries. For example, Intel and Microsoft have been accused in recent years of holding back their next-generation computer chips and software until demand is exhausted for the current generation. Still other producers are accused of using materials and components that will break, wear, rust, or rot sooner than they should. One writer put it this way: "The marvels of modern technology include the development of a soda can which, when discarded, will last forever—and a . . . car, which, when properly cared for, will rust out in two or three years."[8]

Marketers respond that consumers *like* style changes; they get tired of the old goods and want a new look in fashion or a new design in cars. No one has to buy the new look, and if too few people like it, it will simply fail. For most technical products, customers *want* the latest innovations, even if older models still work. Companies that withhold new features run the risk that

Product safety: Following its recall of 6.5 million flawed Firestone tires, product liability and safety concerns have driven Bridgestone/Firestone to the brink of bankruptcy.

competitor will introduce the new feature first and steal the market. For example, consider personal computers. Some consumers grumble that the consumer electronics industry's constant push to produce "faster, smaller, cheaper" models means that they must continually buy new machines just to keep up. Others, however, can hardly wait for the latest model to arrive.

> There was a time not so long ago when planned obsolescence was a troubling ghost in the machine. Four decades ago, consumer advocates described engineers at General Electric who intentionally shortened the life of lightbulbs and automotive engineers who proposed limiting the life span of cars. That was then. In today's topsy-turvy world of personal computers, obsolescence is not only planned, it is extolled by marketers as a principal virtue. Moreover, there has been hardly a peep from consumers, who dutifully line up to buy each new generation of faster, more powerful machines, eager to embrace the promise of simpler, happier, and more productive lives. Today's computer chips are no longer designed to wear out; in fact, they will last for decades or longer. Even so, hapless consumers now rush back to the store ever more quickly, not to replace broken parts but to purchase new computers that will allow them to talk longer, see more vivid colors, or play cooler games.[9]

Thus, companies do not design their products to break down earlier, because they do not want to lose customers to other brands. Instead, they seek constant improvement to ensure that products will consistently meet or exceed customer expectations. Much of so-called planned obsolescence is the working of the competitive and technological forces in a free society—forces that lead to ever-improving goods and services.

Poor Service to Disadvantaged Consumers

Finally, the American marketing system has been accused of poorly serving disadvantaged consumers. For example, critics claim that the urban poor often have to shop in smaller stores that carry inferior goods and charge higher prices. A Consumers Union study compared the food-shopping habits of low-income consumers and the prices they pay relative to middle-income consumers in the same city. The study found that the poor do pay more for inferior goods. The results suggested that the presence of large national chain stores in low-income neighborhoods made a big difference in keeping prices down. However, the study also found evidence of "redlining," a type of economic discrimination in which major chain retailers avoid placing stores in disadvantaged neighborhoods.[10]

Similar redlining charges have been leveled at the insurance, consumer lending, and banking industries. Most recently, home and auto insurers have been accused of assigning higher premiums to people with poor credit ratings. The insurers claim that individuals with bad credit tend to make more insurance claims, and that this justifies charging them higher premiums. However, critics and consumer advocates have accused the insurers of a new form of redlining. Says one writer, "This is a new excuse for denying coverage to the poor, elderly, and minorities."[11]

More recently, lenders and other businesses have been accused of "Weblining," the Internet-age version of redlining:

> As never before, the Internet lets companies identify (or "profile") high- and low-value customers, so firms can decide which product deals, prices, and services it will offer. For the most valued customers, this can mean better information and discounts. Low-value customers may pay the most for the least and sometimes get left behind. In lending, olds-style redlining is unacceptable because it is based on geographic stereotypes, not concrete evidence that specific individuals are poor credit risks. Webliners may claim to have more evidence against the people they snub. But their classifications could also be based on irrelevant profiling data that marketing companies and others collect on the Web. How important to your mortgage status, say, is your taste in paperbacks, political discussion groups, or clothing? Yet all these far-flung threads are getting sewn into online profiles, where they are increasingly intertwined with data on your health, your education loans, and your credit history.[12]

Clearly, better marketing systems must be built to service disadvantaged consumers. Moreover, disadvantaged consumers clearly need consumer protection. The FTC has taken action against merchants who advertise false values, sell old merchandise as new, or charge too much for credit. The commission is also trying to make it harder for merchants to win court judgments against low-income people who were wheedled into buying something.

Marketing's Impact on Society As a Whole

The American marketing system has been accused of adding to several "evils" in American society at large. Advertising has been a special target—so much so that the American Association of Advertising Agencies launched a campaign to defend advertising against what it felt to be common but untrue criticisms.

The American Marketing Association runs ads to counter common advertising criticisms.

False Wants and Too Much Materialism

Critics have charged that the marketing system urges too much interest in material possessions. People are judged by what they *own* rather than by who they *are*. To be considered successful, people must own a large home, two cars, and the latest high-tech gadgets. This drive for wealth and possessions hit new highs in the 1980s, when phrases such as "greed is good" and "shop till you drop" seemed to characterize the times.

In the new millennium, even though many social scientists have noted a reaction against the opulence and waste of the previous decades and a return to more basic values and social commitment, our infatuation with material things continues.

It's hard to escape the notion that what Americans really value is stuff. Since 1987, we've had more shopping malls than high schools. We average six hours a week shopping and only forty minutes playing with our children. Our rate of saving is 2 percent—only a quarter of what it was in the 1950s, when we earned less than half as much in real dollars. In each of the past three years, more U.S. citizens have declared personal bankruptcy than have graduated from college. All this acquisition isn't making us happier; the number of Americans calling themselves "very happy" peaked in 1957.[13]

Nearly two-thirds of adults agree that wearing "only the best designer clothing" conveys status. Even more feel this way about owning expensive jewelry. Big homes are back in vogue, which means Americans have more space to fulfill their acquisitive fantasies, from master bathrooms doubling as spas and gyms to fully wired home entertainment centers.[14]

The critics do not view this interest in material things as a natural state of mind but rather as a matter of false wants created by marketing. Businesses hire Madison Avenue (where the headquarters of many advertising agencies are located) to stimulate people's desires for goods, and Madison Avenue uses the mass media to create materialistic models of the good life. People work harder to earn the necessary money. Their purchases increase the output of American industry, and industry in turn uses Madison Avenue to stimulate more desire for the industrial output. Thus, marketing is seen as creating false wants that benefit industry more than they benefit consumers.

These criticisms overstate the power of business to create needs, however. People have strong defenses against advertising and other marketing tools. Marketers are most effective when they appeal to existing wants rather than when they attempt to create new ones. Furthermore, people

Too much materialism: Our infatuation with material things continues. It's hard to escape the notion that what Americans really value is stuff.

seek information when making important purchases and often do not rely on single sources. Even minor purchases that may be affected by advertising messages lead to repeat purchases only if the product performs as promised. Finally, the high failure rate of new products shows that companies are not able to control demand.

On a deeper level, our wants and values are influenced not only by marketers but also by family, peer groups, religion, ethnic background, and education. If Americans are highly materialistic, these values arose out of basic socialization processes that go much deeper than business and mass media could produce alone. Moreover, some social critics even see materialism as a positive and rewarding force:

> When we purchase an object, what we really buy is meaning. Commercialism is the water we swim in, the air we breathe, our sunlight and our shade. . . . Materialism is a vital source of meaning and happiness in the modern world. . . . We have not just asked to go this way, we have demanded. Now most of the world is lining up, pushing and shoving, eager to elbow into the mall. Getting and spending has become the most passionate, and often the most imaginative, endeavor of modern life. While this is dreary and depressing to some, as doubtless it should be, it is liberating and democratic to many more.[15]

Too Few Social Goods

Business has been accused of overselling private goods at the expense of public goods. As private goods increase, they require more public services that are usually not forthcoming. For example, an increase in automobile ownership (private good) requires more highways, traffic control, parking spaces, and police services (public goods). The overselling of private goods results in "social costs." For cars, the social costs include traffic congestion, air pollution, and deaths and injuries from car accidents.

A way must be found to restore a balance between private and public goods. One option is to make producers bear the full social costs of their operations. The government could require automobile manufacturers to build cars with even more safety features and better pollution control systems. Automakers would then raise their prices to cover extra costs. If buyers found the price of some cars too high, however, the producers of these cars would disappear, and demand would move to those producers that could support the sum of the private and social costs.

A second option is to make consumers pay the social costs. A number of highway authorities around the world are starting to charge "congestion tolls" in an effort to reduce traffic congestion:

> Already, in Southern California, drivers are being charged premiums to travel in underused car pool lanes; Singapore, Norway, and France are managing traffic with varying tolls; peak surcharges are being studied for roads around New York, San Francisco, Los Angeles, and other cities. [Economists] point out that traffic jams are caused when drivers are not charged the costs they impose on others, such as delays. The solution: Make 'em pay.[16]

Interestingly, in San Diego, regular drivers can use the HOV (high-occupancy vehicle) lanes, but they must pay a price based on traffic usage at the time. The toll ranges from $.50 off-peak to $4.00 during rush hour.[17] If the costs of driving rise high enough, consumers will travel at non-peak times or find alternative transportation modes.

Cultural Pollution

Critics charge the marketing system with creating *cultural pollution*. Our senses are being constantly assaulted by advertising. Commercials interrupt serious programs; pages of ads obscure printed matter; billboards mar beautiful scenery. These interruptions continually pollute people's minds with messages of materialism, sex, power, or status. Although most people do not find advertising overly annoying (some even think it is the best part of television programming), some critics call for sweeping changes.

Marketers answer the charges of "commercial noise" with these arguments: First, they hope that their ads reach primarily the target audience. But because of mass-communication channels, some ads are bound to reach people who have no interest in the product and are therefore bored or annoyed. People who buy magazines addressed to their interests—such as *Vogue* or *Fortune*—rarely complain about the ads because the magazines advertise products of interest. Second, ads

Cultural pollution: Our senses are sometimes assaulted by commercial messages.

make much of television and radio free to users and keep down the costs of magazines and newspapers. Many people think commercials are a small price to pay for these benefits. Finally, today's consumers have alternatives. For example, they can zip and zap TV commercials or avoid them altogether on many cable or satellite channels. Thus, to hold consumer attention, advertisers are making their ads more entertaining and informative.

Too Much Political Power

Another criticism is that business wields too much political power. "Oil," "tobacco," "auto," and "pharmaceuticals" senators support an industry's interests against the public interest. Advertisers are accused of holding too much power over the mass media, limiting their freedom to report independently and objectively. One critic has asked, "How can [most magazines] afford to tell the truth about the scandalously low nutritional value of most packaged foods . . . when these magazines are being subsidized by such advertisers as General Foods, Kellogg's, Nabisco, and General Mills? . . . The answer is *they cannot and do not.*"[18]

American industries do promote and protect their own interests. They have a right to representation in Congress and the mass media, although their influence can become too great. Fortunately, many powerful business interests once thought to be untouchable have been tamed in the public interest. For example, Standard Oil was broken up in 1911, and the meatpacking industry was disciplined in the early 1900s after exposures by Upton Sinclair. Ralph Nader caused legislation that forced the automobile industry to build more safety into its cars, and the Surgeon General's Report resulted in cigarette companies putting health warnings on their packages.

More recently, giants such as AT&T, R.J. Reynolds, Intel, and Microsoft have felt the impact of regulators seeking to balance the interests of big business against those of the public. Moreover, because the media receive advertising revenues from many different advertisers, it is easier to resist the influence of one or a few of them. Too much business power tends to result in counterforces that check and offset these powerful interests.

Marketing's Impact on Other Businesses

Critics also charge that a company's marketing practices can harm other companies and reduce competition. Three problems are involved: acquisitions of competitors, marketing practices that create barriers to entry, and unfair competitive marketing practices.

Critics claim that firms are harmed and competition reduced when companies expand by acquiring competitors rather than by developing their own new products. The large number of acquisitions and rapid pace of industry consolidation over the past several decades have caused concern that vigorous young competitors will be absorbed and that competition will be reduced. In virtually every major industry—retailing, entertainment, financial services, utilities, transportation, automobiles, telecommunications, health care—the number of major competitors is shrinking. Consider the glut of acquisitions in the food industry during just the past two years: "The consolidation frenzy led to Unilever's buying Bestfoods, Philip Morris's snatching Nabisco, General Mills' swallowing Pillsbury, Kellogg's taking over Keebler and PepsiCo's seizing of Quaker Oats."[19]

Acquisition is a complex subject. Acquisitions can sometimes be good for society. The acquiring company may gain economies of scale that lead to lower costs and lower prices. A well-managed company may take over a poorly managed company and improve its efficiency. An industry that was not very competitive might become more competitive after the acquisition. But acquisitions can also be harmful and, therefore, are closely regulated by the government.

Critics have also charged that marketing practices bar new companies from entering an industry. Large companies can use patents and heavy promotion spending, and can tie up suppliers or dealers to keep out or drive out competitors. Those concerned with antitrust regulation recognize that some barriers are the natural result of the economic advantages of doing business on a large scale. Other barriers could be challenged by existing and new laws. For example, some critics have proposed a progressive tax on advertising spending to reduce the role of selling costs as a major barrier to entry.

Finally, some firms have in fact used unfair competitive marketing practices with the intention of hurting or destroying other firms. They may set their prices below costs, threaten to cut off business with suppliers, or discourage the buying of a competitor's products. Various laws work to prevent such predatory competition. It is difficult, however, to prove that the intent or action was really predatory. In recent years, Wal-Mart, American Airlines, Intel, and Microsoft have all been accused of various predatory practices. Take Microsoft, for example:

> Competitors and regulators have accused giant Microsoft of predatory "bundling" practices. That's the term used to describe Microsoft's practice of continually adding new features to Windows, the operating system installed on more than 90 percent of America's desktop computers. Because customers are essentially locked in to Windows, it's easy for the company to get them to use its other software—even if competitors make better products. That dampens competition, reduces choice, and could retard innovation. For example, in its zeal to become a leader not just in operating systems but on the Internet, the company bundled its Internet Explorer browser into its Windows software. This move sparked an antitrust suit by the government, much to the delight of Microsoft's rivals. After all, Web-browsing innovator Netscape has seen its market share plummet as it tries to sell what Microsoft now gives away for free.[20]

Although competitors and the government charge that Microsoft's actions are predatory, the question is whether this is unfair competition or the healthy competition of a more efficient company against the less efficient.

Citizen and Public Actions to Regulate Marketing

Because some people view business as the cause of many economic and social ills, grassroots movements have arisen from time to time to keep business in line. The two major movements have been *consumerism* and *environmentalism*.

Consumerism

American business firms have been the target of organized consumer movements on three occasions. The first consumer movement took place in the early 1900s. It was fueled by rising prices, Upton Sinclair's writings on conditions in the meat industry, and scandals in the drug industry. The second consumer movement, in the mid-1930s, was sparked by an upturn in consumer prices during the Great Depression and another drug scandal.

The third movement began in the 1960s. Consumers had become better educated, products had become more complex and potentially hazardous, and people were unhappy with American institutions. Ralph Nader appeared on the scene to force many issues, and other well-known writers accused big business of wasteful and unethical practices. President John F. Kennedy declared that consumers had the right to safety and to be informed, to choose, and to be heard. Congress investigated certain industries and proposed consumer-protection legislation. Since then, many consumer groups have been organized and several consumer laws have been passed. The consumer movement has spread internationally and has become very strong in Europe.[21]

But what is the consumer movement? **Consumerism** is an organized movement of citizens and government agencies to improve the rights and power of buyers in relation to sellers. Traditional *sellers' rights* include:

Consumerism
An organized movement of citizens and government agencies to improve the rights and power of buyers in relation to sellers.

- The right to introduce any product in any size and style, provided it is not hazardous to personal health or safety; or, if it is, to include proper warnings and controls.
- The right to charge any price for the product, provided no discrimination exists among similar kinds of buyers.
- The right to spend any amount to promote the product, provided it is not defined as unfair competition.
- The right to use any product message, provided it is not misleading or dishonest in content or execution.
- The right to use any buying incentive schemes, provided they are not unfair or misleading.

Traditional *buyers' rights* include:

- The right not to buy a product that is offered for sale.
- The right to expect the product to be safe.
- The right to expect the product to perform as claimed.

Comparing these rights, many believe that the balance of power lies on the seller's side. True, the buyer can refuse to buy. But critics feel that the buyer has too little information, education, and protection to make wise decisions when facing sophisticated sellers. Consumer advocates call for the following additional consumer rights:

- The right to be well informed about important aspects of the product.
- The right to be protected against questionable products and marketing practices.
- The right to influence products and marketing practices in ways that will improve the "quality of life."

Each proposed right has led to more specific proposals by consumerists. The right to be informed includes the right to know the true interest on a loan (truth in lending), the true cost per unit of a brand (unit pricing), the ingredients in a product (ingredient labeling), the nutritional value of foods (nutritional labeling), product freshness (open dating), and the true benefits of a product (truth in advertising). Proposals related to consumer protection include strengthening consumer rights in cases of business fraud, requiring greater product safety, and giving more

Consumer desire for more information led to putting ingredients, nutrition, and dating information on product labels.

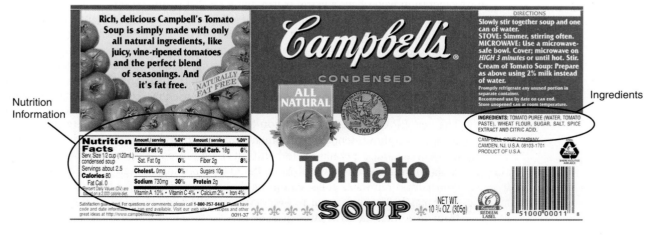

power to government agencies. Proposals relating to quality of life include controlling the ingredients that go into certain products and packaging, reducing the level of advertising "noise," and putting consumer representatives on company boards to protect consumer interests.

Consumers have not only the *right* but also the *responsibility* to protect themselves instead of leaving this function to someone else. Consumers who believe they got a bad deal have several remedies available, including contacting the company or the media; contacting federal, state, or local agencies; and going to small-claims courts.

Environmentalism

Environmentalism

An organized movement of concerned citizens and government agencies to protect and improve people's living environment.

Whereas consumerists consider whether the marketing system is efficiently serving consumer wants, environmentalists are concerned with marketing's effects on the environment and with the costs of serving consumer needs and wants. **Environmentalism** is an organized movement of concerned citizens, businesses, and government agencies to protect and improve people's living environment. Environmentalists are not against marketing and consumption; they simply want people and organizations to operate with more care for the environment. The marketing system's goal, they assert, should not be to maximize consumption, consumer choice, or consumer satisfaction, but rather to maximize life quality. And "life quality" means not only the quantity and quality of consumer goods and services, but also the quality of the environment. Environmentalists want environmental costs included in both producer and consumer decision making.

The first wave of modern environmentalism in the United States was driven by environmental groups and concerned consumers in the 1960s and 1970s. They were concerned with damage to the ecosystem caused by strip-mining, forest depletion, acid rain, loss of the atmosphere's ozone layer, toxic wastes, and litter. They also were concerned with the loss of recreational areas and with the increase in health problems caused by bad air, polluted water, and chemically treated food.

The second environmentalism wave was driven by government, which passed laws and regulations during the 1970s and 1980s governing industrial practices impacting the environment. This wave hit some industries hard. Steel companies and utilities had to invest billions of dollars in pollution control equipment and costlier fuels. The auto industry had to introduce expensive emission controls in cars. The packaging industry had to find ways to reduce litter. These industries and others have often resented and resisted environmental regulations, especially when they have been imposed too rapidly to allow companies to make proper adjustments. Many of these companies claim they have had to absorb large costs that have made them less competitive.

Environmental sustainability

A management approach that involves developing strategies that both sustain the environment and produce profits for the company.

The first two environmentalism waves are now merging into a third and stronger wave in which companies are accepting responsibility for doing no harm to the environment. They are shifting from protest to prevention, and from regulation to responsibility. More and more companies are adopting policies of **environmental sustainability**—developing strategies that both sustain the environment and produce profits for the company. According to one strategist, "The challenge is to develop a *sustainable global economy:* an economy that the planet is capable of supporting indefinitely. . . . [It's] an enormous challenge—and an enormous opportunity."[22]

Sustainability is a crucial but difficult goal. John Browne, chairman of giant oil company BP, recently asked this question: "Is genuine progress still possible? Is development sustainable? Or is one strand of progress—industrialization—now doing such damage to the environment that the next generation won't have a world worth living in?"[23] Browne sees the situation as an opportunity. Five years ago, BP broke ranks with the oil industry on environmental issues. "There are good commercial reasons to do right by the environment," says Browne. Under his leadership, BP has become active in public forums on global climate issues and has worked to reduce emissions in exploration and production. It has begun marketing cleaner fuels and invested significantly in exploring alternative energy sources, such as photovoltaic power and hydrogen. At the local level, BP recently opened "the world's most environmentally friendly service station" near London:

The new BP Connect service station features an array of innovative green initiatives that show BP's commitment to environmental responsibility. The station runs entirely on renewable energy and generates up to half of its own power, using solar panels installed on the roofs and three wind turbines. More than 60 percent of the water needed for the restrooms comes from rainwater collected on the shop roof, and water for hand washing is heated by solar panels. The site's vapor recovery systems collect and recycle even the fuel vapor released from customers' tanks as pump gas. BP has planted landscaping around the site with indige-

Environmental sustainability: BP recently opened "the world's most environmentally friendly service station" near London, featuring an array of innovative green initiatives.

nous plant species. And, to promote biodiversity awareness, the company has undertaken several initiatives to attract local wildlife to the area, such as dragonflies and insect-feeding birds. The wildflower turf under the wind farm will even provide a habitat for bumble bees.[24]

Figure 20.1 shows a grid that companies can use to gauge their progress toward environmental sustainability. At the most basic level, a company can practice *pollution prevention.* This involves more than pollution control—cleaning up waste after it has been created. Pollution prevention means eliminating or minimizing waste before it is created. Companies emphasizing prevention have responded with "green marketing" programs—developing ecologically safer products, recyclable and biodegradable packaging, better pollution controls, and more energy-efficient operations (see Real Marketing 20.2). They are finding that they can be both

FIGURE 20.1
The environmental sustainability grid

	Internal	External
Tomorrow	**New environmental technology** Is the environmental performance of our products limited by our existing technology base? Is there potential to realize major improvements through new technology?	**Sustainability vision** Does our corporate vision direct us toward the solution of social and environmental problems? Does our vision guide the development of new technologies, markets, products, and processes?
Today	**Pollution prevention** Where are the most significant waste and emission streams from our current operations? Can we lower costs and risks by eliminating waste at the source or by using it as useful input?	**Product stewardship** What are the implications for product design and development if we assume responsibility for a product's entire life cycle? Can we add value or lower costs while simultaneously reducing the impact of our products?

Source: Stuart L. Hart, "Beyond Greening: Strategies for a Sustainable World," *Harvard Business Review,* January–February 1997, p. 74. Copyright © 1997 by the President and Fellows of Harvard College; all rights reserved. Reprinted by permission of *Harvard Business Review.*

real marketing 20.2

Environmental Farsightedness Today Pays Off Tomorrow

On Earth Day 1970, a newly emerging environmentalism movement made its first large-scale effort to educate people about the dangers of pollution. This was a tough task: At the time, most folks weren't all that interested in environmental problems. These days, however, environmentalism has broad public support. People hear and read daily about a growing list of environmental problems—global warming, acid rain,

A positive sign.

Mc Donald's Earth Effort

Corporate environmentalism: Enlightened companies are taking action not because someone is forcing them, but because it is the right thing to do.

depletion of the ozone layer, air and water pollution, hazardous waste disposal, the buildup of solid wastes—and they are calling for solutions.

The new environmentalism has caused many consumers to rethink what products they buy and from whom. Nearly 87 percent

of Americans are concerned about the environment. Roper Starch calls the core group of environmentally conscious consumers "greenback greens," noting that they are more likely to support environmental causes with their pocketbooks than to roll up their sleeves to volunteer. Such consumer attitudes have sparked a major marketing thrust—*green marketing*—the movement by companies to develop and market environmentally responsible products and themselves practice the three *R*s of waste management: reducing, reusing, and recycling waste.

McDonald's provides a good example. It used to purchase Coca-Cola syrup in plastic bags encased in cardboard, but now the syrup is delivered as gasoline is, pumped directly from tank trucks into storage vats at restaurants. The change saved 68 million pounds of packaging a year. All napkins, bags, and tray liners in McDonald's restaurants are made from recycled paper, as are its carry-out drink trays and even the stationery used at headquarters. For a company the size of McDonald's, even small changes can make a big difference. For example, just making its drinking straws 20 percent lighter and trimming the size of its napkins saves the company 2 million pounds of waste per year.

In an effort to reduce energy use, McDonald's even invited folks from outside the business, including several people from the Environmental Defense Fund (EDF), to suggest ways that the chain could make its restaurants more energy efficient. As a result, McDonald's built five "TEEM" restaurants (The Energy-Efficient McDonald's) as models of energy efficiency. One such restaurant in Detroit can draw heat from 50 feet below ground level to keep customers warm through the winter. Beyond simply conserving resources, each store saves up to $4,000 each year on energy bills.

Producers in other industries are also responding to environmental concerns. For

example, Herman Miller, the large office-furniture manufacturer, set a trend in the furniture industry when it began using tropical woods from sustainably managed sources, altering even its classic furniture lines. But it went even further by reusing packaging, recapturing solvents used in staining, and burning fabric scraps and sawdust to generate energy for its manufacturing plant. In 2001, Herman Miller recycled 23 million pounds of waste and reused another 21 million pounds for fuel to heat its main site. These moves not only help the environment, they also save Herman Miller $750,000 a year on energy and landfill costs. Such actions earned Herman Miller the 2001 Waste Wise Program Award from the EPA.

Service providers are going green, too. Studies indicate that 85 percent of travelers are willing to pay as much as 8 percent more to stay in an environmentally friendly hotel. They would prefer to check into someplace like the Sheraton Rittenhouse Hotel in Philadelphia, for example. All of the hotel's furniture is made of wood harvested from managed forests, and all of the carpets, draperies, paint, and wallpaper are free of toxic chemicals. The bedsheets and paper goods are produced without toxic bleaches or dyes. A six-story central atrium houses bamboo trees, which grow at a rate of one meter each day and produce oxygen at a rate 35 percent higher than most other plants. The walls of the atrium are fashioned from old issues of *Wall Street Journal* and soybeans, while the floor is made from engineered bamboo.

Even retailers are jumping onto the green bandwagon. For example, Winmark Corporation has developed a $100 million business selling used equipment through retail chains such as Play It Again (used sporting goods and equipment), Once Upon a Child (used children's clothes, toys, and furniture), Music Go Round (used musical instruments), and Plato's Closet ("gently used" brand name clothing and accessories). And Wal-Mart is opening "eco-friendly" stores in which the air-conditioning systems use non-ozone-depleting refrigerant, rainwater is collected from parking lots and rooftops for landscaping, skylights supplement fluorescent lighting adjusted by photo sensors, and the storefront sign is solar powered.

The growth of the Internet has given the green movement a real boost. "The Internet has armed the busy, yet environmentally-conscious consumer with a new method of environmental activism: shopping," notes one analyst.

Online charity malls like Greater Good. com, ShopForChange, and iGive allow consumers to buy goods and have a small percentage of their purchase go to a charity of the choice, green or otherwise. Then there are click-to-donate sites, like The Rain Forest Site (www. therainforestsite.com), where clicking on a button automatically sends a donation to the Nature Conservancy, courtesy of merchants who pay for banner ads on the site. Other mall-like sites, such as EthicalShopper.com, GreenHome.com, and EcoMall.com, offer environmentally friendly products, from chamomile shampoo to nonchlorine bleach. Also sprouting up are individual vendors, like BlueDolphin.com, which sells recycled paper and office supplies, and EcoBayy. com, which sells environmentally safe baby products.

"Whether they buy from the expanding number of dot-coms specializing in enviro-friendly products, or frequent mainstream merchants through charity mall sites that donate a portion of sales to green causes," says the analyst, "e-commerce is expanding the opportunity to 'do the right thing' for Mother Earth."

During the early phase of the new environmentalism, environmentalists and regulators became concerned that companies were going overboard with their use of terms such as *recyclable, degradable, compostable,* and *environmentally responsible.* Perhaps of equal concern was that, as more and more marketers used green-marketing claims, more and more consumers would view them as little more than gimmicks. Now environmentalism appears to be moving into a more mature phase—broader, deeper, and more sophisticated. Gone are the hastily prepared environmental pitches and products designed to capitalize on or exploit growing public concern. "Dressing up ads with pictures of eagles and trees will no longer woo an environmentally sophisticated audience," says an environmentalist. "People want to know that companies are incorporating environmental values into their manufacturing processes, products, packaging, and the very fabric of their corporate cultures."

Some companies have responded to consumer environmental concerns by doing only what is required to avert new regulations or to keep environmentalists quiet. Enlightened companies are taking action not because someone is forcing them to, or to reap short-run profits, but because it is the right thing to do. They believe that environmental farsightedness today will pay off tomorrow—for both the customer and the company.

Sources: Quotes and other information from Robert Rehak, "Green Marketing Awash in Third Wave," *Advertising Age,* November 22, 1993, p. 22; Lisa E. Phillips, "Green Attitude," *American Demographics,* April 1999, pp. 46–47; Rebecca Gardyn, "Saving the Earth, One Click at a Time," *American Demographics,* January 2001, pp. 30–33; Michael Malley, "Turning Green Practices into Greenbacks," *Hotel and Motel Management,* May 17, 1999, p. 8; Amy Zuber, "Go, T.E.E.M.! New McDonald's Units Conserve Energy, Save Money," *Nation's Restaurant News,* March 13, 2000, p. 30; "The 100 Best Corporate Citizens for 2002," accessed online at www. business-ethics. com, August 2002; "Welcome to Winmark—Home of the World's Most Unique Retail Brands," accessed online at www.winmarkcorporation.com, September 2002; and "McDonald's and the Environment," accessed online at www. mcdonalds. com/corporate/social/environment, August 2002.

green *and* competitive. Consider how the Dutch flower industry has responded to its environmental problems:

Intense cultivation of flowers in small areas was contaminating the soil and groundwater with pesticides, herbicides, and fertilizers. Facing increasingly strict regulation, . . . the Dutch understood that the only effective way to address the problem would be to develop a closed-loop system. In advanced Dutch greenhouses, flowers now grow in water and rock wool, not in soil. This lowers the risk of infestation, reducing the need for fertilizers and pesticides, which are delivered in water that circulates and is reused. The . . . closed-loop system also reduces variation in growing conditions, thus improving product quality. Handling costs have gone down because the flowers are cultivated on specially designed platforms. . . . The net result is not only dramatically lower environmental impact but also lower costs, better product quality, and enhanced global competitiveness.[25]

At the next level, companies can practice *product stewardship*—minimizing not just pollution from production but all environmental impacts throughout the full product life cycle. Many companies are adopting *design for environment (DFE)* practices, which involve thinking ahead in the design stage to create products that are easier to recover, reuse, or recycle. DFE not only helps to sustain the environment, it can be highly profitable:

Consider Xerox Corporation's Asset Recycle Management (ARM) program, which uses leased Xerox copiers as sources of high-quality, low-cost parts and components for new machines. A well-developed [process] for taking back leased copiers combined with a sophisticated remanufacturing process allows . . . components to be reconditioned, tested, and then reassembled into "new" machines. Xerox estimates that ARM savings in raw materials, labor, and waste disposal in 1995 alone were in the $300 million to $400 million range. . . . By redefining product-in-use as part of the company's asset base, Xerox has discovered a way to add value and lower costs. It can continually provide lease customers with the latest product upgrades, giving them state-of-the-art functionality with minimum environmental impact.[26]

At the third level of environmental sustainability, companies look to the future and plan for *new environmental technologies.* Many organizations that have made good headway in pollution prevention and product stewardship are still limited by existing technologies. To develop fully sustainable strategies, they will need to develop new technologies. Monsanto is doing this by shifting its agricultural technology base from bulk chemicals to biotechnology. By controlling plant growth and pest resistance through bioengineering rather than through the application of pesticides or fertilizers, Monsanto hopes to fulfill its promise of environmentally sustainable agriculture.[27]

Finally, companies can develop a *sustainability vision,* which serves as a guide to the future. It shows how the company's products and services, processes, and policies must evolve and what new technologies must be developed to get there. This vision of sustainability provides a framework for pollution control, product stewardship, and environmental technology.

Most companies today focus on the lower-left quadrant of the grid in Figure 20.1, investing most heavily in pollution prevention. Some forward-looking companies practice product stewardship and are developing new environmental technologies. Few companies have well-defined sustainability visions. Emphasizing only one or a few cells in the environmental sustainability grid in Figure 20.1 can be shortsighted. For example, investing only in the bottom half of the grid puts a company in a good position today but leaves it vulnerable in the future. In contrast, a heavy emphasis on the top half suggests that a company has good environmental vision but lacks the skills needed to implement it. Thus, companies should work at developing all four dimensions of environmental sustainability. Hewlett-Packard is doing just that:

> Hewlett-Packard has evolved through three distinct phases of environmental sustainability over the past two decades. In the 1980s, the environmental concerns were primarily pollution control and prevention, with a focus on reducing emissions from existing manufacturing processes. . . . In the 1990s, the focus shifted to . . . a product stewardship function, which focused on developing global processes for tracking and managing regulatory compliance issues, customer inquiry response systems, information management, public policy shaping, product take-back programs, green packaging, and integrating "design for the environment" and life cycle analysis into product development processes. Today, sustainability is about developing technologies that actually contribute a positive impact to environmental challenges. [However,] HP has recognized that pollution prevention and product stewardship have become baseline market expectations. To be an environmental leader in the 21st century, HP needs to integrate environmental sustainability into its fundamental business [vision and] strategy.[28]

Environmentalism creates some special challenges for global marketers. As international trade barriers come down and global markets expand, environmental issues are having an ever greater impact on international trade. Countries in North America, Western Europe, and other developed regions are developing stringent environmental standards. In the United States, for example, more than two dozen major pieces of environmental legislation have been enacted since 1970, and recent events suggest that more regulation is on the way. A side accord to the North American Free Trade Agreement (NAFTA) set up a commission for resolving environmental matters. The European Union recently passed "end-of-life" regulations that require carmakers to recycle or reuse at least 80 percent of their old automobiles by 2006. And the EU's Eco-Management and Audit Scheme provides guidelines for environmental self-regulation.[29]

However, environmental policies still vary widely from country to country, and uniform worldwide standards are not expected for many years. Although countries such as Denmark, Germany, Japan, and the United States have fully developed environmental policies and high public expectations, major countries such as China, India, Brazil, and Russia are in only the early stages of developing such policies. Moreover, environmental factors that motivate consumers in one country may have no impact on consumers in another. For example, PVC soft drink bottles cannot be used in Switzerland or Germany. However, they are preferred in France, which has an

FIGURE 20.2
Major marketing decision areas that may be called into question under the law

Selling decisions
Bribing?
Stealing trade secrets?
Disparaging customers?
Misrepresenting?
Disclosure of customer rights?
Unfair discrimination?

Advertising decisions
False advertising?
Deceptive advertising?
Bait-and-switch advertising?
Promotional allowances and services?

Channel decisions
Exclusive dealing?
Exclusive territorial distributorships?
Tying agreements?
Dealer's rights?

Product decisions
Product additions and deletions?
Patent protection?
Product quality and safety?
Product warranty?

Packaging decisions
Fair packaging and labeling?
Excessive cost?
Scarce resource?
Pollution?

Price decisions
Price-fixing?
Predatory pricing?
Price discrimination?
Minimum pricing?
Price increases?
Deceptive pricing?

Competitive relations decisions
Anticompetitive acquisition?
Barriers to entry?
Predatory competition?

extensive recycling process for them. Thus, international companies are finding it difficult to develop standard environmental practices that work around the world. Instead, they are creating general policies and then translating these policies into tailored programs that meet local regulations and expectations.

Public Actions to Regulate Marketing

Citizen concerns about marketing practices will usually lead to public attention and legislative proposals. New bills will be debated—many will be defeated, others will be modified, and a few will become workable laws.

Many of the laws that affect marketing are listed in Chapter 4. The task is to translate these laws into the language that marketing executives understand as they make decisions about competitive relations, products, price, promotion, and channels of distribution. Figure 20.2 illustrates the major legal issues facing marketing management.

Business Actions Toward Socially Responsible Marketing

At first, many companies opposed consumerism and environmentalism. They thought the criticisms were either unfair or unimportant. But by now, most companies have grown to accept the new consumer rights, at least in principle. They might oppose certain pieces of legislation as inappropriate ways to solve specific consumer problems, but they recognize the consumer's right to information and protection. Many of these companies have responded positively to consumerism and environmentalism in order to serve consumer needs better.

Enlightened marketing
A marketing philosophy holding that a company's marketing should support the best long-run performance of the marketing system; its five principles include consumer-oriented marketing, innovative marketing, value marketing, sense-of-mission marketing, and societal marketing.

Enlightened Marketing

The philosophy of **enlightened marketing** holds that a company's marketing should support the best long-run performance of the marketing system. Enlightened marketing consists of five principles: *consumer-oriented marketing, innovative marketing, value marketing, sense-of-mission marketing,* and *societal marketing.*

Consumer-Oriented Marketing

Consumer-oriented | **marketing**
The philosophy of enlightened marketing that holds that the company should view and organize its marketing activities from the consumer's point of view.

Consumer-oriented marketing means that the company should view and organize its marketing activities from the consumer's point of view. It should work hard to sense, serve, and satisfy the needs of a defined group of customers. Every successful company that we've discussed in this text has had this in common: an all-consuming passion for delivering superior value to carefully chosen customers. Only by seeing the world through its customers' eyes can the company build lasting and profitable customer relationships.

Innovative Marketing

Innovative marketing
A principle of enlightened marketing that requires that a company seek real product and marketing improvements.

The principle of **innovative marketing** requires that the company continuously seek real product and marketing improvements. The company that overlooks new and better ways to do things will eventually lose customers to another company that has found a better way. An excellent example of an innovative marketer is Colgate-Palmolive:

> Colgate has become somewhat of a new-product machine in recent years. Worldwide, new products contribute 35 percent of Colgate's revenues, up from 26 percent five years earlier. In the United States, new products account for 58 percent of sales, up from 27 percent. The American Marketing Association (AMA) recently named Colgate-Palmolive its new-product marketer of the year. Colgate took the honors by launching an abundance of innovative and highly successful new consumer products, including Colgate Total toothpaste. Total is perhaps the best example of the company's passion for continuous improvement. Marketing research showed shifts in consumer demographics and concerns—a growing population of aging, health-conscious, and better-educated consumers. For these consumers, Total became a breakout brand that provides a combination of benefits, including cavity prevention, tartar control, fresh breath, and long-lasting effects. The company also launched an innovative marketing program for the new product, which included advertising in health magazines targeting educated consumers who have high involvement in the health of their mouth and teeth. Consumers responded by making Colgate-Palmolive the toothpaste market leader for the first time since 1962. It now captures a 35 percent market share versus Procter & Gamble's 25 percent.[30]

Value Marketing

Value marketing
A principle of enlightened marketing that holds that a company should put most of its resources into value-building marketing investments.

According to the principle of **value marketing,** the company should put most of its resources into value-building marketing investments. Many things marketers do—one-shot sales promotions, minor packaging changes, advertising puffery—may raise sales in the short run but add less *value* than would actual improvements in the product's quality, features, or convenience. Enlightened marketing calls for building long-run consumer loyalty by continually improving the value consumers receive from the firm's marketing offer.

Sense-of-Mission Marketing

Sense-of-mission marketing
A principle of enlightened marketing that holds that a company should define its mission in broad social terms rather than narrow product terms.

Sense-of-mission marketing means that the company should define its mission in broad *social* terms rather than narrow *product* terms. When a company defines a social mission, employees feel better about their work and have a clearer sense of direction. For example, defined in narrow product terms, Ben & Jerry's mission might be "to sell ice cream and frozen yogurt." However, the company states its mission more broadly as one of "linked prosperity," including product, economic, and social missions (see www.benjerrys.com/mission.html). Reshaping the basic task of selling consumer products into the larger mission of serving the interests of consumers, employees, and others in the company's various "communities" gives Ben & Jerry's a vital sense of purpose. Like Ben & Jerry's, many companies today are undertaking socially responsible actions and building concern for their communities into their underlying cultures (see Real Marketing 20.3).

Societal Marketing

Societal marketing
A principle of enlightened marketing that holds that a company should make marketing decisions by considering consumers' wants, the company's requirements, consumers' long-run interests, and society's long-run interests.

Following the principle of **societal marketing,** an enlightened company makes marketing decisions by considering consumers' wants and interests, the company's requirements, and society's long-run interests. The company is aware that neglecting consumer and societal long-run interests is a disservice to consumers and society. Alert companies view societal problems as opportunities.

real marketing 20.3

Mission: Social Responsibility

In a recent poll, 92 percent of consumers said they believe it's important for companies to be good corporate citizens. More than three-quarters responded that they would switch brands and retailers when price and quality are equal for a product associated with a good cause. As a result, cause-related marketing by companies has increased more than 500 percent during the past decade.

Today, acts of good corporate citizenship abound. For example, American Express's Charge Against Hunger program—through which the company donated 3 cents from every transaction made during the traditional holiday season—raised more than $21 million for hunger relief in the United States. Maxwell House, a division of Kraft Foods, created a partnership with Habitat for Humanity to build 100 homes in as many days, while working to raise awareness for the organization. Post Cereal celebrated its one hundredth anniversary by donating to Second Harvest—the nation's largest network of hunger-relief charities—enough cereal to feed more than 1 million people. In addition, Post partnered with grocery retailers to sponsor a 100-day food drive across the United States, supported by national and local ads to increase hunger awareness and to encourage consumer participation in the drive.

It seems that almost every company has a pet cause. Alarm company ADT gives away personal-security systems to battered women. Avon Products helps fund the fight against breast cancer—since 1993, it has raised more than $165 million for this cause. Dow donates employees' time and home construction materials to Habitat for Humanity. Coca-Cola sponsors local Boys and Girls Clubs, and Barnes & Noble promotes literacy.

Beyond aligning with good causes, socially responsible companies care about and serve the communities in which they operate. Take Saturn Corporation, for example:

As its slogan states, Saturn is "A different kind of company. A different kind of car."

The company claims to focus more on its employees, customers, and communities than on revenues and bottom lines. Saturn's CEO notes that "a part of Saturn's business philosophy is to meet the needs of our neighbors." An example of this philosophy in action is Saturn Playgrounds, a company program for employee involvement and community betterment. The goal is to provide young children in poor communities with a safe, fun environment during nonschool hours as an alternative to gangs, drugs, and crime. Backed by Saturn retailers, local Saturn employees and customers join with community members to build a community playground in a single day. So far, the Saturn Playgrounds project has built over 100 playgrounds and two Little League parks across the country. Saturn also supports the Journey of Hope, an annual cross-country bicycle trip in which 70 college students cycle from coast to coast to raise funds and

Socially responsible companies care about and serve their communities. Saturn's many community initiatives include its Saturn Playground project and support for Journey of Hope.

(continued)

awareness on behalf of people with disabilities. Saturn supplies several station wagons that lead the routes and carry gear. At many stops along the trek, Saturn retailers provide meals for the team and host special events, such as wheelchair basketball games and special puppet shows, to help teach kids about people with disabilities.

Each year, *Business Ethics* magazine selects its 100 Best Corporate Citizens, companies that excel at serving their various local, national, and global communities as well as shareholders and customers. Here are examples of companies heading up recent *Business Ethics* best-100 lists:

IBM. The top company for 2002, this technology giant—330,000 employees strong, in 164 countries—received high praise for its diversity policies and for its community giving programs. IBM gives more than just money. Of the more than $126 million donated last year, less than one-third was in cash. The remainder consisted of technology and technical services, the core of what IBM knows best. Moreover, last year, IBM employees contributed 4 million hours of time in a wide range of community projects. Says IBM's vice president of corporate community relations, "With checkbook philanthropy, you could contribute a lot of money and accomplish very little. I think that in the new model, being generous is incredibly important, but the most important aspect of this new model is using our many resources to achieve something of lasting value in the communities where we live, work, and do business."

Procter & Gamble. The top company for 2001, P&G scored especially high in service to its international communities. P&G markets 300 consumer packaged-goods brands to nearly 5 billion consumers in 140 countries, with some 50 percent of revenues coming from overseas. It operates 93 manufacturing facilities in 44 countries outside the United States and has been generous in international grants and gifts in these communities, including earthquake relief in Turkey, community-building projects in Japan, plus contributions for schools in China, school computers in Romania, special education in Malaysia, and shore protection in France. P&G contributes more than $75 million worldwide each year to support such causes.

The St. Paul Companies. The St. Paul, the $7.5 billion Minnesota-based insurer, gained *Business Ethics'* top score for "community," based on its commitment to development of its home communities of St. Paul and Minneapolis. Last year, the company donated an impressive 2 percent of net earnings to support community-building efforts. Its Leadership Initiatives in Neighborhoods program, now in its 16th year, provides grants to current and emerging leaders to develop their leadership potential. Since 1998, The St. Paul has pledged more than $2.2 million to increase the number of teachers of color in Twin Cities urban schools, enhance the retention of talented educators, and better prepare teachers for urban classrooms. St. Paul employee committees are empowered to award grants in the communities where they live and work. And The St. Paul's arts and diversity committee collaborates with United Arts, a local nonprofit organization, on local arts programming related to various cultures, perspectives, and diversity issues. "Increasingly, companies and employees are caring about their communities and want to be part of a greater cause," says St. Paul's chairman and CEO. "They want to do the right thing . . . to take positive actions that make life better for everyone."

Pitney Bowes. This business equipment maker, headquartered in Stamford, Connecticut, also invests in local economic development as a part of its corporate culture. For example, it decided to keep its headquarters in a deteriorating section of Stamford's South End, and to work with grassroots organizations to improve the community. The company donated property near its headquarters for an affordable housing complex and has participated in a down-payment assistance program for home ownership. Pitney Bowes also supports the grassroots South End Neighborhood Revitalization Zone Initiative, which empowers community residents to make decisions about the neighborhood. "Because a lot of the people who live here are low-income," says Polly O'Brien, director of community affairs, "it's not always easy for them to complain about property owners who don't keep places clean or up to code." The program gives these people voice. "To us, it's very easy to sit and write a check, but it doesn't have the same impact for self-sufficiency as if you partner with people," said O'Brien. "It's really their success."

Social responsibility is no longer viewed as the enemy of good business. Instead, it's at the forefront of sound business practice. "The term 'corporate citizenship' is coming into broader use these days," says the editor of *Business Ethics*, "as awareness grows that business has responsibilities beyond profits." Moreover, doing what's good for a company's communities can also be good for the company. A recent study shows that, on average, companies that make the list of best corporate citizens score 10 percent higher on *Business Week's* rankings of financial performance than the remaining companies in the S&P 500. These good corporate citizens also rank higher on *Fortune* magazine's list of most admired companies. The differences were "strikingly large," says the researcher overseeing the study. "This may be the most concrete evidence now available that good citizenship really does pay off on the bottom line."

Sources: "Saturn Dealers Build Six New Playgrounds in One Weekend," *PR Newswire,* June 4, 1997; "Saturn Playgrounds," accessed online at www.saturnbp.com/mysaturn/mycommunity, September 2002; Tom Klusmann, "The 100 Best Corporate Citizens in 2000," *Business Ethics,* March–April 2000; Philip Johansson, "The 100 Best Corporate Citizens for 2001," *Business Ethics,* March–April 2001; Cynthia Wagner, "Economics: Evaluating Good Corporate Citizenship," *The Futurist,* July–August 2001, p. 16; "The 100 Best Corporate Citizens for 2002," *Business Ethics,* April 2002; and information accessed online at www.avoncompany. com/women/avoncrusade, August 2002. For more information and examples, see the *Business Ethics* Web site at www.business-ethics.com.

FIGURE 20.3
Societal classification
of products

Immediate satisfaction

	Low	High
Long-run consumer benefit High	Salutary products	Desirable products
Low	Deficient products	Pleasing products

Deficient products
Products that have neither
immediate appeal nor long-
run benefits.

Pleasing products
Products that give high
immediate satisfaction but
may hurt consumers in the
long run.

Salutary products
Products that have low appeal
but may benefit consumers in
the long run.

Desirable products
Products that give both high
immediate satisfaction and
high long-run benefits.

A societally oriented marketer wants to design products that are not only pleasing but also beneficial. The difference is shown in Figure 20.3. Products can be classified according to their degree of immediate consumer satisfaction and long-run consumer benefit. **Deficient products,** such as bad-tasting and ineffective medicine, have neither immediate appeal nor long-run benefits. **Pleasing products** give high immediate satisfaction but may hurt consumers in the long run. An example is cigarettes. **Salutary products** have low appeal but may benefit consumers in the long run; for instance, seat belts and air bags. **Desirable products** give both high immediate satisfaction and high long-run benefits, such as a tasty *and* nutritious breakfast food.

Examples of desirable products abound. Philips Lightings Earth Light compact fluorescent lightbulb provides good lighting at the same time that it gives long life and energy savings. Toyota's gas-electric hybrid Prius gives both a quiet ride and fuel efficiency. Maytag's front-loading Neptune washer provides superior cleaning along with water savings and energy efficiency. And Herman Miller's Avian office chair is not only attractive and functional but also environmentally responsible:

Herman Miller, one of the world's largest office furniture makers, has received numerous awards for environmentally responsible products and business practices. In 1994 the company formed an Earth Friendly Design Task Force responsible for infusing the company's design process with its environmental values. The task force carries out life-cycle analyses on the company's products, including everything from how much of a product can be made from recycled materials to how much of the product itself can be recycled at the end of its useful life. For example, the company's Avian chair is designed for the lowest possible ecological impact and 100 percent recyclability. Herman Miller reduced material used in the chair by using gas-assist injection molding for the frame, which resulted in hollow frame members (like the bones of birds, hence the chair's name). The frame needs no paint or other finish. All materials are recyclable. No ozone-depleting materials are used. The chair is shipped partially

Herman Miller's Earth Friendly Design Task Force infuses the company's design process with its environmental values. For example, the Avian chair is designed for the lowest possible ecological impact and 100 percent recyclability.

assembled, thus reducing the packaging and energy needed to ship it. Finally, a materials schematic is imbedded in the bottom of the seat to help recycle the chair at the end of its life. This is truly a desirable product—it's won awards for design and function *and* for environmental responsibility.[31]

Companies should try to turn all of their products into desirable products. The challenge posed by pleasing products is that they sell very well but may end up hurting the consumer. The product opportunity, therefore, is to add long-run benefits without reducing the product's pleasing qualities. The challenge posed by salutary products is to add some pleasing qualities so that they will become more desirable in the consumers' minds.

Marketing Ethics

Conscientious marketers face many moral dilemmas. The best thing to do is often unclear. Because not all managers have fine moral sensitivity, companies need to develop *corporate marketing ethics policies*—broad guidelines that everyone in the organization must follow. These policies should cover distributor relations, advertising standards, customer service, pricing, product development, and general ethical standards.

The finest guidelines cannot resolve all the difficult ethical situations the marketer faces. Table 20.1 lists some difficult ethical situations marketers could face during their careers. If marketers choose immediate sales-producing actions in all these cases, their marketing behavior might well be described as immoral or even amoral. If they refuse to go along with *any* of the actions, they might be ineffective as marketing managers and unhappy because of the constant moral tension. Managers need a set of principles that will help them figure out the moral importance of each situation and decide how far they can go in good conscience.

But *what* principle should guide companies and marketing managers on issues of ethics and social responsibility? One philosophy is that such issues are decided by the free market and legal system. Under this principle, companies and their managers are not responsible for making moral judgments. Companies can in good conscience do whatever the system allows.

A second philosophy puts responsibility not on the system but in the hands of individual companies and managers. This more enlightened philosophy suggests that a company should

---

TABLE 20.1   SOME MORALLY DIFFICULT SITUATIONS IN MARKETING

1. You work for a cigarette company and up to now have not been convinced that cigarettes cause cancer. However, recent public policy debates now leave no doubt in your mind about the link between smoking and cancer. What would you do?

2. Your R&D department has changed one of your products slightly. It is not really "new and improved," but you know that putting this statement on the package and in advertising will increase sales. What would you do?

3. You have been asked to add a stripped-down model to your line that could be advertised to pull customers into the store. The product won't be very good, but salespeople will be able to switch buyers up to higher-priced units. You are asked to give the green light for this stripped-down version. What would you do?

4. You are thinking of hiring a product manager who just left a competitor's company. She would be more than happy to tell you all the competitor's plans for the coming year. What would you do?

5. One of your top dealers in an important territory recently has had family troubles, and his sales have slipped. It looks like it will take him a while to straighten out his family trouble. Meanwhile you are losing many sales. Legally, you can terminate the dealer's franchise and replace him. What would you do?

6. You have a chance to win a big account that will mean a lot to you and your company. The purchasing agent hints that a "gift" would influence the decision. Your assistant recommends sending a fine color television set to the buyer's home. What would you do?

7. You have heard that a competitor has a new product feature that will make a big difference in sales. The competitor will demonstrate the feature in a private dealer meeting at the annual trade show. You can easily send a snooper to this meeting to learn about the new feature. What would you do?

8. You have to choose between three ad campaigns outlined by your agency. The first (a) is a soft-sell, honest information campaign. The second (b) uses sex-loaded emotional appeals and exaggerates the product's benefits. The third (c) involves a noisy, irritating commercial that is sure to gain audience attention. Pretests show that the campaigns are effective in the following order: c, b, and a. What would you do?

9. You are interviewing a capable female applicant for a job as salesperson. She is better qualified than the men just interviewed. Nevertheless, you know that some of your important customers prefer dealing with men, and you will lose some sales if you hire her. What would you do?

have a "social conscience." Companies and managers should apply high standards of ethics and morality when making corporate decisions, regardless of "what the system allows." History provides an endless list of examples of company actions that were legal and allowed but were highly irresponsible. Consider the following example:

> Prior to the Pure Food and Drug Act, the advertising for a diet pill promised that a person taking this pill could eat virtually anything at any time and still lose weight. Too good to be true? Actually the claim was quite true; the product lived up to its billing with frightening efficiency. It seems that the primary active ingredient in this "diet supplement" was tapeworm larvae. These larvae would develop in the intestinal tract and, of course, be well fed; the pill taker would in time, quite literally, starve to death.[32]

Each company and marketing manager must work out a philosophy of socially responsible and ethical behavior. Under the societal marketing concept, each manager must look beyond what is legal and allowed and develop standards based on personal integrity, corporate conscience, and long-run consumer welfare. A clear and responsible philosophy will help the company deal with knotty issues such as the one faced recently by 3M:

> In late 1997, a powerful new research technique for scanning blood kept turning up the same odd result: Tiny amounts of a chemical 3M had made for nearly 40 years were showing up in blood drawn from people living all across the country. If the results held up, it meant that virtually all Americans may be carrying some minuscule amount of the chemical, called perfluorooctane sulfonate (PFOS), in their systems. Even though they had yet to come up with definitive answers—and they insisted that there was no evidence of danger to humans—the company reached a drastic decision. In mid-2000, although under no mandate to act, 3M decided to phase out products containing PFOS and related chemicals, including its popular Scotchgard fabric protector. This was no easy decision. Since there was as yet no replacement chemical, it meant a potential loss of $500 million in annual sales. 3M's voluntary actions drew praise from regulators. "3M deserves great credit for identifying the problem and coming forward," says an Environmental Protection Agency administrator. "It took guts," comments another government scientist. "The fact is that most companies . . . go into anger, denial, and the rest of that stuff. [We're used to seeing] decades-long arguments about whether a chemical is really toxic." For 3M, however, it shouldn't have been all that difficult a decision—it was simply the right thing to do.[33]

As with environmentalism, the issue of ethics provides special challenges for international marketers. Business standards and practices vary a great deal from one country to the next. For example, whereas bribes and kickbacks are illegal for U.S. firms, they are standard business practice in many South American countries. One recent study found that companies from some nations were much more likely to use bribes when seeking contracts in emerging-market nations. The most flagrant bribe-paying firms were from Russia and China, with Taiwan and South Korea close behind. The least corrupt were companies from Australia, Sweden, Switzerland, Austria, and Canada.[34] The question arises as to whether a company must lower its ethical standards to compete effectively in countries with lower standards. In one study, two researchers posed this question to chief executives of large international companies and got a unanimous response: No.[35]

For the sake of all of the company's stakeholders—customers, suppliers, employees, shareholders, and the public—it is important to make a commitment to a common set of shared standards worldwide. For example, John Hancock Mutual Life Insurance Company operates successfully in Southeast Asia, an area that by Western standards has widespread questionable business and government practices. Despite warnings from locals that Hancock would have to bend its rules to succeed, the company set out strict guidelines. "We told our people that we had the same ethical standards, same procedures, same policies in these countries that we have in the United States, and we do," says Hancock Chairman Stephen Brown. "We just felt that things like payoffs were wrong—and if we had to do business that way, we'd rather not do business." Hancock employees feel good about the consistent levels of ethics. "There may be countries where you have to do that kind of thing," says Brown. "We haven't found that country yet, and if we do, we won't do business there."[36]

Many industrial and professional associations have suggested codes of ethics, and many companies are now adopting their own codes. For example, the American Marketing Association, an international association of marketing managers and scholars, developed the code of ethics shown in Table 20.2. Companies are also developing programs to teach managers

TABLE 20.2   AMERICAN MARKETING ASSOCIATION CODE OF ETHICS

Members of the American Marketing Association are committed to ethical, professional conduct. They have joined together in subscribing to this Code of Ethics embracing the following topics:

Responsibilities of the Marketer
Marketers must accept responsibility for the consequences of their activities and make every effort to ensure that their decisions, recommendations, and actions function to identify, serve, and satisfy all relevant publics: customers, organizations and society.

Marketers' Professional Conduct Must Be Guided By
1. The basic rule of professional ethics: not knowingly to do harm;
2. The adherence to all applicable laws and regulations;
3. The accurate representation of their education, training and experience; and
4. The active support, practice, and promotion of this Code of Ethics.

Honesty and Fairness
Marketers shall uphold and advance the integrity, honor, and dignity of the marketing profession by:
1. Being honest in serving consumers, clients, employees, suppliers, distributors, and the public;
2. Not knowingly participating in conflict of interest without prior notice to all parties involved; and
3. Establishing equitable fee schedules including the payment or receipt of usual, customary, and/or legal compensation for marketing exchanges.

Rights and Duties of Parties in the Marketing Exchange Process
Participants in the marketing exchange process should be able to expect that:
1. Products and services offered are safe and fit for their intended uses;
2. Communications about offered products and services are not deceptive;
3. All parties intend to discharge their obligations, financial and otherwise, in good faith; and
4. Appropriate internal methods exist for equitable adjustment and/or redress of grievances concerning purchases.

It Is Understood That the Above Would Include, but Is Not Limited to, the Following Responsibilities of the Marketer:
In the Area of Product Development and Management
- disclosure of all substantial risks associated with product or service usage;
- identification of any product component substitution that might materially change the product or impact on the buyer's purchase decision;
- identification of extra cost-added features.

In the Area of Promotions
- avoidance of false and misleading advertising;
- rejection of high-pressure manipulations or misleading sales tactics;
- avoidance of sales promotions that use deception or manipulation.

In the Area of Distribution
- not manipulating the availability of a product for purpose of exploitation;
- not using coercion in the marketing channel;
- not exerting undue influence over the reseller's choice to handle a product.

In the Area of Pricing
- not engaging in price fixing;
- not practicing predatory pricing;
- disclosing the full price associated with any purchase.

In the Area of Marketing Research
- prohibiting selling or fundraising under the guise of conducting research;
- maintaining research integrity by avoiding misrepresentation and omission of pertinent research data;
- treating outside clients and suppliers fairly.

Organizational Relationships
Marketers should be aware of how their behavior may influence or impact on the behavior of others in organizational relationships. They should not demand, encourage, or apply coercion to obtain unethical behavior in their relationships with others, such as employees, suppliers, or customers. They should:
1. Apply confidentiality and anonymity in professional relationships with regard to privileged information;
2. Meet their obligations and responsibilities in contracts and mutual agreements in a timely manner;
3. Avoid taking the work of others, in whole, or in part, and representing this work as their own or directly benefiting from it without compensation or consent of the originator or owner;
4. Avoid manipulation to take advantage of situations to maximize personal welfare in a way that unfairly deprives or damages the organization of others.

Any AMA member found to be in violation of any provision of this Code of Ethics may have his or her Association membership suspended or revoked.

Source: Reprinted with permission from American Marketing Association Code of Ethics, published by the American Marketing Association.

about important ethics issues and help them find the proper responses. They hold ethics workshops and seminars and set up ethics committees. Further, most major U.S. companies have appointed high-level ethics officers to champion ethics issues and to help resolve ethics problems and concerns facing employees.

PricewaterhouseCoopers (PwC) is a good example. In 1996, PwC established an ethics office and comprehensive ethics program, headed by a high-level chief ethics officer. The ethics program begins with a code of conduct, called "The Way We Do Business." PwC employees learn about the code of conduct and about how to handle thorny ethics issues in a comprehensive ethics training program, called "Navigating the Grey." The program also includes an ethics help line and continuous communications at all levels. "Ethics is in everything we say and do," says PwC's CEO, Samuel DiPiazza. Last year alone, the PwC training program involved 40,000 employees, and the help line received over 1,000 calls from people asking for guidance in working through difficult ethics dilemmas.[37]

Ethics programs: PricewaterhouseCoopers established a comprehensive ethics program, which begins with a code of conduct, called "The Way We Do Business." Says PwC's CEO, "Ethics is in everything we say and do."

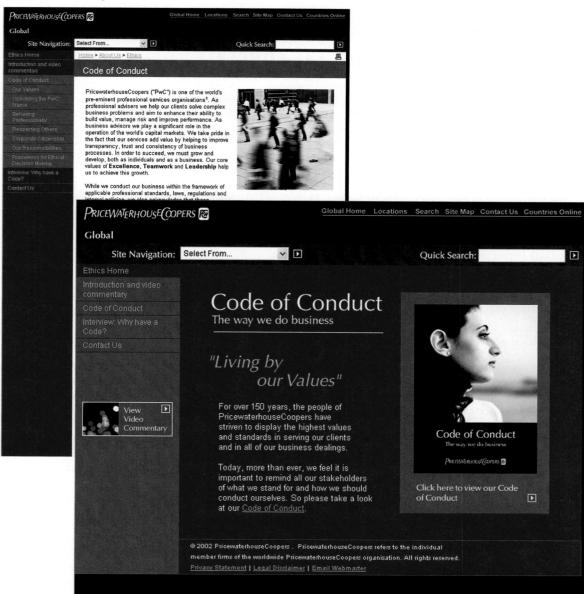

Many companies have developed innovative ways to educate employees about ethics:

Citicorp has developed an ethics board game, which teams of employees use to solve hypothetical quandaries. General Electric employees can tap into specially designed software on their personal computers to get answers to ethical questions. At Texas Instruments, employees are treated to a weekly column on ethics over an electronic news service. One popular feature: a kind of Dear Abby mailbag, answers provided by the company's ethics officer, . . . that deals with the troublesome issues employees face most often.[38]

Still, written codes and ethics programs do not ensure ethical behavior. Ethics and social responsibility require a total corporate commitment. They must be a component of the overall corporate culture. According to PwC's DiPiazza, "I see ethics as a mission-critical issue . . . deeply imbedded in who we are and what we do. It's just as important as our product development cycle or our distribution system. . . . It's about creating a culture based on integrity and respect, not a culture based on dealing with the crisis of the day. . . . We ask ourselves every day, 'Are we doing the right things?' "[39]

The future holds many challenges and opportunities for marketing managers as they move into the new millennium. Technological advances in every area, from telecommunications, information technology, and the Internet to health care and entertainment, provide abundant marketing opportunities. However, forces in the socioeconomic, cultural, and natural environments increase the limits under which marketing can be carried out. Companies that are able to create new customer value in a socially responsible way will have a world to conquer.

LOOKING BACK: REVIEWING THE CONCEPTS

In this chapter, we've closed with many important concepts involving marketing's sweeping impact on individual consumers, other businesses, and society as a whole. You learned that responsible marketers discover what consumers want and respond with the right products, priced to give good value to buyers and profit to the producer. A marketing system should sense, serve, and satisfy consumer needs and improve the quality of consumers' lives. In working to meet consumer needs, marketers may take some actions that are not to everyone's liking or benefit. Marketing managers should be aware of the main *criticisms of marketing*.

1. Identify the major social criticisms of marketing.
Marketing's *impact on individual consumer welfare* has been criticized for its high prices, deceptive practices, high-pressure selling, shoddy or unsafe products, planned obsolescence, and poor service to disadvantaged consumers. Marketing's *impact on society* has been criticized for creating false wants and too much materialism, too few social goods, cultural pollution, and too much political power. Critics have also criticized marketing's *impact on other businesses* for harming competitors and reducing competition through acquisitions, practices that create barriers to entry, and unfair competitive marketing practices.

2. Define *consumerism* and *environmentalism* and explain how they affect marketing strategies.
Concerns about the marketing system have led to *citizen action movements*. *Consumerism* is an organized social movement intended to strengthen the rights and power of consumers relative to sellers. Alert marketers view it as an opportunity to serve consumers better by providing more consumer information, education, and protection. *Environmentalism* is an organized social movement seeking to minimize the harm done to the environment and quality of life by marketing practices. The first wave of modern environmentalism was driven by environmental groups and concerned consumers, whereas the second wave was driven by government, which passed laws and regulations governing industrial practices impacting the environment.

Moving into the twenty-first century, the first two environmentalism waves are merging into a third and stronger wave in which companies are accepting responsibility for doing no environmental harm. Companies now are adopting policies of *environmental sustainability*—developing strategies that both sustain the environment and produce profits for the company.

3. Describe the principles of socially responsible marketing.
Many companies originally opposed these social movements and laws, but most of them now recognize a need for positive consumer information, education, and protection. Some companies have followed a policy of *enlightened marketing*, which holds that a company's marketing should support the best long-run performance of the marketing system. Enlightened marketing consists of five principles: *consumer-oriented marketing, innovative marketing, value marketing, sense-of-mission marketing*, and *societal marketing*.

4. Explain the role of ethics in marketing.
Increasingly, companies are responding to the need to provide company policies and guidelines to help their managers deal with questions of *marketing ethics*. Of course, even the best guidelines cannot resolve all the difficult ethical decisions that individuals and firms must make. But there are some principles that marketers can choose among. One principle states that such issues should be decided by the free market and legal system. A second and more enlightened principle puts responsibility not on the system but in the hands of individual companies and managers. Each firm and marketing manager must work out a philosophy of socially responsible and ethical behavior. Under the societal marketing concept, managers must look beyond what is legal and allowable and develop standards based on personal integrity, corporate conscience, and long-term consumer welfare.

Because business standards and practices vary from country to country, the issue of ethics poses special challenges for international marketers. The growing consensus among today's marketers is that it is important to make a commitment to a common set of shared standards worldwide.

REVIEWING THE KEY TERMS

Consumerism 641
Consumer-oriented marketing 648
Deficient products 651
Desirable products 651
Enlightened marketing 647

Environmental sustainability 642
Environmentalism 642
Innovative marketing 648
Pleasing products 651
Salutary products 651

Sense-of-mission marketing 648
Societal marketing 648
Value marketing 648

DISCUSSING THE CONCEPTS

1. Marketing receives much criticism, some justified and much not. Which of the major criticisms of marketing discussed in the chapter do you think are most justified? Which are least justified?

2. You have been invited to appear along with an economist on a panel assessing marketing practices in the soft drink industry. You are surprised when the economist opens the discussion with a long list of criticisms of marketing (focusing especially on the unnecessarily high marketing costs and deceptive promotional practices). Abandoning your prepared comments, you set out to defend marketing in general and the soft drink industry in particular. How would you respond to the economist's attack?

3. Comment on the state of consumers' rights on the Internet and in e-commerce. Design a "Bill of Rights" that would protect consumers while they shop for products and services on the Internet. Consider such issues as government regulation, ease and convenience of use, solicitation, privacy, and cost-efficient commerce.

4. Figure 20.1 shows a grid that companies can use to gauge their progress toward environmental sustainability. Where

do most firms begin on the grid? Which cells are most difficult to achieve?

5. What is the basic philosophy supporting enlightened marketing? List and briefly describe each of the five principles of enlightened marketing. Cite several examples of firms that practice enlightened marketing.

6. Compare the marketing concept, discussed in Chapter 1, with the principle of societal marketing. Should all marketers adopt the societal marketing concept? Why or why not?

7. Products can be classified according to their degree of immediate consumer satisfaction and long-run consumer benefit. Give an example of a product in each of the four cells of Figure 20.3. Prepare a brief strategy statement for marketing each of the examples you give.

8. You are the marketing manager for a small firm that makes kitchen appliances. While conducting field tests, you discover a design flaw in one of your most popular models that could potentially cause harm to a small number of consumers. However, a product recall would likely bankrupt your company, leaving all of the employees (including you) jobless. What would you do?

APPLYING THE CONCEPTS

1. The "greening of America" has much more to do with lifestyles than forestry management. Adopting a "green" lifestyle means that consumers demand products and services that are environmentally responsible. As consumers turn to the green lifestyle, companies respond with environmentally responsible products and programs. McDonald's, Wal-Mart, and Proctor & Gamble are just a few of the companies that have adopted a more green way of thinking and acting. Visit the Corporate/Social Responsibility/Environment section of the McDonald's Web site (www.mcdonalds.com) and the Internet Green Marketplace Web site (www.envirolink.org) for more information.

   a. Assume that you are a marketing manager for Crayola Crayons (www.crayola.com) and formulate a "green policy" that will make your product both competitive and environmentally responsible. As you formulate this policy, consider the product itself, packaging, distribution, promotion, and merchandising with distributors.

   b. Visit the McDonald's Web site. What is the company's specific green policy? Comment on the appropriateness of this policy.

   c. One organization that has been at the center of promoting a green policy to corporations is Greenpeace (www.greenpeace.org). Do you find Greenpeace's pro-

   posals to be radical? Explain. How might Greenpeace react to the policies you devised for Crayola?

2. As business and marketing become more complicated, judging what is fair and honest becomes more difficult for consumer and marketer alike. In some industries and areas of business practice, rules and regulations governing marketing are reasonably well established and understood. However, in the expanding world of Internet marketing, established regulations are few and far between. The wide-open spaces of the Internet have been characterized as the "old West" of the twenty-first century, where self-rule abounds. While it is certain that the state of regulation will change, it is unclear when and to what extent. Understanding current laws and regulations pertaining to Internet practices, and anticipating future regulatory issues and actions, are extremely important for today's marketing manager. Take a look at the following Web sites: (a) Federal Trade Commission (www.ftc.gov), (b) Federal Communications Commission (www.fcc.gov), (c) FedWorld Information Network (www.fedworld.gov), (d) Consumer Information Center (www.pueblo.gsa.gov), and (e) National Archives and Records Administration (www.nara.gov). Then answer the following questions:

   a. How easy is it to find information about laws and regulations relating to marketing on the Internet? What problems did you encounter in your search? As an entrepreneur wishing to build a marketing Web site, where could you go to research the laws that govern the site's content?

b. The Internet offers consumers great opportunities but also potential difficulties, frustrations, and dangers. Offsetting its wonders, the Web is flooded with less-desirable elements such as spam mail, pornography, and unscrupulous offers and schemes. As a marketing manager of a firm that sells via the Internet, you want to interact with your consumers in a positive and uncluttered environment. What organizations should be involved in regulating Internet usage and commerce? What regulations would you propose? What difficulties do you see in implementing those regulations?

 DIGITAL CONNECTIONS

CONNECTING MARKETERS WITH CONSUMERS THROUGH FEEDBACK

Are you fed up with products and services that don't live up to marketing promises? Have you considered complaining but been discouraged by the lack of response you've gotten in the past? A new day has dawned for the disgruntled consumer. Now, with the help of the Internet, consumers can band together to air their complaints through chat rooms, Web boards, and complaint Web sites. When thousands of voices join together, the results can be amazing. Visit these Web sites: www.planetfeedback.com; www.complaint.com; and www.bbbonline.org. Then answer the following questions:

FOR DISCUSSION

1. As a consumer, think about problems you have had in the past with products or services. Lodge a complaint online to one of the Web sites mentioned. What response did you receive? Did anyone contact you? Did you get further information? Did you find others with similar complaints?

2. Critique the future of complaint Web sites. Will these sites effectively police the Internet? Are these sites a good alternative to federal or state regulation?

3. How can complaint Web sites be misused? Can they harm honest merchants? Find one example in which you think this has happened.

4. Assume that you are the marketing manager for a newly established Internet company. Design a complaint policy that will ensure quick response, accuracy of complaint reporting, accountability, fairness, and genuine concern for the consumer. How would you promote this policy?

Two Hands: Doing Well by Doing Good

With the motto "We make a living by what we get, we make a life by what we give," Linda Brunini founded Two Hands in 1992. The company creates whimsical jewelry and gifts inspired by the drawings of children with disabilities. It donates 1 percent of net sales each year to organizations that support disadvantaged children. The business model has found success—Two Hands was profitable in its first year.

After viewing the Two Hands video, visit www.twohandsinc.com to learn more. Then answer the following questions about socially responsible marketing:

1. Two Hands was founded with the goal of giving back to the community while operating a successful merchandising business. Is the company's focus appropriately balanced between the two bottom lines of mission and profit?

2. How might a business's social mission support its marketing and sales success? How might it detract from such success? Should corporations be evaluated on corporate citizenship in addition to traditional measures such as sales and stock performance?

3. How does a company's approach to social responsibility affect your impression of it? Are you more likely to support a business that invests in community programs? How could Two Hands better leverage its community involvement to benefit its customers, the charities it supports, and its own financial success?

Vitango: Fighting Malnutrition

Imagine teaching an elementary school class in which students are constantly inattentive and falling asleep—not because they are bored but because they are malnourished. In many countries, this is not an unusual problem. Two billion people around the globe suffer from anemia—an iron deficiency. Iron deficiency leads to reduced resistance to disease, lowers learning ability in children, and contributes to the death of one out of five pregnant mothers. Two hundred million children do not get enough vitamin A. As a result, 250,000 of them go blind each year; vitamin A deficiency is also a contributing factor in the deaths of 2.2 million children under five each year from diarrhea. Many malnourished children suffer from zinc deficiency, which leads to growth failure and infections. Close to 2 billion people do not get enough iodine, and iodine deficiency is the leading cause of preventable mental retardation in the world. If they only used the ordinary table salt found in homes and restaurants all across the United States, this wouldn't happen.

What can U.S. businesses do about this deplorable situation? Quite a bit. Companies such as Coca-Cola and Procter & Gamble have invested millions of dollars in research on micronutrients. They are learning how to fortify everyday food and beverages with additional minerals and vitamins to wipe out deficiencies and keep schoolchildren around the world alert and mentally prepared for school.

Fortified foods are common in the United States. Iodine has been added to ordinary table salt for decades, milk contains vitamin D and calcium, and cornflakes list all the micronutrients found in them on the box. A quick check of your pantry reveals that many drinks and other foods have vitamins and minerals added to them. Thus, adding micronutrients to foods is not new or unusual in this country.

What are new are the efforts of companies to identify specific deficiencies and to develop new technologies for adding micronutrients to foodstuffs in order to eliminate or reduce the deficiencies in specific countries. A good example is a Coca-Cola beverage product called Vitango in Botswana.

Coca-Cola spent years developing a powdered beverage that, when mixed with water, looks and tastes like a sweeter version of Hi-C. The beverage is fortified with 12 vitamins and with minerals that are chronically lacking in the diets of people in developing countries. Coke tested this product in Botswana in Project Mission. Every day for eight weeks, nurses visited schools where they mixed the beverage and passed out paper cups of the "new Hi-C." At the end of the test period, levels of iron and zinc in the children's blood levels had grown. Some parents noted that their children had become more attentive at school. After the Botswana tests, Coca-Cola also ran tests in Peru to determine how well the nutrients are absorbed into the bloodstream.

Coca-Cola, however, is not yet ready to launch Vitango. One issue is the powdered product form. Given the impurities of much of the water in Africa, Coca-Cola wants to package Vitango in a ready-to-drink formula, not in the powdered version now available. That will require reformulation that could actually drive down the price.

P&G has also developed micronutrient-enriched drinks for distribution in developing countries. In the 1990s, P&G developed its own proprietary technology for iron, vitamin A, and iodine fortification, which it called GrowthPlus. GrowthPlus was the basic ingredient in a product called Nutridelight that P&G launched in the Philippines. Unfortunately, it didn't sell well—primarily because it was priced at 50 percent above the market price of other powdered drinks.

More recently, P&G has launched another product, Nutristar, in Venezuela. Sold at most food stores, it contains eight vitamins and five minerals, comes in flavors such as mango and passion fruit, and promises to produce "taller, stronger, and smarter kids." To date, Nutristar is doing quite well. One reason is that it's available at McDonald's, where it is chosen by consumers with about half of all Happy Meals sold. P&G is also offering free samples in schools.

The major problem with both Coca-Cola's and P&G's nutritional products is price. These products were expensive to develop because of long lead times, the need to enlist the help of nutritional experts around the world, and the need to develop products that appeal to the local population's tastes. If offered at "reasonable" prices, they would be out of the reach of the world's desperately poor, the group that needs them most. Consider P&G's Vitango. The poor people in other countries are *not* eating at McDonald's. In countries such as Botswana, they are barely existing on cornmeal and rice. They simply cannot afford to buy fortified sweetened drinks or, for that matter, any sweetened drinks.

How can P&G and Coca-Cola market such products without pricing them too high for the intended market? Learning its lesson in the Philippines, P&G priced Nutristar about 25 percent higher than other powdered drinks and 30 percent below carbonated soft drinks. Even so, that's still too high for the poverty-stricken. Coca-Cola originally planned to sell Vitango for about 20 cents for an eight-ounce liquid serving but then realized that this price was too high. That's part of the reason for continuing developmental work on the product.

One solution to the pricing problem is to work with governments, but many of them are too poor to be able to afford the products. Or they lack the resources to educate their people on the merits of fortified foods. Enter GAIN—the Global Alliance for Improved Nutrition—an international consortium set up by

(continued)

the Bill and Melissa Gates charitable foundation. GAIN offers companies assistance in lobbying for favorable tariffs and tax rates and for speedier regulatory review of new products in targeted countries. It also gives local governments money to increase the demand for fortified foods, including large-scale public relations campaigns or a government "seal of approval." This program is receiving $70 million over five years beginning in May 2002. Such actions should help Coca-Cola and P&G by educating target populations about the value of fortified foods and beverages so that they will buy such products.

Of course, Coca-Cola and P&G can work with governments on their own, but their actions may be distrusted. After all, these are "for-profit" organizations whose motives may be suspect. GAIN has the advantage that it's a not-for-profit.

While GAIN seems like a wonderful resource for helping malnourished peoples, it does have its critics. They point out that selling or giving away fortified foods does not solve the underlying problem of poverty. Nor does it teach people good nutritional habits. Moreover, in addition to their vitamins and minerals, many of the "fortified" foods also contain overly large amounts of fat, sugar, and salt. So, for example, whereas the foods might help reduce iron deficiency, they could also lead to obesity. Some observers claim that it would be better to teach people how to grow fruits and vegetables. The problem is that people will die from malnutrition before poverty is eliminated or trees bear fruit.

Other issues must also be addressed. A fortified beverage such as Vitango will help in dealing with malnutrition but can't eliminate it. People will still need to eat a variety of other foods, which makes education very important. Remember that these products contain no juice. They are intended as supplements, not as substitutes for a proper diet. Lack of understanding about how to use products has landed other companies, such as Nestlé with its infant formula, in trouble when they were used inappropriately.

Given all these problems, why would Coca-Cola and P&G develop these products in the first place? One answer is future sales and profits. Products such as Nutristar and Vitango could create a basis from which to launch other Coca-Cola or P&G products, such as snack foods or juice drinks. As sales of carbonated beverages around the world have slowed, these fortified drinks pose a growth opportunity for the companies. Another answer is goodwill, and not just goodwill for the companies involved. September 11, 2001, taught us in the United States that our country is the focus of both the world's envy and its hatred. Efforts to help share our wealth of technology and research in ways that improve the lot of other peoples may be a major deterrent to future attacks and the growth of terrorism. By helping other nations of the world, U.S. corporations can help create environments where freedom can flourish. One writer insists that when U.S. corporations help people as consumers to buy the goods and services that our companies sell, they also enhance our government's ability to sell our country.

QUESTIONS FOR DISCUSSION

1. Which of the textbook's criticisms of marketing's impact on individual consumers, if any, are found in the cases of Vitango and Nutristar?
2. Which of the criticisms of marketing's impact on society as a whole are found in the Vitango and Nutristar case?
3. Could Vitango and Nutristar be considered enlightened marketing? Why or why not?
4. Are the development and marketing of such products as fortified foods and beverages ethical and socially responsible?
5. How should Coca-Cola proceed with the marketing of Vitango?

Sources: Jill Bruss, "Reaching the World," *Beverage Industry,* December 2001, p. 28+; Rance Crain, "U.S. Marketers Must Develop Products to Help Third World," *Advertising Age,* December 3, 2001, p. 20; Betsy McKay, "Drinks for Developing Countries," *Wall Street Journal,* November 27, 2001, pp. B1, B6; Rachel Zimmerman, "Gates Fights Malnutrition with Cheese, Ketchup Incentives," *Wall Street Journal,* May 9, 2002, p. B1.

Case Pilot Case for Part 4: Managing Marketing

The City Harborfront Preservation Society (CHPS): Managing Marketing

Late one afternoon, Guy Purkis sat down in his City Harborfront Preservation Society (CHPS) office to review the developments of the day because his bank was pressuring him to pay overdue accounts. As he gazed out over the panoramic view from his 21st floor office, Guy realized that he needed to quickly develop the first formal marketing plan and budget requested by the new board Chairperson, Rose Koffie, a retired marketing executive.

The CHPS was established as a not-for-profit organization using volunteers to help raise funds for a variety of harborfront-related projects (e.g., printing historical books and donating money to help restore historically-relevant properties). The CHPS's ultimate goal was to own property and a museum featuring unique boating-related artifacts, models, displays, and hands-on work-in-progress projects (e.g., old boats or sunken wrecks being restored). While researching for ways to do a marketing plan, Guy heard of an association comprising organizations like the CHPS that were successful in marketing and funding their harborfront activities.

Directors were appointed for five years, met monthly, belonged to a local yacht club, and were retired business people with significant community influence who nominated close friends to replace them when their term expired.

Guy, CHPS's Executive Director for the past 10 years, was hired as the first part-time employee when the organization was founded 11 years ago. Now 33, Guy was the son of the original Board Chairperson and graduated from City University the year he started with the CHPS. His job was to set up the office, help manage and train volunteers, market and promote CHPS, and handle any administrative duties.

In his second year with CHPS, when he was promoted to Executive Director, Guy began marketing the organization and started fund-raising. Every year the staff and volunteers organized three fund-raising projects (e.g., bingos, celebrity auctions, sail-a-thons, business-to-business canvassing, win-a-boat lotteries) with the most successful project so far raising $39,000 (after expenses) while the least successful lost $73,000.

Guy also hired two friends from the university as full-time administrative assistants, making them responsible for coordinating the 15 to 20 volunteers and for preparing CHPS flyers and promotional materials. To help improve their image, Guy convinced the Board to move to more prestigious offices and negotiated a long-term lease that CHPS's new landlord had just announced could be renegotiated.

Almost 90 percent of the CHPS budget was raised through government grants, but the government recently announced plans to drastically reduce this support. The CHPS's raised $30,000 in its first year, reached a record high of $560,000 five years ago, and currently had $170,000 in revenues and $250,000 in expenses (i.e., $144,000 for wages, $62,000 for rent, $10,000 for marketing, and $34,000 for other costs).

Guy knew he needed to develop a marketing plan to help CHPS improve and wondered just how best to proceed or whom he should ask for help.

Case Pilot Challenge

Marketing managers must realize that doing business with different cultures, or in foreign countries, may require changes in promotions, pricing, distribution, products, and services. Equally important, marketing managers must think about the social or ethical implications related to their efforts. The last two chapters of the text, in Part 4, deal with the variables and issues related to global marketing and to the increasing importance of the role that ethics has in the marketplace.

In the CHPS case, above, Guy is faced with a variety of challenging issues. Try your marketing management skills, visit www.prenhall.com/casepilot/, and see if you can find the answers to the following:

a)   What are some of the ethical issues in this case?

b)   What is one way marketing differs for a not-for-profit organization versus a traditional business?

c)   What role does fundraising play in the organization's marketing?

Measuring and Forecasting Demand

When a company finds an attractive market, it must estimate that market's current size and future potential carefully. This appendix presents the principles and tools for measuring and forecasting market demand.

To develop effective targeting strategies, and to manage their marketing efforts effectively, companies must be good at both measuring *current* market demand and forecasting *future* demand. The company can lose a lot of profit by overestimating or underestimating the market. Overly optimistic estimates of current or future demand can result in costly overcapacity or excess inventories. Underestimating demand can mean missed sales and profit opportunities.

Measuring Current Market Demand

Marketers will want to estimate three different aspects of current market demand—*total market demand, area market demand,* and *actual sales and market shares.*

Estimating Total Market Demand

Total market demand

The volume of a product or service that would be bought by a defined customer group in a defined geographic area in a defined time period in a defined marketing environment under a defined level and mix of industry marketing effort.

The **total market demand** for a product or service is the total volume that would be bought by a defined consumer group in a defined geographic area in a defined time period in a defined marketing environment under a defined level and mix of industry marketing effort. Total market demand is not a fixed number but a function of the stated conditions. For example, next year's total market demand for ice cream in the United States will depend on how much the makers of Breyers, Häagen-Dazs, Ben & Jerry's, and other brands spend on marketing. It will also depend on many environmental factors, ranging from the level of consumer health concerns to the weather in key market areas. The demand for the premium ice cream brands will be affected by economic conditions.

Figure A1.1 shows the relationship between total market demand and various market conditions. The horizontal axis shows different possible levels of industry marketing expenditures in a given time period. The vertical axis shows the resulting demand level. The curve shows the estimated level of market demand at varying levels of industry marketing effort. Some minimum level of sales would take place without any marketing expenditures. Greater marketing expenditures would yield higher levels of demand, first at an increasing rate, and then at a decreasing rate. Marketing efforts above a certain level would not cause much more demand. This upper limit of market demand is called **market potential.** The industry market forecast shows the expected

Market potential

The upper limit of market demand.

FIGURE A1.1
Market demand

Market demand in the specified period

Market demand as a function of industry marketing expenditures

level of market demand corresponding to the planned level of industry marketing effort in the given environment.

Primary demand

The total demand for all brands of a given product or service.

Companies selling in mature markets often take **primary demand**—total demand for all brands of a given product or service—as given. They concentrate their marketing resources on building **selective demand**—demand for *their* brand of the product or service. For example, in the United States, where Coca-Cola faces a mature soft drink market, it directs most of its marketing energies toward building consumer preference for Coke, Diet Coke, Sprite, and its other brands. However, in countries such as China or Russia, which are characterized by huge but largely untapped market potential, Coca-Cola attempts to build the primary demand for soft drinks, as well as preference for its own brands.

Selective demand

The demand for given brand of a product or service.

Companies have developed various practical methods for estimating total market demand. We will illustrate two here. Suppose Sony Music USA wants to estimate the total annual sales of recorded compact disks. A common way to estimate total market demand is as follows:

$$Q = n \times q \times p$$

where Q = total market demand

n = number of buyers in the market

q = quantity purchased by an average buyer per year

p = price of an average unit

Thus, if there are 100 million buyers of compact disks each year, the average buyer buys 6 disks a year, and the average price is $14, then the total market demand for disks is $8.4 billion ($= 100{,}000{,}000 \times 6 \times \$14$).

A variation of this approach is the *chain ratio method*. This method involves multiplying a base number by a chain of adjusting percentages. For example, suppose that Sony wants to estimate demand for its new line of premium digital cameras, which store a large number of high-quality digital images, which are later transferred to a personal computer to be resized, cropped, enhanced, grouped, and printed. Sony's new digital cameras are priced higher than previous digital models and ordinary 35mm cameras. Thus, Sony first plans to target only serious amateur photographers who have home computers and enough money to afford the new cameras. Sony can make a U.S. demand estimate using a chain of calculations like the following:

Total number of U.S. households
× The percentage of U.S. households containing one or more serious amateur photographers
× The percentage of these household owning a personal computer
× The percentage of PC-owning households with enough discretionary income to buy Sony's new digital camera

This simple chain of calculations would provide only a rough estimate of potential demand. However, more detailed chains involving additional segments and other qualifying factors would yield more accurate and refined estimates.

Estimating Area Market Demand

Companies face the problem of selecting the best sales territories and allocating their marketing budget optimally among these territories. Therefore, they need to estimate the market potential of different cities, states, and countries. Two major methods are available: the *market buildup method,* which is used primarily by business goods firms, and the *market factor index method,* which is used primarily by consumer goods firms.

Market Buildup Method

Market buildup method

A forecasting method that identifies market factors that correlate with market potential and combines them into a weighted index.

The **market buildup method** calls for identifying all the potential buyers in each market and estimating their potential purchases. Suppose a manufacturer of mining instruments developed an instrument that can be used in the field to test the actual proportion of gold or silver in metal-bearing ores. By using it, miners would not waste their time digging deposits of ore containing too little gold or silver to be commercially profitable. The manufacturer wants to price the instrument at $1,000. It sees each mine as buying one or more instruments, depending on the mine's size. The company wants to determine the market potential for this instrument in each mining state. It would hire a salesperson to cover each state that has a market potential of over $300,000. The company wants to start by finding the market potential in Colorado.

To estimate the market potential in Colorado, the manufacturer can consult the North American Industrial Classification System (NAICS) developed by the U.S. Bureau of the Census.[1] The NAICS is the government's coding system that classifies industries, for purposes of data collection and reporting, according to the processes they use to produce goods and services. Each major industrial group is assigned to a two-digit code—mining bears the code number 21. Within mining are further breakdowns (the gold-ore-and silver-ore mining category has the code number 21222). Finally, gold and silver ores are subdivided into further NAICS groups, with six-digit code numbers (gold is 212221 and silver is 212222).

Next the manufacturer can turn to the U.S. Census of Mining to determine the number of gold- and silver-mining operations in each state, their locations within the state, and the number of employees, annual sales, and net worth. Suppose that in consulting the census for Colorado, the company finds the data located in columns 1 and 2 of Table A1.1. It can then prepare the market potential estimate shown. Column 1 classifies mines into three groups based on the number of employees. Column 2 shows the number of mines in each group. Column 3 shows the potential number of instruments that mines in each size class might buy. Column 4 shows the unit market potential (column 2 times column 3). Finally, column 5 shows the dollar market potential, given that each instrument sells for $1,000. In this example, Colorado has a market potential of $370,000. Therefore, the mining instrument manufacturer would hire one salesperson for Colorado. In the same way, companies in other industries can use the market buildup method to estimate market potential in specific market areas.

TABLE A1.1   MARKET BUILDUP METHOD USING NAICS: INSTRUMENT POTENTIAL IN COLORADO

NAICS	(1) Number of Employees	(2) Number of Mines	(3) Potential Number of Instruments per Size Class	(4) Unit Market Potential	(5) Dollar Market Potential (at $1,000 Each)
212221	Under 10	40	1	40	
(gold ore mining)	10 to 50	20	2	40	
	Over 50	<u>10</u>	3	<u>30</u>	
		70		110	$110,000
212222	Under 10	80	1	80	
(silver ore mining)	10 to 50	50	2	100	
	Over 50	<u>20</u>	4	<u>80</u>	
		150		260	<u>$260,000</u>
					$370,000

Market Factor Index Method

Consumer goods companies also have to estimate area market potentials. Consider the following example: A manufacturer of men's dress shirts wishes to evaluate its sales performance relative to market potential in several major market areas, starting with Indianapolis. It estimates total national potential for dress shirts at about $2 billion per year. The company's current nationwide sales are $140 million, about a 7 percent share of the total potential market. Its sales in the Indianapolis metropolitan area are $1,100,000. It wants to know whether its share of the Indianapolis market is higher or lower than its national 7 percent market share. To find this out, the company first needs to calculate market potential in the Indianapolis area.

Market factor index method

A forecasting method that calls for identifying the potential buyers in each market and estimating their potential purchases.

A common method for calculating area market potential is the **market factor index method,** which identifies market factors that correlate with market potential and combines them into a weighted index. An excellent example of this method is called the *buying power index,* which is published each year by *Sales & Marketing Management* magazine in its *Survey of Buying Power.*[2] This survey estimates the buying power, or "ability to buy," for each region, state, and metropolitan area of the nation. The buying power index is based on three factors: the area's share of the nation's *population, effective buying income,* and *retail sales.* The buying power index (BPI) for a specific area is given by

$$BPI = .2 \times \text{percentage of national population in the area}$$
$$+ .5 \times \text{the percentage of effective buying income in the area}$$
$$+ .3 \times \text{percentage of national retail sales in the area}$$

Using this index, the shirt manufacturer looks up the Indianapolis metropolitan area and finds that this market has .5596 percent of the nation's population, .5984 percent of the nation's effective buying income, and .6594 percent of the nation's retail sales. Thus, the buying power index for Indianapolis is:

$$BPI = (.2 \times .5596) + (.5 \times .5984) + (.3 \times .6594) = .6089$$

That is, Indianapolis should account for .6089 percent of the nation's total potential demand for dress shirts. Because the total national potential is $2 billion each year, total potential in Indianapolis equals $2 billion × .006089 = $12,178,000. Thus, the company's sales in Indianapolis of $1,100,000 amount to a $1,100,000 / $12,178,000 = 9.03 percent share of area market potential. Comparing this with its 7 percent national share, the company appears to be doing better in Indianapolis than in other parts of the country.

Many companies compute additional area demand measures. Marketers now can refine state-by-state and city-by-city measures down to census tracts or ZIP codes. Census tracts are small areas about the size of a neighborhood, and ZIP code areas (designated by the U.S. Post Office) are larger areas, often the size of small towns. Information on population size, family income, and other characteristics is available for each type of unit. Marketers can use this data to estimate demand in neighborhoods or other smaller geographic units within large cities.

Estimating Actual Sales and Market Shares

Besides estimating total and area demand, a company will want to know the actual industry sales in its market. Thus, it must identify its competitors and estimate their sales.

Industry's trade associations often collect and publish total industry sales, although not individual company sales. In this way, each company can evaluate its performance against the industry as a whole. Suppose the company's sales are increasing at a rate of 5 percent a year and industry sales are increasing at 10 percent. This company actually is losing its relative standing in the industry.

Another way to estimate sales is to buy reports from marketing research firms that audit total sales and brand sales. For example, Nielsen Media Research audits retail sales in various product categories in supermarkets and drugstores and sells this information to interested companies. A company can obtain data on total product category sales as well as brand sales. It can compare its performance with that of the total industry or any particular competitor to see whether it is gaining or losing in its relative standing.[3]

Forecasting Future Demand

Forecasting
The art of estimating future demand by anticipating what buyers are likely to do under a given set of conditions.

Forecasting is the art of estimating future demand by anticipating what buyers are likely to do under a given set of future conditions. Very few products or services lend themselves to easy forecasting. Those that do generally involve a product with steady sales, or sales growth, in a stable competitive situation. But most markets do not have stable total and company demand, so good forecasting becomes a key factor in company success.

Companies commonly use a three-stage procedure to arrive at a sales forecast. First they make an *environmental forecast,* followed by an *industry forecast,* followed by a *company sales forecast.* The environmental forecast calls for projecting inflation, unemployment, interest rates, consumer spending and saving, business investment, government expenditures, net exports, and other environmental events important to the company. The result is a forecast of gross domestic product, which is used along with other indicators to forecast industry sales. Then the company prepares its sales forecast by assuming that it will win a certain share of industry sales.

Companies use several specific techniques to forecast their sales. Table A1.2 lists many of these techniques. All forecasts are built on one of three information bases: what people say, what people do, or what people have done. The first basis—*what people say*—involves surveying the opinions of buyers or those close to them, such as salespeople or outside experts. It includes three methods: surveys of buyer intentions, composites of sales force opinions, and expert opinion. Building a forecast on *what people do* involves putting the product into a test market to assess buyer response. The final basis—*what people have done*—involves analyzing records of past buying behavior or using time-series analysis or statistical demand analysis.

Survey of Buyers' Intentions

One way to forecast what buyers will do is to ask them directly. Surveys are especially valuable if the buyers have clearly formed intentions, will carry them out, and can describe them to interviewers. However, this is sometimes not the case, and marketers must be careful when using consumer survey data to make forecasts.

Several research organizations conduct periodic surveys of consumer buying intentions. These organizations ask questions such as the following:

Do you intend to buy an automobile within the next six months?										
0	.1	.2	.3	.4	.5	.6	.7	.8	.9	1.0
No chance		Slight chance		Fair chance		Good chance		Strong chance		For certain

This is called a *purchase probability scale.* In addition, the various surveys ask about the consumer's present and future personal finances, and his or her expectations about the economy. The various bits of information are combined into a *consumer sentiment measure* (such as the one managed by the Survey Research Center of the University of Michigan) or a *consumer confidence*

TABLE A1.2	**COMMON SALES FORECASTING TECHNIQUES**
Based On	**Methods**
What people say	Surveys of buyers' intentions
	Composite sales force opinions
	Expert opinion
What people do	Test markets
What people have done	Past-sales analysis
	Leading indicators

measure (such as Sindlinger and Company's). Consumer durable-goods companies subscribe to these indexes to help them anticipate major shifts in consumer buying intentions so that they can adjust their production and marketing plans accordingly.

For *business buying,* various agencies carry out intention surveys about plant, equipment, and materials purchases. The two best-known surveys are conducted by the U.S. Department of Commerce and McGraw-Hill. Most of the estimates have been within 10 percent of the actual outcomes.

Composite of Sales Force Opinions

When buyer interviewing is impractical, the company may base its sales forecasts on information provided by the sales force. The company typically asks its salespeople to estimate sales by product for their individual territories. It then adds up the individual estimates to arrive at an overall sales forecast.

Few companies use their sales force's estimates without some adjustments. Salespeople are biased observers. They may be naturally pessimistic or optimistic, or they may go to one extreme or another because of recent sales setbacks or successes. Furthermore, they are often unaware of larger economic developments, and they do not always know how their company's marketing plans will affect future sales in their territories. They may understate demand so that the company will set a low sales quota. They may not take the time to prepare careful estimates or may not consider it worthwhile.

Assuming these biases can be countered, a number of benefits can be gained by involving the sales force in forecasting. Salespeople may have better insights into developing trends than any other group. After participating in the forecasting process, the salespeople may have greater confidence in their quotas and more incentive to achieve them. Also, such "grassroots" forecasting provides estimates broken down by product, territory, customer, and salesperson.

Expert Opinion

Companies can also obtain forecasts by turning to experts. Experts include dealers, distributors, suppliers, marketing consultants, and trade associations. Thus, auto companies survey their dealers periodically for their forecasts of short-term demand. Dealer estimates, however, are subject to the same strengths and weaknesses as sales force estimates.

Many companies buy economic and industry forecasts from well-known firms. These forecasting specialists are in a better position than the company to prepare economic forecasts because they have more data available and more forecasting expertise.

Occasionally companies will invite a special group of experts to prepare a forecast. The experts may be asked to exchange views and come up with a group estimate (group discussion method). Or they may be asked to supply their estimates individually, with the company analyst combining them into a single estimate. Finally, they may supply individual estimates and assumptions that are reviewed by a company analyst, revised, and followed by further rounds of estimation (called the Delphi method).

Experts can provide good insights on which to base forecasts, but they can also be wrong. For example, in 1943, IBM chairman Thomas J. Watson predicted, "I think there's a world market for about five computers." A short time later, *Popular Mechanics* sagely observed that "Computers in the future may weigh no more than 1.5 tons." As recently as 1981, Bill Gates, a founder of Microsoft, proclaimed that "640K ought to be enough for anybody." In 1876, Western Union asserted, "This 'telephone' has too many shortcomings to be seriously considered as a means of communication. The device is inherently of no value to us." And in 1946, Daryl F. Zanuck, head of 20th Century Fox, made this pronouncement: "TV won't be able to hold on to any market it captures after the first six months. People will soon get tired of staring at a plywood box every night."[4] Where possible, the company should back up experts' opinions with estimates obtained using other methods.

Test Marketing

Where buyers do not plan their purchases carefully or where experts are not available or reliable, the company may want to conduct a direct test market. A direct test market is especially useful in forecasting new-product sales or established-product sales in a new distribution channel or territory. Test marketing is discussed in Chapter 10.

Past-Sales Analysis

Sales forecasts can be developed on the basis of past sales. *Time-series analysis* consists of breaking down past time series into four components (trend, cycle, seasonal, and erratic), and projecting these components into the future. *Exponential smoothing* consists of projecting the next period's sales by combining an average of past sales and the most recent sales, giving more weight to the latter. *Statistical demand analysis* consists of measuring the impact level of each of a set of causal factors (e.g., income, marketing expenditures, price) on the sales level. Finally, *econometric analysis* consists of building sets of equations that describe a system and proceeding to statistically fit the parameters.

Leading Indicators

Leading indicators

Time series that change in the same direction but in advance of company sales.

Many companies try to forecast their sales by finding one or more **leading indicators**—other time series that change in the same direction but in advance of company sales. For example, a plumbing supply company might find that its sales lag behind the housing starts index by about four months. The housing starts index would then be a useful leading indicator. The National Bureau of Economic Research has identified 12 of the best leading indicators, and their values are published monthly in the *Survey of Current Business* (see www.bea.doc.gov/bea/pubs.htm).

KEY TERMS

Forecasting A-5
Leading indicators A-7
Market buildup method A-3

Market factor index method A-4
Market potential A-1
Primary demand A-2

Selective demand A-2
Total market demand A-1

Marketing Arithmetic

One aspect of marketing not discussed within the text is marketing arithmetic. The calculation of sales, costs, and certain ratios is important for many marketing decisions. This appendix describes three major areas of marketing arithmetic: the *operating statement, analytic ratios,* and *markups and markdowns.*

Operating Statement

Balance sheet

A financial statement that shows assets, liabilities, and net worth of a company at a given time.

Operating statement (profit-and-loss statement, income statement)

A financial statement that shows company sales, cost of goods sold, and expenses during a given period of time.

The operating statement and the balance sheet are the two main financial statements used by companies. The **balance sheet** shows the assets, liabilities, and net worth of a company at a given time. The **operating statement** (also called **profit-and-loss statement** or **income statement**) is the more important of the two for marketing information. It shows company sales, cost of goods sold, and expenses during a specified time period. By comparing the operating statement from one time period to the next, the firm can spot favorable or unfavorable trends and take appropriate action.

Table A2.1 shows the 2002 operating statement for Dale Parsons Men's Wear, a specialty store in the Midwest. This statement is for a retailer; the operating statement for a manufacturer would be somewhat different. Specifically, the section on purchases within the "cost of goods sold" area would be replaced by "cost of goods manufactured."

The outline of the operating statement follows a logical series of steps to arrive at the firm's $25,000 net profit figure:

Net sales	$300,000
Cost of goods sold	− 175,000
Gross margin	$125,000
Expenses	− 100,000
Net profit	$ 25,000

Gross sales

The total amount that a company charges during a given period of time for merchandise.

The first part details the amount that Parsons received for the goods sold during the year. The sales figures consist of three items: *gross sales, returns and allowances,* and *net sales.* **Gross sales** is the total amount charged to customers during the year for merchandise purchased in Parsons's store. As expected, some customers returned merchandise because of damage or a change of mind. If the customer gets a full refund or full credit on another purchase, we call this a *return.* Or the customer may decide to keep the item if Parsons will reduce the price. This is called an *allowance.* By subtracting returns and allowances from gross sales, we arrive at net sales—what Parsons earned in revenue from a year of selling merchandise:

Gross sales	$325,000
Returns and allowances	− 25,000
Net sales	$300,000

The second major part of the operating statement calculates the amount of sales revenue Dale Parsons retains after paying the costs of the merchandise. We start with the inventory in the

TABLE A2.1	OPERATING STATEMENT: DALE PARSONS MEN'S WEAR, YEAR ENDING DECEMBER 31, 2002			
Gross sales				$325,000
Less: Sales returns and allowances				25,000
Net sales				$300,000
Cost of goods sold				
Beginning inventory, January, at cost			$ 60,000	
Gross purchases	$165,000			
Less: Purchase discounts	15,000			
Net purchases	$150,000			
Plus: Freight-in	10,000			
Net cost of delivered purchases		$160,000		
Cost of goods available for sale		$220,000		
Less: Ending inventory, December 31, at cost		$ 45,000		
Cost of goods sold				$175,000
Gross margin				$125,000
Expenses				
Selling expenses				
Sales, salaries, and commissions	$ 40,000			
Advertising	5,000			
Delivery	5,000			
Total selling expenses		$ 50,000		
Administrative expenses				
Office salaries	$ 20,000			
Office supplies	5,000			
Miscellaneous (outside consultant)	5,000			
Total administrative expenses		$ 30,000		
General expenses				
Rent	$ 10,000			
Heat, light, telephone	5,000			
Miscellaneous (insurance, depreciation)	5,000			
Total general expenses		$ 20,000		
Total expenses				$100,000
Net profit				$ 25,000

Cost of goods sold

The net cost to the company of goods sold.

store at the beginning of the year. During the year, Parsons bought $165,000 worth of suits, slacks, shirts, ties, jeans, and other goods. Suppliers gave the store discounts totaling $15,000, so that net purchases were $150,000. Because the store is located away from regular shipping routes, Parsons had to pay an additional $10,000 to get the products delivered, giving the firm a net cost of $160,000. Adding the beginning inventory, the cost of goods available for sale amounted to $220,000. The $45,000 ending inventory of clothes in the store on December 31 is then subtracted to come up with the $175,000 **cost of goods sold.** Here again we have followed a logical series of steps to figure out the cost of goods sold:

Amount Parsons started with (beginning inventory)	$ 60,000
Net amount purchased	+150,000
Any added costs to obtain these purchases	+ 10,000
Total cost of goods Parsons had available for sale during year	$220,000
Amount Parsons had left over (ending inventory)	− 45,000
Cost of goods actually sold	$175,000

Gross margin

The difference between net sales and cost of goods sold.

The difference between what Parsons paid for the merchandise ($175,000) and what he sold it for ($300,000) is called the **gross margin** ($125,000).

In order to show the profit Parsons "cleared" at the end of the year, we must subtract from the gross margin the *expenses* incurred while doing business. *Selling expenses* included two sales employees, local newspaper and radio advertising, and the cost of delivering merchandise to customers after alterations. Selling expenses totaled $50,000 for the year. *Administrative expenses* included the salary for an office manager, office supplies such as stationery and business cards, and miscellaneous expenses including an administrative audit conducted by an outside consultant. Administrative expenses totaled $30,000 in 2002. Finally, the general expenses of rent, utilities, insurance, and depreciation came to $20,000. Total expenses were therefore $100,000 for the year. By subtracting expenses ($100,000) from the gross margin ($125,000), we arrive at the net profit of $25,000 for Parsons during 2002.

Analytic Ratios

Operating ratios
Ratios of selected operating statement items to net sales that allow marketers to compare the firm's performance in one year with that in previous years (or with industry standards and competitors in the same year).

The operating statement provides the figures needed to compute some crucial ratios. Typically these ratios are called **operating ratios**—the ratio of selected operating statement items to net sales. They let marketers compare the firm's performance in one year to that in previous years (or with industry standards and competitors in the same year). The most commonly used operating ratios are the *gross margin percentage,* the *net profit percentage,* the *operating expense percentage,* and the *returns and allowances percentage.*

Ratio	Formula	Computation from Table A1.1
Gross margin percentage	$= \dfrac{\text{gross margin}}{\text{net sales}}$	$= \dfrac{\$125,000}{\$300,000} = 42\%$
Net profit percentage	$= \dfrac{\text{net profit}}{\text{net sales}}$	$= \dfrac{\$25,000}{\$300,000} = 8\%$
Operating expense percentage	$= \dfrac{\text{total expenses}}{\text{net sales}}$	$= \dfrac{\$100,000}{\$300,000} = 33\%$
Returns and allowances percentage	$= \dfrac{\text{returns and allowances}}{\text{net sales}}$	$= \dfrac{\$25,000}{\$300,000} = 8\%$

Another useful ratio is the *stockturn rate* (also called *inventory turnover rate*). The stockturn rate is the number of times an inventory turns over or is sold during a specified time period (often one year). It may be computed on a cost, selling price, or units basis. Thus the formula can be:

$$\text{Stockturn rate} = \frac{\text{cost of goods sold}}{\text{average inventory at cost}}$$

or

$$\text{Stockturn rate} = \frac{\text{selling price of goods sold}}{\text{average selling price of inventory}}$$

or

$$\text{Stockturn rate} = \frac{\text{sales in units}}{\text{average inventory in units}}$$

We will use the first formula to calculate the stockturn rate for Dale Parsons Men's Wear:

$$\frac{\$175,000}{(\$60,000 + \$45,000)\,/\,2} = \frac{\$175,000}{\$52,500} = 3.3$$

That is, Parsons's inventory turned over 3.3 times in 2002. Normally, the higher the stockturn rate, the higher the management efficiency and company profitability.

Return on investment (ROI)
A common measure of managerial effectiveness—the ratio of net profit to investment.

Return on investment (ROI) is frequently used to measure managerial effectiveness. It uses figures from the firm's operating statement and balance sheet. A commonly used formula for computing ROI is:

$$\text{ROI} = \frac{\text{net profit}}{\text{sales}} \times \frac{\text{sales}}{\text{investment}}$$

You may have two questions about this formula: Why use a two-step process when ROI could be computed simply as net profit divided by investment? And what exactly is "investment"?

To answer these questions, let's look at how each component of the formula can affect the ROI. Suppose Dale Parsons Men's Wear has a total investment of $150,000. Then ROI can be computed as follows:

$$\text{ROI} = \frac{\$25,000 \text{ (net profit)}}{\$300,000 \text{ (sales)}} \times \frac{\$300,000 \text{ (sales)}}{\$150,000 \text{ (investment)}}$$

$$= 8.3\% \times 2 = 16.6\%$$

Now suppose that Parsons had worked to increase his share of market. He could have had the same ROI if his sales had doubled while dollar profit and investment stayed the same (accepting a lower profit ratio to get higher turnover and market share):

$$\text{ROI} = \frac{\$25,000 \text{ (net profit)}}{\$600,000 \text{ (sales)}} \times \frac{\$600,000 \text{ (sales)}}{\$150,000 \text{ (investment)}}$$

$$= 4.16\% \times 4 = 16.6\%$$

Parsons might have increased its ROI by increasing net profit through more cost cutting and more efficient marketing:

$$\text{ROI} = \frac{\$50,000 \text{ (net profit)}}{\$300,000 \text{ (sales)}} \times \frac{\$300,000 \text{ (sales)}}{\$150,000 \text{ (investment)}}$$

$$= 16.6\% \times 2 = 33.2\%$$

Another way to increase ROI is to find some way to get the same levels of sales and profits while decreasing investment (perhaps by cutting the size of Parsons's average inventory):

$$\text{ROI} = \frac{\$25,000 \text{ (net profit)}}{\$300,000 \text{ (sales)}} \times \frac{\$300,000 \text{ (sales)}}{\$75,000 \text{ (investment)}}$$

$$= 8.3\% \times 4 = 33.2\%$$

What is "investment" in the ROI formula? *Investment* is often defined as the total assets of the firm. But many analysts now use other measures of return to assess performance. These measures include *return on net assets (RONA), return on stockholders' equity (ROE),* or *return on assets managed (ROAM).* Because investment is measured at a point in time, we usually compute ROI as the average investment between two time periods (say, January 1 and December 31 of the same year). We can also compute ROI as an "internal rate of return" by using discounted cash flow analysis (see any finance textbook for more on this technique). The objective in using any of these measures is to determine how well the company has been using its resources. As inflation, competitive pressures, and cost of capital increase, such measures become increasingly important indicators of marketing and company performance.

Markups and Markdowns

Markup

The percentage of the cost or price of a product added to cost in order to arrive at a selling price.

Markdown

A percentage reduction from the original selling price.

Retailers and wholesalers must understand the concepts of **markups** and **markdowns.** They must make a profit to stay in business, and the markup percentage affects profits. Markups and markdowns are expressed as percentages.

There are two different ways to compute markups—on *cost* or on *selling price:*

$$\text{Markup percentage on cost} = \frac{\text{dollar markup}}{\text{cost}}$$

$$\text{Markup percentage on selling price} = \frac{\text{dollar markup}}{\text{selling price}}$$

Dale Parsons must decide which formula to use. If Parsons bought shirts for $15 and wanted to mark them up $10 to a price of $25, his markup percentage on cost would be $10/$15 = 67.7%.

If Parsons based markup on selling price, the percentage would be $10/$25 = 40%. In figuring markup percentage, most retailers use the selling price rather than the cost.

Suppose Parsons knew his cost ($12) and desired markup on price (25%) for a man's tie, and wanted to compute the selling price. The formula is:

$$\text{Selling price} = \frac{\text{cost}}{1 - \text{markup}}$$

$$\text{Selling price} = \frac{\$12}{.75} = \$16$$

As a product moves through the channel of distribution, each channel member adds a markup before selling the product to the next member. This "markup chain" is shown for a suit purchased by a Parsons customer for $200:

		$ Amount	% of Selling Price
Manufacturer	Cost	$ 108	90%
	Markup	12	10
	Selling price	120	100
Wholesaler	Cost	120	80
	Markup	30	20
	Selling price	150	100
Retailer	Cost	150	75
	Markup	50	25
	Selling price	200	100

The retailer whose markup is 25 percent does not necessarily enjoy more profit than a manufacturer whose markup is 10 percent. Profit also depends on how many items with that profit margin can be sold (stockturn rate) and on operating efficiency (expenses).

Sometimes a retailer wants to convert markups based on selling price to markups based on cost, and vice versa. The formulas are:

$$\text{Markup percentage on selling price} = \frac{\text{markup percentage on cost}}{100\% + \text{markup percentage on selling cost}}$$

$$\text{Markup percentage on cost} = \frac{\text{markup percentage on selling price}}{100\% - \text{markup percentage on selling price}}$$

Suppose Parsons found that his competitor was using a markup of 30 percent based on cost and wanted to know what this would be as a percentage of selling price. The calculation would be:

$$\frac{30\%}{100\% + 30\%} = \frac{30\%}{130\%} = 23\%$$

Because Parsons was using a 25 percent markup on the selling price for suits, he felt that his markup was suitable compared with that of the competitor.

Near the end of the summer, Parsons still had an inventory of summer slacks in stock. Therefore, he decided to use a *markdown,* a reduction from the original selling price. Before the summer, he had purchased 20 pairs at $10 each, and he had since sold 10 pairs at $20 each. He marked down the other pairs to $15 and sold 5 pairs. We compute his *markdown ratio* as follows:

$$\text{Markdown percentage} = \frac{\text{dollar markdown}}{\text{total net sales in dollars}}$$

The dollar markdown is $25 (5 pairs at $5 each) and total net sales are $275 (10 pairs at $20 + 5 pairs at $15). The ratio, then, is $25/$275 = 9%.

Larger retailers usually compute markdown ratios for each department rather than for individual items. The ratios provide a measure of relative marketing performance for each department and can be calculated and compared over time. Markdown ratios can also be used to compare the performance of different buyers and salespeople in a store's various departments.

KEY TERMS

Balance sheet A-9
Cost of goods sold A-10
Gross margin A-10
Gross sales A-9

Markdown A-12
Markup A-12
Operating ratios A-11

Operating statement (or profit-and-loss statement or income statement) A-9
Return on investment (ROI) A-11

References

CHAPTER 1

1. See Stewart Alsop, "I'm Betting on Amazon," *Fortune,* April 30, 2001, p. 48; Robert D. Hof, "Amazon.com: The Wild World of E-Commerce," *Business Week,* December 14, 1998, p. 106; Kathleen Doler, "Interview: Jeff Bezos, Founder and CEO of Amazon.com Inc.," *Upside,* September 1998, pp. 76–80; Susan Stellin and Geoffrey Colvin, "Shaking Hands on the Web," *Fortune,* May 14, 2001, p. 54; Nick Wingfield, "Leading the News: Amazon's Loss Narrows Sharply on 21% Sales Rise," *Wall Street Journal,* April 24, 2002, p. A3; Leslie Kaufman, "Amazon II: Will This Smile Last?" *Wall Street Journal,* May 19, 2002, p. 3.1; and "About Amazon.com," accessed online at www.amazon.com, June 2002.

2. The American Marketing Association offers this definition: "*Marketing* is the process of planning and executing the conception, pricing, promotion, and distributing of ideas, goods, and services to create exchanges that satisfy individual and organizational objectives."

3. Jack Neff, "Humble Try," *Advertising Age,* February 18, 2002, pp. 3, 12.

4. See Theodore Levitt's classic article, "Marketing Myopia," *Harvard Business Review,* July–August 1960, pp. 45–56. For more recent discussions, see Dhananjayan Kashyap, "Marketing Myopia Revisited: 'A Look Through the 'Colored Glass of a Client,'" *Marketing and Research Today,* August 1996, pp. 197–201; Colin Grant, "Theodore Levitt's Marketing Myopia," *Journal of Business Ethics,* February 1999, pp. 397–406; Jeffrey M. O'Brien, "Drums in the Jungle," *MC Technology Marketing Intelligence,* March 1999, pp. 22–30; and Hershell Sarbin, "Overcoming Marketing Myopia," *Folio,* May 2000, pp. 55–56.

5. See B. Joseph Pine II and James Gilmore, "Welcome to the Experience Economy," *Harvard Business Review,* July–August 1998, p. 99; Jane E. Zarem, *Folio,* "Experience Marketing," Fall 2000, pp. 28–32; and Stephen E. DeLong, "The Experience Economy," *Upside,* November 2001, p. 28.

6. Erika Rasmusson, "Marketing More than a Product," *Sales & Marketing Management,* February 2000, p. 99.

7. For more discussion on demand states, see Philip Kotler, *Marketing Management: Analysis, Planning, Implementation, and Control,* 11th ed. (Upper Saddle River, N.J.: Prentice Hall, 2003), p. 6.

8. Ralph Waldo Emerson offered this advice: "If a man . . . makes a better mousetrap . . . the world will beat a path to his door." Several companies, however, have built better mousetraps yet failed. One was a laser mousetrap costing $1,500. Contrary to popular assumptions, people do not automatically learn about new products, believe product claims, or willingly pay higher prices.

9. See Barry Farber and Joyce Wycoff, "Customer Service: Evolution and Revolution," *Sales & Marketing Management,* May 1991, p. 47; and Kevin Lawrence, "How to Profit from Customer Complaints," *The Canadian Manager,* Fall 2000, pp. 25, 29.

10. Kotler, *Marketing Management,* p. 19.

11. Gary Hamel and C. K. Prahalad, "Seeing the Future First," *Fortune,* September 5, 1994, pp. 64–70; Philip Kotler, *Kotler on Marketing.* (New York: Free Press, 1999), pp. 20–24; and Anthony W. Ulwick, "Turn Customer Input into Innovation," *Harvard Business Review,* January 2002, pp. 91–97.

12. See "Leaders of the Most Admired," *Fortune,* January 29, 1990, pp. 40–54; Thomas A. Stewart, "America's Most Admired Companies," *Fortune,* March 2, 1998, pp. 70–82; and Scott Hensley, "Marketers Increasingly Dispute Health Claims of Rival's Products," *Wall Street Journal,* April 4, 2002, p. B1.

13. See Erika Rasmusson, "Complaints Can Build Relationships," *Sales & Marketing Management,* September 1999, p. 89; "King Customer," *Selling Power,* October 2000, pp. 124–125; and Renee Houston Zemansky and Jeff Weiner, "Just Hang On to What You Got," *Selling Power,* March 2002, pp. 60–64.

14. Information accessed online at www.stew-leonards.com, July 2002.

15. See Libby Estell, "This Call Center Accelerates Sales," *Sales & Marketing Management,* February 1999, p. 72; Mark McMaster, "A Lifetime of Sales," *Sales & Marketing Management,* September 2001, p. 55; and Lauren Keller Johnson, "The Real Value of Customer Loyalty," *MIT Sloan Management Review,* Winter 2002, pp. 14–17.

16. See Brain O'Reilly, "They've Got Mail!" *Fortune,* February 7, 2000, pp. 101–112; and Rick Brooks, "FedEx, UPS Join Forces to Stave Off foreign Push into U.S. Markets," *Wall Street Journal,* February 1, 2001, p. B1.

17. For more on customer satisfaction, see Regina Fazio Marcuna, "Mapping the World of Customer Satisfaction,"

Harvard Business Review, May–June 2000, p. 30; David M. Szymanski, "Customer Satisfaction: A Meta-Analysis of the Empirical Evidence," *Academy of Marketing Science Journal,* Winter 2001, pp. 16–35; and Vikas Mittal and Wagner Kamakura, "Satisfaction, Repurchase Intent, and Repurchase Behavior: Investigating the Moderating Effect of Customer Characteristics," *Journal of Marketing Research,* February 2001, pp. 131–142.

18. For more on this measure and for recent customer satisfaction scores, see Eugene W. Anderson and Claes Fornell, "Foundations of the American Customer Satisfaction Index," *Total Quality Management,* September 2000, pp. S869–S882; and Claes Fornell, "The Science of Satisfaction," *Harvard Business Review,* March 2001, pp. 120–121. Cited facts accessed online at the ACSI Web site at www.bus.umich.edu/research/nqrc/acsi.html, July 2002.

19. Thomas O. Jones and W. Earl Sasser Jr., "Why Satisfied Customers Defect," *Harvard Business Review,* November–December 1995, pp. 88–99. Also see Thomas A. Stewart, "A Satisfied Customer Isn't Enough," *Fortune,* July 21, 1997, pp. 112–113.

20. Jones and Sasser, "Why Satisfied Customers Defect," p. 91. For other examples, see Roger Sant, "Did He Jump or Was He Pushed?" *Marketing News,* May 12, 1997, pp. 2, 21. Also see Denny Hatch and Ernie Schell, "Delight Your Customers," *Target Marketing,* April 2002, pp. 32–39.

21. Erin Stout, "Keep Them Coming Back for More," *Sales & Marketing Management,* February 2002, pp. 51–52.

22. See Kotler, *Kotler on Marketing,* pp. 129–139; Don Peppers and Martha Rogers, "Growing Revenues with Cross-Selling," *Sales & Marketing Management,* February 1999, p. 24; Phil Zinkewicz, "Travelers Agents Begin Getting Access to Citicorp Products," *Rough Notes,* February 1999, pp. 22, 26; and Tara Siegel, "Citigroup Is Ready to Realize Benefits of Cross Selling," *Wall Street Journal,* March 15, 1999, p. B11.

23. See Roland T. Rust, Valerie A. Zeithaml, and Katherine A. Lemon, *Driving Customer Equity.* (New York: Free Press, 2000); and Roland T. Rust, Katherine A. Lemon, and Valerie A. Zeithaml, "Where Should the Next Marketing Dollar Go?" *Marketing Management,* September–October 2001, pp. 24–28.

24. This example is adapted from Rust, Lemon, and Zeithaml, "Where Should the Next Marketing Dollar Go?" *Marketing Management,* p. 25.

25. Leonard L. Berry and A. Parasuraman, *Marketing Services: Competing Through Quality* (New York: Free Press, 1991), pp. 136–142. Also see Richard Cross and Janet Smith, *Customer Bonding: Pathways to Lasting Customer Loyalty* (Lincolnwood, Ill.: NTC Business Books, 1995); and Michelle L. Roehm, Ellen Bolman Pullins, and Harpeer A. Roehm, "Building Loyalty-Building Programs for Packaged Goods Brands," *Journal of Marketing Research,* May 2002, pp. 202–213.

26. See Mary M. Long and Leon G. Schiffman, "Consumption Values and Relationships: Segmenting the Market for Frequency Programs," *Journal of Consumer Marketing,* 2000,

p. 214+; and Naras V. Eechambadi, "Keeping Your Existing Customers Loyal," *Inter@ction Solutions,* February 2002, pp. 26–28. Examples based on information accessed online at www.hog.com and www.swatch.com, September 2002.

27. Michael J. Weiss, "Online America," *American Demographics,* March 2001, pp. 53–60; Taylor, Humphrey, "Internet Penetration at 66% of Adults (137 Million) Nationwide," *The Harris Poll,* April 17, 2002; and "Internet Users Will Top 1 Billion in 2005," press release, Computer Industry Almanac Inc., March 12, 2002, and accessed online at www.c-i-a.com.

28. Robert D. Hof, "The 'Click Here' Economy," *Business Week,* June 22, 1998, pp. 122–128.

29. Robert D. Hof, "Survive and Prosper," *Business Week,* May 14, 2001, p. EB60.

30. Steve Hamm, "E-Biz: Down but Hardly Out," *Business Week,* March 26, 2001, pp. 126–130; and "B2B E-Commerce Headed for Trillions," March 6, 2002, accessed online at cyberatlas.internet.com.

31. See Rick Brooks, "Unequal Treatment: Alienating Customers Isn't Always a Bad Idea, Many Firms Discover," *Wall Street Journal,* January 7, 1999, p. A1; Erika Rasmusson, "Wanted: Profitable Customers," *Sales & Marketing Management,* May 1999, pp. 28–34; Peter Cockburn, "CRM for Profit," *Tele-communications,* December 2000, pp. 89–93; and Chris Serres, "Banks Get Customers' Numbers," *Raleigh News & Observer,* March 19, 2002, pp. A1, A4.

32. Kotler, *Kotler on Marketing,* p. 20.

33. Thor Valdmanis, "Alliances Gain Favor over Risky Mergers," *USA Today,* February 4, 1999, p. 3B. Also see Gabor Gari, "Leveraging the Rewards of Strategic Alliances," *Journal of Business Strategy,* April 1999, pp. 40–43; Rosabeth Moss Kanter, "Why Collaborate?" *Executive Excellence,* April 1999, p. 8; and Matthew Schifrin, "Partner or Perish," *Forbes,* May 21, 2001, pp. 26–28.

34. See Ben & Jerry's full mission statement online at www.benjerry.com. For more reading on environmentalism, see Stuart L. Hart, "Beyond Greening: Strategies for a Sustainable World," *Harvard Business Review,* January–February 1997, pp. 67–76; and Peter M. Senge, Goran Carstedt, and Patrick L. Porter, "Innovating Our Way to the Next Industrial Revolution," *MIT Sloan Management Review,* Winter 2001, pp. 24–38. For more on marketing and social responsibility, see "Can Doing Good Be Good for Business?" *Fortune,* February 2, 1998, pp. 148G–148J; Sankar Sen and C. B. Bhattacharya, "Does Doing Good Always Lead to Doing Better? Consumer Reactions to Corporate Social Responsibility," *Journal of Marketing Research,* May 2001, pp. 225–243; Thea Singer, "Can Business Still Save the World?" *Inc.,* April 30, 2001, pp. 58–71; and Lois A. Mohr, Deborah J. Webb, and Katherine E. Harris, "Do Consumers Expect Companies to Be Socially Responsible? The Impact of Corporate Social Responsibility on Buying Behavior," *Journal of Consumer Affairs,* Summer 2001, pp. 45–72.

35. Example abstracted from Alison Stein Wellner, "Oh Come All Ye Faithful," *American Demographics,* June 2001, pp. 52–55.

36. For other examples, and for a good review of nonprofit marketing, see Philip Kotler and Alan R. Andreasen, *Strategic Marketing for Nonprofit Organizations,* 5th ed. (Upper Saddle River, N.J.: Prentice Hall, 1996); Philip Kotler and Karen Fox, *Strategic Marketing for Educational Institutions* (Upper Saddle River, N.J.: Prentice Hall, 1995); Norman Shawchuck, Philip Kotler, Bruce Wren, and Gustave Rath, *Marketing for Congregations: Choosing to Serve People More Effectively,* (Nashville: Abingdon Press, 1993); William P. Ryan, "The New Landscape for Nonprofits," *Harvard Business Review,* January–February 1999, pp. 127–136; and Don Akchin, "Nonprofit Marketing: Just How Far Has It Come?" *Nonprofit World,* January–February 2001, pp. 33–35.

37. Trevor Jensen, "USPS Brings a New Campaign," *Adweek,* February 25, 2002, p. 2. For more on social marketing, see Philip Kotler, Ned Roberto, and Nancy R. Lee, *Social Marketing: Improving the Quality of Life,* 2nd ed. (Upper Saddle River, N.J.: Prentice Hall, 2002).

CHAPTER 2

1. Robert C. Ford, Cherrill P. Heaton, and Stephen W. Brown, "Delivering Excellent Service: Lessons from the Best Firms," *California Management Review,* Fall 2001, pp. 39–56; Tim O'Brien, "North American Parks Finish 2001 on Par with Last Year," *Amusement Business,* December 24, 2001, pp. 18, 22; "Who Owns What?" *Columbia Journal Review,* posted February 19, 2002 at www.cjr.org; Geraldine Fabrikant, "Disney Profit Picture Shows Weakness, but There Are Encouraging Signs, Too," *New York Times,* April 26, 2002, p. C2; and information accessed online at Disney.go.com/corporate/, June 2002.

2. For a more detailed discussion of corporate- and business-level strategic planning as they apply to marketing, see Philip Kotler, *Marketing Management: Analysis, Planning, Implementation, and Control,* 11th ed. (Upper Saddle River, N.J.: Prentice Hall, 2003), Chapter 4.

3. For these and other examples, see Romauld A. Stone, "Mission Statements Revisited," *SAM Advanced Management Journal,* Winter 1996, pp. 31–37; Orit Gadiesh and James L. Gilbert, "Frontline Action," *Harvard Business Review,* May 2001; and "eBay Community," accessed online at www.ebay.com/community/aboutebay/community/index.html, June 2002.

4. Digby Anderson, "Is This the Perfect Mission Statement?" *Across the Board,* May–June 2001, p. 16.

5. Stone, "Mission Statements Revisited," p. 33.

6. See Gilbert Fuchsberg, "'Visioning' Mission Becomes Its Own Mission," *Wall Street Journal,* January 7, 1994, B1, B3; and Sal Marino, "Where There Is No Visionary, Companies Falter," *Industry Week,* March 15, 1999, p. 20. For more on mission statements, see Barbara Bartkus, Myron Glassman, and R. Bruce McAfee, "Mission Statements: Are They Smoke and Mirrors?" *Business Horizons,* November–December 2000, pp. 23–28; George S. Day, "Define Your Business," *Executive Excellence,* February 2001, p. 12; and Gerhard Gschwandtner, "Job One: What's at the Heart of Your Brand?" *Selling Power,* April 2002, pp. 73–76.

7. See Gary Hamel, "Reinvent Your Company," *Fortune,* June 20, 2000, pp. 98–112; "Fortune 500," *Fortune,* April 16, 2001, pp. F1–F2; and "America's Most Admired: What's So Great About GE?" *Fortune,* March 4, 2002, pp. 65–67.

8. For more on strategic planning, see John A. Byrne, "Strategic Planning," *Business Week,* August 26, 1996, pp. 46–51; Pete Bogda, "Fifteen Years Later, the Return of 'Strategy,'" *Brandweek,* February 1997, p. 18; Ian Wilson, "Strategic Planning for the Millennium: Resolving the Dilemma," *Long Range Planning,* August 1998, pp. 507–513; Tom Devane, "Ten Cardinal Sins of Strategic Planning," *Executive Excellence,* October 2000, p. 15; Dave Lefkowith, "Effective Strategic Planning," *Management Quarterly,* Spring 2001, pp. 7–11; and Stan Abraham, "The Association of Strategic Planning: Strategy Is Still Management's Core Challenge," *Strategy & Leadership,* 2002, pp. 38–42.

9. H. Igor Ansoff, "Strategies for Diversification," *Harvard Business Review,* September–October 1957, pp. 113–124. Also see Philip Kotler, *Kotler on Marketing* (New York: Free Press, 1999), pp. 46–48.

10. Nelson D. Schwartz, "Still Perking After All These Years," *Fortune,* May 24, 1999, pp. 203–210; Louise Lee, "Now Starbucks Uses Its Bean," *Business Week,* February 14, 2000, pp. 92–94; Stephane Fitch, "Latte Grande, Extra Froth," *Forbes,* March 19, 2001, p. 58; and Jacqueline Doherty, "Make It Decaf," *Barrons,* May 20, 2002, pp. 20–21.

11. Leslie Brokaw, "The Secrets of Great Planning," *Inc.,* October 1992, p. 152; and Kotler, *Marketing Management,* Chapter 3.

12. Bradford McKee, "Think Ahead, Set Goals, and Get Out of the Office," *Nation's Business,* May 1993, p. 10. For more on small business strategic planning, see Wendy M. Beech, "In It for the Long Haul," *Black Enterprise,* March 1998, p. 25; Nancy Upton, Elisabeth J. Teal, and Joe T. Felan, "Strategic and Business Planning Practices of Fast Growth Family Firms," *Journal of Small Business Management,* January 2001, pp. 60–72; and Jennifer Keeney, "How to Prepare for the Dawn of a New Economy," *FSB: Fortune Small Business,* April 2002, pp. 10–13.

13. Michael E. Porter, *Competitive Advantage: Creating and Sustaining Superior Performance* (New York: Free Press, 1985); and Michel E. Porter, "What Is Strategy?" *Harvard Business Review,* November–December 1996, pp. 61–78. Also see Jim Webb and Chas Gile, "Reversing the Value Chain," *Journal of Business Strategy,* March–April 2001, pp. 13–17.

14. John C. Narver and Stanley F. Slater, "The Effect of a Market Orientation on Business Profitability," *Journal of Marketing,* October 1990, pp. 20–35. Also see Susan Foreman, "Interdepartmental Dynamics and Market Orientation," *Manager Update,* Winter 1997, pp. 10–19; and Kotler, *Kotler on Marketing,* p. 20.

15. Kotler, *Kotler on Marketing,* pp. 20–22.

16. David Stires, "Fallen Arches," *Fortune,* April 29, 2002, pp. 74–76.

17. Myron Magnet, "The New Golden Rule of Business," *Fortune,* February 21, 1994, pp. 60–63. For more on supply chain management and strategic alliances, also Gabor Gari, "Leveraging

the Rewards of Strategic Alliances," *Journal of Business Strategy,* April 1999, pp. 40–43; Hau Lee "Survey: Chain Reaction," *The Economist* February 2002, pp. S13–S15; and Kotler, *Marketing Management,* pp. 70–71.

18. The four *Ps* classification was first suggested by E. Jerome McCarthy, *Basic Marketing: A Managerial Approach* (Homewood, Ill.: Irwin, 1960). For more discussion of this classification scheme, see Walter van Waterschoot and Christophe Van den Bulte, "The 4P Classification of the Marketing Mix Revisited," *Journal of Marketing,* October 1992, pp. 83–93; Michael G. Harvey, Robert F. Lusch, and Branko Cavarkapo, "A Marketing Mix for the 21st Century," *Journal of Marketing Theory and Practice,* Fall 1996, pp. 1–15; and Don E. Schultz, "Marketers: Bid Farewell to Strategy Based on Old 4Ps," *Marketing News,* February 12, 2001, p. 7.

19. Accessed online at Ad Age Dataplace, www.adage.com/dataplace, June 2002.

20. Robert Lauterborn, "New Marketing Litany: 4P's Passé; C-Words Take Over," *Advertising Age,* October 1, 1990, p. 26. Also see Kotler, *Marketing Management,* Chapter 1.

21. For a good discussion of gaining advantage through implementation effectiveness versus strategic differentiation, see "What Is Strategy," pp. 61–78. Also see Charles H. Noble and Michael P. Mokwa, "Implementing Marketing Strategies: Developing and Testing a Managerial Theory," *Journal of Marketing,* October 1999, pp. 57–73.

22. Brian Dumaine, "Why Great Companies Last," *Business Week,* January 16, 1995, p. 129. See James C. Collins and Jerry I. Porras, *Built to Last: Successful Habits of Visionary Companies* (New York: HarperBusiness, 1995); Rob Goffee and Gareth Jones, *The Character of a Corporation: How Your Company's Culture Can Make or Break Your Business* (New York: HarperBusiness, 1998); and Thomas A. Atchison, "What Is Corporate Culture?" *Trustee,* April 2002, p. 11.

23. Joseph Winski, "One Brand, One Manager," *Advertising Age,* August 20, 1987, p. 86. Also see Jack Neff, "P&G Redefines the Brand Manager," *Advertising Age,* October 13, 1997, pp. 1, 18; James Bell, "Brand Management for the Next Millennium," *Journal of Business Strategy,* March–April 1998, p. 7; and Kevin Lane Keller, *Strategic Brand Management,* 2nd ed. (Upper Saddle River, N.J.: Prentice Hall, 2003).

24. See Roland T. Rust, Valerie A. Zeithaml, and Katherine N. Lemon, *Driving Customer Equity: How Lifetime Customer Value Is Reshaping Corporate Strategy* (New York: Free Press, 2000); and Rust, Lemon, and Zeithaml, "Where Should the Next Marketing Dollar Go?" *Marketing Management,* September–October 2001, pp. 24–28.

25. For details, see Kotler, *Marketing Management,* Chapter 22.

CHAPTER 3

1. Erick Schonfeld, "Schwab Puts It All Online," *Fortune,* December 7, 1998, pp. 94–100; Glenn Coleman, "The Battle for Your Money," *Money,* December 1999, pp. 134–140; Louise Lee, "David S. Pottruck," *Business Week,* September 27, 1999, p. EB51; Clinton Wilder, "Leaders of the Net Era," *Informationweek,* November 27, 2000, pp. 44–56; Elizabeth Corcoran, "The E Gang," *Forbes,* July 24, 2000, pp. 145–172; Adam Morgan, "Ten Ways to Knock Down a Giant, *Marketing,* January 11, 2001, p. 19; John Gorham, "Charles Schwab, Version 4.0," *Forbes,* January 8, 2001, pp. 88–95; Mercedes M. Cardona, "Online Brokers Shift Gears to Retention, Not Trading," *Advertising Age,* April 16, 2001, p. 6; and Louise Lee, "Schwab vs. Wall Street," *Business Week,* June 3, 2002, pp. 65–71.

2. See Taylor, Humphrey, "Internet Penetration at 66% of Adults (137 Million) Nationwide," *The Harris Poll,* April 17, 2002; and "Internet Users Will Top 1 Billion in 2005," press release, Computer Industry Almanac Inc., March 12, 2002, accessed online at www.c-i-a.com.

3. Robyn Greenspan, "The Web as a Way of Life," accessed online at cyberatlas.interent.com, May 21, 2002.

4. Jaime Wold, "Your Very Own Breakfast Cereal," *New York Times,* December 9, 2001, p. 6.10. For other examples, including B2B examples, see Stefan Thomke and Eric Von Hippel, "Customers as Innovators," *Harvard Business Review,* April 2002, pp. 74–81.

5. See Jerry Wind and Arvid Rangaswamy, "Customerization: The Next Revolution in Mass Customization," *Journal of Interactive Marketing,* Winter 2001, pp. 13–32; and Yoram Wind and Vijay Mahajan, "Convergence Marketing," *Journal of Interactive Marketing,* Spring 2002, pp. 64–79.

6. John A. Byrne, "Management by the Web," *Business Week,* August 28, 2000, pp. 84–96.

7. Alan Mitchell, "Internet Zoo Spawns New Business Models," *Marketing Week,* January 21, 1999, pp. 24–25. Also see Philip Kotler, *Marketing Moves: A New Approach to Profits, Growth, and Renewal* (Boston: Harvard Business School Press, 2002).

8. Paola Hjelt, "Flying on the Web in a Turbulent Economy," *Business Week,* April 30, 2001, pp. 142–148.

9. Information accessed online at www.gegxs.com/gxs/aboutus, June 2002.

10. See Greenspan, "The Web as a Way of Life."

11. Frederick F. Reichheld and Phil Schefter, "E-Loyalty: Your Secret Weapon on the Web," *Harvard Business Review,* July–August 2000, pp. 105–113.

12. See Robert D. Hof, "How E-Biz Rose, Fell, and Will Rise Anew," *Business Week,* May 13, 2002, pp. 64–72; and Beth Cox, "E-Commerce Goes on a Roll," April 26, 2002, accessed online at www.atnewyork.com/news/article.php/1016561.

13. "Blue Collar Occupations Moving Online," accessed online at www.cyberatlas.internet.com, April 12, 2001.

14. Roger O. Crockett, "A Web That Looks Like the World," *Business Week,* March 22, 1999, p. EB46–EB47. Also see "True Colors," *American Demographics,* April 2001, pp. 14–15; and Michael Pastore, "Online Consumers Now the Average Consumer," July 12, 2001.

15. See "A Nation Online: How Americans Are Expanding Their Use of the Internet," Department of Commerce, February 2002; Michael Pastore, "Internet Key to Communication Among Youth," January 25, 2002, accessed online at

cyberatlas.internet.com; and John Fetto, "Teen Chatter," *American Demographics,* April 2002, p. 14.

16. See Joanne Cleaver, "Surfing for Seniors," *Marketing News,* July 19, 1999, pp. 1, 7; Sara Teasdale Montgomery, "Senior Surfers Grab Web Attention," *Advertising Age,* July 10, 2000, p. S4; Hassan Fattah, "Hollywood, the Internet, and Kids," *American Demographics,* May 2001, pp. 51–56; and Michael Pastore, "Online Seniors Enthusiastic About Internet Use," September 10, 2001, accessed online at cyberatlas.internet.com.

17. Michael J. Weiss, "Online America," *American Demographics,* March 2001, pp. 53–60; and "'Cyberchondriacs' Prowl the Web," *Business Journal,* May 1, 2002, accessed online at www.bizjournals.com.

18. Information accessed online at www.quickenloans.quicken.com, June 2002.

19. See Steve Hamm, "E-Biz: Down but Hardly Out," *Business Week,* March 26, 2001, pp. 126–130; and "B2B E-Commerce Headed for Trillions," March 6, 2002, accessed online at cyberatlas.internet.com.

20. Peter Loftis, "E-Commerce: Business to Business— Exchanges: Making It Work," *Wall Street Journal,* February 2002, p. R16.

21. Darnell Little, "Let's Keep This Exchange to Ourselves," *Business Week,* December 4, 2000, p. 48. Also see Eric Young, "Web Marketplaces That Really Work," *Fortune/CNET Tech Review,* Winter 2002, pp. 78–86.

22. Facts from eBay annual reports and other information accessed at www.ebay.com, July 2002.

23. Cathy Bowen, "Behind the Spree in Payments for C2C," *Credit Card Management,* April 2000, pp. 28–34. Also see Eryn Brown, "How Can a Dot-Com Be This Hot?" *Fortune,* January 21, 2002, pp. 78–84.

24. Gary M. Stern, "You Got a Complaint?" *Link-Up,* September–October 2001, p. 28; and Bob Tedeschi, "In the Current Internet Wilderness, Some Consumer Community Sites Are Hanging On, and Even Making Money," *New York Times,* January 7, 2002, p. C6.

25. Heather Green, "How to Reach John Q. Public," *Business Week,* March 26, 2001, pp. 132–134. Also see Ellen Florian, "Dot-Com Deathwatch: Dead and (Mostly) Gone," *Fortune,* December 24, 2001, pp. 46–47.

26. Bradley Johnson, "Out-of-Sight Spending Collides with Reality," *Advertising Age,* August 7, 2000, pp. S4–S8.

27. Gary Hamel, "Is This All You Can Build with the Net? Think Bigger," *Fortune,* April 30, 2001, pp. 134–138.

28. See Ann Weintraub, "For Online Pet Stores, It's Dog-Eat-Dog," *Business Week,* March 6, 2000, pp. 78–80; "Death of a Spokespup," *Adweek,* December 11, 2000, pp. 44–46; Jacques R. Chevron, "Name Least of Pet.com's Woes," *Advertising Age,* January 22, 2001, p. 24; and Norm Alster, "Initial Offerings Take a Turn to the Traditional," *New York Times,* May 19, 2002, p. 3.4.

29. Hamm, "E-Biz: Down but Hardly Out," p. 127; and "Business Brief—Staples Inc.: Net Income Falls 5.2% but Its Internet Unit Posts a Pretax Profit," *Wall Street Journal,* August 22, 2001, p. B4.

30. See Chuck Martin, *Net Future* (New York: McGraw-Hill, 1999), p. 33.

31. "E-Commerce Trudges Through Current Slowdown," accessed online at www.cyberatlas.internet.com, May 22, 2001.

32. Sharon Gaudin, "The Site of No Return," *DataMation,* accessed at www.internet.com, May 28, 2002.

33. Laurie Freeman, "Why Internet Brands Take Offline Avenues," *Marketing News,* July 1999, p. 4; and Paul C. Judge, "The Name's the Thing," *Business Week,* November 15, 1999, pp. 35, 39.

34. John Deighton, "The Future of Interactive Marketing," *Harvard Business Review,* November–December 1996, p. 154.

35. Don Peppers and Martha Rogers, "Opening the Door to Consumers," *Sales & Marketing Management,* October 1998, pp. 22–29; Mike Beirne, "Marketers of the Next Generation: Silvio Bonvini," *Brandweek,* November 8, 1999, p. 64; Jack Neff, "P&G vs. Martha," *Advertising Age,* April 8, 2002, p. 24; Hassan Fattah and Pamela Paul, "Gaming Gets Serious," *American Demographics,* May 2002, pp. 38–43; and information from www.candystand.com, June 2002.

36. Jeffrey F. Rayport and Bernard J. Jaworski, *e-Commerce* (New York: McGraw-Hill, 2001), p. 116.

37. Lisa Bertagnoli, "Getting Satisfaction," *Marketing News,* May 7, 2001, p. 11.

38. For these and other examples, see William M. Bulkeley, "E-Commerce (A Special Report): Cover Story—Pass It On: Advertisers Discover They Have a Friend in 'Viral' Marketing," *Wall Street Journal,* January 14, 2002, p. R6.

39. Eilene Zimmerman, "Catch the Bug," *Sales & Marketing Management,* February 2001, pp. 78–82. Also see Ellen Neuborne, "Viral Marketing Alert," *Business Week,* March 19, 2001, p. EB8.

40. Devin Leonard, "Madison Ave. Fights Back," *Fortune,* February 5, 2001, pp. 150–154. Also see "Internet Advertising Revenue Totaled $1.7 Billion for Q4 2001," Interactive Advertising Bureau press release, May 23, 2002, accessed online at www.iab.com; and Stephanie Miles, "Online-Ad Slump Continues, but Sector Has Bright Spots," *Wall Street Journal,* June 5, 2002, p. B4.

41. Rob Norton, "The Bright Future of Web Advertising," *Ecompany Now,* June 2001, pp. 50–60. Also see "Summit Participants Agree Online Poised for Growth," *Advertising Age,* April 1, 2002, p. C6.

42. Information from the iVillage Metrics section of www.ivillage.com, April 2002; and Dennis Callaghan, "Brands to Watch: Paul Allen: MyFamily.com," *MC Technology Marketing Intelligence,* February 2000, pp. 44–46; and "MyFamily.com See Record Growth Surpassing 700,000 Paid Subscriptions," press release accessed online at www.MyFamily.com, June 12, 2002.

43. See Thane Peterson, "E-I-E-I-E-Farming," *Business Week,* May 1, 2000, p. 202; "Survival of the Fittest," *Agri Marketing,*

March 2002, pp. 18–24; and www.agriculture.com. For more reading on Web communities, see Robert V. Kozinets, "The Field Behind the Screen: Using Netnography to Marketing Research in Online Communities," *Journal of Marketing Research*, February 2002, pp. 61–72.

44. Arlene Weintraub, "When E-Mail Ads Aren't Spam," *Business Week*, October 16, 2000, pp. 112–113.

45. Erika Rasmusson, "Tracking Down Sales," *Sales & Marketing Management*, June 1998, p. 19.

46. See Robert Sales, "IFN Launches Infogate, Targets Online Equities Market Data Users," *Wall Street & Technology*, May 2000, p. 84.

47. Elizabeth Corcoran, "The E Gang," *Fortune*, July 24, 2000, p. 145.

48. Michael Porter, "Strategy and the Internet," *Harvard Business Review*, March 2001, pp. 63–78.

49. Timothy J. Mullaney, "Break Out the Black Ink," *Business Week*, May 13, 2002, pp. 74–76.

50. See Peter Han and Angus Maclaurin, "Do Consumers Really Care About Online Privacy?" *Marketing Management*, January–February 2002, pp. 35–38.

51. See Adam Clymer, "Senator Prevents Action on Online Privacy Bill," *New York Times*, May 17, 2002, p. A16.

52. See Jennifer DiSabatino, "FTC OKs Self-Regulation to Protect Children's Privacy," *Computerworld*, February 12, 2001, p. 32.

53. Bob Tedeschi, "Everybody Talks About Online Privacy, but Few Do Anything About It," *New York Times*, June 3, 2002, p. C6.

54. See "Seventy Percent of US Consumers Worry About Online Privacy, but Few Take Protective Action, Reports Jupiter Media Metrix," Jupiter Media Metrix press release, June 3, 2002, accessed online at www.jmm.com.

55. "VeriSign Signs Pact with eBay to Fight Fraud on Auction Site," *Wall Street Journal*, May 8, 2002, p. A9; and the Internet Fraud Complaint Center Annual Report, accessed online at www.ifccfbi.gov, August 2002.

56. See Benjamin M. Compaine, *The Digital Divide: Facing a Crisis or Creating a Myth?* (Boston: MIT Press, 2001); Lisa J. Servon, *Bridging the Digital Divide: Technology, Community, and Public Policy* (Oxford, England: Blackwell Publishers, 2002); and Blaise Cronin, "The Digital Divide," *Library Journal*, February 15, 2002, p. 48.

57. "13-Year-Old Bids over $3M for Items in eBay Auctions," *USA Today*, April 30, 1999, p. 10B.

CHAPTER 4

1. Quotes from James R. Rosenfield, "Millennial Fever," *American Demographics*, December 1997, pp. 47–51; Keith Naughton and Bill Vlasic, "The Nostalgia Boom: Why the Old Is New Again," *Business Week*, March 23, 1998, pp. 58–64, Keith Naughton, "VW Rides a Hot Streak," *Newsweek*, May 22, 2000, pp. 48–50; and Marc Peyser, "Everything Old Is . . . Even Older," *Newsweek*, May 6, 2002, p. 14. Also see James R. Rosenfield, "Millenial Fever Revisited," *Direct Marketing*, June 2000, pp. 44–47; "Volkswagen Is Awarded Two Best Car Picks from *Money Magazine*," VW press release, April 4, 2001, accessed online at www.vw.com; Jeff Green, "Heavy Traffic on Memory Lane," *Business Week*, January 15, 2001, p. 40; and Sholnn Freeman and Beth Demain Reigber, "The VW Bus Is Back," *Wall Street Journal*, June 12, 2002, p. D1.

2. Jennifer Lach, "Dateline America: May 1, 2025," *American Demographics*, May 1999, pp. 19–20. Also see Tom Weir, "Staying Stuck on the Web," *Supermarket Business*, February 15, 2001, pp. 15–16.

3. See Sarah Lorge, "The Coke Advantage," *Sales & Marketing Management*, December 1998, p. 17.

4. World POPClock, U.S. Census Bureau, accessed online at www.census.gov, July 2002. This Web site provides continuously updated projections of the U.S. and world populations.

5. North South Centre website, www.nscentre.org/english/en_news/SW2000/GEW2000-Tip%201_datas.htm, accessed online June 2002.

6. Sally D. Goll, "Marketing: China's (Only) Children Get the Royal Treatment," *Wall Street Journal*, February 8, 1995, pp. B1, B3; James L. Watson, "China's Big Mac Attack," *Foreign Affairs*, May–June 2000, pp. 120–134; Mark Dunn, "Feeding China's Little Emperors: Food, Children, and Social Change," *China Business Review*, September–October 2000, p. 32.

7. U.S. Census Bureau projections and POPClock Projection, U.S. Census Bureau, accessed online at www.census.gov, July 2002.

8. Lach, "Dateline America: May 1, 2025," p. 19.

9. See Joan Raymond, "The Joy of Empty Nesting," *American Demographics*, May 2000, pp. 49–54; David Rakoff, "The Be Generation," *Adweek*, March 5, 2001, pp. SR18–SR22; and Gene Koretz, "Bless the Baby Boomers," *Business Week*, June 10, 2002, p. 30.

10. See Janus Dietz, "When Gen X Meets Aging Baby Boomers," *Marketing News*, May 10, 1999, p. 17; Tammy Joyner, "Gen X-ers Focus on Life Outside the Job Fulfillment," *The Secured Lender*, May–June 2000, pp. 64–68; Judi E. Loomis, "Generation X," *Rough Notes*, September 2000, pp. 52–54; and Jean Chatzky, "Gen Xers Aren't Slackers After All," *Time*, April 8, 2002, p. 87.

11. See Ken Gronback, "Marketing to Generation Y," *DSN Retailing Today*, July 24, 2000, p. 14.

12. Accessed online at www.growingupdigital.com/FLecho.html, October 1999. Also see Douglas Tapscott, *Growing Up Digital: The Rise of the Net Generation* (New York: McGraw-Hill, 1999); Christine Y. Chen, "Chasing the Net Generation," *Fortune*, September 4, 2000, pp. 295–298; and Pamela Paul, "Getting Inside Gen Y," *American Demographics*, September 2001, pp. 43–49.

13. See Gronback, "Marketing to Generation Y," p. 14; "Study Compares Gen Y to Boomers," *Home Textiles Today*, September 11, 2000, p. 14; and Rebecca Gardyn, "Grandaughters of Feminism," *American Demographics*, April 2001, pp. 43–47.

14. See J. Walker Smith and Ann Clurman, *Rocking the Ages* (New York: HarperBusiness, 1998); Mercedes M. Cardona, "Hilfiger's New Apparel Lines Getting Individual Efforts,"

Advertising Age, February 8, 1999, p. 24; and Alison Stein Wellner, "Generational Divide," *American Demographics,* October 2000, pp. 53–58.

15. Alison Stein Wellner, "The American Family in the 21st Century," *American Demographics,* August 2001, p. 20.

16. Information on household composition accessed online at www.census.gov/population/projections/nation/hh-fam/ table5n.txt, July 2002.

17. "How Far Have We Come? Fast Facts on Women and Work," accessed online at www.iVillage.com, June 21, 2001.

18. For these and other examples, see Kelly Shermach, "Niche Malls: Innovation for an Industry in Decline," *Marketing News,* February 26, 1996, p. 1; and Sue Shellenbarger, "'Child-Care Cams': Are They Good News for Working Parents?" *Wall Street Journal,* August 19, 1998, p. B1.

19. U.S. Census Bureau, "Geographical Mobility: Population Characteristics," May 2001, accessed online at www.census. gov/prod/2001pubs/p20-538.pdf.

20. See Kevin Heubusch, "Small Is Beautiful," *American Demographics,* January 1998, pp. 43–49; Brad Edmondson, "A New Era for Rural Americans," *American Demographics,* September 1997, pp. 30–31; Kenneth M. Johnson and Calvin L. Beale, "The Rural Rebound," *Wilson Quarterly,* Spring 1998, pp. 16–27; Alison Stein Wellner, "Size Doesn't Matter," *American Demographics,* May 2001, pp. 23–24; and Roderick J. Harrison, "The New White Flight," *American Demographics,* June 2002, pp. 20–24.

21. Lauri J. Flynn, "Not Just a Copy Shop Any Longer, Kinko's Pushes Its Computer Services," *New York Times,* July 6, 1998, p. D1. Also see Carol Leonetti Dannhauser, "Who's in the Home Office," *American Demographics,* June 1999, pp. 50–56; David Bouchier, "Working from Home, I Think," *New York Times,* January 20, 2002, PLI.13; and John Fetto, "You *Can* Take It with You," *American Demographics,* February 2002, pp. 10–11.

22. U.S. Census Bureau, "Educational Attainment in the United States (Update)," March 2000, accessed online at www.census.gov/population/socdemo/education/p20-536/ p20-536.pdf.

23. See Fabian Linden, "In the Rearview Mirror," *American Demographics,* April 1984, pp. 4–5; Peter Francese, "America at Mid-Decade," *American Demographics,* February 1995, pp. 23–29; Rebecca Piirto Heath, "The New Working Class," *American Demographics,* January 1998, pp. 51–55; and *Digest of Education Statistics 1997,* National Center for Education Statistics, January 1998, at http://nces01.ed.gov/pubs/ digest97.

24. The statistics in this paragraph were obtained from Chuck Paustian, "Anybody Can Do It," *Marketing News,* March 26, 2001, p. 23; and U.S. Census Bureau reports accessed online at www.census.gov, June 2002.

25. Adapted from an example in Laurel Wentz, "Bank of America Goes Multicultural," *Advertising Age,* April 15, 2002, p. 3.

26. For these and other examples, see Laura Koss-Feder, "Out and About," *Marketing News,* May 25, 1998, pp. 1, 20; Jennifer Gilbert, "Ad Spending Booming for Gay-Oriented Sites," *Advertising Age,* December 6, 1999, p. 58; John Fetto, "In Broad Daylight," *American Demographics,* February 2001, pp. 16, 20; Robert Sharoff, "Diversity in the Mainstream," *Marketing News,* May 21, 2001, pp. 1, 13; David Goetzl, "Showtime, MTV Gamble on Gay Net," *Advertising Age,* January 14, 2002, p. 4; and Kristi Nelson, "Canada's Gay TV Network Gets Ready for U.S.," *Electronic Media,* Chicago, May 6, 2002.

27. For these and other examples, see "Marketing to Americans with Disabilities," *Packaged Facts,* New York, 1997; Dan Frost, "The Fun Factor: Marketing Recreation to the Disabled," *American Demographics,* February 1998, pp. 54–58; Michelle Wirth Fellman, "Selling IT Goods to Disabled End-Users," *Marketing News,* March 15, 1999, pp. 1, 17; Alison Stein Wellner, "The Internet's Nest Niche," *American Demographics,* September 2000, pp. 18–19; Alan Hughes, "Taking the 'Dis' Out of Disability," *Black Enterprise,* March 2002, p. 102; and information accessed online at Volkswagen's Web site (www.vw.com), June 2002.

28. James W. Hughes, "Understanding the Squeezed Consumer," *American Demographics,* July 1991, pp. 44–50. For more on consumer spending trends, see Cheryl Russell, "The New Consumer Paradigm," *American Demographics,* April 1999, pp. 50–58.

29. For an excellent summary, see Michael J. Weiss, "Inconspicuous Spending," *American Demographics,* April 2002, pp. 31–39.

30. See Alison Stein Wellner, "The Money in the Middle," *American Demographics,* April 2000, pp. 56–64.

31. Debra Goldman, "Paradox of Pleasure," *American Demographics,* May 1999, pp. 50–53. Also see Kate Fitzgerald, "Luxury Marketing," *Advertising Age,* August 14, 2000, pp. S1, S6.

32. David Leonhardt, "Two-Tier Marketing," *Business Week,* March 17, 1997, pp. 82–90. Also see "MarketLooks: The U.S. Affluent Market," a research report by Packaged Facts, January 1, 2002.

33. For more discussion, see the "Environmentalism" section in Chapter 20. Also see Michael E. Porter and Claas van der Linde, "Green *and* Competitive: Ending the Stalemate," *Harvard Business Review,* September–October 1995, pp. 120–134; Stuart L. Hart, "Beyond Greening: Strategies for a Sustainable World," *Harvard Business Review,* January–February 1997, pp. 67–76; Forest L. Reinhardt, "Bringing the Environment Down to Earth," *Harvard Business Review,* July–August 1999, pp. 149–157; "Earth in the Balance," *American Demographics,* January 2001, p. 24; and Subhabrata Bobby Banerjee, "Corporate Environmentalism: The Construct and Its Measurement," *Journal of Business Research,* March 2002, pp. 177–191.

34. "'Different' 2002 May See U.S. R&D Spending Up 3.5%," *Research Technology Management,* March–April 2002, pp. 7–8.

35. Also see V. Kasturi Rangan, Sohel Karim, and Sheryl K. Sandberg, "Do Better at Doing Good," *Harvard Business Review,* May–June 1996, pp. 42–54; Julie Garrett and Lisa Rochlin, "Cause Marketers Must Learn to Play by Rules," *Marketing News,* May 12, 1997, p. 4; and Sarah Lorge, "Is

Cause-Related Marketing Worth It?" *Sales & Marketing Management,* June 1998, p. 72.

36. For more on Yankelovich Monitor, see http://secure.yankelovich.com/solutions/monitor/y-monitor.asp.

37. See Cyndee Miller, "Trendspotters: 'Dark Ages' Ending; So Is Cocooning," *Marketing News,* February 3, 1997, pp. 1, 16.

38. See Jesse Wong and Erik Guyot, "Asian Flag Maker Says Old Glory Means New Cash," *Wall Street Journal,* October 15, 2001, p. A19; and "A Run on Patriotism," *Warehousing Management,* November 2001, p. 5.

39. For these and other examples, see Patricia Callahan and Amy Merrick, "Greeting-Card Firms Hasten to Serve Nation's New Mood—Sales Surge Shifts Focus to Patriotism, but Taste Remains Paramount Concern," *Wall Street Journal,* October 4, 2001; William Grimes, "On Menus Everywhere, a Big Slice of Patriotism," *New York Times,* October 24, 2001, p. F1; "What's Hot: Patriotism," *DSN Retailing Today,* January 7, 2002, p. 23; Eleena de Lisser, "Shoes, Diapers Salute the Flag," *Wall Street Journal,* February 5, 2002, p. B1; and Karen Springen, "Glory Days," *Newsweek,* February 11, 2002, p. 10.

40. Steve Jarvis, "Red, White, and Blues," *Marketing News,* May 27, 2002, pp. 1, 9.

41. See Debbie Howell, "Health Food, Like Bell Bottoms, Puts Mojo Back in Mass," *DSN Retailing Today,* April 16, 2001, pp. 21–22.

42. Myra Stark, "Celestial Season," *Brandweek,* November 16, 1998, pp. 25–26. Also see Jennifer Harrison, "Advertising Joins the Journal of the Soul," *American Demographics,* June 1997, pp. 22–28; David B. Wolfe, "The Psychological Center of Gravity," *American Demographics,* April 1998, pp. 16–19; Richard Cimino and Don Lattin, "Choosing My Religion," *American Demographics,* April 1999, pp. 60–65; and Pamela Paul, "Convictions and Contradictions," *American Demographics,* June 2002, p. 17.

43. Philip Kotler, *Kotler on Marketing* (New York: Free Press, 1999), p. 3.

44. See Carl P. Zeithaml and Valerie A. Zeithaml, "Environmental Management: Revising the Marketing Perspective," *Journal of Marketing,* Spring 1984, pp. 46–53.

45. Howard E. Butz Jr. and Leonard D. Goodstein, "Measuring Customer Value: Gaining the Strategic Advantage," *Organizational Dynamics,* Winter 1996, pp. 66–67.

CHAPTER 5

1. See "Coke 'Family' Sales Fly as New Coke Stumbles," *Advertising Age,* January 17, 1986, p. 1; Jack Honomichl, "Missing Ingredients in 'New' Coke's Research," *Advertising Age,* July 22, 1985, p. 1; Leah Rickard, "Remembering New Coke," *Advertising Age,* April 17, 1995, p. 6; Rick Wise, "Why Things Go Better with Coke," *Journal of Business Strategy,* January–February 1999, pp. 15–19; and "Beyond Colas and Beyond," *Beverage Industry,* March 2002, pp. 10–18.

2. See Philip Kotler, *Kotler on Marketing* (New York: Free Press, 1999), p. 73.

3. Christina Le Beau, "Mountains to Mine," *American Demographics,* August 2000, pp. 40–44. Also see Joseph M. Winski, "Gentle Rain Turns into Torrent," *Advertising Age,* June 3, 1991, p. 34; David Shenk, *Data Smog: Surviving the Information Glut* (San Francisco: HarperSanFrancisco, 1997); Diane Trommer, "Information Overload—Study Finds Intranet Users Overwhelmed with Data," *Electronic Buyers' News,* April 20, 1998, p. 98; and Stewart Deck, "Data Storm Ahead," *CIO,* April 15, 2001, p. 97.

4. Alice LaPlante, "Still Drowning!" *Computer World,* March 10, 1997, pp. 69–70; and Jennifer Jones, "Looking inside," *InfoWorld,* January 7, 2002, pp. 22–26.

5. See Geoffrey Brewer, "The Customer Stops Here," *Sales & Marketing Management,* March 1998, pp. 31–36; and Andy Patrizio, "Home-Grown CRM," *Insurance & Technology,* February 2001, pp. 49–50.

6. For these and other examples, see Stan Crock, "They Snoop to Conquer," *Business Week,* October 28, 1996, p. 172; and James Curtis, "Behind Enemy Lines," *Marketing,* May 24, 2001, pp. 28–29.

7. See Suzie Amer, "Masters of Intelligence," *Forbes,* April 5, 1999, p. 18.

8. Bruce Hager, "Dumpster Raids? That's Not Very Ladylike, Avon," *Business Week,* April 1, 1991, p. 32; and "Andy Serwer, "P&G's Covert Operation," *Fortune,* September 17, 2001, pp. 42–44.

9. "Company Sleuth Uncovers Business Info for Free," *Link-Up,* January–February 1999, pp. 1, 8.

10. Curtis, "Behind Enemy Lines," pp. 28–29.

11. For more on marketing and competitive intelligence, see David B. Montgomery and Charles Weinberg, "Toward Strategic Intelligence Systems," *Marketing Management,* Winter 1998, pp. 44–52; Morris C. Attaway Sr., "A Review of Issues Related to Gathering and Assessing Competitive Intelligence," *American Business Review,* January 1998, pp. 25–35; and Conor Vibert, "Secrets of Online Sleuthing," *Journal of Business Strategy,* May–June 2001, pp. 39–42.

12. For more on research firms that supply marketing information, see Jack Honomichl, "Honomichl 50," special section, *Marketing News,* June 10, 2002, pp. H1–H43.

13. Justin Martin, "Ignore Your Customer," *Fortune,* May 1, 1995, pp. 121–126; and "Even Executives Are Losing Their Offices," *HR Magazine,* March 1998, p. 77. Also see Gerry Khermouch, "Consumers in the Mist," *Business Week,* February 26, 2001, p. 92; and Lawrence Osborne, "Consuming Rituals of the Suburban Tribe," *New York Times Magazine,* January 13, 2002, pp. 6, 29.

14. Adapted from Rebecca Piirto Heather, "Future Focus Groups," *American Demographics,* January 1994, p. 6. For more on focus groups, see Holly Edmunds, *The Focus Group Research Handbook* (Lincolnwood, Ill.: NTC Business Books, 1999); and R. Kenneth Wade, "Focus Groups' Research Role Is Shifting," *Marketing News,* March 4, 2002, p. 47.

15. Sarah Schafer, "Communications: Getting a Line on Customers," *Inc. Technology,* 1996, p. 102. Also see Alison

Stein Wellner, "I've Asked You Here Because . . . ," *Business Week,* August 14, 2000, p. F14; and Steve Jarvis, "Two Technologies Vie for Piece of Growing Focus Group Market, *Marketing News,* May 27, 2002, p. 4.

16. Adapted from examples in Gary H. Anthes, "Smile, You're on Candid Computer," *Computerworld,* December 3, 2001, p. 50.

17. Kate Maddox, "CRM to Outpace Other IT Spending," *B to B,* March 11, 2002, pp. 2, 33.

18. For these and other examples, see "What've You Done for Us Lately?" *Business Week,* September 14, 1998, pp. 142–148; Sara Sellar, "Dust Off That Data," *Sales & Marketing Management,* May 1999, pp. 71–72; Kotler, *Kotler on Marketing,* p. 29; Marc L. Songini, "Fedex Expects CRM System to Deliver," *Computerworld,* November 6, 2000, p. 10; Leslie Berger, "Business Intelligence: Insights from the Data Pile," *New York Times,* January 13, 2002, p. A9; and Geoffrey James, "Profit Motive," *Selling Power,* March 2002, pp. 68–73.

19. Darrell K. Rigby, "Avoid the Four Perils of CRM," *Harvard Business Review,* February 2002, pp. 101–109.

20. Michael Krauss, "At Many Firms, Technology Obscures CRM," *Marketing News,* March 18, 2002, p. 5.

21. Robert McLuhan, "How to Reap the Benefits of CRM," *Marketing,* May 24, 2001, p. 35; Sellar, "Dust Off That Data," p. 72; and Stewart Deck, "Data Mining," *Computerworld,* March 29, 1999, p. 76. Also see Eric Almquist, Carla Heaton, and Nick Hall, "Making CRM Make Money," *Marketing Management,* May–June 2002, pp. 16–21.

22. Ravi Kalakota and Marcia Robinson, *E-Business: Roadmap for Success* (Reading, Mass: Addison-Wesley, 1999).

23. "Business Bulletin: Studying the Competition," *Wall Street Journal,* March 19, 1995, pp. A1, A5.

24. Alison Stein Wellner, "Research on a Shoestring," *American Demographics,* April 2001, pp. 38–39.

25. See Nancy Levenburg and Tom Dandridge, "Can't Afford Research? Try Miniresearch," *Marketing News,* March 31, 1997, p.19; and Nancy Levenburg, "Research Resources Exist for Small Businesses," *Marketing News,* January 4, 1999, p. 19.

26. Jack Honomichl, "Honomichl Global 25," special section, *Marketing News,* August 13, 2001, pp. H1–H23; and the AC Nielsen Web page, accessed online at www.acnielsen.com, July 2002.

27. Many of the examples in this section, along with others, are found in Subhash C. Jain, *International Marketing Management,* 3d ed. (Boston: PWS-Kent, 1990), pp. 334–339. Ken Gofton, "Going Global with Research," *Marketing,* April 15, 1999, p. 35; Naresh K. Malhotra, *Marketing Research,* 3d ed. (Upper Saddle River, N.J.: Prentice Hall, 1999), chapter 23; and Tim R. V. Davis and Robert B. Young, "International Marketing Research," *Business Horizons,* March–April 2002, pp. 31–38.

28. Jain, *International Marketing Management,* p. 338. Also see Alvin C. Burns and Ronald F. Bush, *Marketing Research,* 3d ed. (Upper Saddle River, N.J.: Prentice Hall, 2000), pp. 317–318.

29. Steve Jarvis, "Status Quo = Progress," *Marketing News,* April 29, 2002, pp. 37–38.

30. Clare Saliba, "U.S. Ends DoubleClick Privacy Probe," *E-Commerce Times,* January 23, 2001, accessed online at www.ecommercetimes.com/perl/story/?id=6917; Mark McMaster, "Too Close for Comfort," *Sales & Marketing Management,* July 2001, pp. 43–48; and "DoubleClick Settles Online-Privacy Suits, Plans to Ensure Protections, Pay Legal Fees," *Wall Street Journal,* April 1, 2002, p. B8.

31. See William O. Bearden, Charles S. Madden, and Kelly Uscategui, "The Pool Is Drying Up," *Marketing Research,* Spring 1998, pp. 26–33; Craig Frazier, "What Are Americans Afraid Of?" *American Demographics,* July 2001, pp. 43–49; and Steve Jarvis, "CMOR Finds Survey Refusal Rate Still Rising," *Marketing News,* February 4, 2002, p. 4.

32. John Schwartz, "Chief Privacy Officers Forge Evolving Corporate Roles," *New York Times,* February 12, 2001, p. C1; and J. Michael Pemberton, "Chief Privacy Officer: Your Next Career?" *Information Management Journal,* May–June 2002, pp. 57–58.

33. Schwartz, "Chief Privacy Officers Forge Evolving Corporate Rules," p. C1. Also see Stephen F. Ambrose Jr., and Joseph W. Gelb, "Consumer Privacy Regulation and Litigation," *Business Lawyer,* May 2001, pp. 1157–1178.

34. Cynthia Crossen, "Studies Galore Support Products and Positions, but Are They Reliable?" *Wall Street Journal,* November 14, 1991, pp. A1, A9. Also see Allan J. Kimmel, "Deception in Marketing Research and Practice: An Introduction," *Psychology and Marketing,* July 2001, pp. 657–661.

35. For example, see Betsy Peterson, "Ethics Revisited," *Marketing Research,* Winter 1996, pp. 47–48; and O C Ferrell, Michael D. Hartline, and Stephen W. McDaniel, "Codes of Ethics Among Corporate Research Departments, Marketing Research Firms, and Data Subcontractors: An Examination of a Three-Communities Metaphor," *Journal of Business Ethics,* April 1998, pp. 503–516. For discussion of a framework for ethical marketing research, see Naresh K. Malhotra and Gina L. Miller, "An Integrated Model of Ethical Decisions in Marketing Research," *Journal of Business Ethics,* February 1998, pp. 263–280; and Kumar C. Rallapalli, "A Paradigm for Development and Promulgation of a Global Code of Marketing Ethics," *Journal of Business Ethics,* January 1999, pp. 125–137.

CHAPTER 6

1. Richard A. Melcher, "Tune-Up Time for Harley," *Business Week,* April 8, 1997, pp. 90–94; Ian P. Murphy, "Aided by Research, Harley Goes Whole Hog," *Marketing News,* December 2, 1996, pp. 16, 17; Linda Sandler, "Workspaces: Harley Shop," *Wall Street Journal,* April 21, 1999, p. B20; Robert Francis, "Leaders of the Pack," *Brandweek,* June 26, 2000, pp. 28–38; Joseph Webber, "Harley Investors May Get a Wobbly Ride," *Business Week,* February 11, 2002, p. 65; Karl Greenberg, "Harley-Davidson Hogs the Spotlight with New Ad, 100th Anniversary Bash," *Brandweek,* February 25, 2002, p. 9; and the Harley-Davidson Web site at www.Harley-Davidson.com, September 2002.

2. World POPClock, U.S. Census Bureau, www.census.gov, September 2002. This Web site provides continuously updated projections of the U.S. and world populations.

3. For this and the following example, see Philip R. Cateora, *International Marketing*, 8th ed. (Homewood, Ill.: Irwin, 1993), chapter: 4; Warren J. Keegan and Mark S. Green, *Global Marketing*, 2nd ed. (Upper Saddle River, N.J.: Prentice Hall, 2000), pp. 129–130; and Warren J. Keegan, *Global Marketing Management*, 7th ed. (Upper Saddle River, N.J.: Prentice Hall, 2002), pp. 68–69.

4. Statistics from Joan Raymond, "¿Tienen Numeros?" *American Demographics*, March 2002, pp. 22–25; and U.S. Census Bureau reports accessed online at www.census.gov, July 2002.

5. See Roberta Bernstein, "Food for Thought," *American Demographics*, May 2000, pp. 39–42; Jack Neff, "Suavitel Generates Waft of Success," *Advertising Age*, February 21, 2000, p. S4; Catherine P. Taylor, "BarbieLatina Says 'Hola' to Net," *Advertising Age*, October 1, 2001, p. 54; and Laurel Wentz, "Doors Opening Wide," *Advertising Age*, May 6, 2002, p. 24.

6. Calmetta Y. Coleman, "Attention Shoppers: Target Makes a Play for Minority Group Sears Has Cultivated," *Wall Street Journal*, April 12, 1999, p. A1; and Robert Sharoff, "Diversity in the Mainstream," *Marketing News*, May 21, 2001, pp. 1, 13+.

7. "The U.S. African American Market," Packaged Facts, January 2002.

8. See "L'eggs Joins New Approach in Marketing to African-American Women," *Supermarket Business*, June 1998, p. 81; and David Whelan, "Black Boom in the Burbs," *American Demographics*, July 2001, pp. 20–21.

9. See David Kiley, "Black Surfing," *Brandweek*, November 17, 1997, p. 36; Kim Cleland, "Narrow-Marketing Efforts Winning the Internet Savvy," *Advertising Age*, November 16, 1998, p. S26; Alan Hughes, "Narrowing the Divide," *Black Enterprise*, May 2002, p. 26; and a list of most popular African American Web sites at www.freemaninstitute.com/AfAmSites.htm, July 2002.

10. Drawn from U.S. Census Bureau reports accessed online at www.census.gov, July 2002. Also see Bernstein, "Food for Thought," p. 40.

11. Louise Lee, "Speaking the Customer's Language—Literally," *Business Week*, September 25, 2000, p. 178.

12. See Christy Fisher, "Marketers Straddle Asian-America Curtain," *Advertising Age*, November 7, 1994; Lis A. Yorgey, "Asian Americans," *Target Marketing*, July 1999, pp. 75, 80; Larry Moskowitz, "Missed Opportunity," *Pharmaceutical Executive*, April 2001, pp. 168–172; and Doug Desjardins, "Pacific Northwest Chains Hone Asian Assortments," *DSN Retailing Today*, May 6, 2002, p. 19.

13. See Kendra Parker, "Reaping What They've Sown," *American Demographics*, December 1999, pp. 34–38; and Ilana Polyak, "The Center of Attention," *American Demographics*, November 2000, pp. 30–32.

14. See Rick Adler, "Stereotypes Won't Work with Seniors Anymore," *Advertising Age*, November 11, 1996, p. 32; Richard Lee, "The Youth Bias in Advertising," *American Demographics*, January 1997, pp. 47–50; D. Allen Kerr, "Where There's Gray, There's Green," *Marketing News*, May 25, 1998, p. 2; Heather Chaplin, "Centrum's Self-Inflicted Silver Bullet," *American Demographics*, March 1999, pp. 68–69; and "Fewer Seniors in the 1990s but Their Ranks Are Set to Explode," *Business Week*, May 28, 2001, p. 30.

15. For more on social class, see Leon G. Schiffman and Leslie L. Kanuk, *Consumer Behavior*, 6th ed. (Upper Saddle River, N.J.: Prentice Hall, 1997), chap. 13; Rebecca Piirto Heath, "The New Working Class," *American Demographics*, January 1998, pp. 51–55; and Linda P. Morton, "Segmenting Publics by Social Class," *Public Relations Quarterly*, Summer 1999, pp. 45–46.

16. Michael Witte, "Buzz-z-z Marketing," *Business Week*, July 30, 2001, pp. 50–56.

17. See Darla Dernovsek, "Marketing to Women," *Credit Union Magazine*, October 2000, pp. 90–96; and Sharon Goldman Edry, "No Longer Just Fun and Games," *American Demographics*, May 2001, pp. 36–38.

18. David Leonhardt, "Hey Kids, Buy This," *Business Week*, June 30, 1997, pp. 62–67; and Jean Halliday, "Automakers Agree, Winning Youth Early Key to Future," *Advertising Age*, April 1, 2002, p. S16.

19. Tobi Elkin, "Sony Marketing Aims at Lifestyle Segments," *Advertising Age*, March 18, 2002, pp. 3, 72.

20. This and other examples of companies using VALS 2 can be found in Rebecca Piirto, "Measuring Minds in the 1990s," *American Demographics*, December 1990, pp. 35–39; and Rebecca Piirto, "VALS the Second Time," *American Demographics*, July 1991, p. 6. For good discussions of other lifestyle topics, see Michael R. Solomon, *Consumer Behavior*, 5th ed. (Upper Saddle River, N.J.: Prentice Hall, 2002), chapter 6.

21. See Paul C. Judge, "Are Tech Buyers Different?" *Business Week*, January 26, 1998, pp. 64–65, 68; Josh Bernoff, Shelley Morrisette, and Kenneth Clemmer, "The Forrester Report," Forrester Research, Inc., 1998; and the Forrester Web site at www.forrester.com, July 2001.

22. Stuart Elliot, "Sampling Tastes of a Changing Russia," *New York Times*, April 1, 1992, pp. D1, D19; and Tom Miller, "Global Segments from 'Strivers' to 'Creatives,'" *Marketing News*, July 20, 1998, p. 11. For an excellent discussion of cross-cultural lifestyle systems, see Philip Kotler, Gary Armstrong, John Saunders, and Veronica Wong, *Principles of Marketing*, 3rd European ed. (London: Prentice Hall Europe, 2001), pp. 202–204.

23. Jennifer Aaker, "Dimensions of Measuring Brand Personality," *Journal of Marketing Research*, August 1997, pp. 347–356. Also see Aaker, "The Malleable Self: The Role of Self-Expression in Persuasion," *Journal of Marketing Research*, May 1999, pp. 45–57; and Swee Hoon Ang, "Personality Influences on Consumption: Insights from the Asian Economic Crisis," *Journal of International Consumer Marketing*, 2001, pp. 5–20.

24. See Myron Magnet, "Let's Go for Growth," *Fortune,* March 7, 1994, p. 70; Aaker, "The Malleable Self", Leon G. Shiffman and Leslie Lazar Kanuk, *Consumer Behavior,* 7th ed. (Upper Saddle River, N.J.: Prentice Hall, 2000, pp. 111–118; and Swee Hoon Ang, "Personality Influences on Consumption."

25. Charles Pappas, "Ad Nauseam," *Advertising Age,* July 10, 2000, pp. 16–18.

26. Jill Venter, "Milk Mustache Campaign Is a Hit with Teens," *St. Louis Post-Dispatch,* April 1, 1998, E1; Dave Fusaro, "The Milk Mustache," *Dairy Foods,* April 1997, p. 75; Judann Pollack, "Milk: Kurt Graetzer," *Advertising Age,* June 30, 1997, p.S1; Gay Verne, "Milk, the Magazine," *American Demographics,* February 2000, pp32–33; Rebecca Flass, "California Processors Vote to Continue 'Got Milk,'" *Adweek,* March 26, 2001, p. 5; and Kate Fitzgerald, "Milk Tailors Effort to Teens," *Advertising Age,* February 18, 2002, p. 16.

27. See Henry Assael, *Consumer Behavior and Marketing Action* (Boston: Kent Publishing, 1987), chap. 4. An earlier classification of three types of consumer buying behavior—routine response behavior, limited problem solving, and extensive problem solving—can be found in John A. Howard and Jagdish Sheth, *The Theory of Consumer Behavior* (New York: John Wiley, 1969), pp. 27–28. Also see John A. Howard, *Consumer Behavior in Marketing Strategy* (Upper Saddle River, N.J.: Prentice Hall, 1989).

28. For more on word-of-mouth sources, see Philip Kotler, *Marketing Management,* 11th ed. (Upper Saddle River, N.J.: Prentice Hall, 2003), pp. 574–575.

29. See Leon Festinger, *A Theory of Cognitive Dissonance* (Stanford, Calif.: Stanford University Press, 1957); Schiffman and Kanuk, *Consumer Behavior,* pp. 219–220; Jeff Stone, "A Radical New Look at Cognitive Dissonance," *American Journal of Psychology,* Summer 1998, pp. 319–326; Thomas R. Schultz, Elene Leveille, and Mark R. Lepper, "Free Choice and Cognitive Dissonance Revisited: Choosing 'Lesser Evils' Versus 'Greater Goods,'" *Personality and Social Psychology Bulletin,* January 1999, pp. 40–48; and Jillian C. Sweeney, Douglas Hausknecht, and Geoffrey N. Soutar, "Cognitive Dissonance After Purchase: A Multidimensional Scale," *Psychology & Marketing,* May 2000, pp. 369–385; and Patti Williams and Jennifer L. Aaker, "Can Mixed Emotions Peacefully Coexist?" March 2002, pp. 636–649.

30. See Frank Rose, "Now Quality Means Service Too," *Fortune,* April 22, 1991, pp. 97–108; Chip Walker, "Word of Mouth," *American Demographics,* July 1995, p. 40; Thomas O. Jones and W. Earl Sasser Jr., "Why Satisfied Customers Defect," *Harvard Business Review,* November–December 1995, pp. 88–99; Roger Sant, "Did He Jump or Was He Pushed?" *Marketing News,* May 12, 1997, pp. 2, 21; Vikas Mittal and Wagner Kamakura, "Satisfaction, Repurchase Intent, and Repurchase Behavior: Investigating the Moderating Effect of Customer Characteristics," *Journal of Marketing Research,* February 2001, pp. 131–142; and Denny Hatch and Ernie Schell, "Delight Your Customers," *Target Marketing,* April 2002, pp. 32–39.

31. The following discussion draws heavily from Everett M. Rogers, *Diffusion of Innovations,* 3rd ed. (New York: Free Press, 1983). Also see Hubert Gatignon and Thomas S. Robertson, "A Propositional Inventory for New Diffusion Research," *Journal of Consumer Research,* March 1985, pp. 849–867; Rogers, *Diffusion of Innovations,* 4th ed. (New York: Free Press, 1995); Marnik G. Dekiple, Philip M. Parker, and Milos Sarvary, "Global Diffusion of Technological Innovations: A Coupled-Hazard Approach," *Journal of Marketing Research,* February 2000, pp. 47–59; Peter J. Danaher, Bruce G.S. Hardie, and William P. Putsis, "Marketing-Mix Variables and the Diffusion of Successive Generations of a Technological Innovation," *Journal of Marketing Research,* November 2001, pp. 501–514; and Eun-Ju Lee, Jinkook Lee, and David W. Schumann, "The Influence of Communication Source and Mode on Consumer Adoption of Technological Innovations," *Journal of Consumer Affairs,* Summer 2002, pp. 1–27.

CHAPTER 7

1. Portions adapted from Thomas V. Bonoma, "Major Sales: Who Really Does the Buying," *Harvard Business Review,* May–June 1982. Copyright © 1982 by the President and Fellows of Harvard College; all rights reserved. Quotes from John Huey, "The Absolute Best Way to Fly," *Fortune,* May 30, 1994, pp. 121–128; Anthony Bianco, "Gulfstream's Pilot," *Business Week,* April 14, 1997, pp. 64–76; and Joshua Cooper Ramo, "Friendly Skies," *Time,* January 8, 2001, p. 46. Also see "My First Gulfstream," *Vanity Fair,* October 1998, pp. 236–258; and David Rimmer, "Business Jets Push GA to Record Highs," *Business & Commercial Aviation,* March 2002, p. 11.

2. See Kate Macarthur, "Teflon Togs Get $40 Million Ad Push," *Advertising Age,* April 8, 2002, p. 3.

3. Sarah Lorge, "Purchasing Power," *Sales & Marketing Management,* June 1998, pp. 43–46.

4. This quote and the following example are from John H. Sheridan, "An Alliance Built on Trust," *Industry Week,* March 17, 1997, pp. 66–70; and Gary S. Vasilash, "Leveraging the Supply Chain for Competitive Advantage," *Automotive Design & Production,* April 2002, pp. 50–51.

5. "Keeping Up with Your Industry," *Insights,* February 2000, p. 1, ChemStation newsletter access online at www.chemstation.com.

6. Patrick J. Robinson, Charles W. Faris, and Yoram Wind, *Industrial Buying Behavior and Creative Marketing* (Boston: Allyn & Bacon, 1967). Also see Erin Anderson, Weyien Chu, and Barton Weitz, "Industrial Purchasing: An Empirical Exploration of the Buyclass Framework," *Journal of Marketing,* July 1987, pp. 71–86; and Michael D. Hutt and Thomas W. Speh, *Business Marketing Management,* 7th ed. (Upper Saddle River, N.J.: Prentice Hall, 2001), pp. 56–66.

7. See Philip Kotler, *Marketing Management,* 11th ed. (Upper Saddle River, N.J.: Prentice Hall, 2003), pp. 219–220.

8. Frederick E. Webster Jr. and Yoram Wind, *Organizational Buying Behavior* (Upper Saddle River, N.J.: Prentice Hall, 1972), pp. 78–80. Also see James C. Anderson and James A. Narus, *Business Market Management: Understanding, Creating and Delivering Value* (Upper Saddle River, N.J.:

Prentice Hall, 1998), chap. 3; and Hutt and Speh, *Business Marketing Management*, pp. 73–77.

9. Webster and Wind, *Organizational Buying Behavior*, pp. 33–37. Also see Edward G. Brierty, Robert W. Eckles, and Robert R. Reeder, *Business Marketing*, 3rd ed. (Upper Saddle River, N.J.: Prentice Hall, 1998), chap. 3.

10. Thomas V. Bonoma, "Major Sales: Who Really Does the Buying," *Harvard Business Review*, May–June 1982, p. 114. Also see Ajay Kohli, "Determinants of Influence in Organizational Buying: A Contingency Approach," *Journal of Marketing*, July 1989, pp. 50–65; and Jeffrey E. Lewin, "The Effects of Downsizing on Organizational Buying Behavior: An Empirical Investigation," *Academy of Marketing Science*, Spring 2001, pp. 151–164.

11. Robinson, Faris, and Wind, *Industrial Buying Behavior*, p. 14.

12. Unless otherwise noted, quotes and spending information in this section are from Michael A. Verespej, "E-Procurement Explosion," *Industry Week*, March 2002, pp. 24–28.

13. See Verespej, "E-Procurement Explosion," pp. 25–28; Andy Reinhardt, "Extranets: Log On, Link Up, Save Big," *Business Week*, June 22, 1998, p. 134; "To Byte the Hand That Feeds," *The Economist*, January 17, 1998, pp. 61–62; Ken Brack, "Source of the Future," *Industrial Distribution*, October 1998, pp. 76–80; James Carbone, "Internet Buying on the Rise," *Purchasing*, March 25, 1999, pp. 51–56; "E-Procurement: Certain Value in Changing Times," *Fortune*, April 30, 2001, pp. S2-S3; and "Benchmark Survey: E-Procurement Adoptions Progress Slowly and Steadily," *Purchasing*, June 20, 2002, p. S8.

14. Paul E. Goulding, "Q&A: Making Uncle Sam Your Customer," *Financial Executive*, May–June 1998, pp. 55–57.

15. Kotler, *Marketing Management*, 11th ed., p. 237.

16. For more on U.S. government buying, see Richard J. Wall and Carolyn M. Jones, "Navigating the Rugged Terrain of Government Contracts," *Internal Auditor*, April 1995, p. 32; Wallace O. Keene, "New Bright Spot in Acquisition Reform," *Public Manager*, Spring 1999, pp. 45–46; and Ellis Booker, "Wartime or Not, Government Contracting a Complex Mission," *B to B*, October 15, 2001, p. 8.

17. See Ellen Messmer, "Feds Buy Online," *Network World*, April 15, 1996, p. 35; "Government Surges Forward with Plans for Electronic Shopping Mall," *Supply Management*, March 18, 1999, p. 9; Christina Couret, "Online Shopping Offers Governments 'Net' Gain," *American City and County*, January 1999, pp. 20–23; Messmer, "The Feds Get into Online Buying," *Network World*, March 5, 2001, p. 67; and Patrick E. Clarke, "DLA Shifting from Managing Supplies to Managing Suppliers," May 30, 2002, accessed online at www.dla.mil.

CHAPTER 8

1. See Kerri Walsh, "Soaps and Detergents," *Chemical Week*, January 23, 2002, pp. 24–27; and information accessed online at www.pg.com and www.tide.com, July 2002.

2. These and other examples found in Nelson D. Schwartz, "Still Perking After All These Years," *Fortune*, May 24, 1999, pp. 203–210; and www.usaopoly.com, July 2002.

3. See Bruce Hager, "Podunk Is Beckoning," *Business Week*, December 2, 1991, p. 76; David Greisling, "The Boonies Are Booming," *Business Week*, October 9, 1995, pp. 104–110; Mike Duff, "Home Depot Drops Villager's Hareware for New Concept," *DSN Retailing Today*, April 22, 2002, pp. 5, 28; and Stephanie Thompson, "Wal-Mart Tops List for New Food Lines, *Advertising Age*, April 29, 2002, pp. 4, 61.

4. Accessed online at www.olay.com, July 2002.

5. Carmetta Y. Coleman, "Eddie Bauer's Windows Add Electronics." *Wall Street Journal*, November 28, 2000, p. B10; and Karen M. Kroll, "Plasma Video Screens Prove Customer Hit in Eddie Bauer," *Stores*, February 2001, pp. 74–75.

6. Pat Sloan and Jack Neff, "With Aging Baby Boomers in Mind, P&G, Den-Mat Plan Launches," *Advertising Age*, April 13, 1998, pp. 3, 38.

7. Alice Z. Cuneo, "Advertisers Target Women, but Market Remains Elusive," *Advertising Age*, November 10, 1997, pp. 1, 24; and Laura Q. Hughes and Alice Z. Cuneo, "Lowes Retools Image in Push Toward Women," *Advertising Age*, February 26, 2001, pp. 3, 51.

8. Michael McCarthy, "Marketers, NFL Focus on Game's Audience of 40 Million Women," *USA Today*, January 25, 2001, p. 1; and Sam Walker, "Super Bowl XXXVI: The NFL Tackles Mom," *Wall Street Journal*, February 1, 2002, p. W1.

9. Michelle Orecklin, "What Women Watch," *Time*, May 13, 2002, pp. 65–66; and information accessed online at www.iVillage.com and www.oxygen.com, July 2002.

10. Amanda Beeler, "Heady Rewards for Loyalty," *Advertising Age*, August 14, 2000, p. S8; and information accessed at www.neimanmarcus.com/store/sitelets/incircle/index.jhtml, July 2002.

11. Brian Bremner, "Looking Downscale Without Looking Down," *Business Week*, October 8, 1990, pp. 62–67; Dan Hogsett, "Family Dollar Drives 1Q Profits," *Home Textiles Today*, January 14, 2002, p. 16; and Debbie Howell, "Humbled Dollar General Rebounds with Verve," *DSN Retailing Today*, April 8, 2002, p. 7.

12. "Lifestyle Marketing," *Progressive Grocer*, August 1997, pp. 107–110; and Philip Kotler, *Marketing Management: Analysis, Planning, Implementation, and Control*, 11th ed. (Upper Saddle River, N.J.: Prentice Hall, 2003), pp. 291–292.

13. Laurie Freeman and Cleveland Horton, "Spree: Honda's Scooters Ride the Cutting Edge," *Advertising Age*, September 5, 1985, pp. 3, 35; "Scooter Wars," *Cycle World*, February 1998, p. 26; Jonathon Welsh, "Transport: The Summer of the Scooter: Boomers Get a New Retro Toy," *Wall Street Journal*, April 13, 2001, p. W1; and Honda's Web site at www.hondamotorcycle.com/scooter, July 2002.

14. See Mark Maremont, "The Hottest Thing Since the Flashbulb," *Business Week*, September 7, 1992; Bruce Nussbaum, "A Camera in a Wet Suit," *Business Week*, June 2, 1997, p. 109; Dan Richards, "The Smartest Disposable Cameras," *Travel Holiday*, December 1998, p. 20; "Point and Click," *Golf Magazine*, February 1999, p. 102; and Todd Wasserman, "Kodak Rages in Favor of the Machines," *Brandweek*, February 26, 2001, p. 6.

15. See Warren Thayer, "Target Heavy Buyers!" *Frozen Food Age,* March 1998, pp. 22–24; Jennifer Ordonez, "Cash Cows: Hamburger Joints Call Them 'Heavy Users,'" *Wall Street Journal,* January 12, 2000, p. A1; and Brian Wonsink and Sea Bum Park, "Methods and Measures That Profile Heavy Users," *Journal of Advertising Research,* July–August 2000, pp. 61–72.

16. Kendra Parker, "How Do You Like Your Beef?" *American Demographics,* January 2000, pp. 35–37.

17. Daniel S. Levine, "Justice Served," *Sales & Marketing Management,* May 1995, pp. 53–61.

18. For more on segmenting business markets, see John Berrigan and Carl Finkbeiner, *Segmentation Marketing: New Methods for Capturing Business* (New York: HarperBusiness, 1992); Rodney L. Griffith and Louis G. Pol, "Segmenting Industrial Markets," *Industrial Marketing Management,* no. 23, 1994, pp. 39–46; Stavros P. Kalafatis and Vicki Cheston, "Normative Models and Practical Applications of Segmentation in Business Markets," *Industrial Marketing Management,* November 1997, pp. 519–530; James C. Anderson and James A. Narus, *Business Market Management* (Upper Saddle River, N.J.: Prentice Hall, 1999), pp. 44–47; and Andy Dexter, "Egotists, Idealists, and Corporate Animals—Segmenting Business Markets, *International Journal of Marketing Research,* First Quarter 2002, pp. 31–51.

19. Cyndee Miller, "Teens Seen as the First Truly Global Consumers," *Advertising Age,* March 27, 1995, p. 9; and Warren J. Keegan, *Global Marketing Management* (Upper Saddle River, N.J.: Prentice Hall, 2002), p. 194.

20. Shawn Tully, "Teens: The Most Global Market of All," *Fortune,* May 16, 1994, pp. 90–97; "MTV Hits 100 Million in Asia," *New Media Markets,* January 28, 1999, p. 12; and Brett Pulley and Andrew Tanzer, "Sumner's Gemstone," *Forbes,* February 21, 2000, pp. 106–111. For more on international segmentation, see V Kumar and Anish Nagpal, "Segmenting Global Markets: Look Before You Leap," *Marketing Research,* Spring 2001, pp. 8–13.

21. See Michael Porter, *Competitive Advantage* (New York: Free Press, 1985), pp. 4–8, 234–236. For more recent discussions, see Leyland Pitt, "Total E-clipse: Five New Forces for Strategy in the Digital Age," *Journal of General Management,* Summer 2001, pp. 1–15; and Stanley Slater and Eric Olson, "A Fresh Look at Industry and Market Analysis," *Business Horizons,* January–February 2002, p. 15–22.

22. Nina Munk, "Why Women Find Lauder Mesmerizing," *Fortune,* May 25, 1998, pp. 97–106; and Christine Bittar, "New Faces, Same Name," *Brandweek,* March 11, 2002, pp. 28–34.

23. Arlene Weintraub, "Chairman of the Board," *Business Week,* May 28, 2001, p. 94.

24. Paul Davidson, "Entrepreneurs Reap Riches from Net Niches," *USA Today,* April 20, 1998, p. B3; and information accessed online at www.ostrichesonline.com, July 2002.

25. For a collection of articles on one-to-one marketing and mass customization, see James H. Gilmore and B. Joseph Pine, *Markets of One: Creating Customer-Unique Value Through Mass Customization* (Boston: Harvard Business School Press, 2001).

26. See Philip Kotler, *Kotler on Marketing* (New York: Free Press, 1999), pp. 149–150.

27. See Jerry Wind and Arvid Rangaswamy, "Customerization: The Next Revolution in Mass Customization," *Journal of Interactive Marketing,* Winter 2001, pp. 13–32.

28. Sony A. Grier, "The Federal Trade Commission's Report on the Marketing of Violent Entertainment to Youths: Developing Policy-Tuned Research," *Journal of Public Policy and Marketing,* Spring 2001, pp. 123–132; and Greg Winter, "Tobacco Company Reneged on Youth Ads, Judge Rules," *New York Times,* June 7, 2002, p. A18.

29. See "PowerMaster," *Fortune,* January 13, 1992, p. 82; Herbert Rotfeld, "The FTC and Marketing Abuse," *Marketing News,* March 17, 1997, p. 4; and George G. Brenkert, "Marketing to Inner-City Blacks: PowerMaster and Moral Responsibility," *Business Ethics Quarterly,* January 1998, pp. 1–18.

30. Joseph Turow, "Breaking Up America: The Dark Side of Target Marketing," *American Demographics,* November 1997, pp. 51–54; and Bette Ann Stead and Jackie Gilbert, "Ethical Issues in Electronic Commerce," *Journal of Business Ethics,* November 2001, pp. 75–85.

31. For interesting discussion of finding ways to differentiate marketing offers, see Ian C. MacMillan and Rita Gunther McGrath, "Discovering New Points of Differentiation," *Harvard Business Review,* July–August 1997, pp. 133–145; and Girish Punj and Junyean Moon, "Positoning Options for Achieving Brand Association: A Psychological Categorization Framework," *Journal of Business Research,* April 2002, pp. 275–283.

32. See Kotler, *Kotler on Marketing,* pp. 59–63.

33. See Bobby J. Calder and Steven J. Reagan, "Brand Design," in Dawn Iacobucci, ed., *Kellogg on Marketing* (New York: John Wiley, 2001) p. 61.

34. The Palm Pilot and Mountain Dew examples are from Alice M. Tybout and Brian Sternthal, "Brand Positioning," in Iacobucci, ed., *Kellogg on Marketing,* p. 54.

CHAPTER 9

1. Excerpt adapted from Penelope Green, "Spiritual Cosmetics. No Kidding," *New York Times,* January 10, 1999, p. 1. Also see Elizabeth Wellington, "The Success of Smell," *The News & Observer,* June 11, 2001, p. E1; Mary Tannen, "Cult Cosmetics," *New York Times Magazine,* Spring 2001, p. 96; and Sandra Yin, "The Nose Knows," *American Demographics,* February 2002, pp. 14–15.

2. See B. Joseph Pine and James H. Gilmore, *The Experience Economy* (New York: Free Press, 1999); Jane E. Zarem, "Experience Marketing," *Folio: The Magazine for Magazine Management,* Fall 2000, pp. 28–32; and Scott Mac Stravic, "Make Impressions Last: Focus on Value," *Marketing News,* October 23, 2000, pp. 44–45.

3. See Mark Hyman, "The Yin and Yang of the Tiger Effect," *Business Week,* October 16, 2000, p. 110; "Finance and Economics: A Tiger Economy," *The Economist,* April 14, 2001, p. 70; Hillary Cassidy, "Target, Tiger Swing TV Deal with

TCG," *Brandweek*, December 2001, p. 11, and Kate Fitzgerald, "Buick Rides the Tiger," *Advertising Age*, April 15, 2002, p. 41.

4. Check out the tourism Web pages of these states at www.TravelTex.com, www.michigan.org, and www.iloveny.state.ny.us.

5. See Philip Kotler, Irving J. Rein, and Donald Haider, *Marketing Places: Attracting Investment, Industry, and Tourism to Cities, States, and Nations* (New York: Free Press, 1993), pp. 202, 273. Additional information accessed online at www.ireland.travel.ie and www.ida.ie, August 2002.

6. Accessed online at www.social-marketing.org/aboutus.html, August 2002.

7. Alan R. Andreasen, Rob Gould, and Karen Gutierrez, "Social Marketing Has a New Champion," *Marketing News*, February 7, 2000, p. 38; and www.social-marketing.org, August 2002.

8. Quotes and definitions from Philip Kotler, *Kotler on Marketing* (New York: Free Press, 1999), p. 17; and www.asq.org, June 2002. For more on quality, see John Dalrymple and Eileen Drew, "Quality: On the Threshold or the Brink?" *Total Quality Management*, July 2000, pp. S697–S703; and Rui Sousa and Christopher A. Voss, "Quality Management Re-Visited: A Reflective Review and Agenda for Future Research," *Journal of Operations Management*, February 2002, pp. 91–109.

9. See Roland T. Rust, Anthony J. Zahorik, and Timothy L. Keiningham, "Return on Quality (ROQ): Making Service Quality Financially Accountable," *Journal of Marketing*, April 1995, pp. 58–70; Dan Bridget, "ISO 9000 Changes the Quality Focus," *Quality*, April 2000, pp. 52–56; and Thomas J. Douglas and William Q. Judge, "Total Quality Management Implementation and Competitive Advantage," *Academy of Management Journal*, February 2001, pp. 158–169.

10. See "Hot R.I.P.: The Floppy Disk," *Rolling Stone*, August 20, 1998, p. 86; Bob Woods, "iMac Drives Apple's Q2 Results," *Computer Dealer News*, April 30, 1999, p. 39; Pui-Wing Tam, "Designing Duo Helps Shape Apple's Fortunes," *Wall Street Journal*, July 18, 2001, p. B1; Robert Dwek, "Apple Pushes Design to Core of Marketing," *Marketing Week*, January 24, 2002, p. 20; and "John Markoff, "Apple Computer Beats Earnings Estimates in Second Quarter," *New York Times*, April 18, 2002, p. C7.

11. Adapted from information found in Mark Schwanhausser, "Thinking Outside the Wallet," *The News & Observer*, May 12, 2002, p. 12E; and "Discover on the Go," *Credit Card Management*, May 2002, p. 9. For other examples, see "Best Product Designs of the Year," *Business Week*, July 8, 2002, pp. 82–94.

12. See Joan Holleran, "Packaging Speaks Volumes," *Beverage Industry*, February 1998, p. 30; "Packaging—A Silent Salesman," *Retail World*, August 28–September 8, 2000, p. 23; and Elliot Young, "Is It Time to Upgrade Your Packaging?" *Beverage Industry*, April 2002, p. 52.

13. Robert M. McMath, "Chock Full of (Pea)nuts," *American Demographics*, April 1997, p. 60.

14. Bro Uttal, "Companies That Serve You Best," *Fortune*, December 7, 1987, p. 116. For an excellent discussion of sup-

port services, see James C. Anderson and James A. Narus, "Capturing the Value of Supplementary Services," *Harvard Business Review*, January–February 1995, pp. 75–83.

15. See Heather Green, "A Cyber Revolt in Health Care," *Business Week*, October 19, 1998, pp. 154–156; Bob Wallace and George V. Hulme, "The Modern Call Center," *Informationweek*, April 9, 2001, pp. 38–46; Alice Dragoon, "Put Your Money Where Your Mouthpiece Is," *Darwin*, February 2002, p. 60–65; and David L. Margulius, "Smarter Call Centers: At Your Service?" *New York Times*, March 14, 2002, p. G1.

16. Ann Marie Kerwin, "Brands Pursue Old, New Money," *Advertising Age*, June 11, 2001, pp. S1, S11.

17. Information accessed online at www.marriott.com, August 2002.

18. Information about P&G's product lines accessed at www.pg.com and www.crest.com, August 2002.

19. "McAtlas Shrugged," *Foreign Policy*, May–June 2001, pp. 26–37.

20. See Philip Kotler, *Marketing Management*, 11th ed. (Upper Saddle River, N.J.: Prentice Hall, 2003), p. 419.

21. Scott Davis, *Brand Asset Management: Driving Profitable Growth Through Your Brands* (San Francisco: Jossey-Bass, 2000); and David C. Bello and Morris. B. Holbrook, "Does an Absence of Brand Equity Generalize Across Product Classes?" *Journal of Business Research*, October 1995, p. 125.

22. Gerry Khermouch, "The Best Global Brands," *Business Week*, August 6, 2001, pp. 50–64.

23. Andrew Pierce and Eric Almquist, "Brand Building May Face a Test," *Advertising Age*, April 9, 2001, p. 22. Also see Don E. Schultz, "Mastering Brand Metrics," *Marketing Management*, May–June 2002, pp. 8–9.

24. See Roland T. Rust, Katherine N. Lemon, and Valerie A. Zeithaml, *Driving Customer Equity: How Lifetime Customer Value Is Reshaping Corporate Strategy* (New York: Free Press, 2000); Katherine N. Lemon, Roland T. Rust, and Valerie A. Zeithaml, "What Drives Customer Equity," *Marketing Management*, Spring 2001, pp. 20–25; and Rust, Lemon, and Zeithaml, "Where Should the Next Marketing Dollar Go?" *Marketing Management*, September–October 2001, pp. 24–28.

25. See Davis, *Brand Asset Management*.

26. Marc Gobe, *Emotional Branding* (New York: Allworth Press, 2001).

27. See Paul N. Bloom, Gregory T. Gundlach, and Joseph P. Cannon, "Slotting Allowances and Fees: School of Thought and the Views of Practicing Managers," *Journal of Marketing*, April 2000, pp. 92–108; Ira Teionwitz, "FTC Pinpoints Slotting Fees," *Advertising Age*, February 26, 2001, p. 52; and Julie Forster, "The Hidden Cost of Shelf Space," *Business Week*, April 15, 2002, p. 103.

28. Warren Thayer, "Loblaws Exec Predicts: Private Labels to Surge," *Frozen Food Age*, May 1996, p. 1; "President's Choice Continues Brisk Pace," *Frozen Food Age*, March 1998, pp. 17–18; David Dunne and Chakravarthi Narasimhan, "The New Appeal of Private Labels," *Harvard Business Review*, May–June 1999, pp. 41–52; "New Private Label

Alternatives Bring Changes to Supercenters, Clubs," *DSN Retailing Today,* February 5, 2001, p. 66; and information from www.presidentschoice.ca, July 2002.

29. See Gerda Gallop-Goodman, "What's in a Name," *American Demographics,* August 2000, p. 26. For more reading on store brands, see David Dunne and Chakravarthi Narasimham, "The New Appeal of Private Labels," *Harvard Business Review,* May–June 1999, pp. 41–52; Kusum L. Ailawadi, Scott Neslin, and Karen Gedenk, "Pursuing the Value-Conscious Consumer: Store Brands Versus National Promotions," *Journal of Marketing,* January 2001, pp. 71–89; and Pradeep K. Chintagunta, "Investigating Category Pricing Behavior at a Retail Chain," *Journal of Marketing Research,* May 2002, pp. 141–151.

30. See Doug Desjardins, "Popularized Entertainment Icons Continue to Dominate Licensing," *DSN Retailing Today,* July 9, 2001, p. 4; Emily Scardino, "Entertainment Licensing: Adding Equity Sells Apparel Programs," *DSN Retailing Today,* June 4, 2001, pp. A10–A12; Patricia Winters Lauro, "Licensing Deals Are Putting Big Brand Name into New Categories at the Supermarket," *New York Times,* June 18, 2002, p. C14; and Derek Manson, "Spidy Cents," *Money,* July 2002, p. 40.

31. See Terry Lefton, "Warner Brothers' Not Very Looney Path to Licensing Gold," *Brandweek,* February 14, 1994, pp. 36–37; Robert Scally, "Warner Builds Brand Presence, Strengthens 'Tunes' Franchise," *Discount Store News,* April 6, 1998, p. 33; "Looney Tunes Launched on East Coast," *Dairy Foods,* April 2001, p. 9; and "Looney Tunes Entering 696 Publix Super Markets," *Dairy Foods,* April 2002, p. 11.

32. See Laura Petrecca, " 'Corporate Brands' Put Licensing in the Spotlight," *Advertising Age,* June 14, 1999, p. 1; and Bob Vavra, "The Game of the Name," *Supermarket Business,* March 15, 2001, pp. 45–46.

33. Phil Carpenter, "Some Cobranding Caveats to Obey," *Marketing News,* November 7, 1994, p. 4; Gabrielle Solomon, "Co-Branding Alliances: Arranged Marriages Made by Marketers," *Fortune,* October 12, 1998, p. 188; "Kmart Licensing Will Continue," *New York Times,* March 21, 2002, p. C5; and Daniel Kadlac, "Martha's New Ruffle," *Time,* July 1, 2002, p. 39.

34. For more on the use of line and brand extensions and consumer attitudes toward them, see Deborah Roedder John, Barbara Loken, and Christopher Joiner, "The Negative Impact of Extensions: Can Flagship Brands Be Eroded?" *Journal of Marketing,* January 1998, pp. 19–32; Zeynep Gurrhan-Canli and Durairaj Maheswaran, "The Effects of Extensions on Brand Name Dilution and Enchancement," *Journal of Marketing,* November 1998, pp. 464–473; Vanitha Swaminathan, Richard J. Fox, and Srinivas K. Reddy, "The Impact of Brand Extension Introduction on Choice," *Journal of Marketing,* October 2001, pp. 1–15; Paul A. Bottomly and Stephen J. S. Holden, "Do We Really Know How Consumers Evaluate Brand Extensions? Empirical Generalizations Based on Secondary Analysis of Eight Studies," *Journal of Marketing Research,* November 2001, pp. 494–500; and Kalpesh Kaushik Desai and Kevin Lane Keller, "The Effect of Ingredient

Branding Strategies on Host Brand Extendibility," *Journal of Marketing,* January 2002, pp. 73–93.

35. "Top 100 Megabrands by Total Measured Advertising Spending," *Advertising Age,* July 16, 2001, p. S2.

36. See Donald D. Tosti and Roger D. Stotz, "Busiling Your Brand from the Inside Out," *Marketing Management,* July–August 2001, pp. 29–33.

37. See Kevin Lane Keller, "The Brand Report Card," *Harvard Business Review,* January 2000, pp. 147–157.

38. Steve Jarvis, "Refocus, Rebuild, Reeducate, Refine, Rebrand," *Marketing News,* March 26, 2001, pp. 1, 11; and "Top 10 Wireless Phone Brands," *Advertising Age,* June 24, 2002, p. S-18.

39. See Ronald Henkoff, "Service Is Everybody's Business," *Fortune,* June 27, 1994, pp. 48–60; Valerie Zeithaml and Mary Jo Bitner, *Services Marketing* (New York: McGraw-Hill, 1999), pp. 8–9; Allen Sinai, "Services in the U.S. Economy," accessed at http://usinfor.state.gov/journals/ites/0496/ijee/ej10.htm; and "Gross Domestic Product," news release, U.S. Bureau of Economic Analysis, June 29, 2001, accessed at www.bea.gov/bea/newsrel/gdp101f.htm.

40. See James L. Heskett, Thomas O. Jones, Gary W. Loveman, W. Earl Sasser Jr., and Leonard A. Schlesinger, "Putting the Service-Profit Chain to Work," *Harvard Business Review,* March–April, 1994, pp. 164–174; and James L. Heskett, W. Earl Sasser Jr., and Leonard A. Schlesinger, *The Service Profit Chain: How Leading Companies Link Profit and Growth to Loyalty, Satisfaction, and Value* (New York: Free Press, 1997). Also see Anthony J. Rucci, Steven P. Kirn, and Richard T. Quinn, "The Employee-Customer-Profit Chain at Sears," *Harvard Business Review,* January–February 1998, pp. 83–97; and Eugene W. Anderson and Vikas Mittal, "Strengthening the Satisfaction-Profit Chain," *Journal of Service Research,* November 2000, pp. 107–120.

41. See Louise Lee, "Schwab vs. Wall Street," *Business Week,* June 3, 2002, pp. 65–71.

42. For discussions of service quality, see A. Parasuraman, Valerie A. Zeithaml, and Leonard L. Berry, "A Conceptual Model of Service Quality and Its Implications for Future Research," *Journal of Marketing,* Fall 1985, pp. 41–50; Zeithaml, Berry, and Parasuraman, "The Behavioral Consequences of Service Quality," *Journal of Marketing,* April 1996, pp. 31–46; Thomas J. Page Jr., "Difference Scores Versus Direct Effects in Service Quality Measurement," *Journal of Service Research,* February 2002, pp. 184–192; and Richard A. Spreng; James J. Jiang, Gary Klein, and Christopher L. Carr, "Measuring Information System Service Quality: SERVQUAL from the Other Side, *MIS Quarterly,* June 2002, pp. 145–166.

43. See James L. Heskett, W. Earl Sasser Jr., and Christopher W. L. Hart, *Service Breakthroughs* (New York: Free Press, 1990).

44. See Stephen S. Tax, Stephen W. Brown, and Murali Chandrashekaran, "Customer Evaluations of Service Complaint Experiences: Implications for Relationship Marketing," *Journal of Marketing,* April 1998, pp. 60–76; Stephen W. Brown, "Practicing Best-in-Class Service Recovery," *Marketing Management,* Summer 2000, pp. 8–9;

and James G. Maxham III, "Service Recovery's Influence on Consumer Satisfaction, Positive Word-of-Mouth, and Purchase Intentions," *Journal of Business Research,* October 2001, p. 11; and David E Bowen, "Internal Service Recovery: Developing a New Construct," *Measuring Business Excellence,* 2002, p. 47.

45. See Paula Mergenbagen, "Product Liability: Who Sues?" *American Demographics,* June 1995, p. 48; "A Primer on Product Liability Laws," *Purchasing,* May 6, 1999, pp. 32–34; Pamela L. Moore, "The Litigation Machine," *Business Week,* January 29, 2001, pp. 115–123; and "Jury Awards in Product Liability Cases Increasing in Recent Years," *Chemical Market Reporter,* February 12, 2001, p. 5.

46. See James A. Bruen, "Product Liability: The Role of the Product Steward," *Risk Management,* February 2002, p. 34.

47. See Philip Cateora, *International Marketing,* 8th ed. (Homewood, Ill.: Irwin, 1993), p. 270; and David Fairlamb, "One Currency—But 15 Economies," *Business Week,* December 31, 2001, p. 59.

48. Information accessed online at www.deutsche-bank.com, July 2002.

49. Information accessed online at www.interpublic.com and www.mccann.com, July 2002.

50. See Carla Rapoport, "Retailers Go Global," *Fortune,* February 20, 1995, pp. 102–108; "Top 200 Global Retailers," *Stores,* January 1998, pp. S5–S12; Jeffery Adler, "The Americanization of Global Retailing," *Discount Merchandiser,* February 1998, p. 102; Mike Troy, "The World's Largest Retailer," *Chain Store Age,* June 2001, pp. 47–49; Mike Troy, "The Super Growth Leaders—Wal-Mart: Global Dominance Puts Half Trillion in Sight," *DSN Retailing Today,* December 10, 2001, p. 17; and "Wal-Mart: International Expansion," *Home Textiles Today,* April 12, 2002, p. 84.

CHAPTER 10

1. Quotes, extracts, and other information from Jay Greene, "Microsoft: How It Became Stronger Than Ever," *Business Week,* June 4, 2001, pp. 74–85; Brent Schlender, "Microsoft: The Beast Is Back," *Fortune,* June 11, 2001, pp. 74–86; Robin Peek, "Microsoft Introduces .Net My Services," *Information Today,* November 2001, p. 40; Greene, "On to the Living Room," *Business Week,* January 21, 2002, pp. 68–72; Greene, "Ballmer's Microsoft," *Business Week,* June 17, 2002, pp. 66–76; and Brent Schlender, "All You Need Is Love, $50 Billion, and Killer Software Code-Named Longhorn," *Fortune,* July 8, 2002, pp. 56–68.

2. For these and other examples, see Cliff Edwards, "Where Have All the Edsels Gone?" *Greensboro News Record,* May 24, 1999, p. B6; Simon Romero, "Once Proudly Carried, and Now Mere Carrion," *New York Times,* November 22, 2001, p. G5; and Kelly Carroll, "Satellite Telephony: Not for the Consumer," *Telephony,"* March 4, 2002, p. 17.

3. See Philip Kotler, *Kotler on Marketing* (New York: Free Press, 1999), p. 51; Martha Wirth Fellman, "Number of New Products Keeps Rising," *Marketing News,* March 29, 1999,

p. 3; Eric Berggren and Thomas Nacher, "Why Good Ideas Go Bust," *Management Review,* February 2000, pp. 32–36; Eric Berggren, "Introducing New Products Can Be Hazardous to Your Company: Use the Right New-Solutions Delivery Tools," *Academy of Management Executive,* August 2001, p. 92; and Bruce Tait, "The Failure of Marketing 'Science,'" *Brandweek,* April 8, 2002, pp. 20–22.

4. Gary Hamel, "Innovation's New Math," *Fortune,* July 9, 2001, pp. 130–131.

5. See Tim Stevens, "Idea Dollars," *Industry Week,* February 16, 1998, pp. 47–49; William E. Coyne, "How 3M Innovates for Long-Term Growth," *Research Technology Management,* March–April 2001, pp. 21–24; and Michael Arndt, "3M: A Lab for Growth," *Business Week,* January 21, 2002, pp. 50–51.

6. Paul Lukas, "Marketing: The Color of Money and Ketchup," *Fortune,* September 18, 2000, p. 38; and ". . . And Adds a Ketchup Mystery Bottle for Kids," *Packaging Digest,* April 2002, p. 4.

7. Pam Weisz, "Avon's Skin-So-Soft Bugs Out," *Brandweek,* June 6, 1994, p. 4; and information accessed online at www.avon.com, August 2002.

8. Stefan Thomke and Eric von Hippel, "Customers as Innovators: A New Way to Create Value," *Harvard Business Review,* April 2002, pp. 74–81.

9. Anthony W. Ulwick, "Turn Customer Input into Innovation," *Harvard Business Review,* January 2002, pp. 91–97.

10. Kotler, *Kotler on Marketing,* pp. 43–44. For more on developing new-product ideas, see Andrew Hargadon and Robert I. Sutton, "Building an Innovation Factory," *Harvard Business Review,* May–June 2000, pp. 157–166.

11. Brian O'Reilly, "New Ideas, New Products," *Fortune,* March 3, 1997, pp. 61–64. Also see Michael Schrage, "Getting Beyond the Innovation Fetish," *Fortune,* November 13, 2000, pp. 225–232.

12. See John McCormick, "The Future Is Not Quite Now," *Automotive Manufacturing & Production,* August 2000, pp. 22–24; "DaimlerChrysler Unveils NECAR 5 Methanol-Powered Fuel Cell Vehicle," *Chemical Market Reporter,* November 13, 2000, p. 5; Dale Buss, "Green Cars," *American Demographics,* January 2001, pp. 57–61; Catherine Greenman, "Fuel Cells: Clean, Reliable (and Pricey) Electricity," *New York Times,* May 10, 2001, p. G8; and Stuart F. Brown, "A Wild Vision for Fuel-Cell Vehicles," *Fortune,* April 1, 2002, p. 72.

13. See Raymond R. Burke, "Virtual Reality Shopping: Breakthrough in Marketing Research," *Harvard Business Review,* March–April 1996, pp. 120–131; Mike Hoffman, "Virtual Shopping," *Inc,* July 1998, p. 88; Christopher Ryan, "Virtual Reality in Marketing," *Direct Marketing,* April 2001, pp. 57–62; and Patrick Waurzyniak, "Going Virtual," *Manufacturing Engineering,* May 2002, pp. 77–88.

14. Adrienne Ward Fawcett, "Oreo Cones Make Top Grade in Poll," *Advertising Age,* June 14, 1993, p. 30; Becky Ebenkamp, "The New Gold Standards," *Brandweek,* April 19, 1999, p. 34; Ebencamp, "It's Like Cheers and Jeers, Only for Brands," *Brankweek,* March 19, 2001; and Ebenkamp, "The Focus Group Has Spoken," *Brandweek,* April 23, 2001, p. 24.

15. Examples adapted from those found in Faye Rice, "Secrets of Product Testing," *Fortune*, November 28, 1994, pp. 172–174; Linda Grant, "Gillette Knows Shaving—And How to Turn Out Hot New Products," *Fortune*, October 14, 1996, pp. 207–210; and Emily Nelson, "Focus Groupies: P&G Keeps Cincinnati Busy with All Its Studies—While Her Sons Test Old Spice, Linda Geil Gets Swabbed," *Wall Street Journal*, January 24, 2002, p. A1.

16. Judann Pollack, "Baked Lays," *Advertising Age*, June 24, 1996, p. S2; and Jack Neff and Suzanne Bidlake, "P&G, Unilever Aim to Take Consumers to the Cleaners," *Advertising Age*, February 12, 2001, pp. 1, 2.

17. The McDonald's, Nabisco, and other examples can be found in Robert McMath, "To Test or Not to Test," *Advertising Age*, June 1998, p. 64; and Bret Thron, "Lessons Learned: Menu Miscues," *Nation's Restaurant News*, May 20, 2002, pp. 102–104. Also see Jerry W. Thomas, "Skipping Research a Major Error," *Marketing News*, March 4, 2002, p. 50.

18. Jack Neff, "Is Testing the Answer?" *Advertising Age*, July 9, 2001, p. 13.

19. For information on BehaviorScan, visit www.behaviorscan.com.

20. Emily Nelson, "Colgate's Net Rose 10% in Period, New Products Helped Boost Sales," *Wall Street Journal*, February 2, 2001, p. B6.

21. For a good review of research on new-product development, see Rajesh Sethi, "New Product Quality and Product Development Teams," *Journal of Marketing*, April 2000, pp. 1–14; Rajesh Sethi, Daniel C. Smith, and C. Whan Park, "Cross-Functional Product Development Teams, Creativity, and the Innovativeness of New Consumer Products," *Journal of Marketing Research*, February 2001, pp. 73–85; Shikhar Sarin and Vijay Mahajan, "The Effect of Reward Structures on the Performance of Cross-Functional Product Development Teams," *Journal of Marketing*, April 2001, pp. 35–54; Avan R. Jassawalla and Hemant C. Sashittal, "The Role of Senior Management and Team Leaders in Building Collaborative New Product Teams," *Engineering Management Journal*, June 2001, pp. 33–39; and Joseph M. Bonner, Robert W. Ruekert, and Orville C. Walker Jr., "Upper Management Control of New Product Development Projects and Project Performance," *Journal of Product Innovation Management*, May 2002, pp. 233–245.

22. Laurie Freeman, "Study: Leading Brands Aren't Always Enduring," *Advertising Age*, February 28, 2000, p. 26.

23. See David Stipp, "The Theory of Fads," *Fortune*, October 14, 1996, pp. 49–52; "Fads vs. Trends," *The Futurist*, March–April 2000, p. 67; Irma Zandl, "How to Separate Trends from Fads," *Brandweek*, October 23, 2000, pp. 30–33; and "Scooter Fad Fades, as Warehouses Fill and Profits Fall," *Wall Street Journal*, June 14, 2001, p. B4.

24. For interesting discussions of how brand performance is affected by the product life-cycle stage at which the brand enters the market, see Venkatesh Shankar, Gregory S. Carpenter, and Lekshman Krishnamurthi, "The Advantages of Entry in the Growth Stage of the Product Life Cycle: An Empirical Analysis," *Journal of Marketing Research*, May 1999, pp. 269–276; William Boulding and Markus Christen, "First-Mover Disadvantage," *Harvard Business Review*, October 2001, pp. 20–21; and William T. Robinson and Sungwook Min, "Is the First to Market the First to Fail? Empirical Evidence for Industrial Goods Businesses," *Journal of Marketing Research*, February 2002, p. 120.

25. Mark McMaster, "Putting a New Spin on Old Products," *Sales & Marketing Management*, April 2001, p. 20; and www.rollwipes.com, July 2002.

26. Michael Hartnett, "Cracker Jack: Chris Neugent," *Advertising Age*, June 26, 2000, p. S22.

27. For a more comprehensive discussion of marketing strategies over the course of the product life cycle, see Philip Kotler, *Marketing Management*, 11th ed. (Upper Saddle River, N.J.: Prentice Hall, 2003), chapter 10.

CHAPTER 11

1. Thomas T. Nagle and Reed K. Holden, *The Strategy and Tactics of Pricing*, 3rd ed. (Upper Saddle River, N.J.: Prentice Hall, 2002), p. 1.

2. Excerpts from "Business: It Was My Idea," *The Economist*, August 15, 1998, p. 54; Karl Taro Greenfeld, "Be Your Own Barcode," *Time*, July 10, 2000, pp. 96–97; Ben Rosier, "The Price Is Right," *Marketing*, February 22, 2001, p.26; and www.priceline.com, July 2002. See also Julia Angwin, "Priceline Founder Closes Online Bidding Site for Gas and Groceries," *Wall Street Journal*, October 6, 2000, p. B1; "Priceline.com Tops Forecast for Quarter, but Its Shares Fall," *New York Times*, February 5, 2002, p. C12; and "Priceline.com's Online 'Reach' Up 810% vs. a Year Ago," June 7, 2002, accessed online at www.priceline.com.

3. Dean Foust, "Raising Prices Won't Fly," *Business Week*, June 3, 2002, p. 34.

4. Philip Kotler, *Marketing Management*, 11th ed. (Upper Saddle River, N.J.: Prentice Hall, 2003), p. 470.

5. See David J. Schwartz, *Marketing Today: A Basic Approach*, 3rd ed. (New York: Harcourt Brace Jovanovich, 1981), pp. 270–273.

6. See Amy E. Cortese, "Good-Bye to Fixed Pricing?" *Business Week*, May 4, 1998, pp. 71–84; Robert D. Hof, "The Buyer Always Wins," *Business Week*, March 22, 1999, pp. EB26–EB28; Robert D. Hof, "Going, Going, Gone," *Business Week*, April 12, 1999, pp. 30–32; and Michael Vizard, Ed Scannell, and Dan Neel, "Suppliers Toy with Dynamic Pricing," *InfoWorld*, May 14, 2001, p. 28.

7. For an excellent discussion of factors affecting pricing decisions, see Nagle and Holden, *The Strategy and Tactics of Pricing*, chap. 1.

8. See Timothy M. Laseter, "Supply Chain Management: The Ins and Outs of Target Costing," *Purchasing*, March 12, 1998, pp. 22–25; John K. Shank and Joseph Fisher, "Case Study: Target Costing as a Strategic Tool," *Sloan Management Review*, Fall 1999, pp. 73–82; and Melanie Wells, "On His Watch," *Forbes*, February 18, 2002, pp. 93–94.

9. Brian Dumaine, "Closing the Innovation Gap," *Fortune,* December 2, 1991, pp. 56–62; and information accessed online at www.johnsoncontrols.com/metasys, July 2002.

10. Here accumulated production is drawn on a semilog scale so that equal distances represent the same percentage increase in output.

11. Joshua Rosenbaum, "Guitar Maker Looks for a New Key," *Wall Street Journal,* February 11, 1998, p. B1; and information accessed online at www.gibson.com, July 2002.

12. See Nagle and Holden, *The Strategy and Tactics of Pricing,* chap. 4.

13. Information accessed online at www.greenmountain.com, October 2002.

14. The arithmetic of markups and margins is discussed in Appendix 2, "Marketing Math."

15. See Philip Kotler, *Kotler on Marketing* (Upper Saddle River, N.J.: Prentice Hall, 1999), p. 54.

16. Erin Stout, "Keep Them Coming Back for More," *Sales & Marketing Management,* February 2002, pp. 51–52.

17. See Mike Troy, "Kmart: 2. Drop EDLP—Continue Promoting the Value Message, *DSN Retailing Today,* March 11, 2002, p. 33; and Laura Heller, "Simple Messages Reinforce EDLP," *DSN Retailing Today,* June 10, 2002, p. 129.

CHAPTER 12

1. Quotes and other information from Tobi Elkin, "Rare Prime-Time Teaser Campaign Gets mLife Off to a Running Start," *Advertising Age,* April 15, 2002, p. S4; Brian McDonough, "AT&T Wireless Pushes mLife with mMode," *Wireless NewsFactor,* April 17, 2002, accessed online at www.wirelessnewsfactor.com; Jay Wrolstad, "AT&T Reveals 'mLife' Mystery," *Wireless NewsFactor,* February 4, 2002, accessed online at www.wirelessnewsfactor.com; Stephanie Mehta, "That Old Sinking Feeling," *Fortune,* December 10, 2001, p. 34; Christopher Saunders, "What Is mLife? Ask AT&T Wireless," February 1, 2002, accessed online at www. atnewyork.com/news/article.php/8471_966711; John Gaffney, "AT&T's mLife in Hell," *Marketing Focus,* February 11, 2002, accessed online at www.business2.com/articles/web/print/0,1650,37798,FF.html; and Peter Elstrom, Heather Green, Roger O. Crockett, Charles Haddad, and Catherine Yang, "What Ails Wireless?" *Business Week,* April 1, 2002, p. 60.

2. For a comprehensive discussion of pricing strategies, see Thomas T. Nagle and Reed K. Holden, *The Strategy and Tactics of Pricing,* 3rd ed. (Upper Saddle River, N.J.: Prentice Hall, 2002).

3. Philip Kotler, *Marketing Management,* 11th ed. (Upper Saddle River, N.J.:Prentice Hall, 2003), p. 474; Kara Swisher, "Electronics 2001: The Essential Guide." *Wall Street Journal,* January 5, 2001; and Cliff Edwards, "HDTV: High-Anxiety Television," *Business Week,* June 10, 2002, pp. 142–146.

4. Seanna Browder, "Nintendo: At the Top of Its Game," *Business Week,* June 9, 1997, pp. 72–73; N'Gai Croal, "Game Wars 5.0," *Newsweek,* May 28, 2001, pp. 65–66; "Console Competition Lowers Opening Price Points," *DSN Retailing Today,* March 25, 2002, p. 18; and Khanh T. L. Tran, "Microsoft to Spend $2 Billion on Xbox Videogame," *Wall Street Journal,* May 21, 2002, p. D5.

5. E. M. Phillips, "Capitalizing on Your Wood By-Products," *FDM,* March 2002, pp. 48–51.

6. Susan Krafft, "Love, Love Me Doo," *American Demographics,* June 1994, pp. 15–16; Damon Darlin, "Zoo Doo," *Forbes,* May 22, 1995, p. 92; and the Zoo Doo Web site, www.zoodoo.com, July 2002.

7. See Nagle and Holden, *The Strategy and Tactics of Pricing,* pp. 244–247; and Stefan Stremersch and Gerard J. Tellis, "Strategic Bundling of Products and Prices: A New Synthesis for Marketing," *Journal of Marketing Research,* January 2002, pp. 55–72.

8. Quotes in this section are from Susan Greco, "Are Your Prices Right?" *Inc.,* January 1997, pp. 88–89; Robert G. Cross, *Revenue Management: Hard-Core Tactics for Market Domination* (New York: Broadway Books, 1998); and Joe Sharkey, "Hotels Take a Lesson from Airline Pricing," *New York Times,* December 17, 2000, p. 4-3. Also see Ramarao Desiraju and Steven M. Shugan, "Strategic Service Pricing and Yield Management," *Journal of Marketing,* January 1999, pp. 44–56; James Schembari, "More and More, We Get Less and . . . ," *New York Times,* January 14, 2001, p. 4-2; and Sheryl E. Kimes, "Perceived Fairness of Yield Management," *Cornell Hotel and Restaurant Administration Quarterly,* February 2002, p. 21.

9. Example adapted from Greco, "Are Your Prices Right?" *Inc.,* p. 88.

10. For more reading on reference prices and psychological pricing, see Robert M. Schindler and Patrick N. Kirby, "Patterns of Right-Most Digits Used in Advertised Prices: Implications for Nine-Ending Effects," *Journal of Consumer Research,* September 1997, pp. 192–201; Dhruv Grewal, Kent B. Monroe, Chris Janiszewski, and Donald R. Lichtenstein, "A Range Theory of Price Perception," *Journal of Consumer Research,* March 1999, pp. 353–368; Tridib Mazumdar and Purushottam Papatla, "An Investigation of Reference Price Segments," *Journal of Marketing Research,* May 2000, pp. 246–258; Indrajit Sinha and Michael Smith, "Consumers' Perceptions of Promotional Framing of Price," *Psychology & Marketing,* March 2000, pp. 257–271; and Tulin Erdem, Glenn Mayhew, and Baohong Sun, "Understanding Reference-Price Shoppers: A Within- and Across-Category Analysis," *Journal of Marketing Research,* November 2001, pp. 445–457.

11. Tim Ambler, "Kicking Price Promotion Habit Is Like Getting Off Heroin—Hard," *Marketing,* May 27, 1999, p. 24. Also see Robert Gray, "Driving Sales at Any Price?" *Marketing,* April 11, 2002, p. 24.

12. Adapted from Andrew Park and Peter Burrows, "Dell, the Conqueror," *Business Week,* September 24, 2001, pp. 92–102. See also Andy Serwer, "Dell Does Domination," *Fortune,* January 21, 2002, pp. 70–75; and Gary McWilliams, "Dell Computer's Kevin Rollins Becomes a Driving Force," *Wall Street Journal,* April 4, 2002, p. B6.

13. Philip R. Cateora, *International Marketing*, 7th ed. (Homewood, Ill.: Irwin, 1990), p. 540. Also see S. Tamer Cavusgil, "Pricing for Global Markets," *Columbia Journal of World Business*, Winter 1996, pp. 66–78; Barbara Stottinger, "Strategic Export Pricing: A Long and Winding Road," *Journal of International Marketing*, 2001, pp. 40–63; and Warren J. Keegan, *Global Marketing Management* (Upper Saddle River, N.J.: Prentice Hall, 2002), chap. 12.

14. See John Greenwald, "Cereal Showdown," *Time*, April 29, 1996, p. 60; "Cereal Thriller," *The Economist*, June 15, 1996, p. 59; Terril Yue Jones, "Outside the Box," *Forbes*, June 14, 1999, pp. 52–53; and "Kellogg Concedes Top Spot to General Mills," *New York Times*, February 22, 2001, p. C4.

15. Jeff Ansell, "Luvs," *Advertising Age*, June 30, 1997, p. S16; and Jack Neff, "Kimberly-Clark Looses 'Bounty Killer,'" *Advertising Age*, April 2, 2001, p. 34.

16. For an excellent discussion of these issues, see Dhruv Grewel and Larry D. Compeau, "Pricing and Public Policy: A Research Agenda and Overview of Special Issue," *Journal of Marketing and Public Policy*, Spring 1999, pp. 3–10.

17. Ralph Blumenthal, "Ex-Executive of Christie's Tells of Collusion Scheme," *New York Times*, November 15, 2001, p. D1; and Paul Hofheinz, "EU Accuses Auction Houses of Running Price-Fixing Cartel," *Wall Street Journal*, April 22, 2002, p. B6.

18. David Barboza, "Archer Daniels Executive Said to Tell of Price-Fixing Talks with Cargill Counterpart," *New York Times*, June 17, 1999, p. 6; Stephen Labaton, "The World Gets Tough on Fixing Prices," *New York Times*, June 3, 2001, p. 3.1; and Scott Kilman, "Court Reinstates Suit Alleging Archer Rigged Sweetener Market," *Wall Street Journal*, June 19, 2002, p. D2.

19. Holman W. Jenkins Jr., "Business World: Flying the 'Angry' Skies," *Wall Street Journal*, April 29, 1998, p. A23.

20. Excerpts from Dan Carney, "Predatory Pricing: Cleared for Takeoff," *Business Week*, May 14, 2001, p. 50.

21. Mike France, "Does Predatory Pricing Make Microsoft a Predator?" *Business Week*, November 23, 1998, pp. 130–132.

22. Grewel and Compeau, "Pricing and Public Policy: A Research Agenda and Overview of Special Issue," p. 8.

23. For more on public policy and pricing, see Louis W. Stern and Thomas L. Eovaldi, *Legal Aspects of Marketing Strategy* (Upper Saddle River, N.J.: Prentice Hall, 1984), chap. 5; Robert J. Posch, *The Complete Guide to Marketing and the Law* (Upper Saddle River, N.J.: Prentice Hall, 1988), chap. 28; Joseph P. Guiltinan and Gregory Gunlach, "Aggressive and Predatory Pricing: A Framework for Analysis," *Journal of Marketing*, July 1996, pp. 87–102; Bruce Upbin, "Vindication," *Forbes*, November 17, 1997, pp. 52–56; Grewel and Compeau, "Pricing and Public Policy: A Research Agenda and Overview of Special Issue," pp. 3–10; and Nagle and Holden, *The Strategy and Tactics of Pricing*, chap. 14.

CHAPTER 13

1. Quotes and other information from Donald V. Fites, "Make Your Dealers Your Partners," *Harvard Business Review*, March–April 1996, pp. 84–95; and DeAnn Weimer, "A New Cat on the Hot Seat," *Business Week*, March 1998, pp. 56–62; Mark Tatge, "Caterpillar Reports 26% Jump in Net Despite Weak Sales," *Wall Street Journal*, April 19, 2000, p. A8; Joseph T. Hallinan, "Caterpillar Beats Estimates, Says 2001 Will Hurt," *Wall Street Journal*, January 19, 2001, p. B6; Sandra Ward, "The Cat Comes Back," *Barron's*, February 25, 2002, pp. 21–24; and information accessed online at www.cat.com, July 2002.

2. For definitions and a complete discussion of distribution channel topics, see Anne T. Coughlin, Erin Anderson, Louis W. Stern, and Adel El-Ansary, *Marketing Channels*, 6th ed. (Upper Saddle River, N.J.: Prentice Hall, 2001), pp. 2–3.

3. See Drew Villard, "Franchisees Fight with Parents Over Internet Sales," *Sacramento Business Journal*, February 16, 2001, pp. 34+; Rochelle Garner, "Mad as Hell," *Sales & Marketing Management*, June 1999, pp. 55–61; Chuck Moozakis, "Herman Miller Builds Three-Pronged Strategy—Furniture Company Tailors Web Efforts to Size of Customer," *Internetweek*, June 11, 2001, pp. PG61–PG62; David Rocks, "Herman Miller," *Business Week*, October 29, 2001, p. EB23; and Kate Macarthur, "McD's Boss Blasts Chain 'Naysayers,'" *Advertising Age*, March 18, 2002, p. 1.

4. William Keenan Jr., "Sales and Marketing—(Pet) Food for Thought," *Industry Week*, March 5, 2001, accessed online at www.industryweek.com/columns/asp/columns.asp?columnid=750; and "P&G Plans Overhaul of Iams Brand," *Marketing Week*, May 30, 2002, p. 6.

5. Coughlin, Anderson, Stern, and El-Ansary, *Marketing Channels*, 6th ed., p. 160.

6. "Business Floating on Air," *The Economist*, May 19, 2001, pp. 56–57; Richard Heller, "Galician Beauty," *Forbes*, May 28, 2001, p. 98; Carlta Vitzthum, "Just-in-Time Fashion—Spanish Retailer Zara Makes Low-Cost Lines in Weeks by Running Its Own Show," *Wall Street Journal*, May 18, 2001, p. B1; and Miguel Helft, "Fashion Fast Forward," *Business 2.0*, May 2002, p. 60.

7. See Ilan Alon, "The Use of Franchising by U.S.-Based Retailers," *Journal of Small Business Management*, April 2001, pp. 111–122; James H. Amos Jr., "Franchising, More than Any Act of Government, Will Strengthen the Global Economy," *Franchising World*, May–June 2001, p. 8; and "Answers to the 21 Most Commonly Asked Questions About Franchising," accessed online at the International Franchise Association Web Site: www.franchise.org, July 2002.

8. See Subhash C. Jain, *International Marketing Management*, 3rd ed. (Boston: PWS-Kent Publishing, 1990), pp. 489–491; and Warren J. Keegan, *Global Marketing Management* (Upper Saddle River, N.J.: Prentice Hall, 2002), pp. 403–404.

9. See Aruna Chandra and John K. Ryans Jr. "Why India Now?" *Marketing Management*, March–April 2002, pp. 43–45; Dana James, "Dark Clouds Should Part for International Marketers," *Marketing News*, January 7, 2002, pp. 9, 13; and Laurie Sullivan, "China Remains Tough Turf for Independent Distributors," *EBN*, July 8, 2002, p. 1.

10. For more on channel relationships, see James A. Narus and James C. Anderson, "Rethinking Distribution," *Harvard*

Business Review, July–August 1996, pp. 112–120; James C. Anderson and James A. Narus, *Business Market Management* (Upper Saddle River, N.J.: Prentice Hall, 1999), pp. 276–288; Jonathon D. Hibbard, Nirmalya Kumar, and Louis W. Stern, "Examining the Impact of Destructive Acts in Marketing Channel Relationships," *Journal of Marketing Research,* February 2001, pp. 45–61; and Stavros P. Kalafatis, "Buyer–Seller Relationships Among Channels of Distribution," *Industrial Marketing Management,* April 2002, pp. 215–228.

11. Cathy Ciccolella, "GE to Offer Online Dealer Support with CustomerNet," *Twice,* April 21, 1997, p. 88; Cathy Ciccolella, "GE Online Support Wins Dealers Over," *Twice,* February 9, 1998, p. 38; Mitch Betts, "GE Appliance Park Still an IT Innovator," *Computerworld,* January 29, 2001, pp. 20–21; and "What Is GE CustomerNet?" accessed online at www.geappliances.com/buildwithge/index_cnet.htm, August 2002.

12. See Heather Harreld and Paul Krill, "Channel Management," *InfoWorld,* October 8, 2001, pp. 46–52; and Barbara Darrow, "Comergent Revs Up PRM, *Crn,* April 8, 2002, p. 60.

13. For a full discussion of laws affecting marketing channels, see Coughlin, Anderson, Stern, and El-Ansary, *Marketing Channels,* chap. 12.

14. James R. Stock, "The Seven Deadly Sins of Reverse Logistics," *Material Handling Management,* March 2001, pp. MHS5–MHS11; and Martin Piszczalksi, "Logistics: A Difference Between Winning and Losing," *Automotive Manufacturing & Production,* May 2001, pp. 16–18.

15. Shlomo Maital, "The Last Frontier of Cost Reduction," *Across the Board,* February 1994, pp. 51–52; and "Wal-Mart to Expand Supercenters to California," *BusinessJournal,* May 15, 2002, accessed online at http://sanjose.bizjournals.com.

16. John Huey, "Wal-Mart: Will It Take Over the World?" *Fortune,* January 30, 1989, pp. 52–64; Mike Troy, "Wal-Mart: Behind the Scenes Efficiency Keeps Growth Curve on Course," *DSN Retailing Today,* June 4, 2001, pp. 80, 91; and "Wal-Mart Centers Benefit from Quick Start," accessed online at www.dtae.org/quickstart/News7/walmart.html, July 2002.

17. J. William Gurley, "Why Dell's War Isn't Dumb," *Fortune,* July 9, 2001, pp. 134–136.

18. Bob Verdisco, "The Coming Retail Revolution," *DSN Retailing Today,* May 6, 2002, p. 12

19. For statistics on freight shipments, see *United States 1997 Economic Census: Transportation,* U.S. Department of Transportation, issued December 1999, accessed. online at www.bts.gov.

20. Kay Moody, Managing Director of Strategic Planning and Intranet Development of FedEx, "Getting Down to Business on the Net at FedEx," presentation to The Information Management Forum, April 19–20, 1999 (Figure 9).

21. Judy Strauss and Raymond Frost, *E-Marketing,* 2nd ed. (Upper Saddle River, N.J.: Prentice Hall, 2001), p. 193; Jean Kinsey, "A Faster, Leaner Supply Chain: New Uses of Information Technology," *American Journal of Agricultural Economics,* November 15, 2000, pp. 1123+.

22. See Robert E. Danielson, "CPFR: Improving Your Business Without Being Limited by Technology," *Apparel Industry Magazine,* February 2000, pp. 56–57; and Ben A. Chaouch, "Stock Levels and Delivery Rates in Vendor-Managed Inventory Programs," *Production and Operations Management,* Spring 2001, pp. 31–44.

23. Tom Stein and Jeff Sweat, "Killer Supply Chains—Six Companies Are Using Supply Chains to Transform the Way They Do Business," *Information Week,* November 11, 1998, p. 36; Susan Reda, "Internet-EDI Initiatives Show Potential to Reinvent Supply Chain Management," *Stores,* January 1999, pp. 26–27; and Craig A. Hill and Gary D. Scudder, "The Use of Electronic Data Interchange for Supply Chain Coordination in the Food Industry," *Journal of Operations Management,* August 2002, pp. 375–387.

24. See Lara L. Sowinski, "Supply Chain Management and Logistics Software," *World Trade,* February 2001, pp. 34–36; Marc L. Songini, "PeopleSoft Pushes CRM, Supply Chain Software," *Computerworld,* May 6, 2002, p. 19; and Amy Rogers, "Supply Chain Players Toss a Few Barbs as Competition Heats Up," *Crn,* April 22, 2002, pp. 29–30.

25. Sandra J. Skrovan, "Partnering with Vendors: The Ties that Bind," *Chain Store Executive,* January 1994, p. 6MH; and Susan Caminiti, "After You Win, the Fun Begins," *Fortune,* May 2, 1994, p. 76.

26. Reed Stith, "Customer-Driven Supply Chain," *Frontline Solutions,* May 2002, p. 40.

27. Mike Verespej, "Logistics' New Look? Now It's Service," *Frontline Solutions,* June 2002, pp. 24–33.

28. Ibid., p. 24.

CHAPTER 14

1. Quotes and information in this Home Depot tale are from Patricia Sellers, "Companies That Serve You Best," *Fortune,* May 31, 1993, pp. 74–88; Thomas H. Nodine, "Home Depot's Leading Indicators of Value," *Harvard Business Review,* March–April 1999, p. 100; Bernie Marcus, Arthur Blank, and Bob Andelman, *Built from Scratch: How a Couple of Regular Guys Grew the Home Depot from Nothing to $30 Billion* (New York: Random House, 1999); "Retailer of the Year Awards: The Home Depot—Best Trained Sales Staff," *Home Textiles Today,* March 26, 2001, p. SS4; Mike Troy, "Motivating Your Workforce: A Home Depot Case Study," *DSN Retailing Today,* June 10, 2002, p. 29; and Chad Terhune and Dan Morse, "Refinishing Home Depot," *Wall Street Journal,* June 25, 2002, p. B1.

2. See Bob Tedeschi, "The History of Online Grocery Shopping: First as Web Farce, Now a Lucrative Field for Older Companies," *New York Times,* May 6, 2002, p. C7.

3. See "2002 SOI Highlights," National Association of Convenience Stores, accessed online at www.cstorecentral.com, August 2002.

4. Richard Turcsik and Jenny Summerour, "David vs. Goliath," *Progressive Grocer,* March 2001, p. 7; Laura Heller, "Wal-Mart Outprices Atlanta Competition," *DSN Retailing,* June 18,

2001, pp. 1, 42; and Mike Duff, "Supercenters Take Lead in Food Retailing," *DSN Retailing Today,* May 6, 2002. pp. F8–F9.

5. See Ray A. Smith, "Outlet Centers Go Upmarket with Amenities," *Wall Street Journal,* June 6, 2001, p. B12; and Mervyn Rothstein, "At a Shoppers' Mecca, Now, Retail for Locals," *New York Times,* April 10, 2002, p. C6.

6. Wendy Zellner, "Warehouse Clubs: When the Going Gets Tough . . . " *Business Week,* July 16, 2001, p. 60; and "Warehouse Clubs Lead Growth," *Chain Store Age,* May 2002, p. 160.

7. See David Stires, "Fallen Arches," *Fortune,* April 29, 2002, pp. 74–76; and Anne Smith, "Landmark 16,000th Subway Restaurant Opens," press release, March 2002, accessed online at www.subway.com.

8. Quotes and information from Shelly Branch, "How Target Got Hot," *Fortune,* May 24, 1999, pp. 169–174; "Target Works Its Market Magic," *DSN Retailing Today,* April 2, 2001, pp. 43, 64; and Constance L. Hayes, "Can Target Survive in Wal-Mart's Cross Hairs?" *New York Times,* June 9, 2002, 3.1.

9. Myron Magnet, "Let's Go for Growth," *Fortune,* March 7, 1994, pp. 60–72. Also see Dierdre Donahue, "Bookstores: A Haven for the Intellect," *USA Today,* July 10, 1997, pp. D1, D2; and Christina Nifong, "Beyond Browsing," *Raleigh News & Observer,* May 25, 1999, p. E1.

10. "Mall of America Starts 10th Year Celebration," *Home Textiles Today,* June 24, 2002, p. 42; and "The History of Mall of America," accessed online at www.mallofamerica.com, September 2002.

11. Andrea Bermudez, "Bijan Dresses the Wealthy for Success," *Apparel News.Net,* December 1–7, 2000, accessed online at www.apparelnews.net/Archieve/120100/News/newsfeat.htm.

12. John Fetto, "Mall Rats," *American Demographics,* March 2002, p. 10; Robert Berner and Gerry Khermouch, "Retail Reckoning," *Business Week,* December 10, 2001, pp. 71–77; and Matt Valley, "The Remalling of America," *National Real Estate Investor,* May 2002, pp. 18–24.

13. Dean Starkman, "The Mall, Without the Haul—'Lifestyle Centers' Slip Quietly into Upscale Areas, Mixing Cachet and 'Curb Appeal,'" *Wall Street Journal,* July 25, 2001, p. B1.

14. Amy Barrett, "A Retailing Pacesetter Pulls Up Lame," *Business Week,* July 12, 1993, pp. 122–123.

15. See Malcolm P. McNair and Eleanor G. May, "The Next Revolution of the Retailing Wheel," *Harvard Business Review,* September–October 1978, pp. 81–91; Stephen Brown, "The Wheel of Retailing: Past and Future," *Journal of Retailing,* Summer 1990, pp. 143–147; Stephen Brown, "Variations on a Marketing Enigma: The Wheel of Retailing Theory," *Journal of Marketing Management,* 7, no. 2, 1991, pp. 131–155; Jennifer Negley, "Retrenching, Reinventing and Remaining Relevant," *Discount Store News,* April 5, 1999, p. 11; and Don E. Schultz, "Another Turn of the Wheel," *Marketing Management,* March–April 2002, pp. 8–9.

16. Charles Haddad, "Office Depot's E-Diva," *Business Week,* August 6, 2001, pp. EB22–EB24; and Meryl Davids Landau, "Sweet Revenge," *Chief Executive,* May 2002, pp. 58–62.

17. Excerpt adapted from Alice Z. Cuneo, "What's in Store?" *Advertising Age,* February 25, 2002, pp. 1, 30–31.

18. See "The Fortune 500," *Fortune,* April 15, 2002, p. F1.

19. Regina Fazio Maruca, "Retailing: Confronting the Challenges That Face Bricks-and-Mortar Stores," *Harvard Business Review,* July–August 1999, pp. 159–168. Also see Marshall L. Fisher, Ananth Raman, and Anna Sheen McClelland, "Rocket Science Retailing Is Almost Here: Are You Ready?" *Harvard Business Review,* July–August 2000, pp. 115–124.

20. James Cox, "Red-Letter Day as East Meets West in the Aisles," *USA Today,* September 11, 1996, p. B1; and "International Operations Data Sheet," July 2002, accessed online at www.walmartstores.com.

21. Carla Rapoport, "Retailers Go Global," *Fortune,* February 20, 1995, pp. 102–108; Joseph H. Ellis, "Global Retailing's Winners and Losers," *Chain Store Age,* December 1997, pp. 27–29; "Global Retailing in the Connected Economy," *Chain Store Age,* December 1999, pp. 69–82; and "Top 200 Global Retailers," *Stores,* October 2000, pp. G6–G15.

22. Adapted from Tim Craig, "Carrefour: At the Intersection of Global," *DSN Retailing Today,* September 18, 2000, p. 16. Additional information from Richard Tomlinson, "Who's Afraid of Wal-Mart?" *Fortune,* June 26, 2000, pp. 186–196; and www.carrefour.com, July 2002.

23. Nifong, "Beyond Browsing," p. E1. Also see Fred Brock, "Catering to the Elderly Can Pay Off," *New York Times,* February 2002, p. 3.11.

24. Kathleen Cholewka, "Standing Out Online: The Five Best E-Marketing Campaigns," *Sales & Marketing Management,* January 2001, pp. 51–58.

25. "McKesson: Online Annual Report 2001," accessed online at www.mckesson.com/wt/ar_2001.php, August 2001; and "Supply Management Online," accessed online at www.mckesson.com, August 2002.

26. Facts accessed online at www.supervalu.com, September 2002.

CHAPTER 15

1. Quotes, excerpts, and other information from Dale Hayes, "It's Easy Being 'Brown,'" *NECG Edge,* May–June 2002, pp. 5–7; "UPS Launches Biggest, 'Brownest' Ad Campaign Ever," February 7, 2002, accessed online at www.pressroom. ups.com; Roger Morton, "Small Parcel's Big 3," *Transportation & Distribution,* March 2002, pp. 71–75; John Beystehner, "Managing the Brand for Strategic Alignment," June 3, 2002, accessed online at www.pressroom.ups.com; Jim Kelly, "The Living, Breathing Brand: The Human Side of Competitive Advantage," accessed online at www.pressroom.ups.com, July 2002; Fiona Kerr, "UPS Logistics Interview with Tim Geiken, UPS Vice President of E-Commerce Marketing," accessed online at www.eyefortransport.com, July 2002; and Kristin S. Krause, "One UPS Face," *Traffic World,* March 4, 2002, p. 31.

2. The first four of these definitions are adapted from Peter D. Bennett, *Dictionary of Marketing Terms* (Chicago: American Marketing Association, 1995).

3. Don E. Schultz, "New Media, Old Problem: Keep Marcom Integrated," *Marketing News*, March 29, 1999, p. 11.

4. Fabian Robinson and Rebecca Rohan, "Developing a Brand," *Black Enterprise*, May 2002, pp. 47–48.

5. See Don E. Schultz, Stanley I. Tannenbaum, and Robert F. Lauterborn, *Integrated Marketing Communication* (Chicago: NTC, 1992), chaps. 3 and 4. Also see James R. Ogdan, *Developing a Creative and Innovative Integrated Marketing Communications Plan* (Upper Saddle River, N.J.: Prentice Hall, 1998); and David Picton and Amanda Broderick, *Integrated Marketing Communications* (New York: Financial Times Management, 1999).

6. P. Griffith Lindell, "You Need Integrated Attitude to Develop IMC," *Marketing News*, May 26, 1997, p. 6. For more discussion of intergrated marketing communications, see Stephen J. Gould, "The State of IMC Research and Applications," *Journal of Advertising Research*, September–October 2000, pp. 22–23; Don E. Schultz, "Summit Explores Where IMC, CRM Meet," *Marketing News*, March 4, 2002, p. 11; and Schultz, "Marcom Model Reverses Traditional Pattern," *Marketing News*, April 1, 2002, p. 8.

7. Carolyn Setlow, "Humorous, Feel-Good Advertising Hits Home with Consumers," *DSN Retailing Today*, April 22, 2002, p. 14.

8. Susanne Craig, "E*Trade to Cut Marketing Even as Its Losses Narrow," *Wall Street Journal*, April 12, 2001, p. B13; "Ad Notes," *Wall Street Jounral*, January 31, 2001, p. B2; John Helyar, "At E*Trade, Growing Up Is Hard to Do," *Fortune*, March 18, 2002, pp. 88–90; and "Amazing Feat," *Advertising Age*, May 6, 2002, p. S1.

9. S. Mark McMaster, "Lessons from the Marlboro Man," *Sales and Marketing Management*, February 2002, pp. 44–46.

10. For these and other examples, see Pamela Paul, "Color by Numbers," *American Demographics*, February 2002, pp. 31–35.

11. Adapted from Jean Halliday, "Creating Max Buzz for New BMW Mini," *Advertising Age*, June 17, 2002, p. 12.

12. For more on advertising spending by company and industry, see the Advertising Age Data Center at www.adage.com.

13. For more on setting promotion budgets, see J. Thomas Russell and W. Ronald Lane, *Kleppner's Advertising Procedure*, 15th ed. (Upper Saddle River, N.J.: Prentice Hall, 2002), pp. 145–149; and Kissan Joseph and Vernon J. Richardson, "Free Cash Flow, Agency Costs, and the Affordability Method of Advertising Budgeting," *Journal of Marketing*, January 2002, pp. 94–107.

14. David Allen, "Excessive Use of the Mirror," *Management Accounting*, June 1966, p. 12. Also see Laura Petrecca, "4A's Will Study Financial Return on Ad Spending," *Advertising Age*, April 7, 1997, pp. 3, 52; and Dana W. Hayman and Don E. Schultz, "How Much Should You Spend on Advertising," *Advertising Age*, April 26, 1999, p. 32.

15. Bill Carter, "After Super Bowl, 'Survivor' Is the Season's Top Hit on TV," *New York Times*, January 30, 2001, p. C8; Joe Flint, "Oscar Ratings Fall, but the Program Finishes on Time," *Wall Street Journal*, March 27, 2001, p. B8; and Stuart Elliott, "Despite Millions of Viewers, the Super Bowl Is Not Quite So for Madison Avenue," *New York Times*, February 1, 2002, p. C2.

16. Michele Marchetti, "What a Sales Call Costs," *Sales & Marketing Management*, September 2000, p. 80.

17. Based on Matthew P. Gonring, "Putting Integrated Marketing Communications to Work Today," *Public Relations Quarterly*, Fall 1994, pp. 45–48. Also see Philip Kotler, *Marketing Management*, 11th ed. (Upper Saddle River, N.J.: Prentice Hall, 2003), pp. 583–584.

18. See "Fostering Renewal: New Logging Method Found to Be More Environmentally Friendly—And Less Expensive," accessed online at www.caterpillar.com, August 2002; and information accessed online at www.statefarm.com/gna/gna.htm, August 2002.

19. For more on the legal aspects of promotion, see Russell and Lane, *Kleppner's Advertising Procedure*, chap. 25; and Douglas J. Dalrymple, William L. Cron, and Thomas E. DeCarlo, *Sales Management*, 7th ed. (New York: Wiley, 2001), chap. 6.

CHAPTER 16

1. Quotes and other information from Lisa Bertagnoli, "Duck Campaign Is Firm's Extra Insurance," *Marketing News*, August 27, 2001, pp. 5–6; "AFLAC's Duck Is Endearing to Customers, Bottom Line," *Best's Review*, November 2000, p. 100; Meg Green, "Duck Preens Feathers for Dental Pitch," *Best's Review*, July 2001, p. 38; Bethany McLean, "Duck and Coverage," *Fortune*, August 13, 2001, pp. 142–143; and Stuart Elliott, "Why a Duck? Because It Sells Insurance," *New York Times*, June 24, 2002, p. C11.

2. Information on U.S. and international advertising spending accessed online at the Ad Age Dataplace, www.adage.com, August 2002; and the International Advertising Association Web page at www.iaaglobal.org, August 2002. Also see "100 Leading National Advertisers," *Advertising Age*, June 24, 2002, p. S-2; and "Media," *Marketing News*, July 8, 2002, p. 15.

3. See Andrew Ehrenberg, Neil Barnard, and John Scriven, "Justifying Our Advertising Budgets," *Marketing & Research Today*, February 1997, pp. 38–44; Dana W. Hayman and Don E. Schultz, "How Much Should You Spend on Advertising?" *Advertising Age*, April 26, 1999, p. 32; J. Thomas Russell and W. Ronald Lane, *Kleppner's Advertising Procedure*, 15th ed. (Upper Saddle River, N.J.: Prentice Hall, 2002), pp. 145–149; and Kissan Joseph and Vernon J. Richardson, "Free Cash Flow, Agency Costs, and the Affordability Method of Advertising Budgeting," *Journal of Marketing*, January 2002, pp. 94–107.

4. Information from Gary Levin, "'Meddling' in Creative More Welcome," *Advertising Age*, April 9, 1990, pp. S4, S8; Eleftheria Parpis, "TBWA: Absolut," *Adweek*, November 9, 1998, p. 172; Sarah Theodore, "Absolut Secrets," *Beverage Industry*, July 2000, p. 50; Hillary Chura, "TBWA Juggles Spirits Accounts," *Advertising Age*, April 8, 2002, pp. 6, 29; and the Q&A section at www.absolut.com, August 2002.

5. "Swimming the Channels," *American Demographics*, June 1998, p. 37; and information accessed online at www.magazine.org, July 2002.

6. Charles Pappas, "Ad Nauseam," *Advertising Age,* July 10, 2000, pp. 16–18.

7. Wayne Friedman, "TV Networks' New Reality," *Advertising Age,* September 24, 2001, pp. 1, 70; and Steven McClellan, "Super Bowl Runneth Over," *Broadcast & Cable,* June 24, 2002, p. 4.

8. Wayne Friedman, "PVR Users Skip Most Ads: Study," *Advertising Age,* July 1, 2002, pp. 4, 46.

9. Edward A. Robinson, "Frogs, Bears, and Orgasms: Think Zany if You Want to Reach Today's Consumers," *Fortune,* June 9, 1997, pp. 153–156. Also see Chuck Ross, "MBC Blasts Beyond the 15-Minute Barrier," *Advertising Age,* August 7, 2000, p. 3; and Tobi Elkin, "Courting Craftier Consumers," July 1, 2002, p. 28.

10. *Newsweek* and *Business Week* cost and circulation data accessed online at http:/mediakit.businessweek.com and www.newsweekmediakit.com, August 2002.

11. See Ariane Herrera, "AAAA Survey Finds Three Percent Drop in Cost to Produce 30—Second TV Commercials," news release, American Association of Advertising Agencies, December 13, 2001, accessed online at www.aaaa.org.

12. Information on advertising agency income and billings from the Advertising Age Data Center, accessed online at http://adage.com/dataplace, August 2002.

13. Patricia Winters Lauro, "New Method of Agency Payments Drive a Stake Through the Heart of the Old 15% Commission," *New York Times,* April 2, 1999, p. 2. Also see Jack Neff, "P&G Hammers Last Nail into Commission Coffin," *Advertising Age,* September 20, 1999, p. 4; and John Tylee, "Nestle Rings Death-Knell on Agency Commission," *Campaign,* October 12, 2001, p. 1.

14. See "U.K. Tobacco Ad Ban Will Include Sports Sponsorship," *AdAgeInternational.com,* May 1997; "Coca-Cola Rapped for Running Competition in India," *AdAgeInternational.com,* February 1997; Naveen Donthu, "A Cross Country Investigation of Recall of and Attitude Toward Comparative Advertising," *Journal of Advertising,* 27, June 22, 1998, p. 111; and John Shannon, "Comparative Ads Call for Prudence," *Marketing Week,* May 6, 1999, p. 32.

15. Cannondale Associates, "2002 Trade Promotion Spending and Merchandising Industry Study," (Wilton, Conn: Cannondale Associates, May 2002), p. 13.

16. Kenneth Hein, "Coke Puts New Twist on Plain Vanilla Sampler, Summer Tours," *Brandweek,* July 1, 2002, p. 35.

17. Debra Aho Williamson, "P&G's Reformulated Pert Plus Builds Consumer Relationships," *Advertising Age,* June 28, 1999, p. 52.

18. "DSN Charts: Coupons," *Discount Store News,* May 3, 1999, p. 4. Also see Jack Neff, "Coupons Get Clipped," *Advertising Age,* November 5, 2001, pp. 1, 47.

19. See "Electronic Coupon Clipping," *USA Today,* May 11, 1999, p. 1B; Cara Beardi, "Catalina Expands in Cyberworld," *Advertising Age,* January 22, 2001, p.19; and Roger O. Crockett, "Penny-Pinchers' Paradise," *Business Week,* January 22, 2001, p. EB12.

20. See Kate Bertrand, "Premiums Prime the Market," *Advertising Age's Business Marketing,* May 1998, p. S6; and Paul Nolan, "Promotions Come Alive with the Sound of Music," *Potentials,* April 1999, p. 10. For other examples, see Elinor Dumont, "Today's Version of the Toaster," *Bank Marketing,* September 2001, pp. 12–14; and Kenneth Hein, "Frito-Lay Supplies Pieces to the Star Wars Puzzle," *Brandweek,* March 25, 2002, p. 10.

21. See "Power to the Key Ring and T-Shirt," *Sales & Marketing Management,* December 1989, p. 14; Chad Kaydo, "Your Logo Here," *Sales & Marketing Management,* April 1998, pp. 65–70; and Bill Prickett, "Promotional Products 2001 Sales—A Diverse Market," news release, Promotional Products Association International, June 17, 2002, accessed online at www.ppai.org.

22. See Richard Szathmary, "Trade Shows," *Sales & Marketing Management,* May 1992, pp. 83–84; Srinath Gopalakrishna, Gary L. Lilien, Jerome D. Williams, and Ian Sequeira, "Do Trade Shows Pay Off?" *Journal of Marketing,* July 1995, pp. 75–83; Peter Jenkins, "Making the Most of Trade Shows," *Nation's Business,* June 1999, p. 8; and Ben Chapman, "The Trade Show Must Go On," *Sales & Marketing Management,* June 2001, p. 22.

23. Adapted from Scott Cutlip, Allen Center, and Glen Broom, *Effective Public Relations,* 8th ed. (Upper Saddle River, N.J.: Prentice Hall, 1999), chap. 1.

24. Diane Brady, "Wizard of Marketing," *Business Week,* July 24, 2000, pp. 84–87. Also see Dick Lynch, "The Magic of 'Harry Potter,'" *Advertising Age,* December 10, 2001, p. 26; and Stephen Brown, "Marketing for Muggles: The Harry Potter Way to Higher Profits," *Business Horizons,* January–February 2002, pp. 6–14.

25. For this and the following examples, including the Segway example, see Jack Neff, "Ries' Thesis: Ads Don't Build Brands, PR Does," *Advertising Age,* July 15, 2002, pp. 14–15.

26. Al Ries and Laura Ries, "First Do Some Publicity," *Advertising Age,* February 8, 1999, p. 42. Also see Al Ries and Laura Ries, *The Fall of Advertising and the Rise of PR* (New York: HarperBusiness, 2002).

27. Portions adapted from Kate Fitzgerald, "Marketing on the Move," *Advertising Age,* March 18, 2002, p. 59; and Scott Hume, Janice Matsumoto, Allison Perlik, and Margaret Sheridan, "Krispy Kreme's Movable Feast," *Restaurants & Institutions,* June 1, 2002, p. 26.

28. See Mark Gleason, "Edelman Sees Niche in Web Public Relations," *Advertising Age,* January 20, 1997, p. 30; Michael Krauss, "Good PR Critical to Growth on the Net," *Marketing News,* January 18, 1999, p. 8; Steve Jarvis, "How the Internet Is Changing Fundamentals of Publicity," *Marketing News,* July 17, 2000, p. 6; and G. A. Markin, "Why Doesn't the Press Call?" *Public Relations Quarterly,* Spring 2002, pp. 9–10.

CHAPTER 17

1. Quotes from Andy Cohen, "Top of the Charts: Lear Corporation," *Sales & Marketing Management,* July 1998,

p. 40. Also see "Lear Corporation," *Sales & Marketing Management,* July 1999, p. 62; Fara Warner, "Lear Won't Take a Back Seat," *Fast Company,* June 2001, pp. 178–185; Judy Bocklage and Paul Welitzkin, "Lear Profit Soared in First Period, But Borg-Warner Swung to Loss, *Wall Street Journal,* April 23, 2002, p. D5; "America's 25 Best Sales Forces," *Sales & Marketing Management,* accessed online at www.salesandmarketing.com, July 2002; and "This Is Lear," accessed online at www.lear.com, July 2002.

2. See Bill Kelley, "How to Sell Airplanes, Boeing Style," *Sales & Marketing Management,* December 9, 1985, pp. 32–34; Andy Cohen, "Boeing," *Sales & Marketing Management,* October 1997, p. 68; and Stanley Holmes, "Rumble over Tokyo," *Business Week,* April 2, 2001, pp. 80–81. Quote from Laurence Zuckerman, "Selling Airplanes with a Smile," *New York Times,* February 17, 2002, p. 3.2.

3. Geoffrey Brewer, "Love the Ones You're With," *Sales & Marketing Management,* February 1997, pp. 38–45. Also see Edward F. Moltzen and Jennifer Hagendorf, "IBM Unleashes E-Business Army," *Computer Reseller News,* January 24, 2000, pp. 3, 8.

4. Michele Marchetti, "What a Sales Call Costs," *Sales & Marketing Management,* September 2000, p. 80.

5. See Martin Everett, "Selling by Telephone," *Sales & Marketing Management,* December 1993, pp. 75–79. Also see Terry Arnold, "Telemarketing Strategy," *Target Marketing,* January 2002, pp. 47–48.

6. Geoffrey Brewer, "Lou Gerstner Has His Hands Full," *Sales & Marketing Management,* May 8, 1998, pp. 36–41; and Michelle Cioci, "Marketing to Small Businesses," *Sales & Marketing Management,* December 2000, pp. 94–100.

7. See "A Phone Is Better than a Face," *Sales & Marketing Management,* October 1987, p. 29. Also see Brett A. Boyle, "The Importance of the Industrial Inside Sales Force: A Case Study," *Industrial Marketing Management,* September 1996, pp. 339–348; Victoria Fraza, "Upgrading Inside Sales," *Industrial Distribution,* December 1997, pp. 44–49; Michele Marchetti, "Look Who's Calling," *Sales & Marketing Management,* May 1998, pp. 43–46; and "Climax Portable Machine Tools Case Study," accessed online at www.selltis.com/case_climax.html, August 2002.

8. Rick Mullin, "From Lone Wolves to Team Players," *Chemical Week,* January 14, 1998, pp. 33–34; and James P. Morgan, "Cross-Functional Buying: Why Teams Are Hot," *Purchasing,* April 5, 2001, pp. 27–32.

9. Robert Hiebeler, Thomas B. Kelly, and Charles Ketteman, *Best Practices: Building Your Business with Customer-Focused Solutions* (New York: Arthur Andersen/Simon & Schuster, 1998), pp. 122–124. For more on team selling, also see Mark A. Moon and Susan Forquer Gupta, "Examining the Formation of Selling Centers: A Conceptual Framework," *Journal of Personal Selling and Sales Management,* Spring 1997, pp. 31–41; and Christian Homburg, John P. Workman Jr., and Ove Jensen, "A Configurational Perspective on Key Account Management, *Journal of Marketing,* April 2002, pp. 38–60.

10. See Geoffrey Brewer, "Mind Reading: What Drives Top Salespeople to Greatness?" *Sales & Marketing Management,* May 1994, pp. 82–88; Barry J. Farber, "Success Stories for Salespeople," *Sales & Marketing Management,* May 1995, pp. 30–31; Roberta Maynard, "Finding the Essence of Good Salespeople," *Nation's Business,* February 1998, p. 10; Jeanie Casison, "Closest Thing to Cloning," *Incentive,* June 1999, p. 7; Nicholas T. Miller, "Finding the Key to Sales Excellence: What Do High Performers Do?" *Commercial Lending Review,* March 2002, p. 17.

11. See "To Test or Not to Test," *Sales & Marketing Management,* May 1994, p. 86; Elena Harris, "Reduce Recruiting Risks," *Sales & Marketing Management,* May 2000, p. 18; and Erin Stout, "Recruiting and Hiring for Less," *Sales & Marketing Management,* May 2002, p. 61.

12. Robert Klein, "Nabisco Sales Soar After Sales Training," *Marketing News,* January 6, 1997, p. 23. Also see Malcolm Fleschner, "Training: How to Find the Best Training Solutions for Your Sales Team," *Selling Power,* June 2001, pp. 93–97; and Christine Galea, "2002 Sales Training Survey," *Sales & Marketing Management,* July 2002, pp. 34–37.

13. Adapted from "SMM's Best of Sales and Marketing: Best Trained Sales Force—Cisco Systems," *Sales & Marketing Magazine,* September 2001, pp. 28–29. Also see Kevin Brass, "Pushing E-Learning," *Sales & Marketing Magazine,* March 2002, p. 56; Mark McMaster, "Express Train," *Sales & Marketing Magazine,* May 2002, pp. 46–54; and "E-Learning for the Sales Force," accessed online at www.cisco.com, August 2002.

14. See Christen P. Heide, "All Levels of Sales Reps Post Impressive Earnings," press release, www.dartnell.com, May 5, 1997; "Dartnell's 30th Sales Force Compensation Survey," Dartnell Corporation, August 1999; and Christine Galea, "2002 Salary Survey," *Sales & Marketing Management,* May 2002, pp. 32–36.

15. Geoffrey Brewer, "Brain Power," *Sales & Marketing Management,* May 1997, pp. 39–48; Don Peppers and Martha Rogers, "The Price of Customer Service," *Sales & Marketing Management,* April 1999, pp. 20–21; Michelle Marchetti, "Pay Changes Are on the Way," *Sales & Marketing Management,* August 2000, p. 101; and Erin Stout, "Is Your Pay Plan on Target?" *Sales & Marketing Management,* January 2002, p. 18.

16. David Prater, "The Third Time's the Charm," *Sales & Marketing Management,* September 2000, pp. 101–104. For more on sales force automation (SFA), see Chris Pullig, James G. Maxham III, and Joseph F. Hair Jr., "Sales-force Automation Systems: An Exploratory Examination of Organizational Factors Associated with Effective Implementation and Sales-Force Productivity," *Journal of Business Research,* May 2002, pp. 401–415.

17. Melinda Ligos, "Point, Click, and Sell," *Sales & Marketing Management,* May 1999, pp. 51–56; Tim Wilson, "Salespeople Leverage the Net," *Internetweek,* June 4, 2001, pp. PG11, PG13; Amy J. Morgan and Scott A. Inks, "Technology and the Sales Force: Increasing Acceptance of Sales Force Automation," *Industrial Marketing Management,* July 2001,

pp. 463–472; and Eilene Zimmerman, "Casting the New Wide," *Sales & Marketing Management,* April 2002, pp. 50–56.

18. Christine Neuberger, "Incentives to Perform, *Selling Power Sourcebook,* 2002, pp. 12–16.

19. Bob Donath, "Delivering Value Starts with Proper Prospecting," *Marketing News,* November 10, 1997, p. 5. Also see "Skills Workshop: Prospecting," *Selling Power,* October 2000, pp. 54–56; and Steve Atlas, "Prospecting at Large Companies," *Selling Power,* January–February 2002, pp. 30–32.

20. David Stamps, "Training for a New Sales Game," *Training,* July 1997, pp. 46–52; and Erin Stout, "Throwing the Right Pitch," *Sales & Marketing Management,* April 2001, pp. 61–63. Also see Mary E. Shoemaker and Mark C. Johlke, "An Examination of a Crucial Selling Skill: Asking Questions," *Journal of Managerial Issues,* Spring 2002, pp. 118–131.

21. Betsey Cummings, "Do Customers Hate Salespeople?" *Sales & Marketing Management,* June 2001, pp. 44–51; and Don Chambers, "Draw Them In," *Selling Power,* March 2001, pp. 51–52.

22. "Briefcase Full of Views: Johnson & Johnson Uses Virtual Reality to Give Prospects an Inside Look at Its Products," *American Demographics,* April 1997; and information accessed online at www.sterrad.com/ASP.htm, August 2002.

23. For these and other direct-marketing statistics in this section, see "Direct Marketing Sales and Advertising Expenditures Increase Despite Challenging Year," June 11, 2002, accessed online at www.the-dma.org/cgi/dispnewsstand?article= 718++++++.

24. Carol Krol, "Pizza Hut's Database Makes Its Couponing More Efficient," *Advertising Age,* November 30, 1998, p. 27; Dana Blakenhorn, "Marketers Hone Targeting," *Advertising Age,* June 18, 2001, p. T16; and Thomas H. Davenport, "How Do They Know Their Customers So Well?" *MIT Sloan Management Review,* Winter 2001, pp. 63–73.

25. For these and other examples, see Jonathan Berry, "A Potent New Tool for Selling: Database Marketing," *Business Week,* September 4, 1994, pp. 56–62; Weld F. Royal, "Do Databases Really Work?" *Sales & Marketing Management,* October 1995, pp. 66–74; Daniel Hill, "Love My Brand," *Brandweek,* January 19, 1998, pp. 26–29; "FedEx Taps Into Data Warehousing," *Advertising Age's Business Marketing,* January 1999, p. 25; and Harriet Marsh, "Dig Deeper into the Database Goldmine," *Marketing,* January 11, 2001, pp. 29–30.

26. Betsy Spethmann, "Can We Talk?" *American Demographics,* March 1999, pp. 42–44. Also see Tricia Campbell, "Database Marketing for the Little Guys," *Sales & Marketing Management,* June 1999, p. 69.

27. *Economic Impact: U.S. Direct Marketing Today Executive Summary,* Direct Marketing Association, 2001.

28. Matthew L. Wald, "Third Area Code Is Added in the Land of the Toll-Free," *New York Times,* April 4, 1998, p. 10; and "AT&T Offers Toll-Free Number Availability Tool Online," *Direct Marketing,* May 2001, p. 24.

29. See Ira Teinowitz, "FTC Opens Hearings on 'Do Not Call' Plan," *Advertising Age,* June 10, 2002, p. 65; and "FTC Extends Comment Period on National 'Do-Not-Call' Registry and Other Proposals," Direct Marketing Association press release, March 29, 2002, accessed online at www.the-dma.org/cgi/ dispnewsstand?article=643++++++.

30. *Economic Impact: U.S. Direct Marketing Today Executive Survey,* Direct Marketing Association, 2001. Also see Cara B. Dipasquale, "Direct-Mail Sector Staying the Course," *Advertising Age,* March 11, 2002, p. 16.

31. Hallie Mummert, "The Year's Best Bells and Whistles," *Target Marketing,* November 2000, pp. TM3–TM5; and Susan Reda, "Software Package Seeks to Revive CD-ROMs as Consumer Marketing Technology," *Stores,* November 2000, pp. 66–70.

32. "DMA Study Shows the Internet Generates 13 Percent of Catalog Sales," DMA press release, June 4, 2001, accessed online at /www.the-dma.org/cgi/disppressrelease?article= 102++++++.

33. "DMA Study: In Slowing Economy, Catalog Sales Growth Continues to Outpace Overall Retail Growth," DMA press release, June 4, 2001, accessed online at www.the-dma.org/cgi/disppressrelease?article = 101++++++.

34. "Catalog Study Now Available," *Business Forms, Labels, and Systems,* June 20, 2001, p. 24; Richard S. Hodgson, "It's Still the Catalog Age," *Catalog Age,* June 2001, p. 156; and J.C. Penney 100th Anniversary: Rewriting the Book on Catalog Sales," *Chain Store Age,* June 2002, p. 68.

35. Lillian Vernon 2002 Annual Report, accessed online at www.lillianvernon.com/pdf/LV-AR_2002_final.pdf.

36. Molly Prior, "Lands' End Crosses Threshold of Internet Retailing Excellence," *DSN Retailing Today,* November 6, 2000, pp. 6, 52; Carol Sliwa, "Clothing Retailer Finds Worldwide Business on the Web," *Computerworld,* April 30, 2001, p. 40; and Sherry Chiger, "Sixth Annual Electronic Marketing Survey," *Catalog Age,* June 2002, pp. 71–76.

37. Example adapted in part from Moira Pascale, "Archie's Online Boom," *Catalog Age,* August 1999, p. 10. Other information accessed online at www.mcphee.com, August 2002.

38. Ron Donoho, "One-Man Show," *Sales & Marketing Management,* June 2001, pp. 36–42.

39. Erika Brown, "Ooh! Aah!" *Forbes,* March 8, 1999, p. 56. Also see Shirley Leung, "Grill Sales Slow but Big Payouts Flow to Foreman," *Wall Street Journal,* February 2, 2001, p. B1; and Jane Bennett Clark, Robert Frick, Matt Popowksy, and Daniel Kohan, "As Seen on TV," *Kiplinger's Personal Finance,* July 2002, p. 99.

40. Suzanne Vranica, "Blue Chips Using Ads with 1-800 Numbers," *Wall Street Journal,* November 30, 2001, p. B8.

41. See Steve Sullivan, "Shopping Channels: Less Hard Sell," *Broadcasting & Cable,* November 27, 2000, pp. 86–90; and Bob Tedeschi, "Television Shopping Channels May Become the Big Winners in the Competition for Online Sales," *New York Times,* April 16, 2001, p. C4.

42. "Lining Up for Interactive Kiosks," *Nation's Business,* February 1998, p. 46; Warren S. Hersch, "Kiosks Poised to Be a Huge Growth Market," *Computer Reseller News,* May 18, 1998, p. 163; Catherine Yang, "No Web Site Is an Island," *Business Week,* March 22, 1999, p. EB38; "Kiosk: Disney Store," *Chain Store Age,* December 2000, p. 14A; and Larry Beck, "The Kiosk's Ship Has Come In," *DSN Retailing Today,* February 19, 2001, p. 14.

43. "Interactive: Ad Age Names Finalists," *Advertising Age,* February 27, 1995, pp. 12–14.

44. Yang, "No Web Site Is an Island," p. EB38.

45. "Sweepstakes Groups Settles with States," *New York Times,* June 27, 2001, p. A14; and "PCH Reaches $34 Million Sweepstakes Settlement with 26 States," *Direct Marketing,* September 2001, p. 6.

46. Jennifer Lee, "Welcome to the Database Lounge," *New York Times,* March 21, 2002, p. G1.

47. Larry Dobrow, "Tread Carefully on Privacy," *Advertising Age,* October 29, 2001, p. S6. Also see Stephen F. Ambrose Jr. and Joseph W. Gelb, "Consumer Privacy Regularion and Legislation," *Business Lawyer,* May 2002, pp. 1231–1256.

48. Debbie A, Connon, "The Ethics of Database Marketing," *Information Management Journal,* May–June 2002, pp. 42–44.

CHAPTER 18

1. Quotes from Gordon Moore, Andrew Grove, and Craig Barrett, "Inside Intel," *Executive Excellence,* February 2000, p. 10; Andy Reinhardt, "The New Intel," *Business Week,* March 13, 2000, pp. 110–124; and George Anders, "How Intel Puts Innovation Inside," *Fast Company,* March 2002, pp. 122–124. Also see Cliff Edwards, "Intel Inside the War Room," *Business Week,* April 30, 2001, p. 40; Tobi Elkin, "Intel Inside at 10," *Advertising Age,* April 30, 2001, p. 4; Jennifer DoSabatino, "Intel Sticks with R&D and Productions Spending Plans," *Computerworld,* March 4, 2002, p. 21; Darrell Dunn, "Intel Is Swinging for the Fences in the Communications IC Market," *Ebn,* March 18, 2002, p. 29; and Jay Palmer, "Back to the Future," *Barron's,* June 17, 2002, pp. 13–14.

2. Andy Serwer, "Kodak: In the Noose," *Fortune,* February 4, 2002, pp. 147–148.

3. See Jonathan Gaw, "Britannica Gives In and Gets Online," *Los Angeles Times,* October 19, 2000, p. A1; "Encyclopaedia Britannica Makes Some Changes," *Link-Up,* July–August 2001, pp.1,6; and Peter Jacso, "Britannica Concise Encyclopaedia, *Link-Up,* May–June 2002, pp. 16–17. For more on identifying competitors, see Bruce H. Clark and David B. Montgomery, "Managerial Identification of Competitors," *Journal of Marketing,* July 1999, pp. 67–83.

4. Jeffrey F. Rayport and Bernard J. Jaworski, *e-Commerce* (New York: McGraw-Hill, 2001), p. 53.

5. Laura Johannes, "Health & Technology: Bausch & Lomb Gets Approval for Lens," *Wall Street Journal,* November 27, 2001, p. B7; and Gene G. Marcial, "Bausch: Look Closer," *Business Week,* February 5, 2001, p. 127.

6. Andy Reinhardt, "Intel Is Taking No Prisoners," *Business Week,* July 12, 1999, p. 38; and Brent Schlender, "Intel Unleashes Its Inner Attila," *Fortune,* October 15, 2001, pp. 169–184.

7. See Michael Porter, *Competitive Advantage* (New York: Free Press, 1985), chap. 6.

8. For more on competitor analysis, see Philip Kotler, *Marketing Management,* 11th ed. (Upper Saddle River, N.J.: Prentice Hall, 2003), chap. 9.

9. Sam Hill and Glenn Rifkin, *Radical Marketing* (New York: HarperBusiness, 1999). Also see Tim Christiansen, "Radical Marketing," *Academy of Marketing Science Journal,* Summer 2000, p. 140.

10. Michael E. Porter, *Competitive Strategy: Techniques for Analyzing Industries and Competitors* (New York: Free Press, 1980), chap. 2; and Porter, "What Is Strategy?" *Harvard Business Review,* November–December 1996, pp. 61–78. Also see James Surowiecki, "The Return of Michael Porter," *Fortune,* February 1, 1999, pp. 135–138.

11. See Michael Treacy and Fred Wiersema, "Customer Intimacy and Other Value Disciplines," *Harvard Business Review,* January–February 1993, pp. 84–93; Michael Treacy and Fred Wiersema, "How Market Leaders Keep Their Edge," *Fortune,* February 6, 1995, pp. 88–98; Michael Treacy and Fred Wiersema, *The Discipline of Market Leaders: Choose Your Customers, Narrow Your Focus, Dominate Your Market* (Perseus Press, 1997); Fred Wiersema, *Customer Intimacy: Pick Your Partners, Shape Your Culture, Win Together* (Knowledge Exchange, 1998); and Fred Wiersema, *New Market Leaders: Who's Winning and How in the Battle for Customers?* (New York: Free Press, 2001).

12. For more discussion on defense and attack strategies, see Philip Kotler, *Marketing Management,* 11th ed., pp. 254–272. Also see Eric K. Clemons and Jason A. Santamaria, "Maneuver Warfare: Can Modern Military Strategy Lead You to Victory?" *Harvard Business Review,* April 2002, pp. 57–65.

13. Erika Rasmusson, "The Jackpot," *Sales & Marketing Management,* June 1998, pp. 35–41; and Christina Binkley, "'Wheel' Deal to Unite Makers of Slot Machines," *Wall Street Journal,* July 10, 2001, p. A3.

14. Jack Neff, "Unilever Cedes Laundry War," *Advertising Age,* May 27, 2002, pp. 1, 47.

15. Amy Barrett, "Dial Succeeds by Stepping in Bigger Footsteps," *Business Week,* June 13, 1994, pp. 82–83; Seth Lubove, "Cleaning Up," *Forbes,* December 28, 1998, p. 110; Harlan S. Byrne, "Building a Cleaner Machine," *Barron's,* April 15, 2002, p. 29; and "Dial: Company Profile," accessed online at www.dialcorp.com, July 2002.

16. "Logitech Posts Record Q$ to Finish Best Year Ever," Logitech press release, April 24, 2002, accessed online at www.logitech.com.

17. Janet Bigham Bernstel, "Switch to the Niche," *Bank Marketing,* January–February 2002, pp. 12–17.

18. Jim Kirk, "Company Finds Itself, Finds Success: Alberto-Culver Adopts Strategy of Knowing Its Strengths and

Promoting Small Brands, Rather Than Tackling Giants," *Chicago Tribune,* January 22, 1998, Business Section, p. 1; and "Alberto Culver Reports Double-Digit Sales and Profit Growth Rates for Second Quarter, First Half," *PRNewswire,* April 25, 2002, accessed online at www.alberto.com.

CHAPTER 19

1. Mark L. Clifford and Nicole Harris, "Coke Pours into Asia," *Business Week,* October 28, 1996, pp. 72–77; Mark Gleason, "Sprite Is Riding Global Ad Effort to No. 4 Status," *Advertising Age,* November 18, 1996, p. 30; Lauren R. Rublin, "Chipping Away," *Barron's,* June 12, 2000, pp. 31–34; Betsy McKay, "Coca-Cola Restructuring Effort Has Yet to Prove Effective," *Asian Wall Street Journal,* March 2, 2001; Hillary Chura and Richard Linnett, "Coca-Cola Readies Global Assault," *Advertising Age,* April 2, 2001, pp. 1, 34; Sean Mehegan, "Soft Drinks," *Adweek,* April 23, 2001, p. SR24; Daniel Rogers, "Coke's Local World Cup Tactics," *Marketing,* May 30, 2002, p. 15; and "Our Company," accessed online at www.coca-cola.com, August 2002.

2. John Alden, "What in the World Drives UPS?" *International Business,* April 1998, pp. 6–7; Karen Pennar, "Two Steps Forward, One Step Back," *Business Week,* August 31, 1998, p.116; Michelle Wirth Fellman, "A New World for Marketers," *Marketing News,* May 10, 1999, p. 13; Alan Greenspan, "International Trade: Globalization vs. Protectionism," *Vital Speeches of the Day,* April 15, 2001, pp. 386–388, and *International Trade Statistics 2001,* GTO, p. 1, accessed online at www.wto.org/english/res_e/statis_e/its2001_e/its01_toc_e.htm, August 2002.

3. Gail Edmondson, "See the World, Erase Its Borders," *Business Week,* August 28, 2000, pp. 113–114.

4. "The Unique Japanese," *Fortune,* November 24, 1986, p. 8; and James D. Southwick, "Addressing Market Access Barriers in Japan Through the WTO," *Law and Policy in International Business,* Spring 2000, pp. 923–976. For more on nontariff and other barriers, see Warren J. Keegan and Mark C. Green, *Principles of Global Marketing* (Upper Saddle River, N.J.: Prentice Hall, 2000), chap. 8.

5. See Douglas Harbrecht and Owen Ullmann, "Finally GATT May Fly," *Business Week,* December 29, 1993, pp. 36–37; Ping Deng, "Impact of GATT Uruguay Round on Various Industries," *American Business Review,* June 1998, pp. 22–29; Helene Cooper, "U.S. Seeks a New Rounds of WTO Talks," *Wall Street Journal,* July 18, 2001, p. A12; Michael Finger, Julio J. Nogues, "The Unbalanced Uruguay Outcome: The New Areas in Future WTO Negotiations," *World Economy,* March 2002, pp. 321–340; and *WTO Annual Report 2002,* accessed online at www.wto.org.

6. Information about the European Union from "The European Union at a Glance," accessed online at http://europa.eu.int, August 2002.

7. Stanley Reed, "We Have Liftoff! The Strong Launch of the Euro Is Hailed Around the World," *Business Week,* January 18, 1999, pp. 34–37; Allyson L. Stewart-Allen, "Changeover to Euro Has Hidden Expenses," *Marketing News,* July 30, 2001, p. 6; and "Finance and Economics: Up for Adoption: Central Europe and the Euro," *The Economist,* June 1, 2002, pp. 69–70.

8. For more on the European Union, see "Around Europe in 40 Years," *The Economist,* May 31, 1997, p. S4; "European Union to Begin Expansion," *New York Times,* March 30, 1998, p. A5; Joan Warner, "Mix Us Culturally? It's Impossible," *Business Week,* April 27, 1998, p. 108; and Paul J. Deveney, "World Watch," *Wall Street Journal,* May 20, 1999, p. A12.

9. Charles J. Whalen, "NAFTA's Scorecard: So Far, So Good," *Business Week,* July 9, 2001, pp. 54–56; Geri Smith, "Betting on Free Trade: Will the Americas Be One Big Market?" *Business Week,* April 23, 2001, pp. 60–62; Ernesto Zedillo, "Commentary: Free Trade Is the Best Diplomacy," *Forbes,* July 23, 2001, p. 49; and Fay Hansen, "World Trade Update," *Business Finance,* March 2002, pp. 9–11.

10. Larry Rohter, "Latin America and Europe to Talk Trade," *New York Times,* June 26, 1999, p. 2; and Bernard Malamud and Wayne A. Label, "The Merco: A Common Currency for Mercosur and Latin America," *American Business Review,* June 2002, pp. 132–139.

11. David Woodruff, "Ready to Shop Until They Drop," *Business Week,* June 22, 1998, pp. 104–108. Also see John Fahy, Graham Hooley, Tony Cox, Jozsef Beracs, et al., "The Development and Impact of Marketing Capabilities in Central Europe," *Journal of International Business Studies,* First Quarter 2000, pp. 63–81; and "Card-Carrying Consumers," *Country Monitor,* July 15, 2002, p. 5.

12. Virginia Postrel, "The Wealth of Nations Depends on How Open They Are to International Trade," *New York Times,* May 17, 2001, p. C2.

13. Dan West, "Countertrade," *Business Credit,* April 2001, pp. 64–67. Also see Dan West, "Countertrade," *Business Credit,* April 2002, pp. 48–51.

14. For this and other examples, see Louis Kraar, "How to Sell to Cashless Buyers," *Fortune,* November 7, 1988, pp. 147–154; Nathaniel Gilbert, "The Case for Countertrade," *Across the Board,* May 1992, pp. 43–45; Darren McDermott and S. Karen Witcher, "Bartering Gains Currency," *Wall Street Journal,* April 6, 1998, p. A10; Anne Millen Porter, "Global Economic Meltdown Boosts Barter Business," *Purchasing,* February 11, 1999, pp. 21–25; S. Jayasankaran, "Fire-Fighting," *Far Eastern Economic Review,* May 31, 2001, p. 52; and Dalia Marin and Monika Schnitzer, "The Economic Institution of International Barter," *Economic Journal,* April 2002, pp. 293–316.

15. Rebecca Piirto Heath, "Think Globally," *Marketing Tools,* October 1996, pp. 49–54; and "The Power of Writing," *National Geographic,* August 1999, pp. 128–129.

16. For other examples, see *Dun & Bradstreet's Guide to Doing Business Around the World* (Upper Saddle River, N.J.: Prentice Hall, 2000); Betsy Cummings, "Selling Around the World," *Sales & Marketing Management,* May 2001, p. 70; James K. Sebenius, "The Hidden Challenge of Cross-Border Negotiations," *Harvard Business Review,* March 2002, pp. 76–85; and Philip

Kotler, *Marketing Management,* 11th ed. (Upper Saddle River, N.J.: Prentice Hall, 2003), chap. 7.

17. Pete Engardio, Manjeet Kripalani, and Alysha Webb, "Smart Globalization," *Business Week,* August 27, 2001, pp. 132–136.

18. Elisabeth Rosenthal, "Buicks, Starbucks and Fried Chicken. Still China?" *New York Times,* February 25, 2002, p. A4.

19. Walter LaFeber, *Michael Jordan and the New Global Capitalism* (New York: W. W. Norton, 1999), p. 23.

20. Henry Jenkins, "Culture Goes Global," *Technology Review,* July–August 2001, p. 89.

21. Moises Naim, "McAtlas Shrugged," *Foreign Policy,* May–June 2001, pp. 26–37; and Suh-Kyung Yoon, "Look Who's Going Native," *Far Eastern Economic Review,* February 1, 2001, pp. 68–69.

22. Paulo Prada and Bruce Orwall, "A Certain 'Je Ne Sais Quoi' at Disney's New Park—Movie-Themed Site Near Paris Is Multilingual, Serves Wine—and Better Sausage Variety," *Wall Street Journal,* March 12, 2002, p. B1.

23. Charles A. Coulombe, "Global Expansion: The Unstoppable Crusade," *Success,* September 1994, pp. 18–20; "Amway Hopes to Set Up Sales Network in India," *Wall Street Journal,* February 17, 1998, p. B8; Gerald S. Couzens, "Dick Devos," *Success,* November 1998, pp. 52–57; information accessed online at www.amway.com/OurStory/o-hist.asp, August 2002; and information accessed online at www.amway.com/infocenter/i-mediFact.asp, August 2002.

24. See "Crest, Colgate Bare Teeth in Competition for China," *Advertising Age International,* November 1996, p. I3; and Jack Neff, "Submerged," *Advertising Age,* March 4, 2002, p. 14.

25. Robert Neff, "In Japan, They're Goofy About Disney," *Business Week,* March 12, 1990, p. 64; "In Brief: E*Trade Licensing Deal Gives It an Israeli Link," *American Banker,* May 11, 1998; John Engen, "Going Going Global," *USBanker,* February 2000, pp. 22S–25S; "Cowboys and Samuri: The Japanizing of Universal," *Wall Street Journal,* March 22, 2001, p. B1; Chester Dawson, "Will Toyko Embrace Another Mouse?" *Business Week,* September 10, 2001; and Bruce Orwall, "Eisner Contends Disney Is Primed for Turnaround," *Wall Street Journal,* August 9, 2002, p. B1.

26. See Cynthia Kemper, "KFC Tradition Sold Japan on Chicken," *Denver Post,* June 7, 1998, p. J4; and Milford Prewitt, "Chains Look for Links Overseas," *Nation's Restaurant News,* February 18, 2002, pp. 1, 6.

27. See Theodore Levitt, "The Globalization of Markets," *Harvard Business Review,* May–June 1983, pp. 92–102; David M. Szymanski, Sundar G. Bharadwaj, and Rajan Varadarajan, "Standardization Versus Adaptation of International Marketing Strategy: An Empirical Investigation," *Journal of Marketing,* October 1993, pp. 1–17; Ashish Banerjee, "Global Campaigns Don't Work; Multinationals Do," *Advertising Age,* April 18, 1994, p. 23; Cyndee Miller, "Chasing Global Dream," *Marketing News,* December 2, 1996, pp. 1, 2; and Jeryl Whitelock and Carole Pimblett, "The Standardization Debate in International Marketing," *Journal of Global Marketing,* 1997, p. 22.

28. See "In India, Beef-Free Mickie D," *Business Week,* April 7, 1995, p. 52; Jeff Walters, "Have Brand Will Travel," *Brandweek,* October 6, 1997, pp. 22–26; and David Barboza, "From Abroad, McDonald's Finds Value in Local Control," *New York Times,* February 12, 1999, p. 1; Nanette Byrnes, "Brands in a Bind," *Business Week,* August 28, 2000, pp. 234–238; and Suh-Kyung Yoon, "Look Who's Going Native," *Far Eastern Economic Review,* February 1, 2001, pp. 68–69.

29. For more, see Warren J. Keegan, *Global Marketing Management,* 7th ed. (Upper Saddle River, N.J.: Prentice Hall, 2002), pp. 346–351.

30. Lawrence Donegan, "Heavy Job Rotation: MTV Europe Sacks 80 Employees in the Name of 'Regionalisation,'" *The Guardian,* November 21, 1997, p. 19; "MTV Hits 100 Million in Asia," *New Media Markets,* January 28, 1999, p. 12; Brett Pulley and Andrew Tanzer, "Sumner's Gemstone," *Forbes,* February 21, 2000, pp. 106–111; Sally Beatty and Carol Hymowitz, "Boss Talk: How MTV Stays Tuned Into Teens," *Wall Street Journal,* March 21, 2000, p. B1; and Kerry Capell, "MTV's World: Mando-Pop. Mexican Hip Hop. Russian Rap. It's All Fueling the Biggest Global Channel," *Business Week,* February 18, 2002, pp. 81–84.

31. Bernd H. Schmitt and Yigang Pan, "In Asia, the Supernatural Means Sales," *New York Times,* February 19, 1995, pp. 3, 11; Sally Taylor, "Tackling the Curse of Bad Feng Shui," *Publishers Weekly,* April 27, 1998, p. 24; Michael Schrage, "Sorry About the Profits, Boss. My Feng Shui Is Off," *Fortune,* November 27, 2000, p. 306; and Barry Janoff, "East Meets West," *Progressive Grocer,* January 2001, pp. 47–49.

32. Kate MacArthur, "Coca-Cola Light Employs Local Edge," *Advertising Age,* August 21, 2000, pp. 18–19.

33. See Alicia Clegg, "One Ad One World?" *Marketing Week,* June 20, 2002, pp. 51–52.

34. See Michael Oneal, "Harley-Davidson: Ready to Hit the Road Again," *Business Week,* July 21, 1986, p. 70; "EU Proposes Dumping Change," *East European Markets,* February 14, 1997, pp. 2–3; and Dobrin R. Kolev and Thomas J. Pruse, "Dumping and Double Crossing: The (In)effectiveness of Cost-Based Trade Policy Under Incomplete Information," *International Economic Review,* August 2002, pp. 895–918.

35. Sarah Ellison, "Revealing Price Discrepencies, the Euro Aids Bargain-Hunters," *Wall Street Journal,* January 30, 2002, p. A15.

36. See Patrick Powers, "Distribution in China: The End of the Beginning," *China Business Review,* July–August, 2001, pp. 8–12; and Drake Weisert, "Coca-Cola in China: Quenching the Thirst of a Billion," *China Business Review,* July–August 2001, pp. 52–55.

37. Richard Tomlinson, "The China Card," *Fortune,* May 25, 1998, p. 82; and Paul Mooney, "Deals on Wheels," *Far East Economic Review,* May 20, 1999, p. 53.

CHAPTER 20

1. Portions adapted from Thea Singer, "Can Business Still Save the World?" *Inc,* April 30, 2001, pp. 58–71. Other information

from Harriot Marsh, "Has the Body Shop Lost Its Direction for Good?" *Marketing*, May 10, 2001, p. 19; Mike Hoffman, "Ben Cohen: Ben & Jerry's Homemade, Established in 1978," *Inc*, April 30, 2001, p. 68; Sarah Ellison, "Body Shop Hopes for New Image with an Omnilife Deal—Possible Takeover Could Spruce Up Brand That Has Lost Its Appeal over the Years," *Wall Street Journal*, June 8, 2001, p. B4; Sarah Ellison, "Body Shop's Two Founders to Step Aside; Sale Talks End," *Wall Street Journal*, February 13, 2002, p. A15; and Renee Volpini, "Fight Global Warming with Ice Cream, Music and Activism," Ben & Jerry's press release, April 2, 2002, accessed online at http://lib.benjerry.com/pressrel/press040202osw.html.

2. See Greg Winter, "Tobacco Producers Are Willing to Talk with Justice Department," *New York Times*, June 22, 2001, p. C1; and Gordan Fairclough, "Study Slams Philip Morris Ads Telling Teens Not to Smoke—How a Market Researcher Who Dedicated Years to Cigarette Sales Came to Create Antismoking Ads," *Wall Street Journal*, May 29, 2002, p. B1.

3. James Heckman, "Don't Shoot the Messenger: More and More Often, Marketing Is the Regulators' Target," *Marketing News*, May 24, 1999, pp. 1, 9; "Sweepstakes Group Settles with States," *New York Times*, June 27, 2001, p. A.14; "Business Brief—Publishers Clearing House: Payment of $34 Million Set to Settle with 26 States," *Wall Street Journal*, June 27, 2001, p. B8; and "PCH Reaches $34 Million Sweepstakes Settlement with 26 States," *Direct Marketing*, September 2001, p. 6.

4. "Palm Settles Deceptive Ad Charges," *New York Times*, March 7, 2002, p. 6.

5. Theodore Levitt, "The Morality (?) of Advertising," *Harvard Business Review*, July–August 1970, pp. 84–92. For counterpoints, see Heckman, "Don't Shoot the Messenger," pp. 1, 9.

6. Sandra Pesmen, "How Low Is Low? How Free Is Free?" *Advertising Age*, May 7, 1990, p. S10; and Karolyn Schuster, "The Dark Side of Nutrition," *Food Management*, June 1999, pp. 34–39.

7. David Welch, "Firestone: Is This Brand Beyond Repair?" *Business Week*, June 11, 2001, p. 48. Also see Ken Belson and Micheline Maynard, "Big Recall Behind It, Tire Maker Regains Its Footing," *New York Times*, August 10, 2002, p. 1.

8. Cliff Edwards, "Where Have All the Edsels Gone?" *Greensboro News Record*, May 24, 1999, p. B6. For a thought-provoking short case involving planned obsolescence, see James A. Heely and Roy L. Nersesian, "The Case of Planned Obsolescence," *Management Accounting*, February 1994, p. 67. Also see Joel Dryfuss, "Planned Obsolescence Is Alive and Well," *Fortune*, February 15, 1999, p. 192; and Atsuo Utaka, "Planned Obsolescence and Marketing Strategy," *Managerial and Decision Economics*, December 2000, pp. 339–344.

9. Adapted from John Markoff, "Is Planned Obsolesence Obsolete?" *New York Times*, February 17, 2002, p. 4, 6.

10. See Judith Bell and Bonnie Maria Burlin, "In Urban Areas: Many More Still Pay More for Food," *Journal of Public Policy and Marketing*, Fall 1993, pp. 268–270; Kathryn Graddy and Diana C. Robertson, "Fairness of Pricing Decisions," *Business Ethics Quarterly*, April 1999, pp. 225–243; Gordon Matthews, "Does Everyone Have the Right to Credit?" *USBanker*, April 2001, pp. 44–48.

11. See Brian Grow and Pallavi Gogoi, "A New Way to Squeeze the Weak?" *Business Week*, January 28, 2002, p. 92.

12. Marcia Stepanek, "Weblining," *Business Week*, April 3, 2000, pp. EB26–EB43. Also see Karin Helperin, "Wells Fargo Online Service Accused of Redlining," *Bank Systems & Technology*, September 2000, p. 19.

13. John De Graaf, "The Overspent American/Luxury Fever," *Amicus Journal*, Summer 1999, pp. 41–43.

14. Carolyn Setlow, "Profiting from America's New Materialism," *Discount Store News*, April 17, 2000, p. 16. For interesting discussions on materialism and consumption, see Mark Rotella, Sarah F. Gould, Lynn Andriani, and Michael Scharf, "The High Price of Materialism," *Publishers Weekly*, July 1, 2002, p. 67; and LinChiat Chang and Robert M. Arkin, "Materialism as an Attempt to Cope with Uncertainty," *Psychology & Marketing*, May 2002, pp. 389–406.

15. James Twitchell, "Two Cheers for Materialism," *Wilson Quarterly*, Spring 1999, pp. 16–26. Also see Twitchell, *Lead Us into Temptation: The Triumph of American Materialism* (New York: Columbia University Press, 1999); and Twitchell, *Living It Up: Our Love Affair with Luxury* (New York: Columbia University Press, 2002).

16. Kim Clark, "Real-World-O-Nomics: How to Make Traffic Jams a Thing of the Past," *Fortune*, March 31, 1997, p. 34. Also see Marianne Jakevich, "Mixed Reviews for the HOV Lanes," *American City & County*, October 2001, pp. 60–64+.

17. Lee Hultgreen and Kim Kawada, "San Diego's Interstate 15 High-Occupancy/Toll Lane Facility Using Value Pricing," *ITE Journal*, June 1999, pp. 22–27.

18. From an advertisement for *Fact* magazine, which does not carry advertisements.

19. Greg Winter, "Hershey Is Put on the Auction Block," *New York Times*, July 26, 2002, p. 5.

20. Adapted from information found in Steve Hamm, "Microsoft's Future," *Business Week*, January 19, 1998, pp. 58–68; and Dan Carney and Mike France, "The Microsoft Case: Tying It All Together," *Business Week*, December 3, 2001, pp. 68–69.

21. For more on the evolution of consumerism, see Paul N. Bloom and Stephen A. Greyser, "The Maturing of Consumerism," *Harvard Business Review*, November–December 1981, pp. 130–139, Robert J. Samualson, "The Aging of Ralph Nader," *Newsweek*, December 16, 1985, p. 57; Douglas A. Harbrecht, "The Second Coming of Ralph Nader," *Business Week*, March 6, 1989, p. 28; George S. Day and David A. Aaker, "A Guide to Consumerism," *Marketing Management*, Spring 1997, pp. 44–48; Benet Middleton, "Consumerism: A Pragmatic Ideology," *Consumer Policy Review*, November/December, 1998, pp. 213–217; and Penelope Green, "Consumerism and Its Malcontents," *New York Times*, December 17, 2000, p. 9.1.

22. Stuart L. Hart, "Beyond Greening: Strategies for a Sustainable World," *Harvard Business Review*, January–February 1997, pp. 66–76. Also see James L. Kolar, "Environmental

Sustainability: Balancing Pollution Control with Economic Growth," *Environmental Quality Management,* Spring 1999, pp. 1–10; and Trevor Price and Doug Probert, "The Need for Environmentally Sustainable Developments," *International Need for Environmentally-Sustainable Developments,* 2002, pp. 1–22.

23. Peter M. Senge, Goran Carstedt, and Patrick L. Porter, "Innovating Our Way to the Next Industrial Revolution," *MIT Sloan Management Review,* Winter 2001, pp. 24–38.

24. Based on information from "BP Launches World's Greenest Service Station," BP press release, April 25, 2002, accessed online at www.bp.com/centres/press/media_resources/press_release/index.asp; and www.bp.com/centres/press/hornchurch/index.asp, September 2002.

25. Michael E. Porter and Claas van der Linde, "Green *and* Competitive: Ending the Stalemate," *Harvard Business Review,* September–October 1995, pp. 120–134.

26. Hart, "Beyond Greening," p. 72. For other examples, see Jacquelyn Ottman, "Environmental Winners Show Sustainable Strategies," *Marketing News,* April 27, 1998, p. 6. Also see "Environment, Health, and Safety 2000 Progress Report," Xerox Corporation, accessed online at http://www2.xerox.com/downloads/ehs2000pdf.

27. Hart, "Beyond Greening," p. 73; Carl Pope, "Billboards of the Garden Wall," *Sierra,* January/February 1999, pp. 12–13; and Hendrik A. Verfaille, "A New Pledge for a New Company," *Executive Speeches,* February–March 2001, pp. 10–13.

28. Lynelle Preston, "Sustainability at Hewlett-Packard: From Theory to Practice," *California Management Review,* Spring 2001, pp. 26–36.

29. See John Audley, *Green Politics and Global Trade: NAFTA and the Future of Environmental Politics* (Washington, D.C.: Georgetown University Press, 1997); Lars K. Hallstrom, "Industry Versus Ecology: Environment in the New Europe," *Futures,* February 1999, pp. 25–38; Joe McKinney, "NAFTA: Four Years Down the Road," *Baylor Business Review,* Spring 1999, pp. 22–23; Andreas Diekmann and Axel Franzen, "The Wealth of Nations and Environmental Concern," *Environment and Behavior,* July 1999, pp. 540–549; "EMAS-Newsletter: The Eco-Management and Audit Scheme," June 2002, accessed online at http://europa.eu.int/comm/environment/emas; and Michelle Conlin and Paul Raeburn, "Industrial Evolution," *Business Week,* April 8, 2002, pp. 70–72.

30. Michelle Wirth Fellman, "New Product Marketer of 1997," *Marketing News,* March 30, 1998, pp. E2, E12; Mercedes M. Cardona, "Colgate Boosts Budget to Further 5-Year Plan," *Advertising Age,* May 15, 2000, p. 6; and Emily Nelson, "Colgate's Net Rose 10 Percent in Period, New Products Helped Boost Sales," *Wall Street Journal,* February 2, 2001, p. B6.

31. Information accessed online at www.HermanMiller.com, October 2001. See also Jacquelyn A. Ottman, "Green Marketing: Wake Up to the Truth About Green Consuming," *In Business,* May–June 2002, p. 31.

32. Dan R. Dalton and Richard A. Cosier, "The Four Faces of Social Responsibility," *Business Horizons,* May–June 1982, pp. 19–27.

33. Joseph Webber, "3M's Big Cleanup," *Business Week,* June 5, 2000, pp. 96–98. Also see Kara Sissell, "3M Defends Timing of Scotchgard Phaseout," *Chemical Week,* April 11, 2001, p. 33; and Peck Hwee Sim, "Ausimont Targets Former Scotchgard Markets," *Chemical Week,* August 7, 2002, p. 32.

34. Barbara Crossette, "Russia and China Top Business Bribers," *New York Times,* May 17, 2002, p. A10.

35. John F. Magee and P. Ranganath Nayak, "Leaders' Perspectives on Business Ethics," *Prizm,* Arthur D. Little, Inc., Cambridge, Mass., First Quarter, 1994, pp. 65–77. Also see Turgut Guvenli and Rajib Sanyal, "Ethical Concerns in International Business: Are Some Issues More Important than Others?" *Business and Society Review,* Summer 2002, pp. 195–206.

36. Ibid., pp. 71–72. Also see Thomas Donaldson, "Values in Tension: Ethics Away from Home," *Harvard Business Review,* September–October 1996, pp. 48–62; Patrick E. Murphy, "Character and Virtue Ethics in International Marketing: An Agenda for Managers, Researchers, and Educators," *Journal of Business Ethics,* January 1999, pp. 107–124; and Gopalkrishnan, "International Exchanges as the Basis for Conceptualizing Ethics in International Business," *Journal of Business Ethics,* February 2001, pp. 3–25.

37. See Samuel A. DiPiazza, "Ethics in Action," *Executive Excellence,* January 2002, pp. 15–16.

38. Kenneth Labich, "The New Crisis in Business Management," *Fortune,* April 20, 1992, pp. 167–176, here p. 176.

39. DiPiazza, "Ethics in Action," p. 15.

Credits

Industries, Inc.; 326 Used with permission of Information Resources Inc.; 327 Colgate-Palmolive Company; 329 Used with permission of 3M; 331 Courtesy of Hershey®s; 334 Frank Siteman, Stock Boston; 336 (Both) Used with permission from Frito-Lay, Inc.

CHAPTER 11: 342 Courtesy of Priceline.com; 346 Courtesy of Cnet and MySimon.com; 349 Courtesy of Four Seasons Hotels; 350 Courtesy of Swatch Ltd.; 353 © 1999 Kinko's, Inc. All rights reserved; 355 Courtesy of Gibson Guitar; 356 Courtesy of Green Mountain Energy Company; 360 Courtesy of Sanford Corp. and Parker Pens; 362 Reprinted courtesy of Caterpillar, Inc.

CHAPTER 12: 368 Simon Wilkinson, Getty Images, Inc.; Courtesy of Dell Computer Corporation; 373 Images courtesy of Nintendo America, Inc.; 374 (Left & Right) Zoo Doo Compost Company, Inc.; 377 D. Young-Wolff, PhotoEdit; 379 (Top) Tim Boyle, Getty Images Inc.—Hulton Archive Photos; 379 (Bottom) AP/Wide World Photos; 380 Tim Boyle, Getty Images, Inc.— Hulton Archive Photos; 382 Michael Newman, PhotoEdit; 387 Courtesy of Kimberly Clark; 388 Courtesy of AARP

CHAPTER 13: 400 Courtesy of Palm, Inc.; 401 © 1995–2001 FedEx. All rights reserved; 404 Courtesy of L.L. Bean and Martin Williams Advertising; 406 (Right) Jan Staller, TimePix; 406 (Left) AP/Wide World Photos; 407 Cereal Partners U.K.; 410 Sunflower Travel; 412 Geico; 413 Dan Rubin; 415 Charles Gupton, Stock Boston; 416 Courtesy of GE; 417 Copyright 1994–2000 Hewlett-Packard Company. Reproduced with permission; 422 Courtesy of Roadway Express; 424 Oracle Corporation; 425 Churchill & Klehr Photography; 426 © Ryder Systems Inc.

CHAPTER 14: 434 Home Depot Inc.; 439 (Right) Churchill & Klehr Photography; 439 (Left) Bonnie Kamin, PhotoEdit; 440 Davis Barber; 443 Katherine Lambert; 445 Courtesy of the Target Corporation; 446 Peter Brandt; 448 (All) Courtesy Mall of America; 449 Courtesy of Office Depot; 453 Courtesy © 2002 Sony Corporation Entertainment America Inc.; 454 W.W. Grainger, Inc.; 457 Fleming Companies, Inc.; 459 McKesson

CHAPTER 15: 464 Courtesy of UPS; 468 HFM; 470 Courtesy of The Saturn Corporation; 473 © Houghton Mifflin Company and Mullen. All rights reserved; 474 Courtesy of Volkswagen and Arnold Worldwide. Photography provided by permission of Bill Cash, photographer; 477 Listerine and Bill Aron, PhotoEdit; 479 (Left) Frederick M. Brown/AFP/Corbis, CORBIS; 479 (Middle) AFP Photo/FREDERICK M. BROWN/CORBIS, CORBIS; 479 (Right) CORBIS; 481 Courtesy of Revlon; 484 Michael Newman, PhotoEdit; 487 Courtesy of State Farm

CHAPTER 16: 492 Aflac; 496 The Pillsbury Company; 498 (Both) Under permission by V&S Vin & Spirit AB. Absolut country of Sweden Vodka and logo, Absolut, Absolut bottle design, and Absolut calligraphy are trademarks owned by V & S Vin & Spirit AB. © 2003 V & S Vin & Spirit AB; 499 (Both) Courtesy of TiVo; 500 (Both) Courtesy of Kraft and Altoids; 502 Courtesy of Apple Computer and Janie Porche. Photography courtesy of Mark Lipson, photographer; 505 (Left) Spencer Grant,

PhotoEdit; 505 (Middle) Michael J. Treola, AP/Wide World Photos; 505 (Right) CORBIS; 506 Courtesy of Hallmark; 509 (All) Courtesy of the DaimlerChrysler Corporation; 511 Lladro Collectors Society; 512 Courtesy of Catalina Marketing; 514 Jeff Scheid, Getty Images, Inc.—Liaison; 516 John Storey Photography; 518 Courtesy of Nike

CHAPTER 17: 524 Courtesy of Lear Corporation; 527 Gabe Palmer, Corbis/Stock Market; 531 DuPont & Company; 532 Jon Feingersh/CORBIS, CORBIS; 533 Getty Images, Inc.; 534 AP/Wide World Photos; 536 (Both) Cisco Systems; 539 Rob Nelson, Black Star; 540 American Express Incentive Services; 542 Courtesy of Advanced Sterilization Products, Irvine, CA; 545 Courtesy of Dell Computer Corporation; 547 Courtesy of Masterfoods and MyPetStop.com; 549 Courtesy of the Carolina Cookie Company™; 552 Frank LaBua; 554 Salton, Inc.; 556 Courtesy of the Direct Marketing Association

CHAPTER 18: 564 Steve Raymer/CORBIS, CORBIS; 568 Encyclopedia Britannica; 570 (All) General Electric Company; 572 Courtesy of Johnson & Johnson; 575 Courtesy of Hohner, Inc.; 576 The Times, Rex Features USA Ltd.; 579 WD-40; 581 Courtesy of Pepsico; 582 Dial Corporation; 583 Melvin Calderon, Getty Images, Inc.—Liaison; 585 First Commerce Bank

CHAPTER 19: 592 © Arthur Meyerson. Courtesy of Coca Cola. "COCA COLA", the "COCA COLA" Contour Bottle, the Red Disc icon and "ALWAYS COCA COLA" are trademarks of the Coca-Cola Company; 595 (Left) Jeffrey Aaronson, Network Aspen; 595 (Right) Pablo Bartholomew, Getty Images, Inc.—Liaison; 597 (Both) Courtesy of Dell Computer Corporation; 600 Keith Dannemiller/CORBIS SABA; 602 Joseph Polleross/Regina Maria Anzenberger; 603 Cary S. Wolinsky, Cary Sol Wolinsky/Trillium Studios; 605 (Left) Michael S. Yamashita/CORBIS, CORBIS; 605 (Right) Eugene Hoshiko, AP/Wide World Photos; 607 Peter Blakely, Corbis/SABA Press Photos, Inc.; 610 © Walt Disney Attractions Japan, Ltd.; 611 (Left) Donald Dietz, Stock Boston; 611 (Right) D. Bartruff, The Image Works; 613 Douglas E. Curran, Agence France-Presse AFP; 615 (Both) Courtesy of Bernard Matussiere; 617 Courtesy of the Audiovisual Library, European Commission; 619 Fritz Hoffmann

CHAPTER 20: 626 Used with permission of Wild Planet Inc., used with permission of Honest Tea, used with permission of Village Real Estate Services, and used with permission of Worldwise, courtesy of Ben & Jerry's, Reproduced with kind permission from The Body Shop International plc; 630 Churchill & Klehr Photography; 631 AP/Wide World Photos; 633 (Both) Enrico Ferorelli; 635 AP/Wide World Photos; 636 (Both) Courtesy of the American Association of Advertising Agencies; 637 Susan Werner, Getty Images, Inc.—Stone; 639 Lester Lefkowitz/CORBIS, CORBIS; 641 Campbell Soup; 643 (Both) BP p.l.c.; 644 McDonald's; 649 Copyright 1998 GM Corp. Used with permission of GM Media Archives. All rights reserved; 651 Herman Miller, Inc.; 655 Courtesy of PricewaterhouseCoopers LLP

Glossary

Adapted marketing mix An international marketing strategy for adjusting the marketing-mix elements to each international target market, bearing more costs but hoping for a larger market share and return.

Administered VMS A vertical marketing system that coordinates successive stages of production and distribution, not through common ownership or contractual ties, but through the size and power of one of the parties.

Adoption process The mental process through which an individual passes from first hearing about an innovation to final adoption.

Advertising Any paid form of nonpersonal presentation and promotion of ideas, goods, or services by an identified sponsor.

Advertising agency A marketing services firm that assists companies in planning, preparing, implementing, and evaluating all or portions of their advertising programs.

Advertising objective A specific communication task to be accomplished with a specific target audience during a specific period of time.

Advertising specialty Useful article imprinted with an advertiser's name, given as a gift to consumers.

Affordable method Setting the promotion budget at the level management thinks the company can afford.

Age and life-cycle segmentation Dividing a market into different age and life-cycle groups.

Agent A wholesaler who represents buyers or sellers on a relatively permanent basis, performs only a few functions, and does not take title to goods.

Allowance Promotional money paid by manufacturers to retailers in return for an agreement to feature the manufacturer's products in some way.

Alternative evaluation The stage of the buyer decision process in which the consumer uses information to evaluate alternative brands in the choice set.

Approach The step in the selling process in which the salesperson meets the customer for the first time.

Attitude A person's consistently favorable or unfavorable evaluations, feelings, and tendencies toward an object or idea.

B2B (business-to-business) e-commerce Using B2B trading networks, auction sites, spot exchanges, online product catalogs, barter sites, and other online resources to reach new customers, serve current customers more effectively, and obtain buying efficiencies and better prices.

B2C (business-to-consumer) e-commerce The online selling of goods and services to final consumers.

Baby boomers The 78 million people born during the baby boom, following World War II and lasting until the early 1960s.

Balance sheet A financial statement that shows assets, liabilities, and net worth of a company at a given time.

Basing-point pricing A geographical pricing strategy in which the seller designates some city as a basing point and charges all customers the freight cost from that city to the customer.

Behavioral segmentation Dividing a market into groups based on consumer knowledge, attitude, use, or response to a product.

Belief A descriptive thought that a person holds about something.

Benchmarking The process of comparing the company's products and processes to those of competitors or leading firms in other industries to find ways to improve quality and performance.

Benefit segmentation Dividing the market into groups according to the different benefits that consumers seek from the product.

Brand A name, term, sign, symbol, or design, or a combination of these, intended to identify the goods or services of one seller or group of sellers and to differentiate them from those of competitors.

Brand equity The positive differential effect that knowing the brand name has on customer response to the product or service.

Brand extension Using a successful brand name to launch a new or modified product in a new category.

Brand personality The specific mix of human traits that may be attributed to a particular brand.

Break-even pricing (target profit pricing) Setting price to break even on the costs of making and marketing a product; or setting price to make a target profit.

Broker A wholesaler who does not take title to goods and whose function is to bring buyers and sellers together and assist in negotiation.

Business analysis A review of the sales, costs, and profit projections for a new product to find out whether these factors satisfy the company's objectives.

Business buyer behavior The buying behavior of the organizations that buy goods and services for use in the production of other products and services or for the purpose of reselling or renting them to others at a profit.

Business buying process The decision process by which business buyers determine which products and services their organizations need to purchase, and then find, evaluate, and choose among alternative suppliers and brands.

Business portfolio The collection of businesses and products that make up the company.

Buyer-readiness stages The stages consumers normally pass through on their way to purchase, including awareness, knowledge, liking, preference, conviction, and purchase.

Buyers The people who make an actual purchase.

Buying center All the individuals and units that participate in the business buying-decision process.

Buzz marketing Cultivating opinion leaders and getting them to spread information about a product or service to others in their communities.

By-product pricing Setting a price for by-products in order to make the main product's price more competitive.

C2B (consumer-to-business) e-commerce Online exchanges in which consumers search out sellers, learn about their offers, and initiate purchases, sometimes even driving transaction terms.

C2C (consumer-to-consumer) e-commerce Online exchanges of goods and information between final consumers.

Captive-product pricing Setting a price for products that must be used along with a main product, such as blades for a razor and film for a camera.

Cash refund offer (rebate) Offer to refund part of the purchase price of a product to consumers who send a "proof of purchase" to the manufacturer.

Catalog marketing Direct marketing through print, video, or electronic catalogs that are mailed to select customers, made available in stores, or presented online.

Category killer Giant specialty store that carries a very deep assortment of a particular line and is staffed by knowledgeable employees.

Causal research Marketing research to test hypotheses about cause-and-effect relationships.

Chain stores Two or more outlets that are owned and controlled in common, have central buying and merchandising, and sell similar lines of merchandise.

Channel conflict Disagreement among marketing channel members on goals and roles—who should do what and for what rewards.

Channel level A layer of intermediaries that performs some work in bringing the product and its ownership closer to the final buyer.

Click-and-mortar companies Traditional brick-and-mortar companies that have added e-marketing to their operations.

Click-only companies The so-called dot-coms, which operate only online without any brick-and-mortar market presence.

Closing The step in the selling process in which the salesperson asks the customer for an order.

Co-branding The practice of using the established brand names of two different companies on the same product.

Cognitive dissonance Buyer discomfort caused by postpurchase conflict.

Commercialization Introducing a new product into the market.

Communication adaptation A global communication strategy of fully adapting advertising messages to local markets.

Competition-based pricing Setting prices based on the prices that competitors charge for similar products.

Competitive advantage An advantage over competitors gained by offering consumers greater value, either through lower prices or by providing more benefits that justify higher prices; An advantage over competitors gained by offering consumers greater value than competitors offer.

Competitive marketing strategies Strategies that strongly position the company against competitors and that give the company the strongest possible strategic advantage.

Competitive-parity method Setting the promotion budget to match competitors' outlays.

Competitor analysis The process of identifying key competitors; assessing their objectives, strategies, strengths and weaknesses, and reaction patterns; and selecting which competitors to attack or avoid.

Competitor-centered company A company whose moves are mainly based on competitors' actions and reactions.

Complex buying behavior Consumer buying behavior in situations characterized by high consumer involvement in a purchase and significant perceived differences among brands.

Concentrated (niche) marketing A market-coverage strategy in which a firm goes after a large share of one or a few segments or niches.

Concept testing Testing new-product concepts with a group of target consumers to find out if the concepts have strong consumer appeal.

Consumer buyer behavior The buying behavior of final consumers—individuals and households who buy goods and services for personal consumption.

Consumer market All the individuals and households who buy or acquire goods and services for personal consumption.

Consumer-oriented marketing The philosophy of enlightened marketing that holds that the company should view and organize its marketing activities from the consumer's point of view.

Consumer product Product bought by final consumer for personal consumption.

Consumerism An organized movement of citizens and government agencies to improve the rights and power of buyers in relation to sellers.

Contests, sweepstakes, games Promotional events that give consumers the chance to win something—such as cash, trips, or goods—by luck or through extra effort.

Contract manufacturing A joint venture in which a company contracts with manufacturers in a foreign market to produce the product or provide its service.

Contractual VMS A vertical marketing system in which independent firms at different levels of production and distribution join together through contracts to obtain more economies or sales impact than they could achieve alone.

Convenience product Consumer product that the customer usually buys frequently, immediately, and with a minimum of comparison and buying effort.

Convenience store A small store, located near a residential area, that is open long hours seven days a week and carries a limited line of high-turnover convenience goods.

Conventional distribution channel A channel consisting of one or more independent producers, wholesalers, and retailers, each a separate business seeking to maximize its own profits even at the expense of profits for the system as a whole.

Corporate VMS A vertical marketing system that combines successive stages of production and distribution under single ownership—channel leadership is established through common ownership.

Corporate Web site A Web site designed to build customer goodwill and to supplement other sales channels, rather than to sell the company's products directly.

Cost of goods sold The net cost to the company of goods sold.

Cost-plus pricing Adding a standard markup to the cost of the product.

Countertrade International trade involving the direct or indirect exchange of goods for other goods instead of cash.

Coupon Certificate that gives buyers a saving when they purchase a specified product.

Cultural environment Institutions and other forces that affect society's basic values, perceptions, preferences, and behaviors.

Culture The set of basic values, perceptions, wants, and behaviors learned by a member of society from family and other important institutions.

Customer database An organized collection of comprehensive data about individual customers or prospects, including geographic, demographic, psychographic, and behavioral data.

Customer-centered company A company that focuses on customer developments in designing its marketing strategies and on delivering superior value to its target customers.

Customer equity The total combined customer lifetime values of all of the company's customers.

Customer lifetime value The value of the entire stream of purchases that the customer would make over a lifetime of patronage.

Customer perceived value The difference between total customer value and total customer cost.

Customer relationship management (CRM) Managing detailed information about individual customers and carefully managing customer "touch points" in order to maximize customer loyalty.

Customer relationship management The overall process of building and maintaining profitable customer relationships by delivering superior customer value and satisfaction.

Customer sales force structure A sales force organization under which salespeople specialize in selling only to certain customers or industries.

Customer satisfaction The extent to which a product's perceived performance matches a buyer's expectations.

Customer value analysis Analysis conducted to determine what benefits target customers value and how they rate the relative value of various competitors' offers.

Customerization Leaving it to individual customers to design the marketing offering—allowing customers to be prosumers rather than only consumers.

Deciders People in the organization's buying center who have formal or informal power to select or approve the final suppliers.

Decline stage The product life-cycle stage in which a product's sales decline.

Deficient products Products that have neither immediate appeal nor long-run benefits.

Demand curve A curve that shows the number of units the market will buy in a given time period, at different prices that might be charged.

Demands Human wants that are backed by buying power.

Demarketing Marketing to reduce demand temporarily or permanently; the aim is not to destroy demand but only to reduce or shift it.

Demographic segmentation Dividing the market into groups based on demographic variables such as age, gender, family size, family life cycle, income, occupation, education, religion, race, gender, and nationality.

Demography The study of human populations in terms of size, density, location, age, gender, race, occupation, and other statistics.

Department store A retail organization that carries a wide variety of product lines—typically clothing, home furnishings, and household goods; each line is operated as a separate department managed by specialist buyers or merchandisers.

Derived demand Business demand that ultimately comes from (derives from) the demand for consumer goods.

Descriptive research Marketing research to better describe marketing problems, situations, or markets, such as the market potential for a product or the demographics and attitudes of consumers.

Desirable products Products that give both high immediate satisfaction and high long-run benefits.

Differentiated (segmented) marketing A market-coverage strategy in which a firm decides to target several market segments and designs separate offers for each.

Direct investment Entering a foreign market by developing foreign-based assembly or manufacturing facilities.

Direct-mail marketing Direct marketing through single mailings that include letters, ads, samples, foldouts, and other "salespeople with wings" sent to prospects on mailing lists.

Direct marketing Direct connections with carefully targeted individual consumers to both obtain an immediate response and cultivate lasting customer relationships; Direct communications with carefully targeted individual consumers to obtain an immediate response.

Direct marketing channel A marketing channel that has no intermediary levels.

Direct-response television marketing Direct marketing via television, including direct-response television advertising and home shopping channels.

Discount A straight reduction in price on purchases during a stated period of time.

Discount store A retail institution that sells standard merchandise at lower prices by accepting lower margins and selling at higher volume.

Disintermediation The displacement of traditional resellers from a marketing channel by radical new types of intermediaries.

Dissonance-reducing buying behavior Consumer buying behavior in situations characterized by high involvement but few perceived differences among brands.

Distribution center A large, highly automated warehouse designed to receive goods from various plants and suppliers, take orders, fill them efficiently, and deliver goods to customers as quickly as possible.

Diversification A strategy for company growth through starting up or acquiring businesses outside the company's current products and markets.

Downsizing Reducing the business portfolio by eliminating products or business units that are not profitable or that no longer fit the company's overall strategy.

Dynamic pricing Charging different prices depending on individual customers and situations.

E-business The use of electronic platforms—intranets, extranets, and the Internet—to conduct a company's business.

E-commerce Buying and selling processes supported by electronic means, primarily the Internet.

Economic community A group of nations organized to work toward common goals in the regulation of international trade.

Economic environment Factors that affect consumer buying power and spending patterns.

E-marketing The marketing side of e-commerce—company efforts to communicate about, promote, and sell products and services over the Internet.

Embargo A ban on the import of a certain product.

Engel's laws Differences noted over a century ago by Ernst Engel in how people shift their spending across food, housing, transportation, health care, and other goods and services categories as family income rises.

Enlightened marketing A marketing philosophy holding that a company's marketing should support the best long-run performance of the marketing system; its five principles include consumer-oriented marketing, innovative marketing, value marketing, sense-of-mission marketing, and societal marketing.

Environmental management perspective A management perspective in which the firm takes aggressive actions to affect the publics and forces in its marketing environment rather than simply watching and reacting to them.

Environmental sustainability A management approach that involves developing strategies that both sustain the environment and produce profits for the company.

Environmentalism An organized movement of concerned citizens and government agencies to protect and improve people's living environment.

Exchange The act of obtaining a desired object from someone by offering something in return.

Exchange controls Government limits on the amount of foreign exchange with other countries and on the exchange rate against other currencies.

Exclusive distribution Giving a limited number of dealers the exclusive right to distribute the company's products in their territories.

Experience curve (learning curve) The drop in the average per-unit production cost that comes with accumulated production experience.

Experimental research The gathering of primary data by selecting matched groups of subjects, giving them different treatments, controlling related factors, and checking for differences in group responses.

Exploratory research Marketing research to gather preliminary information that will help define problems and suggest hypotheses.

Exporting Entering a foreign market by selling goods produced in the company's home country, often with little modification.

Extranet A network that connects a company with its suppliers and distributors.

Factory outlet Off-price retailing operation that is owned and operated by a manufacturer and that normally carries the manufacturer's surplus, discontinued, or irregular goods.

Fad A fashion that enters quickly, is adopted with great zeal, peaks early, and declines very quickly.

Fashion A currently accepted or popular style in a given field.

Fixed costs Costs that do not vary with production or sales level.

FOB-origin pricing A geographical pricing strategy in which goods are placed free on board a carrier; the customer pays the freight from the factory to the destination.

Focus group interviewing Personal interviewing that involves inviting 6 to 10 people to gather for a few hours with a trained interviewer to talk about a product, service, or organization. The interviewer "focuses" the group discussion on important issues.

Follow-up The last step in the selling process, in which the salesperson follows up after the sale to ensure customer satisfaction and repeat business.

Forecasting The art of estimating future demand by anticipating what buyers are likely to do under a given set of conditions.

Franchise A contractual association between a manufacturer, wholesaler, or service organization (a franchiser) and independent businesspeople (franchisees) who buy the right to own and operate one or more units in the franchise system.

Franchise organization A contractual vertical marketing system in which a channel member, called a franchiser, links several stages in the production-distribution process.

Freight-absorption pricing A geographical pricing strategy in which the seller absorbs all or part of the freight charges in order to get the desired business.

Gatekeepers People in the organization's buying center who control the flow of information to others.

Gender segmentation Dividing a market into different groups based on gender.

General need description The stage in the business buying process in which the company describes the general characteristics and quantity of a needed item.

Generation X The 45 million people born between 1965 and 1976 in the "birth dearth" following the baby boom.

Generation Y The 72 million children of the baby boomers, born between 1977 and 1994.

Geographic segmentation Dividing a market into different geographical units such as nations, states, regions, counties, cities, or neighborhoods.

Global firm A firm that, by operating in more than one country, gains R&D, production, marketing, and financial advantages in its costs and reputation that are not available to purely domestic competitors.

Government market Governmental units—federal, state, and local—that purchase or rent goods and services for carrying out the main functions of government.

Gross margin The difference between net sales and cost of goods sold.

Gross sales The total amount that a company charges during a given period of time for merchandise.

Group Two or more people who interact to accomplish individual or mutual goals.

Growth-share matrix A portfolio-planning method that evaluates a company's strategic business units in terms of their market growth rate and relative market share. SBUs are classified as stars, cash cows, question marks, or dogs.

Growth stage The product life-cycle stage in which a product's sales start climbing quickly.

Habitual buying behavior Consumer buying behavior in situations characterized by low consumer involvement and few significant perceived brand differences.

Handling objections The step in the selling process in which the salesperson seeks out, clarifies, and overcomes customer objections to buying.

Horizontal marketing system A channel arrangement in which two or more companies at one level join together to follow a new marketing opportunity.

Idea generation The systematic search for new-product ideas.

Idea screening Screening new-product ideas in order to spot good ideas and drop poor ones as soon as possible.

Income segmentation Dividing a market into different income groups.

Independent off-price retailer Off-price retailer that is either owned and run by entrepreneurs or is a division of a larger retail corporation.

Indirect marketing channel Channel containing one or more intermediary levels.

Individual marketing Tailoring products and marketing programs to the needs and preferences of individual customers—also labeled "markets-of-one marketing," "customized marketing," and "one-to-one marketing."

Industrial product Product bought by individuals and organizations for further processing or for use in conducting a business.

Influencers People in an organization's buying center who affect the buying decision; they often help define specifications and also provide information for evaluating alternatives.

Information search The stage of the buyer decision process in which the consumer is aroused to search for more information; the consumer may simply have heightened attention or may go into active information search.

Innovative marketing A principle of enlightened marketing that requires that a company seek real product and marketing improvements.

Inside sales force Inside salespeople who conduct business from their offices via telephone or visits from prospective buyers.

Institutional market Schools, hospitals, nursing homes, prisons, and other institutions that provide goods and services to people in their care.

Integrated direct marketing Direct-marketing campaigns that use multiple vehicles and multiple stages to improve response rates and profits.

Integrated logistics management The logistics concept that emphasizes teamwork, both inside the company and among all the marketing channel organizations, to maximize the performance of the entire distribution system.

Integrated marketing communications (IMC) The concept under which a company carefully integrates and coordinates its many communications channels to deliver a clear, consistent, and compelling message about the organization and its products.

Intensive distribution Stocking the product in as many outlets as possible.

Interactive marketing Marketing by a service firm that recognizes that perceived service quality depends heavily on the quality of buyer–seller interaction.

Intermarket segmentation Forming segments of consumers who have similar needs and buying behavior even though they are located in different countries.

Intermodal transportation Combining two or more modes of transportation.

Internal databases Electronic collections of information obtained from data sources within the company.

Internal marketing Marketing by a service firm to train and effectively motivate its customer-contact employees and all the supporting service people to work as a team to provide customer satisfaction.

Internet The vast and burgeoning global web of computer networks with no central management or ownership; A vast public web of computer networks, which connects users of all types all around the world to each other and to an amazingly large "information repository." The internet makes up one big "information highway" that can dispatch bits at incredible speeds from one location to another.

Intranet A network that connects people within a company to each other and to the company network.

Introduction stage The product life-cycle stage in which the new product is first distributed and made available for purchase.

Joint ownership A joint venture in which a company joins investors in a foreign market to create a local business in which the company shares joint ownership and control.

Joint venturing Entering foreign markets by joining with foreign companies to produce or market a product or service.

Leading indicators Time series that change in the same direction but in advance of company sales.

Learning Changes in an individual's behavior arising from experience.

Licensing A method of entering a foreign market in which the company enters into an agreement with a licensee in the foreign market, offering the right to use a manufacturing process, trademark, patent, trade secret, or other item of value for a fee or royalty.

Lifestyle A person's pattern of living as expressed in his or her activities, interests, and opinions.

Line extension Using a successful brand name to introduce additional items in a given product category under the same brand name, such as new flavors, forms, colors, added ingredients, or package sizes.

Local marketing Tailoring brands and promotions to the needs and wants of local customer groups—cities, neighborhoods, and even specific stores.

Macroenvironment The larger societal forces that affect the microenvironment—demographic, economic, natural, technological, political, and cultural forces.

Management contracting A joint venture in which the domestic firm supplies the management know-how to a foreign company that supplies the capital; the domestic firm exports management services rather than products.

Manufacturers' sales branches and offices Wholesaling by sellers or buyers themselves rather than through independent wholesalers.

Markdown A percentage reduction from the original selling price.

Market The set of all actual and potential buyers of a product or service.

Market buildup method A forecasting method that identifies market factors that correlate with market potential and combines them into a weighted index.

Market-centered company A company that pays balanced attention to both customers and competitors in designing its marketing strategies.

Market challenger A runner-up firm that is fighting hard to increase its market share in an industry.

Market development A strategy for company growth by identifying and developing new market segments for current company products.

Market factor index method A forecasting method that calls for identifying the potential buyers in each market-and estimating their potential purchases.

Market follower A runner-up firm that wants to hold its share in an industry without rocking the boat.

Market leader The firm with the largest market share in an industry.

Market nicher A firm that serves small segments that the other firms in its industry overlook or ignore.

Market penetration A strategy for company growth by increasing sales of current products to current market segments without changing the product.

Market-penetration pricing Setting a low price for a new product in order to attract a large number of buyers and a large market share.

Market positioning Arranging for a product to occupy a clear, distinctive, and desirable place relative to competing products in the minds of target consumers.

Market potential The upper limit of market demand.

Market segment A group of consumers who respond in a similar way to a given set of marketing efforts.

Market segmentation Dividing a market into distinct groups of buyers who have distinct needs, characteristics, or behavior and who might require separate products or marketing mixes; Dividing a market into distinct groups with distinct needs, characteristics, or behavior who might require separate products or marketing mixes.

Market-skimming pricing Setting a high price for a new product to skim maximum revenues layer by layer from the segments willing to pay the high price; the company makes fewer but more profitable sales.

Marketing A social and managerial process whereby individuals and groups obtain what they need and want through creating and exchanging products and value with others.

Marketing audit A comprehensive, systematic, independent, and periodic examination of a company's environment, objectives, strategies, and activities to determine problem areas and opportunities and to recommend a plan of action to improve the company's marketing performance.

Marketing channel (distribution channel) A set of interdependent organizations involved in the process of making a product or service available for use or consumption by the consumer or business user.

Marketing communications mix (promotion mix) The specific mix of advertising, personal selling, sales promotion, and public relations a company uses to pursue its advertising and marketing objectives.

Marketing concept The marketing management philosophy that holds that achieving organizational goals depends on determining the needs and wants of target markets and delivering the desired satisfactions more effectively and efficiently than competitors do.

Marketing control The process of measuring and evaluating the results of marketing strategies and plans and taking corrective action to ensure that objectives are achieved.

Marketing environment The actors and forces outside marketing that affect marketing management's ability to build and maintain successful relationships with target customers.

Marketing implementation The process that turns marketing strategies and plans into marketing actions in order to accomplish strategic marketing objectives.

Marketing information system (MIS) People, equipment, and procedures to gather, sort, analyze, evaluate, and distribute needed, timely, and accurate information to marketing decision makers.

Marketing intelligence The systematic collection and analysis of publicly available information about competitors and developments in the marketing environment.

Marketing intermediaries Firms that help the company to promote, sell, and distribute its goods to final buyers; they include resellers, physical distribution firms, marketing service agencies, and financial intermediaries.

Marketing logistics (physical distribution) The tasks involved in planning, implementing, and controlling the physical flow of materials, final goods, and related information from points of origin to points of consumption to meet customer requirements at a profit.

Marketing management The art and science of choosing target markets and building profitable relationships with them.

Marketing mix The set of controllable tactical marketing tools—product, price, place, and promotion—that the firm blends to produce the response it wants in the target market.

Marketing offer Some combination of products, services, information, or experiences offered to a market to satisfy a need or want.

Marketing process The process of (1) analyzing marketing opportunities, (2) selecting target markets, (3) developing the marketing mix, and (4) managing the marketing effort.

Marketing research The systematic design, collection, analysis, and reporting of data relevant to a specific marketing situation facing an organization.

Marketing strategy The marketing logic by which the business unit hopes to achieve its marketing objectives.

Marketing strategy development Designing an initial marketing strategy for a new product based on the product concept.

Marketing Web site A Web site that engages consumers in interactions that will move them closer to a direct purchase or other marketing outcome.

Markup The percentage of the cost or price of a product added to cost in order to arrive at a selling price.

Maturity stage The stage in the product life cycle in which sales growth slows or levels off.

Merchant wholesaler Independently owned business that takes title to the merchandise it handles.

Microenvironment The actors close to the company that affect its ability to serve its customers—the company, suppliers, marketing intermediaries, customer markets, competitors, and publics.

Micromarketing The practice of tailoring products and marketing programs to the needs and wants of specific individuals and local customer groups—includes local marketing and individual marketing.

Mission statement A statement of the organization's purpose—what it wants to accomplish in the larger environment.

Modified rebuy A business buying situation in which the buyer wants to modify product specifications, prices, terms, or suppliers.

Motive (drive) A need that is sufficiently pressing to direct the person to seek satisfaction of the need.

Multichannel distribution system A distribution system in which a single firm sets up two or more marketing channels to reach one or more customer segments.

Natural environment Natural resources that are needed as inputs by marketers or that are affected by marketing activities.

Need recognition The first stage of the buyer decision process, in which the consumer recognizes a problem or need.

Needs A state of felt deprivation.

New product A good, service, or idea that is perceived by some potential customers as new.

New-product development The development of original products, product improvements, product modifications, and new brands through the firm's own R&D efforts.

New task A business buying situation in which the buyer purchases a product or service for the first time.

Nonpersonal communication channels Media that carry messages without personal contact or feedback, including major media, atmospheres, and events.

Nontariff trade barriers Nonmonetary barriers to foreign products, such as biases against a foreign company's bids, or product standards that go against a foreign company's product features.

Objective-and-task method Developing the promotion budget by (1) defining specific objectives; (2) determining the tasks that must be performed to achieve these objectives; and (3) estimating the costs of performing these tasks. The sum of these costs is the proposed promotion budget.

Observational research The gathering of primary data by observing relevant people, actions, and situations.

Occasion segmentation Dividing the market into groups according to occasions when buyers get the idea to buy, actually make their purchase, or use the purchased item.

Off-price retailer Retailer that buys at less-than-regular wholesale prices and sells at less than retail. Examples are factory outlets, independents, and warehouse clubs.

Online advertising Advertising that appears while consumers are surfing the Web, including banner and ticker ads, interstitials, skyscrapers, and other forms.

Online databases Computerized collections of information available from online commercial sources or via the Internet.

Online (Internet) marketing research Collecting primary data through Internet surveys and online focus groups.

Open trading networks Huge e-marketspaces in which B2B buyers and sellers find each other online, share information, and complete transactions efficiently.

Operating ratios Ratios of selected operating statement items to net sales that allow marketers to compare the firm's performance in one year with that in previous years (or with industry standards and competitors in the same year).

Operating statement (profit-and-loss statement, income statement) A financial statement that shows company sales, cost of goods sold, and expenses during a given period of time.

Opinion leader Person within a reference group who, because of special skills, knowledge, personality, or other characteristics, exerts influence on others.

Optional-product pricing The pricing of optional or accessory products along with a main product.

Order-routine specification The stage of the business buying process in which the buyer writes the final order with the chosen supplier(s), listing the technical specifications, quantity needed, expected time of delivery, return policies, and warranties.

Outside sales force (or field sales force) Outside salespeople who travel to call on customers.

Packaging The activities of designing and producing the container or wrapper for a product.

Partner relationship management Working closely with partners in other company departments and outside the company to jointly bring greater value to customers.

Partnering with marketing intermediaries Coca-Cola provides Wendy's much more than just soft drinks. It also pledges powerful marketing support.

Patronage reward Cash or other award for the regular use of a certain company's products or services.

Percentage-of-sales method Setting the promotion budget at a certain percentage of current or forecasted sales or as a percentage of the unit sales price.

Perception The process by which people select, organize, and interpret information to form a meaningful picture of the world.

Performance review The stage of the business buying process in which the buyer rates its satisfaction with suppliers, deciding whether to continue, modify, or drop them.

Personal communication channels Channels through which two or more people communicate directly with each other, including face to face, person to audience, over the telephone, or through the mail.

Personal selling Personal presentation by the firm's sales force for the purpose of making sales and building customer relationships.

Personality A person's distinguishing psychological characteristics that lead to relatively consistent and lasting responses to his or her own environment.

Pleasing products Products that give high immediate satisfaction but may hurt consumers in the long run.

Point of purchase (POP) promotion Display and demonstration that takes place at the point of purchase or sale.

Political environment Laws, government agencies, and pressure groups that influence and limit various organizations and individuals in a given society.

Portfolio analysis A tool by which management identifies and evaluates the various businesses making up the company.

Positioning statement A statement that summarizes company or brand positioning—it takes this form: To (target segment and need) our (brand) is (concept) that (point-of-difference).

Postpurchase behavior The stage of the buyer decision process in which consumers take further action after purchase, based on their satisfaction or dissatisfaction.

Preapproach The step in the selling process in which the salesperson learns as much as possible about a prospective customer before making a sales call.

Premium Good offered either free or at low cost as an incentive to buy a product.

Presentation The step in the selling process in which the salesperson tells the "product story" to the buyer, highlighting customer benefits.

Price The amount of money charged for a product or service, or the sum of the values that consumers exchange for the benefits of having or using the product or service.

Price elasticity A measure of the sensitivity of demand to changes in price.

Price pack (cents off deal) Reduced price that is marked by the producer directly on the label or package.

Primary data Information collected for the specific purpose at hand.

Primary demand The total demand for all brands of a given product or service.

Private brand (or store brand) A brand created and owned by a reseller of a product or service.

Private trading networks (PTNs) B2B trading networks that link a particular seller with its own trading partners.

Problem recognition The first stage of the business buying process, in which someone in the company recognizes a problem or need that can be met by acquiring a good or a service.

Product Anything that can be offered to a market for attention, acquisition, use, or consumption that might satisfy a want or need.

Product adaptation Adapting a product to meet local conditions or wants in foreign markets.

Product bundle pricing Combining several products and offering the bundle at a reduced price.

Product concept The idea that consumers will favor products that offer the most quality, performance, and features and that the organization should therefore devote its energy to making continuous product improvements; A detailed version of the new-product idea stated in meaningful consumer terms.

Product development A strategy for company growth by offering modified or new products to current market segments; Developing the product concept into a physical product in order to ensure that the product idea can be turned into a workable product.

Product invention Creating new products or services for foreign markets.

Product life cycle (PLC) The course of a product's sales and profits over its lifetime. It involves five distinct stages: product development, introduction, growth, maturity, and decline.

Product line A group of products that are closely related because they function in a similar manner, are sold to the same customer groups, are marketed through the same types of outlets, or fall within given price ranges.

Product line pricing Setting the price steps between various products in a product line based on cost differences between the products, customer evaluations of different features, and competitors' prices.

Product/market expansion grid A portfolio-planning tool for identifying company growth opportunities through market penetration, market development, product development, or diversification.

Product mix (or product assortment) The set of all product lines and items that a particular seller offers for sale.

Product position The way the product is defined by consumers on important attributes—the place the product occupies in consumers' minds relative to competing products.

Product quality The ability of a product to perform its functions; it includes the product's overall durability, reliability, precision, ease of operation and repair, and other valued attributes.

Product sales force structure A sales force organization under which salespeople specialize in selling only a portion of the company's products or lines.

Product specification The stage of the business buying process in which the buying organization decides on and specifies the best technical product characteristics for a needed item.

Production concept The idea that consumers will favor products that are available and highly affordable.

Promotional pricing Temporarily pricing products below the list price, and sometimes even below cost, to increase short-run sales.

Proposal solicitation The stage of the business buying process in which the buyer invites qualified suppliers to submit proposals.

Prospecting The step in the selling process in which the salesperson identifies qualified potential customers.

Psychographic segmentation Dividing a market into different groups based on social class, lifestyle, or personality characteristics.

Psychological pricing A pricing approach that considers the psychology of prices and not simply the economics; the price is used to say something about the product.

Public Any group that has an actual or potential interest in or impact on an organization's ability to achieve its objectives.

Public relations Building good relations with the company's various publics by obtaining favorable publicity, building up a good "corporate image," and handling or heading off unfavorable rumors, stories, and events.

Pull strategy A promotion strategy that calls for spending a lot on advertising and consumer promotion to build up consumer demand. If the strategy is successful, consumers will ask their retailers for the product, the retailers will ask the wholesalers, and the wholesalers will ask the producers.

Purchase decision The buyer's decision about which brand to purchase.

Push strategy A promotion strategy that calls for using the sales force and trade promotion to push the product through channels. The producer promotes the product to wholesalers, the wholesalers promote to retailers, and the retailers promote to consumer

Quota A limit on the amount of goods that an importing country will accept in certain product categories.

Reference prices Prices that buyers carry in their minds and refer to when they look at a given product.

Retailer Business whose sales come *primarily* from retailing.

Retailing All activities involved in selling goods or services directly to final consumers for their personal, nonbusiness use.

Return on investment (ROI) A common measure of managerial effectiveness—the ratio of net profit to investment.

Sales force management The analysis, planning, implementation, and control of sales force activities. It includes setting and designing sales force strategy; and recruiting, selecting, training, supervising, compensating, and evaluating the firm's salespeople.

Sales promotion Short term incentives to encourage the purchase or sale of a product or service.

Sales quota A standard that states the amount a salesperson should sell and how sales should be divided among the company's products.

Salesperson An individual acting for a company by performing one or more of the following activities: prospecting, communicating, servicing, and information gathering.

Salutary products Products that have low appeal but may benefit consumers in the long run.

Sample A segment of the population selected for marketing research to represent the population as a whole.

Secondary data Information that already exists somewhere, having been collected for another purpose.

Segmented pricing Selling a product or service at two or more prices, where the difference in prices is not based on differences in costs.

Selective demand The demand a given brand of a product or service.

Selective distribution The use of more than one, but fewer than all, of the intermediaries who are willing to carry the company's products.

Selling concept The idea that consumers will not buy enough of the organization's products unless the organization undertakes a large-scale selling and promotion effort.

Selling process The steps that the salesperson follows when selling, which include prospecting and qualifying, preapproach, approach, presentation and demonstration, handling objections, closing, and follow-up.

Sense-of-mission marketing A principle of enlightened marketing that holds that a company should define its mission in broad social terms rather than narrow product terms.

Sequential product development A new-product development approach in which one company department works to complete its stage of the process before passing the new product along to the next department and stage.

Service Any activity or benefit that one party can offer to another that is essentially intangible and does not result in the ownership of anything.

Service inseparability A major characteristic of services—they are produced and consumed at the same time and cannot be separated from their providers, whether the providers are people or machines.

Service intangibility A major characteristic of services—they cannot be seen, tasted, felt, heard, or smelled before they are bought.

Service perishability A major characteristic of services—they cannot be stored for later sale or use.

Service-profit chain The chain that links service firm profits with employee and customer satisfaction.

Service variability A major characteristic of services—their quality may vary greatly, depending on who provides them and when, where, and how.

Shopping center A group of retail businesses planned, developed, owned, and managed as a unit.

Shopping product Consumer good that the customer, in the process of selection and purchase, characteristically compares on such bases as suitability, quality, price, and style.

Simultaneous (or team-based) product development An approach to developing new products in which various company departments work closely together, overlapping the steps in the product-development process to save time and increase effectiveness.

Single-source data systems Electronic monitoring systems that link consumers' exposure to television advertising and promotion (measured using television meters) with what they buy in stores (measured using store checkout scanners).

Social classes Relatively permanent and ordered divisions in a society whose members share similar values, interests, and behaviors.

Social marketing The design, implementation, and control of programs seeking to increase the acceptability of a social idea, cause, or practice among a target group.

Societal marketing A principle of enlightened marketing that holds that a company should make marketing decisions by considering consumers' wants, the company's requirements, consumers' long-run interests, and society's long-run interests.

Societal marketing concept The idea that the organization should determine the needs, wants, and interests of target markets and deliver the desired satisfactions more effectively and efficiently than do competitors in a way that maintains or improves the consumer's and society's well being.

Specialty product Consumer product with unique characteristics or brand identification for which a significant group of buyers is willing to make a special purchase effort.

Specialty store A retail store that carries a narrow product line with a deep assortment within that line.

Standardized marketing mix An international marketing strategy for using basically the same product, advertising, distribution channels, and other elements of the marketing mix in all the company's international markets.

Straight product extension Marketing a product in a foreign market without any change.

Straight rebuy A business buying situation in which the buyer routinely reorders something without any modifications.

Strategic business unit (SBU) A unit of the company that has a separate mission and objectives and that can be planned independently from other company businesses.

Strategic group A group of firms in an industry following the same or a similar strategy.

Strategic planning The process of developing and maintaining a strategic fit between the organization's goals and capabilities and its changing marketing opportunities. It involves defining a clear company mission, setting supporting objectives, designing a sound business portfolio, and coordinating functional strategies.

Style A basic and distinctive mode of expression.

Subculture A group of people with shared value systems based on common life experiences and situations.

Supermarket Large, low-cost, low-margin, high-volume, self-service store that carries a wide variety of food, laundry, and household products.

Superstore A store much larger than a regular supermarket that carries a large assortment of routinely purchased food and nonfood items and offers services such as dry cleaning, post offices, photo finishing, check cashing, bill paying, lunch counters,

Supplier search The stage of the business buying process in which the buyer tries to find the best vendors.

Supplier selection The stage of the business buying process in which the buyer reviews proposals and selects a supplier or suppliers.

Supply chain management Managing upstream and downstream value-added flows of materials, final goods, and related information among suppliers, the company, resellers, and final consumers.

Survey research The gathering of primary data by asking people questions about their knowledge, attitudes, preferences, and buying behavior.

Systems selling Buying a packaged solution to a problem from a single seller, thus avoiding all the separate decisions involved in a complex buying situation.

Target costing Pricing that starts with an ideal selling price, then targets costs that will ensure that the price is met.

Target market A set of buyers sharing common needs or characteristics that the company decides to serve.

Target marketing The process of evaluating each market segment's attractiveness and selecting one or more segments to enter.

Tariff A tax levied by a government against certain imported products.

Team selling Using teams of people from sales, marketing, engineering, finance, technical support, and even upper management to service large, complex accounts.

Technological environment Forces that create new technologies, creating new product and market opportunities.

Telephone marketing Using the telephone to sell directly to customers.

Territorial sales force structure A sales force organization that assigns each salesperson to an exclusive geographic territory in which that salesperson sells the company's full line.

Test marketing The stage of new-product development in which the product and marketing program are tested in more realistic market settings.

Third-party logistics (3PL) provider An independent logistics provider that performs any or all of the functions required to get its client's product to market.

Total costs The sum of the fixed and variable costs for any given level of production.

Total market demand The volume of a product or service that would be bought by a defined customer group in a defined geographic area in a defined time period in a defined marketing environment under a defined level and mix of industry marketing effort.

Transaction A trade of values between two parties.

Undifferentiated (mass) marketing A market-coverage strategy in which a firm decides to ignore market segment differences and go after the whole market with one offer.

Uniform-delivered pricing A geographical pricing strategy in which the company charges the same price plus freight to all customers, regardless of their location.

Unsought product Consumer product that the consumer either does not know about or knows about but does not normally think of buying.

Users Members of the buying organization who will actually use the purchased product or service.

Value analysis An approach to cost reduction in which components are studied carefully to determine if they can be redesigned, standardized, or made by less costly methods of production.

Value-based pricing Setting price based on buyers' perceptions of value rather than on the seller's cost.

Value chain The series of departments that carry out value-creating activities to design, produce, market, deliver, and support a firm's products.

Value-delivery network The network made up of the company, suppliers, distributors, and ultimately customers who "partner" with each other to improve the performance of the entire system.

Value marketing A principle of enlightened marketing that holds that a company should put most of its resources into value-building marketing investments.

Value pricing Offering just the right combination of quality and good service at a fair price.

Value proposition The full positioning of a brand—the full mix of benefits upon which it is positioned.

Variable costs Costs that vary directly with the level of production.

Variety-seeking buying behavior Consumer buying behavior in situations characterized by low consumer involvement but significant perceived brand differences.

Vertical marketing system (VMS) A distribution channel structure in which producers, wholesalers, and retailers act as a unified system. One channel member owns the others, has contracts with them, or has so much power that they all cooperate.

Viral marketing The Internet version of word-of-mouth marketing—e-mail messages or other marketing events that are so infectious that customers will want to pass them along to friends.

Wants The form taken by a human need as shaped by culture and individual personality.

Warehouse club Off-price retailer that sells a limited selection of brand-name grocery items, appliances, clothing, and a hodgepodge of other goods at deep discounts to members who pay annual membership fees.

Web communities Web sites upon which members can congregate online and exchange views on issues of common interest.

Webcasting The automatic downloading of customized information of interest to recipients' PCs, affording an attractive channel for delivering Internet advertising or other information content.

Wheel-of-retailing concept A concept of retailing that states that new types of retailers usually begin as low-margin, low-price, low-status operations but later evolve into higher-priced, higher-service operations, eventually becoming like the conventional retailers they replaced.

Whole-channel view Designing international channels that take into account all the necessary links in distributing the seller's products to final buyers, including the seller's headquarters organization, channels among nations, and channels within nations.

Wholesaler A firm engaged *primarily* in wholesaling activity.

Wholesaling All activities involved in selling goods and services to those buying for resale or business use.

Word-of-mouth influence Personal communication about a product between target buyers and neighbors, friends, family members, and associates.

Zone pricing A geographical pricing strategy in which the company sets up two or more zones. All customers within a zone pay the same total price; the more distant the zone, the higher the price.

Index

Subject

Name/Organization/Brand/Company Index